Scientific Evidence

Third Edition

PAUL C. GIANNELLI
Albert J. Weatherhead III and Richard W. Weatherhead Professor of Law

Case Western Reserve University
School of Law
Cleveland, Ohio

EDWARD J. IMWINKELRIED
Professor of Law

University of California at Davis
School of Law
Davis, California

Volume 1

LEXIS®
LAW PUBLISHING

P.O. Box 7587, Charlottesville, VA 22906-7587

www.lexispublishing.com

Customer Service: 800/562-1197

Library of Congress Catalog Card No. 99-67624
Two-Volume Set ISBN 0-327-04985-5
Volume 1 ISBN 0-327-04983-9

6238111

DEDICATION

Professor Giannelli dedicates his work on this project to Sue, Michael, and Adam.

Professor Imwinkelried dedicates his work on this project to Cindy, Molly, and Ken; his late parents, Mr. and Mrs. John Imwinkelried; and his late parents-in-law, Mary Jane Clark and Lyman (Brownie) Clark.

SUMMARY OF CONTENTS

Volume 1

Volume 2

TABLE OF CONTENTS

Volume 1

Page

Page

PREFACE

When the last edition was in press, the United States Supreme Court handed down *Daubert v. Merrell Dow Pharmaceuticals, Inc.*, and as a result the way courts dealt with scientific and expert evidence changed dramatically. In the intervening years, the Court has filled in some of the gaps left by *Daubert*. In *General Electric Co. v. Joiner*, the Court addressed the standard for appellate review of *Daubert* decisions. In *Kumho Tire Co. v. Carmichael,* the Court extended the *Daubert* reliability requirement to nonscientific expert testimony. In addition, the Court reviewed a constitutional challenge based on polygraph evidence in *United States v. Scheffer*.

In 1999 in *Kumho Tire Co.* the Court once again affirmed its determination to improve the quality of expert testimony in federal trials: "The objective of [*Daubert's* gatekeeping] requirement is to ensure the reliability and relevancy of expert testimony. It is to make certain that an expert, whether basing testimony upon professional studies or personal experience, employs in the courtroom the same level of intellectual rigor that characterizes the practice of an expert in the relevant field." As forceful as these words are, the Court's actions may speak even louder: When the dust settled at the end of each case in its expert testimony trilogy—*Daubert*, *Joiner*, and *Kumho*, the Court had upheld the exclusion of the proffered expert testimony. (It is true that in *Daubert*, the Court remanded. However, on remand, the court of appeals again excluded the evidence, and the Supreme Court denied certiorari.)

In addition, reports concerning the misuse of scientific evidence have become far too prevalent. In West Virginia, the head serologist at the State Police crime laboratory falsified test results in hundreds of cases over a ten-year period. He reported inconclusive results as conclusive, repeatedly altered laboratory records, failed to report conflicting results, failed to conduct additional testing to resolve conflicting results, and reported scientifically impossible or improbable results. Defendants were sentenced to long prison terms based upon his testimony. An investigation indicated that his superiors regarded him as "pro-prosecution." More damning was evidence that his "superiors may have ignored or concealed complaints of his misconduct" and that state laboratory procedures "undoubtedly contributed to an environment within which [his] misconduct escaped detection."

In Texas, a pathologist was convicted of faking autopsies. As many as 20 death penalty cases may be involved. Again, what is troubling is that he had worked closely with prosecutors and police for years and "shaded things to follow along with the police theory of the case." As the special prosecutor remarked: "If the prosecution theory was that death was caused by a Martian death ray, then that was what he reported." When defense attorneys argued that prosecutors were involved in a coverup, they were indicted. But the defense was not the only side hurt by this misconduct. This "expert" also declared that a murder victim had died of natural causes.

ACKNOWLEDGMENTS

With one exception, each chapter of this text that discusses a specific scientific technique has been reviewed by an outside expert. Their opinions provided invaluable suggestions and criticisms which substantially improved the text. The authors, however, did not accept all their suggestions and the text, along with any errors, remains the responsibility of the authors. The authors wish to express their great appreciation to the following persons who reviewed our drafts for the various editions of the treatise:

Dr. Gordon Barland, Department of Defense Polygraph Institute, Ft. McClellan, Ala. (Chapter 8);

Professor Jules B. Gerard, School of Law, Washington University, St. Louis, Mo. (Chapter 9, first edition);

Dr. Oscar Tosi, Ph.D., Sc.D., Professor and Director Emeritus, Speech, Hearing & Voice Identification Laboratories Michigan State University, East Lansing, Mich. (Chapter 10, first and second editions); Bruce E. Koenig, Supervisory Special Agent (retired), Technical Services Division, F.B.I., Quantico, Va. (Chapter 10);

Dr. S.S. Krishnan, Scientific Director (retired), Medical Physics Laboratory, The Toronto Hospital, Toronto, Canada (Chapter 11, first and second editions);

Dr. Martin Orne, Institute of Pennsylvania Hospital and University of Pennsylvania, Philadelphia, Pa.; Dr. Robert A. Karlin, Rutgers University, and Anita Lipton, False Memory Foundation. (Chapter 12);

Dr. Lowell J. Levine, Medicolegal Investigations Unit, New York State Police, Albany, N.Y. (Chapter 13);

John Cayton, Chief, Firearms Section, Regional Criminalistics Laboratory, Kansas City, Mo. (Chapter 14);

Robert D. Koons and Donald G. Havekost, F.B.I. Laboratory. (Chapter 14);

Professor David Kaye, College of Law, Arizona State University, Tempe, Ariz., and Professor Edward Spitznagel, Jr., Mathematics Department, Washington University, St. Louis, Mo. (Chapter 15);

Clarence Phillips, retired Senior Fingerprint Instructor, F.B.I. and Robert Hazen, retired Supervisory Fingerprint Specialist, F.B.I. Academy, Quantico, Va. (Chapter 16);

Dr. Robert Allen, Director, Human Identification Laboratory, H.A. Chapman Institute of Medical Genetics, Children's Medical Center, Tulsa, Okla., Dr. Hugh Chaplin, Jr., Director, Barnes Blood Bank, Washington University School of Medicine, St. Louis, Mo., and Professor David Kaye, College of Law, Arizona State University, Tempe, Ariz. (Chapter 17);

Dr. George Duncan, DNA Specialist, Crime Laboratory, Broward Sheriff's Office, Fort Lauderdale, Fl. (Chapter 18);

Dr. Michael Graham, St. Louis University School of Medicine, St. Louis, Mo. (Chapter 19);

Dr. Alphonse Poklis, Director, Toxicology Laboratory, Medical College of Virginia, Richmond, Va. (Chapter 20);

James Kelly, Kelly & Associates, Decatur, Ga. (Chapter 21);

Dr. Kurt Dubowski, Distinguished Professor of Medicine, College of Medicine, University of Oklahoma, Oklahoma City, Okla. (Chapter 22);

Prof. Jay Siegel, School of Criminal Justice, Michigan State University, Mr. Joseph Bono, Supervisory Chemist, Drug Enforcement Administration Special Testing and Research Laboratory, McLean, Va., and Robert Shapiro, Provost, United States Naval Academy, Annapolis, Md. (Chapter 23);

John T. Wilson, Chief Criminalist, Regional Criminalistics Laboratory, Kansas City, Mo. (Chapter 24);

Prof. Donald Land, Chemistry Department, University of California at Davis, and Dr. John Fairing, Scanning Microscopy International, Ballwin, Mo. (Chapter 25);

Special Agent David Campbell, North Carolina State Bureau of Investigation, Cary, N.C., and the late Captain John Imwinkelried, Retired, San Francisco Fire Department, San Francisco, Cal. (Chapter 26);

Professor John B. Kwasnoski, Western New England Technical Consultants, Ludlow, Ma., and James Dedman III, Director of Training, National College of District Attorneys, Houston, Tx. (Chapter 27);

Professor John B. Kwasnoski, Western New England Technical Consultants, Ludlow, Ma. (Chapter 28).

Professor Imwinkelried wishes to express his appreciation to all the students in his Scientific Evidence classes at the University of San Diego, Washington University, and the University of California at Davis; their seminar papers were of tremendous assistance in preparing his chapters. He would like to extend special thanks to Don Latorraca who assisted him in preparing the first edition. Likewise, he expresses his gratitude to Ms. Jody Willson and Mr. Michael Wilcox, his research assistants on the third edition. Finally, Ms. Beth House, Ms. Ann Graham, and Ms. Glenda McGlashan of the U.C.D. Law School staff deserve special thanks.

ACKNOWLEDGEMENTS

Professor Giannelli wishes to express his appreciation to: Albert J. Weatherhead III and the Weatherhead family; research assistants: Jill Zyskowski and Karen Ross (third edition); Sue Williams, Julie Chiodo, Margaret Russell, and Sally Walters (second edition); secretarial: Ellie Ettinger, and Betty Kaye; library research: Judy Kaul. He also wishes to express his appreciation to those who have taught his students in his Scientific Evidence seminar: Dr. Elizabeth Balraj, Dr. Amanda Jenkins, and Linda Luke of the Cuyahoga Coroner's office; Mary Kelly, Charles Sikora, and Joe Serowik of Cleveland Police Crime Laboratory; Special Agent John Sommer, F.B.I.; Dr. Elizabeth Robinson and Dr. James Simmelink, School of Dentistry, Case Western Reserve University; Tom Bader, F.B.I. (retired); Dick Stimson, Westshore Enforcement Bureau (retired); Dale Laux, Ohio Bureau of Investigation; and James Wooley, Assistant U.S. Attorney.

CHAPTER 1

SCIENTIFIC EVIDENCE*

* The sections in this chapter were revised and renumbered in this edition.

§ 1-1. In General.

The reliability of evidence derived from a scientific theory or principle depends upon three factors: (1) the validity[1] of the underlying theory, (2) the validity of the technique applying that theory, and (3) the proper application of the technique on a particular occasion. In short, neither an invalid technique nor a valid technique improperly applied will produce reliable results.

The first two factors — the validity of the underlying theory and validity of the technique — are distinct issues.[2] One could accept, for example, the validity of the premise underlying "voiceprint" identification — voice uniqueness — but still question whether the voiceprint technique can identify that uniqueness.[3] Similarly, the underlying psychological and physiological principles of polygraph testing could be acknowledged without endorsing the proposition that a polygraph examiner can detect deception by means of the polygraph technique.[4] The validity of a scientific principle and the validity of the technique applying that principle may be established through judicial notice,[5] legislative recognition,[6] stipulation,[7] or the presentation of evidence, including expert testimony.[8]

The third requirement — the proper application of a scientific technique on a particular occasion — raises a number of additional issues: (a) the condition of any instrumentation used in the technique, (b) adherence to proper procedures,

---

1. Although courts use the terms "validity" and "reliability" interchangeably, the terms have distinct meanings in scientific jargon. "Validity" refers to the ability of a test to measure what it is supposed to measure — its accuracy. "Reliability" refers to whether the same results are obtained in each instance in which the test is performed — its consistency. Validity includes reliability, but the converse is not necessarily true. *See* Barland, *The Reliability of Polygraph Chart Evaluations, in* LEGAL ADMISSIBILITY OF THE POLYGRAPH 120, 121 (N. Ansley ed. 1975); Abrams, *Polygraph Validity and Reliability: A Review*, 18 J. FORENSIC SCI. 313, 323 (1973); Latin, Tannehill & White, *Remote Sensing Evidence and Environmental Law*, 64 CALIF. L. REV. 1300, 1384-85 (1976). Although the Supreme Court acknowledged this distinction in Daubert v. Merrell Dow Pharmaceuticals, Inc., 570 U.S. 579, 590 n.9 (1993), it declared that its concern was "evidentiary reliability — that is, trustworthiness."

2. "If the validity of a scientific principle is a prerequisite to its admission into evidence, then consistency requires that evidence of the ability of a machine [radar] to employ that scientific principle reliably must also precede admission of the machine's results into evidence." City of Seattle v. Peterson, 39 Wash. App. 524, 527, 693 P.2d 757, 758 (1985).

3. For a discussion of voiceprint evidence, *see* Chapter 10. *See also* Giannelli, *The Admissibility of Novel Scientific Evidence: Frye v. United States, A Half-Century Later*, 80 COLUM. L. REV. 1197, 1210 (1980).

4. For a discussion of polygraph evidence, *see* Chapter 8.

5. *See* § 1-2 *infra.*

6. *See* § 1-3 *infra.*

7. *See* § 1-4 *infra.*

8. *See* § 1-5 to 1-7 *infra.*

and (c) the qualifications of both the person conducting the procedure and the person interpreting the results.[9]

§ 1-2. Judicial Notice.

Once a scientific principle is sufficiently established, a court may take judicial notice of the validity of that principle.[10] As the Supreme Court has noted: "[T]heories that are so firmly established as to have attained the status of scientific law, such as the laws of thermodynamics, properly are subject to judicial notice under Fed. Rule Evid. 201."[11] Similarly, a court may take judicial notice of the validity of the technique applying the principle.[12] In either case the effect is the same: judicial notice relieves the offering party of the burden of producing evidence on these issues.

Several bite mark cases illustrate this point. For example, the New York Court of Appeals has written: "The reliability of bite mark evidence as a means of identification is sufficiently established in the scientific community to make such evidence admissible in a criminal case, without separately establishing scientific

---

9. *See* § 1-11 *infra.*

10. *See generally* 2 C. McCormick, Evidence ch. 33 (4th ed. 1992); Keeffe, Landis & Shaad, *Sense and Nonsense About Judicial Notice*, 2 Stan. L. Rev. 664, 670-71 (1950); Kleri, *Judicial Notice of Scientific Facts*, 15 Cleve.-Marshall L. Rev. 140 (1966); Korn, *Law, Fact, and Science in the Courts*, 66 Colum. L. Rev. 1080, 1088-90, 1107-08 (1966); Strong, *Questions Affecting the Admissibility of Scientific Evidence*, 1970 U. Ill. L.F. 1, 6-9. *See also* Steward v. State, 652 N.E.2d 490, 499 (Ind. 1995) ("[R]eliability may be established either by judicial notice or, in its absence, by the proponent of the scientific testimony providing sufficient foundation...").

11. Daubert v. Merrell Dow Pharmaceuticals, Inc., 509 U.S. 579, 593 n.11 (1993). *See also* Izer v. State, 236 Ga. App. 282, 282-83, 511 S.E.2d 625, 627 (1999) (laser-based speed measuring device not subject to judicial notice; "[O]nce a procedure or technology has been recognized in a substantial number of courts, or has been utilized for a significant period of time and expert testimony has been received thereon in case after case, a trial court may take judicial notice of the devices's reliability and acceptance. The trial court does not have to keep reinventing the wheel; a once novel technology can and does become commonplace") (citations omitted).

12. Sometimes only the underlying principle is subject to judicial notice. For example, a court could take judicial notice of the underlying principle of radar (the Doppler Effect) but not its application in a new type of radar, *i.e.*, moving radar. *E.g.*, State v. Doles, 70 Ohio App. 2d 35, 38, 433 N.E.2d 1290, 1292 (1980) (moving radar not subject to judicial notice); State v. Hanson, 85 Wis. 2d 233, 244, 270 N.W.2d 212, 217 (1978) (moving radar not subject to judicial notice).

reliability in each case ...."[13] As this case indicates, courts may not use the term "judicial notice"—yet, the effect is the same.[14]

The principles underlying many scientific techniques, including radar,[15] intoxication tests,[16] fingerprints,[17] palm prints,[18] firearms identification,[19] handwriting comparisons,[20] DNA profiling,[21] blood-spatter evidence,[22] as well as

---

13. People v. Middleton, 54 N.Y.2d 42, 45, 429 N.E.2d 100, 101, 444 N.Y.S.2d 581, 582 (1981). *See also* State v. Richards, 166 Ariz. App. 576, 579, 804 P.2d 109, 112 (1990) ("[B]ite mark evidence is admissible without a preliminary determination of reliability..."); State v. Armstrong, 369 S.E.2d 870, 877 (W. Va. 1988) (judicially noticing the reliability of bite mark evidence).

14. *See also* Fugate v. Commonwealth, 993 S.W.2d 931 (Ky. 1999) ("DNA comparison analysis using the RFLP and PCR methods is admissible without being the subject of a pretrial *Daubert* hearing. However, the evidence in question is still subject to challenge at trial").

15. *E.g.,* United States v. Dreos, 156 F. Supp. 200, 208 (D. Md. 1957); State v. Tomanelli, 153 Conn. 365, 370-71, 216 A.2d 625, 629 (1966); Commonwealth v. Whynaught, 377 Mass. 14, 17, 384 N.E.2d 1212, 1215 (1979); State v. Calvert, 682 S.W.2d 474, 477 (Mo. 1984); State v. Dantonio, 18 N.J. 570, 576, 115 A.2d 35, 39 (1955); People v. Knight, 72 N.Y.2d 481, 484, 530 N.E.2d 1273, 1274, 534 N.Y.S.2d 353, 354 (1988) (judicial notice of moving radar); People v. Magri, 3 N.Y.2d 562, 566, 147 N.E.2d 728, 730, 170 N.Y.S.2d 335, 337 (1958); State v. Buchtel, 24 Ohio App. 3d 72, 72, 493 N.E.2d 318, 319 (1985) (judicial notice of K-55 radar). *But see* State v. Doles, 70 Ohio App. 2d 35, 38, 433 N.E.2d 1290, 1292 (1980) (moving radar not subject to judicial notice); Seattle v. Peterson, 39 Wash. App. 524, 528, 693 P.2d 757, 759 (1985) (CMI radar not subject to judicial notice); State v. Hanson, 85 Wis. 2d 233, 244, 270 N.W.2d 212, 217 (1978) (moving radar not subject to judicial notice).

See also Adkins v. Dirickson, 523 F. Supp. 1281, 1283 (E.D. Pa. 1981) (judicial notice of tachograph); State v. Finkle, 128 N.J. Super. 199, 207, 319 A.2d 733, 737 (judicial notice of VASCAR), *aff'd,* 66 N.J. 139, 329 A.2d 65 (1974), *cert. denied,* 423 U.S. 836 (1975). For a discussion of radar evidence, *see* Chapter 28.

16. *E.g.,* State v. Young, 8 Haw. App. 145, 795 P.2d 285, 292 (1990) (Intoxilyzer), *cert. denied,* 833 P.2d 901 (Hawaii 1990); People v. Stringfield, 37 Ill. App. 2d 344, 346, 185 N.E.2d 381, 382 (1962) (breathalyzer); Schultz v. State, 106 Md. App. 145, 151, 664 A.2d 60, 62 (1995) (Horizontal Gaze Nystagmus); State v. Miller, 64 N.J. Super. 262, 268-69, 165 A.2d 829, 832-33 (A.D. 1960) (drunkometer); People v. Donaldson, 36 A.D.2d 37, 40, 319 N.Y.S.2d 172, 176 (1971) (breathalyzer). *But see* State v. Torres, 976 P.2d 20, 33 (N.M. 1999) ("[J]udicial notice of the evidentiary reliability of HGN testing would be inappropriate at this time"). For a discussion of intoxication tests, *see* Chapter 22.

17. *E.g.,* Piquett v. United States, 81 F.2d 75, 85 (7th Cir.), *cert. denied,* 298 U.S. 664 (1936); State v. Rogers, 233 N.C. 390, 397, 64 S.E.2d 572, 577 (1951); Grice v. State, 142 Tex. Crim. 4, 11, 151 S.W.2d 211, 216 (1941). For a discussion of fingerprints, *see* Chapter 16.

18. *E.g.,* State v. Inman, 350 A.2d 582, 588-89 (Me. 1976).

19. *E.g.,* State v. Hackett, 215 S.C. 434, 445, 55 S.E.2d 696, 701 (1949). For a discussion of firearms identification, *see* Chapter 14.

20. *E.g.,* Greenberg Gallery, Inc. v. Bauman, 817 F. Supp. 167, 172 n.5 (D.D.C. 1993) ("It can be judicially noted that handwriting, like fingerprints, are subject to established objective tests, expert opinions about which are admissible"), *aff'd,* 36 F.3d 127 (D.C. Cir. 1994); Adams v. Ristine, 138 Va. 273, 283, 122 S.E. 126, 128 (1924); Fenelon v. State, 195 Wis. 416, 428-29, 217 N.W. 711, 715 (1928). For a discussion of questioned document examinations, *see* Chapter 21.

other procedures[23] have all been judicially recognized in this fashion. If, however, a scientific technique is not well-accepted, it is not a proper subject for judicial notice. Thus, in *State v. Fuller*,[24] the court refused to judicially notice the reliability of certain marijuana identification tests.

Professor McCormick referred to this type of judicial notice as judicial notice of facts capable of certain verification.[25] Similarly, Federal Evidence Rule 201(b) provides that a court may judicially notice an adjudicative fact that is "not subject to reasonable dispute in that it is ... capable of accurate and ready determination by resort to sources whose accuracy cannot reasonably be questioned." Some commentators have questioned whether Rule 201 applies to judicial notice of a scientific principle because this use of judicial notice involves decisions concerning the admissibility of evidence and Federal Rule 104(a) provides that in

---

21. *E.g.*, United States v. Beasley, 102 F.3d 1440, 1448 (8th Cir. 1996) ("[T]he reliability of the PCR method of DNA analysis is sufficiently well established to permit the courts of this circuit to take judicial notice of it in future cases"), *cert. denied*, 520 U.S. 1246 (1997); Moore v. State, 323 Ark. 529, 545, 915 S.W.2d 284, 293 (1996) ("The Court therefore takes judicial notice of the general theory and reliability as well as the techniques of DNA profiling"); Hayes v. State, 660 So. 2d 257, 262, 264 (Fla. 1995) ("We have recently made it clear that Florida utilizes the *Frye* test..."; courts may take judicial notice on some aspects of DNA; but correcting for band-shifting is not generally accepted, citing NAS 1992 report); Fugate v. Commonwealth, 993 S.W.2d 931 (Ky. 1999) ("DNA comparison analysis using the RFLP and PCR methods is admissible without being the subject of a pretrial *Daubert* hearing. However, the evidence in question is still subject to challenge at trial"); State v. Vandebogart, 139 N.H. 145, 652 A.2d 671, 678 (1994) ("[T]rial courts may henceforth take judicial notice that the DNA interim ceiling principle has attained general acceptance"); Taylor v. State, 889 P.2d 319, 338 (Okla. Crim. App. 1995) ("[F]rom this point forward, trial courts faced with DNA profiling evidence produced through these means [RFLP] need not conduct a *Daubert* pretrial admissibility hearing"); State v. Woodall, 385 S.E.2d 253, 260 (W. Va. 1989) (judicial notice of DNA). *See also* National Academy of Sciences, DNA Technology in Forensic Science 149 (1992). For a discussion of DNA evidence, *see* Chapter 17.

22. *E.g.*, People v. Haywood, 209 Mich. App. 217, 530 N.W.2d 497, 501 (judicial notice of the general acceptance of blood spatter evidence), *appeal dismissed*, 450 Mich. 928, 543 N.W.2d 317 (1995); State v. Moore, 458 N.W.2d 90, 98 n.6 (Minn. 1990) ("Because the techniques involved in the [blood spatter] analysis are based on the well-settled sciences of chemistry and physics, the reliability of the technique may be appropriate for judicial notice").

23. *E.g.*, United States v. Lopez, 328 F. Supp. 1077, 1085 (E.D.N.Y. 1971) (gate-flux magnetometer); People v. Lopez, 228 Ill. App. 3d 1061, 593 N.E.2d 647, 656 (1992) (electrophoresis as a method of detecting genetic markers); Brown v. Commonwealth, __ S.W.2d __, 1999 Ky. App. Lexis 17 ("Frequently, ... physical syndromes not only characterize a disease or disorder but provide insight into the cause of the condition as well"; "We ... take judicial notice of the fact that 'shaken baby syndrome' has been adequately analyzed and recognized in the scientific literature to permit testimony about it by a properly qualified expert").

24. 15 Kan. App. 2d 34, 38, 802 P.2d 599, 602 (1990) ("The record in this case establishes the State made no showing that the tests used were so generally accepted that the court should take judicial notice of the reliability of the tests"). *See also* State v. Lewis, 736 P.2d 70, 73 (Haw. App. 1987) (judicial notice of beam attenuator as acceptable reference for testing intoxilyzer improper).

25. 2 C. McCormick, *supra* note 10, § 330.

making such determinations a court is not bound by the rules of evidence (except privileges). Thus, Rule 201 along with its procedural requirements would not apply.[26]

Scope of Judicial Notice

Judicial notice extends only to recognizing the validity of the underlying principle and the validity of the technique applying that principle. A court should not judicially notice the proper application of the technique on a particular occasion because such a fact is not an indisputable fact capable of certain verification.[27] Moreover, judicial notice of the proper application of the technique would infringe upon a defendant's right to a jury trial and right of confrontation. Thus, in a case in which judicial notice of the reliability of palmprint evidence was upheld, the Maine Supreme Court stated:

> While the Justice took judicial notice of the scientific principle of the capacity for identification by comparison of two sets of palm prints, he properly left to the jury to decide what confidence they should place in the securing and preservation of the print on the floor and the defendant's prints which were used for comparison and the process of comparison as conducted by these officers, the competence and the reliability of the expert witness and the credibility of the witnesses. He did not take from the jury the essential decision of whether the print on the floor near the victim's shoulder was or was not made by the defendant's palm.[28]

Procedure

When judicial notice of facts capable of accurate and ready determination is taken, the party requesting judicial notice has the responsibility of providing the

---

26. *See* 1 C. Mueller & L. Kirkpatrick, Federal Evidence § 51 , at 269 (2d ed. 1994); *but see* 21 C. Wright & K. Graham, Federal Practice and Procedure 498 (1977) (A judge "ought to be bound by Rule 201 in deciding whether he can take the question of scientific validity out of the hands of the jury"). Rule 201 also would not apply if judicial notice of a scientific fact is considered a "legislative," rather than an "adjudicative," fact. The rule applies only to adjudicative facts. *See* Fed. R. Evid. 201(b) advisory committee's note ("deciding whether evidence should be admitted ... [is] essentially nonadjudicative in nature"); Strong, *supra* note 10, at 8.

27. *See* Strong, *supra* note 10, at 18-20.

28. State v. Inman, 350 A.2d 582, 589 (Me. 1976). In People v. Middleton, 54 N.Y.2d 42, 45, 429 N.E.2d 100, 101, 444 N.Y.S.2d 581, 582 (1981), the court pointed out that taking judicial notice of the reliability of bitemark evidence was "subject, of course, to the establishment by foundation evidence of the authenticity of the materials used and propriety of the procedure followed in the particular case." *See also* State v. Tomanelli, 153 Conn. 365, 371, 216 A.2d 625, 629 (1966) (judicial notice does not extend to accuracy of a particular instrument).

court with "sources whose accuracy cannot reasonably be questioned."[29] These sources need not be admissible in evidence.[30] With scientific evidence, such sources are typically legal and scientific publications.[31] In addition, the opposing party should be provided "an opportunity to be heard as to the propriety of taking judicial notice and the tenor of the matter noticed."[32]

Jury Instructions

In many cases there is no need to instruct the jury concerning judicial notice of the validity of a scientific technique because the admissibility determination is made solely by the court. Occasionally, however, an instruction is given. For example, the Maine Supreme Court has upheld the use of an instruction informing the jury that the trial court had taken judicial notice of the reliability of palmprint comparisons and that "the fingerprint method of identification is accurate and no two sets of fingerprints or palmprints are exactly alike."[33]

If Federal Rule 201 applies in this context, subsection (g) of the rule governs instructions on judicially noticed facts. It provides: "In a criminal case, the court shall instruct the jury that it may, but is not required to, accept as conclusive any fact judicially noticed." In other words, a judicially noticed fact is not binding upon the jury in a criminal case. This provision was inserted in the Federal Rules because Congress was concerned that requiring the jury to accept a judicially noticed fact would violate a defendant's right to a jury trial.[34]

§ 1-3. Legislative Recognition.

In some cases the validity of a scientific technique is recognized by statute. At one time most of these provisions involved motor vehicle codes and paternity cases. Radar,[35] intoxication tests,[36] and blood tests[37] are often subject to

---

29. FED. R. EVID. 201(b)(2). *See also* 2 C. MCCORMICK, *supra* note 10, § 330, at 395 (It "is the task of counsel to find and to present in argument and briefs such references, excerpts and explanations as will convince the judge that the fact is certain and demonstrable").

30. Wigmore states that "any source whatever that suffices to satisfy [the judge's] mind in making a ruling" is acceptable. 9 J. WIGMORE, EVIDENCE § 2568a, at 538 (3d ed. 1940) (listing "official records, encyclopedias, any book or articles" as examples).

31. *E.g.*, State v. Inman, 350 A.2d 582, 589 (Me. 1976) (citing text on palmprints); People v. Middleton, 54 N.Y.2d 42, 49, 429 N.E.2d 100, 103, 444 N.Y.S.2d 581, 584 (1981) (citing articles on bite mark comparisons).

32. FED. R. EVID. 201(e). *See also* 1 C. MUELLER & L. KIRKPATRICK, *supra* note 26, § 53.

33. State v. Inman, 350 A.2d 582, 588 (Me. 1976).

34. H.R. Rep. No. 650, 93d Cong., 2d Sess., *reprinted in* 1974 U.S. Code Cong. & Ad. News 7075, 7080 (A "mandatory instruction to a jury in a criminal case to accept as conclusive any fact judicially noticed is inappropriate because [it is] contrary to the spirit of the Sixth Amendment right to jury trial"). *See also* 1 C. MUELLER & L. KIRKPATRICK, *supra* note 6, § 55.

35. *E.g.*, MD. CTS. & JUD. PROC. CODE ANN. § 10-301 (1988); VA. CODE ANN. § 46.2-882 (Michie 1991). *See also* Note, *Radar Speed Detection: Homing in on New Evidentiary Problems*,

legislative regulation.[38] As noted in the previous section, these techniques are typically subject to judicial notice as well. Like judicial notice, legislative "notice" or recognition relieves the proponent of the burden of introducing evidence on the validity issue.[39] Frequently, these statutes specify additional requirements for admissibility, such as periodic testing as a prerequisite for introducing breathalyzer results in evidence.[40]

Recent enactments, however, have extended legislative recognition to more controversial techniques — for example, polygraph,[41] hypnosis,[42] rape trauma syndrome,[43] and battered wife syndrome[44] evidence. Many of these techniques would not be subject to judicial notice because their validity is not indisputable.

The most important of these statutes deal with DNA evidence.[45] The DNA statutes vary widely. Interpreting the state DNA statute, the Maryland Court of

---

48 FORDHAM L. REV. 1138, 1149 n.76 (1980) (listing statutes). For a discussion of radar, *see* Chapter. 28.

36. *E.g.*, ARK. CODE. ANN. § 5-65-202 (Michie 1987); MD. CTS. & JUD. PROC. CODE ANN. § 10-302 to 307 (1988); OHIO REV. CODE ANN. § 4511.19 (Baldwin 1991); UTAH CODE ANN. § 41-6-44.3 (1987); UNIF. CHEMICAL TEST FOR INTOXICATION ACT, 9 U.L.A. 61 (Supp. 1967); UNIF. VEHICLE CODE § 11-902.2(a) (rev. ed. 1975). For a discussion of intoxication tests, *see* Chapter 22.

37. *E.g.*, ARK. CODE ANN. § 9-10-108 (Michie 1987) (paternity cases); NEV. REV. STAT. § 56.020 (1989) (criminal cases). *See also* UNIF. PARENTAGE ACT § 11 & 12(3), 9A U.L.A. 601 (1979) (paternity cases). For a discussion of blood tests, *see* Chapter 17.

38. *See also* People v. Williams, 164 Cal. App. 2d Supp. 858, 862, 331 P.2d 251, 254 (1958) (legislative recognition of Nalline test for narcotic use).

39. *But see* Izer v. State, 236 Ga. App. 282, 284, 511 S.E.2d 625, 628 (1999) ("[T]he inclusion of laser-based devices in the [statutory] definition of 'speed detection device,' without more, does not vitiate the state's burden of satisfying the requirements applicable to 'novel scientific evidence'").

40. *See Ex parte* Mayo, 652 So. 2d 201, 209 (Ala. 1994) (administrative rules concerning alcohol breath testing promulgated by Department of Public Health did not satisfy statute which required adoption by Department of Forensic Sciences); Commonwealth v. Barbeau, 411 Mass. 782, 785, 585 N.E.2d 1392, 1394 (1992). *See also* § 1-11(A) *infra* (proper working order requirement).

41. *E.g.*, CAL. EVID. CODE § 351.1 (West 1992) (polygraph admissible by stipulation); N.M. EVID. R. 707 (polygraph results admissible even without stipulation). For a discussion of polygraph evidence, *see* Chapter 8.

42. *E.g.*, CAL. EVID. CODE § 795 (West Supp. 1992); OR. REV. STAT. 136.675-.695 (1991). For a discussion of hypnosis, *see* Chapter 12.

43. *E.g.*, ILL. ANN. STAT. ch. 38, § 115-7.2 (Smith-Hurd 1992). For a discussion of RTS, *see* Chapter 9.

44. *E.g.*, MO. ANN. STAT. § 563.033 (1992); OHIO REV. CODE §§ 2901.06, 2945.39, 2945.392 (Anderson 1991). For a discussion of BWS, *see* Chapter 9.

45. *E.g.*,CONN. GEN. STAT. § 54-86k(a) (1994) (specifying that DNA testing is a reliable scientific technique and may be admitted in a criminal case); Ind. Code § 35-37-4-13 (1991); LA. REV. STAT. ANN. § 15:441.1 (West 1989); MD. CTS. & JUD. PROC. CODE ANN. § 10-915 (1991); MINN. STAT. § 634.25 (1992); TENN. CODE ANN. § 24-7-117(a) (1991); VA. CODE ANN. § 19.2-

Appeals ruled that the use of the phrase "is admissible to prove ... identity" meant that DNA evidence along with population statistics are automatically admissible:

> § 10-915 precludes generalized challenges to the admissibility of DNA evidence, except for constitutional challenges. It therefore eliminates both traditional *Frye-Reed* or "inverse *Frye-Reed*" hearings and individualized balancing of probative value against prejudicial effect. The statute does, however, permit case-specific challenges to the manner in which a particular test was conducted. Although these particularized challenges ordinarily will go to the weight of the evidence rather than its admissibility, the trial judge retains discretion to exclude evidence if it is so unreliable that it would not be helpful to the factfinder.[46]

The only condition the statute imposes on admissibility relates to the statute's discovery requirement.[47] In *State v. Begley*[48] the Tennessee Supreme Court ruled that the state's DNA statute was enacted "to ease the admissibility of DNA evidence in Tennessee." Consequently, DNA evidence was not subject to analysis under *Daubert*. The Virginia DNA statute has been interpreted to permit the trial court to balance probative value against prejudicial effect.[49]

In *Ex parte Turner*[50] the Alabama Supreme Court ruled that the state's DNA statute had superseded the "*Frye*-plus" test adopted in *Ex parte Perry*[51] and had substituted the *Daubert* reliability test in its place.

Constitutional Issues

The interpretation of these statutes may raise constitutional questions. For example, in *State v. Vega*[52] the Ohio Supreme Court held that once a scientific technique (intoxilyzer) has been legislatively recognized "an accused may not make a general attack upon the reliability and validity of the breath testing instrument."[53] This is wrong. It is one thing to legislate the admission of a certain

---

270.5 (Michie 1991); WASH. REV. CODE ANN. § 43.43.752 (West 1989). For a discussion of DNA evidence, *see* Chapter 17.

46. Armstead v. State, 342 Md. 38, 66, 673 A.2d 221, 235 (1996).

47. 673 A.2d at 229.

48. 956 S.W.2d 471, 476 (Tenn. 1997) ("McDaniel held that the pre-Rules of Evidence test of *Frye* ... was superseded by the adoption of Tennessee Rules of Evidence 702 and 703"; The Court also ruled that the PCR method as well as RFLP method came within the statute).

49. *See* VA. CODE ANN. § 19.2-270.5 (Michie 1995); Satcher v. Commonwealth, 244 Va. 220, 421 S.E.2d 821, 835 (1992), *cert. denied*, 507 U.S. 933 (1993).

50. 733 So. 2d 497 (Ala. 1998) (ALA. CODE § 36-18-30) .

51. 586 So. 2d 242 (Ala. 1991). *See* § 1-9 *infra* (*Frye-Daubert* "Plus").

52. 12 Ohio St. 3d 185, 465 N.E.2d 1303 (1984).

53. *Id.* at 190, 465 N.E.2d at 1308. *Accord* Columbus v. Day, 24 Ohio App. 3d 173, 174, 493 N.E.2d 1002, 1003 (1985).

category of evidence, it is quite another thing to preclude the accused from attacking such evidence.

Federal Rule 104(e) provides that a judge's ruling on admissibility does not limit the "right of a party to introduce before the jury evidence relevant to weight or credibility." In *Crane v. Kentucky*[54] the U.S. Supreme Court cited Rule 104(e) in holding that a trial judge's decision to admit a confession does not deprive an accused of the right to contest the reliability of the confession before the jury. According to the Court, a contrary rule deprives the accused of a fair trial: "Whether rooted directly in the Due Process Clause ... or in the Compulsory Process or Confrontation Clauses of the Sixth Amendment ..., the Constitution guarantees criminal defendants 'a meaningful opportunity to present a complete defense.'"[55] Several courts have accepted this argument.[56]

§ 1-4. Stipulations.

In some cases the validity of a scientific technique may be established by stipulation. For example, many courts have admitted polygraph evidence if the prosecution and defense stipulate prior to trial that the results of the polygraph examination are admissible.[57] As one court has noted:

> [T]he primary effect of the stipulation is that it operates as a waiver of objection or challenge to the validity of the basic theory of polygraph testing and eliminates the necessity of or the opportunity for the parties to establish a foundation in each case to satisfy the trial court of the basic theory and validity of polygraphs.[58]

§ 1-5. Expert Testimony: *Frye v. United States*.

A novel scientific technique is rarely so well established that a court would take judicial notice of its validity the first time evidence derived from the technique is offered at trial.[59] Accordingly, the validity of a new technique is

---

54. 476 U.S. 683 (1986).

55. *Id.* at 690 (quoting California v. Trombetta, 467 U.S. 479, 485 (1984)).

56. *E.g.,* Barcott v. Dept. of Public Safety, 741 P.2d 226, 228-29 (Alaska 1987); People v. Thompson, 215 Cal. App. 3d Supp. 7, 14, 265 Cal. Rptr. 105, 109 (1989); State v. Lowther, 740 P.2d 1017, 1021 (Haw. 1987). *See also* Imwinkelried & Scofield, *The Recognition of an Accused's Constitutional Right to Introduce Expert Testimony Attacking the Weight of Prosecution Science Evidence: The Antidote for the Supreme Court's Mistaken Assumption in* California v. Trombetta, 33 ARIZ. L. REV. 59 (1991).

57. For a discussion of polygraph stipulations, *see* § 8-4(C) *infra*.

58. State v. Dean, 103 Wis. 2d 228, 246, 307 N.W.2d 628, 637 (1981).

59. Although rare, it is possible for a court to take judicial notice of the validity of a new technique in a case of first impression. *See* United States v. Lopez, 328 F. Supp. 1077, 1085 (E.D.N.Y. 1971) (judicial notice of validity of magnetometer; expert testimony also received).

typically established through the introduction of evidence, including expert testimony. There are three different tests for determining the admissibility of innovative scientific evidence. One approach treats the validity of the underlying principle and the validity of the technique as aspects of relevancy. This relevancy approach is discussed in section 1-6. A second approach, known as the reliability test, is discussed in section 1-7. A third approach, which requires the proponent of a novel technique to establish its general acceptance in the scientific community, is based on *Frye v. United States*,[60] decided in 1923.

In *Frye* the D.C. Circuit considered the admissibility of polygraph evidence as a case of first impression. The court wrote:

> Just when a scientific principle or discovery crosses the line between the experimental and demonstrable stages is difficult to define. Somewhere in this twilight zone the evidential force of the principle must be recognized, and while the courts will go a long way in admitting expert testimony deduced from a well recognized scientific principle or discovery, the thing from which the deduction is made must be sufficiently established to have gained general acceptance in the particular field in which it belongs.[61]

The court went on to hold that the polygraph had "not yet gained such standing and scientific recognition among physiological and psychological authorities."[62] Thus, under the *Frye* standard, it is not enough that a qualified expert, or even several experts, testifies that a particular technique is valid. *Frye* imposes a special burden: the technique must be generally accepted by the relevant scientific community.

The *Frye* court, in its brief two-page opinion, neither cited authority nor offered an explanation for adopting the general acceptance test.[63] Nevertheless, the general acceptance standard became the majority rule[64] in both federal[65] and

---

60. 293 F. 1013 (D.C. Cir. 1923). For a discussion of facts of the *Frye* case, *see* Starrs, *A Still-Life Watercolor: Frye v. United States*, 27 J. FORENSIC SCI. 684 (1982).

61. 293 F. at 1014. *See* Moenssens, *Polygraph Test Results Meet Standards for Admissibility as Evidence, in* LEGAL ADMISSIBILITY OF THE POLYGRAPH 14, 15 (N. Ansley ed. 1975) (The general acceptance test is "probably the most widely quoted portion of any decision involving novel scientific test results").

62. 293 F. at 1014.

63. Unlike *Daubert*, *Frye* was rarely cited in civil cases. Moreover, it was rarely cited in the decades immediately after it was decided. *See* Loevinger, *Science As Evidence*, 35 JURIMETRICS J. 153, 157 n.19 (Winter 1995) (*Frye* cited 4 times from 1930-39, 2 times from 1940-49, 20 times from 1950-59, 21 times from 1960-69, 100 citations from 1970-79, 470 times from 1980-89, 350 times from 1990-93).

64. *See* United States v. Alexander, 526 F.2d 161, 163 n.3 (8th Cir. 1975) (The "federal courts of appeals continue to subscribe to [the] 'general scientific acceptability' criterion"); United States v. Skeens, 494 F.2d 1050, 1053 (D.C. Cir. 1974) (*Frye* "has been followed uniformly in this and other Circuits ..."); Reed v. State, 283 Md. 374, 382, 391 A.2d 364, 368 (1978) ("This criterion of

state courts[66] until 1993 when the U.S. Supreme Court rejected *Frye* in *Daubert v. Merrell Dow Pharmaceuticals, Inc.*[67] *Frye,* however, still retains significant support in a minority of states.[68] It is known as the *Kelly-Frye* rule in California,[69] *Reed-Frye* in Maryland,[70] and *Davis-Frye* in Michigan.[71]

In addition to polygraph evidence, the *Frye* test has been used to determine the admissibility of evidence derived from voiceprint analysis,[72] neutron activation

---

'general acceptance' in the scientific community has come to be the standard in almost all the courts in the country which have considered the question of the admissibility of scientific evidence").

65. *E.g.,* United States v. Gillespie, 852 F.2d 475, 481 (9th Cir. 1988) (play therapy with anatomically correct dolls); United States v. Christophe, 833 F.2d 1296, 1299 (9th Cir. 1987) (eyewitness identification); United States v. Sanchez, 829 F.2d 757, 759 (9th Cir. 1987) (forward-looking infrared device); United States v. Kozminski, 821 F.2d 1186, 1194-95 (6th Cir. 1987) ("captivity syndrome"), *aff'd,* 487 U.S. 931 (1988); United States v. St. Pierre, 812 F.2d 417, 420 (8th Cir. 1987) (sexual offender profile); United States v. Shorter, 809 F.2d 54, 59-61 (D.C. Cir.) (compulsive gambler), *cert. denied,* 484 U.S. 817 (1987); United States v. Carmel, 801 F.2d 997, 999 (7th Cir. 1986) (compulsive gambler); United States v. Metzger, 778 F.2d 1195, 1203 (6th Cir. 1985) (thin-layer chromatography of explosive residue), *cert. denied,* 477 U.S. 906 (1986); United States v. Smith, 776 F.2d 892, 898 (10th Cir. 1985) (Intoxilyzer); United States v. Distler, 671 F.2d 954, 961-62 (6th Cir.) (gas chromatograph/FID/FPD), *cert. denied,* 454 U.S. 827 (1981); United States v. Tranowski, 659 F.2d 750, 756 (7th Cir. 1981) (astronomical calculations); United States v. Hendershot, 614 F.2d 648, 654 (9th Cir. 1980) (shoeprint lifting technique); United States v. Kilgus, 571 F.2d 508, 510 (9th Cir. 1978) (Forward Looking Infrared System); United States v. Brown, 557 F.2d 541, 559 (6th Cir. 1977) (ion microprobic analysis); United States v. Bowers, 534 F.2d 186, 193 (9th Cir.) (tool mark identification), *cert. denied,* 429 U.S. 942 (1976); United States v. Fishman, 743 F. Supp. 713, 716 (N.D. Cal. 1990) (9th Circuit follows *Frye*).

66. *E.g.,* Adams v. State, 484 So. 2d 1160, 1162 (Ala. Crim. App. 1985) (Alabama follows *Frye*); Contreras v. State, 718 P.2d 129, 136 (Alaska 1986) (*Frye* survives enactment of Rules of Evidence); State v. Miller 202 Conn. 463, 484, 522 A.2d 249, 260 (1987) (Connecticut follows *Frye*); Ibn-Thomas v. United States, 407 A.2d 626, 637 (D.C. 1979) (battered wife syndrome), *aff'd,* 455 A.2d 893 (D.C. 1983); People v. Barbara, 400 Mich. 352, 404, 255 N.W.2d 171, 194 (1977) (polygraph); Alsbach v. Bader, 700 S.W.2d 823, 828 (Mo. 1985) (Missouri follows *Frye*); State v. Reynolds, 235 Neb. 662, 681, 457 N.W.2d 405, 418 (1990) (Nebraska follows *Frye* test)..

67. 509 U.S. 579 (1993). For a discussion of *Daubert, see* § 1-7 *infra* (reliability approach).

68. For a listing of *Frye* jurisdictions, *see* § 1-15 *infra.*

69. People v. Kelly, 17 Cal. 3d 24, 30-31, 549 P.2d 1240, 1244-45, 130 Cal. Rptr. 144, 148-49 (1976).

70. Reed v. State, 283 Md. 374, 381-82, 391 A.2d 364, 368 (1978). *See also* Goldstein v. State, 339 Md. 563, 573-74, 664 A.2d 375, 380-81 (1995) (principles underlying laser-based speed detection devices are generally accepted under *Reed/Frye* standard; *Frye* limited to theories and processes in general; no need for *Frye* hearing for every new device).

71. People v. Davis, 343 Mich. 348, 370, 72 N.W.2d 269 (1955).

72. *E.g.,* United States v. Smith, 869 F.2d 348, 351 (7th Cir. 1989); United States v. Addison, 498 F.2d 741, 743 (D.C. Cir. 1974); People v. Kelly, 17 Cal. 3d 24, 30-31, 549 P.2d 1240, 1244-45, 130 Cal. Rptr. 144, 148-49 (1976); Reed v. State, 283 Md. 374, 381-82, 391 A.2d 364, 368 (1978); People v. Tobey, 401 Mich. 141, 144, 257 N.W.2d 537, 538 (1977); Commonwealth v. Topa, 471 Pa. 223, 231, 369 A.2d 1277, 1281 (1977).

analysis,[73] gunshot residue tests,[74] fingerprints,[75] bite mark comparisons,[76] psycholinguistics,[77] truth serum,[78] scanning electron microscopic analysis,[79] hypnosis,[80] blood analysis,[81] hair analysis,[82] intoxication testing,[83] instrumental analysis,[84] and numerous other forensic techniques.[85]

---

73. *E.g.*, United States v. Stifel, 433 F.2d 431, 441 (6th Cir. 1970), *cert. denied,* 401 U.S. 994 (1971); State v. Coolidge, 109 N.H. 403, 421-22, 260 A.2d 547, 560 (1969), *rev'd on other grounds,* 403 U.S. 443 (1971); State v. Stout, 478 S.W.2d 368, 371 (Mo. 1972).

74. *See* State v. Smith, 50 Ohio App. 2d 183, 193, 362 N.E.2d 1239, 1246 (1976) (modified Harrison-Gilroy technique not generally accepted).

75. *E.g.*, People v. Eyler, 133 Ill. 2d 173, 211, 549 N.E.2d 268, 285-86 (1989) (fingerprint enhancing by superglue technique), *cert. denied,* 498 U.S. 881 (1990); State v. Hayden, 950 P.2d 1024 (Wash. App. 1998) (digitally enhanced evidence of latent fingerprints satisfies *Frye*).

76. *E.g.*, People v. Slone, 76 Cal. App. 3d 611, 623, 143 Cal. Rptr. 61, 68 (1978); People v. Milone, 43 Ill. App. 3d 385, 394-98, 356 N.E.2d 1350, 1356-60 (1976); State v. Sager, 600 S.W.2d 541, 573 (Mo. App.), *cert. denied,* 450 U.S. 910 (1980).

77. *See* United States v. Hearst, 412 F. Supp. 893, 895 (N.D. Cal. 1976), *aff'd on other grounds,* 563 F.2d 1331 (9th Cir. 1977), *cert. denied,* 435 U.S. 1000 (1978).

78. *E.g.*, United States v. Solomon, 753 F.2d 1522, 1526 (9th Cir. 1985); Lindsey v. United States, 237 F.2d 893, 896 (9th Cir. 1956); People v. Cox, 85 Mich. App. 314, 316-17, 271 N.W.2d 216, 217 (1978); State v. Sinnott, 24 N.J. 408, 423, 132 A.2d 298, 306 (1957); Henderson v. State, 94 Okla. Crim. 45, 52, 55, 230 P.2d 495, 502, 505, *cert. denied,* 342 U.S. 898 (1951). *See also* Ramona v. Superior Court, 57 Cal. App.4th. 107, 121, 66 Cal. Rptr. 2d 766, 776 (1997) ("[T]he use of sodium AMYTAL to retrieve repressed memories of child sexual molestation is a scientific technique or method which is subject to the *Kelly* requirements of reliability and acceptance by the relevant scientific community") (no general acceptance).

79. *See* People v. Palmer, 80 Cal. App. 3d 239, 252, 145 Cal. Rptr. 466, 472 (1978).

80. *E.g.*, State *ex rel.* Collins v. Superior Court, 132 Ariz. 180, 195-99, 644 P.2d 1266, 1281-85 (1982); People v. Shirley, 31 Cal. 3d 18, 51-54, 641 P.2d 775, 794-96, 181 Cal. Rptr. 243, 263-65, *cert. denied,* 459 U.S. 859 (1982); State v. Collins, 296 Md. 670, 702, 464 A.2d 1028, 1044 (1983); People v. Gonzales, 415 Mich. 615, 622-25, 329 N.W.2d 743, 745-47 (1982), *modified,* 417 Mich. 968, 336 N.W.2d 751 (1983); State v. Palmer, 210 Neb. 206, 218, 313 N.W.2d 648, 655 (1981); State v. Hurd, 86 N.J. 525, 536, 432 A.2d 86, 91 (1981); People v. Hughes, 59 N.Y.2d 523, 543, 453 N.E.2d 484, 494, 466 N.Y.S.2d 255, 265 (1983); Commonwealth v. Nazarovitch, 496 Pa. 97, 101, 436 A.2d 170, 172 (1981).

81. *E.g.*, People v. Morris, 53 Cal. 3d 152, 206-08, 807 P.2d 949, 981, 279 Cal. Rptr. 720, 751-52 (electrophoretic analysis of dried blood), *cert. denied,* 502 U.S. 959 (1991); Cramer v. Morrison, 88 Cal. App. 3d 873, 886, 153 Cal. Rptr. 865, 872-73 (1979) (HLA); Huntingdon v. Crowley, 64 Cal. 2d 647, 653, 656, 414 P.2d 382, 388, 390, 51 Cal. Rptr. 254, 260, 262 (1966) (Kell-Cellano blood grouping tests); State v. Washington, 229 Kan. 47, 53-55, 622 P.2d 986, 991-93 (1981) (multisystem blood testing); State v. Fenney, 448 N.W.2d 54, 57-58 (Minn. 1989); Rawlings v. State, 740 P.2d 153, 161 (Okla. Crim. 1987); People v. Young, 425 Mich. 470, 473-76, 391 N.W.2d 270, 271-72 (1986) (electrophoretic analysis of dry blood); Commonwealth v. Khamphouseane, 434 Pa. Super. 93, 97, 642 A.2d 490, 492 (1994) (Human Leukocyte Antigen (HLA) testing to establish paternity in a statutory rape case generally accepted), *app. denied*, 538 Pa. 666, 649 A.2d 669 (1994); State v. Adams, 418 N.W.2d 618, 620-21 (S.D. 1988). *See also* Note, *The Admissibility of Electrophoretic Methods of Genetic Marker Bloodstain Typing Under the Frye Standard,* 11 OKLA. CITY U. L. REV. 773 (1986).

82. *E.g.,* United States v. Brady, 595 F.2d 359, 363 (6th Cir.), *cert. denied,* 444 U.S. 862 (1979); People v. Watkins, 78 Mich. App. 89, 96, 259 N.W.2d 381, 385 (1977).

83. *E.g.,*Seewar v. Summerdale, 601 So. 2d 198, 200 (Ala. Crim. App. 1992) (Intoxilyzer 5000 generally accepted); Rivers v. Black, 259 Ala. 528, 531, 68 So. 2d 2, 4 (1953) (drunkometer); Ballard v. State, 955 P.2d 931, 938 (Alaska App. 1998) ("Of the courts that have resolved this issue, most have held that HGN evidence does not satisfy *Frye* if the HGN test results are introduced to establish that the person tested had a particular level of blood alcohol. However, these same courts hold the HGN evidence satisfies *Frye* if the HGN test results are admitted for the more modest purpose of indicating that the person has consumed alcohol and is potentially under the influence"); People v. Leahy, 8 Cal. 4th 587, 612, 882 P.2d 321, 334, 34 Cal. Rptr. 2d 663, 679 (1994) (Horizontal Gaze Nystagmus [HGN] must satisfy *Frye* test; remanded on this issue); Connecticut v. Merritt, 36 Conn. App. 76, 647 A.2d 1021, 1028 (1994) (HGN test must satisfy *Frye* test); People v. Hood, 265 Ill. App. 3d 232, 245, 638 N.E.2d 264, 274 (1994) (HGN satisfies *Frye*); State v. Witte, 251 Kan. 313, 836 P.2d 1110, 1121 (1992) ("HGN evidence requires a *Frye* foundation for admissibility"); Wilson v. State, 124 Md. App. 543, 723 A.2d 494 (1999) ("We clarify and reemphasize here that HGN *test results*, although satisfying *Frye* for limited purpose, *are inadmissible to estimate BAC in any manner*, including estimates of BAC over .10%"); Schultz v. State, 106 Md. App. 145, 150, 664 A.2d 60, 62 (1995) (HGN test generally accepted but evidence inadmissible because no foundation laid to show officer was qualified to administer the test and interpret its results); People v. Morse, 325 Mich. 270, 274, 38 N.W.2d 322, 324 (1949) (drunkometer); People v. Berger, 217 Mich. App. 213, 217, 551 N.W.2d 421, 423 (1996) (HGN generally accepted); State v. Klawitter, 518 N.W.2d 577, 585 (Minn. 1994) (HGN satisfies *Frye*); Montoya v. Metropolitan Court, 98 N.M. 616, 617, 651 P.2d 1260, 1261 (1982) (breath sample retesting); People v. Quinn, 153 Misc. 2d 139, 580 N.Y.S.2d 818, 826 (Cty. Ct. 1991) (Protocol used by "Drug Recognition Expert" satisfies *Frye* test; 12-step evaluation includes horizontal gaze nystagmus, one-leg stand test, finger-to-nose test); State v. Barker, 366 S.E.2d 642, 645 (W. Va. 1988) (HGN); State v. Helmer, 278 N.W.2d 808, 812 (S.D. 1979) (breathalyzer); State v. Canaday, 90 Wash. 2d 808, 814, 585 P.2d 1185, 1188 (1978) (breathalyzer ampoule retesting); State v. Cissne, 72 Wash. App. 677, 865 P.2d 564, 569 (1994) ("[T]he *Frye* standard applies to the admission of evidence based on HGN testing..."). *See generally* Honts & Amato-Henderson, *Horizontal Gaze Nystagmus Test: The State of the Science in 1995*, 71 N.D. L. REV. 671 (1995).

84. *E.g.,* Medley v. United States, 155 F.2d 857, 860 (D.C. Cir.) (spectroscopic analysis), *cert. denied,* 328 U.S. 873 (1946); United States v. Bruno, 333 F. Supp. 570, 574 (E.D. Pa. 1971) (chromatographic analysis of ink); Jones v. United States, 548 A.2d 35, 46 (D.C. 1988) (EMIT drug test); People v. Williams, 54 Cal. Rptr. 2d 521, 527 (1996) (segmentation [computer and mathematical enhancement] for photographic identification is generally accepted); Goldstein v. State, 339 Md. 563, 573-74, 664 A.2d 375, 380-81 (1995) (principles underlying laser-based speed detection devices are generally accepted under *Reed/Frye* standard; *Frye* limited to theories and processes in general; no need for *Frye* hearing for every new device); People v. Roraback, 662 N.Y.S.2d 327, 331 (A.D.) (Fourier Transform Infrared Spectrophotometer analysis of safe lining cement subject to *Frye*), *appeal. denied*, 691 N.E.(2d) 649 (N.Y.1977).

85. *E.g.,* United States v. Traficant, 566 F. Supp. 1046, 1047 (N.D. Ohio 1983) (psychological stress evaluation); People v. Ashmus, 54 Cal. 3d 932, 970-72, 820 P.2d 214, 233-35, 2 Cal. Rptr. 2d 112, 131-33 (1991) (electrophoretic analysis of dried semen stains), *cert. denied*, 506 U.S. 841 (1992); People v. Williams, 164 Cal. App. 2d Supp. 858, 860, 331 P.2d 251, 253 (1958) (Nalline test for narcotic use); People v. Acri, 277 Ill. App. 3d 1030, 1034, 662 N.E.2d 115, 117 (1996) ("There is no 'general acceptance' of the reliability of uncorroborated [canine] alerts in the field of arson investigation"); Cobey v. State, 73 Md. App. 233, 244, 533 A.2d 944, 950 (1987)

In addition, the general acceptance test has been employed in determining the admissibility of various aspects of DNA profiling, including RFLP,[86] PCR-DQA,[87] PCR-polymarkers,[88] STRs,[89] statistical probabilities,[90] and so forth.[91]

(chromosome variant analysis method of proving paternity), *cert. denied,* 312 Md. 127, 538 A.2d 778 (1988); People v. Wesley, 103 Mich. App. 240, 303 N.W.2d 194 (1981) (fingernail comparison); People v. Lauro, 91 Misc. 2d 706, 712, 398 N.Y.S.2d 503, 507 (1977) (trace metal detection technique).

86. *E.g.,* United States v. Two Bulls, 918 F.2d 56, 61 (8th Cir. 1990) (rejecting DNA evidence), *vacated after defendant's death,* 925 F.2d 1127 (8th Cir. 1991); United States v. Yee, 134 F.R.D. 161, 166 (N.D. Ohio 1991) (accepting DNA evidence); Brim v. State, 695 So. 2d 268 (Fla. 1997) ("It is clear that the DNA testing process consists of two distinct steps and that both steps must satisfy the requirements of *Frye*"); Commonwealth v. Curnin, 409 Mass. 218, 219, 565 N.E.2d 440, 441 (1991) (rejecting DNA evidence); People v. Wesley, 83 N.Y.2d 417, 424-25, 633 N.E.2d 451, 455-56, 611 N.Y.S.2d 97, 101-02 (1994) (Lifecodes DNA method generally accepted at time of trial (1988-89); record supports view that visual matching was accepted by the scientific community in 1988); State v. Ford, 301 S.C. 485, 392 S.E.2d 781 (1990) (accepting DNA evidence); State v. Cauthron, 120 Wash. 2d 879, 846 P.2d 502 (1993) (general scientific theory underlying forensic use of DNA identification evidence and the RFLP test were generally accepted in the relevant scientific communities). *See generally* Lander & Budowle, *DNA Fingerprinting Dispute Laid to Rest,* 371 NATURE 735 (1994).

87. *E.g.,* Harmon v. State, 908 P.2d 434, 440-41 (Alaska 1995) (both RFLP and PCR satisfy the *Frye* test; statistical analysis accompanying each form of DNA testing also generally accepted); State v. Tankersley, 191 Ariz. 359, 365, 956 P.2d 486, 492 (1998) ("PCR technology is generally accepted within the relevant scientific community for use on crime scene evidence. Furthermore, we observe that the DQ-alpha marker system is generally accepted means of distinguishing DNA"); Murray v. State, 692 So. 2d 157 (Fla. 1997) (DNA-PCR not generally accepted); State v. Hill, 257 Kan. 774, 785, 895 P.2d 1238, 1247 (1995) (DNA-PCR generally accepted); State v. Russell, 125 Wash. 2d 24, 54-55, 882 P.2d 747, 768 (1994) (PCR-DQA generally accepted; the Cetus kit is only one means of PCR testing and need not be shown to be generally accepted), *cert. denied,* 514 U.S. 1129 (1995).

88. *E.g.,* People v. Pope, 284 Ill. App. 3d 695, 672 N.E.2d 1321 (1996) (PCR-DQ alpha and polymarkers as well as statistics generally accepted), *cert. denied,* 171 Ill.2d 579, 677 N.E.2d 970 (1997); State v. Harvey, 151 N.J. 117, 169, 699 A.2d 596, 621 (1997) (DNA-polymarkers and dot-intensity analysis for mixed-blood sample admissible).

89. *E.g.,* People v. Allen, 72 Cal. App. 4th 1093, 85 Cal. Rptr. 2d 655 (1999) (STRs testing generally accepted).

90. *E.g.,* State v. Johnson, 186 Ariz. 329, 335, 922 P.2d 294, 300 (1996) (en banc) (modified ceiling principle generally accepted); State v. Sivri, 231 Conn. 115, 646 A.2d 169, 189-92 (1994) (while DNA generally accepted, case remanded to decide if population frequency calculations are generally accepted); Lindsey v. People, 892 P.2d 281 (Colo. 1995) (en banc) (DNA statistics generally accepted); People v. Miller, 173 Ill. 2d 167, 670 N.E.2d 721 (1996) (RFLP statistics), *cert. denied,* 520 U.S. 1157 (1997); State v. Colbert, 257 Kan. 896, 909, 896 P.2d 1089, 1097 (1995) (DNA statistics generally accepted); Keirsey v. State, 106 Md. App. 551, 575, 665 A.2d 700, 712 (Ct. Spec. App. 1995) (*Frye* does not apply to the "product rule" or the ceiling principle; both may be used to support statistical projection), *cert. denied,* 520 U.S. 1191 (1997); State v. Bloom, 516 N.W.2d 159, 167 (Minn. 1994) (interim ceiling method admissible); State v. Freeman, 253 Neb. 385, 405, 571 N.W.2d 276, 289 (1997) (DNA statistics admissible); State v. Vandebogart, 139 N.H. 145, 652 A.2d 671, 675 (1994) (interim ceiling principle satisfies *Frye* test); State v.

Frye has also been applied to social science techniques such as the battered woman syndrome,[92] rape trauma syndrome,[93] child abuse accommodation syndrome,[94] profile evidence,[95] psychiatric evidence,[96] and the like.[97]

The next sections focus on specific aspects of the *Frye* test.

§ 1-5(A). Rationale for the *Frye* Test.

The principal justification for the general acceptance standard is that it tends to ensure the reliability of scientific evidence. The D.C. Circuit has stated: "The requirement of general acceptance in the scientific community assures that those

---

Marcus, 294 N.J. Super. 267, 287, 683 A.2d 221, 231 (App. Div. 1996) ("product rule in DNA analysis is generally accepted"), *cert. denied,* 724 A.2d 803 (N.J. 1997); Commonwealth v. Blasioli, 552 Pa. 149, 167, 713 A.2d 1117, 1127(1998) ("[T]he product rule has gained general acceptance across the disciplines of population genetics, human genetics and population demographics"); State v. Copeland, 130 Wash. 2d 244, 922 P.2d 1304 (1996) (en banc) (product rule generally accepted); State v. Buckner, 125 Wash. 2d 915, 918, 890 P.2d 460, 462 (1995) (en banc) (ceiling principle generally accepted, but testimony that only one Caucasian in 19.25 billion (4 times the present population of the Earth) inadmissible).

91. *E.g.,* State v. Harvey, 151 N.J. 117, 169, 699 A.2d 596, 621 (1997) (DNA-polymarkers and dot-intensity analysis for mixed-blood sample admissible) ("In criminal cases we continue to apply the general acceptance or *Frye* test for determining the scientific reliability of expert testimony").

92. *E.g.,* State v. Riker, 123 Wash. 2d 351, 869 P.2d 43, 48-50 (1994) (en banc) (BWS generally accepted but only in a long-term relationship).

93. *E.g.,* Spencer v. General Elec. Co., 688 F. Supp. 1072, 1076 (E.D. Va. 1988), *aff'd,* 894 F.2d 651 (4th Cir. 1990); State v. Marks, 231 Kan. 645, 654, 647 P.2d 1292, 1299 (1982).

94. *E.g.,*Hadden v. State, 690 So. 2d 573 (Fla. 1997) (CSAAS not generally accepted as a diagnostic tool).

95. *E.g.,* State v. Hardwick, 905 P.2d 1384, 1388 (Ariz. App. 1995) (child molester profile not generally accepted); State v. Cavallo, 88 N.J. 508, 517, 443 A.2d 1020, 1024 (1982) (psychological profile of rapist not generally accepted).

96. *E.g.,* United States v. Lewellyn, 723 F.2d 615, 619 (8th Cir. 1983); Hughes v. Mathews, 576 F.2d 1250, 1258 (7th Cir.) , *cert. denied,* 439 U.S. 801 (1978).

97. *E.g.,* People v. Lowitzki, 285 Ill. App. 3d 770, 674 N.E.2d 859 (1996) (pathological gambling), *cert. denied,* 679 N.E.2d 383 (1997); Staggs v. Commonwealth, 877 S.W.2d 604, 606 (Ky. 1993) (use of art therapy to conclude that child had been sexually abused by her father fails *Frye* test); People v. Wernick, 89 N.Y.2d 111, 674 N.E.2d 322, 651 N.Y.S.2d 392 (1996) (neonaticide syndrome not generally accepted).

Some commentators have argued that *Frye* should be applied to expert prediction testimony of dangerousness in capital cases. Note, *People v. Murtishaw: Applying the Frye Test to Psychiatric Predictions of Dangerousness in Capital Cases*, 70 CALIF. L. REV. 1069, 1084-90 (1982). *See also* Dix, *Expert Prediction Testimony in Capital Sentencing: Evidentiary and Constitutional Considerations*, 19 AM. CRIM. L. REV. 1, 12-15 (1981). In Barefoot v. Estelle, 463 U.S. 880 (1983), the Supreme Court upheld the constitutionality of admitting such testimony.

most qualified to assess the general validity of a scientific method will have a determinative voice."[98] The Washington Supreme Court stated it this way:

> Where novel scientific evidence is at issue, the additional *Frye* inquiry allows the judiciary to defer to the scientists precisely where to do so recognizes both the need for admissibility of novel scientific evidence where it is sufficiently accepted, and the need to protect against novel scientific evidence which has not even gained general acceptance in the relevant field. The trial court's gatekeeper role under *Frye* involves by design a conservative approach, requiring careful assessment of the general acceptance of the theory and methodology of novel science, thus helping to ensure, among other things, that "pseudoscience" is kept out of the courtroom.[99]

Other rationales have also been offered in support of *Frye*. First, this test guarantees that "a minimal reserve of experts exists who can critically examine the validity of a scientific determination in a particular case."[100] Second, the *Frye* test "may well promote a degree of uniformity of decision. Individual judges whose particular conclusions may differ regarding the reliability of particular scientific evidence, may discover substantial agreement and consensus in the scientific community."[101] Third, "[w]ithout the *Frye* test or something similar, the reliability of an experimental scientific technique is likely to become a central issue in each trial in which it is introduced, as long as there remains serious disagreement in the scientific community over its reliability. Again and again, the examination and cross-examination of expert witnesses will be protracted and time consuming ... and proceedings may well degenerate into trials of the technique itself."[102]

§ 1-5(B). Application of the *Frye* Test.

The general acceptance test requires a two-step analysis: first, identifying the field in which the underlying principle falls,[103] and second, determining whether

---

98. United States v. Addison, 498 F.2d 741, 743-44 (D.C. Cir. 1974). *See also* People v. Barbara, 400 Mich. 352, 405, 255 N.W.2d 171, 194 (1977) ("It therefore is best to adhere to a standard [*Frye*] which in effect permits the experts who know most about a procedure to experiment and to study it. In effect, they form a kind of technical jury, which must first pass on the scientific status of a procedure before the lay jury utilizes it in making its findings of fact").

99. State v. Copeland, 130 Wash. 2d 244, 259, 922 P.2d 1304, 1314 (1996) (en banc).

100. United States v. Addison, 498 F.2d 741, 744 (D.C. Cir. 1974).

101. People v. Kelly, 17 Cal. 3d 24, 31, 549 P.2d 1240, 1244-45, 130 Cal. Rptr. 144, 148-49 (1976).

102. Reed v. State, 283 Md. 374, 388, 391 A.2d 364, 371-72 (1978).

103. *See* People v. Collins, 94 Misc. 2d 704, 708, 405 N.Y.S.2d 365, 368 (Sup. Ct. 1978) ("At the threshold of determining whether the technique meets the test of acceptance in the scientific

that principle has been generally accepted by members of the identified field. Because neither step is free of difficulties, commentators have called the *Frye* test "remarkably vague,"[104] "undefinable,"[105] and "not enlightening."[106] In addition, the applicability of *Frye* to non-novel scientific evidence is an issue.[107]

Selection of the Proper Field

Many scientific techniques do not fall within the domain of a single academic discipline or professional field. Consequently, selecting the proper field may prove troublesome. Voiceprint,[108] polygraph,[109] bite mark,[110] psycholinguistic,[111] DNA,[112] and remote sensing evidence[113] all illustrate this problem. The problem is further compounded because the selection of the appropriate field will often affect whether a novel technique satisfies the general acceptance test. As the Second Circuit remarked: "Selection of the 'relevant scientific community' appears to influence the result."[114]

---

community, is the question of defining that community"); State v. Jones, 130 Wash. 2d 302, 307, 922 P.2d 806, 809 (1996) (en banc) ("The relevant inquiry, however, is acceptance by scientists, not by the courts or legal commentators").

104. 22 C. Wright & K. Graham, *supra* note 26, at 87. *See also* 1 D. Louisell & C. Mueller, Federal Evidence 821 (1977).

105. Strong, *supra* note 10, at 14.

106. C. McCormick, Evidence 490 (2d ed. 1972).

107. *See* § 1-5(D) *infra*.

108. *See* People v. King, 266 Cal. App. 2d 437, 456, 72 Cal. Rptr. 478, 490 (1968) ("Communication by speech does not fall within any one established category of science. Its understanding requires a knowledge of anatomy, physiology, physics, psychology and linguistics").

109. *See* Moenssens, *supra* note 61, at 17-18 ("*Frye,* rather arbitrarily, relegates the polygraph to the discipline of psychology, a field in which it has unquestionably great application, but which is not necessarily the only field concerned or the best to develop the process"); Note, *The Emergence of the Polygraph at Trial*, 73 Colum. L. Rev. 1120, 1123 (1973).

110. *Compare* People v. Milone, 43 Ill. App. 3d 385, 395, 356 N.E.2d 1350, 1357 (1976) (citing the "medical profession" as the relevant field), *with* People v. Slone, 76 Cal. App. 3d 611, 625, 143 Cal. Rptr. 61, 69 (1978) (citing "dentistry" as the relevant field).

111. *See* Comment, *Stylistics Evidence in the Trial of Patricia Hearst*, 1977 Ariz. St. L.J. 387, 399 ("[A] discipline such as stylistics contains elements from many established sciences such as mathematics, computer science, psychology, and linguistics...").

112. Note, *The Admissibility of DNA Typing: A New Methodology*, 79 Geo. L.J. 313, 319 (1990) (Relevant fields for DNA "could include molecular biology, genetics, environmental biology, physical anthropology, evolutionary biology, population genetics, and statistics").

113. *See* Latin, Tannehill & White, *supra* note 1, at 1368 ("Remote sensing ... is not a self-contained or easily recognizable discipline if evaluated in terms of the formal academic training of its proponents").

114. United States v. Williams, 583 F.2d 1194, 1198 (2d Cir. 1978), *cert. denied,* 439 U.S. 1117 (1979).

One of the leading cases defining the relevant field for the purpose of applying the *Frye* test is *People v. Williams*,[115] in which the validity of the Nalline test for detecting narcotic use was considered.[116] Because the prosecution's own experts conceded that the "medical profession generally [was] unfamiliar with the use of Nalline,"[117] the technique could not have satisfied the *Frye* test if the medical profession had been selected as the appropriate field. Nevertheless, the court upheld the admissibility of the evidence because the test had been "generally accepted by those who would be expected to be familiar with its use."[118] So long as the subfield is sufficiently large that the *Frye* objective of obtaining a consensus judgment of the scientific community can be met, the *Williams* approach is not inconsistent with *Frye*. If, however, the field is defined too narrowly or knowledgeable experts are excluded from the field, this approach undercuts the rationale for the *Frye* test.[119]

Degree of Acceptance

Once the relevant field has been identified, it becomes necessary to determine whether the technique has been "generally accepted" by members of that field. The percentage of those in the field who must accept the technique has never been clearly delineated. For example, one court has defined general acceptance as "widespread; prevalent; extensive though not universal."[120] Another court has conceded that "a degree of scientific divergence of view is inevitable,"[121] without elaborating on how much divergence would be dispositive.[122] As one commentator has remarked: "The resulting standard, something greater than

115. 164 Cal. App. 2d Supp. 858, 331 P.2d 251 (1958).

116. Dilation of the pupils after the injection of Nalline indicates the recent use of narcotics. *Id.* at 860, 331 P.2d at 252-53.

117. *Id.* at 862, 331 P.2d at 253.

118. *Id.*, 331 P.2d at 254. This approach was adopted by a number of courts. *See* Hodo v. Superior Court, 30 Cal. App. 3d 778, 790-91, 106 Cal. Rptr. 547, 554 (1973); Commonwealth v. Lykus, 367 Mass. 191, 203, 327 N.E.2d 671, 677-78 (1975); People v. Rogers, 86 Misc. 2d 868, 881, 385 N.Y.S.2d 228, 237 (Sup. Ct. 1976).

119. *See* Reed v. State, 283 Md. 374, 399, 391 A.2d 364, 377 (1978) ("The purpose of the *Frye* test is defeated by an approach which allows a court to ignore the informed opinions of a substantial segment of the scientific community which stands in opposition to the process in question"); Giannelli, *supra* note 3, at 1210.

120. United States v. Zeiger, 350 F. Supp. 685, 688 (D.D.C.), *rev'd*, 475 F.2d 1280 (D.C. Cir. 1972).

121. Commonwealth v. Lykus, 367 Mass. 191, 204 n.6, 327 N.E.2d 671, 678 n.6 (1975).

122. Some courts apply a "substantial acceptance" test. *See* United States v. Williams, 443 F. Supp. 269, 273 (S.D.N.Y. 1977) (acceptance by a "substantial section of the scientific community"), *aff'd*, 583 F.2d 1194 (2d Cir. 1978), *cert. denied*, 439 U.S. 1117 (1979); Commonwealth v. Devlin, 365 Mass. 149, 153 n.3, 310 N.E.2d 353, 356 n.3 (1974) ("substantial authority" required).

acceptance by the expert himself but less than by all experts in the field, is obviously somewhat lacking in definiteness."[123] The California Supreme Court has provided the most definitive statement on this issue. According to that court, *Frye* is "met if use of the technique is supported by a clear majority of the members of [the scientific] community."[124]

Multi-step Procedures

An additional issue arises in multiple-step procedures, such as DNA profiling which consists of a molecular biology component (declaring a match) and a population genetics component (statistical calculations). In *Murray v. State,*[125] the Florida Supreme Court ruled that both components are subject to the *Frye* test. Similarly, the Arizona Supreme Court has sated: "Arizona's application of *Frye* has historically required general acceptance of both a scientific principle and the technique applying it. ... In the present case, PCR amplification and DQ-alpha testing must each be generally accepted as capable of producing valid, reliable results."[126]

New Developments

A related issue concerns subsequent developments or variants of a technique. For example, the general acceptance of stationary radar should not automatically lead to the admissibility of moving radar.[127] Similarly, general acceptance of RFLP(DNA) does not mean that PCR(DNA), or a particular type of PCR such as DQalpha, polymarkers, or D1S80,[128] is necessarily admissible. At some point,

---

123. Strong, *supra* note 10, at 11.

124. People v. Guerra, 37 Cal. 3d 385, 418, 690 P.2d 635, 656, 208 Cal. Rptr. 162, 183 (1984). *See also* State v. Marcus, 294 N.J. Super. 267, 287, 683 A.2d 221, 231 (App. Div. 1996) ("For scientific evidence to be admissible, we only require that the scientific technique or procedure be accepted as scientifically reliable, not that it produce results which are beyond all legitimate debate"), *cert. denied,* 724 A.2d 803 (N.J. 1997).

125. 692 So. 2d 157, 163 (Fla. 1997) ("[T]he techniques and methods utilized in both steps of the DNA testing process must satisfy the *Frye* test"). *See also* Brim v. State, 695 So. 2d 268, 270 (Fla. 1997) ("It is clear that the DNA testing process consists of two distinct steps and that both steps must satisfy the requirements of *Frye*").

126. State v. Tankersley, 191 Ariz. 359, 364-65, 956 P.2d 486, 491-92(1998) (PCR-DQA admitted).

127. *See* State v. Doles, 70 Ohio App. 2d 35, 38, 433 N.E.2d 1290, 1292 (1980) (moving radar device not subject to judicial notice); Seattle v. Peterson, 39 Wash. App. 524, 528, 693 P.2d 757, 759 (1985) (CMI radar not subject to judicial notice); State v. Hanson, 85 Wis. 2d 233, 244, 270 N.W.2d 212, 217 (1978) (moving radar not subject to judicial notice).

128. *See* text accompanying notes 86-91 *supra.*

however, the new developments may become rather unimportant.[129] Nevertheless, establishing the general acceptance of such refinements should also not be difficult or burdensome.

§ 1-5(C). Acceptance of the Theory.

Whether the proponent of novel scientific evidence must establish general acceptance of both the underlying theory as well as the technique applying that theory remains uncertain.[130] Although a number of cases refer to general acceptance of the "procedure,"[131] "technology,"[132] or "scientific technique,"[133] some commentators[134] and courts appear to require that the underlying theory also be generally accepted. For example, the D.C. Circuit has stated, "The *Frye* standard ... requires that the '[theory] from which the deduction is made be sufficiently established to have gained general acceptance in the particular field in which it belongs.'"[135] This approach would present problems for a technique that has been validated empirically, but whose underlying theory has not been established or understood completely. With such techniques, there may be no general acceptance of the underlying theory.

Empirical validation should be recognized as an acceptable method of establishing the validity of a new technique.[136] Many techniques, such as

---

129. *See* State v. Russell, 125 Wash. 2d 24, 54-55, 882 P.2d 747, 768 (1994) (PCR-DQA generally accepted; the Cetus kit is only one means of PCR testing and need not be shown to be generally accepted), *cert. denied,* 514 U.S. 1129 (1995).

130. *But see* Commonwealth v. Blasioli, 552 Pa. 149, 153, 713 A.2d 1117, 1119 (1998) ("This Court has generally required that both the theory and technique underlying novel scientific evidence must be generally accepted").

131. People v. Law, 40 Cal. App. 3d 69, 84, 114 Cal. Rptr. 708, 718 (1974).

132. United States v. Stifel, 433 F.2d 431, 438 (6th Cir. 1970), *cert. denied,* 401 U.S. 994 (1971).

133. Reed v. State, 283 Md. 374, 385, 391 A.2d 364, 370 (1978).

134. *See* National Academy of Sciences, On the Theory and Practice of Voice Identification 41 (1970) ("The language of *Frye* seems to require acceptance of the underlying theory and not just of the technique itself"); 22 C. Wright & K. Graham, *supra* note 26, at 95 ("As in *Frye,* the decisions turn on the scientific acceptance of the theory ...").

135. United States v. Addison, 498 F.2d 741, 743 (D.C. Cir. 1974) (brackets in original). *See also* United States v. Alexander, 526 F.2d 161, 163 n.3 (8th Cir. 1975) (*Frye* requires "general acceptance in the relevant scientific community of the theory underlying such technique").

136. *See* 22 C. Wright & K. Graham, *supra* note 26, at 95 ("It would be rational to rely upon a scientific device to determine deception if experiments proved that it worked, even though there was a dispute about why it worked"); Tarlow, *Admissibility of Polygraph Evidence in 1975: An Aid in Determining Credibility in a Perjury Plagued System,* 26 Hastings L.J. 917, 922 (1975) ("[T]here does not appear to be general scientific acceptance of a theory to explain all the phenomenon of aspirin. But even though aspirin's theoretical underpinnings may never be elucidated to the satisfaction of the scientific community, the fact is that it works. So does the polygraph").

fingerprint identification, have gained admissibility in this way. Empirical validation, however, raises additional questions. First, how much empirical research is sufficient? Many courts[137] believed the two-year voiceprint study sponsored by the Law Enforcement Assistance Administration[138] was sufficient validation of that technique. The National Academy of Sciences report on voiceprints,[139] however, casts doubt on that assumption. Second, "how much extrapolation to untested situations should be permitted?"[140] For example, the original voiceprint study was based on undisguised male voices. Is that research sufficient validation for the application of the technique to disguised voices or female voices?[141]

§ 1-5(D). Non-Novel Scientific Techniques.

Jurisdictions that follow *Frye* do not necessarily apply the general acceptance test to all types of "scientific" evidence. For example, in *People v. Marx*,[142] a California appellate court avoided applying the *Frye* test to bitemark comparisons. According to the court, the *Frye* test "finds its rational basis in the degree to which the trier of fact must accept, on faith, scientific hypotheses not capable of proof or disproof in court and not even generally accepted outside the courtroom."[143] The court went on to hold that bite mark evidence did not involve blind acceptance by the jury. The basis on which the expert reached his conclusions — models, photographs, and X-rays — were shown to the trier of fact, and the expert's conclusions were verifiable by the court. Thus, the "court did not have to sacrifice its independence and common sense in evaluating" the evidence.[144]

Similarly, the Arizona Supreme Court has ruled that the "*Frye* analysis is not applicable to footprint [comparisons]."[145] Other examples involve taggants in

---

137. *E.g.*, United States v. Williams, 583 F.2d 1194 (2d Cir. 1978), *cert. denied*, 439 U.S. 1117 (1979); United States v. Baller, 519 F.2d 463 (4th Cir.), *cert. denied*, 423 U.S. 1019 (1975); Commonwealth v. Lykus, 367 Mass. 191, 327 N.E.2d 671 (1975).

138. MICHIGAN STATE POLICE, VOICE IDENTIFICATION RESEARCH (1972). For a discussion of voiceprints, *see* Chapter 10.

139. NATIONAL ACADEMY OF SCIENCES, *supra* note 134.

140. *Id.* at 43.

141. *See* State *ex rel.* Trimble v. Hedman, 291 Minn. 442, 458, 192 N.W.2d 432, 441 (1971) (voiceprint identification of female voice upheld); People v. Law, 40 Cal. App. 3d 69, 84-85, 114 Cal. Rptr. 708, 718 (1974) (identification of disguised voice excluded).

142. 54 Cal. App. 3d 100, 126 Cal. Rptr. 350 (1975).

143. *Id.* at 110, 126 Cal. Rptr. at 355-56.

144. *Id.* at 111, 126 Cal. Rptr. at 356.

145. State v. Murray, 184 Ariz. 9, 906 P.2d 542, 562 (1995) (en banc), *cert. denied*, 518 U.S. 1011 (1996).

explosives,[146] tracking dogs,[147] narcotic detection dogs,[148] use of x-rays to identify remains,[149] and the like.[150]

§ 1-5(E). Methods of Establishing General Acceptance.

The offering party has the burden of establishing general acceptance,[151] which "can be an elusive premise to prove."[152] Determining general acceptance usually involves the presentation of expert testimony, consideration of scientific and legal literature, and other judicial opinions.

Typically, the general acceptance of a scientific technique is established through expert testimony; the testimony usually encompasses both the validity of the technique and its general acceptance in the scientific community. Several courts, however, have imposed additional requirements. First, some courts have required corroboration of expert testimony with regard to a novel technique's general acceptance. In rejecting voiceprint evidence, the California Supreme Court questioned "whether the testimony of a single witness alone is ever sufficient to represent, or attest to, the views of an entire scientific community regarding the reliability of a new technique."[153] Similarly, the Pennsylvania

146. *See* United States v. McFillin, 713 F.2d 57, 60 (4th Cir. 1981) (identification of color-coded "taggants" in explosive not a novel scientific technique).

147. *See* State v. Roscoe, 145 Ariz. 212, 700 P.2d 1312, 1319 (1984) (*Frye* does not apply to dog tracking evidence).

148. *See* People v. Sommer, 12 Cal. App. 4th 1642, 16 Cal. Rptr. 2d 165, 173 (1993) (narcotic detection dog not subject to *Frye* test); People v. Brooks, 950 P.2d 649, 652 (Colo. App. 1997) (*Frye* does not apply to dog-tracking evidence; such evidence "does not involve seemingly infallible scientific devices, processes, or theories. Likewise, it does not involved the manipulation of physical evidence with a scientific instrument or require obscure technical or scientific jargon"); People v. Roraback, 662 N.Y.S.2d 327, 331 (A.D. 1997) ("[T]here is no scientific principle or procedure at issue here. The use of a trained canine is an investigative rather than a scientific procedure. Thus, a *Frye* hearing was unnecessary ...") (internal citations omitted).

149. *See* Commonwealth v. Devlin, 365 Mass. 149, 154-55, 310 N.E.2d 353, 357 (1974) (identification of skeletal remains by x-ray comparison); People v. Powell, 97 Mich. App. 287, 291-94, 294 N.W.2d 262, 265 (1980) (torso identification by x-ray comparison).

150. *See Ex parte* Dolvin, 391 So. 2d 677, 679 (Ala. 1980) (*Frye* does not apply to comparison of skeletal remains with inter vivos photographs); Williams v. State, 710 So. 2d 24, 32 (Fla. App.) ("[B]ecause the general portion of the DRE [Drug Recognition Evaluation] protocol is not scientific, and because the use of the HGN test to establish the presence of alcohol has already gained general acceptance in the scientific community ... *Frye* is inapplicable"), *rev. denied,* 725 So. 2d 111 (1998).

151. Murray v. State, 692 So. 2d 157, 161 (Fla. 1997) (burden on proponent to prove general acceptance of both underlying scientific principle and testing procedures).

152. Windmere, Inc. v. International Ins. Co., 105 N.J. 373, 379, 522 A.2d 405, 408 (1987).

153. People v. Kelly, 17 Cal. 3d 24, 37, 549 P.2d 1240, 1248, 130 Cal. Rptr. 144, 152 (1976). *See also* People v. Leahy, 8 Cal. 4th 587, 609, 882 P.2d 321, 334, 34 Cal. Rptr. 2d 663, 676 (1994) ("[T]estimony by police officers regarding the mere *administration* of the [Horizontal Gaze Nystagmus] test is insufficient to meet the general acceptance standard...").

Supreme Court held that the "testimony of one expert ... cannot satisfy [the *Frye*] standard."[154]

Second, several courts have required that testimony of general acceptance be given by "impartial experts."[155] For example, the Michigan Supreme Court rejected voiceprint evidence because "the reputations and careers" of the experts who testified about the general acceptance of the technique were "built on their voiceprint work," and therefore they were not "disinterested and impartial."[156]

In addition to expert testimony, courts have relied upon scientific and legal publications when ascertaining the general acceptance of novel scientific techniques.[157] This represents a type of judicial notice. Courts using these publications are not judicially noticing the validity of the technique.[158] Instead, they are taking judicial notice of various publications, both legal and scientific, in determining whether general acceptance has been achieved.[159]

Finally, some courts have considered prior judicial decisions in determining whether general acceptance has been achieved.[160] Judicially noticing the testimony of experts reported in published opinions seems appropriate;[161] it is the equivalent of judicially noticing expert opinions in scientific journals. Some

---

154. Commonwealth v. Topa, 471 Pa. 223, 232, 369 A.2d 1277, 1282 (1977).

155. *See* State *ex rel.* Collins v. Superior Court, 132 Ariz. 180, 199, 644 P.2d 1266, 1285 (1982); People v. Kelly, 17 Cal. 3d 24, 38, 549 P.2d 1240, 1249, 130 Cal. Rptr. 144, 153 (1976) (questioning whether the leading proponent of voiceprints could "fairly and impartially ... assess the position of the scientific community").

156. People v. Tobey, 401 Mich. 141, 146, 257 N.W.2d 537, 539 (1977).

157. *E.g.,* United States v. Stifel, 433 F.2d 431, 441 (6th Cir. 1970), *cert. denied,* 401 U.S. 994 (1971); People v. Kelly, 17 Cal. 3d 24, 35-36, 549 P.2d 1240, 1247-48, 130 Cal. Rptr. 144, 151-52 (1976); Commonwealth v. Lykus, 367 Mass. 191, 199 n.3, 204, 327 N.E.2d 671, 676 n.3, 678 (1975); State v. Cavallo, 88 N.J. 508, 521, 443 A.2d 1020, 1026 (1982); Commonwealth v. Blasioli, 552 Pa. 149, 167, 713 A.2d 1117, 1126-27(1998) ("At the *Frye* hearing in this case, the Commonwealth presented evidence of general acceptance of the product rule in the relevant scientific disciplines. Such evidence included citation to numerous scientific texts and journals and the testimony of professors of human genetics and statistics from prominent universities").

158. For a discussion of judicial notice, *see* § 1-2 *supra.*

159. In some cases, general acceptance has been established solely by this means. *See* People v. Palmer, 80 Cal. App. 3d 239, 252-53, 145 Cal. Rptr. 466, 472-73 (1978) (scanning electron microscopic analysis). The problems associated with this approach are discussed in Giannelli, *supra* note 3, at 1217-18.

160. *E.g.,* People v. Palmer, 80 Cal. App. 3d 239, 252, 145 Cal. Rptr. 466, 472 (1978); Commonwealth v. Lykus, 367 Mass. 191, 204, 327 N.E.2d 671, 678 (1975); People v. Rogers, 86 Misc. 2d 868, 873, 385 N.Y.S.2d 228, 232 (Sup. Ct. 1976).

161. *See* People v. Kelly, 17 Cal. 3d 24, 34, 549 P.2d 1240, 1247, 130 Cal. Rptr. 144, 151 (1976) (citing expert's testimony in Hodo v. Superior Court, 30 Cal. App. 3d 778, 106 Cal. Rptr. 547 (1973)); Commonwealth v. Lykus, 367 Mass. 191, 199 n.3, 327 N.E.2d 671, 676 n.3 (1975) (citing expert's testimony in United States v. Addison, 498 F.2d 741 (D.C. Cir. 1974)); Commonwealth v. Topa, 471 Pa. 223, 230 n.2, 369 A.2d 1277, 1281 n.2 (1977) (citing expert's testimony in Worley v. State, 263 So. 2d 613 (Fla. App. 1972)).

cases, however, go beyond this practice; they "seem to adopt an approach to the *Frye* test that emphasizes previous court decisions, considering general acceptance not only by scientists but also by courts."[162] For example, one court concluded: "Thus it would appear that inasmuch as the admissibility of [voiceprint] evidence to identify voices has received general judicial recognition, it is no longer considered novel within the *Frye* test and consequently the test is inapplicable."[163] This use of prior judicial decisions undercuts the rationale supporting *Frye* — that those most qualified to judge the validity of a technique should have the determinative voice.[164]

§ 1-5(F). Scope of Appellate Review.

The courts are divided over the proper standard for reviewing a trial court's decision concerning the general acceptance test.[165] Some courts take the position that the "determination of 'general acceptance' is primarily a question of fact for the trial court subject to an appellate court's determination that the trial court has not abused its discretion."[166] The abuse of discretion standard has been criticized for contributing to the "essential vagueness" of the general acceptance standard.[167]

In contrast, other courts take the position that the general acceptance issue is a question of law, subject to de novo review on appeal.[168] This appears to have

---

162. NATIONAL ACADEMY OF SCIENCES, *supra* note 134, at 45.

163. United States v. Mavia, 728 F. Supp. 1471, 1478 (D. Haw. 1990).

164. *See* Giannelli, *supra* note 3, at 1218-19.

165. *See also* § 1-7(H) *infra* (scope of appellate review under *Daubert*).

166. People v. Marx, 54 Cal. App. 3d 100, 109, 126 Cal. Rptr. 350, 355 (1975). *Accord* Hodo v. Superior Court, 30 Cal. App. 3d 778, 784-85, 106 Cal. Rptr. 547, 550 (1973); People v. Miller, 173 Ill. 2d 167, 187, 670 N.E.2d 721, 731 (1996) ("The decision of whether to admit expert testimony about a new scientific technique is committed to the sound discretion of the trial court") (over strong dissent on this issue), *cert. denied*, 520 U.S. 1157 (1997).

167. 1 D. LOUISELL & C. MUELLER, FEDERAL EVIDENCE 821 (1977).

168. *See* State v. Johnson, 186 Ariz. 329, 334, 922 P.2d 294, 299 (1996) (en banc) ("Under *Frye*, this court conducts a de novo review to determine whether a scientific principle used as a basis for expert testimony is generally accepted in the relevant scientific community"); People v. Ashmus, 54 Cal. 3d 932, 971, 820 P.2d 214, 234, 2 Cal. Rptr. 2d 112, 132 (1992) ("On appeal, a *Kelly-Frye* ruling is reviewed independently"), *cert. denied*, 506 U.S. 841 (1992); People v. Law, 40 Cal. App. 3d 69, 74-75, 114 Cal. Rptr. 708, 711 (1974) ("Unquestionably, the trial court enjoys great latitude in determining the qualification of an expert.... While there have been some statements that the same amount of discretion rests in the trial court to determine whether a new scientific test or process has passed from the experimental into the demonstrable stage and has received general acceptance by recognized experts in the scientific field in which it belongs, ... there is a view that the latter issue is one of law ..."); Brim v. State, 695 So. 2d 268, 274 (Fla. 1997) ("[T]he standard of review in cases such as these should be de novo. This means that the trial judge's ruling will be reviewed as a matter of law rather than by an abuse-of-discretion standard");

been the view of the D.C. Circuit,[169] the progenitor of *Frye*. In support of this view, courts have pointed out that there is no reason to defer to a trial court in this context: "The answer to the question about the reliability of a scientific technique or process does not vary according to the circumstances of each case. It is therefore inappropriate to view this threshold question of reliability as a matter within each trial judge's individual discretion."[170] Moreover, the "abuse of discretion" standard would undercut one of the rationales supporting the general acceptance test, *i.e.*, uniformity of decision. The Washington Supreme Court explained the appellate court's role as follows:

> Review of admissibility under *Frye* is de novo and involves a mixed question of law and fact. The reviewing court will undertake a searching review which may extend beyond the record and involve consideration of scientific literature as well as secondary legal authority. A key reason for consideration of such material is that it is impractical in many instances for a true cross-section of scientists to testify at a hearing. Moreover, materials that are not available until after a *Frye* hearing may be considered.[171]

Time of General Acceptance

Another issue concerns the time at which general acceptance must be achieved. Some courts have held that general acceptance at the time of trial is determinative.[172] In contrast, other courts have ruled that general acceptance at the time of appeal is the critical time. According to the New Jersey Supreme Court,

---

Murray v. State, 692 So. 2d 157, 164 (Fla. 1997) ("Under the de novo standard of review we have in this area of law ...").

169. *See* United States v. Addison, 498 F.2d 741, 744 (D.C. Cir. 1974) ("neither the court's opinion nor the record satisfy the *Frye* standard of admissibility" as applied to voiceprint evidence); United States v. Zeiger, 475 F.2d 1280 (D.C. Cir. 1972) (per curiam) (holding polygraph evidence did not satisfy the *Frye* test), *rev'g* 350 F. Supp. 685, 692 (D.D.C. 1972).

170. Reed v. State, 283 Md. 374, 381, 391 A.2d 364, 367 (1978).

171. State v. Copeland, 130 Wash. 2d 244, 255-56, 922 P.2d 1304, 1312-13 (1996) (en banc) (citations omitted).

172. *E.g.*, Lindsey v. People, 892 P.2d 281, 290 n.25 (Colo. 1995) (*Frye* "requires nothing more than general acceptance at the time the evidence is admitted"); Commonwealth v. Blasioli, 552 Pa. 149, 167 n. 26, 713 A.2d 1117, 1127 n.26 (1998) (noting "a split among *Frye* jurisdictions as to whether the test should be applied to determine general agreement in the scientific community as of the time of trial or as of the time of appellate review. ... [W]e find the evidence in this case sufficient to establish general acceptance as of the time of trial"); People v. Wesley, 83 N.Y.2d 417, 424-25, 633 N.E.2d 451, 455-56, 611 N.Y.S.2d 97, 101-02 (1994) (Lifecodes DNA method generally accepted at time of trial (1988-89); record supports view that visual matching was accepted by the scientific community in 1988). *See also* United States v. Bonds, 12 F.3d 540, 552 (6th. Cir. 1993) ("We grant the Government's motion to strike the NRC Report because this report

> In the rapidly changing world of modern science, continuing research may affect the scientific community's acceptance of a novel technology. By reviewing post-trial publications, an appellate court can account for the rapid pace of new technology. The continuing review also recognizes that general acceptance may change between the time of trial and the time of appellate review.[173]

Another court stated it this way: "If the result obtained is the product of invalid scientific theory, there is no good reason to accept it simply because we were fooled at the inception of the inquiry."[174]

§ 1-5(G). Criticisms of the *Frye* Test.

Notwithstanding its widespread judicial adoption, an increasing number of courts have rejected the general acceptance test. Commentators also criticized the test as "infamous,"[175] "a sport,"[176] "archaic,"[177] and "antiquated on the day of its pronouncement."[178]

In addition to the criticisms concerning the difficulties of applying the *Frye* test discussed above, the test has been attacked on other grounds.[179] One criticism is that the general acceptance test is applied selectively.[180] Part of the problem involves defining what types of evidence should be classified as "scientific" for the purpose of applying *Frye*.[181] For example, in *State v. Hall*[182] the Iowa Supreme Court wrote:

---

was not available to the magistrate judge at the *Frye* hearing and was not before the magistrate judge or the district court judge when they ruled on the motions to suppress").

173. State v. Harvey, 151 N.J. 117, 168, 699 A.2d 596, 620 (1997) (DNA-polymarkers and dot-intensity analysis for mixed-blood sample admissible) ("In criminal cases we continue to apply the general acceptance or *Frye* test for determining the scientific reliability of expert testimony") (footnote omitted).

174. State v. Bible, 175 Ariz. 549, 586, 858 P.2d 1152, 1189 n.33 (1993), *cert. denied*, 511 U.S. 1046 (1994).

175. Tarlow, *supra* note 136, at 923.

176. 22 C. WRIGHT & K. GRAHAM, *supra* note 26, at 87.

177. Moenssens, *supra* note 61, at 19.

178. Conrad, *Landmarks and Hallmarks in Scientific Evidence*, *in* SOURCEBOOK IN CRIMINALISTICS 37, 38 (C. Hormachea ed. 1974).

179. *See also* § 1-7(I) *infra* (criticism of *Daubert* test).

180. *See* C. MCCORMICK, EVIDENCE 490 (2d ed. 1972) (*Frye* test "highly selective"); Boyce, *Judicial Recognition of Scientific Evidence in Criminal Cases*, 8 UTAH L. REV. 313, 314 (1964).

181. *See* 22 C. WRIGHT & K. GRAHAM, *supra* note 26, at 87 n.10 ("What is 'scientific evidence' to which the test applies? When a witness testifies that he saw the defendant throw a rock at the victim, the inferences to be drawn from this testimony involve a number of principles of physics, but few courts would apply the *Frye* test").

182. 297 N.W.2d 80 (Iowa 1980) (en banc), *cert. denied*, 450 U.S. 927 (1981).

> Despite [the *Frye* test's] apparent simplicity, distinguishing "scientific" evidence from other areas of expert testimony is a difficult determination in many instances .... The instant case illustrates this difficulty of classifying evidence as scientific or non-scientific. The defendant says the study of blood flight characteristics is itself a science. The witness, on the other hand, testified it was based primarily upon physics and mathematics, which impart accuracy and predictability to the study.[183]

Cases involving the admissibility of hypnotically refreshed testimony offer another illustration. Some courts have applied *Frye* in this context,[184] while other courts have held *Frye* inapplicable. According to the latter courts, *Frye* is limited to expert testimony and hypnotically-refreshed testimony involves lay witnesses.[185]

This definitional problem, however, cannot explain a number of other cases. For example, in *State v. Fields*[186] the Missouri Supreme Court upheld the admissibility of evidence based upon the paraffin test without referring to the *Frye* standard. According to the court, admission is permitted if the examiner is qualified, the test is conducted according to usual standards, and the opponent is provided an adequate opportunity to cross-examine the expert.[187] Several years later, the same court employed the *Frye* test in excluding the results of a blood examination by neutron activation analysis,[188] without explaining why activation analysis, but not the paraffin test, should be required to satisfy the more demanding *Frye* test.[189]

Another criticism of the general acceptance test is that it precludes the admission of reliable evidence. As two commentators have pointed out: "A literal reading of *Frye v. United States* would require that the courts always await the passing of a 'cultural lag' during which period the new method will have had sufficient time to diffuse through scientific discipline and create the requisite body of scientific opinion needed for acceptability."[190] Critics of *Frye* assert that this delay "precludes too much relevant evidence for purposes of the fact

---

183. *Id.* at 85. *See* People v. Sommer, 12 Cal. App. 4th 1642, 16 Cal. Rptr. 2d 165, 173 (1993) (narcotic detection dog not subject to *Frye* test).

184. *See* note 80 *supra.*

185. *See* United States v. Valdez, 722 F.2d 1196, 1201 (5th Cir. 1984); State v. Armstrong, 110 Wis. 2d 555, 568, 329 N.W.2d 386, 393, *cert. denied,* 461 U.S. 946 (1983).

186. 434 S.W.2d 507 (Mo. 1968).

187. *Id.* at 516.

188. State v. Stout, 478 S.W.2d 368, 371 (Mo. 1972).

189. For other examples of inconsistent application of *Frye, see* Giannelli, *supra* note 3, at 1219-21.

190. Maletskos & Spielman, *Introduction of New Scientific Methods in Court, in* LAW ENFORCEMENT, SCIENCE & TECHNOLOGY 957, 958 (S.A. Yefsky ed. 1967).

determining process."[191] In contrast, courts favoring the general acceptance test recognize its conservative nature but believe that this aspect does not involve an "unwarranted cost."[192] The California Supreme Court has gone further, stating that the "primary advantage ... of the *Frye* test lies in its essentially conservative nature."[193] The criticism that the *Frye* test is too conservative begs the question. The question is not whether the *Frye* test is conservative (which it is), but whether other standards will better accomplish the objective of preventing the admission of unreliable scientific evidence.

Still another criticism of *Frye* is that it rests upon an invalid assumption, *i.e.*, that jurors are overwhelmed by scientific evidence. For example, in excluding voiceprint evidence under the *Frye* test, the D.C. Circuit emphasized that scientific evidence may "assume a posture of mystic infallibility in the eyes of a jury of laymen."[194] Commentators, however, have argued that the available empirical research on jury reaction to different types of scientific evidence does not support the D.C. Circuit's assumption.[195]

The *Frye* test also has been criticized because it entrusts the validity issue to the scientific community: "In testing for admissibility of a particular type of scientific evidence, whatever the scientific 'voting' pattern may be, the courts cannot in any event surrender to scientists responsibility for determining the reliability of that evidence."[196] This criticism also begs the question. Under *Frye,* courts, not scientists, control the admissibility issue. A court created the *Frye* test, and courts continue to use it. Whether the courts should follow a test giving the scientific community such a "determinative voice" is another question. But proponents of *Frye* can argue that courts have not surrendered responsibility but rather have exercised that responsibility prudently by deferring to those best capable of judging the validity of scientific evidence.

---

191. United States v. Sample, 378 F. Supp. 44, 53 (E.D. Pa. 1974). *See also* Coppolino v. State, 223 So. 2d 68, 75 (Fla. App. 1968) (concurring opinion) ("Society need not tolerate homicide until there develops a body of medical literature about some particular lethal agent"), *app. dismissed,* 234 So. 2d 120 (Fla. 1969), *cert. denied,* 399 U.S. 927 (1970).

192. United States v. Addison, 498 F.2d 741, 743 (D.C. Cir. 1974).

193. People v. Kelly, 17 Cal. 3d 24, 31, 549 P.2d 1240, 1245, 130 Cal. Rptr. 144, 149 (1976). *See also* Reed v. State, 283 Md. 374, 385-86, 391 A.2d 364, 370 (1978).

194. United States v. Addison, 498 F.2d 741, 744 (D.C. Cir. 1974).

195. *See* Imwinkelried, *The Standard for Admitting Scientific Evidence: A Critique From the Perspective of Juror Psychology*, 28 VILL. L. REV. 554 (1983); Note, *The Frye Doctrine and Relevancy Approach Controversy: An Empirical Evaluation*, 74 GEO. L.J. 1769 (1986).

196. United States v. Williams, 583 F.2d 1194, 1198 (2d Cir. 1978), *cert. denied,* 439 U.S. 1117 (1979). *Accord* State v. Hall, 297 N.W.2d 80, 84-85 (Iowa 1980), *cert. denied,* 450 U.S. 927 (1981).

Finally, "[p]erhaps the most important flaw in the *Frye* test is that by focusing attention on the general acceptance issue, the test obscures critical problems in the use of a particular technique."[197]

§ 1-6. Expert Testimony: The Relevancy Approach.

One alternative approach to *Frye* is to treat scientific evidence in the same way as other evidence, weighing its probative value against countervailing dangers and considerations.[198] Professor McCormick advocated this position. In his 1954 text, he wrote:

> "General scientific acceptance" is a proper condition upon the court's taking judicial notice of scientific facts, but not a criterion for the admissibility of scientific evidence. Any relevant conclusions which are supported by a qualified expert witness should be received unless there are other reasons for exclusion. Particularly, its probative value may be overborne by the familiar dangers of prejudicing or misleading the jury, unfair surprise and undue consumption of time.[199]

As applied, this test often means that qualifying the expert automatically qualifies the technique. Such an approach provides an insufficient threshold standard for admissibility. "The major flaw in the relevancy analysis ... is its failure to recognize the distinctive problems of scientific evidence.... [T]he judge frequently is forced to defer to an expert, thereby permitting admissibility based on the views of a single individual in some cases."[200]

In 1993 the U.S. Supreme Court in *Daubert v. Merrell Dow Pharmaceuticals, Inc.*,[201] ruled that the Federal Rules of Evidence had displaced the *Frye* test. In its place the Court substituted a reliability test.[202] *Daubert* implicitly rejects the relevancy approach; the Supreme Court wrote: "[U]nder the Rules the trial judge must ensure that any and all scientific testimony or evidence admitted is not only relevant, but reliable."[203]

---

197. Giannelli, *supra* note 3, at 1226.

198. For a discussion of the origin of the relevancy approach, *see* Giannelli, *Daubert: Interpreting the Federal Rules of Evidence*, 15 CARDOZO L. REV. 1999 (1994).

199. C. MCCORMICK, EVIDENCE 363-64 (1954). For a discussion of McCormick's view, *see* Giannelli, *supra* note 3, at 1233-35.

200. Giannelli, *supra* note 3, at 1250. *Id.* at 1245 ("[I]t seems questionable whether the relevancy approach will adequately protect against the misuse of unreliable scientific evidence").

201. 509 U.S. 579 (1993).

202. The *Daubert* reliability test is discussed in § 1-7 *infra*.

203. 509 U.S. at 589.

Nevertheless, some jurisdictions have retained the relevancy approach. In *State v. Peters*[204] the Wisconsin Court of Appeals, in upholding the admissibility of DNA evidence, stated that Wisconsin follows neither *Frye* nor *Daubert*: "Once the relevancy of the evidence is established and the witness is qualified as an expert, the reliability of the evidence is a weight and credibility issue for the fact finder and any reliability challenges must be made through cross-examination or by other means of impeachment." Similarly, in *State v. Donner*,[205] an intoxication case, the same court wrote:

> [B]efore *Daubert*, the *Frye* test was not the law in Wisconsin. To that extent, Wisconsin law and *Daubert* coincide. Beyond that, Wisconsin law holds that "any relevant conclusions which are supported by a qualified witness should be received unless there are other reasons for exclusion." Stated otherwise, expert testimony is admissible in Wisconsin if relevant and will be excluded only if the testimony is superfluous or a waste of time.
>
> Assuming that *Daubert* in its application represents something beyond *Walstad*, we observe that we ... are bound to follow our supreme court case law.[206]

The relevancy approach requires a three-step analysis: first, ascertaining the probative value of the evidence; second, identifying any countervailing dangers or considerations; and third, balancing the probative value against the identified dangers or considerations.

Probative Value

The first step of the relevancy approach is to assess the probative value of the proffered evidence. Federal Rule 401 defines relevant evidence as "evidence having any tendency to make the existence of any fact that is of consequence to the determination of the action more probable or less probable than it would be without the evidence." The probative value of scientific evidence depends on its reliability,[207] and since most judges do not possess the scientific background to

---

204. 192 Wis. 2d 674, 534 N.W.2d 867 (App. 1995) (DNA admissible notwithstanding the absence of Native Americans from the database used to project the likelihood of a coincidental DNA match), *rev. denied*, 537 N.W.2d 572 (Wis. 1995).

205. 192 Wis. 2d 305, 531 N.W.2d 369 (App.), *rev. denied*, 534 N.W.2d 86 (Wis. 1995).

206. *Id.* at 316, 531 N.W.2d at 374 (internal citations omitted) (*quoting* State v. Walstad, 119 Wis. 2d 483, 518, 351 N.W.2d 469, 487 (1984)).

207. *See* United States v. Ridling, 350 F. Supp. 90, 94-95 (E.D. Mich. 1972) ("The acceptance of the basic theory [of the polygraph] is a part of the process of making the evidence relevant"); United States v. DeBetham, 348 F. Supp. 1377, 1384 (S.D. Cal. 1972) ("This is not to say the polygraph may escape all requirements of demonstrating its reliability, since that is an integral part of whatever probative value the technique may possess"), *aff'd*, 470 F.2d 1367 (9th Cir.), *cert. denied*, 412 U.S. 707 (1973); State v. Williams, 388 A.2d 500, 504 (Me. 1978) ("proffered evidence [voiceprints] is sufficiently reliable to be held relevant").

determine reliability, the trial judge is often forced to depend on expert testimony to ascertain probative value.[208]

Countervailing Dangers

The second step of the relevancy approach is to identify any countervailing dangers or considerations. Federal Rule 403 provides: "Although relevant, evidence may be excluded if its probative value is substantially outweighed by the danger of unfair prejudice, confusion of issues, or misleading the jury, or by considerations of undue delay, waste of time, or needless presentation of cumulative evidence." The principal danger of scientific evidence is its potential to mislead the jury; that is, such evidence may "assume a posture of mystic infallibility in the eyes of a jury of laymen."[209] Accordingly, "an exaggerated popular opinion of the accuracy of a particular technique [may make] its use prejudicial or likely to mislead the jury."[210] Similarly, a particular technique may pose the danger of misleading the jury because the jury will be required to rely totally on the expert's opinion, thus forcing it "to sacrifice its independence and common sense in evaluating [the evidence]."[211]

Balancing Probative Value Against Dangers

The final step of the relevancy approach is balancing the probative value against the identified dangers or other considerations. The balancing task under Federal Rule 403 permits exclusion of evidence only when the probative value is substantially outweighed by the identified dangers. Moreover, the standard of review on appeal is whether the trial court abused its discretion.[212] Some cases

---

208. *See* Strong, *supra* note 10, at 22 ("[I]n the case of scientific evidence the court will generally be forced to accept the probative value of the evidence as what a qualified expert testifies it to be ..."). *See also* State v. Dean, 103 Wis. 2d 228, 265, 307 N.W.2d 628, 646 (1981) (The "burden on the trial court to assess polygraph evidence may outweigh any probative value the polygraph evidence may have").

209. United States v. Addison, 498 F.2d 741, 744 (D.C. Cir. 1974). *See also* United States v. Alexander, 526 F.2d 161, 168 (8th Cir. 1975) ("When polygraph evidence is offered ..., it is likely to be shrouded with an aura of near infallibility, akin to the ancient oracle of Delphi"); People v. King, 266 Cal. App. 2d 437, 461, 72 Cal. Rptr. 478, 493 (1968) ("[J]urors must not be misled by an 'aura of certainty which often envelops a new scientific process, obscuring its currently experimental nature'").

210. United States v. Baller, 519 F.2d 463, 466 (4th Cir.), *cert. denied,* 423 U.S. 1019 (1975).

211. People v. Marx, 54 Cal. App. 3d 100, 110, 126 Cal. Rptr. 350, 356 (1975) ("[T]he trier of fact is required to rely on the testimony of the polygrapher, verified at most by marks on a graph, to which the expert's hypothesis gives some relevant meaning. Similar total reliance on the expert's assumptions is required for voice spectrogram"); State v. Hall, 297 N.W.2d 80, 86 (Iowa 1980) (blood flight characteristics) ("Such observations are largely based on common sense, and in fact, lie close to the ken of average laymen"), *cert. denied,* 450 U.S. 927 (1981).

212. *See* 22 C. Wright & K. Graham, *supra* note 26, at 309-10.

emphasize that an instruction alerting the jury to the potential dangers of misuse may be helpful if the trial court admits the evidence.[213]

§ 1-7. Expert Testimony: The Reliability (*Daubert*) Approach.

As noted earlier, the U.S. Supreme Court ruled in 1993 that the Federal Rules of Evidence displaced the *Frye* test.[214] The case, *Daubert v. Merrell Dow Pharmaceuticals, Inc.*,[215] involved the admissibility of expert testimony concerning whether Bendectin, an anti-nausea drug, causes birth defects. In place of *Frye,* the Court substituted a reliability test. Such a standard, in the Court's view, was derived from Rule 702, which uses the terms "scientific" and "knowledge."

> [I]n order to qualify as "scientific knowledge," an inference or assertion must be derived by the scientific method. Proposed testimony must be supported by appropriate validation — i.e., "good grounds," based on what is known. In short, the requirement that an expert's testimony pertain to "scientific knowledge" establishes a standard of evidentiary reliability.[216]

Although the *Daubert* decision resolved many issues, like most landmark cases, it left many questions unanswered. These issues are addressed in subsequent sections.

Novel Scientific Evidence

The *Daubert* Court commented that "[a]lthough the *Frye* decision itself focused exclusively on 'novel' scientific techniques, we do not read the requirements of Rule 702 to apply specially or exclusively to unconventional evidence."[217] Nevertheless, related issues arise—*i.e.*, whether the technique is

---

213. *See* United States v. Williams, 583 F.2d 1194, 1200 (2d Cir. 1978), *cert. denied,* 439 U.S. 1117 (1979); United States v. Baller, 519 F.2d 463, 467 (4th Cir.), *cert. denied,* 423 U.S. 1019 (1975). *But see* National Academy of Sciences, *supra* note 134, at 47 ("Such an instruction fails to assist the jurors in their task, but attempts to impress on them its importance"); State v. Dean, 103 Wis. 2d 228, 276-78, 307 N.W.2d 628, 652-53 (1981) (questioning effectiveness of instruction on polygraph evidence).

214. *See* § 1-5 *supra.*

215. 509 U.S. 579 (1993).

216. *Id.* at 590. *See also* United States v. Bush, 44 M.J. 646, 651-52 (A.F.C.M.R. 1996) ("If we may put *Daubert, Gipson,* and Mil. R. Evid. 702 in the vernacular, the judge's first responsibility is to filter from the trier of fact 'junk science.' ... In short, MS/MS hair analysis is a far cry from palmistry, phrenology or chicken guts, and clears the pseudoscience hurdle easily"), *aff'd*, 47 M.J. 305 (C.A.A.F. 1997), *cert. denied,* 118 S. Ct. 1048 (1998).

217. 509 U.S. at 593 n.11. *See also* State v. Torres, 976 P.2d 20, 30 (N.M. 1999) ("The better view ... is that the *Alberico-Daubert* standard is not limited to novel scientific theories. ... Indeed, in some contexts 'novelty' may be nothing more than an antonym for 'general acceptance.' For these

"scientific." In contrast to other courts, the Tennessee Supreme Court rejected the argument that police officer testimony concerning the horizontal gaze nystagmus test was not "scientific" because it involves only an officer's objective observations of the subject's physical characteristics. In the court's view, "the HGN test does differ fundamentally from other field sobriety tests because the witness must necessarily explain the underlying scientific basis of the test in order for the testimony to be meaningful to a jury."[218]

Science & Law

In *Daubert*, the Supreme Court addressed the overarching issue of the relationship between law and science, an issue raised in the numerous amici briefs.[219] The Court wrote:

> It is true that open debate is an essential part of both legal and scientific analyses. Yet there are important differences between the quest for truth in the courtroom and the quest for truth in the laboratory. Scientific conclusions are subject to perpetual revision. Law, on the other hand, must resolve disputes finally and quickly. The scientific project is advanced by broad and wide ranging consideration of a multitude of hypotheses, for those that are incorrect will eventually be shown to be so, and that in itself is an advance. Conjectures that are probably wrong are of little use, however, in the project of reaching a quick, final, and binding legal judgment — often of great consequence — about a particular set of events in the past.[220]

§ 1-7(A). Procedural Issues.

The *Daubert* standard raises many of the same procedural issues as does *Frye*.[221] Under the *Daubert* analysis, the trial court must make a preliminary determination of admissibility pursuant to Federal Rule 104(a).[222] This task

---

reasons, a finding that the scientific principles underlying HGN testing are generally accepted (or no longer a novelty) does not necessarily preclude consideration of other factors relevant to the *Alberico-Daubert* inquiry"); Hartman v. State, 946 S.W.2d 60, 63 (Tex. Crim. App. 1997) (intoxilizer) ("We ... see no value in having a different standard of admissibility for novel scientific evidence"). *See also* § 1-5(D) *supra* (application of *Frye* to non-novel scientific evidence).

218. State v. Murphy, 953 S.W.2d 200, 202 (Tenn. 1997).

219. *See* 509 U.S. at 598 (C.J. Rehnquist, dissenting in part) ("Twenty-two amicus briefs have been filed in the case, and indeed the Court's opinion contains no fewer than 37 citations to amicus briefs and other secondary sources").

220. 509 U.S. at 596-97.

221. *See* § 1-5(E) *supra* (methods of proof).

222. FED. R. EVID. 104(a) ("Preliminary questions concerning ... the admissibility of evidence shall be determined by the court ...").

"entails a preliminary assessment of whether the reasoning or methodology underlying the testimony is scientifically valid and of whether that reasoning or methodology properly can be applied to the facts in issue."[223] As with most evidence issues, the burden of persuasion on the admissibility issue rests with the proponent of the evidence. In *Daubert,* the Court wrote: "These matters should be established by a preponderance of proof."[224]

In an earlier case, Judge Becker pointed out that the most efficient procedure for determining admissibility under this approach is an in limine hearing, at which time the trial court may consider offers of proof, affidavits, stipulations, or learned treatises.[225]

In *Kumho Tire Co. v. Carmichael,*[226] the Supreme Court addressed several procedural issues. The Court had previously ruled that a trial court's decision concerning the *Daubert* reliability requirement was subject to appellate review only for an abuse of discretion.[227] In *Kumho*, the Court ruled that appellate courts must accord trial judges discretion in other respects. There are two aspects to this ruling. First, substantively, "whether *Daubert's* specific factors are, or are not, reasonable measures of reliability in a particular case is a matter that the law grants the trial judge broad latitude to determine."[228] Second, the judge also has discretion concerning the procedural aspects of this inquiry. The trial court is not required to hold a "*Daubert* hearing" every time expert testimony is challenged.[229]

The Adversary Process

Unlike the *Frye* test, the other approaches do not attempt to assure the complete reliability of scientific evidence prior to admission. Although some evidence will be screened out by a court applying these approaches, some innovative techniques will gain admissibility, at which time any deficiencies in the technique should be exposed through traditional adversary trial procedures. For example, in admitting voiceprint evidence, the Fourth Circuit commented: "Unless an exaggerated popular opinion of the accuracy of a particular technique

223. 509 U.S. at 592-93.

224. 509 U.S. at 592 n.10. *See also* United States v. Williams, 95 F.3d 723, 729 (8th Cir. 1996) ("It is the burden of the party offering the expert testimony to lay a foundation for its admission"), *cert. denied,* 519 U.S. 1082 (1997); Daubert v. Merrell Dow Pharmaceuticals, Inc., 43 F.3d 1311, 1316 (9th Cir.) ("[T]he party presenting the expert must show that the expert's findings are based on sound science"), *cert. denied,* 516 U.S. 869 (1995).

225. United States v. Downing, 753 F.2d 1224, 1241 (3d Cir. 1985).

226. 119 S. Ct. 1167 (1999).

227. *See* General Electric Co. v. Joiner, 522 U.S. 136, 138-39 (1997).

228. 119 S. Ct. at 1176.

229. *See* Berger, *Procedural Paradigms for Applying the Daubert Test,* 78 MINN. L. REV. 1345 (1994).

makes its use prejudicial or likely to mislead the jury, it is better to admit relevant scientific evidence in the same manner as other expert testimony and allow its weight to be attacked by cross-examination and refutation."[230]

The *Daubert* Court also stressed the importance of the adversary system in dealing with scientific evidence. The Supreme Court rejected the argument that jettisoning *Frye* would necessarily lead to cases in which "befuddled juries are confounded by absurd and irrational pseudoscientific assertions." According to the Court, this represents an "overly pessimistic" view of the "capabilities of the jury, and of the adversary system."[231] The Court noted that "[v]igorous cross-examination, presentation of contrary evidence, and careful instruction on the burden of proof are the traditional and appropriate means of attacking shaky but admissible evidence."[232]

Thus, the adequacy of these alternate approaches depends, in large measure, on full discovery, the opportunity to re-examine evidence, and the appointment of defense experts.[233] Without these safeguards, cross-examination and refutation are difficult, if not impossible.

§ 1-7(B). *Daubert* Factors.

In performing the *Daubert* "gatekeeping function," the trial court may consider a number of factors. The Court identified five factors. These enumerated factors, however, are neither dispositive nor exhaustive.[234] Indeed, the Court emphasized that the Rule 702 standard is "a flexible one."[235] Thus, it is not surprising that the *Daubert* factors do not apply to every scientific technique[236] or non-scientific evidence.[237]

---

230. United States v. Baller, 519 F.2d 463, 466 (4th Cir.), *cert. denied,* 423 U.S. 1019 (1975). *Accord* United States v. Williams, 583 F.2d 1194, 1200 (2d Cir. 1978), *cert. denied,* 439 U.S. 1117 (1979); United States v. Ridling, 350 F. Supp. 90, 95-96 (E.D. Mich. 1972) ("The evidence is admitted for its worth, and the expert who attempts to make more from it than he should seldom survives a good cross-examination"). *But see* United States v. Wilson, 361 F. Supp. 510, 513 (D. Md. 1973) ("The cross-examination of an expert poses a formidable task; it is the rare attorney who knows as much as the expert"); State v. Dean, 103 Wis. 2d 228, 274, 307 N.W.2d 628, 650-51 (1981) ("Cross-examination ... may not in all situations provide a sufficient basis for the jury to assess the competence of the witness and the merits of the test").

231. 590 U.S. at 596.

232. *Id.* (citing Rock v. Arkansas, 483 U.S. 44, 61 (1987)).

233. These issues are discussed in detail in Chapter 3 (discovery) & Chapter 4 (securing expert assistance).

234. 509 U.S. at 593 ("Many factors will bear on the inquiry, and we do not presume to set out a definitive checklist or test").

235. *Id.* at 594.

236. *E.g.,* Kannankeril v. Terminix, Inc., 128 F.3d 802, 809 (3d Cir. 1997) (peer review and publication not determinative where expert opinion based on "widely accepted scientific

Method vs. Conclusion

One issue should be addressed before examining the *Daubert* factors. In *Daubert*, the Court had written that the "focus, of course, must be solely on principles and methodology, not on the conclusions that they generate."[238] In *General Electric Co. v. Joiner*,[239] the plaintiff argued that the district court had erred because it had disagreed with the conclusions (not the methods) that the experts had drawn from scientific studies. The Court in its first post-*Daubert* decision responded: "[C]onclusions and methodology are not entirely distinct from one another. Trained experts commonly extrapolate from existing data. But nothing in either *Daubert* or the Federal Rules of Evidence requires a district court to admit opinion evidence which is connected to existing data only by the *ipse dixit* of the expert. A court may conclude that there is simply too great an analytical gap between the data and the opinion proffered."[240]

In *Joiner*, the district court had not applied a lax standard; it had scrutinized the underlying scientific basis (*i.e.*, animal and epidemiological studies) of the experts' opinions. The Supreme Court also took a close look at the evidence, finding that the animal studies were "so dissimilar" to the facts presented in this litigation and the epidemiological studies "were not a sufficient basis for the experts' opinions."[241]

Testing & Testability

The first *Daubert* factor is whether the scientific theory or technique can be or has been tested. Citing scientific authorities, the Court noted that a hallmark of science is empirical testing. The Court pointed out that "[o]rdinarily, a key question to be answered ... will be whether [the technique or theory] can be (and

---

knowledge"); Tyus v. Urban Search Management, 102 F.3d 256 (7th. Cir. 1996) (*Daubert* factors do not neatly apply to sociologist), *cert. denied,* 520 U.S. 1251 (1997).

237. *See* § 1-7(D) *infra* (technical evidence).

238. 509 U.S. at 595. *See In re* Paoli R.R. Yard PCB Litigation, 35 F.3d 717, 745, 748 (3d Cir. 1994) ("any step that renders the analysis unreliable ... renders the expert's testimony inadmissible. This is true whether the step completely changes a reliable methodology or merely misapplies that methodology"; "But we think that this distinction has only limited practical import. When a judge disagrees with the conclusions of an expert, it will generally be because he or she thinks that there is a mistake at some step in the investigative or reasoning process of that expert. If the judge thinks that the conclusions of some other expert are correct, it will likely be because the judge thinks that the methodology and reasoning process of the other expert are superior to the first expert"), *cert. denied*, 513 U.S. 1190 (1995); Chesebro, *Taking Daubert's "Focus" Seriously: The Methodology/Conclusion Distinction*, 15 CARDOZO L. REV. 1745 (1994).

239. 522 U.S. 136, 118 S. Ct. 512 (1997). *See also* § 1-7(H) *infra* (scope of appellate review; discussing *Joiner*).

240. 118 S. Ct. at 519.

241. *Id.* at 518.

has been) tested."[242] The Court quoted Hempel: "[T]he statements constituting a scientific explanation must be capable of empirical test."[243] And then Popper: "[T]he criterion of the scientific status of a theory is its falsifiability, or refutability, or testability."[244]

Peer Review & Publication

Second, whether a theory or technique has been subjected to peer review and publication is, in the Court's view, "a relevant, though not dispositive, consideration in assessing the scientific validity."[245] The peer review and publication process increase the likelihood that flaws in methodology will be detected. "'Good science' is a commonly accepted term used to describe the scientific community's system of quality control which protects the community and those who rely upon it from unsubstantiated scientific analysis. It mandates that each proposition undergo a rigorous trilogy of publication, replication and verification before it is relied upon."[246]

The peer review process has its limitations. A former editor of the Journal of the American Medical Association has observed: "Peer review is far from being a 'perfect sausage machine for grinding out the truth.' ... 'Just because peer review

---

242. 509 U.S. at 592.

243. C. HEMPEL, PHILOSOPHY OF NATURAL SCIENCE 49 (1966). The Court also quoted from Green, *Expert Witnesses and Sufficiency of Evidence in Toxic Substances Litigation: The Legacy of Agent Orange and Bendectin Litigation*, 86 NW. U. L. REV. 643, 645 (1992) ("Scientific methodology today is based on generating hypotheses and testing them to see if they can be falsified; indeed, this methodology is what distinguishes science from other fields of human inquiry").

244. K. POPPER, CONJECTURES AND REFUTATIONS: THE GROWTH OF SCIENTIFIC KNOWLEDGE 37 (5th ed. 1989). *But see* T. KUHN, THE STRUCTURE OF SCIENTIFIC REVOLUTIONS 7 (2d ed. 1970) ("[A] new theory, however special its range of application, is seldom or never just an increment to what is already known. Its assimilation requires the reconstruction of prior theory and the reevaluation of prior fact, an intrinsically revolutionary process"); Schwartz, *A "Dogma of Empiricism" Revisited: Daubert v. Merrell Dow Pharmaceuticals, Inc. and the Need to Resurrect the Philosophical Insight of Frye v. United States*, 10 HARV. J. LAW & TECHNOLOGY 149, 152 (1997) ("[T]he *Daubert* decision rests on a basic misunderstanding of the history and philosophy of science. In contrast, this analysis will imply that the much-maligned *Frye* standard is grounded in a fundamental philosophical insight").

245. 509 U.S. at 594. *See also* State v. MacDonald, 718 A.2d 195, 199 (Me. 1998) (expert testimony that accused suffered from a post-traumatic stress disorder called "adult children of alcoholics syndrome" that made her more likely to confess to a crime she did not commit to protect a loved one; "[Given] the dearth of scientific support for and the questionable value to the jury") (not recognized by DSM-IV, based only on his empirical observations, lack of published studies); Fugate v. Commonwealth, 993 S.W.2d 931 (Ky. 1999) ("It is clear that the PCR method of DNA analysis has been subjected to extensive peer review. One court has estimated that over 4,000 published scientific articles exist addressing the merits of the method").

246. Brief of the New England Journal of Medicine, et al., as Amici Curiae in Support of Respondent, Daubert v. Merrell Dow Pharmaceuticals, Inc. (1993), at 2.

is about a review of scientific data doesn't mean that it is itself a scientific process.'"[247] An amici brief in *Daubert*, filed on behalf of several scientists, questioned the peer review system, even going as far as to argue that cross-examination may be as rigorous and reliable a method of truth-determination as peer review.[248] In their view, the peer review system is not intended to yield "the truth" and publication does not mean that an article's content is "generally accepted" or represents a "consensus" position of the relevant academic community.[249] In addition, they noted that peer review journals do not replicate or verify experiments; nor do they warrant that the information contained in an article is valid or otherwise amounts to "good science."[250] They also pointed out that often only two referees are selected and that these individuals spend on average "2.4 hours" reviewing each manuscript.[251] Even with these limitations, peer review remains a potent safeguard.

Error Rate

Third, the *Daubert* Court stated that a technique's "known or potential rate of error" is another relevant factor.[252] The Court cited two voiceprint cases. In *United States v. Williams,*[253] the Second Circuit had rejected the *Frye* rule and admitted voiceprint evidence. The court recognized "the potential rate of error" as "[o]ne indicator of evidential reliability."[254] Citing a Michigan State study, the court noted that the false identification error rate was 6.3%, a rate reduced to 2.4% when doubtful comparisons are eliminated.[255] However, a subsequent National Academy of Sciences [NAS] Report concluded that the reported error rates were generally inadequate for forensic applications[256] and not "valid over

247. L.A. Times, May 22, 1989, pt. 11, at 3 (quoting Elizabeth Knoll).

248. Brief of Amici Curiae Daryl E. Chubin, Edward J. Hackett, David Michael Ozonoff, Richard W. Clapp, Daubert v. Merrell Dow Pharmaceuticals, Inc., 509 U.S. 579 (1993), at 28 ("[T]he peer review system should not be regarded as more rigorous and reliable than the jury system's use of cross-examination").

249. *Id.* at 6 ("[C]onversely, the fact that ideas and information have not been published in a peer review journal does not mean that they are not 'generally accepted', or that they are 'generally rejected', or that they cannot represent 'good science'").

250. *Id.* ("For these reasons, the courts should not rely exclusively on peer review literature, but should consider peer review literature in conjunction with other materials and with expert testimony").

251. *Id.* at 12.

252. 509 U.S. at 594.

253. 583 F.2d 1194 (2d Cir. 1978), *cert. denied*, 439 U.S. 1117 (1979).

254. *Id.* at 1198.

255. *Id.*

256. NATIONAL RESEARCH COUNCIL, ON THE THEORY AND PRACTICE OF VOICE IDENTIFICATION 60 (1979) ("Estimates of error rates now available pertain to only a few of the many combinations of conditions encountered in real-life situations. These estimates do not constitute a generally

the range of conditions usually met in practice."[257] Thus, the question is not whether error rates are important, but rather how to determine whether they are valid. The Second Circuit accepted the proffered error rates without question.

United States v. Smith,[258] decided in 1989, is the other voiceprint case cited in *Daubert*. The *Smith* court discounted the NAS Report by pointing out that the Report took no position on the admissibility issue.[259] The NAS committee believed its report should be limited to scientific, not legal, issues; the latter were beyond its expertise.[260] That does not, however, undermine the Report's largely negative conclusions. In addition, the Seventh Circuit relied on a 1986 FBI survey. The FBI used 2000 voice identification comparisons that its examiners had made over a 15-year period to determine the error rate under field conditions.[261] Meaningful decisions were made in 34.8 percent of the comparisons (696 cases).[262] The false identification error rate was reported as 0.31 percent (1 case) and the false elimination error rate was 0.53 percent (2 cases).

Again, as in *Williams*, the court accepted the FBI survey at face value. No attempt to evaluate the quality of the survey was undertaken. The court was apparently unaware that some speech scientists had criticized the survey for failing to specify the precise method used by the FBI examiners and the criteria for determining examiner proficiency: "To date, no evidence has been published to suggest that *any* examiner has passed objective and independent evaluations before being certified."[263] A more fundamental objection concerned the criterion for determining "ground truth":

---

adequate basis for a judicial or legislative body to use in making judgments concerning the reliability and acceptability of aural-visual voice identification in forensic applications").

257. "The presently available experimental evidence about error rates consists of results from a relatively small number of separate, uncoordinated experiments. These results alone cannot provide estimates of error rates that are valid over the range of conditions usually met in practice." *Id.* at 58. The Report also commented: "All the scientific results and forensic experiences to date, taken together, do not constitute an adequate objective basis for determining the error rates to be expected for voice identification testimony given in forensic cases generally." *Id.* at 68-69.

258. 869 F.2d 348 (7th Cir. 1989).

259. *Id.* at 353 n.7.

260. *See* Rothstein, Book Review, 17 AM. CRIM. L. REV. 153, 154 (1979) ("The [NAS] report is a scientific work, not a legal document").

261. Koenig, *Spectrographic Voice Identification: A Forensic Survey*, 9 J. ACOUSTICAL SOC'Y AM. 2088 (1986).

262. *Id.* at 2090. "Most of the no or low confidence decisions were due to poor recording quality and/or an insufficient number of comparable words. Decisions were also affected by high-pitched voices (usually female) and some forms of voice disguise." *Id.*

263. Shipp et al., *Some Fundamental Considerations Regarding Voice Identification*, 82 J. ACOUSTICAL SOC'Y AM. 687 (1987).

> Identification or elimination "consistent with interviews and other evidence in the investigation" is not an adequate standard to confirm the accuracy of such decisions. Any technique such as this must be proven to be valid and reliable by some independent means before it can be used. Here, the technique is used to support the guilt or innocence of an individual, while the determination of such guilt or innocence is then used to show that the technique is proper. The data provided in this report cannot do both.[264]

In short, the field agents decided for themselves if there was an error. This is a very basic point, one which seriously undercuts the value of the survey.[265]

There are other problems. The *Smith* court did not recognize factual differences between its case and the prior voiceprint cases. The defendant, Tamara Smith, had an identical twin named Tanya. The expert testified that it was "highly probable" that the voice on several recordings was one twin and not the other. In other words, the examination involved a "closed" test, one in which the examiner determines which of several known voice samples is the same as an unknown sample. In contrast, the research cited by the court involved "open" tests, in which the examiner does not know if the unknown sample was made by the speaker of the known sample. In addition, unlike the research relied upon by the court, the expert did not make a positive identification. If anything, these factors support admissibility. The important point, however, is that the court was unaware of them. Apparently, the court was also unaware that the FBI precludes its examiners from testifying in court,[266] a fact that places the FBI survey in a very different light.[267]

---

264. *Id.* The FBI survey did acknowledge that one limitation of the survey was the fact that "investigators are not always correct in their evaluation of a suspect's involvement." Koenig, *FBI Survey, supra* note 261, at 2090. *See also* Koenig et al., *Reply to "Some Fundamental Considerations Regarding Voice Identification,"* 82 J. ACOUSTICAL SOC'Y AM. 688, 689 (1987) (FBI reply to this criticism).

265. This issue is not new; it has long been a disputed issue in the evaluation of polygraph field tests. *See* Chapter 8.

266. Koenig, *Spectrographic Voice Identification*, 13 CRIME LAB. DIGEST 105, 116 (1986).

267. Interestingly, the court admitted the evidence under the *Frye* test. *Smith*, 869 F.2d at 351 ("[T]his circuit has continued to affirm (and to apply) the *Frye* standard"). This is surprising because the FBI survey had acknowledged that voiceprint identification "has yet to find approval among most scientists in phonetics, linguistics, engineering, and related disciplines as a positive test in comparing voice samples," Koenig, *FBI Survey, supra* note 261, at 2088. Three years later, the New York Court of Appeals commented: "[T]here is marked conflict in the judicial and legal authorities as to the reliability of the procedure. New York courts are split on the issue of admissibility .... The legal scholarship on the admissibility of voice spectrograph is likewise conflicting...." People v. Jeter, 80 N.Y.2d 818, 600 N.E.2d 214, 216, 587 N.Y.S.2d 583 (1992) (citations omitted).

Maintenance of Standards

Fourth, the *Daubert* Court identified the "existence and maintenance of standards controlling the technique's operation" as another indicia of trustworthiness, again citing the *Williams* case.[268] The certification procedures of the International Association of Voice Identification are cited as an example in *Williams*. Most members of this group, however, were police officers, not scientists.[269] As the NAS Report later noted, this Association "as presently constituted does not possess the broad base of representation usually considered appropriate and perhaps essential for a national certifying board."[270] The Second Circuit simply did not appreciate that it was citing an association of technicians, rather than scientists.

General Acceptance

Finally, the Supreme Court noted that "general acceptance" remains a factor in assessing reliability. Although the Court rejected "general acceptance" as the sole criterion for admissibility, it recognized its relevance as a legitimate factor in assessing the reliability of scientific evidence. The Court commented: "Widespread acceptance can be an important factor in ruling particular evidence admissible, and 'a known technique that has been able to attract only minimal support within the community' ... may properly be viewed with skepticism."[271]

Post-Daubert Factors

In *General Electric Co. v. Joiner*,[272] the Supreme Court appears to have added another factor: whether "there is simply too great an analytical gap between the data and the opinion proffered." [273]

§ 1-7(C). Other Reliability Factors.

As noted in the last section, the *Daubert* Court stated that the enumerated factors were neither dispositive nor exhaustive[274] and emphasized that the Rule

---

268. 509 U.S. at 594. *See* United States v. Williams, 583 F.2d 1194, 1198 (2d Cir. 1978) (noting professional organization's standards governing "voiceprints"), *cert. denied,* 439 U.S. 1117 (1979).

269. A. Moenssens & F. Inbau, Scientific Evidence in Criminal Cases 580 (2d ed. 1978) ("Except for [Dr.] Tosi, no scientists were among its early members; the majority of them are still police officers who have been trained by either Kersta or Tosi to become 'voiceprint' technicians").

270. NAS Report, *supra* note 256, at 65.

271. 509 U.S. at 594.

272. 522 U.S. 136 (1997).

273. *Id.* at 146.

274. 509 U.S. at 593 ("Many factors will bear on the inquiry, and we do not presume to set out a definitive checklist or test").

702 standard is "a flexible one."[275] In a footnote, the Court noted that several authorities had proposed additional factors for assessing reliability.[276] *United States v. Downing*[277] was one of these. In that case Judge Becker wrote:

> In our view, Rule 702 requires that a district court ruling upon the admission of (novel) scientific evidence, *i.e.*, evidence whose scientific fundamentals are not suitable for judicial notice, conduct a preliminary inquiry focusing on (1) the soundness and reliability of the process or technique used in generating the evidence, (2) the possibility that admitting the evidence would overwhelm, confuse, or mislead the jury, and (3) the proffered connection between the scientific research or test result to be presented, and the particular disputed factual issues in the case.[278]

The Supreme Court also cited Judge Weinstein and Professor Berger's treatise; those authors listed the following factors: (1) the technique's general acceptance in the field, (2) the expert's qualifications and stature, (3) the use which has been made of the new technique, (4) the potential rate of error, (5) the existence of specialized literature, (6) the novelty of the new invention, and (7) the extent to which the technique relies on the subjective interpretation of the expert.[279]

The Court also cited an article written by Justice Mark McCormick of the Iowa Supreme Court, in which he specified eleven factors:

> (1) the potential error rate in using the technique, (2) the existence and maintenance of standards governing its use, (3) presence of safeguards in the characteristics of the technique, (4) analogy to other scientific techniques whose results are admissible, (5) the extent to which the technique has been accepted by scientists in the field involved, (6) the nature and breadth of the inference adduced, (7) the clarity and simplicity with which the technique can be described and its results explained, (8) the extent to which the basic data are verifiable by the court and the jury, (9) the availability of other experts to test and evaluate the technique, (10) the

---

275. *Id.* at 594.

276. *Id.* at 595 n.12 ("A number of authorities have presented variations on the reliability approach, each with its own slightly different factors.... To the extent that they focus on the reliability of evidence as ensured by the scientific validity of its underlying principles, all these versions may well have merit, although we express no opinion regarding any of their particular details").

277. 753 F.2d 1224 (3d Cir. 1985).

278. *Id.* at 1237.

279. 3 J. WEINSTEIN & M. BERGER, WEINSTEIN'S EVIDENCE § 702[03], at 702-41 to -42 (1988).

probative significance of the evidence in the circumstances of the case, and (11) the care with which the technique was employed in the case.[280]

Courts have identified other factors.[281] For example, on remand in *Daubert*, the Ninth Circuit excluded the plaintiff's evidence on the grounds that the underlying research had been conducted in anticipation of litigation and was therefore not valid. The court saw an important difference between experts who "testify about matters naturally and directly out of research they have conducted independent of the litigation" and those who "have developed their opinions expressly for purposes of testifying." [282]

§ 1-7(D). Application of *Daubert* to "Technical" Expert Evidence.

In interpreting Rule 702, the Supreme Court in *Daubert* dealt only with "scientific" evidence.[283] Rule 702, however, also includes the terms "technical" and "specialized" knowledge. That alternate phrasing raised two issues: (1) whether *Daubert*'s reliability requirement extended to these other types of expert testimony, and (2) if so, whether the factors set forth in *Daubert* for judging reliability applied in this context.[284] In 1999, the Court in *Kumho Tire Co. v. Carmichael*[285] answered both questions in the affirmative. *Kumho* involved a civil case—a tire blow-out accident, in which the Court upheld the trial court's

---

280. McCormick, *Scientific Evidence: Defining a New Approach to Admissibility*, 67 IOWA L. REV. 879, 911-12 (1982).

281. *E.g.,* Sheehan v. Daily Racing Form, Inc., 104 F.3d 940, 942 (7th Cir.) (whether expert "is being as careful as he would be in his regular professional work outside his paid litigation consulting"), *cert. denied*, 521 U.S. 1104 (1997); Braun v. Lorillard Inc., 84 F.3d 230, 234 (7th Cir.) (did experts "adhere to the same standards of intellectual rigor that are demanded in their professional work"), *cert. denied*, 519 U.S. 992 (1996); Claar v. Burlington N.R.R., 29 F.3d 499 (9th Cir. 1994) (evidence excluded where expert failed to consider other obvious cause for plaintiff's condition); Sterling v. Velsicol Chem. Corp., 855 F.2d 1188 (6th. Cir. 1988) (field of "clinical ecology" not known to reach reliable results).

282. Daubert v. Merrell Dow Pharmaceuticals, Inc., 43 F.3d 1311, 1317 (9th Cir.) , *cert. denied,* 516 U.S. 869 (1995).

283. 509 U.S. at 590 n.8 ("Our discussion is limited to the scientific context because that is the nature of the expertise offered here").

284. *See* 509 U.S. at 600 (C.J. Rehnquist, dissenting in part) ("Does all of this dicta apply to an expert seeking to testify on the basis of 'technical or other specialized knowledge' ... or are the 'general observations' limited only to 'scientific knowledge'? What is the difference between scientific knowledge and technical knowledge; does Rule 702 actually contemplate that the phrase 'scientific, technical, or specialized knowledge' be broken down into numerous subspecies of expertise ..."). *See also* Imwinkelried, *The Next Step After Daubert: Developing a Similar Epistemological Approach to Ensuring the Reliability of Nonscientific Expert Testimony*, 15 CARDOZO L. REV. 2271 (1994).

285. 119 S. Ct. 1167 (1999).

decision to exclude engineering testimony concerning the cause of the blow-out. However, the decision applies to criminal cases as well.

Prior to *Kumho*, most courts had held that some type of reliability assessment should be applied in this context.[286] For example, Judge Karen Moore, writing for the Sixth Circuit, commented: "[A]lthough '*Daubert* dealt with scientific experts, its language relative to the "gatekeeper" function of federal judges is applicable to all expert testimony offered under Rule 702.'"[287] In another case, she looked directly to Rule 702: "[I]t is thus clear that a district court has the duty to decide not only whether evidence is relevant but also whether it is reliable. But this conclusion does not come from the *Daubert* opinion itself; rather, it comes from the Federal Rules of Evidence."[288] This is the correct result; otherwise, the simple expedient of labeling a technique as "technical" could avoid any judicial scrutiny concerning the reliability of testimony based on that technique.[289]

286. *But see* State v. Trager, 158 Or. App. 399, 974 P.2d 750 (1999) (physician's differential diagnosis that victim had been sexually abused was technical, not scientific, evidence and thus did not have to meet the standards of *Brown*; The diagnosis was not a syndrome or profile because it did not draw its convincing force from generalizations based on empirical data or an empirical study).

287. United States v. Thomas, 74 F.3d 676, 681 (6th Cir.), *cert. denied*, 517 U.S. 1162 (1996). *See also* United States v. Kayne, 90 F.3d 7, 11 (1st Cir. 1996) ("The fact that the subject matter [value of coins] is not 'scientific' is no bar to admissibility of expert testimony"), *cert. denied*, 519 U.S. 1055 (1997); Cummins v. Lyle Indus., 93 F.3d 362, 367 n.2 (7th Cir. 1996) (design engineer); Ventura v. Titan Sports, Inc., 65 F.3d 725, 733 (8th Cir. 1995) (economist), *cert. denied,* 516 U.S. 1174 (1996); United States v. Alzanki, 54 F.3d 994, 1005-06 (1st Cir. 1995) (victimologist), *cert. denied,* 516 U.S. 1111 (1996); United States v. Velasquez, 64 F.3d 844, 849-52 (3d Cir. 1995); United States v. Dorsey, 45 F.3d 809, 813-14 (4th Cir. 1995), *cert. denied,* 517 U.S. 1219 (1996); Deimer v. Cincinnati Sub-Zero Products, Inc., 58 F.3d 341, 343-45 (7th Cir. 1995); Sorenson v. Shaklee Corp., 31 F.3d 638, 649 (8th Cir.1994); United States v. Quinn, 18 F.3d 1461, 1465 (9th Cir.), *cert. denied*, 512 U.S. 1242 (1994). *But see* Iacobelli Construction, Inc. v. County of Monroe, 32 F.3d 19, 25 (2d Cir. 1994).

288. United States v. Jones, 107 F.3d 1147, 1156, 1158 (6th Cir.) ("If that [*Daubert*] framework were to be extended to outside the scientific realm, many types of relevant and reliable expert testimony — that derived substantially from practical experience would be excluded. Such a result truly would turn *Daubert*, a case intended to relax the admissibility requirements for expert scientific evidence, on its head"), *cert. denied,* 521 U.S. 1127 (1997).

289. *See* Moore v. Ashland Chemical, Inc., 126 F.3d 679, 685 (5th Cir. 1997) ("[T]he requirements that *Daubert* found to be inherent in Rule 702, viz., that the trial judge must ensure that the expert's evidence is not only relevant, but reliable, must be applicable to 'technical, or other specialized knowledge,' as well as to scientific testimony. Otherwise, Rule 702 would not place limits on the admissibility of non-scientific expert testimony comparable to those it imposes on purportedly scientific evidence. Moreover, the *Daubert* opinion at several points clearly implies that it is drawing on principles of the Federal Rules that are generally applicable to all types of expert testimony"), *cert. denied*, 119 S. Ct. 1454 (1999); Watkins v. Telsmith, Inc., 121 F.3d 984, 991 (5th. Cir. 1997) ("[I]t seems exactly backwards that experts who purport to rely on general engineering principles and practical experience might escape screening by the district court simply by stating that their conclusions were not reached by any particular method or technique");

A proposed 1998 amendment to Rule 702 adopts the same position.[290] Proposed Rule 702 adds the following clause: "provided that (1) the testimony is sufficiently based upon reliable facts or data, (2) the testimony is the product of reliable principles and methods, and (3) the witness has applied the principles and methods reliably to the facts of the case."[291] The advisory committee note states that the "amendment does not distinguish between scientific and other forms of expert testimony. The trial court's gatekeeping function applies to testimony by any expert."[292]

In *Kumho*, the Supreme Court stated that "*Daubert's* general holding—setting forth the trial judge's general 'gatekeeping' obligation—applies not only to testimony based on 'scientific' knowledge, but also to testimony based on 'technical' and 'other specialized' knowledge."[293] The Court reached this conclusion based on (1) a textual analysis of Rule 702 and (2) the evidentiary rationale that underlying *Daubert*, *i.e.*, that the Federal Rules grant experts special latitude unavailable to other witnesses on the assumption that expert testimony has a reliable basis. In addition, the Court observed that the proposed distinction between scientific and nonscientific expert testimony was unmanageable:

> [I]t would prove difficult, if not impossible, for judges to administer evidentiary rules under which a gatekeeping obligation depended upon a distinction between "scientific" knowledge and "technical" or "other specialized" knowledge. There is no clear line that divides the one from the others. Disciplines such as engineering rest upon scientific knowledge. Pure scientific theory itself may depend for its development upon observation and properly engineered machinery. And conceptual efforts to distinguish the two are unlikely to produce clear legal lines capable of application in particular cases.[294]

Once the Court in *Kumho* decided that the reliability requirement applied to all expert testimony, it had to reach the question of the methodology for assessing that reliability—in particular, whether the factors cited in *Daubert* also applied in this context.[295] The pre-*Kumho* courts that had grappled with the applicability of

---

American Trial Lawyers, *Standards and Procedures for Determining the Admissibility of Expert Testimony after Daubert*, 157 F.R.D. 571, 579 (1994) ("Whether the testimony concerns economic principles, accounting standards, property valuation or other non-scientific subjects, it should be evaluated by reference to the 'knowledge and experience' of that particular field").

290. *See* § 1-10 *infra* (Uniform-Federal Rules Jurisdictions).

291. 181 F.R.D. 144 (1999).

292. *Id.* at 149. The target date is December 1, 2000. 64 Crim. L. (BNA) 478 (Mar. 24, 1999).

293.119 S. Ct. at 1171.

294. *Id.* at 1174.

295. *See* § 1-7(B).

the *Daubert* factors had embraced a multitude of approaches. The Hawaii Supreme Court distinguished "scientific" and "technical" knowledge in this way: "[E]xpert testimony deals with 'technical knowledge' when it involves the mere technical application of well-established scientific principles and procedures. In such a situation, because the underlying scientific principles and procedures are of proven validity/reliability, it is unnecessary to subject technical knowledge to the same type of full-scale reliability determination required for scientific knowledge. Thus, although technical knowledge, like all expert testimony, must be both relevant and reliable, its reliability may be presumed."[296] Therefore, although the court ruled that technical expert testimony must be reliable, it undercut the significance of that ruling by making technical evidence presumptively admissible. The court effectively shifted the burden of proof on the reliability requirement to the opposing party.

The Fifth Circuit took a different approach, commenting that "the *Daubert* Court defined 'scientific knowledge' in terms of 'hard science' or 'Newtonian science.'"[297] The court further wrote:

> [U]nder Rule 702, an opinion based on other technical or specialized knowledge, must be grounded in the principles, methods and procedures of the particular field of knowledge involved. Every discipline employs a body of methods, rules, and postulates, i.e., methodology, both in its ordinary functions and in developing and adopting new concepts, techniques, and analogues. Therefore, the "knowledge" of each discipline, under Rule 702, is both its principles and methodology and the theories, techniques or inferences produced through its methodology. Thus, the proffered opinion of any expert in a field of knowledge, in order to be evidentiarily reliable, must either be based soundly on the current knowledge, principles and methodology of the expert's discipline or be soundly inferred or derived therefrom.[298]

Kumho Tire resolved this split in authority, at least in federal practice. The Supreme Court observed: "[A] trial court may consider one or more of the specific factors that *Daubert* mentioned when doing so will help determine that

296. State v. Fukusaku, 85 Haw. 462, 473, 946 P.2d 32, 43 (1997).

297. Moore v. Ashland Chemical, Inc., 126 F.3d 679 (5th Cir. 1997) (citing Imwinkelried, *The Next Step After Daubert, Developing a Similar Epistemological Approach to Ensuring the Reliability of Nonscientific Expert Testimony*, 15 CARDOZO L. REV. 2271 (1994).), *cert. denied,* 119 S. Ct. 1454 (1999). *See also* Comment, *Inconsistent Gatekeeping in Federal Courts: Application of Daubert v. Merrell Dow Pharmaceuticals, Inc. to Nonscientific Expert Testimony*, 30 LOY. L.A. L. REV. 1379 (1997).

298. 126 F.3d at 686-87. "[T]he hard science techniques or methods that become the '*Daubert* factors' generally are not appropriate for assessing the evidentiary reliability of a proffer of expert clinical medical testimony." *Id.* at 688.

testimony's reliability. But, as the Court stated in *Daubert*, the test of reliability is 'flexible,' and *Daubert's* list of specific factors neither necessarily nor exclusively applies to all experts or in every case."[299] The Court also noted:

> [W]e can neither rule out, nor rule in, for all cases and for all time the applicability of the factors mentioned in *Daubert*, nor can we now do so for subsets of cases categorized by category of expert or by kind of evidence. ...
>
> *Daubert* itself is not to the contrary. It made clear that its list of factors was meant to be helpful, not definitive. Indeed, those factors do not all necessarily apply even in every instance in which the reliability of scientific testimony is challenged. It might not be surprising in a particular case, for example, that a claim made by a scientific witness has never been the subject of peer review, for the particular application at issue may never previously have interested any scientist. Nor, on the other hand, does the presence of *Daubert's* general acceptance factor help show that an expert's testimony is reliable where the discipline itself lacks reliability, as, for example, do theories grounded in any so-called generally accepted principles of astrology or necromancy.[300]

The Supreme Court also addressed related procedural issues. The Court had previously ruled that a trial court's decision concerning the *Daubert* reliability requirement was subject to appellate review only for an abuse of discretion.[301] In *Kumho*, the Court ruled that appellate courts must accord trial judges discretion in other respects. There are two aspects to this ruling. First, substantively, "whether *Daubert's* specific factors are, or are not, reasonable measures of reliability in a particular case is a matter that the law grants the trial judge broad latitude to determine."[302] Second, the judge also has discretion concerning the procedural aspects of this inquiry. The trial court is not required to hold a "*Daubert* hearing" every time expert testimony is challenged.[303]

§ 1-7(E). Application of *Daubert* to Forensic Science Techniques.

Courts have applied the *Daubert* reliability test to a wide variety of forensic techniques: drug analysis,[304] intoxication tests,[305] and other types of evidence.[306]

299.119 S. Ct. at 1171.

300. *Id.* at 1175.

301. *See* General Electric Co. v. Joiner, 522 U.S. 136, 138-39 (1997).

302. 119 S. Ct. at 1176.

303. *See* Berger, *Procedural Paradigms for Applying the Daubert Test*, 78 MINN. L. REV. 1345 (1994).

304. *E.g.,*United States v. Cruz, 127 F.3d 791, 801 (9th. Cir. 1997) (chemical analysis of methamphetamine), *cert. denied*, 118 S. Ct. 896 (1998); United States v. Muldrow, 19 F.3d 1332, 1337 (10th Cir.) (forensic chemist testimony satisfies *Daubert*), *cert. denied*, 513 U.S. 862 (1994);

Numerous decisions apply *Daubert* to DNA profiling, including RFLP,[307] PCR-DQA,[308] PCR-polymarkers,[309] PCR-D1S80,[310] STRs,[311] mitochondrial DNA,[312] statistical probabilities,[313] and so forth. [314]

United States v. McCaskey, 9 F.3d 368, 380 (5th Cir. 1993) (Fourier Transform Infrared Spectrophotometer cocaine test), *cert. denied*, 511 U.S. 1042 (1994); United States v. Bynum, 3 F.3d 769, 773 (4th Cir. 1993) (gas chromatographic analysis of cocaine), *cert. denied*, 510 U.S. 1132 (1994); United States v. Bush, 47 M.J. 305, 311 (C.A.A.F. 1997) (mass-spectrometry hair analysis for detection of drug use), *cert. denied*, 118 S. Ct. 1048 (1998).

305. *E.g.,*United States v. Iron Cloud, 171 F.3d 587, 590-91 (8th Cir. 1999) ("By denying Iron Cloud's request for a *Daubert* hearing on the reliability of the PBT [Portable Breath Test], the judge took the accuracy of the PBTs for granted and he ignored established procedure. Contrary to the court's statements concerning the reliability of the PBT, the PBT has not been established as reliable. PBTs are used in the field for screening purposes. ... The mere fact that a test has been used for a long time does make it reliable"); State v. Torres, 976 P.2d 20, 30 (N.M. 1999) ("Today we adopt the majority view that the results of HGN testing constitute scientific evidence that must meet the standard of evidentiary reliability articulated in *Alberico* and *Daubert*"); State v. Helms, 345 N.C. 578, 582, 504 S.E.2d 293, 295 (1998) ("Until there is sufficient scientifically reliable evidence as to the correlation between intoxication and nystagmus, it is improper to permit a lay person [police officer] to testify as to the meaning of HGN test results"); State v. Hofer, 512 N.W.2d 482, 484 (S.D. 1994) ("[G]eneral acceptance in the scientific community is no longer required"; validity of intoxilyzer "beyond scientific dispute"). *But see* Hulse v. State, 961 P.2d 75, 94, 95 (Mont. 1998) ("[T]he *Daubert* test should only be used to determine the admissibility of novel scientific evidence"; "[T]he HGN test is not novel scientific evidence. Therefore, to determine the admissibility of HGN test results, a district court need not employ the *Daubert* standard"; "nothing in the evidence establishes that Officer Kennedy had special training or education or adequate knowledge qualifying him as an expert to explain the correlation between alcohol consumption and nystagmus, the underlying scientific basis of the HGN test").

306. *E.g.,* United States v. Davis, 103 F.3d 660, 673 (8th Cir. 1996) (bullet composition comparison by Inductively Coupled Plasma-Atomic Emission Spectrometry (ICP) admitted), *cert. denied*, 520 U.S. 1258 (1997); United States v. Jones, 24 F.3d 1177, 1180 (9th Cir. 1994) (voice comparison technique that witness developed and no other expert used failed *Daubert*); United States v. Quinn, 18 F.3d 1461, 1465 (9th Cir. 1994) (use of photogrammetry to determine height of robber in bank surveillance films admissible under *Daubert*; "full evidentiary hearing" on *Daubert* issues not required), *cert. denied*, 512 U.S. 1242 (1994); State v. Buller, 517 N.W.2d 711, 713 (Iowa 1994) (trained dog's detection of fire accelerant admitted; Iowa rejected *Frye* prior to *Daubert*); State v. Dennis, 129 N.C. App. 686, 500 S.E.2d 765 (1998) (Phadebas methodology used to detect the presence of amylase, an enzyme found in saliva as well as other substances, admissible).

307. *E.g.,* Taylor v. State, 889 P.2d 319, 328, 332 (Okla. Crim. App. 1995) ("[T]he time is right for this Court to abandon the *Frye* test and adopt the more structured and yet flexible admissibility standard set forth in *Daubert*") (RFLP match and statistical calculations admissible).

308. *E.g.,* United States v. Hicks, 103 F.3d 837, 844-46 (9th Cir. 1996) (PCR admissible), *cert. denied*, 520 U.S. 1193 (1997); Ingram v. State, 699 N.E.2d 261, 263 (Ind. 1998) ("a proper foundation had been established as the scientific principles of PCR analysis"); Fugate v. Commonwealth, 993 S.W.2d 931 (Ky. 1999) ("DNA comparison analysis using the RFLP and PCR methods is admissible without being the subject of a pretrial *Daubert* hearing. However, the evidence in question is still subject to challenge at trial"); State v. Stills, 125 N.M. 66, 74, 957 P.2d 51, 59 (1998) ("We hold that PCR evidence is admissible in New Mexico Courts"); Bolin v. State,

In *United States v. Bonds*[315] DNA evidence had been admitted at trial under the *Frye* test. On appeal, the Sixth Circuit ruled that DNA evidence also satisfied the *Daubert* standard, which it perceived to be a less-demanding standard.[316] In contrast, the Eighth Circuit imposed a more demanding standard, even though it also admitted DNA evidence:

---

114 Nev. 503, 960 P.2d 784, 800 (1998) ("DNA results obtained through the use of the PCR technique are admissible for use within the forensic context. Further, ... DNA statistical probability calculations need not take into account genetic population substructure to be valid ..."), *cert. denied,* 119 S. Ct. 117 (1999); State v. Lyons, 324 Or. 256, 924 P.2d 802 (1996) (PCR admissible); State v. Lyons, 324 Or. 256, 924 P.2d 802 (1996) (PCR admissible). *See also* Smith & Gordon, The *Admission of DNA Evidence in State and Federal Court*, 65 FORDHAM L. REV. 2465 (1997).

309. *E.g.,*United States v. Beasley, 102 F. 3d 1440, 1448 (8th Cir. 1996) (PCR, DQalpha and Polymarkers admissible), *cert. denied*, 520 U.S. 1246 (1997); Smith v. State, 702 N.E.2d 668, 672 (Ind. 1998) ("PM and D1S80 tests are scientifically reliable").

310. *E.g.,* United States v. Gaines, 979 F. Supp. 1429 (S.D. Fla. 1997) (PCR DQA, PM, D1S80, and amelogenin admitted); Smith v. State, 702 N.E.2d 668, 672 (Ind. 1998) ("PM and D1S80 tests are scientifically reliable").

311. *E.g.,* Commonwealth v. Rosier, 425 Mass. 807, 685 N.E.2d 739 (1997) (DNA-STRs).

312. State v. Council, 515 S.E.2d 508 (1999).

313. *E.g.,* United States v. Davis, 40 F.3d 1069, 1075 (10th Cir. 1994) (FBI method and statistical probability evidence admitted), *cert. denied*, 514 U.S. 1088 (1995); United States v. Chischilly, 30 F.3d 1144, 1153 (9th Cir. 1994) (FBI statistics based on its Native American database admissible, even though defendant's Navajo tribe may be underrepresented), *cert. denied*, 513 U.S. 1132 (1995); Commonwealth v. Lanigan, 419 Mass. 15, 26, 641 N.E.2d 1342, 1349 (1994) (DNA statistics based on NAS Report "ceiling principle" admissible) ("We accept the basic reasoning of the *Daubert* opinion ..."); State v. Moore, 885 P.2d 457, 471-72 (Mont. 1994) (RFLP analysis admitted, objections to lab's methods affects only weight; PCR analysis admitted, contamination issue affects only weight); State v. Anderson, 118 N.M. 284, 881 P.2d 29, 47 (1994) (FBI random match probability statistics admissible).

314. *E.g.,* United States v. Black Cloud, 101 F.3d 1258, 1261 (8th Cir. 1996) (DNA for paternity admitted; "We review a district court's decision on whether to admit evidence for an abuse of discretion"); United States v. Lowe, 954 F. Supp. 401 (D. Mass. 1996) (RFLP chemiluminescence admissible), *cert. denied,* 119 S. Ct. 270 (1998); United States v. Gaines, 979 F. Supp. 1429 (S.D. Fla. 1997) (PCR DQA1, PM, D1S80, and amelogenin admitted); United States v. Shea, 957 F. Supp. 331 (D.N.H. 1997), *cert. denied,* 119 S. Ct. 1480 (1999); Griffith v. State, 976 S.W.2d 241 (Tex. App. 1998) (probability of paternity was 99.99% based on Bayes' Theorem admissible and does not violate presumption of innocents).

315. 12 F.3d 540 (6th Cir. 1993).

316. The court wrote:

> Thus, because the theory, methodology, and reasoning used by the FBI lab to declare matches of DNA samples and to estimate statistical probabilities are scientifically valid and helpful to the trier of fact, we affirm the district court's conclusion that they are admissible under Rule 702.... Our conclusion is not altered by the fact that there are numerous substantive, heated disputes over the procedures that the FBI used and over the accuracy of the results that these procedures produced. We find that the DNA testimony easily meets the more liberal test set out by the Supreme Court in *Daubert.*

12 F.3d at 568.

> We believe that the reliability inquiry set forth in *Daubert* mandates that there be a preliminary showing that the expert properly performed a reliable methodology in arriving at his opinion.... [*Daubert*] suggests that the inquiry extends beyond simply the reliability of the principles or methodologies in the abstract. In order to determine whether scientific testimony is reliable, the court must conclude that the testimony was derived from the application of a reliable methodology or principle in the particular case.
>
> ...
>
> Thus, we conclude that the court should make an initial inquiry into the particular expert's application of the scientific principle or methodology in question. The court should require the testifying expert to provide affidavits attesting that he properly performed the protocols involved in DNA profiling.[317]

Handwriting

Daubert has also had an impact on handwriting comparison. In *United States v. Starzecpyzel*[318] a federal district court held that forensic document examinations (FDE) lacked a valid scientific basis: "In sum, the testimony at the *Daubert* hearing firmly established that forensic document examination, despite the existence of a certification program, professional journals and other trappings of science, cannot, after *Daubert*, be regarded as 'scientific ... knowledge.'"[319] The court added: "[W]hile scientific principles may relate to aspects of handwriting analysis, they have little or nothing to do with the day-to-day tasks performed by FDEs.... [T]his attenuated relationship does not transform the FDE into a scientist."[320]

The court went on to hold, however, that Rule 702 requirements limiting expert testimony to that which assists the trier of fact and is offered by a qualified expert must nevertheless be satisfied: "[T]his court concludes that adequate guidance can be found within Rule 702 to conduct a meaningful inquiry into the reliability of the expertise claimed by FDEs."[321] After the court found the testimony to be sufficiently reliable, it considered the risk of unfair prejudice. Because of FDE's use of terms such as "laboratory" and references to authorities with titles that may contain the words "science" or "scientific," there is a risk that jurors may bestow upon FDE's the aura of the infallibility of science. In addition,

---

317. United States v. Martinez, 3 F.3d 1191, 1197-98 (8th Cir. 1993), *cert. denied*, 510 U.S. 1062 (1994). *See* § 1-9, *infra*, *Frye-Daubert* "Plus."

318. 880 F. Supp. 1027 (S.N.Y. 1995).

319. *Id.* at 1038.

320. *Id.* at 1041.

321. *Id.* at 1043.

FDEs may use a standard, nine-level scale of probability that expresses their opinion regarding genuineness in very precise terms. Such overly fine distinctions are inappropriate in forensic document examination where it is conceded that conclusions are drawn, in large part, on subjective criteria.[322]

In the court's view, these problems did not preclude admission because several procedures can attenuate these risks. First, a jury instruction should be given, stating that "FDEs offer practical rather than scientific expertise."[323] Second, the court may restrict testimony relating to the existence of the nine-level scale. Finally, the defense is entitled "to attack the reliability of forensic document examination, ... to attack the expertise of each testifying FDE, [and] to introduce the testimony of their own FDE...."[324] Subsequent developments are discussed in Chapter 21.

Hair Comparisons

In *Williamson v. Reynolds*,[325] an expert testified that hair samples were "microscopically consistent." However, the "expert did not explain which of the 'approximately' 25 characteristics were consistent, any standards for determining whether the samples were consistent, how many persons could be expected to share this same combination of characteristics, or how he arrived at his conclusions." Moreover, "[t]his court has been unsuccessful in its attempts to locate *any* indication that expert hair comparison testimony meets *any* of the requirements of *Daubert*."[326] The court went on to state: "Although the hair expert may have followed procedures accepted in the community of hair experts, the human hair comparison results in this case were, nonetheless, scientifically unreliable."[327] Finally, the prosecutor stated in closing argument, "[T]here's a match." The state court also misinterpreted the evidence, writing that the "hair evidence placed [petitioner] at the decedent's apartment." The federal district court concluded that the "prosecutor's mischaracterization of the hair evidence

---

322. *Id.* at 1048.

323. *Id.* at 1049. The court attached a draft jury instruction to the end of the opinion. *Id.* at 1050-51.

324. *Id.* at 1050. *See also* United States v. Jones, 107 F.3d 1147, 1160 (6th Cir.) ("In short, expert handwriting analysis is a field of expertise under the Federal Rules of Evidence. This decision, however, does not guarantee the reliability or admissibility of this type of testimony in a particular case"), *cert. denied,* 521 U.S. 1127 (1997).

325. 904 F. Supp. 1529, 1558 (E.D. Okla. 1995).

326. *Id.* at 1557.

327. *Id.* at 1558.

misled the jury...."[328] The Tenth Circuit reversed because the district court had used the wrong standard for habeas review.[329]

In contrast, the Hawaii Supreme Court has ruled that "[b]ecause the scientific principles and procedures underlying hair and fiber evidence are well-established and of proven reliability, the evidence in the present case can be treated as 'technical knowledge.' Thus, an independent reliability determination was unnecessary."[330] Other developments are discussed in Chapter 24.

Polygraph Evidence

The initial post-*Daubert* cases excluded polygraph evidence.[331] However, in *United States v. Posado*,[332] the defendants offered the results of a polygraph examination at a suppression hearing. The Fifth Circuit stated that "the rationale underlying this circuit's per se rule against admitting polygraph evidence did not survive *Daubert*."[333] The court further commented: "There can be no doubt that tremendous advances have been made in polygraph instrumentation and technique in the years since *Frye*.... Current research indicates that, when given under controlled conditions, the polygraph technique accurately predicts truth or deception between seventy and ninety percent of the time."[334] The court, however, limited its ruling, noting that:

> [W]e do not now hold that polygraph examinations are scientifically valid or that they will always assist the trier of fact.... We merely remove the obstacle of the per se rule against admissibility, which was based on

---

328. *Id.* at 1557.

329. Williamson v. Ward, 110 F.3d 1508, 1512 (10th Cir. 1997) (due process, not *Daubert*, standard applies in habeas proceedings).

330. State v. Fukusaku, 85 Haw. 462, 474, 946 P.2d 32, 44 (1997). *See also* McGrew v. State, 682 N.E.2d 1289, 1292 (Ind. 1997) (hair comparison admissible, more a matter of observation by persons with specialized knowledge than a matter of scientific principles); McCarty v. State, 904 P.2d 110, 125 (Okla. Crim. App. 1995) (admitting evidence).

331. *E.g.*, United States v. Black, 831 F. Supp. 120, 123 (E.D.N.Y. 1993) ("After evaluating the standard set forth in the *Daubert* case, premised on Rule 702 of the Federal Rules of Evidence, the Court believes that nothing in *Daubert* would disturb the settled precedent that polygraph evidence is neither reliable nor admissible"); Paxton v. State, 867 P.2d 1309, 1323 n.3 (Okla. Crim. App. 1993) (even after *Daubert*, polygraph inadmissible at least where no new evidence to overcome presumption of unreliability introduced), *cert. denied*, 513 U.S. 886 (1994).

332. 57 F.3d 428 (5th Cir. 1995).

333. *Id.* at 429. *See also* United States v. Cordoba, 104 F.3d 225, 227-28 (9th Cir. 1997) (noting that its former per se rule of exclusion is inconsistent with *Daubert*). *But see* United States v. Kwong, 69 F.3d 663, 668-69 (2d Cir. 1995) ("the 'legal Pandora's box' which the Fifth Circuit opened in *United States v. Posado* ... is not yet agape in this Circuit"; "The record before us simply does not provide the proper opportunity to explore the validity of polygraph evidence under Rule 702"), *cert. denied*, 517 U.S. 1115 (1996).

334. *Id.* at 434.

antiquated concepts about the technical ability of the polygraph and legal precepts that have been expressly overruled by the Supreme Court.[335]

Federal Rule 403 would also govern admissibility. Two factors were cited by the court as counterbalancing any prejudicial effect. First, the prosecution was contacted before the exam and offered an opportunity to participate in the exam. Second, the evidence was not offered before a jury but rather before the judge.

Two district courts thereafter admitted polygraph evidence: *United States v. Galbreth*[336] and *United States v. Crumby.*[337] The state cases have not been influenced by this development; several have reaffirmed the rule of categorical inadmissibility.[338] Other developments are discussed in Chapter 8.

§ 1-7(F). Application of *Daubert* to Social Science Techniques.

Daubert has also been applied to psychological testimony concerning eyewitness identifications,[339] the child sexual abuse accommodation syndrome,[340]

---

335. *Id.*

336. 908 F. Supp. 877, 895 (D.N.M. 1995) ("In conclusion, having determined that Dr. Raskin's testimony is based on 'scientific knowledge' that 'will assist the trier of fact' the Court finds that such testimony is sufficiently reliable and relevant to be admissible under FED. R. EVID. 702").

337. 895 F. Supp. 1354, 1363 (D.C. Ariz. 1995) ("A polygrapher is an expert in determining credibility. If a party can lay the proper foundation to qualify such a witness, then the requirements of Rule 608(a) will be met. The polygrapher will not testify that he knows of the subject's reputation for honesty, but that as an expert in determining credibility, with respect to this case, the subject has demonstrated a character for truthfulness.... [Although] the polygraph evidence's primary purpose is to show credibility, ... it also is evidence that shows Defendant was willing to take a polygraph and, in fact, passed the examination").

338. *E.g.,* State v. Porter, 241 Conn. 57, 698 A.2d 739 (1997) (adopting *Daubert* and excluding polygraph results under Rule 403), *cert. denied,* 523 U.S. 1058 (1998); People v. Gard, 158 Ill. 2d 191, 632 N.E.2d 1026, 1032 (1994) ("[T]he use of polygraph evidence ... is no less repugnant to and no less an affront to the integrity of the judicial process when the examination has been given to a witness ... than it is when the examination has been given to the defendant himself"); State v. Beard, 461 S.E.2d 486, 493 (W. Va. 1995) ("[W]e remain convinced that the reliability of such examinations is still suspect and not generally accepted within the relevant scientific community. Therefore, any speculation that our position in *Frazier* regarding polygraph admissibility is in question due to the *Daubert/Wilt* rulings is put to rest today").

339. *E.g.,*United States v. Hall, 165 F.3d 1095, 1104 (7th Cir.) ("This Court has a long line of cases which reflect our disfavor of expert testimony on the reliability of eyewitness identification"), *cert. denied,* 119 S. Ct. 2381 (1999); United States v. Smith, 156 F.3d 1046, 1053-54 (10th Cir. 1998) ("[E]xpert testimony on eyewitness identification may properly be admitted under *Daubert* in certain circumstances .... In this admittedly close case, we hold only that the district court did not abuse its discretion in excluding the testimony under the circumstances"), *cert. denied,* 119 S. Ct. 844 (1999); United States v. Smith, 122 F.3d 1355, 1359 (11th Cir.) ("[I]t is as true after *Daubert* as it was before that a district court does not abuse its discretion in excluding such testimony"), *cert. denied*, 118 S. Ct. 614 (1997); United States v. Kime, 99 F.3d 870 (8th Cir. 1996), *cert. denied*, 520 U.S. 1220 (1997); United States v. Rincon, 28 F.3d 921, 926 (9th Cir.) (psychologist's

mens rea,[341] and to forensic anthropologist testimony that a defendant was not the person in a surveillance photograph.[342] In *United States v. Hall*,[343] the Seventh Circuit ruled that the trial court erred when it excluded expert testimony on false confessions:

> This ruling overlooked the utility of valid social science. Even though the jury may have had beliefs about the subject, the question is whether those beliefs were correct. Properly conducted social science research often shows that commonly held beliefs are in error. Dr. Ofshe's testimony, assuming its scientific validity, would have let the jury know that a phenomenon known as false confessions exists, how to recognize it, and how to decide whether it fits the facts of the case being tried.[344]

Similarly, in *United States v. Shay*,[345] the First Circuit reversed the trial court's exclusion of psychiatric testimony that the defendant's inculpatory statements were caused by pseudologia fantastica, a mental disorder that makes the person a pathological liar who makes false statements without regard to their consequences.

In *Borawick v. Shay*,[346] a civil case, the plaintiff had no memory of child abuse for 20 years, and then after hypnotic-therapy, she accused her aunt and uncle of sexual abuse when she was age 4 and 7. The Second Circuit, in a case of first impression,[347] ruled the evidence inadmissible under the "totality of circumstances" approach. "We do not believe that *Daubert* is directly applicable to the issue here since *Daubert* concerns the admissibility of data derived from scientific techniques or expert opinions."[348] Nevertheless, "[e]ven though *Daubert* does not provide direct guidance, our decision today is informed by the principles underlying the Supreme Court's holding.... [B]y loosening the strictures on scientific evidence set by *Frye*, *Daubert* reinforces the idea that there should be a presumption of admissibility."[349]

---

testimony on vagaries of eyewitness identifications failed *Daubert*), *cert. denied*, 513 U.S. 1029 (1994).

340. State v. Foret, 628 So. 2d 1116, 1127 (La. 1993) (syndrome inadmissible).

341. Cecil v. Commonwealth, 888 S.W.2d 669, 675 (Ky. 1994).

342. United States v. Dorsey, 45 F.3d 809, 815 (4th Cir.) (inadmissible), *cert. denied*, 515 U.S. 1168 (1995).

343. 93 F.3d 1337 (7th Cir. 1996), *cert. denied*, 119 S. Ct. 2381 (1999).

344. *Id.* at 1345.

345. 57 F.3d 126 (1st Cir. 1995).

346. 68 F.3d 597 (2d Cir. 1995), *cert. denied*, 517 U.S. 1219 (1996). *See also* United States v. Shahzade, 923 F. Supp. 286 (D. Mass. 1996) (repressed memory syndrome satisfies *Daubert*).

347. *Id.* at 600 ("the admissibility of testimony about memories of childhood sexual abuse that are recalled for the first time in adulthood following the use of hypnosis as part of psychotherapy").

348. *Id.* at 610.

349. *Id.*

In *United States v. Powers*,[350] the Fourth Circuit ruled that the penile plethysmograph as a method to measure sexual arousal failed the *Daubert* test. "First, the Government proffered evidence that the scientific literature addressing penile plethysmography does not regard the test as a valid diagnostic tool because, although useful for treatment of sex offenders, it has no accepted standards in the scientific community. Second, the government also introduced evidence before the judge that a vast majority of incest offenders who do not admit their guilt, such as Powers, show a normal reaction to the test."[351] The court also excluded evidence that the defendant did not fit the profile of a fixated pedophile, on the grounds that the evidence was irrelevant; the defendant was charged with statutory rape of his daughter (incest abuse) and not with being a pedophile.[352]

Several state cases have also used *Daubert* in this context. In *State v. Shuck*,[353] the Tennessee Supreme Court ruled that a neuropsychologist's testimony concerning a defendant's acute susceptibility to inducement in support of an entrapment defense was admissible. In *State v. VanNatta*,[354] the Oregon court of appeals ruled that expert testimony of the defendant's submissive personality in support of a duress defense was inadmissible because a defendant's individual personality was not the relevant issue.

§ 1-7(G). Rule 403 & "Fit" Requirement.

The *Daubert* Court recognized that Rule 702 also required that expert testimony be "helpful." In the Court's view, this "condition goes primarily to

---

350. 59 F.3d 1460 (4th Cir. 1995), *cert. denied*, 516 U.S. 1077 (1996).

351. *Id.* at 1471. *See also* State v. Spencer, 119 N.C. App. 662, 667-68, 459 S.E.2d 812, 815-16 (1995) (rejecting defense expert's claim that device is 95 percent accurate; court's review of professional literature shows penile plethysmograph is not a reliable indicator of sexual deviancy), *rev. denied*, 341 N.C. 655 (1995). Nevertheless, courts continue to uphold the use of the device as a condition of parole. Walrath v. Getty, 71 F.3d 679 (7th Cir. 1995).

352. *Id.* at 1472.

353. 953 S.W.2d 662 (Tenn. 1997). *See also* United States v. Newman, 849 F.2d 156, 165 (5th Cir. 1988); United States v. McLernon, 746 F.2d 1098, 1115 (6th Cir. 1984) ("expert testimony concerning a defendant's predisposition may be invaluable in an entrapment case"); United States v. Benveniste, 564 F.2d 335, 339 (9th Cir. 1977); United States v. Hill, 655 F.2d 512, 516 (3d Cir. 1981) ("Testimony by an expert concerning a defendant's susceptibility to influence may be relevant to an entrapment defense"), *cert. denied*, 464 U.S. 1039 (1984).

354. 149 Or. App. 587, 945 P.2d 1062 (1997), *rev. denied*, 952 P.2d 61 (Or. 1997).

relevance."[355] Citing *United States v. Downing*,[356] the Court noted that this "consideration has been aptly described by Judge Becker as one of 'fit.'"[357]

The Court also noted that "scientific validity for one purpose is not necessarily scientific validity for other, unrelated purposes."[358] An example is the use of hypnotically-refreshed testimony in criminal trials. Hypnosis has been recognized as valid for a number of therapeutic purposes but not as a method of producing accurate recollection of past events, which was how it was used in court.[359]

At the end of the opinion, the Court cited Rule 403 and the trial court's authority to exclude scientific evidence where its probative value is outweighed by unfair prejudice, confusion of issues, or misleading the jury.[360]

§ 1-7(H). Scope of Appellate Review

In *General Electric Co. v. Joiner*,[361] the Supreme Court adopted an abuse-of-discretion standard for reviewing a trial court's admissibility decision under *Daubert*. The trial court had excluded the plaintiff's expert testimony, applying a rather demanding admissibility standard. The Court wrote: "We hold ... that abuse of discretion is the proper standard by which to review a district court's decision to admit or exclude scientific evidence. We further hold that, because it was within the District Court's discretion to conclude that the studies upon which the experts relied were not sufficient, whether individually or in combination, to

---

355. 509 U.S. at 591.

356. 753 F.2d 1224, 1242 (3d Cir. 1985).

357. *Id.* at 1242 ("An additional consideration under Rule 702— is whether expert testimony proffered in the case is sufficiently tied to the facts of the case that it will aid the jury in resolving a factual dispute").

358. 509 U.S. at 579 (citing Starrs, *Frye v. United States Restructured and Revitalized: A Proposal to Amend Federal Evidence Rule 702*, 26 JURIMETRICS J. 249, 258 (1986)).

359. *See* State v. Mack, 292 N.W.2d 764, 768 (Minn. 1980) (For hypnosis to be "therapeutically useful, it need not produce historically accurate memory"). For a discussion of hypnosis, *see* Chapter 12.

360. 509 U.S. at 595 (quoting Weinstein, *Rule 702 of the Federal Rules of Evidence is Sound; It Should Not be Amended*, 138 F.R.D. 631, 632 (1991) ("Expert evidence can be both powerful and quite misleading because of the difficulty in evaluating it. Because of this risk, the judge in weighing possible prejudice against probative force under Rule 403 of the present rules exercises more control over experts than over lay witnesses")). *See also* United States v. Hall, 165 F.3d 1095, 1106 (7th Cir.) ("[T]he district court considered the reliability and potential helpfulness of Dr. Wells' testimony, balanced the proffered testimony against cases in which we have expressed a strong disfavor towards the admission of such evidence, and concluded that Dr. Wells' testimony would not assist the trier of fact under Rule 702"), *cert. denied,* 119 S. Ct. 2381 (1999).

361. 522 U.S. 136, 118 S. Ct. 512 (1997). *See* § 1-5(F) *supra* (scope of appellate review for *Frye* test).

support their conclusion that Joiner's exposure to PCBs contributed to his cancer, the District Court did not abuse its discretion in excluding their testimony."[362]

In *Kumho Tire Co. v. Carmichael,*[363] the Court again ruled that appellate courts must accord trial judges discretion in applying *Daubert*. There are two aspects to this ruling. First, substantively, "whether *Daubert's* specific factors are, or are not, reasonable measures of reliability in a particular case is a matter that the law grants the trial judge broad latitude to determine."[364] Second, the judge also has discretion concerning the procedural aspects of this inquiry. The trial court is not required to hold a "*Daubert* hearing" every time expert testimony is challenged

The problem with this approach is the inevitable lack of consistency, one court finding polygraph evidence reliable and another finding the exact opposite.[365] In contrast, the Massachusetts Supreme Judicial Court has stated that "[i]n considering the issue of scientific validity, our review is de novo because a trial judge's conclusion will have applicability beyond the facts of the case before him."[366]

§ 1-7(I). Criticisms of the *Daubert* Test

Like *Frye* before it, the *Daubert* decision has come under vigorous attack. Although the Supreme Court unanimously rejected *Frye,* Chief Justice Rehnquist, joined by Justice Stevens, dissented in part because he believed that the factors specified in the majority opinion were unnecessary to the judgment and were also "vague and abstract."[367] Because of the "unusual subject matter," he believed that the Court should "proceed with great caution in deciding more than we have to, because our reach can so easily exceed our grasp."[368] Along the same vein, he questioned whether judges were equipped to apply the concept of "falsifiability" and observed that they should not be required to become "amateur scientists."[369]

---

362. 118 S. Ct. at 519.

363. 119 S. Ct. 1167 (1999).

364. *Id.* at 1176.

365. *See generally* Faigman, *Appellate Review of Scientific Evidence Under Daubert and Joiner*, 48 HASTINGS L.J. 969 (1997); Jonakait, *The Standard of Appellate Review for Scientific Evidence: Beyond Joiner and Scheffer*, 32 U.C. DAVIS L. REV. 289 (1999).

366. Commonwealth v. Vao Sok, 425 Mass. 787, 683 N.E.2d 671, 677 (1997) (PCR - DQA, PM, and D1S80). *See also* State v. Torres, 976 P.2d 20, 29 (N.M. 1999) ("[T]he threshold question of whether the trial court applied the correct evidentiary rule or standard is subject to de novo review on appeal").

367. 509 U.S. at 598.

368. *Id.* at 599.

369. *Id.* at 600-01.

The initial reviews of the decision questioned whether the opinion provided much guidance.[370] As one commentary observed, "Astonishingly, all parties expressed satisfaction with the *Daubert* decision — the lawyers for the plaintiff and defense, and scientists who wrote amicus briefs."[371] On remand, the Ninth Circuit opinion contained an extended discussion of the Supreme Court's decision under the label "Brave New World."[372]

Professor Graham, a noted authority, did not pull any punches when he wrote: "In attempting to understand the application of *Daubert* by the trial and appellate courts since 1993 ... one can easily become confused and frustrated. *Daubert* is a very, very incomplete case if not a very, very bad decision. It has resulted in a series of conflicting and confusing if not conflicted and confused opinions."[373] We disagree.

Courts retaining *Frye* have also begun to compare the two approaches, finding *Daubert* wanting. The Washington Supreme Court has declared:

> The State maintains that this court should abandon *Frye* and adopt *Daubert*. The State argues that *Frye* is difficult to apply. While *Frye* may be difficult to apply in some contexts, this is a result of the complexity of the particular science at issue, the extent to which the scientific community has made its view known, and the extent of any dispute in the scientific community. The same, or similar problems, arise under *Daubert*, including questions of testability, the extent to which the scientific technique or method is accepted by the scientific community, and drawing the line between legitimate science and "junk" science, along with other questions. Questions of admissibility of complex, controversial scientific techniques or methods, like those involving DNA evidence, are going to be difficult under either standard.[374]

The two standards are also discussed in the next section.

---

370. *See* Stewart, *A New Test: Decision Creates Uncertain Future for Admissibility of Expert Testimony*, A.B.A. J. 48, 48 (Nov. 1993) ("The catch ... is that no one is exactly sure what the new standard is"); Dyk & Castanias, *Daubert Doesn't End Debate on Experts*, NAT'L L.J. 17, 17 (Aug. 2, 1993) ("[T]he opinion of the court, in rejecting the existing standard, has created considerable confusion").

371. Foster et al., *Policy Forum: Science and the Toxic Tort*, 261 SCIENCE 1509, 1614 (Sept. 17, 1993).

372. Daubert v. Merrell Dow Pharmaceuticals, Inc., 43 F.3d 1311, 1316 (9th Cir.) ("Our responsibility, then, unless we badly misread the Supreme Court's opinion, is to resolve disputes among respected, well-credentialed scientists about matters squarely within their expertise, in areas where there is not scientific consensus as to what is and what is not 'good science,' and occasionally to reject such expert testimony because is was not 'derived by the scientific method.' Mindful of our position in the hierarchy of the federal judiciary, we take a deep breath and proceed with this heady task"), *cert. denied,* 516 U.S. 869 (1995).

373. M. GRAHAM, HANDBOOK OF FEDERAL EVIDENCE §702.5 (3d ed. 1992) (Supp. 1996).

374. State v. Copeland, 130 Wash. 2d 244, 258, 922 P.2d 1304, 1314 (1996) (en banc).

§ 1-8. Comparison of *Frye* & *Daubert*.

One question raised by the *Daubert* opinion is whether the Supreme Court intended its reliability test to be more permissive than the *Frye* test. There is some language in the opinion that points in this direction,[375] and a number of courts have adopted this position.[376] The polygraph cases are a good example. In *United States v. Posado*,[377] the Fifth Circuit stated that "the rationale underlying this circuit's per se rule against admitting polygraph evidence did not survive *Daubert*."[378]

There is, however, language in *Daubert* that points the other way,[379] particularly the Court's emphasis on the "gatekeeper" function of the trial court. In *General Electric Co. v. Joiner*,[380] a later case, the Court commented: "Thus, while the Federal Rules of Evidence allow district courts to admit a *somewhat* broader range of scientific testimony than would have been admissible under *Frye*, they leave in place the 'gatekeeper' role of the trial judge in screening such evidence."[381] Moreover, federal courts examining handwriting and hair analysis have questioned the admissibility of previously admitted evidence, thereby undercutting the notion that *Daubert* is a more permissive standard.[382]

Even if a jurisdiction adopts *Daubert*, a scientific technique's admissibility status may not change. Some commentators have argued that "[i]n practice ... courts today all tend to admit the same evidence whether or not they

---

375. *See* 509 U.S. at 589 ("Given the Rules' permissive backdrop and their inclusion of a specific rule on expert testimony that does not mention 'general acceptance,' the assertion that the Rules somehow assimilated *Frye* is unconvincing. *Frye* made 'general acceptance' the exclusive test for admitting expert scientific testimony. That austere standard, absent from, and incompatible with the Federal Rules of Evidence, should not be applied in federal trials").

376. *E.g.*, United States v. Kwong, 69 F.3d 663, 668 (2d Cir. 1995) (polygraph) ("The Federal Rules of Evidence, although concededly more liberal than the *Frye* test, still require a determination that the proffered scientific evidence is both relevant and reliable"), *cert. denied*, 517 U.S. 1115 (1996); Borawick v. Shay, 68 F.3d 597, 610 (2d Cir. 1995) ("[B]y loosening the strictures on scientific evidence set by *Frye*, *Daubert* reinforces the idea that there should be a presumption of admissibility of evidence"), *cert. denied*, 517 U.S. 1229 (1996); United States v. Bonds, 12 F.3d 540, 568 (6th Cir. 1993) ("We find that the DNA testimony easily meets the more liberal test set out by the Supreme Court in *Daubert*").

377. 57 F.3d 428 (5th Cir. 1995).

378. *Id.* at 429. *See* § 1-7(E) *supra* (forensic science techniques).

379. *See* 509 U.S. at 590 ("[I]n order to qualify as 'scientific knowledge,' an inference or assertion must be derived by the scientific method. Proposed testimony must be supported by appropriate validation — *i.e.*, 'good grounds,' based on what is known. In short, the requirement that an expert's testimony pertain to 'scientific knowledge' establishes a standard of evidentiary reliability").

380. 522 U.S. 136 (1997).

381. *Id.* at 142 (emphasis added).

382. *See* § 1-7(E) *supra* (forensic science techniques).

purport to apply the *Frye* standard."[383] This view is suspect, however. *Frye* played a determinative role in the voiceprint cases. As several courts have observed: "[W]hen the *Frye* test has been applied, courts have tended to exclude expert voice identification evidence based on spectrography. The courts are equally likely to admit the evidence when the *Frye* test is not applied."[384]

With other techniques, however, the admissibility standard has not made a difference. For example, few cases have excluded bite mark comparisons, including both courts that applied the general acceptance standard and those that employed other analyses.[385] Similarly, courts in jurisdictions that rejected *Frye* before *Daubert* was decided had excluded evidence based on controversial techniques. For example, in *State v. Brown*[386] the Oregon Supreme Court rejected the *Frye* test but then went on to exclude polygraph evidence under the Oregon Rules of Evidence.[387] In addition, a Delaware court spurned *Frye* but nevertheless excluded hypnotically-refreshed testimony under the Delaware Rules.[388] The same result has occurred in several truth serum cases.[389]

---

383. Weinstein, *Improving Expert Testimony*, 20 U. RICH. L. REV. 473, 478 (1986). *See also* Saltzburg, *Symposium on Science and The Rules of Evidence*, 99 F.R.D. 187, 209 (1983) ("The two approaches are essentially the same, despite the frequency with which they are assumed to differ. The question that is more significant is how much success a scientific claim must have before courts will rely upon it. The answer to this question is the same under *Frye* or the relevancy approach").

384. State v. Free, 493 So. 2d 781, 785 (La. App. 1986), *cert. denied*, 499 So. 2d 83 (1987). *See also* State v. Gortarez, 141 Ariz. 254, 686 P.2d 1224, 1236 n.6 (1984) ("Some courts, generally following the *Frye* rule, refuse to allow spectrographic evidence.... Other courts, generally following modifications of *Frye* or not mentioning it at all, have allowed spectrographic evidence").

385. *See* Chapter 13 (bite mark comparisons).

386. 687 P.2d 751 (Or. 1984) (en banc).

387. *Id.* at 775 ("Notwithstanding the usual deference to trial court discretion, we as an appellate court retain our role to determine the admissibility of scientific evidence under the Oregon Evidence Code"). *See also* State v. Catanese, 368 So. 2d 975, 981 (La. 1979) ("[A]fter engaging in a balancing process at *the appellate level* similar to that recommended by McCormick and other writers, we conclude that at present in our court system the probative value [of polygraph evidence] is so outweighed by the reasons for its exclusion that the evidence should not be admitted..."); State v. Thompson, 381 So. 2d 823, 824 (La. 1980) (rejecting voice stress analysis).

388. State v. Davis, 490 A.2d 601, 605 (Del. Super. 1985) ("[T]he State has not demonstrated that hypnotic recall is sufficiently reliable to be admitted as evidence"); Bundy v. State, 471 So. 2d 9, 18 (Fla. 1985), *cert. denied*, 479 U.S. 894 (1986).

389. *See* Zeigler v. State, 402 So. 2d 365, 373 (Fla. 1981), *cert. denied*, 455 U.S. 1035 (1982); Harper v. State, 249 Ga. 519, 292 S.E.2d 389, 395-96 (1982) (rejecting *Frye* rule but nevertheless excluding truth serum evidence as unreliable).

§ 1-9. *Frye-Daubert* "Plus."

Commentators have argued that some of the DNA cases had engrafted an additional requirement onto the *Frye* standard. This approach has been labeled "*Frye* Plus."[390] For example, in *People v. Castro*[391] the court set forth a three-pronged analysis. According to the court, the admissibility of DNA evidence depends upon a showing that (1) the underlying theory has been generally accepted, (2) the procedures implementing the theory has been generally accepted, and (3) the testing laboratory has followed these procedures.[392] The court wrote that "given the complexity of the DNA multi-system identification tests and the powerful impact that they may have on a jury, passing muster under *Frye* alone is insufficient to place this type of evidence before a jury."[393] The court went on to conclude that the prosecution had satisfied the first two prongs but not the third: "In a piercing attack upon each molecule of evidence presented, the defense was successful in demonstrating to this court that the testing laboratory failed in its responsibility to perform the accepted scientific techniques and experiments in several major respects."[394]

In *United States v. Two Bulls,*[395] the Eighth Circuit adopted the same approach.[396] "We fail to see that this analysis is *sui generis* or that it in any way allows intrusion of the court into deciding problems of weight vis-a-vis admissibility."[397] Moreover, the court believed that this approach was fully

---

390. Goldberg, *A New Day for DNA?*, 78 A.B.A.J. 84, 84 (Apr. 1992) (quoting attorney Angela Byne).

391. 144 Misc. 2d 956, 545 N.Y.S.2d 985 (Sup. Ct. 1989).

392. *Id.* at 959, 545 N.Y.S.2d at 987.

393. *Id.* at 960, 545 N.Y.S.2d at 987. In People v. Wesley, 83 N.Y.2d 417, 611 N.Y.S.2d 97, 104, 633 N.E.2d 451, 458 (1994), the New York Court of Appeals held that case-specific errors generally go to the weight of the evidence, not its admissibility.

In rejecting the three-pronged test, the Maryland Court of Appeals adopted an intermediate approach: "Although these particularized challenges ordinarily will go to the weight of the evidence rather than its admissibility, the trial judge retains discretion to exclude evidence if it is so unreliable that it would not be helpful to the factfinder." Armstead v. State, 342 Md. 38, 66, 673 A.2d 221, 235 (1996).

394. 144 Misc. 2d at 974, 545 N.Y.S.2d at 996. In *Ex Parte* Turner, 733 So. 2d 497 (Ala. 1998), the Alabama Supreme Court ruled that the state's DNA statute, Ala. Code § 36-18-30, superseded the *Frye*-plus test adopted in *Ex Parte* Perry, 586 So. 2d 242 (Ala. 1991), and adopted *Daubert* in its place. *See also* State v. Houser, 241 Neb. 525, 490 N.W.2d 168, 181 (1992) ("[T]he trial court, in determining admissibility of DNA evidence, must first be satisfied, and find, as to the general acceptance of relevant DNA theories in the scientific community, and must be satisfied as to the acceptance and validity of the methodology of testing DNA used. The trial court then determines if specific procedures were properly followed in the case before the court").

395. 918 F.2d 56 (8th Cir. 1990), *vacated after defendant's death,* 925 F.2d 1127 (8th Cir. 1991).

396. *Id.* at 61.

397. *Id.* at 60.

justified: "Because DNA evidence is so new and the resulting prejudice to the defendant is sufficiently great, it is imperative that the court satisfy itself that there exists a sufficient foundational basis as to the overall admissibility of the evidence. This must be done before the government exposes the jury to the lab results."[398] The Second Circuit, however, rejected this approach in *United States v. Jakobetz*.[399] The court referred to this "elevated standard"[400] as "even more stringent than that in *Frye*."[401]

However, even after the Supreme Court rejected the *Frye* test in *Daubert*,[402] the Eighth Circuit continued to impose this additional requirement. The court wrote:

> We believe that the reliability inquiry set forth in *Daubert* mandates that there be a preliminary showing that the expert properly performed a reliable methodology in arriving at his opinion.... [*Daubert*] suggests that the inquiry extends beyond simply the reliability of the principles or methodologies in the abstract. In order to determine whether scientific testimony is reliable, the court must conclude that the testimony was derived from the application of a reliable methodology or principle in the particular case.
>
> Thus, we conclude that the court should make an initial inquiry into the particular expert's application of the scientific principle or methodology in question. The court should require the testifying expert to provide affidavits attesting that he properly performed the protocols involved in DNA profiling.[403]

In short, *Daubert* "plus."

The Arkansas Supreme Court also rejected the *Frye* test and nevertheless adopted the three-prong test.[404] Texas has also followed this approach: "To be considered reliable, evidence of a scientific theory must satisfy the following three criteria: (a) the underlying theory must be valid; (b) the technique applying the theory must be laid; and (c) the technique must have been properly applied on

---

398. *Id.*

399. 955 F.2d 786 (2d Cir.), *cert. denied,* 506 U.S.834 (1992).

400. *Id.* at 795.

401. *Id.* at 794. The Second Circuit also rejected *Frye.*

402. *See* § 1-7 *supra.*

403. United States v. Martinez, 3 F.3d 1191, 1197-98 (8th Cir. 1993), *cert. denied,* 510 U.S. 1062 (1994).

404. Moore v. State, 323 Ark. 529, 547, 915 S.W.2d 284, 294 (1996) ("DNA profiling evidence should no longer be viewed as novel scientific evidence requiring a preliminary inquiry beyond the showing that the expert properly performed a reliable methodology in creating the DNA profiles"; "*Daubert* ... adopted a reliability approach to Rule 702, comparable to the relevancy approach of *Prater* in which reliability is the critical element").

the occasion in question."[405] In addition, Texas has required the proponent of novel scientific evidence to establish its reliability by "clear and convincing" evidence.[406]

In *United States v. Galbreth*,[407] the district court wrote an extensive opinion on the polygraph, concluding that the evidence in that case was admissible. The court also discussed the *Daubert* "plus" issue: "It is not entirely clear whether *Daubert* requires as a prerequisite to admissibility that the proponent establish the validity of the specific application of a scientific technique."[408] "[A]fter reviewing the case law addressing this issue in the context of other forensic laboratory techniques and after careful consideration of the testimony presented at the hearing regarding the polygraph technique, the Court holds that in the context of polygraph evidence, such scrutiny is imperative to a faithful application of *Daubert*."[409] The court went on to rule "that in addition to establishing the scientific validity of the polygraph technique in the abstract, the proponent of the proposed testimony must also prove that the specific examination was conducted properly by a competent examiner."[410]

As noted earlier in this chapter, the third prong in *Castro* is a logical step in establishing the reliability of scientific evidence.[411] A valid technique improperly applied will produce erroneous results. This requirement, however, need not be tied to the *Frye* test. It could be required in a jurisdiction that has rejected *Frye*. Moreover, as discussed in section 1-11, *infra*, this issue predates the DNA cases. Compliance with the third prong can be decided only on a case by case basis.[412] One commentator has argued that the third prong ought to be a condition of admissibility, but that the burden on this issue could be allocated to the defense.[413]

---

405. Campbell v. State, 910 S.W.2d 475, 478 (Tex. Crim. App. 1995) (en banc) (DNA-PCR evidence) (citing Kelly v. State, 824 S.W.2d 568, 573 (Tex. Crim. App. 1992)), *cert. denied*, 517 U.S. 1140 (1996). *See also* Hartman v. State, 946 S.W.2d 60, 62 (Tex. Crim. App. 1997) (intoxilizer).

406. *Id.* at 478.

407. 908 F. Supp. 877 (D.N.M. 1995).

408. *Id.* at 880-81.

409. *Id.* at 881.

410. *Id.* at 882.

411. *See* § 1-1 *supra*.

412. *See* NATIONAL ACADEMY OF SCIENCES, DNA TECHNOLOGY IN FORENSIC SCIENCE 134 (1992) (This assumption — "that the analytical work done for a particular trial comports with proper procedure — can be resolved only case by case and is always open to question, even if the general reliability of DNA typing is fully accepted in the scientific community").

413. Imwinkelried, *The Debate in the DNA Cases Over the Foundation for the Admission of Scientific Evidence: The Importance of Human Error as a Cause of Forensic Misanalysis*, 69 WASH. U. L.Q. 19 (1991).

§ 1-10. Uniform-Federal Rules Jurisdictions.

After the Federal Rules of Evidence were adopted in 1975, courts[414] and commentators[415] divided over whether the Federal Rules had superseded the *Frye* test. The issue was not addressed in the Advisory Committee's Notes,[416] the congressional committee reports,[417] or the hearings on the Federal Rules.[418] Proponents of *Frye* argued that since *Frye* had been the established rule prior to the adoption of the Federal Rules and since there was no indication in the legislative history suggesting that *Frye* had been superseded, the general acceptance test remained intact.

Other courts, both federal[419] and state,[420] disagreed. The proponents of the view that the Federal Rules of Evidence superseded the *Frye* test focused on the

---

414. *See* Ellis v. International Playtex, Inc., 745 F.2d 292, 304 n.15 (4th Cir. 1984) (Although it has expressed concerns about *Frye,* the Fourth Circuit continues to apply it in certain circumstances); Barrel of Fun, Inc. v. State Farm Fire & Cas. Co., 739 F.2d 1028, 1031 n.9 (5th Cir. 1984) (Fifth Circuit continues to apply *Frye* even if its applicability after Federal Rules is unresolved); United States v. Hope, 714 F.2d 1084, 1087 n.3 (11th Cir. 1983) (Eleventh Circuit has yet to decide whether *Frye* survives the Federal Rules).

415. *Compare* 1 D. LOUISELL & C. MUELLER, FEDERAL EVIDENCE 818 (1977) (*Frye* probably survives enactment of Federal Rules) and M. GRAHAM, HANDBOOK OF FEDERAL EVIDENCE § 703.2 (3d ed. 1991), *with* 3 J. WEINSTEIN & M. BERGER, *supra* note 279, ¶ 702[03] (Federal Rule's failure to incorporate *Frye* indicates its abandonment) and 22 C. WRIGHT & K. GRAHAM, *supra* note 26, at 92 (*Frye* repealed by Federal Rules).

416. The Advisory Committee's Notes are reprinted at 56 F.R.D. 183 (1973).

417. H.R. Rep. No. 650, 93d Cong., 2d Sess., *reprinted in* 1974 U.S. Code Cong. & Ad. News 7075; S. Rep. No. 1277, 93d Cong., 2d Sess., *reprinted in* 1974 U.S. Code Cong. & Ad. News 7051; H.R. Rep. No. 1597, 93d Cong., 2d Sess., *reprinted in* 1974 U.S. Code Cong. & Ad. News 7098 (conference report).

418. *Proposed Rules of Evidence: Hearings Before the Special Subcomm. on Reform of Federal Criminal Laws of the House Comm. on the Judiciary,* 93d Cong., 1st Sess. (1973); *Rules of Evidence: Hearings Before the Senate Comm. on the Judiciary,* 93d Cong., 2d Sess. (1974).

419. *E.g.,* United States v. Jakobetz, 955 F.2d 786, 794 (2d Cir.) (DNA evidence), *cert. denied,* 506 U.S. 834 (1992); United States v. Ferri, 778 F.2d 985, 988 (3d Cir. 1985) (innersole shoe comparison), *cert. denied,* 476 U.S. 1172 (1986); United States v. Downing, 753F.2d 1224, 1238 (3d Cir. 1985) (psychological testimony on eyewitness identifications); United States v. Williams, 583 F.2d 1194, 1198 (2d Cir. 1978) (voiceprints), *cert. denied,* 439 U.S. 1117 (1979); United States v. Baller, 519 F.2d 463, 466 (4th Cir.) (voiceprints), *cert. denied,* 423 U.S. 1019 (1975); United States v. Gipson, 24 M.J. 246, 251 (C.M.A. 1987) (polygraph).

420. *E.g.,* Brenk v. State, 311 Ark. 579, 847 S.W.2d 1, 9 (1993) (luminol testing inadmissible even though *Frye* not applied); Prater v. State, 307 Ark. 180, 185, 820 S.W.2d 429, 431 (1991) (DNA evidence); Santiago v. State, 510 A.2d 488, 489 (Del. 1986) (blood-alcohol analysis by gas chromatography); Walen v. State, 434 A.2d 1346, 1354 (Del. 1980) (semen test), *cert. denied,* 455 U.S. 910 (1982); Bundy v. State, 455 So. 2d 330, 341 (Fla. 1984) (Florida has never explicitly adopted *Frye*); Harper v. State, 249 Ga. 519, 524-25, 292 S.E.2d 389, 395 (1982) (truth serum); Andrews v. State, 533 So. 2d 841 (Fla. App. 1988) (DNA evidence), *rev. denied,* 542 So. 2d 1332 (Fla. 1989); State v. Montalbo, 828 P.2d 1274, 1280 (Haw. 1992) (DNA evidence); State v. Rodgers, 119 Idaho 1047, 1049, 812 P.2d 1208, 1210 (1991) (blood spatter analysis); State v.

language of Rules 401, 402, and 702.[421] For example, in *State v. Williams*[422] the Supreme Judicial Court of Maine ruled that the Maine Rules of Evidence, which are patterned after the Federal Rules, "do not purport to establish a special standard to govern the admissibility of testimony involving newly ascertained, or applied, scientific principles."[423] Federal Rule 702, which governs the admissibility of expert testimony, was also cited as evidence of *Frye's* repeal. In *State v. Hall*[424] the Iowa Supreme Court concluded that the *Frye* test "is inconsistent with modern concepts of evidence, such as embodied in the Federal Rules of Evidence, which provide that '[i]f scientific, technical, or other specialized knowledge will assist the trier of fact to understand the evidence or to determine the fact in issue, a witness may testify thereto in the form of an opinion or otherwise.'"[425]

Klindt, 389 N.W.2d 670, 672-73 (Iowa 1986) (enzyme blood analysis); State v. Hall, 297 N.W.2d 80, 85 (Iowa 1980) (blood flight characteristics), *cert. denied,* 450 U.S. 927 (1981); State v. Catanese, 368 So. 2d 975 (La. 1979) (polygraph), *rev'd,* 385 So. 2d 295 (La. 1980); State v. Williams, 388 A.2d 500, 504 (Me. 1978) (voiceprints); Barmeyer v. Montana Power Co., 657 P.2d 594, 598 (Mont. 1983) (corrosion analysis); State v. Dorsey, 88 N.M. 184, 539 P.2d 204 (1975) (polygraph); State v. Pennington, 327 N.C. 89, 98, 393 S.E.2d 847, 852 (1990) (DNA evidence); State v. Williams, 4 Ohio St. 3d 53, 56-58, 446 N.E.2d 444, 446-48 (1983) (voiceprints); State v. Brown, 297 Or. 404, 687 P.2d 751, 759 (1984) (polygraph); State v. Kersting, 50 Or. App. 461, 469, 623 P.2d 1095, 1100 (1981) (hair analysis), *aff'd on other grounds,* 290 Or. 350, 638 P.2d 1145 (1982); State v. Wheeler, 496 A.2d 1382 (R.I. 1985) (voiceprints); Kelly v. State, 824 S.W.2d 568, 571-72 (Tex. Crim. App. 1992) (DNA evidence); Jones v. State, 716 S.W.2d 142, 145 (Tex. App. 1986) (ion-pair extraction/gas chromatography-mass spectrometry); Phillips v. Jackson, 615 P.2d 1228, 1233-34 (Utah 1980) (HLA blood test); O'Dell v. Commonwealth, 234 Va. 672, 695-96, 364 S.E.2d 491, 504 (multisystem electrophoretic blood test), *cert. denied,* 488 U.S. 871 (1988); State v. Walstad, 119 Wis. 2d 483, 514-16, 351 N.W.2d 469, 485-86 (1984) (breathalyzer ampoule retesting); Cullin v. State, 565 P.2d 445, 456-57 (Wyo. 1977) (polygraph). *See also* Hopkins v. State, 579 N.E.2d 1297, 1305 (Ind. 1991) (concurring opinion) (*Frye* not conclusively adopted in Indiana).

421. Rule 401 defines relevant evidence as "evidence having any tendency to make the existence of any fact that is of consequence to the determination of the action more probable or less probable than it would be without the evidence." Rule 402 provides that "[a]ll relevant evidence is admissible, except as otherwise provided by the Constitution of the United States, by Act of Congress, by these rules, or by other rules prescribed by the Supreme Court pursuant to statutory authority." Because scientific evidence could be shown to be reliable and thus relevant under Rule 401 without regard to its general acceptance in the scientific community and because none of the exceptions enumerated in Rule 402 applies, the Federal Rules provide a standard of admissibility that is inconsistent with the *Frye* test.

422. 388 A.2d 500 (Me. 1978).

423. *Id.* at 503.

424. 297 N.W.2d 80 (Iowa 1980) (en banc), *cert. denied,* 450 U.S. 927 (1981).

425. *Id.* at 84. *Accord* United States v. Downing, 753 F.2d 1224, 1235 (3d Cir. 1985); Barmeyer v. Montana Power Co., 657 P.2d 594, 598 (Mont. 1983) (*Frye* test "not in conformity with the spirit of the new rules of evidence"); State v. Williams, 4 Ohio St. 3d 53, 58, 446 N.E.2d 444, 448 (1983) ("Rules of Evidence establish adequate preconditions for admissibility of expert

In *Daubert v. Merrell Dow Pharmaceuticals, Inc.*,[426] a 1993 decision, the Supreme Court rejected *Frye* as inconsistent with the Federal Rules. In place of *Frye,* the Court substituted a "reliability" test based on Rule 702.

State Jurisdictions

Daubert's effect on state jurisdictions depends on several factors. *Daubert* rests on an interpretation of the Federal Rules of Evidence, a federal statute.[427] As a statutory rather than a constitutional case, *Daubert* is not binding on the states, which are therefore free to continue to follow *Frye*.[428] This is true even in the nearly 40 jurisdictions that have adopted evidence rules based on the Federal Rules.

A number of jurisdictions have rejected *Frye* in favor of the *Daubert* approach.[429] Other courts, now citing *Daubert* favorably, had already discarded *Frye*.[430] In contrast, still other courts have retained the *Frye* test. For example, the Arizona Supreme Court declined to follow *Daubert*, noting that it was "not bound by the United States Supreme Court's non-constitutional construction of the Federal Rules of Evidence when we construe the Arizona Rules of Evidence."[431] The court also remarked: "Our rules ... are court-enacted. While the United States Supreme Court considers congressional purpose, this court when construing a rule we have adopted must rely on text and our own intent in adopting or amending the rule in the first instance."[432] Moreover, the U.S.

---

testimony"); State v. Brown, 297 Or. 404, 687 P.2d 751, 759 (1984); State v. Walstad, 119 Wis. 2d 483, 516, 351 N.W.2d 469, 486 (1984) ("The *Frye* concept is alien to the Wisconsin law of evidence").

426. 509 U.S. 579, 589 (1993) ("Given the Rules' permissive backdrop and their inclusion of a specific rule on expert testimony that does not mention 'general acceptance,' the assertion that the Rules somehow assimilated *Frye* is unconvincing. *Frye* made 'general acceptance' the exclusive test for admitting expert scientific testimony. That austere standard, absent from and incompatible with the Federal Rules of Evidence, should not be applied in federal trials"). The *Daubert* test is discussed in § 1-7 *supra.*

427. 509 U.S. at 587 ("We interpret the legislatively-enacted Federal Rules of Evidence as we would any statute").

428. The Uniform Rules of Evidence (1953) contained a relevancy provision similar to that found in the Federal Rules, and yet jurisdictions adopting the Uniform Rules nonetheless adhered to the *Frye* test. *See* UNIF. R. EVID. 1(2) (1953) (relevant evidence); People v. Kelly, 17 Cal. 3d 24, 549 P.2d 1240, 130 Cal. Rptr. 144 (1976); State v. Hurd, 86 N.J. 525, 432 A.2d 86 (1981).

429. *See* § 1-13 *infra* (*Daubert* jurisdictions).

430. *See* § 1-14 *infra* (pre-*Daubert* reliability jurisdictions).

431. State v. Bible, 858 P.2d 1152, 1183 (Ariz. 1993), *cert. denied,* 511 U.S. 1046 (1994). *See* § 1-15 *infra* (*Frye* jurisdictions).

432. *Id. See also State v. Dean*, 246 Neb. 869, 882, 884, 523 N.W.2d 681, 692-93 (1994) ("[N]otwithstanding that our rule 702 parallels the federal rule 702, *Daubert* does not apply to state court decisions. The increasing prevalence of expert evidence cautions against the admission of scientific evidence which is still the subject of dispute and controversy in the relevant scientific

Supreme Court has adopted an unpersuasive and much-criticized "plain meaning" construction in interpreting the Federal Rules, which is not binding on the states.[433]

Codification

Daubert may provide the impetus to amend Federal Rule 702 or its state counterparts. In 1986 several commentators offered amendments.[434] In 1991 the Civil Rules Committee proposed an amendment that required expert testimony be

---

communities.... We thus adhere to the *Frye* standard...."; laser trajectory analysis not a novel technique; "[A]iming a laser beam through bullet holes [in a mobile home] to reconstruct a bullet's path is no less reliable than inserting a dowel into a bullet hole to demonstrate its path"), *cert. denied*, 515 U.S. 1123 (1995); Commonwealth v. Blasioli, 552 Pa. 149, 153 n.1, 713 A.2d 1117, 1119 n.1 (1998) ("Pennsylvania courts are not bound by the Federal Rules of Evidence, and, for the present, this Court has continued to employ the *Frye* standard ..."); State v. Cissne, 72 Wash. App. 677, 865 P.2d 564, 569 ("[U]ntil such time as our Supreme Court abandons *Frye* and interprets ER 702 in the same manner as *Daubert* interpreted Fed. R. Evid. 702, we are bound by ... previous decisions"), *rev. denied*, 124 Wash. 2d 1006, 887 P.2d 1288 (1994).

433. *See* Becker & Orenstein, *The Federal Rules of Evidence After Sixteen Years —The Effect of "Plain Meaning" Jurisprudence, The Need for an Advisory Committee on the Rules of Evidence, and Suggestions for Selective Revision of the Rules*, 60 Geo. Wash. L. Rev. 857, 863 (1992) (commenting on "the potential mischief that can result from a rigid plain meaning analysis of the Rules"); Jonakait, *The Supreme Court, Plain Meaning, and the Changed Rules of Evidence*, 68 Tex. L. Rev. 745, 786 (1990) ("Inevitably, ... the plain-meaning standard will produce worse evidence law by freezing evidence into a literalistic mold, by eliminating its dynamism, and by mandating results without any attempt to satisfy the policy goals of evidence law"); Weissenberger, *The Supreme Court and the Interpretation of the Federal Rules of Evidence*, 53 Ohio St. L.J. 1307, 1338 (1992) (The Court's approach "has recast the method of interpreting evidentiary principles in a manner that ignores the wisdom of the common-law history of the Federal Rules of Evidence and the capability of enlightened growth").

434. Professor Lederer proposed adding the word "reliable" before the phrase "scientific, technical, or other specialized knowledge" in Rule 702. Lederer, *Resolving the Frye Dilemma : A Reliability Approach*, 26 Jurimetrics J. 240 (1986).

Professor Berger proposed adding a second sentence to the rule: "When the witness seeks to testify about a scientific principle or technique that has not previously been accorded judicial recognition, the testimony shall be admitted if the court determines that its probative value outweighs the dangers specified in Rule 403." Berger, *A Relevancy Approach to Novel Scientific Evidence*, 26 Jurimetrics J. 245 (1986).

Professor Starrs proposed adding a second sentence to Rule 702: "In the case of expert testimony based upon a scientific theory or technique, the court shall find that the theory or technique in question is scientifically valid for the purposes for which it is tendered." Starrs, *Frye v. United States Restructured and Revitalized: A Proposal to Amend Federal Evidence Rule 702*, 26 Jurimetrics J. 249 (1986).

Commentaries on the various proposals were later discussed at the ABA's annual conference in August 1986. *Rules for Admissibility of Scientific Evidence*, 115 F.R.D. 79 (1987).

based on "reasonably reliable" information,[435] a provision that apparently embodied a modified *Frye* rule. The drafting committee note states: This standard "does not mandate a return to the strictures of *Frye v. United States*.... However, the court is called upon to reject testimony that is based upon premises lacking any significant support and acceptance within the scientific community."[436] This proposal was later withdrawn. A 1998 proposed amendment to Rule 702 also attempts to address this issue.[437]

There are few models in other jurisdictions. Initial state adoptions of the Federal Rules were simply "silent regarding the viability of *Frye*."[438] Several states later addressed this issue in their Rules. Michigan Rule 702 requires expert testimony be based on "recognized" scientific, technical, or other knowledge. Indiana Rule 702(b) provides that "[e]xpert scientific testimony is admissible only if the court is satisfied that the scientific principles upon which the expert testimony rests are reliable." Hawaii Rule 702 contains an additional provision: "In determining the issue of assistance to the trier of fact, the court may consider the trustworthiness and validity of the scientific technique or mode of analysis employed by the proffered expert."[439] Ohio Rule 702 is more comprehensive.[440]

---

435. *Preliminary Draft of Proposed Amendments to the Federal Rules of Civil Procedure and the Federal Rules of Evidence*, 137 F.R.D. 53, 156 (1991) ("Testimony providing scientific, technical, or other specialized information, in the form of an opinion or otherwise, may be permitted only if (1) the information is reasonably reliable and will substantially assist the trier of fact to understand the evidence or to determine a fact in issue, and (2) the witness is qualified as an expert by knowledge, skill, experience, training, or education to provide such testimony"). *See generally* Giannelli, *"Junk Science": The Criminal Cases*, 84 J. CRIM. L. & CRIMINOLOGY 105 (1993).

436. 137 F.R.D. at 157.

437. This proposal adds the following clause: "provided that (1) the testimony is sufficiently based upon reliable facts or data, (2) the testimony is the product of reliable principles and methods, and (3) the witness has applied the principles and methods reliably to the facts of the case. 181 F.R.D. 144-52 (1999) (submitted to the Standing Committee in June, 1998).

438. 2 G. JOSEPH & S. SALTZBURG, THE FEDERAL RULES OF EVIDENCE IN THE STATES, RULE 702, at 17 (1992).

439. A proposed New York rule, which was never adopted, explicitly adopts the "*Frye* plus" approach. Proposed N.Y. R. EVID. 702(b) provides:

> Scientific testimony. Testimony concerning scientific matters, or testimony concerning the result of a scientific procedure, test or experiment is admissible provided: (1) there is general acceptance within the scientific community of the validity of the theory or principle underlying the matter, procedure, test or experiment; (2) there is general acceptance within the relevant scientific community that the procedure, test or experiment is reliable and produces accurate results; and (3) the particular test, procedure or experiment was conducted in such a way as to yield an accurate result. Upon request of a party, a determination pursuant to this subdivision shall be made before the commencement of trial.

NEW YORK STATE LAW REVISION COMM'N, A CODE OF EVIDENCE FOR THE STATE OF NEW YORK (1991) (submitted to the 1991-92 session of the Legislature by Gov. Mario Cuomo).

Ohio Rule 702(C)(1) offers alternative ways to establish the validity of a scientific theory; it may either be "objectively verifiable" or "widely accepted." Rule 702(C)(3) addresses the *Frye-Daubert* "plus" issue; the proponent must establish that the technique was applied correctly in the particular case.[441]

§ 1-11. Proper Application of a Scientific Technique.

The previous sections dealt with establishing the validity of a scientific technique. Even if the validity of a technique is established, the reliability of evidence derived from that technique will depend on whether the technique was properly applied on the particular occasion involved in the case. "Proper application" requires an examination into a number of factors: (1) if instrumentation was used in the technique, whether the instruments were in proper working order at the time the technique was employed; (2) whether proper procedures were followed at that time; and (3) whether the person using the technique and the person interpreting the results were properly qualified.

The Tennessee Supreme Court's approach to intoxication test evidence offers an instructive illustration. The court has stated the admissibility requirements as follows:

> First, the testing operator must testify that the test used followed Tennessee Bureau of Investigation standards. Second, the operator must be certified in accordance with those standards. Third, the machine must be certified, tested regularly for accuracy, and working properly. Fourth, the motorist must be personally observed for the requisite twenty minutes before taking the test. Fifth, the operator must follow the instrument's

---

440. Ohio Rule 702 reads:

A witness may testify as an expert if all of the following apply:

> (A) The witness' testimony either relates to matters beyond the knowledge or experience possessed by lay persons or dispels a misconception common among lay persons;
> (B) The witness is qualified as an expert by specialized knowledge, skill, experience, training, or education regarding the subject matter of the testimony;
> (C) The witness' testimony is based on reliable scientific, technical, or other specialized information. To the extent that the testimony reports the result of a procedure, test, or experiment, the testimony is reliable only if all of the following apply:
> (1) The theory upon which the procedure, test, or experiment is based is objectively verifiable or is validly derived from widely accepted knowledge, facts, or principles;
> (2) The design of the procedure, test, or experiment reliably implements the theory;
> (3) The particular procedure, test, or experiment was conducted in a way that will yield an accurate result.

See 1 P. GIANNELLI & B. SNYDER, BALDWIN'S OHIO PRACTICE: EVIDENCE § 702.9 (1996).

441. *See* § 1-9 *supra.*

prescribed operational procedure. Lastly, the operator must identify the test results offered in evidence.[442]

The Court rejected the argument that a failure to satisfy these requirements should affect the weight, not the admissibility, of the evidence.

These requirements are discussed in the subsequent sections.

§ 1-11(A). Proper Working Order Requirement.

If a scientific procedure involves instrumentation, the accuracy of results derived from that procedure depends on the functioning of the instrument at the time the procedure is used. Similarly, if a procedure involves the use of reagents or chemicals, the condition of those substances at the time the procedure is used may affect the results.[443]

The courts are divided over whether a showing of an instrument's accuracy affects the admissibility or only the weight of the evidence. Some courts require that the proponent establish the proper working condition of the instrument as a prerequisite to admissibility. For example, this requirement has been applied to polygraph,[444] intoxication,[445] voiceprint,[446] and radar evidence[447] as well as other

---

442. State v. Bobo, 909 S.W.2d 788, 790 (Tenn. 1995) (citing State v. Sensing, 843 S.W.2d 412, 418 (Tenn. 1992)). *See also* State v. Taylor, 694 A.2d 907, 911 (Me. 1997) ("[T]he HGN test's reliability must be established before its results are admissible in evidence ...").

443. One court wrote:

> Because an intoxication test conducted with chemicals of inferior quality could bring to bear a practically conclusive presumption of guilt against an innocent person, it is essential that the officially promulgated methods, procedures and techniques include a thorough analysis of the chemicals by a chemist under laboratory conditions to insure that they are of proper composition, strength and volume at the time a test is conducted.

State v. Goetz, 374 So. 2d 1219, 1220 (La. 1979). *See also* Lauderdale v. State, 548 P.2d 376 (Alaska 1976) (spot checking of ampoules); Cody v. Texas, 548 S.W.2d 401, 404-05 (Tex. Crim. App. 1977) (proof of properly compounded chemicals in breathalyzer test); State v. Baker, 56 Wash. 2d 846, 854, 355 P.2d 806, 811 (1960) (equilibrating device to check ampoules).

444. *See* United States v. Ridling, 350 F. Supp. 90, 93 (E.D. Mich. 1972) ("the recording device or polygraph [must] be in good operating condition").

445. *See* People v. Adams, 59 Cal. App. 3d 559, 561, 131 Cal. Rptr. 190, 191 (1976) ("In general the foundational prerequisites for admissibility of [breathalyzer] testing results are that (1) the particular apparatus utilized was in proper working order ..."); Commonwealth v. Barbeau, 411 Mass. 782, 784, 585 N.E.2d 1392, 1394 (1992) (statute and regulations mandate a "periodic testing program"); Gailey v. Director of Revenue, 717 S.W.2d 240, 242 (Mo. App. 1986) ("The testing officer ... testified he had a Type III permit, and that he followed the authorized 'checklist,' which sets forth the proper mode of operating the breathalyzer machine"); State v. Gerber, 206 Neb. 75, 90, 291 N.W.2d 403, 411 (1980) ("[T]esting device or equipment [must be] in proper working order at the time of conducting the test"); Mentor v. Giordano, 9 Ohio St. 2d 140, 146, 224 N.E.2d 343, 347 (1967) ("There [was] no evidence that the Breathalyzer ... was in proper working order

types of scientific evidence.[448] This requirement is imposed by statute in some jurisdictions.[449] In contrast, other courts have held that the condition of any instrumentation affects the weight of the evidence, not its admissibility.[450]

Various methods of proof have been used to establish the condition of instruments employed in scientific procedures. For example, the condition of radar has been established by the use of tuning forks,[451] periodic maintenance,[452] and test runs by a vehicle with a calibrated speedometer.[453] Periodic maintenance may be shown by the use of business and official records.[454] In addition, evidence

---

..."). *See also* Annot., *Necessity and Sufficiency of Proof that Tests of Blood Alcohol Concentration Were Conducted in Conformance With Prescribed Methods*, 96 A.L.R.3D 745 (1980).

446. *See* People v. Tobey, 60 Mich. App. 420, 429, 231 N.W.2d 403, 408 (1975) ("Proof of a scientific or mechanical instrument's accuracy and proper use is a requisite for the admission of the results derived from such devices"), *rev'd on other grounds,* 401 Mich. 141, 257 N.W.2d 537 (1977).

447. *E.g.,* Commonwealth v. Whynaught, 377 Mass. 14, 18-19, 384 N.E.2d 1212, 1215 (1979); State v. Calvert, 682 S.W.2d 474, 477 (Mo. 1984); State v. Shelt, 46 Ohio App. 2d 115, 119, 346 N.E.2d 345, 348 (1976); State v. Doria, 135 Vt. 341, 342, 376 A.2d 751, 752 (1977); People v. Donohoo, 54 Ill. App. 3d 375, 377-78, 369 N.E.2d 546, 548 (1977).

448. *See* Villegas v. Bryson, 16 Ariz. App. 456, 458, 494 P.2d 61, 63 (1972) (tachograph); State v. Stevens, 467 S.W.2d 10, 23 (Mo.) (neutron activation analysis), *cert. denied,* 404 U.S. 994 (1971); State v. Fields, 434 S.W.2d 507, 516 (Mo. 1968) ("paraffin" test). *See also* J. WIGMORE, SCIENCE OF JUDICIAL PROOF 450 (3d ed. 1937) ("The particular apparatus used ... must be in good condition for accurate work").

449. *E.g.,* ARK. CODE. ANN. § 5-65-202 (Michie 1987) (intoxication tests); FLA. STAT. ANN. § 316.1905(1) (West 1992) (defendant may attack radar equipment credibility); MD. CTS. & JUD. PROC. CODE ANN. § 10-304(e) (1987) (intoxication tests); NEB. REV. STAT. § 39-669.11 (1991) (intoxication tests must be performed according to approved methods).

450. *See* Adkins v. Dirickson, 523 F. Supp. 1281, 1287 (E.D. Pa. 1981) (tachograph); State v. Shimon, 243 N.W.2d 571, 573 (Iowa 1976); People v. Dusing, 5 N.Y.2d 126, 128, 155 N.E.2d 393, 394, 181 N.Y.S.2d 493, 495 (1959); People v. Abdallah, 82 Ill. App. 2d 312, 316, 226 N.E.2d 408, 410 (1967); State v. Dantonio, 18 N.J. 570, 580, 115 A.2d 35, 40 (1955) (dictum).

451. *E.g.,* People v. Walker, 199 Colo. 475, 480, 610 P.2d 496, 500 (1980); State v. Tomanelli, 153 Conn. 365, 372, 216 A.2d 625, 630 (1966); State v. Readding, 160 N.J. Super. 238, 243, 389 A.2d 512, 515 (1978); State v. McDonough, 302 Minn. 468, 470, 225 N.W.2d 259, 260 (1975); State v. Doles, 70 Ohio App. 2d 35, 39, 433 N.E.2d 1290, 1293 (1980).

452. *E.g.,* East Cleveland v. Ferell, 168 Ohio St. 298, 303, 154 N.E.2d 630, 633 (1958); People v. Jones, 10 Misc. 2d 1067, 1075-76, 171 N.Y.S.2d 325, 334 (City Ct. 1958). *See also* Commonwealth v. Barbeau, 411 Mass. 782, 785, 585 N.E.2d 1392, 1394 (1992) (statute and regulations mandate a "periodic testing program" for breathalyzer).

453. *E.g.,* State v. Calvert, 682 S.W.2d 474, 477 (Mo. 1984); Honeycutt v. Commonwealth, 408 S.W.2d 421, 423 (Ky. App. 1966); State v. Graham, 322 S.W.2d 188, 197 (Mo. App. 1959); East Cleveland v. Ferell, 168 Ohio St. 298, 303, 154 N.E.2d 630, 633 (1958); Whitehead v. Lynchburg, 213 Va. 742, 742-43, 195 S.E.2d 858, 859 (1973).

454. *E.g.,* Wester v. State, 528 P.2d 1179, 1183 (Alaska 1974) (calibration certificate for breathalyzer admitted as official record), *cert. denied,* 423 U.S. 836 (1975); People v. Stribel, 199 Colo. 377, 380, 609 P.2d 113, 116 (1980) (record of calibration test for breathalyzer admitted as business record); People v. Black, 84 Ill. App. 3d 1050, 1053, 406 N.E.2d 23, 25 (1980)

of habit may be sufficient to establish the proper working condition of an instrument.[455]

In jurisdictions that require the condition of instrumentation to be established as a prerequisite to admissibility, the trial court is not bound by the rules of evidence in deciding this issue,[456] and the burden of proof is a preponderance of the evidence.[457]

§ 1-11(B). Proper Procedure Requirement.

The accuracy of results obtained from scientific evidence also depends on whether proper procedures were followed. Again, the courts are divided over whether the proponent of scientific evidence must establish adherence to proper procedures as a condition of admissibility. Some courts hold that failure to show adherence to accepted procedures results in the exclusion of the evidence. For example, one court has stated: "It is widely recognized that the party offering the results of laboratory tests must ... vouch for its correct administration in the particular case."[458] Cases involving polygraph,[459] voiceprint,[460] radar,[461] DNA,[462]

(certification decal for breathalyzer admitted as a public record); State v. Ward, 15 Ohio St. 3d 355, 358, 474 N.E.2d 300, 302 (1984) (calibration report of intoxilyzer admitted as a public record). *See also* People v. Gower, 42 N.Y.2d 117, 121, 366 N.E.2d 69, 71, 397 N.Y.S.2d 368, 370 (1977) (breathalyzer reports admissible as business records).

Some jurisdictions provide for the admissibility of testing certificates by statute. *See* FLA. STAT. ANN. § 316.1905(3)(b) (West 1992) (radar); PA. STAT. ANN. tit. 75, § 3368(d) (Bisel 1992); Commonwealth v. Perdok, 411 Pa. 301, 192 A.2d 221 (1963) (radar certificate statute).

455. *See* United States v. Lopez, 328 F. Supp. 1077, 1086 (E.D.N.Y. 1971) (custom and practice sufficient to establish condition of fluxgate magnetometer). *See also* FED. R. EVID. 406 (habit evidence).

456. *See* FED. R. EVID. 104(a).

457. *See* Daubert v. Merrell Dow Pharmaceuticals, Inc., 509 U.S. 579, 592 n.10 (1993) ("These matters should be established by a preponderance of proof"); United States v. Williams, 95 F.3d 723, 729 (8th Cir. 1996) ("It is the burden of the party offering the expert testimony to lay a foundation for its admission"), *cert. denied*, 519 U.S. 1082 (1997); 1 J. WIGMORE, EVIDENCE § 18, at 841-44 (Tillers rev. 1983).

458. United States v. Bruno, 333 F. Supp. 570, 574 (E.D. Pa. 1971) (chromatographic analysis of ink).

459. *See* United States v. Ridling, 350 F. Supp. 90, 93 (E.D. Mich. 1972) ("For a test to be successful, it is important ... that appropriate scientific methods be used in connection with the questioning of the [polygraph] subject ...").

460. *See* People v. Kelly, 17 Cal. 3d 24, 30, 549 P.2d 1240, 1244, 130 Cal. Rptr. 144, 148 (1976) ("The proponent of the [voiceprint] evidence must demonstrate that correct scientific procedures were used in the particular case").

461. *See* United States v. Dreos, 156 F. Supp. 200, 208 (D. Md. 1957) ("proper operative procedures were followed").

462. The DNA cases are discussed in §1-9 *supra* (*Daubert-Frye* "Plus"). *See also* Smith v. State, 702 N.E.2d 668, 673 (Ind. 1998) (DNA) ("[T]he lab was accredited by the American Society of Crime Lab Directors in 1990. Furthermore, the lab runs its tests under controlled conditions,

as well as other types of scientific evidence[463] have taken the same position. Proper procedures are sometimes prescribed by statute or administrative regulation.[464]

In contrast, other courts have held that "[o]bjections to the manner in which the analysis was conducted go to the weight rather than to the admissibility of the evidence."[465] In one case, the California Supreme Court stated that "[c]areless testing affects the weight of the evidence and not its admissibility, and must be attacked on cross-examination or by other expert testimony."[466] An intermediate appellate court, however, held that this language was not intended "to overrule the long-established" California requirement that "requires proof that correct scientific procedures were used in a particular case."[467]

In jurisdictions that require a showing that proper procedures were followed as a prerequisite to admissibility, the trial court is not bound by the rules of evidence in deciding the issue, and the burden of proof is a preponderance of the evidence.[468]

§ 1-11(C). Qualifications of Operators and Interpreters.

If the person conducting a scientific technique is not qualified, the results obtained may not be reliable. Thus, courts have held that the person performing a

---

follows specific protocols, and conducts quality testing on the kits and the analysts. Any concerns in this respect go to the weight of the evidence, not its admissibility").

463. *E.g.*, Fuenning v. Superior Court, 139 Ariz. 590, 680 P.2d 121 (1983) (blood alcohol test); State v. Fields, 434 S.W.2d 507, 516 (Mo. 1968) ("paraffin" test); State v. Helmer, 278 N.W.2d 808, 812-13 (S.D. 1979) (breathalyzer).

464. *See Ex parte* Mayo, 652 So. 2d 201, 209 (Ala. 1994) (administrative rules concerning alcohol breath testing promulgated by Department of Public Health did not satisfy statute which required adoption by Department of Forensic Sciences); Fuenning v. Superior Court, 139 Ariz. 590, 680 P.2d 121, 133 (1983) (intoxication test statute); State v. Krause, 405 So. 2d 832, 834 (La. 1981) (intoxication test statute); State v. Gerber, 206 Neb. 75, 85-86, 291 N.W.2d 403, 409 (1980) (statute "establishes two requirements that must be met in order for the results of a Breathalyzer test to be admissible. It must appear (1) that the test has been performed according to methods approved by the Department of Health"); Cincinnati v. Sand, 43 Ohio St. 2d 79, 85-86, 330 N.E.2d 908, 912 (1975) (intoxication test statute).

465. State v. Johnson, 539 S.W.2d 493, 501 (Mo. App. 1976) (neutron activation analysis), *cert. denied,* 430 U.S. 934 (1976). *Accord* United States v. Stifel, 433 F.2d 431, 438 (6th Cir. 1970) (NAA), *cert. denied,* 401 U.S. 994 (1971); United States v. Kelly, 420 F.2d 26, 28 (2d Cir. 1969) (NAA); United States v. Zeiger, 350 F. Supp. 685, 691 (D.D.C.) (polygraph), *rev'd per curiam,* 475 F.2d 1280 (D.C. Cir. 1972); State v. Stevens, 467 S.W.2d 10, 23 (Mo.) (NAA), *cert. denied,* 404 U.S. 994 (1971).

466. People v. Farmer, 47 Cal. 3d 888, 913, 765 P.2d 940, 956, 254 Cal. Rptr. 508, 524 (admitting footprint evidence), *cert. denied,* 490 U.S. 1107 (1989).

467. People v. Axell, 235 Cal. App. 3d 836, 862, 1 Cal. Rptr. 2d 411, 427 (1991) (admitting DNA evidence).

468. *See* notes 456 & 457 *supra* and accompanying text.

test or operating an instrument must be properly qualified.[469] The standard for determining the qualifications of experts is discussed in Chapter 5.

In many instances, the person who conducts the test also interprets the results. Firearms and fingerprint identifications are illustrative techniques. In contrast, other scientific procedures involve two experts. In this situation, courts must "differentiate between ability to operate an instrument or perform a test and the ability to make an interpretation drawn from use of the instrument."[470] For example, a technician operates the X-ray machine but is not qualified to interpret the results. Similarly, a police officer could qualify as an expert in the operation of a breathalyzer but would not have the requisite expertise to interpret the results.[471] A physician or other expert would have to testify about the relationship between the alcohol content of the breath and the effect on the brain, unless a statute created a presumption of intoxication when the alcohol concentration reached a specified level[472] or defined the substantive offense as driving with a specified breath-alcohol concentration.[473]

---

469. *See* United States v. Dreos, 156 F. Supp. 200, 208 (D. Md. 1957) (radar equipment "manned by a competent operator"); State v. Fields, 434 S.W.2d 507, 516 (Mo. 1968) ("paraffin" test); State v. Taylor, 694 A.2d 907, 912 (Me. 1997) ("A proper foundation shall consist of evidence that the officer or administrator of the HGN test is trained in the procedure and the test was properly administered") (footnote omitted); State v. Gerber, 206 Neb. 75, 90, 291 N.W.2d 403, 411 (1980) ("the person giving and interpreting the [breathalyzer] test [must be] properly qualified"); State v. Crowder, 285 N.C. 42, 50, 203 S.E.2d 38, 44 (1974) (police officer who collected evidence for atomic absorption analysis "qualified by training and experience to perform that simple task"); 3 J. WIGMORE, EVIDENCE § 795, at 245 (Chadbourn Rev. 1970) ("The witness operating the [X-ray machine] and taking the photograph must be qualified for that work by training and experience"); Strong, *supra* note 10, at 16.

470. People v. King, 266 Cal. App. 2d 437, 457, 72 Cal. Rptr. 478, 491 (1968).

471. *See* State v. Taylor, 694 A.2d 907, 909 (Me. 1997) ("Officer Green also testified that he knows how to administer the test properly although he is unaware of the scientific basis for it"); State v. James, 68 Ohio App. 2d 227, 229, 428 N.E.2d 876, 878 (1980) (state trooper qualified to operate Intoxilyzer but not qualified to express an opinion on other aspects of blood-alcohol testing); State v. Priester, 301 S.C. 165, 167-68, 391 S.E.2d 227, 228 (1990) (lab technologist not qualified to testify about the effect of alcohol on the brain); Durham v. State, 710 S.W.2d 176, 179 (Tex. App. 1986) (qualification on operation of Intoxilyzer did not qualify witness to express opinion about effect of alcohol on blood levels); French v. State, 484 S.W.2d 716, 719 (Tex. Crim. App. 1972) ("an officer may administer a breath test even though he is not otherwise qualified to interpret the results ...").

472. *See* OHIO REV. CODE ANN. § 4511.19 (Baldwin 1991). *See generally* Latin, Tannehill & White, *supra* note 1, at 1366-67, 1370; Strong, *supra* note 10, at 9 n.27.

473. For a discussion of intoxication tests, *see* Chapter 22.

Horizontal gaze nystagmus (HGN) cases illustrates this point. A police officer may be qualified to conduct a HGN test, an intoxication test, but not be qualified to interpret the results. According to one court,

> [The officer's] opinion that appellant was under the influence of alcohol, to the extent it was based on the nystagmus test, rests on scientific principles well beyond his knowledge, training, or education. Without some understanding of the processes by which alcohol ingestion produces nystagmus, how strong the correlation is, how other possible causes might be masked, what margin of error has been shown in statistical surveys, and a host of other relevant factors, [the officer's] opinion on causation, notwithstanding his ability to recognize the symptom, was unfounded.[474]

§ 1-12. Constitutional Issues.

The admissibility of scientific evidence in criminal cases may be affected by constitutional considerations. Typically, the issue has arisen in polygraph and hypnosis cases.[475] The main argument focuses on an accused's constitutional right to introduce defense evidence, notwithstanding restrictive evidentiary rules such as the *Frye* test.[476]

The right to present a defense is based principally on two Supreme Court cases, although more recent cases also recognize such a right.[477] In *Washington v.*

---

474. People v. Williams, 3 Cal. App. 4th 1326, 1334, 5 Cal. Rptr. 2d 130, 135 (1992). *See also* State v. Torres, 976 P.2d 20, 33 (N.M. 1999) ("Officer Bowdich was not qualified to testify about the scientific bases of HGN testing, and although his testimony lent support for a conclusion that the test was widely used ... his testimony did not explain how the test proved intoxication").

475. This issue, however, has been raised in other contexts. *See* Patrick v. State, 295 Ark. 473, 476-77, 750 S.W.2d 391, 392-93 (1988) (due process violated by exclusion of defense intoxication tests); State v. Cavallo, 88 N.J. 508, 529, 443 A.2d 1020, 1030 (1982) (no violation to exclude evidence of psychological profile of rapists).

476. In addition to the "right to present evidence" argument considered in the text, defendants have argued that Brady v. Maryland, 373 U.S. 83 (1963), requires the admission of polygraph evidence. In *Brady* the Court ruled that the prosecution must disclose favorable material defense evidence upon request. *See* § 8-5 *infra*.

477. *See* Crane v. Kentucky, 476 U.S. 683, 690 (1986) ("Whether rooted directly in the Due Process Clause ... or in the Compulsory Process or Confrontation Clauses of the Sixth Amendment ..., the Constitution guarantees criminal defendants 'a meaningful opportunity to present a complete defense'"); Ake v. Oklahoma, 470 U.S. 68, 76 (1985) ("[W]hen a State brings its judicial power to bear on an indigent in a criminal proceeding, it must take steps to assure that the defendant has a fair opportunity to present his defense"); California v. Trombetta, 467 U.S. 479, 485 (1984) ("We have long interpreted [the due process] standard of fairness to require that criminal defendants be afforded a meaningful opportunity to present a complete defense"). *See also* Michigan v. Lucas, 500 U.S. 145 (1991); Taylor v. Illinois, 484 U.S. 400, 422 (1988); Rock v. Arkansas, 483 U.S. 44, 49 (1987).

Texas[478] the Court held that a state evidentiary rule, which made the testimony of an unconvicted accomplice incompetent if offered by the defense, violated the compulsory process guarantee.[479] In short, the Compulsory Process Clause overrode a state evidentiary rule that precluded the accused from introducing defense evidence. Moreover, the Court used broad language in explaining the purpose of the compulsory process clause: "The right to offer the testimony of witnesses, and to compel their attendance, if necessary, is in plain terms the right to present a defense, the right to present the defendant's version of the facts as well as the prosecution's to the jury so it may decide where the truth lies."[480] An Ohio trial court, in *State v. Sims,*[481] found an implied right to present defense evidence in the compulsory process guarantee, which, it concluded, compelled admission of defense polygraph evidence.

The second Supreme Court case is *Chambers v. Mississippi,*[482] in which the Court held that state evidentiary rules that precluded the accused from introducing critical and reliable evidence violated due process. In that case, Mississippi's "voucher rule" and hearsay rule prevented the defendant from introducing out-of-court statements by a third party admitting to the murder that Chambers was charged with committing.[483] Like *Washington v. Texas*, *Chambers* can be viewed as a case in which constitutional demands overrode state evidentiary rules: "Broadly construed, [*Chambers*] appears to recognize that the accused in a criminal proceeding has a constitutional right to introduce any exculpatory evidence, unless the state can demonstrate that it is so inherently unreliable as to leave the trier of fact no rational basis for evaluating its truth."[484]

---

478. 388 U.S. 14 (1967).

479. *See generally* Westen, *The Compulsory Process Clause*, 73 MICH. L. REV. 71 (1974); Westen, *Compulsory Process II*, 74 MICH. L. REV. 192 (1975).

480. 388 U.S. at 19. *See also* United States v. Valenzuela-Bernal, 458 U.S. 858 (1982).

481. 52 Ohio Misc. 31, 369 N.E.2d 24 (C.P. 1977). *See also* Comment, *Polygraph Admission Through Compulsory Process*, 16 AKRON L. REV. 761 (1983).

482. 410 U.S. 284 (1973).

483. The Court subsequently applied *Chambers* in Green v. Georgia, 442 U.S. 95 (1979).

484. Westen, *The Compulsory Process Clause*, 73 MICH. L. REV. 71, 151-52 (1974). In a 1985 case, a federal district court wrote that "[a] part of the due process guarantee is that an individual not suffer punitive action as a result of an inaccurate scientific procedure." Higgs v. Wilson, 616 F. Supp. 226, 230 (W.D. Ky. 1985) (use of the EMIT urinalysis drug test without a confirmatory test in prison disciplinary proceedings violates due process), *vacated and remanded on other grounds*, 793 F.2d 1291 (6th Cir. 1986), *aff'd in part, vacated in part, and remanded in part on other grounds sub nom.*, Higgs v. Bland, 888 F.2d 443 (6th Cir. 1989). *See also* Armstead v. State, 342 Md. 38, 87, 673 A.2d 221, 245 (1996) (citing Dowling v. United States, 493 U.S. 342, 353 (1990)) ("[T]he essence of the due process 'fundamental fairness' inquiry is whether there was a balanced, fully explored presentation of the evidence. This balance in turn depends on the jury's ability to weigh the evidence, and the defendant's opportunity to challenge the evidence").

Chambers was relied upon in *State v. Dorsey*,[485] in which a New Mexico appellate court upheld the admission of defense sponsored polygraph evidence. The right to present defense evidence was also relied upon in *McMorris v. Israel*,[486] in which the defendant offered to stipulate to the admission of a polygraph results. Although stipulated polygraph results were admissible under state law,[487] the prosecutor, without offering any explanation, refused to enter into a stipulation. In granting habeas corpus relief, the Seventh Circuit wrote: "Where credibility is as critical as in the instant case, the circumstances are such as to make the polygraph evidence materially exculpatory within the meaning of the Constitution."[488] Despite *McMorris* and similar cases, most courts have rejected the argument that admission of polygraph evidence is constitutionally required.[489]

In *United States v. Sheffer*[490] the U.S. Supreme Court held that adoption of the per se rule of exclusion of polygraph evidence was not unconstitutional. The Court acknowledged, once more, the right to present a defense, albeit a qualified right. "A defendant's right to present relevant evidence is not unlimited, but rather is subject to reasonable restrictions."[491] In the Court's view, evidence "rules do not abridge an accused's right to present a defense so long as they are not 'arbitrary' or disproportionate to the purposes they are designed to serve. Moreover, we have found the exclusion of evidence to be unconstitutionally

---

485. 87 N.M. 323, 325, 532 P.2d 912, 914-15, *aff'd,* 88 N.M. 184, 539 P.2d 204 (1975). *See generally* Churchwell, *The Constitutional Right to Present Evidence: Progeny of Chambers v. Mississippi*, 19 CRIM. L. BULL. 131 (1983); Clinton, *The Right to Present a Defense: An Emergent Constitutional Guarantee in Criminal Trials*, 9 IND. L. REV. 711, 810-15 (1976); Note, *Compulsory Process and Polygraph Evidence: Does Exclusion Violate a Criminal Defendant's Due Process Rights?*, 12 CONN. L. REV. 324 (1980); Note, *Admission of Polygraph Results: A Due Process Perspective*, 55 IND. L.J. 157 (1979).

486. 643 F.2d 458 (7th Cir. 1981), *cert. denied,* 455 U.S. 967 (1982).

487. At the time of trial, polygraph evidence was admissible pursuant to stipulation in Wisconsin. State v. Stanislawski, 62 Wis. 2d 730, 216 N.W.2d 8 (1974). After *McMorris* was decided, however, the Wisconsin Supreme Court overruled *Stanislawski,* holding that polygraph evidence was inadmissible even in the case of a stipulation. State v. Dean, 103 Wis. 2d 228, 307 N.W.2d 628 (1981).

488. 643 F.2d at 462. The court, however, rested its decision on narrower grounds; that is, the prosecution's refusal to stipulate without offering a valid ground for the refusal deprived the defendant of due process: "From all that appears, [the prosecutor] was acting solely for tactical reasons in the belief that a test would not be helpful to his case. If the prosecutor refuses and states reasons, it then becomes the duty of the court to determine whether the reasons offered rise above the purely tactical considerations presented in a given case." *Id.* at 466.

489. *See* § 8.5(D) *infra* (listing cases). *See* United States v. Lech, 895 F. Supp. 582 , 586 (S.D.N.Y. 1995) ("Lech has no constitutional right to introduce evidence whose probative value is substantially outweighed by its tendency to confuse and mislead a jury").

490. 523 U.S. 303, 118 S. Ct. 1261 (1998).

491. *Id.* at 1264.

arbitrary or disproportionate only where it has infringed upon a weighty interest of the accused."[492]

Justice Thomas, writing for the majority, identified three interests that support the per se rule: (1) ensuring that only reliable evidence is introduced at trial, (2) preserving the jury's role in determining credibility, and (3) avoiding litigation of collateral issues. As to reliability, the opinion noted that "the scientific community remains extremely polarized about the reliability of polygraph techniques."[493] The opinion also observed that "[n]othing in *Daubert* foreclosed, as a constitutional matter, per se exclusionary rules for certain types of expert or scientific evidence."[494] Justice Thomas also cited the preservation of the jury's role in determining the credibility. "By its very nature, polygraph evidence may diminish the jury's role in making credibility determinations."[495] A third reason supporting the per se rule of exclusion is, in Justice Thomas's view, the avoidance of litigation on collateral issues, which "prolongs criminal trials and threatens to distract the jury from its central function of determining guilt or innocence."[496]

Interestingly, Justice Kennedy along with three other Justices rejected the second and third interests. In his concurring opinion, Justice Kennedy pointed out that Federal Rule 704 abolishes the ultimate issue rule and thus the "invading the province of the jury" argument has been rejected under most modern evidence codes. Significantly, he also wrote:

> I doubt, though, that the rule of per se exclusion is wise, and some later case might present a more compelling case for introduction of the testimony than this one does. Though the considerable discretion given to the trial court in admitting and excluding scientific evidence is not a constitutional mandate, see *Daubert* . . . there is some tension between that rule and our holding today. And, as Justice Stevens points out [in dissent], there is much inconsistency between the Government's extensive use of polygraph to make vital security determinations and the argument it makes here, stressing the inaccuracy of these tests.[497]

Hypnotic Evidence

The right to present defense evidence also has arisen in cases in which hypnotically induced statements have been offered in evidence. The California Supreme Court rejected a defendant's constitutional argument that the exclusion

492. *Id.*
493. *Id.* at 1265.
494. *Id.* at 1266.
495. *Id.* at 1267.
496. *Id.*
497. *Id.* at 1269.

of these out-of-court statements denied him the right to present defense evidence under *Chambers*. According to the court, "the trial court's ruling did not elevate a fastidious adherence to the technicalities of the law of evidence over the right to a fair trial. For here, unlike *Chambers,* there was no solid assurance that the hearsay statements were reliable."[498]

Defendant's Right to Testify

The above cases must be distinguished from *Rock v. Arkansas.*[499] In that case the trial court excluded a murder defendant's testimony because she had been hypnotized, a ruling that was upheld by the Arkansas Supreme Court. The U.S. Supreme Court reversed. The Court began its analysis by recognizing an accused's right to testify. "At this point in the development of our adversary system, it cannot be doubted that a defendant in a criminal case has the right to take the witness stand and to testify in his or her own defense."[500] This right is based on due process, the right of compulsory process, the right to counsel, and the privilege against self-incrimination.

Two limitations in the Court's opinion are noteworthy. First, the Court did not rule that the defendant's testimony was automatically admissible. It recognized that an approach less restrictive than Arkansas's rule of per se exclusion may satisfy constitutional guarantees: "The State would be well within its powers if it established guidelines to aid trial courts in the evaluation of posthypnosis testimony and it may be able to show that testimony in a particular case is so unreliable that exclusion is justified."[501] Second, the Court explicitly limited its decision to the testimony of the accused: "This case does not involve the admissibility of testimony of previously hypnotized witnesses other than criminal defendants and we express no opinion on that issue."[502]

§ 1-13. *Daubert* Jurisdictions.

Alabama. *Ex parte Turner*, 733 So. 2d 497 (Ala. 1998) (the state's DNA statute, Ala. Code § 36-18-30, superseded the *Frye*-plus test adopted in *Ex parte Perry*, 586 So. 2d 242 (Ala. 1991), and adopted *Daubert* in its place. *Frye*, however, remains the rule for other types of scientific evidence).

---

498. People v. Blair, 25 Cal. 3d 640, 665, 602 P.2d 738, 753, 159 Cal. Rptr. 818, 833 (1979). *See also* Greenfield v. Robinson, 413 F. Supp. 1113, 1120-21 (W.D. Va. 1976). For a discussion of hypnosis, *see* Chapter 12.

499. 483 U.S. 44 (1987).

500. *Id.* at 49.

501. *Id.* at 61.

502. *Id.* at 58 n.15. For a further discussion of *Rock, see* Chapter 12.

Alaska. *State v. Coon,* 974 P.2d 386, 402-03 (Alaska 1999) (sound spectrograph; "voiceprints") ("We adopt the *Daubert* standard for determining the admissibility of scientific evidence. We hold that the voice spectrograph analysis evidence was admissible under *Daubert* and the Alaska Rules of Evidence in this case.").

Connecticut. *State v. Porter*, 241 Conn. 57, 698 A.2d 739, 751 (1997) (polygraph) ("[O]ur reasons for adopting *Daubert* ...."), *cert. denied,* 118 S. Ct. 1384 (1998).

Indiana. *Steward v. State*, 652 N.E.2d 490, 498 (Ind. 1995) ("The concerns driving *Daubert* coincide with the express requirement of Indiana Rule of Evidence 702(b) that the trial court be satisfied of the reliability of the scientific principles involved. Thus, although not binding upon the determination of state evidentiary law issues, the federal evidence law of *Daubert* and its progeny is helpful to the bench and bar in applying Indiana Rule of Evidence 702(b).").

Kentucky. *Fugate v. Commonwealth*, 993 S.W.2d 931 (Ky. 1999) ("This Court adopted the *Daubert* formula for admitting scientific evidence in *Mitchell* ..."); *Mitchell v. Commonwealth*, 908 S.W.2d 100, 101 (Ky. 1995) (rejects *Frye* for *Daubert*) (DNA previously admitted under the *Frye* test; "we adopt the standard of review set forth in *Daubert*."); *Cecil v. Commonwealth*, 888 S.W.2d 669, 675 (Ky. 1994) (clinical psychologist testimony on mens rea properly admitted under *Daubert*).

Massachusetts. *Commonwealth v. Vao Sok*, 425 Mass. 787, 683 N.E.2d 671, 677 (1997) (DNA PCR - DQA1, PM, and D1S80); *Commonwealth v. Rosier*, 425 Mass. 807, 685 N.E.2d 739 (1997) (DNA-STRs); *Commonwealth v. Lanigan*, 419 Mass. 15, 26, 641 N.E.2d 1342, 1349 (1994) (DNA statistics based on NAS Report "ceiling principle" admissible) ("We accept the basic reasoning of the *Daubert* opinion ...."). *See also Commonwealth v. Sands*, 424 Mass. 184, 675 N.E.2d 370, 371 (1997) ("[A] party seeking to introduce ... scientific theory is generally accepted within the relevant scientific community, or by showing that the theory is reliable or valid through other [*Daubert*] means.") (foundation for HGN test must be laid).

New Hampshire. *State v. Hungerford*, 142 N.H. 110, 121, 697 A.2d 916, 922 (1997) (repressed memories) ("Also helpful are the considerations enunciated by the United States Supreme Court in *Daubert* ...."); *but see* State v. Vandebogart, 136 N.H. 365, 374, 616 A.2d 483, 489 (1992) ("We adopted the *Frye* standard in *Coolidge* ....").

New Mexico. *State v. Alberico*, 116 N.M. 156, 861 P.2d 192 (1993).

Oklahoma. *Taylor v. State*, 889 P.2d 319, 328, 332 (Okla. Crim. App. 1995) ("[T]he time is right for this court to abandon the *Frye* test and adopt the more structured and yet flexible admissibility standard set forth in *Daubert*") (DNA (RFLP) match and statistical calculations admissible).

South Dakota. *State v. Schweitzer*, 533 N.W.2d 156, 159 (S.D. 1995) (*Daubert* recognized in *Hofer*; DNA statistics admissible); *State v. Hofer*, 512 N.W.2d 482, 484 (S.D. 1994) ("[G]eneral acceptance in the scientific community is no longer required"; validity of intoxilyzer "beyond scientific dispute"); *State v. Loftus*, 573 N.W.2d 167, 173 (S.D. 1997) ("In *State v. Hofer*, we departed from adherence to the former *Frye* rule ... And adopted the new standard set forth by the United States Supreme Court in *Daubert* ....") (use of product rule in DNA statistical analysis is reliable).

Tennessee. *State v. Begley*, 956 S.W.2d 471, 475 n. 9 (Tenn. 1997) ("*McDaniel* held that the pre-Rules of Evidence test of *Frye* ... was superseded by the adoption of Tennessee Rules of Evidence 702 and 703.") (DNA-PCR).

West Virginia. *State v. Beard*, 194 W. Va. 740, 746, 461 S.E.2d 486, 493 (1995) (polygraph evidence still inadmissible under *Daubert/Wilt* standard); *Wilt v. Buracker*, 191 W. Va. 39, 46-47, 443 S.E.2d 196, 203 (1993) ("*Daubert's* analysis of Federal Rule 702 should be followed in analyzing the admissibility of expert testimony under 702 of West Virginia Rules of Evidence"; excluded economist's calculations of hedonic damages), *cert. denied*, 511 U.S. 1129 (1994).

§ 1-14. Pre-*Daubert* Reliability Jurisdictions.

Arkansas. *Moore v. State*, 323 Ark. 529, 547, 915 S.W.2d 284, 294 (1996) (DNA evidence no longer novel; "*Daubert* ... adopted a reliability approach to Rule 702, comparable to the relevancy approach of *Prater* in which reliability is the critical element.").

Delaware. *Nelson v. State*, 628 A.2d 69, 73 (Del. 1993) ("Our decisions [in prior cases] are consistent with the Supreme Court's decision in *Daubert*") (DNA admissible only with statistical probability).

Georgia. *Carr v. State*, 267 Ga. 701, 482 S.E.2d 314, 317 (1997) (dog alert to fire accelerant not shown "with verifiable certainty" to be accurate and reliable).

Hawaii. *State v. Fukusaku*, 85 Haw. 462, 946 P.2d 32 (1997).

Iowa. *Hutchison v. American Family Mut. Ins. Co.*, 514 N.W.2d 882, 885 (Iowa 1994) (*Daubert* consistent with Iowa precedents).

Louisiana. *State v. Quatrevingt*, 670 So. 2d 197 (La.) (ruling band-shifting in DNA analysis not reliable), *cert. denied*, 519 U.S. 927 (1996); *State v. Foret*, 628 So. 2d 1116, 1123 (La. 1993) ("Past decisions of this court have espoused similar sentiments [as *Daubert*] ....") (child abuse accommodation syndrome excluded).

Maine. *State v. Taylor*, 694 A.2d 907, 910 (Me. 1997) (horizontal gaze nystagmus) (citing *State v. Williams*, 388 A.2d 500, 504 (Me. 1978)).

Military. *United States v. Buenaventura*, 40 M.J. 519, 525 (A.C.M.R. 1994) (child sexual abuse syndrome) (Court of Military Appeals' approach "closely parallels" *Daubert*), *rev'd on other grounds*, 45 M.J. 72 (1996).

Montana. *State v. Cline*, 909 P.2d 1171, 1177, 1178 (Mont. 1996) ("[T]his Court has adopted the standard set forth in *Daubert*.... *Daubert* test should only be used to determine the admissibility of novel scientific evidence"; "[T]he State established the necessary foundation regarding the issue of determining the age of fingerprints"); *State v. Moore*, 268 Mont. 20, 42, 885 P.2d 457, 471 (1994) (DNA-PCR admitted) ("[T]he guidelines set forth in *Daubert* are consistent with our previous holding in *Barmeyer* concerning the admission of expert testimony of novel scientific evidence, and we, therefore, adopt the *Daubert* standard ....").

North Carolina. *State v. Goode*, 341 N.C. 513, 461 S.E.2d 631 (1995) (bloodstain pattern interpretation admissible under N.C. approach which is consistent with *Daubert*).

Oregon. *State v. O'Key*, 321 Or. 285, 306, 899 P.2d 663, 680 (1995) (en banc) ("Both *Daubert* and *Brown* allow *Frye*'s 'general acceptance' standard to be considered as one factor in the trial court's decision about admissibility.... Faced with a proffer of expert scientific testimony, an Oregon trial court ... should, therefore, find *Daubert* instructive"; HGN intoxication test is scientifically valid). *See also State v. Lyons*, 324 Or. 256, 260 n. 1, 924 P.2d 802, 804 n.1 (1996) (DNA-PCR).

South Carolina. *State v. Council,* 515 S.E.2d 508, 517 (1999) (mitochondrial DNA) ("[T]his Court has never adopted [the *Frye*] standard.") ("While this Court does not adopt *Daubert*, we find the proper analysis for determining admissibility of scientific evidence is now under the SCRE [Rules 702 and 403]. ... The trial judge should apply the *Jones* factors to determine reliability.") (citing *State v. Jones*, 273 S.C. 723, 259 S.E.2d 120 (1979) ((1) publications and peer review of the technique, (2) prior application of the method to the type of evidence involved in the case, (3) the quality control procedures used to ensure reliability, and (4) the consistency of the method with recognized scientific laws and procedures).

Texas. *E.I. Du Pont de Nemours & Co. v. Robinson*, 923 S.W.2d 549, 554 (Tex. 1995) (noting that there are "professional experts" who sometimes put forth "junk science," comments that *Daubert* properly strengthens the role of trial judge as gatekeeper in civil cases); *Hartman v. State*, 946 S.W.2d 60, 63 (Tex. Crim. 1997) (Texas follows *State v. Kelly*, 824 S.W.2d 568 (Tex. Crim. 1992), and *Daubert*).

Utah. *State v. Cosby*, 927 P.2d 638, 642 (Utah 1996) ("If there is a noteworthy difference between the two opinions, it is perhaps that our opinion in *Rimmasch* provides a detailed and rigorous outline for trial courts to follow when making determinations concerning the admissibility of scientific evidence. *Rimmasch*, 775 P.2d at 403 ("[T]he trial court should carefully explore each logical link in the chain that leads to expert testimony given in court and determine its reliability.") The Supreme Court in *Daubert*, on the other hand, emphasized a more flexible approach ....").

Vermont. *State v. Brooks*, 162 Vt. 26, 643 A.2d 226 (1993) (*Daubert* consistent with Vermont precedents).

Wyoming. *Springfield v. State*, 860 P.2d 435, 442-43 (Wyo. 1993) (DNA).

§ 1-15. *Frye* Jurisdictions.

Alabama. *Ex parte Turner*, 733 So. 2d 497 (Ala. 1998) (the state's DNA statute, Ala. Code § 36-18-30, superseded the *Frye*-plus test adopted in *Ex parte Perry*, 586 So. 2d 242 (Ala. 1991), and adopted *Daubert* in its place. *Frye*, however, remains the rule for other types of scientific evidence).

Arizona. *State v. Tankersley*, 191 Ariz. 359, 364, 956 P.2d 486, 491(1998) (PCR-DQA admitted) ("Although not raised below, the state asks this court to abandon the *Frye* test in favor of the current federal [*Daubert*] standard for determining the admissibility of new scientific evidence. ... We decline to do so"); *State v. Hummert*, 188 Ariz. 119, 127, 933 P.2d 1187, 1195 (1997) ("Although compliance with *Frye* is necessary when the scientist reaches a conclusion by applying a scientific theory or process based on the work or discovery of others, under Rules 702 and 703 experts may testify concerning their own experimentation and observation and opinions based on their own work without first showing general acceptance."); *State v. Johnson*, 186 Ariz. 329, 331, 922 P.2d 294, 296 (1996) (en banc) (DNA) ("[T]he *Frye* rule, which has been followed without causing significant problems since it was first adopted in 1962, remains the rule in Arizona."); *State v. Bible*, 175 Ariz. 549, 858 P.2d 1152, 1183 (1993) (DNA), *cert. denied*, 511 U.S. 1046 (1994).

California. *People v. Leahy*, 8 Cal. 4th 587, 604, 882 P.2d 321, 323, 34 Cal. Rptr. 2d 663, 673 (1994) (Horizontal Gaze Nystagmus must satisfy *Frye* test) (The "*Kelly* formulation [of *Frye* under Cal. Evid. Code] survived *Daubert* ....").

Colorado. *Lindsey v. People*, 892 P.2d 281, 288 (Colo. 1995) (en banc) (applying *Frye*; DNA statistics generally accepted despite "subgroup" debate) (noting *Daubert* "issue not now before us") ("Despite the criticisms leveled at *Frye*, this standard is not far removed from the evaluation required under FRE 702."). *Id.* at 289 n. 23 (concurrence argued for *Daubert* test).

Florida. *Murray v. State*, 692 So. 2d 157, 164 (Fla. 1997); *Hayes v. State*, 660 So. 2d 257, 262 (Fla. 1995) ("We have recently made it clear that Florida utilizes the *Frye* test...."; courts may take judicial notice on some aspects of DNA; but correcting for band-shifting is not generally accepted, citing NAS 1992 report). *See also Flanagan v. State*, 625 So. 2d 827, 829 n.2 (Fla. 1993) (despite *Daubert*, "Florida continues to adhere to the *Frye* test ....") (sex offender profile excluded); *Brim v. State*, 695 So. 2d 268, 270 (Fla. 1997) ("It is clear that the DNA testing process consists of two distinct steps and that both steps must satisfy the requirements of *Frye*."); *Hadden v. State*, 690 So. 2d 573 , 577 (Fla. 1997) (child sexual abuse accommodation syndrome "testimony in child-abuse prosecutions must be subjected to *Frye* test"; not generally accepted as a diagnostic tool).

Illinois. *People v. Miller*, 173 Ill. 2d 167, 187, 670 N.E.2d 721, 731 (1996) ("Illinois follows the *Frye* standard for the admission of novel scientific evidence."), *cert. denied*, 520 U.S. 1157 (1997); *People v. Lowitzki*, 285 Ill. App. 3d 770, 777, 674 N.E.2d 859, 863 (1996) ("[T]he admissibility of new scientific techniques must be evaluated under the *Frye* 'general acceptance' standard. Although this standard has been superseded in federal court by the perhaps more liberal Federal Rules of Evidence..., the *Frye* standard remains the appropriate standard in Illinois."), *appeal denied*, 679 N.E.2d 383 (Ill. 1997).

Kansas. *State v. Colbert*, 257 Kan. 896, 909, 896 P.2d 1089, 1097 (1995) (DNA profile statistics generally accepted); *State v. Hill*, 257 Kan. 774, 783, 895 P.2d 1238, 1245 (1995) ("Kansas has repeatedly applied *Frye*") (DNA-PCR admissible because generally accepted); *State v. Warden*, 257 Kan. 94, 113, 891

P.2d 1074, 1088 (1995) (facilitated communication (autistic child testimony against molester) not scientific evidence; therefore, *Frye* does not control).

Maryland. *Burral v. State,* 352 Md. 707, 738, 724 A.2d 65, 80 (1999) (Despite *Daubert*, "we have not abandoned *Frye* or *Reed.*"); *Goldstein v. State*, 339 Md. 563, 573-77, 664 A.2d 375, 380-81 (1995) (principles underlying laser-based speed detection devices are generally accepted under *Reed/Frye* standard; *Frye* limited to theories and processes in general; no need for *Frye* hearing for every new device); *United States Gypsum Co. v. Baltimore*, 336 Md. 145, 182, 647 A.2d 405, 423 (1994) (asbestos evidence). *See also Williams v. State*, 342 Md. 724, 679 A.2d 1106 (1996) (DNA-PCR not covered by state statute; therefore, it must satisfy the *Frye-Reed* test).

Michigan. *People v. Lee*, 212 Mich. App. 228, 262, 537 N.W.2d 233, 249 n. 17 (1995) (applying *Davis-Frye* rule until Supreme Court changes) (PCR-DNA evidence would be admissible under the "more relaxed" *Daubert* standard because it is admissible under the "more rigorous" *Davis-Frye* standard), *app. denied*, 554 N.W.2d 12 (Mich. 1996).

Mississippi. *Young v. City of Brookhaven*, 693 So. 2d 1355, 1360-61 (Miss. 1997) ("[T]his Court finds that the HGN test is not generally accepted within the scientific community and cannot be used as scientific evidence to prove intoxication ....")

Missouri. *State v. Kinder*, 942 S.W.2d 313, 327 (Mo. 1996) ("[W]e hold that the [DNA] product rule is generally accepted in the scientific community...."), *cert. denied,* 118 S. Ct. 149 (1997). *See also State v. Huchting*, 927 S.W.2d 411 (Mo. App. 1996) (DNA generally accepted under *Frye*).

Nebraska. *State v. Freeman*, 253 Neb. 385, 405, 571 N.W.2d 276, 289 (1997) ("The *Frye* test has been used in Nebraska and was formally adopted in *State v. Reynolds* ...."); *State v. Dean*, 246 Neb. 869, 882, 884, 523 N.W.2d 681, 692-93 (1994) ("[N]otwithstanding that our rule 702 parallels the federal rule 702, *Daubert* does not apply to state court decisions. The increasing prevalence of expert evidence cautions against the admission of scientific evidence which is still the subject of dispute and controversy in the relevant scientific communities.... We thus adhere to the *Frye* standard...."; laser trajectory analysis not a novel technique; "[A]iming a laser beam through bullet holes [in a mobile home] to reconstruct a bullet's path is no less reliable than inserting a dowel into a bullet hole to demonstrate its path."), *cert. denied*, 515 U.S. 1123 (1995).

New Jersey. *State v. Harvey*, 151 N.J. 117, 169, 699 A.2d 596, 621 (1997) (DNA-polymarkers and dot-intensity analysis for mixed-blood sample admissible) ("In criminal cases we continue to apply the general acceptance or *Frye* test for determining the scientific reliability of expert testimony.").

New York. *People v. Wernick*, 89 N.Y.2d 111, 674 N.E.2d 322, 651 N.Y.S.2d 392 (1996) ("This Court has often endorsed and applied the well-recognized rule of *Frye*...."; neonaticide syndrome not generally accepted); *People v. Wesley*, 83 N.Y.2d 417, 424, 633 N.E.2d 451, 455, 611 N.Y.S.2d 97, 101 (1994) (Lifecodes DNA method generally accepted).

Pennsylvania. *Commonwealth v. Blasioli*, 552 Pa. 149, 153, 713 A.2d 1117, 1119 (1998) ("In determining whether novel scientific evidence is admissible in criminal trials, Pennsylvania courts apply the test set forth in *Frye* ..."); *Commonwealth v. Crews*, 536 Pa. 508, 518 n. 2, 640 A.2d 395, 400 n. 2 (1994) ("*Daubert* relaxes, somewhat, the impediments to admission of novel scientific evidence.... Whether or not the rationale of *Daubert* will supersede or modify the *Frye* test in Pennsylvania is left to another day.").

Washington. *State v. Copeland*, 130 Wash. 2d 244, 261, 922 P.2d 1304, 1315 (1996) (en banc) ("reaffirm our adherence to the *Frye* standard where novel scientific evidence is concerned"); *Reese v. Stroh*, 128 Wash. 2d 300, 308, 907 P.2d 282, 286 (1995) (en banc) (expert testimony in a civil case concerning causation "does not implicate *Frye*"; "While we acknowledge the invitation to adopt the federal test for reliability under Fed. R. Evid. 702 as outlined in *Daubert*, we decline to do so in this case."); *State v. Riker*, 123 Wash. 2d 351, 360 n. 1, 869 P.2d 43, 48 n. 1 (1994) (en banc) (battered person syndrome generally accepted but only in a long-term relationship; court will "continue to adhere to the view that the *Frye* analysis is a threshold inquiry to be considered in determining the admissibility of evidence under ER 702"; however, "many of the 'general observations' made [in *Daubert*] may be of use to trial judges in making the threshold *Frye* determination.").

§ 1-16. Selected Bibliography.

1 D. Louisell & C. Mueller, Federal Evidence § 105 (1977).

3 J. Weinstein & M. Berger, Weinstein's Evidence § 702[03] (1992).

22 C. Wright & K. Graham, Federal Practice and Procedure § 5168 (1978).

Allen, *Expertise and the Daubert Decision*, 84 J. Crim. L. & Criminology 1157 (1994).

Berger, *Novel Forensic Evidence: The Need for Court-Appointed Experts After Daubert*, 1 Shepard's Expert and Scientific Evidence Quarterly 487 (1994).

Bernstein, *Junk Science in the United States and the Commonwealth*, 21 Yale J. Int'l Law 123 (1996).

Black, *A Unified Theory of Scientific Evidence*, 56 Fordham. L. Rev. 595 (1988).

Black, Ayala & Saffran-Brinks, *Science and the Law in the Wake of Daubert: A New Search for Scientific Knowledge*, 72 TEX. L. REV. 715 (1994).

Bohan & Heels, *The Case Against Daubert: The New Scientific Evidence "Standard" and the Standards of the Several States*, 40 J. FORENSIC SCI. 1030 (1995).

Development in the Law — Confronting the New Challenges of Scientific Evidence, 108 HARV. L. REV. 1509 (1995).

Giannelli, *"Junk Science": The Criminal Cases*, 84 J. CRIM. L. & CRIMINOLOGY 105 (1993).

Giannelli, *Daubert and Forensic Science*, 1 SHEPARD'S EXPERT AND SCIENTIFIC EVIDENCE QUARTERLY 457 (1994).

Giannelli, *Daubert: Interpreting the Federal Rules of Evidence*, 15 CARDOZO L. REV. 1999 (1994).

Giannelli, *The Admissibility of Novel Scientific Evidence: Frye v. United States, A Half-Century Later*, 80 COLUM. L. REV. 1197 (1980).

Graham, *Daubert v. Merrell Dow Pharmaceuticals, Inc.: No Frye, Now What?*, 30 CRIM. L. BULL. 153 (1994).

Gross, *Substance and Form in Scientific Evidence: What Daubert Didn't Do*, 3 SHEPARD'S EXPERT AND SCIENTIFIC EVIDENCE QUARTERLY 129 (1995).

Imwinkelried, *A Comparative Law Analysis of the Standard for Admitting Scientific Evidence: The United States Stands Alone*, 42 FORENSIC SCI. INT'L 15 (1989).

Imwinkelried, *A New Era in the Evolution of Scientific Evidence: A Primer on Evaluating the Weight of Scientific Evidence*, 23 WM. & MARY L. REV. 261 (1981).

Imwinkelried, *Judge Versus Jury: Who Should Decide Questions of Preliminary Facts Conditioning the Admissibility of Scientific Evidence?*, 25 WM. & MARY L. REV. 577 (1984).

Imwinkelried, *The Daubert Standard for Validating Scientific Evidence: Linking Us to the Scientific Past*, 1 SHEPARD'S EXPERT AND SCIENTIFIC EVIDENCE QUARTERLY 493 (1994).

Imwinkelried, *The Standard for Admitting Scientific Evidence: A Critique from the Perspective of Juror Psychology*, 28 VILL. L. REV. 554 (1983).

Jonakait, *Real Science and Forensic Science*, 1 SHEPARD'S EXPERT AND SCIENTIFIC EVIDENCE QUARTERLY 435 (1994).

Kreiling, *Scientific Evidence: Toward Providing the Lay Trier with the Comprehensible and Reliable Evidence Necessary to Meet the Goals of the Rules of Evidence*, 32 ARIZ. L. REV. 915 (1990).

McCormick, *Scientific Evidence: Defining a New Approach to Admissibility*, 67 IOWA L. REV. 879 (1982).

O'Connor, *The Supreme Court's Philosophy of Science: Will the Real Karl Popper Please Stand Up?*, 35 JURIMETRICS J. 263 (1995).

Poulter, *Daubert and Scientific Evidence: Assessing Evidentiary Reliability in Toxic Tort Litigation*, 1993 UTAH L. REV. 1307.

Saks, *Implications of the Daubert Test for Forensic Identification Science*, 1 SHEPARD'S EXPERT AND SCIENTIFIC EVIDENCE QUARTERLY 427 (1994).

Schwartz, *A 'Dogma of Empiricism' Revisited: Daubert v. Merrell Dow Pharmaceuticals, Inc. and the Need to Resurrect the Philosophical Insight of Frye v. United States*, 10 HARV. J. LAW & TECH. 149 (1997).

Strong, *Questions Affecting the Admissibility of Scientific Evidence*, 1970 U. ILL. L.F. 1.

Annotations

Annot., *Reliability of scientific technique and its acceptance within scientific community as affecting admissibility, at federal trial, of expert testimony as to result of test or study based on such technique — modern cases*, 105 A.L.R. FED. 299 (1991).

CHAPTER 2

CONSTITUTIONAL LIMITATIONS ON OBTAINING EVIDENCE FOR SCIENTIFIC ANALYSIS

§ 2-1. In General.

Through the examination of trace evidence, many scientific techniques can establish a link between a suspect and the scene of a crime. Blood, semen, hair, fibers, soil, and fingerprints have all been used in this manner. In addition, bite marks, gunshot residues, handwriting, and voice exemplars have been used to connect a suspect and a crime.

These techniques often require the suspect's cooperation, ranging from his passive presence for fingerprinting or blood extraction to his active participation in providing voice or handwriting samples. This contact between the police and a suspect has spawned litigation. Several constitutional provisions are implicated: (1) the privilege against compulsory self-incrimination, (2) the right to counsel, (3) the right to be free from unreasonable searches and seizures, and (4) due process. This chapter examines these issues.

§ 2-2. Self-Incrimination.

The fifth amendment[1] to the U.S. Constitution prohibits compulsory self-incrimination.[2]

Testimonial vs. Physical Evidence

The leading case on the applicability of the fifth amendment privilege to the collection of physical evidence is *Schmerber v. California.*[3] While being treated at a hospital for injuries sustained in an automobile collision, Schmerber was arrested for driving under the influence of alcohol. At the direction of the investigating police officer, a physician obtained a blood sample from Schmerber. Although the defendant objected to this procedure on the advice of counsel, his blood was extracted and analyzed for alcoholic content. Before the Supreme Court, Schmerber argued that the extraction of blood violated the privilege against self-incrimination. Rejecting this argument, the Court held that the privilege covers only *communicative or testimonial evidence,* not *physical or real evidence.* According to the Court:

> It is clear that the protection of the privilege reaches an accused's communications, whatever form they might take.... On the other hand, both federal and state courts have usually held that it offers no protection against compulsion to submit to fingerprinting, photographing, or measurements, to write or speak for identification, to appear in court, to stand, to assume a stance, to walk, or to make a particular gesture. The distinction which has emerged, often expressed in different ways, is that the privilege is a bar against compelling "communications" or "testimony," but that compulsion which makes a suspect or accused the source of "real or physical evidence" does not violate it.[4]

The Court cited Justice Holmes' opinion in *Holt v. United States,*[5] in which compelled modeling of a blouse found at the crime scene was held to be outside the scope of the privilege: "[T]he prohibition of compelling a man in a criminal court to be witness against himself is a prohibition of the use of physical or moral

---

1. *See* Malloy v. Hogan, 378 U.S. 1, 8 (1964) (privilege against compulsory self-incrimination applies to the states).

2. For a general discussion of the fifth amendment, *see* 1 E. Imwinkelried, P. Giannelli, F. Gilligan & F. Lederer, Courtroom Criminal Evidence ch. 17 (3d ed. 1998); 1 C. McCormick, Evidence ch. 13 (4th ed. 1992); C. Whitebread & C. Slobogin, Criminal Procedure ch. 15 (3d ed. 1993); 8 J. Wigmore, Evidence §§ 2250-84 (McNaughton rev. 1961).

3. 384 U.S. 757 (1966).

4. *Id.* at 763-64.

5. 218 U.S. 245 (1910).

compulsion to extort communications from him, not an exclusion of his body as evidence when it may be material."[6]

Subsequent Supreme Court cases reaffirmed the testimonial-physical evidence distinction recognized in *Schmerber.* In *United States v. Wade,*[7] the Court held that compelling an accused to exhibit his person for observation was compulsion "to exhibit his physical characteristics, not compulsion to disclose any knowledge he might have"[8] and thus not proscribed by the privilege. In *Gilbert v. California,*[9] the Court concluded that the compelled production of a "mere handwriting exemplar, in contrast to the content of what is written, like the voice or body itself, is an identifying physical characteristic outside [the fifth amendment's] protection."[10] Similarly, in *United States v. Dionisio,*[11] the Court ruled that compelling a defendant to speak for the purpose of voice analysis did not violate the fifth amendment because the "voice recordings were to be used solely to measure the physical properties of the witnesses' voices, not for the testimonial or communicative content of what was to be said."[12]

Pennsylvania v. Muniz,[13] decided in 1990, involved evidence of slurred speech and lack of muscular coordination revealed by an arrestee during sobriety tests.[14] Muniz was requested to perform a horizontal gaze nystagmus test, a walk-and-turn test, and a one-leg-stand test. A videotape of his performance was shown at trial. The Supreme Court wrote:

> Under *Schmerber* and its progeny, ... any slurring of speech and other

---

6. *Id.* at 252-53. For a detailed discussion of the testimonial evidence limitation, *see* 1 C. McCormick, *supra* note 2, § 124; C. Whitebread & C. Slobogin, *supra* note 2, § 15.04; 8 J. Wigmore, *supra* note 2, §§ 2263-65; Arenella, *Schmerber and the Privilege Against Self-Incrimination: A Reappraisal,* 20 Am. Crim. L. Rev. 31 (1982); Dann, *The Fifth Amendment Privilege Against Self-Incrimination: Extorting Physical Evidence From a Suspect,* 43 S. Cal. L. Rev. 597 (1970); Easton, *Bodily Samples and the Privilege Against Self-Incrimination,* 1991 Crim. L. Rev. 18; Geyh, *The Testimonial Component of the Right Against Self-Incrimination,* 36 Cath. U. L. Rev. 611 (1987).

7. 388 U.S. 218 (1967).

8. *Id.* at 222.

9. 388 U.S. 263 (1967).

10. *Id.* at 266-67. *Accord* United States v. Euge, 444 U.S. 707, 718 (1980) ("Compulsion of handwriting exemplars ... [not] testimonial evidence protected by the Fifth Amendment privilege against self incrimination"); United States v. Mara, 410 U.S. 19, 22 n.* (1973) (handwriting exemplars).

11. 410 U.S. 1 (1973).

12. *Id.* at 7. *See also* Fisher v. United States, 425 U.S. 391, 408 (1976).

13. 496 U.S. 582 (1990).

14. A traffic stop by itself does not amount to custody under *Miranda.* Therefore, incriminating statements made to the police before arrest are admissible. Berkemer v. McCarty, 468 U.S. 420 (1984). Such statements are testimonial, but without custody there is no "compulsion" within the meaning of the fifth amendment. Accordingly, *Miranda* warnings are not required. For example, Muniz's verbal admissions during the roadside dexterity tests were admissible. 496 U.S. at 588 n.3.

> evidence of lack of muscular coordination revealed by Muniz's responses to Officer Hosterman's direct questions constitute nontestimonial components of those responses. Requiring a suspect to reveal the physical manner in which he articulates words, like requiring him to reveal the physical properties of the sound produced by his voice, see *Dionisio* ..., does not, without more, compel him to provide a "testimonial" response for purposes of the privilege.[15]

The Court also held that routine booking questions fell outside the protection of the fifth amendment.[16] Muniz's inability to answer when requested to state the date of his sixth birthday, however, amounted to a testimonial response and should have been excluded.[17]

Under *Schmerber* and its progeny, obtaining evidence for most forensic techniques is free from fifth amendment concerns because these techniques involve physical, not testimonial, evidence.[18] Thus, the lower courts have applied *Schmerber* to cases involving handwriting exemplars,[19] fingerprints,[20] voice exemplars,[21] dental impressions,[22] urine samples,[23] sobriety tests,[24] gunshot

---

15. 496 U.S. at 592. "[I]n order to be testimonial, an accused's communication must itself, explicitly or implicitly, relate a factual assertion or disclose information." Doe v. United States, 487 U.S. 201, 210 (1988).

16. Muniz was asked his name, address, height, weight, eye color, date of birth, and current age. Four justices stated that these routine booking questions were not testimonial. Four other justices disagreed but believed routine booking questions fell within an exception to the fifth amendment.

17. When asked if he knew the date of his sixth birthday, Muniz responded: "No, I don't." 496 U.S. at 586.

18. A suspect's refusal to submit to a nontestimonial identification procedure may result in a contempt citation. *See* United States v. Rudy, 429 F.2d 993, 994 (9th Cir. 1970) (handwriting samples); United States v. Hammond, 419 F.2d 166, 168 (4th Cir. 1969) (lineup), *cert. denied,* 397 U.S. 1068 (1970); United States v. Doe (Devlin), 405 F.2d 436, 438-39 (2d Cir. 1968) (handwriting exemplar).

19. *E.g., In re* Special Fed. Grand Jury, 809 F.2d 1023, 1027-28 (3d Cir. 1987) (requiring backhand slant exemplars); United States v. Richardson, 755 F.2d 685, 685-86 (8th Cir. 1985); United States v. Shively, 715 F.2d 260, 268-69 (7th Cir. 1983), *cert. denied,* 465 U.S. 1007 (1984); United States v. Cotner, 657 F.2d 1171, 1173 (10th Cir. 1981); Palmer v. United States, 530 F.2d 787, 789 (8th Cir. 1976); United States v. Greene, 722 F. Supp. 1221, 1223 (E.D. Pa. 1989). Some courts, however, have held that an order requiring a defendant to provide handwriting samples of words as "dictated" violates the fifth amendment (*see infra*).

20. *E.g., In re* Doe, 860 F.2d 40, 46 (2d Cir. 1988); United States v. Thomann, 609 F.2d 560, 562 (1st Cir. 1979); *In re* Maguire, 571 F.2d 675, 677 (1st Cir.) (court may order the use of reasonable force to compel fingerprinting), *cert. denied,* 436 U.S. 911 (1978); State v. Taylor, 422 So. 2d 109, 116 (La. 1982); State v. Burch, 490 So. 2d 552, 554 (La. App. 1986) (fingerprinting defendant in open court before the judge is permissible); Commonwealth v. Jefferson, 445 Pa. 1, 281 A.2d 852 (1971).

21. *E.g.,* Burnett v. Collins, 982 F.2d 922 (5th Cir. 1993) (live voice exemplar in presence of jury); United States v. Delaplane, 778 F.2d 570, 575 (10th Cir. 1985), *cert. denied,* 479 U.S. 827

residues,[25] hair samples,[26] and other techniques.[27] Recent cases have focused on DNA samples for databanking.[28] Nevertheless, the testimonial-physical evidence distinction has raised a number of issues, which are discussed below.

(1986); *In re* Grand Jury Proceedings (Hellmann), 756 F.2d 428, 431 (6th Cir. 1985); United States v. Williams, 704 F.2d 315, 320 (6th Cir.) (live voice exemplar in presence of jury), *cert. denied,* 464 U.S. 991 (1983); United States v. Franks, 511 F.2d 25, 32 (6th Cir.), *cert. denied,* 422 U.S. 1042 (1975); Fuller v. State, 858 S.W.2d 528, 531-32 (Tex. App. 1993) (trial court order requiring defendant to repeat words used by assailant for the purpose of voice identification does not violate state constitution); State v. Hubanks, 173 Wis. 2d 1, 496 N.W.2d 96 (App. 1992) (defendant's refusal to provide in-court voice exemplar of specific words was a proper subject of jury instruction concerning such refusal), *cert. denied,* 510 U.S. 830 (1993). ***But see*** United States v. Olvera, 30 F.3d 1195, 1198 (9th Cir.) (requiring the defendant to speak in the presence of jury the words uttered during a robbery violated due process under the facts of this case), *cert. denied,* 513 U.S. 1031 (1994). *See generally* Note, *The Constitutional Framework Limiting Compelled Voice Exemplars: Exploration of the Current Constitutional Boundaries of Government Power Over a Criminal Defendant,* 33 San Diego L. Rev. 349 (1996).

22. *E.g.,* United States v. Maceo, 873 F.2d 1, 5-6 (1st Cir.) (examination of teeth), *cert. denied,* 493 U.S. 840 (1989); United States v. Holland, 378 F. Supp. 144, 154 (E.D. Pa.), *aff'd sub nom.,* Appeal of Ehly, 506 F.2d 1050 (3d Cir. 1974), *cert. denied,* 420 U.S. 994 (1975); State v. Evans, 44 Conn. App. 307, 689 A.2d 494, 501 ("[B]ecause the order to display one's teeth, whether prior to or at trial, does not involve communications or testimony, the defendant's claim is not of constitutional magnitude..."), *app. denied,* 692 A.2d 819 (Conn. 1997); State v. Asherman, 193 Conn. 695, 710-14, 478 A.2d 227, 239-40 (1984), *cert. denied,* 470 U.S. 1050 (1985); State v. Thornton, 253 Ga. 524, 525, 322 S.E.2d 711, 712 (1984) (state constitution); People v. Milone, 43 Ill. App. 3d 385, 392, 356 N.E.2d 1350, 1355 (1976); Brewer v. State, 725 So. 2d 106, 130 (Miss.) ("[T]he trial court's admission of the dental impression into evidence was proper as the impression was nothing more than evidence identifying a physical characteristic—very similar to fingerprints ..."), *cert. denied,* 119 S. Ct. 1270 (1998); State v. Sapsford, 22 Ohio App. 3d 1, 3, 488 N.E.2d 218, 220 (1983).

23. *E.g.,* United States v. Edmo, 140 F.3d 1289, 1292 (9th Cir. 1998) ("Being required to comply with Officer Boone's request for a urine sample did not deprive Edmo of his Fifth Amendment privilege ..."); Lucero v. Gunter, 17 F.3d 1347, 1350 (10th Cir. 1994) ("[U]rine samples used for drug testing constitute nontestimonial evidence and therefore do not implicate Plaintiff's Fifth Amendment right against self-incrimination"); Murray v. Haldeman, 16 M.J. 74, 80-81 (C.M.A. 1983); McKenna v. State, 671 S.W.2d 138, 139 (Tex. App. 1984).

24. *E.g.,* State v. Theriault, 696 P.2d 718, 719 (Ariz. App. 1984) (field sobriety test); People v. Saturday, 135 Ill. App. 3d 1052, 482 N.E.2d 1124 (1985); State v. Beeland, 487 So. 2d 703 (La. App. 1986); Commonwealth v. Hayes, 544 Pa. 46, 674 A.2d 677 (1996) (field sobriety tests — horizontal gaze nystagmus test, walk-and-turn test, heal-to-toe test, and one-leg-stand test — do not fall within state constitutional privilege); Commonwealth v. Romesburg, 353 Pa. Super. 215, 218, 509 A.2d 413, 415 (1986) (state constitution); State v. Roadifer, 346 N.W.2d 438, 440 (S.D. 1984) (dexterity test); State v. Maze, 16 Kan. App. 2d 527, 825 P.2d 1169, 1173 (1992) ("recitation of the alphabet is not testimonial"). Some courts disagree concerning the recitation of the alphabet (*see infra*).

25. State v. Ulrich, 187 Mont. 347, 354, 609 P.2d 1218, 1222 (1980) (GSR swabbings); Commonwealth v. Monahan, 378 Pa. Super. 623, 632, 549 A.2d 231, 235 (1988) (GSR swabbings).

26. *E.g.,* United States v. Dougall, 919 F.2d 932, 935 (5th Cir. 1990), *cert. denied,* 501 U.S. 1234 (1991); United States v. Ingram, 797 F. Supp. 705, 707 (E.D. Ark. 1992).

Attempts to Disguise

In *People v. Tai*,[29] a California appellate court ruled that testimony by a questioned document expert that the defendant had attempted to disguise his writing did not violate the fifth amendment. The exemplars, in the expert's opinion, "were not naturally written and were written with the intent to disguise."[30] The court concluded: "Just as a defendant's refusal to provide a handwriting exemplar is admissible evidence of consciousness of guilt, so too is opinion evidence of a defendant's efforts to disguise his handwriting on an exemplar. Since a defendant has no privilege to refuse to provide a court-ordered handwriting exemplar, his or her attempts to alter or disguise this physical characteristic is admissible evidence of consciousness of guilt."[31] The court cited two federal cases as precedent.[32]

Recitation of Alphabet

In *State v. Maze*,[33] the Kansas court of appeals ruled that "recitation of the alphabet is not testimonial in that it does not require a suspect to communicate any personal beliefs or knowledge."[34] In contrast, the Florida Supreme Court in *Allred v. State*[35] ruled that evidence of the defendant's incorrect recitation of the alphabet, when stopped for driving under the influence, violates the state constitution: "Failure to accurately recite the alphabet 'discloses information'

---

27. *E.g.*, People v. Thomas, 180 Cal. App. 3d 47, 52, 225 Cal. Rptr. 277, 279 (1986) (saliva, hair, and blood); State v. Edwards, 463 So. 2d 551, 554 (Fla. App. 1985) (blood-alcohol test); Commonwealth v. Billings, 42 Mass. App. 261, 264 n.7, 676 N.E.2d 62, 64 n.7 ("the defendant's lifting his foot to show ... the bottom of his sneaker was nontestimonial"), *cert. denied*, 679 N.E.2d 558 (Mass. 1997). *See also* 8 J. Wigmore, *supra* note 2, § 2265 (listing other cases).

28. *E.g.*, Shaffer v. Saffle, 148 F.3d 1180, 1181 (10th Cir.) (Oklahoma statute) ("We rejected the Fifth Amendment self-incrimination claim because DNA samples are not testimonial in nature"), *cert. denied*, 119 S. Ct. 520 (1998); Schlicher v. (NPN) Peters, I & I, 103 F.3d 940 (10th Cir. 1996) (Kansas statute); Boling v. Romer, 101 F.3d 1336, 1340 (10th Cir. 1996) (Colorado statute). The Fourth Amendment issues are discussed in § 2-4(D) *infra*.

29. 37 Cal. App. 4th 990, 44 Cal. Rptr. 2d 253 (1995).

30. *Id.* at 996, 44 Cal. Rptr. 2d at 256.

31. *Id.* at 998, 44 Cal. Rptr. 2d at 258 (citations omitted).

32. United States v. Wolfish, 525 F.2d 457, 461 (2d Cir. 1975) (prosecution closing argument that defendant's efforts to disguise his handwriting, as testified to by an expert, was evidence of guilt did not violate the fifth amendment), *cert. denied*, 423 U.S. 1059 (1976); United States v. Stembridge, 477 F.2d 874, 876 (5th Cir. 1973) ("The accused has not been permitted to frustrate the prosecution's right to this evidence by simply refusing to give the required exemplars.... [I]f an accused were free to disguise his writing, without any sanctions, exemplars would be worthless. Hence it is not improper for the prosecution to show that the defendant attempted to avoid providing a valid handwriting sample by intentionally distorting his handwriting").

33. 16 Kan. App. 2d 527, 825 P.2d 1169 (1992).

34. *Id.* at 1173.

35. 622 So. 2d 984 (Fla. 1993).

beyond possible slurred speech; it is the *content* (incorrect recitation) of the speech that is being introduced, rather than merely the *manner* (slurring) of speech."[36]

Dictation for Handwriting

In *United States v. Wade*,[37] the court ruled that requiring a defendant to provide handwriting exemplars pursuant to dictation violated the fifth amendment. In reaching this conclusion, the court discussed the underlying distinction between "testimonial" and non-testimonial evidence. Providing an exemplar, by itself, merely recorded "purely physical or real properties." Such evidence does not require the defendant to reveal his "consciousness of the facts and the operations of his mind in expressing it."[38] Providing exemplars does not compel the defendant to "disclose any knowledge he might have."[39] Obtaining an exemplar by dictation differs because the act of producing the exemplar has testimonial aspects: "[T]he production of an exemplar pursuant to oral dictation would allow the defendant's spelling and choice of form for writing numbers, or 'the content of what is written,' to be admitted into evidence. Thus, a dictated handwriting exemplar would require Wade to demonstrate his cognitive abilities. Because it requires Wade to reveal his thought processes, which have communicative qualities, the dictated exemplar is prohibited by the Fifth Amendment."[40] The court also noted that the two federal cases on this issue had reached opposing conclusions.[41] Finally, the court distinguished a case in which the defendant was required to write an alias believed to have been used by the culprit.[42] The court discerned a difference between the two cases: "Unlike the present case, the exact spelling or form of the sample requested ... was not an

---

36. *Id.* at 987. *Accord*, Vickers v. State, 878 S.W.2d 329, 330 (Tex. App. 1994) ("In this case, Vickers' responses to the State's request that he recite the alphabet ... showed that his mind was confused. Consequently, we hold that his response was testimonial in nature and that it should have been suppressed").

37. 1995 U.S. Dist. LEXIS 11066 (S.D.N.Y. 1995).

38. Doe v. United States, 487 U.S. 201, 210-11 (1988).

39. *Id.* at 222.

40. 1995 U.S. Dist. LEXIS 11066 at *6 (S.D.N.Y. 1995) (quoting *Gilbert* at 266-67) ("the Government requests that Wade provide non-physical evidence having content in the form of spelling idiosyncra[s]ies and the manner in which he writes numbers").

41. *Compare* United States v. Campbell, 732 F.2d 1017, 1021 (1st Cir. 1984) (dictation requires "a testimonial message in addition to a physical display"; a defendant could not be compelled to take the stand to take a spelling test), *with* United States v. Fester, 544 F.2d 353 (9th Cir. 1976), *cert. denied*, 429 U.S. 1099 (1977) (no violation).

42. United States v. Jacobowitz, 877 F.2d 162 (2d Cir. 1989). *See also* United States v. Doe, 405 F.2d 436, 438 (2d Cir. 1968).

issue because the government had instructed the defendant as to the content of the exemplar."[43]

State Constitutions

An accused may be able to rely on state law.[44] A state is always free to provide a defendant with greater self-incrimination protection than is afforded by federal law.[45] For example, the self-incrimination clause of the Georgia Constitution turns on a distinction between "passive" and "active" participation in the incriminatory act. Passive submission while evidence is obtained does not violate the clause. Thus, fingerprints could be compelled. Compelled active participation, such as requiring a suspect to place a foot in a cast, however, is prohibited.[46]

§ 2-2(A). Refusal to Take Intoxication Tests.

In *South Dakota v. Neville*,[47] the Supreme Court considered whether the admission into evidence of a defendant's refusal to submit to a blood-alcohol test violated the fifth amendment. Instead of relying on the testimonial-physical evidence distinction, the Court rested its decision on different grounds. According to the Court, refusal to take the test did not amount to "compulsion" within the meaning of the privilege: "[A] refusal to take a blood-alcohol test, after a police officer has lawfully requested it, is not an act coerced by the officer, and thus is not protected by the privilege against self-incrimination."[48] The Court further explained that the

> respondent concedes, as he must, that the State could legitimately compel the suspect, against his will, to accede to the test. Given, then, that the offer

43. 1995 U.S. Dist. LEXIS 11066 at *9 (S.D.N.Y. 1995).

44. *See generally* C. WHITEBREAD & C. SLOGOGIN, *supra* note 2, ch. 34; Brennan, *State Constitutions and the Protection of Individual Rights*, 90 HARV. L. REV. 489 (1977).

45. *Id.* Most state courts, however, interpret their constitutions to provide the same protection as provided by the federal constitution. *E.g.*, State v. Bertram, 591 A.2d 14 (R.I. 1991) (handwriting samples); McCune, *Self-Incrimination Protection Under The Alaska Constitution: A Descriptive Analysis*, 12 ALASKA L. REV. 43 (1995).

46. Creamer v. State, 229 Ga. 511, 192 S.E.2d 350 (1972) (surgical removal of bullet; Georgia Constitution provides greater self-incrimination protection than U.S. Constitution), *cert. dismissed,* 410 U.S. 975 (1973); Green v. State, 260 Ga. 625, 627, 398 S.E.2d 360, 362 (1990) ("[T]he use of a substance naturally excreted by the human body [urine] does not violate a defendant's right against self-incrimination under the Georgia Constitution"), *cert. denied,* 500 U.S. 935 (1991).

47. 459 U.S. 553 (1983). *See also* Uviller, *Self-Incrimination by Inference: Constitutional Restrictions on the Evidentiary Use of a Suspect's Refusal to Submit to a Search*, 81 J. CRIM. L. & CRIMINOLOGY 37 (1990); Note, *Self-Incrimination Issues in the Context of Videotaping Drunk Drivers: Focusing on the Fifth Amendment*, 10 HARV. J. L. & PUB. POLICY 631 (1987).

48. 459 U.S. at 564.

> of taking a blood-alcohol test is clearly legitimate, the action becomes no *less* legitimate when the State offers a second option of refusing the test, with the attendant penalties for making the choice.[49]

In addition, the Court held that failure to warn Neville that his refusal could be used against him did not violate due process.[50]

Some courts have reached a different result under state law.[51] For instance, the Supreme Judicial Court of Massachusetts has written: "It does not logically follow, however, that, because test results are not testimonial, refusal evidence falls in the same category."[52] The court went on to conclude: "[I]f refusal evidence has relevance to any issue essential to the prosecution's case, it is because it is reflective of the knowledge, understanding, and thought process of the accused."[53] Consequently, evidence of refusal to take a breathalyzer test violates the state self-incrimination clause. In a later case, the court ruled that evidence of a defendant's refusal to submit to a gunshot residue test also violated the state constitution. "If the fact that the defendant refused to allow the hand-swabbing demonstrates consciousness of guilt, such refusal rises to the level of a self-accusation."[54]

---

49. *Id.* at 563.

50. *Id.* at 566. A number of courts have reached the same result on state constitutional grounds. *See* Cox v. People, 735 P.2d 153, 157 (Colo. 1987); McDonnell v. Commissioner of Pub. Safety, 473 N.W.2d 848, 855 (Minn. 1991); Ricks v. State, 611 So. 2d 212, 216 (Miss. 1992); State v. Neasbitt, 735 P.2d 337, 338 (Okla. Crim. App. 1987); Commonwealth v. Hayes, 544 Pa. 46, 55, 674 A.2d 677, 682 (1996) (field sobriety tests are nontestimonial); State v. Hoenscheid, 374 N.W.2d 128, 129-30 (S.D. 1985); Farmer v. Commonwealth, 12 Va. App. 337, 404 S.E.2d 371, 372-73 (1991) (en banc). *See generally* Craddick, *Blood-Alcohol Tests: Neville and Its Progeny*, 20 Crim. L. Bull. 493 (1984); Annot., *Admissibility in Criminal Case of Evidence that Accused Refused to Take Test of Intoxication*, 26 A.L.R.4th 1112 (1983).

51. *E.g.*, State v. Denney, 130 N.H. 217, 223, 536 A.2d 1242, 1245 (1987) (admission of defendant's refusal without warning violates state due process); State v. Beaton, 516 N.W.2d 645, 649 (N.D. 1994) (self-incrimination clause of the state constitution precludes the admission of a defendant's "words of refusal" but not the fact of refusal); State v. Satrom, 524 N.W.2d 92 (N.D. 1994) (same).

52. Opinion of the Justices to the Senate, 412 Mass. 1201, 591 N.E.2d 1073, 1077-78 (1992) ("In the ordinary case a prosecutor would seek to introduce refusal evidence to show, and would argue if permitted, that a defendant's refusal is the equivalent of his statement, 'I have had so much to drink that I know or at least suspect that I am unable to pass the test'").

53. *Id.*, 591 N.E.2d at 1078. The Massachusetts Constitution contains an additional clause; it prohibits compelling a person to "furnish evidence against himself." The court has ruled that this provision requires a "broader interpretation" than that of the fifth amendment. *Id.* at 1078. *See also* Commonwealth v. McGrail, 419 Mass. 774, 780, 647 N.E.2d 712, 715 (1995) (evidence of refusal to submit to field sobriety tests violates state self-incrimination clause).

54. Commonwealth v. Lydon, 413 Mass. 309, 597 N.E.2d 36, 40 (1992).

In *State v. Fish*,[55] the Oregon Supreme Court ruled the use of evidence of a defendant's refusal to submit to a field sobriety test violates the state constitution. The tests differed from the blood-alcohol test in *Neville*. The court wrote:

> Some of the field sobriety tests involve verbal statements that communicate information regarding an individual's state of mind. Many of the field sobriety tests authorized by [the statute] draw upon the individual's memory, perception, and ability to communicate, i.e., his or her testimonial capacity. For example, the tests involve counting, answering questions relating to the individual's residence and date of birth, estimating a period of time, and reciting the alphabet. There can be no doubt that those aspects of the field sobriety tests require the individual to communicate information to the police about the individual's beliefs, knowledge, or state of mind. Accordingly, we conclude that at least those aspects of the field sobriety tests are clearly "testimonial" under ... the Oregon Constitution.[56]

§ 2-2(B). Polygraph Examinations.

Some types of forensic techniques may implicate the fifth amendment. As the Supreme Court has noted, the "distinction between real or physical evidence, on the one hand, and communications or testimony, on the other, is not readily drawn in many cases."[57] Polygraph testing and psychiatric examinations are examples.[58] The Court in *Schmerber* commented on the fifth amendment aspects of polygraph examinations:

> Some tests seemingly directed to obtain "physical evidence," for example, lie detector tests measuring changes in body function during interrogation, may actually be directed to eliciting responses which are essentially testimonial. To compel a person to submit to testing in which an effort will be made to determine his guilt or innocence on the basis of physiological responses, whether willed or not, is to evoke the spirit and history of the Fifth Amendment.[59]

---

55. 321 Or. 48, 893 P.2d 1023 (1995) (en banc).

56. *Id.* at 60, 893 P.2d at 1030 (citations omitted). *See also* State v. Nielsen, 147 Or. App. 294, 307, 936 P.2d 374, 382 (*Fish* not applicable to multi-task divided attention tests (walk-and-turn, one-leg-stand, and modified Romberg) because the "purpose of the test is not ... to obtain answers to the questions put to the subject; it is instead to determine whether the person can perform the physical tasks as requested while at the same time attempting to answer the questions"), *rev. denied*, 950 P.2d 892 (Or. 1997).

57. South Dakota v. Neville, 459 U.S. 553, 561 (1983).

58. *Id.* at 561 n.12.

59. 384 U.S. at 764.

Courts that have admitted polygraph evidence have recognized the applicability of the privilege in this context:[60] "The polygraph results are essentially testimonial in nature and therefore a defendant could not be compelled initially to take such an examination on the Commonwealth's motion."[61]

§ 2-2(C). Psychiatric Examinations.

In *Estelle v. Smith,*[62] the Supreme Court held that the fifth amendment privilege protected against compelled disclosures during a court-ordered psychiatric examination. A psychiatrist, after interviewing Smith, testified about Smith's future dangerousness during the penalty stage of a capital case. The Court rejected the state's argument that the defendant's communications to the psychiatrist were nontestimonial. According to the Court, the "prognosis as to future dangerousness rested on statements [the defendant] made, and remarks he omitted, in reciting the details of the crime."[63] The Court continued by saying that a "criminal defendant, who neither initiates a psychiatric evaluation nor attempts to introduce any psychiatric evidence, may not be compelled to respond to a psychiatrist if his statements can be used against him at a capital sentencing proceeding."[64] However, for the reasons discussed below, if the accused uses psychiatric evidence, the privilege is considered waived.[65]

The Supreme Court distinguished two other types of psychiatric examinations. If the examination had been limited to a routine *competency* examination to determine whether the defendant understood the charges against him and was capable of assisting in his defense, "no Fifth Amendment issue would have arisen."[66] An examination to determine an accused's competency to stand trial involves a limited and neutral purpose not adverse to the defendant.[67]

---

60. For a discussion of the fifth amendment issues involving polygraph testing, *see* § 8-7 *infra.*

61. Commonwealth v. A Juvenile, 365 Mass. 421, 431, 313 N.E.2d 120, 127 (1974).

62. 451 U.S. 454 (1981).

63. *Id.* at 464.

64. *Id.* at 468. *See also* Powell v. Texas, 492 U.S. 680 (1989) (per curiam) (psychiatric evidence on future dangerousness based on an in-custody psychiatric exam without notice to counsel violates the self-incrimination clause and the right to counsel).

65. *See* Lagrone v. State, 942 S.W.2d 602, 612 (Tex. Crim. App. 1997) ("[W]hen the defense demonstrates the intent to put on future dangerousness expert testimony, trial courts may order defendants to submit to an independent, state-sponsored psychiatric exam prior to the actual presentation of the defense's expert testimony"), *cert. denied*, 118 S. Ct. 305 (1997).

66. 451 U.S. at 465.

67. *See* 1 C. McCormick, *supra* note 2, § 136, at 505 ("This is apparently because a finding of competency simply removes a potential bar to trial of the accused and thus does not constitute 'incrimination' within the meaning of the Fifth Amendment privilege").

In addition, the Court indicated that a *sanity* examination is also different. When an insanity defense is asserted, a defendant may be required to submit to examination by a prosecution psychiatrist.[68]

§ 2-3. Right to Counsel.

The sixth amendment guarantees an accused the right to counsel.[69] This right has not been limited to trial but has been extended to certain pretrial proceedings such as the preliminary hearing[70] and, under some circumstances, to identification procedures[71] and interrogations.[72] Although defendants have argued that the right to counsel applies when evidence is obtained from them for scientific analysis, this argument has not been successful for two reasons: (1) the right to counsel often has not attached at the time the evidence is obtained by the police, and (2) this type of police conduct does not raise right to counsel concerns

---

68. 451 U.S. at 465. In Buchanan v. Kentucky, 483 U.S. 402, 422-23 (1987), the Supreme Court commented: "[I]f a defendant requests such an evaluation or presents psychiatric evidence, then, at the very least, the prosecution may rebut this presentation with evidence from the reports of the examination that the defendant requested. The defendant would have no Fifth Amendment privilege against the introduction of this psychiatric testimony by the prosecution." *See also* Powell v. Texas, 492 U.S. 680, 684 (1989) (where an accused asserts a mental-status defense, he waives the right to raise a Fifth Amendment challenge to the prosecution's use of a psychiatric report); Schnieder v. Lylnaugh, 835 F.2d 570, 575-76 (5th Cir 1988) ("[A] defendant who puts his mental state at issue with psychological evidence may not then use the Fifth Amendment to bar the state from rebutting in kind. ... It is unfair and improper to allow a defendant to introduce favorable psychological testimony and then prevent the prosecution from resorting to the most effective and in most instances the only means of rebuttal: other psychological testimony"); United States v. White, 21 F. Supp. 2d 1197, 1200 (E.D. Cal. 1998) ("[V]irtually all circuits addressing this issue in cases where a defendant has interposed the defense of insanity have uniformly held that a court-ordered psychiatric examination does not violate the Fifth Amendment's privilege against self-incrimination"); State v. Schackart, 175 Ariz. 494, 858 P.2d 639, 645 (1993) (Privilege does not bar a compelled psychiatric examination by a state expert if an accused intends to introduce expert testimony concerning lack of intent; "To hold otherwise would deprive the state of the only adequate means to contest the conclusions of a defense psychiatric expert"), *cert. denied*, 511 U.S. 1046 (1994); Commonwealth v. Morley, 545 Pa. 420, 429, 681 A.2d 1254, 1258 (1996) (state constitution); State v. Martin, 950 S.W.2d 20, 24 (Tenn. 1997) ("Virtually every federal and state court jurisdiction has held that where a defendant raises an insanity defense, the Fifth Amendment right against self-incrimination is not violated by a court-ordered psychiatric examination or by the prosecution's use of evidence from the examination to rebut evidence introduced by the defendant").

69. *See* Gideon v. Wainwright, 372 U.S. 335 (1963) (right to counsel applies to the states).

70. *See* Coleman v. Alabama, 399 U.S. 1 (1970).

71. *See* Moore v. Illinois, 434 U.S. 220 (1977); Kirby v. Illinois, 406 U.S. 682 (1972); United States v. Wade, 388 U.S. 218 (1967).

72. *See* Kuhlmann v. Wilson, 477 U.S. 436 (1986); United States v. Henry, 447 U.S. 264 (1980); Brewer v. Williams, 430 U.S. 387 (1977); Massiah v. United States, 377 U.S. 201 (1964).

because it does not involve a "critical stage" in the proceedings for sixth amendment purposes.

Attachment of the Right to Counsel

The Supreme Court has held that the right to counsel attaches only after the "initiation of adversary judicial criminal proceedings — whether by way of formal charge, preliminary hearing, indictment, information, or arraignment."[73] An arrest, by itself, does not trigger the right to counsel. Frequently, evidence submitted for scientific analysis is obtained from defendants during the investigatory stage, prior to commencement of formal criminal proceedings, and thus before the right to counsel attaches. Cases involving handwriting exemplars,[74] gunshot residues,[75] teeth impressions,[76] and urine samples[77] have been decided on this basis.

Similarly, although the Supreme Court has yet to decide the issue,[78] most courts hold that a person arrested for driving while intoxicated does not have a federal constitutional right to counsel when deciding whether to take a blood-alcohol test.[79] In some jurisdictions, however, a right to *consult* counsel may be

---

73. Kirby v. Illinois, 406 U.S. 682, 689 (1972). *Accord* United States v. Gouveia, 467 U.S. 180, 187-88 (1984); Moore v. Illinois, 434 U.S. 220, 227-29 (1977); Brewer v. Williams, 430 U.S. 387, 398 (1977).

74. *E.g.,* Lazoda v. Maggy, 900 F. Supp. 596, 604 (N.D.N.Y. 1995) (request for handwriting exemplars and fingerprints; "right to counsel does not attach until the filing of formal charges"); United States v. Richardson, 837 F. Supp. 570, 573-75 (S.D.N.Y. 1993).

75. State v. Ulrich, 187 Mont. 347, 609 P.2d 1218 (1980) (GSR swabbings taken before right to counsel attached).

76. Spence v. State, 795 S.W.2d 743, 752-53 (Tex. Crim. App. 1990) (en banc) (teeth impressions taken before right to counsel attached), *cert. denied,* 499 U.S. 932 (1991); State v. Howe, 136 Vt. 53, 63, 386 A.2d 1125, 1131 (1978) (right to counsel had not attached at time dental impressions taken).

77. United States v. Edmo, 140 F.3d 1289, 1293 (9th Cir. 1998) (request for urine sample; possession of a firearm while using a controlled substance; no right to counsel "until adversary proceedings had been initiated against him"); Lucero v. Gunter, 17 F.3d 1347, 1351 (10th Cir. 1994) ("Plaintiff was asked to submit to a urinalysis before the beginning of formal adversary criminal proceedings").

78. In Nyflot v. Minnesota Comm'r of Pub. Safety, 474 U.S. 1027 (1985), the Supreme Court dismissed for lack of a substantial question an appeal raising the right to counsel issue, a disposition that has far more significance than a denial of certiorari. Justice White, with Justice Stevens, dissented and wrote: "Most of the courts that have considered this issue have rejected the argument that the Sixth Amendment right to counsel covers the stage at which the decision whether to consent to the blood alcohol test must be made. A few, however, have found that the Sixth Amendment right to counsel does extend to this stage. Other courts have found a right to counsel based on state law, or on general due process guarantees. Given these varying results, I would note probable jurisdiction to settle the question presented." *Id.* at 1029 (internal citations omitted).

79. *See* Roberts v. Maine, 48 F.3d 1287, 1290 (1st Cir. 1995) (The "right to counsel had not attached at the time [refusal to take blood/alcohol test] of the alleged violation of his Sixth

guaranteed by a state constitution[80] or statute.[81] The right includes the right to consult in a confidential manner.[82]

In *Roberts v. Maine*,[83] the First Circuit found a unique situation where the refusal to permit an arrestee to contact his attorney violated due process, *i.e.*, lacked fundamental fairness. While handcuffed at the police station, Roberts was asked to take a blood/alcohol test and was informed that if he refused to submit to the test, his drivers license would be suspended and his refusal would be used against him at trial. He was not told that his failure to take the test would result in a 48-hour term of incarceration. Roberts asked to call his attorney, but the request was refused. "Roberts thus had to make a decision with irrevocable consequences

---

Amendment rights"); McVeigh v. Smith, 872 F.2d 725 (6th Cir. 1989); Langelier v. Coleman, 861 F.2d 1508, 1510 n.3 (11th Cir. 1988); State v. Cichowski, 203 Conn. 97, 102, 523 A.2d 503, 506 (1987); Brank v. State, 528 A.2d 1185, 1190 (Del. 1987) (no due process right to consult attorney); State v. Ankney, 109 Idaho 1, 5-6, 704 P.2d 333, 337-38 (1985); State v. Bristor, 236 Kan. 313, 322, 691 P.2d 1, 7 (1984); Commonwealth v. Brazelton, 404 Mass. 783, 785, 537 N.E.2d 142, 143 (1989); State v. Schulze, 116 Wash. 2d 154, 804 P.2d 566, 570-71 (1991) (en banc) (right to counsel under state and federal constitutions had not attached at time defendant submitted to mandatory blood test in vehicular homicide case); Wheeler v. State, 705 P.2d 861, 864 (Wyo. 1985). For a further discussion of this issue, *see* § 22-7(E) *infra*.

80. *E.g.*, Brosan v. Cochran, 307 Md. 662, 668-69, 516 A.2d 970, 974 (1986) (state due process right to face-to-face consultation with attorney); Friedman v. Comm'r of Pub. Safety, 473 N.W.2d 828, 832 (Minn. 1991) (state constitution); State v. White, 504 N.W.2d 211 (Minn. 1993) (limited state constitutional right to consult counsel does not include the right to appointed counsel at state expense for indigents); Ruffenach v. Comm'r of Pub. Safety, 528 N.W.2d 254, 256 (Minn. App. 1995) (discussing driver's limited right to consult with counsel before deciding whether to take the implied consent test); State v. Spencer, 305 Or. 59, 74-75, 750 P.2d 147, 156 (1988) (en banc) (state constitution).

See also Heles v. South Dakota, 530 F. Supp. 646, 653 (D.S.D.) (due process right to counsel), *rev'd on other grounds,* 682 F.2d 201 (8th Cir. 1982); Murphy, *Constitutional Bases for a Right of Access to Counsel at the Pre-Trial Stages of Drunk Driving Prosecutions: A Study in Conflicting Rights*, 4 N. ILL. U. L. REV. 203 (1984); Comment, *Public Outcry v. Individual Rights: Right to Counsel and the Drunk Driver's Dilemma*, 69 MARQ. L. REV. 278 (1986); Annot., *Denial of Accused's Request for Initial Contact with Attorney — Drunk Driving Cases*, 18 A.L.R.4TH 705 (1982).

81. *E.g.*, Whisehunt v. State, 746 P.2d 1298, 1298 (Alaska 1987); Kuntz v. State Hwy. Comm'r, 405 N.W.2d 285, 290 (N.D. 1987); State v. Garvey, 595 A.2d 267, 268 (Vt. 1991).

82. *See* City of Mandan v. Jewett, 517 N.W.2d 640, 642 (N.D. 1994) (limited statutory right to consult with counsel before DUI test includes a reasonable opportunity to talk privately with counsel); State v. Penrod, 133 Or. App. 454, 457-58, 892 P.2d 729, 731 (1995) ("[C]onfidentiality is inherent in the [state constitutional] right to consult with counsel; to hold otherwise would effectively render the right meaningless.... [I]f the consultation with counsel must occur during the 15-minute observation period, the police may justifiably limit the privacy aspect of the right.... Similarly, if there is evidence that fully accommodating an arrestee's request for a private consultation would unreasonably delay, and thus interfere with, the proper administration of the test, then the arrestee's right to a confidential conversation may also be limited").

83. 48 F.3d 1287 (1st Cir. 1995).

for his sentence after the state provided him with inaccurate information with which he was expected to make that decision. Under this combination of circumstances, it is incumbent upon the state to honor a reasonable request to call an attorney. Refusing to provide this simple safeguard violated Roberts' right to due process."[84]

Critical Stage

The right to counsel often does not apply for a second reason. Neither the obtaining of evidence for scientific analysis nor the analysis itself is a "critical" stage within the meaning of the sixth amendment. The leading cases are *United States v. Wade*[85] and *Gilbert v. California.*[86]

In *Wade,* the Supreme Court held that the right to counsel applied to lineup identifications. According to the Court, a lineup presents "grave potential for prejudice ... which may not be capable of reconstruction at trial, and [the] presence of counsel itself can often avert prejudice and assure a meaningful confrontation at trial."[87] The Court, however, distinguished eyewitness identification procedures from the scientific analysis of physical evidence:

> The Government characterizes the lineup as a mere preparatory step in the gathering of the prosecution's evidence, not different — for Sixth Amendment purposes — from various other preparatory steps, such as systemized or scientific analyzing of the accused's fingerprints, blood sample, clothing, hair, and the like. We think there are differences which preclude such stages being characterized as critical stages at which the accused has the right to the presence of his counsel. Knowledge of the techniques of science and technology is sufficiently available, and the variables in techniques few enough, that the accused has the opportunity for a meaningful confrontation of the Government's case at trial through the ordinary processes of cross-examination of Government's expert witnesses and the presentation of the evidence of his own experts. The denial of a right to have his counsel present at such analyses does not therefore violate the Sixth Amendment; they are not critical stages since there is minimal risk that his counsel's absence at such stages might derogate from his right to a fair trial.[88]

In *Gilbert* the defendant contended that his right to counsel had been violated when he was compelled to provide handwriting exemplars in the absence of an

84. *Id.* at 1292.
85. 388 U.S. 218 (1967).
86. 388 U.S. 263 (1967).
87. 388 U.S. at 236.
88. *Id.* at 227-28.

attorney. Whereas *Wade* focused on the time of the forensic analysis, *Gilbert* focused on the time the evidence was obtained from the suspect. Nevertheless, the result was the same; the right to counsel did not apply. The Court in *Gilbert* found significant differences between conducting a lineup and obtaining exemplars:

> The taking of the exemplars was not a "critical" stage of the criminal proceedings entitling petitioner to the assistance of counsel. Putting aside the fact that the exemplars were taken before the indictment and appointment of counsel, there is minimal risk that the absence of counsel might derogate from his right to a fair trial. Cf. *United States v. Wade*.... If, for some reason, an unrepresentative exemplar is taken, this can be brought out and corrected through the adversary process at trial since the accused can make an unlimited number of additional exemplars for analysis and comparison by government and defense handwriting experts. Thus, "the accused has the opportunity for a meaningful confrontation of the [State's] case at trial through the ordinary processes of cross-examination of the [State's] expert [handwriting] witnesses and the presentation of the evidence of his own [handwriting] experts." *United States v. Wade*....[89]

Hence, unlike eyewitness identification procedures, the adversary process is thought to afford a criminal defendant an adequate opportunity to confront and challenge scientific evidence. The ability to discover and reexamine the prosecution's evidence, to cross-examine the state's witnesses at trial, and to present defense experts minimizes the need for counsel. Moreover, as one court has remarked: "Not only is the taking of the exemplars not at a critical stage of the proceedings entitling an accused to the assistance of counsel, but Appellant has pointed to no function counsel could perform, were he present, save the futile advice not to give the sample."[90]

Accordingly, courts have held the right to counsel does not apply when gunshot residues,[91] fingerprints,[92] palm prints,[93] blood,[94] hair,[95] teeth

---

89. 388 U.S. at 267. The Court approvingly cited *Gilbert* in United States v. Euge, 444 U.S. 707, 718 (1980) (handwriting exemplars), and in United States v. Ash, 413 U.S. 300, 318 n.10 (1973) (photographic identification conducted without defendant present).

90. Lewis v. United States, 382 F.2d 817, 819 (D.C. Cir.) (handwriting exemplars), *cert. denied,* 389 U.S. 962 (1967).

91. *E.g.,* State v. Odom, 303 N.C. 163, 167, 277 S.E.2d 352, 355, *cert. denied,* 454 U.S. 1052 (1981); People v. Mullings, 110 A.D.2d 720, 721, 488 N.Y.S.2d 36, 37 (1985).

92. *E.g.,* Ward v. United States, 486 F.2d 305, 306 (5th Cir. 1973), *cert. denied,* 416 U.S. 990 (1974); United States v. McNeal, 463 F.2d 1180, 1181 (5th Cir. 1972); United States v. Gibson, 444 F.2d 275, 277 (5th Cir. 1971); Woods v. United States, 397 F.2d 156, 156 (9th Cir. 1968); Pearson v. United States, 389 F.2d 684, 686 (5th Cir. 1968); Lindsey v. State, 331 So. 2d 797, 801 (Ala. Crim. App. 1976); State v. Jones, 467 So. 2d 147, 149-50 (La. App. 1985).

impressions,[96] breath samples,[97] and other types of evidence[98] are obtained from defendants.

However, polygraph examinations raise a different issue. Because such examinations implicate the fifth amendment,[99] *Miranda* and its right to counsel requirement apply.[100] In addition, after the commencement of judicial adversary proceedings, the sixth amendment right to counsel would be applicable to polygraph examinations.[101] Moreover, under some circumstances, the right to counsel would also apply to psychiatric examinations.[102]

§ 2-4. Search & Seizure.

The fourth amendment guarantees the right to be free from unreasonable governmental searches and seizures. In some cases, evidence which may be

---

93. *E.g.,* United States v. Sanders, 477 F.2d 112, 113 (5th Cir.), *cert. denied,* 414 U.S. 870 (1973); State v. Jones, 467 So. 2d 147, 149-50 (La. App. 1985).

94. *E.g.,* Schmerber v. California, 384 U.S. 757, 765-66 (1966); United States v. Bullock, 71 F.3d 171, 177 (5th Cir. 1995) ("the taking of blood and hair samples are not critical confrontations"), *cert. denied,* 517 U.S. 1126 (1996); United States v. Puckett, 907 F.2d 581, 583 (5th Cir. 1990); United States v. Sheard, 473 F.2d 139, 148 (D.C. Cir. 1972), *cert. denied,* 412 U.S. 943 (1973); United States v. Smith, 470 F.2d 377, 379-80 (D.C. Cir. 1972); Brown v. State, 29 Md. App. 1, 10, 349 A.2d 359, 365 (1975); State v. Kalakosky, 121 Wash. 2d 525, 852 P.2d 1064, 1069 (1993) ("[T]he taking of nontestimonial physical evidence [blood for DNA testing] is not usually a critical stage at which the right to counsel attaches").

95. *E.g.,* United States v. Bullock, 71 F.3d 171, 177 (5th Cir. 1995) ("the taking of blood and hair samples are not critical confrontations"); United States v. Dougall, 919 F.2d 932, 935 (5th Cir. 1990), *cert. denied,* 501 U.S. 1234 (1991); United States v. Jackson, 448 F.2d 963, 971 (9th Cir. 1971), *cert. denied,* 405 U.S. 924 (1972); Henry v. United States, 432 F.2d 114, 119 (9th Cir. 1970), *cert. denied,* 400 U.S. 1011 (1971); State v. Brierly, 109 Ariz. 310, 319, 509 P.2d 203, 212 (1973) (en banc).

96. *E.g.,* United States v. Maceo, 873 F.2d 1, 4-5 (1st Cir.) (examination of teeth), *cert. denied,* 493 U.S. 840 (1980); Brewer v. State, 725 So. 2d 106, 130 (Miss. 1998) ("[T]he taking of the dental impression was like the taking of fingerprints —which this Court has held not be a critical stage so as to require counsel's presence"), *cert. denied,* 119 S. Ct. 1270 (1998); State v. Howe, 136 Vt. 53, 63, 386 A.2d 1125, 1131 (1978) (dental impression).

97. *E.g.,* McNulty v. Curry, 42 Ohio St. 2d 341, 328 N.E.2d 798 (1975) (breathalyzer); State v. Greene, 128 N.H. 317, 320, 512 A.2d 429, 431 1986).

98. *E.g.,* United States v. Cotner, 657 F.2d 1171, 1173 (10th Cir. 1981) (handwriting exemplars); United States v. Kim, 577 F.2d 473, 481 (9th Cir. 1978) (voice identification); United States v. Love, 482 F.2d 213, 216 (5th Cir.) (bomb nitrate swabbings), *cert. denied,* 414 U.S. 1026 (1973); United States v. Smith, 470 F.2d 377, 380 (D.C. Cir. 1972) (benzidine swabbing of penis for blood analysis).

99. *See* § 2-2(B) *supra.*

100. *See* § 8-8 *infra.*

101. *See* State v. Jones, 19 Wash. App. 850, 578 P.2d 71 (1978) (confession obtained after polygraph examination violated right to counsel).

102. *See* Estelle v. Smith, 451 U.S. 454, 469-73 (1981) (right to counsel attached when psychiatric examination involved issue of defendant's future dangerousness in a capital case).

subjected to scientific analysis is seized from a specific location.[103] In other situations the evidence is seized from a suspect. The cases involving the latter situation are discussed in this section.[104]

Typically, there are two distinct fourth amendment issues raised when physical evidence is obtained from a suspect for the purpose of scientific analysis. First, there is a "seizure" of the person, which brings the suspect under the control of the police. Second, there is a subsequent search and seizure of physical characteristics, biological specimens, or trace evidence from this previously seized suspect.[105]

§ 2-4(A). Seizure of the Person.

Before trace evidence or physical characteristics can be obtained from a suspect, the suspect either must consent or be detained under some form of government control.[106] Such control raises the question whether the person has been "seized" within the meaning of the fourth amendment. Evidence submitted for scientific analysis has been collected from suspects at the time of arrest,[107] during pretrial incarceration,[108] during detention on less than probable cause,[109] and pursuant to grand jury subpoenas[110] and administrative summonses.[111] If the

---

103. *E.g.,* Cardwell v. Lewis, 417 U.S. 583 (1974) (seizure of suspect's car for paint chip and mark comparison); Coolidge v. New Hampshire, 403 U.S. 443 (1971) (seizure of suspect's car). The evidence obtained from the car in *Coolidge* was subjected to neutron activation analysis. State v. Coolidge, 109 N.H. 403, 408-09, 260 A.2d 547, 552 (1969).

104. The most comprehensive text on the fourth amendment is W. LAFAVE, SEARCH AND SEIZURE (3d ed. 1996). *See also* E. IMWINKELRIED, P. GIANNELLI, F. GILLIGAN & F. LEDERER, COURTROOM CRIMINAL EVIDENCE (3d ed. 1998).

105. "[T]he obtaining of physical evidence from a person involves a potential Fourth Amendment violation at two different levels — the 'seizure' of the 'person' necessary to bring him into contact with government agents ... and the subsequent search for and seizure of the evidence." United States v. Dionisio, 410 U.S. 1, 8 (1973) (voice exemplar). *See also* Skinner v. Railway Labor Executives' Ass'n, 489 U.S. 602, 616 (1989) (blood and urine tests); Cupp v. Murphy, 412 U.S. 291 (1973) (fingernail scrapings); Schmerber v. California, 384 U.S. 757 (1966) (blood sample).

106. If the suspect voluntarily consents to appear at the stationhouse and provide the evidence, the fourth amendment requirements are satisfied. *See* note 162 *infra.*

107. *See* Schmerber v. California, 384 U.S. 757 (1966) (blood). *See also* Cupp v. Murphy, 412 U.S. 291 (1973) (fingernail scrapings; probable cause existed although suspect not formally placed under arrest).

108. *See* Edwards v. United States, 415 U.S. 800 (1974) (examination of clothing for paint chips).

109. *See* Wise v. Murphy, 275 A.2d 205 (D.C. 1971) (en banc) (lineup); *In re* Fingerprinting of M.B., 125 N.J. Super. 115, 309 A.2d 3 (1973) (fingerprints).

110. *See* United States v. Dionisio, 410 U.S. 1 (1973) (voice exemplars); United States v. Mara, 410 U.S. 19 (1973) (handwriting exemplars).

111. *See* United States v. Euge, 444 U.S. 707 (1980) (IRS summons to compel handwriting exemplars).

initial seizure of the person violates fourth amendment requirements, evidence recovered in the subsequent search of that person may be excluded at trial as "fruit of the poisonous tree."[112]

§ 2-4(A)(1). Arrest.

An arrest is a "seizure" of the person within the meaning of the fourth amendment.[113] Generally, if the arrest is valid, the seizure of physical evidence from the person incident to the arrest is also valid.[114] While the arrest of a person in a public place does not require the issuance of an arrest warrant,[115] it does require *probable cause* that a crime has been committed by the arrestee.[116] For example, in *Schmerber v. California*[117] the defendant was arrested for driving while under the influence of alcohol before blood was extracted. The Court held that probable cause for the arrest existed based on the arresting officer's observation of the defendant at both the scene of the accident and the hospital; the officer testified that the defendant's eyes were glassy and bloodshot and that he smelled liquor on the defendant's breath.[118] The Court considered the constitutionality of the initial seizure (the arrest) before turning to the fourth amendment implications of withdrawing blood from the suspect.[119]

In *Davis v. Mississippi*[120] the Supreme Court considered the constitutionality of a detention during which fingerprints were obtained from the defendant. Although fingerprints and palm prints were found on the window used by an assailant to gain entry into a rape victim's house, the victim could not provide any description of her attacker other than his race and approximate age. The police conducted a dragnet procedure in which numerous young African-

---

112. The "fruit of the poisonous tree" doctrine, however, is subject to several exceptions. *See generally* 5 W. LAFAVE, *supra* note 104, § 11.4; 2 E. IMWINKELRIED, P. GIANNELLI, F. GILLIGAN & F. LEDERER, *supra* note 104, ch. 22.

113. *See generally* 3 W. LAFAVE, *supra* note 104, § 5.1; 2 E. IMWINKELRIED, P. GIANNELLI, F. GILLIGAN & F. LEDERER, *supra* note 104, ch. 20.

114. *See* § 2-4(B)(2) *infra* (search incident to arrest).

115. United States v. Watson, 423 U.S. 411 (1976). Arrests in private dwellings, however, raise different issues. Steagald v. United States, 451 U.S. 204 (1981) (search warrant required for arrest of defendant found in a third party's house); Payton v. New York, 445 U.S. 573 (1980) (arrest warrant required for arrest of defendant found in his own house). *See generally* 3 W. LAFAVE, *supra* note 104, § 6.1; 2 E. IMWINKELRIED, P. GIANNELLI, F. GILLIGAN & F. LEDERER, *supra* note 104, ch. 22.

116. For a discussion of the probable cause requirement, *see* 2 W. LAFAVE, *supra* note 104, § 3.1; 2 E. IMWINKELRIED, P. GIANNELLI, F. GILLIGAN & F. LEDERER, *supra* note 104, ch. 19.

117. 384 U.S. 757 (1966).

118. *Id.* at 768-69.

119. *Id.* at 768-71. *See also* Cupp v. Murphy, 412 U.S. 291 (1973) (fingernail scrapings; probable cause existed although suspect not formally placed under arrest).

120. 394 U.S. 721 (1969).

American males, including Davis, were detained and fingerprinted. Subsequently, Davis was seized a second time and another set of fingerprints was obtained; these prints were used for comparison with the crime scene prints and introduced at trial. The Court ruled that the detention, based neither on probable cause nor a warrant, was illegal. Consequently, the fingerprint evidence was suppressed.

Similarly, in *Hayes v. Florida*[121] the Supreme Court held that the transportation and investigative detention of a defendant for the purpose of obtaining fingerprints violated the fourth amendment in the absence of probable cause or judicial authorization.[122]

§ 2-4(A)(2). Detention on Less Than Probable Cause.

In *Terry v. Ohio*,[123] the Supreme Court first recognized that the detention of a suspect on less than probable cause may satisfy fourth amendment requirements. The importance of *Terry* and its progeny, defining the scope of the "stop and frisk" doctrine,[124] to the collection of physical evidence for the purpose of scientific analysis turns on dictum in *Davis v. Mississippi*.[125] As noted previously, the Court in *Davis* held that detention of a suspect on less than probable cause, during which fingerprints were obtained, was unconstitutional. However, the Court commented:

> Detentions for the sole purpose of obtaining fingerprints are no less subject to the constraints of the Fourth Amendment. It is arguable, however, that, because of the unique nature of the fingerprinting process, such detentions might, under narrowly defined circumstances, be found to comply with the Fourth Amendment even though there is no probable cause in the traditional sense.... Detention for fingerprinting may constitute a much less serious intrusion upon personal security than other types of police searches and detentions. Fingerprinting involves none of the probing into an individual's private life and thoughts that marks an interrogation or search. Nor can fingerprint detention be employed repeatedly to harass any individual, since the police need only one set of each person's prints. Furthermore, fingerprinting is an inherently more reliable and effective crime solving tool than eyewitness identifications or confessions and is not subject to such abuses as the improper lineup and the "third degree." Finally, because there is no danger of destruction of fingerprints, the limited detention need not

---

121. 470 U.S. 811 (1985).

122. *Id.* at 816.

123. 392 U.S. 1 (1968).

124. *See generally* 4 W. LAFAVE, *supra* note 104, §§ 9.1-9.6; 2 E. IMWINKELRIED, P. GIANNELLI, F. GILLIGAN & F. LEDERER, *supra* note 104, ch. 22.

125. 394 U.S. 721 (1969).

> come unexpectedly or at an inconvenient time. For this same reason, the general requirement that the authorization of a judicial officer be obtained in advance of detention would seem not to admit of any exception in the fingerprinting context.
>
> We have no occasion in this case, however, to determine whether the requirements of the Fourth Amendment could be met by narrowly circumscribed procedures for obtaining, during the course of a criminal investigation, the fingerprints of individuals for whom there is no probable cause to arrest....[126]

The invitation contained in this dictum did not go unanswered. A number of statutes and court rules providing for detentions on less than probable cause for the purpose of nontestimonial identification procedures[127] have been adopted[128] or proposed.[129] For example, an Arizona statute provides for the issuance of judicial orders for obtaining "fingerprints, palm prints, footprints, measurements, handwriting, handprinting, sound of voice, blood samples, urine samples, saliva samples, hair samples, comparative personal appearance, or photographs of an individual."[130] Such an order may be issued if the following conditions are satisfied:

---

126. *Id.* at 727-28.

127. For a discussion of this issue, *see* 4 W. LAFAVE, *supra* note 104, § 9.6(b); 2 E. IMWINKELRIED, P. GIANNELLI, F. GILLIGAN & F. LEDERER, *supra* note 104, ch. 20. Dix, *Nonarrest Investigatory Detentions in Search and Seizure Law*, 1985 DUKE L.J. 849; Israel, *Legislative Regulation of Searches and Seizures*, 73 MICH. L. REV. 222, 238-41, 310-14 (1974); Uviller, *The Acquisition of Evidence for Criminal Prosecution: Some Constitutional Premises and Practices in Transition*, 35 VAND. L. REV. 501, 524-25 (1982); Comment, *Detention for Taking Physical Evidence Without Probable Cause*, 14 ARIZ. L. REV. 132 (1972); Comment, *People v. Harris, Rule 41.1, and the Constitutionality of Investigatory Detentions on Less Than Probable Cause*, 61 U. COLO. L. REV. 815 (1990); Note, *Detention to Obtain Physical Evidence Without Probable Cause: Proposed Rule 41.1 of the Federal Rules of Criminal Procedure*, 72 COLUM. L. REV. 712 (1972); Comment, *The Constitutionality of Compulsory Identification Procedures on Less Than Probable Cause: Reassessing the Davis Dictum*, 89 DICK. L. REV. 501 (1985); Note, *DNA Typing: A New Investigatory Tool*, 1989 DUKE L.J. 474; Note, *Proposed Federal Rule of Criminal Procedure 41.1*, 56 MINN. L. REV. 667 (1972); Comment, *Criminal Law and Procedure Nontestimonial Identification Orders Without Probable Cause*, 12 WAKE FOREST L. REV. 387 (1976); Note, *Constitutional Limitations on the Taking of Body Evidence*, 78 YALE L.J. 1074 (1969).

128. *See* ARIZ. REV. STAT. ANN. § 13-3905; Colo. R. Crim. P. 41.1; IDAHO CODE § 19-625; NEB. REV. STAT. § 29-3301 to 3307; N.C. GEN. STAT. § 15A-271 to -282; UTAH CODE ANN. § 77-8-1(1) (lineups only); VT. R. CRIM. P. 41.1.

129. MODEL CODE OF PRE-ARRAIGNMENT PROCEDURE art. 170 (Proposed Official Draft 1975); UNIF. R. CRIM. P. 436 (Approved Draft 1974); FED. R. CRIM. P. 41.1 (Proposed Draft), 52 F.R.D. 462 (1971).

130. ARIZ. REV. STAT. ANN. § 13-3905(D).

1. Reasonable cause for belief that a specifically described criminal offense punishable by at least one year in the state prison has been committed.
2. Procurement of evidence of identifying physical characteristics from an identified or particularly described individual may contribute to the identification of the individual who committed such offense.
3. Such evidence cannot otherwise be obtained by the investigating officer from either the law enforcement agency employing the affiant or the criminal identification division of the Arizona department of public safety.[131]

The Arizona courts have upheld the constitutionality of this provision.[132] Similarly, the Colorado rule on nontestimonial identification procedures also has been upheld.[133]

Unlike other provisions, the Arizona statute does not specify the quantum of evidence required to subject a person to such an order. In contrast, an Idaho statute provides that a nontestimonial identification order may be issued if "[r]easonable grounds exist, which may or may not amount to probable cause, to believe that the ... individual committed the criminal offense."[134] In other words, the "reasonable suspicion" test of *Terry v. Ohio*.

The Supreme Court has yet to decide the constitutionality of such provisions. In *Hayes v. Florida*,[135] however, the Court noted that it had "not abandon[ed] the suggestion in *Davis* ... that under circumscribed procedures, the Fourth Amendment might permit the judiciary to authorize the seizure of a person on less than probable cause and his removal to the police station for the purpose of fingerprinting."[136] The Court also noted that the state courts were divided on this

---

131. ARIZ. REV. STAT. ANN. § 13-3905(A).

132. *See* State v. Via, 146 Ariz. 108, 704 P.2d 238 (1985), *cert. denied*, 475 U.S. 1048 (1986); State v. Grijalva, 111 Ariz. 476, 533 P.2d 533 (en banc), *cert. denied,* 423 U.S. 873 (1975) (photographs, fingerprints and hair samples); Long v. Garrett, 22 Ariz. App. 397, 527 P.2d 1240 (1974) (handwriting exemplar).

133. *See* People v. Madson, 638 P.2d 18, 31-32 (Colo. 1981) (en banc) (handwriting exemplars). *See also* People v. Davis, 669 P.2d 130, 133-35 (Colo. 1983) (nontestimonial order for photographs, fingerprints, and voice exemplar based on informant's tip upheld); People v. Harris, 729 P.2d 1000, 1002 (Colo. App. 1986), *aff'd*, 762 P.2d 651 (Colo.), *cert. denied*, 488 U.S. 985 (1988).

134. IDAHO CODE § 19-625(B). *See also* COLO. R. CRIM. P. 41.1(c)(2) ("reasonable grounds, not amounting to probable cause to arrest, to suspect that the person ... committed the offense"); N.C. GEN. STAT. § 15A-273(2) ("reasonable grounds to suspect"); UTAH CODE ANN. § 77-8-1(1) ("reason to believe"); VT. R. CRIM. P. 41.1(c)(2) ("reasonable grounds ... to suspect").

The Nebraska statute has been construed to require probable cause. State v. Evans, 215 Neb. 433, 442, 338 N.W.2d 788, 794 (1983).

135. 470 U.S. 811 (1985).

136. *Id.* at 817.

issue. For example, some courts have refused to uphold the issuance of such orders,[137] while other courts have sanctioned their use.[138]

Two points deserve attention. First, in *Hayes* the Court strongly indicated that "a brief detention in the field for the purpose of fingerprinting," based on reasonable suspicion, would be constitutional.[139] Second, the dicta in *Davis* and *Hayes* involved fingerprinting, which the Court emphasized was not an intrusive procedure. The issuance of a nontestimonial identification order for more intrusive procedures, such as the extraction of blood, may conflict with *Schmerber v. California,*[140] in which the Court required a more demanding standard.[141]

In *United States v. Ingram*[142] a prosecutor requested a court order to compel the defendant, who had been released on bail, to provide hair samples. The court ruled that such an order implicated the fourth amendment in two respects — the compulsion of the defendant to appear and the seizure of the hair. Both intrusions had to be justified by reasonable suspicion (not probable cause): The prosecution "will only need to show a reasonable suspicion, based upon specific and articulable facts and the inferences rationally drawn from those facts, that (1) Mr. Ingram has committed a crime, and (2) that the taking of hair samples will provide evidence connecting him to the crime that he allegedly committed."[143] In addition, a neutral judicial officer would determine whether this standard had been satisfied: "The requirement of prior judicial approval will best safeguard the individual's privacy interests without placing a significant burden on prosecutors or the court system."[144]

---

137. *See* United States v. Jennings, 468 F.2d 111, 115 (9th Cir. 1972) (fingerprints); *In re* September 1981 Term Grand Jury, 104 Ill. App. 3d 94, 99-100, 432 N.E.2d 625, 630 (1982) (probable cause required for blood and hair samples); People v. Marshall, 69 Mich. App. 288, 300, 244 N.W.2d 451, 457 (1976) (detention order for hair and blood samples must be based on probable cause); State v. Evans, 215 Neb. 433, 441, 338 N.W.2d 788, 794 (1983) (probable cause required for fingerprints and palmprints); *In re* Investigation into the Death of Abe A., 56 N.Y.2d 288, 291, 437 N.E.2d 265, 266, 452 N.Y.S.2d 6, 7 (1982) (probable cause required for blood sample); *In re* Armed Robbery, 99 Wash.2d 106, 112, 659 P.2d 1092, 1096 (1983) (lineup).

138. *See* Wise v. Murphy, 275 A.2d 205, 213-16 (D.C. 1971) (en banc) (lineups); State v. Hall, 93 N.J. 552, 561-63, 461 A.2d 1155, 1160, *cert. denied,* 464 U.S. 1008 (1983); *In re* Fingerprinting of M.B., 125 N.J. Super. 115, 121-22, 309 A.2d 3, 6 (1973) (fingerprints).

139. 470 U.S. at 816.

140. 384 U.S. 757 (1966).

141. *See* People v. Marshall, 69 Mich. App. 288, 297-98, 244 N.W.2d 451, 456 (1976) ("No judicial precedent was found, however, which sanctioned the use of a court order on less than probable cause in order to take blood samples from a suspect's person. Indeed, the constitutionality of such a procedure appears doubtful in light of *Schmerber v. California*"). *See also* § 2-4(B)(3) *infra.*

142. 797 F. Supp. 705 (E.D. Ark. 1992).

143. *Id.* at 717.

144. *Id.*

The South Carolina Supreme Court has interpreted the state search warrant statute to permit nontestimonial identification orders, including orders for blood, saliva, head hair, pubic hair, and fingerprints. The statute requires "(1) probable cause to believe the suspect has committed the crime, (2) a clear indication that relevant material evidence will be found, and (3) the method used to secure it is safe and reliable."[145]

§ 2-4(A)(3). Grand Jury Subpoenas & Administrative Summonses.

Another method by which evidence may be obtained from a suspect is the grand jury subpoena. In *United States v. Dionisio*[146] the defendant challenged the use of a grand jury subpoena to obtain voice exemplars, arguing that an appearance before a grand jury pursuant to a subpoena was a "seizure" of the person within the meaning of the fourth amendment. The Supreme Court rejected this argument, holding that the "compulsion exerted by a grand jury subpoena differs from the seizure effected by an arrest or even an investigative 'stop'."[147]

> The latter is abrupt, is effected with force or the threat of it and often in demeaning circumstances, and, in the case of arrest, results in a record involving social stigma. A subpoena is served in the same manner as other legal process; it involves no stigma whatever; if the time for appearance is inconvenient, this can generally be altered; and it remains at all times under the control and supervision of a court.[148]

In short, since the fourth amendment is not implicated, requirements such as probable cause do not apply. Courts have upheld the use of a grand jury subpoena to obtain handwriting exemplars,[149] fingerprints,[150] hair samples,[151] shoe and foot prints,[152] as well as other evidence of identification.[153]

---

145. *In re* Investigation of Death of Melinda Renee Snyder, 417 S.E.2d 572, 574 (S.C. 1992). *See also* State v. Register, 419 S.E.2d 771 (S.C. 1992) (probable cause not established).

146. 410 U.S. 1 (1973).

147. *Id.* at 10.

148. *Id.* (quoting United States v. Doe (Schwartz), 457 F.2d 895, 898 (2d Cir. 1972), *cert. denied,* 410 U.S. 941 (1973)).

149. *E.g.,* United States v. Mara, 410 U.S. 19, 21-22 (1973); United States v. Richardson, 755 F.2d 685, 685-86 (8th Cir. 1985).

150. *E.g., In re* Grand Jury Proceedings (Schofield), 507 F.2d 963, 967 (3d Cir.), *cert. denied,* 421 U.S. 1015 (1975). *See also In re* Melvin, 550 F.2d 674, 677 (1st Cir. 1977); Doe v. State, 634 So. 2d 613, 615 (Fla. 1994) (per curiam) (statutorily authorized prosecutor subpoena for fingerprint and handwriting exemplars is not unconstitutional).

151. *E.g., In re* Grand Jury Proceedings (Mills), 686 F.2d 135, 139 (3d Cir.), *cert. denied,* 459 U.S. 1020 (1982).

152. United States v. Ferri, 778 F.2d 985, 995-96 (3d Cir. 1985) (shoe and foot prints), *cert. denied,* 476 U.S. 1172 (1986).

The use of a grand jury subpoena to obtain blood samples, however, presents a different question. Such an under-the-skin intrusion raises significant fourth amendment issues. One federal district court has ruled that a grand jury subpoena for blood and saliva samples must be based on reasonable suspicion.[154] A different district court disagreed, holding that the use of a subpoena for this purpose is improper; a warrant based upon probable cause is required. According to this court, "[t]o allow the United States to use a Rule 17(c) subpoena for this purpose would abrogate T.S.'s Fourth Amendment rights and, thus, transform the subpoena into an instrument by which an illegal search and seizure is effectuated."[155]

Several state courts have also addressed this issue. After holding that the state constitution provides greater protection than its federal counterpart, the Illinois Supreme Court examined a subpoena that required blood, head and pubic hair, and finger and palm prints. The court ruled that "some showing of individualized suspicion as well as relevance must be made before physical evidence of a noninvasive nature, such as an in-person appearance in a lineup or fingerprinting, is demanded of a witness. This may be done through an affidavit by the State's Attorney."[156] Pubic hair samples, however, are different. They come from "the most private part of the human body" and "a demand for pubic hair represents a considerable intrusion into personal privacy."[157] Accordingly, probable cause and a warrant are required. Head hairs also raise privacy concerns. While the color and texture of the hair are readily observable, an "individual does not ordinarily have the expectation that others will cut, pull or comb his hair without his permission."[158] Thus, the probable cause requirement applies here as well.

---

153. *E.g., In re* Grand Jury Proceedings (Hellmann), 756 F.2d 428, 431 (6th Cir. 1985) (voice exemplar); *In re* Maguire, 571 F.2d 675 (1st Cir.) (lineup), *cert. denied,* 436 U.S. 911 (1978); *In re* Rodgers, 359 F. Supp. 576, 577 (E.D.N.Y. 1973) (photographs); *In re* Toon, 364 A.2d 1177, 1180 (D.C. 1976) (lineup), *cert. denied,* 429 U.S. 1099 (1977).

154. Henry v. Ryan, 775 F. Supp. 247 (N.D. Ill. 1991).

155. *In re* Grand Jury Proceedings (T.S.), 816 F. Supp. 1196, 1205 (W.D. Ky. 1993).

156. *In re* May 1991 Will County Grand Jury, 152 Ill. 2d 381, 604 N.E.2d 929, 935-36 (1992).

157. *Id.* at 936.

158. *Id.* at 938. *See also* People v. Payne, 282 Ill. App. 3d 307, 311, 667 N.E.2d 643, 646 ("Based on *Will County Grand Jury*, we find that a showing of relevance and individualized suspicion is necessary for the grand jury to compel production of dental impressions. The taking of dental impressions falls in line with the category of noninvasive physical evidence described in *Will County Grand Jury* including lineups, fingerprints, palm prints, voice exemplars and handwriting exemplars. Unlike the cases where probable cause has been required, for example the taking of blood or hair samples, having dental impressions made does not involve an actual taking or removal of evidence from the body and does not violate an individual's bodily integrity by diminishing the body to any degree"), *cert. denied*, 675 N.E.2d 638 (Ill. 1996).

The Oklahoma Court of Criminal Appeals has held, as a matter of state law, that a grand subpoena for blood samples requires probable cause and a subpoena for finger and palm prints requires a reasonable and individualized suspicion.[159]

The Massachusetts Supreme Judicial Court has ruled that a grand jury subpoena for blood samples was subject to the reasonableness requirement, though not necessarily the probable cause requirement. In the court's view, "A grand jury must have a reasonable basis for believing (have probable cause for believing, if you wish) that a blood sample will provide test results that will significantly aid (in this case perhaps indispensably aid) the grand jury in their investigation of circumstances in which there is good reason to believe a crime was committed."[160] In this case, it was reasonable to believe that either the father or brother had raped a 21-year-old woman who was profoundly retarded and autistic.

Administrative Summons

The Supreme Court also has considered whether an administrative summons may be used to obtain evidence of physical characteristics. In *United States v. Euge*[161] the Court ruled that the Internal Revenue Service was statutorily authorized to issue summonses compelling a taxpayer to provide handwriting exemplars. Furthermore, the Court found no constitutional impediment to this procedure.

§ 2-4(B). Search & Seizure of Physical Evidence.

Even if a suspect's detention is constitutionally permissible, the question remains whether the search of that person is also permissible. The initial inquiry is whether there is, in fact, a search within the meaning of the fourth amendment. If there is a "search," the next question is whether the search complies with fourth amendment constraints such as the warrant and probable cause requirements.[162]

---

159. Woolverton v. Multicounty Grand Jury, 859 P.2d 1112 (Okla. Crim. App. 1993). *See also* Einesman, *Vampires Among Us: Does a Grand Jury Subpoena For Blood Violate the Fourth Amendment?*, 22 AM. J. CRIM. L. 327 (1995).

160. *In re* Grand Jury Invest., 427 Mass. 221, 226, 692 N.E.2d 56, 60, *cert. denied,* 119 S. Ct. 171 (1998).

161. 444 U.S. 707 (1980).

162. If a suspect consents, neither a warrant nor probable cause is required. *See* Brent v. White, 398 F.2d 503, 505 (5th Cir. 1968) (consent to blood extraction), *cert. denied,* 393 U.S. 1123 (1969); United States *ex rel.* Parson v. Anderson, 354 F. Supp. 1060, 1088 (D. Del. 1972) (consent to blood extraction, pubic combing, and fingernail scraping), *aff'd,* 481 F.2d 94 (3d Cir.), *cert. denied,* 414 U.S. 1072 (1973).

However, the consent must be valid. *See* Graves v. Beto, 301 F. Supp. 264, 266 (E.D. Tex. 1969) (consent not valid where defendant deceived as to purpose of blood test), *aff'd,* 424 F.2d 524,

§ 2-4(B)(1). Physical Characteristics.

The leading case on defining which governmental activities are "searches" within the meaning of the fourth amendment is *Katz v. United States.*[163] *Katz* substituted a privacy approach for the traditional property approach to this issue.[164] According to the Court: "[T]he Fourth Amendment protects people, not places. What a person knowingly exposes to the public, even in his own home or office, is not a subject of Fourth Amendment protection.... But what he seeks to preserve as private, even in an area accessible to the public, may be constitutionally protected."[165] The *Katz* rationale played a major role in two cases which involved the compelled production of voice and handwriting exemplars by means of a grand jury subpoena.

In *United States v. Dionisio,*[166] after ruling that the compelled appearance of a person before a grand jury was not a "seizure" within the meaning of the fourth amendment,[167] the Court considered whether the taking of a voice exemplar constituted a search:

> The physical characteristics of a person's voice, its tone and manner, as opposed to the content of a specific conversation, are constantly exposed to the public. Like a man's facial characteristics, or handwriting, his voice is repeatedly produced for others to hear. No person can have a reasonable expectation that others will not know the sound of his voice, any more than he can reasonably expect that his face will be a mystery to the world.[168]

Accordingly, there was no search. In *United States v. Mara*[169] the Court reached the same conclusion with respect to handwriting: "Handwriting, like speech, is repeatedly shown to the public, and there is no more expectation of privacy in the physical characteristics of a person's script than there is in the tone of his voice."[170]

---

525 (5th Cir.), *cert. denied,* 400 U.S. 960 (1970). *See generally* 3 W. LAFAVE, *supra* note 104, § 8.2(n); 2 E. IMWINKELRIED, P. GIANNELLI, F. GILLIGAN & F. LEDERER, *supra* note 104, ch. 20.

163. 389 U.S. 347 (1967).

164. *See generally* 1 W. LAFAVE, *supra* note 104, § 2.1; 2 E. IMWINKELRIED, P. GIANNELLI, F. GILLIGAN & F. LEDERER, *supra* note 104, ch. 18.

165. 389 U.S. at 351.

166. 410 U.S. 1 (1973).

167. *See* § 2-4(A)(3) *supra.*

168. *Id.* at 14. *Accord* United States v. Franks, 511 F.2d 25, 32 (6th Cir.), *cert. denied,* 422 U.S. 1042 (1975).

169. 410 U.S. 19 (1973).

170. *Id.* at 21. *Accord* United States v. Euge, 444 U.S. 707, 718 (1980) ("Compulsion of handwriting exemplars is neither a search or seizure subject to Fourth Amendment protections...").

Invasive Procedures

All evidence of physical characteristics, however, is not beyond fourth amendment protection. In *Schmerber v. California,*[171] decided before *Dionisio,* the Supreme Court held that the extraction of blood for the purpose of scientific analysis "plainly constitutes searches of the 'persons'"[172] within the meaning of the fourth amendment. In *Dionisio* the Court distinguished, rather than overruled, *Schmerber:* "The required disclosure of a person's voice is thus immeasurably further removed from the Fourth Amendment protection than was the intrusion into the body effected by the blood extraction in *Schmerber.*"[173]

The difference between *Dionsio* and *Schmerber* turns on the bodily intrusion involved in the extraction of blood samples. In *Skinner v. Railway Labor Executives' Ass'n,*[174] the Court wrote that "it is obvious that this physical intrusion, penetrating beneath the skin, infringes an expectation of privacy that society is prepared to recognize as reasonable."[175] In addition, an ensuing chemical analysis of the blood sample to obtain physiological data "is a further invasion"[176] of privacy interests — informational privacy. Under this view, the analysis of breath to determine intoxication "implicates similar concerns about bodily integrity" and thus constitutes a search.[177]

The Court in *Skinner* also considered the collection of urine samples. Even though this procedure does not involve a bodily intrusion, the Court held that it was a search. Like blood, the chemical analysis of urine can "reveal a host of private medical facts," including whether a person is epileptic, pregnant, or diabetic. Moreover, the manner of collection, which may involve visual or aural monitoring of urination, "itself implicates privacy interests."[178]

---

171. 384 U.S. 757 (1966).

172. *Id.* at 767.

173. 410 U.S. at 14.

174. 489 U.S. 602 (1989).

175. *Id.* at 616.

176. *Id.*

177. *Id.* at 616-17. *See also* Burnett v. Anchorage, 806 F.2d 1447, 1449 (9th Cir. 1986) ("[T]he administration of a breath test is a search within the meaning of the Fourth Amendment ..."); Commonwealth v. Quarles, 229 Pa. Super. 363, 377, 324 A.2d 452, 460 (1974) ("[W]here a person is pursuant to the implied consent law held or transported so that either his blood or breath may be tested, and the test is administered, the requirements of the Fourth Amendment must be satisfied as to ... the subsequent testing and seizure of evidence").

178. 489 U.S. at 617. *See also* Forbes v. Trigg, 976 F.2d 308, 312 (7th Cir. 1992) ("Urine tests are searches for Fourth Amendment purposes, and prison inmates retain protected privacy rights in their bodies..."), *cert. denied*, 507 U.S. 950 (1993).

In another case, *Cupp v. Murphy,*[179] the Court considered the legality of seizing fingernail scrapings from a suspect. After finding that the defendant had been detained on probable cause, the Court stated:

> The inquiry does not end here, however, because Murphy was subjected to a search as well as a seizure of his person. Unlike the fingerprinting in *Davis,* the voice exemplar obtained in *United States v. Dionisio* ..., or the handwriting exemplar obtained in *United States v. Mara* ..., the search of the respondent's fingernails went beyond mere "physical characteristics ... constantly exposed to the public," *United States v. Dionisio* ..., and constituted the type of "severe, though brief, intrusion upon cherished personal security" that is subject to constitutional scrutiny.[180]

In sum, any procedure more intrusive than the obtaining of physical characteristics generally exposed to the public (fingerprints, voice, or handwriting) implicates the fourth amendment. Accordingly, taking shoe prints,[181] examining teeth,[182] and inspecting hands under ultraviolet light[183] are not considered searches. In contrast, taking hair samples generally has been characterized as a search,[184] as has the taking of saliva samples.[185]

---

179. 412 U.S. 291 (1973).

180. *Id.* at 295.

181. *See* United States v. Ferri, 778 F.2d 985, 995-96 (3d Cir. 1985), *cert. denied,* 476 U.S. 1172 (1986). *See also* Commonwealth v. Billings, 42 Mass. App. 261, 265, 676 N.E.2d 62, 65 ("The physical characteristics of the soles of a person's shoes, like one's voice, face, and handwriting, are constantly exposed to the public. Footprints on the ground are visible for all to see. People display the soles of their shoes when they cross their legs, climb stairs, or put their feet up on furniture"), *cert. denied,* 679 N.E.2d 558 (Mass. 1997).

182. *See* United States v. Holland, 378 F. Supp. 144, 154 (E.D. Pa. 1974) (dental examination not a search), *cert. denied,* 420 U.S. 994 (1975).

183. *See* United States v. Kenaan, 496 F.2d 181, 182-83 (1st Cir. 1974); United States v. Richardson, 388 F.2d 842, 845 (6th Cir. 1968); Williams v. Lancaster, 639 F. Supp. 377, 382 (E.D. Pa. 1986); United States v. DeMarsh, 360 F. Supp. 132, 137 (E.D. Wis. 1973); *but see* People v. Santistevan, 715 P.2d 792, 795 (Colo.) (ultraviolet inspection of hands a search), *cert. denied,* 479 U.S. 965 (1986).

184. *See* Bouse v. Bussey, 573 F.2d 548, 550 (9th Cir. 1977); United States v. D'Amico, 408 F.2d 331, 333 (2d Cir. 1969); State v. Sharpe, 284 N.C. 157, 162-63, 200 S.E.2d 44, 47-48 (1973); Barber v. Rubin, 72 A.D.2d 347, 354, 424 N.Y.S.2d 453, 458 (1980); State v. McCumber, 622 P.2d 353, 360 (Utah 1980). *See also In re* May 1991 Will County Grand Jury, 152 Ill. 2d 381, 604 N.E.2d 929, 935-38 (1992) (both pubic and head hair protected by state constitution).

But see In re Grand Jury Proceedings (Mills), 686 F.2d 135, 139 (3d Cir.) (seizure of facial and head hair not a search), *cert. denied,* 459 U.S. 1020 (1982). *See generally* 1 W. LAFAVE, *supra* note 104, § 2.6(a); 2 E. IMWINKELRIED, P. GIANNELLI, F. GILLIGAN & F. LEDERER, *supra* note 104, ch. 18.

§ 2-4(B)(2). Searches Incident to or After Arrest.

If obtaining physical evidence from a legally detained suspect is considered a search,[186] that search must satisfy constitutional requirements. In other words, if the fourth amendment applies, questions are raised concerning the existence of probable cause and the necessity of obtaining a warrant.

One of the major exceptions to the warrant requirement is the search incident to arrest doctrine.[187] Under this exception, once a suspect has been arrested based upon probable cause, a search of the arrestee's person and the area within his immediate control is permitted. In *Chimel v. California*[188] the Supreme Court set forth a twofold justification for this exception: (1) protection of the arresting officer and (2) prevention of the destruction of evidence.[189]

---

185. In United States v. Nicolosi, 885 F. Supp. 50, 55 (E.D. N.Y. 1995), the court wrote:

> A saliva sample can provide a significant amount of genetic identity information and it is generally not an item in the public domain. Yet, expectorating is not viewed with the same disfavor nor concealed behind closed doors as urinating; consider the commonplace sight of athletes expectorating on national television on a daily basis....
>
> It is typically the case that a saliva sample is obtained by swabbing the inside of the subject's mouth with a pad of some sort. Such a scenario, wherein a citizen is directed to submit to an intrusion into his body, is properly viewed as implicating his dignitary interests. This factor, combined with the private identifying information contained in the sample suggests that a proper compliance with the requirement of the Fourth Amendment is mandated.

See also Commonwealth v. Blasioli, 685 A.2d 151, 156 (Pa. Super. 1996) ("We believe that a person has an expectation of privacy that includes the taking of his saliva, as he does with his blood, breath, and urine") (state and federal constitution), *app. granted*, 548 Pa. 36, 693 A.2d 584 (1997).

186. Obtaining evidence of some physical characteristics (voice, handwriting, fingerprints) is not considered a search. *See* § 2-4(B)(1) *supra.*

187. *See generally* 3 W. LAFAVE, *supra* note 104, § 5.2 ; 2 E. IMWINKELRIED, P. GIANNELLI, F. GILLIGAN & F. LEDERER, *supra* note 104, ch. 20.

188. 395 U.S. 752 (1969). The Court wrote:

> When an arrest is made, it is reasonable for the arresting officer to search the person arrested in order to remove any weapons that the latter might seek to use in order to resist arrest or effect his escape. Otherwise, the officer's safety might well be endangered, and the arrest itself frustrated. In addition, it is entirely reasonable for the arresting officer to search for and seize any evidence of the arrestee's person in order to prevent its concealment or destruction. And the areas into which an arrestee might reach in order to grab a weapon or evidentiary items must, of course, be governed by a like rule.

Id. at 762-63.

189. The probable cause to arrest must precede the search incident to arrest (but not necessarily the formal arrest). In other words, the fruit of the search may not be used as the basis of the probable cause for the arrest. In Smith v. Ohio, 494 U.S. 541 (1990) (per curiam), probable cause to arrest did not exist until the officer looked into a paper bag and saw contraband:

Several Supreme Court cases involving the seizure of evidence for the purpose of scientific analysis have involved the search incident to arrest theory. In *Cupp v. Murphy*[190] the Court upheld a search and seizure of fingernail scrapings under the *Chimel* doctrine. During the voluntary stationhouse questioning of the defendant about his wife's strangulation murder, the police observed a dark spot on the defendant's finger, which they believed to be blood. Despite the defendant's protests, fingernail scrapings were taken. The scrapings contained traces of skin and blood as well as fabric from the victim's garments. The facts of *Cupp v. Murphy* are somewhat unusual because the defendant was not formally placed under arrest at the time the scrapings were removed.[191] Nevertheless, the Court assumed probable cause for an arrest existed and held that the "rationale of *Chimel,* in these circumstances, justified the police in subjecting him to the very limited search necessary to preserve the highly evanescent evidence they found under his fingernails."[192]

In *United States v. Edwards*[193] the defendant was arrested at night and then incarcerated in a local jail for attempting to break into a post office. Investigation at the scene revealed paint chips at a window. The following morning, the police seized the defendant's clothes. Examination of the clothes disclosed paint chips, which matched those found at the scene of the crime. The Supreme Court held that the delayed search of the clothing was constitutional, notwithstanding the absence of a warrant. According to the Court, the established rule is that:

> [O]nce the accused is lawfully arrested and is in custody, the effects in his possession at the place of detention that were subject to search at the time and place of his arrest may lawfully be searched and seized without a warrant even though a substantial period of time has elapsed between the arrest and subsequent administrative processing, on the one hand, and the taking of the property for use as evidence, on the other. This is true where the clothing or effects are immediately seized upon arrival at the jail, held under the defendant's name in the "property room" of the jail, and at a later time searched and taken for use at the subsequent criminal trial. The result

---

> As we have had occasion in the past to observe, "[i]t is axiomatic that an incident search may not precede an arrest and serve as its justification. The exception for searches incident to arrest permits the police to search a lawfully arrested person and areas within his immediate control. ... [I]t does not permit the police to search any citizen without a warrant or probable cause so long as an arrest immediately follows.

Id. at 543. *Smith* should be distinguished from cases where probable cause to arrest preceded the search incident to arrest but not the formal arrest. *See infra.*

190. 412 U.S. 291 (1973).

191. The Court indicated that a more extensive search would have been permissible if the defendant had been placed under arrest. *Id.* at 296.

192. *Id.* at 296.

193. 415 U.S. 800 (1974).

is the same where the property is not physically taken from the defendant until sometime after his incarceration.[194]

The Court also wrote: "Nor is there any doubt that clothing or other belongings may be seized upon arrival of the accused at the place of detention and later subjected to laboratory analysis or that the test results are admissible at trial."[195]

The seizure of gunshot residue,[196] fingerprints,[197] bomb residue,[198] hair,[199] urine,[200] as well as other types of physical evidence[201] has been upheld as incident

---

194. *Id.* at 807-08. *See also* 3 W. LAFAVE, *supra* note 104, § 5.3(d); 2 E. IMWINKELRIED, P. GIANNELLI, F. GILLIGAN & F. LEDERER, *supra* note 104, ch. 20.

195. 415 U.S. at 803-04. *See also* Illinois v. LaFayette, 462 U.S. 640 (1983) (stationhouse inventory of detainee's clothes and possessions upheld).

196. *See* State v. Ulrich, 187 Mont. 347, 609 P.2d 1218, 1221 (1980); State v. Riley, 201 W. Va. 708, 717, 500 S.E.2d 524, 533 (1997) (swabbing a murder arrestee's hands and face for gunpowder residue was reasonable in light of the limited intrusion and the ready destructibility of the evidence).

197. *See* Napolitano v. United States, 340 F.2d 313, 314 (1st Cir. 1965); Smith v. United States, 324 F.2d 879, 882 (D.C. Cir. 1963), *cert. denied,* 377 U.S. 954 (1964); State v. Inman, 301 A.2d 348, 354 (Me. 1973); Commonwealth v. Young, 524 Pa. 373, 388, 572 A.2d 1217, 1224 (1990).

The obtaining of fingerprints, however, is probably not a search within the meaning of fourth amendment because a person does not have a reasonable expectation of privacy with respect to fingerprints. *See* § 2-4(B)(1) *supra.*

198. *See* United States v. Bridges, 499 F.2d 179, 180 (7th Cir.) (swabbing of hands for bomb residue), *cert. denied,* 419 U.S. 1010 (1974); United States v. Kenaan, 496 F.2d 181, 183 (1st Cir. 1974) (ultraviolet inspection of hands for bomb residue); United States v. Love, 482 F.2d 213, 216 (5th Cir.), *cert. denied,* 414 U.S. 1026 (1973).

199. *See* United States v. Weir, 657 F.2d 1005, 1007 (8th Cir. 1981); United States v. D'Amico, 408 F.2d 331, 333 (2d Cir. 1969) (clipping of head hair of an in-custody defendant not unreasonable); United States *ex rel.* Parson v. Anderson, 354 F. Supp. 1060, 1087 (D. Del. 1972) (hair combings), *aff'd,* 481 F.2d 94 (3d Cir.), *cert. denied,* 414 U.S. 1072 (1973); State v. Brierly, 109 Ariz. 310, 319, 509 P.2d 203, 212 (1973) (en banc) (head hair); Commonwealth v. Tarver, 369 Mass. 302, 307, 345 N.E.2d 671, 675 (1975) (head, chest, and pubic hair); People v. Rankins, 81 Mich. App. 694, 265 N.W.2d 792 (1978) (pubic hair); State v. Cobb, 295 N.C. 1, 19-20, 243 S.E.2d 759, 770 (1978) (pubic hair); State v. Sharpe, 284 N.C. 157, 160-64, 200 S.E.2d 44, 47-49 (1973) (hair).

But see Bouse v. Bussey, 573 F.2d 548, 550 (9th Cir. 1977) (warrant required for removal of hair); United States v. Allen, 337 F. Supp. 1041, 1043 (E.D. Pa. 1972) (warrant required for removal of hair); State v. Gammill, 2 Kan. App. 2d 627, 628-29, 585 P.2d 1074, 1077-78 (1978) (plucking of pubic hair constituted a bodily intrusion requiring a warrant); People v. Lovett, 85 Mich. App. 534, 538, 272 N.W.2d 126, 127 (1978) (warrant required for semen and pubic hair samples); Barber v. Rubin, 72 A.D.2d 347, 424 N.Y.S.2d 453 (1980) (court order for hair removal upheld); Commonwealth v. Robson, 461 Pa. 615, 629, 337 A.2d 573, 580 (magistrate authorized removal of pubic hair), *cert. denied,* 423 U.S. 934 (1975).

200. *See* United States v. Edmo, 140 F.3d 1289, 1292 (9th Cir. 1998) ("[R]equiring an arrestee to submit to a urine test is reasonable under the Fourth Amendment. It is a less intrusive search than withdrawal of blood from the human body. It involves no risk of trauma or pain. Like alcohol in the blood system, traces of controlled substances in the urine will also disappear over time"); Ewing v.

to a lawful arrest. More intrusive searches, such as those involving bodily intrusions, require greater justification.[202]

Finally, court orders directing suspects to submit to nontestimonial identification procedures *after* arrest or indictment have been upheld.[203] Moreover, nontestimonial examinations are found in pretrial discovery provisions in many jurisdictions.[204]

§ 2-4(B)(3). Bodily Intrusions.

The Supreme Court has shown a greater concern for searches involving bodily intrusions than for other types of searches. For example, in *Schmerber v. California*[205] the Court considered the constitutionality of extracting blood for the purpose of blood-alcohol analysis. The Court rejected the notion that the extraction of blood would automatically be encompassed by the search incident to arrest doctrine. According to the Court, the justifications underlying the search incident to arrest rule

> have little applicability with respect to searches involving intrusions beyond the body's surface. The interests in human dignity and privacy which the Fourth Amendment protects forbid any such intrusions on the mere chance that desired evidence might be obtained. In the absence of a *clear indication* that in fact such evidence will be found, these fundamental human interests

State, 160 Ind. App. 138, 148-49, 310 N.E.2d 571, 578 (1974) (en banc). *But see* People v. Williams, 192 Colo. 249, 257, 557 P.2d 399, 406 (1976) (*Schmerber* "clear indication" standard required for urine sample).

201. *E.g.,* Burnett v. Anchorage, 806 F.2d 1447, 1450 (9th Cir. 1986) (breathalyzer examination); United States v. Smith, 470 F.2d 377, 379 (D.C. Cir. 1972) (benzidine swabbings of penis for blood); Brent v. White, 398 F.2d 503, 505 (5th Cir. 1968) (penis scraping for blood), *cert. denied,* 393 U.S. 1123 (1969); United States *ex. rel.* Parson v. Anderson, 354 F. Supp. 1060, 1087 (D. Del. 1972) (fingernail scrapings), *aff'd,* 481 F.2d 94 (3d Cir.), *cert. denied,* 414 U.S. 1072 (1973); People v. Lovett, 85 Mich. App. 534, 539, 272 N.W.2d 126, 127 (1978) (saliva); Alvarez v. State, 857 S.W.2d 143 (Tex. App. 1993) (nasal secretions later determined to contain crack cocaine obtained in a lawful search incident to arrest). *See generally* 3 W. LAFAVE, *supra* note 104, § 5.3(c).

202. *See* § 2-4(B)(3) *infra* (bodily intrusions).

203. *See* United States v. Mitchell, 556 F.2d 371, 382 (6th Cir.), *cert. denied,* 434 U.S. 925 (1977); Adams v. United States, 399 F.2d 574, 579 (D.C. Cir. 1968), *cert. denied,* 393 U.S. 1067 (1969). *See also* 3 W. LAFAVE, *supra* note 104, § 9.6(c).

204. *See* ABA STANDARDS FOR CRIMINAL JUSTICE, STANDARD 11-2.3 (3d ed. 1996). For a discussion of this type of discovery, *see* § 3-16 *infra. See also* Standard 11-3.1 (obtaining nontestimonial information from third parties).

205. 384 U.S. 757 (1966).

> require law officers to suffer the risk that such evidence may disappear unless there is an immediate search.[206]

The Court further considered the necessity of securing a warrant based on probable cause as a prerequisite to the extraction of blood. It found the purpose underlying the warrant requirement — the intervention of a neutral detached magistrate between the police and the citizen — applicable to bodily intrusions: "The importance of the informed, detached and deliberate determinations of the issue whether or not to invade another's body in search of evidence of guilt is indisputable and great."[207] Nevertheless, because the alcohol content of blood diminishes with the passage of time, the Court recognized an "emergency" exception to the warrant requirement, which was necessary to preclude the destruction of evidence.

The emergency exception recognized in *Schmerber,* however, would not apply in other contexts — for example, when blood is sought for the purpose of genetic testing, including DNA profiling, a physical characteristic that remains constant.[208]

At one time, the Ninth Circuit had held that the arrest must precede or at least be substantially contemporaneous with the seizure of blood,[209] but the court later abandoned that position.[210] As long as there was probable cause, a formal arrest should not be required.[211]

---

206. *Id.* at 769-70 (emphasis added). *See also* United States v. Allen, 337 F. Supp. 1041, 1043 (E.D. Pa. 1972) (warrant required for hair removal and X-ray because such procedures involve bodily intrusions); People v. Williams, 192 Colo. 249, 257, 557 P.2d 399, 406 (1976) (en banc) ("clear indication" standard required for urine sample); State v. Anonymous, 32 Conn. Sup. 306, 317, 353 A.2d 789, 795 (1976) (X-ray covered by *Schmerber*); State v. Gammill, 2 Kan. App. 2d 627, 628, 585 P.2d 1074, 1077 (1978) (plucking of pubic hair constitutes a bodily intrusion requiring a warrant).

207. 384 U.S. at 770.

208. *See* Graves v. Beto, 301 F. Supp. 264, 265 (E.D. Tex. 1969), *aff'd,* 424 F.2d 524 (5th Cir.), *cert. denied,* 400 U.S. 960 (1970); Mills v. State, 28 Md. App. 300, 307, 345 A.2d 127, 132 (1975), *aff'd,* 28 Md. 262, 363 A.2d 491 (1976). *See also* Barlow v. Ground, 943 F.2d 1132, 1138-39 (9th Cir. 1991) (warrantless blood extraction to test for AIDS-causing HIV virus unconstitutional); State v. Gammill, 2 Kan. App. 2d 627, 628, 585 P.2d 1074, 1077 (1978) (hair follicle, no emergency as in *Schmerber*); State v. Jones, 895 P.2d 643 (Nev. 1995) (warrantless extraction of blood to test for cocaine violates fourth amendment due to lack of exigent circumstances as in *Schmerber*; cocaine and its metabolites remain in the user's blood for 6-14 hours after ingestion).

209. *See* United States v. Harvey, 701 F.2d 800, 805 (9th Cir. 1983). *See generally* Note, *United States v. Harvey: Blood Alcohol Analysis and the Fourth Amendment*, 1984 DET. C.L. REV. 1023.

210. *See* United States v. Chapel, 55 F.3d 1416, 1419 (9th Cir. 1995) ("Before a law enforcement officer may lawfully take a blood sample without consent or a warrant, he or she must have probable cause to believe that the suspect has committed an offense of which the current state of one's blood will constitute evidence.... The requirement of a contemporaneous arrest adds nothing

Search Warrants

A search warrant, as distinguished from an arrest warrant, may be used to obtain blood samples. This would require probable cause that (1) the subject committed a crime and (2) blood analysis results would be evidence of that crime. The Washington Supreme Court has ruled that additional safeguards are not required: "neither notice nor an adversarial hearing are constitutionally mandated prior to the issuance of a search warrant to obtain a blood sample from a suspect."[212] In contrast, Massachusetts requires a hearing.[213]

Private Searches

The fourth amendment does not apply to a private search,[214] such as the withdrawal of blood for medical purposes by medical personnel.[215] A similar rule has been applied to a government-employed doctor at a Public Health Service hospital, when the tests were conducted for purely medical reasons.[216]

Manner of Conducting Search

Schmerber is also important because the Court held that the scientific procedure chosen as well as the manner in which it is performed are both subject

---

to the constitutional protection; the probable cause threshold in these circumstances remains the same"), *cert. denied*, 516 U.S. 1065 (1996).

211. *See* State v. Cocio, 147 Ariz. 277, 283, 709 P.2d 1336, 1344 (1985) (en banc) (formal arrest not required for seizure of blood sample); People v. Deltoro, 214 Cal. App. 3d 1417, 1422-25, 263 Cal. Rptr. 305, 307-10 (1989) (same); People v. Sutherland, 683 P.2d 1192, 1195-96 (Colo. 1984) (en banc); State v. Baker, 502 A.2d 489, 492-93 (Me. 1985) (same); State v. Milligan, 304 Or. 659, 669, 748 P.2d 130, 136 (1988) (en banc) (same).

212. State v. Kalakosky, 121 Wash. 2d 525, 852 P.2d 1064, 1070 (1993).

213. The Supreme Judicial Court of Massachusetts ruled in *In re* Lavigne, 418 Mass. 831, 835-36, 641 N.E.2d 1328, 1331 (1994), that the common law permits the issuance of a warrant for the extraction of blood for DNA testing if the prosecution establishes that there is probable cause to believe that a person has committed a crime (murder) and the blood would aid the investigation. The person, however, has a right to a hearing, at which time the judge should weigh the seriousness of the crime, the importance of the evidence to the investigation, and the unavailability of less intrusive means against the person's right to be free from bodily intrusions.

214. *See* 2 E. Imwinkelried, P. Giannelli, F. Gilligan & F. Lederer, *supra* note 104, ch. 18.

215. People v. Perlos, 436 Mich. 305, 316-17, 462 N.W.2d 310, 315 (1990) (fourth amendment not implicated when blood is withdrawn at hospital for medical purposes even though implied consent law makes the result admissible). *See also* State v. Hardy, 1997 Tex. Crim. App. Lexis 91 (Tex. Crim. App. 1997) ("[I]n the case of blood test results obtained by subpoena, where the tests were conducted by medical personnel solely for medical purposes, the person's interest in bodily integrity is not present"). Nevertheless, in some jurisdictions the physician-patient privilege may apply.

216. United States v. Attson, 900 F.2d 1427, 1429-34 (9th Cir.), *cert. denied,* 498 U.S. 961 (1990).

to the fourth amendment's reasonableness requirement. With respect to the procedure, the Court commented, "we are satisfied that the test chosen to measure petitioner's blood alcohol level was a reasonable one. Extraction of blood samples for testing is a highly effective means of determining the degree to which a person is under the influence of alcohol."[217] The Court also found that the "record shows that the test was performed in a reasonable manner. Petitioner's blood was taken by a physician in a hospital environment according to accepted medical practices."[218]

§ 2-4(B)(4). Surgical Procedures.

The most intrusive procedures that have been challenged on fourth amendment grounds involve the surgical removal of bullets from suspects for the purpose of firearms identification.[219] The Supreme Court considered the issue in *Winston v. Lee.*[220] According to the Court:

> The reasonableness of surgical intrusions beneath the skin depends on a case-by-case approach, in which the individual's interests in privacy and security are weighed against society's interests in conducting the procedure. In a given case, the question whether the community's need for evidence outweighs the substantial privacy interests at stake is a delicate one admitting of few categorical answers.[221]

---

217. 384 U.S. at 771.

218. *Id. See generally* Note, *Shed Thou No Blood: The Forcible Removal of Blood Samples From Drunk Driving Suspects*, 60 S. CAL. L. REV. 1115 (1987).

219. *See generally* Bacigal, *Dodging a Bullet, but Opening Old Wounds in Fourth Amendment Jurisprudence*, 16 SETON HALL. L. REV. 597 (1986); Dunbar, *Under the Knife: The Constitutionality of Surgical Removal of Bullets from Nonconsenting Criminal Defendants*, 36 MED. TRIAL TECH. Q. 184 (1990); Tolley & Hull, *Court Ordered Surgery to Retrieve Evidence in Georgia in Light of the United States Supreme Court Decision in Winston v. Lee,* 37 MERCER L. REV. 1005 (1986); Note, *Bodily Intrusion in Search of Evidence: A Study in Fourth Amendment Decisionmaking*, 62 IND. L.J. 1181 (1987); Comment, *Analyzing the Reasonableness of Bodily Intrusions*, 68 MARQ. L. REV. 130 (1984); Note, *The Fourth Amendment and Surgical Searches: Invasion of the Bullet Snatchers*, 9 NOVA L. REV. 331 (1985); Annot., *Admissibility in Criminal Case, of Physical Evidence Obtained Without Consent by Surgical Removal From Person's Body*, 41 A.L.R.4TH 60 (1985).

220. 470 U.S. 753 (1985).

221. *Id.* at 760. In United States v. Crowder, 543 F.2d 312 (D.C. Cir. 1976) (en banc), *cert. denied,* 429 U.S. 1062 (1977), the defendant was ordered to undergo minor surgery for the removal of bullet fragments from his arm. The D.C. Circuit upheld the removal of the bullet under the circumstances of that case. The court cited the following factors:

> (1) the evidence sought was relevant, could have been obtained in no other way, and there was probable cause to believe that the operation would produce it; (2) the operation was minor, was performed by a skilled surgeon, and every possible precaution was taken to guard against any surgical complications, so that the risk of permanent injury was minimal; (3)

The Court relied principally on two factors to determine that surgery would be unconstitutional in *Winston*. First, the Court referred to the risk to the defendant's health as a "crucial factor."[222] For example, "a search for evidence of a crime may be unjustifiable if it endangers the life or health of the suspect."[223] The Court later noted that the record showed uncertainty about the medical risks involved.[224] Other cases have permitted *minor* surgery,[225] while precluding more serious procedures.[226]

Second, the Court found that the prosecution's need for the evidence was not compelling. There was substantial additional evidence that could be introduced to establish the defendant's guilt;[227] the victim made a positive and spontaneous identification of the accused, and the accused had been found with a bullet wound near the scene of the crime soon after its commission.

The Court mentioned, but did not rely, on two other factors. First, because the accused had been provided with a full adversary hearing and appellate review, the Court declined to consider whether less protective safeguards were constitutionally acceptable.[228] Second, the Court noted that some question had been raised about the probative value of the evidence since the bullet's markings may have corroded. The Court, however, stated that it had given little weight to this factor due to the absence of lower court findings on the issue.[229] One court has held surgery unreasonable because the probative value of the evidence

---

> before the operation was performed the District Court held an adversary hearing at which the defendant appeared with counsel; (4) thereafter and before the operation was performed the defendant was afforded an opportunity for appellate review by this court.

Id. at 316.

222. 470 U.S. at 761.

223. *Id.*

224. *Id.* at 763-64.

225. *See* Johnson v. State, 521 So. 2d 1006, 1014-15 (Ala. Crim. App. 1986), *aff'd,* 521 So. 2d 1018, *cert. denied,* 488 U.S. 876 (1988); State v. Martin, 404 So. 2d 960, 962-63 (La. 1981); Creamer v. State, 229 Ga. 511, 515, 192 S.E.2d 350, 353 (1972), *cert. dismissed,* 410 U.S. 975 (1973); Allison v. State, 129 Ga. App. 364, 365, 199 S.E.2d 587, 588-89 (1973), *cert. denied,* 414 U.S. 1145 (1974); Hughes v. State, 56 Md. App. 12, 18-20, 466 A.2d 533, 536, *cert. denied,* 298 Md. 394, 470 A.2d 353 (1983); State v. Richards, 585 S.W.2d 505, 506 (Mo. App. 1979); Andrews v. Love, 763 P.2d 714 (Okla. Crim. App. 1988), *cert. denied,* 489 U.S. 1082 (1989); State v. Allen, 277 S.C. 595, 603, 291 S.E.2d 459, 463 (1982).

226. *See* Bowden v. State, 256 Ark. 820, 510 S.W.2d 879 (1974) (removal of bullet from spinal canal); People v. Smith, 80 Misc. 2d 210, 362 N.Y.S.2d 909 (Sup. Ct. 1974) (removal of bullet as major bodily intrusion).

227. 470 U.S. at 766-67.

228. *Id.* at 763 n.6. *See* State v. Overstreet, 551 S.W.2d 621, 628 (Mo. 1977) (en banc) (minor surgery unconstitutional in absence of court approval).

229. 470 U.S. at 766 n.10.

remained doubtful due to the possible alteration of the bullet's rifling striations by the chemical effect of bodily fluids over a four-year period.[230]

In *Curry v. State*,[231] the court held that a trial court's order requiring the surgical removal of a bullet from the accused's leg violated the fourth amendment. The court first concluded that "the State's compelling need to retrieve evidence of a crime is, alone, insufficient to justify an intrusion into the body of a living human being. There must also be proof that the surgical procedure required to accomplish the seizure is reasonable, *i.e.*, unsubstantial."[232] The court held that the risks of surgery were too high:

> [D]efendant's physician testified that the bullet was buried deep within the muscle of his patient's left leg; that the projectile was close to vital bodily components; that there was no medical reason to remove the bullet and that the procedure required to retrieve the evidence posed an unnecessary risk to defendant's health, including the possibility of infection and paralysis. Under these circumstances and in light of the overwhelming wealth of alternative evidence supporting the State's case, the trial court's order requiring surgical removal of the bullet from defendant's leg oversteps defendant's Fourth Amendment right to be secure in his person.[233]

Therefore, the testimony concerning the accused's resistance was inadmissible.

Interestingly, in one case in which surgical removal was upheld,[234] the retrieved bullet did not match the suspect firearm.[235] In another case, the court ruled that the state's failure to provide a defendant with funds for surgery did not violate the right to compulsory process.[236]

§ 2-4(C). Drug Testing.

The Supreme Court first considered the constitutionality of drug testing procedures in a pair of 1989 cases. Both cases involved regulatory or administrative searches. Unlike law enforcement searches, such procedures are intended to achieve governmental objectives other than the detection or prevention of crime.

---

230. Doe v. State, 409 So. 2d 25, 27 (Fla. App. 1981), *rev. denied,* 418 So. 2d 1280 (Fla. 1982).

231. 217 Ga. App. 623, 458 S.E.2d 385 (1995).

232. *Id.* at 625, 458 S.E.2d at 386.

233. *Id.* at 625-26, 458 S.E.2d at 387.

234. Creamer v. State, 232 Ga. 136, 205 S.E.2d 240 (1972), *cert. dismissed,* 410 U.S. 975 (1973).

235. Emmett v. Ricketts (Creamer), 397 F. Supp. 1025, 1033 n.14 (N.D. Ga. 1975).

236. People v. Wilkerson, 123 Ill. App. 3d 527, 533-34, 463 N.E.2d 139, 144-45 (1984).

In *Skinner v. Railway Labor Executives' Ass'n,*[237] the Court considered regulations issued by the Federal Railway Administration. The regulations mandated blood and urine tests for railroad employees who are involved in major accidents and permitted testing for employees who violate safety rules. The Court rejected the contention that permissive inspections by private railroads, which were authorized by the regulations, were private searches outside the purview of the fourth amendment.[238] Moreover, blood, breath, and urine collection and testing procedures were searches within the meaning of the fourth amendment.[239] However, the Court found that the toxicological testing procedures were reasonable. The Court balanced the need for the search against the invasion of privacy involved. The railroad employees "discharge duties fraught with ... risks of injury to others" and "can cause great human loss before any signs of impairment becomes noticeable to supervisors or others."[240]

In a companion case, *National Treas. Employees Union v. Von Raab,*[241] the Court upheld an employee drug testing program, which included urinalysis, for federal customs officials who were transferred or promoted to positions involving the interdiction of illegal drugs or who were required to carry a firearm. Note that in both *Skinner* and *Von Raab* neither probable cause, reasonable suspicion, nor a warrant was required. These cases, however, do not sanction all governmentally sponsored drug-testing procedures.

In *Vernonia Sch. Dist. 47J v. Acton,*[242] the Supreme Court upheld drug testing of high school students in sporting events, but in *Chandler v. Miller*[243] the Court struck down a Georgia's requirement that candidates for designated state offices pass a urinalysis drug test within 30 days prior to qualifying for nomination. This provision did not fit within the closely guarded category of constitutionally permissible suspicionless searches.

§ 2-4(D). DNA Databanks.

A number of jurisdictions have enacted DNA statutes that require blood samples from persons convicted of crimes, or a specific category of crime, such as violent or sex crimes. Such provisions have been challenged on fourth

237. 489 U.S. 602 (1989).

238. *Id.* at 615-16 (The regulations "are clear indices of the Government's encouragement, endorsement, and participation, and suffice to implicate the Fourth Amendment").

239. *See* discussion of *Skinner* in § 2-4(B)(1) *supra.*

240. 489 U.S. at 628.

241. 489 U.S. 656 (1989).

242. 515 U.S. 646 (1995). *See also* Willis v. Anderson, 158 F.3d 415 (7th Cir. 1998) (mandatory drug testing of high school student suspended for fighting violates 4th Amendment), *cert. denied,* 119 S. Ct. 1254 (1999).

243. 520 U.S. 305 (1997).

amendment grounds. In *State v. Olivas*[244] the Washington Supreme Court rejected a fourth amendment challenge to a DNA identification sex offender law. According to the court, this provision constituted a valid regulatory search under *Skinner*. The Fourth Circuit reached the same result but under a different fourth amendment analysis – the diminished privacy rights of convicted persons.[245]

The Ninth Circuit upheld an Oregon statute that required all persons convicted of murder or a sexual offense to provide blood samples for a DNA databank.[246] The court wrote:

> Taking into account all of the factors discussed above — the reduced expectations of privacy held by persons convicted of one of the felonies to which [the statute] applies, the blood extractions' relatively minimal intrusion into these person's privacy interests, the public's incontestable interest in preventing recidivism and identifying and prosecuting murderers and sexual offenders, and the likelihood that a DNA data bank will advance this interest — we conclude that [the statute] is reasonable and therefore constitutional under the Fourth Amendment.[247]

The court also noted that the statute left prison officials no discretion to choose which person must submit and also prohibited the use of this information for illegitimate purposes.

---

244. 122 Wash. 2d 73, 856 P.2d 1076 (1993).

245. Jones v. Murray, 962 F.2d 302 (4th Cir.), *cert. denied*, 506 U.S. 977 (1992). *See also* Sanders v. Coman, 864 F. Supp. 496, 499-501 (E.D.N.C. 1994) (forcible drawing of blood for DNA databank violates neither the fourth, eighth, or fourteenth amendments).

246. Rise v. State of Oregon, 59 F.3d 1556 (9th Cir. 1995), *cert. denied*, 517 U.S. 1161 (1996). *See also* Shaffer v. Saffle, 148 F.3d 1180, 1181 (10th Cir. 1998) (Oklahoma statute) ("[W]hile obtaining DNA samples implicates Fourth Amendment concerns, it is reasonable in light of an inmate's diminished privacy rights, the minimal intrusion involved, and the legitimate government interest in using DNA to investigate and prosecute crimes"); Schlicher v. (NPN) Peters, I & I, 103 F.3d 940 (10th Cir. 1996) (Kansas statute) (same); Boling v. Romer, 101 F.3d 1336, 1340 (10th Cir. 1996) ("[W]hile obtaining and analyzing the DNA or saliva of an inmate convicted of a sex offense is a search and seizure implicating Fourth Amendment concerns, it is a reasonable search and seizure. This is so in light of an inmate's diminished privacy rights; the minimal intrusion of saliva and blood tests; and the legitimate government interest in the investigation and prosecution of unsolved and future criminal acts by the use of DNA in a manner not significantly different from the use of fingerprints") (also rejecting Fifth Amendment, due process, equal protection, and cruel and unusual punishment claims); *In re* Maricopa County Juvenile Action, 930 P.2d 496 (Ariz. App. 1996) (juvenile sex offenders).

247. 59 F.3d at 1562. *See generally* Krent, *Of Diaries and Data Banks: Use Restrictions Under the Fourth Amendment*, 74 TEX. L. REV. 49 (1995); Note, *Criminal DNA Data Banks: Revolution for Law Enforcement or Threat to Individual Privacy?*, 22 AM. J. CRIM. L. 461 (1995).

§ 2-5. Due Process.

The seizure of evidence for the purpose of scientific analysis has been challenged on due process grounds in several cases. In *Rochin v. California,*[248] decided in 1952, the Supreme Court held that the forcible stomach pumping of a suspect to recover narcotic pills "shock[ed] the conscience"[249] and did not comport with traditional ideas of fair play and decency,[250] thereby violating due process.

The Court distinguished *Rochin* in a later case, *Breithaupt v. Abram.*[251] In that case the Court upheld the compelled extraction of blood in the face of a due process challenge. In distinguishing the extraction of stomach contents from the extraction of blood, the *Breithaupt* Court emphasized that the latter procedure, "under the protective eye of a physician," was a routine and scientifically accurate method and therefore did not involve the "brutality" and "offensiveness" present in *Rochin.*[252] This ruling was reaffirmed in *Schmerber v. California.*[253]

The *Rochin* and *Breithaupt* decisions predated the applicability of the Bill of Rights to the states through the due process clause of the fourteenth amendment,[254] and thus the continued validity of an independent due process analysis in these cases is questionable. Such issues no longer need be addressed in terms of due process but rather as possible violations of specific constitutional guarantees enumerated in the Bill of Rights.[255] For example, according to the Court in *Schmerber,* the manner in which evidence is obtained from a suspect is subject to the reasonableness clause of the fourth amendment.[256] This requirement would seem to encompass virtually all cases that are vulnerable to attack on due process grounds.[257]

---

248. 342 U.S. 165 (1952).

249. *Id.* at 172.

250. *Id.* at 173.

251. 352 U.S. 432 (1957).

252. *Id.* at 435.

253. 384 U.S. 757 (1966).

254. The fourth amendment exclusionary rule was applied to the states in Mapp v. Ohio, 367 U.S. 643 (1961).

255. This may explain why *Rochin* has not played a major role in subsequent cases. *See* Yanez v. Romero, 619 F.2d 851, 854 (10th Cir.) ("We do not say that the Supreme Court's decision in *Rochin* has eroded, but we do say that it has been applied in a positive way quite infrequently"), *cert. denied,* 449 U.S. 876 (1980). However, in a later case the Supreme Court, citing *Rochin,* commented that the "Due Process Clause imposes limitations on the government's ability to coerce individuals into participating in criminal prosecutions." Doe v. United States, 487 U.S. 201, 214 n.13 (1988).

256. 384 U.S. at 771.

257. *See* People v. Bracamonte, 15 Cal. 3d 394, 404-05, 540 P.2d 624, 631, 124 Cal. Rptr. 528, 535 (1975) (en banc) (forced ingestion of emetic solution violated fourth amendment). *But see* Yanez v. Romero, 619 F.2d 851, 853 (10th Cir.) (*Rochin's* due process "prohibition ... is somewhat

§ 2-6. Selected Bibliography.

E. IMWINKELRIED, P. GIANNELLI, F. GILLIGAN & F. LEDERER, COURTROOM CRIMINAL EVIDENCE (3d ed. 1998)
W. LAFAVE, SEARCH AND SEIZURE (3d ed. 1996).
W. LAFAVE & J. ISRAEL, CRIMINAL PROCEDURE (1984).
C. MCCORMICK, EVIDENCE (4th ed. 1992).
C. WHITEBREAD & C. SLOBOGIN, CRIMINAL PROCEDURE (3d ed. 1993).

---

broader than the limitation provided by the Fourth Amendment"), *cert. denied,* 449 U.S. 876 (1980); United States v. Ingram, 797 F. Supp. 705, 707 (E.D. Ark. 1992) ("Unlike the stomach pumping discussed in *Rochin,* taking a hair sample would not 'offend even hardened sensibilities' or elicit comparison to 'the rack and screw'"); State v. Strong, 493 N.W.2d 834, 836 (Iowa 1992) (Fourth Amendment, rather than *Rochin*, applied to stomach-pumping for crack cocaine).

CHAPTER 3

DISCOVERY*

§ 3-1. In General.

There is little question that pretrial discovery is critical when scientific evidence is admitted at trial. The ABA Standards note that the "need for full and fair disclosure is especially apparent with respect to scientific proof and the testimony of experts. This sort of evidence is practically impossible for the adversary to test or rebut at trial without an advance opportunity to examine it closely."[1] The first National Academy of Sciences DNA report recommended "open" discovery: "The prosecutor has a strong responsibility to reveal fully to defense counsel and experts retained by the defendant all material that might be necessary in evaluating the evidence."[2] As one court put it, "[T]here are no scientific grounds for withholding information in the discovery process."[3]

---

*The sections in this chapter were revised and renumbered in this edition.

1. ABA STANDARDS RELATING TO DISCOVERY AND PROCEDURE BEFORE TRIAL 66 (Approved Draft 1970). *See also* FED. R. CRIM. P. 16 advisory committee's note (1975), *reprinted* at 62 F.R.D. 312 (1974) ("[I]t is difficult to test expert testimony at trial without advance notice and preparation"); Giannelli, *Criminal Discovery, Scientific Evidence, and DNA*, 44 VAND. L. REV. 791 (1991).

2. NATIONAL RESEARCH COUNCIL, DNA TECHNOLOGY IN FORENSIC SCIENCE 146 (1992).

3. State v. Tankersley, 191 Ariz. 359, 368, 956 P.2d 486, 495 (1998).

Traditionally, criminal discovery has been far more limited than civil discovery. Opponents of liberal discovery argue that criminal discovery will encourage perjury, lead to the intimidation of witnesses, and, because of the fifth amendment, be a one-way street.[4] With scientific evidence, however, the traditional arguments against criminal discovery lose whatever force they might otherwise have. The first argument fails because "it is virtually impossible for evidence or information of this kind to be distorted or misused because of its advance disclosure."[5] Also, there is no evidence that experts have been intimidated, probably because the evidence could be retested or another expert could testify about the examination.[6] Finally, the self-incrimination clause as presently interpreted by the Supreme Court presents little impediment to prosecution discovery of scientific proof.[7]

In addition, due process concerns are eliminated by extensive defense discovery of scientific evidence. As the Supreme Court has noted, due process "speak[s] to the balance of forces between the accused and his accuser."[8] There are over three hundred crime laboratories in this country, eighty percent under the control of the police,[9] and most laboratories examine only evidence submitted by law enforcement agencies.[10] In contrast, criminal defendants, who are typically indigent, do not have access to such resources.[11] Thus, it is not surprising that a commentator would write: "[T]he inequality of investigative resources between prosecution and defense is likely to have its maximum impact

---

4. 2 C. Wright, Federal Practice and Procedure § 252, at 36-37 (2d ed. 1982).

5. ABA Standards Relating to Discovery, *supra* note 1, at 67.

6. 2 W. LaFave & J. Israel, Criminal Procedure § 19.3, at 490 (1984) ("Once the report is prepared, the scientific expert's position is not readily influenced, and therefore disclosure presents little danger of prompting perjury or intimidation"). *See also* People v. Beeler, 9 Cal. 4th 953, 979, 891 P.2d 153, 168, 39 Cal. Rptr. 2d 607, 622 (1995) (en banc) (autopsy report admitted as business record through the testimony of a pathologist who had not performed the autopsy; the pathologist who had conducted the autopsy "had apparently left the coroner's office under unfavorable conditions"), *cert. denied*, 516 U.S. 1053 (1996).

7. For a discussion of the fifth amendment issues, *see* § 3-15 *infra*.

8. Wardius v. Oregon, 412 U.S. 470, 474 (1973). *See also* Ross v. Moffitt, 417 U.S. 600, 609 (1974) ("'Due process' emphasizes fairness between the State and the individual dealing with the State ..."); Lassiter v. Department of Social Servs., 452 U.S. 18, 28 (1981) (the "adversary system presupposes that accurate and just results are most likely to be obtained through the equal contest of opposed interests ...").

9. Peterson, Mihajlovic & Bedrosian, *The Capabilities, Uses, and Effects of the Nation's Criminalistics Laboratories*, 30 J. Forensic Sci. 10, 11 (1985) ("Seventy-nine percent of all [257 out of 319] laboratories responding to our survey are located within law enforcement/public safety agencies").

10. *Id.* at 13 ("Fifty-seven percent ... would *only* examine evidence submitted by law enforcement officials"). *See also* Federal Bureau of Investigation, Handbook of Forensic Science ix (rev. ed. 1994) (FBI lab services available only to duly constituted state, county, and municipal law enforcement agencies).

11. For a discussion of the right to a defense expert, *see* Chapter 4.

in the presentation of evidence which must be analyzed and developed in the laboratory or hospital."[12]

The importance of complete discovery is illustrated by the infamous case of *In re Investigation of the W. Va. State Police Crime Lab., Serology Div.*[13] At the request of a prosecutor, the West Virginia Supreme Court appointed a judge to investigate the "willful false testimony" of the head serologist of the state police crime laboratory. The report by the judge states:

> The acts of misconduct on the part of Zain included (1) overstating the strength of results; (2) overstating the frequency of genetic matches on individual pieces of evidence; (3) misreporting the frequency of genetic matches on multiple pieces of evidence; (4) reporting that multiple items of evidence had been tested, when only a single item had been tested; (5) reporting inconclusive results as conclusive; (6) repeatedly altering laboratory records; (7) grouping results to create the erroneous impression that genetic markers had been obtained from all samples tested; (8) failing to report conflicting results; (9) failing to conduct or to report conducting additional testing to resolve conflicting results; (10) implying a match with a suspect when testing supported only a match with the victim; and (11) reporting scientifically impossible or improbable results.[14]

While defense discovery is not a complete cure for type of abuse, it would go a long way toward that goal.[15]

§ 3-2. Defense Discovery.

Because discovery is primarily governed by statutes, rules, or common-law precedents, there is a wide variation among jurisdictions as to the types of

---

12. Rezneck, *The New Federal Rules of Criminal Procedure*, 54 GEO. L.J. 1276, 1278 (1966). *See also* State v. Cook, 43 N.J. 560, 567, 206 A.2d 359, 363 (1965) (pretrial discovery "lessen[s] the imbalance which may result from the State's early and complete investigation in contrast to [defendant's] ... late and limited investigation"); Krantz, *Pretrial Discovery in Criminal Cases: A Necessity for Fair and Impartial Justice*, 42 NEB. L. REV. 127, 131-32 (1963).

13. 438 S.E.2d 501 (W. Va. 1993).

14. *Id.* at 503 (quoting report). *See also* Giannelli, *The Abuse of Scientific Evidence in Criminal Cases: The Need for Independent Crime Laboratories*, 4 VA. J. SOC. POLICY & L. 439 (1997).

15. *See* Rowe, *Commentary, in* CONVICTED BY JURIES, EXONERATED BY SCIENCE: CASE STUDIES IN THE USE OF DNA EVIDENCE TO ESTABLISH INNOCENCE AFTER TRIAL xvii-xviii (Connors et al. 1996) (discussing the exoneration of 28 convicts through the use of DNA technology—some of whom had been sentenced to death) ("It is also clear that in case after case, defense counsel failed to review the case notes of the prosecution's forensic serologists. Even a layperson would have seen the Fred Zain's written reports and sworn testimony were contradicted by his case notes. Again, one has to reflect on the likelihood that numerous innocent persons are presently incarcerated because of the inadequacy of their attorneys") [hereinafter cited as CONVICTED BY JURIES, EXONERATED BY SCIENCE].

materials that are discoverable. A number of jurisdictions follow current Federal Rule 16. Other jurisdictions pattern their discovery rules on the original ABA Standards.[16] Still other jurisdictions have adopted the 1966 version of the Federal Rule 16. A number of jurisdictions do not fall into any discernible category, while some jurisdictions deal with discovery under common-law precedents.[17]

The most common discovery provisions relating to scientific evidence concern laboratory reports[18] and the inspection, including the retesting, of evidence.[19] In 1993, the requirement of a summary of an expert's testimony was added to the federal rule.[20]

Two other points are noteworthy. First, courts have inherent power to order discovery.[21] Second, although the Supreme Court has written that "[t]here is no general constitutional right to discovery in a criminal case,"[22] constitutional considerations play an important role in this area of law.[23]

Generally, discovery is initiated by the defense, either through a request to the prosecution or a discovery motion to the court. With some scientific techniques, however, the prosecution may be required to provide notice to the defense, even in the absence of a discovery request or motion. Hypnosis is an example; most courts require the prosecution to notify the defense if a witness has been

---

16. The original ABA STANDARDS RELATING TO DISCOVERY were published in 1970. A second edition was published in 1980. The third edition of the ABA STANDARDS was published in 1996.

17. *E.g.,* Wing v. State, 490 P.2d 1376, 1382 (Okla. Crim. 1971) (scientific reports are discoverable), *cert. denied,* 406 U.S. 919 (1972).

18. *See* § 3-3 *infra.*

19. *See* § 3-7 *infra.*

20. *See* § 3-5 *infra.*

21. *See* United States v. Nobles, 422 U.S. 225, 231 (1975) ("Decisions of this Court repeatedly have recognized the federal judiciary's inherent power to require the prosecution to produce the previously recorded statements of its witnesses ..."); United States v. Beckford, 962 F. Supp. 748, 756 (E.D. Va. 1997) ("Hence, it seems rather clear that the inherent powers of courts to fashion rules of discovery has been incorporated in the Rules by FED. R. CRIM. P. 57(b)"); United States v. Kloepper, 725 F. Supp. 638, 640 (D. Mass. 1989) (district court has inherent authority to order handwriting exemplars and fingerprints of defendant be produced even though not specifically listed in Rule 16). *See also* Hewitt & Bell, *Beyond Rule 16: The Inherent Power of the Federal Court to Order Pretrial Discovery in Criminal Cases*, 7 U.S.F. L. REV. 233 (1973).

22. Weatherford v. Bursey, 429 U.S. 545, 559 (1977).

23. The Court has recognized a limited due process right to the disclosure and preservation of exculpatory and material evidence under certain circumstances. *See* §§ 3-12 & 13 *infra.* In Pennsylvania v. Ritchie, 480 U.S. 39, 55-58 (1987), a plurality of the Court reaffirmed this position. In a concurring opinion, Justice Blackmun, who cast the deciding vote, indicated that the confrontation clause as well as due process applied to criminal discovery: "In my view, there might well be a confrontation violation if, as here, a defendant is denied pretrial access to information that would make possible effective cross-examination of a crucial prosecution witness." *Id.* at 61-62. Two other Justices agreed with this analysis, while two others dissented on procedural grounds.

subjected to pretrial hypnosis.[24] For example, in *Orndorff v. Lockhart*[25] the court ruled that the failure to notify the defense that a witness had been hypnotized violated the Confrontation Clause because it deprived the accused of the opportunity to cross-examine the witness on this issue.

§ 3-3. Scientific Reports.

Virtually all jurisdictions provide for the disclosure of scientific reports in the possession of the prosecution. Scientific reports also are discoverable under the ABA Standards[26] and the Uniform Rules.[27]

Federal Criminal Rule 16(a)(1)(D) governs defense discovery of the "results or reports of physical or mental examinations, and of scientific tests or experiments."[28] Under this provision, scientific reports are discoverable if they are either material[29] to the preparation of the defense or are intended for use by

---

24. *See* United States v. Miller, 411 F.2d 825, 832 (2d Cir. 1969); State *ex rel.* Collins v. Superior Court, 132 Ariz. 180, 210, 644 P.2d 1266, 1296 (1982); People v. Tait, 99 Mich. App. 19, 26-27, 297 N.W.2d 853, 856 (1980); State v. Hurd, 86 N.J. 525, 543, 432 A.2d 86, 95 (1981); Gee v. State, 662 P.2d 103, 105 (Wyo. 1983); State v. Armstrong, 110 Wis. 2d 555, 571-72, 329 N.W.2d 386, 395, *cert. denied*, 461 U.S. 946 (1983). For a further discussion of hypnosis, *see* Chapter 12.

25. 998 F.2d 1426 (8th Cir. 1993), *cert. denied*, 511 U.S. 1060 (1994). *See also* E. CONNORS, T. LUNDREGAN, N. MILLER & T. MCEWEN, CONVICTED BY JURIES, EXONERATED BY SCIENCE: CASE STUDIES IN THE USE OF DNA EVIDENCE TO ESTABLISH INNOCENCE AFTER TRIAL 15 &18 (1996) ("In *Honaker*, the defendant's attorney alleged that the government intentionally kept exculpatory evidence from the defense, including information that two of the government's witnesses were secretly hypnotized to enhance their testimony and the prosecution's criminalist was never told that Honaker had a vasectomy (and could not have been the source of the sperm in the victim"); Fricker, *State Falters in Retrial of Escaped Con*, 81 A.B.A. J. 38, 40 (June 1995) ("The defense was not told of the hypnosis during the first trial, and the tape of that session has since been erased").

26. 2 ABA STANDARDS FOR CRIMINAL JUSTICE 11-2.1(a)(iv) (3d ed. 1996) ("Any reports or statements made by experts in connection with the case, including results of physical or mental examinations and of scientific tests, experiments, or comparisons") [hereinafter cited as ABA STANDARDS].

27. UNIF. R. CRIM. P. 421(a) (Approved Draft 1974) ("expert reports"). *See also* NATIONAL ADVISORY COMMISSION ON CRIMINAL JUSTICE STANDARDS AND GOALS, COURTS, Standard 4.9(3) (1973).

28. *See generally* 8 MOORE'S FEDERAL PRACTICE § 16.05[3] (1992); 2 C. WRIGHT, *supra* note 2, § 254; Burns, *Pretrial Discovery in the Federal Courts*, *in* 1 CRIMINAL DEFENSE TECHNIQUES ch. 10 (S. Allen, I. Rosen, E. Smolinsky & D. Winston eds. 1992).

29. *See* United States v. Miller, 161 F.3d 977, 986 (6th Cir. 1998) ("Counsel for the government indicated that the exemplars were taken as part of an independent investigation, and they were not evidence in defendant's case. The government contends the results of the handwriting tests were neither material to the defense, nor were they intended for use by the government, and therefore, they did not have to be disclosed under Rule 16. We agree"), *cert. denied*, 119 S. Ct. 1275 (1999); United States v. Holloway, 971 F.2d 675, 679 (11th Cir. 1992) (inconclusive handwriting and fingerprint reports not material), *cert. denied*, 507 U.S. 962 (1993).

the prosecution as evidence in its case-in-chief at trial. The prosecution's obligation under Rule 16 extends to reports which, even if unknown, could be ascertained by the exercise of due diligence. According to the Advisory Committee's Note (1966), the defendant "is not required to designate" the type of report sought. The 1975 amendments made discovery mandatory rather than discretionary and provide for discovery requests to the prosecution rather than by motion to the court.

The types of reports covered by Rule 16 are broad. The 1966 Committee's Note specifically mentioned reports of "fingerprint and handwriting comparisons." One commentator, writing at the time, has provided a more comprehensive list:

> [R]esults of ballistics tests, fingerprint comparisons; handwriting analyses; autopsy reports; medical examinations of victims of crime — such as complainants in sex cases; blood tests; urinalyses; analyses of fibers, paints, and other materials; and other chemical analyses, such as tests for the presence of narcotics. In short, to the extent that the government utilizes modern scientific techniques for crime detection, the findings will be available to the defendant.[30]

The cases support this interpretation; they include reports on fingerprints,[31] footprints,[32] palm prints,[33] drug analysis,[34] handwriting,[35] as well as sundry other techniques.[36] The courts are divided over the disclosure of polygraph reports,[37] an issue the Supreme Court has address in the context of the *Brady* rule.[38]

---

30. Rezneck, *The New Federal Rules of Criminal Procedure*, 54 GEO. L.J. 1276, 1278 (1966). *See also* DEL. SUPER. CT. CRIM. R. 16(A)(2) ("reports of autopsies, ballistics tests, fingerprint analyses, handwriting analyses, blood, urine and breath tests"); VA. S. CT. R. 3A:11(b)(1)(i) ("reports of autopsies, ballistics tests, fingerprint analyses, handwriting analyses, blood, urine and breath tests and other scientific reports").

31. *E.g.*, United States v. Edmonson, 962 F.2d 1535, 1545-46 (10th Cir. 1992), *cert. denied*, 521 U.S. 1128 (1997); United States v. Beaver, 524 F.2d 963, 966 (5th Cir. 1975), *cert. denied,* 425 U.S. 905 (1976); United States v. Feola, 651 F. Supp. 1068, 1143-46 (S.D.N.Y. 1987) (fingerprint, hair and fiber analysis), *aff'd,* 875 F.2d 857 (2d Cir.), *cert. denied,* 493 U.S. 834 (1989).

32. United States v. Hemmer, 729 F.2d 10, 12 (1st Cir. 1984) (fingerprint, handwriting, and footprint examinations).

33 United States v. O'Shea, 450 F.2d 298, 300 (5th Cir. 1971).

34. *E.g.,* United States v. Boney, 572 F.2d 397, 403 (2d Cir. 1978) (comparison of drug tablets); United States v. Eisler, 567 F.2d 814, 816-17 (8th Cir. 1977) (heroin); United States v. Penix, 516 F. Supp. 248, 258 (W.D. Okla. 1981) (cocaine).

35. *E.g.,*United States v. Holloway, 971 F.2d 675, 679 (11th Cir. 1992) (inconclusive handwriting and fingerprint reports not material), *cert. denied*, 507 U.S. 962 (1993); United States v. Mavrokordatos, 933 F.2d 843, 847 (10th Cir. 1991) (handwriting report).

36. *E.g.,* United States v. Price, 75 F.3d 1440, 1445 (10th Cir.) ("The record shows the prosecution turned over its entire investigative files, including all reports and test results issued by the [Kansas Bureau of Investigation] laboratories"), *cert. denied,* 517 U.S. 1239 (1996); United

Oral Reports

There are several major deficiencies in many of the discovery rules on scientific reports. One is that they may not cover oral reports. Prior to 1993 when the expert testimony "summary" rule was adopted,[39] nothing in Federal Rule 16 required that a report be made or, if made, that it be written, even if a scientific test was performed.[40] In *United States v. Shue*[41] the Seventh Circuit had ruled that the accused was not entitled to the verbal report of an FBI photographic expert who compared pictures of Shue with those of a bank robber. Unknown to the defense, the expert made the comparison the night before he testified. Similarly, a police officer in *United States v. Johnson*[42] testified as an Emergency Medical Technician without pretrial notice to the defense. Although the defense argued that the testimony was "highly prejudicial" because it contradicted an important

---

States v. Gowen, 32 F.3d 1466, 1469-70 (10th Cir. 1994) (diagnostic interview and testing results of expert on post-traumatic stress disorder [PTSD]), *cert. denied*, 513 U.S. 1173 (1995); United States v. Longie, 984 F.2d 955, 958 (8th Cir. 1993) (medical report and photographs); United States v. Fontaine, 575 F.2d 970, 974-75 (1st Cir.) (voice test comparison), *cert. denied*, 439 U.S. 851 (1978); United States v. Kelly, 420 F.2d 26, 28 (2d Cir. 1969) (neutron activation analysis results); United States v. Feola, 651 F. Supp. 1068, 1143-46 (S.D.N.Y. 1987) (fingerprint, hair and fiber analysis), *aff'd*, 875 F.2d 857 (2d Cir.), *cert. denied*, 493 U.S. 834 (1989); United States v. Ahmad, 53 F.R.D. 186, 189 (D.C. Pa. 1971) (all reports made in connection with case). *See also* Annot., *Reports of Tests, Experiments, or Analyses as Subject to Discovery by Defendant under Rule 16 of Federal Rules of Criminal Procedure*, 110 A.L.R. FED. 313 (1992).

37. *See* United States v. Williams, 792 F. Supp. 1120, 1132 (S.D. Ind. 1992) (polygraph reports are "work product" and thus not discoverable); Patrick v. State, 329 Md. 24, 35-36, 617 A.2d 215, 220 (1992) ("[T]he reports of State experts who have conducted polygraph examinations, whether the results are exculpatory of the accused's guilt or not, constitute discoverable 'scientific tests' within the contemplation of the [discovery] rule"); State v. Davis, 62 Ohio St. 3d 326, 341-42, 581 N.E.2d 1362, 1376 (1991) (polygraph test result is not a scientific report under OHIO R. CRIM. P. 16), *cert. dismissed*, 506 U.S. 803 (1992).

38. *See* § 3-12 *infra.*

39. *See* § 3-5 *infra.*

40. As a matter of practice most crime laboratories prepare reports. One commentator has written:

> An additional practice of some laboratories merits discussion. This practice is that of examiners not writing results in official report form unless they are informed by the prosecutor that the case is going to trial. The principal justification for this procedure is the high volume of cases to be analyzed and the time required to prepare written case reports. The argument is made, "What is the point in taking the time to prepare an official report if the case may be dismissed or may result in a guilty plea?" To allow the prosecutor discretion over what laboratory examinations appear in report form puts the defendant at a distinct disadvantage.

Peterson, *Ethical Issues in the Collection, Examination, and Use of Physical Evidence*, *in* FORENSIC SCIENCE 35, 41 (G. Davies ed. 1986).

41. 766 F.2d 1122, 1135 (7th Cir. 1985), *cert. denied*, 484 U.S. 956 (1987).

42. 713 F.2d 654 (11th Cir. 1983), *cert. denied*, 456 U.S. 1030 (1984).

aspect of the defense case, the Eleventh Circuit merely noted that there was no right to a witness list and Rule 16 was not implicated because "no ... reports were made in this case."[43] In contrast, several state jurisdictions explicitly provide for the discovery of oral reports.[44]

Insufficient Information

The principal problem with most discovery provisions on scientific reports is that the typical laboratory report is inadequate; it reveals only the results of the examination performed.[45] Frequently, other critical information is not disclosed. Several examples are discussed below.[46]

---

43. *Id.* at 659. *See also* United States v. Smith, 101 F.3d 202, 210 (1st Cir. 1996) ("[W]here the test result in question consisted of the expert's unrecorded comparison of the test-firing casings with those at the crime scene, Rule 16(a)(1)(D) did not obligate the government to produce in advance the expert's conclusions"), *cert. denied*, 520 U.S. 1160 (1997); United States v. Messerlian, 832 F.2d 778, 795 (3d Cir. 1987) (noting but not deciding whether oral reports are discoverable under Rule 16), *cert. denied,* 485 U.S. 988 (1988); United States v. Glaze, 643 F.2d 549, 551-52 (8th Cir. 1981) (unwritten results of field test for drugs not disclosed); Stewart v. Commonwealth, 245 Va. 222, 236, 427 S.E.2d 394, 404 (State discovery rule on scientific reports does not apply to oral reports of experts; blood spatter expert examined evidence on eve of trial and "discussed his conclusions with the Commonwealth's Attorney but submitted nothing in writing"), *cert. denied*, 510 U.S. 848 (1993). The same rule applies to oral reports by defense experts. *See* note 292 *infra.*

44. *See* ME. R. CRIM. P. 16(c)(4) ("If an expert witness whom the state intends to call in any proceeding has not prepared a report of examination or tests, the court, upon motion, may order that the expert prepare and the attorney for the state serve a report stating the subject matter on which the expert is expected to testify, the substance of the facts to which the expert is expected to testify and a summary of the expert's opinions and the grounds for each opinion"); MD. R. CRIM. P. 4-263(b)(4) (1992) (requiring the production of the "substance of any such oral [expert] report and conclusion").

45. *E.g.,* United States v. Parker, 491 F.2d 517, 525 (8th Cir. 1973) (BND lab report reproduced), *cert. denied,* 416 U.S. 989 (1974). *See also* Allis, *Limitations on Prosecutorial Discovery of the Defense Case in Federal Courts: The Shield of Confidentiality*, 50 S. CAL. L. REV. 461, 475 n.51 (1977) ("Many criminal defense attorneys suspect that the unusual brevity of reports by FBI fingerprint and handwriting experts (*e.g.*, often one or two short sentences) may be partially explained by the fact that defense counsel is entitled to copies of them prior to trial").

46. For a further discussion, *see* Giannelli, *Criminal Discovery, Scientific Evidence, and DNA*, 44 VAND. L. REV. 791 (1991). There are exceptions to the cases in the text. For example, in one case a trial court ordered discovery of:

> The reports of any scientific tests, examinations or experiments, or physical or mental examinations, or copies thereof, including but not limited to: (1) a statement of all material or other information or sources considered by the examiner in arriving at an opinion, the methodology used, and the findings and conclusions of the examiner, (2) a resume and curriculum vitae of the examiner's qualifications, experience, subject matter of the examiner's testimony, and prior occasions of testimony as an expert, and (3) any worksheets, photographs, notes, or other things used to assist the examiner in reaching an opinion and recording the process and methodology of reaching an opinion.

First, the reports rarely indicate the procedure used in the analysis. A laboratory report concluding that an examined substance is marijuana may not specify whether this conclusion is based upon a visual examination, the Duquenois-Levine test, thin-layer chromatography, or some other test. Without this information, it is difficult for counsel to prepare adequately for trial.[47] Similarly, a report stating that a seized substance is "Heroin HCl"[48] is not very informative. Some types of evidence present the examiner with a choice among a variety of testing techniques. Drug tests range from preliminary screening examinations, such as color change and micro crystal tests, to extremely specific and sophisticated analysis, such as infrared spectrophotometry. Different laboratories use different protocols, and some experts make positive identifications based only on preliminary screening tests.[49] This information is critical, and there is no reason to keep it hidden.

Second, the analyst's qualifications are frequently not provided with the report. Indeed, the report may not even be signed. The credentials of the expert are significant for two reasons. First, the opposing party needs to know if the expert is qualified (1) to prepare for cross-examination, (2) to decide whether to retain his or her own expert, and (3) to determine whether independent testing is desirable. Second, a surprising number of expert witnesses have lied about their credentials.[50] In one case a serologist testified that he had a master's degree in science, "whereas in fact he never attained a graduate degree."[51] In another case the death penalty was vacated when it was discovered that a prosecution expert, who "had testified in many cases," had lied about her professional qualifications:

United States v. Cadet, 727 F.2d 1453, 1459-60 (9th Cir. 1984).

47. For a discussion of drug identification testing, *see* Chapter 23.

48. United States v. Parker, 491 F.2d 517, 525 (8th Cir. 1973) (Bureau of Narcotics and Dangerous Drugs lab report), *cert. denied*, 416 U.S. 989 (1974). *See also* United States v. Davis, 14 M.J. 847, 848 n.3 (A.C.M.R. 1982) ("[M]ost laboratory reports only state general conclusions . . .").

49. "On the basis of a test that shows only the compound in question is a member of a sizable class, some forensic chemists are prepared to take the stand and state their opinion that the substance is methamphetamine (or THC, or cocaine, or whatever)." M. Saks & R. Van Duizend, The Use of Scientific Evidence in Litigation 7-8 (1983).

50. *E.g.*, Maddox v. Lord, 818 F.2d 1058, 1062 (2d Cir. 1987) (serologist testified falsely about academic credentials); Kline v. State, 444 So. 2d 1102, 1104 (Fla. App. 1984) (psychologist convicted of perjury for claiming he had a doctorate during Ted Bundy trial); People v. Alfano, 95 Ill. App. 3d 1026, 1028-29, 420 N.E.2d 1114, 1116 (1983) (arson expert testified falsely about academic credentials); State v. Elder, 199 Kan. 607, 607-09, 433 P.2d 462, 463-64 (1967) (lab technician convicted of perjury for misrepresenting educational background); State v. DeFronzo, 59 Ohio Misc. 113, 116, 394 N.E.2d 1027, 1030 (C.P. 1978) (lab analyst pleaded guilty to 8 counts of falsification for misstating academic credentials).

See also Saks, *Prevalence and Impact of Ethical Problems in Forensic Science*, 34 J. Forensic Sci. 772 (1989) (listing other cases); Annotation, *Perjury or Wilfully False Testimony of Expert Witness as Basis for New Trial on Ground of Newly Discovered Evidence*, 38 A.L.R.3d 812 (1971).

51. Doepel v. United States, 434 A.2d 449, 460 (D.C. App.), *cert. denied*, 454 U.S. 1037 (1981).

"she had never fulfilled the educational requirements for a laboratory technician."[52] Discovery is a remedy for this type of abuse.[53]

Third, courts have disagreed about what constitutes a "scientific report" for purposes of discovery. The Georgia Supreme Court has held that microspectrophotometer graphs are not scientific reports and therefore are not discoverable.[54] Similarly, the Ninth Circuit has ruled that log notes made by a chemist in preparing his final report were not discoverable as scientific reports.[55] In contrast, the Louisiana Court of Appeals adopted a more enlightened approach when faced with a discovery request for notes, diagrams, printouts, and other records. According to the court, "[f]undamental fairness and due process require that the defense be given the opportunity, prior to trial, to examine the basis from which an expert reaches his conclusion."[56] This problem is overcome if such documents are independently discoverable[57] or, as in the federal system, a summary of the expert's testimony is required.[58] In any event, this material should be disclosed.

Other instances where critical information has been omitted from reports are not hard to find. For example, in *Harrison v. State*[59] the state turned over an "autopsy report, which did not state any opinion as to the instruments that caused the victim's injuries."[60] Nevertheless, at trial the pathologist testified about a number of factors not disclosed to the defense: temporal relationship of certain injuries to the victim's death and his opinion that the murder victim had been raped. The Mississippi Supreme Court held: "This Court cannot countenance or condone the willful withholding of crucial evidence during discovery."[61] Not all courts would reach this result.

Similarly, in *Driscoll v. Delo*,[62] a capital murder case, the laboratory report indicated that blood traces on Driscoll's knife were type A, which matched the

---

52. Commonwealth v. Mount, 435 Pa. 419, 422, 257 A.2d 578, 579 (1969).

53. *See* Starrs, *Mountebanks Among Forensic Scientists, in* 2 FORENSIC SCIENCE HANDBOOK 1, 31 (R. Saferstein ed. 1988). *See also* CONVICTED BY JURIES, EXONERATED BY SCIENCE, *supra* note 15, at 62-63 (discussing the exoneration of 28 convicts through the use of DNA technology—some of whom had been sentenced to death; "Subsequently, the chief prosecution expert who conducted the serology tests pleaded guilty to perjury charges that alleged he lied about his qualifications and training").

54. Williams v. State, 251 Ga. 749, 754, 312 S.E.2d 40, 51 (1983). *See also* Griffin v. State, 183 Ga. App. 386, 358 S.E.2d 917 (1987) (latent fingerprint card not a scientific report).

55. United States v. Iglesias, 881 F.2d 1519, 1523-24 (9th Cir. 1989), *cert. denied,* 493 U.S. 1088 (1990).

56. State v. Burgess, 482 So. 2d 651, 653 (La. App. 1985).

57. *See* § 3-4 *infra.*

58. *See* § 3-5 *infra.*

59. 635 So. 2d 894 (Miss. 1994) (en banc).

60. *Id.* at 898.

61. *Id.* at 898.

62. 71 F.3d 701, 707 (8th Cir. 1995), *cert. denied,* 519 U.S. 910 (1996).

blood of a prison guard who had been injured by a stab wound but did not match the blood type of a murdered guard whose blood type was O. To explain the absence of type O blood, the prosecution offered several theories, one of which was that the presence of the type O blood was "masked" by the type A blood. The chief serologist of the state crime laboratory testified about this theory at trial. Only in a subsequent habeas proceeding was it revealed that the serologist had performed another test in which "masking" was not a problem. This test revealed that there was no type O blood on the knife. "The jury was never informed that the lattes test was performed or that no type O blood was on the knife.... In its closing argument, the state made much of the masking theory, turning unfavorable serology evidence into neutral evidence at worst."[63]

Reciprocal Discovery

If a defendant requests discovery of scientific reports pursuant to Rule 16, the prosecution is entitled, upon request, to reciprocal discovery of defense reports.[64] Prosecution discovery, however, extends only to reports the defendant intends to introduce as evidence in chief or which have been prepared by an expert who the defense intends to call as a witness, provided the reports relate to that expert's testimony.[65]

State Jurisdictions

State rules governing defense discovery of scientific reports vary widely. A number of jurisdictions follow current Federal Rule 16 and make discovery mandatory upon request.[66] Other jurisdictions pattern their discovery rules on the original ABA Standards,[67] which also require disclosure of scientific reports.[68] Still other jurisdictions have adopted the 1966 version of the Federal Rule 16, which required a motion to the court and made discovery of scientific reports discretionary.[69] A number of jurisdictions do not fall into any discernible

---

63. *Id.* at 708.

64. FED. R. CRIM. P. 16(b)(1)(B).

65. *See* § 3-15 *infra.*

66. *E.g.,* ME. R. CRIM. P. 16(b)(2)(B); N.M. R. CRIM. P. 5-501(A)(4); OHIO R. CRIM. P. 16(B)(1)(d) (mandatory but motion required); TENN. R. CRIM. P. 16(a)(1)(D) (mandatory upon request).

67. The original ABA STANDARDS RELATING TO DISCOVERY were published in 1970. A second edition was published in 1980 and the third edition in 1996.

68. *E.g.,* ALASKA R. CRIM. P. 16(b)(iv); COLO. R. CRIM. P. 16(a)(III); FLA. R. CRIM. P. 3.220(b)(x); ILL. ANN. STAT. ch. 110a, § 412(a)(iv) (Smith-Hurd Supp. 1985); MO. R. CRIM. P. 25.03(A)(5); OR. REV. STAT. § 135.815(3) (1991); VT. R. CRIM. P. 16(a)(2)(C) (mandatory upon request).

69. *E.g.,* ARK. R. CRIM. P. 17.4(a) (court may require disclosure of "other relevant materials and information upon a showing of materiality"); IDAHO CODE § 19-1309(1)(b) (1987); KY. R. CRIM. P.

category,[70] while some jurisdictions deal with discovery under common-law precedents.[71]

§ 3-4. Graphs, Lab Notes & Related Documents.

Many discovery rules include provisions concerning the discovery of documents in the government's possession, and these may provide a basis for obtaining material, such as bench notes and graphs, that may not be part of the final report.[72] For example, in *United States v. Zanfordino*[73] the defendant requested disclosure of laboratory notes and materials used by FBI experts who reported on a footprint comparison. The trial court ruled that these materials came within Rule 16(a)(1)(C), which permits discovery of documents and tangible objects that are material to the preparation of the defense:

> A narrow view of Rule 16(a)(1)(C) is inappropriate; failure to provide reasonably available material that might be helpful to the defense and which does not pose any risks to witnesses or to ongoing investigation is contrary to requirements of due process and to the purposes of the Confrontation Clause. If an expert is testifying based in part on undisclosed sources of

---

7.24(1)(b); NEV. R. CRIM. P. § 174.235(2) (1987); WYO. R. CRIM. P. 18(a)(2) (discretionary on motion).

70. *E.g.*, CONN. GEN. STAT. ANN. § 54-86a (West Supp. 1992) (on motion; discretionary); DEL. SUPER. CT. R. CRIM. P. 16(a)(2) (on request); IOWA CODE ANN. § 813.2 R. 13(a)(b) (1979) (on motion; discretionary); KAN. STAT. ANN. § 22-3212(1)(b) (1981) (on request); LA. CODE CRIM. PROC. ANN. art. 719 (West 1981) (on motion; mandatory); MINN. R. CRIM. P. 9.01(1)(4) (on request); MONT. CODE ANN. § 46-15-302(3)(a) (1981) (on motion; discretionary); NEB. REV. STAT. § 29-1912(1)(e) (1989) (on motion); N.J. R. CRIM. P. 3:13-3(a)(4) (on request); N.Y. CRIM. PROC. LAW § 240.20(1)(c) (1982) (on request); N.C. GEN. STAT. § 15A-903(e) (1988) (on motion; mandatory); PA. R. CRIM. P. 305(B)(1)(e) (on request; mandatory); R.I. SUPER. CT. R. 16(a)(5) (on request); TEX. CRIM. PROC. CODE art. 39.14 (1979) (on motion; discretionary); VA. SUP. CT. R. 3A:11(b)(1)(ii) (on motion; mandatory); W. VA. CODE § 62-1B-2(2) (1989) (on motion; discretionary); WIS. STAT. ANN. § 971.23(5) (West 1985) (on motion; discretionary).

71. *E.g.*, Wing v. State, 490 P.2d 1376, 1382 (Okla. Crim. 1971) (scientific reports are discoverable), *cert. denied,* 406 U.S. 919 (1972).

72. *See* United States v. Armstrong, 517 U.S. 456, 463 (1996) ("We hold that Rule 16(a)(1)(C) authorizes defendants to examine Government documents material to the preparation of their defense against the Government's case-in-chief, but not to the preparation of selective-prosecution claims"); Price v. State, 269 Ga. 222, 223, 498 S.E.2d 262, 264 (1998) ("This Court and the court of appeals have previously refused to allow defendants access to such graphs and other data. Those cases, however, were interpreting the former criminal discovery provisions .... The current discovery rule regarding chemical testing in DUI cases ... is broader and grants defendants access to 'full information concerning the test.' Under this provision, the results generated by the use of the chromatograph are discoverable").

73. 833 F. Supp. 429 (S.D.N.Y. 1993).

information, cross-examination vouchsafed by that Clause would be unduly restricted.[74]

Similarly, in *United States v. Yee,*[75] a DNA case, the defense sought production of matching criteria, environmental insult studies, population data, and proficiency tests. The federal magistrate granted the motion based on Rule 16(1)(a)(C). He ruled that "predicate materials" were discoverable under this provision.[76] Other cases are in accord.[77] Numerous courts have recognized the need for pretrial discovery in DNA cases,[78] with several courts specifying extensive discovery.[79]

---

74. *Id.* at 432. *See also* § 3-7 *infra* (Inspection & Retesting).

75. 129 F.R.D. 629 (N.D. Ohio 1990).

76. *Id.* at 635. *See also* United States v. Iglesias, 881 F.2d 1519, 1527 (9th Cir. 1989) (dissenting opinion), *cert. denied,* 493 U.S. 1088 (1990). *See generally* Annot., *Books, Papers, and Documents Subject to Discovery by Defendant under Rule 16 of Federal Rules of Criminal Procedure,* 108 A.L.R. Fed. 381 (1992).

77. *E.g.,* United States v. Green, 144 F.R.D. 631, 639 (W.D.N.Y. 1992) (Rule 16 covers "not only all scientific reports but also all findings, scientific or technical data upon which such reports are based"); State v. Feldman, 254 N.J. Super. 754, 758-59, 604 A.2d 242, 244 (1992) (data base for Automated Fingerprint Information System (AFIS) and curriculum vitae of operator discoverable); State v. Cunningham, 108 N.C. App. 185, 195, 423 S.E.2d 802, 808 (1992) (like Fed. R. 16, the state discovery statute entitles "a criminal defendant to pretrial discovery of not only conclusory laboratory reports, but also of any tests performed or procedure utilized by chemist to reach such conclusions"; also includes bench notes and graphs). *But see* State v. Dykes, 252 Kan. 556, 561, 847 P.2d 1214, 1217-18 (Kan. 1993) (denial of request for the data base used to determine DNA match did not deny a fair trial; defense argued that accused's "substantial" Cherokee ancestry made this data important).

78. *See Ex parte* Perry, 586 So. 2d 242, 255 (Ala. 1991) (specifying extensive discovery for DNA cases); State v. Schwartz, 447 N.W.2d 422, 427 (Minn. 1989) ("[F]air trial and due process rights are implicated when data relied upon by a laboratory in performing tests are not available to the opposing party for review and cross examination").

79. People v. Castro, 144 Misc. 2d 956, 545 N.Y.S.2d 985 (Sup. Ct. 1989), recognized the need for extensive discovery: "The proponent, whether defense or prosecution, must give discovery to the adversary, which must include: 1) Copies of autorads, with the opportunity to examine the originals. 2) Copies of laboratory books. 3) Copies of quality control tests run on material utilized. 4) Copies of reports by the testing laboratory issued to proponent. 5) A written report by the testing laboratory setting forth the method used to declare a match or non-match, with actual size measurements, and mean or average size measurement, if applicable, together with standard deviation used. 6) A statement by the testing lab, setting forth the method used to calculate the allele frequency in the relevant population. 7) A copy of the data pool for each loci examined. 8) A certification by the testing lab that the same rule used to declare a match was used to determine the allele frequency in the population. 9) A statement setting forth observed contaminants, the reasons therefore, and tests performed to determine the origin and the results thereof. 10) If the sample is degraded, a statement setting forth the tests performed and the results thereof. 11) A statement setting forth any other observed defects or laboratory errors, the reasons therefore and the results thereof. 12) Chain of custody documents." *Id.* at 978-79, 545 N.Y.S.2d at 999.

A similar result was reached, but on constitutional grounds, in *People v. Davis*.[80] Lifecodes, a private DNA laboratory, refused to disclose the statistical data underlying a DNA probability estimate. The court reversed: "The rule is plain that where the prosecution is permitted to call a witness, expert or not, who testifies as to a fact in issue or a conclusion to be drawn, the defendant is entitled to examine the underlying data, the basis for the testimony' or else the defendant suffers undue prejudice."[81]

Laboratory Notes

Courts are divided over whether laboratory notes are discoverable. In the trial of Timothy Spencer, the first person executed based on DNA evidence,[82] the defense sought discovery of the prosecution expert's "work notes," which formed the basis of his report. The motion was denied, a ruling upheld by the Virginia Supreme Court.[83] This ruling is indefensible. The ABA Standards provide for the discovery of such notes[84] as do a number of jurisdictions.[85] According to one

---

See also State v. Charles, 617 So. 2d 895, 896 (La. 1993) ("(1) The State is directed to designate which of the three DNA test reports and results it intends to introduce at trial; (2) Should the State designate either of the first two DNA test reports and results received by the defense, the trial court's original *ex parte* order is reinstated, and the state is hereby ordered to provide to the defense the following documents and evidence required by the defendant's expert: (a) The computations which were performed in order to calculate the probability of a match; (b) The evidence on which the state's laboratory relied to reach the following two assumptions (i) that the genotypes in each system are in Hardy-Weinberg equilibrium proportions; and (ii) all four systems are independently distributed in the populations; (c) How the tables used by the laboratory were obtained in order to reach its conclusion that the genotypes in each system are in Hardy-Weinberg equilibrium proportions and all four systems are independently distributed in the population; (d) How many individuals were used to calculate the frequencies in each column of the tables and how those individuals can be characterized demographically; and (e) What evidence was used to reach a conclusion that a bin width of 1/8% is reasonable including a scientific explanation of just what was analyzed and how it was analyzed. (3) Should the State designate the last DNA report and results therefrom (received by defense counsel on April 6, 1993), the State is hereby ordered to produce for use by the defense experts all information, including but not limited to reports, summaries, documents, and written evidence of surveys and studies conducted which indicate the frequency of the alleles in each of the three races referred to in the report and the denominator for each frequency").

80. 196 A.D.2d 597, 601 N.Y.S.2d 174 (1993).

81. *Id.* at 175 (citations omitted).

82. *Murderer Put to Death in Virginia: First U.S. Execution Based on DNA Tests*, N.Y. TIMES, Apr. 28, 1994.

83. Spencer v. Commonwealth, 384 S.E.2d 785, 791 (Va. 1989).

84. 2 ABA STANDARDS FOR CRIMINAL JUSTICE 11-23 (1986 Supp.) ("Rough notes" may be discoverable where relevant "to an assessment (1) of the appropriateness of the testing methods selected, (2) of the competence of the tester, (3) of the care in the execution of the test, or (4) of some other factor bearing on the credibility of the expert's results").

court, "[f]undamental fairness and due process require that the defense be given the opportunity, prior to trial, to examine the basis from which an expert reaches his conclusion."[86]

§ 3-5. Summary of Expert Testimony.

To rectify some of the problems discussed above, Federal Rule 16 was amended in 1993 to require the government, upon defense request, to disclose a written summary of the testimony of the experts it intends to use during its case-in-chief. The summary must describe the witness's opinions, the bases and reasons for the opinions, and the witness's qualifications.[87] The amendment is intended to "expand federal criminal discovery" in order to "minimize surprise that often results from unexpected expert testimony, [to] reduce the need for continuances, and to provide the opponent with a fair opportunity to test the merit of the expert's testimony through focused cross-examination."[88] The prosecution is entitled to reciprocal discovery if the defense invokes this provision.[89] This rule supersedes the work-product rule[90] but does not apply to rebuttal experts.[91]

---

85. *See* People v. DaGata, 86 N.Y.2d 40, 44-45, 652 N.E.2d 932, 935, 629 N.Y.S.2d 186, 189 (1995) (The "10 pages of [DNA] notes used by the FBI in preparation of the report ... clearly fall within the statute as '[a]ny written report or document or portion thereof ... concerning a ... scientific test.' According to the record, the FBI had no problem with providing those notes but wanted a court order.... Moreover, the People specified no good reason to deny defendant access to the notes..."); People v. Slowe, 125 Misc. 2d 591, 591-92, 479 N.Y.S.2d 962, 963-64 (Co. Ct. 1984) (discovery includes lab notes and checklists formalized by protocol or routine).

86. State v. Burgess, 482 So. 2d 651, 653 (La. App. 1985). *See also* Rowe, CONVICTED BY JURIES, EXONERATED BY SCIENCE, *supra* note 15, at xvii-xviii (discussing the exoneration of 28 convicts through the use of DNA technology—some of whom had been sentenced to death; "It is also clear that in case after case, defense counsel failed to review the case notes of the prosecution's forensic serologists. Even a layperson would have seen the Fred Zain's written reports and sworn testimony were contradicted by his case notes. Again, one has to reflect on the likelihood that numerous innocent persons are presently incarcerated because of the inadequacy of their attorneys").

87. FED. R. CRIM. P. 16(a)(1)(E). The rule was amended in 1997 to clarify the prosecution and defense reciprocal discovery obligations, including obligations triggered by CRIM. R. 12.2 (notice of intent to introduce expert testimony concerning the accused's mental condition).

88. FED. R. CRIM. P. 16 advisory committee's note, *reprinted at* 147 F.R.D. at 473.

89. FED. R. CRIM. P. 16(b)(1)(C).

90. *See* United States v. Thompson, 923 F. Supp. 144, 145 (S.D. Ind. 1996) ("The language of Rule 16(a)(2) is clear — the dictates of paragraph (E) in subdivision (a)(1) take precedence over (a)(2)'s [work product] disclosure exemption"). *See* § 3-20 *infra* (work product).

91. *See* United States v. Richmond, 153 F.R.D. 7, 8 (D. Mass. 1994) ("The Rule, by its explicit terms, does not require disclosure of any experts to be called in rebuttal").

Application of the rule raises several issues. First, although the rule does not apply to lay witnesses,[92] the prosecution should not "subvert" this rule by offering expert opinion as lay opinion testimony.[93]

Second, the timeliness of disclosure may be problem. The drafters state that "[a]lthough no specific timing requirements are included, it is expected that the parties will make their requests and disclosures in a timely fashion."[94] In *United States v. Richmond*[95] the district court rejected the prosecution's offer to produce an expert summary three days before trial. The court noted that "it is hard to imagine a situation in which the government would not learn of the need for expert testimony until the trial is underway except as rebuttal testimony."[96] Moreover, the court stated that "disclosure three days before trial is absurd."[97] In cases where the prosecution's preparation has not reached the point where a summary can be prepared, the summary may be submitted subsequently – provided the defense receives it 45 days before trial.

A third issue concerns the following statement in the drafters' notes: "In some instances, a generic description of the likely witness and that witness's qualifications may be sufficient, *e.g.*, where a DEA laboratory chemist will testify, but it is not clear which particular chemist will be available."[98] One would

---

92. *See* United States v. Ortega, 150 F.3d 937, 943 (8th Cir. 1998) ("Special Agent Dillow and Trooper Banasik were listed on the government's witness list, not on its expert witness list, but they were allowed to testify both as fact witnesses and, over the defendant's objection, as experts with specialized knowledge of drug-relate activities. ... These complaints ring hollow in light of Ortega's failure even to request a continuance to allow him an opportunity to pursue these avenues"), *cert. denied,* 119 S. Ct. 837 (1999); United States v. Hicks, 103 F.3d 837, 841 (9th Cir. 1996) (Rule 16(a)(1)(E) does "not apply to witnesses who may offer lay opinion testimony or to summary witnesses who testify under Federal Rule of Evidence 1006"), *cert. denied,* 520 U.S. 1193 (1997); United States v. Hardwell, 80 F.3d 1471, 1495 (10th Cir.) ("Rule 16(a)(1)(E) requires disclosure of experts' opinions. It does not require disclosure of the opinions of lay witnesses"), *cert. denied,* 118 S. Ct. 1570 (1998); United States v. DiMarzo, 80 F.3d 656, 659 (1st Cir.) ("[Agent's] response expressed neither a lay *nor* an expert *opinion,* as distinguished from a statement of fact was to what [the agent] had witnessed during his 29 years in law enforcement"), *cert. denied,* 519 U.S. 904 (1996).

93. United States v. Figueroa-Lopez, 125 F.3d 1241, 1246 (9th Cir. 1997), *cert. denied,* 118 S. Ct. 1823 (1998).

94. 147 F.R.D. at 473.

95. 153 F.R.D. 7 (D. Mass. 1994).

96. *Id.* at 8.

97. *Id.*

98. 147 F.R.D. at 474-75. An earlier version of the amendment contained different language. It required "a written report prepared and *signed by the witness* that includes a complete statement of all opinions to be expressed and the basis and reasons therefor, the data or other information relied upon in forming such opinions, any exhibits to be used as a summary of or support for such opinions, and the qualifications of the witness." Weinstein, *Rule 702 of the Federal Rules of Evidence is Sound; It Should Not be Amended,* 138 F.R.D. 631, 635 (1992) (emphasis added).

hope that the "particular chemist" would be the one who performed the analysis, *i.e.*, has personal knowledge. Otherwise, confrontation problems may arise.[99]

A fourth issue relates to the scope of discovery under the rule. The drafters noted that the summary includes the bases of the expert's opinion, which "should cover not only written and oral reports, tests, reports, and investigations, but any information that might be recognized as a legitimate basis for an opinion under Federal Rules of Evidence 703, including opinions of other experts."[100] In *United States v. Jackson*[101] the Seventh Circuit held that a written summary concerning the drug courier profile met the minimum requirements ("barely") and cautioned: "[W]e strongly encourage the government to offer more specific descriptions of the opinions of the witnesses, foundations for their testimony, and their qualifications."[102]

Finally, in one case, *United States v. Crass*,[103] the defense asked whether expert testimony concerning the use of guns in the drug trade would be offered. The prosecution responded in the negative. At trial a prosecution expert testified about the street value of drugs. The First Circuit ruled that the "duty to disclose under Rule 16 is triggered by a proper request" and the expert "police testimony proffered by the government did not come within the pretrial motion submitted by the defense, because it directly related to the street value of the seized drugs and only indirectly to the purpose for which Crass kept the guns."[104] The lesson here is that the defense request should encompass *all* experts.

---

99. If a chemist without personal knowledge testifies, the basis of the testimony may violate FED. R. EVID. 703 (discussed in Chapter 5), which does not permit "summary" experts. If the expert is merely reading the laboratory report, hearsay and confrontation issues arise. *See* Chapter 6 (admissibility of lab reports).

100. 147 F.R.D. at 475.

101. 51 F.3d 646 (7th Cir. 1995). *See also* United States v. Yoon, 128 F.3d 515, 526 (7th Cir. 1997) ("These letters set forth Agent Wolverton's qualifications and experience in the area of suspected check-kiting.... Moreover, the government tendered to the defense copies of a transcript from an unrelated trial in which Agent Wolverton had previously testified as to the methodology and the bases he uses for analyzing check-kiting").

102. *Id.* at 651. *See also* United States v. Price, 75 F.3d 1440, 1445-46 (10th Cir.) ("Price was certainly entitled to witness, including expert witness, information under amended rule 16(a)(1)(E)"), *cert. denied*, 517 U.S. 1239 (1996); United States v. Basinger, 60 F.3d 1400, 1407 (9th Cir. 1995) (citing Rule 16(a)(1)(E), the court stated that it "will only reverse a conviction because of a discovery violation if the district court abused its discretion and that error resulted in prejudice to the defendant's substantial rights").

103. 50 F.3d 81 (1st Cir. 1995).

104. *Id.* at 83.

§ 3-6. Witness Lists.

A number of jurisdictions require the prosecution to provide the defense with the names of the witnesses it intends to call at trial.[105] These provisions extend to expert witnesses. Unfortunately, they may not require that a witness be designated as an expert,[106] a practice that greatly undermines the value of such a list.

In other jurisdictions defense discovery does not include the right to a witness list. Federal Rule 16 is an example.[107] However, the 1993 "summary" rule, in effect, provides for notice with respect to experts.[108]

If a scientific report is prepared in a "no witness list" jurisdiction, the defense can anticipate that the expert who prepared the report will be a witness. If, however, a report is not prepared, the defense may have no notice that an expert will testify for the prosecution at trial and thus may be unprepared to challenge the testimony.[109] For example, in the Wayne Williams trial the prosecution had an expert from the Royal Canadian Mounted Police analyze hairs and fibers, which played a prominent role in the case.[110] The expert examined samples for eleven days and then testified from personal notes. He did not, however, prepare a report of his analysis. The Georgia Supreme Court ruled that the failure to prepare a report was not error; under the state discovery provisions, scientific reports were discoverable only if they existed.[111]

---

105. *E.g.*, ALASKA R. CRIM. P. 16(b)(1)(i); COLO. R. CRIM. P. 16I (a)(1)(V); FLA. R. CRIM. P. 3.220(b)(1)(i); MINN. R. CRIM. P. 9.01(I)(1)(a).

106. *See* Knoedler v. State, 69 Md. App. 764, 768-69, 519 A.2d 811, 812-13 (Spec. App. 1987) (state need not categorize proposed witness as an expert); State v. Caulder, 75 Or. App. 457, 458-60, 706 P.2d 1007, 1008-09 (state need not disclose that witness will testify as an expert), *rev. denied,* 300 Or. 451, 712 P.2d 110 (1985).

107. *E.g.*, United States v. Holland, 884 F.2d 354, 357 (8th Cir. 1989) (Rule 16 does not require disclosure of prospective witnesses, including experts), *cert. denied,* 493 U.S. 997 (1989); United States v. Taylor, 707 F. Supp. 696, 702-03 (S.D.N.Y. 1989) (witness list, including expert witnesses, not discoverable). In 1974 Congress rejected a provision that would require the disclosure of witness lists. *See* 2 W. LAFAVE & J. ISRAEL, *supra* note 6, at 493.

108. *See* § 3-5 *supra.*

109. *See also* § 3-3 *supra.*

110. *See* Williams v. State, 251 Ga. 749, 755, 312 S.E.2d 40, 99-100 (1983) (Smith, J., dissenting).

111. *Id.* at 754, 312 S.E.2d at 50. *See also* Stewart v. Commonwealth, 245 Va. 222, 230, 427 S.E.2d 394, 400 (There is no constitutional right to "a list of [state] expert witnesses, statements of their qualifications, and a description of their expected testimony and copies of any reports prepared by those experts"), *cert. denied,* 510 U.S. 848 (1993); Law v. State, 251 Ga. 525, 528, 307 S.E.2d 904, 906 (1983).

§ 3-7. Inspection & Retesting.

Many jurisdictions provide for defense inspection of documents and tangible objects. Both the ABA Standards[112] and Uniform Rules[113] contain comparable provisions. The commentary to the original ABA Standards states: "Materials discoverable under this standard include: movies, weapons, bullets, footprint impressions obtained by use of plaster and the like, articles of clothing, materials found at the scene of the offense (such as narcotics, paint scrapings, hair, tools, or other equipment), receipts, financial records, charts, diagrams and other visual aids."[114]

Federal Rule 16

In federal trials, Criminal Rule 16(a)(1)(C) governs defense inspection of tangible objects.[115] This provision covers all tangible objects in the possession, custody, or control of the government which (1) are material to the preparation of the defense, (2) are intended for use by the prosecution as evidence in chief at trial, or (3) were obtained from or belong to the defendant.[116] The 1975 amendments made inspection mandatory, rather than discretionary, and deleted a requirement that the request be "reasonable." As with scientific reports, there is a continuing duty to disclose[117] and sanctions for violations of the rule rest within the trial court's discretion.[118] If a defense request for discovery is made pursuant to Rule 16, the prosecution is entitled to inspect tangible objects that the defendant intends to introduce as evidence in chief at trial.[119]

---

112. ABA STANDARDS 11-2.1(a)(v), *supra* note 16, ("Any tangible objects, including books, papers, documents, photographs, buildings, places, or other objects which pertain to the case or which were obtained for or belong to the defendant").

113. UNIF. R. CRIM. P. 421(a) (Approved Draft 1974) ("[T]he prosecuting attorney shall allow the defendant at any reasonable time and in any reasonable manner to inspect, photograph, copy, or have reasonable tests made"). *See also* NATIONAL ADVISORY COMMISSION ON CRIMINAL JUSTICE STANDARDS AND GOALS, COURTS, STANDARD 4.9(4) (1973).

114. ABA STANDARDS RELATING TO DISCOVERY, *supra* note 1, at 69.

115. *See generally* 8 MOORE'S FEDERAL PRACTICE § 16.05[4] (1992); 2 C. WRIGHT, *supra* note 2, § 254; Burns, *Pretrial Discovery in the Federal Courts, in* 1 CRIMINAL DEFENSE TECHNIQUES ch. 10 (S. Allen, I. Rosen, E. Smolinsky & D. Winston eds. 1992).

116. *See* United States v. Buchanan, 585 F.2d 100, 101 (5th Cir. 1978) (handwriting exemplars); United States v. Gordon, 580 F.2d 827, 836-37 (5th Cir. 1978) (product of experiment), *cert. denied,* 439 U.S. 1079 (1979); Government of Virgin Islands v. Testamark, 570 F.2d 1162, 1164-65 (3d Cir. 1978) (blood sample); United States v. Reid, 43 F.R.D. 520, 521 (N.D. Ill. 1967) (drugs); United States v. Lloyd, 992 F.2d 348, 351 (D.C. Cir. 1993) ("This materiality standard normally 'is not a heavy burden,' ... ; rather, evidence is material as long as there is a strong indication that it will 'play an important role in uncovering admissible evidence, aiding witness preparation, corroborating testimony, or assisting impeachment or rebuttal'").

117. *See* § 3-18 *infra.*

118. *See* § 3-19 *infra.*

119. *See* § 3-15 *infra*

Although Rule 16 does not explicitly provide for testing or retesting of physical evidence, the courts have interpreted the rule to include this right. For example, the Fifth Circuit has observed: "In cases involving a controlled substance, courts have held a concomitant part of the examination or inspection to be the right of the accused to have an independent chemical analysis performed on the seized substance."[120] The right to retest encompasses substances subjected to neutron activation analysis.[121] There is little question that the same rule applies to DNA evidence[122] as well as other techniques.[123] Indeed, in one case the trial court required the prosecution to make government laboratory facilities available for retesting by defense expert.[124]

---

120. United States v. Gaultney, 606 F.2d 540, 545 (5th Cir. 1979), *rev'd on other grounds sub nom.* Steagald v. United States, 451 U.S. 204 (1981). *Accord* United States v. Dukes, 139 F.3d 469, 477 (5th Cir. 1998) ("The Government does not dispute Dukes's right to inspect and test the evidence pursuant to FED. R. CRIM. P 16(a)(1)(C). Rather, it contends that Dukes could have had the cocaine base tested had he complied with the DEA procedures for doing so"); United States v. Butler, 988 F.2d 537, 543 (5th Cir.) ("Because the substance alleged to be cocaine base was obtained from Butler and because the government intended to use the substance as evidence at trial, ... the [trial] court erred in refusing to grant appellant's motion to test a sample of the substance"), *cert. denied*, 510 U.S. 956 (1993); United States v. Vaughn, 736 F.2d 665, 666 (11th Cir. 1984) ("Defendants could have obtained their own analysis of the [cocaine] samples"); United States v. Sullivan, 578 F.2d 121, 124 (5th Cir. 1978) (right of inspection "includes the right to have an expert examine the narcotics before trial"); United States v. Pollack, 402 F. Supp. 1310, 1312 (D. Mass. 1975); United States v. Mastrobuono, 271 F. Supp. 197, 197 (S.D.N.Y. 1967); United States v. Acarino, 270 F. Supp. 526, 528 (E.D.N.Y. 1967); United States v. Bentvena, 193 F. Supp. 485, 498 (S.D.N.Y. 1960); United States v. Lopez, 26 F.R.D.174 (S.D.N.Y. 1960); United States v. Taylor, 25 F.R.D. 225, 226 (E.D.N.Y. 1960); United States v. Tirado, 25 F.R.D. 270, 272 (S.D.N.Y. 1958).

121. *See* United States v. Stifel, 433 F.2d 431, 441 (6th Cir. 1970) ("[I]f the government sees fit to use this time-consuming, expensive means of factfinding, it must both allow time for a defendant to make similar tests, and in the instance of an indigent defendant, a means to provide for payment for same"), *cert. denied,* 401 U.S. 994 (1971); United States v. Kelly, 420 F.2d 26, 29 (2d Cir. 1969) (a "fair opportunity for the defense to run its own neutron activation tests of the material" must be provided).

122. *See* NATIONAL RESEARCH COUNCIL, DNA TECHNOLOGY IN FORENSIC SCIENCE 146 (1992) ("The prosecutor has a strong responsibility to reveal fully to defense counsel and experts retained by the defendant all material that might be necessary in evaluating the evidence").

123. *See also* United States v. Hrubik, 280 F. Supp. 481, 481 (D. Alaska 1968) (motion to retest water sample granted).

124. United States v. Bockius, 564 F.2d 1193, 1196 (5th Cir. 1977).

Supervision of Retesting

The court, of course, may impose reasonable safeguards on such retesting.[125] The Rhode Island Supreme Court has provided the following guidelines for retesting:

> A defendant who desires to analyze an article or substance should file a motion setting forth the circumstances of the proposed analysis, the identity of the expert who will conduct such analysis, his qualifications, and scientific background. The court may then, in its discretion, provide for appropriate safeguards, including, where necessary, the performance of such tests at the state laboratory under the supervision of the state's analyst.[126]

In *Prince v. Superior Court*[127] the trial judge ordered that a DNA sample be divided between the prosecution and defense for testing and that a representative of the state be present at the defense testing. The appellate court reversed, holding such an order violated the defendant's right to effective assistance of counsel.

State Jurisdictions

Like provisions for the discovery of scientific reports, state provisions governing the inspection of tangible objects vary widely. Some states follow the current Federal Rule 16,[128] while others follow the ABA Standards,[129] the 1966 version of Federal Rule 16,[130] or common-law precedents. Several state provisions explicitly provide for the retesting of physical evidence,[131] and other courts have interpreted their inspection provisions to include this right.[132] A New

---

125. *See* United States v. Dukes, 139 F.3d 469, 477 (5th Cir.) ("The Government does not dispute Dukes's right to inspect and test the evidence pursuant to FED. R. CRIM. P. 16(a)(1)(C). Rather, it contends that Dukes could have had the cocaine base tested had he complied with the DEA procedures for doing so"), *cert. denied,* 119 S. Ct. 215 (1998).

126. State v. Faraone, 425 A.2d 523, 526 (R.I. 1981).

127. 8 Cal. App. 4th 1176, 1179, 10 Cal. Rptr. 2d 855, 857 (1992).

128. *See* note 66 *supra.*

129. *See* note 67 *supra.*

130. Discovery under the 1966 version of Rule 16 was discretionary upon a motion to the court. It also required that a request for inspection be "reasonable" and "material."

131. *E.g.,* IOWA CODE ANN. § 813.2, R. 13(2)(b)(1) (1979); LA. CODE CRIM. P. art. 718 (West 1981); N.C. GEN. STAT. § 15A-903(e) (1983); OHIO REV. CODE ANN. § 2925.51(E) (Baldwin 1991) (drug cases); WIS. STAT. ANN. § 971.23(5) (West 1985). *See also* UNIF. R. CRIM. P. 421(a) (Approved Draft 1974).

132. *E.g.,* James v. Commonwealth, 482 S.W.2d 92, 94 (Ky. 1972); State v. Migliore, 261 La. 722, 737, 260 So. 2d 682, 688 (1972); State v. Cloutier, 302 A.2d 84, 89 (Me. 1973); People v. White, 40 N.Y.2d 797, 798, 358 N.E.2d 1031, 1032, 390 N.Y.S.2d 405, 406 (1976); People v. Green, 123 Misc. 2d 648, 657, 474 N.Y.S.2d 171, 173-74 (1984) (hazardous waste); State v. Gaddis, 530 S.W.2d 64, 69 (Tenn. 1975); Terrell v. State, 521 S.W.2d 618, 618 (Tex. Crim. App.

York statute establishes a procedure under which a defendant may petition the court to order DNA testing in certain circumstances.[133]

Constitutional Right to Retest

In addition to discovery provisions, the right to retest physical evidence is supported by constitutional principles. In one case a defendant's request for inspection of a murder weapon and bullet was denied by a state court. The Fifth Circuit granted habeas relief. According to the court, "[f]undamental fairness is violated when a criminal defendant ... is denied the opportunity to have an expert of his choosing, bound by appropriate safeguards imposed by the Court, examine a piece of critical evidence whose nature is subject to varying expert opinion."[134]

In rejecting a due process right to retest, several courts have reasoned that the defendant's opportunity to cross-examine the prosecution's expert witnesses provides sufficient protection for an accused.[135] As explained in Chapter 4, this rationale is not persuasive.[136] There is a significant difference between attacking the opinion of an opponent's expert through cross-examination and attacking that opinion through the testimony of a defense expert, and mistakes, even with

---

1975). *See also* Annot., *Right of Accused in State Courts to Have Expert Inspect, Examine, or Test Physical Evidence in Possession of Prosecution — Modern Cases*, 27 A.L.R.4TH 1188 (1984).

133. N.Y. Crim. Pro. § 440.301(1-a). *See also* People v. Chichester, 162 Misc. 2d 658, 659, 618 N.Y.S.2d 201, 202 (Cty. Ct. 1994) (convicted defendant has right to use DNA testing, at his own expense, on physical evidence that is in the possession of the prosecutor's office).

134. Barnard v. Henderson, 514 F.2d 744, 746 (5th Cir. 1975). *Accord* White v. Maggio, 556 F. 2d 1352, 1357 (5th Cir. 1977); Gayle v. State, 591 So. 2d 153, 154-55 (Ala. Crim. App. 1991) (due process and state discovery rule recognize right to retest); Warren v. State, 292 Ala. 71, 75, 288 So. 2d 826, 830 (1973); McNutt v. Superior Court, 133 Ariz. 7, 9, 648 P.2d 122, 124 (1982); People v. Backus, 23 Cal. 3d 360, 384, 590 P.2d 837, 851, 152 Cal. Rptr. 710, 724 (1979); Sabel v. State, 248 Ga. 10, 17, 282 S.E.2d 61, 68 (1981); Patterson v. State, 238 Ga. 204, 206, 232 S.E.2d 233, 234, *cert. denied,* 431 U.S. 970 (1977); Jackson v. State, 243 So. 2d 396, 398 (Miss. 1970); State v. Hanson, 278 N.W.2d 198, 200 (S.D. 1979); State v. Adkins, 280 S.E.2d 293, 295-96 (W. Va. 1981); State v. McArdle, 194 S.E.2d 174, 178-79 (W. Va. 1973). *See also* Gray v. Rowley, 604 F.2d 382, 384 (5th Cir. 1979) (evidence not "critical"), *cert. denied,* 445 U.S. 944 (1977); State v. Koennecke, 274 Or. 169, 179, 545 P.2d 127, 133 (1976) (right to retest conditioned on preliminary showing that results will be favorable to defendant); State v. Faraone, 425 A.2d 523, 526 (R.I. 1981); Montoya, *A Theory of Compulsory Process Clause Discovery Rights* 70 IND. L. J. 845, 880-84 (1995).

135. *See* Frias v. State, 547 N.E.2d 809, 813 (Ind. 1989), *cert. denied,* 495 U.S. 921 (1990); People v. Anderson, 88 Mich. App. 513, 516-17, 276 N.W.2d 924, 926 (1979); People v. Bell, 74 Mich. App. 270, 275, 253 N.W.2d 726, 729 (1977); Commonwealth v. Dorsey, 266 Pa. Super. 442, 451-52, 405 A.2d 516, 521 (1979).

136. *See* § 4-5(E) *infra.*

commonplace techniques such as fingerprint and firearms identification, have occurred.[137]

In *State v. Pulaski County Circuit Court*[138] the Arkansas Supreme Court ruled that a trial court lacks the authority, constitutional or otherwise, to compel the prosecution to submit blood, hair, and saliva samples to the FBI for DNA testing. The court did not, however, consider whether the defense could move for the appointment of a defense expert to conduct the DNA tests.

Right to Have Expert Present at Test

In some cases the defense may request to have a defense expert present during the prosecution testing. For example, in *People v. Monagas*,[139] the defendant moved for an order to permit its expert to be present when the FBI performed DNA testing. The court denied the motion. As a practical matter, the FBI "indicated that it would refuse to allow unauthorized personnel into its laboratory. The laboratory operates under a strict security system which precludes the presence of outsiders without clearance, and any breach of that security would compromise the laboratory's effectiveness with respect to hundreds of cases. The entire testing process will take three to four months...."[140]

This tactic may backfire, however. What is the expert's role here? If the defense expert is present and does not object to the testing procedures, the prosecution can use the defense expert's silence as an imprimatur for the test results — whether the defense expert testifies or not. If the defense expert criticizes the testing at trial, the prosecution can ask on cross-examination why the expert did not object at the time of the testing? Here, the prosecutor could argue that, had the defense expert been interested in valid test results, the expert would have raised such concerns during the test. This is similar to the problem that defense attorneys face when they represent a client at a lineup — *i.e.*, whether defense counsel waives any objection by not asserting it at the lineup.[141]

§ 3-8. Consumptive Testing.

A related issue concerns the defendant's right to have a defense expert present when the government conducts scientific tests which consume evidence and thus

---

137. *See* Giannelli, *Criminal Discovery, Scientific Evidence, and DNA*, 44 VAND. L. REV. 791, 816-19 (1991).

138. 316 Ark. 514, 872 S.W.2d 414 (1994) (per curiam).

139. 161 Misc. 2d 898, 615 N.Y.S.2d 633 (Sup. Ct. 1994).

140. *Id.* at 899-900, 615 N.Y.S.2d at 634.

141. *See* 1 W. LAFAVE & J. ISRAEL, CRIMINAL PROCEDURE § 7.3(c), at 576 (1984); Gilligan, *Eyewitness Identification*, 58 MIL. R. REV. 183, 201 (1972); Panel Discussion, *The Role of the Defense Lawyer at a Line-up in Light of the Wade, Gilbert and Stovall Decisions*, 4 CRIM. L. BULL. 273, 290 (1968).

make retesting impossible. This right is recognized by statute in a few jurisdictions,[142] and several courts have commented that such a practice is the preferred procedure.[143]

In addition, this procedure may be constitutionally required under certain circumstances.[144] For example, the Colorado Supreme Court in commenting on the due process issues raised by destructive testing has written: "[I]t may be incumbent on the state to contact the defendant to determine whether he wishes his expert to be present during the tests."[145] In a later case, *People v. Garries,*[146] the Court suppressed bloodstain evidence because it was destroyed in testing. The state had neither photographed the test results nor provided the defense with the opportunity to have its own expert present during analysis.[147]

As *Garries* indicates, there may be other ways to satisfy due process in this context—in lieu of the presence of defense experts. In *State v. Thomas*[148] the West Virginia Supreme Court ruled that if the prosecution conducts complicated tests (electrophoretic blood test) that consume all the tested substance, the state must "preserve as much documentation of the test as is reasonably possible to allow for a full and fair examination of the results by a defendant and his experts."[149]

A Colorado statute specifies the factors that a court should consider in determining whether the results of a laboratory test should be admitted when a sufficient quantity of the tested substance cannot be preserved for independent testing. These factors include, among other things, whether other testing methods

142. *See* OHIO REV. CODE ANN. § 2925.51(E) (Baldwin 1991) (drug cases). *See also* UNIF. R. CRIM. P. 421(a) (Approved Draft 1974); ABA STANDARDS 11-3.2.(a), *supra* note 15 (party must notify the opponent if it intends to destroy any object).

143. *See* United States v. Bridges, 499 F.2d 179, 185 (7th Cir. 1974); United States v. Love, 482 F.2d 213, 220 (5th Cir.), *cert. denied,* 414 U.S. 1026 (1973); State v. Herrera, 365 So. 2d 399, 401 (Fla. App. 1979), *cert. denied,* 373 So. 2d 459 (Fla. 1979); State v. Carlson, 267 N.W.2d 170, 175 n.4 (Minn. 1978).

144. *See also* Commonwealth v. Gliniewicz, 398 Mass. 744, 749, 500 N.E.2d 1324, 1327 (1986) ("[T]he defendants received no notice of the impending tests, and thus were not able to have their own expert present to observe and potentially to refute the subjective aspects of the [blood test]"); State v. Gaddis, 530 S.W.2d 64, 69 (Tenn. 1975) ("When such a situation arises, good faith demands that no test or analysis be made except by agreement between the District Attorney and defense counsel, or until such time as defense counsel may arrange to have his own expert present at the test"); State v. Wright, 87 Wash. 2d 783, 793, 557 P.2d 1, 7 (1976) ("[B]efore any testing or disposition of evidence occurs, the defendant should be given notice of the type of evidence involved and its planned disposition").

145. People v. Gomez, 198 Colo. 105, 112, 596 P.2d 1192, 1197 (1979) (heroin), *cert. denied,* 455 U.S. 943 (1982).

146. 645 P.2d 1306 (Colo. 1982).

147. *Id.* at 1309-10.

148. 187 W. Va. 686, 421 S.E.2d 227 (W. Va. 1992).

149. *Id.* at 688, 421 S.E.2d at 229.

were available, whether used test samples should have been preserved, whether quantitative testing was necessary, and whether it would have been reasonable to contact the defendant to determine if he wanted an expert present during the test.[150]

The tactics of requesting the presence of a defense expert are discussed in the previous section.

Consumptive Testing by the Defense

In *State v. Cosey*,[151] the defense exhausted, during DNA testing, the remaining testable semen specimen that had been obtained from the crime scene. This precluded the prosecution from performing additional, more sophisticated DNA testing similar to that performed by the defense. The defendant neither intended to use the DNA tests at trial nor call the analyst as a witness. The Louisiana Supreme Court ruled that "fundamental fairness and the extraordinary circumstances presented by this case dictate that the prosecution be allowed to obtain copies of the test results in question."[152]

§ 3-9. Depositions.

A majority of jurisdictions do not permit discovery depositions in criminal cases. Instead, criminal depositions generally are limited to preserving the testimony of a witness who may be unavailable for trial.[153] Several jurisdictions,[154] however, do permit discovery depositions,[155] and these

---

150. COLO. REV. STAT. § 16-3-309 (1986).

151. 652 So. 2d 993 (La. 1995) (per curiam).

152. *Id.* at 994.

153. *E.g.*, FED. R. CRIM. P. 15(a); COLO. R. CRIM. P. 15(a); IDAHO R. CRIM. P. 15; WYO. R. CRIM. P. 17(a). *See generally* 2 W. LAFAVE & J. ISRAEL, *supra* note 6, § 19.3(k); 8 MOORE'S FEDERAL PRACTICE ch. 15 (1983); 2 C. WRIGHT, *supra* note 2, §§ 241-45.

154. ALASKA R. CRIM. P. 15(a) (either party may file a motion for discovery deposition); ARIZ. R. CRIM. P. 15.3(a)(2) (either party may file a motion for deposition upon showing that it is "material to the case or necessary adequately to prepare a defense or investigate the offense"); FLA. R. CRIM. P. 3.220(h) (defendant may depose witnesses; court approval not required); IND. CODE ANN. § 35-37-4-3 (West 1986) (either side may depose witness; court approval not required); IOWA CODE ANN. § 813.2, R. 12(1), (3) (West Supp. 1983) (defendant may depose witness for discovery); MO. R. CRIM. P. 25.12 (defendant may depose witness; court approval not required); NEB. REV. STAT. § 29-1917 (1989) (either party in felony case may file deposition motion); N.H. REV. STAT. ANN. §517:13 (II) (Supp. 1991) (court discretion); TEX. CODE CRIM. PROC. art. 39.02 (1979) (defendant may depose witnesses upon showing of good reason); VT. R. CRIM. P. 15(a) (either party may depose witnesses; court approval not required); WASH. SUPER. CT. R. 4.6(a) (parties may depose witness who refuses to discuss case). *See also* UNIF. R. CRIM. P. 431(a)(2) (Approved Draft 1974).

155. *See generally* Hill, *Pretrial Discovery of Prosecution Witnesses in State Courts*, *in* 1A CRIMINAL DEFENSE TECHNIQUES § 11.04 (S. Allen, I. Rosen, E. Smolinsky, & D. Winston eds.

provisions would apply to experts.[156] Moreover, Federal Evidence Rule 706(a), which has been adopted in many jurisdictions, provides for the deposition of court-appointed experts.[157]

Several Ohio decisions recognize the right to depose prosecution experts, even though Ohio Criminal Rule 15 apparently limits depositions to the preservation of testimony. For example, the Ohio Supreme Court has written: "In Ohio, it is not questioned that through pretrial discovery under Crim. R. 16 the defense may obtain the name of the individual responsible for conducting the calibration test [of the breathalyzer], and determine through deposition under Crim. R. 15 whether such an individual utilized the proper methods in calibrating the machine."[158] In addition, the Maine Supreme Court has allowed interrogatories of a prosecution expert.[159]

§ 3-10. Examination of Alleged Victim.

Several cases discuss a defendant's right to an involuntary physical or psychological examination of alleged rape or child abuse victims.

Physical Examinations

Courts have adopted several approaches to physical examinations.[160] Some courts recognize a due process right to such an examination.[161] Others allow an examination if the defendant can demonstrate a compelling need. For example, the New Jersey Supreme Court recognized a trial court's inherent power to order a physical examination but only when there is a substantial need:

1992); Langrock, *Vermont's Experiment in Criminal Discovery*, 53 A.B.A.J. 732 (1967); Note, *Discovery Depositions: A Proposed Right for Criminal Defendants*, 51 S. CAL. L. REV. 467 (1978).

156. *E.g.*, Ford v. Commonwealth, 665 S.W.2d 304, 310 (Ky. 1983) ("lengthy pre-trial deposition" of forensic serologist).

157. For a discussion of court-appointed experts, *see* § 4-8 *infra*.

158. State v. Walker, 53 Ohio St. 2d 192, 197, 374 N.E.2d 132, 135 (1978). *Accord* State v. Spikes, 67 Ohio St. 2d 405, 411, 423 N.E.2d 1122, 1128 (1981) (Rule 15 permits deposition of preparers of hospital report); State v. Cross, 48 Ohio App. 2d 357, 360, 357 N.E.2d 1103, 1105-06 (1975) (chemist may be deposed).

159. State v. Rolls, 389 A.2d 824, 828 n.4 (Me. 1978) (enzyme blood analysis). *See also* United States v. Sanchez-Galvez, 33 F.3d 829, 833 (7th Cir. 1994) (defendants deposed a DEA agent who testified about drug transactions).

160. *See* Montoya, *A Theory of Compulsory Process Clause Discovery Rights*, 70 IND. L. J. 845, 884-88 (1995); Comment, *A Fourth Amendment Approach to Compulsory Physical Examinations of Sex Offense Victims*, 57 U. CHI. L. REV. 873 (1990).

161. "In these circumstances and limited to the facts of this case, we hold that appellant, as a matter of due process and fairness, was entitled at least to have the alleged victim examined by an independent gynecologist in preparation for trial." Turner v. Commonwealth, 767 S.W.2d 557, 559 (Ky. 1988), *cert. denied*, 493 U.S. 901 (1989).

> Courts may order the physical examination of a child sex-abuse victim only when satisfied that the defendant has made a sufficient showing that such an examination can produce competent evidence that has substantial probative worth, and if admitted and believed by the trier of fact, that evidence could refute or neutralize incriminating evidence or impugn the credibility of prosecution witnesses. Further, the court must be satisfied that the defendant's need clearly outweighs the possible harmful consequences to the alleged victim.[162]

Still other courts refuse to recognize such a right under any conditions because the "order requiring complainant to submit to a physical examination was clearly outside the scope of discovery authorized by the statute [and thus] the judge had no authority to issue that order and it is void."[163]

In a different context, a Florida appellate court ruled that a prosecution witness could not be compelled to produce fingerprint and hair samples to support defendant's claim that the witness tampered with the crime scene before the police arrived.[164]

Psychological Examinations

A similar diversity of opinion exists concerning involuntary psychological or psychiatric examinations.[165] Some courts hold that trial courts lack authority to order such examinations.[166] Others use a "substantial need" test.[167] Defendants

---

162. State v. D.R.H., 127 N.J. 249, 604 A.2d 89, 95 (1992). *Accord* People v. Chard, 808 P.2d 351, 353-54 (Colo. 1991), *cert. denied,* 502 U.S. 863 (1991).

163. *E.g.,* State *ex rel.* Wade v. Stephens, 724 S.W.2d 141, 144-45 (Tex. Crim. App. 1987).

164. Burlett v. Hamwi, 626 So. 2d 1040 (Fla. Ct. App. 1993).

165. *See* Annot., *Necessity or Permissibility of Mental Examination to Determine Competency or Credibility of Complainant in Sexual Offense Prosecutions,* 45 A.L.R.4TH 310 (1986).

166. State v. Gabrielson, 464 N.W.2d 434, 436 (Iowa 1990). In State v. Horn, 337 N.C. 449, 543-54, 446 S.E.2d 52, 53-54 (1994), the N.C. Supreme Court ruled that a trial court lacks authority to compel an unwilling witness to submit to a psychiatric examination. The Court, however, did note that the trial court has other alternatives: (1) appointment of a defense mental health expert to review findings of psychological evaluations already performed on the victim; (2) preclude admission of prosecution's psychological evidence; and (3) dismissal of the case.

167. Government of Virgin Islands v. Leonard A., 922 F.2d 1141, 1143-44 (3d Cir. 1991); State v. R.W., 104 N.J. 14, 21, 514 A.2d 1287, 1291 (1986); State v. Redd, 642 A.2d 829, 835 (Del. Super. 1993) (The "'substantial need' criterion is an amplification of, and is not inconsistent with, Delaware's 'compelling' reasons standard"); State v. Camejo, 641 So. 2d 109, 113 (Fla. App. 1994) (per curiam) ("Florida law accords with the majority rule in other jurisdictions that trial courts have the inherent power to order psychological examinations.... [C]redibility may be a reason to order such an examination, but only if *there is strong and compelling evidence*"), *approved,* 660 So. 2d 242 (Fla. 1995); Keeney v. State, 109 Nev. 220, 226, 850 P.2d 311, 315 (1993) ("it would be error to preclude a defendant from having an alleged child-victim examined by an expert in psychiatry or psychology if: (1) the State has employed such an expert; (2) the victim is not shown by compelling reasons to be in need of protection; (3) evidence of the crime has little or no corroboration beyond

have challenged a refusal to order an examination on constitutional grounds. The Ninth Circuit, however, has ruled that a trial court's refusal to order a psychiatric examination of two young sexual assault victims to determine whether they exhibited signs of Rape Trauma Syndrome did not violate due process.[168]

A different issue may be presented if the state uses an expert. The Nevada Supreme Court has held: "Unless competent evidence presents a compelling reason to protect the victim, it is error to deny a defendant the assistance of a defense psychologist or psychiatrist to examine the child-victim and testify at trial when the State is provided such assistance."[169] Basing its decision on due process, the Illinois Supreme Court has held that "unless the victim consents to an examination by an expert chosen by the defendant, the State may not introduce testimony from an *examining* expert that the victim of an alleged sexual assault suffers from a 'recognized and accepted form of post-traumatic stress syndrome.'"[170]

§ 3-11. Subpoenas; Right of Access.

The Sixth Amendment provides: "In all criminal prosecutions, the accused shall enjoy the right ... to have compulsory process for obtaining witnesses in his favor." Criminal Rule 17 implements this right. Subpoenas are typically used where evidence is in the control of a third party and thus beyond most discovery rules.

In addition the Compulsory Process Clause, there is a due process right of access. *Pennsylvania v. Ritchie*[171] involved a defendant's right of access to confidential files. Ritchie was charged with raping and sexually abusing his daughter. The case was initially referred to the state youth services agency (CYS). Prior to trial, Ritchie attempted to subpoena the agency's records. CYS claimed the records were privileged under state law, and the trial court refused to

---

the testimony of the victim; and (4) there is a reasonable basis for believing that the victim's mental or emotional state may have affected his or her veracity"). *See also* Griego v. State, 111 Nev. 444, 893 P.2d 995, 999 (1995) (applying *Keeney* factors).

168. Gilpin v. McCormick, 921 F.2d 928, 931 (9th Cir. 1990).

169. Lickey v. State, 827 P.2d 824, 826 (Nev. 1992).

170. People v. Wheeler, 151 Ill.2d 298, 312, 602 N.E.2d 826, 833 (1992). *See also* State v. Maday, 507 N.W.2d 365, 372 (Wis. App. 1993) ("When the state manifests an intent during its case-in-chief to present testimony of one or more experts, who have personally examined a victim of an alleged sexual assault, and will testify that the victim's behavior is consistent with the behaviors of other victims of sexual assault, a defendant may request a psychological examination of the victim"), *rev. dismissed,* 510 N.W.2d 139 (Wis. 1993); State v. Schaller, 199 Wis. 2d 23, 34, 544 N.W.2d 247, 252 (App. 1995) (*Maday* distinguished; prosecution witnesses here did not examine the alleged victim but simply described characteristics of battered women), *rev. denied,* 546 N.W.2d 469 (Wis. 1996).

171. 480 U.S. 39 (1987).

order disclosure.[172] The Supreme Court preferred to evaluate Ritchie's claim under a due process, rather than a compulsory process, analysis. Due process requires the prosecution to turn over evidence in its possession that is both favorable to the accused and material to guilt or punishment. Citing the *Brady* rule,[173] the plurality wrote: "Evidence is material only if there is a reasonable probability that, had the evidence been disclosed to the defense, the result of the proceeding would have been different."[174] Although the state's interest in confidentiality is strong, this interest does not necessarily mean that disclosure should be precluded in all circumstances. If material to a criminal defendant's defense, the records should be disclosed. Consequently, the case was remanded: "Ritchie is entitled to have the CYS file reviewed by the trial court to determine whether it contains information that probably would have changed the outcome of his trial."[175]

---

172. Ritchie's conviction was overturned when the Pennsylvania Supreme Court ruled that the Confrontation and Compulsory Process Clauses required full access to the records. The U.S. Supreme Court affirmed in part, reversed in part, and remanded the case for further proceedings. Ritchie claimed that denying him access to the records interfered with his right to cross-examine his daughter at trial. A plurality of the Court rejected this argument:

> The opinions of this Court show that the right of confrontation is a trial right, designed to prevent improper restrictions on the types of questions that defense counsel may ask during cross-examination. ... The ability to question adverse witnesses, however, does not include the power to require the pretrial disclosure of any and all information that might be useful in contradicting unfavorable testimony. Normally the right to confront one's accusers is satisfied if defense counsel receives wide latitude at trial to question witnesses.

Id. at 52. In a concurring opinion, Justice Blackmun, who cast the deciding vote, disagreed with the plurality: "In my view, there might well be a confrontation violation if, as here, a defendant is denied pretrial access to information that would make possible effective cross-examination of a crucial prosecution witness." *Id.* at 61-62. In dissent Justices Brennan and Marshall agreed:

> The creation of a significant impediment to the conduct of cross-examination thus undercuts the protections of the Confrontation Clause, even if that impediment is not erected at the trial itself. In this case, the foreclosure of access to prior statements of the testifying victim deprived the defendant of material crucial to the conduct of cross-examination.

Id. at 71. Justices Stevens and Scalia dissented on procedural grounds. *Id.* at 72-78.

173. *See* § 3-12 *infra.*

174. 480 U.S. at 57 (citation omitted).

175. *Id.* at 58. The Court, however, did not believe that the defense attorney had a right to examine the records. The defendant's interest in a fair trial can be protected by an in camera review by the trial court. Full disclosure to the defense would "sacrifice unnecessarily the Commonwealth's compelling interest in protecting its child abuse information." *Id.* at 60.

Prosecution Subpoenas

The prosecution also has subpoena power. In *State v. DeMarco*[176] a N.J. appellate court ruled that the prosecution may not compel discovery of DNA reports prepared by the defendant's expert witness for other clients in unrelated cases. The prosecution issued a subpoena for all of Dr. Blake's DNA reports that indicated the existence of unexplained contamination. The court indicated that the work-product rule would not apply and that applying the attorney-client privilege to reports generated outside of New Jersey would be problematic. Nevertheless, the court issued a protective order under its discovery rule. "Although we do not determine the applicability of the privileges or *Mingo's* Sixth Amendment [right to counsel] analysis, their underlying policies inform our view of the issue. Dr. Blake's reports contain private and critical information which should be shielded from undue public exposure. Moreover, litigators, public and private, should have access to the assistance of retained experts with a minimum of risk that their reports, which otherwise have not been placed in the public domain, will surface in unrelated litigation." [177]

The right to counsel, including the *Mingo* case, is discussed in a later section.[178]

§ 3-12. Constitutional Duty to Disclose Evidence.

In *Brady v. Maryland*[179] the Supreme Court recognized the prosecution's constitutional duty to disclose favorable defense evidence.[180] The Court wrote: "[T]he suppression by the prosecution of evidence favorable to an accused upon request violates due process where the evidence is material either to guilt or to punishment, irrespective of the good faith or bad faith of the prosecution."[181] In order to establish a *Brady* violation, the defendant must show that (1) the prosecution failed to disclose evidence, (2) the evidence was favorable to the defense, and (3) the evidence was material.[182]

---

176. 275 N.J. Super. 311, 646 A.2d 431 (1994) (per curiam).

177. *Id.* at 332, 646 A.2d at 436-37.

178. *See* § 5-10 *infra.*

179. 373 U.S. 83 (1963).

180. *See generally* 2 W. LaFave & J. Israel, *supra* note 6, § 19.5; 8 Moore's Federal Practice § 16.06 (1992); C. Whitebread & C. Slogogin, Criminal Procedure ch. 24 (3d ed. 1993); McDaniel & Greenblatt, *Brady Strategies and Tactics, in* 1A Criminal Defense Techniques ch. 23 (S. Allen, I. Rosen, D. Winston, & E. Smolinsky eds. 1992); Babcock, *Fair Play: Evidence Favorable to an Accused and Effective Assistance of Counsel*, 34 Stan. L. Rev. 1133 (1982); Note, *The Prosecutor's Duty of Disclose: From Brady to Agurs and Beyond*, 69 J. Crim. L. & Criminology 197 (1978).

181. 373 U.S. at 87.

182. Moore v. Illinois, 408 U.S. 786, 794-95 (1972).

United States v. Agurs

In *United States v. Agurs*[183] the Court recognized three different situations in which *Brady* applies.[184] The first situation involves cases in which the undisclosed evidence involves perjured testimony and the prosecution knew, or should have known, of the perjury.[185] A defense request is unnecessary in this situation.[186]

This category is based on several cases decided by the Court before *Agurs.*[187] One of these cases, *Miller v. Pate,*[188] involved the misuse of "scientific" evidence. Prior to trial, a defense request for the inspection of physical evidence that the prosecution intended to introduce at trial was denied. At trial, a prosecution expert testified that stains on underwear shorts were type A blood, which matched the defendant's blood type. The prosecution repeatedly referred to this "crucial testimony" in closing argument. At a subsequent federal habeas corpus hearing, the defense had the opportunity to examine the shorts and discovered that the stains were paint, not blood. In addition, the proceedings revealed that the prosecutor was aware of this fact at the time of trial. The Supreme Court reversed, holding that "the Fourteenth Amendment cannot tolerate a state criminal conviction obtained by the knowing use of false evidence."[189]

The second situation involves cases, such as *Brady,* in which a pretrial request for specific evidence is made.[190] According to the Court, "if the subject matter of such a request is material, or indeed if a substantial basis for claiming materiality exists, it is reasonable to require the prosecutor to respond either by furnishing the information or by submitting the problem to the trial judge."[191] Significantly,

---

183. 427 U.S. 97 (1976).

184. Prior to *Agurs* the Court decided several other *Brady* cases. *See* Moore v. Illinois, 408 U.S. 786 (1972) (suppressed evidence not material); Giglio v. United States, 405 U.S. 150 (1972) (prosecution's failure to correct perjurious denial of promises of leniency violated *Brady* even though the prosecutor who tried the case was unaware of the promises); Giles v. Maryland, 386 U.S. 66 (1967) (remanded).

185. 427 U.S. at 103.

186. Under these circumstances, the conviction must be set aside if there is any reasonable likelihood that the false testimony could have affected the judgment of the jury. *Id.*

187. *See* Donnelly v. DeChristoforo, 416 U.S. 637 (1974); Giglio v. United States, 405 U.S. 150 (1972); Miller v. Pate, 386 U.S. 1 (1967); Napue v. Illinois, 360 U.S. 264 (1959); Alcorta v. Texas, 355 U.S. 28 (1957); Pyle v. Kansas, 317 U.S. 213 (1942); Mooney v. Holohan, 294 U.S. 103 (1935).

188. 386 U.S. 1 (1967).

189. *Id.* at 7. A later investigation established that the stains were both blood and paint. *See The Vindication of A Prosecutor*, 59 J. CRIM. L., CRIMINOLOGY & POLICE SCI. 335 (1968).

190. 427 U.S. at 104.

191. *Id.* at 106.

the Court added: "When the prosecutor receives a specific and relevant request, the failure to make any response is seldom, if ever, excusable."[192]

The third situation involves cases in which the defense either makes no request or a general request for "all *Brady* material" or "anything exculpatory." Under these circumstances, the prosecutor's duty is limited to disclosing information that is "obviously exculpatory in character."[193] Nevertheless, for the first time, the Court acknowledged the prosecutor's duty to disclose favorable evidence even in the absence of a defense request.

United States v. Bagley

In *United States v. Bagley*[194] the Court undercut the distinction made in *Agurs* between the second situation (specific request) and third situation (general or no request). The Court ruled that the same standard of "materiality" applies in both situations. In these two situations, the omitted evidence is material "only if there is a reasonable probability that, had the evidence been disclosed to the defense, the result of the proceeding would have been different."[195]

Kyles v. Whitley

In *Kyles v. Whitley*[196] the Court reversed a first degree murder conviction due to a *Brady* violation, noting that in *Bagley* it had "disavowed any difference between exculpatory and impeachment evidence for *Brady* purposes, and it abandoned the distinction between the second and third *Agurs* circumstances, *i.e.*, the 'specific-request' and 'general- or no-request' situations."[197] The Court went on to explain that *Bagley* had addressed four aspects of the "materiality" requirement. First, that requirement did not mean that the defendant had to show that the undisclosed evidence would have resulted in an acquittal.[198] Second, the

---

192. *Id.*

193. *Id.* at 107. After *Agurs* the Court found no *Brady* violation in Weatherford v. Bursey, 429 U.S. 545 (1977), because *Brady* is limited to exculpatory evidence.

194. 473 U.S. 667 (1985).

195. *Id.* at 682. Only Justice O'Connor joined in this part of Justice Blackmun's opinion. Nevertheless, three concurring Justices indicated that the "reasonable probability" standard of materiality covered "all instances of prosecutorial failure to disclose evidence favorable to the accused." *Id.* at 685 (White, J., concurring).

196. 514 U.S. 419 (1995).

197. *Id.* at 432. The Court also commented: "The prosecution's affirmative duty to disclose evidence favorable to a defendant can trace its origins to early 20th-century strictures against misrepresentation and is of course most prominently associated with this Court's decision in *Brady*...." *Id.*

198. *Id.* at 434 ("*Bagley's* touchstone of materiality is a 'reasonable probability' of a different result, and the adjective is important. The question is not whether the defendant would more likely than not have received a different verdict with the evidence, but whether in its absence he received a fair trial, understood as a trial resulting in a verdict worthy of confidence. A 'reasonable

Bagley materiality requirement is "not a sufficiency of evidence test. A defendant need not demonstrate that after discounting the inculpatory evidence in light of the undisclosed evidence, there would not have been enough left to convict." Third, once a reviewing court has found constitutional error "there is no need for further harmless-error review."[199] Fourth, the materiality standard focuses on the "suppressed evidence considered collectively, not item-by-item."[200]

The Court also observed: "On the one side, showing that the prosecution knew of an item of favorable evidence unknown to the defense does not amount to a *Brady* violation, without more. But the prosecution, which alone can know what is undisclosed, must be assigned the consequent responsibility to gauge the likely net effect of all such evidence and make disclosure when the point of 'reasonable probability' is reached. This in turn means that the individual prosecutor has a duty to learn of any favorable evidence known to the others acting on the government's behalf in the case, including the police."[201] If in doubt, the prosecutor should disclose: "This means, naturally, that a prosecutor anxious about tacking too close to the wind will disclose a favorable piece of evidence.... This is as it should be."[202]

Wood v. Bartholomew

In *Wood v. Bartholomew*,[203] the Supreme Court ruled that a lower court was wrong in concluding that the prosecution's failure to turn over the results of a polygraph examination of a key witness violated *Brady*. Polygraph results were inadmissible under state law, even for impeachment, in the absence of a stipulation. "Disclosure of the polygraph results, then, could have had no direct effect on the outcome of trial, because respondent could have made no mention of them either during argument or while questioning witnesses."[204] The possibility that the undisclosed information would have led the defense counsel to additional avenues of discovery was, in the Court's view, speculative.

---

probability' of a different result is accordingly shown when the Government's evidentiary suppression 'undermines confidence in the outcome of the trial'") (citing *Bagley*, 473 U.S. at 678).

199. *Id.* at 435.

200. *Id.* at 436.

201. *Id.* at 436.

202. *Id.* at 439. *See* Berger v. United States, 295 U.S. 78, 88 (1935) (the prosecutor's interest "in a criminal prosecution is not that it shall win a case, but that justice shall be done").

203. 516 U.S. 1 (1995) (per curiam). Defendant admitted participation in a robbery in which a person was shot and killed. The issue was whether the killing was premeditated murder or a lesser form of murder. The defendant claimed that the weapon fired accidentally. Two prosecution witnesses, the defendant's brother and the brother's girlfriend, took polygraph examinations prior to trial. Their answers were consistent with their trial testimony. When asked about their own involvement in the robbery, the examiner found her answers to be "inconclusive" and the brother's "deceptive." Neither examination was disclosed to the defense.

204. *Id.* at 10.

Moreover, at the habeas proceeding the trial defense counsel testified that he had made a strategic decision to limit the cross-examination of the brother. Accordingly, "it is not 'reasonably likely' that disclosure of the polygraph results — inadmissible under state law — would have resulted in a different outcome at trial."[205] Other courts have reached different results depending on the circumstances.[206]

Strickler v. Greene

The Court's latest decision, *Strickler v. Greene*,[207] once again pointed out that there "are three components of a true *Brady* violation: The evidence at issue must be favorable to the accused, either because it is exculpatory, or because it is impeaching; that evidence must have been suppressed by the State, either willfully or inadvertently; and prejudice must have ensued."[208] In this case, the Court found that the suppressed evidence was exculpatory. The materials consisted of notes taken by a detective during his interviews with an eyewitness and letters written by the witness to the detective. "They cast serious doubt on [the witness's] confident assertion of her 'exceptionally good memory.'"[209] The Court held, however, that the accused had not established prejudice.[210]

---

205. *Id.* at 11.

206. *E.g.*, United States v. Minsky, 963 F.2d 870, 875 (6th Cir. 1992) ("The government did not even provide the defense with a copy of Brown's polygraph test until the second day of trial. Moreover, the government never provided the defense with copies of the FBI 302s. The defense therefore could not understand the significance of the polygraph results..."); Jacobs v. Singletary, 952 F.2d 1282, 1289 (11th Cir. 1992) (failure to disclose statement made to polygraph examiner violated *Brady*); Galloway v. Brewer, 525 F.2d 369, 371 (8th Cir. 1975), *cert. denied,* 424 U.S. 974 (1976) (right of confrontation requires disclosure of polygraph examiner's notes); United States v. MacEntee, 713 F. Supp. 829, 831 (E.D. Pa. 1989) (polygraph results discoverable under *Brady* even though not admissible); Carter v. Rafferty, 621 F. Supp. 533, 558 (D.N.J. 1985) (failure to disclose polygraph results violates due process), *aff'd in relevant part,* 826 F.2d 1299 (3d Cir. 1987), *cert. denied,* 484 U.S. 1011 (1988); People v. Bass, 84 Ill. App. 3d 624, 630, 405 N.E.2d 1182, 1187 (1980) (failure to disclose polygraph results violates due process); State v. Carter, 85 N.J. 300, 310, 426 A.2d 501, 506 (1981) (remand to determine whether failure to provide polygraph results violated *Brady*).

207. 119 S. Ct. 1936 (1999).

208. *Id.* at 1948.

209. *Id.* at 1944.

210. Nevertheless, the Court added a significant comment: "We certainly do not criticize the prosecution's use of the open file policy. We recognize that this practice may increase the efficiency and the fairness of the criminal process. We merely note that, if a prosecutor asserts that he complies with *Brady* through an open file policy, defense counsel may reasonably rely on that file to contain all materials the State is constitutionally obligated to disclose under *Brady*." *Id.* at 1949 n.23.

Scientific Evidence Cases

Brady issues involving the use of scientific evidence are common. They have arisen in cases in which the prosecution has failed to disclose the results of firearms,[211] fingerprint,[212] handwriting,[213] blood and urine,[214] voice,[215] hair,[216] and other examinations.[217] A number of cases have involved the failure to reveal the results of examinations of rape victims.[218]

---

211. *E.g.,* Barbee v. Warden, Maryland Penitentiary, 331 F.2d 842, 846 (4th Cir. 1964) (failure to disclose "ballistics" report showing defendant's gun did not fire murder bullet violated due process); State v. Hurd, 520 S.W.2d 158, 165 (Mo. App. 1975) (failure to disclose "ballistics" and other reports violated *Brady*). *See also* McMullen v. Maxwell, 3 Ohio St. 2d 160, 168, 209 N.E.2d 449, 455-56 (1965).

212. *E.g.,* Barbee v. Warden, Maryland Penitentiary, 331 F.2d 842, 846 (4th Cir. 1964) (failure to disclose negative fingerprint report violated due process); State v. Sahlie, 245 N.W.2d 476, 478-79 (S.D. 1976) (failure to disclose fingerprint reports violated *Brady*).

213. *E.g.,* United States v. Hauff, 473 F.2d 1350, 1354 (7th Cir.) (failure to disclose inconclusive handwriting report did not violate due process), *cert. denied,* 412 U.S. 907 (1973).

214. *E.g.,* Smith v. Secretary of Dep't of Cors., 50 F.3d 801, 832 (10th Cir.) ("Even without medical tests of the clothing to evaluate whether the substance was in fact blood, the mere fact that Mr. Newell had these clothes in his car would itself have been a subject for cross-examination.... In spite of this initial decision, no tests were ever performed and the clothes were never made available to the defense to allow it to conduct independent tests. Under these circumstances, the State may not now claim that whatever exculpatory value the clothes possessed was speculative"), *cert. denied,* 516 U.S. 905 (1995); Clay v. Black, 479 F.2d 319, 320 (6th Cir. 1973) (failure to disclose bloodstain report violated *Brady*); People v. Drake, 64 Mich. App. 671, 680-83, 236 N.W.2d 537, 542-43 (1975) (remanded to determine whether failure to disclose blood and urine analyses violated *Brady*).

215. *E.g.,* United States v. Fontaine, 575 F.2d 970, 974 (1st Cir. 1978) (voice comparison test not material within meaning of *Brady*). *See also* Commonwealth v. Topa, 471 Pa. 223, 234-35, 369 A.2d 1277, 1283 (1977) (Roberts, J., concurring) (failure to disclose voice exemplars violates *Brady*).

216. *E.g.,* Norris v. Slayton, 540 F.2d 1241, 1243-44 (4th Cir. 1976) (failure to disclose neutral report of hair analysis did not violate *Brady*); United States *ex rel.* Lewis v. Lane, 656 F. Supp. 181, 189 (C.D. Ill. 1987) (failure to disclose hair analysis did not violate due process), *cert. denied,* 488 U.S. 829 (1988); Smith v. United States, 363 A.2d 667, 668 (D.C. 1976) (report of negative hair analysis not exculpatory within meaning of *Brady*).

217. *E.g.,* United States v. Lehman, 756 F.2d 725, 729 (9th Cir. 1985) (remanded to determine whether footprint report contained exculpatory information), *cert. denied,* 474 U.S. 994 (1985), *appeal after remand,* 792 F.2d 899, *cert. denied,* 479 U.S. 868 (1986); Patler v. Slayton, 503 F.2d 472, 479 (4th Cir. 1974) (failure to disclose various scientific reports did not violate *Brady*); United States v. Stifel, 594 F. Supp. 1525, 1543 (N.D. Ohio 1984) (failure to disclose neutron activation analysis tests violated due process); Emmett v. Ricketts, 397 F. Supp. 1025, 1038 (N.D. Ga. 1975) (failure to disclose hypnosis violated *Brady*); State v. Hurd, 520 S.W.2d 158, 165 (Mo. App. 1975) (failure to disclose chemical and physical examination reports violated *Brady*); Commonwealth v. Stickle, 484 Pa. 89, 98-101, 398 A.2d 957, 962-63 (1979) (failure to disclose report on gasoline vapors and tire track comparison did not violate *Brady*).

218. *E.g.,* Hilliard v. Spalding, 719 F.2d 1443, 1447 (9th Cir. 1983) (prosecution must disclose exculpatory sperm test results); United States *ex rel.* Raymond v. Illinois, 455 F.2d 62, 66-67 (7th

United States v. Stifel[219] illustrates the importance of *Brady* material. The prosecution charged Stifel with murdering his former girlfriend's fiancé by sending a bomb through the mail. Crucial prosecution evidence involved neutron activation analysis (NAA) performed on bomb debris (vinyl tape, metal cap, cardboard mailing tube, and paper gummed label) and similar items obtained from Stifel's place of employment. The prosecution expert testified that the label and cardboard tube were "of the same type and same manufacture."[220] The metal cap and tape were "of the same manufacture" and from the "same batch" — one day's manufacturing production.[221] The Sixth Circuit upheld the admissibility of the NAA evidence. After his conviction, Stifel filed a request under the Freedom of Information Act. The FOIA material revealed the existence of another suspect in the bombing and discrepancies about the background tests on the vinyl tape.[222] As a result, Stifel filed a post-conviction petition, alleging a *Brady* violation. He argued that the expert, when cross-examined, had failed to disclose that additional tests had been performed on the tape. The court disagreed that the expert had misrepresented the facts on this issue but noted the misleading character of this information in granting relief: "[H]ad the defense known of the November 1968 tests performed by [the expert] on tape obtained from Plymouth Rubber Company, it could have used this evidence to further impeach the credibility of [the expert's] scientific methods."[223]

Nelson v. Zant[224] is another example. The critical evidence in the case was a hair found on the victim's body. The state's expert testified that the hair not only could have come from the defendant but that it could only have come from about 120 people in the entire Savannah area. The prosecution failed to disclose that the FBI had also examined the hair and concluded that the hair was not suitable for comparison purposes. On review, the prosecution argued that the hair was not "material" within the meaning of *Brady*. The Georgia Supreme Court reversed.

Cir. 1971) (failure to disclose test showing absence of sperm violated *Brady*), *cert. denied,* 409 U.S. 885 (1972); United States v. Poole, 379 F.2d 645, 647 (7th Cir. 1967) (failure to disclose report showing absence of semen required reversal); Ayres v. State, 436 A.2d 800, 802 (Del. 1981) (failure to disclose results of fingernail scraping examination, hair analysis, and other tests in sufficient time violated *Brady*); State v. Gammill, 2 Kan. App. 2d 627, 632, 585 P.2d 1074, 1079-80 (1978) (failure to disclose results of microscopic examination of vaginal aspirations was improper).

219. 433 F.2d 431 (6th Cir. 1970), *cert. denied,* 401 U.S. 994 (1971).

220. *Id.* at 436.

221. *Id.*

222. United States v. Stifel, 594 F. Supp. 1525 (N.D. Ohio 1984).

223. *Id.* at 1543.

224. 261 Ga. 358, 405 S.E.2d 250 (1991).

DNA Cases

Brady issues have also arisen in DNA cases. In *Sadler v. State*[225] the court ruled that the prosecution's failure to disclose an inconclusive DNA report violated the *Brady* rule. The defense argued that receipt of the report would have allowed it to: "(1) have hired an expert to analyze the report; (2) used it for comparison purposes; (3) be better prepared for cross-examination; (4) be able to cross-examine the people who collected and transported the semen; and (5) had their own DNA tests performed."[226] The court held that the failure to disclose the report was error but not a material error.

A different *Brady* issue arose in *People v. Davis*.[227] In this case Lifecodes, a private DNA laboratory, refused to disclose the statistical data underlying a DNA probability estimate. The court reversed: "The rule is plain that where the prosecution is permitted to call a witness, expert or not, who testifies as to a fact in issue or a conclusion to be drawn, the defendant is entitled to examine the underlying data, the basis for the testimony' or else the defendant suffers undue prejudice."[228]

"Exculpatory" Requirement

Brady requires that the suppressed evidence be favorable or exculpatory. This requirement has proved troublesome. The Seventh Circuit has held that an inconclusive handwriting report "was not exculpatory, but merely not inculpatory."[229] Similarly, the Fourth Circuit characterized a report showing that hair from a rape defendant was not found at the scene of the crime as a "neutral" report.[230] In another case, however, the Fourth Circuit expressed a different view:

---

225. 846 P.2d 377 (Okla. Crim. App. 1993). *See also* NATIONAL RESEARCH COUNCIL, DNA TECHNOLOGY IN FORENSIC SCIENCE 146 (1992) ("The prosecutor has a strong responsibility to reveal fully to defense counsel and experts retained by the defendant all material that might be necessary in evaluating the [DNA] evidence").

226. 846 P.2d at 382.

227. 196 A.D.2d 597, 601 N.Y.S.2d 174 (1993), *app. denied*, 617 N.Y.S.2d 145 (N.Y. 1994).

228. *Id.* at 598, 601 N.Y.S.2d at 175. *See also* State v. Schwartz, 447 N.W.2d 422, 427 (Minn. 1989) ("[F]air trial and due process rights are implicated when data relied upon by a laboratory in performing tests are not available to the opposing party for review and cross examination").

229. United States v. Hauff, 473 F.2d 1350, 1354 (7th Cir.), *cert. denied*, 412 U.S. 907 (1973).

230. Norris v. Slayton, 540 F.2d 1241, 1244 (4th Cir. 1976). *See also* United States v. Gillings, 156 F.3d 857, 860 (8th Cir. 1998) ("Although we do not condone the government's delay in disclosing the laboratory report and the fingerprint photographs to defense counsel, we do not agree with defendant that this delay amounted to a violation of *Brady* .... The laboratory report and the fingerprint photographs were not necessarily favorable to the defense. The laboratory report was neutral evidence; it reported only that no latent fingerprints had been found on the plastic bags and film canister found in the jacket. The fingerprint photograph were of fingerprints found in Ms. Walton's apartment and were not identified as defendant's. The fingerprint photographs were neutral and speculative evidence ...") (citations omitted).

"[S]uch a characterization [as neutral] often has little meaning; evidence such as this may, because of its neutrality, tend to be favorable to the accused. While it does not by any means establish his absence from the scene of the crime, it does demonstrate that a number of factors which *could* link the defendant to the crime do not."[231]

"Materiality" Requirement

In *Bell v. Coughlin*,[232] the prosecution failed to turn over FBI ballistics test results to the defense. "The results of the FBI tests were mixed. The lab positively matched a cartridge shell (B3) to the .45 caliber pistol but reported that no conclusion could be reached with respect to the two bullets (J/R2 and J/R4) in its possession.... Thus, although the results of the FBI tests may be characterized as mixed, they clearly contained exculpatory material."[233] The court went on to rule, however, that the results were not "material" within the meaning of *Brady*.

---

231. Patler v. Slayton, 503 F.2d 472, 479 (4th Cir. 1974) (FBI lab report on shoeprint, soil sample, hair sample, murder weapon, and clothing). *See also* State v. Resh, 124 Ohio App. 3d 694, 704, 707 N.E.2d 531 (1997) ("Had the defense counsel been informed of these [negative] test results, he could have contacted Wraxall for an explanation. Indeed, after the SERI report came to light, Resh corresponded with Wraxall, who told him in a letter that the results of the DNA test and the absence of genetic markers, which are very durable, suggested to him that the stain was not blood. In fact, Wraxall stated that he could not even confirm that the stains were of human origin. This evidence would have directly counteracted Dale Laux's unrebutted testimony at trial that the stains were human blood. Thus, the report is relevant and exculpatory"); Commonwealth v. Hawk, 551 Pa. 71, 79, 709 A.2d 373, 373 (1998) ("The results of the rape kit tests, showing a lack of semen and foreign pubic hair, were consistent with Hawk's assertion that he did not engage in sexual intercourse with the victim. Further, although the forensic scientist could not state conclusively that no intercourse occurred, her testimony concerning the possibility that no intercourse occurred would have supported a reasonable inference that Hawk did not have sexual intercourse with the victim. Because the competing allegations in this case rested on testimonial evidence, scientific evidence corroborative of Hawk's denial of sexual intercourse would have been highly probative of his credibility ... "). Note, *The Prosecutor's Duty to Disclose: From Brady to Agurs and Beyond*, 69 J. CRIM. L. & CRIMINOLOGY 197, 209 (1978) ("Where results are negative in that they fail to associate the defendant with the crime, they should be considered favorable. However, where the results are inconclusive because, for example, there is insufficient material to test, then those results are of so innocuous a character that they need not be disclosed").

232. 820 F. Supp. 780 (S.D.N.Y.), *aff'd*, 17 F.3d 390 (2d Cir. 1993), *cert. denied*, 512 U.S. 1210 (1994).

233. *Id.* at 786-87. *See also* Gordon v. Thornberg, 790 F. Supp. 374, 375 n.1 (D.R.I. 1992) (The accused's "shoes had been sent to the FBI laboratory for analysis; the FBI noted no presence of flammable substances on the shoes. Subsequently, the shoes were sent to the University of Rhode Island's crime laboratory. The URI crime lab found gasoline on the shoes. When the existence of the negative FBI lab report became known, the state granted Mr. Gordon's motion for a mistrial").

"Timeliness" Requirement

The *Brady* rule does not necessarily require pretrial disclosure; instead, disclosure at trial may be sufficient if made in sufficient time for the defense to use the information.[234] Nevertheless, delayed disclosure occurs far too often.[235]

Police Control

The cases make clear that the prosecution is also responsible for exculpatory evidence in the hands of the police. In one case the California Supreme Court commented:

> In this case, the uncontroverted record confirms that neither petitioner nor anyone acting on his behalf received a copy of the worksheet. At the reference hearing, Fitzpatrick acknowledged the lab "worked closely with the District Attorney's Office in assisting it in the prosecution of cases"; and there is no serious dispute that in these circumstances it was part of the investigative "team." The prosecutor thus had the obligation to determine if the lab's files contained any exculpatory evidence, such as the worksheet, and disclose it to petitioner. ... Any other rule would leave the defendant's due process rights to the fortuity of a subordinate agency's procedural protocol, which the Supreme Court has squarely rejected. "[A]ny argument for excusing a prosecutor from disclosing what he does not happen to know about boils down to a plea to substitute the police for the prosecutor, and even for the courts themselves, as the final arbiters of the government's obligation to ensure fair trials." Whether or not he actually did examine the files, the lab personnel's knowledge is imputed.[236]

---

234. United States v. Scarborough, 128 F.3d 1373, 1376 (10th Cir. 1997) ("The late disclosure of this exculpatory information [negative fingerprint report] is troubling, and it highlights the need for vigilance by prosecutors in ensuring that government agents are informed of and respect *Brady* requirements"); State v. Goode, 341 N.C. 513, 536, 461 S.E.2d 631, 645 (1995) ("Given that the prosecutor notified defendant of the evidence four days before trial and knew of it himself no sooner, the trial court's ordering a recess to permit defendant to locate material on the subject or another expert witness was well within the due exercise of the discretion permitted the court under the circumstances"); *Ex parte* Mowbray, 943 S.W.2d 461, 465 (Tex. Crim. App. 1996) ("State's counsel early on recognized the potential lethal effect of MacDonell's testimony on their theory of the case, and beginning in November and continuing until May they engaged in a deliberate course of conduct to keep MacDonell's findings and opinions from Applicant's counsel until the last days before trial. Even then they caused Applicant's counsel to believe MacDonell would be a witness and available for cross-examination") (due process violation), *cert. denied,* 521 U.S. 1120 (1997).

235. Ayres v. State, 436 A.2d 800, 802 (Del. 1981) (failure to disclose results of fingernail scraping examination, hair analysis, and other tests in sufficient time violated *Brady*).

236. *In re* Brown, 17 Cal. 4th 873, 880-81, 952 P.2d 715, 719, 72 Cal. Rptr. 2d 698, 702 (citing *Kyles*, 514 U.S. at 438), *cert. denied,* 119 S. Ct. 438 (1998).

§ 3-13. Constitutional Duty to Preserve Evidence.

Brady's due process disclosure requirement includes the right to have the evidence preserved, at least under certain circumstances.[237] The seminal case is *United States v. Bryant,*[238] in which narcotics agents failed to retain a tape recording of a critical conversation between an undercover agent and the defendants. The D.C. Circuit wrote: "It is most consistent with the purposes of [*Brady,* Rule 16, and the Jencks Act] safeguards to hold that the duty of disclosure attaches in some form once the Government has first gathered and taken possession of the evidence in question. Otherwise, disclosure might be avoided by destroying vital evidence before prosecution begins or before defendants hear of its existence."[239] In addition to due process, the right of preservation may be supported by the compulsory process[240] and right of confrontation guarantees.[241]

---

237. *See generally* 2 LAFAVE & J. ISRAEL, *supra* note 6, § 19.5(h); Comment, *The Prosecution's Duty to Preserve Evidence Before Trial,* 72 CALIF. L. REV. 1019 (1984); Note, *The Right to Independent Testing: A New Hitch in the Preservation of Evidence Doctrine,* 75 COLUM. L. REV. 1355 (1975); Comment, *Judicial Response to Government Loss or Destruction of Evidence,* 39 U. CHI. L. REV. 542 (1972); Comment, *Criminal Procedure: Government Has Duty to Implement Effective Guidelines to Preserve Discoverable Evidence,* 1971 DUKE L.J. 644; Note, *The Prosecutor's Duty to Disclose: From Brady to Agurs and Beyond,* 69 J. CRIM. L. & CRIMINOLOGY 197, 220-24 (1978).

238. 439 F.2d 642 (D.C. 1971), *aff'd after remand,* 448 F.2d 1182 (1971). The Court in *Bryant* relied on United States v. Augenblick, 393 U.S. 348 (1969), in which the Supreme Court stated that "the Government bore the burden of producing [Jencks Act material] or explaining why it could not do so." *Id.* at 355-56.

239. 439 F.2d at 651 ("Hence we hold that before a request for discovery has been made, the duty of disclosure is operative as a duty of preservation. Only if evidence is carefully preserved during the early stages of investigation will disclosure be possible later"). *Accord* Government of Virgin Islands v. Testamark, 570 F.2d 1162, 1166 (3d Cir. 1978); United States v. Harris, 543 F.2d 1247, 1252 (9th Cir. 1976); People *ex rel.* Gallagher v. District Court, 656 P.2d 1287, 1291 (Colo. 1983).

240. *See* Government of Virgin Islands v. Testamark, 570 F.2d 1162, 1166 (3d Cir. 1978) ("Loss or destruction of relevant evidence ... may also deny a defendant the right to compulsory process"); Westen, *The Compulsory Process Clause,* 73 MICH. L. REV. 71, 174-75 n.485 (1974) ("The government's failure to preserve material evidence in the defendant's favor ... violates his right of compulsory process because it precludes him from effectively producing the evidence in court"). *But see* People v. Eddington, 53 Mich. App. 200, 207-09, 218 N.W.2d 831, 835-36 (1974) (lost evidence cases raise no compulsory process issue).

241. *See* Johnson v. State, 249 So. 2d 470, 472 (Fla. App. 1971) (confrontation right to reexamine incriminatory bullet), *writ discharged,* 280 So. 2d 673 (Fla. 1973); People v. Taylor, 54 Ill. App. 3d 454, 457-58, 369 N.E.2d 573, 576 (1977) (confrontation and due process rights to preservation of heroin for independent examination).

But see People v. Triplett, 68 Mich. App. 531, 538-41, 243 N.W.2d 665, 669-71 (1976) (no confrontation violation where gun and slugs inadvertently destroyed); People v. Eddington, 53 Mich. App. 200, 207-09, 218 N.W.2d 831, 835-36 (1974) (no confrontation violation where glass particles lost).

Once recognized by the courts, the right of preservation was extensively litigated in scientific evidence cases. Defendants have successfully argued that this right has been violated by the prosecution's failure to preserve drugs,[242] bullets,[243] a fingertip,[244] blood,[245] urine,[246] trace metal detection results,[247] as well as physical evidence of arson,[248] rape,[249] and homicide.[250] Consumption of the

---

242. *E.g.,* People v. Clements, 661 P.2d 267, 273 (Colo. 1983) (failure to preserve nondangerous materials used to manufacture drugs violates due process); People v. Gomez, 198 Colo. 105, 111-12, 596 P.2d 1192, 1197 (1979) (consumption of heroin in unnecessary tests violates due process), *cert. denied,* 455 U.S. 943 (1982); Stipp v. State, 371 So. 2d 712 (Fla. App. 1979) (consumption of cocaine); People v. Dodsworth, 60 Ill. App. 3d 207, 210, 376 N.E.2d 449, 451 (1978) (consumption of MDA); People v. Taylor, 54 Ill. App. 3d 454, 457-58, 369 N.E.2d 573, 576 (1977) (consumption of heroin); Green v. Commonwealth, 684 S.W.2d 13, 16 (Ky. 1984) (consumption of drugs); People v. Wagstaff, 107 A.D.2d 877, 879, 484 N.Y.S.2d 264, 266 (1985) (destruction of marijuana). *But see* Schwartz v. State, 177 Ind. App. 258, 265, 379 N.E.2d 480, 486-87 (1978) (suppression denied where no showing retest of LSD would be exculpatory).

243. *See* Johnson v. State, 249 So. 2d 470, 472 (Fla. App. 1971), *writ discharged,* 280 So. 2d 673 (Fla. 1973). *But see* People v. Triplett, 68 Mich. App. 531, 538-41, 243 N.W.2d 665, 669-71 (1976) (inadvertent destruction of revolver and slugs not a constitutional violation); State v. Grady, 38 N.C. App. 152, 157, 247 S.E.2d 624, 627 (1978) (no constitutional violation where defendant failed to show materiality of lost bullet), *appeal dismissed,* 296 N.C. 107, 249 S.E.2d 806 (1978).

244. *See* People v. Morgan, 199 Colo. 237, 242, 606 P.2d 1296, 1298 (1980).

245. *See* People v. Collins, 730 P.2d 293, 297-99 (Colo. 1986); People v. Garries, 645 P.2d 1306, 1308 (Colo. 1982); State v. Swanson, 222 Mont. 357, 722 P.2d 1155, 1158 (1986); State v. Kersting, 50 Or. App. 461, 475, 623 P.2d 1095, 1103-04 (1981); State v. Lovato, 94 N.M. 780, 781, 617 P.2d 169, 171 (1980). *But see* People v. Howard, 130 Ill. App. 3d 1042, 474 N.E.2d 1345, 1353 (1985); State v. Casele, 198 N.J. Super. 462, 487 A.2d 765 (1985).

246. *See* People v. Moore, 34 Cal. 3d 215, 217, 666 P.2d 419, 423, 193 Cal. Rptr. 404, 406 (1983).

247. *See* People *ex rel.* Gallagher v. District Court, 656 P.2d 1287, 1292 (Colo. 1983).

248. *See* State v. Hannah, 120 Ariz. 1, 2, 583 P.2d 888, 889 (1978) (inadvertent destruction of arson evidence violates due process). *But see* People v. Brown, 194 Colo. 553, 556, 574 P.2d 92, 94 (1978) (no constitutional violation where good faith efforts to preserve arson evidence shown and investigator was available for examination).

249. *See* Hilliard v. Spalding, 719 F.2d 1443, 1447 (9th Cir. 1983) (failure to preserve sperm sample); Deberry v. State, 457 A.2d 744, 747 (Del. 1983) (failure to preserve clothing for blood analysis violates *Brady*); State v. Havas, 95 Nev. 706, 708, 601 P.2d 1197, 1198 (1979) (failure to preserve victim's clothing required dismissal). *But see* Johnston v. Pittman, 731 F.2d 1231, 1234-35 (5th Cir. 1984) (allowing rape pack to spoil did not violate due process); State v. Smoot, 99 Idaho 855, 860, 590 P.2d 1001, 1006 (1978) (failure to preserve seminal fluid samples not error in absence of fault); State v. Vaster, 99 Wash. 2d 44, 54, 659 P.2d 528, 534 (1983) (inadvertent destruction of seminal fluid sample did not violate due process).

250. *See* People v. Shepard, 701 P.2d 49 (Colo. 1985) (vehicle destroyed); State v. Wright, 87 Wash. 2d 783, 791, 557 P.2d 1, 67 (1976) (victim's clothing destroyed). *See also* People v. Harmes, 38 Colo. App. 378, 381, 560 P.2d 470, 473 (1976) (failure to preserve videotape of alleged assault violated due process).

evidence during testing, if justified, was permitted.[251] Nevertheless, the scope of this right remained uncertain.

People v. Hitch

At one time the leading case on this issue was *People v. Hitch* (1974),[252] which involved the preservation of breathalyzer ampoules.[253] The defendant argued that destruction of the ampoule after the administration of the test deprived him of due process. The California Supreme Court agreed, holding that if "there is a reasonable possibility that [the ampoules] would constitute favorable evidence, ... then such evidence must be disclosed."[254] The court also wrote: "[T]he test ampoule, its contents and the reference ampoule customarily used in the test constitute material evidence on the issue of the driver's guilt or innocence of the charge of driving a vehicle under the influence of intoxicating liquor. We conclude that the investigative agency involved in the test has a duty to preserve and disclose such evidence."[255]

Hitch soon became controversial. For example, some courts questioned the usefulness of retesting. The Washington Supreme Court commented that "ampoule retesting procedures are not generally accepted" as valid and thus "expert testimony based on scientific retesting of used breathalyzer ampoules is inadmissible."[256] In contrast, the Arizona Supreme Court concluded that preservation of an ampoule would provide some useful information.[257]

---

251. *E.g.,* Lee v. State, 511 P.2d 1076, 1077 (Alaska 1973); State v. Herrera, 365 So. 2d 399, 400 (Fla. App. 1979); State v. Atkins, 369 So. 2d 389, 390 (Fla. App. 1979); Partain v. State, 238 Ga. 207, 208, 232 S.E.2d 46, 46 (1977); State v. Lightle, 210 Kan. 415, 416, 502 P.2d 834, 836 (1972); Hanson v. State, 684 S.W.2d 337, 343 (Mo. App. 1984). *See* § 3-8 *supra.*

252. 12 Cal. 3d 641, 527 P.2d 361, 117 Cal. Rptr. 9 (1974).

253. For a further discussion of this issue, *see* § 22-7(D), *infra. See generally* Note, *The Right to Independent Testing: A New Hitch in the Preservation of Evidence Doctrine*, 75 COLUM. L. REV. 1355 (1975); Note, *Washington's New DWI Statute: Does Due Process Mandate Preservation of Breathalyzer Ampoules?*, 16 GONZ. L. REV. 357 (1981); Note, *The Prosecutor's Duty of Disclose: From Brady to Agurs and Beyond*, 69 J. CRIM. L. & CRIMINOLOGY 197, 222-24 (1978); Note, *Preservation of Material Evidence in California: Does Hitch Survive Trombetta?*, 13 HASTINGS CONST. L.Q. 147 (1985); Note, *Breathalyzers: Should the State be Required to Preserve the Ampoules?*, 15 LAND & WATER L. REV. 299 (1980); Comment, *California v. Trombetta: Holding Our Breath on the Duty to Preserve*, 12 WESTERN ST. U. L. REV. 309 (1984); Note, *The Defendant's Right to Independent Analysis of the Breathalyzer Ampoule: The Probable Virginia Response*, 21 WM. & MARY L. REV. 219 (1979); Annot., *Destruction of Ampoule Used in Alcohol Breath Test as Warranting Suppression of Result of Test,* 19 A.L.R.4TH 509 (1983).

254. 12 Cal. 3d at 649, 527 P.2d at 367, 117 Cal. Rptr. at 15.

255. *Id.* at 652, 527 P.2d at 369, 117 Cal. Rptr. at 17.

256. State v. Canaday, 90 Wash. 2d 808, 814, 585 P.2d 1185, 1188 (1978). Other courts rejecting *Hitch* include: Edwards v. Oklahoma, 429 F. Supp. 668, 670 (W.D. Okla. 1976), *rev'd on other grounds,* 577 F.2d 1119 (10th Cir. 1978); State v. Phillipe, 402 So. 2d 33, 34 (Fla. App. 1981), *petition denied,* 412 So. 2d 469 (Fla. 1982); People v. Stark, 73 Mich. App. 332, 338, 251

The California Supreme Court abandoned *Hitch* in *People v. Johnson* (1989).[258] According to the court, *Hitch* was based on federal due process notions, and a 1984 U.S. Supreme Court's decision, had adopted a more restrictive test for determining a due process violation in this context: *California v. Trombetta.*[259]

California v. Trombetta

Some techniques, such as the intoxilyzer, do not use ampoules. In this situation, several courts had required the preservation of additional breath samples.[260] In *California v. Trombetta* (1984),[261] however, the U.S. Supreme

---

N.W.2d 574, 577 (1977); State v. Shutt, 116 N.H. 495, 497, 363 A.2d 406, 408 (1976); People v. Santiago, 116 Misc. 2d 340, 349, 455 N.Y.S.2d 511, 517 (1982); State v. Larson, 313 N.W.2d 750, 756 (N.D. 1981); Edwards v. State, 544 P.2d 60, 64 (Okla. Crim. App. 1975); State v. Newton, 274 S.C. 287, 291-92, 262 S.E.2d 906, 909 (1980); State v. Helmer, 278 N.W.2d 808, 812 (S.D. 1979); Turpin v. State, 606 S.W.2d 907, 917-18 (Tex. Crim. App. 1980); State v. Walstad, 119 Wis. 2d 483, 351 N.W.2d 469 (1984).

257. Scales v. City Court, 122 Ariz. 231, 233, 594 P.2d 97, 99 (1979) ("(1) the volume of the solution in the ampoule can be measured; (2) the sulphuric acid content can be measured; (3) nitric acid content can be determined; (4) the thickness of the glass wall of the ampoule can be measured; (5) any imperfection in the glass can be detected; (6) the existence of any foreign substance either on the outside or the inside of the ampoule can be determined"). *Accord* Lauderdale v. State, 548 P.2d 376, 381 (Alaska 1976). *See also* WIS. STAT. ANN. § 343.305(10)(d) (West 1985) (requiring ampoule preservation).

258. 47 Cal. 3d 1194, 767 P.2d 1047, 255 Cal. Rptr. 569 (1989), *cert. denied,* 494 U.S. 1058 (1990). *See also* People v. Medina, 51 Cal. 3d 870, 893-94, 799 P.2d 1282, 1296-97, 274 Cal. Rptr. 849, 863-64 (1990) (failure to retain bottle from which fingerprint taken did not violate due process), *aff'd on other grounds,*505 U.S. 437 (1992).

259. 467 U.S. 479 (1984).

260. *E.g.,* Champion v. Department of Pub. Safety, 721 P.2d 131, 133 (Alaska 1986) (license revocation proceeding); Municipality of Anchorage v. Serrano, 649 P.2d 256, 259 (Alaska App. 1982) (breathalyzer); State v. Kemp, 168 Ariz. 334, 335-36, 813 P.2d 315, 317 (1991) (advice on right to independent test not required when blood extracted rather than breath); State v. Velasco, 165 Ariz. 480, 488-89, 799 P.2d 821, 829-30 (1990) (silica-gel method of preserving breath sample in intoxilyzer testing satisfied state's preservation requirement); State *ex rel.* Dean v. City Court, 163 Ariz. 510, 514, 789 P.2d 180, 184 (1990) (offering suspect option of blood test with preservation of sample or breath test without preservation of sample satisfies state due process); Baca v. Smith, 124 Ariz. 353, 354, 604 P.2d 617, 618 (1979) (gas chromatograph intoximeter); Garcia v. District Court, 197 Colo. 38, 41, 589 P.2d 924, 926 (1979) (breathalyzer and gas chromatograph). *See also* VT. STAT. ANN. tit. 23, § 1203(a)(d) (1991) (requiring 45-day preservation of blood and breath samples).

But see People v. Miller, 52 Cal. App. 3d 666, 668, 125 Cal. Rptr. 341, 342 (1975) (intoxilyzer); State v. Young, 228 Kan. 355, 363, 614 P.2d 441, 447 (1980) (gas chromatograph intoximeter); Montoya v. Metropolitan Court, 98 N.M. 616, 617, 651 P.2d 1260, 1261 (1982); State v. Larson, 313 N.W.2d 750, 756 (N.D. 1981) (breathalyzer).

261. 467 U.S. 479 (1984).

Court ruled that due process did not impose such a requirement. According to the Court:

> Whatever duty the Constitution imposes on the States to preserve evidence, that duty must be limited to evidence that might be expected to play a significant role in the suspect's defense. To meet this standard of constitutional materiality, ... [the] evidence must both possess an exculpatory value that was apparent before the evidence was destroyed, and also be of such a nature that the defendant would be unable to obtain comparable evidence by other reasonably available means.[262]

The Court held that neither of these conditions was satisfied. Given the reliability of the intoxilyzer, "breath samples were much more likely to provide inculpatory [rather] than exculpatory evidence."[263] Moreover, alternative methods of attacking the intoxilyzer results were available; the defendant had the right under state law to inspect the intoxilyzer, the right to introduce evidence to show possible interference with the machine's measurements, and the right to cross-examine the police concerning operator error.[264]

Arizona v. Youngblood

In *Arizona v. Youngblood* (1988)[265] the Supreme Court again addressed the failure to preserve evidence issue — semen in a sexual assault case. The Court adopted a "good faith" requirement. While good faith is not a requirement in the *Brady*-suppression cases, the Court ruled it determinative in a failure to preserve situation: "We therefore hold that unless a criminal defendant can show bad faith on the part of the police, failure to preserve potentially useful evidence does not constitute a denial of due process of law."[266] The bad faith requirement turns on "the police's knowledge of the exculpatory value of the evidence at the time it was lost or destroyed."[267] Moreover, due process is not violated "when the police fail to use a particular investigatory tool."[268]

---

262. *Id.* at 488-89.

263. *Id.* at 489.

264. *Id.* at 490.

265. 488 U.S. 51 (1988). *See generally* Note, *The Role of Police Culpability in Leon and Youngblood*, 76 VA. L. REV. 1213, 1223 n.59 (1990) ("Of course, there is the additional difficulty of proving that the police knew the evidence to be exculpatory. Few officers will be willing to admit they destroyed evidence they knew to be exculpatory").

266. *Id.* at 58.

267. *Id.* at 57 n. *.

268. *Id.* at 59.

"Bad Faith" Requirement

The "bad faith" test has been applied often. Some courts have found "bad faith destruction,"[269] while numerous courts have not."[270]

269. *E.g.*, United States v. Bohl, 25 F.3d 904, 906 (10th Cir. 1994) (Government denied defendants "a meaningful opportunity to present a defense by intentionally disposing of potentially exculpatory and highly probative evidence in the face of [defendants'] repeated requests for pretrial access to that evidence"); United States v. Cooper, 983 F.2d 928, 932 (9th Cir. 1993) (bad faith destruction of methamphetamine lab equipment violates due process); United States v. Belcher, 769 F. Supp. 201, 204 (W.D. Va. 1991) (due process violated when state intentionally destroys marihuana without first testing it; *Youngblood's* bad faith test not applicable); People v. Walker, 628 N.E.2d 971, 973 (Ill. App. 1993) (destruction of clothing satisfies demanding *Youngblood* test; items destroyed within six weeks of crime based on improper authorization), *app. denied,* 633 N.E.2d 13 (1994); State v. Jordan, 73 Ohio App. 3d 524, 531, 597 N.E.2d 1165, 1167 (1992) ("By destroying and then substituting other evidence and securing indictments based upon it, the police actions in themselves constituted a [due process] violation...").

270. *E.g.*, United States v. Alston, 112 F.3d 32, 35 (1st Cir. 1997) ("Here, no basis exists for a charge of bad faith or negligence. To see if the weapon had been used in other crimes was simply good police work. And the test firing, so long as the unjamming and rust removal were admitted, properly helped to confirm that the gun was 'designed' to expel a bullet by explosion. The only disadvantage of which Alston might fairly complain is that the cleaning and repair work tended to undermine his scienter argument [felon in possession of a firearm]; and there is no reason to think that the ATF anticipated the scienter defense"), *cert. denied,* 118 S. Ct. 568 (1997); Villafuerte v. Stewart, 111 F.3d 616, 625 (9th Cir. 1997) ("Nor did the failure to conduct tests on the semen sample violate Villafuerte's due process rights. The record contains no evidence that the semen sample could have had exculpatory value which was apparent at the time the officers failed to perform the tests"), *cert. denied,* 118 S. Ct. 860 (1998); United States v. Deaner, 1 F.3d 192, 201 (3d Cir. 1993) (destruction of rotting marijuana was negligent at most); Jones v. McCaughtry, 965 F.2d 473, 477-78 (7th Cir.) (failure to preserve non-motile sperm was not in bad faith), *cert. denied,* 506 U.S. 929 (1992); Paradis v. Arave, 954 F.2d 1483, 1488-89 (9th Cir. 1991) (no due process violation where panties negligently lost), *cert. denied,* 513 U.S. 1117 (1995); United States v. McKie, 951 F.2d 399, 403 (D.C. Cir. 1991) (crack cocaine lost after lab tests: no bad faith, not likely to be exculpatory); United States v. Westerdahl, 945 F.2d 1083, 1087 (9th Cir. 1991) (no constitutional duty to perform more sophisticated tests; reasonable to return evidence to innocent owner after examination); Carlson v. State, 945 F.2d 1026, 1029 (8th Cir. 1991) (no bad faith when entire blood sample consumed; "sample was very small and the test was run twice because the first [test] result was less than certain"); United States v. Sandoval, 913 F. Supp. 494, 497 (S.D. Tex. 1995) ("[T]here is no indication ... that the agents destroyed the marijuana to circumvent disclosure requirements or for any other improper motive"); State v. Youngblood, 173 Ariz. 502, 508, 844 P.2d 1152, 1158 (1993) (destruction of semen evidence did not violate state constitution; bad faith required); State v. Baldwin, 224 Conn. 347, 364, 618 A.2d 513, 522 (Conn. 1993) (mistaken destruction of narcotic vials); State v. Dulaney, 493 N.W.2d 787, 791 (Iowa 1992) (routine destruction of blood sample was not in bad faith); State v. Mabe, 412 S.E.2d 386, 388 (S.C. 1991) (no bad faith in destruction of cocaine).

"Materiality" Requirement

Some courts have concluded that *Youngblood* applies only to "material exculpatory evidence."[271] Moreover, the availability of alternative evidence affects the materiality requirement.[272]

State Constitutions

A significant number of state courts have rejected *Youngblood's* bad faith test as a matter of state constitutional law.[273] The Alaska Supreme Court has commented: "Since a defendant must provide the state with potentially incriminating evidence at the risk of criminal penalties, we hold that due process requires that the defendant be given an opportunity to challenge the reliability of that evidence in the simplest and most effective way possible, that is, an independent test."[274] The court went on to hold that explicit notice of the right to

---

271. State v. Wittenbarger, 124 Wash. 2d 467, 477, 880 P.2d 517, 522 (1994) (en banc) (maintenance and repair records of BAC Verifier Data Master "did not rise to the level of 'material exculpatory evidence' and are, at best, only potentially useful to the defense"). *See also* Grisby v. Blodgett, 130 F.3d 365, 371 (9th Cir. 1997) ("The duty to preserve evidence is limited to material evidence, *i.e.*, evidence whose exculpatory value was apparent before its destruction and that is of such nature that the defendant cannot obtain comparable evidence from the other sources. ... Grisby's counsel was aware of the carpet and had the opportunity to test it; the police never interfered with his ability to do so. The prosecutor even joined in a motion to acquire the carpet from the apartment owners, in part because of Grisby's proposed tests").

272. *See* State v. Berkley, 567 A.2d 915, 917-18 (Me. 1989) (arson charge based in part on chemical analysis of soil samples; the destruction of the soil samples prevented the defendant from obtaining them; evidence admissible because defendant could have taken independent soil samples or presented evidence at trial to impeach the State's test results).

273. *See also* State v. Morales, 232 Conn. 707, 726, 657 A.2d 585, 594 n.20 (1995) ("Apparently only Arizona and California ... have concluded that their state charters offer the same limited degree of protection as the federal constitution"; "Like our sister states, we conclude that the good or bad faith of the police in failing to preserve potentially useful evidence [semen stains that could have been tested for DNA] cannot be dispositive of whether a criminal defendant has been deprived of due process of law. Accordingly, we, too, reject the litmus test of bad faith on the part of the police, which the United States Supreme Court adopted under the federal constitution in *Youngblood*"); Commonwealth v. Henderson, 411 Mass. 309, 311, 582 N.E.2d 496, 497 (1991) ("The rule under the due process provisions of the Massachusetts Constitution is stricter than that stated in the *Youngblood* opinion"); Commonwealth v. Sasville, 35 Mass. App. 15, 24, 616 N.E.2d 476, 482 (1993) (dismissal of indictment because destruction of fetus of fourteen-year-old rape complainant was grossly negligent and prejudicial); State v. Osakalumi, 194 W. Va. 758, 766, 461 S.E.2d 504, 512 (1995) ("As a matter of state constitutional law, we find that fundamental fairness requires this Court to evaluate the State's failure to preserve potentially exculpatory evidence in the context of the entire record"); State v. Delisle, 162 Vt. 293, 310, 648 A.2d 632, 643 (1994) (*Youngblood* decision "too narrow because it limits due process violations to only those cases in which a defendant can demonstrate bad faith, even though the negligent loss of evidence may critically prejudice a defendant").

274. Gundersen v. Anchorage, 792 P.2d 673, 676 (Alaska 1990).

an independent test and an offer to assist in obtaining one as an alternative to preservation of a breath sample would also satisfied due process requirements.[275] Similarly, the Hawaii Supreme Court rejected the bad faith test as too restrictive because it precludes courts "in cases where no bad faith is shown, from inquiring into the favorableness of the evidence or the prejudice suffered by the defendant as a result of its loss."[276]

Other state courts have also gone their own way. The Alabama Supreme Court has recognized an exception to the bad faith test where the evidence is so critical to the defense as to make a criminal trial without it "fundamentally unfair."[277] The court applied that exception in a toxic waste dumping prosecution where the sole evidence in the case, the samples tested, were not preserved. The Delaware Supreme Court rejected *Youngblood* and set forth a three-pronged analysis: (1) the degree of negligence or bad faith involved, (2) the importance of the missing evidence, considering the probative value and reliability of secondary or substitute evidence that remains available, and (3) the sufficiency of the other evidence used at trial to sustain conviction.[278] The Illinois Supreme Court ruled that the good faith destruction of evidence could nevertheless violate due process if the state had notice from a defense discovery request.[279]

§ 3-14. Duty to Gather Evidence.

The cases recognizing a duty to preserve a separate breath sample for defense testing are, in effect, requiring the procurement of defense evidence, not merely the preservation of existing evidence. Several cases have considered the broader

---

275. *Id.* at 676-78. *See also* Thorne v. Department of Public Safety, 774 P.2d 1326, 1331 n.9 (Alaska 1989) ("We have construed the Alaska Constitution's Due Process Clause to not require a showing of bad faith").

276. State v. Matafeo, 71 Haw. 183, 187, 787 P.2d 671, 673 (1990).

277. *Ex parte* Gingo, 605 So. 2d 1237, 1241 (Ala. 1992), *cert. denied*, 506 U.S. 1049 (1993). *See also* Gurley v. State, 639 So. 2d 557 (Ala. Crim. App. 1993) (failure to preserve murder victim's wallet for defense testing violates state constitution).

278. Hammond v. State, 569 A.2d 81, 87 (Del. 1989) ("We remain convinced that fundamental fairness, as an element of due process, requires the State's failure to preserve evidence that could be favorable to the defendant '[to] be evaluated in the context of the entire record.' ... When evidence has not been preserved, the conduct of the State's agents is a relevant consideration, but it is not determinative") (quoting *Agurs* 427 U.S. at 97).

279. People v. Newberry, 166 Ill. 2d 310, 317, 652 N.E.2d 288, 292 (1995) (mistaken destruction of drugs) ("Here, unlike *Youngblood* and *Trombetta*, the police destroyed the disputed substance after defense counsel had requested access to it in his discovery motion. Where evidence is requested by the defense in a discovery motion, the State is on notice that the evidence must be preserved, and the defense is not required to make an independent showing that the evidence has exculpatory value in order to establish a due process violation.... If the State proceeds to destroy the evidence, appropriate sanctions may be imposed even if the destruction is inadvertent").

issue of whether a defendant has a right to an adequate police investigation.[280] Although most courts have refused to recognize such a right,[281] when a defense request is made and a reliable test is available, a strong argument for recognizing the government's duty to conduct such test exists. For example, in one case the defense requested that a homicide victim's hands be analyzed by trace metal detection analysis.[282] The police refused to conduct the test, and the Colorado Supreme Court reversed on due process grounds: "Under the circumstances here we conclude that at a minimum the prosecution had the duty to preserve the hands in a condition suitable for testing and to make available to the defendant an opportunity for independent trace metal testing of the victim's hands before burial."[283]

In *State v. Ware*[284] the New Mexico Supreme Court drew a distinction between failure to preserve evidence once gathered and failure to collect evidence during the investigation of a crime scene. The police had taken a photograph of a bloody rock in lieu of taking blood samples. The court wrote:

> While we recognize the rule that police officers generally have no duty to collect all potential evidence from a crime scene, we conclude that this rule is not absolute. We do not condone shoddy and inadequate police investigation procedures at the expense of a criminal defendant's right to a

---

280. *See* Note, *Toward a Constitutional Right to an Adequate Police Investigation: A Step Beyond Brady*, 53 N.Y.U. L. REV. 835 (1978).

281. *E.g.*, United States v. Henson, 486 F.2d 1292, 1298 n.3 (D.C. Cir. 1973) (failure to conduct fingerprint analysis); March v. State, 859 P.2d 714, 716 (Alaska App. 1993) ("Officers investigating a crime need not track down every conceivable investigative lead and seize every scintilla of evidence regardless of its apparent importance ... or run the risk of denying a defendant due process ...") (citations omitted); State v. Rivera, 152 Ariz. 507, 512, 733 P.2d 1090, 1095 (1987) ("The State has no corresponding duty, however, to gather blood alcohol evidence for the defense to use in corroborating the defense's own evidence"); State v. Rhodes, 112 Ariz. 500, 504, 543 P.2d 1129, 1133 (1975) (failure to take fingerprints); *In re* Alexander B., 220 Cal. App. 3d 1572, 1579, 270 Cal. Rptr. 342, 345 (1990) ("The police have no obligation to gather up all evidence which might eventually prove useful to the defense"); Bryant v. State, 268 Ind. 498, 499, 376 N.E.2d 1123, 1124 (1978) (failure to perform gunshot residue tests); State v. Steffes, 500 N.W.2d 608, 612 (N.D. 1993) (state has no duty to collect particular evidence at the crime scene); State v. Simpson, 611 S.W.2d 556, 560 (Mo. App. 1981) (state has no obligation to conduct hair and fingerprint analyses).

282. For a discussion of trace metal detection, *see* § 14-14 *infra*.

283. People *ex rel.* Gallagher v. District Court, 656 P.2d 1287, 1292 (Colo. 1983). *See also* Evans v. Superior Court, 11 Cal. 3d 617, 522 P.2d 681, 114 Cal. Rptr. 121 (1974) (due process requires prosecution to honor defense request for a lineup); Comment, ABA STANDARD 11-3.2(b), *supra* note 15 (recognizing court's authority to order scientific tests favorable to the defense).

284. 118 N.M. 319, 881 P.2d 679 (1994).

> fair trial. In some cases, the State's failure to gather evidence may amount to suppression of material evidence.[285]

The court then adopted a two-part test: The evidence must be material to the defense and the officers must have acted in bad faith, in which case suppression of the prosecution's evidence may be ordered. If the officers were grossly negligent in failing to gather the evidence, "the trial court may instruct the jury that it can infer that the material evidence not gathered from the crime scene would be unfavorable to the State."[286] In addition, the defense is entitled to cross-examine on deficiencies in the investigation. In *Daniels v. State*,[287] the Nevada Supreme Court adopted the *Ware* position.

§ 3-15. Prosecution Discovery.

Prosecution discovery of scientific reports and inspection of tangible objects is widely sanctioned.[288] In some jurisdictions, prosecution discovery is permitted only if the defense first seeks discovery from the prosecution.[289] In other jurisdictions, prosecution discovery is not conditioned on defense discovery.[290] Federal Rule 16 is an example of the former model; it requires only reciprocal

---

285. *Id.* at 684.

286. *Id.* at 685.

287. 114 Nev. 261, 956 P.2d 111 (1998).

288. *See generally* 2 W. LaFave & J. Israel, *supra* note 6, § 19.4; 8 Moore's Federal Practice § 16.06 (1992); 2 C. Wright, *supra* note 2, §§ 255-56; Allis, *Limitations on Prosecutorial Discovery of the Defense Case in Federal Courts: The Shield of Confidentiality*, 50 So. Cal. L. Rev. 461 (1977); Blumenson, *Constitutional Limitations on Prosecutorial Discovery*, 18 Harv. C.R.-C.L. L. Rev. 123 (1983); Esqueda, *Michigan Strives To Balance The Adversarial Process And Seek The Truth With Its New Reciprocal Criminal Discovery Rule*, 74 U. Det. Mercy L. Rev. 317 (1997); Mosteller, *Discovery Against the Defense: Tilting the Adversarial Balance*, 74 Calif. L. Rev. 1567 (1986); Myers, *Reciprocal Discovery Violations: Visiting The Sins Of The Defense Lawyer On The Innocent Client*, 33 Am. Crim. L. Rev. 1277 (1996); Slobogin, *Discovery By the Prosecution in the United States: A Balancing Approach*, 36 Crim. L.Q. 423 (1994); Tomlinson, *Constitutional Limitations on Prosecutorial Discovery*, 23 San Diego L. Rev. 993 (1986); Williams, *Sidestepping Scott: Modifying Criminal Discovery In Alaska*, 15 Alaska L. Rev. 33 (1998); Note, *Prosecutorial Discovery Under Proposed Rule 16*, 85 Harv. L. Rev. 994 (1972); Annot., *Right of Prosecution to Discovery of Case-Related Notes, Statements and Report — State Cases*, 23 A.L.R.4th 799 (1983).

289. *E.g.*, Del. Super. Ct. Crim. R. 16(b); Fla. R. Crim. P. 3.220(d)(2)(ii); Iowa Code Ann. § 813.2, R. 13(3) (West Supp. 1992); Kan. Stat. Ann. § 22-3212(3) (1988); Ky. R. Crim. P. 7.24(3) (court discretion); La. Code Crim. Proc. art. 724 & 725 (West 1981); N.J. R. Crim. P. 3.13-3(b); N.D. R. Crim. P. 16(b); R.I. Super. Ct. Crim. R. 16(b); Tenn. R. Crim. P. 16(b)(1); Va. S. Ct. R. 3A:11(c); Wyo. R. Crim. P. 18(d).

290. *E.g.*, Alaska R. Crim. P. 16(c)(4); Ill. Ann. Stat. ch. 110a, § 413(c) (Smith-Hurd Supp. 1985); Me. R. Crim. P. 16A(c) & (d); Minn. R. Crim. P. 9.02; Mo. R. Crim. P. 25.05(A)(1); N.M. R. Crim. P. 5-502(a) (mandatory); Or. Rev. Stat. § 135.835(2) (1991); Wash. Super. Ct. Crim. R. 4.7(g).

discovery. Thus, if the defense obtains discovery of either tangible objects or scientific reports, the prosecution is entitled to discovery of scientific reports within the possession or control of the defendant which the defense intends to introduce as evidence in chief at trial or which were prepared by an expert whom the defense intends to call at trial, provided the reports relate to the expert's testimony.[291] Oral reports are not subject to disclosure under this provision.[292] However, if the defense requests a summary of prosecution expert testimony pursuant to Rule 16(a)(1)(E), reciprocal discovery is required under Rule 16(b)(1)(C).[293]

Self-Incrimination

The Supreme Court addressed the constitutionality of prosecution discovery in *Williams v. Florida,*[294] which involved a state statute requiring the defense to notify the prosecution of its intention to offer an alibi defense and to provide the names of its alibi witnesses. The defendant argued that the statute violated the Self-incrimination Clause. Rejecting this argument, the Court found that the statute did not amount to "compulsion" within the meaning of the fifth amendment: "At most, the rule only compelled petitioner to accelerate the timing of his disclosure, forcing him to divulge at an earlier date information that the petitioner from the beginning planned to divulge at trial."[295]

The "accelerated discovery" rationale applies to prosecution discovery of scientific reports that the defense intends to introduce at trial[296] but not to reports prepared by experts who will not be called as witnesses.[297] In *Binegar v. Eighth*

---

291. Similarly, if the defense obtains discovery of either tangible objects or scientific reports, the prosecution is entitled to discovery of documents and tangible objects which are within the possession, custody, or control of the defendant and which the defendant intends to introduce as evidence in chief. FED. R. CRIM. P. 16(b)(1)(A); State v. Nichols, 877 S.W.2d 722, 730 (Tenn. 1994) ("[W]hen a psychologist or psychiatrist does not prepare a summary report, but instead relies on extensive memoranda to record not only observations and hypotheses but also evaluations, such records are discoverable under [the reciprocal discovery rule]"), *cert. denied,* 513 U.S. 1114 (1995).

292. *E.g.,* United States v. Peters, 937 F.2d 1422, 1425 (9th Cir. 1991); United States v. Matta, 937 F.2d 567, 565-66 (11th Cir. 1991); State v. Genotti, 220 Conn. 796, 601 A.2d 1013, 1019 (1992).

293. *See* § 3-5 *supra.*

294. 399 U.S. 78 (1970).

295. *Id.* at 85.

296. *See* 2 W. LAFAVE & J. ISRAEL, *supra* note 6, § 19.4, at 525 ("[A]ny self-incrimination claim could be met by the accelerated disclosure rationale since the defendant either intends to use the report itself or call the expert who will testify as to its contents").

297. *See* People *ex rel.* Bowman v. Woodward, 63 Ill. 2d 382, 388, 349 N.E.2d 57, 60 (1976). *See also* 2 W. LAFAVE & J. ISRAEL, *supra* note 6, at 526.

Judicial District Court,[298] the Nevada Supreme Court ruled that a discovery statute violated the fifth amendment because it had "a greater effect than simply compelling the defendant to accelerate the timing of disclosures that the defendant intended to divulge at trial.... Under [one provision], the defendant would be forced to disclose witness statements and the results or reports of mental and physical examinations and scientific tests or experiments, even if the defendant never intended to introduce the statements or materials at trial."[299] Moreover, some state courts reject the *Williams* rationale as a matter of state constitutional law.[300]

There is, however, a second ground for rejecting a fifth amendment challenge. The Self-incrimination Clause prohibits only compulsion directed at the suspect. According to the Supreme Court, "the Fifth Amendment privilege against self-incrimination, being personal to the defendant, does not extend to the testimony or statements of third parties called as witnesses at trial."[301] Accordingly, compelling a defense counsel to reveal scientific reports would not necessarily violate the privilege.[302]

---

298. 112 Nev. 544, 915 P.2d 889 (1996).

299. *Id.* at 551, 915 P.2d at 894.

300. *E.g.,* Scott v. State, 519 P.2d 774, 785 (Alaska 1974); State v. Summerville, 948 P.2d 469 (Alaska 1997) (reaffirming *Scott*). *See also* Williams, *Sidestepping Scott: Modifying Criminal Discovery In Alaska*, 15 ALASKA L. REV. 33 (1998).

At one time California also followed this approach. *See In re* Misener, 698 P.2d 637, 213 Cal. Rptr. 569 (1985); People v. Collie, 30 Cal. 3d 43, 634 P.2d 534, 177 Cal. Rptr. 458 (1981). This position was subsequently overturned by constitutional amendment. Izazaga v. Superior Court, 54 Cal. 3d 356, 363, 815 P.2d 304, 308, 285 Cal. Rptr. 231, 235 (1991); Woods v. Superior Court, 25 Cal. App. 4th 178, 185-86, 30 Cal. Rptr. 2d 182, 184-86 (1994) (reciprocal discovery statute requires disclosure of the raw results of standardized psychological and intelligence tests administered and relied upon by a defense expert the defense intends to call at trial; not a fifth amendment violation); Hines v. Superior Court, 20 Cal. App. 4th 1818, 1823, 25 Cal. Rptr. 2d 712, 714 (1993) (defense not required to disclose expert's random notes, interview notes, preliminary drafts of report, etc.); Sandeffer v. Superior Court, 18 Cal. App. 4th 672, 678, 22 Cal. Rptr. 2d 261, 264 (1993) (defense not required to disclose identity of, or reports from, an expert that defense has not yet determined to call as a witness).

301. United States v. Nobles, 422 U.S. 225, 234 (1975) (compelled production of defense investigator's notes does not violate fifth amendment because it involved no compulsion of the defendant); Gipson v. State, 609 P.2d 1038, 1044 (Alaska 1980) (compelled disclosure of defense firearm expert's report does not violate the fifth amendment); Izazaga v. Superior Court, 54 Cal. 3d 356, 815 P.2d 304, 285 Cal. Rptr. 231 (1991).

302. *See* 2 W. LAFAVE & J. ISRAEL, *supra* note 6, § 19.4, at 525 ("Self-incrimination objections to disclosure of scientific reports have uniformly been rejected on the ground that 'no disclosure of any kind, by defendant, is involved in this issue'"); Mosteller, *supra* note 288, 74 CALIF. L. REV. 1567, 1656 (1986) (the fifth amendment "does not protect against such disclosures because the lawyer, not the defendant, is compelled to respond").

Due Process

The Supreme Court left several issues unresolved in *Williams*. The discovery statute in that case provided for liberal defense discovery, and the Court indicated that a due process issue would have been presented if reciprocal defense discovery had not been provided.[303] In *Wardius v. Oregon*,[304] which also involved a notice of alibi rule, the Court confronted this issue. The statute in *Wardius* made no provision for reciprocal defense discovery. The Court held that prosecution discovery under these circumstances violated due process: "[T]he Due Process Clause of the Fourteenth Amendment forbids enforcement of alibi rules unless reciprocal discovery rights are given to criminal defendants."[305] Accordingly, due process precludes prosecution discovery of scientific reports and evidence in the absence of reciprocal defense discovery.[306]

Other rules also provide for prosecution discovery and apply to expert testimony. Federal Rule 26.2 provides for the production of prior statements of a witness after the witness has testified on direct examination. This provision, which relates to trial discovery, would apply to the prior statements of defense and prosecution expert witnesses.

§ 3-16. Nontestimonial Identifications Orders.

Some state discovery provisions track the ABA Standards and provide for the production of nontestimonial identification evidence.[307] The ABA Standards permit the prosecution to obtain fingerprint, handwriting, and voice exemplars as well as specimens of blood, urine, saliva, breath, hair, and nails from the

---

303. 399 U.S. at 82 n.11.

304. 412 U.S. 470 (1973).

305. *Id.* at 472.

306. *See* State v. Lucious, 270 Ga. 361, 1999 Ga. LEXIS 587, * 7 (Ga. 1999) ("Applying this due process standard to the act, we find that the Act furthers legitimate State interests by establishing a closely symmetrical scheme of discovery in criminal cases that maximizes the presentation of reliable evidence, minimizes the risk that a judgment will be predicated on incomplete or misleading evidence, and fosters fairness and efficiency in criminal proceedings. Because the Act provides for reciprocal discovery in criminal felony cases with any imbalance favoring the defendant, the act does not violate the due process clause of the United States or Georgia constitutions").

307. ALASKA R. CRIM. P. 16(c)(1) & (2); ARIZ. R. CRIM. P. 15.2(a); COLO. R. CRIM. P. 16(II)(a); FLA. R. CRIM. P. 3.220(b)(1); ILL. ANN. STAT. ch. 110a, § 413(a) (Smith-Hurd 1976); IOWA CODE ANN. § 810 (West 1979); ME. R. CRIM. P. 16A(a); WASH. SUPER. CT. R. 4.7(b)(2). The constitutionality of using nontestimonial identification procedures before arrest or indictment is discussed at § 2-4(A)(2) *supra*.

defendant.[308] In addition, courts possess inherent authority to order such discovery.[309]

§ 3-17. Insanity Defense.

Federal Rule 12.2 requires pretrial notice to the prosecution if the defendant intends to rely on an insanity defense or introduce expert testimony concerning his mental condition.[310] This rule also permits the court to order a psychiatric examination of the defendant. The rule also applies when the defendant offers the battered women syndrome defense.[311] The application of the privilege against self-incrimination in this context is discussed in Chapter 2.

§ 3-18. Continuing Duty to Disclose.

Federal Rule 16(c) recognizes a "continuing duty to disclose" scientific reports if, prior to or during trial, new reports are prepared. For example, in *United States v. Kelly*[312] neutron activation tests were conducted after the trial court ordered discovery of scientific reports. The defense, however, was not informed of the tests until trial. After recognizing the prosecution's continuing duty to disclose the results of scientific tests, the Second Circuit wrote: "The course of the government smacks too much of a trial by ambush, in violation of the spirit of the rules. A new trial is required, with a fair opportunity for the defense to run its own neutron activation tests of the material...."[313]

In *State v. Scudder*[314] the Ohio Supreme Court found that the prosecution's failure to disclose a DNA frequency report after the initial disclosure of a DNA matching report was an inadvertent mistake that did not hinder the defense, who had their own DNA experts testing samples.

---

308. ABA STANDARDS 11-2.3, *supra* note 15.

309. United States v. Kloepper, 725 F. Supp. 638, 639-41 (D. Mass. 1989) (handwriting exemplars, fingerprints, and palm prints).

310. *See* 2 W. LAFAVE & J. ISRAEL, *supra* note 6, § 19-4(c); Annot., *Notice to Government of Defense Based Upon Defendant's Mental Condition at Time of Alleged Crime, and Court-Ordered Psychiatric Examination Thereon, Under Rule 12.2, Fed. Rules of Criminal Procedure*, 63 A.L.R. FED. 552 (1983).

311. United States v. Vega-Penarete, 137 F.R.D. 233, 235 (E.D.N.C. 1991). For a discussion of the BWS, *see* Chapter 9.

312. 420 F.2d 26 (2d Cir. 1969).

313. *Id.* at 29. *See also* United States v. Barrett, 703 F.2d 1076, 1080-81 (9th Cir. 1983); United States v. Boney, 572 F.2d 397, 403 (2d Cir. 1978) (drug report); United States v. Bockius, 564 F.2d 1193, 1197-98 (5th Cir. 1977) (polarimeter test); State v. Wilson, 30 Ohio St. 3d 99, 100-02, 507 N.E.2d 1109, 1110-12 (1987) (failure to update NAA report resulted in "trial by ambush"); Acevedo v. State, 467 So. 2d 220, 224 (Miss. 1985) (state violated continuing duty to disclose regarding gunshot residue test).

314. 71 Ohio St. 3d 263, 269-70, 643 N.E.2d 524, 530 (1994), *cert. denied*, 515 U.S. 1164 (1995).

§ 3-19. Discovery Abuses & Sanctions.

One of the most common abuses is the late disclosure of discovery material. For example, in *United States v. Wicker*[315] the testimony of a prosecution expert was excluded because the laboratory report had not been disclosed in a timely manner. But exclusion of the expert's testimony is not an automatic remedy in this context.[316]

Federal Criminal Rule 16(d)(2) governs the sanctions that may be imposed for violations of the rule. The sanctions include ordering discovery, granting continuances, and prohibiting the introduction of the undisclosed evidence. In addition, the court "may enter such other order as it deems just under the circumstances." The choice of sanction rests within the discretion of the trial court, and appellate courts will reverse only for an abuse of discretion and a showing of prejudice.[317] In exercising its discretion, the trial court should consider three factors: (1) the reason for the violation, including whether the prosecution acted in bad faith; (2) the extent of prejudice to the defendant; and

---

315. 848 F.2d 1059.

316. *E.g.,* United States v. Cardales, 168 F.3d 548, 555-56 (1st Cir. 1999) (During direct exam of prosecution witness, "the witness disclosed for the first time the existence of a laboratory test showing that the [ship's] carpet tested negative for the presence of marijuana"; mistrial not required because defense counsel "effectively cross-examined the government witness who disclosed the report, and used the test results in its closing argument"), *petition for cert. filed* (1999); United States v. Longie, 984 F.2d 955, 958 (8th Cir. 1993) ("Because the government did not learn of this evidence [medical report and photographs] until a late date and acted expeditiously to deliver it to the defense, we conclude that the government did not act in bad faith in failing to disclose the evidence sooner"); United States v. Edmonson, 962 F.2d 1535, 1545-46 (10th Cir. 1992) (fingerprint report prepared a month after trial commenced but promptly provided to defense at that time demonstrated good faith), *cert. denied,* 521 U.S. 1128 (1997); Commonwealth v. Montgomery, 533 Pa. 491, 497, 626 A.2d 109, 112 (1993) (results of semen test conducted on first day of trial and promptly turned over to defense; no violation of discovery rule unless results deliberately withheld).

317. *See* United States v. Dukes, 139 F.3d 469, 476 (5th Cir.) ("We review alleged discovery violations under the abuse of discretion standard"), *cert. denied,* 119 S. Ct. 215 (1998); United States v. Mavrokordatos, 933 F.2d 843, 847 (10th Cir. 1991) (finding an abuse of discretion); United States v. Wicker, 848 F.2d 1059, 1061-62 (10th Cir. 1988) (excluding testimony of prosecution expert); United States v. Merritt, 736 F.2d 223, 229 (5th Cir. 1984) (no prejudice demonstrated); United States v. Hemmer, 729 F.2d 10, 13 (1st Cir. 1984) (no prejudice demonstrated); United States v. Shively, 715 F.2d 260, 269 (7th Cir. 1983) (harmless error); United States v. Boney, 572 F.2d 397, 403 (2d Cir. 1978) (no abuse of discretion where trial court offered a continuance); United States v. Eisler, 567 F.2d 814, 817 (8th Cir. 1977) (no abuse of discretion where trial court excluded expert testimony and report); United States v. Bockius, 564 F.2d 1193, 1196 (5th Cir. 1977) (no abuse where court ordered that government laboratory facilities be made available to defense); United States v. Kelly, 420 F.2d 26, 29 (2d Cir. 1969) (new trial ordered).

See also Annot., *Exclusion of Evidence in State Criminal Action for Failure of Prosecution to Comply with Discovery Requirements as to Physical or Documentary Evidence or the Like — Modern Cases,* 27 A.L.R.4TH 105 (1984).

(3) the feasibility of curing the prejudice with a continuance.[318] Appellate courts frequently cited the failure of the defense to request a continuance in finding that delayed disclosure was not prejudicial.[319]

Defense Sanctions

Sanctions also apply to the defense. In *Williams* the Supreme Court declined to determine whether the exclusion of defense evidence would be a constitutionally permissible sanction for violating a discovery rule.[320] In *Taylor v. Illinois*[321] the Court held that exclusion of defense evidence as a discovery sanction is constitutional under certain circumstances, *i.e.*, a willful and blatant violation. Subsequently, the Court reaffirmed this position in *Michigan v. Lucas*.[322] Both cases, however, state that exclusion under some circumstances is unconstitutional.[323]

In the second Oklahoma bombing trial, the defense did not list the name of Dr. Whitehurst nor provide the required summary of his testimony.[324] The trial court precluded him from testifying. The Tenth Circuit upheld the sanction because the circumstances suggested that either counsel "changed their mind about the value of his testimony, or waited to the last minute to attempt to call him to provide the defense with a tactical advantage."[325]

---

318. United States v. Wicker, 848 F.2d 1059, 1061 (10th Cir. 1988).

319. United States v. Ortega, 150 F.3d 937, 943 (8th Cir. 1998) ("Special Agent Dillow and Trooper Banasik were listed on the government's witness list, not on its expert witness list, but they were allowed to testify both as fact witnesses and, over the defendant objection, as experts with specialized knowledge of drug-relate activities. ... These complaints ring hollow in light of Ortega's failure even to request a continuance to allow him an opportunity to pursue these avenues"); United States v. Appleby, 975 F.2d 1384, 1387 (8th Cir. 1992) (finding no abuse of discretion in allowing handwriting expert to testify where expert was not disclosed until a week into trial but defendant requested no continuance to hire his own expert").

320. 399 U.S. at 83 n.14. *See* § 3-15 *supra*.

321. 484 U.S. 400 (1988).

322. 500 U.S. 145 (1991).

323. *See* State v. Delgado, 174 Ariz. 252, 260, 848 P.2d 337, 345 (Ariz. App. 1993) (exclusion of defense rebuttal witness constituted error; critical witness and any surprise to state partly due to the state's own late disclosure); People v. Pronovost, 773 P.2d 555, 558-59 (Colo. 1989) (exclusion of defense expert as a discovery sanction violated defendant's right to present evidence); State v. Passino, 640 A.2d 547, 552 (Vt. 1994) ("[T]he trial court should have imposed a sanction less severe than exclusion of [DNA] evidence for defense counsel's failure to comply with notice requirements.... The trial court's sanction unduly trammeled defendant's right to present evidence ...").

324. United States v. Nichols, 169 F.3d 1255 (10th Cir. 1999).

325. *Id.* at 1268. The court also commented:

> We find no evidence in the record to suggest Dr. Whitehurst was a actually prevented from offering his testimony. Indeed, the record reflects Dr. Whitehurst was difficult to intimidate, having already given a three-day, pro-defense pretrial deposition, written scores of letters

§ 3-20. Work Product.

The Supreme Court in *United States v. Nobles*[326] held the work product privilege applicable to both the pretrial and trial stages of criminal proceedings.[327] Although *Nobles* involved a defense investigator, its rationale would extend to expert witnesses. The Court wrote:

> At its core, the work product doctrine shelters the mental processes of the attorney, providing a privileged area within which he can analyze and prepare his client's case. But the doctrine is an intensely practical one, grounded in the realities of litigation in our adversary system. One of those realities is that attorneys often must rely on the assistance of investigators and other agents in the compilation of materials in preparation for trial. It is therefore necessary that the doctrine protect material prepared by agents for the attorney as well as those prepared by the attorney himself.[328]

The Court also held that calling a witness at trial waives the work product privilege.[329]

Federal Rule 16 recognizes the work product privilege for both the prosecution[330] and the defense.[331] However, the privilege does not apply to scientific and medical reports that are otherwise discoverable.[332] Prosecution discovery of scientific reports under Rule 16 extends only to reports which the defense intends to introduce at trial and to reports prepared by an expert whom the defense intends to call at trial. Accordingly, Rule 16 is consistent with *Nobles'* waiver analysis. The reports of defense experts who are consulted but

---

> criticizing the FBI's conduct in this and other cases, and testified as defense witness for Mr. McVeigh.

Id. at 1269.

326. 422 U.S. 225 (1975).

327. *Id.* at 238-39. *See generally* Feldman, *Work Product in Criminal Practice and Procedure*, 50 U. CIN. L. REV. 495 (1981).

328. 422 U.S. at 238-39.

329. *Id.* at 239. *See also* Woods v. Superior Court, 25 Cal. App. 4th 178, 185, 30 Cal. Rptr. 2d 182, 187 (1994) ("[E]lecting to present the expert as a witness destroys the work-product privilege"), *review denied*, 1994 Cal. LEXIS 4376 (Cal. Aug. 11, 1994).

330. FED. R. CRIM. P. 16(a)(2). *See* United States v. Armstrong, 517 U.S. 456, 463 (1996) ("Under Rule 16(a)(1)(C), a defendant may examine documents material to his defense, but, under Rule 16(a)(2), he may not examine Government work product in connection with his case").

331. FED. R. CRIM. P. 16(b)(2).

332. *But see* United States v. Williams, 792 F. Supp. 1120, 1132 (S.D. Ind. 1992) (polygraph reports are "work product" and thus not discoverable); Williams v. State, 251 Ga. 749, 752, 312 S.E.2d 40, 50 (1983) (handwritten notes of experiments of experts are work product and not discoverable).

not used as witnesses do not fall within the waiver rule.[333] In addition, such reports may be protected by the attorney-client privilege or the right to counsel.[334]

A federal district court applied the work product rule to preclude a defense "ballistics" expert from being called as a prosecution witness.[335] Although the court acknowledged that it was entering "relatively uncharted waters and the case-law is an insufficient and contradictory navigational aid,"[336] it found that the opinions that the prosecution sought to introduce "were developed at the request of, and in consultation with, the defendants' attorneys for use within those attorney's [sic] internal strategic processes."[337] The court also noted that "exhaustive research has disclosed no criminal case in which a federal court has permitted the government to elicit testimony from a defendant's consultative expert concerning that expert's efforts or opinions undertaken or developed at the request of a defense attorney in preparation for a criminal trial."[338]

In *State v. Cosey*,[339] the defense exhausted, during DNA testing, the remaining testable crime scene semen specimen, which precluded the prosecution from performing additional, more sophisticated DNA testing similar to that performed by the defense. The defendant neither intended to use the DNA tests at trial nor call the analyst as a witness. The Louisiana Supreme Court ruled that "fundamental fairness and the extraordinary circumstances presented by this case dictate that the prosecution be allowed to obtain copies of the test results in question."[340]

§ 3-21. Selected Bibliography.

2 W. LAFAVE & J. ISRAEL, CRIMINAL PROCEDURE ch. 19 (1984).
8 MOORE'S FEDERAL PRACTICE ch. 16 (1983).
2 C. WRIGHT, FEDERAL PRACTICE AND PROCEDURE 251-61 (2d ed. 1982).

---

333. *See* State *ex rel.* Richardson v. Randall, 660 S.W.2d 699, 701 (Mo. 1983) (prosecution not entitled to discovery of name of handwriting expert who was consulted but not called as a witness by the defense); Mosteller, *supra* note 288, at 1657 (noting division of authority on this issue).

334. *See* § 5-9 *infra* (attorney-client privilege).

335. United States v. Walker, 910 F. Supp. 861, 864 (N.D.N.Y. 1995) ("[T]he government should be precluded from eliciting testimony from the defenses' experts concerning the efforts they undertook at the request of defendants' attorneys, or the opinions and conclusions they developed at the behest of defendants' attorneys, unless the government first makes a showing of substantial need of that testimony and inability to obtain the substantial equivalent of that testimony without undue hardship.... The Court's conclusion is grounded in a practical application of the 'work-product' doctrine").

336. *Id.* at 866.

337. *Id.* at 865.

338. *Id.* at 864.

339. 652 So. 2d 993 (La. 1995) (per curiam).

340. *Id.* at 994.

Burns, *Pretrial Discovery in Federal Courts*, *in* 1 CRIMINAL DEFENSE TECHNIQUES ch. 10 (S. Allen, I. Rosen, E. Smolinsky & D. Winston eds. 1992).

Giannelli, *The Abuse of Scientific Evidence in Criminal Cases: The Need for Independent Crime Laboratories*, 4 VA. J. SOC. POLICY & L. 439 (1997).

Giannelli, *Criminal Discovery, Scientific Evidence, and DNA*, 44 VAND. L. REV. 791 (1991).

McDonald, *Brady: Strategies and Tactics*, *in* 1A CRIMINAL DEFENSE TECHNIQUES 23 (S. Allen, I. Rosen, E. Smolinsky & D. Winston eds. 1983).

Montoya, *A Theory of Compulsory Process Clause Discovery Rights*, 70 IND. L. J. 845 (1995).

Comment, *The Right to Independent Testing: Boon for Defendant — Burden for Prosecution?*, 74 KY. L.J. 231 (1985).

Annotations

Annot., *Consumption or destruction of physical evidence due to testing or analysis by prosecution's expert as warranting suppression of evidence or dismissal of case against accused in state court*, 40 A.L.R.4TH 594 (1985).

Annot., *Necessity or permissibility of mental examination to determine competency or credibility of complainant in sexual offense prosecution*, 45 A.L.R.4TH 310 (1986).

Annot., *Prosecution's failure to preserve potentially exculpatory evidence as violating criminal defendant's due process rights under Federal Constitution — Supreme Court cases*, 102 L. ED. 2D 1041 (1990).

Annot., *Books, papers, and documents subject to discovery by defendant under Rule 16 of Federal Rules of Criminal Procedure*, 108 A.L.R. FED. 381 (1992).

Annot., *Reports of tests, experiments, or analyses as subject to discovery by defendant under Rule 16 of Federal Rules of Criminal Procedure*, 110 A.L.R. FED. 313 (1992).

CHAPTER 4

SECURING EXPERT ASSISTANCE*

§ 4-1. In General.

In many criminal cases, securing the services of experts to examine evidence, to advise counsel, and to testify at trial is critical. As the ABA Standards note: "The quality of representation at trial ... may be excellent and yet valueless to the defendant if his defense requires the assistance of a psychiatrist or handwriting expert and no such services are available."[1] As early as 1929 Justice Cardozo commented: "[U]pon the trial of certain issues, such as insanity or forgery, experts are often necessary both for the prosecution and for defense.... [A]

*The sections in this chapter were revised and renumbered in this edition.

1. ABA STANDARDS RELATING TO PROVIDING DEFENSE SERVICES 5-1.4 (2d ed. 1980) (commentary). The third edition of the ABA STANDARDS FOR CRIMINAL JUSTICE 5-1.4 (3d ed. 1992) has been published. *See also* ABA CRIMINAL JUSTICE MENTAL HEALTH STANDARD 7-1.1 (2d ed. 1989) (discussing differences between a consulting and testifying expert).

defendant may be at an unfair disadvantage, if he is unable because of poverty to parry by his own witnesses the thrusts of those against him."[2]

§ 4-2. Prosecution & Defense Access to Experts.

Obtaining expert assistance is generally not difficult for the prosecution. The prosecution has access to the services of state, county, or metropolitan crime laboratories.[3] In addition, federal forensic laboratories often provide their services to state law enforcement agencies. For example, the services of the FBI Laboratory are "available without charge to all duly constituted state, county, and municipal law enforcement agencies of the United States and its territorial possessions."[4] These services, which are provided without charge, include both the examination of evidence and the court appearance of the expert.

---

2. Reilly v. Berry, 250 N.Y. 456, 461, 166 N.E. 165, 167 (1929). Judge Jerome Frank wrote:

> The best lawyer in the world cannot competently defend an accused person if the lawyer cannot obtain existing evidence crucial to the defense, e.g., if the defendant cannot pay the fee of an investigator to find a pivotal missing witness or a necessary document, or that of an expert accountant or mining engineer or chemist.... In such circumstances, if the government does not supply the funds, justice is denied the poor — and represents but an upper-bracket privilege.

United States v. Johnson, 238 F.2d 565, 572 (2d Cir. 1956) (dissent), *vacated*, 352 U.S. 565 (1957). *See also National Advisory Commission on Criminal Justice Standards and Goals, Courts* 280 (1973).

3. Most states have established crime laboratories. *E.g.*, IOWA CODE ANN. § 691.1; KAN. STAT. ANN. § 21-2502; LA. REV. STAT. ANN. § 40:2261; MONT. CODE ANN. § 44-3-301; N.D. CENT. CODE § 19-01-10; OHIO REV. CODE ANN. § 307.75; TENN. CODE ANN. § 38-6-103; VA. CODE § 2.1-426; WIS. STAT. ANN. § 165.75.

See also ABA STANDARDS RELATING TO THE PROSECUTION FUNCTION AND THE DEFENSE FUNCTION 3-2.4 (b) (3d ed. 1993) ("[T]he prosecutor should also be provided with funds for the employment of qualified experts as needed for particular cases"). The accompanying commentary states: "The prosecutor must also be provided with expert scientific assistance to keep pace with the need for effective investigation and prosecution of criminal activities. The value of a modern crime laboratory such as that maintained by the FBI, in the investigation and solution of crime, is universally recognized. ... In addition, public funds should be provided for the employment of the services of psychiatrists, pathologists, chemists, document analysts, ballistics experts, and other experts ...." For a listing of crime laboratories, *see* R. FOX & C. CUNNINGHAM, CRIME SCENE SEARCH AND PHYSICAL EVIDENCE HANDBOOK 174-85 (1974). *See also* PRESIDENT'S COMM. ON LAW ENFORCEMENT & ADMINISTRATION OF JUSTICE, THE CHALLENGE OF CRIME IN A FREE SOCIETY 255 (1967) (crime laboratories are "the oldest and strongest link between science and technology and criminal justice"); Stone, *Capabilities of Modern Forensic Laboratories*, 25 WM. & MARY L. REV. 659 (1984).

4. Williams, *The FBI Laboratory — Its Availability and Use by Prosecutors from Investigation to Trial*, 28 U. KAN. CITY L. REV. 95, 99 (1960). *See also* FEDERAL BUREAU OF INVESTIGATION, HANDBOOK OF FORENSIC SCIENCE ix (rev. ed. 1994); 28 C.F.R. § 0.85(g) (authorizing the FBI lab "to provide, without cost, technical and scientific assistance ..., for all duly constituted law enforcement agencies, ... which may desire to avail themselves of the service"); *FBI Announces*

Forensic laboratory services, however, are not generally available to criminal defendants. A survey of approximately 300 crime laboratories revealed that "fifty-seven percent ... would only examine evidence submitted by law enforcement officials."[5] This may account for the disparity between the defense and prosecution use of experts. In their jury study, Kalven and Zeisel commented: "Again, the imbalance between prosecution and defense appears. In 22 percent of the cases the prosecution has the only expert witness, whereas in only 3 percent of the cases does the defense have such an advantage."[6] The voiceprint cases offer another illustration. As a National Academy of Sciences report noted, a "striking fact about the trials involving voicegram evidence to date is the very large proportion in which the only experts testifying were those called by the state."[7]

A number of sources indicate that the lack of defense experts continues to be a problem.[8] In 1990, the *National Law Journal* published the results of a six-month investigation of the defenses of capital murder cases in the South. One of the "key findings" of this investigation concerned defense experts: "Judges routinely

---

New Forensic Examination Policy, 63 FBI LAW ENFORCEMENT BULL. 7 (May 1994) ("Effective July 1, 1994, the FBI Laboratory will no longer accept evidence from State and local law enforcement agencies for forensic examination in cases involving property crime investigations, except those cases that involve personal injury or for crimes that were intended to cause personal injury"); Gordon v. Thornberg, 790 F. Supp. 374, 376-77 (D.R.I. 1992) (Freedom of Information Act request for FBI lab report).

5. Peterson, Mihajlovic, & Bedrosian, *The Capabilities, Uses, and Effects of the Nation's Criminalistics Laboratories*, 30 J. FORENSIC SCI. 10, 13 (1985).

6. H. KALVEN & H. ZEISEL, THE AMERICAN JURY 139 (1966).

7. NATIONAL RESEARCH COUNCIL, ON THE THEORY AND PRACTICE OF VOICE IDENTIFICATION 49 (1979). *See also* People v. Chapter, 13 Crim. L. Rep. (BNA) 2479 (Cal. Super. 1973) ("In approximately eighty percent of the twenty-five [voiceprint] cases in which such expert testimony/opinion was admitted there was no opposing expert testimony on the issue of reliability and general acceptability of the scientific community ...").

8. *See* Fricker, *State Falters in Retrial of Escaped Con*, 81 A.B.A. J. 38, 38-39 (June 1995) ("The court-appointed defense lawyers in the first trial were denied money for independent forensic tests because the judge said the county could not afford it"; "OSBI chemists testified that one blood stain on the mattress in Munson's room was Type O and another was Type A, the same type as Munson's and [the victim's blood. One test showed that the Type A blood contained genetic markers that were in [the victim's] blood as well [as] that of 11 percent of the population. However, the chemist admitted on cross-examination that the genetic marker reading could be produced by two old stains that were mixed. The Texas pathologist who testified in the first trial that [the victim] had been killed by a .22-caliber bullet, Dr. Ralph Erdmann, has since had his license revoked and has entered guilty pleas to seven felonies relating to phony or unperformed autopsies. The prosecution did not call Erdmann to testify again. Instead, testifying for the defense, Forth Worth pathologist ... said X-rays of [the victim's] skull indicate she had been shot at least twice by larger bullets").

deny lawyers' requests for expert/investigative fees."[9] Another article reports: "In recent DNA cases in Oklahoma and Alabama, .. the defense did not retain any experts, because the presiding judge had refused to authorize funds."[10] In addition, a 1992 study of indigent defense systems noted that the "greatest disparities occur in the areas of investigators and expert witnesses, with the prosecutors possessing more resources."[11]

If a defendant has sufficient financial resources, there are sources for obtaining expert assistance.[12] If the defendant is indigent, however, the picture is altered, often drastically. A number of statutory provisions, state and federal, attempt to provide expert assistance to indigent defendants.[13] Typically, there are also specific statutes for mental competency and insanity defense cases.[14] Experts may also be appointed in post-conviction proceedings.[15] Finally, trial courts have the authority to appoint experts to assist them.[16]

In addition, the U.S. Supreme Court has recognized a due process right to defense experts, at least under certain circumstances.[17] Nevertheless, whether these sources are adequate remains questionable.

---

9. Coyle et al., *Fatal Defense: Trial and Error in the Nation's Death Belt*, NAT'L L.J., June 11, 1990, at 30. As part of the investigation, sixty death row trial lawyers were interviewed. "54.2% felt courts provided inadequate investigation and expert funds." *Id.* at 40. One attorney, who was appointed to represent a death row inmate in Georgia, had his request for the appointment of an expert denied. He commented: "There's an economic presumption of guilt.... The district attorney has all the resources of the state crime lab, and we have to go hat in hand to the judge and the DA on every request." *Id.* at 38.

See also A Study of Representation in Capital Cases in Texas, 56 TEX. B.J. 333, 408 (Apr. 1993) (Report of The Spangenberg Group prepared for the Texas State Bar) ("There is a serious underfunding of essential expert services and other expenses in capital trials and appeals").

10. Neufeld & Colman, *When Science Takes the Witness Stand*, 262 SCI. AM. 46, 53 (May 1990).

11. R. HANSON, INDIGENT DEFENDERS: GET THE JOB DONE AND DONE WELL 100 (1992) (study by the National Center for State Courts).

12. *See* NATIONAL DIRECTORY OF EXPERT WITNESSES (1997). In addition, there are several organizations that assist in securing experts. These include: The American Academy of Forensic Sciences, 410 North 21st Street, Suite 203, Colorado Springs, CO. 80904; Technical Advisory Service for Attorneys (1-800-523-2319), Law and Technology Associates, 575 Madison Avenue, New York, NY 10022.

13. *See* §§ 4-3 and 4-4 *infra.*

14. *See* § 4-7 *infra.*

15. *See* § 4-9 *infra.*

16. *See* § 4-8 *infra.*

17. *See* § 4-5 *infra.* Other constitutional bases for the right to expert assistance are discussed in § 4-6 *infra.*

§ 4-3. Federal Criminal Justice Act.

In federal trials, the Criminal Justice Act (CJA)[18] provides for expert assistance for indigent defendants. Section (e)(1) of the Act reads:

> Counsel for a person who is financially unable to obtain investigative, expert, or other services necessary for an adequate representation may request them in an *ex parte* application. Upon finding, after appropriate inquiry in an *ex parte* proceeding, that the services are necessary and the person is financially unable to obtain them, the court, or the United States magistrate if the services are required in connection with a matter over which he has jurisdiction, shall authorize counsel to obtain the services.[19]

The Act limits expenses for expert services to $1,000.00 unless the court certifies that a greater amount is "necessary to provide fair compensation for services of an unusual character or duration."[20] Until 1986 the maximum had been $300.[21]

Psychiatrists are the most common expert requested pursuant to the CJA —at least when judged by the reported cases.[22] Other requests have involved

---

18. 18 U.S.C. § 3006(A). *See generally* Oaks, *Obtaining Compensation and Defense Services Under the Federal Criminal Justice Act, in* 1 CRIMINAL DEFENSE TECHNIQUES ch. 7 (1999); Kutak, *The Criminal Justice Act of 1964*, 44 NEB. L. REV. 703 (1965); Oaks, *Improving the Criminal Justice Act*, 55 A.B.A. J. 217 (1969).

19. 18 U.S.C. § 3006(A)(e)(1). *See also* 3 C. WRIGHT, FEDERAL PRACTICE AND PROCEDURE § 740 (2d ed. 1982); Annot., *Construction and application of provision in subsection (e) of Criminal Justice Act of 1964 (18 U.S.C. § 3006A(e)) concerning right of indigent defendant to aid in obtaining services of investigator or expert*, 6 A.L.R. FED. 1007 (1971).

20. 18 U.S.C. § 3006(A)(e)(3). The Act also specifies that $300.00 may be expended without prior authorization. Such an expenditure, however, is "subject to later review." 18 U.S.C. § 3006(A)(e)(2). *See also* United States v. Bryant, 311 F. Supp. 726 (D.D.C. 1970) (amount over $300.00 reimbursable under FED. R. CRIM. P. 17(b)).

21. *See* H.R. Rep. No. 417, 99th Cong., 2d Sess. 6, reprinted in 1986 U.S. Code Cong. & Admin. News 6165, 6178.

22. *E.g.,* United States v. Roman, 121 F.3d 136, 143 (3d Cir. 1997) ("In appropriate cases a court can order that such funds be provided [for a psychiatrist] to assist an indigent defendant in preparing for sentencing"; not an abuse of discretion to deny request in this case), *cert. denied*, 522 U.S. 1061 (1998); United States v. Castro, 15 F.3d 417, 422 (5th Cir.) (defendant "never provided the district court with any evidence, aside from his drug addiction, to support his request for psychiatric evaluation"), *cert. denied*, 513 U.S. 841 (1994); United States v. Smith, 987 F.2d 888, 891 (2d Cir.) (error to deny request for psychiatric assistance for duress defense and "incomplete duress" defense for sentencing guidelines), *cert. denied*, 510 U.S. 875 (1993); United States v. Rinchack, 820 F.2d 1557, 1563-64 (11th Cir. 1987); United States v. Crews, 781 F.2d 826, 833-34 (10th Cir. 1986) ("an indigent defendant raising an insanity defense is entitled to the aid of a psychiatrist"); United States v. Reason, 549 F.2d 309, 311 (4th Cir. 1977); United States v. Bass, 477 F.2d 723, 726 (9th Cir. 1973); United States v. Theriault, 440 F.2d 713, 714 (5th Cir. 1971), *cert. denied*, 411 U.S. 984 (1973); United States v. Taylor, 437 F.2d 371, 373 (4th Cir. 1971). *See also* Annot., *Right of federal indigent criminal defendant to obtain independent psychiatric*

polygraph examiners,[23] psychologists for eyewitness identification testimony,[24] fingerprint experts,[25] handwriting examiners,[26] accountants,[27] as well as other experts.[28] These are the typical experts in criminal litigation. Less common are

---

examination pursuant to subsection (e) of Criminal Justice Act of 1964, as amended (18 U.S.C. § 3006(e)), 40 A.L.R. FED. 707 (1978).

See generally Lewin, *Mental Disorder and the Federal Indigent,* 11 S.D. L. REV. 198 (1966); Note, *An Indigent Criminal Defendant's Constitutional Right to a Psychiatric Expert,* 1984 U. ILL. L. REV. 481; Comment, *Developing Standards for Psychiatric Assistance for Indigents Under the Criminal Justice Act,* 59 IOWA L. REV. 726 (1974); Note, *Criminal Law: Indigent Defendant's Right to Independent Psychiatrist,* 7 TULSA L.J. 137 (1971); Note, *Criminal Procedure: The Indigent's Right to Psychiatric Assistance at Trial,* 20 WAYNE L. REV. 1365 (1974); Note, *The Criminal Justice Act of 1964: The Defendant's Right to an Independent Psychiatric Examination,* 28 WASH. & LEE L. REV. 443 (1971).

23. *E.g.,* United States v. Penick, 496 F.2d 1105, 1109 (7th Cir.) (request granted in part and denied in part), *cert. denied,* 419 U.S. 897 (1974). *See generally* Annot., *Right of indigent criminal defendant to polygraph test at public expense,* 11 A.L.R.4TH 733 (1982).

24. *E.g.,* United States v. Labansat, 94 F.3d 527, 530 (9th Cir. 1996) ("Counsel can easily expose through cross-examination and closing argument the unreliability, if any, of delayed eyewitness identification"), *cert. denied,* 519 U.S. 1140 (1997); United States v. Larkin, 978 F.2d 964, 971 (7th Cir. 1992), *cert. denied,* 507 U.S. 935 (1993); United States v. George, 975 F.2d 1431, 1432 (9th Cir. 1992); United States v. Brewer, 783 F.2d 841, 842-43 (9th Cir.) (not error to refuse to appoint psychologist to testify about unreliability of eyewitness identifications), *cert. denied,* 479 U.S. 831 (1986); United States v. Purham, 725 F.2d 450, 454 (8th Cir. 1984) (same); United States v. Sims, 617 F.2d 1371, 1375 (9th Cir. 1980) (same); United States v. Fosher, 590 F.2d 381, 382 (1st Cir. 1979) (same).

25. *E.g.,* United States v. Walborn, 730 F.2d 192, 194 (5th Cir.) (denial of request not error), *cert. denied,* 469 U.S. 842 (1984); United States v. Patterson, 724 F.2d 1128, 1131 (5th Cir. 1984) (denial of request error); United States v. Durant, 545 F.2d 823, 829 (2d Cir. 1976) (denial of request error).

26. *E.g.,* United States v. Perrera, 842 F.2d 73, 76-77 (4th Cir.) (denial of request not error), *cert. denied,* 488 U.S. 837 (1988); United States v. Sailer, 552 F.2d 213 (8th Cir.) (no abuse of discretion to deny request under circumstances of case), *cert. denied,* 431 U.S. 959 (1977).

27. *E.g.,* United States v. Lefkowitz, 125 F.3d 608, 620 (8th Cir. 1997) (due process not violated when court limited accused to "$169,000 in accountant expert fees under the Criminal Justice Act"), *cert. denied,* 118 S. Ct. 1527 (1998); United States v. Sloan, 65 F.3d 861, 864 (10th Cir. 1995) (request for CPA to examine defendant's financial status to show lack of drug dealing denied where prosecution conceded that defendant had no funds), *cert. denied,* 516 U.S. 1097 (1996); United States v. Kennedy, 64 F.3d 1465, 1469-73 (10th Cir. 1995) (request of $18,000 for Arthur Anderson accounting firm to conduct an audit denied where defendant granted $5,000 for a metals industry expert and $7,500 for a "Ponzi scheme" expert); United States v. Hope, 901 F.2d 1013, 1021 n.13 (11th Cir. 1990) (denial of request not error), *cert. denied,* 498 U.S. 1041 (1991).

28. *E.g.,* United States v. Cannon, 88 F.3d 1495, 1504 (8th Cir. 1996) (request for chemist concerning composition of cocaine and cocaine base for sentencing denied); United States v. Manning, 79 F.3d 212, 218-19 (1st Cir.) (request for retired police officer to testify about inadequacies of police investigation, failure to test broken glass of window for fingerprints and to trace origins of pipe bomb components denied; adding in n.4 that "[t]his is not to say, however, that expert opinion on the adequacy of a police investigation can never be necessary to an indigent defendant's defense"), *cert. denied,* 519 U.S. 853 (1996); United States v. Sloan, 65 F.3d 861, 864

requests for optometrists,[29] addictionologists,[30] theologists,[31] linguists,[32] hypnotists,[33] sexual offender profilers,[34] jury selection experts,[35] and psychiatrists to examine alleged child sex abuse victims.[36]

The general purpose of the Criminal Justice Act is to "achieve more meaningful and effective representation for defendants in Federal criminal cases."[37] In interpreting section (e), the courts have identified a number of purposes: (1) "to redress the imbalance in the criminal process when the resources of the United States Government are pitted against an indigent

---

(10th Cir. 1995) (request for medical doctor to show defendant was not a drug "user" denied where prosecution conceded this fact), *cert. denied*, 516 U.S. 1097 (1996); United States v. Scott, 48 F.3d 1389, 1395-96 (5th Cir.) (request for voice identification expert waived by lack of timely motion), *cert. denied*, 516 U.S. 902 (1995); United States v. Greschner, 802 F.2d 373, 376 (10th Cir. 1986) (request for penologist denied), *cert. denied,* 480 U.S. 908 (1987); United States v. Harris, 542 F.2d 1283 (7th Cir. 1976) (request for clinical psychologist to assist in jury selection and request for urban sociologist denied).

29. *See* United States v. Childress, 58 F.3d 693, 732 (D.C. Cir.) (request for optometrist at $200.00 per hour to bolster defendant's claim that he did not wear glasses and therefore was not person involved in a drug conspiracy denied where probative value is slight and request reinstated only two hours before trial), *cert. denied*, 516 U.S. 1098 (1995); United States v. Moss, 544 F.2d 954, 961 (8th Cir. 1976) (request for optometrist denied), *cert. denied*, 429 U.S. 1077 (1977).

30. United States v. Bailey, 112 F.3d 758, 767 (4th Cir.) (forensic pathologist, forensic psychologist, addictionologist, and blood-hair-fiber expert provided), *cert. denied*, 522 U.S. 896 (1997).

31. United States v. Bauer, 75 F.3d 1366, 1376 (9th Cir. 1996) (request for a theologian to testify on use of marijuana for religious purposes, for defense under Religious Freedom Restoration Act of 1993, remanded for determinations whether defendant is in fact a Rastafarian and whether a reasonable attorney would engage the services of a theology expert if the defendant had financial means), *cert. denied*, 519 U.S. 1131 (1997), on remand, United States v. Bauer, 84 F.3d 1549, 1559 (9th Cir.) (request for theology expert for defense under the Religious Freedom Restoration Act), *cert. denied,* 519 U.S. 901 (1996).

32. United States v. Ingle, 157 F.3d 1147, 1152 (8th Cir. 1998) (denying request for rhetorician as expert on the voluntariness of his tape recorded admissions to cellmates; "[L]inguistic issues of this kind have often been found inappropriate for expert testimony"); United States v. Valverde, 846 F.2d 513, 514 (8th Cir. 1988) (request for linguist denied).

33. United States v. Bercier, 848 F.2d 917, 919 (8th Cir. 1988) (denial of request not error).

34. United States v. St. Pierre, 812 F.2d 417, 420 (8th Cir. 1987) (request for expert to determine whether defendant fits sexual offender profile denied).

35. United States v. Nelson, 137 F.3d 1094, 1101 n.2 (9th Cir.) ("Appellants cannot demonstrate that a reasonably competent counsel would have requested funds for these studies because a study of the prejudice against Hispanics and the poor is not relevant to overcoming the lack of a prima facie showing of underrepresentation [under the 'fair cross-section' requirement for trial by jury]"), *cert. denied,* 119 S. Ct. 232 (1998).

36. United States v. Spotted War Bonnet, 882 F.2d 1360, 1362 (8th Cir. 1989) (request for psychiatrist to examine alleged child sex abuse victims denied), *cert. denied*, 112 U.S. 1187 (1992).

37. H.R. Rep. No. 1546, 91st Cong., 2d Sess. 4, reprinted in 1970 U.S. Code Cong. & Ad. News 3982, 3984.

defendant;"[38] (2) "to place indigent defendants as nearly as may be on a level of equality with nonindigent defendants in the defense of criminal cases;"[39] and (3) "to accord federal prisoners full constitutional rights under Due Process and the Sixth Amendment."[40] These purposes are not the same. The first is based on due process, the second on an equal protection rationale, and the third, in part, on the right to counsel.[41]

Standard for Appointment

A defendant seeking CJA funds must meet a two-pronged test: "(1) The accused must satisfy the court that financial inability prevents him from obtaining the services he requests; and (2) The accused must show need for such services to present an adequate defense."[42] Specifically, the statute requires expert "services necessary for an adequate defense."[43]

Courts have stated this standard in different ways. The First Circuit requires a defendant to show that the proffered expert testimony is "pivotal" or "critical" to the defense.[44] The Fifth Circuit has ruled that "where the government's case rests heavily on a theory most competently addressed by expert testimony, an indigent defendant must be afforded the opportunity to prepare and present his defense to such a theory with the assistance of his own expert pursuant to section 3006A(e)."[45] According to the Ninth Circuit, the statute requires expert services when "a reasonable attorney would engage such services for a client having the independent financial means to pay for them."[46] The Second Circuit concurs.[47]

---

38. United States v. Durant, 545 F.2d 823, 827 (2d Cir. 1976).

39. United States v. Tate, 419 F.2d 131, 132 (6th Cir. 1969). *Accord* United States v. Schappel, 445 F.2d 716, 721 n.13 (D.C. Cir. 1971).

40. Mason v. Arizona, 504 F.2d 1345, 1352 (9th Cir. 1974), *cert. denied,* 420 U.S. 936 (1975). *Accord* Proffitt v. United States, 582 F.2d 854, 857 (4th Cir. 1978), *cert. denied,* 447 U.S. 910 (1980).

41. *See* § 4-6 *infra.*

42. United States v. Schultz, 431 F.2d 907, 908 (8th Cir. 1970). *Accord* United States v. Sailer, 552 F.2d 213, 215 (8th Cir.), *cert. denied,* 431 U.S. 959 (1977). *See* § 4-10 *infra* (indigency determinations).

43. 18 U.S.C. § 3006(A)(e)(1).

44. United States v. Manning, 79 F.3d 212, 218 (1st Cir.), *cert. denied,* 519 U.S. 853 (1996).

45. United States v. Patterson, 724 F.2d 1128, 1130 (5th Cir. 1984). *Accord* United States v. Williams, 998 F.2d 258, 263 (5th Cir. 1993), *cert. denied,* 510 U.S. 1099 (1994).

46. United States v. Bass, 477 F.2d 723, 725 (9th Cir. 1973). This standard was derived from Judge Wisdom's concurring opinion in United States v. Theriault, 440 F.2d 713, 717 (5th Cir. 1971), *cert. denied,* 411 U.S. 984 (1972). *See also* United States v. Labansat, 94 F.3d 527, 530 (9th Cir. 1996) ("Labansat must show that the lack of an expert deprived him of effective assistance of counsel. He must demonstrate both that a reasonably competent counsel would have required the assistance of the requested expert for a paying client, and that he was prejudiced by the lack of expert assistance. Prejudice must be shown by clear and convincing evidence"), *cert. denied,* 519 U.S. 1140 (1997); United States v. Bauer, 75 F.3d 1366, 1376 (9th Cir. 1996) (request for a

The Eleventh Circuit has stated that "necessary" means the trial court can reject an application for appointment if it concludes that the accused "does not have a plausible claim or defense."[48]

Courts have also commented upon the scope of assistance provided by the CJA. An adequate defense includes both "pretrial and trial assistance to the defense as well as potential trial testimony."[49] It includes "preparation for cross-examination of a government expert as well as presentation of an expert defense witness."[50] Thus, the admissibility of expert testimony is not necessarily a determinative factor.[51] Finally, the Act also applies to sentencing hearings.[52]

Ex parte *Applications*

Both the application for defense services and the proceedings to determine whether to grant the request are *ex parte*. As one court has noted: "The manifest

---

theologian to testify on use of marijuana for religious purposes, for defense under Religious Freedom Restoration Act of 1993, remanded for determinations whether defendant is in fact a Rastafarian and whether a reasonable attorney would engage the services of a theology expert if the defendant had financial means), *cert. denied*, 519 U.S. 1131 (1997); United States v. Armstrong, 621 F.2d 951, 956 (9th Cir. 1980); United States v. Sims, 617 F.2d 1371, 1375 (9th Cir. 1980); United States v. Hartfield, 513 F.2d 254, 257 (9th Cir. 1975); Brinkley v. United States, 498 F.2d 505, 509-10 (8th Cir. 1974).

47. United States v. Salameh, 152 F.3d 88, 118 (2d Cir. 1998) (World Trade Center bombing) (received $35,000 in CJA funds for five experts: DNA, explosives, computers, linguistics, and culture (sociologists); *Durant* standard applied: would attorney independently engage expert for a paying client; "While the district judge should entertain such requests with liberal attitude, he is nevertheless 'obligated to exercise his discretion ...'"), *cert. denied,* 119 S. Ct. 1273 (1999);United States v. Smith, 987 F.2d 888, 891 (2d Cir.) (Second Circuit adopted *Bass* test), *cert. denied*, 510 U.S. 785 (1993);United States v. Durant, 545 F.2d 823, 827 (2d Cir. 1976).

48. United States v. Rinchack, 820 F.2d 1557, 1564 (11th Cir. 1987); United States v. Alden, 767 F.2d 314, 318-19 (7th Cir. 1984) ("plausible defense" standard used along with "private attorney" standard).

49. United States v. Bass, 477 F.2d 723, 726 (9th Cir. 1973). *Accord* United States v. Sims, 617 F.2d 1371, 1373 (9th Cir. 1980).

50. United States v. Durant, 545 F.2d 823, 827 (2d Cir. 1976).

51. *See* United States v. Sims, 617 F.2d 1371, 1375 n.3 (9th Cir. 1980) ("While the admissibility or acceptance of a particular type of expert's field of study may be a factor in considering the 'necessity' ... of appointing an expert, to hold that it was the only factor would be inconsistent with the underlying purpose of the Criminal Justice Act"). *But see* United States v. Fosher, 590 F.2d 381, 384 (1st Cir. 1979); United States v. Penick, 496 F.2d 1105, 1110 (7th Cir.), *cert. denied,* 419 U.S. 897 (1974).

52. *E.g.,* United States v. Roman, 121 F.3d 136, 143 (3d Cir. 1997) ("In appropriate cases a court can order that such funds be provided [for a psychiatrist] to assist an indigent defendant in preparing for sentencing"; not an abuse of discretion to deny request in this case), *cert. denied*, 522 U.S. 1061 (1998); United States v. Smith, 987 F.2d 888, 891 (2d Cir.) (error to deny request for psychiatric assistance for duress defense and "incomplete duress" defense for sentencing guidelines), *cert. denied*, 510 U.S. 875 (1993).

purpose of requiring that the inquiry be *ex parte* is to insure that the defendant will not have to make a premature disclosure of his case."[53] In effect, this provision permits the expert to "be a partisan witness. His conclusions need not be reported in advance of trial to the court or to the prosecution."[54] A defendant's failure to object to the presence of the prosecutor or the lack of an *ex parte* hearing is subject to plain error analysis.[55]

Procedural Issues

The failure to make a timely request for an expert constitutes a wavier.[56] The courts of appeal use an "abuse of discretion" standard when reviewing a trial court's appointment decision.[57]

---

53. Marshall v. United States, 423 F.2d 1315, 1318 (10th Cir. 1970). *Accord* United States v. Gonzales, 150 F.3d 1246, 1259 (10th Cir. 1998) ("The CJA, which requires that a defendant reveal a high degree of detail about his or her reasons for requesting assistance other than counsel in preparing for trial, recognizes that confidentiality of that detail is vital to the proper functioning of the CJA process") (citations omitted), *cert. denied,* 119 S. Ct. 918 (1999); Lawson v. Dixon, 3 F.3d 743, 751 (4th Cir. 1993) (The CJA "has been interpreted as virtually guaranteeing that decisions on expert-appointment motions will be made, as that statute requires, 'after appropriate inquiry in an *ex parte* proceeding'"), *cert. denied*, 510 U.S. 1171 (1994); United States v. Lawson, 653 F.2d 299, 304 (7th Cir. 1981), *cert. denied,* 454 U.S. 1150 (1982); United States v. Durant, 545 F.2d 823, 826 n.5 (2d Cir. 1976); United States v. Sutton, 464 F.2d 552, 553 (5th Cir. 1972); United States v. Chavis, 476 F.2d 1137, 1141 (D.C. Cir. 1973); United States v. Hamlet, 456 F.2d 1284, 1284 (5th Cir. 1972), *cert. denied,* 414 U.S. 1026 (1973). *See also* United States v. Bailey, 112 F.3d 758, 768 (4th Cir.) (not error in this case to unseal *ex parte* motions for experts), *cert. denied*, 522 U.S. 896 (1997).

54. United States v. Bass, 477 F.2d 723, 726 (9th Cir. 1973). *Accord* United States v. Theriault, 440 F.2d 713, 715 (5th Cir. 1971), *cert. denied,* 411 U.S. 984 (1973).

55. *See* United States v. Pofahl, 990 F.2d 1456, 1472 (5th Cir.) (lack of hearing), *cert. denied,* 510 U.S. 996 (1993); United States v. Greschner, 802 F.2d 373, 380 (10th Cir. 1986) (prosecutors present), *cert. denied*, 480 U.S. 908 (1987).

56. *See* United States v. Childress, 58 F.3d 693, 732 (D.C. Cir. 1995) (request denied where withdrawn and reinstated only two hours before trial), *cert. denied*, 516 U.S. 1098 (1996); United States v. Scott, 48 F.3d 1389, 1396 (5th Cir.) ("counsel never referred to the statute, or to Scott's financial ability to procure an expert. The request made by counsel was for 'time to employ' an [voice identification] expert, not for permission to employ an expert at government expense"), *cert. denied*, 516 U.S. 902 (1995); United States v. Patterson, 438 F.2d 328, 329 (5th Cir. 1971) ("The rights established by 18 U.S.C.A. 3006A(e) are procedural, and the failure to make a timely motion or request waives the necessity for the court's consideration of an appointment of an expert witness").

57. *E.g.*, United States v. Cannon, 88 F.3d 1495, 1504 (8th Cir. 1996) (district court has wide discretion); United States v. Manning, 79 F.3d 212, 218 (1st Cir.), *cert. denied*, 516 U.S. 1097 (1996); United States v. Sloan, 65 F.3d 861, 864 (10th Cir. 1995), *cert. denied*, 516 U.S. 1097 (1996); United States v. Kennedy, 64 F.3d 1465, 1470 (10th Cir. 1995); United States v. Childress, 58 F.3d 693, 732 (D.C. Cir. 1995), *cert. denied*, 516 U.S. 1098 (1996).

Fee determinations are considered administrative, rather than judicial, functions.[58] Moreover, a defense attorney is not personally liable for funds expended under the CJA.[59]

§ 4-4. State Statutes.

A number of state statutes and rules provide for expert assistance for indigent defendants.[60] These provisions, however, differ in many respects. Some explicitly provide for the services of experts,[61] while others mention only investigative services.[62] Still others refer to the reimbursement of reasonable or necessary expenses incurred by attorneys representing indigent defendants.[63]

---

58. *See* United States v. Gonzales, 150 F.3d 1246, 1251-52, 1255 n.11, 1257 (10th Cir. 1998) (newspaper seeks CJA vouchers) ("Requests for compensation for these services are submitted on CJA form 31 for death penalty cases and on form 21 for all other cases. These forms require information as to the type of services performed, such as psychiatric, fingerprint, or ballistics, and an itemization of services rendered and expenses incurred. These forms are also generally submitted at the end of trial except in capital cases .... In addition to the information contained on [the] forms ... the applicants must submit backup documentation, including detailed time sheets specifying the specific services performed and receipts for expenses incurred"; "[T]here is much support for the replacement of judges with an independent administrative board, which would handle the judiciary's present functions in administering the CJA. *See generally* COMMITTEE TO REVIEW THE CRIMINAL JUSTICE ACT, JUDICIAL CONFERENCE OF THE UNITED STATES, FINAL REPORT, 1993 WL 69540, at *35-39 (Jan. 29, 1993)"; "It is the judge who protects the interests of the public fisc in a process that has traditionally been closed to the prosecution"), *cert. denied,* 119 S. Ct. 918 (1999); United States v. Bloomer, 150 F.3d 146, 148 (2d Cir. 1998) (orders concerning fee determinations for services already rendered by an expert under § 3006A are not appealable orders: "[F]ee determinations concerning services already rendered are administrative, rather than judicial, determinations. ... Section 3006A does not provide for governmental involvement in the appointment of an expert, by way of notice or otherwise; applications for appointment of an expert are *ex parte* and nonadversarial").

59. *See* United States v. Silva, 140 F.3d 1098 (7th Cir. 1998) (attorney not personally liable for fees of an expert appointed and authorized under CJA; Applied Forensics Technologies International, Inc., examined suspicious audio tapes for $9,250 for copies and $27,000 for originals).

60. *See* N. LEFSTEIN, CRIMINAL DEFENSE SERVICES FOR THE POOR app. B (1982) (listing state statutes), Moriarty, *Liberty, Justice ... and Experts For All,* 6 LAW & EQUALITY 247, 269-72 (1988).

61. *E.g.,* HAWAII REV. STAT. § 802-7; IOWA CODE ANN. § 813.2 R. 19(4); KAN. STAT. ANN. § 22-4508; MINN. STAT. ANN. § 611.21(a); N.H. REV. STAT. ANN. § 604-A:6; N.Y. COUNTY LAW § 722-c; N.C. GEN. STAT. § 7A-454; OHIO REV. CODE ANN. § 2929.024; OR. REV. STAT. § 135.055(3)-(4); TEX. CRIM. P. CODE ANN. § 26.05(a); WASH. SUPER. CT. CRIM. R. 3.1(f).

62. *E.g.,* ALASKA STAT. § 18.85.100 (*see also* ALASKA R. CRIM. P. 39 (reasonable cost of investigation); ALASKA ADMIN. R. 12(g) (expert witness fees); UTAH CODE ANN. § 77-32-303.

63. *E.g.,* ALA. CODE § 15-12-21(d); DEL. CODE ANN. tit. 29, § 4605; IDAHO CODE § 19-860(b); S.C. CODE ANN. § 17-3-80.

The coverage of these provisions also differs. Some are limited to capital cases.[64] One statute applies only in drug prosecutions.[65] Moreover, some statutes provide for the payment of reasonable expenses[66] while others specify a maximum amount.[67] A number of the latter statutes provide for expenses above the maximum in extraordinary circumstances.[68] The procedures specified for obtaining expert assistance also vary. A number of statutes, like the Criminal Justice Act, provide for *ex parte* proceedings.[69] Other statutes are silent on this point. Some statutes also apply to the appointment of experts in post-conviction proceedings.[70]

Some statutory provisions permit the defense to submit evidence for analysis.[71]

---

64. *E.g.*, ARIZ. REV. STAT. ANN. § 13-4013(B) (capital cases); ILL. ANN. STAT. ch. 38, § 113-3(d) (capital cases); TENN. CODE ANN. § 40-14-207(b) (capital cases). *See also* CAL. PENAL CODE § 987.9 (capital and life sentence cases). *See generally* Comment, *The Constitutional Right to Assistance in Addition to Counsel in a Death Penalty Case*, 23 DUQ. L. REV. 753 (1985).

65. OHIO REV. CODE ANN. § 2925.51 (controlled substance cases).

66. *E.g.*, FLA. STAT. ANN. § 914.06; IOWA CODE ANN. § 813.2 R. 19(4); KAN. STAT. ANN. § 22-4508; WASH. SUPER. CT. CRIM. R. 3.1(f).

67. *E.g.*, ILL. ANN. STAT. ch. 38, § 113-3(d) ($250 maximum in capital cases); MINN. STAT. ANN. § 611.21 ($1,000 maximum); S.C. CODE ANN. § 17-3-80 ($2,000 maximum); W. VA. CODE § 29-21-13a(c) ($1,500 maximum).

68. *E.g.*, MINN. STAT. ANN. § 611.21(b) ($1,000 unless services are of unusual character or duration); N.H. REV. STAT. ANN. § 604-A:6 ($300 unless nature or quantity reasonably merits greater compensation); N.Y. COUNTY LAW § 722-c ($300 maximum unless extraordinary circumstances); W. VA. CODE § 29-21-13a(c) ($1,500 maximum unless good cause shown).

69. *E.g.*, KAN. STAT. ANN. § 22-4508; MINN. STAT. ANN. § 611.21(a); N.Y. COUNTY LAW § 722-c; OR. REV. STAT. § 135.055(3); TENN. CODE ANN. § 40-14-207(b); WIS. STAT. ANN. § 165.79 (results of state laboratory analysis for defense privileged).

See also People v. Berryman, 6 Cal. 4th 1048, 1071, 864 P.2d 40, 53, 25 Cal. Rptr. 2d 867, 880 (1993) (statute that specifies that application for expert funds be confidential does not preclude cross-examination of criminalist about compensation), *cert. denied*, 513 U.S. 1076 (1995); *Ex parte* Lexington County, 442 S.E.2d 589, 593 (S.C. 1994) (statute requires an *ex parte* hearing; a county has no standing to participate in this hearing).

70. *See* Owens v. State, 908 S.W.2d 923, 929 (Tenn. 1995) (TENN. CODE ANN. § 40-14-207(b), applies to capital post-conviction cases). *But see* Davis v. State, 912 S.W.2d 689, 696 (Tenn. 1995) (Statute does not apply in non-capital post-conviction cases; also no constitutional right: "In the absence of a Constitutional right to counsel, there can be no Constitutional right to support services at state expense"). *See also* People v. Chichester, 162 Misc. 2d 658, 659, 618 N.Y.S.2d 201, 202 (Co. Ct. 1994) (convicted defendant has right, at his own expense, to use DNA testing on physical evidence in the possession of the prosecutor's office).

71. *E.g.*, IOWA CODE ANN. § 691.1; N.D. CENT. CODE § 19-01-10; WIS. STAT. ANN. § 165.79. At one time Virginia had a comparable provision. *See generally* Note, *Exploring the Limits of Brady v. Maryland: Criminal Discovery as a Due Process Right in Access to Police Investigations and State Crime Laboratories*, 15 U. RICH. L. REV. 189, 208-10 (1980).

§ 4-5. Due Process: *Ake v. Oklahoma*.

Prior to 1985 the U.S. Supreme Court had considered an indigent's right to expert services only once. In *United States ex rel. Smith v. Baldi*[72] a murder defendant argued that "the assistance of a psychiatrist was necessary to afford him adequate counsel"[73] in the presentation of his insanity defense and thus the state was obligated to provide such assistance. In rejecting this argument, the Supreme Court stated, "We cannot say that the State has that duty by constitutional mandate."[74]

Smith, however, was not a convincing precedent. First, it could easily be distinguished on the facts. Two defense psychiatrists had examined Smith, and consequently the Supreme Court's opinion could be read as rejecting only a right to additional experts.[75] More importantly, *Smith* was decided in 1953, and its continued vitality after the Warren Court's revolution in criminal procedure during the 1960s seemed suspect. Indeed, the Fifth Circuit had noted that the "*Baldi* decision ... was severely undercut by the [Supreme] Court's decision in *Griffin v. Illinois*."[76] Moreover, in 1981 the Supreme Court in *Little v. Streater*[77] ruled that an indigent defendant in a paternity action, a "quasi-criminal" proceeding, had the right to a blood grouping test at state expense. In 1983, the Court in *Barefoot v. Estelle*[78] upheld the admissibility of expert testimony of future dangerousness in capital cases. In so ruling, the Court wrote that the "jurors should not be barred from hearing the views of the State's psychiatrists along with opposing views of the defendant's doctors."[79] In a footnote the Court noted that there was no "contention that, despite petitioner's claim of indigence, the court refused to provide an expert for petitioner."[80]

Nevertheless, some courts continued to refuse to recognize a right to expert assistance. For example, the Mississippi Supreme Court concluded: "Neither the United States Constitution nor the Mississippi Constitution requires that the Nation or State furnish an indigent defendant with the assistance of a psychiatrist. The only assistance that they require is the assistance of legal counsel."[81] In 1985,

---

72. 344 U.S. 561 (1953).

73. *Id.* at 568.

74. *Id.*

75. *See* Bush v. McCollum, 231 F. Supp. 560, 564 (N.D. Tex. 1964) (court distinguished *Smith* because two defense psychiatrists had testified in that case), *aff'd,* 344 F.2d 672 (5th Cir. 1965).

76. Pedrero v. Wainwright, 590 F.2d 1383, 1390 n.6 (5th Cir.), *cert. denied*, 444 U.S. 943 (1979). *See also* United States ex *rel.* Huguley v. Martin, 325 F. Supp. 489, 493 (N.D. Ga. 1971). For a discussion of *Griffin, see* § 4-6(B), *infra.*

77. 452 U.S. 1 (1981).

78. 463 U.S. 880 (1983).

79. *Id.* at 898-99.

80. *Id.* at 899 n.5.

81. Phillips v. State, 197 So. 2d 241, 244 (Miss. 1967). *See also* Stockton v. Commonwealth, 227 Va. 124, 140-41, 314 S.E.2d 371, 382 (1984) (There is "no constitutional right to the

however, the U.S. Supreme Court recognized, for the first time, a due process right to expert assistance; that case was *Ake v. Oklahoma.*[82]

Ake v. Oklahoma

Ake was charged with capital murder. At arraignment, his conduct was "so bizarre" that the trial judge ordered, *sua sponte,* a mental evaluation. Ake was found incompetent to stand trial but later recovered due to antipsychotic drugs. When the prosecution resumed, Ake's attorney requested a psychiatric evaluation at state expense to prepare an insanity defense. Citing *Smith*, the trial court refused. Thus, although insanity was the only contested issue at trial, no psychiatrists testified on this issue, and Ake was convicted. In the penalty stage, the prosecution relied on state psychiatrists, who testified that Ake was "dangerous to society," in seeking the death sentence. This testimony stood unrebutted because Ake could not afford an expert. On review, the Supreme Court overturned Ake's conviction.

The Court quickly dismissed the precedential value of *Smith*. Since defense psychiatrists had testified in *Smith*, the Court held that *Smith* did not stand for the broad proposition that there was no constitutional right to a psychiatric examination, but at most, stood for "the proposition that there is no constitutional right to more psychiatric assistance than the defendant in *Smith* had received."[83] More importantly, the Court recognized that *Smith* had been decided "at a time when indigent defendants in state courts had no constitutional right to even the presence of counsel."[84] Thus, according to the Court, *Smith* did not preclude consideration of "whether fundamental fairness today requires a different result."[85]

The Court's due process analysis relied on a three-pronged test derived from *Matthews v. Eldridge.*[86]

> Three factors are relevant to this determination. The first is the private interest that will be affected by the action of the State. The second is the governmental interest that will be affected if the safeguard is to be provided. The third is the probable value of the additional or substitute

---

appointment, at public expense, of an investigator to assist in his defense.... When a trial court employs an investigator at public expense, it is 'an act of judicial grace not constitutionally required'"). Other cases are summarized in Annot., *Right of indigent defendant in criminal case to aid of state by appointment of investigator or expert*, 34 A.L.R.3D 1256 (1970).

82. 470 U.S. 68 (1985). Ake was later retried and convicted. He again raised a right to expert assistance issue; this time the issue involved the appointment of a psychiatrist for a competency hearing. Ake v. State, 778 P.2d 460, 464-65 (Okla. Crim. App. 1989).

83. 470 U.S. at 85.

84. *Id.*

85. *Id.*

86. 424 U.S. 319 (1976).

> procedural safeguards that are sought, and the risk of an erroneous deprivation of the affected interest if those safeguards are not provided.[87]

Applying these factors, the Court found that a defendant's interest in the accuracy of a criminal trial that places his life or liberty at risk "is almost uniquely compelling."[88] In contrast, the state's only interest is economic. Although the state claimed that the cost of providing expert assistance would result in "a staggering burden to the State," the Court dismissed this argument, pointing out (1) that many other jurisdictions provided psychiatric assistance to indigent defendants and (2) that its holding was limited to "one competent psychiatrist."[89] Finally, the Court considered the probable value of the assistance sought and the risk of error if it was not provided. The Court concluded that the need for expert assistance was critical and the risk of error "extremely high"[90] if assistance was not provided.

The Court used different formulae to state its holding.[91] In one passage, the Court wrote: "[W]hen a State brings its judicial power to bear on an indigent in a criminal proceeding, it must take steps to assure that the defendant has a fair opportunity to present his defense."[92] This fair opportunity mandates that an accused be provided with the "basic tools of an adequate defense."[93] In another passage, the Court elaborated on what it meant by a "fair opportunity" and "basic tools" for an adequate defense: "We hold that when a defendant has made a preliminary showing that his sanity at the time of the offense is likely to be a significant factor at trial, the Constitution requires that a State provide access to a psychiatrist's assistance on this issue, if the defendant cannot otherwise afford one."[94]

The facts met this standard: (1) Ake's only defense was insanity. (2) His bizarre behavior at the arraignment, just four months after the crime, prompted the trial court to order sua sponte a mental examination. (3) A state psychiatrist declared Ake incompetent to stand trial. (4) He was found competent six weeks later only if he stayed on Thorazine, an antipsychotic drug. (5) The state's

---

87. 470 U.S. at 77.

88. *Id.* at 78.

89. *Id.* at 79.

90. *Id.* at 82.

91. The Supreme Court used the three-pronged test set forth in *Matthews v. Eldridge* to determine whether a right to expert assistance was constitutionally required but that is not the test the Court fashioned for applying the right. *See* Johnson v. Gibson, 169 F.3d 1239, 1246 (10th Cir. 1999) ("The [*Ake*] first and second prongs of this test are easily satisfied .... Thus, the critical factor in assessing whether a particular expert is a required 'basic tool' of an adequate defense is the third prong of the test that deals with probable value and risk of error associated with the additional assistance").

92. 470 U.S. at 76.

93. *Id.* at 77 (quoting Britt v. North Carolina, 404 U.S. 226 (1971)).

94. *Id.* at 74.

psychiatric testimony acknowledged the severity of Ake's mental illness and the possibility that it "might have begun many years earlier." (6) The burden of producing evidence of insanity rested, under state law, with the defendant. In a footnote, however, the Court commented: "We express no opinion as to whether any of these factors, alone or in combination, is necessary to make this finding."[95]

In addition, the Court found a due process violation for the denial of expert assistance at the death penalty hearing, at which state experts testified about Ake's future dangerousness.

While the *Ake* decision settled the core issue by recognizing a right to expert assistance, it left a number of important issues unresolved. These issues are discussed in the following sections.

§ 4-5(A). Noncapital Cases.

In his concurring opinion, Chief Justice Burger emphasized that *Ake* involved a capital case: "The facts of the case and the question presented confine the actual holding of the Court. In capital cases the finality of the sentence imposed warrants protections that may or may not be required in other cases."[96] Some courts initially accepted this limitation, one writing that "*Ake* does not reach noncapital cases."[97]

Although *Ake* involved a capital defendant, nothing in the majority opinion suggested that the newly-recognized right to expert assistance was limited to death penalty cases. Justice Rehnquist, the lone dissenter, implicitly acknowledged that the majority opinion was not so limited. He criticized the majority because "the constitutional rule announced by the Court is far too broad. I would limit the rule to capital cases."[98] Moreover, the Court in *Little v. Streater*,[99] a prior civil case, had ruled that an indigent defendant in a paternity action had the right to a blood grouping test at state expense.

Most courts assume that *Ake* applies to noncapital cases. As the Eighth Circuit has noted, "Nor do we draw a decisive line for due-process purposes between capital and noncapital cases."[100]

---

95. *Id.* at 86 n.12.

96. *Id.* at 87.

97. Isom v. State, 488 So. 2d 12, 13 (Ala. Crim. App. 1986). *Accord* McCord v. State, 507 So. 2d 1030, 1033 (Ala. Crim. App. 1987). *But see Ex parte* Sanders, 612 So. 2d 1199, 1201-02 (Ala. 1993) ("ballistics" expert; no mention of noncapital limitation).

98. 470 U.S. at 87. At one point in the *Ake* opinion, the Court spoke of the "interest in the accuracy of a criminal proceeding that places an individual's life *or liberty* at risk..." 470 U.S. at 78 (emphasis added).

99. 452 U.S. 1, 16-17 (1981).

100. Little v. Armontrout, 835 F.2d 1240, 1243 (8th Cir. 1987) (en banc) (error to fail to appoint hypnotist), *cert. denied,* 487 U.S. 1210 (1988). *See also* Cowley v. Stricklin, 929 F.2d 640, 643 (11th Cir. 1991) (prison term imposed); State v. Barnett, 909 S.W.2d 423, 427-28 (Tenn. 1995)

§ 4-5(B). Misdemeanor Cases.

If *Ake* applies to noncapital cases, there is a need to establish another baseline — e.g., all felony cases. One commentator has argued that the right to expert assistance should extend to all cases in which imprisonment is imposed,[101] which is the standard used for the right to counsel.[102] In *Elmore v. State,*[103] the court assumed that *Ake* applied in a DUI misdemeanor case, in which the defendant was sentenced to 180 days confinement probated for two years. Nevertheless, the court found that the requisite showing had not been made.[104]

§ 4-5(C). Nonpsychiatric Experts.

Ake involved psychiatric experts in an insanity defense case, and although the importance of expert testimony in this type of trial played a critical role in the decision, the Court's rationale extends to prosecutions involving other types of experts. Indeed, the Court not only held that Ake had the right to expert assistance for the insanity defense but also on the "future dangerousness" issue raised in the penalty stage.[105] Moreover, in a later case, *Caldwell v. Mississippi,*[106]

("Certainly, there is no explicit language in the *Ake* decision limiting its application to capital cases.... [O]nly one jurisdiction has concluded that *Ake* does not apply outside the capital case context. Marlow v. State, 538 So. 2d 804 (Ala. Crim. App. 1988).... The due process principle of fundamental fairness applies to all criminal prosecutions, and does not rest upon the severity of the sanction sought or imposed"); State v. Taylor, 939 S.W.2d 148, 152 (Tex. Crim. App. 1996) ("[W]e have also extended — at least implicitly — the due process protections recognized in *Ake* beyond the capital context").

101. Note, *Expert Services and the Indigent Criminal Defendant: The Constitutional Mandate of Ake v. Oklahoma,* 84 MICH. L. REV. 1326, 1329 (1986).

102. *See* Argersinger v. Hamlin, 407 U.S. 25, 33 (1972) ("The requirement of counsel may well be necessary for a fair trial even in a petty offense prosecution. We are by no means convinced that legal and constitutional questions involved in a case that actually leads to imprisonment even for a brief period are any less complex than when a person can be sent off for six months or more"); Scott v. Illinois, 440 U.S. 367, 373 (1979) ("[T]he central premise of *Argersinger* — that actual imprisonment is a penalty different in kind from fines or the mere threat of imprisonment — is eminently sound and warrants adoption of actual imprisonment as the line defining the constitutional right to appointment of counsel").

103. 968 S.W.2d 462 (Tex. App. 1998).

104. *See also* Rey v. State, 897 S.W.2d 333, 346 (Tex. Crim. App. 1995) (concurring) ("The interest in accuracy is considerably less in noncapital cases, especially in lower level felony or misdemeanor cases where the accused, if convicted, faces a short period of incarceration, or even a fine and/or a probated sentence. In such cases, the accused's burden of proof to support his request for a state-funded expert should be clear and convincing evidence and great weight should be given to the State's concern for cost").

105. "[D]ue process requires access to a psychiatric examination on relevant issues, to the testimony of the psychiatrist, and to assistance in preparation at the sentencing phase." 470 U.S. at 84. The right to a defense expert to rebut expert testimony of future dangerousness was foreshadowed in Barefoot v. Estelle, 463 U.S. 880 (1983). In upholding the use of such testimony, the Court declined to consider a trial court's refusal to appoint fingerprint and ballistics experts because the defendant had not made a sufficient showing of need. The Court, however, gave no indication that fingerprint or ballistic experts were beyond the scope of *Ake*. In addition, the Court in *Little v. Streater*,[107] a prior case, had ruled that an indigent defendant in a civil paternity action had the right to a blood grouping test at state expense.

Nevertheless, some early cases adopted a restrictive position. For example, the Alabama Supreme Court rejected a defense request for the appointment of a forensic pathologist by noting that "there is nothing contained in the *Ake* decision to suggest that the United States Supreme Court was addressing anything other than psychiatrists and the insanity defense."[108] In contrast, the Eighth Circuit ruled that "there is no principled way to distinguish between psychiatric and nonpsychiatric experts. The question in each case must be not what field of science or expert knowledge is involved, but rather how important the scientific issue is in the case, and how much help a defense expert could have given."[109] The Alabama Supreme Court later ruled that an indigent was entitled to a DNA expert under *Ake*.[110]

---

the Court wrote that the "jurors should not be barred from hearing the views of the State's psychiatrists along with opposing views of the defendant's doctors." *Id.* at 898-99. In a footnote the Court noted that there was no "contention that, despite petitioner's claim of indigence, the court refused to provide an expert for petitioner." *Id.* at 899 n.5.

106. 472 U.S. 320, 323 n.1 (1985). *See* Johnson v. Oklahoma, 484 U.S. 878 (1987) (J. Marshall with J. Brennan dissenting to denial of certiorari) (Court should decide "the important question of whether and when an indigent defendant is entitled to non-psychiatric expert assistance").

107. 452 U.S. 1, 16-17 (1981).

108. *Ex parte* Grayson, 479 So. 2d 76, 82 (Ala.), *cert. denied,* 474 U.S. 865 (1985). *Accord* Stafford v. Love, 726 P.2d 894, 896 (Okla. 1986); Plunkett v. State, 719 P.2d 834, 839 (Okla. Crim. App.) (no right to bloodstain expert) ("Such a risk in other areas of scientific evidence is not necessarily present because the scientific expert is often able to explain to the jury how a conclusion was reached, the defense counsel can attack that conclusion, and the jury can then decide whether the conclusion had a sound basis"), *cert. denied,* 479 U.S. 1019 (1986).

109. Little v. Armontrout, 835 F.2d 1240, 1243 (8th Cir. 1987) (en banc) (error to fail to appoint hypnotist), *cert. denied,* 487 U.S. 1210 (1988). *See also* Rey v. State, 897 S.W.2d 333 (Tex. Crim. App. 1995) (en banc) ("*Ake* is not limited to psychiatric experts").

110. *Ex parte* Dubose, 662 So. 2d 1189, 1192-94 (Ala. 1995) ("[N]or have our cases interpreting *Ake* specifically ruled that the holding of *Ake* was limited to cases involving a psychiatrist.... [W]e conclude that the principles enunciated in *Ake*, and grounded in the due process guarantee of fundamental fairness, apply in a case of nonpsychiatric expert assistance...") (citing Alabama cases involving requests for experts for change of venue motions, semen tests, race bias, jury polling, jury selection, death-qualified juries, and fingerprints). *See also Ex parte* Moody, 684 So. 2d 114, 119 (Ala. 1996) ("Alabama Courts have extended *Ake* to other types of expert witnesses necessary to the defense") (citing DNA and ballistic experts); *Ex parte* Sanders, 612 So. 2d 1199, 1201 (Ala. 1993) ("ballistics" expert).

Numerous cases have recognized a right to assistance outside the insanity defense context, including such areas as toxicology,[111] pathology,[112] fingerprinting,[113] hypnosis,[114] serology,[115] DNA profiling,[116] ballistics,[117]

---

111. Bright v. State, 265 Ga. 265, 455 S.E.2d 37, 50-51 (1995) (failure to appoint toxicologist to explain effects of a history of cocaine use at death penalty hearing violated *Ake*), *cert. denied*, 116 S. Ct. 196 (1995).

112. *E.g.,* Sommers v. Commonwealth, 843 S.W.2d 879, 883-85 (Ky. 1992) (failure to appoint defense pathologist and arson expert violated state statute which implements due process right); State v. Ballard, 333 N.C. 515, 518, 428 S.E.2d 178, 180 (*Ake* applies to pathologists, medical experts, fingerprint examiners, and investigators), *cert. denied*, 510 U.S. 984 (1993); Rey v. State, 897 S.W.2d 333 (Tex. Crim. App. 1995) (forensic pathologist).

113. *E.g.,* People v. Lawson, 163 Ill. 2d 187, 230, 644 N.E.2d 1172, 1192 (1994) (shoeprint and fingerprint expert); State v. Carmouche, 527 So. 2d 307 (La. 1988); State v. Bridges, 325 N.C. 529, 533-34, 385 S.E.2d 337, 339 (1989); State v. Moore, 321 N.C. 327, 343-45, 364 S.E.2d 648, 656-57 (1988). *See generally* Annot., *Right of indigent defendant in state criminal case to assistance of fingerprint expert*, 72 A.L.R.4TH 874 (1989).

114. Little v. Armontrout, 835 F.2d 1240, 1243 (8th Cir. 1987) (en banc), *cert. denied,* 487 U.S. 1210 (1988).

115. State v. Carmouche, 527 So. 2d 307 (La. 1988) (serologists appointed).

116. *E.g., Ex parte* Dubose, 662 So. 2d 1189, 1192-93 (Ala. 1995); Prater v. State, 307 Ark. 180, 200, 820 S.W.2d 429, 439 (1991) (Trial court erred when it declined to appoint a defense expert "because of a shortage of county funds") (basis for right to defense expert not specified); Cade v. State, 658 So. 2d 550, 555 (Fla. App.), *rev. denied*, 663 So. 2d 631 (Fla. 1995); Polk v. State, 612 So. 2d 381, 393-94 (Miss. 1992) (appendix guidelines for future DNA cases) ("It is also imperative that no defendant have [DNA] evidence admitted against him without the benefit of an independent expert witness to evaluate the data on his behalf." *Ake* requires defendant "be allowed reasonable funds for access to an expert who can independently evaluate the evidence presented against him by the State, analyze it, and present that analysis at trial").

But see People v. Leonard, 224 Mich. App. 569, 581, 569 N.W.2d 663, 669 ("[O]nly two courts have held that whenever the prosecution intends to introduce DNA evidence against a defendant at trial, the defendant has a due process right to an appointment of a DNA expert to assist in his defense"), *app. denied*, 456 Mich. 888, 570 N.W.2d 659 (1997); State v. Huchting, 927 S.W.2d 411, 420 (Mo. App. 1996) ("[W]e disagree with his contention that the average attorney is ill-equipped to defend against [DNA] evidence. To the contrary, law libraries — *i.e.*, law journals, practitioners' guides, annotated law reports, CLE materials, etc. — are teeming with information and advice for lawyers preparing to deal with DNA evidence in trial. Even a cursory perusal of the literature in this area reveals copious lists of questions for defense attorneys to use in cross-examinations and other strategies for undermining the weight of DNA evidence"); Husske v. Commonwealth, 252 Va. 203, 476 S.E.2d 920 (1996) (under *Ake*, "basic tools may include the appointment of non-psychiatric experts" but defendant failed to show a particularized need for a DNA expert; also no prejudice because defendant confessed), *cert. denied*, 519 U.S. 1154 (1997).

See also NATIONAL RESEARCH COUNCIL, DNA TECHNOLOGY IN FORENSIC SCIENCE 147, 149 (National Academy of Sciences Press, 1992) ("Defense counsel must have access to adequate expert assistance, even when the admissibility of the results of analytical techniques is not in question, because there is still a need to review the quality of the laboratory work and the interpretation of results"; "Because of the potential power of DNA evidence, authorities must make funds available to pay for expert witnesses...").

117. *Ex parte* Sanders, 612 So. 2d 1199, 1201 (Ala. 1993).

handwriting,[118] bite marks,[119] blood spatter,[120] the "battered wife syndrome,"[121] as well as other types of expertise.[122]

§ 4-5(D). Role of Expert: Neutral or Partisan.

Ake fails to specify clearly the role of the expert — whether the appointment of a neutral expert, who reports to the court, satisfies *Ake*, or whether a partisan defense expert is required.[123] At one point in the opinion the Court stated that the defendant had the right to "one competent psychiatrist"[124] when an insanity defense is raised. It also held that the right to expert assistance did not include the "right to choose a psychiatrist of his personal liking or to receive funds to hire his own."[125] Neither of these passages, however, is conclusive, and other passages point toward a partisan role. According to the Court, the accused is guaranteed "access to a competent psychiatrist who will conduct an appropriate examination and assist in evaluation, preparation, and presentation of the defense."[126] This expert would "conduct a professional examination on issues relevant to the defense, to help determine whether the insanity defense is viable, to present testimony, and to assist in preparing the cross-examination of a State's psychiatric witnesses."[127] In *Tuggle v. Netherland*[128] the Supreme Court, in a

---

118. People v. Dickerson, 239 Ill. App. 3d 951, 958, 606 N.E.2d 762, 767 (1992).

119. Thornton v. State, 255 Ga. 434, 435, 339 S.E.2d 240, 241 (1986).

120. James v. State, 613 N.E.2d 15, 21-22 (Ind. 1993). *But see* Stewart v. Commonwealth, 427 S.E.2d 394, 405 (Va.) ("Stewart cites no cases that indicate such assistance [blood spatter expert] is required in order to provide the constitutionally required 'basic tools of an adequate defense'"), *cert. denied*, 510 U.S. 848 (1993).

121. Dunn v. Roberts, 963 F.2d 308, 314 (10th Cir. 1992); Doe v. Superior Court, 39 Cal. App. 4th 538, 545, 45 Cal. Rptr. 2d 888, 892 (1995) ("The problem in this case is that the record is insufficient to determine whether Jane has access to a 'competent' psychiatrist or psychologist.... But this is not a run-of-mill case and the request is for someone with experience in a particular specialty [battered woman syndrome & post-traumatic stress syndrome]").

122. *E.g.*, State v. Coker, 412 N.W.2d 589, 590 (Iowa 1987) (intoxication expert); State v. Ballard, 333 N.C. 515, 518, 428 S.E.2d 178, 180 (1993) (*Ake* applies to pathologists, medical experts, fingerprint examiners, and investigators), *cert. denied*, 510 U.S. 984 (1993).

See generally Annot., *Right of indigent defendant in state criminal case to assistance of chemist, toxicologist, technician, narcotics expert, or similar nonmedical specialist in substance analysis*, 74 A.L.R.4TH 388 (1989); Annot., *Right of indigent defendant in state criminal case to assistance of expert in social attitudes*, 74 A.L.R.4TH 330 (1989).

123. *See Ake*, 470 U.S. at 92 (J. Rehnquist, dissenting) ("I see no reason why the defendant should be entitled to an opposing view, or to a 'defense' advocate"). *See also* Vickers v. Arizona, 497 U.S. 1033, 1036 (1990) (J. Marshall dissenting from denial of certiorari) ("*Ake* requires the appointment of a psychiatrist who will assist in the preparation of the defense, not one who will merely give an independent assessment to the judge or jury").

124. 470 U.S. at 79.

125. *Id.* at 83.

126. *Id.*

127. *Id.* at 82.

1995 per curiam opinion, referred to *Ake* as providing for an "independent psychiatrist."[129] The Court also wrote: "The *Ake* error prevented petitioner from developing his own psychiatric evidence to rebut the Commonwealth's evidence and to enhance his defense in mitigation. As a result, the Commonwealth's psychiatric evidence went unchallenged, which may have unfairly increased its persuasiveness in the eyes of the jury."[130]

The lower courts split on this issue. The Fifth Circuit has ruled that a "court-appointed psychiatrist, whose opinion and testimony is available to both sides, satisfies [the accused's] rights."[131] The Tenth Circuit rejected that view:

> That duty [to appoint a psychiatrist] cannot be satisfied with the appointment of an expert who ultimately testifies contrary to the defense on the issue of competence. The essential benefit of having an expert in the first place is denied the defendant when the services of the doctor must be shared with the prosecution. In this case, the benefit sought was not only the testimony of a psychiatrist to present the defendant's side of the case, but also the assistance of an expert to interpret the findings of an expert witness and to aid in the preparation of his cross-examination. Without that assistance, the defendant was deprived of the fair trial due process demands.[132]

Other federal decisions support this view.[133] The Eighth Circuit has also rejected the notion that the right to subpoena state experts is an appropriate consideration:

---

128. 516 U.S. 10 (1995) (per curiam) (state presented psychiatric testimony of "future dangerousness" in penalty phase of capital case; Court remanded for determination "whether harmless-error analysis is applicable to this case"), *on remand*, 79 F.3d 1386, 1396 (4th Cir.) (finding harmless error), *cert. denied*, 519 U.S. 894 (1996).

129. *Id.* at 12.

130. *Id.* at 13.

131. Granviel v. Lynaugh, 881 F.2d 185, 191 (5th Cir. 1989) ("The state is not required to permit defendants to shop around for a favorable expert.... He has no right to the appointment of a psychiatrist who will reach biased or only favorable conclusions"), *cert. denied,* 495 U.S. 963 (1990); Commonwealth v. Reid, 537 Pa. 167, 642 A.2d 453, 457 (*Ake* contemplates appointment of neutral expert), *cert. denied*, 510 U.S. 904 (1994).

132. United States v. Sloan, 776 F.2d 926, 929 (10th Cir. 1985). *Accord* Castro v. Oklahoma, 71 F.3d 1502, 1515 (10th Cir. 1995) ("Dr. Hamilton's refusal to testify on Mr. Castro's behalf in and of itself makes his assistance inadequate. In explicating the right to expert psychiatric assistance at sentencing, the Court in *Ake* specifically noted part of the expert's role included taking the stand.... Dr. Hamilton's informal agreement with counsel specifically included a stipulation he would not be called to testify"); Dunn v. Roberts, 963 F.2d 308 (10th Cir. 1992); Lilles v. Saffle, 945 F.2d 333, 340 (10th Cir. 1991), *cert. denied,* 502 U.S. 1066 (1992); United States v. Austin, 933 F.2d 833, 841 (10th Cir. 1991).

133. *E.g.,* Cowley v. Stricklin, 929 F.2d 640, 643 (11th Cir. 1991); Smith v. McCormick, 914 F.2d 1153, 1157 (9th Cir. 1990) ("The right to psychiatric assistance does not mean the right to place the report of a 'neutral' psychiatrist before the court; rather it means the right to use the

"[T]he ability to subpoena a state examiner and to question that person on the stand does not amount to the expert assistance required by *Ake*."[134]

Many state cases are in accord.[135] For example, in *De Freece v. State*[136] the Texas Court of Criminal Appeals ruled that the appointment of a "disinterested" court expert did not satisfy the demands of *Ake*. The court explained:

> In an adversarial system due process requires at least a reasonably level playing field at trial. In the present context that means more than just an examination by a "neutral" psychiatrist. It also means the appointment of a psychiatrist to provide technical assistance to the accused, to help evaluate the strength of his defense, to offer his own expert diagnosis at trial if it is favorable to that defense, and to identify the weaknesses in the State's case, if any, by testifying himself and/or preparing counsel to cross-examine opposing experts. We recognize that the accused is not entitled to a psychiatrist of his choice, or even to one who believes the accused was insane at the time of the offense. *Ake* makes this much clear. But even a psychiatrist who ultimately believes the accused was sane can prove invaluable by pointing out contrary indicators and exposing flaws in the diagnoses of State's witnesses.[137]

---

services of a psychiatrist in whatever capacity defense counsel deems appropriate — including to decide, with the psychiatrist's assistance, not to present to the court particular claims of mental impairment"); Williamson v. Reynolds, 904 F. Supp. 1529, 1561-62 (E.D. Okla. 1995) ("As science has increasingly entered the courtroom and begun to play an enlarging role in criminal prosecutions, the importance of the expert witness has also grown.... This court disagrees that cross-examination of the State's experts was an acceptable substitute for Petitioner's own experts.... [W]hen forensic evidence and expert testimony are critical parts of the criminal prosecution of an indigent defendant, due process requires the State to provide an expert who is not beholden to the prosecution"), *rev'd on other grounds*, Williamson v. Ward, 110 F.3d 1508, 1522 (10th Cir. 1997) (due process, not *Daubert*, standard applies in habeas proceedings); Buttrum v. Black, 721 F. Supp. 1268, 1312-13 (N.D. Ga. 1989) ("*Ake* contemplates a psychiatrist who will work closely with the defense by conducting an independent examination, testifying if necessary, and preparing for the sentencing phase of the trial"), *aff'd*, 908 F.2d 695 (11th Cir. 1990).

134. Starr v. Lockhart, 23 F.3d 1280, 1289 (8th Cir.), *cert. denied*, 513 U.S. 995 (1994).

135. *See* Binion v. Commonwealth, 891 S.W.2d 383, 386 (Ky. 1995); Harrison v. State, 635 So. 2d 894, 902 (Miss. 1994) (en banc) ("Due process and fundamental fairness required the lower court to allow the defense access to an independent pathologist ..."); Polk v. State, 612 So. 2d 381, 393-94 (Miss. 1992) (DNA) (*Ake* requires defendant "be allowed reasonable funds for access to an expert who can independently evaluate the evidence presented against him by the State, analyze it, and present that analysis at trial").

136. 848 S.W.2d 150, 159 (Tex. Crim. App.) ("We reject the notion that a 'court's expert' necessarily fulfills the role of psychiatric assistant to the indigent accused envisioned by *Ake*.... In [this] context the phrase 'court's expert' is an oxymoron"), *cert. denied*, 510 U.S. 905 (1993).

137. *Id.*

The court also rejected the notion that an "admirable" cross-examination of the prosecution expert or the opportunity to subpoena an expert justified the failure to appoint a defense expert.[138]

In *State v. Taylor*,[139] the same court again addressed this issue, albeit in a different context. At the defendant's request, the trial court appointed a DNA expert to examine semen in a rape case. The expert reported that the defendant's DNA fell within a class of persons (one to 12 million random match) that could have deposited the semen. The report was also sent to the prosecutor, who immediately adopted the expert as a prosecution witness. The court of appeals reversed, holding that this expert was not a defense expert under *Ake*. The court wrote: "[The expert] furnished her inculpatory scientific conclusions to all parties, including the prosecution. If [the expert] was genuinely appellant's DNA expert, then her conclusions were the work-product of defense counsel and would never have been provided to the prosecutor."[140] Significantly, the court recognized that *Ake* encompasses more than a *testifying* defense expert; it requires a *consulting* expert — "due process, at a minimum, requires expert aid in an evaluation of a defendant's case in an effort to present it in the best possible light to the jury."[141]

In an insightful opinion, the Alabama Supreme Court recognized the distinction between a partisan expert and an expert of the defense's choice. The *Ake* right is analogous to the right to counsel where the right to legal representation does not necessarily include the right to counsel of "choice."[142] The court wrote: "Similarly, an indigent defendant is not entitled to legal counsel of his choice, when counsel is to be paid by public funds, but rather is entitled to competent legal representation."[143] The court went on to hold that "an indigent defendant is not entitled to the expert of his particular choice, but is entitled to a competent expert in the field of expertise that has been found necessary to the defense."[144]

---

138. *Id.* at 160-61.

139. 939 S.W.2d 148 (Tex. Crim. App. 1996).

140. *Id.* at 152. The court also observed that due process does "not require a defendant to be furnished with a testifying expert who would unequivocally support an exculpatory theory of the defense. Thus, a defendant is not entitled to 'shop' for experts — at the State's expense — until he unearths a person who supports his theory of the case." *Id.*

141. *Id.* at 153.

142. *See generally* 2 W. LaFave & J. Israel, Criminal Procedure § 11.4 (1984) (choice of counsel).

143. *Ex parte* Moody, 684 So. 2d 114, 121-22 (Ala. 1996).

144. *Id.* at 121.

§ 4-5(E). Standard for Appointment.

The defendant has the burden of establishing the need for expert assistance. According to *Ake,* the accused must make a "preliminary showing" that an issue requiring expert assistance is "likely to be a significant factor at trial."[145] In a later case, *Caldwell v. Mississippi,*[146] the Court declined to consider a trial court's refusal to appoint fingerprint and "ballistics" experts because the defendant had "offered little more than undeveloped assertions that the requested assistance would be beneficial."[147]

The precise dimensions of this threshold showing are not clear. As one court has noted, "the *Ake* decision fails to establish a bright line test for determining when a defendant has demonstrated that sanity at the time of the offense will be a significant factor at the time of trial."[148] A line must be drawn someplace between a defense expert on "demand"[149] and a showing that an expert is "absolutely necessary."[150]

Some reasonable threshold showing is necessary because the system cannot afford defense experts on "demand."[151] Moreover, the incentives tend to foster

---

145. 470 U.S. at 74.

146. 472 U.S. 320 (1985).

147. *Id.* at 323 n.1.

148. Volson v. Blackburn, 794 F.2d 173, 176 (5th Cir. 1986). *See also* Cade v. State, 658 So. 2d 550, 553-54 (Fla. App.) ("[W]e have reviewed the developing law in other jurisdictions. Although this has been of some help, we are bound to conclude that determining 'abuse of discretion' in this context has typically boiled down to an *ad hoc* exercise of intuition by the appellate court that there was a substantial risk that the failure to supply the defendant with an expert deprived the defendant of a fair trial.... Since there has been no clear guidance given by the United States Supreme Court in constitutional terms, the approach taken by state courts varies.... The federal courts have been no more precise.... Some federal courts have been liberal in applying this test.... It does appear that since ours is a system that relies largely on the adversarial system for truth-seeking, it is dangerous to give all the tools to the state and hope it will do the right thing and always do it well"), *rev. denied*, 663 So. 2d 631 (1995).

149. Moore v. Kemp, 809 F.2d 702, 712 (11th Cir.) (en banc) ("due process does not require the government automatically to provide indigent defendants with expert assistance upon demand"), *cert. denied*, 481 U.S. 1054 (1987).

150. *Ex parte* Moody, 684 So. 2d 114, 119 (Ala. 1996) ("To meet this standard, the indigent defendant must show, with reasonable specificity, that the expert is absolutely necessary to answer a substantial issue or question raised by the state or to support a critical element of the defense").

151. The Fifth Circuit has ruled that "neither the bare assertion that the defendant was insane at the time of the offense, nor evidence of mental problems generally is sufficient to make the threshold showing required by *Ake*." Williams v. Collins, 989 F.2d 841, 845 (5th Cir. 1993). Instead, *Ake* requires "a factual showing sufficient to give the trial court reasonable ground to doubt his sanity at the time of the offense." *Id. See also* Yohey v. Collins, 985 F.2d 222, 227 (5th Cir. 1993) (habeas relief denied because request for ballistics expert was based on "speculative" theory and there was no evidence that the autopsy results were inaccurate or subject to disagreement between experts); Scott v. Louisiana, 934 F.2d 631, 633 (5th Cir. 1991) (non-psychiatric experts should be appointed only if evidence is both critical to conviction and subject to varying expert

boilerplate motions for expert assistance. First, failure to make an *Ake* request waives the issue for appeal[152] and may also result in a claim of ineffective counsel in subsequent proceedings.[153] Second, the request may give the defense leverage in plea bargaining. Third, denial of the request provides another issue for an appeal in the event of conviction. In short, because the defense does not pay for the expert, there is little "downside" to making an *Ake* request. *State v. Mason,*[154] a capital case, is illustrative. The defendant received state funds for the services of a private investigator, a forensic psychiatrist, a forensic pathologist, and for DNA and blood testing services. He requested, but did not receive, funds to hire a soils and trace evidence expert, a shoeprint expert, an eyewitness identification expert, a homicide investigation expert, a mass media expert, a forensic psychologist, a statistical DNA expert, and a firearms expert.

Consequently, a threshold standard is needed to separate the wheat from the chaff.[155] However, if the threshold standard is set too high, the defendant is placed in a "Catch-22" situation, in which the standard "demand[s] that the defendant possess already the expertise of the witness sought."[156]

A number of courts have adopted a "reasonable probability" standard. In *Moore v. Kemp,*[157] the Eleventh Circuit stated "that a defendant must show the

---

opinions); Wainwright v. Norris, 872 F. Supp. 574, 584-87 (E.D. Ark. 1994) ($500 for ballistics and gunshot residue expert satisfied *Ake* even though defense requested another $1000; moreover, failure to appoint expert sociologist to testify on prison life at capital sentencing did not violate due process), *aff'd in part, rev'd in part,* 80 F.3d 1126 (8th Cir.), *cert. denied,* 519 U.S. 968 (1996).

152. *See infra.*

153. *See* § 4-6(A) *infra.*

154. 82 Ohio St. 3d 144, 694 N.E.2d 932, *cert. denied,* 119 S. Ct. 624 (1998).

155. *See* Rogers v. Gibson, 173 F.3d 1278, 1287 (10th Cir. 1999) ("Petitioner asked the trial court for a state-appointed forensic expert to counter the state's anticipated evidence regarding hair and fiber samples and the medical examiner's report. Counsel stated that he needed the expert assistance to review the potential evidence, evaluate its weight and discover any exculpatory evidence. ... Petitioner merely speculates that the requested assistance would have been beneficial"); Moore v. Reynolds, 153 F.3d 1086, 111-12 (10th Cir. 1998) (ballistics expert to counter state expert who linked shell casings found at the crime to the .22 rifle Moore left with brother-in-law after the crime; in penalty stage—sociologist to testify to rate of recidivism among capital murders, parole and probation expert to testify concerning whether Moore was capable of rehabilitation and whether he could someday become a productive member of society; requests are "entirely speculative"), *cert. denied,* 119 S. Ct. 1266 (1999).

156. State v. Moore, 321 N.C. 327, 364 S.E.2d 648, 657 (1988).

157. 809 F.2d 702 (11th Cir.) (en banc), *cert. denied,* 481 U.S. 1054 (1987). *See also* Little v. Armontrout, 835 F.2d 1240, 1244 (8th Cir. 1987) (en banc) ("[T]he defendant must show a reasonable probability that an expert would aid in his defense, and that denial of expert assistance would result in an unfair trial"), *cert. denied,* 487 U.S. 1210 (1988); State v. Touchet, 642 So. 2d 1213, 1216 (La. 1994) (adopting the *Moore* standard and then commenting: "To meet this standard, a defendant must ordinarily establish, with a reasonable degree of specificity, that the assistance is required to answer a substantial issue or question that is raised by the prosecution's case or to support a critical element of the defense"); State v. Gonderman, 531 N.W.2d 11, 12 (N.D. 1995)

trial court that there exists a reasonable probability both [1] that an expert would be of assistance to the defense and [2] that denial of expert assistance would result in a fundamentally unfair trial."[158] While the first prong of the "reasonable probability" standard is defensible, the second prong erects a formidable obstacle. It is one thing to make a pretrial showing that assistance is needed; it is quite another to make a *pretrial* showing that the trial would be fundamentally unfair without the expert assistance. This becomes more obvious when the court spelled out the requisite showing: "Thus, if a defendant wants an expert to assist his attorney in confronting the prosecution's proof—by preparing counsel to cross-examine the prosecution's experts or by providing rebuttal testimony—he must inform the court of the nature of the prosecution's case and how the requested expert would be useful. At the very least, he must inform the trial court about the nature of the crime and the evidence linking him to the crime."[159] The main problem with the rebuttal situation referred to in this quotation is the lack of adequate defense discovery. The court acknowledged this problem in a footnote[160] but appears unaware that such discovery is often not available.[161]

Several other formulations have been offered. For example, the Tenth Circuit requires the defendant to show a "clear and genuine" issue, "one that constitutes a 'close' question which may well be decided one way or the other."[162] Other courts require a showing of "particularized need." This "threshold showing is to

---

(failure to appoint "nocturnal penile study" expert to establish accused's impotence in sex abuse cases did not violate due process).

158. 809 F.2d at 712 ("*Ake* and *Caldwell*, taken together, hold that a defendant must demonstrate something more than a mere possibility of assistance from a requested expert; due process does not require the government automatically to provide indigent defendants with expert assistance upon demand. Rather, a fair reading of these precedents is that a defendant must show the trial court that there exists a reasonable probability both that an expert would be of assistance to the defense and that denial of expert assistance would result in a fundamentally unfair trial").

159. *Id.* at 712 ("By the same token, if the defendant desires the appointment of an expert so that he can present an affirmative defense, such as insanity, he must demonstrate a substantial basis for the defense, as the defendant did in *Ake*. In each instance, the defendant's showing must also include a specific description of the expert or experts desired; without this basic information, the court would be unable to grant the defendant's motion, because the court would not know what type of expert was needed. In addition, the defendant should inform the court why the particular expert is necessary").

160. *Id.* at 712 n.10 ("In a jurisdiction still employing 'trial by ambush,' the defendant might have to ask the court to make the prosecutor disclose the theory of his case and the results of any tests that may have been performed by government experts or at the government's request").

161. For a discussion of discovery, *see* Chapter 3.

162. Rogers v. Gibson, 173 F.3d 1278, 1285 n.5 (10th Cir. 1999) (psychiatrist in capital case; Tenth Circuit requires "clear and genuine" and "close question"; Under *Castro*, automatic right if state offers evidence of future dangerousness in a capital case even if not through an expert; "We have rejected a narrow interpretation of *Ake* ...").

be determined on a case-by-case basis" considering "all facts and circumstances."[163]

Instead of parsing the various formulations of the *Ake* standard, a more informative approach may be to focus on the factors relevant to the appointment decision.

Cross-Examination

Appellate courts often cite the fact that the defense cross-examination of the prosecution expert was good, and therefore no defense expert was needed.[164] Several courts have gone further, one writing: "[D]efense trial counsel exhibited an understanding of the scientific evidence, and effectively and comprehensively cross-examined the prosecution's experts. Defense counsel's undergraduate degree is in chemistry with a minor in biophysics."[165] Another court has declared: "we disagree with his contention that the average attorney is ill-equipped to defend against [DNA] evidence. To the contrary, law libraries — i.e., law journals, practitioners' guides, annotated law reports, CLE materials, etc. — are teeming with information and advice for lawyers preparing to deal with DNA evidence in trial. Even a cursory perusal of the literature in this area reveals

163. State v. Barnett, 909 S.W.2d 423, 431 (Tenn. 1995) (*Ake* "does not require the appointment of a psychiatrist who will reach conclusions that the defendant wishes. What is important is that the defendant have access to, and the assistance of, a competent, independent psychiatric expert..."). *See also* State v. Harvest, 967 S.W.2d 829 (Tenn. Crim. App. 1997) (accused established a "particularized need" for a psychiatrist; institutionalized at mental health facilities his entire adult life; prior acquittal by reason of insanity); Husske v. Commonwealth, 476 S.E.2d 920 (Va. 1996) (under *Ake*, "basic tools may include the appointment of non-psychiatric experts" but defendant failed to show a particularized need for a DNA expert; also no prejudice because defendant confessed), *cert. denied*, 519 U.S. 1154 (1997).

164. *See* Plunkett v. State, 719 P.2d 834, 839 (Okla. Crim. App. 1986) (no right to bloodstain expert) ("Such a risk in other areas of scientific evidence is not necessarily present because the scientific expert is often able to explain to the jury how a conclusion was reached, the defense counsel can attack that conclusion, and the jury can then decide whether the conclusion had a sound basis"), *cert. denied*, 479 U.S. 1019 (1986); Weatherspoon v. State, 732 So. 2d 158, 161 (Miss. 1999) ("If the State had produced an expert at trial to substantiate the claims of Officer Wyman, then the denial of an expert in support of the defendant's testimony would require close examination. However, Weatherspoon enjoyed full cross-examination of the State witness and adequately rebutted Officer Wyman's testimony. Weatherspoons's problem was credibility, not accessibility to expert assistance"; also accused's offer to take polygraph test inadmissible).

In rejecting a due process right to retest evidence, several courts have reasoned that the defendant's opportunity to cross-examine the prosecution's expert witnesses provides sufficient protection for an accused. *See* Frias v. State, 547 N.E.2d 809, 813 (Ind. 1989), *cert. denied*, 495 U.S. 921 (1990); People v. Anderson, 276 N.W.2d 924, 926 (Mich. App. 1979); People v. Bell, 253 N.W.2d 726, 729 (Mich. App. 1977); Commonwealth v. Dorsey, 405 A.2d 516, 521 (Pa. Super. 1979).

165. People v. Leonard, 224 Mich. App. 569, 585, 569 N.W.2d 663, 671, *app. denied*, 570 N.W.2d 659 (Mich. 1997).

copious lists of questions for defense attorneys to use in cross-examinations and other strategies for undermining the weight of DNA evidence."[166]

There are several problems with this view. First, the same rationale could be applied to prosecutors seeking to have an accused who raises an insanity defense examined by a prosecution expert. There are numerous texts and CLE materials on this subject, and yet virtually every jurisdiction has procedures permitting an examination of the accused by a state psychiatrist.[167]

Second, there is a significant difference between attacking the opinion of an opponent's expert through cross-examination and attacking that opinion through the testimony of a defense expert.[168] In *Daubert* the Supreme Court did not cite cross-examination by itself; it noted that "[v]igorous cross-examination, *presentation of contrary evidence*, and careful instruction on the burden of proof are the traditional and appropriate means of attacking shaky but admissible evidence."[169] Similarly, the National Academy of Sciences report stated that "[m]ere cross examination by a defense attorney inexperienced in the science of DNA testing will not be sufficient."[170] A forensic scientist agrees: "If cross-examination is to be the only way to discover misleading or inadequate testimony by forensic scientists, then too much is being expected from it."[171]

---

166. State v. Huchting, 927 S.W.2d 411, 420 (Mo. App. 1996).

167. *See* FED. R. CRIM. P. 12.2(c) (court-ordered psychiatric examination to determine sanity at time of offense). *See* § 2-2(B) *supra*.

168. *See* United States v. Wilson, 361 F. Supp. 510, 513 (D. Md. 1973) ("The cross-examination of an expert poses a formidable task; it is the rare attorney who knows as much as the expert") (polygraph evidence); State v. Dean, 307 N.W.2d 628, 650-51 (Wis. 1981) ("[C]ross-examination ... may not in all situations provide a sufficient basis for the jury to assess the competence of the witness and the merits of the test") (polygraph evidence).

169. 509 U.S. at 596 (emphasis added) (citing Rock v. Arkansas, 483 U.S. 44, 61 (1987)). In 1983, the Court in Barefoot v. Estelle, 463 U.S. 880 (1983), upheld the admissibility of expert testimony of future dangerousness in capital cases. In so ruling, the Court wrote that the "jurors should not be barred from hearing the views of the State's psychiatrists *along with opposing views of the defendant's doctors*." *Id.* at 898-99 (emphasis added). For a discussion of *Daubert*, *see* Chapter 1.

170. DNA report, *supra* note 116, at 160.

171. Lucas, *The Ethical Responsibilities of the Forensic Scientist: Exploring the Limits*, 34 J. FORENSIC SCI. 719, 724 (1989). Lucas is the Director, The Centre of Forensic Sciences, Ministry of the Solicitor General, Toronto, Ontario. One commentator rejects, almost out of hand, the argument that the "searing test of a rigorous cross-examination" is a sufficient safeguard in this context. He writes: "All that one can say to such an argument is that the lawyers who make it should know better, and, if they do know better, as they must if they are experienced trial lawyers, they should have more conscience than to perpetuate such a myth." Ingraham, *The Ethics of Testimony: Conflicting Views on the Role of the Criminologist as Expert Witness*, *in* EXPERT WITNESSES 179, 183 (P. Anderson & L. Winfree eds. 1987).

Many courts recognize this point. For instance, in *De Freece v. State*[172] the Texas Court of Criminal Appeals rejected the notion that an "admirable" cross-examination of the prosecution expert justified the failure to appoint a defense expert.[173]

Timeliness & Specificity

The threshold showing should include procedural requirements such as timeliness[174] and reasonable specificity.[175] As one court stated: "Defense counsel should not have to attempt to train himself in the technical subject before being allowed the assistance of an expert; nevertheless, just by virtue of the lawyer's role, some level of understanding is expected."[176] The court went on to state: "Counsel should be able to articulate a basis for requiring an expert beyond telling the judge that the subject is 'complicated.' This would seem to be especially true of forensic sciences commonly involved in criminal cases, such as fingerprinting, ballistics, handwriting and DNA identification. Counsel should be expected at least to know what is in the legal literature and in case law about the topic."[177]

The Illinois Supreme Court has held that the defendant is not required to identify a specific expert or estimate that expert's fees. The court found a constitutional violation because a shoeprint and fingerprint expert was "necessary

---

172. 848 S.W.2d 150, 159 (Tex. Crim. App.) ("We reject the notion that a 'court's expert' necessarily fulfills the role of psychiatric assistant to the indigent accused envisioned by *Ake*.... In [this] context the phrase 'court's expert' is an oxymoron"), *cert. denied*, 510 U.S. 905 (1993).

173. *Id.* at 160-61. *See also* Williamson v. Reynolds, 904 F. Supp. 1529, 1562 (E.D. Okla. 1995) ("This court disagrees that cross-examination of the State's experts was an acceptable substitute for Petitioner's own experts.... [W]hen forensic evidence and expert testimony are critical parts of the criminal prosecution of an indigent defendant, due process requires the State to provide an expert who is not beholden to the prosecution"), *rev'd on other grounds*, Williamson v. Ward, 110 F.3d 1508, 1522 (10th Cir. 1997) (due process, not *Daubert*, standard applies in habeas proceedings); People v. Lawson, 163 Ill.2d 187, 227, 644 N.E.2d 1172, 1191 (1994) (defense counsel's cross-examination was not sufficient).

174. *See* Cade v. State, 658 So. 2d 550, 554 (Fla. App.) ("[T]he request was made timely. Also, there was specificity: The expert sought to be appointed was identified, the tasks to be performed were outlined, the hourly rate was provided and an estimate of fees was made ($3,000.00)"), *rev. denied*, 663 So. 2d 631 (Fla. 1995).

175. *See also Ex parte* Moody, 684 So. 2d 114, 119 (Ala. 1996) ("To meet this standard, the indigent defendant must show, with reasonable specificity, that the expert is absolutely necessary to answer a substantial issue or question raised by the state or to support a critical element of the defense"); State v. Touchet, 642 So. 2d 1213, 1216 (La. 1994) ("To meet this standard, a defendant must ordinarily establish, with a reasonable degree of specificity, that the assistance is required to answer a substantial issue or question that is raised by the prosecution's case or to support a critical element of the defense").

176. Cade v. State, 658 So. 2d 550, 555 (Fla. App.), *rev. denied*, 663 So. 2d 631 (Fla. 1995).

177. *Id.* at 555.

to proving a crucial issue in the case."[178] Nevertheless, courts should expect more.[179]

Preliminary Assessment

Some courts have denied a request because it was exploratory[180] or speculative.[181] A valid exploratory request should be distinguished from one that is merely a shot-in-the-dark. There are times when an *Ake* request, of necessity, must be exploratory—an attorney may need an expert to determine if there is a meritorious scientific issue in the case. For example, faced with blood spatter evidence for the first time, a lawyer cannot assess whether there is a basis for challenging such evidence. Thus, despite the exploratory nature of the request, an expert should be provided.[182]

Harrison v. State,[183] a bite mark case in which the accused received the death penalty for the murder of a ten-year-old girl, offers another illustration. A prosecution expert testified that the defendant had bitten the victim more than forty times, but the trial court nevertheless rejected a defense request for an expert. To demonstrate a "particularized need" for a defense expert, the trial judge required that the expert first review the evidence and write an affidavit. Without pay, however, most experts will not review the evidence or prepare an

---

178. People v. Lawson, 163 Ill.2d 187, 227, 644 N.E.2d 1172, 1191 (1994).

179. According to two commentators, a motion for the appointment of an expert should include: (1) The type of expert necessary; (2) The assistance the expert will provide to the defense; (3) The name, qualifications, fees, etc. of the desired expert; (4) The reasonableness of the expert's fees and other costs; (5) The objective bases for the request (specific factual reasons for why an expert is necessary); (6) The subjective bases for the request (personal observations of your client such as possible emotional problems or drug addiction, etc. about which you wish to have an expert testify); (7) The legal necessity for the expert's testimony, *i.e.*, what element will it attack; (8) The legal entitlement to an independent expert; and, (9) The inadequacy of available government experts. Hollander & Baldwin, *Expert Testimony in Criminal Trials: Creative Uses, Creative Attacks*, 15 CHAMPION 6, 12 (Dec. 1991). *See also* Dubose v. State, 662 So. 2d 1156 (Ala. Crim. App. 1993), (containing excerpts of affidavit on necessity of funds for DNA experts and expected fees of $10,000 to $30,000), *aff'd*, 662 So. 2d 1189 (Ala. 1995).

180. James v. State, 613 N.E.2d 15, 21 (Ind. 1993) ("whether the purpose of the expert is exploratory only").

181. Yohey v. Collins, 985 F.2d 222, 227 (5th Cir. 1993) (habeas relief denied because request for ballistics expert was based on "speculative" theory and there was no evidence that autopsy results were inaccurate or subject to disagreement between experts).

182. James v. State, 613 N.E.2d 15, 21 (Ind. 1993) ("[k]nowledge concerning cross-examination of blood spatter experts is not the kind of experience that defense counsel would normally be expected to possess"). *But see* Stewart v. Commonwealth, 427 S.E.2d 394, 405 (Va. 1993) ("Stewart cites no cases that indicate such assistance [blood spatter expert] is required in order to provide the constitutionally required 'basic tools of an adequate defense'"), *cert. denied*, 510 U.S. 848 (1993).

183. 635 So. 2d 894 (Miss. 1994).

affidavit. By the time of the appeal, an expert had been found, and he concluded that the "marks were not from bites."[184]

A limited *Ake* right should be recognized for a preliminary analysis if a good faith showing is made.[185] Here, a two-step process should be adopted. Enough money for an initial assessment should be authorized, with the understanding that further funds may be forthcoming based on the expert's affidavit that expert testimony is required.

Novelty

There is a special need for defense experts when novel scientific evidence is introduced. Paradoxically, there is often a lack of defense experts in these cases due to the novelty. With such evidence, there is often a delay before independent experts appreciate how science is being used in the courtroom.[186] For example, "voiceprint" evidence was introduced in the early 1970s.[187] A decade later, a National Academy of Sciences report noted that a "striking fact about the trials involving voicegram evidence to date is the very large proportion in which the only experts testifying were those called by the state."[188] The report also concluded that the reported error rates were generally inadequate for forensic

184. Moss, *Death, Habeas and Good Lawyers: Balancing Fairness and Finality*, 78 A.B.A. J. 83, 85 (Dec. 1992). The defense attorney noted that it is difficult to obtain good lawyers for three reasons: "Fees may be restricted, judges are reluctant to spend money on experts, and standards are lax for trial counsel." *Id.* at 84.

185. One pre-*Ake* court commented: "In the nature of things it may be difficult, in advance of trial, for counsel representing an indigent defendant to demonstrate an undoubted need for such funds. However, he can at least advise the court as to the general lines of inquiry he wishes to pursue, being as specific as possible." Puett v. Superior Court, 96 Cal. App. 3d 936, 939, 158 Cal. Rptr. 266, 267 (1979).

186. One of the justifications for the *Frye* rule, which requires the scientific technique gain "general acceptance" in the scientific community as a prerequisite to admissibility, focuses on this point: The *Frye* test guarantees that "a minimal reserve of experts exists who can critically examine the validity of a scientific determination in a particular case." United States v. Addison, 498 F.2d 741, 743-44 (D.C. Cir. 1974). For a discussion of *Frye*, *see* Chapter 1.

187. For a discussion of voiceprints, *see* Chapter 10.

188. NATIONAL RESEARCH COUNCIL , ON THE THEORY AND PRACTICE OF VOICE IDENTIFICATION 49 (1979). *See also* People v. Chapter, 13 Crim. L. Rep. (BNA) 2479 (Cal. Super. 1973) ("In approximately eighty percent of the twenty-five [voiceprint] cases in which such expert testimony/opinion was admitted there was no opposing expert testimony on the issue of reliability and general acceptability of the scientific community ...").

applications[189] and not "valid over the range of conditions usually met in practice."[190]

The early DNA cases repeated this pattern. There was no defense expert in *Andrews v. State*,[191] the first reported appellate case considering the admissibility of DNA evidence. Nor was there a defense expert in *Spencer v. Commonwealth*,[192] the first execution case.[193] At trial, the prosecution experts "testified unequivocally that there was no disagreement in the scientific community about the reliability of DNA print testing,"[194] and there was "no dissent whatsoever in the scientific community."[195] Later events completely undermined these statements.[196] Other examples of trial court refusals to appoint DNA experts include *Ex parte Dubose*[197] and *Prater v. State*.[198] Courts should not use the lack of defense experts as proof that a technique is accepted in the scientific community.

Testimony By Prosecution Experts

The appearance of a prosecution expert is, of course, a relevant factor in determining whether to appoint a defense expert. As Justice Cardozo noted, "a defendant may be at an unfair disadvantage, if he is unable because of poverty to parry by his own witnesses the thrusts of those against him."[199] Several cases illustrate this point.

---

189. *Id.* at 60 ("Estimates of error rates now available pertain to only a few of the many combinations of conditions encountered in real-life situations. These estimates do not constitute a generally adequate basis for a judicial or legislative body to use in making judgments concerning the reliability and acceptability of aural-visual voice identification in forensic applications").

190. "The presently available experimental evidence about error rates consists of results from a relatively small number of separate, uncoordinated experiments. These results alone cannot provide estimates of error rates that are valid over the range of conditions usually met in practice." *Id.* at 58. The Report also commented: "All the scientific results and forensic experiences to date, taken together, do not constitute an adequate objective basis for determining the error rates to be expected for voice identification testimony given in forensic cases generally." *Id.* at 68-69.

191. 533 So. 2d 841 (Fla. App. 1988), *rev. denied,* 542 So. 2d 1332 (Fla. 1989).

192. 238 Va. 295, 384 S.E.2d 785 (1989), *cert. denied,* 493 U.S. 1093 (1990).

193. *Murderer Put to Death in Virginia: First U.S. Execution Based on DNA Tests*, N.Y. TIMES, Apr. 28, 1994, at A1.

194. 384 S.E.2d at 792.

195. *Id.* at 797.

196. *See* Giannelli, *The DNA Story: An Alternative View*, 88 J. CRIM. L.& CRIMINOLOGY 380 (1997).

197. 662 So. 2d 1189, 1192-93 (Ala. 1995) (*Ake* due process violation for failure to provide indigent defendant with funds for DNA expert).

198. 820 S.W.2d 429, 439 (Ark. 1991) (trial judge denied motion for appointment of defense expert because no available funds; reversed).

199. Reilly v. Berry, 250 N.Y. 456, 461, 166 N.E. 165, 167 (1929).

In *Washington v. State*,[200] a capital case, the Oklahoma Court of Criminal Appeals ruled that a defendant was not entitled to the appointment of a defense expert, even though a prosecution expert had testified that the defendant had made the bite mark found on a murder victim. Moreover, the prosecution expert conceded that he had used a novel method of comparison that no one else had ever used. He also testified that only "one in a billion people" had a particular characteristic shared by the defendant.[201] The basis for this astounding statistic is not revealed. This result is indefensible.

In *Sommers v. Commonwealth*,[202] the Kentucky Supreme Court ruled that the trial court erred by failing to appoint a defense pathologist and arson expert. The prosecution called six experts. The court cited a number of factors, including a defense affidavit indicating that the state's witnesses had demonstrated an *unwillingness to cooperate with the defense*.[203]

The presence of a prosecution expert, however, should not automatically require the appointment of a defense expert. In virtually every homicide case, a forensic pathologist or other expert will testify as to the cause of death. If the accused asserts an alibi defense or an affirmative defense such as insanity, the cause of death may not be disputed and thus a defense pathologist may not be required.

Absence of Prosecution Experts

In one case, the Eighth Circuit indicated that the absence of a prosecution expert is a relevant factor in deciding the appointment issue, and it may have been in that case.[204] The absence of a prosecution expert, however, should not necessarily mean that there is no need for a defense expert. The most obvious examples involve affirmative defenses, such as insanity (as in *Ake*), battered woman syndrome in self-defense cases,[205] or psychological expertise in

---

200. 836 P.2d 673, 677 (Okla. Crim. App. 1992).

201. *Id.* at 678 (Parks, J., concurring in part, dissenting in part).

202. 843 S.W.2d 879 (Ky. 1992) (violation of state statute, which implements due process right).

203. *Id.* at 884-85.

204. Mendoza v. Leapley, 5 F.3d 341, 342 (8th Cir. 1993) (denial of request for appointment of psychologist to testify that accused's personality was inconsistent with that of a child rapist; "The State did not present psychological evidence, so Mendoza did not need an expert in order to respond to damaging evidence of the same type").

205. *See* Dunn v. Roberts, 963 F.2d 308, 314 (10th Cir. 1992); Doe v. Superior Court, 39 Cal. App. 4th 538, 545, 45 Cal. Rptr. 2d 888, 892 (1995) ("The problem in this case is that the record is insufficient to determine whether Jane has access to a 'competent' psychiatrist or psychologist.... But this is not a run-of-mill case and the request is for someone with experience in a particular specialty [battered woman syndrome & post-traumatic stress syndrome]"), *rev. denied* (1996).

entrapment cases.[206] Another example would be cases in which a prosecution witness had been hypnotized.[207] In these circumstances, a defense expert may be needed to explain how hypnosis may have affected a lay witness's testimony.

The Eighth Circuit explained it this way: "We see no rational reason that a defendant be allowed an *Ake* expert only if the prosecution is relying on an opposing expert. Often, one party needs expert testimony to explain that conditions are other than they superficially seem to be, while the opposing party is content with the lay person's unaided assessment of the situation."[208]

Centrality of the Evidence

Courts often focus on whether the requested expert testimony concerns an issue that is "crucial,"[209] "critical,"[210] "central,"[211] or the like.[212] For instance, the Illinois Supreme Court found a constitutional violation because a shoeprint and

---

206. *See* United States v. Newman, 849 F.2d 156, 165 (5th Cir. 1988); United States v. McLernon, 746 F.2d 1098, 1115 (6th Cir. 1984) ("expert testimony concerning a defendant's predisposition may be invaluable in an entrapment case"); United States v. Benveniste, 564 F.2d 335, 339 (9th Cir. 1977); United States v. Hill, 655 F.2d 512, 516 (3d Cir. 1981) ("Testimony by an expert concerning a defendant's susceptibility to influence may be relevant to an entrapment defense"), *cert. denied*, 464 U.S. 1039 (1984); State v. Shuck, 953 S.W.2d 662 (Tenn. 1997).

207. *See* Little v. Armontrout, 835 F.2d 1240, 1243 (8th Cir. 1987) (en banc) (error to fail to appoint hypnotist), *cert. denied*, 487 U.S. 1210 (1988).

208. Starr v. Lockhart, 23 F.3d 1280, 1290 n.8 (8th Cir.) *cert. denied*, 513 U.S. 995 (1994). *See also* Castro v. Oklahoma, 71 F.3d 1502, 1514 (10th Cir. 1995) ("The *Ake* duty was triggered here by the State's presentation of *any* evidence of Mr. Castro's future dangerousness or continuing threat to society.... There is no necessity for the State to offer psychiatric testimony or evidence during the sentencing phase of a capital trial for its *Ake* duty to apply").

209. *See* Sommers v. Commonwealth, 843 S.W.2d 879, 883-85 (Ky. 1992) (failure to appoint defense pathologist and arson expert violated state statute that implements due process right; the cause of death and the genesis of the fire were matters of crucial dispute, resolvable only through circumstantial evidence and expert opinion).

210. *See* Scott v. Louisiana, 934 F.2d 631, 633 (5th Cir. 1991) (non-psychiatric experts should be appointed only if evidence is both critical to conviction and subject to varying expert opinions); *Ex parte* Dubose, 662 So. 2d 1189, 1194-95 (Ala. 1995) (*Ake* expert is required only when the evidence "(1) [is] 'critical' ... the only evidence linking the accused with the crime or proving an element of the corpus delicti").

211. *See* Cade v. State, 658 So. 2d 550, 555 (Fla. App.) (whether the DNA evidence was central to the prosecution's case), *rev. denied*, 663 So. 2d 631 (Fla. 1995).

212. *See Ex parte* Moody, 684 So. 2d 114, 119 (Ala. 1996) ("To meet this standard, the indigent defendant must show, with reasonable specificity, that the expert is absolutely necessary to answer a substantial issue or question raised by the state or to support a critical element of the defense"); Scott v. State, 593 N.E.2d 198, 200 (Ind. 1992) ("Another consideration for the trial court is whether the expert services will go toward answering a substantial question or simply an ancillary one. For example, if the State's principal evidence linking the defendant to the crime is sufficiently technical that it is commonly the subject of expert testimony, the trial court should strongly consider providing an expert") (citation omitted).

fingerprint expert was "necessary to proving a crucial issue in the case."[213] Perhaps "relative importance"[214] is a more apt phrase. *Ake* itself used the phrase "likely to be a significant factor at trial."[215] Although this factor is obviously relevant, it is difficult to articulate a more helpful standard.

Complexity

The complexity of a scientific technique will often support the appointment of a defense expert. In the leading neutron activation analysis case, the Sixth Circuit noted: "[I]f the government sees fit to use this time consuming, expensive means of fact finding, it must both allow time for a defendant to make similar tests, and in the instance of an indigent defendant, a means to provide for payment for same."[216]

DNA profiling also exemplifies this factor. In *Ex parte Dubose*[217] the court wrote: "Given the complexity of DNA technology, it is doubtful that a defense attorney will have the requisite knowledge to effectively [examine such evidence] without expert assistance." Another court identified the "highly technical" nature of DNA evidence as a factor in the appointment decision.[218] Several courts[219] and commentators[220] as well as the National Academy of Sciences report recognize the need for defense experts in this context. The report states: "Defense counsel must have access to adequate expert assistance, even when the admissibility of the results of analytical techniques is not in question

213. People v. Lawson, 163 Ill.2d 187, 227, 644 N.E.2d 1172, 1191 (1994).

214. Harrison v. State, 635 So. 2d 894, 901 (Miss. 1994) (en banc) (the "relative importance of the testimony offered by the State's experts is one factor to consider in assessing the fairness of the trial").

215. 470 U.S. at 74.

216. United States v. Stifel, 433 F.2d 431, 441 (6th Cir. 1970), *cert. denied,* 401 U.S. 994 (1971).

217. 662 So. 2d 1189, 1196 (Ala. 1995). *See also* Rey v. State, 897 S.W.2d 333, 338 (Tex. Crim. App. 1995) (en banc) (affidavit of forensic pathologist questioning prosecution expert's conclusions submitted; "The nature of an expert's field and the importance and complexity of the issue will bear directly upon whether the appointment of an expert will be helpful").

218. Cade v. State, 658 So. 2d 550, 554 (Fla. App.) ("whether the evidence is highly technical"), *rev. denied*, 663 So. 2d 631 (Fla. 1995).

219. *E.g.,* Polk v. State, 612 So. 2d 381, 393-94 (Miss. 1992) (appendix guidelines for future DNA cases) ("It is also imperative that no defendant have [DNA] evidence admitted against him without the benefit of an independent expert witness to evaluate the data on his behalf"; *Ake* requires defendant "be allowed reasonable funds for access to an expert who can independently evaluate the evidence presented against him by the State, analyze it, and present that analysis at trial").

220. *See* Comment, *Defense Access to State-Funded DNA Experts: Considerations of Due Process*, 85 CAL. L. REV. 1803 (1997); Comment, *Genetics and Justice: An Indigent Defendant's Right to DNA Expert Assistance*, 1998 U. CHI. L. FORUM 396.

because there is still a need to review the quality of the laboratory work and the interpretation of results."[221]

This view, however, is not universally accepted. The Michigan court of appeals observed: "[O]nly two courts have held that whenever the prosecution intends to introduce DNA evidence against a defendant at trial, the defendant has a due process right to an appointment of a DNA expert to assist in his defense."[222] This position is problematic even when DNA profiling becomes routine.[223] The importance of defense DNA experts is illustrated by the *O.J. Simpson* trial, where a prosecution expert, a leading population geneticist, made a simple computation mistake that was revealed only during cross-examination.[224]

Routine Tests

The recognition of complexity as an appropriate *Ake* factor does not necessarily mean that defense experts are not needed when the prosecution offers the results of routine tests. As illustrated by several fingerprint cases, even the most basic techniques are subject to error. For example, in *Imbler v. Craven*[225] the expert failed to observe an exculpatory fingerprint in a murder case, in which the death penalty was imposed. In another murder case, *State v. Caldwell*,[226] the

---

221. NATIONAL RESEARCH COUNCIL, DNA TECHNOLOGY IN FORENSIC SCIENCE 147 (National Academy of Sciences Press, 1992). The Report also stated: "Because of the potential power of DNA evidence, authorities must make funds available to pay for expert witnesses...." *Id.* at 149.

222. People v. Leonard, 224 Mich. App. 569, 580, 569 N.W.2d 663, 669, *app. denied*, 570 N.W.2d 659 (Mich. 1997). *Accord* State v. Huchting, 927 S.W.2d 411, 420 (Mo. App. 1996) ("[W]e disagree with his contention that the average attorney is ill-equipped to defend against [DNA] evidence. To the contrary, law libraries — *i.e.*, law journals, practitioners' guides, annotated law reports, CLE materials, etc. — are teeming with information and advice for lawyers preparing to deal with DNA evidence in trial. Even a cursory perusal of the literature in this area reveals copious lists of questions for defense attorneys to use in cross-examinations and other strategies for undermining the weight of DNA evidence"); Husske v. Commonwealth, 476 S.E.2d 920 (Va. 1996) (under *Ake*, "basic tools may include the appointment of non-psychiatric experts" but defendant failed to show a particularized need for a DNA expert; also no prejudice because defendant confessed), *cert. denied*, 519 U.S. 1154 (1997).

223. The novelty of DNA evidence is a distinct factor and is discussed earlier. *See also* Prater v. State, 820 S.W.2d 429, 439 (Ark. 1991) (Trial court erred when it declined to appoint a defense expert "because of a shortage of county funds") (basis for right to defense expert not specified).

224. *See* Kaye, *Cross-Examining Science*, 36 JURIMETRICS J. vii (Winter 1996) (editor's page); Horgan, *High Profile: The Simpson Case Raises the Issue of DNA Reliability*, SCI. AM., Oct. 1994, at 33, 36.

225. 298 F. Supp. 795 (C.D. Cal. 1969), *aff'd*, 424 F.2d 631 (9th Cir.), *cert. denied*, 400 U.S. 865 (1970).

226. 322 N.W.2d 574 (Minn. 1982).

court wrote: "The fingerprint expert's testimony was damning—and it was false."[227]

Several firearms identification cases are also instructive. In February 1989 the L.A. Police arrested Rickey Ross for the murder of three prostitutes. An expert, the head of the Department's Firearms Identification Division, made a *positive* identification after comparing the murder bullets and a bullet fired from Ross' 9 mm Smith & Wesson.[228] Based on the same evidence, however, a defense expert reached the opposite conclusion—Ross' gun could *not* have fired the fatal bullets. Two independent experts came to yet another conclusion: there was insufficient evidence to draw any conclusions. The case against Ross was dropped.[229]

Differing Opinions; Subjectivity

Several courts have emphasized that the need for expert assistance increases if a technique often involves differing expert opinions.[230] For example, in a DNA case, the Indiana Supreme Court upheld a trial judge's denial of funds for a DNA expert. The court wrote: "Psychiatry is an extremely uncertain field dealing with the mysteries of the human mind where expert opinions can be expected to and

227. *Id.* at 586. *See* Starrs, *A Miscue in Fingerprint Identification: Causes and Concerns*, 12 J. POLICE SCI. & ADMIN. 287 (1984).

228. One of the defense attorneys later admitted, "I suppose I was like the average citizen. They said it was a match, I thought it was like a fingerprint." Baker & Lieberman, *Faulty Ballistics in Deputy's Arrest; Eagerness to "Make" Gun Cited in LAPD Lab Error*, L.A. TIMES, May 22, 1989, at 1, col. 1; Freed, *LAPD Probing What Went Wrong With Ballistics Tests on Ross' Gun*, L.A. TIMES, May 16, 1989, at 26, col. 1.

229. This was not the first time that the L.A. crime laboratory had stumbled. A prior misidentification occurred in the investigation of Sirhan Sirhan for the assassination of Bobby Kennedy: "In [People v. Sirhan] seven independent examiners were appointed by the presiding judge of the Superior Court of Los Angeles County to reexamine the purported firearms bullet comparison post trial. The examiners were unanimous in their findings that the identification testified to at the grand jury indictment and in the trial were misrepresented in that the purported identification of bullets lodged in victim Kennedy . . . with Sirhan's gun were non-existent. In both of these cases discovery and cross examination were lacking." Bradford, *Forensic Firearms Identification: Competence or Incompetence*, 5 FORUM 14 (July/August 1978). In a third case, *In re* Kirschke, 53 Cal. App.3d 405, 125 Cal. Rptr. 680 (1975), *cert. denied,* 429 U.S. 820 (1976), the firearms identification expert made a conclusive identification. On appeal the court concluded that the expert had "negligently presented false demonstrative evidence in support of his ballistics testimony." 125 Cal. Rptr. at 682.

230. *See* Williams v. Collins, 989 F.2d 841, 845 (5th Cir. 1993); Yohey v. Collins, 985 F.2d 222, 227 (5th Cir. 1993) (habeas relief denied because request for ballistics expert was based on "speculative" theory and no evidence that autopsy results were inaccurate or subject to disagreement between experts); Scott v. Louisiana, 934 F.2d 631, 633 (5th Cir. 1991) (non-psychiatric experts should be appointed only if evidence is both critical to conviction and subject to varying expert opinions); James v. State, 613 N.E.2d 15, 21 (Ind. 1993) (blood spatter expert) ("whether the nature of the expert testimony involves precise physical measurements and chemical testing, the results of which were not subject to dispute...").

do differ widely. In contrast, the neutral [DNA] experts here were testifying to the results of a test 'involving precise, physical measurements and chemical testing.'"[231] This argument is problematic. The Alabama Supreme Court reached the opposite conclusion concerning DNA. The court recognized that one factor in the appointment decision is whether the evidence "is subject to varying expert opinions" but then observed: "Given the complexity of DNA technology, it is doubtful that a defense attorney will have the requisite knowledge to effectively [examine such evidence] without expert assistance."[232]

In addition, courts often do not seem to appreciate the degree of subjectivity associated with scientific evidence. Firearms identification is an example. Even though based on objective data (striation marks on a bullet), the conclusion about a match comes down to the examiner's subjective judgment.[233] Questioned documents,[234] bite marks,[235] and even fingerprints[236] fall into the same category. DNA evidence also involves subjectivity if a "match" is declared based only on "eye-balling" the autorads.[237]

Admissibility of Expert Testimony

If the expert testimony is not admissible, there is generally no need for a defense expert. There are, however, some important exceptions—for example, requests for defense polygraph experts. While the majority of courts still exclude polygraph results, a number of post-*Daubert* cases may represent an evolving trend toward admissibility.[238] In any event, the polygraph is used extensively in criminal practice, albeit on the periphery of the trial. Many jurisdictions admit polygraph evidence upon stipulation.[239] Similarly, courts have admitted polygraph evidence in suppression hearings, sentencing hearings, motions for new trial proceedings, and prison disciplinary hearings.[240] Moreover, some courts

---

231. Harrison v. State, 644 N.E.2d 1243, 1253 (Ind. 1995) (quoting James v. State, 613 N.E.2d 15, 21 (Ind. 1993)), *cert. denied*, 519 U.S. 933 (1996).

232. *Ex parte* Dubose, 662 So. 2d 1189, 1194-95, 1196 (Ala. 1995).

233. *See* Chapter 14.

234. *See* Chapter 21.

235. *See* Chapter 13.

236. *See* Chapter 16.

237. *See* Thompson & Ford, *DNA Typing: Acceptance and Weight of the New Genetic Identification Tests*, 75 VA. L. REV. 45, 88 (1989) ("There are currently no formal standards for determining what constitutes a match between two DNA prints. Whether a match is declared between two prints is a subjective judgment for the forensic expert").

238. *See* Giannelli, *Polygraph Evidence: Post-Daubert*, 49 HASTINGS L.J. 895 (1998).

239. *See* § 8-4(C) *infra* (discussing admissibility by stipulation).

240. *See* § 8-6 *infra* (discussing admissibility in proceedings other than trials).

have enforced plea bargains based on polygraph results.[241] In short, the polygraph is an integral part of modern criminal process.

Expert Advisor vs. Trial Witness

In some situations an expert is needed as an advisor both before and during trial, even if the expert does not testify. The Court in *Ake* recognized this point, when it wrote that the expert would "conduct a professional examination on issues relevant to the defense, to help determine whether the insanity defense is viable, to present testimony, and *to assist in preparing the cross-examination* of a State's psychiatric witnesses."[242] In other words, the court recognized that *Ake* encompasses more than a *testifying* defense expert; it requires a *consulting* expert—"due process, at a minimum, requires expert aid in an evaluation of a defendant's case in an effort to present it in the best possible light to the jury."[243]

Federal Rule of Evidence 615, which governs the sequestration of witnesses, implicitly recognizes the need for consulting experts in this circumstance. The rule recognizes an exception to the sequestration rule for witnesses whose presence in court is essential to the presentation of a party's case. According to the drafters, this category "contemplates such persons as an agent who handled the transaction being litigated or an expert needed to advise counsel in the management of the litigation."[244]

Cost

In *Ex parte Moody*[245] the court stated that the "anticipated costs of such an expert"[246] was a relevant consideration. Although some cases mention cost,[247]

---

241. In some cases prosecutors have gone beyond stipulating to the admissibility of test results and have agreed to dismiss charges if the defendant passes a polygraph examination. *See* § 8-9 *infra* (discussing pretrial agreement cases). *See also* United States v. Santiago-Gonzalez, 66 F.3d 3, 6 n.1 (1st Cir. 1995) (polygraph used to measure defendant's requirement to be truthful under a plea agreement).

242. 470 U.S. at 82 (emphasis added).

243. State v. Taylor, 939 S.W.2d 148, 153 (Tex. Crim. App. 1996).

244. FED. R. EVID. 615 advisory committee's note. *See also* 1 MCCORMICK, EVIDENCE § 50, at 190 (4th ed 1992) ("An example of a witness whose presence may be essential is an expert witness"); 6 WIGMORE, EVIDENCE § 1841, at 475 n.4 (Chadbourn rev. 1976).

245. 684 So. 2d 114 (Ala. 1996).

246. *Id.* at 122. *See also* Fricker, *State Falters in Retrial of Escaped Con*, 81 A.B.A. J. 38, 38-39 (June 1995) ("The court-appointed defense lawyers in the first trial were denied money for independent tests because the judge said the county could not afford it").

247. *E.g.*, Wainwright v. Norris, 872 F. Supp. 574, 584-87 (E.D. Ark. 1994) ($500 for ballistics and gunshot residue expert satisfied *Ake* even though defense requested another $1000; moreover, failure to appoint expert sociologist to testify on prison life at capital sentencing did not violate due process), *aff'd in part, rev'd in part*, 80 F.3d 1126 (8th Cir.), *cert. denied*, 519 U.S. 968 (1996); Dubose v. State, 662 So. 2d 1156 (Ala. Crim. App. 1993), *aff'd*, 662 So. 2d 1189 (Ala. 1995)

few explicitly state that cost is a germane factor. This may be because the *Ake* Court summarily dismissed cost as a relevant factor.[248] The expenses can be quite high.[249]

Other Factors

In addition to the above factors, the Florida Court of Appeals noted that the cases had suggested additional factors: (1) whether the remaining evidence against the defendant is overwhelming, (2) whether the scientific evidence is impressive to a jury, and (3) whether the literature and case law suggest it is vulnerable to attack.[250]

§ 4-5(F). Right to an Effective Expert.

Several defendants have argued that *Ake* includes the right to *effective* expert assistance. Indeed, the Court in *Ake* did refer to the right to "one competent psychiatrist." Nevertheless, the lower courts have frequently rejected this argument.[251] According to the Fourth Circuit: "To inaugurate a constitutional or procedural rule of an ineffective expert witness in lieu of the constitutional standard of an ineffective attorney ... is going further than the federal procedural demands of a fair trial and the constitution require."[252] The Seventh Circuit

(containing excerpts of affidavit on necessity of funds for DNA experts and expected fees of $10,000 to $30,000); Cade v. State, 658 So. 2d 550, 555 (Fla. App.) (specificity of the request, *i.e.*, the expert sought was identified, the tasks to be performed were outlined, the hourly rate was provided and an estimate of fees was made ($3,000.00)), *rev. denied*, 663 So. 2d 631 (Fla. 1995).

248. *See* text accompanying note 89 *supra*.

249. *See* United States v. Salameh, 152 F.3d 88, 118 (2d Cir. 1998) (World Trade Center bombing) (received $35,000 in CJA funds for five experts: DNA, explosives, computers, linguistics, and culture (sociologists)"), *cert. denied,* 119 S. Ct. 1273 (1999); United States v. Silva, 140 F.3d 1098 (7th Cir. 1998) (attorney not personally liable for fees of an expert appointed and authorized under CJA; Applied Forensics Technologies International, Inc., examined suspicious audio tapes for $9,250 for copies and $27,000 for originals); State v. Barror, 1997 WL 614983 (Ohio App. 6 Dist.) ($800 for expert on interviewing techniques too costly in a child abuse case, which rested entirely on the testimony of 5-year-old daughter). *See also* Scheck, *The Use of DNA Evidence in Death Penalty Cases*, 23 HOFSTRA L. REV. 627, 639 (1995) ($2,000-3,000).

250. Cade v. State, 658 So. 2d 550, 555 (Fla. App.), *rev. denied*, 663 So. 2d 631 (Fla. 1995).

251. *E.g.,* Provenzano v. Singletary, 148 F.3d 1327, 1334 (11th Cir. 1998) ("We did speculate in *Clisby* that under certain limited circumstances due process might require the trial court to intervene to ensure that a defendant receives the assistance of a competent mental health expert, but we held that there was no indication the examination of the psychiatrist in that case was anything less than adequate"), *cert. denied,* 1999 U.S. LEXIS 4564 (1999); Skaggs v. Parker, 27 F. Supp. 2d 952, 965 (W.D. Ky. 1998) ("Sometime after trial and conviction, Skaggs discovered that [the defense insanity expert] had testified falsely concerning his credentials and that he was not a licensed clinical psychologist"; defense attorney selected the expert without making any investigation of his credentials).

252. Waye v. Murray, 884 F.2d 765, 766-67 (4th Cir.), *cert. denied,* 492 U.S. 936 (1989).

objected that such a rule would require the federal courts "to engage in a form of 'psychiatric medical malpractice' review."[253] The Ninth Circuit also declined to become enmeshed in such "a psycho-legal quagmire."[254]

These opinions dismiss the issue too quickly. First, the issue may resurface as an ineffective assistance of counsel claim, based on counsel's failure to obtain the appointment of a competent expert.[255] Second, the appointment of an expert in the wrong field does not satisfy *Ake*. For example, in *Castro v. Oklahoma*[256] the Tenth Circuit declined to decide an *Ake* issue based on the expert's competence. Nevertheless, the Court remarked: "We believe a serious question whether Dr. Hamilton was competent to provide expert psychiatric assistance exists. Dr. Hamilton's specialties in child and geriatric psychiatry probably render him unqualified to offer an expert opinion on many of the issues raised in a capital murder trial. A forensic psychiatrist or psychologist is the proper specialist for such a task."[257]

§ 4-5(G). *Ex Parte* Applications.

One procedural issue turns on which view of the expert's role is adopted.[258] If the accused has a right to a partisan expert, the proceedings seeking appointment should be *ex parte*, as they are under the Criminal Justice Act.[259] The *Ake* decision does not explicitly address this issue, although at one point the Court spoke of an "*ex parte* threshold showing."[260] Moreover, several courts have ruled that an application for appointment of an expert should be considered in an *ex parte* hearing: "[I]n making the requisite showing defendant could be placed in a position of revealing his theory of the case. He therefore has a legitimate interest in making that showing *ex parte*."[261]

---

253. Silagy v. Peters, 905 F.2d 986, 1013 (7th Cir. 1990), *cert. denied,* 498 U.S. 1110 (1991).

254. Harris v. Vasquez, 943 F.2d 930, 951 (9th Cir. 1991).

255. *See* Turpin v. Bennett, 270 Ga. 584, 513 S.E.2d 478, 481 (1999) (psychiatrist suffered from AIDS dementia at trial) ("The due process clause ensures that a defendant will be given access to a competent psychiatrist when the defendant's mental state is at issue. ... But this is not to say that a defendant is entitled to the effective assistance of a psychiatrist in addition to the effective assistance of counsel"; effective counsel right applicable) (citation omitted).

256. 71 F.3d 1502 (10th Cir. 1995).

257. *Id.* at 1515. *See also Ex parte* Moody, 684 So. 2d 114, 121 (Ala. 1996) ("entitled to a competent expert in the field of expertise that has been found necessary to the defense"); Burns, *The Right to the Effective Assistance of a Psychiatrist Under Ake v. Oklahoma*, 30 CRIM. L. BULL. 429 (1994); Garcia, *Legal and Ethical Considerations in Using Expert Witnesses in Litigation*, 1 SHEPARD'S EXPERT & SCIENTIFIC EVIDENCE Q. 717 (1994).

258. *See* § 4-5(D) *supra.*

259. *See* § 4-3 *supra.*

260. 470 U.S. at 82.

261. Brooks v. State, 259 Ga. 562, 566, 385 S.E.2d 81, 84 (1989), *cert. denied,* 494 U.S. 1018 (1990). *Accord Ex parte* Moody, 684 So. 2d 114, 120 (Ala. 1996) ("[A]n indigent criminal

Despite the persuasiveness of this reasoning, other courts have rejected the constitutional argument.[262] In addition, the North Carolina Supreme Court has held that an *ex parte* hearing is required for motions to appoint a psychiatrist but not for fingerprint experts.[263] According to the court, the "key difference between a hearing on the question of an indigent defendant's right to a fingerprint expert and one on the question of his right to a psychiatric expert is that the object of adversarial scrutiny is not mere physical evidence, but the defendant himself. The matter is not tactile and objective, but one of an intensely sensitive, personal nature."[264] An open hearing involving an independent psychological evaluation "necessarily impinges upon the defendant's right to the assistance of counsel and his privilege against self-incrimination."[265]

The Louisiana Supreme Court has noted that in criminal cases "*ex parte* treatment is not the rule, but rather the exception, and that, in order to deviate from the general rule of open and contradictory hearings, there must be a showing of good cause."[266] The court then concluded that "although the initial application for funding for expert services will be considered *ex parte*, unless the

---

defendant is entitled to an *ex parte* hearing on whether expert assistance is necessary, based on the Fifth, Sixth, and Fourteenth Amendments...") (discussing reasons for this rule); MacGregor v. State, 733 P.2d 416 (Okla. Crim. App. 1987); Williams v. State, 958 S.W.2d 186, 192-93 (Tex. Crim. App. 1997) ("While the Supreme Court's suggestion that the threshold showing should be made *ex parte* is dicta, it is consistent with the due process principles upon which *Ake* rests.... The problem with requiring this [threshold] showing to be shared with the State at the pretrial stage is that it compels a defendant to disclose to the State his defensive theories or 'work product.' ... [H]e is forced to choose between either forgoing the appointment of an expert or disclosing to the State in some detail his defensive theories or theories about weakness in the State's case. This is contrary to *Ake's* concern that an indigent defendant who is entitled to expert assistance have 'meaningful access to justice,' and undermines the work produce doctrine").

262. *See* State v. Apelt, 176 Ariz. 349, 861 P.2d 634, 650 (1993) (en banc) ("[W]e do not believe that the Fourteenth Amendment's guarantees of due process and equal protection encompass such a right [to an *ex parte* hearing]"), *cert. denied*, 513 U.S. 834 (1994); State v. Floody, 481 N.W.2d 242, 254-56 (S.D. 1992).

263. State v. Phipps, 331 N.C. 427, 449, 418 S.E.2d 178, 190 (1992) ("[T]he decision to grant an *ex parte* hearing is within the trial court's discretion. Though such a hearing may in fact be the better practice, it is not always constitutionally required under *Ake*").

264. State v. Ballard, 333 N.C. 515, 519, 428 S.E.2d 178, 180 (1993), *cert. denied*, 510 U.S. 984 (1993). *See also* State v. Barnett, 909 S.W.2d 423, 428 (Tenn. 1995) ("Our reading of *Ake* convinces us that an *ex parte* hearing is required [at least when a request is for a psychiatric expert].... Indigent defendants who must seek state-funding to hire a psychiatric expert should not be required to reveal their theory of defense when their more affluent counterparts, with funds to hire experts, are not required to reveal their theory of defense, or the identity of experts who are consulted, but who may not, or do not, testify at trial").

265. 333 N.C. at 519, 428 S.E.2d at 180. *Accord* State v. Bates, 333 N.C. 523, 527, 428 S.E.2d 693, 695 (1993) (*Ballard* applies whether expert is a psychiatrist or forensic psychologist), *cert. denied,* 519 U.S. 1131 (1997).

266. State v. Touchet, 642 So. 2d 1213, 1220 (La. 1994).

defendant demonstrates some particularized prejudice to him by state participation in the hearing, the hearing on the funding will be conducted in a contradictory manner."[267] There are, however, criminal proceedings such as grand jury and in camera hearings that are closed. Moreover, what is the prosecutors role here: To deny the adversary the basic tools of the defense? Or, to protect the public fisc?

§ 4-5(H). Harmless Error Analysis.

The courts are divided over whether an *Ake* violation is subject to the harmless doctrine. Most constitutional rights are subject to a harmless error inquiry. However, certain violations are "regarded as so elemental that their existence abrogates the basic structure of a constitutional trial, and which are therefore not subject to harmless error analysis...."[268] The Eighth Circuit has ruled that an *Ake* violation is subject to harmless error analysis.[269] In contrast, the Texas Court of Criminal Appeals held that an *Ake* violation is a "structural" error and therefore not subject to harmless error review.[270]

In *Tuggle v. Netherland*,[271] the U.S. Supreme Court did not decide this issue but stated that it was remanding the case for a determination "whether harmless-error analysis is applicable to this case."[272] On remand, the Fourth Circuit ruled that an *Ake* error is subject to harmless error analysis under *Brecht v. Abrahamson*.[273]

---

267. *Id.*

268. Starr v. Lockhart, 23 F.3d 1280, 1291 (8th Cir.) (citing the following rights as not subject to harmless error analysis: "the right to counsel, trial by a biased judge, exclusion of members of the defendant's race from the grand jury, deprivation of the right to self-representation, and denial of the right to a public trial"), *cert. denied*, 513 U.S. 995 (1994).

269. *Id.* at 1292. *See also* White v. Johnson, 153 F.3d 197, 201 (5th Cir. 1998) ("Three other circuits have expressly concluded that *Ake* error is subject to harmless-error analysis, and we now join them"; *Ake* error is a "trial," not a "structural," error), *cert. denied,* 119 S. Ct. 1048 (1999).

270. Rey v. State, 897 S.W.2d 333, 345 (Tex. Crim. App. 1995) (forensic pathologist) ("We can conceive of few errors that are more structural in nature than one which eliminates a basic tool of an adequate defense and in doing so dramatically affects the accuracy of the jury's determination").

271. 516 U.S. 10, 14 (1995) (per curiam) (state presented psychiatric testimony of "future dangerousness" in penalty phase of capital case but request for defense expert denied in violation of *Ake*; "[N]either the state court nor the Court of Appeals addressed whether harmless-error analysis is applicable to this case. Because this Court customarily does not address such an issue in the first instance, we vacate the judgment ... and remand the case for further proceedings consistent with this opinion").

272. *Id.* at 14.

273. Tuggle v. Netherland, 79 F.3d 1386, 1393 (4th Cir.), *cert. denied*, 519 U.S. 894 (1996). *See also* Castro v. Oklahoma, 71 F.3d 1502, 1514-16 (10th Cir. 1995) (error not harmless); Brewer v. Reynolds, 51 F.3d 1519, 1529 (10th Cir. 1995) (*Ake* subject to harmless error analysis, but disagrees with Eighth Circuit on which harmless error rule applies; *Brecht v. Abrahamson*, rather than *Chapman*, applies on habeas review), *cert. denied*, 516 U.S. 1124 (1996).

§ 4-5(I). Pretrial Motions.

The issues in *Ake* concerned the merits of the trial (insanity issue) and a sentencing issue (future dangerousness) in a capital sentencing proceeding. Moreover, the *Ake* Court spoke of a significant issue "at trial." Nevertheless, experts often provide invaluable assistance on pretrial issues, such as supporting change of venue motions, establishing race bias in jury selection, challenging death-qualified juries, and other issues.[274] Expert assistance may also be needed to challenge a confession.[275]

In *United States v. Moses*,[276] the Sixth Circuit ruled that expert testimony was required under the Child Victim's and Child Witnesses' Rights Act[277] to establish "trauma" in order to excuse a victim from testifying at trial.

§ 4-5(J). Sentencing & Capital Proceedings.

In addition to the insanity defense, *Ake* involved the penalty stage of a capital case—in particular, the issue of future dangerousness, which is an aggravating factor in several jurisdictions.[278] The Tenth Circuit has taken the position that the "*Ake* duty [is] triggered here by the State's presentation of any evidence of Mr. Castro's future dangerousness or continuing threat to society .... There is no necessity for the State to offer psychiatric testimony or evidence during the sentencing phase of a capital trial for its *Ake* duty to apply."[279] Other courts

---

274. *But see* State v. Tison, 129 Ariz. 526, 633 P.2d 335 (1981) (upholding denial of request for a public opinion survey to assist in jury selection in highly publicized criminal trial), *vacated on other grounds*, 481 U.S. 137 (1987).

275. United States v. Ingle, 157 F.3d 1147, 1152 (8th Cir. 1998) (denying request for rhetorician as expert on the voluntariness of his tape recorded admissions to cellmates; "[L]inguistc issues of this kind have often been found inappropriate for expert testimony"). For cases permitting expert testimony on confessions, *see* § 9-9 *infra*.

276. 137 F.3d 894, 900 (6th Cir. 1998) ("[W]hile Bollman may be an expert in social work, we do not find evidence in the record that she qualifies as an expert for purpose of rendering a psychological or psychiatric opinion under [the statute]").

277. 18 U.S.C. § 3509(b)(1)(B)(i).

278. *See also* Tuggle v. Netherland, 516 U.S. 10, 13 (1995) (per curiam) ("The *Ake* error prevented petitioner from developing his own psychiatric evidence to rebut the Commonwealth's evidence and to enhance his defense in mitigation. As a result, the Commonwealth's psychiatric evidence went unchallenged, which may have unfairly increased its persuasiveness in the eyes of the jury"; state presented psychiatric testimony of "future dangerousness" in penalty phase of capital case; Court remanded for determination whether harmless-error analysis applied), *on remand*, 79 F.3d 1386, 1396 (4th Cir.) (finding harmless error), *cert. denied*, 519 U.S. 894 (1996).

279. Castro v. Oklahoma, 71 F.3d 1502, 1514 (10th Cir. 1995). *Accord* Walker v. Attorney General, 167 F.3d 1339, 1348 (10th Cir. 1999) (psychiatrist in capital case) ("[W]e have construed *Ake* broadly. We held in *Brewer* that even when the State did not present expert testimony, the *Ake* requirements apply if the State presented evidence at the sentencing phase concerning the defendant's future dangerousness and the defendant showed that his mental condition could have been a significant mitigating factor. ... [T]he evidence ... presented through the mental health

disagree, limiting *Ake* to cases in which the state introduces expert testimony of future dangerousness.[280]

In addition to "future dangerousness," there are numerous other issues in death penalty cases that may be addressed by experts.[281] For example, mitigation experts are often employed.[282] Similarly, mental condition is often a mitigating factor.[283] In addition to the CJA, another federal statute covers death penalty cases.[284] Some states also have specific statutes in death penalty cases.[285]

Similarly, expert testimony may be important for sentencing in noncapital cases.[286]

---

experts was sufficient to trigger the application of *Ake* ...") (citation omitted); Moore v. Reynolds, 153 F.3d 1086, 1109 n.4, 1110 (10th Cir. 1998) ("Other circuits have narrowly construed *Ake* as creating an entitlement to assistance of a mental health expert during sentencing only when the state offers psychiatric evidence of defendant's future dangerousness"; "Based upon this information, we conclude that Moore has established a likelihood that his mental condition could have been a mitigation factor at the sentencing phase"; but harmless error), *cert. denied,* 119 S. Ct. 1266 (1999); Brewer v. Reynolds, 51 F.3d 1519, 1529 (10th Cir. 1995) (rejecting "a narrow construction of *Ake*"), *cert. denied,* 516 U.S. 1124 (1996).

280. Goodwin v. Johnson, 132 F.3d 162, 188 (5th Cir. 1998) (rehabilitation expert at penalty stage; Fifth Circuit standard requires both critical to conviction and subject to varying expert opinion; "Goodwin acknowledges that his proposed interpretation of *Ake* would entitle every defendant in a Texas capital case to the appointment of a psychiatrist because imposition of the death penalty requires that the state prove [future dangerousness]").

281. Wainwright v. Norris, 872 F. Supp. 574, 584-87 (E.D. Ark. 1994) (failure to appoint expert sociologist to testify on prison life at capital sentencing did not violate due process), *aff'd in part, rev'd in part,* 80 F.3d 1126 (8th Cir.), *cert. denied,* 519 U.S. 968 (1996).

282. James v. State, 613 N.E.2d 15, 21 (Ind. 1993) ("In cases where a defendant faces the death penalty, we also have held that the failure to allow the defendant appropriate resources to retain an expert who would give an opinion concerning the statutory mitigator, may require reversal of the death penalty"). *But see* Moore v. Reynolds, 153 F.3d 1086, 111-12 (10th Cir. 1998) (in penalty stage — request for sociologist to testify to rate of recidivism among capital murder, parole and probation expert to testify concerning whether Moore was capable of rehabilitation and whether he could someday become a productive member of society; request are "entirely speculative"), *cert. denied,* 119 S. Ct. 1266 (1999).

283. *E.g.*, Tuggle v. Netherland, 79 F.3d 1386, 1392 (4th Cir.) (*Ake* violated where psychiatric expert not provided on sentencing), *cert. denied,* 519 U.S. 894 (1996); Starr v. Lockhart, 23 F.3d 1280, 1288 (8th Cir.) (failure to appoint mental health expert on defendant's mental retardation at a death penalty sentencing hearing violated *Ake*), *cert. denied,* 513 U.S. 995 (1994).

284. 21 U.S.C. § 848(q)(9) (expert or other services for guilt or sentence) & (10)(B) ($ 7,500.00 limit unless court certifies greater amount). *See also* United States v. McVeigh, 918 F. Supp. 1452, 1462 (W.D. Okla. 1996) (Oklahoma City bombing; Anti-Drug Abuse Act of 1988 applies to death penalty cases).

285. *See* § 4-4 *supra.*

286. *E.g.*, United States v. Roman, 121 F.3d 136, 143 (3d Cir. 1997) ("In appropriate cases a court can order that such funds be provided [for a psychiatrist] to assist an indigent defendant in preparing for sentencing"; not an abuse of discretion to deny request in this case), *cert. denied,* 522 U.S. 1061 (1998); United States v. Smith, 987 F.2d 888, 891 (2d Cir. 1993) (error to deny request for psychiatric assistance to raise duress defense and incomplete duress defense for sentencing

§ 4-5(K). Other Proceedings.

In addition to criminal cases, other proceedings also may involve the loss of liberty or the loss of fundamental rights. The use of experts is not uncommon in many of these proceedings, several of which are discussed below.

Juvenile Adjudicatory Hearings

In *In re Gault*[287] the Supreme Court held that due process safeguards applied to juvenile adjudicatory hearings, in which delinquency was at issue.[288] Specifically, the Court held that the right to notice, right to counsel, right of confrontation, and the privilege against compelled self-incrimination applied in delinquency hearings. In subsequent cases, the Court held that the constitutional standard of proof in criminal cases (proof beyond a reasonable doubt)[289] and the Double Jeopardy Clause[290] also applied to delinquency cases. Because these proceedings are so closely related to criminal trials, there is little question that *Ake* would apply in delinquency proceedings.

Juvenile court jurisdiction goes beyond delinquency cases and includes dependency, neglect, and abuse cases. The Supreme Court has applied due process standards to such cases when they involve the permanent deprivation of parental rights.[291] Testimony by psychologists, caseworkers, and counselors is often admitted in dependency and neglect cases.[292] Similarly medical testimony concerning the "battered child syndrome" is admissible in physical abuse

---

guidelines), *cert. denied*, 510 U.S. 875 (1993); United States v. Nusz, 809 F. Supp. 814, 816 (D. Kan. 1992) (denial of request for psychologist to determine future dangerousness for sentencing purposes), *aff'd*, 17 F.3d 1437 (10th Cir. 1994).

287. 387 U.S. 1 (1967).

288. Delinquency refers to conduct by a child that would be criminal if committed by an adult.

289. *In re* Winship, 397 U.S. 358 (1970).

290. Illinois v. Vitale, 447 U.S. 410 (1980); Swisher v. Brady, 438 U.S. .204 (1978); Breed v. Jones, 421 U.S. 519 (1975). The Court, however, refused to extend the right to jury trial to juvenile cases. McKeiver v. Pennsylvania, 403 U.S. 528 (1971).

291. *See* Santosky v. Kramer, 455 U.S. 745, 758 (1982) ("In parental rights termination proceedings, the private interest affected is commanding; the risk of error from using a preponderance standard is substantial; and the countervailing governmental interest favoring that standard is comparatively slight"; requiring "clear and convincing" evidence); Lassiter v. Department of Social Services, 452 U.S. 18, 27 (1981) (due process may require the appointment of counsel for indigent parents on a case-by-case basis).

292. *E.g., In re* Webb, 64 Ohio App. 3d 280, 581 N.E.2d 570 (1989) (physician's clinical impression that children had been sexually abused admitted), *motion dismissed*, 48 Ohio St.3d 1061, 549 N.E.2d 1191 (1990); *In re* Brown, 60 Ohio App. 3d 136, 573 N.E.2d 1217 (1989) (social worker's testimony about mother's "past parenting history and her ability to comply with prior reunification plans regarding her other children" admitted).

cases.[293] Consequently, several courts have extended *Ake* to permanent custody proceedings.[294]

Juvenile Court Transfer Hearings

Transfer of jurisdiction refers to the process by which a juvenile court relinquishes jurisdiction and transfers a juvenile case to the criminal courts for prosecution. This process, variously described as waiver, certification, or bind-over, has been a unique part of the juvenile court system since the establishment of the first juvenile court in 1999.[295] In *Kent v. United States*[296] the Supreme Court ruled a transfer proceeding invalid. According to the Court, transfer is a "critically important"[297] stage of the juvenile process and "there is no place in our system of law for reaching a result of such tremendous consequences without ceremony—without hearing, without effective assistance of counsel, without a statement of reasons."[298]

Experts often testify in transfer cases.[299] Some courts, however, have declared that *Ake* does not apply in this context, a rather dubious proposition.[300]

Civil Commitment Proceedings

Because civil commitment proceedings may result in the loss of liberty, they are subject to due process safeguards.[301] For example, in *Addington v. Texas*[302]

---

293. *E.g.,* United States v. Bowers, 660 F.2d 527, 529 (5th Cir. 1981); State v. Durfee, 322 N.W.2d 778, 783-84 (Minn. 1982); State v. Holland, 346 N.W.2d 302, 307-08 (S.D. 1984). Annot., *Admissibility of expert medical testimony on battered child syndrome*, 98 A.L.R.3D 306 (1980).

294. *In re* Shaeffer Children, 85 Ohio App. 3d 683, 621 N.E.2d 426 (1993) (indigent mother entitled to assistance of court appointed psychiatric expert in permanent custody proceeding where her mental health was principal issue); *In re* Brown, No. C-850878, 1986 WL 13385 (1st Ohio App. 1986) ("[The] due process clause of the United States Constitution and the due course of law provision under the Ohio Constitution require the appointment of a psychiatrist to assist an indigent parent in permanent custody proceedings in which the parent's mental condition is at issue").

295. Illinois Juvenile Court Act of 1899. 1899 Ill. Laws 131. As one court has observed: "There is no proceeding for adults comparable directly to the juvenile jurisdiction waiver hearing." Kemplen v. Maryland, 428 F.2d 169, 173 (4th Cir. 1970).

296. 383 U.S. 541 (1966).

297. *Id.* at 556.

298. *Id.* at 554.

299. *E.g.,* State v. Watson, 47 Ohio St.3d 93, 94, 547 N.E.2d 1181 (1989) ("At the hearing, the court clinic psychiatrist ... testified that appellant showed 'no evidence of any psychiatric disorder'"); State v. Parks, 51 Ohio App.3d 194, 197, 555 N.E.2d 671 (1988) ("The social worker ... testified it would be doubtful that the appellant would be amenable to rehabilitation in a juvenile institution").

300. *See* State *ex rel.* a Juvenile v. Hoose, 43 Ohio App.3d 109, 111, 539 N.E.2d 704 (1988) (*Ake* not applicable to transfer hearings because these hearings do not determine guilt or innocence, nor is liberty at stake) (citing State v. R.G.D., 108 N.J. 1, 18, 527 A.2d 834 (1987)).

the Supreme Court ruled that a person committed to a mental institution in a civil proceeding must be shown to be dangerous by "clear and convincing" evidence. By its very nature, these proceedings involve expert testimony: "In civil commitment cases, where the trier of fact is required by statute to determine whether a person is dangerous or likely to be dangerous, expert prediction may be the only evidence available."[303] *Ake* would presumably apply here.

Sex Offender Proceedings

In *Kansas v. Hendricks*[304] the Supreme Court upheld the Kansas Sexually Violent Predator Act in the face of challenges on substantive due process, double jeopardy, and ex post facto grounds. The Court held that the Act's definition of "mental abnormality" satisfied the substantive due process requirements for civil commitment. The Act also provided a number of procedural safeguards. The burden of proof was allocated to the State, and indigents were provided counsel and an examination by a mental health expert. Moreover, the respondent may present and cross-examine witnesses and review documentary evidence. Here, again, expert testimony plays a central role. For example, the California Sexually Violent Predator Act requires that the offender be evaluated by two psychiatrists or psychologists.[305] *Ake* should apply.

§ 4-5(L). Related Issues.

Ake has raised a number of related issues, some of which are discussed below.

Right to Examine Alleged Victim

One issue concerns whether the right to an expert encompasses a right to require an alleged victim to be examined by such an expert. For example, the Nevada Supreme Court has held that "it is error to deny a defendant the

---

301. *See* O'Connor v. Donaldson, 422 U.S. 563 (1975) (due process violated when state continues to confine a mentally ill person who is not dangerous).

302. 441 U.S. 418, 433 (1979).

303. People v. Ward, 71 Cal. App. 4th 368, 83 Cal. Rptr. 2d 828, 832 (1999) (citing People v. Murtishaw, 29 Cal.3d 733, 772, 631 P.2d 446, 175 Cal. Rptr. 738 (1981); People v. Superior Court (Blakely), 60 Cal. App. 4th 202, 215, 70 Cal. Rptr. 2d 388 (1997)).

304. 521 U.S. 346 (1997).

305. West's Ann. Cal. Welf. & Inst. Code § 6601(d). *See also* People v. Ward, 71 Cal. App. 4th 368, 83 Cal. Rptr. 2d 828, 831(1999) ("California distinguished between expert medical opinion and scientific evidence; the former is not subject to the special admissibility rule of *Kelly-Frye. Kelly-Frye* applies to cases involving novel devices or processes, not to expert medical testimony, such as a psychiatrist's prediction of future dangerousness or a diagnosis of mental illness") (citations omitted).

assistance of a defense psychologist or psychiatrist to examine the child-victim and testify at trial when the State is provided such assistance."[306]

Prosecution Use of Defense Experts

A second issue concerns whether the prosecution may use a defense appointed expert at trial if the defense declines to call the expert as a defense witness.[307] This issue is discussed in § 5-9 *infra*.

Prosecution Comment on Failure to Call Experts

Third, the Delaware Supreme Court has ruled that a prosecutor may comment on a defendant's failure to call a fingerprint expert after the defendant had attacked the prosecution's expert.[308] The court ruled that such a comment does not infringe upon the privilege against self-incrimination, nor does it violate due process where an indigent fails to seek funds for a defense expert.[309]

Right to Consult Expert at Trial

Fourth, the New York Court of Appeals, citing *Ake*, ruled that precluding the defense counsel from consulting with his own expert during the cross-examination of the prosecution expert was reversible error.[310]

Presence of Prosecution Expert

In *Prince v. Superior Court*[311] the trial judge ordered that a DNA sample be divided between the prosecution and defense for testing and that a representative

---

306. Lickey v. State, 827 P.2d 824, 826 (1992). *See also* People v. Wheeler, 151 Ill. 2d 298, 312, 602 N.E.2d 826, 833 (1992) (Citing *Ake*, the court wrote that "it is fundamentally unfair that the State was able to present the testimony of an examining expert, but the defendant was limited to the testimony of a nonexamining expert..."); State v. Maday, 507 N.W.2d 365, 370 (Wis. App. 1993) ("Maday complains that the court will be limiting his experts to the presentation of comments on the testimony of the state's experts. His position is that he is denied meaningful cross-examination because he will not have access to the same information used by the state's experts. Without personal clinical interviews, Maday argues, the state has a strategic advantage that he cannot overcome"). For a further discussion of this issue, *see* Chapter 3 (§ 3-10).

307. *See* Smith v. McCormick, 914 F.2d 1153, 1159-60 (9th Cir. 1990) (citing attorney-client privilege in rejecting neutral expert approach). *But see* State v. McDaniel, 485 N.W.2d 630, 633 (Iowa 1992) (prosecution use of defense appointed expert did not violate due process or effective assistance of counsel guarantees).

308. Benson v. State, 636 A.2d 907, 910-11 (Del. 1994).

309. *But see* State v. Cloutier, 628 A.2d 1047, 1049 (Me. 1993) (prosecutor precluded from eliciting testimony that the prosecution chemist had given blood samples to the defense; court had previously rejected the common law missing-witness inference and feared creating a "missing-test-result" inference).

310. People v. Santana, 80 N.Y.2d 92, 100, 600 N.E.2d 201, 205 (1992).

of the state be present at the defense testing. The appellate court reversed, holding that such an order violated the defendant's right to effective assistance of counsel. The court commented: "Effective assistance of counsel includes the assistance of experts in preparing a defense ..., and communication with them in confidence...."[312]

Prosecution Monopoly

Finally, sometimes the only available expertise is controlled by the government. For example, in *People v. Evans*[313] the court ordered the New York City Police Department's Auto Crime Division to assign an experienced officer to assist the defense in inspecting vehicles: "Where the government holds a monopoly of expertise on a matter that reasonably bears on a defense in a criminal action, due process requires that a defendant be afforded access to this expertise."[314]

In another case, the court ordered "the Illinois State crime lab perform the analysis."[315] In still another case the trial court required the prosecution to make government laboratory facilities available for retesting by a defense expert.[316]

§ 4-6. Other Constitutional Rights.

Prior to *Ake* a number of courts had recognized a right to expert assistance but had disagreed on the constitutional basis for this right. The right to effective assistance of counsel, equal protection, due process, and compulsory process had all been relied upon.[317] Because the Supreme Court in *Ake* rested its decision on due process grounds, it did not consider these alternative grounds: "Because we conclude that the Due Process Clause guaranteed to Ake the assistance he requested and was denied, we have no occasion to consider the applicability of the Equal Protection Clause, or the Sixth Amendment, in this context."[318] Even

---

311. 8 Cal. App. 4th 1176, 10 Cal. Rptr. 2d 855 (1992).

312. *Id.* at 1180, 10 Cal. Rptr. 2d at 857.

313. 141 Misc. 2d 781, 534 N.Y.S.2d 640 (Sup. Ct. 1988).

314. *Id.* at 783, 534 N.Y.S.2d at 642.

315. People v. Dickerson, 239 Ill. App. 3d 951, 959, 606 N.E.2d 762, 767 (1992) (handwriting expert).

316. United States v. Bockius, 564 F.2d 1193, 1196 (5th Cir. 1977).

317. The right to confrontation may also support a right to expert assistance. *See* Note, *The Indigent's Right to an Adequate Defense: Expert and Investigative Assistance in Criminal Proceedings*, 55 CORNELL L. REV. 632, 642-43 (1970). *See also* Pennsylvania v. Ritchie, 480 U.S. 39, 61-62 (1987) (J. Blackmun, concurring) ("In my view, there might well be a confrontation violation if, as here, a defendant is denied pretrial access to information that would make possible effective cross-examination of a crucial prosecution witness").

318. 470 U.S. at 87 n.13.

after *Ake*, it is not uncommon to see citations to these other constitutional bases. These additional constitutional bases are discussed below.

Imbalance of Resources

There are other due process lines of cases that might also support a right to expert assistance.[319] *Ake* focused on only one aspect of due process — the right to present a defense. A different due process argument could be based on the state's providing expert assistance to the prosecution and not the defense. In other contexts, the Supreme Court has noted that due process "speak[s] to the balance of forces between the accused and his accuser."[320] Thus, in discussing the right to expert assistance under the Criminal Justice Act, one court noted, "If the fairness of our system is to be assured, indigent defendants must have access to minimal defense aids to offset the advantage presented by the vast prosecutorial and investigative resources available to the Government."[321]

Brady Doctrine

Still another due process argument centers on the prosecutor's duty to disclose favorable evidence to the defense under *Brady v. Maryland.*[322] Some cases regard the failure of the state to provide expert assistance as a denial of the right to exculpatory defense evidence. For example, one court has written: "[T]he denial of a reasonable request to obtain the services of a necessary psychiatric witness is effectually a suppression of evidence violating the fundamental right of due

319. The Court has recognized on more than one occasion that the term "due process" is not self-defining: "For all its consequence, 'due process' has never been, and perhaps can never be, precisely defined.... [T]he phrase expresses the requirement of 'fundamental fairness,' a requirement whose meaning can be as opaque as its importance is lofty." Lassiter v. Department of Social Servs., 452 U.S. 18, 24 (1981).

320. Wardius v. Oregon, 412 U.S. 470, 472 (1973). *See also* Lassiter v. Department of Social Servs., 452 U.S. 18, 28 (1981) (The "adversary system presupposes, accurate and just results are most likely to be obtained through the equal contest of opposed interests ..."); Ross v. Moffitt, 417 U.S. 600, 609 (1974) (Due process "emphasizes fairness between the State and the individual dealing with the State").

321. United States v. Hartfield, 513 F.2d 254, 258 (9th Cir. 1975). *See also* United States v. Stifel, 433 F.2d 431, 441 (6th Cir. 1970) ("[I]f the government sees fit to use this time consuming, expensive means of fact-finding [neutron activation analysis], it must both allow time for a defendant to make similar tests, and in the instance of an indigent defendant, a means to provide for payment for same"), *cert. denied*, 401 U.S. 994 (1971); State v. Johnson, 333 So. 2d 223, 225 (La. 1976) ("Due process and fundamental fairness require that a defendant charged with homicide be given the right to choose his own ballistics expert to examine the alleged murder weapon and bullet in order to rebut testimony of the State's expert witnesses").

322. 373 U.S. 83 (1963). For a further discussion of *Brady*, *see* Chapter 3.

process."[323] The principal problem with this analysis is determining whether the evidence will be exculpatory.[324]

§ 4-6(A). Effective Assistance of Counsel.

In *Gideon v. Wainwright*[325] the Supreme Court held the sixth amendment right to counsel applicable to the states. Accordingly, the state must provide counsel to indigent defendants.[326] The Court noted: "[I]n our adversary system of criminal justice, any person hailed into court, who is too poor to hire a lawyer, cannot be assured a fair trial unless counsel is provided for him."[327] The right to counsel includes the right to effective assistance of counsel.[328]

Several courts have found ineffective assistance where defense counsel has failed to obtain the services of expert witnesses: "The failure of defense counsel to seek such assistance when the need is apparent deprives an accused of adequate representation in violation of his sixth amendment right to counsel."[329] Similarly, another court found ineffectiveness where defense counsel knew that gunshot residue testimony was "critical," but nevertheless "failed to depose ... the State's expert witness, nor bothered to consult with any other expert in the

---

323. United States *ex rel.* Robinson, 345 F.2d 691, 695 (7th Cir. 1965), *aff'd in part, remanded in part on other grounds*, 383 U.S. 375 (1966). *Accord* Bowen v. Eyman, 324 F. Supp. 339, 340 (D. Ariz. 1970) ("refusal to run the tests is tantamount to a suppression of evidence such as there was in *Brady* ..."); State v. Hanson, 278 N.W.2d 198, 200 (S.D. 1979) (citing *Brady* in finding a right to an independent expert).

324. *See* Little v. Streater, 452 U.S. 1 (1981) ("exculpatory evidence").

325. 372 U.S. 335 (1963).

326. Argersinger v. Hamlin, 407 U.S. 25 (1972), extended the right to counsel to all trials, including misdemeanor cases, in which imprisonment is imposed. *See also* Scott v. Illinois, 440 U.S. 367 (1979) (right to counsel attaches with imprisonment).

327. 372 U.S. at 344.

328. *See* Strickland v. Washington, 666 U.S. 668 (1984); United States v. Cronic, 666 U.S. 648 (1984); Powell v. Alabama, 287 U.S. 45, 71 (1932).

329. Proffitt v. United States, 582 F.2d 854, 857 (4th Cir. 1978), *cert. denied,* 447 U.S. 910 (1980). *See also* Rowe, *Commentary, in* CONVICTED BY JURIES, EXONERATED BY SCIENCE: CASE STUDIES IN THE USE OF DNA EVIDENCE TO ESTABLISH INNOCENCE AFTER TRIAL xvii-xviii (Connors et al. 1996) (discussing the exoneration of 28 convicts through the use of DNA technology—some of whom had been sentenced to death; "One problem that DNA testing will not remedy is inadequate legal counsel. In case after case reported here, defense counsel failed to consult competent scientific experts. Even a neophyte forensic serologist would have detected the problems with the prosecution's serological evidence in the Dotson case. It is also clear that in case after case, defense counsel failed to review the case notes of the prosecution's forensic serologists. Even a layperson would have seen that Fred Zain's written reports and sworn testimony were contradicted by his case notes. Again, one has to reflect on the likelihood that numerous innocent persons are presently incarcerated because of the inadequacy of their attorneys").

See also CONNORS ET AL., CONVICTED BY JURIES, EXONERATED BY SCIENCE: CASE STUDIES IN THE USE OF DNA EVIDENCE TO ESTABLISH INNOCENCE AFTER TRIAL 67-68 (1996) ("ineffective counsel at [Piszek's] trial (trial counsel never requested DNA testing").

field.[330] Other cases, both federal[331] and state,[332] have also found incompetence for failing to obtain expert assistance.

---

330. Troedel v. Wainwright, 667 F. Supp. 1456, 1461 (S.D. Fla. 1986), *aff'd*, 828 F.2d 670 (11th Cir. 1987). *See also* Bloom v. Calderon, 132 F.3d 1267, 1278 (9th Cir. 1997) ("Even the third-year law student knew the defense needed a psychiatric expert witness. That witness was to be Dr. Kling. As a result of trial counsel's woefully deficient performance, however, Dr. Kling was not provided with sufficient information and, as a result, his testimony not only failed to help the defense, it significantly hindered it. Kling's report (which he now acknowledges was inaccurate) permitted the prosecution to turn Kling's trial testimony against Bloom, and it gave the prosecution the ammunition it needed to secure guilty verdicts of first degree murder with special circumstances on all three counts"), *cert. denied*, 523 U.S. 1145 (1998).

331. *E.g.*, Baylor v. Estelle, 94 F.3d 1321, 1324 (9th Cir. 1996) ("We have difficulty understanding how reasonably competent counsel would not recognize 'the obvious exculpatory potential of semen evidence in a sexual assault case,' particularly when the criminalist's report plainly indicates that the donor was an ABO nonsecretor whereas Baylor was an ABO type 'O' secretor and that this 'would thus eliminate Baylor as the perpetrator unless a test ... on a liquid semen sample showed that he mimicked a nonsecretor .... Whether or not Stockwell's report was itself conclusive, it was one test away from titling the scale powerfully in Baylor's direction") (citation omitted), *cert. denied*, 520 U.S. 1151 (1997); Glenn v. Tate, 71 F.3d 1204, 1209-11 (6th Cir. 1995) (ineffective assistance in penalty phase of capital murder case for failing to present evidence of defendant's mental retardation/neurological impairment, and by acquiescing to prosecutor's suggestion that experts requested by defense be treated as court-appointed rather than defense experts, and by failing to challenge expert reports), *cert. denied*, 519 U.S. 910 (1996); Driscoll v. Delo, 71 F.3d 701, 709 (8th Cir. 1995) (In a capital murder case whether alleged murder weapon "had blood matching the victim's constituted an issue of the utmost importance. Under these circumstances, a reasonable defense lawyer would take some measures to understand the laboratory tests performed and the inferences that one could logically draw from the results. At the very least, any reasonable attorney under the circumstances would study the state's laboratory report with sufficient care so that if the prosecution advanced a theory at trial that was at odds with the serology evidence, the defense would be in a position to expose it on cross-examination"), *cert. denied*, 519 U.S. 910 (1996); Foster v. Lockhart, 9 F.3d 722, 726 (8th Cir. 1993) (failure to pursue an impotency defense in a rape case); United States v. Tarricone, 996 F.2d 1414, 1418 (2d Cir. 1993) (failure to consult handwriting expert made out a viable claim of ineffectiveness); Sims v. Livesay, 970 F.2d 1575, 1580 (6th Cir. 1992) (failure to have quilt examined for gunshot residue); Wood v. Zahradnick, 578 F.2d 980, 982 (4th Cir. 1978); United States v. Fessel, 531 F.2d 1275, 1279 (5th Cir. 1976) ("[W]hen an insanity defense is appropriate and the defendant lacks funds to secure private psychiatric assistance, it is the duty of his attorney to seek such assistance through the use of [the Criminal Justice Act]"); United States v. Fratus, 530 F.2d 644, 649-50 (5th Cir.), *cert. denied*, 429 U.S. 846 (1976); United States v. Edwards, 488 F.2d 1154, 1164 (5th Cir. 1974); Owsley v. Peyton, 368 F.2d 1002, 1003 (4th Cir. 1966); United States *ex rel.* Foster v. Gilmore, 35 F. Supp. 2d 626, 630 (N.D. Illinois 1999) ("This court finds inexplicable—and wholly ineffective–defense counsel's failure to consult a psychiatric expert prior to or even during the trial"); Halton v. Hesson, 803 F. Supp. 1272, 1276 (M.D. Tenn. 1992) (failure to call psychiatrist); Loe v. United States, 545 F. Supp. 662, 672 (E.D. Va. 1982) (counsel ineffective for failing to request a partisan expert under C.J.A.). *But see* Bonin v. Vasquez, 794 F. Supp. 957, 963-64 (C.D. Cal. 1992) (failure to present psychiatric witness at penalty phase of capital murder trial), *cert. denied*, 516 U.S. 1051 (1996).

If failure to secure expert assistance may constitute ineffective assistance of counsel, then it is but a short step to recognizing that the sixth amendment places an affirmative duty upon the state to provide expert services to indigent defendants upon request.[333] A number of courts have taken that step.[334] "[T]he right to counsel is meaningless if the lawyer is unable to make an effective

---

332. *E.g.*, People v. Frierson, 25 Cal. 3d 142, 163-64, 599 P.2d 587, 598-600, 158 Cal. Rptr. 281, 292-93 (1979); Moore v. State, 827 S.W.2d 213, 214 (Mo. 1992) (counsel ineffective for failing to request serological test); State v. Hicks, 195 Wis. 2d 620, 627-28, 536 N.W.2d 487, 491 (App. 1995) ("Before the trial, [defense counsel] knew that the root tissue of hair specimens could be subject to DNA testing at certain out-of-state laboratories and he knew of the technology used for that testing. He did not discuss this with his client or with the district attorney, or petition the court to have this test performed or do anything to pursue such testing"; failure to obtain DNA analysis was not a strategic or tactical decision).

333. *See* Lickey v. State, 827 P.2d 824, 826 (Nev. 1992) ("If failure to request a psychological examination constitutes grounds for a finding of ineffective counsel, it logically follows that a defendant facing charges of sexual assault of a minor should be afforded an expert psychiatric witness"). *See also* Rogers v. Gibson, 173 F.3d 1278, 1284 (10th Cir. 1999) (psychiatrist in capital case) (*Ake* "principle is derived in significant part from the Fourteenth Amendment's due process guarantee of fundamental fairness, and in part from the Sixth Amendment's guarantee of the 'fundamental right to a fair trial'") (citing *Strickland*).

Support for this view is also found in two Supreme Court cases. *See* United States v. Wade, 388 U.S. 218, 227-28 (1967) (no right to counsel at examination of scientific evidence because "the accused has the opportunity for a meaningful confrontation of the Government's case at trial through the ordinary processes of cross-examination of Government's expert witnesses and the presentation of the evidence of his own experts"); Gilbert v. California, 388 U.S. 263, 267 (1967) (no right to counsel at time handwriting exemplars are obtained because "the accused can make an unlimited number of additional exemplars for analysis and comparison by ... defense handwriting experts").

334. *E.g.*, Matlock v. Rose, 731 F.2d 1236, 1243-44 (6th Cir. 1984); Brinks v. Alabama, 465 F.2d 446, 449 (5th Cir. 1972), *cert. denied*, 409 U.S. 1130 (1979); Hintz v. Beto, 379 F.2d 937, 941 (5th Cir. 1967) ("effective assistance of counsel ... may necessitate a psychiatric examination of a defendant"); Greer v. Beto, 379 F.2d 923, 925 (5th Cir. 1967) (state policy of not providing psychiatric experts for defense "may not ... avoid the federal constitutional right to the effective assistance of counsel"); Corenevsky v. Superior Court, 36 Cal. 3d 307, 319, 682 P.2d 360, 367, 204 Cal. Rptr. 165, 172 (1984) (right to counsel "includes the right to reasonably necessary ancillary defense services"); *In re* Ketchel, 68 Cal. 2d 397, 399, 438 P.2d 625, 627, 66 Cal. Rptr. 881, 883 (1968); Taylor v. Superior Court, 168 Cal. App. 3d 1217, 1218, 215 Cal. Rptr. 73, 74 (1985) (fingerprint expert); People v. Worthy, 109 Cal. App. 3d 514, 518-19, 167 Cal. Rptr. 402, 404-05 (1980); English v. Missildine, 311 N.W.2d 292, 393 (Iowa 1981); State v. Anaya, 456 A.2d 1255, 1262-63 (Me. 1983); State v. Rush, 46 N.J. 399, 416, 217 A.2d 441, 450 (1966); State v. Second Judicial Dist. Court, 85 Nev. 241, 243-44, 453 P.2d 421, 422-23 (1969); State v. Parton, 303 N.C. 55, 66, 277 S.E.2d 410, 418 (1981); State v. Dickamore, 22 Wash. App. 851, 854, 592 P.2d 681, 683 (1979).

But see United States *ex rel.* Huguley v. Martin, 325 F. Supp. 489, 493 (N.D. Ga. 1971); State v. Superior Court, 2 Ariz. App. 458, 409 P.2d 742 (1966).

defense because he has no funds to provide the specialized testimony which the case requires."[335]

A leading pre-*Ake* case was *Williams v. Martin,*[336] in which an indigent murder defendant requested the appointment of an independent forensic pathologist to determine the victim's cause of death. The request was denied by the state trial court. In granting habeas relief, the Fourth Circuit based its decision on the equal protection guarantee and the right to counsel:[337] "There can be no doubt that an effective defense sometimes requires the assistance of an expert witness."[338] Under this theory, an expert should be appointed whenever necessary for counsel to render effective assistance;[339] that is, "whenever the [expert] services are necessary to the preparation and presentation of an adequate defense."[340]

Several post-*Ake* decisions continue to cite the right to counsel in this context. An Iowa court cited the sixth amendment in ruling that a trial court erred in failing to appoint an accident reconstruction expert in a vehicular homicide case: "Effective representation of counsel includes the right to an expert witness."[341] In 1996 the Alabama Supreme Court wrote that the "Sixth Amendment right to assistance of counsel encompasses the right to effective assistance of counsel.... This right includes access to expert witnesses where it is appropriate."[342]

In *Prince v. Superior Court*[343] the trial judge ordered that a DNA sample be divided between the prosecution and defense for testing and that a representative

---

335. Bush v. McCollum, 231 F. Supp. 560, 565 (N.D. Tex. 1964), *aff'd,* 344 F.2d 672 (5th Cir. 1965).

The right to expert assistance is closely related to the right to investigative assistance, which has also been recognized by several courts. *See* Mason v. Arizona, 504 F.2d 1345, 1351 (9th Cir. 1974), *cert. denied*, 420 U.S. 936 (1975) ("effective assistance of counsel guarantee ... requires, when necessary, the allowance of investigative expenses or appointment of investigative assistance for indigent defendants in order to insure effective preparation of their defense by their attorneys"); Davis v. Coiner, 356 F. Supp. 695 (N.D. Va. 1973); United States v. Germany, 32 F.R.D. 421, 423-24 (M.D. Ala. 1963); Lucero v. Superior Court, 122 Cal. App. 3d 484, 176 Cal. Rptr. 62 (1981); State v. Madison, 345 So. 2d 485 (La. 1977). *See generally* Note, *Providing Indigent Criminal Defendants State Paid Investigators*, 13 WAKE FOREST L. REV. 655 (1977).

336. 618 F.2d 1021 (4th Cir. 1980).

337. *Id.* at 1027.

338. *Id.* at 1025. *Williams* is discussed in further detail in § 4-6(B) *infra*.

339. *See* United States v. Fessel, 531 F.2d 1275, 1278 (5th Cir. 1976).

340. Proffitt v. United States, 582 F.2d 854, 857 (4th Cir. 1978), *cert. denied,* 447 U.S. 910 (1980).

341. State v. Van Scoyoc, 511 N.W.2d 628, 630 (Iowa 1993) (expert's testimony relevant to issue of "recklessness" of defendant's conduct). *See also* People v. Gaglione, 26 Cal. App. 4th 1291, 1304, 32 Cal. Rptr. 2d 169, 176 (1994) ("[T]he right to effective assistance of counsel entitles indigent defendants to access to public funds for expert services"), *rev. denied*, 1994 Cal. LEXIS 5769 (Cal. Oct. 27, 1994).

342. *Ex parte* Moody, 684 So. 2d 114, 120 (Ala. 1996) (*citing* United States v. Wright, 489 F.2d 1181, 1188 n.6 (D.C. Cir. 1973)).

343. 8 Cal. App. 4th 1176, 10 Cal. Rptr. 2d 855 (1992).

of the state be present at the defense testing. The appellate court reversed, holding that such an order violated the defendant's right to effective assistance of counsel. The court commented: "Effective assistance of counsel includes the assistance of experts in preparing a defense ..., and communication with them in confidence...."[344]

§ 4-6(B). Equal Protection.

The equal protection argument for the appointment of defense experts has its genesis in *Griffin v. Illinois,*[345] in which an indigent defendant challenged a state practice of conditioning appellate review upon the availability of a transcript that the defendant could not afford. The Supreme Court held that failure to provide a free transcript denied the accused due process and equal protection. According to the Court, "There can be no equal justice where the kind of trial a man gets depends on the amount of money he has."[346] In *Douglas v. California*[347] the Court extended the "*Griffin* principle" to the appointment of counsel for a first appeal as of right. Other cases also echoed this principle: "*Griffin v. Illinois* and its progeny established the principle that the State must, as a matter of equal protection, provide indigent prisoners with the basic tools of an adequate defense or appeal, when those tools are available for a price to other prisoners."[348] (This quotation appears in *Ake*).

Several courts relied on this line of cases when recognizing an indigent's right to expert assistance. For example, one court wrote: "It is obvious that only [the defendant's] inability to pay for the services of a psychiatrist prevented a proper presentation of his case. The Supreme Court has unmistakably held that in criminal proceedings it will not tolerate discrimination between indigents and those who possess the means to protect their rights."[349]

A leading case is *Williams v. Martin,*[350] in which an indigent defendant requested the services of a forensic pathologist to evaluate the victim's cause of

---

344. *Id.* at 1180, 10 Cal. Rptr. 2d at 857.

345. 351 U.S. 12 (1956).

346. *Id.* at 19 (plurality opinion).

347. 372 U.S. 353 (1963).

348. Britt v. North Carolina, 404 U.S. 226, 227 (1971). *See also* Roberts v. LaVallee, 389 U.S. 40, 42 (1967) ("Our decisions for more than a decade now have made clear that differences in access to the instruments needed to vindicate legal rights, when based upon the financial situation of the defendant, are repugnant to the Constitution").

349. Jacobs v. United States, 350 F.2d 571, 573 (4th Cir. 1965). *Accord* Bradford v. United States, 413 F.2d 467, 474 (5th Cir. 1969); People v. Gunnerson, 74 Cal. App. 3d 370, 379, 141 Cal. Rptr. 488, 494 (1977); Pierce v. State, 251 Ga. 590, 592-93, 308 S.E.2d 367, 368-69 (1983); State v. Olin, 103 Idaho 391, 394, 648 P.2d 203, 206 (1982); State v. Anaya, 456 A.2d 1255, 1262-63 (Me. 1983).

350. 618 F.2d 1021, 1027 (4th Cir. 1980). *Williams* is discussed at 49 GEO. WASH. L. REV. 191 (1980); 16 WAKE FOREST L. REV. 1031 (1980).

death in a homicide prosecution. The Fourth Circuit held that the trial court's refusal to appoint an expert "denied [the defendant] equal protection of the law."[351] According to the court, the standard for determining whether expert assistance is constitutionally required is "(a) whether a substantial question requiring expert testimony arose over the cause of death, and (b) whether Williams' defense could be fully developed without professional assistance."[352] The court's examination of the record revealed that a substantial question about the cause of death had existed and that the absence of an expert witness hampered the development of this defense. Significantly, the court held that "[i]t is not incumbent upon Williams to prove ... that an independent expert would have provided helpful testimony at trial. An indigent prisoner ... should not be required to present proof of what an expert would say when he is denied access to an expert."[353]

The principal problem with this line of analysis is the Supreme Court's later cases — in particular, *Ross v. Moffitt,*[354] which undercuts the *Griffin-Douglas* rationale.[355] *Ross* involved the appointment of counsel for discretionary appeals. The Court held that the state's failure to provide counsel in such appeals did not violate the equal protection guarantee. According to the Court, the equal protection clause "'does not require absolute equality or precisely equal advantages.'"[356] Although the Court recognized the disadvantage an indigent suffered in comparison with a nonindigent in this context, it held that the "duty of the State ... is not to duplicate the legal arsenal that may be privately retained by a criminal defendant in a continuing effort to reverse his conviction, but only to assure the indigent defendant an adequate opportunity to present his claims fairly in the context of the State's appellate process."[357] Thus, the focus of the Court's analysis was not on the disparity between indigent and nonindigent, but on whether the indigent had an "adequate opportunity" to present his case.[358]

---

351. 618 F.2d at 1027. The court also found a denial of effective assistance of counsel. *See* § 4-6(A) *supra.*

352. *Id.* at 1026.

353. *Id.* at 1026-27.

354. 417 U.S. 600 (1974).

355. *See* L. TRIBE, AMERICAN CONSTITUTIONAL LAW 1119 (1988) (*Douglas* "effectively sterilized" in *Ross*); Kamisar, *Poverty, Equality and Criminal Procedure: From Griffin v. Illinois and Douglas v. California to Ross v. Moffitt, in* NATIONAL COLLEGE OF DISTRICT ATTORNEYS, CONSTITUTIONAL LAW DESKBOOK 1-79 (3d ed. 1978); 49 GEO. WASH. L. REV. 191 (1980).

356. 417 U.S. at 612 (quoting San Antonio Independent School Dist. v. Rodriguez, 411 U.S. 1, 24 (1973)).

357. *Id.* at 616.

358. The notion that equal protection requires only an "adequate opportunity" for a defendant to present his claims was reaffirmed in United States v. MacCollam, 426 U.S. 317 (1976). *See also* Wainwright v. Torna, 455 U.S. 586 (1982) (Because defendant had no constitutional right to

This approach smacks more of a due process than an equal protection analysis.[359] Earlier, in *Ross,* the Court pointed out that equal protection analysis "emphasizes disparity in treatment by a State between classes of individuals whose situations are arguably indistinguishable," whereas due process analysis "emphasizes fairness between the State and the individual dealing with the State, regardless of how other individuals in the same situation may be treated."[360] Although *Ross* weakens the equal protection argument for expert assistance,[361] it does not completely undercut it. Without an expert witness, an indigent may not have an "adequate opportunity" to present a defense. This standard, however, is similar, if not identical, to the Court's due process analysis in *Ake.*[362]

§ 4-6(C). Compulsory Process.

In *Washington v. Texas*[363] the Supreme Court held that the Compulsory Process Clause applied in state trials. Moreover, the Court adopted a liberal view of the clause; it was not limited to the right to subpoena witnesses but also included the right to present defense evidence: "The right to offer the testimony of witnesses, and to compel their attendance, if necessary, is in plain terms the right to present a defense, the right to present the defendant's version of the facts as well as the prosecution's to the jury so it may decide where the truth lies."[364]

---

counsel under *Ross* for a discretionary appeal, he could not be deprived of the effective assistance of counsel on such an appeal).

359. *See* Kamisar, *supra* note 355, at 1-101. In a later case, the Court noted that "[d]ue process and equal protection principles converge in the Court's analysis in these cases." Bearden v. Georgia, 461 U.S. 660, 665 (1983). In that case the Court held that a sentencing court could not revoke a defendant's probation for failure to pay a fine absent evidence and findings that the defendant was responsible for such failure and that alternative forms of punishment were inadequate. In so holding, the Court preferred to rest its decision on due process grounds. *Id.* at 666 n.8. *See also* Evitts v. Lucey, 469 U.S. 387 (1985) (due process guarantees the right to effective assistance of counsel in an appeal of right).

360. 417 U.S. at 609. *See also* Evitts v. Lucey, 469 U.S. 387, 405 (1985); Bearden v. Georgia, 461 U.S. 660, 665 (1983) (quoting *Ross* on this point).

361. A number of courts have cited *Ross* in upholding denials of requests for expert assistance. Dorsey v. Solomon, 435 F. Supp. 725, 736 (D. Md. 1977); State v. Parton, 303 N.C. 55, 66, 277 S.E.2d 410, 418 (1981); State v. Gray, 292 N.C. 270, 277-78, 233 S.E.2d 905, 911 (1977); Graham v. State, 547 S.W.2d 531, 535 (Tenn. 1977). *See also* Blankenship v. State, 247 Ga. 590, 277 S.E.2d 505 (1981).

362. *See* § 4-5 *supra.* Some courts cite *Ake* in ruling on equal protection challenges to the failure to appoint a defense expert. *See* People v. Stone, 195 Mich. App. 600, 604-05, 491 N.W.2d 628, 630-31 (1992) (accused's interest in appointment of expert is less at sentencing hearing than at trial).

363. 388 U.S. 14 (1967).

364. *Id.* at 19. *See also* United States v. Nixon, 418 U.S. 683, 709 (1974) ("We have elected to employ an adversary system of criminal justice in which the parties contest all issues before a court of law. The need to develop all relevant facts in the adversary system is both fundamental and

Although *Washington* did not involve expert witnesses, "it is scarcely conceivable that defendants could be constitutionally denied the opportunity to call experts to give opinion evidence about such matters as fingerprints, bloodstains, sanity, and other matters that routinely arise in criminal litigation."[365]

Nevertheless, the right to expert assistance based on the compulsory process guarantee is not without limitations. The Court has held that a violation of the Compulsory Process Clause "requires some showing that the evidence lost would be both material and favorable to the defense."[366]

A number of courts have based a defendant's right to expert testimony on the compulsory process guarantee. In *Flores v. Estelle,*[367] for example, the defendant attempted to elicit expert opinion testimony from a state toxicologist who had been subpoenaed by the defense. The expert refused to express an opinion because he had not been retained as an expert witness, and the trial court declined to require him to testify. The reviewing courts agreed "that the trial court erred in refusing to require [the expert] to testify, thereby depriving Flores of effective compulsory process for obtaining witnesses in his favor."[368]

Similarly, in *People v. Watson*[369] an indigent forgery defendant requested the appointment of a handwriting expert. The Illinois Supreme Court held that the refusal to appoint the expert violated the compulsory process guarantee:

> The court recognizes that there is a distinction between the right to call witnesses and the right to have these witnesses paid for by the government, but in certain instances involving indigents, the lack of funds with which to pay for the witness will often preclude him from calling that witness and occasionally prevent him from offering a defense. Thus, although the defendant is afforded the shadow of the right to call witnesses, he is deprived of the substance.[370]

The court went on to conclude that "[w]hether it is necessary to subpoena expert witnesses in order to assure a fair trial will depend upon the facts in each case."[371]

---

comprehensive. The ends of criminal justice would be defeated if judgments were to be founded on a partial or speculative presentation of the facts. The very integrity of the judicial system and public confidence in the system depend on full disclosure of all the facts, within the framework of the rules of evidence. To ensure that justice is done, it is imperative to the function of courts that compulsory process be available for the production of evidence needed either by the prosecution or by the defense").

365. Westen, *Compulsory Process II,* 74 MICH. L. REV. 192, 203 (1975).

366. United States v. Valenzuela-Bernal, 458 U.S. 858, 873 (1982).

367. 492 F.2d 711 (5th Cir. 1974).

368. *Id.* at 712. *See also* English v. Missildine, 311 N.W.2d 292 (Iowa 1981); State v. Sims, 52 Ohio Misc. 31, 369 N.E.2d 24 (C.P. 1977).

369. 36 Ill. 2d 228, 221 N.E.2d 645 (1966).

370. *Id.* at 233, 221 N.E.2d 648.

371. *Id.* at 234, 221 N.E.2d at 648.

Watson was such a case because the "issue of handwriting goes to the heart of the defense" and the expert's testimony "may have been crucial" to that defense.[372] *Watson* was decided prior to the U.S. Supreme Court's decision in *Ake*, which relied on due process grounds. In a subsequent case, the Illinois Supreme Court concluded that its analysis in *Watson* "poses no conflict" with the *Ake* decision.[373]

§ 4-7. Mental Competency & Insanity Defense Statutes.

In *Dusky v. United States*[374] the U.S. Supreme Court set forth the test for determining competency to stand trial: "[T]he test must be whether he has sufficient present ability to consult with his lawyer with a reasonable degree of rational understanding—and whether he has a rational as well as factual understanding of the proceedings against him." Frequently, the appointment of experts to determine whether a defendant is competent to stand trial is governed by a specific statute. For example, a federal district court may order a mental examination to determine competency to stand trial.[375] This expert is a court expert, not a defense expert.

The insanity defense raises different legal issues.[376] Some statutes also authorize mental examinations in this context— e.g., Insanity Defense Act of 1984.[377] An expert appointed under this provision also functions in a different role:

> A psychiatrist appointed under § 4242 at the government's request or on the court's own motion is "expected to be neutral and detached," ... and reports his findings to the court even if the defendant does not wish him to do so. Under the Criminal Justice Act, 18 U.S.C. § 3006A, by contrast, the mental

---

372. *Id.*, 221 N.E.2d at 649. The Illinois courts have interpreted *Watson* on a number of occasions. *See* People v. Walker, 53 Ill. 2d 485, 495, 292 N.E.2d 387, 393 (1973) (no showing that assistance "sufficiently related to the defendant's theory of defense"); People v. Glower, 49 Ill. 2d 78, 82, 273 N.E.2d 367, 370 (1971) (defendant must show assistance "necessary to prove a crucial issue"); People v. Nichols, 70 Ill. App. 3d 748, 753, 388 N.E.2d 984, 988 (1979) (failure to appoint psychiatrist violates *Watson* rule); People v. Vines, 43 Ill. App. 3d 986, 989, 358 N.E.2d 72, 74 (1976) (expert assistance must be necessary to a crucial issue); People v. Clay, 19 Ill. App. 3d 296, 299, 311 N.E.2d 384, 386 (1974) (expert testimony must be "deemed crucial to a proper defense").

373. People v. Lawson, 163 Ill. 2d 187, 644 N.E.2d 1172, 1189 (1994).

374. 362 U.S. 402, 402 (1960).

375. 18 U.S.C. § 4241(b) (mental competency).

376. Mental competency at trial must be distinguished from the insanity defense, which refers to the defendant's mental condition at the time of the offense. Moreover, the policy issues raised by the insanity defense differ substantially from those raised by an accused's competency to stand trial. Insanity concerns a defendant's culpability for his criminal acts; it is a substantive criminal law issue. In contrast, mental competency involves a due process issue. Accordingly, different standards are employed in these two contexts.

377. 18 U.S.C. § 4242(a). *See also* FED. R. CRIM. P. 12.2(c) (court-ordered psychiatric examination to determine sanity at time of offense).

health expert "fills a different role." ... The § 3006A expert's conclusions need not be reported either to the court or to the prosecution.[378]

§ 4-8. Court Appointed Experts.

A trial court has inherent authority to appoint expert witnesses[379] and technical advisors.[380] In many jurisdictions, this authority has been codified in statutes and court rules.[381] Federal Evidence Rule 706(a) is an example.[382] Rule 706(c) provides that the decision whether to disclose to the jury that the expert has been appointed by the court lies within the discretion of the trial court. Rule 706(d) recognizes the right of the parties to call their own experts, notwithstanding the appointment of an expert by the court.

There are several disadvantages associated with the court appointment of expert witnesses. First, if the jury is informed of the appointment, the witness may be cloaked with the authority of the court, at least in the eyes of the jury.[383] The federal drafters acknowledged this problem: "court appointed experts [may] acquire an aura of infallibility to which they are not entitled...."[384] Second, the

378. United States v. Williams, 998 F.2d 258, 263 (5th Cir. 1993) (quoting United States v. Theriault, 440 F.2d 713, 715 (5th Cir. 1971)), *cert. denied*, 510 U.S. 1099 (1994).

379. FED. R. EVID. 706 advisory committee's note, ("The inherent power of a trial judge to appoint an expert of his own choosing is virtually unquestioned"); 1 C. MCCORMICK, EVIDENCE § 17 (4th ed. 1992); Johnson, *Court-Appointed Scientific Expert Witnesses: Unfettering Expertise*, 2 HIGH TECH. L.J. 249 (1988); Lee, *Court-Appointed Experts and Judicial Reluctance: A Proposal to Amend Rule 706 of the Federal Rules of Evidence*, 6 YALE L. & POL'Y REV. 480 (1988); Sink, *The Unused Power of a Federal Judge to Call His Own Expert Witnesses*, 29 S. CAL. L. REV. 195 (1956).

380. Note, *Improving Judicial Gatekeeping: Technical Advisors and Scientific Evidence*, 110 HARV. L. REV. 941 (1997).

381. *See* 2 J. WIGMORE, EVIDENCE § 563 (Chadbourn rev. 1979) (listing rules and statutes). *See also* Annot., *Trial Court's Appointment, in Civil Case, of Expert Witness*, 95 A.L.R.2D 390 (1964). J. CECIL & T. WILLGING, COURT-APPOINTED EXPERTS: DEFINING THE ROLE OF EXPERTS APPOINTED UNDER FEDERAL RULE OF EVIDENCE 706 (Fed. Judicial Center 1993).

382. The rule provides: "The court may on its own motion or on the motion of any party enter an order to show cause why expert witnesses should not be appointed, and may request the parties to submit nominations. The court may appoint any expert witnesses agreed upon by the parties, and may appoint expert witnesses of its own selection. An expert witness shall not be appointed by the court unless the witness consents to act. A witness so appointed shall be informed of the witness' duties by the court in writing, a copy of which shall be filed with the clerk, or at a conference in which the parties shall have opportunity to participate. A witness so appointed shall advise the parties of the witness' findings, if any; the witness' deposition may be taken by any party; and the witness may be called to testify by the court or any party. The witness shall be subject to cross examination by each party, including a party calling the witness."

383. *See* Kian v. Mirro Aluminum Co., 88 F.R.D. 351, 356 (E.D. Mich. 1980). *See generally* Saltzburg, *The Unnecessarily Expanding Role of the American Trial Judge*, 64 VA. L. REV. 1 (1978).

384. FED. R. EVID. 706 advisory committee's note.

motion for the appointment of an expert may disclose a defense theory previously unknown to the prosecution. In contrast, the motion for the appointment of a defense expert under the Criminal Justice Act is *ex parte*, thus precluding prosecution discovery in most cases.[385]

Even though the authority to appoint expert witnesses is firmly established, few courts exercise that authority. In contrast, in the civil-law countries court experts are the tradition.[386] Moreover, one commentator has argued persuasively for the mandatory appointment of all experts.[387]

From a defense perspective, a court-appointed expert is not a *defense* expert.

§ 4-9. Post-Conviction Proceedings.

A 1996 Department of Justice report highlights the need for post-conviction proceedings in light of DNA profiling. The report discusses the exoneration of 28 convicts through the use of DNA technology—some of whom had been sentenced to death.[388]

A federal statute provides for expert services in post-conviction collateral attacks on the validity of federal and state court convictions.[389] Some state statutes also provide for the appointment of experts in these proceedings.[390] A New York statute establishes a procedure under which a convict may petition the

---

385. *See* § 4-3 *supra.*

386. Imwinkelried, *The Court Appointment of Expert Witnesses in the United States: A Failed Experiment*, 8 INT'L J. MED. & L. 601 (1989).

387. Gross, *Expert Evidence*, 1991 WIS. L. REV. 1113.

388. CONNORS ET AL., CONVICTED BY JURIES, EXONERATED BY SCIENCE: CASE STUDIES IN THE USE OF DNA EVIDENCE TO ESTABLISH INNOCENCE AFTER TRIAL (1996). *See generally* Elizabeth V. LaFollette, *State v. Hunt and Exculpatory DNA Evidence: When is a New Trial Warranted*, 74 N.C. L. REV. 1295 (1996).

389. 21 U.S.C. § 848(q)(4)(B) & (q)(9). *See* Fuller v. Johnson, 114 F.3d 491, 503 (5th Cir.) ("[T]he guarantees of section 3006A(e) are distinct in at least one important respect: the statute provides defense expert assistance for preparation for his trial, and provision of those statutory guarantees therefore takes on a constitutional dimension not present in collateral habeas corpus proceedings"), *cert. denied,* 522 U.S. 963 (1997); Lawson v. Dixon, 3 F.3d 743, 750-52 (4th Cir. 1993) (*ex parte* proceedings for appointment are required), *cert. denied,* 510 U.S. 1171 (1994); *In re* Lindsey, 875 F.2d 1502, 1505-08 (11th Cir. 1989); Mosely v. French, 6 F. Supp. 2d 474, 478 (M.D.N.C. 1998) (Under 18 U.S.C. § 848(q)(4)(B) & (q)(9) and CJA, "petitioner wants a forensic pathologist to assist in preparing his contention that trial counsel was ineffective for not obtaining a pathologist").

390. *See* Owens v. State, 908 S.W.2d 923, 929 (Tenn. 1995) (TENN. CODE ANN. § 40-14-207(b), applies to capital post-conviction cases). *But see* Davis v. State, 912 S.W.2d 689, 696 (Tenn. 1995) (Statute does not apply in non-capital post-conviction cases; also no constitutional right: "In the absence of a Constitutional right to counsel, there can be no Constitutional right to support services at state expense").

court for DNA testing in certain circumstances.[391] Several courts have ordered retesting without a specific statute.[392]

§ 4-10. Determining Indigency.

The rights discussed in this chapter are based on a defendant's lack of financial resources. The accused's indigence status is often determined at the time counsel is appointed. Nevertheless, a defendant who has the resources to hire an attorney may not have the funds to hire an expert: "[F]inancial assistance provided by a third party which enables an indigent criminal defendant to have the benefit of private counsel is not relevant to the defendant's right to have expert assistance provided at public expense."[393]

§ 4-11. Selected Bibliography

2 W. LaFave & J. Israel, Criminal Procedure § 11.2 (1984).

C. Whitebread & C. Slobogin, Criminal Procedure § 31.05 (3d ed. 1993).

Burns, *The Right to the Effective Assistance of a Psychiatrist Under Ake v. Oklahoma*, 30 Crim. L. Bull. 429 (1994).

Casey & Keilitz, *An Evaluation of Mental Health Expert Assistance Provided to Indigent Criminal Defendants: Organization, Administration, and Fiscal Management*, 34 N.Y.L. Sch. L. Rev. 19 (1989).

Decker, *Expert Services in the Defense of Criminal Cases: The Constitutional and Statutory Rights of Indigents*, 51 Cin. L. Rev. 574 (1982).

Harris, *Ake Revisited: Expert Psychiatric Witnesses Remain Beyond Reach for Indigent*, 68 N.C. L. Rev. 763 (1990).

Harris, *The Constitution and Truth Seeking: A New Theory on Expert Services for Indigent Defendants*, 83 J. Crim. L. & Criminology 469 (1992).

Hoeffel, *The Dark Side of DNA Profiling: Unreliable Scientific Evidence Meets the Criminal Defendant*, 42 Stan. L. Rev. 465, 519-23 (1990).

Kwall, *The Use of Expert Services by Privately Retained Criminal Defense Attorneys*, 13 Loy. U. Chi. L.J. 1 (1981).

Lee, *In the Wake of Ake v. Oklahoma: An Indigent Criminal Defendant's Lack of Ex parte Access to Expert Services*, 67 N.Y.U. L. Rev. 154 (1992).

Margolin & Wagner, *The Indigent Criminal Defendant and Defense Services: A Search for Constitutional Standards*, 24 Hastings L.J. 647 (1973).

---

391. N.Y. Crim. Pro. § 440.30(1-a). *See also* People v. Chichester, 162 Misc. 2d 658, 659, 618 N.Y.S.2d 201, 202 (Cty. Ct. 1994) (convicted defendant has right to use DNA testing, at his own expense, on physical evidence that is in the possession of the prosecutor's office).

392. *E.g.*, Sewell v. State, 592 N.E.2d 705, 707 (Ind. App. 1992); State v. Thomas, 245 N.J. Super. 428, 435, 586 A.2d 250, 254 (A.D. 1991); People v. Callace, 151 Misc.2d 464, 573 N.Y.S.2d 137 (Co. Ct. 1991); Dabbas v. Vegari, 149 Misc.2d 844, 570 N.Y.S.2d 765 (Sup. Ct. 1990); Commonwealth v. Brison, 421 Pa. Super. 442, 453, 618 A.2d 420, 425 (1992) ("[P]rinciples of justice require us to vacate appellant's conviction and remand to the trial court for the performance of DNA analysis on the samples taken from the victim").

393. Benson v. State, 636 A.2d 907, 910-11 (Del. 1994).

Medine, *The Constitutional Right to Expert Assistance for Indigents in Civil Cases*, 41 HASTINGS L.J. 281 (1990).
Moriarty, *Liberty, Justice ... and Experts for All*, 6 LAW & INEQUALITY 247 (1988).
Petterson, *Indigent Defense: DNA Experts for Indigents*, 18 THE CHAMPION 29 (Dec. 1994).
Comment, *Defense Access to State-Funded DNA Experts: Considerations of Due Process*, 85 CAL. L. REV. 1803 (1997).
Comment, *Genetics and Justice: An Indigent Defendant's Right to DNA Expert Assistance*, U. CHI. L. FORUM 396 (1998).
Note, *The Indigent's Right to an Adequate Defense: Expert and Investigative Assistance in Criminal Proceedings*, 55 CORNELL L. REV. 632 (1970).
Note, *The Constitutional Right to Psychiatric Assistance: Cause for Reexamination of Ake*, 30 AM. CRIM. L. REV. 1329 (1993).
Comment, *Nonpsychiatric Expert Assistance and the Requisite Showing of Need: A Catch-22 in the Post-Ake Criminal Justice System*, 37 EMORY L.J. 995 (1988).
Note, *Witness for the Prosecution: Prosecutorial Discovery of Information Generated by Non-Testifying Defense Psychiatric Experts*, 62 FORDHAM L. REV. 653 (1993).
Note, *An Indigent Criminal Defendant's Constitutional Right to a Psychiatric Expert*, 1984 U. ILL. L. REV. 481.
Note, *Expert Services and the Indigent Criminal Defendant: The Constitutional Mandate of Ake v. Oklahoma*, 84 MICH. L. REV. 1326 (1986).
Note, *Right to Aid in Addition to Counsel for Indigent Criminal Defendants*, 47 MINN. L. REV. 1054 (1963).
Note, *The Right to a Partisan Psychiatric Expert: Might Indigency Preclude Insanity?*, 61 N.Y.U. L. REV. 703 (1986).
Note, *A Question of Competence: The Indigent Criminal Defendant's Right to Adequate and Competent Psychiatric Assistance After Ake v. Oklahoma*, 14 VT. L. REV. 121 (1989).
Comment, *Assistance in Addition to Counsel for Indigent Defendants: The Need for; the Lack of; the Right to*, 16 VILL. L. REV. 323 (1970).
Comment, *Curing the Ake of an Incompetent Expert: A Separate Reviewable Issue?*, 29 SAN DIEGO L. REV. 799 (1992).
Comment, *Criminal Law: Marshaling the Defense — Indigent Defendants Guaranteed Psychiatric Assistance at Trial to Explain Battered Woman Syndrome*, 32 WASHBURN L.J. 249 (1993).

Annotations

Annot., *Construction and application of provision in subsection (e) of Criminal Justice Act of 1964 (18 U.S.C. § 3006A(e)) concerning right of indigent defendant to aid in obtaining services of investigator or expert*, 6 A.L.R. FED. 1007 (1971).
Annot., *Right of federal indigent criminal defendant to obtain independent psychiatric examination pursuant to subsection (e) of Criminal Justice Act of 1964, as amended (18 U.S.C. § 3006(e))*, 40 A.L.R. FED. 707 (1978).
Annot., *Right of indigent defendant in state criminal case to assistance of psychiatrist or psychologist*, 85 A.L.R.4TH 19 (1991).
Annot., *Right of indigent defendant in state criminal case to assistance of fingerprint expert*, 72 A.L.R.4TH 874 (1989).
Annot., *Right of indigent defendant in state criminal case to assistance of ballistics experts*, 71 A.L.R.4TH 638 (1989).
Annot., *Right of indigent criminal defendant to polygraph test at public expense*, 11 A.L.R.4TH 733 (1982).

Annot., *Right of indigent defendant in criminal case to aid of state by appointment of investigator or expert*, 34 A.L.R.3D 1256 (1970).

Annot., *Right of indigent defendant in state criminal case to assistance of chemist, toxicologist, technician, narcotics expert, or similar nonmedical specialist in substance analysis*, 74 A.L.R.4TH 388 (1989).

Annot., *Right of indigent defendant in state criminal case to assistance of expert in social attitudes*, 74 A.L.R.4TH 330 (1989).

Annot., *Right of indigent defendant in state criminal case to assistance of investigator*, 81 A.L.R.4TH 259 (1990).

CHAPTER 5

EXPERT TESTIMONY

§ 5-1. In General.

The admissibility of expert testimony depends on several factors: (1) the subject matter of the testimony, (2) the qualifications of the expert, (3) the conformity of the evidence to a valid explanatory theory, and (4) whether the probative value of the testimony outweighs other considerations.[1] The third factor, which deals with the admissibility of novel scientific evidence, is discussed in Chapter 1.

§ 5-2. Subject Matter of Expert Testimony.

An expert may testify only about a matter that is a proper subject for expert testimony. The subject matter of expert testimony is bounded on two sides, and these boundaries often shift over a period of time. In 1947 Professor Maguire commented on this aspect of expert testimony:

> The field of expertness is bounded on one side by the great area of the commonplace, supposedly within the ken of every person of moderate intelligence, and on the other by the even greater area of the speculative and uncertain. Of course both these boundaries constantly shift, as the former area enlarges and the latter diminishes. Only a few years ago it would have been necessary to take expert evidence on issues with respect to the operation of motor cars, airplanes, or radio which are now so completely

---

1. *See* United States v. Amaral, 488 F.2d 1148, 1153 (9th Cir. 1973); State v. Chapple, 135 Ariz. 281, 291, 660 P.2d 1208, 1218 (1983); Ibn-Tamas v. United States, 407 A.2d 626, 632-39 (D.C. 1979), *appeal after remand,* 455 A.2d 893 (D.C. 1983).

> inside the domain of popular understanding that such evidence would be rejected as superfluous. A century ago purportedly expert evidence on these topics would have been rejected as visionary.[2]

Federal Rule of Evidence 702 provides that expert testimony is admissible if "scientific, technical, or other specialized knowledge will assist the trier of fact to understand the evidence or to determine a fact in issue." The trial court is entrusted with the responsibility of determining whether the proffered testimony is a proper subject for an expert. As the U.S. Supreme Court has noted, the trial judge has "broad discretion in the matter of the admission or exclusion of expert evidence, and his action is to be sustained unless manifestly erroneous."[3] According to the federal drafters, "Rule 702 is broadly phrased. The fields of knowledge which may be drawn upon are not limited merely to the 'scientific' and 'technical' but extend to all 'specialized' knowledge.... Thus within the scope of the rule are not only experts in the strictest sense of the word, *e.g.*, physicians, physicists, and architects, but also the large group sometimes called 'skilled' witnesses, such as bankers or landowners testifying to land values."[4]

The standard adopted by Rule 702 — whether expert testimony will "assist the trier of fact" — is a more liberal formulation of the subject matter requirement than that which is found in many common-law opinions. The common law often phrased the requirement as whether the subject was beyond the comprehension of a layman.[5] In contrast, the test set forth in Rule 702 "is not whether the jury could reach some conclusion in the absence of the expert evidence, but whether the jury is qualified without such testimony 'to determine intelligently and to the best possible degree the particular issue without enlightenment from those having a specialized understanding of the subject.'"[6] This standard is consistent with Wigmore's formulation of the test for expert testimony: "On *this subject* can a

---

2. J. MAGUIRE, EVIDENCE: COMMON SENSE AND COMMON LAW 30 (1947). The boundary between the visionary and expertness areas raises the issue of the admissibility of novel scientific evidence and is discussed in Chapter 1.

3. Salem v. United States Lines Co., 370 U.S. 31, 35 (1962). *See also* Hamling v. United States, 418 U.S. 87, 108 (1974) ("[T]he District Court has wide discretion in its determination to admit and exclude evidence, and this is particularly true in the case of expert testimony"); United States v. Catadeda, 94 F.3d 592, 596 (9th Cir. 1996) ("We have previously held that a district court's refusal to admit evidence from a cultural expert does not constitute an abuse of discretion").

4. FED. R. EVID. 702 advisory committee's note.

5. *E.g.*, Fineberg v. United States, 393 F.2d 417, 421 (9th Cir. 1968) ("beyond the knowledge of the average layman"); Jenkins v. United States, 307 F.2d 637, 643 (D.C. Cir. 1962) ("beyond the ken of the average layman").

6. State v. Chapple, 135 Ariz. 281, 292-93, 660 P.2d 1208, 1219-20 (1983) (quoting Ladd, *Expert Testimony*, 5 VAND. L. REV. 414, 418 (1952)).

jury receive from *this person* appreciable help?"[7] As the Seventh Circuit has noted, the trial court is "not compelled to exclude the expert testimony just because the testimony may, to a greater or lesser degree, cover matters that are within the average juror's comprehension."[8] Undoubtedly, an enlightened application of the common-law rule will often result in the same ruling as would be reached under Rule 702. Nevertheless, the assist-the-jury standard focuses on the correct issue.[9]

Eyewitness Identification Experts

Several examples illustrate the possible difference between the two standards. First, many courts have excluded expert testimony concerning the unreliability of eyewitness identifications because "the trustworthiness in general of eyewitness observations [is] not beyond the ken of the jurors."[10] In *State v. Chapple,*[11] however, the Arizona Supreme Court ruled the trial court erred in excluding such testimony in light of the facts of that case. According to the court,

> [e]ven assuming that jurors of ordinary education need no expert testimony to enlighten them to the danger of eyewitness identification, the offer of proof indicated that [the expert's] testimony would have informed the jury that there are many specific variables which affect the accuracy of identification and which apply to the facts of this case.[12]

Battered Women Syndrome

A second example involves expert testimony concerning the battered woman syndrome. The battered woman syndrome describes a pattern of violence inflicted on a woman by her mate. Typically, evidence of the syndrome is offered

---

7. 7 J. WIGMORE, EVIDENCE § 1923, at 29 (Chadbourn rev. 1978). *See also* Ladd, *supra* note 6, at 418 ("There is no more certain test for determining when experts may be used than the common sense inquiry whether the untrained layman would be qualified to determine intelligently and to the best possible degree the particular issue without enlightenment from those having a specialized understanding of the subject involved in the dispute").

8. United States v. Hall, 93 F.3d 1337, 1342 (7th Cir. 1996) (false confession).

9. *See also* United States v. Rahm, 993 F.2d 1405, 1414 (9th Cir. 1993) ("The average juror would not be capable of interpreting the WAIS-R or MMPI results"); Hampton v. State, 588 N.E.2d 555, 558 (Ind. App. 1992) ("Portions of [blood spatter analysis] were beyond the common knowledge and experience of the average lay person, but portions of it were also inherently understandable").

10. State v. Porraro, 121 R.I. 882, 892, 404 A.2d 465, 471 (1979). Most appellate courts have upheld the discretion of a trial court to exclude expert testimony on this issue. For a further discussion, *see* Chapter 9.

11. 135 Ariz. 281, 660 P.2d 1208 (1983).

12. *Id.* at 293, 660 P.2d at 1220. *See also* United States v. Downing, 753 F.2d 1224, 1231-32 (3d Cir. 1985); United States v. Smith, 736 F.2d 1103, 1106-07 (6th Cir. 1984); People v. McDonald, 37 Cal.3d 351, 369, 690 P.2d 709, 721, 208 Cal. Rptr. 236, 248 (1984).

to support a self-defense claim in a homicide prosecution of the woman for the death of her mate. Some courts have upheld the exclusion of expert testimony on this issue because "the subject of the expert testimony is within the understanding of the jury."[13] In contrast, other courts have held this testimony admissible because it tends to explain two elements of the self-defense claim: (1) the woman's subjective fear of serious injury or death, and (2) the reasonableness of that belief. For example, the battered woman syndrome may explain why a battered woman has not left her mate after the initial beatings.[14] According to these courts, the evidence supplies "an interpretation of the facts which differed from the ordinary lay perception."[15] In so holding, these courts take the position that the test for admission is whether the expert testimony "sheds light" on a relevant issue which a lay person, without expert assistance, would not perceive.[16]

Criminal Modus Operandi Experts

Police officers may offer expert testimony based on their experience. For example, an FBI agent is qualified to testify that a substance is cocaine based on four years of experience during which time he identified cocaine by sight on 35 occasions and his identifications had been confirmed by laboratory analysis in most cases.[17] Indeed, criminals have testified as experts.[18] Testimony by police

---

13. State v. Thomas, 66 Ohio St. 2d 518, 521, 423 N.E.2d 137, 140 (1981). *Thomas* was later overruled. State v. Koss, 49 Ohio St. 3d 213, 217, 551 N.E.2d 970, 974 (1990).

14. *See* State v. Kelly, 97 N.J. 178, 196, 478 A.2d 364, 372 (1984) ("Only by understanding these unique pressures that force battered women to remain with their mates, despite their longstanding and reasonable fear of severe bodily harm and the isolation that being a battered woman creates, can a battered woman's state of mind be accurately and fairly understood").

15. Ibn-Tamas v. United States, 407 A.2d 626, 634-35 (D.C. 1979), *appeal after remand,* 455 A.2d 893 (D.C. 1983).

16. *Id.* at 633. *Accord* Hawthorne v. State, 408 So. 2d 801, 806 (Fla. App. 1982); Smith v. State, 247 Ga. 612, 619, 277 S.E.2d 678, 683 (1981). For a further discussion of the battered woman syndrome, *see* Chapter 9.

17. United States v. Bermudez, 526 F.2d 89, 97-98 (2d Cir. 1975), *cert. denied,* 425 U.S. 970 (1976). *See also* State v. Essick, 67 N.C. App. 697, 698, 314 S.E.2d 268, 270 (1984) (detective better qualified than jury to draw inference that vegetable matter was marijuana). *But see* People v. Park, 72 Ill. 2d 203, 208-11, 380 N.E.2d 795, 798-99 (1978) (deputy sheriff not qualified to identify marijuana). *See generally* DeFoor, *Consumer Testimony as Proof of Identity of the Controlled Substance in a Narcotics Case,* 33 U. FLA. L. REV. 682 (1981).

18. *E.g.,* United States v. Williams, 81 F.3d 1434, 1441 (7th Cir. 1996) ("There was no pretense that he was impartial, or a member of a learned profession. Neither condition is required to qualify a person as an expert witness under the current rules of evidence.... There is not even a paradox in the suggestion that the biggest experts on crime are, often, criminals"), *cert. denied,* 118 S. Ct. 723 (1998); United States v. Johnson, 575 F.2d 1347, 1360-61 (5th Cir. 1978) (experienced marijuana smoker qualified to testify that certain marijuana came from Colombia), *cert. denied,* 440 U.S. 907 (1979).

experts on the modus operandi of various types of crimes, such as counterfeiting,[19] bookmaking,[20] pickpocketing,[21] fraud,[22] organized crime,[23] gang-related crimes,[24] as well as other offenses[25] has been admitted. The most frequent use of this type of testimony involves drug trafficking. Expert testimony has been admitted about the operation of clandestine laboratories,[26] the street value of drugs,[27] the amount of drugs consistent with distribution rather than personal use,[28] strategies of deception,[29] as well as other aspects of the drug

---

19. United States v. Burchfield, 719 F.2d 356, 358 (11th Cir. 1983).

20. United States v. Scavo, 593 F.2d 837, 843-44 (8th Cir. 1979).

21. United States v. Jackson, 425 F.2d 574, 576-77 (D.C. Cir. 1970).

22. *E.g.,* United States v. Alonso, 48 F.3d 1536, 1541 (9th Cir. 1995) (credit card fraud) (police testimony concerning counter-surveillance techniques and defendant's conduct as consistent with techniques; "consistent with" testimony admissible); United States v. Hutchins, 757 F.2d 11, 13 (2d Cir.) (confidence schemes), *cert. denied,* 742 U.S. 1031 (1985); People v. Singh, 37 Cal. App. 4th 1343, 44 Cal. Rptr. 2d 644 (1995) (staged automobile accidents for fraudulent insurance recovery).

23. *E.g.,* United States v. Amuso, 21 F.3d 1251, 1263 (2d Cir.) (FBI agent's testimony concerning common cosa nostra terminology necessary to explain tape recorded evidence), *cert. denied,* 513 U.S. 932 (1994); United States v. Locascio, 6 F.3d 924, 936 (2d Cir. 1993) ("inner workings of the Gambino Family" in the John Gotti trial), *cert. denied,* 511 U.S. 1070 (1994); United States v. Pungitore, 910 F.2d 1084, 1148-49 (3d Cir. 1990) (structure and organization of La Cosa Nostra), *cert. denied,* 500 U.S. 915 (1991).

24. *E.g.,* People v. Gardeley, 14 Cal. 4th 605, 617, 927 P.2d 713, 721, 59 Cal. Rptr. 356, 364 (1996) ("The subject matter of the culture and habits of criminal street gangs, of particular relevance here, meets [the expert witness] criterion") , *cert. denied,* 118 S. Ct. 148 (1997); People v. Valdez, 58 Cal. App.4th 494, 506, 68 Cal. Rptr. 2d 135, 142 (1997) ("In general, where a gang enhancement is alleged, expert testimony concerning the culture, habits, and psychology of gangs is permissible because these subjects are 'sufficiently beyond common experience that the opinion of an expert would assist the trier of fact'").

25. *See generally* Note, *Police Expert Witnesses and the Ultimate Issue Rule,* 44 LA. L. REV. 211 (1983).

26. *See* United States v. Anderson, 61 F.3d 1290, 1297-98 (7th Cir.) (clandestine PCP laboratory), *cert. denied,* 516 U.S. 1000 (1995).

27. *E.g.,* United States v. Nobles, 69 F.3d 172, 183 (7th Cir. 1995) (DEA agent "explained that the 774.9 grams of 94% pure cocaine that Nobles was carrying in his bag, when processed for retail sale, would result in approximately 3 kilograms of 24% pure cocaine, which would sell for roughly $300,000 on the street, and would be enough to provide over 24,000 individual doses of cocaine. [The agent] opined that this large quantity of cocaine could only have been intended for distribution, and not for personal use").

28. *E.g.,* United States v. Valle, 72 F.3d 210, 214 (1st Cir. 1995) (expert testified that "so large a quantity of crack was consistent with distribution as opposed to personal use ... [and] listed the visible characteristics of the prototypical crack addict, and noted that the appellant manifested none of these symptoms"); United States v. Cotton, 22 F.3d 182, 185 (8th Cir. 1994) (admitted detective's "expert opinion that the amount of crack cocaine seized was indicative of distribution"); United States v. Lipscomb, 14 F.3d 1236, 1243 (7th Cir. 1994) (police expert testimony that cocaine was for street level distribution); United States v. Brown, 7 F.3d 648, 653 (7th Cir. 1993)

trade.[30] In addition, expert testimony on various aspects of the tools of the drug trade, including the use of beepers,[31] code words,[32] weapons,[33] duct tape,[34] and the like,[35] has been admitted.

There are, of course, limitations on this type of testimony. For example, *United States v. Garcia*[36] involved the testimony of an FBI language specialist who translated ten telephone conversations and gave his opinion about the meaning of certain phrases used in the conversations. The specialist also testified that the phrase "your old man" referred to the defendant. The Tenth Circuit ruled this testimony improper: "Unlike [the expert's] opinion as to jargon used in the drug trade which may be explained by expert opinion testimony, ... no

---

(based on large amount of drugs seized and other circumstances, DEA agent permitted to testify that accused possessed drugs for sale, not use).

29. *E.g.*, United States v. Garcia, 86 F.3d 394, 400 (5th Cir. 1996) ("The average juror may not be aware that the presence of 166.9 kilograms of cocaine is indicative of a large drug trafficking organization, and may not be aware that large drug trafficking organizations commonly use 'car swaps,' 'stash houses' and conduct 'heat runs'"), *cert. denied*, 117 S. Ct. 752 (1997); United States v. Penny, 60 F.3d 1257, 1265 (7th Cir. 1995) (marshal testified that "drug dealers place coffee beans in door frames in order 'to throw off the dogs for the scent of drugs or cocaine'"), *cert. denied*, 516 U.S. 1121 (1996).

30. *E.g.*, United States v. Boney, 977 F.2d 624, 631 (D.C. Cir. 1992) (police expert testimony about the roles and behavior of drug traffickers, who was a "runner," who was a "holder" — and who was going to "make the sale" — admitted); United States v. Sparks, 949 F.2d 1023, 1026 (8th Cir. 1991) (use of street gangs to distribute drugs), *cert. denied,* 504 U.S. 927 (1992); United States v. Foster, 939 F.2d 445, 451-52 (7th Cir. 1991) (methods used by narcotics traffickers); United States v. Dunn, 846 F.2d 761, 763 (D.C. Cir. 1988) (modus operandi of drug distributors); United States v. Monu, 782 F.2d 1209, 1210-11 (4th Cir. 1986) (narcotics "tool of the trade"); United States v. Ginsberg, 758 F.2d 823, 830 (2d Cir. 1985) (narcotics operations); United States v. Pugliese, 712 F.2d 1574, 1581 (2d Cir. 1983) (agent qualified to testify regarding typical characteristics of heroin addicts); State v. Berry, 140 N.J. 280, 658 N.E.2d 702 (1995) (testimony that drug dealers often use juveniles as drug "mules" and use a "money man" to hold drug proceeds admissible). *See generally* Annot., *Admissibility of Expert Evidence Concerning the Meaning of Narcotics Code Language in Federal Prosecution for Narcotics Dealing — Modern Cases*, 104 A.L.R. FED. 230 (1991).

31. *E.g.*, United States v. Solis, 923 F.2d 548, 550 (7th Cir. 1991).

32. *E.g.*, United States v. Griffith, 118 F.3d 318, 321 (5th Cir. 1997) ("we now have, by one count, 223 terms for marijuana"); United States v. Hoffman, 832 F.2d 1299, 1309-10 (1st Cir. 1987) ; United States v. Ramirez, 796 F.2d 212, 216-17 (7th Cir. 1986).

33. *E.g.*, United States v. Conyers, 118 F.3d 755, 758 (D.C. Cir. 1997) (type of packaging used "consistent with distribution in District of Columbia" and ".357 Magnum is the revolver of choice among local drug dealers").

34. *E.g.*, United States v. Moore, 104 F.3d 377, 384 (D.C. Cir. 1997) ("duct tape such as that found under the hood of Moore's car is often used by people in the drug world to bind hands, legs, and mouths of people who are either being robbed in the drug world or who need to be maintained").

35. *E.g.*, United States v. Parker, 32 F.3d 395, 400 (8th Cir. 1994) (admitted agent's testimony that certain entries in a notebook were "drug notes").

36. 994 F.2d 1499 (10th Cir. 1993).

specialized knowledge is necessary to understand the phrase 'your old man.' Therefore, expert testimony on this point was unnecessary."[37]

The use of police experts has raised other issues. In *United States v. Cruz*[38] the expert testified about the use of intermediaries or brokers in the drug trade. The D.C. Circuit questioned whether such testimony was useful: "That drug traffickers may seek to conceal their identities by using intermediaries would seem evident to the average juror from movies, television crime dramas, and news stories."[39] Moreover, the court believed that the expert's testimony was directed at another purpose: "[T]he credibility of a fact-witness may not be bolstered by arguing that the witness's version of events is consistent with an expert's description of patterns of criminal conduct, at least where the witness's version is not attacked as improbable or ambiguous evidence of such conduct."[40] The Second Circuit distinguished *Cruz* in *Headley v. Tilghman*,[41] in which testimony that the physical evidence seized from an apartment was consistent with evidence that might be found at a distribution house was admitted. The evidence was not used to show a pattern of conduct. As Judge Moore has noted, use of a drug trade expert as both a fact and an expert witness should be carefully circumscribed:

> [W]hen a police officer testifies in two different capacities in the same case, there is a significant risk that the jury will be confused by the officer's dual role.... Although the government should exercise caution when using the same officer as an expert and a fact witness, we refuse to adopt a per se prohibition of this practice. We note that both the district court and the prosecutor should take care to assure that the jury is informed of the dual roles of a law enforcement officer as a fact and an expert witness, so that

---

37. *Id.* at 1506 (evidence admitted as lay opinion testimony).

38. 981 F.2d 659 (2d Cir. 1992).

39. *Id.* at 662.

40. *Id.* at 663. *See also* United States v. Romero, 57 F.3d 565, 571 (7th Cir. 1995) ("While we hesitate to confirm the all-too-pervasive conceit that the average juror in New York is more sophisticated than her midwestern counterpart, we are reluctant to extend the implications of *Castillo* to the instant case.... Nor do jurors necessarily require assistance in drawing conclusions from the presence of scales and baggies, although that is a closer issue. But our society has not progressed (or rather, descended) to the point where the tools of the drug trade are familiar to all"); United States v. Castillo, 924 F.2d 1227, 1231 (2d Cir. 1991), *cert. denied*, 513 U.S. 829 (1994); People v. Kelsey, 194 A.D.2d 248, 253, 606 N.Y.S.2d 621, 624 (1994) (officers' recitation of street dealers' modus operandi crossed the line between providing useful background and tarring the defendant with the crimes of others); Note, *The Admissibility of Ultimate Issue Expert Testimony by Law Enforcement Officers in Criminal Trials*, 93 COLUM. L. REV. 231 (1993).

41. 53 F.3d 472, 476 (2d Cir.) (the "testimony concerning the operation of a typical 'distribution house,' however, was introduced, not to demonstrate a pattern of conduct, but to show that the physical evidence seized from the apartment was consistent with evidence that might be found at a distribution house"), *cert. denied*, 517 U.S. 1162 (1995).

the jury can give proper weight to each type of testimony. In the instant case, the prosecutor did delineate the transition between the examination of Todd as an expert witness and questions relating to his role as a fact witness.[42]

Expert Opinion on the Law

Two other recurring issues are worth noting. The first is whether an expert can testify "on the law," which would include expert opinion testimony applying a legal standard to the facts as well as expert testimony on some aspect of the substantive law. The prevailing rule prohibits such testimony.[43] The Seventh Circuit has recognized that this issue is not as simple as might initially appear:

> The question is this: when can expert witnesses offer legal opinions? In addressing this question, federal courts have not provided uniform answers.... Our own cases have determined that Federal Rules of Evidence 702 and 704 prohibit experts from offering opinions about legal issues that will determine the outcome of a case. That is, they cannot testify about legal issues on which the judge will instruct the jury.... Our cases have also indicated that there are some circumstances in which experts can offer legal opinions, but we have not exhaustively identified them.... Not every court has followed this approach, however; and, some of their opinions do not clearly determine when experts may and may not testify about legal issues.[44]

---

42. United States v. Thomas, 74 F.3d 676, 682-83 (6th Cir.) (expert testified that "drug dealers who sell crack at the 'street' level normally do not keep written records, front drugs to their customers, or use scales, and that they generally do use pagers and carry 'rocks' that sell for approximately twenty dollars each"), *cert. denied*, 517 U.S. 162 (1996). *See also* United States v. Catlett, 97 F.3d 565, 571 (D.C. Cir. 1996) ("[E]very federal court to consider the issue of dual testimony as both a fact and expert witness has concluded that the Federal Rules of Evidence permit such testimony").

43. *E.g.*, Peterson v. City of Plymouth, 60 F.3d 469, 475 (8th Cir. 1995) (expert's "testimony involved only his views concerning the reasonableness of the officers' conduct in light of 'Fourth Amendment standards.' To that end, his testimony was not a fact-based opinion, but a statement of legal conclusion.... The legal conclusions were for the court to make"); Police Retirement System v. Midwest Inv., 940 F.2d 351, 357 (8th Cir. 1991) ("Explaining the law is the judge's job. [The expert's] extensive law-related expert testimony allowed him to usurp the judge's place"); Federal Realty Investment Trust v. Pacific Ins. Co., 760 F. Supp. 533, 538 (D. Md. 1991) ("expert testimony concerning applicable legal standard is improper and inadmissible").

See generally Baker, *The Impropriety of Expert Witness Testimony on the Law*, 40 U. KAN. L. REV. 325 (1992); Ehrhardt, *The Conflict Concerning Expert Witnesses and Legal Conclusions*, 92 W. VA. L. REV. 645 (1990); Note, *Expert Legal Testimony*, 97 HARV. L. REV. 797 (1984).

44. United States v. Sinclair, 74 F.3d 753, 758 n.1 (7th Cir. 1996) ("The potential for jury confusion may be substantial when the evidence refers to legal issues at the heart of other litigation; such evidence can create a distracting trial within a trial"). *See also* United States v. Russo, 74 F.3d

In short, admissibility depends on the purpose for which the testimony is offered.

Expert Opinion on Credibility

Another issue concerns whether expert testimony on the credibility of a witness is admissible.[45] This issue frequently surfaces in cases that admit rape trauma syndrome or child abuse accommodation syndrome.[46] According to the First Circuit, "[r]ather than requiring the wholesale exclusion of expert testimony concerning credibility issues, these cases stand for the more limited proposition that an expert's opinion that another witness is lying or telling the truth is ordinarily inadmissible pursuant to Rule 702 because the opinion exceeds the scope of the expert's specialized knowledge and therefore merely informs the jury that it should reach a particular conclusion.... [T]he Federal Rules of Evidence permit expert testimony to be offered in appropriate circumstances to establish a witness's truthful or untruthful character."[47] The court went on to rule that expert psychiatric testimony that the defendant suffered from "pseudologia fantastica" that caused him to make grandiose statements similar in nature to the statements the prosecution was seeking to use against him was admissible under Rule 702.

In contrast, the Eighth Circuit has stated that "expert testimony going to the issue of credibility is not admissible."[48] Thus, a psychologist in a civil rights action may not testify that an officer in a fatal police shooting suffered from post-traumatic stress syndrome, which impaired the officer's ability to describe an incident. These cases are difficult to reconcile.

1383, 1395 (2d Cir.) (expert "gave no opinion as to whether the appellants had violated the securities laws and did not make any statements about their intent; he simply described certain stock transactions and his opinion of their effect on the market"), *cert. denied*, 117 S. Ct. 293 (1996); United States v. Just, 74 F.3d 902, 905 (8th Cir. 1996) (expert testimony that a "weapon was a 'machinegun'" admissible in a prosecution for illegally possessing and transferring a machinegun); United States v. Duncan, 42 F.3d 97, 103 (2d Cir. 1994) ("This Court has found the distinction between factual conclusions and legal conclusions to be an important one in the context of expert opinion"); United States v. Seago, 39 F.3d 1299, 1309 (5th Cir. 1994) ("Expert testimony may be particularly appropriate when specialized areas of law, such as the insurance and financial matters relevant herein, are at issue.... [Expert] testimony would not be admissible for the purpose of proving what the law is; the declaration of controlling law must come from the court. Rather, it would be admissible as it relates to [a defendant's] understanding and resulting state of mind").

45. *See* Berger, *United States v. Scop: The Common-Law Approach to an Expert's Opinion About a Witness's Credibility Still Does Not Work*, 55 BROOK. L. REV. 559 (1989).

46. For a discussion of CAAS evidence, *see* Chapter 9.

47. United States v. Shay, 57 F.3d 126, 131 (1st Cir. 1995). The court added: "Although a court may not exclude expert testimony simply because it concerns a credibility question or because non-expert testimony was presented on the same issue, it retains ample discretion to exclude or limit such testimony for other reasons [Rule 403]." *Id.* at 134.

48. Westcott v. Crinklaw, 68 F.3d 1073, 1077 (8th Cir. 1995).

§ 5-3. Qualifications of Experts.

Federal Evidence Rule 702 provides that a witness may qualify as an expert by reason of "knowledge, skill, experience, training, or education." Under Federal Rule 104(a),[49] determining a witness's qualifications is a matter for the trial court, and the court's decision is reviewable on appeal only for an abuse of discretion.[50]

Although the trial court is given wide latitude on the qualification issue, there are some rules of thumb. First, because "the rule uses the disjunctive, a person may qualify to render expert testimony in any one of the five ways listed: knowledge, skill, experience, training, or education."[51] Thus, "[q]ualifications which may satisfy the requirements of Evid. R. 702 are multitudinous. ... [T]here is no 'degree' requirement, *per se*. Professional experience and training in a particular field may be sufficient to qualify one as an expert."[52] The rule comports with Wigmore's view; he wrote that the witness's expertise "may have been attained, so far as legal rules go, in any way whatever; all the law requires is that it should have been attained."[53] The federal drafters adopted the same approach: "[T]he expert is viewed, not in a narrow sense, but as a person qualified by 'knowledge, skill, experience, training or education.' Thus within the scope of the rule are not only experts in the strictest sense of the word, *e.g.*

---

49. FED. R. EVID. 104(a) ("Preliminary questions concerning the qualification of a person to be a witness ... shall be determined by the court ..."). *See also* United States v. Gatling, 96 F.3d 1511, 1523 (D.C. Cir. 1996) ("[The defendant] suggests that new expert testimony is *per se* inappropriate rebuttal evidence, but we find no support for this proposition in the case law or in the rules of evidence").

50. *See* Hamling v. United States, 418 U.S. 87, 108 (1974) ("[T]he District Court has wide discretion in its determination to admit and exclude evidence, and this is particularly true in the case of expert testimony"); Salem v. United States Lines Co., 370 U.S. 31, 35 (1962) (Trial judge has "broad discretion in the matter of the admission or exclusion of expert evidence, and his action is to be sustained unless manifestly erroneous").

51. Kopf v. Skyrm, 993 F.2d 374, 377 (4th Cir. 1993).

52. State v. Mack, 73 Ohio St. 3d 502, 511, 653 N.E.2d 329 (1995). *See also* United States v. Kunzman, 54 F.3d 1522, 1530 (10th Cir. 1995) ("Experience alone can qualify a witness to give expert testimony"; banker for 20 years interpreting numbers and bank stamps on checks to show they cleared interstate banking system); *In re* Paoli R.R. Yard PCB Litigation, 916 F.2d 829, 855 (3d Cir. 1990) ("The district court's insistence on a certain kind of degree or background is inconsistent with our jurisprudence in this area"), *cert. denied*, 499 U.S. 961 (1991); Davis v. United States, 865 F.2d 164, 168 (8th Cir 1988) ("Rule 702 does not state a preference for academic training over demonstrated practical experience"); State v. Beuke, 38 Ohio St.3d 29, 43, 526 N..E..2d 274 (1988) ("Although [the investigator] has no degree, his professional experience and training in collecting and preserving evidence was such as to permit the trial court to qualify him as an expert'').

53. 2 J. WIGMORE, EVIDENCE § 556, at 751 (Chadbourn rev. 1979).

physicians, physicists, and architects, but also the large group sometimes called 'skilled' witnesses, such as bankers or landowners testifying to land values."[54]

Second, the expert need not be an "outstanding practitioner in the field in which he professes expertise."[55] Similar qualifications between experts testifying on the same issue are not required.[56]

Third, the expert's qualifications should be based on the nature and extent of the witness's knowledge and not on the witness's "title."[57] In one case, the D.C. Circuit reversed a trial court's ruling that psychologists were not qualified to testify on the issue of insanity because they lacked medical training.[58] The court stated that an expert's qualifications must be based on the nature and extent of the witness's knowledge and not on his "title."[59] On one hand, many psychologists would not be qualified to express an opinion on insanity because their "training and experience may not provide an adequate basis for their testimony."[60] On the other hand, other psychologists, because of their training and experience in the diagnosis and treatment of mental disorders, may be qualified.[61]

Licensing

Licensing in a field in usually not determinative, but some courts have ruled that a witness who does not have the appropriate license is not qualified. In one case, the court held that a witness not licensed to investigate fires under a state

---

54. FED. R.EVID. 702 advisory committee's note.

55. United States v. Barker, 553 F.2d 1013, 1024 (6th Cir. 1977) . In reversing a trial court's ruling that a defense fingerprint expert was unqualified, the Sixth Circuit wrote:

> An expert need not have certificates of training, nor memberships in professional organizations .... Nor need he be, as the trial court apparently required, an outstanding practitioner in the field in which he professes expertise. Comparisons between his professional stature and the stature of witnesses for an opposing party may be made by the jury, if it becomes necessary to decide which of two conflicting opinions to believe. But the only question for the trial judge who must decide whether or not to allow the jury to consider a proffered expert's opinions is, "whether his knowledge of the subject matter is such that his opinion will most likely assist the trier of fact in arriving at the truth."

Id. (quoting Holmgren v. Massey-Ferguson, Inc., 516 F.2d 856, 858 (8th Cir. 1975)).

56. *See* United States v. Madoch, 935 F. Supp. 965, 972 (N.D. Ill. 1996) ("[O]ne expert need not hold the exact same set of qualifications to rebut another expert's testimony.... This Court need not analyze, as Defendant contends it should, whether a psychologist or psychiatrist is more qualified to testify as to the psychological condition of a patient at the time of the offense").

57. Jenkins v. United States, 307 F.2d 637, 643-44 (DC Cir 1962) ("[W]e must examine the reality behind the title 'psychologist'").

58. *Id.* at 643.

59. *Id.* at 644 ("[W]e must examine the reality behind the title 'psychologist'").

60. *Id.*

61. *Id.*

statute was not qualified to testify about the cause of a fire in an arson prosecution.[62]

Expert Testifying Beyond Qualifications

An expert's testimony must relate to the subject matter on which the expert has been qualified. In other words, a witness may be qualified to express an opinion on one matter but not on another.[63] For example, a criminalist may be qualified to testify that no fingerprints were found on an object but not qualified to testify that the absence of fingerprints resulted from the fact that gloves were used or that the prints were wiped away: "The government has failed to show that [the expert's] training qualifies him as an expert with respect to the reason no fingerprints were found ...."[64] In another case a pathologist's testimony that a bruise discovered during an autopsy was consistent with a bite mark was struck, in part, because he was not qualified in forensic dentistry.[65]

Further, a witness may be an expert on one aspect of a scientific technique but not on other aspects. Accordingly, courts must "differentiate between ability to operate an instrument or perform a test and the ability to make an interpretation drawn from use of the instrument."[66] For example, a police officer may be qualified to operate a breathalyzer but not qualified to interpret the results. The training and experience needed to perform these two distinct functions are very different.[67] Similarly, a police officer may be qualified to conduct a horizontal gaze nystagmus test (an intoxication test) but not be qualified to interpret the results. According to one court,

---

62. People v. West, 264 Ill. App. 3d 176, 636 N.E.2d 1239 (1994).

63. J. Maguire, *supra* note 2, at 30-31 ("It goes without saying that an expert qualified to testify upon one topic may be completely unqualified to testify about another as to which he lacks special knowledge, skill, experience, or training, but some applications of this principle take the unwary by surprise").

64. United States v. Booth, 669 F.2d 1231, 1240 (9th Cir. 1981).

65. State v. Adams, 481 A.2d 718, 727-28 (R.I. 1984). In United States v. Navarro, 90 F.3d 1245 (7th Cir. 1996), the agent testified about aspects of narcotics trafficking, including his opinion that Hispanics agree to consent searches more than other persons. The appellate court questioned this testimony: "The qualifications he gave in court do not indicate that he has experience as an expert in hispanic or latino culture, or even with hispanic or latino drug dealers. No foundation was laid in this area; Agent Fanter did not report, for example, that he worked with Hispanic or Latinos, spoke Spanish, or conducted undercover investigations in Hispanic, South American, or North American latino communities." *Id.* at 1262.

66. People v. King, 266 Cal. App. 2d 437, 457, 72 Cal. Rptr. 478, 491 (1968).

67. *See* State v. James, 68 Ohio App. 2d 227, 229, 428 N.E.2d 876, 878 (1980) (state trooper qualified as an expert in the operation of intoxilyzer but did not possess sufficient learning and knowledge about effects of alcohol consumption); State v. Priester, 301 S.C. 165, 167-68, 391 S.E.2d 227, 228 (1990) (lab toxicologist not qualified to testify about the effect of alcohol on the brain); French v. State, 484 S.W.2d 716, 719 (Tex. Crim. App. 1972) ("[A]n officer may administer a breath test even though he is not otherwise qualified to interpret the results ...").

> [The officer's] opinion that appellant was under the influence of alcohol, to the extent it was based on the nystagmus test, rests on scientific principles well beyond his knowledge, training, or education. Without some understanding of the processes by which alcohol ingestion produces nystagmus, how strong the correlation is, how other possible causes might be masked, what margin of error has been shown in statistical surveys, and a host of other relevant factors, [the officer's] opinion on causation, notwithstanding his ability to recognize the symptom, was unfounded.[68]

Stipulations

Frequently, opposing counsel offers to stipulate to the qualifications of an expert. These offers are often rejected because the stipulation deprives the jury of information that makes the expert's opinion more persuasive. In *State v. Colwell*[69] the trial court required the defense counsel to accept the prosecution's offer to stipulate to the qualifications of the defense pathologist. Consequently, the jury was deprived of learning the credentials of the expert, who had a "national reputation" in the field of forensic pathology. In contrast, eleven pages of the transcript were needed to record the qualifications of the prosecution's expert. The Kansas Supreme Court reversed:

> We conclude that an offer by the State to stipulate to the qualifications of an expert witness called by the defendant is merely an offer unless accepted by the defendant. Absent such acceptance, the defendant has the right to present the witness' qualifications to the jury.[70]

§ 5-4. Probative Value vs. Other Factors.

The trial court retains discretionary authority to exclude relevant evidence. Federal Rule of Evidence 403 provides: "Although relevant, evidence may be excluded if its probative value is substantially outweighed by the danger of unfair prejudice, confusion of issues, or misleading the jury, or by considerations of undue delay, waste of time, or needless presentation of cumulative evidence."[71] As one court has noted: "Expert testimony, like any other testimony, may be

---

68. People v. Williams, 3 Cal. App. 4th 1326, 1334, 5 Cal. Rptr. 2d 130, 135 (1992). *But see* People v. Ojeda, 225 Cal. App. 3d 404, 408, 275 Cal. Rptr. 472, 474 (1990) ("The gaze nystagmus test, as do other commonly used field sobriety tests, requires only the personal observation of the officer administering it").

69. 246 Kan. 382, 790 P.2d 430 (1990).

70. *Id.* at 386, 790 P.2d at 434.

71. For a further discussion of Rule 403, *see* § 1-6 *supra*.

excluded if, compared to its probative worth, it would create a substantial danger of undue prejudice or confusion."[72]

The principal danger of scientific evidence is its potential to mislead the jury; that is, such evidence may "assume a posture of mystic infallibility in the eyes of a jury of laymen."[73] Accordingly, "an exaggerated popular opinion of the accuracy of a particular technique [may make] its use prejudicial or likely to mislead the jury."[74] Similarly, a particular technique may pose the danger of misleading the jury because the jury will be required to rely totally on the expert's opinion, thus forcing it "to sacrifice its independence and common sense in evaluating [the evidence]."[75]

Appellate Review

Appellate courts use an "abuse of discretion" standard to review a trial court's decision under Rule 403. Although this standard grants the trial court wide latitude, this discretion is not unlimited. For example, in *United States v. Dwyer*[76] the trial court refused to permit the accused to call a second expert to testify on an insanity defense. Moreover, the trial court refused to explain the basis for its decision despite a defense request for an explanation. The Second Circuit reversed:

---

72. United States v. Schmidt, 711 F.2d 595, 598 (5th Cir. 1983). *See also* Jones v. State, 425 N.E.2d 128, 136-37 (Ind. 1981) (Hunter, J. dissenting) ("extensive and impressive credentials such as those revealed here, together with the testimony of a sophisticated technological nature far beyond the average layman's understanding, may impress a jury and influence inordinately the weight which is attached to the expert testimony").

73. United States v. Addison, 498 F.2d 741, 744 (D.C. Cir. 1974). *See also* United States v. Alexander, 526 F.2d 161, 168 (8th Cir. 1975) ("When polygraph evidence is offered ..., it is likely to be shrouded with an aura of near infallibility, akin to the ancient oracle of Delphi"); People v. King, 266 Cal. App. 2d 437, 461, 72 Cal. Rptr. 478, 493 (1968) ("[J]urors must not be misled by an 'aura of certainty which often envelops a new scientific process, obscuring its currently experimental nature'").

74. United States v. Baller, 519 F.2d 463, 466 (4th Cir.), *cert. denied,* 423 U.S. 1019 (1975). *See also* Weinstein, *Rule 702 of the Federal Rules of Evidence is Sound; It Should Not be Amended,* 138 F.R.D. 631, 632 (1992) ("Expert evidence can be both powerful and quite misleading because of the difficulty in evaluating it. Because of this risk, the judge in weighing possible prejudice against probative force under Rule 403 of the present rules exercises more control over experts than over lay witnesses").

75. People v. Marx, 54 Cal. App. 3d 100, 110, 126 Cal. Rptr. 350, 356 (1975) ("[T]he trier of fact is required to rely on the testimony of the polygrapher, verified at most by marks on a graph, to which the expert's hypothesis gives some relevant meaning. Similar total reliance on the expert's assumptions is required for voice spectrogram"); State v. Hall, 297 N.W.2d 80, 86 (Iowa 1980) (blood flight characteristics) ("Such observations are largely based on common sense, and in fact, lie close to the ken of average laymen").

76. 539 F.2d 924 (2d Cir. 1976).

> Although Rule 403 has placed great discretion in the trial judge, discretion does not mean immunity from accountability .... Unfortunately, where the reasons for a discretionary ruling are not apparent to counsel, they will probably not be apparent to an appellate court. We therefore find it difficult to comprehend the district judge's adamant refusal to respond to defense counsel's inquiries. The spirit of Rule 403 would have been better served had the judge "confront[ed] the problem explicitly, acknowledging and weighing both the prejudice and the probative worth" of the proffered testimony.[77]

Negative Evidence

In *United States v. Thompson*,[78] the defendant claimed that she did not know that cocaine was in her suitcase. The trial court precluded the defense from commenting on the lack of fingerprint evidence. The Ninth Circuit ruled that the trial court had abused its discretion. "When the defense is lack of knowledge, the lack of fingerprint evidence is a relevant fact which may be elicited by defense counsel during direct or cross examination of witnesses, and incorporated into counsel's closing statement."[79] A trial court may, however, limit such argument by precluding speculative inferences about the reliability of police investigative practices or unwarranted comments on the credibility of government witnesses.[80]

§ 5-5. Bases of Expert Opinion Testimony.

Expert witnesses are permitted to express opinions. As the drafters of the Federal Rules noted, however, an expert is not required to testify in the form of opinions, and thus Federal Rule 702 provides that an expert may testify "in the form of an opinion or otherwise." Accordingly, an expert "may give a dissertation or exposition of scientific or other principles relevant to the case, leaving the trier of fact to apply them to the facts."[81]

Expert opinion testimony may be based on three different types of facts: (1) the expert's personal knowledge, (2) assumed facts supported by evidence in the record, typically in the form of a hypothetical question, and (3) information

---

77. *Id.* at 928 (quoting United States v. Robinson, 530 F.2d 1076, 1081 (D.C. Cir. 1976)).

78. 37 F.3d 450 (9th Cir. 1994).

79. *Id.* at 454. *See also* United States v. Poindexter, 942 F.2d 354, 360 (6th Cir.), *cert. denied*, 502 U.S. 994 (1991) ("In every criminal case, the mosaic of evidence that comprises the record before a jury includes both the evidence and the lack of evidence on material matters. Indeed, it is the absence of evidence [fingerprint] upon such matters that may provide the reasonable doubt that moves a jury to acquit").

80. United States v. Hoffman, 964 F.2d 21, 26 (D.C. Cir. 1992) ("It is permissible for a defense attorney to point out to the jury that no fingerprint evidence has been introduced and to argue that the absence of such evidence weakens the Government's case").

81. FED. R. EVID. 702 advisory committee's note.

supplied to the expert outside of the trial. Federal Rule 703 recognizes all three sources.[82] Each basis is discussed in the next sections.

Confrontation Issues

In *Delaware v. Fensterer*[83] the Supreme Court considered a confrontation challenge involving the basis of expert testimony. In that case an FBI analyst testified that hair found at a murder scene had been forcibly removed. He further testified that three methods were available to make this determination, but he could not remember which method he had used to reach his conclusion. According to the Delaware Supreme Court, the expert's lack of memory precluded the defense from testing the basis for the opinion by cross-examination and thus violated the right of confrontation.[84]

The U.S. Supreme Court disagreed and reversed. In the Court's view, "[T]he Confrontation Clause is generally satisfied when the defense is given full and fair opportunity to probe and expose ... infirmities through cross-examination, thereby calling to the attention of the factfinder the reasons for giving scant weight to the witness' testimony."[85] The Court went on to hold that such an opportunity had been provided at trial, noting that the "defense counsel's cross-examination of Agent Robillard demonstrated to the jury that Robillard could not even recall the theory on which his opinion was based."[86] The Court, however, did caution that its decision was limited to the facts presented.[87]

Nevertheless, on remand the Delaware Supreme Court again held the opinion inadmissible, but on evidentiary, rather than constitutional, grounds. According to the court: "While a witness's mere lack of memory as to a particular fact may go only to the weight of that evidence, an expert witness's inability to establish a sufficient basis for his opinion clearly renders the opinion inadmissible under D.R.E. 705."[88]

---

82. FED. R. EVID. 703 provides:

> The facts or data in the particular case upon which an expert bases an opinion or inference may be those perceived by or made known to the expert at or before the hearing. If of a type reasonably relied upon by experts in the particular field in forming opinions or inferences upon the subject, the facts or data need not be admissible in evidence.

83. 474 U.S. 15 (1985).

84. State v. Fensterer, 493 A.2d 959, 964 (Del. 1985).

85. 474 U.S. at 22. *See also* State v. Place, 128 N.H. 75, 77-78, 513 A.2d 321, 323 (1986) (chemist permitted to testify even though he did not remember conducting specific test involved in case).

86. 474 U.S. at 20.

87. "We need not decide whether there are circumstances in which a witness' lapse of memory may so frustrate any opportunity for cross-examination that admission of the witness' direct testimony violates the Confrontation Clause." *Id.* at 20.

88. Fensterer v. State, 509 A.2d 1106, 1109-10 (Del. 1986).

§ 5-5(A). Personal Knowledge.

Expert witnesses frequently express opinions based on their personal observations. For example, the forensic chemist who examines a substance and concludes it is a controlled substance may express an opinion concerning the identity of the substance based on his firsthand knowledge.[89] Similarly, the forensic pathologist who expresses an opinion about the cause of death in a homicide case, after conducting an autopsy, is basing her opinion on personal observation.[90]

§ 5-5(B). Hypothetical Questions.

Experts may also base their opinions on assumed facts that are supported by evidence in the record. In some jurisdictions, an expert who has attended the trial is permitted to assume that the evidence adduced at trial is true and express an opinion based on this evidence.[91] The major deficiency with this procedure is that the jury may not understand which facts the expert is assuming to be true, a problem which is particularly pronounced in a long, complicated trial or where the evidence is conflicting.

An expert also may express an opinion based on assumed facts that are stated in the form of a hypothetical question. The hypothetical question has two principal advantages. First, it informs the jury of the facts upon which the expert's opinion is based. Second, it provides the opposing party with an opportunity to object before an opinion is expressed, if the question contains assumed facts that are not supported by evidence admitted at trial. Despite these advantages, the hypothetical question has been criticized as a cumbersome and unwieldy device which often precludes the expert from fully explaining her opinion to the jury. As one court has noted, "[r]ather than inducing a clear expression of expert opinion and the basis for it, [the hypothetical question] inhibits the expert and forecloses him from explaining his reasoning in a manner that is intelligible to a jury."[92] It has also been criticized "as encouraging partisan bias, affording an opportunity for summing up in the middle of the case, and as complex and time consuming."[93]

---

89. *See* Chapter 23 (drug testing).

90. *See* Chapter 19 (forensic pathology).

91. *See* United States v. Crabtree, 979 F.2d 1261, 1270 (1992) ("Rule 703 ... specifically states that an expert can base his opinion on the facts and data learned from attending the trial and listening to testimony. That is precisely what Agent Turner did; there is little if any difference between counsel disclosing prior testimony to an expert and having an expert listen to such testimony in the courtroom"), *cert. denied,* 510 U.S. 878 (1993); 2 J. WIGMORE, EVIDENCE § 681 (Chadbourn rev. 1979); 1 C. MCCORMICK, EVIDENCE § 14 (4th ed. 1992).

92. Rabata v. Dohner, 45 Wis. 2d 111, 129, 172 N.W.2d 409, 417 (1969).

93. FED. R. EVID. 705 advisory committee's note.

Federal Rules 703 and 705 permit an expert to express an opinion without resort to a hypothetical question, even if the expert lacks personal knowledge of the underlying facts. Thus, in federal practice the hypothetical question is optional rather than mandatory.

If a hypothetical question is used to elicit expert opinion, an issue concerning the adequacy of the facts assumed in the hypothetical may arise. There is a danger that the question will contain a one-sided view of the relevant issues; for example, adverse facts may be omitted from the hypothetical question. In such a case the jury may give undue weight to the expert's opinion without fully appreciating the inadequacy of the underlying factual basis. Because of this problem, some jurisdictions require the hypothetical to include the "material" facts in the case.[94] Other jurisdictions reject this requirement, leaving the opponent with the responsibility of highlighting such omissions during cross-examination or reformulating the hypothetical question to include the omitted facts.[95]

§ 5-5(C). Non-record Facts.

In addition, Rule 703 permits an expert to express an opinion based on information that has not been admitted at trial and, indeed, may be inadmissible: "If of a type reasonably relied upon by experts in the particular field in forming opinions or inferences upon the subject, the facts or data need not be admissible in evidence." An ABA study has commented: "Rule 703 was a controversial rule when enacted, and it remains controversial."[96]

Rule 703 permits an expert to base an opinion on hearsay evidence. According to one court:

> The rationale in favor of the admissibility of expert testimony based on hearsay is that the expert is fully capable of judging for himself what is, or is not, a reliable basis for his opinion. This relates directly to one of the functions of the expert witness, namely to lend his special expertise to the issue before him.[97]

---

94. 1 C. McCormick, *supra* note 91, at 61.

95. *Id.*

96. ABA Section of Litigation, Emerging Problems Under the Federal Rules of Evidence, Rule 703 Discussion at 176 (2d ed. 1991).

97. United States v. Sims, 514 F.2d 147, 149 (9th Cir.), *cert. denied,* 423 U.S. 845 (1975). *See also* Soden v. Freightliner Corp., 714 F.2d 498, 502-03 (5th Cir. 1983) (The inquiry under Rule 703 "must be made on a case-by-case basis and should focus on the reliability of the opinion and its foundation rather than ... on the fact that it was based, technically speaking, upon hearsay").

United States v. Arias[98] illustrates the rule. A chemist, based on a comparison of quaaludes seized from the defendants and quaaludes supplied by DEA agents in Colombia, testified that the seized quaaludes were made by the same machine as the tablets from Colombia. The defendants objected to this testimony on the grounds that the expert's opinion regarding the origin of the Columbian tablets was based on hearsay. The court rejected the argument because "an expert may base his testimony upon the type of hearsay he would normally rely upon in the course of his work.... D.E.A. forensic scientists rely upon agents in the field to submit samples and to establish their authenticity as is shown by the fact that the pill in question was catalogued and kept for sample use by the D.E.A."[99]

Similarly, in *United States v. Lundy*[100] an arson expert testified that a fire had been purposefully set. His opinion was based on his firsthand inspection of the scene and on interviews with witnesses at the scene. The Seventh Circuit ruled the testimony admissible under Rule 703: "[H]earsay and third-party observations that are of a type normally relied upon by an expert in the field are properly utilized by such an expert in developing an expert opinion.... [The expert] presented uncontroverted evidence that interviews with many witnesses to a fire are a standard investigatory technique in cause and origin inquiries."[101]

Syllogistic Analysis

Viewing expert testimony as a syllogism may obviate some of the problems associated with Rule 703.[102] For example, a pathologist may testify that a homicide victim had been shot at close range. The major premise is a general proposition: powder burns on the chest of a victim indicate a close-range entrance wound. The minor premise is the finding of such a wound during the

98. 678 F.2d 1202 (4th Cir.), *cert. denied,* 459 U.S. 910 (1982).

99. *Id.* at 1206.

100. 809 F.2d 392 (7th Cir. 1987).

101. *Id.* at 395 ("In addition, [the expert's] opinion was also based heavily on his own investigation, which ruled out most accidental causes and suggested that an accelerant had been used"). *See also* United States v. Vest, 116 F.3d 1179, 1185 (7th Cir. 1997) ("The subject of these government questions, however, was the credibility of the patients — something not within an expert's area of special competence. With only Vest's records and the patients' statements to the FBI as evidence, the expert was in no better position than a lay person to say whether the patient testified truthfully"), *cert. denied,* 118 S. Ct. 1058 (1998); United States v. Tran Trong Cuong, 18 F.3d 1132, 1143 (4th Cir. 1994) ("The Stevenson report was prepared at the request of the prosecution and thereby is a forensic opinion or report in a criminal case. We question whether Dr. MacIntosh usually relies upon forensic medical opinions or reports in forming his opinions in his field of expertise — family medicine"); People v. Bynum, 257 Ill. App. 3d 502, 629 N.E.2d 724 (1994) (lab technician may testify about composition of seized substance although she relied on computer-generated and computer-stored substance profile graphs used by the testing device).

102. *See* Imwinkelried, *The "Bases" of Expert Testimony: The Syllogistic Structure of Scientific Testimony,* 67 N.C. L. REV. 1 (1988).

autopsy. The conclusion as stated above is derived from these two premises. Rule 703 concerns only the minor premise, which it refers to as the "facts or data in the particular case." A pathologist who did not perform the autopsy could consult the report, view the photographs, and then reach the same conclusion. Under Rule 703 these documents need not be admitted in evidence.

The major premise is not governed by Rule 703. This premise is gleaned from the expert's experience and learning in forensic pathology. Often, it is developed over time and includes much hearsay. Professor Maguire stated it this way: "Progress of expert knowledge demands reliance upon the learning of the past. Almost invariably this learning is recorded in hearsay form. No individual can ever make himself into an expert without absorbing much hearsay — lectures by his teachers, statements in textbooks, reports of experiments and experiences of others in the same field."[103]

There is nothing wrong with relying on this type of "background" hearsay; indeed, the witness would probably not be an expert without it. Thus, an expert who has consulted books or spoken to other experts is acting properly. There is a problem only if the text or other expert's opinion is offered in evidence for the truth of the assertions contained therein. This would raise a hearsay issue. More importantly, Rule 703 does not govern this issue.

Determining Admissibility

The admissibility of expert opinions based on non-record facts under Rule 703 raises several issues. One issue concerns the trial court's role in determining what types of information are reasonably relied upon in a particular field. The federal drafters provided little guidance on this issue. The Advisory Committee's Note merely comments that the "opinion of an 'accidentologist' as to the point of impact in an automobile collision based on statements of bystanders" would not satisfy the requirement.

There are two different approaches to the judge's role. One approach requires the court to make an independent assessment of the reasonableness of the expert's reliance:

> [T]he court may not abdicate its independent responsibilities to decide if the bases meet minimum standards of reliability as a condition of admissibility.... If the underlying data are so lacking in probative force and reliability that no reasonable expert could base an opinion on them, an opinion which rests entirely upon them must be excluded.[104]

---

103. J. MAGUIRE, *supra* note 2, at 29.

104. *In re* "Agent Orange" Product Liability Litigation, 611 F. Supp. 1221, 1245 (E.D.N.Y. 1985), *aff'd,* 818 F.2d 187 (2d Cir. 1987), *cert. denied,* 487 U.S. 1234 (1988). *See also* United States v. Locascio, 6 F.3d 924, 938 (2d Cir. 1993) ("[A] district court is not bound to accept expert

The other approach limits the judge's role to determining what experts in the field consider reasonable. The "proper inquiry is not what the court deems reliable, but what experts in the relevant discipline deem it to be."[105] The Third Circuit added: "In substituting its own opinion as to what constitutes reasonable reliance for that of the experts in the relevant fields the trial court misinterpreted Rule 703."[106] Even under this approach, however, the trial court is not required to accept the testifying expert's view of what is reasonably relied upon by experts in a particular field.[107] The Third Circuit changed positions after the U.S. Supreme Court decided the *Daubert* case.[108] The court noted that its "former view is no longer tenable in light of *Daubert*."[109]

In making this determination, the trial court may consider the testimony of the testifying expert, other experts, learned treatises,[110] and judicially noticeable facts.[111]

Cross-Examination

Rule 703 should be read in conjunction with Rule 705, which permits the expert to express an opinion without first disclosing the underlying basis for that opinion. Rule 705, however, also provides that the expert may be "required to disclose the underlying facts or data on cross-examination." In *United States v. A*

---

testimony based on questionable data simply because other experts use such data in the field"), *cert. denied*, 511 U.S. 1070 (1994).

105. Zenith Radio Corp. v. Matsushita Elec. Indus. Co., 505 F. Supp. 1190 (E.D. Pa. 1980), *aff'd in part and rev'd in part,* 723 F.2d 238 (3d Cir. 1983), *rev'd,* 475 U.S. 574 (1986).

106. *Id.* at 277.

107. *See* Merit Motors, Inc. v. Chrysler Corp., 569 F.2d 666, 673 (D.C. 1977).

108. *Daubert* is discussed in Chapter 1.

109. *In re* Paoli R.R. Yard PCB Litigation, 35 F.3d 717, 748 (3d Cir. 1994), *cert. denied*, 513 U.S. 1190 (1995). The court wrote:

> [I]t is the judge who makes the determination of reasonable reliance, and that for the judge to make the factual determination under Rule 104(a) that an expert is basing his or her opinion on a type of data *reasonably* relied upon by experts, the judge must conduct an independent evaluation into reasonableness. The judge can of course take into account the particular expert's opinion that experts reasonably rely on that type of data, as well as the opinions of other experts as to its reliability, but the judge can also take into account other factors he or she deems relevant.

See also Imwinkelried, *The Meaning of "Facts or Data" in Federal Rule of Evidence 703: The Significance of the Supreme Court's Decision to Rely on Federal Rule 702 in Daubert v. Merrell Dow Pharmaceuticals, Inc.*, 54 MD. L. REV. 352 (1995).

110. United States v. Tranowski, 659 F.3d 750, 755 (7th Cir. 1981).

111. *See* Ambrosini v. Labarraque, 966 F.2d 1464, 1467 (D.C. Cir. 1992) ("In effect, we took judicial notice ... that the chemical, *in vitro, in vivo*, and recalculated epidemiological studies were not of a type reasonably relied on experts in the field").

& S Council Oil Co.,[112] the prosecution required its witness to take a polygraph examination as part of a plea agreement. The witness failed two tests. At trial the prosecution attempted to bolster the witness's credibility by introducing the testimony of a psychiatrist who testified that the witness was able to distinguish reality from imagination. The Fourth Circuit ruled that since the expert must have discounted the polygraph results in reaching his opinion, the defense should have been permitted to cross-examine on this issue:

> Council should have been permitted to fully explore the bases of Rollins' opinion, including inquiry about Jackson's polygraph result. Rule 703 creates a shield by which a party may enjoy the benefit of inadmissible evidence by wrapping it in an expert's opinion; Rule 705 is the cross-examiner's sword, and, within very broad limits, he may wield it as he likes.[113]

Hearsay Use

Another issue concerns how the jury may use the out-of-court information if the expert testifies about the basis for the opinion. Although Rule 703 permits an expert to base an opinion on hearsay information, it does not explicitly recognize a hearsay exception for this information. Under one view, the jury can consider the information only in evaluating the expert's opinion; it cannot use the information substantively, *i.e.*, for the truth of the assertions contained therein.[114] An ABA report comments that "[i]t is important to keep in mind that Rule 703 is not an exception to the rule against hearsay. Even though an expert may disclose to the jury the data he relied upon, the data will not be considered as substantive evidence for purposes of establishing a prima facie case."[115]

Other authorities, however, envision the substantive use of the information,[116] creating, in effect, another hearsay exception. One commentator has written: "For most but not all practical purposes, Rule 703 operates as the equivalent of an additional exception to the rule against hearsay ...."[117] In contrast, another

---

112. 947 F.2d 1128 (4th Cir. 1991).

113. *Id.* at 1135.

114. *E.g.*, United States v. Wright, 783 F.2d 1091, 1100 (D.C. Cir. 1986); United States v. Affleck, 776 F.2d 1451, 1457 (10th Cir. 1985); United States v. Sims, 514 F.2d 147, 149-50 (9th Cir.), *cert. denied,* 423 U.S. 845 (1975). *See generally* Carlson, *Collision Course in Expert Testimony: Limitations on Affirmative Introduction of Underlying Data*, 36 U. FLA. L. REV. 234 (1984); Annot., *Admissibility of Testimony of Expert, as to Basis of his Opinion, to Matters Otherwise Excludible as Hearsay — State Cases*, 89 A.L.R.4TH 456 (1991).

115. ABA SECTION OF LITIGATION, EMERGING PROBLEMS UNDER THE FEDERAL RULES OF EVIDENCE 181 (2d ed. 1991).

116. 2 C. MCCORMICK, *supra* note 91, § 324.3.

117. 2 M. GRAHAM, HANDBOOK OF FEDERAL EVIDENCE § 703.1, at 112 (4th ed. 1996). *See generally* Carlson, *Policing the Bases of Modern Expert Testimony*, 39 VAND. L. REV. 577 (1986);

commentator has argued that "an expert may identify the various sources for her opinion and give a general description of the subjects discussed in the underlying reports. However, the expert may not spread hearsay before the jury except under limited circumstances."[118]

Confrontation Issues

In criminal trials, the use of hearsay evidence as a basis for expert opinion testimony raises confrontation issues. In *United States v. Lawson*[119] the defense objected to the testimony of a prosecution psychiatrist who testified that the defendant was sane. The expert had limited personal contact with the defendant and relied on hearsay information in formulating his opinion. The Seventh Circuit ruled the testimony admissible. According to the court, reliance on staff reports, interviews conducted by other psychiatrists, and background information from military and prosecution records was "clearly of the type that psychiatrists would rely upon in making a similar professional judgment" and thus satisfied the requirements of Rule 703.[120] Although the court also rejected the defendant's confrontation argument, it recognized the cogency of that argument in certain circumstances: "An expert's testimony that was based entirely on hearsay reports, while it might satisfy Rule 703, would nevertheless violate a defendant's constitutional right to confront adverse witnesses. The Government could not, for example, simply produce a witness who did nothing but summarize out-of-court statements made by others."[121]

The Seventh Circuit also rejected a confrontation challenge in a case where a voiceprint expert testified based on spectrograms prepared by a different expert:

> The confrontation clause ... does not forbid reliance at trial by experts upon material prepared by others. It requires, however, that the defendant

---

Rice, *Inadmissible Evidence as a Basis for Expert Opinion Testimony: A Response to Professor Carlson*, 40 VAND. L. REV. 583 (1987); Note, *The Scope of the Reasonable Reliance Requirement of Federal Rule of Evidence 703*, 1988 ILL. L. REV. 1069; Comment, *Fed. R. Evid. 703: A Back Door Entrance for Hearsay and Other Inadmissible Evidence: A Time For Change?*, 63 TEMPLE L. REV. 543 (1990).

118. Carlson, *Experts as Hearsay Conduits: Confrontation Abuses in Opinion Testimony*, 76 MINN. L. REV. 859, 869 (1992).

119. 653 F.2d 299 (7th Cir. 1981), *cert. denied,* 454 U.S. 1150 (1982).

120. *Id.* at 302.

121. *Id.* at 302. *See also* ABA SECTION OF LITIGATION, EMERGING PROBLEMS UNDER THE FEDERAL RULES OF EVIDENCE 181 (2d ed. 1991) ("In criminal prosecutions the defendant's constitutional right to confront and cross-examine adverse witnesses presents a concern not found in civil cases"); ABA Criminal Justice Section, *Federal Rules of Evidence: A Fresh Review and Evaluation*, 120 F.R.D. 299, 371 (1988) ("The back door introduction of the contents of a nontestifying expert's report, without producing the author of the material, can in many cases, impinge on the defendant's Sixth Amendment rights").

> have access to such material, in order that she has an adequate opportunity to prepare her cross-examination.... It is, of course, true that an expert witness may not simply summarize the out-of-court statements of others as his testimony.... That is not, however, what Dr. Nakasone did in this case. He was not ... merely an "understudy" for Lieutenant Smrkovski.[122]

In *State v. Towne*[123] a prosecution expert testified that the defendant was sexually disturbed but not mentally ill. To support his opinion, the expert cited a book that had been written by a friend of his. He also testified that he had spoken by telephone with the author and that the author agreed with his opinion in the case. The Vermont Supreme Court held that the expert's references to the author did not come within the rule allowing an expert to base an opinion upon facts not admissible in evidence but reasonably relied on by experts in the field. Instead, the court found that the witness was in effect "'acting as a conduit' for the other doctor's opinion."[124] According to the court, not only was the opinion hearsay, but it also violated the defendant's right of confrontation.[125]

The distinction recognized by these courts is between an expert who forms his own opinion, albeit based in part on the work of others, and an expert who merely summarizes the work of others. The Eighth Circuit has written: "Fed. R. Evid. 703 does not permit an expert witness to circumvent the rules of hearsay by testifying that other experts, not present in the courtroom, corroborate his views."[126]

---

122. United States v. Smith, 869 F.2d 348, 355 (7th Cir. 1989). *See also* United States v. Wright, 783 F.2d 1091, 1101 (D.C. Cir. 1986) ("Confrontation Clause concerns arise where the rules governing expert testimony are misused in order to bring otherwise inadmissible evidence before the jury without the opportunity for effective cross-examination"); United States v. Affleck, 776 F.2d 1451, 1456-58 (10th Cir. 1985) (no confrontation violation); United States v. Williams, 447 F.2d 1285 (5th Cir. 1971) (testimony of expert on the value of land, based on documents and records not admitted in evidence, did not violate the right of confrontation), *cert. denied,* 405 U.S. 954 (1972); Hull v. State, 687 So. 2d 708, 717 (Miss. 1996) ("Although the State may not impermissibly bolster an expert's conclusion through irrelevant repetitions of corroborative opinions solicited of nontestifying colleagues, the value of face-to-face confrontation in this scenario is low, and this Court declines to create a mechanical confrontation rule in the expert opinion arena"); State v. Henderson, 554 S.W.2d 117, 118-22 (Tenn. 1977) (admission of laboratory report through the testimony of the director of the laboratory violated confrontation right).

123. 142 Vt. 241, 453 A.2d 1133 (1982).

124. *Id.* at 246, 453 A.2d at 1135.

125. Carlson, *supra* note 114, at 248 ("For such support to come from a nontestifying expert insulated from cross-examination presents a difficult, almost impossible situation for the opponent of the evidence").

126. United States v. Grey Bear, 883 F.2d 1382, 1392-93 (8th Cir. 1989), *cert. denied,* 493 U.S. 1047 (1990). *See also* United States v. Tran Trong Cuong, 18 F.3d 1132, 1143 (4th Cir. 1994) ("Essentially, the defendant is subjected to the testimony of a witness whom he may not cross-

Supervising Chemist

A related confrontation issue arises where a supervising chemist identifies a substance based, at least in part, on tests performed by other chemists. Several courts have upheld this practice if the supervising chemist testifies that the tests were performed under his personal supervision.[127] The issue, however, remains problematic. For example, in *Reardon v. Manson*[128] a toxicologist testified based on tests performed by a chemist. The Second Circuit upheld the practice: "Expert reliance upon the output of others does not necessarily violate the confrontation clause where the expert is available for questioning concerning the nature and reasonableness of his reliance.... This is particularly true where the defendants have access to the same sources of information through subpoena or otherwise."[129] The expert, however, worked at a laboratory staffed by three doctorate-level toxicologists and 24 chemists with lesser credentials. With an annual volume of 20,000 tests, the toxicologists had an average of "only a few minutes per day to attend to any given test. Is this adequate involvement to justify testifying to the findings?"[130] Here, the line between an independent expert and a summary witness is blurred.

§ 5-6. Degree of Certitude.

Some jurisdictions require an expert to express an opinion in terms of reasonable scientific probability or certainty.[131] For example, in *State v. Holt*[132]

---

examine, and Dr. MacIntosh bolstered his testimony by claiming that an outstanding doctor, who is also a lawyer and president of the Medical Society, agrees with him").

127. *E.g.,* State v. Reardon, 172 Conn. 593, 597-98, 376 A.2d 65, 67 (1977); Jenkins v. State, 627 N.E.2d 789, 793 (Ind. 1993) (FBI supervisor in DNA unit testified that a lab technician worked with him and performed the actual manipulation of the samples while the expert conducted the statistical analysis; no confrontation violation), *cert. denied,* 513 U.S. 812 (1994); Commonwealth v. Manning, 495 Pa. 652, 660-61, 435 A.2d 1207, 1211-12 (1981) (testimony of supervising toxicologist who identified PCP based on tests performed under his direction admitted); Commonwealth v. Gilliard, 300 Pa. Super. 469, 476, 446 A.2d 951, 954 (1982) (testimony of medical examiner based on toxicologist report admitted); State v. Kreck, 86 Wash. 2d 112, 116-21, 542 P.2d 782, 785-88 (1975); State v. Ecklund, 30 Wash. App. 313, 317-19, 633 P.2d 933, 935-36 (1981). *See also* United States v. Posey, 647 F.2d 1048, 1051 (10th Cir. 1981).

128. 806 F.2d 39, 42 (2d Cir. 1986), *cert. denied,* 481 U.S. 1020 (1987).

129. *Id.* at 42. *See also* United States v. Smith, 869 F.2d 348, 355 (7th Cir. 1989) ("The confrontation clause ... does not forbid reliance at trial by experts upon material prepared by others"); United States v. Coleman, 631 F.2d 908, 914-15 (D.C. Cir. 1980) (court declines to decide this "difficult" question). *But see* Ardoin v. State, 682 S.W.2d 595 (Tex. App. 1984) (statute authorizes custodian to testify about procedures used in test even though he did not conduct the test).

130. M. SAKS & R. VAN DUIZEND, THE USE OF SCIENTIFIC EVIDENCE IN LITIGATION 49 (1983).

131. *See generally* 7 J. WIGMORE, EVIDENCE § 1976 (Chadbourn rev. 1978); Graham, *Expert Witness Testimony and the Federal Rules of Evidence: Insuring Adequate Assurance of*

an expert testified that based on neutron activation analysis two hair samples were "similar *and ... likely* to be from the same source."[133] According to the Ohio Supreme Court, expert testimony is admissible only if the opinion is based upon "reasonable scientific certainty." For that court, reasonable scientific certainty meant that the expert had to testify that the hair sample probably came from the defendant and not that it possibly came from him.[134]

The *Holt* case is wrong. Frequently, experts testify that two samples "could have come from the same source" or "were likely to be from the same source." Such testimony meets the relevancy standard of Federal Rule 401, and there is no requirement in the Federal Rules that an expert's opinion be expressed in terms of "probabilities." For example, in *United States v. Cyphers*[135] the expert testified that hair samples found on items used in a robbery "could have come" from the defendants.[136] The defendants argued that the testimony was inadmissible because the expert did not express his opinion in terms of reasonable scientific certainty. The court wrote: "There is no such requirement.... To the extent *State v. Holt* expresses a contrary view, we find it unpersuasive."[137] Another court wrote that "[f]ar from being the 'leading case' on the subject, as defendant suggests *Holt* is, our research indicates that no other jurisdiction has adopted its rationale in excluding the results of a neutron-activation analysis."[138] Indeed, the Ohio Supreme Court has backed away from *Holt* in later cases.[139]

Trustworthiness, 1986 U. ILL. L. REV. 43, 60-63; Joseph, *Less Than Certain Medical Testimony*, 14 TRIAL 51 (Jan. 1978); Klein, *Expert Testimony in Pharmaceutical Product Liability Acts*, 45 FOOD DRUG. COSM. L.J. 393, 413-24 (1990); Martin, *The Uncertain Rule of Certainty: An Analysis and Proposal for a Federal Rule of Evidence Rule*, 20 WAYNE L. REV. 781 (1974); McElhaney, *Expert Witnesses and the Federal Rules of Evidence*, 28 MERCER L. REV. 463, 477 (1977).

132. 17 Ohio St. 2d 81, 246 N.E.2d 365 (1969).

133. *Id.* at 85, 246 N.E.2d at 368.

134. *Id.* at 86, 246 N.E.2d at 368.

135. 553 F.2d 1064 (7th Cir.), *cert. denied,* 434 U.S. 843 (1977).

136. *Id.* at 1072. *See also* United States v. Davis, 44 M.J. 13, 16 (C.A.A.F. 1996) ("Evidence was also admitted that appellant owned sneakers which 'could have' made these prints").

137. *Id. See also* United States v. Oaxaca, 569 F.2d 518, 526 (9th Cir.) (expert's opinion regarding hair comparison admissible even though expert was less than certain), *cert. denied,* 439 U.S. 926 (1978); United States v. Spencer, 439 F.2d 1047, 1049 (2d Cir. 1971) (expert's opinion regarding handwriting comparison admissible even though expert did not make a positive identification); United States v. Longfellow, 406 F.2d 415, 416 (4th Cir.) (expert's opinion regarding paint comparison admissible, even though expert did not make a positive identification), *cert. denied,* 394 U.S. 998 (1969); State v. Boyer, 406 So. 2d 143, 148 (La. 1981) (reasonable scientific certainty not required where expert testifies concerning the presence of gunshot residue based on neutron activation analysis).

138. People v. Johnson, 114 Ill. 2d 170, 196, 499 N.E.2d 1355, 1366-67 (1986), *cert. denied,* 480 U.S. 951 (1987).

139. *See* State v. D'Ambrosio, 67 Ohio St. 3d 185, 191, 616 N.E.2d 909 (1993) ("While several decisions from this court indicate that speculative opinions by medical experts are inadmissible since they are based on possibilities and not probabilities, . . . we believe that the better practice,

Nevertheless, the "reasonable scientific certainty" requirement is still cited in the cases. "Many courts continue to exclude opinions which fall short of expressing a probability or certainty.... These opinions have been excluded in jurisdictions which have adopted the Federal Rules of Evidence."[140] Another commentator agrees: "there is nevertheless an undercurrent that the expert in federal court express some basis for both the confidence with which his conclusion is formed, and the probability that his conclusion is accurate."[141] Sometimes the phrase seems to be used to exclude speculative opinions, those without a sufficient scientific basis. Indeed, this may explain the Ohio Supreme Court's opinion in *Holt,* which was one of the early cases on neutron activation analysis. If this is the issue, it should be addressed directly and not obscured by the "reasonable scientific certainty" rubric. As one court has noted, "[c]are must be taken, however, to see that the incantation does not become a semantic trap and the failure to voice it is not used as a basis for exclusion without analysis of the testimony itself."[142]

§ 5-7. Ultimate Issue Rule.

At one time both lay and expert witnesses were prohibited from expressing opinions on the ultimate issues in a case. This rule was sometimes justified on the grounds that such opinions "invade the province of the jury" or "usurp the function of the jury."[143]

---

especially in criminal cases, is to let experts testify in terms of possibility. *See* Giannelli, Ohio Evidence Manual (1988) 98, Section 702.05 ... Here [the coroner's] testimony helped the trier of fact to understand that, despite contrary appearances, the size of wound was consistent with the size and shape of State's Exhibit 8A [a knife]. Although [the coroner's] testimony does not prove that State's Exhibit 8A was the murder weapon, we believe that is an issue of sufficiency, not admissibility. Giannelli, *supra.* A piece of relevant evidence need not by itself prove a fact in order to be admissible"). *See also* State v. Allen, 73 Ohio St. 3d 626, 635-36, 653 N.E.2d 675 (1995) (upholding the admissibility of a trace-evidence expert who testified that items burned in the victim's fireplace "could have" had blood on them and it was possible that a black substance found on the bottom of the accused's shoes was ash") (citing *D'Ambrosio*); State v. Hart, 94 Ohio. App. 3d 665, 677, 641 N.E.2d 755 (1994) (forensic medical expert's opinion on whether a sexual assault had occurred or had been attempted "is no longer inadmissible merely because it is not stated to a reasonable medical probability'').

140. Imwinkelried & Scofield, *The Recognition of an Accused's Constitutional Right to Introduce Expert Testimony Attacking the Weight of Prosecution Science Evidence: The Antidote for the Supreme Court's Mistaken Assumption in California v. Trombetta,* 33 ARIZ. L. REV. 59, 69 (1991).

141. Hullverson, *Reasonable Degree of Medical Certainty: A Tort et a Travers,* 31 ST. LOUIS U. L.J. 577, 582 (1987).

142. Schulz v. Celotex Corp., 942 F.2d 204, 208 (3d Cir. 1991).

143. *E.g.,* United States v. Cairns, 434 F.2d 643, 644 (9th Cir. 1970) (defendant argued that opinion "invade[s] the province of the jury"); Linden v. United States, 254 F.2d 560, 566 (4th Cir. 1958) (defendant argued "province of the fact finder was thus invaded").

There are several problems with the ultimate issue rule. First, difficult questions of application are involved in distinguishing "ultimate facts" from other facts.[144] Second, a witness cannot usurp the function of the jury.[145] The jury is not bound by an opinion, even one by an expert,[146] and is instructed that it may disregard the opinion of witnesses, including those of experts.[147] Of course, there is a danger that the jury may be unduly influenced by the opinion of a particular witness, especially an expert; but this problem exists whether the witness is offering an opinion or testifying about observed facts.[148]

Finally, the ultimate issue rule provides an improper standard for determining the admissibility of expert testimony. The standard should be whether the opinion assists the trier of fact, not whether it relates to an ultimate issue. For example, in a forgery case the only contested issue may be whether the defendant forged a check. A questioned document expert, because of her training and experience, may be able to answer that question. In such a case, an opinion on the "ultimate issue" is both desirable and perhaps even necessary to reaching a just result. The expert would not be permitted to testify that the defendant was "guilty." However, the expert may testify, based on the examination of the documents, that the known exemplars and the check were written by the same person ("common authorship").

Federal Rule 704(a)

The modern trend is to abolish the ultimate issue prohibition. Erosion began with expert witnesses,[149] and now includes lay witnesses as well. For example, Federal Rule of Evidence 704, as originally enacted (now 704(a)), abolished the ultimate issue prohibition.[150] As the drafters pointed out, however, Rule 704 does not open the door to all opinions on ultimate issues:

---

144. 1 C. McCORMICK, *supra* note 91, § 12; Ladd, *supra* note 6, at 423.

145. 7 J. WIGMORE, EVIDENCE § 1920, at 18 (Chadbourn rev. 1978) (ultimate issue rule criticized as "a mere bit of empty rhetoric"); Ladd, *supra* note 6, at 424-25.

146. *See* Mason v. United States, 402 F.2d 732, 737 (8th Cir. 1968), *cert. denied,* 394 U.S. 950 (1969); McDaniel v. United States, 343 F.2d 785, 789 (5th Cir.), *cert. denied,* 382 U.S. 826 (1965).

147. *See* 1 E. DEVITT, C. BLACKMAR, M. WOLFF & K. O'MALLEY, FEDERAL JURY PRACTICE AND INSTRUCTIONS § 14.01 (4th ed. 1992) (expert witness instruction).

148. *See* Note, *Opinion Testimony "Invading the Province of the Jury,"* 20 U. CIN. L. REV. 484, 488 (1951).

149. *E.g.,* Feguer v. United States, 302 F.2d 214, 242 (8th Cir.) ("This court has long held generally that an expert, as distinguished from a lay witness, may express his opinion on the ultimate jury question"), *cert. denied,* 371 U.S. 872 (1962).

150. Federal Rule 704(a) provides: "Except as provided in subdivision (b), testimony in the form of an opinion or inference otherwise admissible is not objectionable because it embraces an ultimate issue to be decided by the trier of fact."

> The abolition of the ultimate issue rule does not lower the bars so as to admit all opinions. Under Rules 701 [lay opinions] and 702 [expert opinions], opinions must be helpful to the trier of fact, and Rule 403 provides for exclusion of evidence which wastes time. These provisions afford ample assurances against the admission of opinions which would merely tell the jury what result to reach .... They also stand ready to exclude opinions phrased in terms of inadequately explored legal criteria.[151]

As one court has observed: "No witness should be permitted to give his opinion directly that a person is guilty or innocent, or is criminally responsible or irresponsible."[152]

The federal courts have admitted expert opinion testimony regarding matters that could be considered "ultimate issues."[153] For example, in *United States v. Boney*[154] a police expert testified about the roles and behavior of drug traffickers. In response to a hypothetical question involving the same words, locations, and amounts of cocaine at issue, the expert identified who was a "runner," who was a "holder," and who was going to "make the sale." The D.C. Circuit ruled this testimony admissible; the expert's "testimony, which at most matched particular defendants and their actions with paradigm roles in an illegal enterprise, does not amount to a direct opinion on the defendants' guilt."[155] In short, if the proffered testimony satisfies the requirements of Rules 702 and 403, it should be admitted. The Tenth Circuit, however, has properly noted: "Caution should be the watchword in receiving such evidence in criminal cases."[156]

Rule 704 played a role in *United States v. Sheffer*,[157] in which the Supreme Court held that adoption of a per se rule of exclusion of polygraph evidence is not unconstitutional. Justice Thomas cited the preservation of the jury's role in determining credibility as one factor supporting the majority opinion: "By its very nature, polygraph evidence may diminish the jury's role in making

---

151. FED. R. EVID. 704 advisory committee's note.

152. Grismore v. Consolidated Prods. Co., 232 Iowa 328, 361, 5 N.W.2d 646, 663 (1942).

153. *E.g.,* United States v. Brown, 7 F.3d 648, 653 (7th Cir. 1993) (based on large amount of drugs seized and other circumstances DEA agent permitted to testify that accused possessed drugs for sale, not use); United States v. Fleishman, 684 F.2d 1329, 1335 (9th Cir.) (undercover agent permitted to testify that a person was acting as a "lookout"), *cert. denied,* 459 U.S. 1044 (1982); United States v. Johnson, 637 F.2d 1224, 1246-47 (9th Cir. 1980) (treating physician permitted to testify that a person suffered serious bodily injury).

154. 977 F.2d 624 (D.C. Cir. 1992).

155. *Id.* at 631.*See also* United States v. White, 116 F.3d 903, 922 (D.C. Cir.) ("Notably absent from both the prosecutor's questions and Rawls's answers were the mirroring hypothetical's that have concerned us in other cases"), *cert. denied,* 118 S. Ct. 391 (1997).

156. United States v. Gutierrez, 576 F.2d 269, 275 (10th Cir.), *cert. denied,* 439 U.S. 954 (1978). *See also* United States v. Brown, 776 F.2d 397, 401 (2d Cir. 1985).

157. 118 S. Ct. 1261 (1998).

credibility determinations."[158] In his concurring opinion, Justice Kennedy pointed out that Rule 704 abolished the ultimate issue rule and thus the "invading the province of the jury" argument had been rejected under most modern evidence codes.

Rule 704(b): Mental States

In 1984, Congress amended Rule 704 by adding a new subdivision (b):

> No expert witness testifying with respect to the mental state or condition of a defendant in a criminal case may state an opinion or inference as to whether the defendant did or did not have the mental state or condition constituting an element of the crime charged or of a defense thereto. Such ultimate issues are matters for the trier of fact alone.

Thus, while Rule 704(a) abrogates the ultimate issue rule as a general matter, a special exception applies in criminal cases in which a defendant's mental condition is in issue — for example, where insanity is raised as a defense.[159] Note that the rule does not apply to lay witness testimony.

The application of Rule 704(b) raises several problems.[160] One issue is whether the rule precludes expert testimony which negates mens rea (diminished capacity), such as when specific intent is required, as opposed to testimony on the question of insanity, which is an affirmative defense. Courts have held the rule does not prohibit the former testimony,[161] even though the rule explicitly refers to testimony on "an element" of the offense as well as to defenses.

---

158. *Id.* at 1267.

159. The legislative history contains the following rationale for this rule:

> The purpose of this amendment is to eliminate the confusing spectacle of competing expert witnesses testifying to directly contradictory conclusions as to the ultimate legal issue to be found by the trier of fact. Under this proposal, expert psychiatric testimony would be limited to presenting and explaining their diagnoses, such as whether the defendant had a severe mental disease or defect and what the characteristics of such a disease or defect, if any, may have been.

S. Rep. No. 225, 98th Cong., 2d Sess., *reprinted in* 1984 U.S. Code Cong. & Ad. News 3182, 3412.

160. *See* United States v. Abou-Kassem,78 F.3d 161, 166 (5th Cir.) ("Rule 704(b) violates neither due process nor equal protection"), *cert. denied,* 117 S. Ct. 70 (1996); United States v. Austin, 981 F.2d 1163 (10th Cir. 1992), *cert. denied,* 507 U.S. 1035 (1993).

161. *E.g.,* United States v. Westcott, 83 F.3d 1354, 1358 (11th Cir.) ("The Act does not, however, completely eliminate the use of mental disease or defect evidence outside of attempts to establish the affirmative defense of insanity. The Act does not, by its terms, prohibit psychiatric evidence relevant to issues other than excuse or justification of otherwise criminal conduct.... Psychiatric evidence which negates mens rea thus negates an element of the offense rather than constituting a justification or excuse"), *cert. denied,* 117 S. Ct. 269 (1996); United States v. Cameron, 907 F.2d 1051, 1067 (11th Cir. 1990); United States v. Pohlot, 827 F.2d 889, 905-06 (3d

Second, most courts have held that Rule 704(b) covers experts who are not mental health experts.[162]

A third issue is how close to an ultimate mental issue may the expert's opinion come. For example, one court ruled that testimony in terms of a legal conclusion — whether a defendant was able to appreciate the wrongfulness of his conduct — was improper. In contrast, testimony that the defendant suffered from a mental disease or that such a mental disease would affect a person's ability to appreciate his actions is acceptable.[163] Another court stated the rule this way:

> [E]xpert testimony ... may address the mental illness of Defendant and the characteristics, if any, of that mental illness. Expert testimony may not be introduced, however, with respect to an expert's inference or opinion that, at the time of the alleged crimes, Defendant was (1) sane; (2) insane; (3) lacked substantial capacity to know the wrongfulness of his conduct; or (4) lacked substantial capacity to conform his conduct to the requirements of the law which he is charged with violating.[164]

Cir. 1987), *cert. denied,* 484 U.S. 1011 (1988); United States v. Skodnek, 896 F. Supp. 60, 63 (D. Mass. 1995) ("Nor is psychiatric testimony on mens rea barred by the IDRA. The language of the statute and its legislative history, as many courts have held, establish that Congress intended to bar 'affirmative defenses' that 'excuse' misconduct — not evidence that disproves, an element of the crime itself"). *See generally* Note, *Resurrection of the Ultimate Issue Rule: Federal Rule of Evidence 704(b) and the Insanity Defense*, 72 CORNELL L. REV. 620 (1987); Note, *Punishing the Insane: Restriction of Expert Psychiatric Testimony by Federal Rule of Evidence 704(b)*, 40 U. FLA. L. REV. 541 (1988).

162. *See* United States v. Morales, 108 F.3d 1031, 1036 (9th Cir. 1997) (accountant) ("The language of Rule 704(b) is perfectly plain. It does not limit its reach to psychiatrists and other mental health experts. Its reach extends to all expert witnesses"). The court went on to explain: "[The accountant] was not going to state an opinion or draw an inference that Morales did not intend to make false entries [the ultimate issue]. Rather, she was going to state her opinion as to a predicate matter — that Morales had a weak grasp of bookkeeping principles." *Id.* at 1037. *See also* United States v. Valle, 72 F.3d 210, 215-16 (1st Cir. 1995) ("Rule 704(b) has not been restricted to testimony offered by psychiatrists and other mental health professionals. To the precise contrary, courts have consistently read the rule to apply to cases in which intent is an element of the offense and an expert — whether or not a psychiatrist or other mental health professional — seeks to testify to the defendant's actual intent.... Rule 704(b) prohibits all direct expert testimony concerning a criminal defendant's intent, regardless of the witness's field of expertise, so long as intent is an element of the crime charged").

163. United States v. Kristiansen, 901 F.2d 1463, 1466 (8th Cir. 1990).

164. United States v. Pickett, 604 F. Supp. 407, 410-11 (S.D. Ohio 1985), *aff'd,* 790 F.2d 35 (6th Cir. 1986). *See also* United States v. Brown, 32 F.3d 236, 240 (7th Cir. 1994) (In an insanity case, "Rule 704(b) clearly excludes expert opinion as to the defendant's appreciation for his acts. The testimony in this case, though, is not specific to Brown's mental state, but concerns the characteristics of his mental disorder, which is permitted by Rule 704(b)"); United States v. Thigpen, 4 F.3d 1573, 1580 (11th Cir. 1993) (expert testimony that schizophrenia does not necessarily imply that a person would be unable to appreciate the nature and quality of his acts does not violate Rule 704(b)), *cert. denied,* 512 U.S. 1238 (1994); United States v. Reno, 992 F.2d 739,

The Seventh Circuit in *United States v. Brown*[165] ruled that Rule 704(b) was not violated by testimony of a DEA agent that the accused possessed drugs for sale rather than for personal use. The expert based his opinion on several factors, including the large amount of drugs seized, possession of a weapon, and lack of a pipe or other smoking device that a user would possess. The court concluded: "[T]his testimony merely explained [the expert's] analysis of the facts supporting the inference of an intention to distribute, without directly addressing the issue of Brown's actual mental state."[166]

Similarly, in *United States v. Lipscomb*[167] the Seventh Circuit upheld police expert testimony that seized cocaine was for street level distribution. After acknowledging problems of unfair prejudice when an officer performs the dual role of eyewitness and expert, the court stated:

> [W]hen a law enforcement official states an opinion about the criminal nature of a defendant's activities, such testimony should not be excluded under Rule 704(b) as long as it is made clear, either by the court expressly or in the nature of the examination, that the opinion is based on the expert's knowledge of common criminal practices, and not on some special knowledge of the defendant's mental processes. Relevant in this regard, though not determinative, is the degree to which the expert refers specifically to the "intent" of the defendant....[168]

Some courts have drawn a line between "predicate" matters and ultimate issues. For example, the First Circuit has written: "Though Rule 704(b) bars experts from opining on the ultimate issue of a defendant's felonious intent, the rule does not prohibit experts from testifying to predicate facts from which a jury might infer such intent."[169]

---

743 (7th Cir.) ("While complicated hypothetical questions that restate the legal test for sanity are therefore not allowed, questions regarding the presence of a mental disorder or the characteristics of the disease are clearly allowed"), *cert. denied*, 510 U.S. 971 (1993).

165. 7 F.3d 648 (7th Cir. 1993).

166. *Id.* at 653.

167. 14 F.3d 1236 (7th Cir. 1994).

168. *Id.* at 1242. *See also* United States v. Denniso, 937 F.2d 559, 565 (10th Cir. 1991) ("[The defense expert's] testimony— that alcohol and drug consumption by a person with borderline personality disorder renders that person incapable of forming specific intent — is the type of opinion or inference testimony Rule 704(b) is intended to exclude"), *cert. denied,* 502 U.S. 1037 (1992).

169. United States v. Valle, 72 F.3d 210, 215-16 (1st Cir. 1995). *See also* United States v. Morales, 108 F.3d 1031, 1036 (9th Cir. 1997) ("[The accountant] was not going to state an opinion or draw an inference that Morales did not intend to make false entries [the ultimate issue]. Rather, she was going to state her opinion as to a predicated matter — that Morales had a weak grasp of bookkeeping principles"); United States v. Torres, 53 F.3d 1129, 1141 (10th Cir.) (permissible in a

The D.C. Circuit has ruled, however, that there is a line beyond which expert testimony may not cross:

> This court has never held that the Government may simply recite a list of "hypothetical" facts that exactly mirror the case at hand and then ask an expert to give an opinion as to whether such facts provide an intention to distribute narcotics.... [T]he prosecutor simply restated the facts of this case in his question to Officer Stroud, and, although termed a hypothetical, that question was plainly designed to elicit the expert's testimony about the *intent of the defendant.* Thus, when Officer Stroud responded that the hypothetical subject's possession of the crack cocaine was consistent with "intent to distribute," the admission of that testimony clearly violated Rule 704(b)....[170]

In a different case, the D.C. Circuit ruled that evidence of a defendant's mental retardation is admissible if offered to negate the specific intent required for conspiracy. "The distinction between evidence of a defendant's general 'ability to form a certain intent' and evidence of his intent at the time of the crime, however, is not particularly helpful: Both types of evidence may be relevant to the jury's consideration of whether the government proved that the defendant entertained the requisite intent."[171]

§ 5-8. Experiments.

Expert testimony is often based on experiments, typically out-of-court experiments. Generally, testimony based on an out-of-court experiment is admissible if the experiment is conducted under the same or substantially similar circumstances as those involved in the case.[172]

For example, the results of shotgun tests conducted to determine muzzle-to-target distance have been admitted in evidence.[173] When a shot shell is fired, the

---

drug case to permit IRS agent, after reviewing records, to testify that "defendants' income could not be traced to a legitimate, legal source of income"), *cert. denied*, 515 U.S. 1152 (1995).

170. United States v. Boyd, 55 F.3d 667, 672 (D.C. Cir. 1995).

171. United States v. Childress, 58 F.3d 693, 730 (D.C. Cir. 1995), *cert. denied*, 516 U.S. 1098 (1996).

172. *E.g.*, Persian Galleries, Inc. v. Transcontinental Ins. Co., 38 F.3d 253, 258 (6th Cir. 1994) ("Because the videotaped experiment was substantially similar to the actual conditions at the burglary scene, the district court did not abuse its discretion ..."); Cowens v. Siemens-Elema AB, 837 F.2d 817, 820 (8th Cir. 1988); United States v. Metzger, 778 F.2d 1195, 1204 (6th Cir. 1985), *cert. denied,* 477 U.S. 906 (1986); Robbins v. Whelan, 653 F.2d 47, 49-50 (1st Cir.), *cert. denied,* 454 U.S. 1123 (1981); Jackson v. Fletcher, 647 F.2d 1020, 1026-27 (10th Cir. 1981); Hall v. General Motors Corp., 647 F.2d 175, 180-81 (D.C. Cir. 1980).

173. *E.g.*, West v. State, 200 Ga. 566, 571, 37 S.E.2d 799, 801-02 (1946); State v. Tourville, 295 S.W.2d 1, 6-7 (Mo. 1956), *cert. denied*, 352 U.S. 1018 (1957); State v. Bates, 48 Ohio St. 2d

pellets generally emerge from the muzzle grouped together and then disperse in an ever-increasing pattern as the distance from the muzzle increases. The closer the shotgun is to the target, the smaller the dispersion pattern. By firing a shotgun at different distances, the dispersion pattern for a particular distance may be ascertained and compared to the dispersion pattern present at the crime scene. As one court has commented:

> The results of tests to determine the distance from which a weapon had been fired are admissible into evidence provided the test was conducted under conditions sufficiently similar to the actual conditions involved in the case that they can be fairly said to have probative value and will enlighten, not confuse, the jury.[174]

The relevancy of these experiments depends on the extent to which the conditions existing at the crime can be replicated in the experiment. Because the dispersion pattern differs for different shotguns and different types of ammunition, the identical weapon and the same type of ammunition used in the crime typically are required for this type of test. If the conditions are not substantially similar, the results are not admissible.[175] For example, some courts have excluded dispersion pattern tests on the ground that the target material used in the test was not shown to be similar to human skin tissue.[176] In contrast, other courts have held that admissibility is not affected by this factor.[177]

Under the Federal Rules of Evidence, the admissibility of evidence of out-of-court experiments is governed by Rules 401 to 403, namely, whether the probative value of the evidence is substantially outweighed by the danger of misleading the jury.[178] Note, however, that the "substantially similar standard is a flexible one which, even when construed strictly, does not require that all variables be controlled."[179]

The Tenth Circuit has distinguished between different types of experiments. The court has written:

315, 321-22, 358 N.E.2d 584, 588-89 (1976), *vacated on other grounds*, 438 U.S. 910 (1978); Andrews v. State, 555 P.2d 1079, 1083-84 (Okla. Crim. App. 1976); Williams v. State, 147 Tex. Crim. 178, 184, 179 S.W.2d 297, 300 (1944). For a further discussion of this issue, *see* Chapter 14.

174. Andrews v. State, 555 P.2d 1079, 1083 (Okla. Crim. App. 1976).

175. *E.g.*, Miller v. State, 250 Ind. 656, 236 N.E.2d 585 (1968); Roberts v. State, 117 Tex. Crim. 418, 424-25, 35 S.W.2d 175, 178 (1931).

176. *E.g.*, Roberts v. State, 189 So. 2d 543, 546 (Fla. App. 1966); People v. Cohen, 50 N.Y.2d 908, 409 N.E.2d 921, 431 N.Y.S.2d 446 (1980).

177. *E.g.*, State v. Brooks, 16 Wash. App. 535, 540, 557 P.2d 362, 366 (1976).

178. *See generally* 2 J. WIGMORE, EVIDENCE §§445-60 (Chadbourn rev. 1979).

179. United States v. Metzger, 778 F.2d 1195, 1204 (6th Cir. 1985), *cert. denied,* 477 U.S. 906 (1986). *See also* Persian Galleries, Inc. v. Transcontinental Ins. Co., 38 F.3d 253, 258 (6th Cir. 1994) ("Because the videotaped experiment was substantially similar to the actual conditions at the burglary scene, the district court did not abuse its discretion ...").

> As a general rule, the proponent seeking to admit out-of-court experiments into evidence must demonstrate a "'similarity of circumstances and conditions'" between the tests and the subject of litigation.... "The purpose of the rule is to prevent confusion of the jury...." A recognized exception to this rule exists when the experiment merely illustrates principles used to form an expert opinion.... Therefore, experiments which purport to recreate an accident must be conducted under conditions similar to that accident, while experiments which demonstrate general principles used in forming an expert's opinion are not required to adhere strictly to the conditions of the accident.[180]

The Eighth Circuit recognized that in many cases the "distinction between evidence offered as a reconstruction of the accident and evidence offered to demonstrate scientific principles is very difficult to draw."[181] Nevertheless, the court also wrote:

> [E]xperimental evidence falls on a spectrum and the foundational standard for its admissibility is determined by whether the evidence is closer to simulating the accident or to demonstrating abstract scientific principles. The closer the experiment gets to simulating the accident, the more similar the conditions of the experiment must be to the accident conditions.[182]

§ 5-9. Learned Treatises.

Learned treatises are frequently used in conjunction with expert testimony.[183] In all jurisdictions an expert may be impeached with a learned treatise. There is, however, disagreement as to the conditions under which a treatise may be used for this purpose. Some jurisdictions allow this method of impeachment only when the expert *relies* on the treatise in reaching her opinion. Other jurisdictions permit impeachment if the expert *recognizes* the treatise as an authoritative work, even though the expert did not rely on it. Still other jurisdictions permit impeachment if the treatise is established as a recognized authority *by any means,* including the testimony of other experts or by judicial notice.[184]

---

180. Gilbert v. Cosco, Inc., 989 F.2d 399, 402 (10th Cir. 1993).

181. McKnight v. Johnson Controls, Inc., 36 F.3d 1396, 1402 (8th Cir. 1994).

182. *Id.* (citation omitted).

183. *See generally* 2 C. McCormick, *supra* note 91, § 321; 6 J. Wigmore, Evidence §§ 1690-1700 (Chadbourn rev. 1976); People v. Jakupcak, 275 Ill. App. 3d 830, 837, 656 N.E.2d 442, 488 (1995) ("[The expert] acknowledged, on cross examination, that the traffic reconstruction manual published by the Northwestern University Traffic Institute is an authoritative manual or treatise in the field of accident reconstruction").

184. *See* Fed. R. Evid. 803(18) advisory committee's note.

Under the traditional view, a learned treatise is admissible only for impeachment.[185] Accordingly, the jury's use of a treatise as substantive evidence violates the hearsay rule. In contrast, Federal Rule of Evidence 803(18) recognizes a hearsay exception for learned treatises,[186] thus permitting their substantive use. According to the federal drafters, the "hearsay objection must be regarded as unimpressive when directed against treatises since a high standard of accuracy is engendered by various factors: the treatise is written primarily and impartially for professionals, subject to scrutiny and exposure for inaccuracy, with the reputation of the writer at stake."[187]

There are two limitations recognized by the federal rule. First, a treatise may be used substantively only when an expert is on the stand.[188] This requirement provides an important safeguard because it ensures that a knowledgeable person is available "to explain and assist in the application of the treatise."[189] Second, the treatise may be read to the jury but not received as an exhibit, thus precluding its misuse in the jury room.[190]

§ 5-10. Attorney-Client Privilege.

The attorney-client privilege[191] is designed to protect confidential communications between a client and the attorney. As the Supreme Court has

---

185. Many jurisdictions still follow the traditional rule. *E.g.,* MICH. R. EVID. 707 (treatises "admissible for impeachment purposes only"); OHIO R. EVID. 706 (impeachment only).

186. FED. R.EVID. 803(18) provides:

> To the extent called to the attention of an expert witness upon cross-examination or relied upon by the expert witness in direct examination, statements contained in published treatises, periodicals, or pamphlets on a subject of history, medicine, or other science or art, established as a reliable authority by the testimony or admission of the witness or by other expert testimony or by judicial notice. If admitted, the statements may be read into evidence but may not be received as exhibits.

Although the federal rule is progressive when judged by American standards, it is narrower than the exception recognized in other common-law jurisdictions. *See* Imwinkelried, *A Comparativist Critique of the Interface Between Hearsay and Expert Opinion in American Evidence Law*, 33 B.C. L. REV. 1, 20-22 (1991).

187. FED. R. EVID. 803(18) advisory committee's note.

188. *See* United States v. An Article of Drug, 661 F.3d 742, 745 (9th Cir. 1981) (treatise read by expert during direct examination); Zwack v. State, 757 S.W.2d 66, 67-69 (Tex. App. 1988) (improper to read treatise in absence of an expert).

189. FED. R. EVID. 803(18) advisory committee's note. *See* United States v. Turner, 104 F.3d 217, 221 (8th Cir. 1997) ("In the present case, there was no expert testimony establishing the texts as authoritative").

190. *See* Graham v. Wyeth Labs., 906 F.2d 1399, 1414 (10th Cir.) (permitting treatise in jury room raises danger that jurors will be unduly impressed by treatise), *cert. denied,* 498 U.S. 981 (1990).

191. *See generally* 8 J. WIGMORE, EVIDENCE §§ 2290-2329 (McNaughton rev. 1961).

noted: "Its purpose is to encourage full and frank communication between attorneys and their clients and thereby promote broader public interests in the observance of law and administration of justice. The privilege recognizes that sound legal advice or advocacy serves public ends and that such advice or advocacy depends upon the lawyer being fully informed by the client."[192]

Application of the attorney-client privilege to expert witnesses sometimes arises in scientific evidence cases.[193] Two different uses of experts must be distinguished. First, an expert may be retained for the purpose of testifying at trial. In this situation, the privilege is waived.[194] A "party ought not to be permitted to thwart effective cross-examination of a material witness whom he will call at trial merely by invoking the attorney-client privilege to prohibit pretrial discovery."[195]

Second, an expert may be retained for the purpose of consultation; that is, to provide the attorney with information needed to determine whether a scientific defense is feasible. If such an expert provides an adverse opinion and the defense nevertheless desires to proceed with the defense, typically through the use of other experts, the question arises whether the attorney-client privilege precludes the prosecution from calling the defense-retained expert as a government witness.[196]

Numerous courts have held that the attorney-client privilege covers communications made to an attorney by an expert retained for the purpose of

---

192. Upjohn Co. v. United States, 449 U.S. 383, 389 (1981). *See also* Fisher v. United States, 425 U.S. 391, 403 (1976) ("The purpose of the privilege is to encourage clients to make full disclosure to their attorneys").

193. If the expert is a physician or psychotherapist, the application of a separate privilege may be raised. Many jurisdictions recognize a physician-patient privilege, and some recognize a psychotherapist-patient privilege. However, these privileges are not always applicable for several reasons. Many jurisdictions limit these privileges to civil cases. Others limit them to situations where the patient consults the physician for the purpose of treatment. Finally, others hold the privilege waived under a patient-litigant exception.

194. *See* United States v. Alvarez, 519 F.2d 1036, 1046-47 (3d Cir. 1975); Pouncy v. State, 353 So. 2d 640, 642 (Fla. App. 1977); State v. Mingo, 77 N.J. 576, 584, 392 A.2d 590, 595 (1978). *See also* United States v. Nobles, 422 U.S. 225, 239 (1975) ("Respondent, by electing to present the investigator as a witness, waived the [work product] privilege with respect to matters covered in his testimony").

195. Friedenthal, *Discovery and Use of an Adverse Party's Expert Information*, 14 STAN. L. REV. 455, 464-65 (1962).

196. *See generally* Imwinkelried, *The Applicability of the Attorney-Client Privilege to Non-Testifying Experts: Reestablishing the Boundaries Between the Attorney-Client Privilege and the Work Product Protection*, 68 WASH. L.Q. 19, 21-23 (1990); Saltzburg, *Privileges and Professionals: Lawyers and Psychiatrists*, 66 VA. L. REV. 597 (1980); Note, *Discovery of Attorney-Expert Communications: Current State of, and Suggestions for, Federal and Missouri Practice*, 57 MO. L. REV. 247 (1992) (civil rules); Note, *Protecting the Confidentiality of Pretrial Psychiatric Disclosures: A Survey of Standards*, 51 N.Y.U. L. REV. 409 (1976); Annot., *Compelling Testimony of Opponent's Expert in State Court*, 66 A.L.R.4TH 213 (1988).

providing information necessary for proper representation.[197] This appears to be the majority view.[198] The argument supporting this rule rests on the attorney's need to obtain expert advice. As one court has stated: "Only a foolhardy lawyer would determine tactical and evidentiary strategy in a case with psychiatric issues without the guidance and interpretation of psychiatrists and others skilled in this field."[199] An attorney, however, might not seek such assistance if an expert's adverse opinion could be introduced by the prosecution: "Breaching the attorney-client privilege ... would have the effect of inhibiting the free exercise of a defense attorney's informed judgment by confronting him with the likelihood that, in taking a step obviously crucial to his client's defense, he is creating a potential government witness who theretofore did not exist."[200]

Other courts have rejected the extension of the attorney-client privilege in this context, although their reasons vary. First, some courts limit the privilege to

---

197. *E.g.,* United States v. Alvarez, 519 F.2d 1036, 1046-47 (3d Cir. 1975) (psychiatrist); United States v. Kovel, 296 F.2d 918, 921-22 (2d Cir. 1961) (accountant); United States v. Layton, 90 F.R.D. 520, 525 (N.D. Cal. 1981); (psychiatrist); Bailey v. Meister Brau, Inc., 57 F.R.D. 11, 13 (N.D. Ill. 1972) (financial expert); Houston v. State, 602 P.2d 784, 791 (Alaska 1979) (psychiatrist); People v. Lines, 13 Cal. 3d 500, 514-15, 531 P.2d 793, 802-03, 119 Cal. Rptr. 225, 234-35 (1975) (psychiatrist); Miller v. District Court, 737 P.2d 834 (Colo. 1987) (psychiatrist); Pouncy v. State, 353 So. 2d 640, 642 (Fla. App. 1977) (psychiatrist); People v. Knippenberg, 66 Ill. 2d 276, 283-84, 362 N.E.2d 681, 684 (1977) (investigator); State v. Pratt, 284 Md. 516, 520-22, 398 A.2d 421, 423-24 (1979) (psychiatrist); People v. Hilliker, 29 Mich. App. 543, 546-47, 185 N.W.2d 831, 833-34 (1971) (psychiatrist); State v. Kociolek, 23 N.J. 400, 411-16, 129 A.2d 417, 423-25 (1957) (psychiatrist); State v. Hitopoulus, 279 S.C. 549, 550-51, 309 S.E.2d 747, 748-49 (1983); Commonwealth v. Noll, 443 Pa. Super. 602, 607, 662 A.2d 1123, 1126 (1995) ("[T]he information gathered by [the accident reconstructionist] should be protected by the attorney work product doctrine and the attorney-client privilege"), *app. denied,* 543 Pa. 726, 673 A.2d 333 (1996); State v. Thompson, 329 S.C. 72, 495 S.E.2d 437 (1998) (attorney-client privilege extends to communications between the client and a psychiatrist retained to aid the preparation of a case). *See generally* Annot., *Applicability of Attorney-Client Privilege to Communications Made in Presence of or Solely to or by Third Person,* 14 A.L.R.4TH 594 (1982).

Proposed Federal Rule of Evidence 503, which was not adopted by Congress, also extends the privilege to nontestifying experts. Subdivision (4) defines a representative of an attorney as "one employed to assist the lawyer in the rendition of professional legal services." The Advisory Committee's Note states that this "definition includes an expert employed to assist in rendering legal advice." Advisory Committee's Note, Proposed FED. R. EVID. 503, *reprinted in* 51 F.R.D. 315, 363 (1971).

The ABA CRIMINAL JUSTICE MENTAL HEALTH STANDARDS (1989) adopt the same position. Standard 7-3.3 (b). The Standards restrict prosecutorial access to the results of defense-initiated mental health evaluations of the defendant whenever the defendant does not intend to call the expert as a witness.

198. *See* State v. Pratt, 284 Md. 516, 520, 398 A.2d 421, 423 (1979) (This view is "almost universally accepted").

199. United States *ex rel.* Edney v. Smith, 425 F. Supp. 1038, 1047 (E.D.N.Y. 1976), *aff'd,* 556 F.2d 556 (2d Cir.), *cert. denied,* 431 U.S. 958 (1977).

200. State v. Pratt, 284 Md. 516, 524, 398 A.2d 421, 426 (1979).

communications between the attorney and client. Under this view, experts and other agents are not covered by the privilege.[201] Second, other courts hold that the privilege extends only to confidential communications and thus does not apply to experts who do not rely on the client's confidential communications in reaching their opinions. Under this view, a psychiatrist may be protected by the privilege[202] but not a fingerprint,[203] questioned document expert,[204] or medical examiner.[205] Third, still other courts hold that the privilege is waived when the defense introduces scientific evidence. Accordingly, a defendant who raises an insanity defense waives the privilege with respect to all psychiatrists who have examined the defendant.[206]

---

201. *E.g.,* State v. Carter, 641 S.W.2d 54, 57 (Mo. 1982), *cert. denied,* 461 U.S. 932 (1983); State v. Hamlet, 133 Wash. 2d 314, 323, 944 P.2d 1026, 1031 (1997) ("[N]either the attorney-client privilege nor the Sixth Amendment right to counsel is violated by the ordered disclosure of the name of the nontestifying expert retained by the defense for purposes of a diminished capacity defense ... nor by the State calling that expert as a State's witness to rebut evidence of a diminished capacity defense"). *See also* State v. Schaaf, 169 Ariz. 323, 332, 819 P.2d 909, 918 (1991) ("Even if defendant had not waived this right, we find it to be within the trial court's broad discretion to determine whether an expert witness will be required to testify, even if it was the other party who initially retained the expert witness"), *cert. denied,* 516 U.S. 1129 (1996).

202. In People v. Knuckles, 165 Ill. 2d 125, 650 N.E.2d 974 (1995), the crime was committed nine years earlier, and the defense psychiatrist was the only expert who had examined the accused at that time. First, the court ruled that the attorney-client privilege covered a mental health professional. The scope of the privilege had to be extended to "meet the complexities of modern legal practice." This rule is also supported by an "effective assistance of counsel" argument. Second, the court rejected an automatic waiver rule, under which the privilege is waived if the defendant "puts his mental state in issue." The court held that the privilege is waived only with respect to the testimony and reports of those experts who will testify. Third, the court rejected creating a "public interest" exception for this case.

203. *See* People v. Speck, 41 Ill. 2d 177, 200-01, 242 N.E.2d 208, 221 (1968).

204. *See* United States v. Pipkins, 528 F.2d 559, 563-64 (5th Cir.) (handwriting exemplars given to expert by attorney not within privilege), *cert. denied,* 426 U.S. 952 (1976). *See also* Morris v. State, 59 Md. App. 659, 669, 477 A.2d 1206, 1211 (1984).

205. Rose v. State, 591 So. 2d 195, 197 (Fla. App. 1991) (medical examiner initially hired by the defense) ("[T]he assertion of the privilege in the psychiatric witness cases is based on the confidential communications which may be made to the psychiatrist"). *See also* State v. Richey, 64 Ohio St. 3d 353, 360, 595 N.E.2d 915, 922 (1992) ("Although the prosecutor's use of a defense expert may violate an accused's attorney-client privilege, [the arson expert] did not disclose or rely upon any confidential communications here"), *cert. denied,* 507 U.S. 989 (1993).

206. *See* Gray v. District Court, 884 P.2d 286, 293 (Colo. 1994) (en banc) ("[W]here a defendant tenders his or her mental condition as an issue in the trial, the defendant waives the right to claim the attorney-client and physician/psychologist-patient privileges, and a prosecution's use of testimony of a defense-retained psychiatrist, who is not called by the defendant to testify at trial, is admissible at trial"), *cert. denied,* 514 U.S. 1084 (1995); State v. Carter, 641 S.W.2d 54, 57 (Mo. 1982); People v. Edney, 39 N.Y.2d 620, 624-25, 350 N.E.2d 400, 402-03, 385 N.Y.S.2d 23, 25-26 (1976); State v. Pawlyk, 115 Wash. 2d 457, 470-73, 800 P.2d 338, 345-46 (1990) ("[T]he attorney-client privilege does not extend to the testimony of a psychiatrist" when a defendant raises an insanity defense).

One commentator has argued that the privilege should not be extended to experts because such an approach would convert the narrow privilege into a broad rule of incompetency. Instead, the work product rule should preclude access to a defense expert's opinion unless a substantial showing of need is demonstrated.[207]

Right to Counsel

In addition to the attorney-client privilege, defendants have argued that the sixth amendment right to effective assistance of counsel precludes the use of defense-retained experts by the prosecution. Several courts have accepted this argument:

> A defense attorney should be completely free and unfettered in making a decision as fundamental as that concerning the retention of an expert to assist him. Reliance upon the confidentiality of an expert's advice itself is a crucial aspect of a defense attorney's ability to consult with and advise his client. If the confidentiality of that advice cannot be anticipated, the attorney might well forgo seeking such assistance, to the consequent detriment of his client's cause.[208]

Similarly, a commentator has argued that a "rule allowing any incriminating information developed during defense preparation to be used against the defendant would impair both a vigorous defense effort, which is central to the

---

But see United States v. Alvarez, 519 F.2d 1036, 1046 (3d Cir. 1975); Houston v. State, 602 P.2d 784, 791 (Alaska 1979); State v. Pratt, 284 Md. 516, 522, 398 A.2d 421, 424 (1979).

See also Woods v. Superior Court, 25 Cal. App. 4th 178, 187, 30 Cal. Rptr. 2d 182, 187 (1994) ("[W]hile communications with an expert retained to assist in the preparation of a defense may initially be protected by the attorney-client privilege, the privilege is waived where as here the expert is identified, a substantial portion of his otherwise privileged evaluation is disclosed in his report, and the report is released"), *rev. denied*, 1994 Cal. LEXIS 4376 (Cal. Aug. 11, 1994).

207. Imwinkelried, *The Applicability of the Attorney-Client Privilege to Non-Testifying Experts: Reestablishing the Boundaries Between the Attorney-Client Privilege and the Work Product Protection*, 68 WASH. L.Q. 19 (1990). *See also* Mosteller, *Discovery Against the Defense: Tilting the Adversarial Balance*, 74 CALIF. L. REV. 1567, 1657-64 (1986); Note, *Must the Show Go On? Defining When One Party May Call or Compel an Opposing Party's Consultative Expert to Testify*, 78 MINN. L. REV. 1191, 1218 (1994) (Proposing a new evidence rule to "allow experts retained as nontestifying witnesses to testify at trial for the adverse party if the proffering party demonstrates a reasonable need for the testimony"). For a further discussion of the work-product rule, *see* Chapter 3 (§ 3.20).

208. State v. Mingo, 77 N.J. 576, 587, 392 A.2d 590, 595 (1978) (handwriting expert). *See also* United States v. Alvarez, 519 F.2d 1036, 1046 (3d Cir. 1975) (psychiatrist); Perez v. People, 745 P.2d 650, 652 (Colo. 1987) (handwriting expert); Hutchinson v. People, 742 P.2d 875, 881 (Colo. 1987) (handwriting expert) ("[A] defense counsel's access to expert assistance is a crucial element in assuring a defendant's right to effective legal assistance ..."); People v. Knippenberg, 66 Ill. 2d 276, 283-85, 362 N.E.2d 681, 684-85 (1977) (investigator).

adversary system, and the defendant-counsel relationship."[209] Notwithstanding the persuasiveness of this argument, some courts have rejected it.[210]

In *Gray v. District Court*,[211] the Colorado Supreme Court distinguished its earlier case, *Hutchinson v. People*,[212] which found a sixth amendment violation where the prosecution used a defense-retained handwriting expert. *Gray* involved an insanity defense, a critical difference in the Court's view: "[P]olicy considerations dictate full disclosure of mental evaluations performed by psychiatrists originally retained by the defense where a defendant asserts a mental status defense, since, unlike a trial to establish guilt, a defendant is the sole source of evidence concerning his mental condition."[213]

In *State v. DeMarco*,[214] a N.J. appellate court ruled that the prosecution may not compel discovery of DNA reports prepared by the defendant's expert witness for other clients in unrelated cases. The prosecution issued a subpoena for all of Dr. Blake's DNA reports that indicated the existence of unexplained contamination. The court indicated that the work-product rule would not apply and that applying the attorney-client privilege to reports generated outside of New Jersey would be problematic. Nevertheless, the court issued a protective order under its discovery rule.

> Although we do not determine the applicability of the privileges or *Mingo's* Sixth Amendment analysis, their underlying policies inform our view of the issue. Dr. Blake's reports contain private and critical information which

---

209. Mosteller, *supra* note 207, at 1668. *See also* 2 W. LaFave & J. Israel, Criminal Procedure §19.4, at 526 (1984) ("[R]equiring disclosure of scientific tests that the defendant does not intend to use may be viewed as an interference with effective assistance of counsel").

210. *E.g.*, Noggle v. Marshall, 706 F.2d 1408, 1414-15 (6th Cir. 1983); Granviel v. Estelle, 655 F.2d 673, 683 (5th Cir. 1981), *cert. denied*, 455 U.S. 1003 (1982); United States *ex rel.* Edney v. Smith, 425 F. Supp. 1038, 1054-55 (E.D.N.Y. 1976), *aff'd*, 556 F.2d 556 (2d Cir.), *cert. denied*, 431 U.S. 958 (1977); State v. McDaniel, 485 N.W.2d 630, 633 (Iowa 1992) (prosecution use of defense appointed expert did not violate due process or effective assistance of counsel); State v. Craney, 347 N.W.2d 668, 676-77 (Iowa), *cert. denied*, 469 U.S. 884 (1984); State v. Schneider, 402 N.W.2d 779, 786-88 (Minn. 1987); State v. Dodis, 314 N.W.2d 233, 240-41 (Minn. 1982); State v. Carter, 641 S.W.2d 54, 59 (Mo. 1982), *cert. denied*, 461 U.S. 932 (1983); Haynes v. State, 103 Nev. 309, 316-18, 739 P.2d 497, 502-03 (1987) (defense-retained psychiatrist); State v. Richey, 64 Ohio St. 3d 353, 360, 595 N.E.2d 915, 922 (1992) ("The prosecutor's use of a defense expert does not violate an accused's Sixth Amendment right to counsel"), *cert. denied*, 507 U.S. 989 (1993); State v. Hamlet, 133 Wash. d 314, 323, 944 P.2d 1026, 1031 (1997) ("[N]either the attorney-client privilege nor the Sixth Amendment right to counsel is violated by the ordered disclosure of the name of the nontestifying expert retained by the defense for purposes of a diminished capacity defense ... nor by the State calling that expert as a State's witness to rebut evidence of a diminished capacity defense"); State v. Pawlyk, 115 Wash. 2d 457, 470-73, 800 P.2d 338, 345-46 (1990).

211. 884 P.2d 286 (Colo. 1994) (en banc), *cert. denied*, 115 S. Ct. 1797 (1995).

212. 742 P.2d 875 (Colo. 1987).

213. 884 P.2d at 295.

214. 275 N.J. Super. 311, 646 A.2d 431 (1994) (per curiam).

should be shielded from undue public exposure. Moreover, litigators, public and private, should have access to the assistance of retained experts with a minimum of risk that their reports, which otherwise have not been placed in the public domain, will surface in unrelated litigation.[215]

§ 5-11. Selected Bibliography.

2 J. WIGMORE, EVIDENCE §§ 555-71, 672-86 (Chadbourn rev. 1979).

Berger, *United States v. Scop: The Common-Law Approach to an Expert's Opinion About a Witness's Credibility Still Does Not Work*, 55 BROOKLYN L. REV. 559 (1989).

Carlson, *Policing the Bases of Modern Expert Testimony*, 39 VAND. L. REV. 577 (1986).

Carlson, *Experts as Hearsay Conduits: Confrontation Abuses in Opinion Testimony*, 76 MINN. L. REV. 859 (1992).

Carlson, *Experts, Judges, and Commentators: The Underlying Debate About an Expert's Underlying Data*, 47 MERCER L. REV. 481 (1996).

Faigman, *Struggling to Stop the Flood of Unreliable Expert Testimony*, 76 MINN. L. REV. 877 (1992).

Graham, *Expert Witness Testimony and the Federal Rules of Evidence: Insuring Adequate Assurance of Trustworthiness*, 1986 U. ILL. L. REV. 43.

Gross, *Expert Evidence*, 1991 WIS. L. REV. 1113.

Imwinkelried, *The "Bases" of Expert Testimony: The Syllogistic Structure of Scientific Testimony*, 67 N.C. L. REV. 1 (1988).

Imwinkelried, *The Applicability of the Attorney-Client Privilege to Non-Testifying Experts: Reestablishing the Boundaries Between the Attorney-Client Privilege and the Work Product Protection*, 68 WASH. L.Q. 19 (1990).

Imwinkelried, *The Meaning of "Facts or Data" in Federal Rule of Evidence 703: The Significance of the Supreme Court's Decision to Rely on Federal Rule 702 in Daubert v. Merrell Dow Pharmaceuticals, Inc.*, 54 MD. L. REV. 352 (1995).

Rice, *Expert Testimony: A Debate Between Logic or Tradition Rather Than Between Deference or Education*, 87 NW. U. L. REV. 1166 (1993).

Rice, *Inadmissible Evidence as a Basis for Expert Opinion Testimony: A Response to Professor Carlson*, 40 VAND. L. REV. 583 (1987).

Weinstein, *Improving Expert Testimony*, 20 U. RICH. L. REV. 473 (1986).

Note, *The Admissibility of Ultimate Issue Expert Testimony by Law Enforcement Officers in Criminal Trials*, 93 COLUM. L. REV. 231 (1993).

Note, *Witness for the Prosecution: Prosecutorial Discovery of Information Generated by Non-Testifying Defense Psychiatric Experts*, 62 FORDHAM L. REV. 653 (1993).

---

215. *Id.* at 322, 646 A.2d at 436-37.

CHAPTER 6

LABORATORY REPORTS

§ 6-1. In General.

Frequently, the most expedient way to introduce scientific evidence at trial is through the admission of a laboratory report. The results of drug analyses,[1] fingerprint examinations,[2] intoxication tests,[3] rape victim examinations,[4] and various other scientific techniques[5] have been admitted in this fashion. Similarly, pathological findings have been introduced through autopsy reports.[6] Some of these reports have been prepared by public agencies, such as police crime

---

1. *E.g.*, United States v. Frattini, 501 F.2d 1234, 1235-36 (2d Cir. 1974) (cocaine); United States v. Parker, 491 F.2d 517, 520-21 (8th Cir. 1973) (heroin), *cert. denied*, 416 U.S. 989 (1974).

2. *E.g.*, United States v. Taylor, 4 U.S.C.M.A. 232, 238-39, 15 C.M.R. 232, 238-39 (C.M.A. 1954).

3. *E.g.*, Kay v. United States, 255 F.2d 476, 480 (4th Cir.) (certificate of blood alcohol test), *cert. denied,* 358 U.S. 825 (1958); State v. Smith, 312 N.C. 361, 381, 323 S.E.2d 316, 318 (1984) (affidavit of breath tests results).

4. *E.g.*, Government of Virgin Islands v. St. Ange, 458 F.2d 981, 82 (3d Cir. 1972) (hospital lab report identifying sperm on vaginal smear); Henson v. State, 332 A.2d 773, 775 (Del. 1975) (hospital record of rape victim examination).

5. *E.g.*, Hardy v. State, 53 Ala. App. 75, 78, 297 So. 2d 399, 402 (1974) (firearms identification report); State v. Taylor, 486 S.W.2d 239, 242 (Mo. 1972) (lab report of examination of burglary debris).

6. *E.g.*, Grover v. State, 41 Md. App. 705, 710-11, 398 A.2d 528, 531 (1979); Burleson v. State, 585 S.W.2d 711, 712-13 (Tex. Crim. App. 1979).

laboratories and medical examiner offices.[7] Others have been prepared by private hospitals.[8]

Refreshing Recollection

The admissibility of laboratory and autopsy reports at trial may raise a number of evidentiary issues. If the analyst testifies, he may use the laboratory report to refresh his recollection.[9] In this situation, however, the analyst's in-court testimony and not the laboratory report is the evidence. The report may be introduced in evidence for impeachment only if offered by the opposing party.[10]

Authentication

The admission of a laboratory report in lieu of the analyst's testimony presents different issues. First, the report must be authenticated.[11] Since, however, most laboratory reports in criminal cases are prepared by government laboratories, they often qualify as self-authenticating documents and thus may be admitted without the testimony of an authenticating witness.[12]

---

7. *E.g.*, United States v. Parker, 491 F.2d 517, 520-21 (8th Cir. 1973) (Bureau of Narcotics and Dangerous Drugs laboratory), *cert. denied,* 416 U.S. 989 (1974); Robertson v. Cox, 320 F. Supp. 900, 900 (W.D. Va. 1970) (medical examiner's office).

8. *See supra* note 4.

9. *E.g.*, United States v. Franklin, 747 F.2d 497, 498 (8th Cir. 1984) (chemists refreshed recollection prior to trial by reviewing reports prepared at the time cocaine tested). *See generally* 1 E. IMWINKELRIED, P. GIANNELLI, F. GILLIGAN & F. LEDERER, COURTROOM CRIMINAL EVIDENCE § 1217 (3d ed. 1998).

10. *See* FED. R. EVID. 612 ("[A]n adverse party is entitled to have the writing produced at the hearing, to inspect it, to cross-examine the witness thereon, and to introduce in evidence those portions which relate to the testimony of the witness").

11. *See* State v. Kraft, 134 N.J. Super. 416, 418, 341 A.2d 373, 374 (1975) (laboratory report not authenticated); Commonwealth v. Cummings, 338 Pa. Super. 149, 153, 487 A.2d 897 (1985) (certificate of accuracy for stopwatch not authenticated). *See generally* 1 E. IMWINKELRIED, P. GIANNELLI, F. GILLIGAN & F. LEDERER, *supra* note 9, ch. 4.

12. *See* FED. R. EVID. 902. *See also* United States v. Davis, 14 M.J. 847, 849 n.2 (A.C.M.R. 1982) ("A laboratory report may also be admitted as an official record when it is accompanied by an authenticating certificate"); Ealy v. State, 685 N.E.2d 1047, 1050 (Ind. 1997) ("Defendant argues that even if the autopsy report was self-authenticating, this, in and of itself, does not provide an exception to the hearsay rules. This is correct. Self-authentication merely relieves the proponent from providing foundational testimony; it is not a hearsay exception").

Best Evidence Rule

Second, the original writing ("best evidence") rule requires that the original be produced or accounted for.[13] An exception, however, is typically recognized for public records, under which certified copies of public records are admissible.[14]

Hearsay and Confrontation

The most serious obstacle to the admission of laboratory reports is the hearsay rule,[15] an issue which typically involves the applicability of the public records, business records, or recorded recollection exceptions. In addition, the admission of these reports against an accused raises confrontation issues. These issues are discussed *infra*.

Foundational Rulings

The analysis of the evidentiary and constitutional issues may differ depending on the purpose for which a laboratory report is offered. If the report is offered on the merits — to establish an essential element of the charged offense — the hearsay and confrontation problems become critical. A laboratory report identifying a substance as cocaine is an example. Sometimes, however, a report is not offered on the merits but rather to establish a foundational requirement for the admissibility of another item of evidence. For example, the proponent of scientific evidence typically is required to show that any instrumentation used in a scientific examination had been in proper working order at the time of the analysis.[16] Thus, the results of an intoxilyzer test are not admissible unless the instrument had been properly calibrated. A report establishing the calibration of

---

13. *See* FED. R. EVID. 1002 ("To prove the content of a writing, recording, or photograph, the original writing, recording, or photograph is required, except as otherwise provided in these rules or by Act of Congress"). *See generally* 1 E. IMWINKELRIED, P. GIANNELLI, F. GILLIGAN & F. LEDERER, *supra* note 9, ch. 15.

14. *See* FED. R. EVID. 1005 ("The contents of an official record ... may be proved by copy, certified as correct in accordance with Rule 902 or testified to be correct by a witness who has compared it with the original"); People v. Brown, 128 Misc. 2d 149, 152, 488 N.Y.S.2d 559, 563 (Co. Ct. 1985) ("Properly certified or authenticated copies of the test results are ... admissible as copies of official records ...").

15. *See* City of Mason v. Murphy, 123 Ohio App.3d 592, 599, 704 N.E.2d 1260, 1264 (1997) ("The letter was hearsay becausc it contained statements made by [the forensic chemist], who did not testify at the trial, and was offered into evidence to prove the truth of the matter asserted, that appellant's blood contained 'a blood ethanol level of 0.26% grams/100ml'. Accordingly, we find that the letter and the contents of the letter were inadmissible evidence because they were hearsay and do not fall within any of the hearsay exceptions").

16. For a discussion of the foundational requirements for the admissibility of scientific evidence, *see* Chapter 1.

intoxilyzer equipment may be offered for this purpose.[17] This type of report differs from a report specifying intoxilyzer test results. In this context, the rules of evidence may not apply. According to Federal Evidence Rule 104(a), a trial court, in deciding preliminary questions of admissibility, "is not bound by the rules of evidence except those with respect to privileges." Accordingly, hearsay evidence is admissible.

§ 6-2. Federal Rules of Evidence.

Prior to the adoption of the Federal Rules of Evidence in 1975, the federal courts generally admitted laboratory reports under the business or public records exceptions to the hearsay rule.[18] The enactment of Federal Rules, however, cast doubt on the admissibility of laboratory reports under these exceptions.

§ 6-2(A). Public Records Exception.

Federal Rule 803(8) recognizes a hearsay exception for public (governmental) records.[19] The public records exception is supported by several rationales. First, because of "the assumption that a public official will perform his duty properly,"[20] public records are considered reliable. Second, "the unlikelihood that

---

17. *E.g.,* State v. Ward, 15 Ohio St. 3d 355, 358, 474 N.E.2d 300, 302 (1984) (calibration report of intoxilyzer admissible as a public record). In Price v. State, 269 Ga. 222, 498 S.E.2d 262 (1998), the Georgia Supreme Court admitted a certificate to establish the qualifications of the blood drawer in a DUI case. A statute authorized the use of the certificate. The court ruled that "[b]ecause the certificate is a public record and thus satisfies the reliability concerns of the confrontation clause" it is admissible. *Id.* at 222, 498 S.E.2d at 263.

18. *E.g.,* United States v. Frattini, 501 F.2d 1234, 1235-36 (2d Cir. 1974) (lab report identifying substance as cocaine); United States v. Parker, 491 F.2d 517, 520-21 (8th Cir. 1973) (lab report identifying substance as heroin), *cert. denied,* 416 U.S. 989 (1974); Government of Virgin Islands v. St. Ange, 458 F.2d 981, 982 (3d Cir. 1972) (hospital lab report identifying sperm on vaginal smear); Kay v. United States, 255 F.2d 476, 480 (4th Cir.) (lab report of blood alcohol test), *cert. denied,* 358 U.S. 825 (1958); United States v. Ware, 247 F.2d 698, 699 (7th Cir. 1957) (lab report identifying substance as heroin).

19. It provides:

> Records, reports, statements, or data compilations, in any form, of public offices or agencies, setting forth (A) the activities of the office or agency, or (B) matters observed pursuant to duty imposed by law as to which matters there was a duty to report, excluding, however, in criminal cases matters observed by police officers and other law enforcement personnel, or (C) in civil actions and proceedings and against the Government in criminal cases, factual findings resulting from an investigation made pursuant to authority granted by law, unless the sources of information or other circumstances indicate lack of trustworthiness.

See generally 1 E. IMWINKELRIED, P. GIANNELLI, F. GILLIGAN & F. LEDERER, *supra* note 9, § 1223 (official records).

20. FED. R. EVID. 803(8) advisory committee's note. *See* Shea v. Depart. of Motor Vehicles, 62 Cal. App. 4th 1057, 1061, 72 Cal. Rptr. 2d 896, 898 (1998) (A forensic alcohol report offered at an

[the official] will remember details independently of the record"[21] makes reliance on the record a necessity in many cases.

Although Rule 803(8) was intended to facilitate the use of public records, its application in criminal cases has spawned a number of problems. Initially, the classification of different kinds of public records can sometimes be troublesome. The rule recognizes three types of public records: (A) records relating to the activities of the public office, (B) records involving matters observed pursuant to a duty, and (C) investigative reports. The distinctions between these subdivisions are not precise and thus there may be an "overlap."[22] Because limitations on admissibility differ depending on the type of public record involved, it is sometimes critical to determine which subdivision applies. Courts have considered both Rule 803(8)(B) and (C) when ruling on the admissibility of laboratory reports.

Rule 803(8)(C): Investigative Records

Rule 803(8)(C) encompasses public records containing "factual findings resulting from an investigation made pursuant to authority granted by law." The federal drafters referred to such records as "evaluative reports."[23] In a leading case, *United States v. Oates,*[24] the Second Circuit wrote that it "seems indisputable" that the chemist's official report and worksheet identifying a substance as heroin can be characterized as "investigative reports."[25] As the rule explicitly provides, investigative reports are not admissible in criminal cases when offered *against the accused*;[26] they are, however, admissible if offered against the prosecution.[27] According to the federal drafters, this result is required

---

administrative hearing prepared by an unsupervised trainee does not fall within the public employee exception to the hearsay rule. "Since a trainee has no official duty to report the test results, his or her results are not entitled to the presumption that official duty was performed"); Manning v. Depart. of Motor Vehicles, 61 Cal. App. 4th 273, 71 Cal. Rptr. 2d 647 (1998) (trainee at lab signed a computer printout attesting to having performed a forensic alcohol test on a sample the day before the sample was received by the lab).

21. FED. R. EVID. 803(8) advisory committee's note.

22. United States v. Oates, 560 F.2d 45, 67 (2d Cir. 1977) ("[T]here may be no sharp demarcation between the records covered by exception 8(B) and those referenced in exception 8(C), ... and indeed there may in some cases be actual overlap ...").

23. FED. R. EVID. 803(8) advisory committee's note.

24. 560 F.2d 45 (2d Cir. 1977).

25. *Id.* at 67. *See also* Bradford Trust Co. v. Merrill Lynch, Pierce, Fenner & Smith, Inc., 805 F.2d 49, 54-55 (2d Cir. 1986) (fingerprint and handwriting reports admissible under Rule 803(8)(C) in a civil case).

26. *But see* State v. Manke, 328 N.W.2d 799, 802-05 (N.D. 1982) (admitting lab report under N.D. EVID. R. 803(8)(C)).

27. *See generally* Annot., *Admissibility Under Rule 803(8)(C) of Federal Rules of Evidence, of "Factual Findings Resulting From Investigation Made Pursuant to Authority Granted by Law,"* 47

"in view of the almost certain collision with confrontation rights which would result from their use against the accused in a criminal case."[28]

Rule 803(8)(B): Matters Observed Pursuant to a Duty

Courts have also considered the admissibility of laboratory reports under Rule 803(8)(B) — reports of matters observed and recorded pursuant to a legal duty. The court in *Oates* concluded that laboratory reports "might also be within the ambit" of this provision,[29] a ruling that required the court to examine Rule 803(8)(B)'s explicit exclusion of police records: "[I]n criminal cases matters observed by police officers and other law enforcement personnel" are inadmissible.[30]

According to the Senate Committee Report, the police records exclusion was based on the belief that "observations by police officers at the scene of the crime or the apprehension of the defendant are not as reliable as observations by public officials in other cases because of the adversarial nature of the confrontation between the police and the defendant in criminal cases."[31] In addition, the legislative history indicates that Congress was concerned with the confrontation problems raised by the use of police records in criminal trials.[32] In *Oates* the court adopted a literal interpretation of the police records exclusion, under which *all* police reports are automatically excluded. According to the court, prosecution laboratory reports fell within this exclusion.[33]

In contrast, other courts adopted a more flexible approach, holding that the police records exclusion does not apply to all police records. For example, the Ninth Circuit held that "Congress did not intend to exclude [police] records of routine, nonadversarial matters."[34] The court focused on the Senate Committee

---

A.L.R. FED. 321 (1980). For a discussion of Rule 803(8)(C) in civil cases, *see* Beech Aircraft Corp. v. Rainey, 488 U.S. 153 (1988).

28. FED. R. EVID. 803(8) advisory committee's note.

29. 560 F.2d at 65.

30. *See generally* Annot., *Construction and Application of Provision of Rule 803(8)(B), Federal Rules of Evidence, Excluding From Exceptions to Hearsay Rule in Criminal Cases Matters Observed by Law Enforcement Officers*, 37 A.L.R. FED. 831 (1978).

31. S. Rep. No. 1277, 93d Cong., 2d Sess. 17, *reprinted in* 1974 U.S. Code Cong. & Ad. News 7051, 7064.

32. *See* United States v. Oates, 560 F.2d 45, 78 (2d Cir. 1977) ("[T]he pervasive fear of the draftsmen and of Congress that interference with an accused's right to confrontation would occur was the reason why in criminal cases evaluative reports of government agencies and law enforcement reports were expressly denied the benefit to which they might otherwise be entitled under FRE 803(8)").

33. *Id.* at 78-89.

34. United States v. Orozco, 590 F.2d 789, 793 (9th Cir.) (customs officer's recording of license plate numbers admissible), *cert. denied*, 442 U.S. 920 (1979). *See also* United States v. Enterline, 894 F.2d 287, 289-91 (8th Cir. 1990) (computer report of identification numbers of stolen vehicles admissible as a routine, nonadversarial record); United States v. Dancy, 861 F.2d 77, 79-80 (5th

Report's language concerning the "adversarial nature of the confrontation" between the police and the defendant "'at the scene of the crime or the apprehension of the defendant.'"[35] One court accepting this view has stated:

> In the case of documents recording routine, objective observations, made as part of the everyday function of the preparing official or agency, the factors likely to cloud the perception of an official engaged in the more traditional law enforcement functions of observation and investigation of crime are simply not present. Due to the lack of any motivation on the part of the recording official to do other than mechanically register an unambiguous factual matter ..., such records are, like other public documents, inherently reliable.[36]

If laboratory reports are considered routine and objective, they may be admissible under this approach.[37] According to one court, a chemist "does no more than seek to establish an intrinsically neutral fact."[38] Another court stated that reports of chemical analyses contain "objective facts rather than expressions of opinion."[39]

However, the characterization of laboratory procedures as routine and objective is not without problems. As noted by a New Jersey court, a laboratory

---

Cir. 1988) (state prison fingerprint card admissible); United States v. Puente, 826 F.2d 1415, 1417-18 (5th Cir. 1987) (Customs Service computer printout of license plates of cars crossing the border admissible); United States v. Wilmer, 799 F.2d 495, 501 (9th Cir. 1986) (breathalyzer calibration certificate admissible), *cert. denied,* 481 U.S. 1004 (1987); United States v. Gilbert, 774 F.2d 962, 964-65 (9th Cir. 1985) (notations on fingerprint card admissible); United States v. Quezada, 754 F.2d 1190, 1194 (5th Cir. 1985) (warrant of deportation admissible); United States v. Coleman, 631 F.2d 908, 910-12 (D.C. Cir. 1980) (chain of custody documents admissible); United States v. Hernandez-Rojas, 617 F.2d 533, 535 (9th Cir.) (warrant of deportation admissible), *cert. denied,* 449 U.S. 864 (1980); United States v. Union Nacional de Trabajadores, 576 F.2d 388, 391 (1st Cir. 1978) (marshall's return on service of injunction admissible); United States v. Grady, 544 F.2d 598, 604 (2d Cir. 1976) (routine recording of serial numbers unrelated to commission of crime admissible).

35. 590 F.2d at 793 (quoting S. Rep. No. 1277, 93d Cong., 2d Sess. 17, *reprinted in* 1974 U.S. Code Cong. & Ad. News 7051, 7064).

36. United States v. Quezada, 754 F.2d 1190, 1194 (5th Cir. 1985).

37. *E.g.,* United States v. DeWater, 846 F.2d 528, 530 (9th Cir. 1988) (intoxilyzer test report admissible as a routine record); State v. Smith, 312 N.C. 361, 381, 323 S.E.2d 316, 327 (1984) (rejecting *Oates* and admitting report of breath analysis tests). *See also* State v. Smith, 66 Or. App. 703, 707, 675 P.2d 510, 512 (1984) (distinguishing *Oates* and admitting certificate of breathalyzer inspections).

38. United States v. Evans, 21 U.S.C.M.A. 579, 582, 45 C.M.R. 353, 356 (C.M.A. 1972) (LSD analysis).

39. Howard v. United States, 473 A.2d 835, 839 (D.C. App. 1984). *See also* Kay v. United States, 255 F.2d 476, 481 (4th Cir.) (certificate of blood alcohol test results involves "an objective fact, not a mere expression of opinion"), *cert. denied,* 358 U.S. 825 (1958).

report identifying a substance as marijuana is "not concerned with routine observations of acts, conditions or events observed or recorded by presumably neutral public officials."[40] Rather, it involves "the examination and evaluation of crucial evidence against a defendant made after the commencement of a criminal prosecution and for use in that prosecution."[41] Similarly, in *Cole v. State*[42] the court ruled that a laboratory report was not a routine, nonadversarial report under the Texas Rules of Evidence: "the reports were not prepared for purposes independent of specific litigation, nor were they ministerial, objective observations of an unambiguous factual nature."[43]

Indeed, the bias of some crime laboratories is well documented.[44] At different times, Professors Peterson,[45] Starrs,[46] and Moenssens[47] have noted this problem. The issue has also surfaced in Britain and Australia.[48] As one commentator has noted, "Many reformers in the United Kingdom believe that a large percentage of the problems that have arisen in the forensic science context are attributable to the fact that English forensic science is almost solely the province of the state."[49]

---

40. State v. Matulewicz, 198 N.J. Super. 474, 477, 487 A.2d 772, 773 (App. Div. 1985).

41. *Id.*

42. 839 S.W.2d 798 (Tex. Crim. App. 1990) (lab report on rape victim examination excluded).

43. *Id.* at 805.

44. *See* Giannelli, *The Abuse of Scientific Evidence in Criminal Cases: The Need for Independent Crime Laboratories*, 4 VA. J. SOC. POLICY & L. 439 (1997).

45. "It also is important to recognize that the police agency controls the formal and informal system of rewards and sanctions for the laboratory examiners. Many of these laboratories make their services available only to law enforcement agencies. All of these factors raise a legitimate issue regarding the objectivity of laboratory personnel." *Symposium on Science and the Rules of Legal Procedure*, 101 F.R.D. 599, 642 (1983) (statement of Professor Joseph Peterson).

46. Starrs, *The Seamy Side of Forensic Science: The Mephitic Stain of Fred Salem Zain*, 17 SCIENTIFIC SLEUTHING REV. 1, 8 (Winter 1993) ("The inbred bias of crime laboratories affiliated with law enforcement agencies must be breached").

47. Moenssens, *Novel Scientific Evidence in Criminal Cases: Some Words of Caution*, 84 J. CRIM. L. & CRIMINOLOGY 1, 6 (1993) (crime labs "may be so imbued with a pro-police bias that they are willing to circumvent true scientific investigation methods for the sake of 'making their point'").

48. *See* Freckelton, *Science and the Legal Culture*, 2 EXPERT EVIDENCE 107, 112 (1993) ("unequivocal evidence that the pro-prosecution orientation of government scientists . . . had not adequately been countered in England"); Wilson, *Lessons from the Antipodes: Lessons from the Successes and Failures of Forensic Science*, 67 FORENSIC SCI. INT'L 79, 82 (1994) ("The 'independence' of forensic science is often largely mythical. A series of case records suggests that scientific testimony is frequently distorted or molded to fit preconceived misassumptions about the nature of the crime or the guilt or innocence of the accused").

49. Bernstein, *Junk Science in the United States and the Commonwealth*, 21 YALE J. INT'L L. 123, 171 (1996).

Other Law Enforcement Personnel

The application of the police records exclusion also turns on the meaning of the phrase "police officers and other law enforcement personnel." In *Oates* the Second Circuit held that chemists employed by the U.S. Customs Service were "law enforcement personnel" within the meaning of the rule. According to the court, "any officer or employee of a governmental agency which has law enforcement responsibilities" is covered by that phrase, and "[c]hemists at the laboratory are, without question, important participants in the prosecutorial effort."[50] Because the legislative history provides no elaboration of the term "other law enforcement personnel," room for disagreement with the *Oates* interpretation remains.[51] Indeed, the *Oates* court labeled the issue a "difficult question."[52]

Since Congress, when enacting this provision, had focused on the "policeman on the beat,"[53] it is arguable that laboratory analysts should not be considered law enforcement personnel. For example, one court commented that a chemist does "not have an interest in the outcome of trials."[54] Many criminalists share this view: "The forensic scientist does not serve as an advocate for the plaintiff, prosecution, or defendant; he serves as an advocate for an opinion or conclusion based on objective physical evidence."[55] Accordingly, a commentator has asserted that a chemist in a laboratory, even a government laboratory, is distinguishable from a policeman at a crime scene, and thus the term "other law enforcement personnel" should be limited to those with "police powers."[56]

---

50. 560 F.2d at 68. *See also* Cole v. State, 839 S.W.2d 798, 803(Tex. Crim. App. 1990) ("[A]s was the case in *Oates,* the role of the chemists in this instance did not terminate with the completion of the chemical analyses and submission of any resulting report, but participation continued until one chemist had testified as a crucial prosecution witness at trial").

51. *See* Manocchio v. Moran, 919 F.2d 770, 777 (1st Cir. 1990) (medical examiner not a law enforcement officer), *cert. denied,* 500 U.S. 910 (1991); United States v. Orozco, 590 F.2d 789, 793 (9th Cir. 1979) (customs inspector at border qualifies as "law enforcement personnel"), *cert. denied,* 439 U.S. 1049 (1978); United States v. Hansen, 583 F.2d 325, 333 (7th Cir.) (city building inspectors not "law enforcement personnel"), *cert. denied,* 439 U.S. 912 (1978); United States v. Ruffin, 575 F.2d 346, 356 (2d Cir. 1978) (IRS personnel who gather data routinely used in criminal prosecutions perform a law enforcement function).

52. 560 F.2d at 67.

53. 120 Cong. Rec. 2387 (1974).

54. Howard v. United States, 473 A.2d 835, 839 (D.C. App. 1984).

55. Stone, *Capabilities of Modern Forensic Laboratories*, 25 WM. & MARY L. REV. 659, 674 (1984).

56. Grant, *The Trustworthiness Standard for Public Records and Reports Hearsay Exception*, 12 W. ST. U. L. REV. 53, 78 (1984).

There are several problems with this view. First, many laboratory examiners are law enforcement officers and thus have "police powers."[57] Second, the modern crime laboratory is an integral part of the law enforcement establishment.[58] "Of the approximately 300 crime laboratories in the United States, over eighty percent are in police departments."[59] Moreover, most laboratories examine only prosecution evidence. A survey of 257 crime laboratories revealed that "[f]ifty-seven percent ... would *only* examine evidence submitted by law enforcement officials."[60]

Autopsy Reports

Some courts distinguish autopsy reports from crime laboratory reports. In a later case, *United States v. Rosa*,[61] the Second Circuit upheld the admissibility of the factual portions of an autopsy report under Federal Rule 803(8)(B). The court ruled that, unlike the customs officials in *Oates*, medical examiner employees were not "other law enforcement personnel": "Unlike Customs, which has responsibility for enforcement of ... customs and narcotics laws, ... the Medical Examiner's Office is required simply to investigate unnatural deaths; it refers a death bearing any indicium of criminality to the appropriate district attorney and has no responsibility for enforcing any laws ...."[62]

In *Ealy v. State*[63] the Indiana Supreme Court held that the admissibility of an autopsy report as a public record depended on three factors, one of which was whether the report was prepared for advocacy purposes or in anticipation of litigation: "As a general rule, the examiners who prepared the autopsy report do

57. *See* NATIONAL ADVISORY COMM'N ON CRIMINAL JUSTICE STANDARDS AND GOALS, POLICE 303 (1974) ("There are ... many police laboratories that have been staffed almost exclusively with sworn personnel").

58. *See* PRESIDENT'S COMM'N ON LAW ENFORCEMENT AND ADMIN. OF JUSTICE, THE CHALLENGE OF CRIME IN A FREE SOCIETY 255 (1967) ("The crime laboratory has been the oldest and strongest link between science and technology and criminal justice").

59. *Symposium on Science and the Rules of Legal Procedure*, 101 F.R.D. 599, 633 (1984) (remarks of Professor Joseph Peterson). *See also* Peterson, Mihajlovic, & Bedrosian, *The Capabilities, Uses, and Effects of the Nation's Criminalistics Laboratories*, 30 J. FORENSIC SCI. 10, 11 (1985) ("Seventy-nine percent of all laboratories responding to our survey are located within law enforcement/public safety agencies").

60. *Id.* at 13 (emphasis in original).

61. 11 F.3d 315 (2d Cir. 1993), *cert. denied*, 511 U.S. 1042 (1994).

62. *Id.* at 332. *Accord* Garcia v. State, 868 S.W.2d 337 (Tex. Crim. App. 1993) (autopsy report admissible under TEX. R. EVID. 803(8)(B); county medical examiner not "other law enforcement personnel").

63. 685 N.E.2d 1047 (Ind. 1997). The other factors were: (1) whether the report involved a material contested issue, and (2) whether the report contained a factual finding. "As applied to the case at bar, the autopsy report was admissible. Under the first step in the analysis, there is nothing in the autopsy report which addresses a materially contested issue in the case. Primarily, there is no argument over the cause of death." *Id.* at 1055.

so for nonadvocacy reasons. They are charged by law with the job of producing public documents relating to deaths. They do not know if a particular case will result in trial, nor do they know who a potential defendant might be.... They have every incentive to do a proper job and their impartially is assumed."[64]

Private Laboratories

In *United States v. Blackburn*[65] the Seventh Circuit ruled that "a private company that conducts tests independently with its own equipment and prepares reports by itself based on those tests, even if at the instance of a governmental agency, is not part of the prosecution team."[66] This conclusion meant not only that the "police records exclusion" rule did not apply but also that the report was not a public record. The admissibility of the report (of lensometer readings for eyeglasses found at a crime scene) was upheld under the federal residual hearsay exception.[67]

Lab Reports Offered by the Defense

The police records exclusion raises an additional issue. On its face, Rule 803(8)(B) would appear to exclude all police records, whether offered by the prosecution or the defense. In this respect, subdivision (B) differs from subdivision (C), which expressly excludes investigative reports in criminal cases only when offered by the prosecution. In *United States v. Smith*[68] the D.C. Circuit addressed this issue: "[T]he apparently absolute language of 803(8)(B) had its origin in congressional concern that use of reports against defendants would be unfair."[69] Accordingly, "803(8)(B) should be read, in accordance with the obvious intent of Congress and in harmony with 803(8)(C) to authorize the admission of the reports of police officers and other law enforcement personnel at the request of the defendant in a criminal case."[70]

---

64. *Id. See also id.* at 1051 n.3 ("The reports do not fall under 8(a) because those who prepare autopsy reports are not law enforcement personnel").

65. 992 F.2d 666 (7th Cir.), *cert. denied*, 410 U.S. 949 (1993).

66. *Id.* at 672.

67. Because the document "was prepared at the request of the FBI, in anticipation of a prosecution against [the accused]," it was inadmissible as a business record. *Id.* at 670 ("Clearly, the report in this case was not kept in the course of a regularly conducted business activity, but rather was specially prepared at the behest of the FBI...").

68. 521 F.2d 957 (D.C. Cir. 1975).

69. *Id.* at 969 n.24.

70. *Id.* at 968 n.24. *See also* OHIO EVID. R. 803(8)(B) (explicitly exempting reports "offered by the defendant" from the police records exclusion); State v. Therriault, 485 A.2d 986, 996-97 (Me. 1984) (police lab report offered by defendant admissible as business record).

§ 6-2(B). Relationship Between Public Records & Other Exceptions.

Another area of uncertainty concerns the relationship between the public records exception and other hearsay exceptions.[71] Several courts have held that documents excludable under the public records exception are not admissible under any other hearsay exception. This interpretation may preclude the admissibility of government laboratory reports as business records[72] or as recorded recollection.[73] In *United States v. Oates*[74] the prosecution argued that the chemist's report was admissible as a business record. Although the Second Circuit recognized that as a general rule hearsay evidence failing to satisfy the requirements of one exception may nonetheless be admissible under another exception,[75] it found that Congress' "clear legislative intent" in excluding police and investigative reports in Rule 803(8) precluded their admission under any other hearsay exception.[76]

Other courts disagree in part with *Oates* and hold that Congress intended to exclude these reports only when offered in lieu of the testimony of the declarant. According to these courts: "The accompanying testimony of the author minimizes the danger of unreliability by giving the trier of fact the opportunity to weigh his credibility and consider the circumstances surrounding preparation of the report."[77] Under this view, if a laboratory report qualifies as recorded

---

71. *See generally* Annot., *Admissibility, Over Hearsay Objection, of Police Observations and Investigative Findings Offered by Government in Criminal Prosecution, Excluded From Public Records Exception to Hearsay Rule Under Rule 803(8)(B) or (C), Federal Rules of Evidence*, 56 A.L.R. FED. 168 (1982).

72. FED. R. EVID. 803(6). For a discussion of the business records exception, *see* §6-2(C) *infra.*

73. FED. R. EVID. 803(5). For a discussion of the recorded recollection exception, *see* §6-2(D) *infra.*

74. 560 F.2d 45 (2d Cir. 1977).

75. *Id.* at 66.

76. *Id.* at 68, 72 & 77. *Accord* United States v. Pinto-Mejia, 720 F.2d 248, 258 (2d Cir. 1983) (certificate of foreign government); United States v. Sims, 617 F.2d 1371, 1377 (9th Cir. 1980) (FBI report); United States v. Cain, 615 F.2d 380, 382 (5th Cir. 1980) (prison escape report); United States v. Ruffin, 575 F.2d 346, 355-56 (2d Cir. 1978) (IRS computer printouts); United States v. American Cyanamid Co., 427 F. Supp. 859, 867 (S.D.N.Y. 1977) (government internal memoranda and letters); Cole v. State, 839 S.W.2d 798 (Tex. Crim. App. 1990) (lab report on rape victim examination excluded). In United States v. Yakobov, 712 F.2d 20, 25-27 (2d Cir. 1983), the Second Circuit ruled *Oates* inapplicable to records admissible under Rule 803(10), absence of a public record.

77. United States v. King, 613 F.2d 670, 673 (7th Cir. 1980) (Social Security forms admitted as business records where the preparers testified). *Accord* United States v. Sokolow, 81 F.3d 397, 405 (3d Cir. 1996) (following *Hayes* and *King*), *cert. denied*, 117 S. Ct. 960 (1997); United States v. Hayes, 861 F.2d 1225, 1230 (10th Cir. 1988) (IRS computer data); United States v. Picciandra, 788 F.2d 39, 44 (1st Cir.) (recorded recollections of DEA agent admitted where he testified), *cert. denied,* 479 U.S. 847 (1986); United States v. Sawyer, 607 F.2d 1190, 1193 (7th Cir. 1979)

recollection, an exception which requires the declarant to testify, or as a business record and the declarant also testifies, the report is admissible.[78]

Some courts, however, go further. In *United States v. Baker*[79] the Eighth Circuit considered the admissibility of laboratory reports under the Federal Rules and concluded, without analysis, that "[w]hen made on a routine basis, laboratory analyses of controlled substances are admissible as business records under Federal Rule of Evidence 803(6)."[80]

In *United States v. Blackburn*[81] the Seventh Circuit also addressed this issue:

> The trouble with the formal structure of the Rule 803 exceptions is that only Rule 803(8) contains this restriction on the use of investigatory documents in criminal cases. None of the other exceptions, such as the business records exception, limit the use of documents in criminal cases. But if a document prohibited under Rule 803(8)(B) or (C) can come into evidence under Rule 803(6), then the 803(8) restrictions are rendered nugatory.[82]

After citing both *Oates* and *Baker*, the court noted that it had "steered a middle course between the Eighth Circuit's wholesale admission of laboratory reports and the Second Circuit's virtual ban."[83] The court ruled that a computer printout of lensometer readings for eyeglasses found at a crime scene was inadmissible as a business record, under Rule 803(6), because the document "was prepared at the request of the FBI, in anticipation of a prosecution against [the accused]."[84] The court went on, however, to admit the report under the residual hearsay exception, then Federal Rule 803(24).[85]

(recorded recollections of IRS agent admitted where agent testified), *cert. denied,* 445 U.S. 943 (1980). *See also* Abdel v. United States, 670 F.2d 73, 75 n.3 (7th Cir. 1982).

78. In *United States v. Coleman,* 631 F.2d 908, 914-15 (D.C. Cir. 1980), the D.C. Circuit upheld the admission of DEA chemical analysis forms where the examining chemist testified about the controlled substance. The court, however, reversed, without reaching the merits, as to those counts where a supervising chemist testified in lieu of the examining chemist.

79. 855 F.2d 1353 (8th Cir. 1988), *cert. denied,* 490 U.S. 1096 (1989).

80. *Id.* at 1359. *See also* United States v. Roulette, 75 F.3d 418, 422 (8th Cir.) (affirming *Baker,* lab report identifying cocaine admissible as business record, no confrontation violation), *cert. denied,* 519 U.S. 853 (1996).

81. 992 F.2d 666 (7th Cir.), *cert. denied,* 510 U.S. 949 (1993).

82. *Id.* at 671.

83. *Id.*

84. *Id.* at 670 ("Clearly, the report in this case was not kept in the course of a regularly conducted business activity, but rather was specially prepared at the behest of the FBI...").

85. *Id.* at 672. *But see* People v. Bridges, 184 A.D.2d 1042, 584 N.Y.S.2d 360 (admission of hospital report indicating presence of motile sperm under business record exception violated right of confrontation), *app. denied,* 605 N.E.2d 878 (N.Y. 1992).

§ 6-2(C). Business Records Exception.

If not precluded by Rule 803(8)(public records exception),[86] government laboratory reports may be admissible as business records under Rule 803(6).[87] In addition, laboratory reports prepared by nongovernmental entities, such as private hospitals, may fall within this exception.[88] Prior to the adoption of the Federal Rules, the admissibility of these reports as business records raised two issues: (1) whether the results reported were properly considered inadmissible opinions, as opposed to facts, and (2) whether the reports were excludable because they were prepared in anticipation of prosecution.[89] Federal Rule 803(6) settles the first issue by expressly providing for the admissibility of "opinions" and "diagnoses."

The second issue, the admissibility of records prepared in anticipation of litigation, remains problematic. Rule 803(6) contains a trustworthiness clause, under which business records are excludable if "the source of information or the method or circumstances of preparation indicate lack of trustworthiness." One

---

86. *See* §6-2(B) *supra.*

87. FED. R. EVID. 803(6) provides:

> Records of regularly conducted activity. A memorandum, report, record, or data compilation, in any form, of acts, events, conditions, opinions, or diagnoses, made at or near the time by, or from information transmitted by, a person with knowledge, if kept in the course of a regularly conducted business activity, and if it was the regular practice of that business activity to make the memorandum, report, record, or data compilation, all as shown by the testimony of the custodian or other qualified witness, unless the source of information or the method or circumstances of preparation indicate lack of trustworthiness. The term "business" as used in this paragraph includes business, institution, association, profession, occupation, and calling of every kind, whether or not conducted for profit.

88. *E.g.,* United States v. McCormick, 54 F.3d 214, 223-24 (5th Cir.) ("urinalysis reports bear substantial indicia of reliability, as they 'are the regular reports of a company whose business it is to conduct such tests, and which expects its clients to act on the basis of its reports.' Still, they are not so inherently reliable as to be automatically admissible in any [parole] revocation hearing") (citations omitted), *cert. denied,* 516 U.S. 902 (1995); United States v. Pierre, 47 F.3d 241, 242 (7th Cir. 1995) (urinalysis reports as written reports of medical tests are "in the main reliable"); United States v. Martin, 984 F.2d 308, 314 (9th Cir. 1993); United States v. Bell, 785 F.2d 640, 643 (8th Cir. 1986) (urinalysis reports are regular reports of a company); United States v. Mendel, 746 F.2d 155, 165-66 (2d Cir. 1984) (documents establishing authenticity of blood test admissible as business records), *cert. denied,* 469 U.S. 1213 (1985); Commonwealth v. Xiong, 428 Pa. Super. 136, 147, 630 A.2d 446, 452 (1993) (notation on physician's report that victim had "no hymen" admissible as a business record because it involves a fact rather than an opinion), *app. denied,* 537 Pa. 609, 641 A.2d 309 (1994); Commonwealth v. Kravontka, 384 Pa. Super. 346, 350-51, 558 A.2d 865, 867-68 (1989) (blood-alcohol test results admissible; no confrontation violation); State v. Ziegler, 114 Wash. 2d 533, 538, 789 P.2d 79, 83 (1990) (physician's records of rape victim's lab test results admissible); State v. Sellers, 39 Wash. App. 799, 695 P.2d 1014, 1019 (1985) (results of lab test of victim's blood type ordered by personal physician admissible).

89. *See* Imwinkelried, *The Constitutionality of Introducing Evaluative Laboratory Reports Against Criminal Defendants,* 30 HASTINGS L.J. 621, 626-29 (1979).

factor affecting reliability is the motivation of the person who prepares the report — whether the record was "prepared with an eye toward litigation."[90] The exclusion of "litigation records" has long been applied to police reports. For example, in *United States v. Ware,*[91] a pre-Federal Rules case, the Seventh Circuit wrote:

> [E]ven if memoranda ... are regularly prepared by law enforcement officers, they lack the necessary earmarks of reliability and trustworthiness. Their source and the nature and manner of their compilation unavoidably dictate that they are inadmissible under [the Federal Business Records Act]. They are also subject to the objection that such utility as they possess relates primarily to prosecution of suspected law breakers, and only incidentally to the systematic conduct of the police business.[92]

Nevertheless, courts applying the "litigation records" exclusion often have not extended it to laboratory reports.[93] For example, in *United States v. Evans*[94] a military court commented: "We are not persuaded that a chemical examiner's report is made principally for the purpose of prosecution."[95] In contrast, in *State v. Henderson*[96] the Tennessee Supreme Court stated that laboratory reports "cannot be said to have been prepared for any reason other than their potential litigation value."[97]

In *United States v. Baker*[98] the Eighth Circuit considered the admissibility of laboratory reports under the Federal Rules and concluded, without analysis, that

90. United States v. Smith, 521 F.2d 957, 966 (D.C. Cir. 1975). As *Smith* notes, the "litigation records" exclusion is derived from Palmer v. Hoffman, 318 U.S. 109 (1943). The Advisory Committee's Note to Rule 803(6) indicates that the trustworthiness clause was intended to codify *Palmer.*

91. 247 F.2d 698 (7th Cir. 1957).

92. *Id.* at 700. *Accord* United States v. Bohrer, 807 F.2d 159, 162-63 (10th Cir. 1986) (IRS contact card prepared for litigation); United States v. Smith, 521 F.2d 957, 966-67 (D.C. Cir. 1975); United States v. Brown, 451 F.2d 1231, 1233-34 (5th Cir. 1971); Sanchez v. United States, 293 F.2d 260, 269 (8th Cir. 1961).

93. *See* United States v. Frattini, 501 F.2d 1234, 1235-36 (2d Cir. 1974); United States v. Ware, 247 F.2d 698, 699 (7th Cir. 1957); *In re* Nelson, 83 Misc. 2d 1081, 1083-84, 374 N.Y.S.2d 982, 984-86 (Fam. Ct. 1975).

94. 21 U.S.C.M.A. 579, 45 C.M.R. 353 (C.M.A. 1972).

95. *Id.* at 582, 45 C.M.R. at 356. *See also* United States v. Strangstalien, 7 M.J. 225, 228 (C.M.A. 1979).

96. 554 S.W.2d 117 (Tenn. 1977).

97. *Id.* at 120. *See also* United States v. Smith, 521 F.2d 957, 967 (D.C. Cir. 1975) (police reports not admissible if offered by the prosecution).

98. 855 F.2d 1353 (8th Cir. 1988), *cert. denied,* 490 U.S. 1096 (1989).

"[w]hen made on a routine basis, laboratory analyses of controlled substances are admissible as business records under Federal Rule of Evidence 803(6)."[99]

In contrast, the Seventh Circuit in *United States v. Blackburn*[100] ruled that a computer printout of lensometer readings for eyeglasses found at a crime scene was inadmissible as a business record, under Rule 803(6), because the document "was prepared at the request of the FBI, in anticipation of a prosecution against [the accused]."[101] The court went on, however, to admit the report under the residual hearsay exception, then Federal Rule 803(24).[102]

Similarly, an Ohio court of appeals held that a casefile containing the results of DNA testing prepared by Cellmark Laboratories was inadmissible. The court stated that, "[w]here a document generally satisfies the elements of Evid. R. 803(6), but was prepared in anticipation of litigation, the underlying rationale of trustworthiness is supplanted by a natural motivation to color the facts in favor of the requesting entity."[103] The court concluded that "[t]he DNA casefile prepared by Cellmark was certainly prepared as part of its business. Yet the casefile was prepared for the sole purpose of litigation and, therefore, lacks the requisite trustworthiness."[104]

§ 6-2(D). Recorded Recollection Exception.

If not precluded by Rule 803(8)(public records exception),[105] laboratory reports may be admissible as recorded recollection under Rule 803(5).[106] For

---

99. *Id.* at 1359. *See also* United States v. Roulette, 75 F.3d 418, 422 (8th Cir.) (affirming *Baker*, lab report identifying cocaine admissible as business record, no confrontation violation), *cert. denied*, 519 U.S. 853 (1996).

100. 992 F.2d 666 (7th Cir.), *cert. denied*, 510 U.S. 949 (1993).

101. *Id.* at 670 ("Clearly, the report in this case was not kept in the course of a regularly conducted business activity, but rather was specially prepared at the behest of the FBI...").

102. *Id.* at 672. *But see* People v. Bridges, 184 A.D.2d 1042, 584 N.Y.S.2d 360 (admission of hospital report indicating presence of motile sperm under business record exception violated right of confrontation), *app. denied*, 605 N.E.2d 878 (N.Y. 1992).

103. State v. Lane, 108 Ohio App. 3d 477, 488, 671 N.E.2d 272, 279 (1995), *app. denied*, 85 Ohio St.3d 1477, 664 N.E.2d 1291 (1996).

104. *Id.* at 488, 671 N.E.2d at 280.

105. *See* §6-2(B) *supra*. *See also* United States v. Sawyer, 607 F.2d 1190, 1193 (7th Cir. 1979) (police records exclusion of Rule 803(8) does not apply where preparer of report testifies and report qualifies as recorded recollection), *cert. denied*, 445 U.S. 943 (1980).

106. FED. R. EVID. 803(5) recognizes a hearsay exception for recorded recollection: "A memorandum or record concerning a matter about which a witness once had knowledge but now has insufficient recollection to enable the witness to testify fully and accurately, shown to have been made or adopted by the witness when the matter was fresh in the witness' memory and to reflect that knowledge correctly. If admitted, the memorandum or record may be read into evidence but may not itself be received as an exhibit unless offered by an adverse party." *See generally* 1 E. IMWINKELRIED, P. GIANNELLI, F. GILLIGAN & F. LEDERER, *supra* note 9, § 1214.

example, in *United States v. Marshall*[107] the Ninth Circuit upheld the admissibility of a chemist's report identifying a substance as cocaine where the chemist testified that he had analyzed the substance and had prepared the report, but had no independent recollection of the tests.[108] The chemist did testify, however, that the report was accurate and was prepared contemporaneously with his examination of the substance.[109]

§ 6-3. State & Military Provisions.

Many state courts have ruled laboratory and autopsy reports admissible under either the business records[110] or public records exceptions[111] to the hearsay rule. In contrast, other courts have excluded these reports.[112]

In addition, some jurisdictions have enacted statutes providing for the admissibility of certain types of reports, such as breathalyzer results.[113] Many of

---

107. 532 F.2d 1279 (9th Cir. 1976).

108. *Id.* at 1285-86.

109. *Id.*

110. *E.g.,* People v. Beeler, 9 Cal. 4th 953, 979, 891 P.2d 153, 168, 39 Cal. Rptr. 2d 607, 622 (1995) (en banc) (autopsy report admitted as business record through the testimony of a pathologist who had not performed the autopsy; the pathologist who had conducted the autopsy "had apparently left the coroner's office under unfavorable conditions," *i.e.*, he "had caused 'quite a bit of consternation' in a prior murder case by basing his conclusion regarding the cause of death on a police report rather than on medical evidence"; also conclusion that victim died due to a bullet wound to the heart was an admissible "diagnosis" under the business records statute; "firmly rooted" hearsay exception for confrontation purposes), *cert. denied*, 516 U.S. 1053 (1996); Henson v. State, 332 A.2d 773, 775 (Del. Super. 1975) (hospital record of rape victim examination); State v. Rhone, 555 S.W.2d 839, 841-42 (Mo. 1977) (lab report of clothing and debris); State v. Taylor, 486 S.W.2d 239, 242 (Mo. 1972) (lab report of debris); People v. Porter, 46 A.D.2d 307, 311, 362 N.Y.S.2d 249, 255 (1974) (blood-alcohol test report); Burleson v. State, 585 S.W.2d 711, 712-13 (Tex. Crim. 1979) (autopsy report); State v. Kreck, 86 Wash. 2d 112, 114-16, 542 P.2d 782, 784-85 (1975) (blood examination report); State v. Ecklund, 30 Wash. App. 313, 319, 633 P.2d 933, 936-37 (1981) (serological report).

111. *E.g.,* Seals v. State, 282 Ala. 586, 604, 213 So. 2d 645, 662-63 (1968) (toxicologist report); People v. Clark, 3 Cal. 4th 41, 159, 833 P.2d 561, 628, 10 Cal. Rptr. 2d 554 (1992) (autopsy report admitted as an official record; examining physician had died; "firmly rooted" hearsay exception for confrontation purposes), *cert. denied*, 507 U.S. 993 (1993); State v. Snider, 168 Mont. 220, 229, 541 P.2d 1204, 1209 (1975) (marijuana report); *In re* Kevin G., 80 Misc. 2d 517, 519, 363 N.Y.S.2d 999, 1002 (Fam. Ct. 1975) (heroin report).

112. *E.g.*, People v. Domin, 71 Mich. App. 315, 316, 248 N.W.2d 250, 251 (1976) (lab report identifying substance as LSD inadmissible hearsay); State v. Russell, 114 N.H. 222, 224, 317 A.2d 781, 782 (1974) (lab report identifying substance as marijuana does not qualify as a business record); Bennett v. State, 448 P.2d 253, 264 (Okla. Crim. 1968) (psychiatric report inadmissible). In addition, several courts have excluded laboratory reports on constitutional grounds, *see* §6-4 *infra.*

113. *See* Wester v. State, 528 P.2d 1179, 1183 (Alaska 1974), *cert. denied,* 423 U.S. 836 (1975); State v. Larochelle, 112 N.H. 392, 394, 297 A.2d 223, 225 (1972).

the cases, however, predate the enactment of the Federal Rules of Evidence and the state adoption of the Federal Rules. The admissibility of laboratory reports in jurisdictions that have adopted the Federal Rules raises the same issues discussed in the preceding section.[114] The Military Rules of Evidence explicitly provide for the admissibility of "forensic laboratory reports" as business[115] and public records.[116]

Notice & Demand Statutes

Some jurisdictions have enacted statutes that provide for the admissibility of laboratory reports if the defendant does not request the presence of the analyst at trial.[117] Other statutes require the prosecution to notify the defense of its intention to use the laboratory report at trial and then provide for the report's admission if the defense does not request the analyst's presence.[118] Failure to serve a copy of the report on the defense as required may render the report inadmissible.[119] A defendant's failure to request the analyst has been construed as a waiver of the right of confrontation.[120] In *Raquepaw v. State*[121] the Nevada Supreme Court ruled that only the accused, and not his attorney, may waive the right of confrontation. Thus, the admission of a certificate reporting intoxilyzer results was error. This is a rather dubious position because lawyers often waive their clients rights in this context.

The details of this type of statute are important; they are not all identical. For example, in *Miller v. State*,[122] the Georgia Supreme Court ruled that a "notice and demand" statute violated the right of confrontation. The Georgia "statute does not

---

114. *See* Cole v. State, 839 S.W.2d 798 (Tex. Crim. App. 1990) (lab report on rape victim examination excluded under Texas Rules of Evidence).

115. MIL. R. EVID. 803(6).

116. MIL. R. EVID. 803(8). *But see* United States v. Broadnax, 23 M.J. 389, 393 (C.M.A. 1987) (excluding handwriting report as too subjective).

117. *E.g.*, IOWA CODE ANN. §691.2; ME. REV. STAT. ANN. tit. 17A, §1112(1).

118. *E.g.*, MD. CTS. & JUD. PROC. CODE ANN. §10-306 (intoxication tests); N.J. STAT. ANN. § 2C:35-19 (controlled substances); OHIO REV. CODE ANN. §2925.51(C) (controlled substances); WASH. R. CRIM. P. 6.13 (lab report admissible if defendant, after receiving notice, does not demand expert's presence seven days before trial).

119. *See* Johnson v. United States, 596 A.2d 511, 514 (D.C. App. 1991) (failure to serve cocaine report on defendant five days before trial renders report inadmissible); State v. Reese, 56 Ohio App. 2d 278, 280, 382 N.E.2d 1193, 1195 (1978) (failure to serve lab report on defendant renders report inadmissible).

120. *See* State v. Davison, 245 N.W.2d 321, 323 (Iowa 1976), *cert. denied,* 430 U.S. 955 (1977); State v. Kramer, 231 N.W.2d 874, 880 (Iowa 1975); State v. Hancock, 317 Or. 5, 854 P.2d 926 (1993) (statute that provides for admission of state police lab report of controlled substances and also subpoena for examiner's appearance does not violate the state or federal constitution). *See also* State v. Christianson, 404 A.2d 999, 1005 (Me. 1979) (confrontation issue not raised).

121. 108 Nev. 1020, 843 P.2d 364 (1992) (per curiam).

122. 266 Ga. 850, 472 S.E.2d 74 (1996).

provide that the filing of an objection to the admission of the certificate will result in the lab analyst's appearance in court. Compare ... where statutes in Maryland, Maine and New Hampshire withstood constitutional challenges because they provided procedures through which a defendant could confront the analyst merely by making a timely filing."[123] The court observed that the "statute also creates a 'Catch-22' barrier between a defendant and his constitutional right.... When a defendant attempts to surmount the barrier, he finds himself in the untenable position of having to identify 'specific grounds' in order to confront the analyst, but being unable to confront the analyst in order to identify the 'specific grounds.'"[124]

In *State v. Clark*[125] the Montana Supreme Court held that Montana Rule 803(8), which authorizes the admission of written reports of the Montana state crime laboratory upon notice and a defense failure to subpoena the analyst,[126] violated the state constitutional provision on the right of confrontation.[127] The court wrote: "In this case, the chemical analysis of the drugs was a critical component of the State's case. The experience, background, and training of the technician, and the method and manner of tests conducted, are all matters which the defendant is entitled to explore through cross-examination in the presence of the fact-finder."[128] The court also rejected the proposition that the right to subpoena the examiner altered the constitutional analysis:

> Contrary to the State's argument, the fact that Clark could have subpoenaed the State's witness if he had so chosen does not remedy the Rule's constitutional deficits. Rather, the Rule effectively required Clark to subpoena and produce the State's expert in order to rightfully take advantage of the protection afforded him under the Confrontation Clause. In reality, the defendant is compelled to produce evidence during his case-in-chief, which in many instances will be incriminating, should he choose to

---

123. *Id.* at 79 (citing Moon v. State, 300 Md. 354, 478 A.2d 695, 703 (1984); State v. Christianson, 404 A.2d 999, 1002 (Me. 1979); State v. Larochelle, 112 N.H. 392, 297 A.2d 223 (1972)).

124. *Id.*

125. 964 P.2d 766 (Mont. 1998).

126. Rule 803, Mil. R. Evid. (Title 26, ch. 10) provides in part: "However, written reports from the Montana state crime laboratory are within the exception to the hearsay rules when the state has notified the court and opposing parties in writing of its intention to offer such report or reports in evidence at trial in sufficient time for the party not offering the report or reports (1) to obtain the depositions before trial of the person or persons responsible for compiling such reports, or (2) to subpoena the attendance of said persons at trial."

127. 964 P.2d at 771 ("Unlike its federal counterpart, the text of Montana's Confrontation Clause specifically guarantees the accused's right 'to meet the witnesses against him face to face'").

128. *Id.*

> test the State's case. Such a result is impermissible in light of the due process guarantees of Article II, Section 17, of the Montana Constitution.[129]

Shifting Burden of Proof

In *Wigglesworth v. Oregon*[130] the Ninth Circuit reviewed an Oregon statute that not only made a drug lab report admissible but also "prima facie evidence" of the reported results. Although the statute recognized the defendant's right to subpoena the criminalist, the court concluded that this procedure "places the defendant in a 'Catch 22' situation – call the criminalist who prepared the report during the defendant's own case, and possibly bolster the prosecution's case, or forego examination of the criminalist and perhaps lose an opportunity to expose a defect in the report's authenticity."[131] The court found a due process violation:

> [T]he only way Wigglesworth could challenge the lab report was to pursue a course of action which carried with it the substantial risk of assisting the prosecution in establishing the report's authenticity. This effectively relieved the state of its burden of proof on an essential element of its case, and denied Wigglesworth due process....[132]

After Wigglesworth's trial, this defect was eliminated when the Oregon Supreme Court interpreted the statute as requiring the prosecution, upon defense request, to call the criminalist during its own case.[133]

§ 6-4. Confrontation Clause.

Even if laboratory reports are admissible under a hearsay exception, the Confrontation Clause may require exclusion. The sixth amendment provides that "[i]n all criminal prosecutions, the accused shall enjoy the right ... to be confronted with the witnesses against him."[134] In *Pointer v. Texas*[135] the Supreme Court held the clause binding upon the states.

---

129. *Id.* at 772-73.

130. 49 F.3d 578, 580 (9th Cir. 1995).

131. *Id.* at 581.

132. *Id.*

133. State v. Hancock, 317 Or. 5, 11-12, 854 P.2d 926, 929 (1993).

134. For discussions of the relationship between the hearsay rule and the Confrontation Clause, *see* 1 E. IMWINKELRIED, P. GIANNELLI, F. GILLIGAN & F. LEDERER, *supra* note 9, § 1315; A. AMAR, THE CONSTITUTION AND CRIMINAL PROCEDURE 129 (1997); Friedman, *Confrontation: The Search for Basic Principles*, 86 GEO. L. J. 1011 (1998); Graham, *The Confrontation Clause, the Hearsay Rule, and Child Sexual Abuse Prosecutions: The State of the Relationship*, 72 MINN. L. REV. 523 (1988); Jonakait, *Restoring the Confrontation Clause to the Sixth Amendment*, 35 UCLA L. REV. 557 (1988); Kirkpatrick, *Confrontation and Hearsay: Exemptions from the Constitutional Unavailability Requirement*, 70 MINN. L. REV. 665 (1986); Kirst, *The Procedural Dimension of Confrontation Doctrine*, 66 NEB. L. REV. 485 (1987); Lilly, *Notes on the Confrontation Clause and*

§ 6-4(A). Supreme Court Framework.

A hearsay declarant is, in effect, a "witness against" the accused. Thus, a literal interpretation of the Confrontation Clause would preclude the prosecution from introducing any hearsay statement, notwithstanding the applicability of a recognized hearsay exception. The Supreme Court has never accepted this interpretation because it "would abrogate virtually every hearsay exception, a result long rejected as unintended and too extreme."[136]

The Confrontation Clause also could be interpreted as requiring only the right to cross-examine in-court witnesses and not out-of-court declarants.[137] Under this view, all hearsay exceptions would satisfy constitutional requirements.[138] The Supreme Court also has rejected this view:

> While it may readily be conceded that hearsay rules and the Confrontation Clause are generally designed to protect similar values, it is quite a different thing to suggest that the overlap is complete and that the Confrontation Clause is nothing more or less than a codification of the rules of hearsay and their exceptions as they existed historically at common law. Our decisions have never established such a congruence; indeed, we have more than once found a violation of confrontation values even though the statements in issue were admitted under an arguably recognized hearsay exception.... The converse is equally true: merely because evidence is admitted in violation of a long-established hearsay rule does not lead to the automatic conclusion that confrontation rights have been denied.[139]

The Court has continued to adhere to this position, noting: "We have been careful 'not to equate the Confrontation Clause's prohibitions with the general rule prohibiting the admission of hearsay statements.'"[140]

Ohio v. Roberts, 36 U. FLA. L. REV. 207 (1984); Westen, *The Future of Confrontation*, 77 MICH. L. REV. 1185 (1979); Westen, *Confrontation and Compulsory Process: A Unified Theory of Evidence for Criminal Cases*, 91 HARV. L. REV. 567 (1978); Younger, *Confrontation*, 24 WASHBURN L.J. 1 (1984).

135. 380 U.S. 400 (1965).

136. Ohio v. Roberts, 448 U.S. 56, 63 (1980).

137. This was apparently Wigmore's view. *See* 5 J. WIGMORE, EVIDENCE §1397 (Chadbourn rev. 1974).

138. *See* Lilly v. Virginia, 119 S. Ct. 1887, 1894 (1999) ("Because that restrictive reading of the Clause's term 'witnesses' would have virtually eliminated the Clause's role in restricting the admission of hearsay testimony, we considered it foreclosed by our prior cases").

139. California v. Green, 399 U.S. 149, 155-56 (1970).

140. White v. Illinois, 502 U.S. 346, 352 (1992) (quoting Idaho v. Wright, 497 U.S. 805, 814 (1990)). *See also* Dutton v. Evans, 400 U.S. 74, 86 (1970) ("It seems apparent that the Sixth Amendment's Confrontation Clause and the evidentiary hearsay rule stem from the same roots. But this Court has never equated the two, and we decline to do so now").

Instead of either of these two approaches, the Court has attempted to steer a middle course, a task that often has proved elusive.[141] The Court's decisions lack consistency, and none have directly dealt with the admissibility of laboratory reports. In *Diaz v. United States*[142] the Court held that an autopsy report "could not have been admitted without the consent of the accused ... because the accused was entitled to meet the witnesses face to face."[143] That case, however, was decided in 1912.

Roberts' Two-Prong Test

In *Roberts v. Ohio,*[144] decided in 1980, the Court identified two values underlying the Confrontation Clause: the "Framers' preference for face-to-face accusation" and an "underlying purpose to augment accuracy in the factfinding process."[145] From these values, the Court derived a two-pronged analysis that focused on (1) the unavailability of the declarant and (2) the reliability of the hearsay statement.[146] The Court wrote:

> In sum, when a hearsay declarant is not present for cross-examination at trial, the Confrontation Clause normally requires a showing that [the declarant] is unavailable. Even then, his statement is admissible only if it bears adequate "indicia of reliability." Reliability can be inferred without more in a case where the evidence falls within a firmly rooted hearsay

141 There does appear to be general agreement that the Confrontation Clause was originally intended to preclude trial by affidavit. In an early confrontation case, the Court wrote: "The primary purpose of the constitutional provision ... was to prevent depositions or *ex parte* affidavits ... being used against the prisoner in lieu of a personal examination and cross-examination of the witnesses." Mattox v. United States, 156 U.S. 237, 242 (1895). *See also* Dutton v. Evans, 400 U.S. 74, 94 (1970) (concurring) (The "paradigmatic evil the Confrontation Clause was aimed at" was "trial by affidavit"); California v. Green, 399 U.S. 149, 156 (1970) ("It is sufficient to note that the particular vice that gave impetus to the confrontation claim was the practice of trying defendants on *evidence* which consisted solely of ex parte affidavits or depositions"); Westen, *supra* note 134, 91 HARV. L. REV. 567, 574-75 (1978) ("Yet it has been understood since the earliest confrontation cases that the prohibition of trials by affidavit lies at the very core of our notions of confrontation").

142. 223 U.S. 442 (1912).

143. *Id.* at 450. *See also* Richardson v. Perales, 402 U.S. 389, 402 (1971) (no due process violation to admit physician's report in social security disability claim hearing).

144. 448 U.S. 56 (1980). *See* Lilly v. Virginia, 119 S. Ct. 1887, 1894 (1999) ("[W]e adhere[] to our general framework, summarized in *Ohio v. Roberts,* that the veracity of hearsay statements is sufficiently dependable to allow the untested admission of such statements against an accused when (1) 'the evidence falls within a firmly rooted hearsay exception' or (2) it contains 'particularized guarantees of trustworthiness' such that adversarial testing would be expected to add little, if anything, to the statements' reliability") (citations omitted).

145. 448 U.S. at 65.

146. "The central concern of the Confrontation Clause is to ensure the reliability of the evidence against a criminal defendant by subjecting it to rigorous testing in the context of an adversary proceeding before the trier of fact." Maryland v. Craig, 497 U.S. 836, 845 (1990).

> exception. In other cases, the evidence must be excluded, at least absent a showing of particularized guarantees of trustworthiness.[147]

This summation of confrontation requirements immediately raised problems. *Roberts* involved the admissibility of a preliminary hearing transcript as former testimony, a hearsay exception that traditionally required a showing of unavailability. Most hearsay exceptions, however, do not require such a showing. Did the Court intend to impose an unavailability requirement on every exception?[148]

Unavailability Prong

This two-pronged approach, requiring both reliability and unavailability, was soon modified.[149] *United States v. Inadi,*[150] which involved the coconspirator exception to the hearsay rule,[151] appeared to limit *Roberts*' unavailability requirement to cases in which former testimony is introduced:

> *Roberts* should not be read as an abstract answer to questions not presented in that case, but rather as a resolution of the issue the Court said it was examining: "the constitutional propriety of the introduction in evidence of the preliminary hearing testimony of a witness not produced at the defendant's subsequent state criminal trial."[152]

---

147. 448 U.S. at 57.

148. *See* Jonakait, *supra* note 134, at 558 (The *Roberts'* "framework was immediately controversial"); Lilly, *supra* note 134, at 224 ("Beneath [*Roberts*'] apparently orthodox disposition ... lies an interpretation of possibly far-reaching significance").

149. The test for unavailability is set forth in Barber v. Page, 390 U.S. 719, 725 (1968), in which the Court held that this requirement is satisfied only if "the prosecutorial authorities have made a good-faith effort to obtain" the presence of the declarant at trial. According to the Court in *Barber*, good-faith effort requires more than a showing that the declarant is beyond the subpoena power of the trial court. The Court in *Roberts* reaffirmed this test and provided the following explanation:

> The law does not require the doing of a futile act. Thus, if no possibility of procuring the witness exists (as, for example, the witness' intervening death), "good faith" demands nothing of the prosecution. But if there is a possibility, albeit remote, that affirmative measures might produce the declarant, the obligation of good faith may demand their effectuation. "The lengths to which the prosecution must go to produce a witness ... is a question of reasonableness." ... The ultimate question is whether the witness is unavailable despite good-faith efforts undertaken prior to trial to locate and present that witness. As with other evidentiary proponents, the prosecution bears the burden of establishing this predicate.

Ohio v. Roberts, 448 U.S. 56, 74-75 (1980).

150. 475 U.S. 387 (1986).

151. The federal version of the coconspirator exemption is found in FED. R. EVID. 801(d)(2)(E) ("a statement by a coconspirator of a party during the course and in furtherance of the conspiracy").

152. 475 U.S. at 392-93 (quoting Ohio v. Roberts, 448 U.S. 56, 58 (1980)).

Roberts, in the Court's view, should not be interpreted "to stand for the radical proposition that no out-of-court statement can be introduced by the government without a showing that the declarant is unavailable."[153] The Court reaffirmed this position in *White v. Illinois*:[154] "*Roberts* stands for the proposition that unavailability analysis is a necessary part of the Confrontation Clause inquiry *only when* the challenged out-of-court statements were made in the course of a prior judicial proceeding."[155] The Court went on to hold that a showing of unavailability was not required when excited utterances[156] or statements made for the purpose of medical diagnosis[157] are offered in evidence. Thus, despite the language in *Roberts*, unavailability is not always demanded. Indeed, *Inadi* and *White* establish blanket rules dispensing with the unavailability requirement for at least some hearsay exceptions—the conspirator admissions exemption in *Inadi* and the excited utterance and medical diagnosis exceptions in *White*. One commentator has suggested that "[t]he former testimony exception will likely stand practically alone as to the requirement that the prosecution demonstrate the hearsay declarant's unavailability."[158]

"Better Evidence" Rationale

The Supreme Court offered two rationales for these rulings. First, the Court reasoned that the coconspirator, excited utterance, and medical diagnosis exceptions differ from the former testimony exception at issue in *Roberts*. According to the *Inadi* Court, unlike former in-court testimony, coconspirator statements "provide evidence of the conspiracy's context that cannot be replicated, even if the declarant testifies to the same matters in court."[159] Similarly, the *White* Court noted that excited utterances and statements made for the purpose of medical diagnosis had substantial probative value that "could not

---

153. *Id.* at 394.

154. 502 U.S. 346 (1992).

155. *Id.* at 354 (emphasis added).

156. The federal version of the excited utterance (spontaneous exclamation) exception is found in FED. R. EVID. 803(2) ("A statement relating to a startling event or condition made while the declarant was under the stress of excitement caused by the event or condition").

157. The federal version of this exception is found in FED. R. EVID. 803(4) ("Statements made for purposes of medical diagnosis or treatment and describing medical history, or past or present symptoms, pain, or sensations, or the inception or general character of the cause or external source thereof insofar as reasonably pertinent to diagnosis or treatment").

158. Haddad, *The Future of Confrontation Clause Developments: What Will Emerge When the Supreme Court Synthesizes the Diverse Lines of Confrontation Decisions?*, 81 J. CRIM. L. & CRIMINOLOGY 77, 82 (1990). *See also* Swift, *Smoke and Mirrors: The Failure of the Supreme Court's Accuracy Rationale in White v. Illinois Requires a New Look at Confrontation*, 22 CAPITAL U. L. REV. 145, 146 (1993) (*White* represents a "blanket rejection of an unavailability requirement in most cases").

159. 475 U.S. at 395.

be duplicated simply by the declarant later testifying in court."[160] In short, the Court believed that the out-of-court statement is "better evidence" than the in-court testimony. "When two versions of the same evidence are available, longstanding principles of the law of hearsay, applicable as well to Confrontation Clause analysis, favor the better evidence."[161]

This argument is flawed because it presupposes that the out-of-court statement *or* the in-court testimony may be introduced at trial, but not both. There is no reason, however, why both cannot be admitted in evidence in most trials. Under the hearsay rule, statements falling within these exceptions are admissible even if the declarant testifies.

"Unnecessary Burden" Rationale

The second reason noted in these cases involved what the Court believed to be an unnecessary burden on the prosecution. The prosecution subpoenas the witnesses it needs, and the defense is guaranteed the same opportunity under the Compulsory Process Clause. An unavailability rule would operate only in those cases in which neither side wanted to call the witness. In the Court's view, the benefit of an unavailability rule is therefore marginal. At the same time, keeping track of additional witnesses would impose "substantial burdens" because the "prosecution would be required to repeatedly locate and keep continuously available each declarant."[162]

Once, again, the Court's opinions are not persuasive. The prosecution has to keep track of the state's witnesses. Typically, this means retaining a witness's name, address, telephone number, and place of employment, and issuing subpoenas when necessary. The incremental burden of keeping track of additional witnesses would often be minimal. The declarant in *Inadi* failed to appear because of car trouble, a rather unimpressive excuse.

The applicability of this factor to lab reports is discussed below.

Reliability Prong

Subsequent decisions also considered the second prong (reliability) mentioned in *Roberts*. Under this prong, a hearsay statement satisfies confrontation requirements either because the statement (1) falls within a "firmly rooted" hearsay exception[163] or (2) possesses "particularized guarantees of

---

160. 502 U.S. at 356.

161. United States v. Inadi, 475 U.S. 387, 394 (1986).

162. White v. Illinois, 502 U.S. 346, 355 (1992).

163. *See* Lilly v. Virginia, 119 S. Ct. 1887, 1894 (1999) ("[T]he question whether the statements fall within a firmly rooted hearsay exception for Confrontation Clause purposes is a question of federal law. Accordingly, it is appropriate to begin our analysis by examining the 'firmly rooted' doctrine and the roots of the 'against penal interest' exception").

trustworthiness." *Bourjaily v. United States*[164] considered a confrontation challenge to coconspirator statements. Tracing the judicial history of the coconspirator exception back over a century and a half, the Court found the exception "firmly enough rooted in our jurisprudence."[165] Accordingly, such statements automatically satisfy confrontation demands for reliability. The Court adopted the same analysis in *White*, writing that there "can be no doubt" that the excited utterance and medical diagnosis hearsay exceptions are "firmly rooted." The Court stated that the excited utterance exception had been recognized for "at least two centuries" and both the Federal Rules of Evidence and nearly "four-fifths" of the states had adopted it.[166]

The Court's automatic acceptance of "firmly rooted" hearsay exceptions is problematic. Although the Court noted that the excited utterance exception had been recognized for "at least two centuries" and had been widely adopted, the Court failed to acknowledge that the exception also has long been criticized.[167]

In addition, the Court's treatment of the medical diagnosis exception is also flawed. As one commentator noted, this exception "is not a centuries' old exception, since it was firmly adopted only eighteen years ago in the Federal Rules of Evidence. The [*White*] opinion does not mention this."[168] The Court's definition of the exception "would seem to include anything the patient chooses to talk about with a doctor!"[169]

However, in its latest decision, *Lilly v. Virginia*,[170] the Court ruled on the admissibility of declarations of penal interest made by an arrested accomplice when offered against an accused. The Court stated "that accomplices' confessions that inculpate a criminal defendant are not within a firmly rooted exception to the hearsay rule as that concept has been defined in our Confrontation Clause jurisprudence."[171]

---

164. 483 U.S. 171 (1987).

165. *Id.* at 183.

166. 502 U.S. at 356 n.8.

167. Swift, *supra* note 158, at 154 (1993) ("What the opinion does not say is that, despite this pedigree, such spontaneous or excited statements are viewed as one of the *least* reliable types of admissible hearsay"). *See also* 2 McCormick, Evidence § 272, at 216 (4th ed 1992) ("The entire basis for the exception is, of course, subject to question. While psychologists would probably concede that excitement minimizes the possibility of reflective self-interest influencing the declarant's statements, they have questioned whether this might be outweighed by the distorting effect of shock and excitement upon the declarant's observation and judgment").

168. Swift, *supra* note 158, at 155.

169. *Id.* at 157.

170. 119 S. Ct. 1887(1999).

171. *Id.* at 1899. In explaining the "firmly rooted" exception doctrine, the Court commented: "This standard is designed to allow the introduction of statements falling within a category of hearsay whose conditions have proven over time 'to remove all temptation to falsehood, and to enforce as strict an adherence to the truth as would the obligation of an oath' and cross-examination at a trial." *Id.* at 1895 (citing *Mattox*, 156 U.S. at 244).

Particularized Guarantees

If a hearsay exception is not "firmly rooted," the sixth amendment requires that "particularized guarantees of trustworthiness" accompany the making of the hearsay statement. This was the Court's holding in *Idaho v. Wright,*[172] which involved the admissibility of a child's statement under a residual hearsay exception. This requirement involves a case-by-case approach that considers the "totality of the circumstances" at the time the statement was made. It precludes consideration of independent corroborating circumstances in determining reliability.[173]

In *Lilly v. Virginia,*[174] the Court rejected an attempt to admit an accomplice's statement inculpating the accused under this doctrine.[175]

Summary

Thus, despite the Court's statements in earlier cases, recent decisions suggest that the right of confrontation has been "deconstitutionalized" into the hearsay rule. "Firmly rooted" exceptions are presumptively reliable, and the test for classifying an exception as "firmly rooted" is not rigorous. At this time the unavailability requirement has been applied only to former testimony. Yet, traditional hearsay law always required unavailability as a prerequisite for the use of former testimony. One commentator has written: "The confrontation clause is

---

172. 497 U.S. 805 (1990).

173. "[T]he relevant circumstances include only those that surround the making of the statement and that render the declarant particularly worthy of belief." 497 U.S. at 819. In rejecting reliance on corroborating proof, the Court wrote: "[T]he use of corroborating evidence to support a hearsay statement's 'particularized guarantees of trustworthiness' would permit admission of a presumptively unreliable statement by bootstrapping on the trustworthiness of other evidence at trial, a result we think at odds with the requirement that hearsay evidence admitted under the Confrontation Clause be so trustworthy that cross-examination of the declarant would be of marginal utility." *Id.* at 823.

174. Lilly v. Virginia, 119 S. Ct. 1887 (1999). The Court noted: "The residual 'trustworthiness' test credits the axiom that a rigid application of the Clause's standard for admissibility might in an exceptional case exclude a statement of an unavailable witness that is incontestably probative, competent, and reliable, yet nonetheless outside of any firmly rooted hearsay exception." *Id.* at 1899-1900.

175. *Id.* at 1901 ("It is abundantly clear that neither the words that Mark spoke nor the setting in which he was questioned provides any basis for concluding that his comments regarding petitioner's guilt were so reliable that there was no need to subject them to adversarial testing in a trial setting. Mark was in custody for his involvement in, and knowledge of, serious crimes and made his statements under the supervision of governmental authorities. He was primarily responding to the officers' leading questions, which were asked without any contemporaneous cross-examination by adverse parties. Thus, Mark had a natural motive to attempt to exculpate himself as much as possible").

no longer a constitutional right protecting the accused, but essentially a minor adjunct to evidence law."[176]

Nevertheless, the Court has not formally adopted this position, and commentators continue to search for the proper interpretation of the Confrontation Clause. One commentator has argued that "[h]earsay statements procured by agents of the prosecution or police should . . . stand on different footing than hearsay created without governmental intrusion. The Confrontation Clause should bar hearsay statements elicited by governmental agents unless the declarant is produced at trial or unless special procedures ... are followed."[177] Another has written: "The confrontation clause gives the accused the right to exclude all out-of-court statements when the declarant is not produced except when the prosecutor establishes the lack of a reasonable probability that the accused's cross-examination of the declarant would have led the jury to weigh the evidence more favorably to the accused."[178]

Whether the business and public records exceptions as applied to laboratory reports are also "firmly rooted" is discussed below, as is the unavailability requirement.

§ 6-4(B). Laboratory Reports.

Lower courts disagree on whether the admission of laboratory reports violates the Confrontation Clause. Many of the cases, however, were decided prior to the Supreme Court's latest confrontation decisions, and thus their precedential value is suspect. Prior to *Roberts* (1980), a number of courts had rejected the constitutional argument,[179] while others had accepted it.[180] This division

---

176. Jonakait, *supra* note 134, at 558. *See also* Berger, *The Deconstitutionalization of the Confrontation Clause: A Proposal for a Prosecutorial Restraint Model*, 76 MINN. L. REV. 557, 557 (1992) (The Supreme Court "has transformed a constitutional guarantee into an evidentiary doctrine 'generally designed to protect similar values,' as the hearsay rule"); Haddad, *supra* note 158, at 80 ("Because of these rules, the confrontation clause offers little protection beyond that afforded by domestic hearsay law").

177. Berger, *supra* note 176, at 561-62. *See also* Swift, *Abolishing the Hearsay Rule*, 75 CAL. L. REV. 495, 514 (1987) ("The crucial point about Burden-Shifting Declarants is that their systematic use allows plaintiffs and prosecutors to present hearsay statements, often in documentary form, without simultaneously producing a witness knowledgeable about the declarant, the statement, or any of her testimonial qualities or circumstances. ... Burden-shifting is a tactical choice").

178. Jonakait, *supra* note 134, at 622.

179. *E.g.*, Kay v. United States, 255 F.2d 476, 480-81 (4th Cir.) (blood alcohol report), *cert. denied*, 358 U.S. 825 (1958); United States *ex rel.* Lurry v. Johnson, 378 F. Supp. 818, 822 (E.D. Pa. 1974) (hospital record of rape victim examination); Robertson v. Cox, 320 F. Supp. 900, 900 (W.D. Va. 1970) (lab report identifying seminal fluid); Henson v. State, 332 A.2d 773, 775 (Del. Super.1975) (hospital record of rape victim examination); Grover v. State, 41 Md. App. 705, 710-11, 398 A.2d 528, 531 (1979) (autopsy report); Commonwealth v. Franks, 359 Mass. 577, 580-81, 270 N.E.2d 837, 839-40 (1971) (hospital report identifying sperm); Commonwealth v. Harvard,

continued after *Roberts*. Some courts have found confrontation violations involving reports on drugs,[181] urinalysis,[182] medical records,[183] and sundry other techniques.[184] However, other courts have arrived at the opposite conclusion, again with repect to a variety of reports, such as those involving drugs,[185] autopsies,[186] intoxication tests,[187] and so forth.[188]

---

356 Mass. 452, 461-62, 253 N.E.2d 346, 351-52 (1969) (marijuana report); State v. Larochelle, 112 N.H. 392, 397, 297 A.2d 223, 226 (1972) (breathalyzer results); Burleson v. State, 585 S.W.2d 711, 712-13 (Tex. Crim. 1979) (autopsy report); Robertson v. Commonwealth, 211 Va. 62, 65, 175 S.E.2d 260, 262 (1970) (seminal fluid report); State v. Kreck, 86 Wash. 2d 112, 116-19, 542 P.2d 782, 785-86 (1975) (blood test report).

180. *E.g.,* Stewart v. Cowan, 528 F.2d 79, 85 (6th Cir. 1976) (ballistics report); Kienlen v. United States, 437 F.2d 843, 848-49 (10th Cir. 1971) (psychiatric report); Phillips v. Neil, 452 F.2d 337, 348 (6th Cir. 1971) (psychiatric report), *cert. denied,* 409 U.S. 884 (1972); People v. Johnson, 11 Ill. App. 3d 395, 401-02, 296 N.E.2d 763, 768 (1973) (psychiatric report); Gregory v. State, 40 Md. App. 297, 325, 391 A.2d 437, 454 (1978) (psychiatric report); State v. Russell, 114 N.H. 223, 224-25, 317 A.2d 781, 782 (1974) (marijuana report); Commonwealth v. McCloud, 457 Pa. 310, 315-17, 322 A.2d 653, 657 (1974) (autopsy report; state constitution); State v. Henderson, 554 S.W.2d 117, 122 (Tenn. 1977) (LSD and marijuana report).

181. *E.g.,* Grantham v. State, 580 So. 2d 53, 58 (Ala. Crim. App. 1991) (marijuana); Miller v. State, 266 Ga. 850, 472 S.E.2d 74 (1996) (marijuana affidavit by forensic drug chemist does not fit within a statutorily recognized hearsay exception; violates confrontation right where unavailability of chemist not shown); *In re* J.H., 244 N.J. Super. 207, 581 A.2d 1347 (A.D. 1990) (lab certificate identifying substance as cocaine).

182. United States v. Martin, 984 F.2d 308 (9th Cir. 1993) (urinalysis report showing presence of cocaine and methadone at revocation of supervised release violated right of confrontation).

183. *E.g.,* Pickett v. Bowen, 798 F.2d 1385, 1387 (11th Cir. 1986) (admission of medical report violated right of confrontation); Moon v. State, 300 Md. 354, 368-73, 478 A.2d 695, 702-04 (1984) (hospital report of alcohol test); People v. Bridges, 184 A.D.2d 1040, 584 N.Y.S.2d 360 (hospital report indicating presence of motile sperm), *app. denied,* 605 N.E.2d 878 (N.Y. 1992).

184. *E.g.,* United States v. McClintock, 748 F.2d 1278, 1290-92 (9th Cir. 1984) (reports on the value of gems), *cert. denied,* 474 U.S. 822 (1985); Stevens v. Bordenkircher, 746 F.2d 342, 348 (6th Cir. 1984) (death certificate).

185. *E.g.,* United States v. Roulette, 75 F.3d 418, 422 (8th Cir.) (cocaine), *cert. denied,* 519 U.S. 853 (1996); United States v. Baker, 855 F.2d 1353, 1360 (8th Cir. 1988) (drug report), *cert. denied,* 490 U.S. 1069 (1989); United States v. Vietor, 10 M.J. 69, 70 (C.M.A. 1980) (marijuana); Howard v. United States, 473 A.2d 835, 840 (D.C. App. 1984) (heroin); State v. Sosa, 59 Wash. App. 678, 681, 800 P.2d 839, 844 (1990) (heroin).

See also Wigglesworth v. Oregon, 49 F.3d 578, 580 (9th Cir. 1995) (dictum) ("If the [cocaine lab] report was admissible under [the public records] exception to the hearsay rule, Wigglesworth's right of confrontation was not violated").

186. *E.g.,* United States v. Rosa, 11 F.3d 315, 333 (2d Cir. 1993) (factual portions of autopsy report), *cert. denied,* 511 U.S. 1042 (1994); Manocchio v. Moran, 919 F.2d 770, 777 (1st Cir. 1990), *cert. denied,* 500 U.S. 910 (1991); People v. Beeler, 9 Cal. 4th 953, 979, 891 P.2d 153, 168, 39 Cal. Rptr. 2d 607, 622 (1995) (en banc) (autopsy report admitted as business record through the testimony of a pathologist who had not performed the autopsy; the pathologist who had conducted the autopsy "had apparently left the coroner's office under unfavorable conditions," *i.e.,* he "had caused 'quite a bit of consternation' in a prior murder case by basing his conclusion regarding the

§ 6-4(C). Indicia of Reliability of Lab Reports.

Several passages in *Roberts* indicate that most statements falling within the public and business records exceptions will satisfy the reliability requirement. In one passage, the Court noted that "[r]eliability can be inferred without more in a case where the evidence falls within a firmly rooted hearsay exception."[189] Both exceptions would appear to qualify as "firmly rooted."[190] Moreover, in another passage the Court stated that "certain hearsay exceptions rest upon such solid foundations that admission of virtually any evidence within them comports with the 'substance of the constitutional protection.'"[191] In an accompanying footnote, the Court cited the business and public records exceptions as examples.[192] *Inadi* and *White* seem to support this analysis. In both cases, the Court simply looked to see how long a hearsay exception had been recognized and how extensively it had been adopted throughout the country.

Some courts have applied the firmly-rooted-exception rationale without much analysis. In *United States v. Baker*[193] the Eighth Circuit held: "When admitting the laboratory reports under the business records exception, the district court acted under a firmly rooted exception."[194] Other courts have reached the same

---

cause of death on a police report rather than on medical evidence"; also conclusion that victim died due to a bullet wound to the heart was an admissible "diagnosis" under the business records statute; "firmly rooted" hearsay exception for confrontation purposes), *cert. denied*, 516 U.S. 1053 (1996); People v. Clark, 3 Cal. 4th 41, 158, 833 P.2d 561, 10 Cal. Rptr. 2d 554 (1992) (examining physician had died), *cert. denied*, 507 U.S. 993 (1993); Ealy v. State, 685 N.E.2d 1047, 1055 (Ind. 1997) ("[I]t is relatively well established that the admission of autopsy reports does not violate a defendant's confrontation rights").

187. *E.g.*, United States v. DeWater, 846 F.2d 528, 530 (9th Cir. 1988) (intoxilyzer test report); Price v. State, 269 Ga. 222, 222, 498 S.E.2d 262, 263 (1998) (statute authorized use of certificate to establish the qualifications of the blood drawer in a DUI case; "Because the certificate is a public record and thus satisfies the reliability concerns of the confrontation clause," it is admissible); State v. Smith, 312 N.C. 361, 365, 323 S.E.2d 316, 318 (1984) (breath tests affidavit); Commonwealth v. Kravontka, 384 Pa. Super. 346, 355, 558 A.2d 865, 870 (1989) (blood-alcohol test).

188. *E.g.*, United States v. Bernard S., 795 F.2d 749 (9th Cir. 1986) (medical records of only peripheral significance); State v. Russo, 3 Conn. App. 137, 485 A.2d 1335, 1339-40 (1985) (hospital report).

189. 448 U.S. at 66.

190. *See* 5 J. Wigmore, Evidence §§1517-61b (business records), §§1630-38a (public records) (Chadbourn rev. 1974).

191. 448 U.S. at 66 (quoting Mattox v. United States, 156 U.S. 237, 244 (1895)).

192. 448 U.S. at 66 n.8.

193. 855 F.2d 1353 (8th Cir. 1988), *cert. denied,* 490 U.S. 1069 (1987).

194. *Id.* at 360. *See also* United States v. DeWater, 846 F.2d 528, 530 (9th Cir. 1988) (intoxilyzer test report admissible as public record, a "firmly rooted" exception); Commonwealth v. Kravontka, 384 Pa. Super. 346, 355, 558 A.2d 865, 870 (1989) (admission of blood-alcohol test as business record; no confrontation violation). *But see* United States v. Bentley, 875 F.2d 1114, 1121-23 (5th Cir. 1989) (dissenting opinion) (constitution violated where lab report summarized an unidentified test by an anonymous technician).

result, using a different analysis. They focus on the existence of particularized guarantees of trustworthiness rather than the "firmly rooted" exception rationale.[195] In *United States v. Rosa*[196] the Second Circuit ruled that admission of factual portions of an autopsy report did not violate the right of confrontation. The court held that even if autopsy reports do not fall within a "firmly rooted" hearsay exception, the factual portions have particularized guarantees of trustworthiness.

In contrast, the Mississippi Supreme Court in *Kettle v. State*[197] ruled that the admission of a laboratory report identifying a substance as cocaine violated the right of confrontation, even though the report may be admissible under the business records exception to the hearsay rule. Upon objection, the defendant "is entitled to have the person who conducted the test testify in person."[198] The court, at least implicitly, recognized that in this context the business record exception is not "firmly rooted."[199]

Reliability Problems

Although business and public records generally may bear adequate indicia of reliability, laboratory reports may not. Laboratory reports typically are prepared in anticipation of prosecution and, although probably rare, they can be falsified. Indeed, the Supreme Court has recognized that "the results of laboratory tests may be contrived,"[200] and in one instance an FBI analyst "reported results of lab tests that he did not in fact conduct."[201]

In West Virginia, the former head serologist of the State Police crime laboratory falsified test results in as many as 134 cases from 1979 to 1989.[202] Defendants, since exonerated, were sentenced to long prison terms based upon his testimony. A judicial inquiry concluded that "as a matter of law, any testimonial or documentary evidence offered by Zain at any time in any criminal

195. *See* Manocchio v. Moran, 919 F.2d 770, 777 (1st Cir. 1990) (autopsy report admissible but not as a "firmly rooted" exception), *cert. denied,* 500 U.S. 910 (1991); State v. Sosa, 59 Wash. App. 678, 800 P.2d 839 (1990) (admission of heroin report not a confrontation violation).

196. 11 F.3d 315, 333 (2d Cir. 1993), *cert. denied*, 511 U.S. 1042 (1994).

197. 641 So. 2d 746 (Miss. 1994).

198. *Id.* at 747.

199. *Id.* at 750 (noting the "firmly rooted hearsay exception" rule but declining to go beyond the "facts of this case").

200. United States v. Ash, 413 U.S. 300, 320 (1973).

201. State v. Ruybal, 408 A.2d 1284, 1285 (Me. 1979). *See also* United States v. Gault, 141 F.3d 1399, 1403 (10th Cir. 1998) ("The DEA agent . . . had admitted to failing to perform the controlled substance tests upon which her reports were based"); State v. DeFronzo, 59 Ohio Misc. 113, 118, 394 N.E.2d 1027, 1031 (C.P. 1978) (Expert represented that certain lab tests were conducted when "no such tests were ever conducted").

202. *In re* Investigation of the W. Va. State Police Crime Lab., Serology Div., 438 S.E.2d 501 (W. Va. 1993).

prosecution should be deemed invalid, unreliable, and inadmissible."[203] The West Virginia Supreme Court opinion adopting this report[204] speaks of "shocking and egregious violations," "corruption of our legal system," and "mock[ing] the ideal of justice under law."[205] The report states:

> The acts of misconduct on the part of Zain included (1) overstating the strength of results; (2) overstating the frequency of genetic matches on individual pieces of evidence; (3) misreporting the frequency of genetic matches on multiple pieces of evidence; (4) reporting that multiple items of evidence had been tested, when only a single item had been tested; (5) reporting inconclusive results as conclusive; (6) repeatedly altering laboratory records; (7) grouping results to create the erroneous impression that genetic markers had been obtained from all samples tested; (8) failing to report conflicting results; (9) failing to conduct or to report conducting additional testing to resolve conflicting results; (10) implying a match with a suspect when testing supported only a match with the victim; and (11) reporting scientifically impossible or improbable results.[206]

More typically, the reports may simply be incorrect. The Laboratory Proficiency Testing Program Report, sponsored by the Law Enforcement Assistance Administration, documented a high incidence of errors.[207] Seventy-one percent of the crime laboratories tested provided unacceptable results in a blood test, 51.4% made errors in matching paint samples, 35.5% erred in a soil examination, and 28.2% made mistakes in firearms identifications. A review of five handwriting comparison proficiency tests showed that, at best, "[d]ocument examiners were correct 57% of the time and incorrect 43% of the time."[208] Despite these results, most crime laboratories are still not subject to mandatory proficiency testing.[209]

Moreover, many conclusions recorded in lab reports are based on subjective judgments,[210] about which experts may disagree.[211] Thus, "[w]ithout the

---

203. *Id.* at 520 (the Report is reprinted after the opinion). In another passage, the report stated that Zain's conduct "strikes at the heart of the integrity of the State's case in every prosecution in which Zain was involved." *Id.* at 519.

204. *Id.* at 508 ("We adopt Judge Holliday's report and order its immediate implementation").

205. *Id.*

206. *Id.* at 516.

207. J. PETERSON, E. FABRICANT & K. FIELD, CRIME LABORATORY PROFICIENCY TESTING RESEARCH PROGRAM (1978).

208. Risinger, Denbeaux & Sax, *Exorcism of Ignorance as a Proxy For Rational Knowledge: The Lessons of Handwriting Identification "Expertise,"* 137 U. PA. L. REV. 731, 748 (1989).

209. *See* Jonakait, *Forensic Science: The Need for Regulation*, 4 HARV. J.L. & TECH. 109 (Spring 1991).

210. *See* United States v. McClintock, 748 F.2d 1278, 1292 (9th Cir. 1984) ("[B]ecause of the various means of evaluation and apparent subjective decisions that enter into the evaluation of testimony of the doctor, it would be difficult to assess the validity of the test upon which the opinions of the doctor expressed in the report were based."[212]

A lab report may be misleading in other respects because it typically provides insufficient information about the analyst and the tests performed.[213] For example, a gunshot residue report indicating that a person recently fired a weapon may be based on the paraffin test, neutron activation analysis, scanning electron microscopy, or some other procedure.[214] Some of these tests are valid, while others are not. Moreover, the qualifications of the analyst are often not included in the report, and in some cases, the supervising chemist may sign the report rather than the analyst who actually conducted the tests.[215] Given these problems, it seems questionable that laboratory reports should routinely be found to possess the requisite reliability.

Autopsy reports may also be misleading. For example, in one case a death certificate based on an autopsy revealed the identity of the body and the cause of death. Later proceedings demonstrated that most of this information was suspect. For example, the conclusion regarding the cause of death — recorded as gunshot wounds — was based not on the autopsy but rather on the statement of a witness as transmitted to the coroner through the police.[216]

§ 6-4(D). Unavailability of the Declarant.

The unavailability requirement presents additional difficulties.[217] While establishing the unavailability of the declarant is not a prerequisite for the admissibility of business and public records,[218] *Roberts* states that the

---

gems, [the defendant's] confrontation of the preparers of the reports may have been valuable to his defense").

211. *See* Commonwealth v. McCloud, 457 Pa. 310, 313, 322 A.2d 653, 655 (1974) (cross-examination important because experts often give conflicting opinions).

212. State v. Stokes, 433 So. 2d 96, 103 (La. 1983) (bitemark analysis report offered by defense held inadmissible as business record).

213. *See* United States v. Davis, 14 M.J. 847, 848 n.3 (A.C.M.R. 1982) (specifying limitations of lab reports).

214. For a discussion of the various gunshot residue tests, *see* Chapter 14.

215. For a discussion of the admissibility of a supervising expert's testimony in lieu of the examining expert's testimony, *see* § 5-4(C), *supra*.

216. Stevens v. Bordenkircher, 746 F.2d 342, 346 (6th Cir. 1984). *See also* People v. Beeler, 9 Cal. 4th 953, 979, 891 P.2d 153, 168, 39 Cal. Rptr. 2d 607, 622 (1995) (en banc) (pathologist who had conducted the autopsy "had apparently left the coroner's office under unfavorable conditions," *i.e.*, he "had caused 'quite a bit of consternation' in a prior murder case by basing his conclusion regarding the cause of death on a police report rather than on medical evidence"), *cert. denied*, 516 U.S. 1053 (1996).

217. *See generally* Note, *Confrontation and the Unavailable Witness: Searching for a Standard*, 18 VAL. U. L. REV. 193 (1983).

218. Following the traditional view, the Federal Rules place the business and public records exceptions in Rule 803, which does not require a showing of the declarant's unavailability.

Confrontation Clause "normally" requires a showing of unavailability. As noted above, however, both *Inadi* and *White* limit the unavailability requirement set forth in *Roberts*. They also establish blanket rules dispensing with the requirement for at least some hearsay exceptions — the coconspirator exception in *Inadi* and the excited utterance and medical diagnosis exceptions in *White*. As noted earlier, the Court offered two reasons for these rulings.

First, these exceptions differed from the former testimony exception at issue in *Roberts*. Unlike former in-court testimony, coconspirator statements "provide evidence of the conspiracy's context that cannot be replicated, even if the declarant testifies to the same matters in court."[219] Similarly, the Court in *White* noted that excited utterances and statements made for the purpose of medical diagnosis had substantial probative value that "could not be duplicated simply by the declarant later testifying in court."[220] This rationale does not apply to laboratory reports. There is nothing inherently trustworthy about their preparation. Nor is there any loss of probative value when the expert testifies in court. The conditions surrounding the making of the report can be "replicated" and "duplicated" at trial.

The second reason noted in these cases involved what the Court believed to be an unnecessary burden on the prosecution. The prosecution subpoenas those witnesses that it needs, and the same opportunity is guaranteed to the defense under the Compulsory Process Clause. Thus, an unavailability rule would operate only in those cases where neither side wanted to call the witness. According to the Court, this would "impose substantial additional burdens on the factfinding process," because the prosecution would "be required to repeatedly locate and keep continuously available each declarant."[221] At least part of this rationale does not apply to laboratory reports. Most reports are prepared by experts working at government crime laboratories. Unlike other witnesses, keeping track of them is not a burdensome task.

Moreover, in other contexts the Supreme Court has repeatedly cited the importance of an accused's right to cross-examine expert witnesses. For example, the Court has written:

> Knowledge of the techniques of science and technology is sufficiently available, and the variables in techniques few enough, that the accused has the opportunity for a meaningful confrontation of the Government's case at trial through the ordinary processes of cross-examination of the Government's expert witnesses ....[222]

---

219. 475 U.S. at 395.

220. 502 U.S. at 356.

221. *Id.* at 742.

222. United States v. Wade, 388 U.S. 218, 227-28 (1967). *See also* Gilbert v. California, 388 U.S. 263, 267 (1967).

Similarly, in refusing to recognize a defendant's right to have breath samples preserved, the Court commented that "as to operator error, the defendant retains the right to cross-examine the law enforcement officer who administered the Intoxilyzer test."[223] Moreover, the Court in *Daubert v. Merrell Dow Pharmaceuticals, Inc.,*[224] stressed the importance of the adversary system in dealing with scientific evidence. The Court noted that "[v]igorous cross-examination, presentation of contrary evidence, and careful instruction on the burden of proof are the traditional and appropriate means of attacking shaky but admissible evidence."[225]

In sum, the Court has emphasized in several different contexts the importance of the right of confrontation when an accused is faced with the results of scientific testing. It would be difficult to reconcile these pronouncements with the view that trial confrontation of laboratory analysts is of small utility.

Compulsory Process

One other aspect of the confrontation cases deserves comment. In upholding the admissibility of laboratory reports in face of a confrontation challenge, a number of courts have cited the defendant's failure to subpoena the analyst.[226] For example, in *State v. Spikes*[227] the Ohio Supreme Court wrote that defense counsel "could have subpoenaed [the preparers] to testify at trial."[228] Both *Inadi* and *White* contain language supporting this view.

This view, however, merges the confrontation and compulsory process guarantees, leaving the accused with only the latter protection. As one commentator has noted:

> The danger here is that the defendant will find himself in a dilemma: if he stands on the claim of error and refuses to invoke his right of compulsory process to produce the witness on his own initiative, the appellate court may conclude that he never had a genuine interest in an in-person examination of the declarant; yet if the defendant tries to mitigate the injury by proceeding

---

223. California v. Trombetta, 467 U.S. 479, 490 (1984). In rejecting a challenge to the admissibility of expert psychiatric testimony of future dangerousness in capital cases, the Court again cited the traditional safeguards of the adversary system, which presumably would include cross-examination: "We are not persuaded ... that the fact-finder and the adversary system will not be competent to uncover, recognize, and take due account of [such testimony's] shortcomings." Barefoot v. Estelle, 463 U.S. 880, 899 (1983).

224. 509 U.S. 579 (1993). For a discussion of *Daubert, see* Chapter 1.

225. *Id.* at 596 (citing Rock v. Arkansas, 483 U.S. 44, 61 (1987)).

226. *E.g.,* United States v. Miller, 23 U.S.C.M.A. 247, 250, 49 C.M.R. 380, 383 (C.M.A. 1974); Burleson v. State, 585 S.W.2d 711, 713 (Tex. Crim. 1979). *See also* State v. Manke, 328 N.W.2d 799, 803-04 (N.D. 1982).

227. 67 Ohio St. 2d 405, 423 N.E.2d 1122 (1981), *appeal dismissed,* 454 U.S. 1131 (1982).

228. *Id.* at 411, 423 N.E.2d at 1128.

> to produce and examine the witness on his own, the appellate court may conclude that the prosecutor's error was harmless. This dilemma is obviously unacceptable, because it would preclude defendants from ever successfully challenging a prosecutor's failure to take the initiative in producing a witness in person.[229]

Thus, the defendant's failure to call the analyst as a witness should not be construed as a waiver of the right to confront the analyst.[230]

In *State v. Clark*[231] the Montana Supreme Court held that Montana Rule 803(8), which authorizes the admission of written reports of the Montana state crime laboratory upon notice and a defense failure to subpoena the analyst,[232] violated the state constitutional provision on the right of confrontation.[233] The court rejected the proposition that the right to subpoena the examiner altered the constitutional analysis: "Contrary to the State's argument, the fact that Clark could have subpoenaed the State's witness if he had so chosen does not remedy the Rule's constitutional deficits. Rather, the Rule effectively required Clark to subpoena and produce the State's expert in order to rightfully take advantage of the protection afforded him under the Confrontation Clause. In reality, the defendant is compelled to produce evidence during his case-in-chief, which in many instance will be incriminating, should he choose to test the State's case. Such a result is impermissible in light of the due process guarantees of Article II, Section 17, of the Montana Constitution."[234]

---

229. Westen, *supra* note 134, 91 HARV. L. REV. at 623-24. *See also* Lilly, *supra* note 134, at 231.

230. *See* Phillips v. Neil, 452 F.2d 337, 348-49 (6th Cir. 1971), *cert. denied,* 409 U.S. 884 (1972); Gregory v. State, 40 Md. App. 297, 328 n.28, 391 A.2d 437, 455 n.28 (1978).

231. 964 P.2d 766 (Mont. 1998).

232. Rule 803, MIL. R. EVID. (Title 26, ch. 10) provides in part: "However, written reports from the Montana state crime laboratory are within the exception to the hearsay rules when the state has notified the court and opposing parties in writing of its intention to offer such report or reports in evidence at trial in sufficient time for the party not offering the report or reports (1) to obtain the depositions before trial of the person or persons responsible for compiling such reports, or (2) to subpoena the attendance of said persons at trial."

233. 964 P.2d at 771 ("Unlike its federal counterpart, the text of Montana's Confrontation Clause specifically guarantees the accused's right 'to meet the witnesses against him face to face'").

234. *Id.* at 772-73.

§ 6-5. Probation & Parole Revocation.

Probation revocation hearings are not part of a criminal prosecution and thus the sixth amendment does not apply in these proceedings.[235] However, because a probationer has a liberty interest at stake, due process requires a qualified right of confrontation.[236] The admission of urinalysis reports is common in these proceedings. According to some courts, the government's interest in minimizing the difficulty and expense of procuring witnesses often outweighs the defendant's interest in confrontation.[237] Nevertheless, some courts have found constitutional violations here.[238]

In *United States v. Grandlund*[239] the Fifth Circuit ruled that five days before the hearing the defendant should be given (1) a copy of the lab report, (2) a copy of the chain of custody report, and (3) an affidavit by a responsible lab employee attesting to the lab procedures, including chain-of-custody routines.

§ 6-6. Selected Bibliography.

E. IMWINKELRIED, P. GIANNELLI, F. GILLIGAN & F. LEDERER, COURTROOM CRIMINAL EVIDENCE ch. 15 (3d ed. 1998)

Alexander, *The Hearsay Exception for Public Records in Federal Criminal Trials*, 47 ALB. L. REV. 699 (1983).

Giannelli, *The Abuse of Scientific Evidence in Criminal Cases: The Need for Independent Crime Laboratories*, 4 VA. J. SOC. POLICY & L. 439 (Spring 1997).

Giannelli, *The Admissibility of Laboratory Reports in Criminal Trials: The Reliability of Scientific Proof*, 49 OHIO ST. L.J. 671 (1988).

Giannelli, *Expert Testimony and the Confrontation Clause*, 21 CAPITAL U. L. REV. 45 (1993).

---

235. *See also* United States v. Washington, 146 F.3d 219, 221 (4th Cir. 1998) (amended cocaine lab report issued by Pennsylvania State Police regional lab sufficiently reliable for sentencing even though dramatically increased the sentence).

236. *See* Young v. Harper, 520 U.S. 143 (1997) (preparole conditional supervision program); Morrissey v. Brewer, 408 U.S. 471, 489 (1972) (defendant has "the right to confront and cross-examine adverse witnesses (unless the hearing officer specifically finds good cause for not allowing confrontation)") (parole revocation hearings); Gagnon v. Scapelli, 411 U.S. 778 (1973) (probation revocation hearing).

237. *See* United States v. McCormick, 54 F.3d 214 (5th Cir.) (numerous indicia that urinalysis reliable, including recognized reliability of urinalysis report as a business record and affidavit from manager attesting to lab procedures), *cert. denied*, 516 U.S. 902 (1995); United States v. Kindred, 918 F.2d 485 (5th Cir. 1990) (defendant did not contest allegation of drug use nor accuracy of urinalysis report).

238. *See* Meeks v. McBride, 81 F.3d 717, 721 (7th Cir. 1996) ("Thus, in light of the discrepancy in the identifying information [prisoner number] on the face of the toxicology [marijuana] report, and the fact that no explanation for that discrepancy has been offered, we conclude that the report lacks sufficient indicia of reliability to support the CAB's decision. Meeks was therefore deprived of his good-time credits ... in violation of his right to due process"); United States v. Martin, 984 F.2d 308 (9th Cir. 1993) (urinalysis report showing presence of cocaine and methadone at revocation of supervised release violated right of confrontation).

239. 71 F.3d 507 (5th Cir. 1995), *cert. denied*, 516 U.S. 1152 (1996).

Grant, *The Trustworthiness Standard for Public Records and Reports Hearsay Exception*, 12 W. St. U. L. REV. 53 (1984).

Imwinkelried, *The Constitutionality of Introducing Evaluative Laboratory Reports Against Criminal Defendants*, 30 HASTINGS L.J. 621 (1979).

Annotations

Annot., *Construction and application of provision of Rule 803(8)(B), Federal Rules of Evidence, excluding from exceptions to hearsay rule in criminal cases matters observed by law enforcement officers*, 37 A.L.R. FED. 831 (1978).

Annot., *Admissibility, over hearsay objection, of police observations and investigative findings offered by government in criminal prosecution, excluded from the public records exception to hearsay rule under Rule 803(8)(B) or (C), Federal Rules of Evidence*, 56 A.L.R. FED. 168 (1982).

Annot., *Admissibility in state court proceedings of police reports under the official record exception to hearsay rule*, 31 A.L.R.4TH 913 (1984).

Chapter 7

CHAIN OF CUSTODY

§ 7-1. Introduction.

Authentication or identification[1] of real evidence refers to the requirement of proving that an item of evidence is genuine, *i.e.*, that it is what its proponent claims it to be.[2] McCormick expressed the requirement in this way: "[W]hen real evidence is offered an adequate foundation for admission will require testimony first that the object offered is *the* object which was involved in the incident, and further that the condition of the object is substantially unchanged."[3] Federal Evidence Rule 901(a) codifies this requirement. It provides: "The requirement of authentication or identification as a condition precedent to admissibility is satisfied by evidence sufficient to support a finding that the matter in question is what its proponent claims."[4]

Recent high profile cases highlight the importance of the authentication requirement. In the O.J. Simpson case, "the defense, in essence, put the crime laboratory on trial."[5] Writing in the aftermath of the Simpson trial, a police chief observed: "[T]he O.J. Simpson case and other recent sensational trials have put

---

1. *See* Giannelli, *Chain of Custody and the Handling of Real Evidence*, 20 AM. CRIM. L. REV. 527 (1983); Imwinkelried, *The Identification of Original, Real Evidence*, 61 MIL. L. REV. 145 (1973). *See also* Anderson, *Chain of Custody Requirements in Admissibility of Evidence*, 37 MONT. L. REV. 144 (1976); Graham, *Relevancy and Exclusion of Relevant Evidence — Real Evidence*, 18 CRIM. L. BULL. 241 (1982); Michael & Adler, *Real Proof*, 5 VAND. L. REV. 344 (1952); Comment, *Preconditions for Admission of Demonstrative Evidence*, 61 NW. U. L. REV. 472 (1966).

2. The term "real evidence" is used in this chapter to describe tangible evidence that is historically connected with a criminal case, as distinguished from evidence, such as a model, which is merely illustrative. *See* 2 C. MCCORMICK, EVIDENCE § 212 (4th ed. 1992).

3. *Id.* at 8.

4. *See In re* Sealed Case, 99 F.3d 1175, 1177 (D.C. Cir. 1996) ("[T]he evidence admitted by the trial court was what the government claimed it to be — the 324 ziplock bags of crack found in the house on the day of the raid. The language of Rule 901 requires no more").

5. E. CONNORS, T. LUNDREGAN, N. MILLER & T. MCEWEN, CONVICTED BY JURIES, EXONERATED BY SCIENCE: CASE STUDIES IN THE USE OF DNA EVIDENCE TO ESTABLISH INNOCENCE AFTER TRIAL xxvi (1996) (Matt L. Rodriguez, Superintendent of Chicago Police).

law enforcement under an intensely powerful microscope, examining our most basic procedures for collecting, processing, and caring for evidence."[6] Similarly, in the JonBenet Ramsey investigation a detective "further contaminated the crime scene by placing a blanket over the body and by allowing 10 people to mill through the house."[7] Moreover, Attorney General Janet Reno has cautioned that "[a]mong the tasks ahead are ... maintaining the highest standards for the collection and preservation of DNA evidence."[8]

Identity of Evidence

In criminal trials, it is often necessary to show that an item seized by the police, such as drugs, was the same item analyzed at the crime laboratory and introduced at trial. There are two principal methods of proving the identity of real evidence: first, establishing that the evidence is "readily identifiable," and second, establishing a "chain of custody." Both methods are discussed later in this chapter.

Condition of Evidence

In addition to showing that the object introduced in evidence is the same object as the one involved in the crime, the proponent of the evidence must show that the object has retained its relevant evidentiary characteristics. Alteration of the item may reduce or negate its probative value and may mislead the jury. Thus, before physical objects are admissible in evidence the proponent must establish that they are in "substantially the same condition as when the crime was committed."[9]

Determining what changes are "substantial" depends on how the changes affect the relevance of the evidence. Radically altered items of evidence may still be admitted if their pertinent features remain unaltered: "Even though the object is not in *exactly* the same condition at trial as at the time in issue — or even in substantially the same condition — the exhibit may still be admitted if the

---

6. *Id.* ("In the post-O.J. Simpson era, the handling of evidence until it reaches the crime laboratory will be as important as the laboratory technology, conditions, or procedures themselves").

7. Brooke, *Bungled JonBenet Case Bursts a City's Majesty*, N.Y. TIMES, Dec. 5, 1997, at A10.

8. E. CONNORS, T. LUNDREGAN, N. MILLER & T. MCEWEN, *supra* note 5, at iii.

9. Gallego v. United States, 276 F.2d 914, 917 (9th Cir. 1960). *Accord* United States v. Harrington, 923 F.2d 1371, 1374 (9th Cir.), *cert. denied*, 502 U.S. 854 (1991); United States v. McKinney, 631 F.2d 569, 571 (8th Cir. 1980); United States v. Aviles, 623 F.2d 1192, 1197 (7th Cir. 1980); United States v. Zink, 612 F.2d 511, 514 (10th Cir. 1980) ("condition is materially unchanged"); United States v. Brown, 482 F.2d 1226, 1228 (8th Cir. 1973); United States v. Lookretis, 422 F.2d 647, 650-51 (7th Cir.), *cert. denied*, 398 U.S. 904 (1970); United States v. S.B. Penick & Co., 136 F.2d 413, 415 (2d Cir. 1943); State v. Johnson, 162 Conn. 215, 232-33, 292 A.2d 903, 912 (1972).

changes can be explained, and they do not destroy the evidentiary value of the object."[10] For example, in *United States v. Skelley*[11] counterfeit bills were admissible even though they apparently changed color due to tests for fingerprints. According to the court, the change in color did not "destroy the relevance of the bills to show their counterfeit character from the identity of serial numbers, and their competence as evidence for this purpose [was] unimpaired by the ... possibility of a change in color."[12]

§ 7-2. Readily Identifiable Evidence.

If an object is easily identified, there may be no need to establish a chain of custody.[13] McCormick refers to such items as "unique and readily identifiable."[14] As one court has noted:

> If an exhibit is directly identified by a witness as the object which is involved in the case, then that direct identification is sufficient. Such is the case with many objects which have special identifying characteristics, such as a number or mark, or are made to have such identifying characteristics by special marks.[15]

---

10. Comment, 61 NW. U.L. REV., *supra* note 1, at 484. *See also* 2 C. MCCORMICK, *supra* note 2, at 8-9 ("It should, however, always be borne in mind that foundational requirements are essentially requirements of logic, and not rules of art. Thus, *e.g.*, even a radically altered item of real evidence may be admissible if its pertinent features remain unaltered").

11. 501 F.2d 447 (7th Cir.), *cert. denied*, 419 U.S. 1051 (1974).

12. *Id.* at 451. *See also* Duke v. State, 257 Ala. 339, 344-45, 58 So. 2d 764, 769 (1952) (shell admissible although sheriff scratched initials on it); Davidson v. State, 208 Ga. 834, 836, 69 S.E.2d 757, 759 (1952) (victim's clothing admissible although washed); Bruce v. State, 268 Ind. 180, 238, 375 N.E.2d 1042, 1073 (1978) (contamination "in no way vitiated the evidentiary value of the exhibits").

13. *See* United States v. Clonts, 966 F.2d 1366, 1368 (10th Cir. 1992) ("If the evidence is unique, readily identifiable and resistant to change, the foundation for admission need only be testimony that the evidence is what it purports to be"), *cert. denied*, 513 U.S. 905 (1994).

14. 2 C. MCCORMICK, *supra* note 2, at 8.

15. State v. Conley, 32 Ohio App. 2d 54, 59, 288 N.E.2d 296, 300 (1971). *See also* United States v. Camuti, 78 F.3d 738, 743 (1st Cir. 1996) ("Chain of custody is one means of authenticating evidence but not the only means ... "); United States v. LePera, 443 F.2d 810, 813 (9th Cir.) ("Counterfeit notes ... printed from a single plate, are unique and identifiable without proof of chain of custody"), *cert. denied*, 404 U.S. 958 (1971); United States v. Blue, 440 F.2d 300, 303 (7th Cir.) ("The chain of custody is not relevant when a witness identifies the object as the actual object about which he has testified"), *cert. denied*, 404 U.S. 836 (1971); Johnson v. State, 620 So. 2d 679, 693 (Ala. Crim. App. 1992) (Chain of custody requirements do not apply with the same force to items that are unique and identifiable in themselves), *rev'd on other grounds*, 620 So. 2d 709 (Ala.), *cert. denied*, 510 U.S. 905 (1993); Lestico v. Kuehner, 204 Minn. 125, 130, 283 N.W. 122, 125 (1938) ("It is utterly immaterial in how many or whose hands the tire had been so long as it could be identified"); State v. Malone, 694 S.W.2d 723, 727 (Mo. 1985) (chain of custody not required if there is a positive identification), *cert. denied*, 476 U.S. 1165 (1986); State

The Federal Rules recognize this method of identification. Rule 901(b)(4), entitled "Distinctive characteristics and the like," provides that "[a]ppearance, contents, substance, internal patterns, or other distinctive characteristics, taken in conjunction with circumstances" may satisfy the authentication requirement.[16] This method of proof is merely an application of the firsthand knowledge[17] and opinion rules[18] — the opinion of a lay witness based on personal observation.

Numerous examples of authenticating readily identifiable objects are found in the cases. All of these examples involve objects whose characteristics somehow make them unique. First, any item imprinted with a serial number, such as a weapon[19] or dollar bill,[20] may be identified by that number.

Second, an object that is inscribed with the initials or markings of a police officer or other person may be readily identifiable. In such cases, the person converts a non-unique object into a readily identifiable one by placing distinctive markings on it. This practice, recommended in crime scene and evidence collection manuals,[21] is well accepted in the cases. Firearms,[22] bullets,[23] shell

---

v. Jones, 342 N.C. 523, 536, 467 S.E.2d 12, 18-19 (1995) ("The State must establish a detailed chain of custody 'only when the evidence offered is not readily identifiable or is susceptible to alteration and there is reason to believe that it may have been altered'") (quoting State v. Campbell, 311 N.C. 386, 389, 317 S.E.2d 391, 392 (1984)).

16. *See* United States v. Georgalis, 631 F.2d 1199, 1206 (5th Cir. 1980) (letters authenticated under Rule 901(b)(4) without need for a chain of custody).

17. *See* FED. R. EVID. 602 ("A witness may not testify to a matter unless evidence is introduced sufficient to support a finding that the witness has personal knowledge of the matter").

18. *See* FED. R. EVID. 701 ("If the witness is not testifying as an expert, the witness' testimony in the form of opinions or inferences is limited to those opinions or inferences which are (a) rationally based on the perception of the witness and (b) helpful to a clear understanding of the witness' testimony or the determination of a fact in issue"); 7 J. WIGMORE, EVIDENCE § 1977 (Chadbourn rev. 1978) (opinion rule as applied to "identity").

19. *E.g.*, United States v. Douglas, 964 F.2d 738, 742 (8th Cir. 1992) ("Smith and Wesson with serial number 79515"); Jackson v. State, 241 Ark. 850, 854, 410 S.W.2d 766, 769 (1967); People v. Soto, 35 Ill. App. 3d 166, 170, 341 N.E.2d 107, 110 (1975); Wolfe v. State, 270 Ind. 81, 86, 383 N.E.2d 317, 318 (1978); State v. Kroeplin, 266 N.W.2d 537, 540 (N.D. 1978).

20. *E.g.*, Calderon v. United States, 269 F.2d 416, 419 (10th Cir. 1959); State v. Conley, 32 Ohio App. 2d 54, 60, 288 N.E.2d 296, 300-01 (1971).

21. *See* F.B.I., HANDBOOK OF FORENSIC SCIENCE 91 (rev. ed. 1994); R. FOX & C. CUNNINGHAM, CRIME SCENE SEARCH AND PHYSICAL EVIDENCE HANDBOOK (1973); C. O'HARA, FUNDAMENTALS OF CRIMINAL INVESTIGATION 79-84 (5th ed. 1980); J. OSTERBURG, THE CRIME LABORATORY 8 (1968).

22. *E.g.*, United States v. Madril, 445 F.2d 827, 828 (9th Cir. 1971) (pistol), *vacated on other grounds*, 404 U.S. 1010 (1972); Lilly v. State, 482 N.E.2d 457, 459 (Ind. 1985); Dixon v. State, 243 Ind. 654, 656-57, 189 N.E.2d 715, 716 (1963) (shotgun); Delahoussaye v. State, 697 S.W.2d 68, 70 (Tex. App. 1985).

23. *E.g.*, Duke v. State, 257 Ala. 339, 344-45, 58 So. 2d 764, 769 (1952); Sims v. State, 243 Ga. 83, 85, 252 S.E.2d 501, 503 (1979); State v. Ross, 275 N.C. 550, 553-54, 169 S.E.2d 875, 878 (1969), *cert. denied*, 397 U.S. 1050 (1970).

casings,[24] currency,[25] laboratory slides,[26] and sundry other objects[27] have been admitted into evidence, at least in part, on this basis.

Third, an object may possess distinctive natural characteristics that may make it readily identifiable.[28] For example, in *United States v. Briddle*[29] the prosecution introduced evidence that a button top found at the scene of a burglary came from the defendant's coat. The police officer described the button as follows:

> It had a picture of a whale on the front of it. It was leather.... And it had a sticky substance on the back, as though it might have been stuck to something.... [I]t was a dark brown in color. Had a whale or fish on it. The tail was up in the air. Split. And I believe it was the left eye of the animal that was up.[30]

The Eighth Circuit held this identification sufficient: "Given the uniqueness of the buttons on Briddle's coat, we think this identification evidence established that the exhibit ... was the button top found at the scene of the burglary."[31]

---

24. *See* Almodovar v. State, 464 N.E.2d 906, 911 (Ind. 1984) (initials scratched on shell casing).

25. *E.g.*, United States v. Capocci, 433 F.2d 155, 157 (1st Cir. 1970) (counterfeit bill); United States v. Bourassa, 411 F.2d 69, 72-73 (10th Cir.) (coin), *cert. denied*, 396 U.S. 915 (1969); Rosemund v. United States, 386 F.2d 412, 412 (10th Cir. 1967) (stolen money).

26. *E.g.*, Gass v. United States, 416 F.2d 767, 770 (D.C. Cir. 1969); Wheeler v. United States, 211 F.2d 19, 22-23 (D.C. Cir. 1953), *cert. denied*, 347 U.S. 1019 (1954); State v. Romo, 66 Ariz. 174, 178-80, 185 P.2d 757, 759-61 (1947).

27. *E.g.*,United States v. Ricco, 52 F.3d 58, 61 (4th Cir.) (detective "identified the vials [of cocaine] using his initials and the case number"), *cert. denied*, 516 U.S. 898 (1995); O'Quinn v. United States, 411 F.2d 78, 80 (10th Cir. 1969) (jar); People v. Horace, 186 Cal. App. 2d 560, 562, 9 Cal. Rptr. 43, 44 (1960) (crowbar); Roland v. State, 137 Ga. App. 796, 798, 224 S.E.2d 846, 848 (1976) (fingerprint cards); State v. Engberg, 109 Idaho 530, 534, 708 P.2d 935, 939 (App. 1985) (seizing officer placed initials on poker machine); People v. Sansone, 42 Ill. App. 3d 512, 514, 356 N.E.2d 101, 103 (1976) (stolen record albums); Johnson v. State, 267 Ind. 415, 420-21, 370 N.E.2d 892, 894-95 (1977) (knife); Fletcher v. State, 253 Ind. 468, 470-71, 255 N.E.2d 217, 219 (1970) (keys and bottles of whiskey); State v. Coleman, 441 S.W.2d 46, 51 (Mo. 1969) (box, watch, and bolt); State v. Ball, 1 Ohio App. 2d 297, 302, 204 N.E.2d 557, 560-61 (catheter), *appeal dismissed*, 176 Ohio St. 481, 200 N.E.2d 325 (1964).

28. *E.g.*, United States v. Reed, 392 F.2d 865, 867 (7th Cir.) ("very unusual looking hat"), *cert. denied*, 393 U.S. 984 (1968); Reyes v. United States, 383 F.2d 734, 734 (9th Cir. 1967) (holdup note "was unique and readily identifiable"); Pinkney v. United States, 363 F.2d 696, 698 (D.C. Cir. 1966) (knife identified by eyewitness after providing accurate description); Jenkins v. United States, 361 F.2d 615, 619 n.6 (10th Cir. 1966) (coin of unusual thickness); Jenkins v. Bierschenk, 333 F.2d 421, 425 (8th Cir. 1964) (joint with abrasion mark); Turner v. State, 178 Ga. App. 888, 889, 345 S.E.2d 99, 101 (1986) (distinctive shirt); State v. Shawley, 334 Mo. 352, 373-74, 67 S.W.2d 74, 85 (1933) (twisted and battered bullet); State v. Augustine, 1 Or. App. 372, 373, 462 P.2d 693, 694 (1969) (stolen auto transmission with "special markings").

29. 443 F.2d 443 (8th Cir.), *cert. denied*, 404 U.S. 942 (1971).

30. *Id.* at 448.

31. *Id.* at 449.

Similarly, in *United States v. Logan*[32] a "gun — the only .25 Titan automatic with a scratched-off serial number that Officer Grimes had ever seized — was admitted into evidence only after Officer Grimes identified it by make, model, size, color, style of its grip, and its scratched-off serial number. We find the government made a prima facie showing of authenticity."[33] Thus, the issue is whether the distinctive characteristics are sufficient to make it unlikely that another object would have the same characteristics.[34] Both *Briddle* and *Logan* involved very distinctive objects; far less distinctive objects have been admitted in evidence.

Witness Uncertainty

A witness's uncertainty in identifying an exhibit is not determinative. In one case, the evidence was admitted because the witness was "pretty sure" that an ax was the same one used in an attack.[35] In another case the court wrote, "[T]he witness' lack of certitude as to whether the objects offered are the ones he saw on a prior occasion goes to the weight the jury should give to the evidence, but lack of certitude does not preclude admissibility."[36]

§ 7-3. Chain of Custody.

The use of a chain of custody to authenticate evidence is well established in criminal trials. Nevertheless, two commentators have written that the governing federal rule "can easily be read as doing away with any chain of custody

---

32. 949 F.2d 1370 (5th Cir. 1991), *cert. denied*, 504 U.S. 925 (1992).

33. *Id.* at 1378.

34. *See* 2 J. Wigmore, Evidence § 411 (Chadbourn rev. 1979).

35. United States v. Johnson, 637 F.2d 1224, 1247-48 (9th Cir. 1980):

> [A]lthough the trial record reveals the identification of the ax made by Papse may not have been entirely free from doubt, the witness did state that he was "pretty sure" this was the weapon Johnson had used against him, that he saw the ax in Johnson's hand, and that he was personally familiar with this particular ax because he had used it in the past. Based on Papse's testimony, a reasonable juror could have found that this ax was the weapon allegedly used in the assault. Papse's ability or inability to specify particular identifying features of the ax, as well as the evidence of the ax's alleged changed condition, should then go to the question of weight to be accorded this evidence, which is precisely what the trial court ruled. In other words, although the jury remained free to reject the government's assertion that this ax had been used in the assault, the requirements for admissibility specified in Rule 901(a) had been met.

36. Howland v. State, 51 Wis. 2d 162, 171, 186 N.W.2d 319, 323 (1971). *Accord* United States v. Drumright, 534 F.2d 1383, 1385 (10th Cir.), *cert. denied*, 429 U.S. 960 (1976); United States v. Capocci, 433 F.2d 155, 157 (1st Cir. 1970); United States v. Rizzo, 418 F.2d 71, 81 (7th Cir. 1969), *cert. denied*, 397 U.S. 967 (1970).

requirement."[37] This seems doubtful. If anything, there is a need for more stringent requirements. The mass processing of immunoassay tests and the increasing volume of DNA testing heighten the importance of proper handling procedures. Indeed, improper labeling was the cause of an error in a DNA proficiency test.[38]

In some situations the proponent must establish a chain of custody. Proof of the chain of custody may be necessary either because the item of evidence is not readily identifiable or because more than simple identification is necessary to establish the item's relevance.

First, a chain of custody is often required for fungible evidence because these items have no unique characteristics. The inability to distinguish between fungible items makes positive identification by observation often impossible.[39] In addition, the nature of these items frequently makes them particularly susceptible to tampering or loss.[40] Nevertheless, the proper handling of fungible evidence — using lock-sealed envelopes[41] or containers that custodians then mark and initial

---

37. 2 S. Saltzburg & M. Martin, Federal Rules of Evidence Manual 478 (5th ed. 1990) (citing Fed. R. Evid. 901(a)). For a further discussion of this issue, *see* § 7-4 *infra.*

38. *See* note 47 *infra.*

39. *See* State v. Conley, 32 Ohio App. 2d 54, 59, 288 N.E.2d 296, 300 (1971) ("One white pill looks much like any other white pill and hence positive identification simply by observation is usually impossible").

40. The "danger of tampering, loss, or mistake with respect to an exhibit is greatest where the exhibit is small and is one which has physical characteristics fungible in nature and similar in form to substances familiar to people in their daily lives." Graham v. State, 253 Ind. 525, 531, 255 N.E.2d 652, 655 (1970). *See also* United States v. Haldeman, 559 F.2d 31, 108 (D.C. Cir. 1976) ("There was never any significant risk, as there would be with a fungible piece of real evidence, such as blood samples, that the tape recordings were inadvertently exchanged with other evidence of a similar type"), *cert. denied,* 431 U.S. 933 (1977); United States v. LePera, 443 F.2d 810, 812-13 (9th Cir.) ("Narcotic drugs are fungible and, being such, evidence of a continuous chain of possession is often necessary ... "), *cert. denied,* 404 U.S. 958 (1971); Brewer v. United States, 353 F.2d 260, 261 (8th Cir. 1965) ("Marijuana is fungible. There is no intrinsic way that one can identify a specimen observed yesterday with the one presented today"); Lucas v. State, 274 Ind. 635, 640, 413 N.E.2d 578, 582 (1980) ("[O]ur rule requiring that the chain of custody be established ... applies with diminishing strictness as the exhibits concerned become decreasingly susceptible to alteration, tampering or substitution").

41. Lock-sealed envelopes "can be opened only by destroying the seals." United States v. Santiago, 534 F.2d 768, 770 (7th Cir. 1976). *See also* United States v. Ricco, 52 F.3d 58, 61 (4th Cir.) (detective "identified the vials [of cocaine] using his initials and the case number"), *cert. denied,* 516 U.S. 898 (1995); United States v. Cox, 923 F.2d 519, 522 (7th Cir. 1991) ("[Detective] Vasquez testified that the marked, sealed evidence envelope he delivered to and retrieved from the lab was the same envelope into which he placed the plastic bag he received from Talley, and that the bag was in the same condition as when he received it from Talley (save the changes and marks made by the lab)").

— makes the evidence readily identifiable and eliminates most problems of misidentification and contamination.[42]

Second, if the relevance of an exhibit depends on its subsequent laboratory analysis, identification by police markings made at the scene does not provide a sufficient foundation. The markings establish that the exhibit in court was the item seized by the police, but a chain of custody may be necessary to establish that the item seized was the item analyzed at the crime laboratory. For example, in *Robinson v. Commonwealth*[43] the court reversed a rape conviction due to a break in the chain of custody: "The mere fact that the blouse and the panties were identified [by the victim at trial] did not prove the chain of possession necessary to validate the F.B.I. analysis of them."[44]

Third, if the condition of the object, not merely its identity, is the relevant issue, a chain of custody may be required to establish that the object had not been altered during police custody. This requirement is a necessary safeguard for evidence that is susceptible to undetected contamination or deterioration, such as blood samples[45] and substances subjected to neutron activation analysis.[46] Contamination problems also arise with DNA evidence. In an early DNA proficiency test, "out of 50 samples, 2 firms each declared 1 false match that could have resulted in the conviction of an innocent person. The errors

---

42. *See* United States v. Pressly, 978 F.2d 1026, 1028 (8th Cir. 1992) ("The officer who seized the substances [cocaine] testified that he marked them at the time of the seizure and that the packages admitted into evidence still bore his marks"); People v. Rivera, 184 A.D.2d 153, 592 N.Y.S.2d 697 (1993) (failure of arresting officer to mark 6 fungible glassine envelopes of heroin at time of seizure resulted in a gap in the chain of custody that required a reversal).

43. 212 Va. 136, 183 S.E.2d 179 (1971).

44. *Id.* at 139, 183 S.E.2d at 181. *See also* United States v. Ladd, 885 F.2d 954, 957 (1st Cir. 1989) ("In short, there was no competent proof to indicate that the sample extracted from Massey's corpse was the one which CSL tested. An important step in the custodial pavane was omitted"); Graham v. State, 253 Ind. 525, 532-34, 255 N.E.2d 652, 655-56 (1970) (wrapper containing white powder initialed at time police took possession but break in chain of custody prior to chemical analysis resulted in reversal).

45. *See* Lynch v. State, 687 S.W.2d 76, 78 (Tex. App. 1985) (chain of custody required for blood in a criminal case); Ritter v. State, 3 Tenn. Crim. App. 372, 462 S.W.2d 247, 249 (1970) ("Blood specimens ... should be handled with the greatest of care and all persons who handle the specimen should be ready to identify it and testify to its custody and unchanged condition"). *Cf.* Virgin Islands v. Testamark, 570 F.2d 1162, 1164 (3d Cir. 1978) (blood sample allowed to spoil). *See also* Glendening & Waugh, *The Stability of Ordinary Blood Alcohol Samples Held Various Periods of Time Under Different Conditions*, 10 J. FORENSIC SCI. 192, 199 (1965) (showing instability of alcohol content in blood samples for different temperatures and storage periods).

46. *See* Comment, *The Evidentiary Uses of Neutron Activation Analysis*, 59 CAL. L. REV. 997, 1013 (1971) ("If two unknowns that are compared to determine whether they came from a common source have both been contaminated in a similar way, it is clear that completely false points of similarity can result"); State v. Johnson, 539 S.W.2d 493, 505 (Mo. App. 1976) (control sample used to establish that NAA sample was uncontaminated), *cert. denied*, 430 U.S. 934 (1977).

apparently arose from sample handling problems."[47] Indeed, in *State v. Hammond*[48] the prosecutor argued unsuccessfully that exculpatory DNA evidence had been contaminated.

§ 7-3(A). Length of Chain.

When a chain of custody is required, either to show the identity of the item or its unchanged condition, it is necessary to determine where the chain begins and ends. Only breaks in possession that occur within the period included in the chain of custody affect admissibility.

The Initial Link

Disputes over the initial link in the chain of custody focus on whether the continuous possession requirement should apply at the time of the incident at issue or at the time when the evidence comes into the possession of its proponent. According to one position, a "chain-of-custody foundation is not required ... for periods before the evidence comes into the possession of law enforcement personnel."[49] The theory underlying this rule is that "the State cannot be charged with the responsibility of accounting for the custody of the exhibit" when it is not in its possession.[50] This rule has been applied in two different types of cases: first, those in which a third party had possession of the object prior to the time it was turned over to the police,[51] and second, those in which the object was not discovered at the crime scene until sometime after the commission of the crime.[52]

This position misconceives the purpose of the chain of custody rule. The rule is not designed to hold the police accountable, but rather to ensure that evidence is relevant. Police accountability is a means to this end. If the relevance of an object depends on its use in a crime, the offering party must establish, through a

---

47. Office of Technology Assessment, U.S. Congress, Genetic Witness: Forensic Uses of DNA Tests 80 (1990) (footnotes omitted); Thompson, *The Myth of DNA Fingerprints*, 9 Cal. Law. 34 (Apr. 1989) (Cellmark official admitted that the "error occurred because a lab technician incorrectly labeled a vial").

48. State v. Hammond, 221 Conn. 264, 604 A.2d 793 (1992).

49. Williams v. State, 269 Ind. 265, 269-70, 379 N.E.2d 981, 984 (1978). *See also* McAnalley v. State, 514 N.E.2d 831, 835 (Ind. 1987); Arnold v. State, 436 N.E.2d 288, 291 (Ind. 1982).

50. Zupp v. State, 258 Ind. 625, 629-30, 283 N.E.2d 540, 543 (1972).

51. *See* Zupp v. State, 258 Ind. 625, 629-30, 283 N.E.2d 540, 543 (1972); Love v. State, 178 Ind. App. 497, 500, 383 N.E.2d 382, 384 (1978); Greenlee v. State, 170 Ind. App. 639, 645, 354 N.E.2d 312, 315-16 (1976).

52. *See* Williams v. State, 269 Ind. 265, 269-70, 379 N.E.2d 981, 984 (1978) (three-hour delay in discovery of revolver); Thornton v. State, 268 Ind. 456, 459-60, 376 N.E.2d 492, 494 (1978) (knife discovered in open field subsequent to arrest).

chain of custody or otherwise, a connection between that object and the crime.[53] For example, if a third party finds a rifle near a crime scene and turns it over to the police several hours or days after the crime, it would be necessary to "account" for the rifle during the time it was in the third party's possession in order to tie the rifle to the place where the crime occurred.

The Final Link

Disagreement over the point at which the chain of custody ends focuses on whether the chain ends when the item is introduced at trial or at an earlier stage, *e.g.*, when a laboratory analyzes the item. Some commentators have read several cases as requiring the prosecution to trace the chain of custody from the time of seizure until the time of trial in all cases.[54] There may be some support for this view in the Advisory Committee's Note to Federal Rule 901, where the drafters refer to "establishing narcotics as taken from an accused and accounting for custody through the period until trial, including laboratory analysis."

The "length" of the chain of custody, however, depends on the purpose for which the evidence is offered. This point is illustrated by *State v. Conley,*[55] which involved a prosecution for the illegal sale of LSD. The drugs were purchased with marked bills whose serial numbers had been recorded. The defendant objected to both the admissibility of the bills and the LSD. The court wrote:

> To identify a particular item ... as being part of a pertinent incident in the past usually requires the showing of a continuous chain of custodians up to the material moment. When a chemical analysis is involved ... the material moment is the moment of analysis, since this provides the basis for the

53. In United States v. White, 569 F.2d 263 (5th Cir.), *cert. denied*, 439 U.S. 848 (1978), the court noted: "This is not a routine chain of custody situation in which the chain is broken between seizure of the evidence from the accused and a subsequent trial. Rather, the alleged break occurred before the government came into possession of the heroin." *Id.* at 266. After citing the rule in the "typical chain of custody cases," the court wrote: "We apply the same rule in the instant case." *Id. See also* United States v. Gelzer, 50 F.3d 1133, 1141 (2d Cir. 1995) ("The government concedes that there was not a 'full' chain of custody established for the revolver alleged to have been used during the robberies and to have been discarded during the car chase. At trial, Officer Staub testified that he found the revolver on Scranton Avenue near the intersection of Picadilly Downs and gave it to Officer Curtis") (evidence admitted); United States v. Cyphers, 553 F.2d 1064, 1073 (7th Cir.) (2 to 3-hour gap before evidence seized), *cert. denied*, 434 U.S. 843 (1977); People v. Brown, 115 A.D.2d 610, 496 N.Y.S.2d 272 (1985) (piece of rug recovered five days after crime held inadmissible).

54. *See* Annot., *Proof of identity of person or thing where object, specimen, or part is taken from a human body, as basis for admission of testimony or report of expert or officer based on such object, specimen, or part*, 21 A.L.R.2D 1216, 1236 (1952).

55. 32 Ohio App. 2d 54, 288 N.E.2d 296 (1971).

> expert testimony and makes that testimony relevant to the case. In the case of many other items, the material moment occurs at the trial.[56]

The court went on to hold that the chain of custody for the marked bills ran from the time the bills were marked until the trial, at which time they were identified. The chain of custody for the drugs differed; it ran from the time of seizure to the time of chemical analysis.

As a matter of relevancy, this approach is sound. The loss or destruction of the drugs after chemical analysis would not affect the relevance of the expert's testimony concerning the nature of the drugs.[57] Moreover, the prosecution generally is not required to introduce real evidence in order to prove its case. As one court has observed:

> It is not always necessary that tangible evidence be physically admitted at a trial.... Even when evidence is available it need not be physically offered. Thus, the grand larceny of an automobile may be established merely on competent testimony describing the stolen vehicle without actually producing the automobile before the trier of fact.[58]

The so-called "best evidence" rule applies only to writings, recordings, and photographs, not to real evidence.[59]

Nevertheless, the Florida Supreme Court has adopted a contrary position. According to the court, "when a defendant is charged with possession of a

---

56. *Id.* at 59-60, 288 N.E.2d at 300. *See also* United States v. Grant, 967 F.2d 81, 83 (2d Cir. 1992) ("In order for the chemist's testimony to be relevant, there must be some likelihood that the substance tested by the chemist was the substance seized at the airport"), *cert. denied*, 507 U.S. 924 (1993).

57. *See* United States v. Bailey, 277 F.2d 560, 565 (7th Cir. 1960) ("Even if the exhibits, including the heroin, had not been introduced in evidence the testimony of the witnesses and the stipulation as to the chemical analysis were sufficient...."); United States v. Sears, 248 F.2d 377, 378 (7th Cir. 1957), *cert. denied*, 355 U.S. 602 (1958); Bean v. United States, 533 F. Supp. 567, 578 (D. Colo. 1980); United States v. Singer, 43 F. Supp. 863, 864 (E.D.N.Y. 1942); People v. Schwartz, 64 Ill. App. 3d 989, 992-93, 382 N.E.2d 59, 63 (1978); People v. Julian, 41 N.Y.2d 340, 343-44, 360 N.E.2d 1310, 1313, 392 N.Y.S.2d 610, 612-13 (1977).

58. Holle v. State, 26 Md. App. 267, 274, 337 A.2d 163, 166 (1975) (stolen marked currency). *Accord* United States v. Kelly, 14 F.3d 1169, 1176 (7th Cir. 1994) ("The government is not required to introduce narcotics in evidence to obtain a narcotics conviction"); United States v. Grant, 967 F.2d 81, 83 (2d Cir. 1992) (heroin), *cert. denied*, 507 U.S. 924 (1993); United States v. Figueroa, 618 F.2d 934, 941 (2d Cir. 1980) (heroin); Chandler v. United States, 318 F.2d 356, 357 (10th Cir. 1963) (whiskey bottles); Ware v. United States, 259 F.2d 442, 444 (8th Cir. 1958) (heroin); Foster v. United States, 212 F.2d 249, 250 (D.C. Cir. 1954) (stolen property); United States v. Adelman, 107 F.2d 497, 498-99 (2d Cir. 1939) (morphine); State v. Lewis, 401 A.2d 645, 648 (Me. 1979) (hypodermic syringe); State v. Kroeplin, 266 N.W.2d 537, 539 (N.D. 1978) (rifle).

59. *See* FED. R. EVID. 1002. *See generally* 1 E. IMWINKELRIED, P. GIANNELLI, F. GILLIGAN & F. LEDERER, COURTROOM CRIMINAL EVIDENCE ch. 15 (3d ed. 1998) (best evidence rule).

controlled substance, that substance, if available, must be introduced into evidence."[60] In support of this rule, the court wrote:

> An absolute rule that a substance may be introduced or not at the discretion of the prosecutor is practically undesirable because of its potential for abuse. For example, such prosecutorial discretion could deliberately or unwittingly be used to confuse defense counsel and thwart the ability to make certain objections, particularly objections to chain of custody....
>
> The state's failure to introduce the substance in evidence against the defendant might put the defendant in the awkward position of introducing it himself should he wish to challenge its authenticity where there has been testimony of its existence as here....[61]

In addition, the loss or destruction of the evidence after laboratory analysis may affect the defendant's right to reexamine the evidence, which could result in the exclusion of expert testimony based on the prior laboratory examination.[62]

§ 7-3(B). Links in Chain.

The "links" in the chain of custody are those persons who have had *physical* custody of the object. Persons who have had access to, but not possession of, the evidence generally need not be accounted for. Such persons are not custodians. As noted by one court: "There is no rule requiring the prosecution to produce as witnesses all persons who were in a position to come into contact with the article sought to be introduced in evidence."[63]

Failure to account for the evidence during possession by a custodian may constitute a critical break in the chain of custody.[64] Some courts have indicated

---

60. G.E.G. v. State, 417 So. 2d 975, 977 (Fla. 1982).

61. *Id.* at 977-78.

62. *See* § 3-13 *supra* (constitutional duty to preserve evidence).

63. Gallego v. United States, 276 F.2d 914, 917 (9th Cir. 1960). *Accord* United States v. Fletcher, 487 F.2d 22, 23 (5th Cir. 1973) (fact that "fifteen persons had access to the evidence room" affects weight, not admissibility), *cert. denied*, 416 U.S. 958 (1974); Reyes v. United States, 383 F.2d 734, 734 (9th Cir. 1967) ("[T]he Government was under no obligation to produce as witnesses all persons who may have handled exhibit 1").

64. *E.g.*, United States v. Panczko, 353 F.2d 676, 679 (7th Cir. 1965) ("There is no evidence as to where or from whom Lieutenant Remkus got the keys"), *cert. denied*, 383 U.S. 935 (1966); Novak v. District of Columbia, 160 F.2d 588, 589 (D.C. Cir. 1947) (evidence failed "to identify the sample from which the analyses were made as being that sample taken from the appellant"); Smith v. United States, 157 F.2d 705 (D.C. Cir. 1946) (witness testified that watch presented in court had been handed to him by police officer at scene but he did not see where officer obtained the watch); United States v. Lewis, 19 M.J. 869 (A.F.C.M.R. 1985) (prosecution failed to show that urine sample analyzed at lab was the sample taken from the defendant); *Ex parte* Garrett, 608 So. 2d 337, 338 (Ala. 1992) (officer who transported marijuana did not identify who received evidence at lab; "This is clearly a case of a missing link in the chain of custody"); People v. Rivera, 184 A.D.2d

that all the links in the chain of custody must testify at trial.[65] The prevalent view, however, is that "the fact of a 'missing link does not prevent the admission of real evidence, so long as there is sufficient proof that the evidence is what it purports to be....'"[66] Thus, while a custodian in the chain of possession need not testify under all circumstances, the evidence should be accounted for during the time it was under that custodian's control. Several recurrent examples of "missing link" cases are discussed below.

Informants

The authentication of evidence by means other than the testimony of custodial links frequently arises in drug cases where an informant who handled the drugs does not testify at trial. In this situation, an undercover officer who accompanied the informant can testify about the informant's handling of the drugs. Thus, a noncustodian with firsthand knowledge may supply evidence of the object's handling while in the custody of the nontestifying informant.[67]

The testimony of a custodial link also may be dispensed with when circumstantial evidence sufficiently connects a defendant with drugs purchased from him by an informant, *i.e.*, a "controlled drug buy." For example, in *Peden v. United States*[68] an informant was searched prior to a drug transaction and provided with marked money.[69] While under surveillance, she met the defendant, and both were immediately arrested and searched.[70] The informant had morphine, and the defendant had the marked money.[71] Although the informant did not

---

153, 592 N.Y.S.2d 697 (1993) (failure of arresting officer to mark 6 fungible glassine envelopes of heroin at time of seizure resulted in a gap in the chain of custody that required a reversal).

65. *E.g.*, People v. Connelly, 35 N.Y.2d 171, 174, 316 N.E.2d 706, 708, 359 N.Y.S.2d 266, 269 (1974) ("[A]dmissibility generally requires that all those who have handled the item 'identify it and testify to its custody and unchanged condition'").

66. United States v. Howard-Arias, 679 F.2d 363, 366 (4th Cir.), *cert. denied*, 459 U.S. 874 (1982). *See also* United States v. Ricco, 52 F.3d 58, 61 (4th Cir.), *cert. denied*, 516 U.S. 898 (1995); United States v. Harrington, 923 F.2d 1371, 1374 (9th Cir.) ("[T]he prosecution was not required to call the custodian of the evidence"), *cert. denied*, 502 U.S. 854 (1991); United States v. Cardenas, 864 F.2d 1528, 1532 (10th Cir.) ("There is no rule that the prosecution must produce all persons who had custody of the evidence to testify at trial"), *cert. denied*, 491 U.S. 909 (1989); People v. Jones, 148 Ill. App. 3d 345, 499 N.E.2d 510, 514 (1986) ("A sufficient chain of custody does not require every person involved in the chain to testify").

67. *E.g.*, United States v. Jones, 404 F. Supp. 529, 542 (E.D. Pa. 1975) (undercover agent observed defendant giving drugs to informant; informant did not testify), *aff'd*, 538 F.2d 321 (3d Cir. 1976).

68. 223 F.2d 319 (D.C. Cir. 1955), *cert. denied*, 359 U.S. 971 (1959).

69. *Id.* at 321.

70. *Id.*

71. *Id.*

testify, the court held the chain sufficient to connect the defendant with the morphine.[72]

Postal Employees

Postal employees who handle evidence sent to a crime laboratory by mail are custodial links. Postal employees rarely, if ever, testify at trial, however. A rule requiring every custodian to testify would necessitate calling all postal employees who handled the evidence. This would "place an impossible burden upon the state."[73] Therefore, courts invoke the presumption that "articles transported by regular United States mail and delivered in the ordinary course of the mails are delivered in substantially the same condition in which they were sent."[74]

Many law enforcement agencies recommend registered mail or other similar means for sending evidence.[75] Furthermore, the FBI recommends stringent packaging requirements for items mailed to its laboratory.[76] Proof that these procedures were followed, and not the presumption of due delivery, assures the reliability of the evidence.

Minor Links

Another category of cases involves what may be called "minor links" — intermediate custodians who had possession for a short period of time and merely passed the evidence along to another link. For example, in one case a chief chemist, who had received a sealed envelope of heroin and then turned it over to

---

72. *Id. See also* United States v. Amaro, 422 F.2d 1078, 1080 (9th Cir. 1970).

73. Trantham v. State, 508 P.2d 1104, 1107 (Okla. Crim. App. 1973).

74. Schacht v. State, 154 Neb. 858, 861, 50 N.W.2d 78, 80 (1951). *See also* Pasadena Research Laboratories, Inc. v. United States, 169 F.2d 375, 382 (9th Cir.) (presumption of regularity applies to postal employees' handling of vials during shipment), *cert. denied*, 335 U.S. 853 (1948); Ver Steegh v. Flaugh, Inc., 251 Iowa 1011, 1018, 103 N.W.2d 718, 723 (1960) (presumption of proper and untampered delivery of evidence by postal authorities); State v. Jordan, 14 N.C. App. 453, 456, 188 S.E.2d 701, 702 (1972); Rogers v. Commonwealth, 197 Va. 527, 531, 90 S.E.2d 257, 259-60 (1955) ("In proving identity legal presumptions may of course be relied upon unless rebutted, *e.g.*, that articles regularly mailed are delivered in substantially the same condition in which they were sent"). *But see* Miller v. State, 484 So. 2d 1203, 1205 (Ala. Crim. App. 1986) (no presumption of delivery where blood specimen placed in agency's "regular outgoing mail" rather than U.S. mail).

75. F.B.I., *supra* note 21, at 103 ("Ship [physical evidence] by U.S. Postal Service, Registered Mail, United Parcel Service, Federal Express, or air freight"). *See also* United States v. Godoy, 528 F.2d 281, 283 (9th Cir. 1975) (narcotics sent by registered mail to laboratory); United States v. Jackson, 482 F.2d 1254, 1266 (8th Cir. 1973) (registered, special delivery, air mail); Brewer v. United States, 353 F.2d 260, 262 (8th Cir. 1965) (registered mail).

76. F.B.I., *supra* note 21, at 103 (use suitable containers, package each item separately, and seal securely).

the examining chemist, did not testify. The court upheld the admissibility of the evidence because the seal was "unbroken when the latter received it."[77]

The category of minor links whose testimony is not required to establish a chain of custody includes not only laboratory personnel[78] but also police officers who receive evidence from a seizing officer and mail[79] or transport[80] it to a laboratory for analysis. In short, "accounting for" all the links in the chain of custody does not necessarily mean all the links need testify at trial.

§ 7-4. Burden and Standard of Proof.

The burden of proving authentication, including a chain of custody, rests with the party offering the evidence.[81] Prior to the adoption of the Federal Rules of Evidence, the courts described the standard of proof in various ways. The most

---

77. United States v. Picard, 464 F.2d 215, 216 n.1 (1st Cir. 1972).

78. *E.g.*, United States v. Williams, 809 F.2d 75, 89-90 (1st Cir. 1986) (lab technician need not testify), *cert. denied*, 482 U.S. 906 (1987); United States v. Glaze, 643 F.2d 549, 552 (8th Cir. 1981) (nontestifying chemist received and transported narcotics to testifying chemist); Gass v. United States, 416 F.2d 767, 770 (D.C. Cir. 1969) (nontestifying nurse transported marked slides from examining physician to pathologist); United States v. Burris, 393 F.2d 81, 82-83 (7th Cir. 1968) (examining chemist, who did not personally receive narcotics, testified about standard laboratory procedure and unbroken seal).

79. *E.g.*, United States v. Jones, 404 F. Supp. 529, 543 (E.D. Pa. 1975) (testimony of officer who mailed heroin to lab not necessary where sealed packages initialed and return receipt introduced), *aff'd*, 538 F.2d 321 (3d Cir. 1976); United States v. Marks, 32 F. Supp. 459, 460 (D. Conn. 1940) (police officer who mailed heroin died prior to trial; officer's handwriting on sealed envelopes identified and package sent by registered mail).

80. *E.g.*, United States v. Gelzer, 50 F.3d 1133, 1141 (2d Cir. 1995) ("At trial, Officer Staub testified that he found the revolver on Scranton Avenue near the intersection of Picadilly Downs and gave it to Officer Curtis. Next, Postal Inspector Morrison testified that he received the revolver from Detective Curtis and sent it to Washington, D.C., for forensic testing"); United States v. Cardenas, 864 F.2d 1528, 1532 (10th Cir.) (officer who carried cocaine to evidence room did not testify), *cert. denied*, 491 U.S. 909 (1989); United States v. Lampson, 627 F.2d 62, 65 (7th Cir. 1980) (deputy sheriff who transported evidence did not testify); United States v. Robinson, 447 F.2d 1215, 1221 (D.C. Cir. 1971) (officer who received evidence from seizing officer and transported it to chemist did not testify), *rev'd on rehearing on other grounds*, 471 F.2d 1082 (D.C. Cir. 1972), *rev'd on other grounds*, 414 U.S. 218 (1973); Bay v. State, 489 N.E.2d 1220, 1223 (Ind. App. 1986) (detective who transported marijuana to lab did not testify); Berendes v. Commissioner of Pub. Safety, 382 N.W.2d 888, 891 (Minn. App. 1986) (evidence of who transported blood sample to lab not necessary); Schram v. Commissioner of Pub. Safety, 359 N.W.2d 632 (Minn. App. 1984) (police officer who transported blood sample to lab did not testify); State v. Goad, 692 S.W.2d 32, 36 (Tenn. Crim. App. 1985) (property room custodian need not testify).

81. *See* United States v. Santiago, 534 F.2d 768, 770 (7th Cir. 1976). *See generally* 1 J. WIGMORE, EVIDENCE § 18, at 841 (Tillers rev. 1983) ("The opponent merely invokes the law; ... the proponent must make the evidence satisfy the law"); Bourjaily v. United States, 483 U.S. 171, 175 (1987) ("We have traditionally required that these [preliminary] matters be established by a preponderance of proof").

common expression of the standard was that the offering party had to establish the identity and condition of the exhibit by a "reasonable probability."[82] Phrases such as "reasonable certainty"[83] and "reasonable assurance"[84] seem only variants of this standard. The reasonable probability standard appears to require no more than the "preponderance of evidence" or "more probable than not" standard,[85] and some courts have explicitly expressed the standard in those terms.[86] Moreover, chain of custody "requirements go to the competency of the evidence, not merely to its credibility."[87] Under this view, the trial court determines whether this standard has been satisfied.[88]

Federal Rules

In contrast, Federal Rule 901(a) requires only that the offering party introduce "evidence sufficient to support a finding that the matter in question is what its

---

82. *E.g.*, United States v. Brown, 482 F.2d 1226, 1228 (8th Cir. 1973) ("reasonable probability the article has not been changed in any important respect"); United States v. Robinson, 447 F.2d 1215, 1220 (D.C. Cir. 1971), *rev'd on other grounds*, 414 U.S. 218 (1973); United States v. Capocci, 433 F.2d 155, 157 (1st Cir. 1970); Gass v. United States, 416 F.2d 767, 770 (D.C. Cir. 1969); West v. United States, 359 F.2d 50, 55 (8th Cir.), *cert. denied*, 385 U.S. 867 (1966); Brewer v. United States, 353 F.2d 260, 262 (8th Cir. 1965); Gallego v. United States, 276 F.2d 914, 917 (9th Cir. 1960); United States v. S.B. Penick & Co., 136 F.2d 413, 415 (2d Cir. 1943); State v. Johnson, 162 Conn. 215, 232, 292 A.2d 903, 911-12 (1972); Doye v. State, 16 Md. App. 511, 519, 299 A.2d 117, 121 (1973).

83. *See* United States v. Jones, 404 F. Supp. 529, 543 (E.D. Pa. 1975); State v. Tillman, 208 Kan. 954, 958-59, 494 P.2d 1178, 1182 (1972); Sorce v. State, 88 Nev. 350, 352-53, 497 P.2d 902, 903 (1972).

84. *See* State v. Cress, 344 A.2d 57, 61 (Me. 1975); State v. Baines, 394 S.W.2d 312, 316 (Mo. 1965), *cert. denied*, 384 U.S. 992 (1966); People v. Julian, 41 N.Y.2d 340, 344, 360 N.E.2d 1310, 1313, 392 N.Y.S.2d 610, 613 (1977).

85. *See* People v. Riser, 47 Cal. 2d 566, 580-81, 305 P.2d 1, 10 ("The requirement of reasonable certainty is not met when some vital link in the chain of possession is not accounted for, because then it is as likely as not that the evidence analyzed was not the evidence originally received"), *appeal dismissed*, 358 U.S. 646 (1959); State v. Serl, 269 N.W.2d 785, 788-89 (S.D. 1978). *See also* People v. Lucas, 12 Cal. 4th 415, 444, 907 P.2d 373, 391, 48 Cal. Rptr. 2d 525, 543 (1995) ("The requirement of reasonable certainty is not met when some vital link in the chain of possession is not accounted for, because then it is as likely as not that the evidence analyzed was not the evidence originally received") (quoting *Riser* and other cases), *cert. denied*, 117 S. Ct. 114 (1996).

86. *See* State v. Henderson, 337 So. 2d 204, 206 (La. 1976); State v. Sears, 298 So. 2d 814, 821 (La. 1974); State v. Williams, 273 So. 2d 280, 281 (La. 1973) ("clear preponderance").

87. State v. Serl, 269 N.W.2d 785, 789 (S.D. 1978).

88. "That determination is to be made by the trial judge, not the jury...." United States v. Brown, 482 F.2d 1226, 1228 (8th Cir. 1973). *Accord* United States v. Daughtry, 502 F.2d 1019, 1021-23 (5th Cir. 1974); United States v. Stevenson, 445 F.2d 25, 27 (7th Cir.), *cert. denied*, 404 U.S. 857 (1971); West v. United States, 359 F.2d 50, 55 (8th Cir.), *cert. denied*, 385 U.S. 867 (1966); Brewer v. United States, 353 F.2d 260, 262 (8th Cir. 1965).

proponent claims." Thus, the trial court decides only whether sufficient evidence has been introduced from which a reasonable jury could find the evidence identified.[89] In other words, the offering party need only make a "prima facie"[90] showing of authenticity to gain admissibility, and the jury decides whether the evidence has been sufficiently identified.[91]

Not only is the prima facie standard less stringent than the "more probable than not" standard, but it also results in a different rule concerning the application of the rules of evidence. Federal Rule 104(a) provides that in deciding preliminary questions of admissibility the trial court "is not bound by the rules of evidence except those with respect to privileges."[92] Accordingly, if the admissibility decision is entrusted to the trial court under the "more probable than not" standard, evidence rules would not be applicable and hearsay could be considered by the court. Rule 104(b), which governs questions of conditional relevancy, is an exception to Rule 104(a), and Rule 901(a) is a specialized application of Rule 104(b).[93] If Rule 104(b) controls, the rules of evidence apply because the jury shares in the authenticity decision.[94] Since the Federal Rules

---

89. *See* Zenith Radio Corp. v. Matsushita Elec. Indus. Co., 505 F. Supp. 1190, 1220 (E.D. Pa. 1980) ("[W]hile the court's power to 'consider' inadmissible evidence under Rule 104(a) is clear, the substantive determination which the court is required to make on the issue of authentication is whether admissible evidence exists which is sufficient to support a jury finding of authenticity .... [O]ur task in ruling on authenticity is limited to determining whether there is substantial admissible evidence to support a finding of authentication by the trier of fact"), *aff'd in part and rev'd in part*, 723 F.2d 238 (3d Cir. 1983), *rev'd*, 475 U.S. 574 (1986).

90. *See* United States v. Johnson, 68 F.3d 899, 903 (5th Cir. 1995) ("Any break in the chain of custody affects the weight, not the admissibility of evidence. Thus, if the district court correctly finds that the government has made a prima facie showing of authenticity, then the evidence is admissible, and issues of authenticity are for the jury to decide"); United States v. Sparks, 2 F.3d 574, 582 (5th Cir. 1993) (Prosecution need only make a "prima facie" showing that bottles of crack seized from accused were the drugs analyzed), *cert. denied*, 510 U.S. 1080 (1994); United States v. Ortiz, 966 F.2d 707, 716 (1st Cir. 1992) (Rule 901(a) "does not erect a particularly high hurdle"), *cert. denied*, 506 U.S. 1063 (1993); United States v. Logan, 949 F.2d 1370, 1377 (5th Cir. 1991) ("we look for a prima facie showing of authenticity" when examining a chain of custody), *cert. denied*, 504 U.S. 925 (1992); United States v. Johnson, 637 F.2d 1224, 1247 (9th Cir. 1980); United States v. Goichman, 547 F.2d 778, 784 (3d Cir. 1976).

91. *See* United States v. Goichman, 547 F.2d 778, 784 (3d Cir. 1976) ("[I]t is the jury who will ultimately determine the authenticity of the evidence, not the court").

92. *See also* United States v. Matlock, 415 U.S. 164, 172-73 (1974) ("[T]he rules of evidence normally applicable in criminal trials do not operate with full force at hearings before the judge to determine the admissibility of evidence").

93. *See* 1 E. IMWINKELRIED, P. GIANNELLI, F. GILLIGAN & F. LEDERER, COURTROOM CRIMINAL EVIDENCE § 134 (3d ed. 1998) (discussing conditional relevance).

94. Zenith Radio Corp. v. Matsushita Elec. Indus. Co., 505 F. Supp. 1190 (E.D. Pa. 1980), *aff'd in part and rev'd in part*, 723 F.2d 238 (3d Cir. 1983), *rev'd*, 475 U.S. 574 (1986).

treat authentication as a matter of conditional relevance, *i.e.*, adopt the prima facie evidence standard, evidence rules apply in this context.[95]

Whether the Federal Rules of Evidence were intended to effect a major change in the chain of custody requirements is unclear. Two commentators have written that "Rule 901(a) can easily be read as doing away with any chain of custody requirement."[96] Several decisions of the Fifth Circuit contain language that supports this view. For example, the court has written that "chain of custody goes to the weight rather than the admissibility of the evidence, and is thus reserved for the jury."[97] The Second Circuit also appears to have adopted this less stringent standard: "Fed. R. Evid. 901 requires that to meet the admissibility threshold the government need only prove a rational basis for concluding that an exhibit is what it is claimed to be."[98]

Other federal courts of appeal, however, continue to apply the pre-Rule's "reasonable probability" standard.[99] Moreover, decisions of the Fifth Circuit also

---

95. For a discussion of this issue, *see* Giannelli, *supra* note 1, at 554-56.

96. 2 S. Saltzburg & M. Martin, Federal Rules of Evidence Manual 478 (5th ed. 1990).

97. Ballou v. Henri Studios, Inc., 656 F.2d 1147, 1154 (5th Cir. 1981). *Accord* United States v. Johnson, 68 F.3d 899, 903 (5th Cir. 1995) ("Any break in the chain of custody affects the weight, not the admissibility of evidence. Thus, if the district court correctly finds that the government has made a prima facie showing of authenticity, then the evidence is admissible, and issues of authenticity are for the jury to decide"); United States v. Crawford, 52 F.3d 1303, 1311 (5th Cir. 1995) ("Any break in the chain of custody affects the weight, not admissibility, of evidence"); United States v. Shaw, 920 F.2d 1225, 1229-30 (5th Cir.) ("any break in the chain of custody of physical evidence does not render the evidence inadmissible but instead goes to the weight that the jury should accord that evidence"), *cert. denied*, 500 U.S. 926 (1991); United States v. Colatriano, 624 F.2d 686, 689 (5th Cir. 1980); United States v. Henderson, 588 F.2d 157, 160 (5th Cir.), *cert. denied*, 440 U.S. 975 (1979).

98. United States v. Hon, 904 F.2d 803, 809 (2d Cir. 1990), *cert. denied*, 498 U.S. 1069 (1991). *But see* United States v. Gelzer, 50 F.3d 1133, 1141 (2d Cir. 1995) ("There was sufficient evidence to establish that it is more likely than not that the revolver offered at trial was the same as that recovered by Officer Staub").

99. *E.g.*, United States v. Gelzer, 50 F.3d 1133, 1141 (2d Cir. 1995) ("There was sufficient evidence to establish that it is more likely than not that the revolver offered at trial was the same as that recovered by Officer Staub"); United States v. Williams, 44 F.3d 614, 618 (7th Cir. 1995) ("reasonable likelihood"); United States v. Miller, 994 F.2d 441, 443 (8th Cir. 1993); United States v. Pazzanese, 982 F.2d 251, 253 (8th Cir. 1992); United States v. Harrington, 923 F.2d 1371, 1374 (9th Cir.), *cert. denied*, 502 U.S. 854 164 (1991); United States v. Cardenas, 864 F.2d 1528, 1532 (10th Cir.), *cert. denied*, 491 U.S. 909 (1989); United States v. Rans, 851 F.2d 1111, 1114 (8th Cir. 1988); United States v. Roberts, 844 F.2d 537, 550 (8th Cir.), *cert. denied*, 488 U.S. 867 (1988); United States v. Williams, 809 F.2d 75, 89 (1st Cir. 1986), *cert. denied*, 482 U.S. 906 (1987); United States v. Jones, 687 F.2d 1265, 1267 (8th Cir. 1982); United States v. Howard-Arias, 679 F.2d 363, 366 (4th Cir.), *cert. denied*, 459 U.S. 874 (1982); United States v. Jackson, 649 F.2d 967, 973 (3d Cir.), *cert. denied*, 454 U.S. 1034 (1981); United States v. Weeks, 645 F.2d 658, 660 (8th Cir. 1981); United States v. Brewer, 630 F.2d 795, 802 (10th Cir. 1980); United States v. Aviles, 623 F.2d 1192, 1198 (7th Cir. 1980); United States v. Luna, 585 F.2d 1, 6 (1st Cir.), *cert. denied*, 439 U.S. 852 (1978).

cite the "reasonable probability" standard as the threshold requirement under Rule 901.[100]

Of course, if the authentication issue involves an essential element of the charged offense, such as in a possession-of-drugs case, the prosecution must establish that a reasonable jury could find — beyond a reasonable doubt — that the drugs seized were the drugs tested or suffer a directed verdict.[101]

State Rules

Some state adaptations of the Federal Rules specifically require a chain of custody. For example, Alaska Rule 901(a) contains a comprehensive provision on this subject.[102] The commentary to Delaware Rule of Evidence 901, which parallels the federal rule, contains the following statement: "It is not intended that this rule abolish the necessity of showing the chain of custody of exhibits in criminal proceedings."[103] The commentary to the Military Rules states that "[t]here appears to be no reason to believe that the rule will change present law as it affects chains of custody for real evidence — especially if fungible."[104]

Application of the Standard of Proof

To satisfy its burden of proof, the prosecution need not eliminate every possibility of substitution, alteration, or tampering. The "mere possibility of a break in the chain does not render the physical evidence inadmissible, but raises

---

100. *See* Ballou v. Henri Studios, Inc., 656 F.2d 1147, 1155 (5th Cir. 1981); United States v. Albert, 595 F.2d 283, 290 (5th Cir.), *cert. denied*, 444 U.S. 963 (1979).

101. *See* 1 E. Imwinkelried, P. Giannelli, F. Gilligan & F. Lederer, Courtroom Criminal Evidence § 2918 (3d ed. 1998) (burden of going forward).

102. Alaska R. Evid. 901(a) reads:

> (1) Whenever the prosecution in a criminal trial offers (A) real evidence which is of such a nature as not to be readily identifiable, or as to be susceptible to adulteration, contamination, modification, tampering, or other changes in form attributable to accident, carelessness, error or fraud, or (B) testimony describing real evidence of the type set forth in (A) if the information on which the description is based was acquired while the evidence was in the custody or control of the prosecution, the prosecution must first demonstrate as a matter of reasonable certainty that the evidence is at the time of trial or was at the time it was observed properly identified and free of the possible taints identified by this paragraph.
>
> (2) In any case in which real evidence of the kind described in subparagraph (1) of this subdivision is offered, the court may require additional proof before deciding whether to admit or exclude evidence under Rule 403.

103. Del. R. Evid. 901 (1994), comment.

104. Mil. R. Evid. 901, analysis.

the question of weight to be accorded by the jury...."[105] In *United States v. Ladd*,[106] the First Circuit stated the rule as follows:

> In the last analysis, the prosecution's chain-of-custody evidence must be adequate — not infallible. Here, some links in the chain were rusty, but none were missing. Without question, the defense succeeded in showing a certain sloppiness, regrettable in a forensic laboratory. Yet the net effect of any such disarray on the authenticity of the evidence depended on what inferences a reasonable factfinder might choose to draw from it. Where, as in this case, a trier chooses among plausible (albeit competing) inferences, appellate courts should not intrude.[107]

Accordingly, the evidence was admissible. The same court, however, ruled that another item of evidence should have been excluded due to a "missing link" that resulted from a discrepancy between laboratory identification numbers: "In short, there was no competent proof to indicate that the sample extracted from Massey's corpse was the one that CSL tested. An important step in the custodial pavane was omitted."[108]

Many discrepancies concerning the weight,[109] number,[110] date,[111] and labeling[112] of evidence often will not result in exclusion. In one case a four-day

---

105. United States v. Jardina, 747 F.2d 945, 951 (5th Cir. 1984), *cert. denied*, 470 U.S. 1058 (1985). *See also* United States v. Allen, 106 F.3d 695, 700 (6th Cir.) ("Merely raising the possibility of tampering is insufficient to render evidence inadmissible"), *cert. denied*, 117 S. Ct. 2467 (1997); United States v. Kelly, 14 F.3d 1169, 1175 (7th Cir. 1994) ("[A]n adequate chain of custody can be shown even if all possibilities of tampering are not excluded").

106. 885 F.2d 954 (1st Cir. 1989).

107. *Id.* at 957. *See also* United States v. Scott, 19 F.3d 1238, 1245 (7th Cir.) ("[T]he government does not need to prove a 'perfect' chain of custody, and any gaps in the chain 'go to the weight of the evidence and not its admissibility.' In this case there was at most a minor gap in the chain of custody"), *cert. denied*, 513 U.S. 857 (1994); Kennedy v. State, 578 N.E.2d 633, 639 (Ind. 1991) ("[T]he State need not establish a perfect chain of custody, and any gaps go to the weight of the evidence and not its admissibility").

108. 885 F.2d at 957.

109. *See* United States v. Godoy, 528 F.2d 281, 283 (9th Cir. 1975); People v. Zipprich, 141 Ill. App. 3d 123, 490 N.E.2d 8, 10-11 (1986); People v. Julian, 41 N.Y.2d 340, 342, 360 N.E.2d 1310, 1312, 392 N.Y.S.2d 610, 612 (1977).

110. *See* United States v. Hon, 904 F.2d 803, 810 (2d Cir. 1990), *cert. denied*, 498 U.S. 1069 (1991); United States v. Clark, 425 F.2d 827, 833 (3d Cir.), *cert. denied*, 400 U.S. 820 (1970).

111. *See* United States v. Robinson, 967 F.2d 287, 291 (9th Cir. 1992) ("government concedes that there is a discrepancy regarding the date of seizure"); United States v. Barcella, 432 F.2d 570, 572 (1st Cir. 1970); State v. Smith, 463 So. 2d 1003, 1005 (La. App. 1985).

112. *See* United States v. Kelly, 14 F.3d 1169, 1175-76 (7th Cir. 1994) (discrepancy in inventory did not preclude admissibility of evidence). *See also In re* Sealed Case, 99 F.3d 1175, 1177 (D.C. Cir. 1996) ("The police investigator at the scene placed all of the narcotics evidence [13 bags seized from defendant and 311 from house] in a raid kit. The tampering described in *Lane*

delay, during which drugs and a gun remained in a police officer's car trunk, did not result in exclusion of the evidence.[113] In another case, *United States v. Stewart*,[114] the D.C. Circuit wrote:

> The government persuasively maintains that it met its burden here because there is no suggestion that the drugs left the vault during the twelve-day period and DEA chemists who analyzed the drug sample found no evidence of tampering. An MPRD officer further testified that, as a general matter, if any signs of tampering are found in items to be delivered to the DEA, or if items are found to be unsealed, the problem is investigated and the evidence is not accepted at the laboratory. Under the circumstances, because the evidence was at no point missing or accessible to unauthorized persons, the delay in transferring the drugs from the vault at the Narcotics Branch to the DEA did not constitute a break in the chain of custody.[115]

In satisfying its burden of proof, the prosecution is frequently aided by the so-called "presumption of regularity."[116] As one court has commented:

> In the absence of any evidence to the contrary, the trial judge was entitled to assume that this official would not tamper with the sack and can or their contents. Where no evidence indicating otherwise is produced, the presumption of regularity supports the official acts of public officers, and courts presume that they have properly discharged their official duties.[117]

---

does not include the repackaging of evidence done in this case"); United States v. Allocco, 234 F.2d 955, 956 (2d Cir.), *cert. denied*, 352 U.S. 931 (1956); Ingle v. State, 176 Ind. App. 695, 707, 377 N.E.2d 885, 892 (1975); State v. Beaudoin, 386 A.2d 731, 733 (Me. 1978); Renner v. Commissioner of Pub. Safety, 373 N.W.2d 628, 632 (Minn. App. 1985).

113. United States v. Logan, 949 F.2d 1370, 1377 (5th Cir. 1991), *cert. denied*, 504 U.S. 925 (1992).

114. United States v. Stewart, 104 F.3d 1377 (D.C. Cir.), *cert. denied*, 117 S. Ct. 1856 (1997).

115. *Id.* at 1383. *See also* Lagrone v. State, 942 S.W.2d 602, 617 (Tex. Crim. App.) ("In the absence of any evidence of tampering, ... we see no reason to prohibit the admission of properly identified evidence just because it has been kept in an evidence room for an extended period of time [31 months] and undergone prior forensic testing"), *cert. denied*, 118 S. Ct. 305 (1997).

116. For a detailed discussion of the presumption of regularity, *see* Giannelli, *supra* note 1, at 558-60.

117. Gallego v. United States, 276 F.2d 914, 917 (9th Cir. 1960). *Accord* United States v. Allen, 106 F.3d 695, 700 (6th Cir. 1997) ("Where there is no evidence indicating tampering with the exhibits occurred, courts presume public officers have discharged their duties properly"); United States v. Scott, 19 F.3d 1238, 1245 (7th Cir.) ("In making this determination, the district court makes a 'presumption of regularity,' presuming that the government officials who had custody of the exhibits discharged their duties properly"), *cert. denied*, 513 U.S. 857 (1994); United States v. Kelly, 14 F.3d 1169, 1175 (7th Cir. 1994) ("When there is no evidence of tampering, a presumption of regularity attends the official acts of public officers in custody of evidence; the courts presume they did their jobs correctly"); United States v. Miller, 994 F.2d 441, 444 (8th Cir. 1993) ("officials

Several cases have extended the presumption to hospital personnel.[118] The presumption of regularity, however, has been criticized. "The presumption of regularity, if it can be dignified as a rule, does not serve as a substitute for evidence when authenticity is, as here, challenged on not insubstantial grounds. At best it may relieve the government of the necessity for offering proof of custody until the integrity of the evidence has been put in issue."[119] In addition, Wigmore observed that the presumption of regularity was "more often mentioned than enforced."[120] In short, the presumption could be deleted from the cases and nothing would change. The prosecution's burden would remain the same.

Appellate Review

The standard on appeal for reviewing a trial court's decision on identification is an abuse of discretion.[121]

---

are entitled to the presumption of integrity"); United States v. Lott, 854 F.2d 244, 250 (7th Cir. 1988); United States v. Olson, 846 F.2d 1103, 1116 (7th Cir.), *cert. denied*, 488 U.S. 850 (1988); United States v. Aviles, 623 F.2d 1192, 1198 (7th Cir. 1980); United States v. Nelson, 603 F.2d 42, 48 (8th Cir. 1979); United States v. Lane, 591 F.2d 961, 962 (D.C. Cir. 1979); United States v. Coades, 549 F.2d 1303, 1309 (9th Cir. 1977); United States v. Daughtry, 502 F.2d 1019, 1021 (5th Cir. 1974); United States v. Brown, 482 F.2d 1226, 1228 (8th Cir. 1973); West v. United States, 359 F.2d 50, 55 (8th Cir.), *cert. denied*, 385 U.S. 867 (1966); State v. Lamp, 322 N.W.2d 48, 59 (Iowa 1982).

118. Gass v. United States, 416 F.2d 767, 770 (D.C. Cir. 1969); Pasadena Research Laboratories, Inc. v. United States, 169 F.2d 375, 381-82 (9th Cir.), *cert. denied*, 335 U.S. 853 (1948).

119. United States v. Starks, 515 F.2d 112, 122 (3d Cir. 1975). *See also* United States v. Lampson, 627 F.2d 62, 65 (7th Cir. 1980) ("The Government's burden ... cannot be diluted by unwarranted presumptions about the evidence it seeks to introduce"); Bauer v. Veith, 374 Mich. 1, 3, 130 N.W.2d 897, 899 (1964) (presumption cannot be used to "supply missing links in the chain").

120. 9 J. WIGMORE, EVIDENCE § 2534, at 488 (3d ed. 1940).

121. *E.g.*, United States v. Ricco, 52 F.3d 58, 61 (4th Cir.), *cert. denied*, 516 U.S. 898 (1995); United States v. Williams, 44 F.3d 614, 618 (7th Cir. 1995); United States v. Scott, 19 F.3d 1238, 1245 (7th Cir.), *cert. denied*, 513 U.S. 857 (1994); United States v. Boykins, 9 F.3d 1278, 1285 (7th Cir. 1993), *cert. denied*, 117 S. Ct. 1271 (1997); United States v. Johnson, 977 F.2d 1360, 1368 (10th Cir. 1992) ("Although the chain of custody for the bottles may not be perfect, we conclude that the district court did not abuse its discretion in admitting this evidence"), *cert. denied*, 506 U.S. 1070 (1993); United States v. Ladd, 885 F.2d 954, 956 (1st Cir. 1989); United States v. Jones, 687 F.2d 1265, 1267 (8th Cir. 1982); United States v. Howard-Arias, 679 F.2d 363, 366 (4th Cir.), *cert. denied*, 459 U.S. 874 (1982); United States v. Mullins, 638 F.2d 1151, 1152 (8th Cir. 1981); United States v. Georgalis, 631 F.2d 1199, 1206 (5th Cir. 1980); United States v. Brewer, 630 F.2d 795, 802 (10th Cir. 1980).

§ 7-5. Methods of Proof.

Absent a stipulation, the chain of custody typically is established, at least in part, by the testimony of the persons (links) who had possession of the object. These witnesses may refresh their recollections by referring to any available documentation.[122]

Stipulations

The stipulation cases are instructive.[123] In one case, the accused challenged the chain of custody despite a stipulation.[124] In another case, the accused was successful in making such a challenge because the stipulation was defective; it failed to state that the material seized from the defendant was the same material tested by the chemist.[125]

Habit & Routine Practice Evidence

The proponent may also introduce evidence of habit or routine practice to establish the chain of custody.[126] Federal Rule 406 provides that "[e]vidence of the habit of a person or of the routine practice of an organization ... is relevant to prove that the conduct of the person or organization on a particular occasion was in conformity with the habit or routine practice." Accordingly, evidence of the standard operating procedures of police departments and laboratories in safeguarding real evidence may be used to establish the chain of custody.[127]

---

122. *See* FED. R. EVID. 612 (use of writings to refresh memory); United States v. Stevenson, 445 F.2d 25, 27 (7th Cir.) (in establishing chain of custody, officers "refreshed their recollection from official records"), *cert. denied*, 404 U.S. 857 (1971).

123. *See* People v. Perine, 82 Ill. App. 3d 610, 612, 402 N.E.2d 847, 849 (1980) (chain of custody stipulated); State v. Lagasse, 410 A.2d 537, 541 (Me. 1980) (stipulation that police maintained proper chain of custody of knife while in their possession). For a discussion of stipulations, *see* 2 E. IMWINKELRIED, P. GIANNELLI, F. GILLIGAN & F. LEDERER, COURTROOM CRIMINAL EVIDENCE ch. 31 (3d ed. 1998).

124. United States v. Clonts, 966 F.2d 1366, 1369 (10th Cir. 1992), *cert. denied*, 513 U.S. 905 (1994).

125. People v. Maurice, 31 Ill. 2d 456, 458, 202 N.E.2d 480, 481 (1964).

126. *See* 1 E. IMWINKELRIED, P. GIANNELLI, F. GILLIGAN & F. LEDERER, COURTROOM CRIMINAL EVIDENCE § 808 (3d ed. 1998) (habit evidence).

127. *See* United States v. Jones, 687 F.2d 1265, 1267 (8th Cir. 1982) (evidence handled by government according to "established procedures"); United States v. Luna, 585 F.2d 1, 6 (1st Cir.) ("normal police procedure"), *cert. denied*, 439 U.S. 852 (1978); United States v. Burris, 393 F.2d 81, 83 (7th Cir. 1968) (chemist testified about standard procedure of laboratory); Brewer v. United States, 353 F.2d 260, 262-63 (8th Cir. 1965) ("normal procedure" described); State v. Conley, 32 Ohio App. 2d 54, 62, 288 N.E.2d 296, 302 (1971) ("standard operating procedure" of laboratory).

The existence of standard operating procedures is sometimes critical. In a civil paternity action filed by the state, an appellate court rejected a chain-of-custody challenge to DNA results because a laboratory supervisor testified that:

> The [chain of custody] document was developed in order to allow the supervisor to confirm the chain of custody without having to bring numerous laboratory personnel to court. Dr. Harmon thoroughly discussed the document and its safety devices. She testified in detail as to her laboratory's procedures for drawing blood samples and assuring proper identification of both the individuals having the test and the blood samples drawn from those individuals. She testified that once the blood samples were received by the laboratory they were checked for any sign of tampering.[128]

Documentary Evidence

Sometimes the chain of custody has been established by documentary evidence.[129] For example, courts have held that laboratory slides and labels on specimen bottles fall within the federal Business Records Act, an exception to the hearsay rule, because they had been prepared by hospital personnel in the regular course of business.[130] Furthermore, the public records and recorded recollection exceptions to the hearsay rule may also apply to chain of custody documents.

These cases, however, predate the adoption of the Federal Rules of Evidence. Federal Rule 803(8)(B), which governs the public records exception, specifically excludes "in criminal cases matters observed by police officers and other law enforcement personnel."[131] According to the legislative history, this exclusion was based on the belief that "observations by police officers at the scene of the crime or the apprehension of the defendant are not as reliable as observations by public officials in other cases because of the adversarial nature of the confrontation between the police and the defendant in criminal cases."[132] The scope of the police records exclusion has divided the courts. Some courts seem to

---

128. J.E.B. v. State, 606 So. 2d 156, 157 (Ala. Civ. App.), *cert. denied*, 1992 Ala. LEXIS 1296 (Ala. Oct. 12, 1992), *rev'd on other grounds*, 508 U.S. 905 (1993).

129. *E.g.*, United States v. Luna, 585 F.2d 1, 6 (1st Cir.) (police "accounted for the evidence, either by official records or by testimony concerning normal police procedure"), *cert. denied*, 439 U.S. 852 (1978); Graham v. State, 253 Ind. 525, 533, 255 N.E.2d 652, 654 (1970) ("police custody records" may be used to establish chain of custody).

130. *See* United States v. Duhart, 496 F.2d 941, 944 (9th Cir.), *cert. denied*, 419 U.S. 967 (1974); Gass v. United States, 416 F.2d 767, 771 (D.C. Cir. 1969); Wheeler v. United States, 211 F.2d 19, 22-23 (D.C. Cir. 1953), *cert. denied*, 347 U.S. 1019 (1954).

131. *See also* MIL. R. EVID. 803(6) & (8) (specifying that "chain of custody documents" are admissible). *See* § 6-2 *supra* (business records exception).

132. S. Rep. No. 1277, 93 Cong., 2d Sess. 17, *reprinted in* 1974 U.S.C.C.A.N. 7051, 7064.

apply a per se rule, under which all police reports are automatically excluded,[133] while others have adopted a more flexible approach. For example, some courts have held that Congress "did not intend to exclude [police] records of routine, nonadversarial matters."[134] Chain of custody records are routine and are often nonadversarial in the sense that they are frequently used at a crime scene before a suspect is identified. Moreover, the systematic use of these documents better ensures the integrity of the evidence than a police officer's memory or case notes.

Another issue concerns the relationship between the public records exception and other hearsay exceptions. Several courts have held that documents subject to exclusion under the public records exception are not admissible under any other hearsay exception.[135] This interpretation would preclude the admissibility of chain of custody documents as business records[136] or as recorded recollection[137] if those documents are inadmissible as police records under Rule 803(8). This view, however, is not accepted by all courts.[138]

United States v. Coleman[139] is one of the few cases dealing with the admissibility of chain of custody documents under the Federal Rules. The defendant contended that police reports are never admissible when offered by the prosecution, and thus DEA forms of chemical analysis and lock-seal envelopes containing notations of the date, time, and location of the sale of heroin and an identification of the seller by a John Doe number were inadmissible. The court rejected this argument, holding that the documents were not unreliable on the ground that they were prepared for the purpose of litigation. Although the court recognized that the forms "have certain indicia of 'police reports,'" it found that the forms and lock-sealed envelopes contained "only skeletal information, and are prepared not solely with an eye towards presentation, but towards preserving a record of the chain of custody."[140]

---

133. *See* United States v. Ruffin, 575 F.2d 346, 356 (2d Cir. 1978); United States v. Oates, 560 F.2d. 45, 67 (2d Cir. 1977).

134. United States v. Hernandez-Rojas, 617 F.2d 533, 535 (9th Cir.), *cert. denied*, 449 U.S. 864 (1980); United States v. Orozco, 590 F.2d 789, 793 (9th Cir.), *cert. denied*, 439 U.S. 1049 (1979).

135. *See* United States v. Oates, 560 F.2d 45 (2d Cir. 1977).

136. Fed. R. Evid. 803(6).

137. Fed. R. Evid. 803(5).

138. Several courts have found the congressional purpose of excluding police reports under Rule 803(8) was intended to apply only when such reports were admitted in lieu of testimony. United States v. King, 613 F.2d 670, 673 (7th Cir. 1980); United States v. Sawyer, 607 F.2d 1190, 1193 (7th Cir. 1979), *cert. denied*, 445 U.S. 943 (1980).

139. 631 F.2d 908 (D.C. Cir. 1980).

140. *Id.* at 912.

Chain of custody documents also may be challenged on confrontation grounds.[141]

§ 7-6. Selected Bibliography.

Giannelli, *Chain of Custody and the Handling of Real Evidence*, 20 AM. CRIM. L. REV. 527 (1983).
Imwinkelried, *The Identification of Original, Real Evidence*, 61 MIL. L. REV. 145 (1973).
Michael & Adler, *Real Proof*, 5 VAND. L. REV. 344 (1952).

Annotations

Annot., *Proof of identity of person or thing where object, specimen, or part is taken from a human body, as basis for admission of testimony or report of expert or officer based on such object, specimen, or part*, 21 A.L.R.2D 1216 (1952).

141. *But see* Payne v. Janasz, 711 F.2d 1305, 1313-14 (6th Cir. 1983) (admission of evidence tag bearing inscription "10001 Cedar Avenue" did not violate right of confrontation). *See* § 6-4 *supra* (confrontation clause).

CHAPTER 8

POLYGRAPH AND DECEPTION TESTS*

§ 8-1. In General.

Since the credibility of witnesses plays such a prominent role in criminal trials, it is not surprising that the development of a scientific technique that can detect deception has long been sought. As Dean Wigmore, the noted evidence scholar, wrote in 1923: "If there is ever devised a psychological test for the valuation of witnesses, the law will run to meet it."[1] Unfortunately, none of the techniques

---

*The sections in this chapter were revised and renumbered in this edition. The authors wish to express their appreciation to Dr. Gordon Barland, Department of Defense Polygraph Institute, who reviewed this chapter.

thus far developed has proved satisfactory for courtroom use. The most important of the deception tests is the polygraph, and this chapter focuses on that technique. In addition, two other deception tests — truth serum testing and voice stress analysis — are also discussed. Hypnosis is discussed in Chapter 12.

This chapter is concerned with the use of polygraph evidence in criminal trials. Polygraph testing, however, raises additional legal issues, such as preemployment screening. The Employee Polygraph Protection Act governs this issue.[2]

§ 8-2. Polygraph Technique.

Modern polygraph procedures developed over a long period of time, commencing around the turn of the century.[3] Today, the field is also known as the psychophysiological detection of deception (PDD). Polygraph testing may be classified by the underlying theory of the test (deception or information test) and by the purpose of the test: specific incident or screening (background).

§ 8-2(A). Theory: CQT & GKT.

The most common polygraph examination today, the "Control (Comparison) Question" technique (CQT), is based upon two premises: (1) the psychological stress caused by the *fear of detection* produces involuntary physiological responses in the autonomic nervous system, and (2) a polygraph examiner, based on these responses as recorded by a polygraph instrument, can detect this

---

1. 2 WIGMORE, EVIDENCE § 875, at 237 (2d ed. 1923).

2. *See* § 8-10 *infra*.

3. For a history of the development of the polygraph and the extent of its present-day use, *see* Barland, *The Polygraph Test in the USA and Elsewhere*, *in* THE POLYGRAPH TEST: LIES, TRUTH AND SCIENCE 73 (A. Gale ed. 1988). The search for a truth detector can be traced back to the 19th Century: CESAR LOMBROSO, L'HOMME CRIMINEL (2d ed. 1895). Early accounts include: Marston, *Systolic Blood Pressure Symptoms of Deception*, 2 J. EXPERIMENTAL PSYCH. 117 (1917); *Psychological Possibilities in the Deception Tests*, 11 J. CRIM. L. & CRIMINOLOGY 551 (1921); LARSON, LYING AND ITS DETECTION (1932); Keeler, *Scientific Methods of Criminal Detection with the Polygraph*, 2 KAN. B. ASS'N 22 (1933); Summers, *Science Can Get the Confession*, 8 FORDHAM L. REV. 335 (1939); Trovillo, *A History of Lie Detection*, 29 J. CRIM. L., CRIMINOLOGY & POLICE SCI. 848 (1939) (part I); 30 CRIM. L., CRIMINOLOGY & POLICE SCI. 104 (1939) (part II).

See also Ansley, *Development of Deception Criteria Prior to 1950*, 28 POLYGRAPH 28 (1999) ("In 1950 th[e] only formal polygraph training was at the Keeler Polygraph Institute, and most examiners were preceptor trained or self-taught. Most of the instruments were two-channel (cardiograph and pneumograph) mechanical units, although there were some with electrodermal units. The most widely used technique was relevant-irrelevant. A few examiners used one or the other of two published Control Question techniques, one published by Summers (1939), and the other by Inbau (1948). Among the many shortcomings in 1950 was a lack of agreement on what constituted deception criteria. Add inadequate chart markings, and that independent analysis of someone else's charts was difficult, and the results were problematic").

deception.[4] The "fear of detection" theory, however, is but one of a number of theories that have been proposed to explain a subject's reactions.[5]

In contrast, a different examination, the "Guilty Knowledge" (GKT) or "Concealed Knowledge" test rests on a markedly different theory. The GKT may be used when important information about a crime has *not* been disclosed to the public. Consequently, only the perpetrator, and not other suspects, will possess this knowledge and react to it during the test. While the CQT is a deception test, the GKT is an "information" test. The requirement of concealed information, however, greatly limits the use of this examination in practice.[6]

§ 8-2(B). Examinations: Specific Incident & Screening.

Polygraph examinations can be divided into two categories based on the purpose of the examination. One type focuses on a *specific incident,* typically a crime or other occurrence involving misconduct. This chapter focuses on this type of examination.

The second type is a "background" examination, involving past conduct over a period of time. The typical pre-employment screening test is an example. Although the use of this type of examination has been greatly limited by the 1988

---

4. A report by the Office of Technology Assessment (OTA) explained:

> The basic theory of polygraph testing is only partially developed. The testing process is complex and not amenable to easy understanding. The most commonly accepted theory at present is that, when the person being examined fears detection, that fear produces a measurable physiological reaction when the person responds deceptively. Thus, in this theory, the polygraph instrument is measuring the fear of detection rather than deception per se. And the examiner infers deception when the physiological response to questions about the crime or unauthorized activity is greater than the response to other questions.

U.S. Congress, Office of Technology Assessment, *Scientific Validity of Polygraph Testing: A Review and Evaluation — A Technical Memorandum,* OTA-TM-H-15 (1983) [hereinafter cited as OTA Report], *reprinted in* 12 POLYGRAPH 196, 201 (1983). *See also* Barland & Raskin, *Detection of Deception, in* ELECTRODERMAL ACTIVITY IN PSYCHOLOGICAL RESEARCH, 417, 445-47 (W. Prokasy & D. Raskin eds. 1973).

5. *See* Davis, *Physiological Responses as a Means of Evaluating Information, in* THE MANIPULATION OF HUMAN BEHAVIOR 142, 160-65 (A. Biderman & Zimmer eds. 1961) (discussing conditioning theories (the conditioned response theory, the conflict theory) and the threat-of-punishment theory).

6. *See* Raskin, *The Polygraph in 1986: Scientific, Professional and Legal Issues Surrounding Application and Acceptance of Polygraph Evidence,* 1986 UTAH L. REV. 29, 31-32 ("[I]t is employed infrequently because the special information necessary to construct a valid concealed information test is typically lacking"). For a discussion of the different techniques, including the "peak of tension" and "guilty knowledge" tests, *see* D. LYKKEN, A TREMOR IN THE BLOOD: USES AND ABUSES OF THE LIE DETECTOR 103-50, 249-307 (1981). *See also* Podlesny, *Is the Guilty Knowledge Polygraph Technique Applicable in Criminal Investigations? A Review of FBI Case Records,* 20 CRIME LAB. DIGEST 57 (July 1993) (concluding that this examination may be of limited practical value in criminal investigations).

federal act,[7] screening tests are still used extensively by federal, state, and local governments, especially in law enforcement. Indeed, in "case studies carried out in Illinois, Ohio, Maryland and Florida it was found that out of 3,576 police applicants given pre-employment polygraph examinations, 58% (2,068) were identified as high risk candidates for police work in that they had behavioral histories of involvement in activities such as felony thefts, burglaries, robberies, the use and sale of illegal drugs, bribery, car thefts, and various sexual offenses."[8]

Other tests are used in the intelligence and national security communities.[9] For example Aldrich Ames, the CIA agent who sold secrets to the Soviet Union, had been tested. Ames "did not 'beat' the polygraph tests; instead, he simply talked the CIA out of believing the results, which showed deception every time he took the test. Since the false positive error rate is approximately 10 percent ... Ames could have argued with some force that the positive results were false."[10]

§ 8-2(C). Instrument.

The physiological responses[11] used in polygraph testing are changes in blood pressure-pulse, respiration, and galvanic skin resistance.[12] The polygraph instrument simultaneously and continuously measures and records these physiological reactions on a graph or chart (polygram). Blood pressure-pulse is measured by a sphygmomanometer (blood pressure cuff) that is placed on the subject's arm; respiration is measured by pneumograph tubes that are fastened

---

7. *See* § 8-10 *infra* (Employee Polygraph Protection Act).

8. *Polygraph: Issues and Answers*, 25 POLYGRAPH 134, 135 (1996) ("According to a recent survey over 60% of the large police departments in the United States use polygraph testing in the pre-employment screening process. Police agencies have found that polygraph testing is a very effective means by which to identify high risk candidates").

9. *See* Department of Defense Polygraph Institute Research Division Staff, *A Comparison of Psychophysiological Detection of Deception Accuracy Rates Obtained Using the Counterintelligence Scope Polygraph and the Test for Espionage and Sabotage Question Formats*, 26 POLYGRAPH 79 (1997). The 1994 DoD report stated: "During fiscal year 1994, DoD investigations obtained unique and significant information from interviews conducted with the aid of the polygraph. In all illustrated instances, the polygraph examination process produced significant security or criminal information which would not otherwise have been secured for the specific investigation. The polygraph examination process was also valuable in helping to establish the innocence of persons charged with serious infractions." Department of Defense Polygraph Program, *1994 Report to Congress, reprinted in* 24 POLYGRAPH 19 (1995). *See also* Department of Defense Polygraph Program, *1993 Report to Congress, reprinted in* 23 POLYGRAPH 61 (1994).

10. *Daubert May Presage New Role for Polygraphs as Evidence*, BNA CRIMINAL PRACTICE MANUAL 195, 201 (1997) (quoting Dr. David Raskin).

11. For a discussion of the psychophysiologic basis of polygraphy, *see* S. ABRAMS, A POLYGRAPH HANDBOOK FOR ATTORNEYS ch. 3 (1977).

12. Some instruments are also equipped to record muscular activity. These tracings may reveal efforts to "beat" the machine and in some cases provide independent deception criteria. J. REID & F. INBAU, TRUTH AND DECEPTION 262 (2d ed. 1977).

around the subject's abdomen and chest; and galvanic skin response is measured by electrodes that are attached to the subject's fingertips.[13]

A quality polygraph instrument can accurately measure and record these responses.[14] The modern instruments are lap top computers. The instrument, however, detects neither deception nor the fear of detection; it provides only a recording of physiological responses. It is the examiner who, based on these recordings, infers deception.

§ 8-2(D). Examiner.

The examiner's role cannot be overstated, because it is the examiner who decides whether there is sufficient indication of deception.[15] The examiner's expertise is critical in (1) determining the suitability of the subject for testing, (2) formulating proper test questions, (3) establishing the necessary rapport with the subject, (4) detecting attempts to mask or create chart reactions, or other countermeasures,[16] (5) stimulating the subject to react, and (6) interpreting the charts.[17]

Even though the examiner is the linchpin of the procedure, proponents acknowledge that there are serious problems on this score. One authority has commented that "a substantial proportion of those who conduct tests in the public

---

13. The galvanic skin resistance or electrodermal response involves the measurement of changes in the flow of electrical current. *Id.* at 275-91. A different method of measuring electrodermal activity, based on skin conductance response (SCR), is now in use. Conductance is the inverse of resistance. Sweat causes the skin's resistance to decrease and conductance to increase. Honts & Barger, *A Comparison of the Relative Utility of Skin Conductance and Skin Resistance Couplers for the Measurement of Electrodermal Activity*, 19 POLYGRAPH 199 (1990).

14. *See* State v. Dean, 103 Wis. 2d 228, 235, 307 N.W.2d 628, 632 (1981) ("A quality machine accurately measures and records these body responses").

15. The OTA report states:

> [T]he polygraph is not simply a machine or instrument that signals whether a person is being truthful or deceptive. The instrument cannot itself detect deception. A polygraph test is very complex and depends heavily on the interaction between the examiner and the individual being tested, and requires that the examiner infer deception or truthfulness based on a comparison of the person's physiological responses to various questions. The quality of the questions asked depends in part on what information the examiner already has about the person being questioned.

OTA Report, *supra* note 4, *reprinted in* 12 POLYGRAPH at 196 (statement of John Gibbons, Director of Office of Technology Assessment).

16. *See* § 8-3(E) *infra* (countermeasures).

17. J. REID & F. INBAU, *supra* note 12, at 5 ("[T]he most important factor involved in the use of any such instrument is the ability, experience, education, and integrity of the examiner himself").

and private sectors lack adequate training and competence."[18] Others have observed that "[p]olygraph examiners in the United States, as a whole, are poorly trained."[19]

Polygraph Schools

The American Polygraph Association (APA)[20] accredits polygraph schools.[21] Graduation from one of these schools should be a minimum requirement. The private schools conduct a seven-week course, while the Department of Defense Polygraph Institute (DoDPI) runs a fourteen-week course. The DoDPI trains all federal polygraph examiners. It "is the only program known to base its curriculum on forensic psychophysiology, and conceptual, abstract, and applied knowledge that meet the requirements of a master's degree-level of study."[22] The qualification standards include a college degree (or equivalent), two-years experience as an investigator, and a six-month internship that includes at least 25 polygraph exams. In addition, 80 hours of continuing instruction are required annually. Outside of federally-trained examiners, few have such qualifications.

Licensing

Twenty-nine states have licensing statutes,[23] a number of which require continuing education (typically twenty hours per year).[24] These provisions

---

18. Raskin, *supra* note 6, 1986 UTAH L. REV. 29, at 66-67. "As bad as the situation is in the federal sector, it is generally worse in the local law enforcement agencies and in the private sector." *Id.* at 68.

19. Honts & Perry, *Polygraph Admissibility*, 16 LAW & HUM. BEHAV. 357, 375 (1992). *See also* Honts & Quick, *The Polygraph in 1995: Progress in Science and the Law*, 71 N.D. L. REV. 987, 998 (1995) ("Given the poor general state of examiner training in the polygraph profession, the assessment of competence of the specific examiner offering evidence is critically important").

20. The APA was founded in 1966. It publishes a quarterly journal entitled POLYGRAPH and a bimonthly newsletter. "The American Polygraph Association (APA) is an international association which represents the polygraph profession in programs which establish standards of ethical practice, techniques, instrumentation, and training. The APA has approximately 2,000 members, of which the majority are in the United States." *Polygraph: Issues and Answers*, *supra* note 8, at 145.

21. The APA has accredited fourteen polygraph schools. One school is in Canada (Canadian Police College Polygraph School). The others are located in the United States, including two government-sponsored schools: DoD Polygraph Institute and the Texas Department of Public Safety Law Enforcement Polygraph School.

22. Department of Defense, Polygraph Program, *Annual Report to Congress* 14 (1996) *reprinted in* 30 POLYGRAPH 240 (1997) [hereinafter DoDPI 1996 Annual Report].

23. *Issues and Answers*, *supra* note 8, at 142.

24. *E.g.*, ALA. CODE § 34-25-21; ARK. CODE. ANN. § 17-39-202 (1987); ILL. ANN. STAT. ch. 111, § 2412; KY. REV. STAT. ANN. § 329.030; LA. REV. STAT. ANN. § 37:2838; MICH. COMP. LAWS ANN. § 338.1710; MISS. CODE ANN. § 73-29-13; NEV. REV. STAT. § 648.110(g); N.D. CENT. CODE § 43-31-07; OKLA. STAT. ANN. tit. 59, § 1458; TEX. REV. CIV. STAT. ANN. art. 4413(29cc) § 8. *See*

presumably play a role in determining the qualifications of experts in those jurisdictions that admit polygraph evidence, either in the discretion of the trial court or by stipulation.[25] Typically, these statutes establish requirements relating to age, citizenship, character, and academic or investigative experience. Requirements governing polygraph schooling and internships are also common.

In some jurisdictions the statute merely establishes an administrative agency, which is responsible for promulgating rules governing examiners.[26] Other provisions go beyond establishing qualification standards and prescribe the types of testing procedures that must be used in the examination. For example, the Nevada statute provides that only examinations conducted with approved instruments, using widely accepted techniques, and at least two charts may be administered.[27]

New Mexico Rule of Evidence, the only admissibility rule of its kind, specifies minimum qualifications to include five years' experience administering or interpreting examinations or equivalent academic training and at least twenty hours of continuing education during the twelve months prior to the examination offered in evidence.[28]

In addition, one authority recommends three years of full-time experience, including 250 forensic cases (not employment screening).[29] The DoD Polygraph Institute, the American Polygraph Association, the American Association of Police Polygraphists, and various regional and state polygraph associations conduct specialized and annual courses.

§ 8-2(E). Procedure.

The specific incident techniques involve several steps, the most important of which are the pretest interview, the examination of the subject while attached to the instrument, and chart interpretation.[30]

The pretest interview serves a variety of critical functions. First, it is used to acquaint the subject with the effectiveness of the technique; this will allay the

---

generally Annot., *Validity and Construction of Statutes Licensing or Otherwise Regulating Operators of Polygraph or Similar Devices*, 32 A.L.R.3D 1324 (1970).

25. *See* Holcomb v. State, 268 Ark. 138, 140, 594 S.W.2d 22, 23 (1980) (stipulation interpreted to require a licensed examiner); State v. Tavernier, 27 Or. App. 115, 118, 555 P.2d 481, 482 (1976) (same).

26. *E.g.*, VA. CODE, §§ 54.1-200 to 54.1-201, 54.1-1800 to 54.1-1806.

27. NEV. REV. STAT. §§ 648.183, 648-185. *See* § 8-4(D) *infra*.

28. *See* N.M. R. EVID. 11-707.

29. Barland, *Standards for the Admissibility of Polygraph Results as Evidence*, 16 U. WEST L.A. L. REV. 37, 44 (1984).

30. Other steps in the technique include a preliminary investigation designed to provide the examiner with as much information as possible about the incident under investigation and the subject of the examination. J. REID & F. INBAU, *supra* note 12, at 11.

apprehensions of the truthful subject and stimulate the deceptive subject's concern about the prospect of detection.[31] Second, the interview is used to assess the suitability of the subject for testing. The examiner may be alerted to some condition, such as a physical ailment,[32] low intelligence,[33] or the use of medication,[34] that may affect the test results. Third, test questions are formulated with the subject's assistance during the interview. The examiner must define and clarify the issues of the test.

A post-test interview is considered important by some authorities.[35] Unlike the pretest interview and the examination itself, the examiner need not remain objective in the post-test interview. Indeed, its principal function is to elicit a confession from subjects considered deceptive, and it is quite effective for this purpose.[36]

§ 8-2(F). Types of Formats: RIT & CQT.

Examiners can use several different types of formats for investigating a specific incident. The early examiners used the "relevant-irrelevant question" (RIT) test. Relevant questions concern the subject matter under investigation. For example: "Did you take $100 from your employer's safe?" (The relevant question is sometimes called the "issue" question.) Irrelevant or neutral questions are used to obtain a subject's normal truthful reactions and chart tracings—*i.e.*, the examinee's physiological tracings while in a state of homeostasis or equilibrium. Examples of irrelevant questions are: "Is your name [subject's name]?" "Are you over 21 years of age?" Both types of questions must be answered "yes" or "no." The responses to the relevant questions are compared with the subject's responses to the irrelevant questions.

The principal criticism of the RIT in this context is its underlying assumption that an innocent person will not react to the relevant questions: "Because relevant questions may produce relatively strong reactions, even when answered truthfully, many innocent subjects would be expected to produce deceptive outcomes on the test."[37] Other authorities disagree, arguing that the RIT test, if properly used, may be useful.[38]

---

31. *Id.* at 13-14.

32. *Id.* at 233.

33. *Id.* at 247.

34. *Id.* at 236.

35. *Id.* at 4.

36. *See* § 8-8 *infra* (confessions).

37. Raskin, *supra* note 6, 1986 UTAH L. REV. at 33. "There is no clear and systematic way to interpret the outcome of a relevant-irrelevant test, and the result is subject to a great deal of error." *Id. See also* Honts & Perry, *Polygraph Admissibility*, 16 LAW & HUM. BEHAV. 357, 359 (1992) ("Almost all of the scientists involved in detection of deception research reject the notion that the

Control Question Technique

The Control Question Technique (CQT) was developed in the 1940s as an improvement of the relevant-irrelevant exam.[39] Control questions concern "an act of wrongdoing *of the same general nature as the main incident under investigation,* and one to which the subject, in all probability, will lie or to which his answer will be of dubious validity in his own mind."[40] For this reason, they are sometimes called "probable lie" questions and are typically general and vague—for example, "Before the age of 25, did you ever steal anything?"

Control questions are designed as a stimulus for the truthful subject. Generally, the truthful person will respond more to the control questions than to the relevant questions because they represent a greater threat to that person. For the same reason, the deceptive person will respond more to the relevant questions than to the control questions. Therefore, the subject's *comparative* responses to the control and relevant questions are the key in the CQT.[41] Recent reports use the term "comparison question test" because the test does not involve "controls" in the scientific sense of that word.

Formulating adequate control questions is not an easy task.[42] As one writer noted, "it is extremely difficult to devise control questions that would ensure the eliciting of stronger reactions in an innocent person than would the relevant

---

relevant-irrelevant test could be a useful discriminator of truth and deception"). The RIT is most often used for background or pre-employment screening but is sometimes used in criminal cases.

38. *See* Barland, *The Polygraph Test in the USA and Elsewhere, in* THE POLYGRAPH TEST: LIES, TRUTH AND SCIENCE 73, 80 (A. Gale ed. 1988).

39. *See* Reid, *A Revised Questioning Technique in Lie Detection Tests*, 37 J. CRIM. L., CRIMINOLOGY & POLICE SCI. 542 (1947).

40. J. REID & F. INBAU, *supra* note 12, at 28. *See also* Raskin, *Science, Competence, and Polygraph Techniques*, 8 CRIM. DEF. 11, 13 (May-June 1981) ("[T]he control question deals with similar subject matter, is very general in nature, covers a long span of time and a large number of possible acts, and it is almost impossible for most people to answer it with an unequivocal 'no' and with certainty that they are being completely truthful").

41. "[I]nnocent subjects are expected to show stronger reactions to the control questions than to the relevant questions, whereas guilty subjects are expected to show the opposite." Kircher & Raskin, *Human Versus Computerized Evaluations of Polygraph Data in a Laboratory Setting*, 73 J. APPLIED PSYCHOL. 291 (1988). *Accord* J. REID & F. INBAU, *supra* note 12, at 63; Orne, *Implications of Laboratory Research for the Detection of Deception, in* LEGAL ADMISSIBILITY OF THE POLYGRAPH 94, 96 (N. Ansley ed. 1975).

42. *See also* Ansley, *Question Formulation*, 27 POLYGRAPH 181, 181 (1998) ("Try to conduct your tests with a single-issue test format, as they tend to be more accurate than multiple issue formats").

questions relating to the crime of which they had been accused."[43] This may explain why there are more false positives than false negatives with the CQT.[44]

There are several different types of CQT.[45] One is the Zone Comparison Technique (ZCT), which includes a number of different formats.[46] The Modified General Question Technique (MGQT) is the other principal technique.[47]

Sequence of Questions

Questions are formulated to elicit either a "yes" or "no" response. There are no surprise questions; the examiner reviews the questions with the subject during the pretest interview to ensure understanding. The examination typically consists of ten to twelve questions. While the subject knows the questions, she does not know the order in which they will be asked. The examination lasts several minutes and is repeated at least one more time; often two or three more examinations are conducted.

The first one or two questions are irrelevant questions. Other irrelevant questions as well as the relevant and control questions are interspersed in the remaining questions. The following example illustrates the control question sequence for the University of Utah format:

1. (Neutral) Do you understand that I will ask only the questions we have discussed?
2. (Pseudo-Relevant) Regarding whether you took that ring, do you intend to answer all of the questions truthfully?
3. (Neutral) Do you live in the United States?
4. (Control) During the first twenty-four years of your life, did you ever take something that did not belong to you?
5. (Relevant) Did you take a ring from the Behavioral Sciences Building on July 1, 1985?
6. (Neutral) Is your name Joanne?
7. (Control) Between the ages of ten and twenty-four, did you ever do anything dishonest or illegal?

---

43. Bull, *What is the Lie-Detection Test?*, *in* THE POLYGRAPH TEST: LIES, TRUTH AND SCIENCE 14 (A. Gale ed. 1988).

44. *Id. See also* Matte, *The Review, Presentation and Assurance of Intended Interpretation of Test Questions is Critical to the Outcome of Polygraph Tests*, 22 POLYGRAPH 299 (1993).

45. "[T]he two most widely used formats are the zone comparison and the modified general question test (MGQT)." Olsen, Harris, Capps & Ansley, *Computerized Polygraph Scoring System*, 42 J. FORENSIC SCI. 61, 61 (1997).

46. *See* Ansley, *The Zone Comparison Test*, 27 POLYGRAPH 108 (1998).

47. *See* Ansley, *The Validity Of the Modified General Question Test (MGQT)*, 27 POLYGRAPH 35 (1998) (MGQT derives name from combination of Army CID and Reid Control Question Technique (Modified)).

8. (Relevant) Did you take that diamond ring from a desk in the Behavioral Sciences Building on July 1?
9. (Neutral) Were you born in the month of February?
10. (Control) Before 1984 did you ever lie to get out of trouble or to cause a problem for someone else?
11. (Relevant) Were you in any way involved in the theft of that diamond ring from the Behavioral Sciences Building last July?[48]

Note that the control and relevant questions are paired.

Other Types of Questions

Some formats contain additional types of questions. For example, a "sacrifice relevant question" may be used as the first relevant question — *e.g.*, "In regard to the theft, do you intend to answer the questions truthfully?" This question is not evaluated because it is assumed that the first introduction of the subject under investigation will trigger a response, even from an innocent person.[49] A "symptomatic" question may also be used — *e.g.*, "Are you convinced that I will not ask you a question that has not already been reviewed?" This question is intended to identify a subject who is concerned with some topic other than the one under investigation.[50]

Directed Lie Control Question

A refinement is the "directed lie" control question. In this procedure, the subject is told to lie to the directed control question[51] — *e.g.*, "Before age 25, did you ever tell a lie?" Subjects are instructed that if their reaction to this question is not sufficiently strong, the test will be inconclusive. In theory, guilty subjects will be unconcerned about this question and focus on the relevant questions. In contrast, innocent subjects will react because they are concerned about an inconclusive result.[52] This approach is not without its detractors.[53]

---

48. Raskin, *supra* note 6, 1986 UTAH L. REV. at 36.

49. *See also* Capps, *Predictive Value of the Sacrifice Relevant*, 20 POLYGRAPH 1 (1991); Horvath, *The Value and Effectiveness of the Sacrifice Relevant Question: An Empirical Assessment*, 23 POLYGRAPH 261 (1994).

50. *See* Capps et al., *Effectiveness of the Symptomatic Question*, 22 POLYGRAPH 285 (1993).

51. *See* Honts & Raskin, *A Field Study of the Validity of the Directed Lie Control Question*, 16 J. POLICE SCI. & ADMIN. 56 (1988).

52. "The directed lie test represents an improvement over the traditional control question test, in that it is more standardized in structure, is easier to administer, requires less manipulation of the subject, and is more readily explained to lawyers, judges and juries, according to Raskin. Most important, it reduces the number of false positives." *BNA Manual*, *supra* note 10, at 199.

Stimulation Test

As part of the examination, a stimulation test is often administered.[54] It is sometimes known as the number test, card test, or stim test. The purpose of the test is to impress the subject with the efficacy of the technique. A wide variety of stimulation tests are used. Reid and Inbau describe a card test that is based on deceiving the subject.[55] Most stimulation tests, such as those used by federal examiners, do not involve trickery.[56]

§ 8-2(G). Methods of Evaluation.

There are three methods of evaluation: global, numerical, and computerized.

Global Evaluation

Global evaluation, the oldest method, involves an overall impression of the charts plus other factors. The most controversial of these other factors is the examiner's "clinical impressions" of the subject during the pretest interview and the examination. In other words, the examiner considers the subject's demeanor ("body language") as well as the recorded reactions of the instrument.[57] Critics contend that such a judgment is "a highly subjective and hence speculative interpretation about the meaning of a complex series of verbal, behavioral and physiological responses."[58]

---

53. *Compare* Matt, *An Analysis of the Psychodynamics of the Directed Lie Control Questions in the Control Question Technique*, 27 POLYGRAPH, 56 (1998), *with* Honts & Gordon, *A Critical Analysis of Matte's Analysis of the Directed Lie*, 27 POLYGRAPH 241 (1998).

54. An issue of POLYGRAPH is devoted to the subject. 7 POLYGRAPH 173-214 (1978).

55. In the card test, the subject is asked to select a card from a deck. The examiner then goes through all the cards, one at a time, asking if each was the one selected. The subject is instructed to answer "no" each time, even when the correct card is shown. The examiner, supposedly based on the polygraph technique, then identifies the correct card. Often the identification is not made through the polygraph technique, but because the cards are marked. J. REID & F. INBAU, *supra* note 12, at 42 & 85.

56. Decker, *The Army Stimulation Test — A Control Procedure*, 7 POLYGRAPH 176, 176 (1978) ("There is absolutely no trickery in this test"). *See also* Widup & Barland, *The Numbers Test, The Effect of the Location of the Numbers Test on Examiner Decision Rates in Criminal Psychophysiological Detection of Deception Tests*, 25 POLYGRAPH 256 (1996).

57. "For example, [the examiner] must look at the polygraph charts, the suspect's demeanor and behavior, the case facts, and whatever other indicators there may be." Barland, *supra* note 29, 16 U. WEST L.A. L. REV. at 39. "The clinical approach minimizes inconclusive results, for such examiners tend to rely upon their analysis of the subject's behavior when the charts are marginal." *Id.* at 40.

58. Kleinmuntz, *The Polygraph as Credible Court Evidence*, THE CHAMPION 14, 16 (Sept.-Oct. 1984). *See also* D. LYKKEN, A TREMOR IN BLOOD, *supra* note 6, ch. 6.

Numerical Evaluation

The numerical approach was developed about 1960.[59] The subject's behavioral reactions are not considered, only the recorded chart reactions. Several different scoring systems are used. The systems developed by the DoD Polygraph Institute[60] and by the University of Utah[61] are similar.[62] The comparative reaction to each pair of relevant and control questions is scored. The scores range from +3 for a dramatic reaction to a control question to -3 for the same type of reaction to the relevant question. Noticeable but small reactions are scored +1 or -1. A lack of a significant reaction is scored 0. Total scores of +6 or higher indicate truthfulness, while total scores of -6 or lower indicate deception. Scores that fall in between are considered inconclusive. This scoring technique is sometimes called the "seven position scale" because there are seven possible values.[63]

The primary advantage of the numerical approach is that it "helps to ensure a rigorous, semi-objective evaluation of the physiological information contained in the charts."[64] Numerical scoring reduces, but does not eliminate, subjectivity.[65]

---

59. Cleve Backster is credited with developing this approach. He is the director of the Backster School of Lie Detection, San Diego. *See* Backster, *New Standards in Polygraph Chart Interpretation, Do the Charts Speak for Themselves?*, 11 LAW & ORDER 67 (1963). *See also* Ansley, *The Zone Comparison Test*, 27 POLYGRAPH 108, 108 (1998) ("In 1961, Cleve Backster published a new test format, called the zone comparison. Like Summers' earlier test it featured pairs of control questions and relevant questions, plus irrelevant questions. All test formats employ one or more irrelevant questions as buffers, and interspersed in the test question sequence as needed to quell responses. Backster added some features, pre-test evaluation, a fixed format, and scoring methodology. His format added two new types of questions, the symptomatic and the sacrifice relevant questions").

60. *See* Swinford, *Manually Scoring Polygraph Charts Utilizing the Seven-Position Numerical Analysis Scale at the Department of Defense Polygraph Institute*, 28 POLYGRAPH 10 (1999).

61. *See* Bell, Raskin, Honts & Kircher, *The Utah Numerical Scoring System*, 28 POLYGRAPH 1, 1 (1999) (Validity of several lab studies: "Excluding inconclusive outcomes, the overall percentage of correct decisions was 91% for guilty subjects and was 89% for innocent subjects"; in one field study the "decisions were 100% correct for both guilty and innocent suspects. In another study, decisions were 92% correct for guilty suspects and 100% for innocents suspects").

62. Raskin, *supra* note 6, 1986 UTAH L. REV. at 37-38.

63. There is also a "three position scale." *See* Krapohl, *A Comparison of 3- and 7-position Scoring Scales with Laboratory Data*, 27 POLYGRAPH 210, 211 (1998) ("There is a family of testing formats under the umbrella term Zone Comparison Technique (ZCT), including the Backster, DoDPI, and Utah. These formats are considered to be the most powerful PDD techniques because the relevant questions are very specific and essentially are rewordings of a single question").

64. Barland, *supra* note 29, 16 U. WEST L.A. L. REV. at 40. *See also* Capps & Ansley, *Numerical Scoring of Polygraph Charts: What Examiners Really Do*, 21 POLYGRAPH 264 (1992); Weaver, *Effects of Differing Numerical Chart Evaluation Systems on Polygraph Examination Results*, 14 POLYGRAPH 34 (1985).

65. *See* Olsen, Harris, Capps & Ansley, *supra* note 45, at 61 & 62 ("Although substantial differences in interpretation are uncommon, practitioners can and do differ in their conclusions"; "Examiners will differ on how they award points").

Moreover, some research indicates that numerical scoring systems are more reliable.[66]

Computer Evaluations

Computerized scoring is the third method.[67] Computers are used in two different ways in polygraph testing—first, as the instrument (hardware), and second, as a specific software application. There are four algorithms currently available: *Polyscore* (Applied Physics Laboratory, Johns Hopkins University),[68] *Computerized Polygraph System* (University of Utah), *Axciton*, and *Identifi*. Computerized scoring is a specific application of numerical scoring.[69] An automated system reduces the risk of human error and minimizes disagreements among examiners.[70] Computer scoring may be used as a quality control procedure or as the principal scorer; the latter is only developmental at this time.

§ 8-2(H). Quality Control Procedures.

Typically, polygraph examinations conducted by federal agencies are independently reviewed by senior examiners. These agencies use numerical scoring, and the quality control reviews are "blind" examinations, *i.e.*, the charts are evaluated without viewing the subject or knowing the field examiner's conclusion.[71] As noted above, computers can also be used for quality control.[72]

---

66. *See* Barland & Podlesny, *Validity and Reliability of Detection of Deception*, 6 POLYGRAPH 1, 18 (1977); Weaver, *The Numerical Evaluation of Polygraph Charts: Evaluation and Comparison of Three Major Systems*, 9 POLYGRAPH 94 (1980).

67. *See* Yankee, *The Current Status of Research in Forensic Psychophysiology and Its Application in the Psychophysiological Detection of Deception*, 40 J. FORENSIC SCI. 63, 64 (1995) (computerized polygraph instruments include: Axciton, Stoelting, and Lafayette).

68. Olsen, Harris, Capps & Ansley, *supra* note 45, at 61.

69. "Dichotomous computer classifications of subjects in the standardization sample were 93% correct. Blind numerical evaluations of the same data by an expert interpreter were 89% correct." Kircher & Raskin, *Human Versus Computerized Evaluations of Polygraph Data in a Laboratory Setting*, 73 J. APPLIED PSYCHOL. 291 (1988). This study used mock crime experiments, and thus its application to field conditions cannot be assumed. *Id.* at 301. In a later field study using U.S. Secret Service examiners, the computer evaluations proved reliable: "[T]he accuracy of human and computer interpretations was higher than the blind interpretations, and it ranged from 95-96% on confirmed truthful subjects and 83-96% on confirmed deceptive subjects." D. RASKIN, J. KIRCHER, C. HONTS & S. HOROWITZ, A STUDY OF THE VALIDITY OF POLYGRAPH EXAMINATIONS IN CRIMINAL INVESTIGATION (May 1988) (Nat'l Inst. of Justice, Grant No. 85-IJ-CX-0040).

70. "[D]isagreements among polygraph examiners are common and limit the validity and utility of the technique in applied settings." Kircher & Raskin, *supra* note 69, 73 J. APPLIED PSYCHOL. at 292.

71. Furgerson, *Polygraph Policy Model for Law Enforcement*, 56 F.B.I. LAW ENFORCEMENT BULL. 7, 14-19 (June 1987) ("Experience has shown the value of quality control as an integral part of law enforcement polygraph usage. In such a program, polygraph charts and documentation are

In the absence of a quality control program, review by an independent examiner becomes critical: "By far the most important single safeguard that should be required prior to admissibility of polygraph evidence is the review of the polygraph examination by an objective, disinterested expert polygraph examiner."[73] Unfortunately, many examinations are conducted without any quality control safeguards.[74]

§ 8-3. Validity of Polygraph Examinations.

The validity of polygraph testing in criminal investigations remains controversial. The question is extremely complex.[75] Critics argue that the physiological responses caused by the fear of detection have not been shown to be different from physiological responses caused by other emotions.[76]

---

reviewed 'in the blind' by another senior and well-qualified examiner to insure that they substantiate the conclusion of the testing examiner as to truth or deception").

72. *See* Wygant, *Scoring in a Computer Age*, 28 POLYGRAPH 77, 80 (1999) ("Anecdotal information suggests that differences are occurring for most examiner's less than 10% of the time; and most of the differences are only one degree (the examiners's manual score indicating a definite result while the computer says it's inconclusive, or the reverse of that").

73. Barland, *supra* note 29, 16 U. WEST L.A. L. REV. at 50.

74. Professor Raskin's account of the *Fay* case illustrates the importance of quality control procedures and examiner qualifications:

> In the celebrated case of Floyd Fay, who was wrongly convicted of murder in 1978 and served two years in prison before the actual perpetrators were apprehended, the five interpreters used different methods to analyze the polygraph tests. The two field polygraph examiners who testified at the trial diagnosed him as deceptive, one using the United States Army numerical scoring system and the other using a global evaluation. Another examiner, a professor of criminology at Michigan State University who employed a global evaluation, said that the test was inconclusive. A private polygraph examiner with a doctoral degree in psychology scored the polygraph charts at +1 (inconclusive) using the United States Army system, and a psychiatry professor at the University of Minnesota said that polygraph tests are of no value. The author [Dr. Raskin] interpreted the charts as truthful (+7).

Raskin, *supra* note 6, 1986 UTAH L. REV. at 39-40.

75. Orne, Thackray & Paskewitz, *On the Detection of Deception*, *in* HANDBOOK OF PSYCHOPHYSIOLOGY 743, 751 (W. Greenfield & R. Sternback eds. 1972) ("No fully satisfactory way is available at this time for evaluating the overall effectiveness of the technique, and it is probable that no such answer will be forthcoming in the near future from real life situations"); Barland & Raskin, *supra* note 4, at 435 ("The question of the validity of the lie detection technique in the field is an extremely complex issue which may never be fully answerable"). *See also The Validity and Reliability of Polygraph Testing*, 26 POLYGRAPH 215 (1997) (compendium of 80 research projects since 1980).

76. Two commentators wrote:

> [T]here is no reason to believe that lying produces distinctive physiological changes that characterize it and only it.... [T]here is no set of responses — physiological or otherwise — that humans emit only when lying or that they produce only when telling the truth.... No doubt when we tell a lie many of us experience an inner turmoil, but we experience a similar

Proponents, however, do not claim that there is a special physiological response that indicates deception. Rather, they believe that *changes* in physiological reactions in response to different types of questions indicate deception.

Two preliminary points are not subject to serious dispute. First, error rates frequently cited by field examiners are suspect because they are often based on the assumption that polygraph results are correct unless proven otherwise.[77] In many instances no systematic follow-up studies have been conducted to verify the examiner's conclusions, verification criteria are not specified, and improper procedures are used to compute the error rate.[78]

Second, polygraph research is an ongoing process and much of it is quite recent. A 1984 Department of Defense study noted that there "has been more scientific research conducted on lie detection in the last six years than in the previous 60 years."[79] In 1988 another authority, Dr. Gordon Barland, wrote: "Only now are superior paradigms being developed which combine the ground truth of the laboratory with the realism of field applications."[80] In 1995, the Director of the Defense Polygraph Institute noted: "The period between 1986 and the present has been one of unparalleled advances in the psychophysiological detection of deception testing procedures and processes."[81]

> turmoil when we are falsely accused of a crime, when we are anxious about having to defend ourselves against accusations, when we are questioned about sensitive topics — and, for that matter, when we are elated or otherwise emotionally stirred.

Kleinmuntz & Szucko, *On the Fallibility of Lie Detection*, 17 LAW & SOC'Y REV. 85, 87 (1982). *See also* D. LYKKEN, A TREMOR IN THE BLOOD: USES AND ABUSES OF THE LIE DETECTOR ch. 4 (1981); Lykken, *The Lie Detector and the Law*, 8 CRIM. DEF. 19, 21 (May-June 1981) ("But people do not all react in the same way when they are lying and, more important, any reaction that you might display when answering deceptively you might also display another time, when you are being truthful").

77. *See* F. INBAU & J. REID, LIE DETECTION AND CRIMINAL INTERROGATION 111 (3d ed. 1953) ("This estimate accords to the lie-detector technique, *when applied under the most favorable conditions*, an accuracy of 95 percent, with a 4 percent margin of indefinite determinations and a 1 per cent margin of possible error").

78. Orne, *supra* note 41, at 103-04; *Validity Panel, in* LEGAL ADMISSIBILITY OF THE POLYGRAPH 155 (N. Ansley ed. 1975) (statement of Gordon Barland).

79. Department of Defense, *The Accuracy and Utility of Polygraph Testing* (1984), *reprinted in* 13 POLYGRAPH 1, 58 (1984). *See also* Raskin, *supra* note 40, at 13 (prior to 1970 very little scientific experimentation had been conducted).

80. Barland, *The Polygraph Test in the USA and Elsewhere, in* THE POLYGRAPH TEST: LIES, TRUTH AND SCIENCE 76 (A. Gale ed. 1988).

81. Yankee, *The Current Status of Research in Forensic Psychophysiology and Its Application in the Psychophysiological Detection of Deception*, 40 J. FORENSIC SCI. 63, 63 (1995).

§ 8-3(A). Purpose of Study.

Some polygraph studies test for validity, while others test for reliability.[82] The term "validity" refers to a test procedure's accuracy, that is, its ability to measure what it is supposed to measure. The term "reliability" refers to its consistency: whether the same results are obtained each time the test is performed. Validity includes reliability, but the converse is not necessarily true.[83] The latter would include a study designed to determine whether a single examiner reaches consistent results over a period of time, or whether several different examiners reach the same conclusion when the same subject is tested.

§ 8-3(B). Field & Laboratory Studies.

There are two different kinds of polygraph validity studies: (1) field studies of actual cases and (2) mock crime experiments, which are laboratory simulations. Both have drawbacks. Field studies depend on establishing a valid criterion for determining guilt or innocence. Some studies use panels of trial attorneys to determine guilt, an approach with obvious problems. Dr. Raskin argued that the best criterion is confirmation by a subject's later confession.[84] Others, however, have pointed out that the confession criterion introduces a number of issues of sampling bias.[85]

Laboratory experimentation has its own limitations. There are important differences between the laboratory and forensic environments that may

---

82. Another purpose (albeit non-scientific) involves an evaluation of the "utility" of the polygraph. Even if polygraph evidence is not admitted at trial, it may nevertheless be sufficiently reliable for other important uses, such as preemployment screening for police departments, national security purposes, and criminal investigations.

83. Barland, *The Reliability of Polygraph Chart Evaluation*, *in* LEGAL ADMISSIBILITY OF THE POLYGRAPH 120, 121 (N. Ansley 1975).

84. Raskin, *supra* note 6, 1986 UTAH L. REV. at 44 (stating that the best available method uses cases in which suspects confess after the polygraph examination, after which the charts are evaluated blindly by independent examiners). *See generally* Honts, *Criterion Development and Validity of the CQT in Field Application*, 27 POLYGRAPH 219 (1998) (field study of 41 Canadian criminal cases examined) (finding numerical scoring system very reliable and CQT very accurate in discriminating between truth tellers and deceivers in field settings); Putnam, *Field Accuracy of Polygraph in the Law Enforcement Environment*, 23 POLYGRAPH 260 (1994) (285 actual cases verified by confession of examinee or by another person, correct in 62 of 65 verified truthful (95%) cases and 219 of 220 verified deceptive (99%) cases).

85. *See* Patrick & Iacono, *Validity of the Control Question Polygraph Test: The Problem of Sampling Bias*, 76 J. APPLIED PSYCHOL. 229 (1991) ("A deceptive polygraph test outcome provides the incentive for an examiner to interrogate a subject, and if the subject confesses, the polygraph outcome is confirmed. (In the ultimate version of this self-fulfilling prophecy, an examiner may accept a minor admission from the subject — one that does not relate specifically to the issue of the polygraph test — as evidence of the subject's guilt")).

undermine the validity of these experiments.[86] The principal difference is that fear of detection is not as strong for experimental subjects.[87] In addition, some laboratory studies fail to replicate field conditions; they use neither experienced examiners nor general population samples as subjects.[88]

§ 8-3(C). Selected Studies.

A number of authorities have questioned the validity of polygraph testing. Dr. Lykken is perhaps the most well-known critic.[89] Other authorities, however, strongly support the validity of polygraph testing, at least under certain conditions.[90]

Understanding the literature on this subject requires an appreciation of a number of additional issues. First, some tests such as the CQT appear to be "more accurate at detecting the deception of the guilty person than detecting the truthfulness of the innocent person."[91] Second, the subject of the test — whether a suspect or victim — may also be important. Apparently, false positives are

---

86. *Validity Panel*, *supra* note 78, at 160-62; Barland & Raskin, *supra* note 4, at 436-45.

87. Lykken, *supra* note 76, at 23 ("Since the emotional impact of such artificial simulations, as well as the importance to the individual of the outcome, is inevitably very different than in real life situations, such laboratory assessments provide no valid basis for estimating the accuracy of the lie test in the field"). Researchers attempt to solve this problem by using cash bonuses. Raskin, *Does Science Support Polygraph Testing?*, *in* THE POLYGRAPH TEST: LIES, TRUTH AND SCIENCE 96, 99 (A. Gale ed. 1988).

88. *See* Ansley, *Simulations and Polygraph Research*, 24 POLYGRAPH 275, 282 (1995) ("If researchers want to know about the validity of polygraph examinations or find data on other aspects of field testing, simulations in the laboratory where they can control the factors under study need to be as much like field conditions as possible").

89. Dr. Lykken's writings include: D. LYKKEN, A TREMOR IN THE BLOOD: USES AND ABUSES OF THE LIE DETECTOR (1981); Lykken, *The Lie Detector and the Law*, 8 CRIM. DEF. 19 (May-June 1981); Lykken, *The Validity of Tests: Caveat Emptor*, 27 JURIMETRICS J. 263 (Spring 1987); Lykken, *The Case Against Polygraph Testing*, *in* THE POLYGRAPH TEST: LIES, TRUTH AND SCIENCE 110 (A. Gale ed. 1988).

Other critics include: Carroll, *How Accurate is Polygraph Lie Detection?*, *in* THE POLYGRAPH TEST: LIES, TRUTH AND SCIENCE 19 (A. Gale ed. 1988); Iacono & Patrick, *Assessing Deception: Polygraph Techniques*, *in* CLINICAL ASSESSMENT OF MALINGERING AND DECEPTION 205 (R. Rogers ed. 1988); Kleinmuntz & Szucko, *A Field Study of the Fallibility of Polygraphic Lie Detection*, 308 NATURE 449 (1984) (the validity of polygraphic interrogation has yet to be established); Kleinmuntz & Szucko, *supra* note 76.

90. *See* S. Abrams, *supra* note 11, at 115; J. REID & F. INBAU, *supra* note 12, at 304; D. Raskin, G. Barland & J. Podlesny, *Validity and Reliability of Detection of Deception* (June 1978); Raskin, *Does Science Support Polygraph Testing?*, *in* THE POLYGRAPH TEST: LIES, TRUTH AND SCIENCE 96, 101 (A. Gale ed. 1988); Barland, *The Polygraph Test in the USA and Elsewhere*, *id.* at 83; Raskin, *supra* note 6, 1986 UTAH L. REV. 29; Raskin & Kircher, *The Validity of Lykken's Criticisms: Fact or Fancy?*, 27 JURIMETRICS J. 271 (Spring 1987).

91. Barland, *The Polygraph Test in the USA and Elsewhere*, *in* THE POLYGRAPH TEST: LIES, TRUTH AND SCIENCE 73 (A. Gale ed. 1988).

more frequent with victims than with suspects.[92] Third, the type of issue involved is important: polygraph examinations involving specific factual issues produce more valid results than those involving mental state issues.[93]

In the fall of 1983, the Office of Technology Assessment of the U.S. Congress submitted a report in which it reviewed and evaluated the research on polygraph validity. The report included the following passage as part of its findings:

> OTA found meaningful scientific evidence of polygraph validity only in the area of criminal investigations. However, even here, there is a wide divergence in the results of the relevant research. Six prior research reviews showed average validity ranging from a low of 64 percent to a high of 98 percent. OTA's own review of 28 studies meeting minimum acceptable scientific criteria found that, for example, correct guilty detections ranged from 17 to 100 percent. Overall, the cumulative research evidence suggests that when used in criminal investigations, the polygraph test detects deception better than chance, but with significant error rates.[94]

In contrast, a 1984 Department of Defense report reached far more favorable conclusions about polygraph validity:

> Thus, the Bersh study, experience of investigators and quality control personnel, and mock crime laboratory studies give different estimates of the accuracy of control question tests in criminal investigations, ranging from about 80% to 95%.... [T]here are no data suggesting that the various polygraph techniques and applications in [the Department of Defense] have high false positive or high false negative error rates.[95]

---

92. Raskin, *Does Science Support Polygraph Testing?*, *in* THE POLYGRAPH TEST: LIES, TRUTH AND SCIENCE 96, 101 (A. Gale ed. 1988); Barland, *The Polygraph Test in the USA and Elsewhere*, *id.* at 83.

93. Barland, *id.* at 83-84; Raskin, *supra* note 6, 1986 UTAH L. REV. at 46-47.

94. OTA Report, *supra* note 4, *reprinted in* 12 POLYGRAPH at 200. For other articles and reports on the validity issue, *see* Abrams, *Polygraph Validity and Reliability: A Review*, 18 J. FORENSIC SCI. 313 (1973); Ansley, A *Compendium on Polygraph Validity*, 12 POLYGRAPH 53 (1983); Horvath, *Detection of Deception: A Review of Field and Laboratory Research*, 5 POLYGRAPH 107 (1976).

95. Department of Defense, *The Accuracy and Utility of Polygraph Testing*, *supra* note 79, *reprinted in* 13 POLYGRAPH at 63. Moreover, a 1982 Gallup poll survey of the Society for Psychological Research reported that 61% of the 155 members responding believed that the polygraph is a useful diagnostic tool when considered with other available information. Gallup Organization, *Survey of Members of the Society for Psychological Research Concerning Their Opinion of Polygraph Test Interpretation*, 13 POLYGRAPH 153, 157 (1984).

A significant problem in interpreting the various reports concerns which studies used scientifically valid methodologies.[96] In 1986 Professor Raskin cited five mock crime studies that he considered valid because they used the control question technique, trained examiners, field techniques, and non-student populations. He concluded: "The combined accuracy of decisions was 95%, with an inconclusive rate of 8%. It should be noted that the majority of errors were false positive errors of diagnosing deception in subjects who were actually truthful. The evaluations misdiagnosed 8% of innocent subjects as deceptive and only 3% of guilty subjects as truthful (false negative errors)."[97] In 1988, Raskin and his colleagues reported the results of a field study on the control question technique as administered by Secret Service personnel. In addition to field examiners, blind interpretation of charts by quality control examiners and computer interpretation were studied. The report concluded: "The accuracy of human and computer interpretations was very high. Decision by the original examiners on individual relevant questions ranged from 91-96% correct on confirmed truthful answers and 85-95% correct on confirmed deceptive answers. Blind interpretation produced somewhat lower accuracies, ranging from 63-85% on truthful answers and 84-94% on deceptive answers."[98]

Nevertheless, the controversy continued. Iacono and Patrick concluded in 1988 that the "best defense one can offer for the continued use of the CQT is that its accuracy is indeterminate."[99] In 1989, Raskin responded: "The voluminous scientific literature indicates that they can be highly accurate when properly employed in appropriate circumstances, but they are also subject to abuse and misinterpretation."[100] A decade later, the debate continued unabated.[101]

---

96. *See* Kircher, Horowitz & Raskin, *Meta-Analysis of Mock Crime Studies of the Control Polygraph Technique*, 12 LAW & HUM. BEHAV. 79 (1988) (differences in subjects, incentives, and decision policies may account for as much as 65% of the observed variance in detection rates).

97. Raskin, *supra* note 6, 1986 UTAH L. REV. at 42 ("These error rates indicate the limitations of the control question technique, even when it is performed under carefully controlled conditions by highly skilled examiners with extensive psychological training and expertise").

98. D. RASKIN, J. KIRCHER, C. HONTS & S. HOROWITZ, A STUDY OF THE VALIDITY OF POLYGRAPH EXAMINATIONS IN CRIMINAL INVESTIGATION (May 1988) (Nat'l Inst. of Justice, Grant No. 85-IJ-CX-0040) ("However, the accuracy of the computer interpretations was higher than the blind interpretations, and it ranged from 95-96% on confirmed truthful suspects and 83-96% on confirmed deceptive subjects. The results provide considerable support for the accuracy of decisions made by the original examiners concerning the outcomes of polygraph tests").

99. Iacono & Patrick, *Assessing Deception: Polygraph Techniques*, *in* CLINICAL ASSESSMENT OF MALINGERING AND DECEPTION 205, 233 (R. Rogers ed. 1988).

100. Raskin, *Polygraph Techniques for the Detection of Deception*, *in* PSYCHOLOGICAL METHODS IN CRIMINAL INVESTIGATIONS AND EVIDENCE 247, 290 (Raskin ed. 1989).

101. 1 D. FAIGMAN, D. KAYE, M. SAKS & J. SANDERS, MODERN SCIENTIFIC EVIDENCE ch. 14 (1997).

§ 8-3(D). Computer Scoring.

A significant recent development involves computer software programs to evaluate polygraph charts. For example, *Polyscore*, developed by Johns Hopkins University Applied Physics Laboratory, is a computerized algorithm for evaluating zone comparison examinations and is based on digitized polygraph data from criminal investigations.[102] The program's evaluation methodology differs from that used by examiners.[103] The validity of the computerized programs will be the next step in the polygraph debate.

§ 8-3(E). Countermeasures.

Another important research issue involves countermeasures or techniques to "beat" the test by a guilty subject. The OTA report commented that the "research on countermeasures has been limited and the results conflicting."[104] But this report is dated.[105] Countermeasures can be divided into two categories: (1) those that change the examinee's general physiological state, such as drugs and biofeedback, and (2) those that produce effects at specific points in the examination, such as mental imagery and physical countermeasures.[106] In addition, countermeasures that may be successful against one type of examination, such as the CQT test, would not necessarily be effective against the concealed information test.[107]

Physical countermeasures appear to pose the greatest threat to the control question technique.[108] To be effective, the subject must produce stronger physiological responses to the control questions than to the relevant questions. Biting the tongue or pressing toes against the floor have produced significant false negative results in laboratory studies. One study concluded that the

---

102. Olsen , Harris, Capps & Ansley, *supra* note 45. In developing the algorithm, real cases, not mock crime data, used. Indicators of deception, called features, were characterized numerically. Examples of features would be expansion of respiration, rapid increase in blood volume, etc. "We sought a set of features that would allow us to separate deceptive and nondeceptive subjects as clearly as possible." *Id.* at 62.

103. The lab started collecting data in 1989. The 1997 article concluded: (1) "Because subject status, for many of the cases in the database, was determined by examiner decision, these results demonstrate that the algorithm is consistent with experienced examiner decisions." (2) "The results indicate that an algorithm has been built that can separate the confirmed truthful and deceptive subjects in this database." (3) "The algorithm does not mimic traditional chart interpretation." *Id.* at 69-70.

104. OTA Report, *supra* note 4, *reprinted in* 12 POLYGRAPH at 201.

105. *See* Krapohl, *A Taxonomy of Polygraph Countermeasures*, 25 POLYGRAPH 35 (1996).

106. Honts, *Interpreting Research on Polygraph Countermeasures*, 15 J. POLICE SCI. & ADMIN. 204 (1987). *See also* Gudjonsson, *How to Defeat the Polygraph Tests*, *in* THE POLYGRAPH TEST: LIES, TRUTH AND SCIENCE 126 (A. Gale ed. 1988).

107. *See* § 8-2(A) *supra* (theory of CQT & GKT).

108. Raskin, *supra* note 6, 1986 UTAH L. REV. at 50-51.

principal threat is subjects who "have received systematic training in countermeasures."[109] Spontaneous countermeasures were not effective. Another study concluded that a polygraph instrument with an activity sensor would detect most attempts at physical countermeasures.[110]

In sum, countermeasures may be divided into three levels of sophistication: low level, mid-level, and high level. Low level countermeasures are those which are not taught. The subject tries whatever comes to mind, making up his tactics while the test is in progress. They are easily detected. Mid-level countermeasures are those that the subject has learned from a semi-authoritative or authoritative source—*e.g.*, books or the Internet. These are more sophisticated, and stand some chance of success if the examiner is not alert. These are becoming increasingly common as more people access the Internet. Nevertheless, they can be detected by trained examiners. High-level countermeasures are those taught by an unethical examiner. As would be expected, these stand the greatest chance of success. None are guaranteed to succeed. These are probably very rare in the criminal setting.

§ 8-3(F). Psychopaths.

The ability of a sociopath or psychopath,[111] a person without a conscience, to "beat" the polygraph has been the subject of several studies. One mock crime experiment with 48 prison inmates revealed that not one of the "guilty" subjects was able to produce a truthful response.[112] In another study, the investigators found that guilty psychopaths were as easily detected as "guilty" nonpsychopaths.[113] However, as with all polygraph procedures, the ability of the examiner is crucial.[114]

In sum, the research has shown that psychopathic personalities perform no differently than other subjects.

---

109. Honts, Raskin, Kircher & Hodes, *Effects of Spontaneous Countermeasures on the Physiological Detection of Deception*, 16 J. POLICE SCI. & ADMIN. 91, 93 (1988).

110. Abrams & Davidson, *Counter-Countermeasures in Polygraph Testing*, 17 POLYGRAPH 16, 19 (1988).

111. *See generally* R. HARE, WITHOUT CONSCIENCE: THE DISTURBING WORLD OF THE PSYCHOPATHS AMONG US (1993).

112. Raskin & Hare, *Psychopathy and Detection of Deception in a Prison Population*, 15 PSYCHOPHYSIOLOGY 126 (1978).

113. Patrick & Iacono, *Psychopathy, Threat, and Polygraph Test Accuracy*, J. APPLIED PSYCH. 347 (1989).

114. *See* Krsnich, *Applications of Polygraph to the Psychopathic Personality*, 26 POLYGRAPH 107 (1997).

§ 8-3(G). Friendly Polygrapher Issue.

The friendly polygrapher hypothesis, first raised by Dr. Martin Orne as an issue worth investigating,[115] suggests that a polygraph examination privately conducted by the defense may not be reliable because the fear of detection is not sufficiently realistic; the defendant knows that failing the test does not result in any adverse consequence. Thus, the possibility of a false negative will increase. This hypothesis, however, has never been established, and "[a]t present, the only research bearing upon this hypothesis does not support it."[116]

§ 8-4. Admissibility.

The introduction of polygraph evidence at trial raises both evidence and constitutional issues, both of which are discussed *infra*.

In addition to the admissibility and constitutional issues, the polygraph technique is worth examining for other reasons. First, the polygraph cases provide a rich history of how courts have grappled with scientific evidence. No other scientific technique has been subject to judicial review for as a long period; it has been 75 years since *Frye v. United States,*[117] the first case, was decided. For the most part, other techniques came to the courts only once, albeit often over a tortuous path; they were accepted or rejected. In contrast, the polygraph seems to fade into the background and then erupt back to the forefront as in the 1970s, 1980s, and now the 1990s with the post-*Daubert* cases.

Second, in many ways the courts' treatment of polygraph evidence has differed radically from its approach to other scientific techniques. The paradoxes are striking. For example, many jurisdictions admit polygraph evidence upon stipulation, even though the stipulation does nothing to enhance the reliability of the evidence, which is the principal reason for exclusion.[118] Similarly, some courts that exclude polygraph evidence at trial admit it in suppression hearings, sentencing hearings, motions for new trial proceedings, and prison disciplinary hearings.[119] Moreover, some courts enforce plea bargains based on polygraph evidence.[120]

---

115. Orne, *supra* note 41.

116. Barland, *supra* note 29, 16 U. WEST L.A. L. REV. at 49. *See also* Raskin, *supra* note 6, 1986 UTAH L. REV. at 63 ("When the 'friendly polygrapher' hypothesis is examined in light of all meaningful scientific data, no credible evidence supports the theory").

117. 293 F. 1013 (D.C. Cir. 1923).

118. *See* § 8-4(C) *infra* (admissibility by stipulation).

119. *See* § 8-6 *infra* (admissibility in proceedings other than trials).

120. In some cases prosecutors have gone beyond stipulating to the admissibility of test results and have agreed to dismiss charges if the defendant passes a polygraph examination. *See* § 8-9 *infra* (discussing pretrial agreements). *See also* United States v. Santiago-Gonzales, 66 F.3d 3, 6 n.1 (1st Cir. 1995) (polygraph used to measure defendant's requirement to be truthful under a plea agreement).

Third, the extensive use of the polygraph by the government raises another paradox — especially for prosecutors challenging its admissibility. The DoD 1994 report stated: "During fiscal year 1994, DoD investigations obtained unique and significant information from interviews conducted with the aid of the polygraph. In all illustrated instances, the polygraph examination process produced significant security or criminal information which would not otherwise have been secured for the specific investigation. The polygraph examination process was also valuable in helping to establish the innocence of persons charged with serious infractions."[121] In 1996, the Department of Defense (DoD) conducted 12,548 polygraph examinations. Sixty-three percent (7,945) involved the DoD Counterintelligence-Scope Polygraph (CSP) Program. The other categories include 21.5% criminal investigations (2,696), 4.6% exculpatory (579), and 10.6% miscellaneous (1,328), the latter includes security investigations, counterintelligence and intelligence operations, and assistance to non-DoD federal agencies.[122] Further, the Department of Defense Polygraph Institute (DoDPI) trains 100 federal examiners a year in a masters level program,[123] as well as allocates funds for polygraph research. Justice Kennedy took note of this point in his concurring opinion in *Scheffer*.[124] "[T]here is much inconsistency between the Government's extensive use of polygraph to make vital security determinations and the argument it makes here, stressing the inaccuracy of these tests."[125]

§ 8-4(A). Historical Overview.

Early Cases

The admissibility of polygraph evidence was first considered and rejected in *Frye v. United States*,[126] the 1923 case in which the D.C. Circuit established the general acceptance test for the admissibility of scientific evidence.[127] According

121. Department of Defense Polygraph Program, *1994 Report to Congress, reprinted in* 24 POLYGRAPH 19 (1995). *See also* Department of Defense Polygraph Program, *1993 Report to Congress, reprinted in* 23 POLYGRAPH 61 (1994).

122. Department of Defense, *Polygraph Program, Annual Report to Congress* 1 (1996) [hereinafter DoDPI 1996 Annual Report].

123. The DoDPI trains all federal polygraph examiners. *See also* Furgerson, *Perspectives on Polygraphs: A Guide to Survival*, 21 POLYGRAPH 164, 164 (1992) (from 1977 to 1992, 115 FBI agents have attended the DoD Polygraph Institute (or its predecessor); they have conducted over 40,000 polygraph exams).

124. *See* § 8-5 *infra* (constitutional argument).

125. 118 S. Ct. at 1269.

126. 293 F. 1013 (D.C. Cir. 1923).

127. For a discussion of the general acceptance test, *see* Chapter 1.

to the court, the polygraph[128] had not gained general acceptance in the fields of psychology and physiology.[129] From *Frye* until the 1970s, polygraph evidence was overwhelmingly rejected by the courts.[130]

1970s Cases

In the early 1970s several trial courts departed from nearly fifty years of precedent and admitted the results of unstipulated polygraph examinations. In *United States v. Ridling,*[131] a federal district court found that "the theory of the polygraph is sound" and "directly relevant" to the issue (perjury) being litigated.[132] The court went on to hold that the results of a polygraph examination conducted by a court-appointed expert would be admissible under certain conditions.[133] Polygraph results were also admitted in *United States v. Zeiger.*[134] The *Zeiger* court held that the "polygraph has been accepted by authorities in the field as being capable of producing highly probative evidence in a court of law when properly used by competent, experienced examiners."[135] In addition, in *People v. Cutter*[136] a California court admitted polygraph evidence during a suppression hearing after finding that the "polygraph now enjoys general acceptance among authorities, including psychologists and researchers ... as well as polygraph examiners."[137] In the next year, a third federal district court, in an extensive opinion, stated that polygraph results would have been admitted if the court had not been bound by precedent.[138] Several other courts also admitted

---

128. The instrument used in *Frye* measured only one physiological response (blood pressure), whereas the modern polygraph measures respiration and galvanic skin resistance in addition to blood pressure. The technique also has been improved through the development of control questions, the pretest interview, and stimulation methods. The early instrument is described in Marston, *Psychological Possibilities in the Deception Tests*, 11 J. CRIM. L. & CRIMINOLOGY 551 (1921).

129. 293 F. at 1014. *See generally* Skolnick, *Scientific Theory and Scientific Evidence: An Analysis of Lie-Detection*, 70 YALE L.J. 694 (1961).

130. People v. Kenny, 167 Misc. 51, 54, 3 N.Y.S.2d 348, 351 (Sup. Ct. 1938), is an exception to the general rule of exclusion. That case, however, was soon undercut by People v. Forte, 279 N.Y. 204, 206, 18 N.E.2d 31, 32 (1938), which reaffirmed the N.Y. Court of Appeals' earlier position excluding the results of polygraph examinations.

131. 350 F. Supp. 90 (E.D. Mich. 1972).

132. *Id.* at 95.

133. Admissibility was conditioned on the selection of a court-appointed expert and the expert's determination that the results indicated either truth or deception. If the appointed expert testified, the defendant's own expert would also be permitted to testify. *Id.* at 99.

134. 350 F. Supp. 685 (D.D.C.), *rev'd,* 475 F.2d 1280 (D.C. Cir. 1972) (per curiam).

135. *Id.* at 690.

136. 12 Crim. L. Rptr. (BNA) 2133 (Cal. Super. Ct. Nov. 6, 1972).

137. *Id.* at 2134.

138. United States v. DeBetham, 348 F. Supp. 1377, 1391 (S.D. Cal.), *aff'd,* 470 F.2d 1367 (9th Cir. 1972), *cert. denied,* 412 U.S. 907 (1973).

polygraph evidence at this time, some were civil cases[139] and others were criminal cases in special circumstances.[140]

In 1974, the Supreme Judicial Court of Massachusetts admitted polygraph evidence without stipulation in *Commonwealth v. A Juvenile*.[141] In 1975, the New Mexico Supreme Court in *State v. Dorsey*[142] held that polygraph results are admissible if (1) the operator is qualified, (2) the testing procedures were reliable, and (3) the test of the particular subject was valid. An Ohio trial court in 1977[143] and a New York trial court in 1979 reached the same result.[144]

The trend in favor of admissibility which these cases seemed to forecast never developed. *Zeiger* was reversed per curiam,[145] while *Ridling* and *Cutter* were never appealed, thus precluding the opportunity for appellate approval. Nevertheless, the judicial approach to polygraph evidence seems to have been altered by these decisions and the attention that they received in the literature.[146] In particular, after these decisions were rendered, a number of courts admitted polygraph results upon stipulation.

By the end of the decade, the cases could be divided into three groups. The first group consisted of those courts that adhered to the traditional position, holding polygraph evidence per se inadmissible. A second group of courts admitted polygraph evidence upon stipulation. Finally, a few courts entrusted the admissibility of polygraph evidence to the discretion of the trial court.

1980s Cases

Developments in the 1980s were mixed. In 1982, a California appellate court in *Witherspoon v. Superior Court*[147] opened the door to the possible admission of polygraph evidence. In 1983, New Mexico adopted Evidence Rule 707, which permits the admission of polygraph evidence. In 1986, the Idaho Supreme Court

---

139. *E.g.,* Walter v. O'Connell, 339 N.Y.S.2d 386, 388 (Queens Civ. Ct. 1972) (civil case); *In re* Stenzel, 336 N.Y.S.2d 839 (Niagara Cty. Fam. Ct. 1972) (civil case).

140. *E.g.,* United States v. Hart, 344 F. Supp. 522, 523-24 (E.D.N.Y. 1971) (*Brady* issue); State v. Watson, 278 A.2d 543, 546 (Hudson Cty. Ct. 1971) (sentencing).

141. 365 Mass. 421, 313 N.E.2d 120 (1974).

142. 88 N.M.184, 539 P.2d 204, 205 (1975).

143. State v. Sims, 52 Ohio Misc. 31, 42, 369 N.E.2d, 24, 32 (C.P. 1977) (citing constitutional grounds).

144. People v. Daniels, 422 N.Y.S.2d 832, 837 (Sup. Ct. 1979).

145. United States v. Zeiger, 475 F.2d 1280 (D.C. Cir. 1972).

146. *See generally* Tarlow, *Admissibility of Polygraph Evidence in 1975: An Aid in Determining Credibility in a Perjury-Plagued System*, 26 HASTINGS L.J. 917 (1975); Note, *The Emergence of the Polygraph at Trial*, 73 COLUM. L. REV. 1120 (1973); Note, *Pinocchio's New Nose*, 48 N.Y.U. L. REV. 339 (1973).

147. 133 Cal. App. 3d 24, 28, 183 Cal. Rptr. 2d 615, 617 (1982) ("[N]o legal reason exists for continuing the judicially developed exclusion of [polygraph] evidence").

in *In re* X[148] ruled polygraph evidence admissible in proceedings under the Child Protective Act. In 1987, the Court of Military Appeals in United *States v. Gipson*[149] ruled polygraph evidence admissible, as did the Eleventh Circuit in 1989.[150]

There were also major setbacks. The California legislature closed the door opened by *Witherspoon*, enacting a statute that permits only the admissibility of stipulated polygraph results.[151] The Supreme Judicial Court of Massachusetts, the court that had decided a landmark case admitting polygraph evidence without stipulation,[152] abruptly changed directions and excluded polygraph evidence.[153] In 1991, Military Rule of Evidence 707 abrogated the *Gipson* decision.[154] In addition, several courts that had recognized the admissibility of stipulated polygraph results retreated, reverting back to the per se exclusion rule.[155] The Wisconsin Supreme Court's decision in *State v. Dean*[156] may be the most significant. The court jettisoned its earlier opinion after the Seventh Circuit held in *McMorris v. Israel*[157] that the prosecution in a stipulation state (Wisconsin) was constitutionally required to justify its refusal to stipulate.[158]

Finally, Congress passed the Employee Polygraph Protection Act[159] in 1988. With limited exceptions, the Act prohibits the use of polygraph tests for preemployment screening or during the course of private employment. Governmental entities are exempt. Although the Act does not apply in criminal cases, it had the effect of putting many polygraphers out of business, including many incompetent ones.

---

148. 714 P.2d 13, 19 (Idaho 1986).

149. 24 M.J. 246, 253-54 (C.M.A. 1987).

150. United States v. Piccinonna, 885 F.2d 1529 (11th Cir. 1989) (en banc).

151. CAL. EVID. CODE § 351.1.

152. *See* note 141 and accompanying text (discussing *A Juvenile*).

153. Commonwealth v. Mendes, 406 Mass. 201, 547 N.E.2d 35 (1989).

154. This rule subsequently become the focus the *Scheffer* decision, in which the U.S. Supreme Court upheld the constitutionality of the per se rule of exclusion. *See* § 8-5 *infra*.

155. *E.g.*, State v. Milano, 297 N.C. 485, 256 S.E.2d 154 (1979), *overruled by* State v. Grier, 307 N.C. 628, 645, 300 S.E.2d 351, 356-61 (1983); State v. Stanislawski, 62 Wis. 2d 730, 216 N.W.2d 8 (1974), *overruled by* State v. Dean, 103 Wis. 2d 228, 297, 307 N.W.2d 628, 653 (Wis. 1981). *See also* Castleberry v. State, 522 P.2d 257 (Okla. Crim. App. 1974), and Jones v. State, 527 P.2d 169 (Okla. Crim. App. 1974), *overruled by* Fulton v. State, 541 P.2d 871, 872 (Okla. Crim. App. 1975).

156. 103 Wis. 2d 228, 297, 307 N.W.2d 628, 653 (Wis. 1981).

157. 643 F.2d 458 (7th Cir. 1981), *cert. denied*, 455 U.S. 967 (1982).

158. *See* § 8-5 *infra* (constitutional arguments).

159. *See* § 8-10 *infra*.

1990s Cases

In 1993, the U.S. Supreme Court decided *Daubert,* and the lower courts, once again, were forced to address polygraph evidence.[160] As explained below, this lead to the rejection of the per se rule of exclusion in several federal courts. In 1998, the Supreme Court in *Scheffer* held that the per se rule of exclusion was not unconstitutional.[161]

§ 8-4(B). Per Se Exclusion.

A majority of states still follow the traditional rule, holding polygraph evidence per se inadmissible.[162] At one time most federal circuit courts also

---

160. For a discussion of *Daubert, see* Chapter 1.

161. *See* § 8-5 *infra.*

162. *E.g.,* Pulakis v. State, 476 P.2d 474, 479 (Alaska 1970); People v. Anderson, 637 P.2d 354, 358 (Colo. 1981); State v. Porter, 241 Conn. 57, 694 A.2d 1262 (1997) (adopting *Daubert* and excluding polygraph results under Rule 403), *cert. denied,* 118 S. Ct. 1384 (1998); State v. Miller, 202 Conn. 463, 486, 522 A.2d 249, 260-61 (1987); State v. Antone, 615 P.2d 101, 109 (Hawaii 1980); People v. Gard, 158 Ill.2d 191, 632 N.E.2d 1026, 1032 (1994) ("[T]he use of polygraph evidence ... is no less repugnant to and no less an affront to the integrity of the judicial process when the examination has been given to a witness ... than it is when the examination has been given to the defendant himself"); People v. Baynes, 88 Ill. 2d 225, 244, 430 N.E.2d 1070, 1079 (1981); Harris v. State, 481 N.E.2d 382, 384 (Ind. 1985); Ice v. Commonwealth, 667 S.W.2d 671, 675 (Ky. 1984); State v. Catanese, 368 So. 2d 975, 981 (La. 1979); Kelley v. State, 288 Md. 298, 302, 418 A.2d 217, 219 (1980); State v. Mitchell, 402 A.2d 479, 482 (Me. 1979); Commonwealth v. Mendes, 406 Mass. 201, 201, 547 N.E.2d 35, 36 (1989); People v. Barbara, 400 Mich. 352, 359, 255 N.W.2d 171, 173 (1977); State v. Anderson, 379 N.W.2d 70, 79 (Minn. 1985), *cert. denied,* 476 U.S. 1141 (1986); State v. Michaeloff, 324 N.W.2d 926, 927 (Minn. 1982); Pennington v. State, 437 So. 2d 37, 40 (Miss. 1983); State v. Staat, 811 P.2d 1261, 1263 (Mont. 1991); State v. Beachman, 616 P.2d 337, 339 (Mont. 1980); State v. Biddle, 599 S.W.2d 182, 185 (Mo. 1980); Mathes v. City of Omaha, 254 Neb. 269, 274, 576 N.W.2d 181, 185 (1998) ("We discern no reason for making admissible in administrative hearings the results of polygraph examinations which are not admissible in criminal cases and therefore hold that the results of such examinations are inadmissible for the purpose of attempting to show deception in a proceeding before an administrative agency of a municipal government"); State v. Steinmark, 195 Neb. 545, 548, 239 N.W.2d 495, 497 (1976); State v. French, 119 N.H. 500, 503, 403 A.2d 424, 426, *cert. denied,* 444 U.S. 954 (1979); State v. Fleming, 350 N.C. 109, 512 S.E.2d 720, 738, 739 (1999) ("Defendant has presented us with no compelling reason to alter our long-standing holdings that evidence concerning polygraph testing is inadmissible"); State v. Grier, 307 N.C. 628, 645, 300 S.E.2d 351, 361 (1983); State v. Olmstead, 261 N.W.2d 880, 886 (N.D.), *cert. denied,* 436 U.S. 918 (1978); Birdsong v. State, 649 P.2d 786, 788 (Okla. Crim. App. 1982); State v. Lyon, 304 Or. 221, 231, 744 P.2d 231, 236 (1987); Commonwealth v. Brockington, 500 Pa. 216, 220, 455 A.2d 627, 629 (1983); State v. Dery, 545 A.2d 1014, 1017 (R.I. 1988); State v. Copeland, 278 S.C. 572, 582, 300 S.E.2d 63, 69 (1982), *cert. denied,* 463 U.S. 1214 (1983); State v. Watson, 248 N.W.2d 398, 399 (S.D. 1976); State v. Land, 681 S.W.2d 589, 592 (Tenn. Crim. App. 1984); Romero v. State, 493 S.W.2d 206, 213 (Tex. Crim. App. 1973); Robinson v. Commonwealth, 231 Va. 142, 156, 341 S.E.2d 159, 167 (1986); Lee v. Commonwealth, 200 Va. 233, 237, 105 S.E.2d 152, 155 (1958);

followed the per se approach.[163] However, as discussed below, the *Daubert* decision has had a significant affect on the federal position.

References to Polygraph

The exclusionary rule extends to evidence that a person was willing to take, took, or refused to take an examination.[164] The reference, however, may not result in a mistrial or in a reversal on appeal.[165]

State v. Beard, 461 S.E.2d 486, 493 (W. Va. 1995) ("[W]e remain convinced that the reliability of such examinations is still suspect and not generally accepted within the relevant scientific community. Therefore, any speculation that our position in *Frazier* regarding polygraph admissibility is in question due to the *Daubert/Wilt* rulings is put to rest today"); State v. Frazier, 252 S.E.2d 39, 49 (W. Va. 1979); State v. Dean, 103 Wis. 2d 228, 279, 307 N.W.2d 628, 653 (1981).

See generally 3A J. WIGMORE, EVIDENCE § 999 (Chadbourn rev. 1970).

163. *E.g.,* United States v. A & S Council Oil Co., 947 F.2d 1128, 1133-34 (4th Cir. 1991); United States v. Hunter, 672 F.2d 815, 817 (10th Cir. 1982); United States v. Clark, 598 F.2d 994, 995 (5th Cir. 1979), *vacated en banc,* 622 F.2d 917 (5th Cir. 1980), *cert. denied,* 449 U.S. 1128 (1981); United States v. Skeens, 494 F.2d 1050, 1053 (D.C. Cir. 1974).

See also Annot., *Modern Status of Rule Relating to Admission of Results of Lie Detector (Polygraph) Test in Federal Criminal Trials,* 43 A.L.R. FED. 68 (1979).

164. *E.g.,* United States v. Gantley 172 F.3d 422, 430 (6th Cir. 1999) ("[T]he jury could not help but suffer some unfair bias against the government by virtue of Gantley's statement regarding his having taken a polygraph examination"); United States v. Murray, 784 F.2d 188, 188-89 (6th Cir. 1986) (comment about polygraph deliberately introduced by experienced FBI agent was prejudicial error); Weatherspoon v. State, 732 So. 2d 158, 162 (Miss. 1999) ("testimony pertaining to a witness's offer to take a polygraph, whether it be a witness for the State or the defense, is not admissible at trial"); State v. Willis, 109 N.C. App. 184, 426 S.E.2d 471 (1993) (examiner's testimony that accused had lied about questions concerning his wife's shooting death was inadmissible, even though the polygraph test was never mentioned); Bennett v. Commonwealth, 29 Va. App. 261, 511 S.E.2d 439, 443- 44 (1999) ("Because a polygraph examination has no proper evidentiary use, neither the results of a polygraph, nor '[e]vidence of a person's willingness or unwillingness to submit to a polygraph' is admissible in court") (citations omitted). *See generally* Annot., *Propriety and Prejudicial Effect of Informing Jury that Witness in Criminal Prosecution Has Taken Polygraph Test,* 15 A.L.R.4TH 824 (1982); Annot., *Propriety and Prejudicial Effect of Informing Jury that Accused Has Taken Polygraph Test, Where Results of Test Would be Inadmissible in Evidence,* 88 A.L.R.3D 227 (1978); Annot., *Propriety and Prejudicial Effect of Comment or Evidence As to Accused's Willingness to Take Lie Detector Test,* 95 A.L.R.2D 819 (1964).

165. *See* Peyton v. United States, 709 A.2d 65, 70 (D.C. App.) ("In determining whether evidence of a lie detector test was so prejudicial that it denied the defendant a fair trial, courts have looked at many factors. The factors that have been considered include: (1) whether the reference to a lie detector was repeated or whether it was a single, isolated statement; (2) whether the reference was solicited by counsel, or was an inadvertent and unresponsive statement; (3) whether the witness making the reference is the principal witness upon whom the entire prosecution depends; (4) whether credibility is a crucial issue; (5) whether a great deal of other evidence exists; and, (6) whether an inference as to the result of the test can be drawn. No single factor is determinative in

Frye Test

Prior to 1993, when *Daubert* was decided, most courts relied upon the *Frye* general acceptance test as the basis for exclusion of polygraph results.[166] The application of this test raised several issues. According to *Frye,* psychology and physiology are the fields in which general acceptance must be achieved.[167] Several decisions had expanded the "field" to include polygraph examiners.[168] In *United States v. Alexander,*[169] however, the Eighth Circuit rejected this view: "Experts in neurology, psychiatry and physiology may offer needed enlightenment upon the basic premises of polygraphy. Polygraphists often lack extensive training in these specialized sciences."[170] A related issue concerned the extent to which the widespread use of the polygraph in law enforcement, security, and industrial activities may be considered evidence of general acceptance. Some courts accorded such evidence considerable weight,[171] while others ignored it.[172] Still other courts rejected *Frye* as the appropriate standard for determining the admissibility of scientific evidence but still excluded polygraph evidence.[173]

Daubert Test

After the U.S. Supreme Court's decision in *Daubert v. Merrell Dow Pharmaceuticals, Inc.*[174] overruled *Frye*, the Fifth Circuit in *United States v.*

---

any case. The factors themselves are not the test, but rather, they help to evaluate whether the defendant was prejudiced") (citations omitted), *cert. denied,* 119 S. Ct. 134 (1998).

166. *E.g.*, Kelley v. State, 288 Md. 298, 302, 418 A.2d 217, 219 (1980); People v. Barbara, 400 Mich. 352, 377, 255 N.W.2d 171, 181 (1977).

167. 293 F. at 1014.

168. *See* United States v. Zeiger, 350 F. Supp. 685, 689 (D.D.C.), *rev'd,* 475 F.2d 1280 (D.C. Cir. 1972); United States v. DeBetham, 348 F. Supp. 1377, 1388 (S.D. Cal.), *aff'd,* 470 F.2d 1367 (9th Cir. 1972), *cert. denied,* 412 U.S. 907 (1973); United States v. Wilson, 361 F. Supp. 510, 511 (D. Md. 1973).

169. 526 F.2d 161 (8th Cir. 1975).

170. *Id.* at 164 n.6. The position advanced in *Alexander* seems inconsistent with an earlier decision of the same court. United States v. Oliver, 525 F.2d 731, 736 (8th Cir. 1975) ("We believe the necessary foundation can be constructed through testimony showing a sufficient degree of acceptance of the science of polygraphy by experienced practitioners in polygraphy and other related experts").

171. *E.g.*, United States v. Piccinonna, 885 F.2d 1529, 1532 (11th Cir. 1989); United States v. Zeiger, 350 F. Supp. 685, 688 (D.D.C.), *rev'd,* 475 F.2d 1280 (D.C. Cir. 1972); United States v. DeBetham, 348 F. Supp. 1377, 1389 (S.D. Cal.), *aff'd,* 470 F.2d 1367 (9th Cir. 1972), *cert. denied,* 412 U.S. 907 (1973); People v. Cutter, 12 Crim. L. Rptr. (BNA) 2133, 2134 (Cal. Super. Ct. Nov. 6, 1972).

172. *E.g.*, United States v. Alexander, 526 F.2d 161 (8th Cir. 1975).

173. *E.g.*, State v. Catanese, 368 So. 2d 975, 979 (La. 1979); State v. Brown, 297 Or. 404, 416-17, 687 P.2d 751, 759 (1984).

174. 509 U.S. 579 (1993). For a further discussion of *Daubert* and *Frye*, *see* Chapter 1.

Posado[175] stated that "the rationale underlying this circuit's per se rule against admitting polygraph evidence did not survive *Daubert*."[176] The court went on to comment that "[t]here can be no doubt that tremendous advances have been made in polygraph instrumentation and technique in the years since *Frye* [1923]. ... Current research indicates that, when given under controlled conditions, the polygraph technique accurately predicts truth or deception between seventy and ninety percent of the time."[177] The court, however, limited its ruling, commenting that

> we do not now hold that polygraph examinations are scientifically valid or that they will always assist the trier of fact .... We merely remove the obstacle of the per se rule against admissibility, which was based on antiquated concepts about the technical ability of the polygraph and legal precepts that have been expressly overruled by the Supreme Court.[178]

The Ninth[179] and Tenth[180] Circuits adopted the same position. Two other circuits had embraced this position prior to *Daubert*; the Seventh Circuit had long abandoned the per se rule[181] and in 1989 the Eleventh Circuit followed suit.[182] The Sixth Circuit also falls in this category, albeit reluctantly.[183]

---

175. 57 F.3d 428 (5th Cir. 1995).

176. *Id.* at 429.

177. *Id.* at 434.

178. *Id. See also* United States v. Pettigrew, 77 F.3d 1500, 1515 (5th Cir. 1996) (trial court did not abuse its discretion in excluding polygraph evidence).

179. *See* United States v. Cordoba, 104 F.3d 225, 227-28 (9th Cir. 1997) (noting that its former per se rule of exclusion is inconsistent with *Daubert*). On remand, the trial court excluded the evidence under *Daubert*. United States v. Cordoba, 991 F. Supp. 1199, 1202 (C.D. Cal. 1998).

180. *See* United States v. Call, 129 F.3d 1402 (10th Cir. 1997), *cert. denied*, 118 S. Ct. 2064 (1998).

181. *See* United States v. Pulido, 69 F.3d 192, 205 (7th Cir. 1995) ("Our decisions acknowledge the considerable scientific and legal debate over polygraph testing and recognize that a trial court deciding whether to admit polygraph evidence 'must engage in a delicate balancing of many factors including probative value, prejudicial effect, confusion of the issues, misleading the jury, and undue delay") (quoting United States v. Olson, 978 F.2d 1472, 1480 (7th Cir. 1992), *cert. denied*, 507 U.S. 997 (1993)).

182. United States v. Piccinonna, 885 F.2d 1529 (11th Cir. 1989). *See also* Barker v. Jackson Nat'l Life Ins. Co., 896 F. Supp. 1159, 1161-62 (N.D. 1995) ("Surprisingly, in the six years since *Piccinonna*, the Eleventh Circuit appears not to have had opportunity to elaborate on the decision, other than to decide that it was not to be applied retroactively").

183. *See* United States v. Thomas, 167 F.3d 299, 308 (6th Cir. 1999) ("This court has never adopted a per se prohibition on the introduction of polygraph evidence. We do, however, generally disfavor admitting the results of polygraph examinations. In one post-*Daubert* decision, we again expressed our long-held opinion that the results of a polygraph are inherently unreliable") (citations omitted) (citing United States v. Scarborough, 43 F.3d 1021, 1026 (6th Cir. 1994)); Conti v. Commissioner, 39 F.3d 658, 663 (6th Cir. 1994) (noting that "unilaterally obtained polygraph evidence is almost never admissible under Evidence Rule 403"), *cert. denied*, 514 U.S. 1082 (1995);

Other circuits take a more cautious approach.[184] Indeed, the Second Circuit wrote that "the 'legal Pandora's box' which the Fifth Circuit opened in *United States v. Posado* ... is not yet agape in this Circuit."[185] In addition, the state cases have not been influenced by this development; several have reaffirmed the rule of categorical inadmissibility,[186] even while citing *Daubert*.[187] Other courts have continued to require stipulations.[188] Nevertheless, *Daubert* has dramatically changed the legal landscape. In this altered climate, some district courts have admitted polygraph evidence[189] — for example, *United States v. Crumby*[190] and

---

United States v. Sherlin, 67 F.3d 1208, 1216-17 (6th Cir. 1995) ("A privately commissioned polygraph test, which was unknown to the government until after its completion, is of extremely dubious probative value").

184. *See* United States v. Williams, 95 F.3d 723, 729 (8th Cir. 1996) (defendant failed to lay a foundation for polygraph admissibility).

185. United States v. Kwong, 69 F.3d 663, 668-69 (2d Cir. 1995) ("The record before us simply does not provide the proper opportunity to explore the validity of polygraph evidence under Rule 702"). *See also* United States v. Pitner, 969 F. Supp. 1246 (W.D. Wash. 1997); United States v. Castillo, 1997 WL 83746 (E.D. Pa. 1997) (polygraph evidence not admissible under EVID. R. 608); Meyers v. Arcudi, 947 F. Supp. 581, 587 (D. Conn. 1996) ("[W]hile the accuracy of the CQT polygraph exam has been tested, there are serious flaws which may underestimate the error rates. ..."); Miller v. Heaven, 922 F. Supp. 495, 503 (D. Kan. 1996) (insufficient showing under *Daubert* and excludable under Rule 403); United States v. Dominguez, 902 F. Supp. 757, 740 (E.D. Mich. 1995) (excluding evidence); United States v. Lech, 895 F. Supp. 582, 585 (S.D.N.Y. 1995) ("[T]he polygraph results here are properly excluded under Rule 403"); United States v. Black, 831 F. Supp. 120, 123 (E.D.N.Y. 1993) ("After evaluating the standard set forth in the *Daubert* case, premised on Rule 702 ..., the Court believes that nothing in *Daubert* would disturb the settled precedent that polygraph evidence is neither reliable nor admissible").

186. *E.g.*, People v. Gard, 158 Ill.2d 191, 632 N.E.2d 1026, 1032 (1994) ("[T]he use of polygraph evidence ... is no less repugnant to and no less an affront to the integrity of the judicial process when the examination has been given to a witness ... than it is when the examination has been given to the defendant himself").

187. *E.g.*, State v. Porter, 241 Conn. 57, 694 A.2d 1262 (1997) (adopting *Daubert* and excluding polygraph results under Rule 403), *cert. denied*, 118 S. Ct. 1384 (1998); State v. Beard, 461 S.E.2d 486, 493 (W. Va. 1995) ("[W]e remain convinced that the reliability of such examinations is still suspect and not generally accepted within the relevant scientific community. Therefore, any speculation that our position in *Frazier* regarding polygraph admissibility is in question due to the *Daubert/Wilt* rulings is put to rest today").

188. *E.g.*, State v. Webber, 918 P.2d 609, 619-20 (Kan. 1996) (citing "the ironclad rule that the results of such examinations are inadmissible absent a stipulation between the parties"); State v. Cosby, 927 P.2d 638, 642 (Utah 1996) (reaffirming the need for a stipulation).

189. *See* United States v. Padilla, 908 F. Supp. 923 (S.D. Fla. 1995) (admitting polygraph evidence offered by the defense); State Farm Fire & Cas. Co., 897 F. Supp. 299 (W.D. La. 1995) (admitting polygraph evidence in a civil case).

190. 895 F. Supp. 1354 (D.C. Ariz. 1995).

United States v. Galbreth.[191] In short, the "trend appears to be moving toward admissibility."[192] These cases are discussed in § 8-4(D) *infra*.

Rationale

The principal argument against the admissibility of polygraph evidence is lack of reliability.[193] Several points are made on this score: the lack of empirical validation,[194] the numerous uncontrollable factors involved in the examination,[195] the subjective nature of the deception determination,[196] and the absence of adequate standards for assessing the qualifications of examiners.[197]

---

191. 908 F. Supp. 877 (D.N.M. 1995).

192. Zehnle, *Polygraph Admissibility in the Post-Daubert Era*, ABA CRIMINAL JUSTICE 11, 13 (Summer 1997).

193. *See* United States v. Gantley, 172 F.3d 422, 430 (6th Cir. 1999) ("Evidence of polygraph examination results is generally inadmissible. The reason for this is 'the general skepticism that pervades the scientific community concerning the reliability of polygraph examination") (citations omitted); United States v. Alexander, 526 F.2d 161, 166 (8th Cir. 1975) ("[W]e are still unable to conclude that there is sufficient scientific acceptability and reliability to warrant the admission of the results of such tests in evidence"); People v. Baynes, 88 Ill. 2d 225, 239, 430 N.E.2d 1070, 1076 (1981) ("[T]he primary obstacle in admission of polygraph evidence, stipulated to or not, has continually and consistently been the instrument's disputed scientific reliability"); State v. Wakefield, 267 Kan. 116, 977 P.2d 941, 954, 955 (1999) ("[P]olygraph tests are too unreliable to be admissible ..."). *Accord* Pulakis v. State, 476 P.2d 474, 479 (Alaska 1970); State v. Briddle, 599 S.W.2d 182, 185 (Mo. 1980); Lee v. Commonwealth, 200 Va. 233, 237, 105 S.E.2d 152, 155 (1958); State v. Frazier, 252 S.E.2d 39, 43-44 (W. Va. 1979).

194. *See* United States v. Wilson, 361 F. Supp. 510, 514 (D. Md. 1973) ("incipient stage of experimental research"); People v. Monigan, 72 Ill. App. 3d 87, 96, 390 N.E.2d 562, 568 (1979) ("[T]he estimate of the degree of accuracy of polygraph tests seem[s] to come from polygraph examiners themselves"); People v. Barbara, 400 Mich. 352, 394-95, 255 N.W.2d 171, 189 (1977) ("[W]e find there is difficulty in empirically verifying polygraphic findings, ... some questions concerning the accuracy figures, ... and an apparent lack of a rational scientific explanation for this phenomenon").

195. *See* People v. Anderson, 637 P.2d 354, 359 (Colo. 1981) ("Several uncontrollable or unascertainable physiological and psychological responses may cause difficulty or error ..."); People v. Baynes, 88 Ill. 2d 225, 236, 430 N.E.2d 1070, 1075 (1981) ("abnormal blood pressure, heart and respiratory irregularities, fatigue, intoxication, rationalization, extreme nervousness, meditative abstraction, controlled breathing, instrument discomfort, uncomfortable room temperature, obesity, hidden muscular contractions, self-inflicted pain, mental incompetence, psychopathy or schizophrenia, ingestion of a sedative, an attempt to suppress a cough, fear induced by suspicion or accusation, or lack of fear of detection").

196. People v. Anderson, 637 P.2d 354, 360 (Colo. 1981) (The polygraph technique, "albeit based on a scientific theory, remains an art with unusual responsibility placed on the examiner"); People v. Monigan, 72 Ill. App. 3d 87, 98, 390 N.E.2d 562, 569 (1979) ("almost total subjectiveness surrounding the use of the polygraph and the interpretation of the results"); State v. Frazier, 252 S.E.2d 39, 48 (W. Va. 1979) ("subjective analysis").

197. *See* People v. Anderson, 637 P.2d 354, 360 (Colo. 1981) ("The absence of adequate qualification standards for the polygraph profession heighten[s] the possibility for grave abuse ...");

Even if the reliability of the technique is established, additional problems are cited as reasons for exclusion — for example, the danger that an opinion concerning the truthfulness of a witness will intrude too much into the jury's historic function of assessing credibility,[198] the danger that the jury will overvalue the expert's testimony,[199] and the possibility that the trial will degenerate into a time-consuming trial of the technique.[200]

In *United States v. Scheffer,*[201] the U.S. Supreme Court held that the per se rule of exclusion of polygraph evidence is not unconstitutional. The Court identified three interests that support the per se rule: (1) ensuring that only reliable evidence is introduced at trial, (2) preserving the jury's role in determining credibility, and (3) avoiding litigation of collateral issues.[202]

State v. Catanese, 368 So. 2d 975, 982 (La. 1979) (lack of judicial and legislative control over competence of examiners).

198. *See* People v. Baynes, 88 Ill. 2d 225, 244, 430 N.E.2d 1070, 1079 (1981) ("A potential trial by polygraph is an unwarranted intrusion into the jury function"); State v. Davis, 407 So. 2d 702, 706 (La. 1981) ("usurps the jury's prerogative on a question involving credibility"); State v. Wakefield, 267 Kan. 116, 977 P.2d 941, 954, 955 (1999) ("[P]olygraph tests ... tend to invade the province of the jury in determining the ultimate question of fact: whether a witness is speaking the truth"); State v. Beachman, 616 P.2d 337, 339 (Mont. 1980) ("It is distinctly the jury's province to determine whether a witness is being truthful").

199. *See* United States v. Alexander, 526 F.2d 161, 168 (8th Cir. 1975) ("When polygraph evidence is offered ..., it is likely to be shrouded with an aura of near infallibility, akin to the ancient oracle of Delphi"); State v. Catanese, 368 So. 2d 975, 981 (La. 1979) ("trier of fact is apt to give almost conclusive weight to the polygraph expert's opinion").

Whether juries will be overawed by polygraph evidence is a matter of dispute. *See generally* Cavoukian & Heslegrave, *The Admissibility of Polygraph Evidence in Court: Some Empirical Findings*, 4 LAW & HUM. BEHAV. 117 (1980); Carlson, Pasano & Jannuzzo, *The Effect of Lie Detector Evidence on Jury Deliberations: An Empirical Study*, 5 J. POLICE SCI. & ADMIN. 148 (1977); Markwart & Lynch, *The Effect of Polygraph Evidence on Mock Jury Decision-Making*, 7 J. POLICE SCI. & ADMIN. 324 (1979).

200. *See* People v. Barbara, 400 Mich. 352, 410, 255 N.W.2d 171, 196 (1977) ("possibility of bogging down trials with collateral matters, perhaps resulting in a trial of the polygraph, or a battle of experts"); State v. Grier, 307 N.C. 628, 643, 300 S.E.2d 351, 359-60 (1983) ("possibility that the criminal proceeding may degenerate into a trial of the polygraph machine"); State v. Dean, 103 Wis. 2d 228, 275, 307 N.W.2d 628, 651 (1981) ("become a trial of the polygraph and the polygraph operator rather than a trial of the defendant's guilt").

201. 523 U.S.303, 118 S. Ct. 1261 (1998). In *Scheffer*, the U.S. Court of Appeals for the Armed Forces had held that Military Rule 707 was unconstitutional as applied in that case. In that court's view, "A *per se* exclusion of polygraph evidence offered by an accused to rebut an attack on his credibility, without giving him an opportunity to lay a foundation under MIL. R. EVID. 702 and *Daubert*, violates his Sixth Amendment right to present a defense. We limit our holding to exculpatory evidence arising from a polygraph examination of an accused, offered to rebut an attack on his credibility." 44 M.J. 442, 445 (C.A.A.F. 1996).

202. *See* § 8-5 *infra* (discussing *Scheffer*)..

§ 8-4(C). By Stipulation.

A substantial minority of courts admit polygraph evidence upon stipulation of the parties.[203] For the most part, this result has been achieved by court decision,[204] although a California statute accomplishes the same result.[205] At one time the trend toward admissibility by stipulation appeared so strong that it seemed only a matter of time before it became the majority rule. Later decisions, however, cast doubt on this possibility. Indeed, several courts that initially admitted polygraph evidence upon stipulation have overruled their earlier decisions and now hold polygraph evidence per se inadmissible.[206]

---

203. *See generally* Katz, *Dilemmas of Polygraph Stipulations*, 14 SETON HALL L. REV. 285 (1984); Note, *Admissibility of Polygraph Data When Both Parties Have Stipulated That It Will Be Admissible*, 13 LAND & WATER L. REV. 613 (1978); Note, *Admissibility of Polygraph Test Results Upon Stipulation of the Parties*, 30 MERCER L. REV. 357 (1978); 47 MO. L. REV. 586 (1982).

204. *See* United States v. Piccinonna, 885 F.2d 1529, 1536 (11th Cir. 1989); Anderson v. United States, 788 F.2d 517, 519 (8th Cir. 1986); Brown v. Darcy, 783 F.2d 1389, 1397 (9th Cir. 1986); United States v. Oliver, 525 F.2d 731, 737 (8th Cir. 1975), *cert. denied,* 424 U.S. 973 (1976); *Ex parte* Clements, 447 So. 2d 695, 698 (Ala. 1984); State v. Montes, 136 Ariz. 491, 499, 667 P.2d 191, 199 (1983); State v. Valdez, 91 Ariz. 274, 283, 371 P.2d 894, 900 (1962); Holcomb v. State, 268 Ark. 138, 139, 594 S.W.2d 22, 23 (1980); Williams v. State, 378 A.2d 117, 120 (Del. 1977); Davis v. State, 520 So. 2d 572, 573-74 (Fla. 1988); State v. Chambers, 240 Ga. 76, 76-77, 239 S.E.2d 324, 325 (1977); State v. Fain, 116 Idaho 82, 86, 774 P.2d 252, 256-57, *cert. denied,* 493 U.S. 917 (1989); Pavone v. State, 273 Ind. 162, 164-66, 402 N.E.2d 976, 978-79 (1980); State v. Marti, 290 N.W.2d 570, 586-87 (Iowa 1980); State v. Wakefield, 267 Kan. 116, 977 P.2d 941, 954, 955 (1999) ("The rule in Kansas is absent a stipulation of the parties, the results of a polygraph examination are too unreliable to be admissible at trial"); State v. Roach, 223 Kan. 732, 735, 576 P.2d 1082, 1086 (1978); Corbett v. State, 584 P.2d 704, 707 (Nev. 1978); State v. McDavitt, 62 N.J. 36, 297 A.2d 849, 854-55 (1972); State v. Souel, 53 Ohio St. 2d 123, 133-34, 372 N.E.2d 1318, 1323-24 (1978); State v. Cosby, 927 P.2d 638, 642 (Utah 1996) (reaffirming the need for a stipulation); State v. Rebeterano, 681 P.2d 1265, 1268-69 (Utah 1984); State v. Renfro, 96 Wash. 2d 902, 905, 639 P.2d 737, 739, *cert. denied,* 459 U.S. 842 (1982); Cullin v. State, 565 P.2d 445, 457 (Wyo. 1977).

See generally 3A J. WIGMORE, EVIDENCE § 999 (Chadbourn rev. 1970); Annot., *Admissibility of Lie Detector Test Taken Upon Stipulation that the Results Will Be Admissible in Evidence*, 53 A.L.R.3D 1005 (1973).

205. *See* CAL. EVID. CODE § 351.1: "Notwithstanding any other provision of law, the results of a polygraph examination, the opinion of a polygraph examiner, or any reference to an offer to take, failure to take, or taking of a polygraph examination, shall not be admitted into evidence in any criminal proceeding ... unless all parties stipulate to the admission of such results." *See also* People v. Kegler, 197 Cal. App. 3d 72, 90, 242 Cal. Rptr. 897, 909 (1987) (stipulation statute does not violate defendant's constitutional rights).

206. *See* State v. Grier, 307 N.C. 628, 645, 300 S.E.2d 351, 356-61 (1983), *overruling* State v. Milano, 297 N.C. 485, 256 S.E.2d 154 (1979); Fulton v. State, 541 P.2d 871, 872 (Okla. Crim. App. 1975), *overruling* Castleberry v. State, 522 P.2d 257 (Okla. Crim. App. 1974), and Jones v. State, 527 P.2d 169 (Okla. Crim. App. 1974); State v. Dean, 103 Wis. 2d 228, 279, 307 N.W.2d 628, 653 (1981), *overruling* State v. Stanislawski, 62 Wis. 2d 730, 216 N.W.2d 8 (1974).

Rationale

Courts rejecting the admissibility of stipulated examinations argue that the stipulation does nothing to enhance the reliability of polygraph evidence, which is the principal reason for exclusion.[207] According to some courts the answer to this objection is that admissibility does not derive "from the fact that the stipulation somehow imbues the evidence with reliability ... but from the fact that the parties are estopped, by their stipulated waiver of the right to object, from asserting the unacceptability of the evidence ...."[208] Other courts that accept stipulated results recognize, at least implicitly, that the technique possesses some degree of validity — at least when the results are admitted under controlled conditions designed both to ensure that the examination is properly administered by a competent examiner and to limit the purpose of admissibility.[209] Finally, some courts justify admission on a combination of these grounds.[210]

The legal theory recognized for admission of stipulated results is sometimes critical. The waiver or estoppel theory could permit the prosecution to introduce polygraph results in its case-in-chief unless the stipulation limits admissibility to impeachment. In contrast, courts permitting admission of stipulated results under controlled conditions typically limit admissibility to credibility, with the result that the evidence is admissible only if the defendant testifies, thereby placing credibility in issue.

---

207. *See* Pulakis v. State, 476 P.2d 474, 479 (Alaska 1970); State v. Grier, 307 N.C. 628, 642, 300 S.E.2d 351, 359 (1983); Commonwealth v. Brockington, 500 Pa. 216, 220, 455 A.2d 627, 629 (1983); Romero v. State, 493 S.W.2d 206, 213 (Tex. Crim. App. 1973); State v. Dean, 103 Wis. 2d 228, 268-69, 307 N.W.2d 628, 648 (1981).

See also People v. Monigan, 72 Ill. App. 3d 87, 88, 390 N.E.2d 562, 563 (1979) (stipulation rejected as contrary to public policy and as an invalid stipulation of law).

208. Wynn v. State, 423 So. 2d 294, 299 (Ala. Crim. App. 1982). *Accord* State v. Marti, 290 N.W.2d 570, 586-87 (Iowa 1980) (estoppel); State v. Rebeterano, 681 P.2d 1265, 1269 (Utah 1984) (estoppel).

209. *E.g.*, United States v. Oliver, 525 F.2d 731, 736 (8th Cir. 1975) ("We believe the necessary foundation can be constructed through testimony showing a sufficient degree of acceptance of the science of polygraphy by experienced practitioners in polygraphy and other related experts"), *cert. denied,* 424 U.S. 973 (1976); State v. Valdez, 91 Ariz. 274, 283, 371 P.2d 894, 900 (1962) (polygraphy "has been developed to a state in which its results are probative enough to warrant admissibility upon stipulation"); Corbett v. State, 584 P.2d 704, 707 (Nev. 1978); State v. McDavitt, 62 N.J. 36, 46, 297 A.2d 849, 854-55 (1972).

210. *See* State v. Renfro, 96 Wash. 2d 902, 906-07, 639 P.2d 737, 739, *cert. denied,* 459 U.S. 842 (1982).

Conditions for Admissibility

The leading case on admissibility by stipulation is *State v. Valdez,*[211] in which the Arizona Supreme Court held that stipulated polygraph results are admissible if the following conditions are met:

> (1) That the county attorney, defendant and his counsel all sign a written stipulation providing for defendant's submission to the test and for the subsequent admission at trial of the graphs and the examiner's opinion thereon on behalf of either defendant or the state.
>
> (2) That notwithstanding the stipulation the admissibility of the test results is subject to the discretion of the trial judge, *i.e.*, if the trial judge is not convinced that the examiner is qualified or that the test was conducted under proper conditions he may refuse to accept such evidence.
>
> (3) That if the graphs and examiner's opinion are offered in evidence the opposing party shall have the right to cross-examine the examiner respecting:
>
> > a. the examiner's qualifications and training;
> >
> > b. the conditions under which the test was administered;
> >
> > c. the limitations of and possibilities for error in the technique of polygraphic interrogation; and
> >
> > d. at the discretion of the trial judge, any other matter deemed pertinent to the inquiry.
>
> (4) That if such evidence is admitted the trial judge should instruct the jury that the examiner's testimony does not tend to prove or disprove any element of the crime with which a defendant is charged but at most tends only to indicate that at the time of the examination defendant was not telling the truth. Further, the jury members should be instructed that it is for them to determine what corroborative weight and effect such testimony should be given.[212]

The *Valdez* conditions have been adopted by many of the courts that admit stipulated polygraph results.[213] Several courts have altered the conditions in some respects. For example, an oral agreement in open court in lieu of a written

---

211. 91 Ariz. 274, 371 P.2d 894 (1962).

212. *Id.* at 283-84, 371 P.2d at 900-01.

213. *E.g.,* Wynn v. State, 423 So. 2d 294, 300 (Ala. Crim. App. 1982); State v. Souel, 53 Ohio St. 2d 123, 134, 372 N.E.2d 1318, 1323 (1978).

agreement is recognized by some courts.[214] In addition, a warning that the defendant is waiving the right against self-incrimination may also be required.[215]

In addition, the trial judge has discretion to exclude the evidence even when a stipulation exists.[216]

Interpretation of Stipulation

The interpretation of stipulations has raised a number of issues,[217] and these cases highlight the importance of drafting the stipulation with care. For example, an agreement to admit the results of a polygraph examination conducted by a competent examiner does not encompass an examination by an examiner who is not licensed under the applicable state statute.[218] An agreement to admit the results of an examination permits the prosecution to use the results in its case-in-chief in the absence of a statement limiting the results to impeachment.[219]

Moreover, some courts have held that the agreement must be strictly construed; thus, when the state failed to comply with a stipulation that required the defense attorney to review all questions, the results of the examination were inadmissible.[220] The argument for construing a stipulation strictly against the state is based on constitutional grounds: "Where an accused waives his constitutional right to remain silent in exchange for an agreement that his statements will not be used under certain conditions which are fulfilled, the bargain made by the State will be enforced."[221]

In *Ivey v. State*[222] stipulated results were admitted even though the accused did not have counsel at the time. The accused was not in custody, had over a week to

---

214. *See* Wynn v. State, 423 So. 2d 294, 299 (Ala. Crim. App. 1982); State v. Marti, 290 N.W.2d 570, 587 (Iowa 1980); State v. Roach, 223 Kan. 732, 736, 576 P.2d 1082, 1086 (1978).

215. *See* Wynn v. State, 423 So. 2d 294, 299 (Ala. Crim. App. 1982).

216. *See* United States v. Wright, 22 F. Supp. 2d 751, 754 (W.D. Tenn. 1998) ("[T]he United States and the Defendant entered into a written stipulation that neither party would contest the admissibility of the examination's results at trial. . . . Nevertheless, whether a prior agreement concerning admissibility existed is not dispositive of whether Defendant's polygraph examination should be excluded from evidence").

217. *E.g.,* Young v. State, 387 So. 2d 512, 512-13 (Fla. App. 1980) (experts in addition to examiner not permitted to testify because their testimony was not part of the stipulation); Porterfield v. State, 150 Ga. App. 303, 257 S.E.2d 372, 373 (1979) (testimony concerning inconclusive results not admissible because not part of the stipulation).

218. Holcomb v. State, 268 Ark. 138, 140, 594 S.W.2d 22, 23 (1980); State v. Tavernier, 27 Or. App. 115, 118, 555 P.2d 481, 482 (1976).

219. White v. State, 269 Ind. 479, 483-84, 381 N.E.2d 481, 484-85 (1978); State v. Baskerville, 139 N.J. Super. 389, 394, 354 A.2d 328, 330 (1976).

220. Chambers v. State, 146 Ga. App. 126, 128, 245 S.E.2d 467, 469 (1978).

221. State v. Fuller, 387 So. 2d 1040, 1041-42 (Fla. App. 1980).

222. 203 Ga. App. 886, 418 S.E.2d 71 (1992).

decide, and twice signed written waivers of the right to remain silent and to the assistance of counsel.

Ineffective Assistance of Counsel

In *People v. Reeder*[223] an appellate court held that a defense counsel "who, in advance of the examination, stipulates that a defendant will submit to a polygraph examination and the results will be admissible at trial demonstrates incompetence."[224] This decision was subsequently vacated and the defendant's incompetency-of-counsel claim rejected.[225] Later cases are in accord. For example, in one case the court held that when counsel agrees to an examination after the defendant insists on his innocence, there is no incompetence.[226]

In *Houston v. Lockhart*[227] the Eighth Circuit found ineffective assistance of counsel where the defense attorney failed to have an oral stipulation reduced to writing and then failed to raise the issue at trial after the prosecutor reneged on the agreement.

§ 8-4(D). Discretionary Admission.

Before the *Daubert* decision, a few trial courts had admitted polygraph evidence even in the absence of a stipulation.[228] After *Daubert*, most federal courts rejected the per se rule of exclusion[229] and, as discussed below, began recognizing the trial court's discretion to admit polygraph evidence.

State Cases

Of the state jurisdictions, New Mexico has gone the furthest in admitting polygraph evidence. In *State v. Dorsey*[230] the New Mexico Supreme Court held that polygraph results are admissible if (1) the operator is qualified, (2) the testing procedures were reliable, and (3) the test of the particular subject was

---

223. 129 Cal. Rptr. 646 (1976).

224. *Id.* at 648.

225. People v. Reeder, 65 Cal. App. 3d 235, 135 Cal. Rptr. 421 (1976).

226. People v. Berry, 118 Cal. App. 3d 122, 134, 173 Cal. Rptr. 137, 143, *cert. denied,* 454 U.S. 966 (1981). *Accord* State v. Sloan, 226 N.J. Super. 605, 612-14, 545 A.2d 230, 233-34 (A.D. 1988). *See generally* Annot., *Adequacy of Defense Counsel's Representation of Criminal Client Regarding Hypnosis and Truth Tests,* 9 A.L.R.4TH 354 (1981).

227. 982 F.2d 1246, 1251-52 (8th Cir. 1993).

228. The following trial courts admitted polygraph evidence at a criminal trial without a stipulation. United States v. Ridling, 350 F. Supp. 90, 99 (E.D. Mich. 1972); People v. Daniels, 422 N.Y.S.2d 832, 837 (Sup. Ct. 1979); State v. Sims, 52 Ohio Misc. 31, 42, 369 N.E.2d 24, 32 (C.P. 1977). *See also In re* X, 110 Idaho 44, 50, 714 P.2d 13, 19 (1986) (polygraph evidence admissible in proceedings under Child Protective Act).

229. *See* § 8-4(B) *supra.*

230. 88 N.M. 184, 539 P.2d 204 (1975).

valid.[231] Currently, New Mexico Evidence Rule 11-707 governs admissibility. This rule permits the admissibility of polygraph evidence in the discretion of the trial court[232] under the following conditions. First, the examination must be conducted by a qualified examiner. Minimum qualifications include five years of experience administering or interpreting examinations (or equivalent academic training) and at least twenty hours of continuing education during the twelve months prior to the examination offered in evidence.[233] Second, the examination must include at least two relevant questions, at least three charts, and be quantitatively scored.[234] Moreover, the pretest interview and actual testing must be recorded on an audio or video recording device.[235] Third, the party intending to offer the evidence generally must provide thirty-day written notice to the other party, including copies of the examiner's report, each chart, the audio or video recording of the pretest interview and actual testing, and a list of any prior examinations taken by the subject.[236]

At one time Massachusetts admitted polygraph evidence without stipulation. In *Commonwealth v. A Juvenile* (1974)[237] the Supreme Judicial Court of Massachusetts held polygraph evidence admissible if the defendant agreed in advance to the admission of test results and the trial judge conducted a "close and searching inquiry" into the qualifications of the examiner, the methods employed in the examination, and the suitability of the defendant for testing.[238] In 1989, however, the court abruptly abandoned the position it had adopted in *A Juvenile* and ruled polygraph evidence inadmissible in criminal trials.[239] According to the court, the "failure of the basic theory of polygraphy to have gained general

---

231. *Id.* at 184-85, 539 P.2d at 205. *See also* State v. Sanders, 117 N.M. 452, 872 P.2d 870 (1994); Tafoya v. Baca, 103 N.M. 56, 60, 702 P.2d 1001, 1005 (1985) (disclosure of test results not required unless defendant intends to offer polygraph evidence); State v. Urioste, 94 N.M. 767, 700, 617 P.2d 156, 159 (1980) (error to preclude cross-examination of examiner concerning chart and scoring); State v. Bell, 90 N.M. 134, 138-39, 560 P.2d 925, 929-30 (1977) (inconclusive results are irrelevant and therefore inadmissible); State v. Aragon, 116 N.M. 291, 861 P.2d 972 (App. 1993).

232. N.M. Evid. R. 11-707(C).

233. N.M. Evid. R. 11-707(B).

234. N.M. Evid. R. 11-707(C).

235. N.M. Evid. R. 11-707(E).

236. N.M. Evid. R. 11-707(D).

237. 365 Mass. 421, 313 N.E.2d 120 (1974).

238. *Id.* at 426, 313 N.E.2d at 124. *See also* Commonwealth v. Wick, 399 Mass. 705, 706-07, 506 N.E.2d 857, 858 (1987); Commonwealth v. Martin, 392 Mass. 161, 162-63, 466 N.E.2d 76 (1984); Commonwealth v. Walker, 392 Mass. 152, 156-59, 506 N.E.2d 71, 75 (1984); Commonwealth v. DiLego, 387 Mass. 394, 397, 439 N.E.2d 807, 808 (1982); Commonwealth v. Vitello, 376 Mass. 426, 450-52, 381 N.E.2d 582, 597-98 (1978); Commonwealth v. Moynihan, 376 Mass. 468, 478-79, 381 N.E.2d 575, 581 (1978); Commonwealth v. Stewart, 375 Mass. 380, 384, 377 N.E.2d 693, 697 (1978); Commonwealth v. Howard, 367 Mass. 569, 573, 327 N.E.2d 736, 739 (1975).

239. Commonwealth v. Mendes, 406 Mass. 201, 547 N.E.2d 35 (1989).

acceptance among physiological and psychological authorities"[240] required it to reevaluate its position.

Federal Cases

Even before *Daubert*, the Seventh Circuit had adopted the discretionary admission approach.[241] In most reported cases, however, trial courts exercise this discretion by excluding polygraph evidence.

In 1989, the Eleventh Circuit, sitting en banc, in *United States v. Piccinonna,*[242] ruled polygraph evidence admissible under certain circumstances, even in the absence of a stipulation.[243] The court went on to specify several conditions for admissibility. Polygraph evidence was admissible to impeach or corroborate the testimony of a witness if: (1) adequate notice was provided; (2) the opposing side had the opportunity to conduct its own test; and (3) the requirements of the Federal Rules of Evidence were satisfied — for example, corroboration was permissible only after impeachment. Even if all three conditions were met, the decision on admissibility was entrusted to the discretion of the trial court.[244]

---

240. *Id.* at 201, 547 N.E.2d at 35-36.

241. *See* United States v. Pulido, 69 F.3d 192, 205 (7th Cir. 1995) ("Our decisions acknowledge the considerable scientific and legal debate over polygraph testing and recognize that a trial court deciding whether to admit polygraph evidence 'must engage in a delicate balancing of many factors including probative value, prejudicial effect, confusion of the issues, misleading the jury, and undue delay'") (quoting United States v. Olson, 978 F.2d 1472, 1480 (7th Cir. 1992), *cert. denied,* 507 U.S. 997 (1993)); United States v. Dietrich, 854 F.2d 1056, 1059 (7th Cir. 1988); United States v. Tucker, 773 F.2d 136, 141 (7th Cir. 1985), *cert. denied,* 478 U.S. 1022 (1986); United States v. Williams, 737 F.2d 594, 611 (7th Cir. 1984); United States v. Feldman, 711 F.2d 758, 767 (7th Cir. 1983); United States v. Black, 684 F.2d 481, 484 (7th Cir.), *cert. denied,* 459 U.S. 1043 (1982); United States v. Rumell, 642 F.2d 213, 215 (7th Cir. 1981) (citing other cases).

242. 885 F.2d 1529 (11th Cir. 1989). *See also* Barker v. Jackson Nat'l Life Ins. Co., 896 F. Supp. 1159, 1161-62 (N.D. 1995) ("Surprisingly, in the six years since *Piccinonna,* the Eleventh Circuit appears not to have had opportunity to elaborate on the decision, other than to decide that it was not be applied retroactively"; "I agree with the Sixth Circuit's decision in *Conti,* that the results of a polygraph unilaterally arranged by one party should ordinarily not be admissible").

243. The Court based its decision on a number of factors:

> Since the *Frye* decision, tremendous advances have been made in polygraph instrumentation and technique. Better equipment is being used by more adequately trained polygraph administrators. Further, polygraph tests are used extensively by government agencies. Field investigative agencies such as the FBI, the Secret Service, military intelligence and law enforcement agencies use the polygraph. Thus, even under a strict adherence to the traditional *Frye* standard, we believe it is no longer accurate to state categorically that polygraph testing lacks general acceptance for use in all circumstances.

885 F.2d at 1532.

244. The trial court could reject the evidence because the examiner was not qualified, the test was poorly administered, or the questions were improper. On remand, the trial court excluded the

In 1987, the Court of Military Appeals[245] ruled polygraph evidence admissible in the discretion of the trial judge. In 1991, however, Military Rule of Evidence 707(a) abrogated this decision.[246] The rule was upheld in *Scheffer*.[247]

Daubert Test

As noted earlier, several federal circuit courts abandoned the per se rule of exclusion in the wake of *Daubert*. A few district courts took advantage of this development and admitted polygraph evidence. Most courts did not.

In *United States v. Crumby*[248] polygraph results were admitted as exculpatory evidence. Dr. Raskin testified that the polygraph was 90 percent accurate and that it is much more likely that inaccurate polygraph results will reflect a truthful individual appearing to be deceptive rather than a deceptive individual appearing to be truthful. The court commented:

> A polygrapher is an expert in determining credibility. If a party can lay the proper foundation to qualify such a witness, then the requirements of Rule 608(a) will be met. The polygrapher will not testify that he knows of the subject's reputation for honesty, but that as an expert in determining credibility, with respect to this case, the subject has demonstrated a character for truthfulness.... [Although] the polygraph evidence's primary purpose is to show credibility, ... it also is evidence that shows Defendant was willing to take a polygraph and, in fact, passed the examination.[249]

In *United States v. Galbreth*,[250] the district court wrote an extensive opinion on the polygraph, discussing validity studies, countermeasures, and the "friendly polygrapher" issue. In addition, the court applied all the *Daubert* factors and concluded that the evidence was admissible:

> In conclusion, having determined that Dr. Raskin's testimony is based on "scientific knowledge" that "will assist the trier of fact" the Court finds that

---

evidence because the questions and answers were irrelevant, and any probative value was outweighed by the danger of misleading the jury. United States v. Piccinonna, 729 F. Supp. 1336 (D.C. Fla. 1990).

245. United States v. Gipson, 24 M.J. 246, 253-54 (C.M.A. 1987).

246. MIL. R. EVID. 707 ("Notwithstanding any other provision of law, the results of a polygraph examination, the opinion of a polygraph examiner, or any reference to an offer to take, failure to take, or taking of a polygraph examination, shall not be admitted into evidence"). *See* S. SALTZBURG, L. SCHINASI & D. SCHLUETER, MILITARY RULES OF EVIDENCE MANUAL 89 (4th ed. 1997).

247. United States v. Scheffer, 523 U.S. 303, 118 S. Ct. 1261 (1998) *See* § 8-5 *infra* (constitutional argument).

248. 895 F. Supp. 1354 (D.C. Ariz. 1995).

249. *Id.* at 1363-64.

250. 908 F. Supp. 877 (D.N.M. 1995).

> such testimony is sufficiently reliable and relevant to be admissible under Fed. R. Evid. 702.
>
> The Court finds that Dr. Raskin's testimony is admissible under Fed. R. Evid. 403. The expert testimony is highly probative of a critical fact in issue, *i.e.*, whether the Defendant possessed the willful mens rea at the time he failed to report certain items of income. This is so, because the accuracy of the test results is approximately 95%. In light of such an elevated accuracy rate, the results of the test are highly probative....[251]

Polygraph evidence, however, continued to be excluded by most federal courts. There are two issues: The first is whether the evidence satisfies Rule 702's reliability standard as enunciated in *Daubert*; abolition of the per se rule does not mean that polygraph evidence is admissible— only that *Daubert*, rather than the per se rule, controls.[252] The second issue is whether the evidence is excludable under Federal Rule 403, which gives trial judges authority to weigh the probative value of evidence against other factors.

Rule 702

Several cases have analyzed polygraph evidence under *Daubert* and found it wanting. For example, in *United States v. Cordoba*,[253] the court commented: "Although capable of testing and subject to peer review, no reliable error rate conclusions are available for real-life polygraph testing. Additionally, there is no general acceptance in the scientific community for the courtroom fact-determinative use proposed here. Finally, there are no reliable and accepted standards *controlling* polygraphy. Without such *controlling* standards, there is no way to ensure proper protocol, or measure the reliability of a polygraph examination. Without such standards, the proposed polygraph evidence is inadmissible because it is not based on reliable 'scientific knowledge.'"[254] Similarly, in *United States v. Orians*,[255] the court found that "four of the five fact[or]s of *Daubert* militate against the admission of the polygraph evidence. The remaining factor, peer review and publication, favors admission. Thus, the

251. *Id.* at 895.

252. For example, in United States v. Call, 129 F.3d 1402 (10th Cir. 1997), *cert. denied,* 118 S. Ct. 2064 (1998), the Tenth Circuit, based on *Daubert*, rejected its categorical rule of exclusion. Nevertheless, the court was quite reticent: "However, our holding does not suggest a newfound enthusiasm for polygraph evidence. We caution that our application of *Daubert* to polygraph evidence does not imply that polygraph examinations satisfy the requirements of Rule 702." *Id.* at 1405.

253. 991 F. Supp. 1199 (C.D. Cal. 1998).

254. *Id.* at 1202.

255. 9 F. Supp. 2d 1168 (D. Ariz 1998).

court concludes that the polygraph evidence should not be admitted in the present case."[256]

In *United States v. Gilliard*,[257] the Eleventh Circuit upheld the exclusion of a hybrid technique that combined the "probable lie" and directed lie techniques, noting: "Considering the paucity of tests and published studies addressing the validity of the hybrid technique, and Gilliard's failure to show that the hybrid technique has gained general acceptance within the relevant scientific community, the district court did not abuse its discretion in finding the Honts Polygraph evidence to be inadmissible under Fed. R. Evid. 702. Furthermore, due to the lack of corroboration by other studies and polygraphers, the district court did not err in declining to assign much weight to the rate of accuracy that Dr. Honts attributed to the hybrid technique."[258]

Rule 403

Courts cite a number of factors when analyzing polygraph evidence under Rule 403. In *United States v. Posado*[259] the Fifth Circuit noted two factors as counterbalancing any prejudicial effect. First, the prosecution was contacted before the exam and was offered an opportunity to participate in the exam. Second, the evidence was proffered before a judge rather than a jury.

Other cases stress the importance of providing the other party with notice of intent to introduce polygraph evidence[260] and the lack of an opposing expert at the examination.[261] In short, unilateral examinations are disfavored.[262] Other cited

---

256. *Id.* at 1174.

257. 133 F.3d 809 (11th Cir. 1998).

258. *Id.* at 815.

259. 57 F.3d 428 (5th Cir. 1995).

260. *See* United States v. Croft, 124 F.3d 1109, 1120 (9th Cir. 1997) (no abuse of discretion to exclude polygraph results when defense waited until trial to provide notice to prosecution).

261. *See* United States v. Gilliard, 133 F.3d 809, 815 (11th Cir. 1998) ("The district court expressed further concern with respect to the fact that a Government representative was not present during the administration of the Honts Polygraph. Although a party is not required to give an adverse party advance notice of, and the opportunity to be present at, a polygraph examination, the absence of such notice and opportunity may be a factor in determining whether admission of the polygraph evidence would unduly prejudice the adverse party. In this case, even though the Government had the opportunity to view a videotape of the Honts Polygraph examination, viewing a videotape is not the same as being present at the examination. The district court could reasonably have concluded that the unilateral nature of the Honts Polygraph hindered the Government's ability to cross examine Gilliard's experts and to have its own experts conduct an independent review of the Honts Polygraph results").

262. *See* United States v. Thomas, 167 F.3d 299, 309 (6th Cir. 1999) ("In this case, Thomas took a private polygraph test administered by an examiner hired by his family, and did not inform the government of his test results until after he had taken the examination. We have repeatedly held that 'unilaterally obtained polygraph evidence is almost never admissible under Evidence Rule 403'") (citations omitted).

factors include: the lack of probative value,[263] the danger of misleading the jury,[264] and the consumption of time.[265]

The trial court's decision is reviewed only for an abuse of discretion.[266]

§ 8-5. Constitutional Arguments for Admissibility.

Several constitutional arguments have been advanced to support the admissibility of polygraph evidence. First, defendants have argued that the constitutional right to present a defense includes the right to introduce favorable polygraph results. Second, defendants have argued for a constitutional right to impeach prosecution witnesses if they have failed government-administered examinations.

Right to Present a Defense

The most common argument focuses on an accused's right to present a defense.[267] In *State v. Dorsey*[268] a New Mexico appellate court reversed a trial

---

263. *See* United States v. Taylor, 154 F.3d 675, 683 (7th Cir.) ("The court, however, excluded the expert testimony because it determined that the expert's application of the technique in this case was not reliable. First, the court was concerned that the expert appeared to use 'stock' questions in the test rather than questions tailored to the circumstances of this case. Second, the expert used a subjective visual scoring technique in calculating the results rather than the more reliable objective numerical scoring system. Finding that those factors lessened the reliability of the test, the court then determined that the probative value of the testimony was significantly outweighed by the danger of unfair prejudice under Rule 403. The reliability problems rendered the probative value minimal according to the district court, and there was a danger that the jury would consider the polygraph test to be conclusive regarding Gaston's veracity. That determination by the court was not an abuse of discretion"), *cert. denied*, 119 S. Ct. 629 (1998).

264. *See* United States v. Cordoba, 104 F.3d 225 (9th Cir. 1996); Maddox v. Cash Loans of Huntsville II, 21 F. Supp. 2d 1336, 1340 (N.D. Ala. 1998) ("The polygraph evidence has questionable probative value at best. Not only is the probative value of the polygraph evidence negligible, its effect would be highly prejudicial and lead to jury confusion. Absent unusual circumstances, expert testimony concerning the truthfulness or credibility of a witness is inadmissible because it invades the jury's province to make credibility determinations").

265. *See* United States v. Gilliard, 133 F.3d 809, 814 (11th Cir. 1998) ("The district court was concerned about the amount of time it would have taken the parties to present evidence pertaining to the Honts Polygraph, and the way in which it would have affected the focus of the trial. Although the actual number of hours and minutes it would take to put on expert testimony should not ordinarily be a controlling factor, a court may consider whether the amount of time needed to present the evidence would shift the focus of a criminal trial from determining guilt or innocence to determining the validity of the of the scientific method at issue").

266. United States v. Jordan, 150 F.3d 895, 900 (8th Cir. 1998) (no abuse of discretion to exclude test of nontestifying codefendant), *cert. denied,* 119 S. Ct. 1153 (1999).

267. For a further discussion of the constitutional argument, *see* Chapter 1. *See generally* Clinton, *The Right to Present a Defense: An Emergent Constitutional Guarantee in Criminal Trials*, 9 IND. L. REV. 713, 810-15 (1976); Note, *Polygraph Admission Through Compulsory Process*, 16 AKRON L. REV. 761 (1983); Note, *Compulsory Process and Polygraph Evidence: Does*

court's exclusion of polygraph evidence, holding that a defendant has a due process right to present critical and reliable defense evidence. In *Jackson v. Garrison*[269] a federal district court held that the exclusion of polygraph evidence denied a defendant a fair trial. In *State v. Sims*[270] an Ohio trial court found an implied right to present defense evidence in the compulsory process guarantee, which, it concluded, compelled the admission of defense polygraph evidence. The precedential value of these cases, however, is not strong. *Jackson* was overruled on appeal,[271] *Dorsey* was affirmed but not on constitutional grounds,[272] and *Sims* is inconsistent with later Ohio cases.[273]

The right to present defense evidence also was cited in *McMorris v. Israel*,[274] in which the defendant offered to stipulate to the admission of a polygraph examination. Although stipulated polygraph results were admissible under state law at that time,[275] the prosecutor, without offering any reasons, refused to stipulate. In granting habeas corpus relief, the Seventh Circuit wrote: "Where credibility is as critical as in the instant case, the circumstances are such as to make the polygraph evidence materially exculpatory within the meaning of the Constitution."[276] The response to *McMorris* was chilly. Chief Justice Rehnquist

---

Exclusion Violate a Criminal Defendant's Due Process Rights?, 12 CONN. L. REV. 324 (1980); Note, *Admission of Polygraph Results: A Due Process Perspective*, 55 IND. L.J. 157 (1979); Note, *State v. Dean: A Compulsory Process Analysis of the Inadmissibility of Polygraph Evidence*, 1984 WIS. L. REV. 237.

268. 87 N.M. 323, 532 P.2d 912, 914-15 (N.M. App.), *aff'd on other grounds,* 88 N.M. 184, 539 P.2d 204 (1975).

269. 495 F. Supp. 9 (W.D.N.C. 1979), *rev'd,* 677 F.2d 371 (4th Cir. 1981).

270. 52 Ohio Misc. 31, 32, 369 N.E.2d 24, 46 (C.P. 1977).

271. Jackson v. Garrison, 677 F.2d 371 (4th Cir. 1981).

272. State v. Dorsey, 88 N.M. 184, 539 P.2d 204 (1975).

273. Although the Ohio Supreme Court accepted the admission of stipulated polygraph results in State v. Souel, 53 Ohio St. 2d 123, 132, 372 N.E.2d 1318, 1323 (1978), it rejected the constitutional arguments for admission in State v. Levert, 58 Ohio St. 2d 213, 215, 389 N.E.2d 848, 850 (1979).

274. 643 F.2d 458 (7th Cir. 1981), *cert. denied,* 455 U.S. 967 (1982).

275. At the time McMorris was tried, Wisconsin admitted stipulated polygraph results. After the Seventh Circuit decision, the Wisconsin Supreme Court overruled its prior decision and held polygraph evidence per se inadmissible. State v. Dean, 103 Wis. 2d 228, 279, 307 N.W.2d 628, 653 (1981).

276. 643 F.2d at 462. The court, however, rested its decision on narrower grounds; that is, the prosecution's refusal to stipulate without offering a valid ground for the refusal deprived the defendant of due process: "From all that appears, [the prosecutor] was acting solely for tactical reasons in the belief that a test would not be helpful to his case. If the prosecutor refuses *and states reasons,* it then becomes the duty of the court to determine whether the reasons offered rise above the purely tactical considerations present in a given case." *Id.* at 466. *See also* Stuart v. Gagnon, 614 F. Supp. 247, 252 (E.D. Wis. 1985) (prosecutor offered legitimate nontactical reason for refusing to stipulate), *aff'd,* 837 F.2d 289 (7th Cir. 1987).

characterized *McMorris* as a "dubious constitutional holding."[277] Most courts rejected the proposition that there is a constitutional right to present polygraph evidence.[278] Moreover, the Seventh Circuit itself noted that *McMorris* applied only where a jurisdiction accepted stipulated polygraph results[279] and did not limit a trial court's discretionary authority to exclude polygraph evidence.[280]

In *United States v. Scheffer*,[281] the U.S. Supreme Court held that the per se rule of exclusion was not unconstitutional. The Court acknowledged once more the right to present a defense, albeit as a qualified right. "A defendant's right to present relevant evidence is not unlimited, but rather is subject to reasonable restrictions."[282] In the Court's view, evidence "rules do not abridge an accused's right to present a defense so long as they are not 'arbitrary' or disproportionate to the purposes they are designed to serve. Moreover, we have found the exclusion of evidence to be unconstitutionally arbitrary or disproportionate only where it has infringed upon a weighty interest of the accused."[283]

---

277. Israel v. McMorris, 455 U.S. 967, 970 (1982) (Rehnquist, J., dissenting from denial of certiorari).

278. *See* Bashor v. Risley, 730 F.2d 1228, 1238 (9th Cir. 1984); United States v. Gordon, 688 F.2d 42, 44 (8th Cir. 1982); Milano v. Garrison, 677 F.2d 374, 375 (4th Cir. 1981); Jackson v. Garrison, 677 F.2d 371, 373 (4th Cir. 1981); United States v. Glover, 596 F.2d 857, 867 (9th Cir.), *cert. denied,* 444 U.S. 860 (1979); Conner v. Auger, 595 F.2d 407, 411 (8th Cir.), *cert. denied,* 444 U.S. 851 (1979); United States v. Bohr, 581 F.2d 1294, 1303 (8th Cir.), *cert. denied,* 439 U.S. 958 (1978); United States v. Gipson, 24 M.J. 246, 252 (C.M.A. 1987); United States v. Lech, 895 F. Supp. 582, 586 (S.D.N.Y. 1995) ("Lech has no constitutional right to introduce evidence whose probative value is substantially outweighed by its tendency to confuse and mislead a jury"); *In re* Aontae D., 25 Cal. App. 4th 167, 176, 30 Cal. Rptr. 2d 176, 181 (1994) ("[T]he first aspect of the due process claim – that polygraph evidence is competent and crucial enough that its absence would significantly impair the defendant's ability to mount a defense – is without support"); People v. Price, 1 Cal. 4th 324, 420, 821 P.2d 610, 663, 3 Cal. Rptr. 2d 106, 159 (1991) ("A party has no due process right to present evidence of test results if the tests used scientific techniques not generally accepted as reliable in the scientific community"); People v. Kegler, 197 Cal. App. 3d 72, 89, 242 Cal. Rptr. 897, 909 (1987); People v. Williams, 123 Mich. App. 752, 757-58, 333 N.W.2d 577, 580 (1983).

279. United States v. Black, 684 F.2d 481, 483 (7th Cir.), *cert. denied,* 459 U.S. 1043 (1982).

280. United States v. Feldman, 711 F.2d 758, 767 (7th Cir.), *cert. denied,* 464 U.S. 939 (1983); United States v. Lupo, 652 F.2d 723, 729 (7th Cir. 1981), *cert. denied,* 457 U.S. 1135 (1982).

281. 523 U.S. 303, 118 S. Ct. 1261 (1998). In *Scheffer,* the U.S. Court of Appeals for the Armed Forces had held that Military Rule 707 was unconstitutional as applied in that case. In that court's view, "A *per se* exclusion of polygraph evidence offered by an accused to rebut an attack on his credibility, without giving him an opportunity to lay a foundation under Mil. R. Evid. 702 and *Daubert*, violates his Sixth Amendment right to present a defense. We limit our holding to exculpatory evidence arising from a polygraph examination of an accused, offered to rebut an attack on his credibility." 44 M.J. 442, 445 (C.A.A.F. 1996).

282. 118 S. Ct. at 1264.

283. *Id.*

Justice Thomas's majority opinion identified three interests that support the per se rule of exclusion: (1) ensuring that only reliable evidence is introduced at trial, (2) preserving the jury's role in determining credibility, and (3) avoiding litigation of collateral issues. As to reliability, the opinion noted that "the scientific community remains extremely polarized about the reliability of polygraph techniques."[284] The opinion also observed that "[n]othing in *Daubert* foreclosed, as a constitutional matter, per se exclusionary rules for certain types of expert or scientific evidence."[285] Justice Thomas also cited the jury's role in determining credibility: "By its very nature, polygraph evidence may diminish the jury's role in making credibility determinations."[286] A third reason, in Justice Thomas's view, is the avoidance of litigation on collateral issues, which "prolongs criminal trials and threatens to distract the jury from its central function of determining guilt or innocence."[287]

Justice Kennedy along with three other Justices rejected the second and third interest. In his concurring opinion, Justice Kennedy pointed out that Federal Rule 704 abolishes the ultimate issue rule and thus the invading-the-province-of-the-jury argument had been rejected under most modern evidence codes. Significantly, he also wrote:

> I doubt, though, that the rule of per se exclusion is wise, and some later case might present a more compelling case for introduction of the testimony than this one does. Though the considerable discretion given to the trial court in admitting and excluding scientific evidence is not a constitutional mandate, see *Daubert* ... there is some tension between that rule and our holding today. And, as Justice Stevens points out [in dissent], there is much inconsistency between the Government's extensive use of polygraph to make vital security determinations and the argument it makes here, stressing the inaccuracy of these tests.[288]

Impeachment of Prosecution Witnesses

In *United States v. A & S Council Oil Co.*[289] the defendant sought "a Confrontation Clause exception to the general inadmissibility of polygraph

---

284. *Id.* at 1265.

285. *Id.* at 1266 n.7.

286. *Id.* at 1267.

287. *Id. See also* Mayabb v. Johnson 168 F.3d 863, 870 (5th Cir. 1999) ("Following *Scheffer*, this court recently held that a Texas court's exclusion of polygraph evidence based on state law did not violate the § 2254 petitioner's federal constitutional rights") (citing *Castillo v. Johnson*); Castillo v. Johnson, 141 F.3d 218, 222 (5th Cir. 1998) ("the trial court's exclusion of polygraph evidence based on state law did not violate Castillo's federal constitutional rights") (citing *Scheffer*), *cert. denied*, 119 S. Ct. 28 (1998).

288. *Id.* at 1269.

289. 947 F.2d 1128 (4th Cir. 1991).

results to accommodate an accused's attacks on the credibility of key government witnesses."[290] The prosecution witness had entered into a plea agreement with the government, which required the witness to take a polygraph examination if requested by the prosecution. The witness also agreed that the results would be admissible against him in a court of law. The witness thereafter failed two polygraph examinations. The defense sought to introduce these examinations as impeachment evidence. Although the Fourth Circuit acknowledged that the facts of the case were "compelling," it felt bound by its prior decisions, which had excluded polygraph results.[291] Accordingly, the court rejected an "exculpatory use" exception for polygraph evidence.

A similar issue was raised in *United States v. Hart,*[292] in which the court ruled that a prosecution witness's negative polygraph results were admissible under *Brady v. Maryland.*[293] The court interpreted *Brady* as requiring the disclosure of "any evidence which may tend to exculpate a defendant."[294] Since the prosecution initially thought the polygraph sufficiently reliable to conduct an examination, it had the burden, according to the court, of explaining why the test results should be excluded at trial.

Subsequent cases, however, generally rejected this reasoning.[295] In *Wood v. Bartholomew,*[296] the U.S. Supreme Court ruled that the prosecution's failure to

---

290. *Id.* at 1133.

291. "The broad exception Council seeks to create for an accused's attacks on government witnesses would ... conflict with [our] precedents." *Id.* at 1134. The court, however, did rule the evidence admissible on a different issue. The prosecution offered the testimony of a psychiatrist to bolster the credibility of the prosecution witness. Since the psychiatrist had considered the polygraph results in forming his opinion, the defense was entitled, under FED. R. EVID. 705, to cross-examine the psychiatrist concerning the untruthful results. *Id.* at 1134-35.

292. 344 F. Supp. 522 (E.D.N.Y. 1971).

293. 373 U.S. 83 (1963). For a discussion of *Brady, see* Chapter 3.

294. 344 F. Supp. at 523.

295. For example, in *United States v. MacEntee,* 713 F. Supp. 829 (E.D. Pa. 1989), the court commented: "The *Hart* court makes an incorrect logical leap. *Brady* ... stands for the principal [sic] that the constitution requires the government to turn over exculpatory information to the defense. Once the government turns over such information, however, the question of whether it may be introduced at trial is governed by the Federal Rules of Evidence, not by *Brady.*" *Id.* at 831. *See also* People v. Price, 1 Cal. 4th 324, 419, 821 P.2d 610, 663, 3 Cal. Rptr. 106, 159 (1991); State v. Christopher, 149 N.J. Super. 269, 275-76, 373 A.2d 705, 708 (A.D. 1977); State v. Waff, 373 N.W.2d 18, 25 (S.D. 1985); Robinson v. Commonwealth, 231 Va. 142, 156, 341 S.E.2d 159, 167 (1986); State v. Young, 89 Wash. 2d 613, 622-23, 574 P.2d 1171, 1177, *cert. denied,* 439 U.S. 870 (1978).

296. 516 U.S. 1 (1995) (per curiam). Defendant admitted participation in a robbery, in which a person was shot and killed. The issue was whether the killing was premeditated murder or a lesser form of murder. The defendant claimed that the weapon fired accidentally. Two prosecution witnesses, the defendant's brother and the brother's girlfriend, took polygraph examinations prior to trial. Their answers were consistent with their trial testimony. When asked about their own

turn over the results of a polygraph examination of a key witness did not violated the *Brady* rule.

The Court ruled that *Brady* had not been violated because polygraph results were inadmissible under state law, even for impeachment, in the absence of a stipulation. "Disclosure of the polygraph results, then, could have had no direct effect on the outcome of trial, because respondent could have made no mention of them either during argument or while questioning witnesses."[297] The possibility that the undisclosed information would have lead the defense counsel to additional avenues of discovery was, in the Court's view, speculative. Moreover, at the habeas proceeding the trial defense counsel testified that he had made a strategic decision to limit the cross-examination of the brother. Accordingly, "it is not 'reasonably likely' that disclosure of the polygraph results — inadmissible under state law — would have resulted in a different outcome at trial."[298]

§ 8-6. Proceedings Other Than Trial.

Courts have admitted polygraph evidence in various criminal proceedings other than trial, such as grand jury proceedings,[299] suppression hearings,[300] sentencing hearings,[301] motions for new trial proceedings,[302] probation revocation

---

involvement in the robbery, the examiner found her answers to be "inconclusive" and the brother's "deceptive." Neither examination was disclosed to the defense.

297. *Id.* at 10.

298. *Id.* at 11.

299. *E.g., In re* Grand Jury Investigation, 791 F. Supp. 192, 194 (S.D. Ohio 1992); United States v. Narciso, 446 F. Supp. 252, 297-98 (E.D. Mich. 1977); United States v. Callahan, 442 F. Supp. 1213, 1218 (D. Minn. 1978), *rev'd,* 596 F.2d 759 (8th Cir. 1979).

300. *E.g.,* People v. Cutter, 12 Crim. L. Rep. (BNA) 2133 (Cal. Super. Ct. Nov. 6, 1972); People v. McKinney, 137 Mich. App. 110, 115, 357 N.W.2d 825, 828 (1984).

301. *E.g.,* State v. Jones, 110 Ariz. 546, 551, 521 P.2d 978, 983, *cert. denied,* 419 U.S. 1004 (1974); State v. Watson, 115 N.J. Super. 213, 218, 278 A.2d 543, 546 (1971). *But see* State v. Anderson 977 P.2d 315, 317 (Mont. 1999) ("Polygraph evidence may not be used in any proceeding in a court of law in Montana. This prohibition encompasses the use of polygraph results during sentencing. This prohibition also encompasses the introduction of polygraph results into evidence via a court-ordered sex offender evaluation"); State v. Council, 335 S.C. 1, 515 S.E.2d 508, 519-20 (1999) ("This Court has consistently held the results of polygraph examinations are generally not admissible because the reliability of the tests is questionable. [T]his Court has declined to admit in mitigation the results of a polygraph exam offered during the penalty phase of a trial") (citations omitted); State v. Copeland, 278 S.C. 572, 582, 300 S.E.2d 63, 69 (1982), *cert. denied,* 463 U.S. 1214 (1983).

302. *E.g.,* State v. Catanese, 368 So. 2d 975, 982-83 (La. 1979); People v. Barbara, 400 Mich. 352, 412-14, 255 N.W.2d 171, 197-99 (1977); People v. Snell, 118 Mich. App. 750, 768, 325 N.W.2d 563, 572 (1982); State v. Yodsnukis, 281 N.W.2d 255, 259-60 (N.D. 1979); State v. Olmstead, 261 N.W.2d 880, 886 (N.D.), *cert. denied,* 436 U.S. 918 (1978). *See generally* Note, *People v. Barbara: The Admissibility of Polygraph Test Results in Support of a Motion for New*

hearings,[303] and prison disciplinary hearings.[304] Polygraph evidence may also be considered in determining probable cause.[305]

Some of these courts distinguish such proceedings from the trial itself. For example, the Michigan Supreme Court has held polygraph evidence admissible on a motion for a new trial although the same evidence is inadmissible at trial.[306] According to the court, polygraph results may be of some assistance to the trial judge in deciding issues that typically arise in proceedings to determine whether a new trial should be granted: "Traditionally, the testimony of recanting or suddenly discovered witnesses has been highly suspect, largely because it is impossible to determine when the truth is being told. The polygraph won't do this either; not even its most ardent proponents would so contend. But it might help."[307] The court also commented that admissibility in this context would provide an "opportunity to test [the] effectiveness of the polygraph."[308]

In *Cassamassima v. State*,[309] the Florida Court of Appeals upheld a requirement that a convicted child molester submit to a polygraph examination as a condition of probation. Even if polygraph evidence could not be relied upon in a probation revocation proceeding, it may nevertheless be used to deter or detect future child abuse. The court held that the state could avoid fifth amendment issues by precluding the use of the examination results in future prosecutions. The concurring opinion took the position that the defendant waived any fifth

---

Trial, 1978 DET. C.L. REV. 347; Note, *Polygraph Examination Results Admissible in Post-Conviction Hearings*, 56 N.C. L. REV.U 380 (1978); 55 U. DET. J. URB. L. 155 (1977).

303. State v. Travis, 867 P.2d 234 (Idaho 1994).

304. *E.g.*, Toussaint v. McCarthy, 926 F.2d 800, 803 (9th Cir.), *cert. denied,* 502 U.S. 874 (1990); Lenea v. Lane, 882 F.2d 1171, 1174 (7th Cir. 1989); Terrell v. Godinez, 966 F. Supp. 679 (N.D. Ill. 1997).

305. *E.g.*, Craig v. Singletary, 127 F.3d 1030, 1046 (11th Cir. 1997) ("Indications of deception on a polygraph examination may be taken into account in determining whether probable cause exists"), *cert. denied,* 523 U.S. 1031 (1998); Bennett v. Grand Prairie, 883 F.2d 400, 405-06 (5th Cir. 1989); State v. Coffey, 309 Or. 342, 345-47, 788 P.2d 424, 425-27 (1990); State v. Cherry, 61 Wash. App. 301, 810 P.2d 990, 942-43 (1991);

306. People v. Barbara, 400 Mich. 352, 411-14, 255 N.W.2d 171, 197-98 (1977).

307. *Id.* at 415, 255 N.W.2d at 199.

308. *Id.*

309. 657 So. 2d 906 (Fla. App. 1995) (en banc). Among the questions was whether he had been alone with a child or had any manner of sexual contact with a child. *See also* State v. Lumley, 267 Kan. 4, 977 P.2d 914, 921 (1999) ("In this case, there was no violation of Lumley's Fifth Amendment protections against self-incrimination. The polygraph question and answer which led to Lumley's revocation referred solely to Lumley's condition of probation that he not be alone with children during the term of his probation. Answering the question truthfully would not have exposed Lumley to prosecution for another crime"; "The polygraph condition helped to monitor compliance and was therefore reasonably related to the defendant's criminal offense. Because this condition was aimed at deterring and discovering criminal conduct most likely to occur during unsupervised contact with young females, the condition was reasonably related to future criminality").

amendment issue by agreeing to the examination as part of a condition for probation.

§ 8-7. Privilege Against Self-Incrimination.

In *Schmerber v. California*[310] the U.S. Supreme Court indicated, albeit in dictum, that compelled submission to a polygraph test would violate the fifth amendment's prohibition against compelled self-incrimination:

> Some tests seemingly directed to obtain "physical evidence," for example, lie detector tests measuring changes in body function during interrogation, may actually be directed to eliciting responses which are essentially testimonial. To compel a person to submit to testing in which an effort will be made to determine his guilt or innocence on the basis of physiological responses, whether willed or not, is to evoke the spirit and history of the Fifth Amendment.[311]

The courts that have admitted polygraph evidence have recognized the applicability of the privilege in this context: "The polygraph results are essentially testimonial in nature and therefore a defendant could not be compelled initially to take such an examination on the Commonwealth's motion."[312] The protection of the privilege also extends to any comment by the prosecution that a defendant had refused to submit to an examination.[313] The defendant, however, may waive the privilege.[314]

A different fifth amendment issue arises when public employees are required to take a polygraph test or lose their job. In *Wiley v. Baltimore*[315] the Fourth Circuit held that requiring police officers to take a polygraph test or face the loss of their jobs did not violate the self-incrimination clause as long as the questions were narrowly and specifically job-related and the officers were not asked to waive the privilege: "[T]he state may compel job-related testimony from an employee in the course of a criminal investigation, provided, of course, that the state does not make direct or derivative use of the employee's statement against the employee in any criminal proceeding."[316]

---

310. 384 U.S. 757 (1966). For a discussion of the fifth amendment, *see* Chapter 2.

311. *Id.* at 764.

312. Commonwealth v. A Juvenile, 365 Mass. 421, 431, 313 N.E.2d 120, 127 (1974).

313. *See* Bowen v. Eyman, 324 F. Supp. 339, 341 (D. Ariz. 1970); MacDonald v. State, 164 Ind. App. 285, 293-94, 328 N.E.2d 436, 441 (1975).

314. *See* Fernandez v. Rodriguez, 761 F.2d 558, 562 (10th Cir. 1985) (agreement to stipulate to admission of polygraph results was not a valid waiver of privilege against self-incrimination); United States v. Oliver, 525 F.2d 731, 734-36 (8th Cir. 1975), *cert. denied,* 424 U.S. 973 (1976); United States v. Ridling, 350 F. Supp. 90, 97 (E.D. Mich. 1972).

315. 48 F.3d 773 (4th Cir.), *cert. denied*, 516 U.S. 825 (1995).

316. *Id.* at 777 (this type of immunity is self-executing).

§ 8-8. Confessions.

It is not uncommon for a defendant to make an incriminatory statement before, during, or after a polygraph examination.[317]

Miranda Warnings

Since polygraph examinations involve testimonial evidence under the fifth amendment privilege,[318] the admissibility of statements made during the examination process often are subject to *Miranda* warnings.[319] *Miranda* warnings, however, are required only if the defendant is in custody[320] and is interrogated.[321] A person who is not under arrest and who voluntarily agrees to take the examination is not "in custody."[322] Moreover, the defendant may waive the right to remain silent and to counsel when agreeing to take a polygraph examination.[323]

Even if the defendant initially asserts the right to counsel after receiving *Miranda* warnings, the defendant may subsequently waive that right by initiating conversations with the police, including a request for a polygraph examination.[324] In *Wyrick v. Fields*[325] the U.S. Supreme Court held that statements made by a defendant during a post-test interview were admissible where the defendant, who was represented by counsel, requested a polygraph examination and was informed of his *Miranda* rights. The Court rejected the argument that new warnings were required prior to the post-test interview. However, not all post-test

---

317. For a general discussion of the law of confessions, *see* 2 E. IMWINKELRIED, P. GIANNELLI, F. GILLIGAN & F. LEDERER, COURTROOM CRIMINAL EVIDENCE ch. 24-27 (3d ed. 1998); 1 W. LAFAVE & J. ISRAEL, CRIMINAL PROCEDURE ch. 6 (1984).

318. *See* § 8-7 *supra.*

319. Miranda v. Arizona, 384 U.S. 436 (1966). *See also* United States v. Little Bear, 583 F.2d 411, 414 (8th Cir. 1978) (tailoring *Miranda* warnings for polygraph examinations).

320. *See* Berkemer v. McCarty, 468 U.S. 420 (1984).

321. *See* Rhode Island v. Innis, 446 U.S. 291 (1980).

322. *E.g.*, Jenner v. Smith, 982 F.2d 329, 335 (8th Cir.) (confession after polygraph exam admissible because defendant was not in custody), *cert. denied*, 510 U.S. 822 (1993).

323. *See* United States v. Iron Thunder, 714 F.2d 765, 771-72 (8th Cir. 1983); Henry v. Dees, 658 F.2d 406, 408 (5th Cir. 1981) (waiver invalid where examiner asked questions of a mentally retarded defendant that went beyond agreement to take examination).

324. *See* Oregon v. Bradshaw, 462 U.S. 1039 (1983).

325. 459 U.S. 42 (1982). *See also* Correll v. Thompson, 63 F.3d 1279, 1287 (4th Cir. 1995) ("Under the reasoning of *Wyrick*, if Correll requested the opportunity to submit to the polygraph examination and knowingly and voluntarily waived his rights prior to taking the test, the later disclosure of the results of the polygraph examination would not have amounted to police-initiated interrogation"), *cert. denied*, 516 U.S. 1035 (1996).

statements are admissible; they are admissible only if the defendant voluntarily and knowingly waives the rights to remain silent and to counsel.[326]

Right to Counsel

In addition to fifth amendment *Miranda* rights, a defendant's admissions during a polygraph examination may be excluded from evidence if they are obtained in violation of the sixth amendment right to counsel[327] or are involuntary under the due process clause.[328]

Limited Admissibility

Some courts hold that polygraph evidence is admissible for the limited purpose of showing the voluntariness of a confession.[329] In one case the defendant offered negative polygraph results to explain why he had confessed. The Illinois Supreme Court ruled that the trial court's exclusion of this evidence "deprived defendant of his fundamental right to a fair opportunity to present a defense.... Defendant has a right, regardless of how substantial or infirm the evidence against him, to familiarize the jury with every circumstance attendant to the State's obtention of his confession."[330] The same court later ruled that the prosecution could introduce the same evidence to show the voluntariness of a confession.[331]

---

326. *See* United States v. Gillyard, 726 F.2d 1426, 1429-30 (9th Cir. 1984) (defendant did not validly waive right to a post-test interrogation by officers other than the examiner). *See generally* 2 E. IMWINKELRIED, P. GIANNELLI, F. GILLIGAN & F. LEDERER, *supra* note 317, ch. 25.

327. *See* Barrera v. Young, 794 F.2d 1264, 1271-72 (7th Cir. 1986) (right to counsel waived); Fields v. Wyrick, 706 F.2d 879, 880-81 (8th Cir. 1983). *See* § 2-3 *supra* (right to counsel).*See generally* 2 E. IMWINKELRIED, P. GIANNELLI, F. GILLIGAN & F. LEDERER, *supra* note 317, ch. 26.

328. *E.g.*, Jenner v. Smith, 982 F.2d 329, 334 (8th Cir.) (confession after polygraph exam not involuntary), *cert. denied*, 510 U.S. 822 (1993); Barrera v. Young, 794 F.2d 1264, 1271-72 (7th Cir. 1986) (same); State v. Craig, 262 Mont. 240, 243, 864 P.2d 1240, 1242 (1993) ("[I]t is not acceptable to this Court for the police to use the results of a polygraph examination to tell a defendant that he lied in order to extract a confession"). *See generally* Annot., *Admissibility in Evidence of Confession Made by Accused in Anticipation of, During, or Following Polygraph Examination*, 89 A.L.R.3D 230 (1979).

329. *See* United States v. Kampiles, 609 F.2d 1233, 1244-45 (7th Cir. 1979), *cert. denied,* 446 U.S. 954 (1980); Annot., *Admissibility of Polygraph Evidence at Trial on Issue of Voluntariness of Confession Made by Accused,* 92 A.L.R.3D 1317 (1979).

330. People v. Melock, 149 Ill.2d 423, 599 N.E.2d 941, 959 (1992).

331. *See* People v. Jefferson, 184 Ill. 2d 486, 495, 705 N.E.2d 56, 61 (1998) ("We conclude that the trial judge correctly permitted the State to present evidence here regarding the circumstances surrounding the defendant's confession, including her agreement to undergo a polygraph examination later that evening. . . . [T]he trial judge in this case correctly permitted the State to rebut the defendant's claim of coercion with polygraph evidence. . . . In this case, the challenged evidence was offered for a limited purpose: to show why the defendant agreed to speak to authorities, after she testified that her statement to authorities was prompted by their promises that

§ 8-9. Pretrial Agreements.

In a few reported cases prosecutors have gone beyond stipulating to the admissibility of test results and have agreed to dismiss charges if the defendant passes a polygraph examination.[332] In some cases the defendant had no obligations under the agreement other than to cooperate in the examination.[333] In other cases the defendant either agreed to admit the test results[334] or to enter a plea to a reduced charge[335] in the event he failed the examination.

A determinative factor in the reported cases has been the existence of a statute requiring court approval for dismissals. When a trial court approved the dismissal or was aware of the agreement, appellate courts have held the prosecutor bound by the agreement on public policy grounds.[336] According to these courts, the agreement represents a "pledge of public faith — a promise made by state officials — and one that should not be lightly disregarded."[337] In contrast, when court approval was required but not obtained, prosecution has been permitted even though a defendant successfully passed the examination.[338]

Notwithstanding the lack of court approval, enforcement of such an agreement may be required on constitutional grounds. In agreeing to take a polygraph examination, the defendant waives his fifth amendment privilege against self-incrimination, and it seems questionable that the state could induce such a waiver by promising to dismiss the charges in the event the defendant passes the examination and then renege on that promise.[339] The Illinois Supreme Court cited the waiver of the privilege in ruling that the state must abide by its agreement to dismiss if the defendant passes a polygraph test.[340]

In another case, a Pennsylvania appellate court enforced an agreement between a police officer and the defendant, which required the dismissal of

---

if she made a statement she would be released from custody and would be allowed to see her daughter and her parents").

332. *See generally* Annot., *Enforceability of Agreement by State Officials to Drop Prosecution if Accused Successfully Passes Polygraph Test,* 36 A.L.R.3D 1280 (1971).

333. *See* People v. Reagan, 395 Mich. 306, 309, 235 N.W.2d 581, 583 (1975); State v. Sanchell, 191 Neb. 505, 509-10, 216 N.W.2d 504, 507-08 (1974) (agreement not binding without court approval), *cert. denied,* 420 U.S. 909 (1975).

334. *See* Butler v. State, 228 So. 2d 421, 424-25 (Fla. App. 1969).

335. *See* State v. Davis, 188 So. 2d 24, 27 (Fla. App. 1966).

336. Butler v. State, 228 So. 2d 421, 424 (Fla. App. 1969); State v. Davis, 188 So. 2d 24, 28 (Fla. App. 1966); People v. Reagan, 395 Mich. 306, 318, 235 N.W.2d 581, 587 (1975).

337. State v. Davis, 188 So. 2d 24, 27 (Fla. App. 1966).

338. State v. Sanchell, 191 Neb. 505, 510, 216 N.W.2d 504, 508 (1974), *cert. denied,* 420 U.S. 909 (1975). *See also* Snead v. State, 415 So. 2d 887, 889 (Fla. App. 1982) (oral agreement with sheriff who lacked authority to enter into such an agreement is not enforceable).

339. *Cf.* Santobello v. New York, 404 U.S. 257 (1971) (enforceability of plea bargain).

340. People v. Stark, 106 Ill.2d 441, 452, 478 N.E.2d 350, 355-56 (1985).

charges if the defendant passed a polygraph test.[341] The court rejected the argument that the officer did not have the authority to make such an agreement. "Fundamental fairness" required the Commonwealth to abide by its commitments.[342] The Pennsylvania Supreme Court reversed because a "non-prosecution agreement between [an accused] and a municipal police officer is not binding upon the District Attorney."[343]

United States v. Santiago-Gonzales[344] involved a plea agreement under which the prosecution was required to move for downward departure under the federal Sentencing Guidelines. The agreement required the defendant to provide truthful information and submit to a polygraph examination. It also contained a clause that if the examiner found the defendant's answers deceptive the agreement was terminated. The First Circuit wrote:

> Defendant does not claim that the examiner's opinion was rooted in bad faith or was based on anything but his own objective interpretation of the examination results. Rather, he argues that because a polygraph examination is an inherently unreliable means of determining truth, and such results are not generally admissible in courts of law, that part of the agreement requiring him to submit to and pass the test should be deemed void.
>
> ... Having agreed to the test, whatever its scientific weaknesses might be, defendant cannot now be heard to say that his own promise was illusory or that he was somehow misled. Nor can he credibly argue that the government's discretionary decision not to file the departure motion was made in bad faith or without rational basis.[345]

In *United States v. Ailsworth,*[346] a district court found that the government had breached a plea agreement by failing to limit the polygraph questions to statements made in the defendant's oral debriefing. The court ordered a second examination in which the government, with the aid of qualified examiner, would refashion the questions. The issue again came before the court when the defense challenged the examiner and requested that the examination be conducted in association with a defense-selected examiner. The court rejected this request,

---

341. Commonwealth v. Scuilli, 423 Pa. Super. 453, 621 A.2d 620 (1993), *rev'd*, 539 Pa. 440, 652 A.2d 1300 (1995).

342. *Id.* at 625 (citing the doctrine of equitable immunity).

343. Commonwealth v. Scuilli, 539 Pa. 440, 652 A.2d 1300 (1995).

344. 66 F.3d 3 (1st Cir. 1995).

345. *Id.* at 6-7. *See also* United States v. Swinehurt, 614 F.2d 853, 857 n.2 (3d Cir.) ("Although the infallibility of polygraphs is arguable, we decline to hold that the Government cannot rely on the tests where the parties agree to such reliance in a plea bargain"), *cert. denied*, 445 U.S. 827 (1980).

346. 899 F. Supp. 511, 518-19 (D. Kan. 1995).

commenting that "such a request is a blatant attempt to modify the terms of the plea agreements and is denied on that basis alone."[347]

§ 8-10. Employee Polygraph Protection Act.

Congress enacted the Employee Polygraph Protection Act in 1988.[348] With limited exceptions, the Act prohibits the use of polygraph tests for preemployment screening or during the course of employment.[349] Governmental entities are exempt. Although the Act does not apply in criminal cases, it had the effect of putting many polygraphers out of business, including many incompetent ones.

§ 8-11. Voice Stress Analysis.

Voice Stress Analysis (VSA) is intended to detect deception.[350] It is based on the theory that a person's voice changes when that person is being deceptive; that is, the emotional stress accompanying the deception will produce physiological responses that can be recorded and analyzed. At one time, the Psychological Stress Evaluation (PSE) was the most widely known type of voice stress analysis.[351] Currently, the Computer Voice Stress Analyzer (CVSA) is the most popular. Although it lacks scientific support, police departments continue to used the device, presumably as a method to obtain confessions.[352]

---

347. United States v. Ailsworth, 914 F. Supp. 426, 429 (D. Kan. 1995).

348. 29 U.S.C. §§ 2001-09 (1991). The Department of Labor has promulgated regulations pursuant to the Act. 29 C.F.R. pt. 801; 56 Fed. Reg. 9046 (1991).

See also Fallin v. Mindis Metals, Inc., 865 F. Supp. 834, 840 (N.D. Ga. 1994) (independent polygraph examiner not an "employer" under the Act); Zeligson, *Polygraph Exams Could Limit Employers' Losses*, NAT'L L.J., Feb. 26, 1996, at C8.

349. *See* Note, *The Employee Polygraph Protection Act of 1988 — Should the Federal Government Regulate the Use of Polygraphs in the Private Sector?*, 58 U. CIN. L. REV. 559 (1989); Note, *The Employee Polygraph Protection Act of 1988: A Balance of Interests*, 75 IOWA L. REV. 539 (1990).

350. *See generally* L. TAYLOR, SCIENTIFIC INTERROGATION ch. 11 (1984); Kenety, *The Psychological Stress Evaluator: The Theory, Validity and Legal Status of an Innovative "Lie Detector,"* 55 IND. L.J. 349 (1980); Ronayne, *Admissibility of Testing by the Psychological Stress Evaluator*, 9 PACE L. REV. 243 (1989); Note, *The Psychological Stress Evaluator: Yesterday's Dream — Tomorrow's Nightmare*, 24 CLEV. ST. L. REV. 299 (1975); Note, *The Psychological Stress Evaluator: A Recent Development in Lie Detector Technology*, 7 U. CAL. DAVIS L. REV. 332 (1974); 13 N.M. L. REV. 703 (1983).

351. Other types are the voice stress analyzer (VSA), the computerized voice stress analyzer (CVSA), the Mark II voice analyzer, and the now defunct Hagoth voice analyzer.

352. *See* Hansen, *Truth Sleuth or Faulty Detector?*, 85 A.B.A. J. 16 (May 1999) ("Yet police are still buying the devices in increasing numbers, says Hughes, whose company counts nearly 700 police agencies as customers, some 100 of them in the last two years alone").

VSA measures changes in frequency modulations of the voice (microtremors), the inaudible component of the voice produced by muscles in speech production. As stress increases, frequency modulation decreases. The procedure involves the audio recording of a person's voice and the transmitting of that recording into a voice stress evaluator. The evaluator receives the electronically transduced speech patterns, analyzes them, and registers the results on chart paper. The examiner then evaluates the chart for indications of stress (decreases in microtremors) and then determines whether deception is present.

Although VAS might be considered a "voice lie detector," it differs from the polygraph in several respects. Unlike the polygraph, a person can be subjected to VAS without being "hooked up" to the evaluator, without knowledge that the test is being conducted, and the evaluation is not limited to "yes" and "no" responses. Another difference is that VSA is based on only one physiological response, while the polygraph uses three different physiological responses.

The validity of VSA is suspect. Independent studies have consistently challenged the validity of this technique. For example, in one study, VAS "failed to perform at a level better than chance expectancy."[353] In another study, researchers found that "in no test of the present study was the VAS-criteria correspondence . . . or the differences between VAS evaluations and chance decisions and between correct and incorrect evaluations significant, as to support the claim for VAS validity as a detector of psychological stress."[354] Another commentator concluded that "the promise of voice stress analysis in the lie detection field is not and may never be a reality. All of the reliable evidence now available shows that none of the voice stress devices is useful in detecting deception...."[355] A 1987 study reached "the inescapable conclusion ...that a device that will permit the detection of lying from the voice analysis alone presently does not exist."[356] A 1998 study concluded that the decisions of

---

353. Timm, *The Efficacy of the Psychological Stress Evaluator in Detecting Deception*, 11 J. POLICE SCI. & ADMIN. 62, 65 (1983).

354. Nachshon & Feldman, *Vocal Indices of Psychological Stress: A Validation Study of the Psychological Stress Evaluator*, 8 J. POLICE SCI. & ADMIN. 40, 50 (1980).

355. Horvath, *Detecting Deception: The Promise and Reality of Voice Stress Analysis*, 27 J. FORENSIC SCI. 340, 349 (1982). *See also* D. LYKKEN, A TREMOR IN BLOOD, *supra* note 6, at 159 ("There is no scientifically credible evidence that the PSE ... can reliably measure difference in 'stress' as reflected in the human voice"). *But see* Chapman, *Psychological Stress Evaluation (Narrative Testing)*, *in* 2 FORENSIC SCIENCES ch. 33 (C. Wecht 1984).

A number of PSE studies are reproduced in *Hearings on the Use of Polygraphs and Similar Devices by Federal Agencies before the Subcomm. on Foreign Affairs and Government Information of the House Comm. on Government Operations*, 93d Cong., 2d Sess. (1974).

356. Hollien, Geison & Hicks, *Voice Stress Evaluators and Lie Detection*, 32 J. FORENSIC SCI. 405, 415 (1987). *See also* Nachshon, Elaad & Amsel, *Validity of the Psychological Stress Evaluator: A Field Study*, 13 J. POLICE SCI. & ADMIN. 275 (1985).

experienced examiners using the Computerized Voice Stress Analyzer were not significantly better than chance.[357]

Admissibility

Several courts have considered the admissibility of VAS evidence. The overwhelming majority have rejected evidence based on this technique. Some courts have held that VAS evidence has not achieved general acceptance in the scientific community and thus is inadmissible under the *Frye* test,[358] while others have simply concluded that VAS is not reliable.[359] One court ruled that exclusion of VAS evidence does not violate a defendant's right to a fair trial.[360]

In contrast to the majority rule, the New Mexico Supreme Court has ruled VAS evidence admissible in the discretion of the trial court, provided the offering party introduces evidence establishing (1) the qualifications of the examiner, (2) the reliability of the testing procedure as approved by authorities in the field, and (3) the validity of the test in the particular case.[361] Thus, the court

---

357. Janniro & Cestaro, *Effectiveness of Detection of Deception Examinations Using the Computer Voice Stress Analyzer*, 27 POLYGRAPH 28, 32 (1998) ("[T]he instrument failed to function in a manner that would allow examiners to discriminate between truthful and deceptive responses from test subjects. . . . Although the CVSA instrument is purported to detect stress in human speech, there is still no unambiguous evidence to support that claim").

358. *E.g.*, Barrel of Fun, Inc. v. State Farm Fire & Cas. Co., 739 F.2d 1028, 1032 (5th Cir. 1984); United States v. Traficant, 566 F. Supp. 1046, 1047 (N.D. Ohio 1983); Neises v. Solomon State Bank, 236 Kan. 767, 774, 696 P.2d 372, 377-78 (1985); United States v. Bothwell, 17 M.J. 684, 688 (A.C.M.R. 1983); Smith v. State, 31 Md. App. 106, 119-20, 355 A.2d 527, 535 (1976); Sabag v. Continental South Dakota, 374 N.W.2d 349, 353 (S.D. 1985) ("no general scientific acceptance").

See also Annot., *Admissibility of Voice Stress Evaluation Test Results or of Statements Made During Test*, 47 A.L.R.4TH 1202 (1986). For a discussion of the *Frye* test, *see* Chapter 1.

359. *E.g.*, Caldwell v. State, 267 Ark. 1053, 1060, 594 S.W.2d 24, 28 (1980); People v. Lippert, 125 Ill. App. 3d 489, 503, 466 N.E.2d 276, 286 (1984); State v. Gaudet, 638 So. 2d 1216, 1222 (La. App.) ("Defendant acknowledges that introduction of [results of voice stress test] is contrary to settled jurisprudence"), *writ denied*, 648 So. 2d 386 (La. 1994); State v. Higginbotham, 554 So. 2d 1308, 1310 (La. App. 1989); State v. Arnold, 533 So. 2d 1311, 1315 (La. App.), *writ denied*, 534 So. 2d 959 (La. 1988); State v. Naas, 409 So. 2d 535, 548 (La. 1981); State v. Thompson, 381 So. 2d 823, 824 (La. 1980); State v. Schouest, 351 So. 2d 462, 469 (La. 1977); State v. Ochalla, 285 N.W.2d 683, 684 (Minn. 1979); State v. Milano, 297 N.C. 485, 500, 256 S.E.2d 154, 163 (1979); People v. Tarsia, 50 N.Y.2d 1, 7, 405 N.E.2d 188, 191, 427 N.Y.S.2d 944, 946 (1980); State v. Makerson, 52 N.C. App. 149, 153, 277 S.E.2d 869, 872 (1981); *c.f.* Heisse v. Vermont, 519 F. Supp. 36, 46 (D. Vt. 1980) (statute limiting licenses to polygraph examiners is rationally based on wider acceptance of reliability).

360. Milano v. Garrison, 677 F.2d 374, 375 (4th Cir. 1981). *See also* State v. Gaudet, 638 So. 2d 1216, 1222 (La. App.) (rejecting argument that exclusion of results of voice stress test violated constitutional right to a fair trial), *writ denied*, 648 So. 2d 386 (La. 1994).

361. Simon Neustadt Family Center, Inc. v. Bludworth, 97 N.M. 500, 504, 641 P.2d 531, 535 (1982).

has adopted the same liberal approach to the admissibility of VAS evidence that it had previously embraced with polygraph evidence.[362]

In addition, the Eleventh Circuit has ruled that requiring a probationer to submit to VAS examinations as a condition of probation is permissible.[363]

§ 8-12. Truth Serum.

So-called "truth serums"[364] involve the use of drugs, such as scopolamine, sodium amytal, sodium pentothal, and brevital sodium, that are central nervous system depressants.[365] These drugs temporarily alter a person's psychological state in such a way as "to induce a relaxed state of mind in which the suspect becomes more talkative and has less emotional control."[366] The efficacy of "truth serums" as a method of lie detection has been viewed with skepticism by many commentators:

> [E]xperimental and clinical findings indicate that only individuals who have conscious and unconscious reasons for doing so are inclined to confess and yield to interrogation under drug influence. On the other hand, some are able to withhold information and some, especially character neurotics, are able to lie. Others are so suggestible they will describe, in response to suggestive questioning, behavior which never in fact occurred. Notwithstanding these limitations, a drug-induced interview may be a valuable adjunct to an otherwise thorough psychiatric examination. In some instances it may enable a psychiatrist to ascertain more quickly the depth and type of mental illness. But drugs are not "truth sera." They lessen inhibitions to verbalization and stimulate unrepressed expression not only of fact but of fancy and suggestion as well. Thus the material produced is not "truth" in the sense that it conforms to empirical fact.[367]

---

362. *See* § 8-4(D) *supra.*

363. Owens v. Kelley, 681 F.2d 1362, 1369-70 (11th Cir. 1982).

364. "The description truth serum is misleading as the drug used is not a serum, and it does not always lead to the truth." MacDonald, *Truth Serum*, 46 J. CRIM. L., CRIMINOLOGY & POLICE SCI. 259 (1955).

365. *See generally* L. TAYLOR, SCIENTIFIC INTERROGATION ch. 10 (1984); Dession, Freedman, Donnelly & Redlich, *Drug-Induced Revelation and Criminal Investigation*, 62 YALE L.J. 315 (1952); Polen, *The Admissibility of Truth Serum Tests in the Courts*, 35 TEMP. L.Q. 401 (1962); Note, *An Analysis of the Limited Legal Value of Truth Serum*, 11 SYRACUSE L. REV. 64 (1959).

366. MacDonald, *supra* note 364, at 259.

367. Dession, Freedman, Donnelly & Redlich, *supra* note 365, at 319. *See also* Geis & Kamm, *Drug Induced Statements*, 10 CLEV.–MARSHALL. L. REV. 313 (1961); Gottschalk, *The Use of Drugs in Interrogation, in* THE MANIPULATION OF HUMAN BEHAVIOR 130 (A. Biderman & H. Zimmer eds. 1961); MacDonald, *supra* note 364.

The courts uniformly reject the admissibility of statements made by a person while under the influence of "truth serum" drugs when those statements are offered to prove the truth of the matter asserted.[368] This rule of exclusion also extends to expert testimony that a defendant was telling the truth while under the influence of such drugs.[369]

A different evidentiary issue arises when an expert offers an opinion about a subject's mental condition based on an examination that included the use of "truth serum" drugs. Some courts permit expert opinion testimony in this situation,[370] although the trial court retains discretion to exclude the drug-induced statements themselves.[371]

Finally, the use of "truth serum" drugs to induce a confession is challengeable on due process grounds. As the U.S. Supreme Court has remarked: "It is difficult to imagine a situation in which a confession would be less the product of a free intellect, less voluntary, than when brought about by a drug having the effect of a 'truth serum.'" [372]

---

368. *E.g.,* United States v. Solomon, 753 F.2d 1522, 1525-26 (9th Cir. 1985); Lindsey v. United States, 237 F.2d 893, 895-96 (9th Cir. 1956); Ramona v. Superior Court, 57 Cal. App. 4th 107, 66 Cal. Rptr. 2d 766, 776 (1997) ("[T]he use of sodium amytal to retrieve repressed memories of child sexual molestation is a scientific technique or method which is subject to the *Kelly* requirements of reliability and acceptance by the relevant scientific community") (no general acceptance); People v. Stiles, 692 P.2d 1124, 1128 (Colo. App. 1984); Fetters v. State, 436 A.2d 796, 800 (Del. 1981); Zeigler v. State, 402 So. 2d 365, 373 (Fla. 1981), *cert. denied,* 455 U.S. 1035 (1982); State v. Linn, 93 Idaho 430, 433, 462 P.2d 729, 732 (1969); State v. Rosencrantz, 110 Idaho 124, 130, 714 P.2d 93, 99 (App. 1986); State v. Adams, 218 Kan. 495, 508, 545 P.2d 1134, 1144 (1976); State v. Foerstel, 674 S.W.2d 583, 593-94 (Mo. App. 1984); State v. Blome, 209 N.J. Super. 227, 238, 507 A.2d 283, 288 (A.D.), *cert. denied,* 104 N.J. 458, 577 A.2d 444 (1986); State v. Delk, 692 S.W.2d 431, 439 (Tenn. Crim. App. 1985); Reed v. State, 644 S.W.2d 479, 482 (Tex. Crim. App. 1983); Cain v. State, 549 S.W.2d 707, 712 (Tex. Crim. App. 1977); Archie v. Commonwealth, 14 Va. App. 684, 420 S.E.2d 718, 723 (1992) ("[T]estimony induced by sodium amytal is generally regarded as unreliable, and many states have excluded testimony regarding statements elicited from a defendant while under the influence of sodium amytal").

See generally 3A J. Wigmore, Evidence § 998 (Chadbourn rev. 1970) (listing cases); Annot., *Admissibility of Physiological or Psychological Truth and Deception Test or its Results to Support Physician's Testimony,* 41 A.L.R.3d 1369 (1972).

369. *E.g.,* Harper v. State, 249 Ga. 519, 526, 292 S.E.2d 389, 396 (1982); People v. Cox, 85 Mich. App. 314, 317, 271 N.W.2d 216, 218 (1978); Merritt v. Commonwealth, 386 S.W.2d 727, 729-30 (Ky. 1965).

370. *See* People v. Cartier, 51 Cal. 2d 590, 601, 335 P.2d 114, 122 (1959); State v. White, 60 Wash. 2d 551, 374 P.2d 942, 950-53 (1962), *cert. denied,* 375 U.S. 883 (1963). *But see* People v. Ford, 304 N.Y. 679, 681-82, 107 N.E.2d 595, 596-97 (1952).

371. *See* People v. Hiser, 267 Cal. App. 2d 47, 61-62, 72 Cal. Rptr. 906, 915-16 (1968); People v. Myers, 35 Ill. 2d 311, 333, 220 N.E.2d 297, 310 (1966), *cert. denied,* 385 U.S. 1019 (1967); State v. Chase, 206 Kan. 352, 357-58, 480 P.2d 62, 67 (1971).

372. Townsend v. Sain, 372 U.S. 293, 307-08 (1963). *See also* People v. Johnson, 32 Cal. App. 3d 988, 1002, 109 Cal. Rptr. 118, 127 (1973).

§ 8-13. Selected Bibliography.

Reports

U.S. Congress Office of Technology Assessment, *Scientific Validity of Polygraph Testing: A Review and Evaluation — A Technical Memorandum* (OTA-TM-H-15 1983), *reprinted in* 12 POLYGRAPH 196 (1983).

Department of Defense, *The Accuracy and Utility of Polygraph Testing* (1984), *reprinted in* 13 POLYGRAPH 1 (1984).

Books

S. ABRAMS, A POLYGRAPH HANDBOOK FOR ATTORNEYS (1977).

D. LYKKEN, A TREMOR IN THE BLOOD: USES AND ABUSES OF THE LIE DETECTOR (1981).

1 D. FAIGMAN, D. KAYE, M. SAKS & J. SANDERS, MODERN SCIENTIFIC EVIDENCE ch. 14 (1997).

A. MOENSSENS, J. STARRS, & C. HENDERSON, SCIENTIFIC EVIDENCE: CIVIL AND CRIMINAL ch. 20 (4th ed. 1995).

J. REID & F. INBAU, TRUTH AND DECEPTION (2d ed. 1977).

THE POLYGRAPH TEST: LIES, TRUTH AND SCIENCE (A. Gale ed. 1988).

Bailey & Barnett, *The Polygraph and the Search for Truth, in* LEGAL MEDICINE ANNUAL 329 (C. Wecht ed. 1972).

Sevilla, *Reliability of Polygraph Examination*, 14 AM. JUR. PROOF OF FACTS 2D 1 (1977).

Articles

Department of Defense Polygraph Program, 21 POLYGRAPH 92 (1992).

Furgerson, *Perspectives on Polygraph: A Guide to Survival*, 21 POLYGRAPH 164 (1992).

Yankee, *The Current Status of Research in Forensic Psychophysiology and Its Application in the Psychophysiological Detection of Deception*, 40 J. FORENSIC SCI. 63 (1995).

Law Review Articles

Barland, *Standards for the Admissibility of Polygraph Results as Evidence*, 16 U. WEST L.A. L. REV. 37 (1984).

Denemark, *The Search For "Scientific Knowledge" in Federal Courts in The Post-Frye Era: Refuting the Assertion that "Law Seeks Justice While Science Seeks Truth,"* 8 HIGH TECH. L. J. 235 (1993).

Giannelli, *Polygraph Evidence: Post-Daubert*, 49 HASTINGS L.J. 895 (1998).

Honts & Perry, *Polygraph Admissibility*, 16 LAW & HUM. BEHAV. 357 (1992).

Honts & Quick, *The Polygraph in 1995: Progress in Science and the Law*, 71 N.D. L. REV. 987 (1995).

Imwinkelried & McCall, *Issues Once Moot: The Other Evidentiary Objections to the Admission of Exculpatory Polygraph Examinations*, 32 WAKE FOREST L. REV. 1045 (1997).

McCall, *Misconceptions and Reevaluation — Polygraph Admissibility After Rock and Daubert*, 1996 U. ILL. L. REV. 363.

Raskin, *The Polygraph in 1986: Scientific, Professional and Legal Issues Surrounding Application and Acceptance of Polygraph Evidence*, 1986 UTAH L. REV. 29.

Rothblatt, *Cross-Examination of Polygraph Expert*, 16 U. WEST L.A. L. REV. 55 (1984).

Sevilla, *Polygraph 1984: Behind the Closed Door of Admissibility*, 16 U. WEST L.A. L. REV. 5 (1984).

Note, *Polygraph Evidence in Federal Courts: Should It Be Admissible?*, 36 AM. CRIM. L. REV. 87 (999).

Note, *Reexamining Polygraph Admissibility*, 56 MO. L. REV. 143 (1991).

Note, *The Truth About Polygraph Evidence in Criminal Trials: The Implications of State v. Mitchell*, 70 N.C. L. REV. 2042 (1992).

Note, *A Critical Look at the Admissibility of Polygraph Evidence in the Wake of Daubert: The Lie Detector Fails the Test*, 46 CATHOLIC U. L. REV. 1247 (1997).

Annotations

Annot., *Modern status of rule relating to admission of results of lie detector (polygraph) test in federal criminal trials*, 43 A.L.R. FED. 68 (1979).

Annot., *Admissibility of lie detector test taken upon stipulation that the results will be admissible into evidence*, 53 A.L.R.3D 1005 (1973).

Annot., *Admissibility of evidence of polygraph test results, or offer or refusal to take test, in action for malicious prosecution*, 10 A.L.R.5TH 663 (1993).

Annot., *Admissibility of polygraph or similar lie detector test results, or willingness to submit to test, on issues of coverage under insurance policy, or insurer's good faith belief that claim was not covered*, 7 A.L.R.5TH 143 (1992).

Annot., *Enforceability of agreement by state officials to drop prosecution if accused successfully passes polygraph test*, 36 A.L.R.3D 1280 (1971).

Annot., *Validity and construction of statutes licensing or otherwise regulating operators of polygraph or similar devices*, 32 A.L.R.3D 1324 (1970).

Annot., *Propriety and prejudicial effect of comment or evidence as to accused's willingness to take lie detector test*, 95 A.L.R.2D 819 (1964).

Annot., *Propriety and prejudicial effect of informing jury that witness in criminal prosecution has taken polygraph test*, 15 A.L.R.4TH 824 (1982).

Annot., *Propriety and prejudicial effect of informing jury that accused has taken polygraph test, where results of test would be inadmissible in evidence*, 88 A.L.R.3D 227 (1978).

Annot., *Right of indigent criminal defendant to polygraph test at public expense*,11 A.L.R.4TH 733 (1982).

Annot., *Admissibility of polygraph evidence at trial on issue of voluntariness of confession made by accused*, 92 A.L.R.3D 1317 (1979).

Annot., *Admissibility in evidence of confession made by accused in anticipation of, during, or following polygraph examination*, 89 A.L.R.3D 230 (1979).

Annot., *Admissibility of lie detector results, or of offer or refusal to take test, in attorney disciplinary proceeding*, 79 A.L.R.4TH 576 (1990).

Annot., *Propriety of conditioning probation on defendant's submission to polygraph or other lie detector testing*, 86 A.L.R.4TH 709 (1991).

Annot., *Admissibility of voice stress evaluation test results or of statements made during test*, 47 A.L.R.4TH 1202 (1986).

CHAPTER 9

PSYCHOLOGICAL AND SOCIAL SCIENCE EVIDENCE

§ 9-1. In General.

The use of social science research in law is now commonplace, although not without controversy. In a seminal article, Walker and Monahan coined the phrase "social frameworks" to describe a new use of this research.[1] The term refers to the use of social science research to provide a context for assisting a jury to decide specific factual issues.[2] For example, social science research concerning the problems associated with eyewitness identifications provides background information that assists a jury in deciding whether the eyewitness's account in a particular case is accurate. This, of course, is but one way that this type of evidence may be used.

This chapter discusses a variety of issues that involve social science research. Many of these issues cluster under the headings of "syndromes" and "profiles."

§ 9-2. Eyewitness Identifications.

Both courts and commentators have noted the problems of eyewitness identifications.[3] For example, in *United States v. Wade,*[4] the U.S. Supreme Court wrote: "The vagaries of eyewitness identification are well-known; the annals of criminal law are rife with instances of mistaken identification."[5]

Although psychological research on eyewitness identification dates back to the turn of the century,[6] most of research is fairly[7] recent. This research emphasizes

---

1. Walker & Monahan, *Social Frameworks: A New Use of Social Science in Law*, 73 VA. L. REV. 559 (1987). *See also* Monahan & Walker, *Empirical Questions Without Empirical Answers*, 1991 WIS. L. REV. 569; Walker & Monahan, *Social Facts: Scientific Methodology as Legal Precedent*, 76 CALIF. L. REV. 877 (1988); Monahan & Walker, *Social Authority: Obtaining, Evaluating, and Establishing Social Science in Law*, 134 U. PA. L. REV. 477 (1986).

2. "We therefore propose a new category, which we term social framework, to refer to *the use of general conclusions from social science research in determining factual issues in a specific case.*" Walker & Monahan, *supra* note 1, 73 VA. L. REV. at 570.

3. *E.g.,* EVALUATING WITNESS EVIDENCE: RECENT PSYCHOLOGICAL RESEARCH AND NEW PERSPECTIVES (S. Lloyd-Bostock & B. Clifford eds. 1983); B. CLIFFORD & R. BULL, PSYCHOLOGY OF PERSON IDENTIFICATION (1978); E. LOFTUS & K. KETCHAM, WITNESS FOR THE DEFENSE: THE ACCUSED, THE EYEWITNESS, AND THE EXPERT WHO PUTS MEMORY ON TRIAL (1991); E. LOFTUS & J. DOYLE, EYEWITNESS TESTIMONY: CIVIL AND CRIMINAL (1987); E. LOFTUS, EYEWITNESS TESTIMONY (1979); A. YARMEY, PSYCHOLOGY OF EYEWITNESS TESTIMONY (1978); EYEWITNESS TESTIMONY: PSYCHOLOGICAL PERSPECTIVES (G. Wells & E. Loftus eds. 1984); Levine & Tapp, *The Psychology of Criminal Identification: The Gap from Wade to Kirby*, 121 U. PA. L. REV. 1079 (1973); CUTLER & PENROD, MISTAKEN IDENTIFICATION: THE EYEWITNESS, PSYCHOLOGY, AND THE LAW (1995); Seelau & Wells, *Applied Eyewitness Research: The Other Mission*, 19 LAW & HUM. BEHAV. 319 (1995) ("[I]t has been estimated that eyewitness evidence plays a major role in over 75,000 cases a year in the U.S. alone, and mistaken eyewitness identification has been identified as the single most important factor leading to false convictions"); LOFTUS & DOYLE, EYEWITNESS TESTIMONY: CIVIL AND CRIMINAL (2d ed. 1992); LOFTUS & KETCHAM, WITNESS FOR THE DEFENSE: THE ACCUSED, THE EYEWITNESS, AND THE EXPERT WHO PUTS MEMORY ON TRIAL (1991).

4. 388 U.S. 218 (1967).

5. *Id.* at 228.

6. *See* H. MUNSTERBERG, ON THE WITNESS STAND: ESSAYS ON PSYCHOLOGY AND CRIME (1908).

the complex nature of human perception and memory. Human memory does not function like a videotape recorder, accurately recording all images which can subsequently be fully retrieved. Rather, it is a constructive process, in which many factors play a part.

The perception and memory process can be divided into three stages. The first is the acquisition stage, during which the event is perceived and entered in the memory. The second is the retention stage — the time between the event and its recollection. The third stage is the retrieval stage during which the information relating to the event is recalled.[8] Inaccuracies can be introduced at all three stages.

In the acquisition stage, the literature indicates that witnesses are more accurate when: (1) exposure time is longer rather than shorter, (2) events are less rather than more violent, (3) witnesses are not subject to extreme stress, (4) witnesses are free from biased expectations, (5) witnesses are young adults rather than children, and (6) witnesses are asked to report on salient aspects of an event rather than peripheral aspects.[9]

Retention of information in memory (second stage) can be influenced by numerous factors. Two principal points emerge from the research.[10] First, the longer the interval between the event and the recollection of the event, the greater the lapse in memory. Moreover, the lapse in memory does not decrease at a uniform rate; it decreases sharply immediately after the event and then more slowly over a period of time.[11] This phenomenon is known as the "curve of forgetting." Second, new information enters the memory between the event and its recollection: "External information provided from the outside can intrude into the witness's memory, as can his own thoughts, and both can cause dramatic changes in his recollection."[12]

Finally, the way in which information is retrieved (third stage) can influence memory. For example, the method of questioning, the type of identification procedure employed, the status of the questioner, and nonverbal communication clues all may distort memory.[13]

---

7. Wells & Loftus, *Eyewitness Research: Then and Now*, *in* EYEWITNESS TESTIMONY: PSYCHOLOGICAL PERSPECTIVES 1, 3 (G. Wells & E. Loftus eds. 1984) ("over 85% of the entire published literature has surfaced since 1978").

8. E. LOFTUS, EYEWITNESS TESTIMONY, *supra* note 3 , at 21.

9. Loftus, *Eyewitness Testimony: Psychological Research and Legal Thought*, *in* 3 CRIME AND JUSTICE: AN ANNUAL REVIEW OF RESEARCH 105, 115-16 (M. Tonry & N. Morris eds. 1981).

10. *Id.* at 119.

11. E. LOFTUS, EYEWITNESS TESTIMONY, *supra* note 3, at 53.

12. *Id.* at 87.

13. Loftus, *supra* note 9, at 110.

Factors

Research has identified a number of factors that may affect eyewitness identifications.

First, cross-racial identifications present special problems.[14] Dr. Elizabeth Loftus, a prominent researcher in this field, noted that people "have greater difficulty in recognizing faces of another race than faces of their own race. This cross-racial identification problem is not due to the fact that people have greater prejudices or less experience with members of the other race."[15]

Second, "weapon focus" frequently interferes with a person's ability to identify faces; that is, when a weapon is used in a crime, the witness's attention will focus on the weapon rather than the facial features of the person holding the weapon.[16]

Third, "unconscious transference" may lead to misidentifications.[17] A witness who has seen an innocent suspect at an earlier time may misidentify that suspect because he "looks familiar." For example, a witness may view a photographic display that includes a picture of an innocent suspect. No identification is made. Later, the witness picks the innocent suspect out of a lineup, unconsciously remembering the face from the photo display.

Fourth, research indicates that the relationship between the accuracy of an identification and a witness's confidence in the identification is not strong.[18] Indeed, two researchers have concluded that "the eyewitness accuracy-confidence relationship is weak under good laboratory conditions and functionally useless in forensically representative settings."[19]

---

14. *See* Platz & Hosch, *Cross Racial/Ethnic Eyewitness Identification: A Field Study*, 18 J. APPLIED SOC. PSYCHOL. 972, 981-83 (1988); Johnson, *Cross-Racial Identification Errors in Criminal Cases*, 69 CORNELL L. REV. 934, 938-39 (1984) ("The impairment in ability to recognize black faces is substantial").

15. E. LOFTUS, EYEWITNESS TESTIMONY, *supra* note 3, at 139.

16. *See* Loftus, Loftus & Messo, *Some Facts About "Weapon Focus,"* 11 LAW & HUM. BEHAV. 55, 61-62 (1987); Maass & Kohnken, *Eyewitness Identification: Simulating the "Weapon Effect,"* 13 LAW & HUM. BEHAV. 397, 405 (1989); Steblay, *A Meta-Analytic Review of the Weapon Focus Effect*, 16 LAW & HUM. BEHAV. 413 (1992).

17. E. LOFTUS, EYEWITNESS TESTIMONY, *supra* note 3, at 142-51.

18. *See* Cutler & Penrod, *Forensically Relevant Moderators of the Relation Between Eyewitness Identification Accuracy and Confidence*, 74 J. APPLIED PSYCHOL. 650 (1989); Deffenbacher, *Eyewitness Accuracy and Confidence: Can We Infer Anything About Their Relationship?*, 4 LAW & HUM. BEHAV. 243, 250-57 (1980).

19. Wells & Murray, *Eyewitness Confidence*, *in* EYEWITNESS TESTIMONY: PSYCHOLOGICAL PERSPECTIVES 155, 165 (G. Wells & E. Loftus eds. 1984).

Jury Impact

The research also reveals that the impact of eyewitness identifications on juries is substantial.[20] In commenting on the research, Dr. Loftus has written that eyewitness testimony "is likely to be believed by jurors, especially when it is offered with a high level of confidence, even though the accuracy of an eyewitness and the confidence of that witness may not be related to one another at all."[21] Another study also emphasized this point: "The results of this study are consistent with a growing body of research which suggests that when jurors assess eyewitness accuracy, they are unlikely to rely on factors that are predictive of eyewitness identification accuracy (*e.g.*, encoding and retrieval conditions). In contrast, jurors seem inclined to evaluate identification accuracy based on factors that appear to have questionable associations with identification accuracy."[22]

§ 9-2(A). Constitutional Issues.

The courts responded to the problems associated with eyewitness identification testimony in a number of different ways. Initially, cross-examination was viewed as an adequate vehicle for alerting the jury to these problems. This changed in 1967 when the U.S. Supreme Court decided a trilogy of cases that imposed constitutional restraints on identification procedures.[23]

In *United States v. Wade*[24] the Court ruled that a defendant had a sixth amendment right to counsel at a lineup. The presence of counsel, according to the Court, assures that a criminal defendant can effectively challenge a subsequent in-court identification based on a suggestive pretrial identification. This ruling, however, was substantially circumscribed in *Kirby v. Illinois* (1972),[25] when the Court held that the right to counsel did not attach until the commencement of judicial adversary proceedings — for example, at the initial appearance before a magistrate. Accordingly, an arrest by itself does not trigger the right to counsel. Since many, if not most, lineups occur prior to the initiation of judicial proceedings, the right to counsel has not played a major role in later cases.

---

20. *See* Brigham & Bothwell, *The Ability of Prospective Jurors to Estimate the Accuracy of Eyewitness Identifications*, 7 LAW & HUM. BEHAV. 19 (1983).

21. E. LOFTUS, EYEWITNESS TESTIMONY, *supra* note 3, at 19.

22. Berman, Narby & Cutler, *Effects of Inconsistent Eyewitness Statements on Mock-Jurors' Evaluations of the Eyewitness, Perceptions of Defendant Culpability and Verdicts*, 19 LAW & HUM. BEHAV. 79, 87 (1995) (finding strategy of highlighting inconsistencies in the eyewitness' recall testimony during cross-examination effective).

23. United States v. Wade, 388 U.S. 218 (1967); Gilbert v. California, 388 U.S. 263 (1967); Stovall v. Denno, 388 U.S. 293 (1967). *See generally* 1 W. LAFAVE & J. ISRAEL, CRIMINAL PROCEDURE § 7.3 (1984); N. SOBEL, EYE-WITNESS IDENTIFICATION: LEGAL AND PRACTICAL PROBLEMS (2d ed. 1972).

24. 388 U.S. 218 (1967).

25. 406 U.S 682 (1972). *See also* Moore v. Illinois, 434 U.S. 220 (1977).

Moreover, the Court ruled in *United States v. Ash*[26] that the right to counsel did not apply at a photographic display, even if the display was conducted after the attachment of the right to counsel.

In addition to the right to counsel, the Supreme Court has reviewed identification procedures under a due process analysis. In 1967 the Court held that an "unnecessarily suggestive" identification procedure violated due process.[27] This due process test, which focused on the procedure itself, was subsequently modified. The new test focuses on the reliability of the actual identification in the case.[28] Thus, an identification based on an unnecessarily suggestive procedure may nevertheless be admissible if found to be reliable. In determining reliability, a number of factors are relevant: the eyewitness's opportunity to view the perpetrator at the time of the crime, the degree of the witness's attention at that time, the accuracy of the witness's initial description, the witness's level of certainty, and the time lapse between the crime and the identification.[29] Empirical research casts doubt on several of these factors: "[P]sychological literature raises serious doubts about the correctness of the Supreme Court's assumption that predictive validity is related to the accuracy of the witness' prior description of a perpetrator and to the confidence the witness has in the accuracy of the identification."[30]

Social science research has also examined identification procedures. For example, one study indicated that sequential rather than simultaneous presentation of suspects in lineups or photographic displays enhances accuracy.[31] A showup (one person lineup) is generally "perceived by most common-law jurisdictions and by most psycho-legal researchers as being highly prejudicial to suspects."[32] Consequently, videotaping lineup identifications has become common in some precincts. The videotape serves as a deterrent against

---

26. 413 U.S. 300 (1973).

27. Stovall v. Denno, 388 U.S. 293 (1967). *See generally* 1 W. LaFave & J. Israel, Criminal Procedure § 7.4 (1984); N. Sobel, Eye-Witness Identification: Legal and Practical Problems (2d ed. 1972).

28. Manson v. Brathwaite, 432 U.S. 98 (1977); Neil v. Biggers, 409 U.S. 188 (1972).

29. 432 U.S. at 98.

30. Penrod & Cutler, *Eyewitness Expert Testimony and Jury Decisionmaking*, 52 Law & Contemp. Probs. 43, 51 (Autumn 1989). *See also* Pigott, Brigham & Bothwell, *A Field Study on the Relationship Between Quality of Eyewitnesses' Descriptions and Identification Accuracy*, 17 J. Police Sci. & Admin. 84, 87 (1990) ("description congruence, description accuracy, and description completeness are not predictive of identification accuracy in a meaningful field setting. It appears that the Supreme Court was wrong in its emphasis on this 'description accuracy' criterion ...").

31. Cutler & Penrod, *Improving the Reliability of Eyewitness Identification: Lineup Construction and Presentation*, 73 J. Applied Psychol. 281 (1988).

32. Yarmey et. al., *Accuracy of Eyewitness Identifications in Showups and Lineups*, 20 Law & Hum. Behav. 459, 459 (1996).

procedural biases, a safeguard against distorted memory, and an objective record of "how quickly — a given witness... made his or her selection — often a better cue than self-expression of confidence."[33]

§ 9-2(B). Jury Instructions.

In addition to constitutional considerations, some courts have attempted to deal with eyewitness identification problems by requiring special cautionary jury instructions. The leading case is *United States v. Telfaire,*[34] which sets forth a recommended instruction.[35] Other courts have adopted the *Telfaire* instruction. The Sixth Circuit requires the instruction when the issue of identity is crucial – "either where no corroboration of the testimony exists, or where the witness' memory has faded by the time of trial, or where there was a limited opportunity for observation."[36] The available research, however, suggests that "the *Telfaire* instructions ineffectively protect the defendant against mistaken conviction."[37]

There are three different approaches in the cases: (1) courts requiring the *Telfaire* instruction;[38] (2) courts that leave the decision on whether to instruct to the discretion of the trial court;[39] and (3) courts that reject *Telfaire*-like instructions, holding that the general instructions on credibility are sufficient.[40]

In *Commonwealth v. Hyatt,*[41] the Supreme Judicial Court of Massachusetts held that giving an instruction on cross-racial identifications may be appropriate,

---

33. Kassin, *Eyewitness Identification Procedures: The Fifth Rule,* 22 LAW & HUM. BEHAV. 649, 651 (1998).

34. 469 F.2d 552 (D.C. Cir. 1972).

35. *Id.* at 558-59.

36. United States v. Tipton, 11 F.3d 602, 606 (6th Cir. 1993), *cert. denied,* 512 U.S. 1212 (1994).

37. Penrod & Cutler, *Eyewitness Expert Testimony and Jury Decisionmaking,* 52 LAW & CONTEMP. PROBS. 43, 82 (Autumn 1989); Ramirez, Semba & Geiselman, *Judge's Cautionary Instructions on Eyewitness Testimony,* 14 AM. J. FORENSIC PSYCH. 31 (1996). *See also* Greene, *Eyewitness Testimony and the Use of Cautionary Instructions,* 8 BRIDGEPORT L. REV. 15 (1987); Note, *Eyewitness Identification Testimony and the Need for Cautionary Jury Instructions in Criminal Cases,* 60 WASH. U. L.Q. 1387 (1983); Annot., *Necessity of, and Prejudicial Effect of Omitting, Cautionary Instruction to Jury as to Reliability of, or Factors to be Considered in Evaluating, Eyewitness Identification Testimony — State Cases,* 23 A.L.R.4TH 1089 (1983).

38. In State v. Dyle, 899 S.W.2d 607 (Tenn. 1995), the Tennessee Supreme Court adopted a modified instruction, which must be given if eyewitness identification is a material issue and if requested by defense counsel.

39. *See* Gunning v. State, 347 Md. 332, 348, 701 A.2d 374, 382 (1997) ("[A]n identification instruction may be appropriate and necessary in certain instances, but the matter is addressed to the sound discretion of the trial judge").

40. Some courts also reject an instruction as an impermissible judicial comment on the evidence, a rule adopted in some state jurisdictions. *See* Conely v. State, 270 Ark. 886, 607 S.W.2d 328, 330 (1980).

41. 419 Mass. 815, 818, 647 N.E.2d 1168, 1171 (1995).

but the trial court had not abused its discretion in not giving the instruction in this case.[42]

§ 9-2(C). Admissibility of Expert Testimony.

The use of expert testimony to inform juries of the problems of eyewitness identifications is another possible approach.[43] Most courts, federal[44] and state,[45]

---

42. *See* State v. Cromedy, 158 N.J. 112, 132, 727 A.2d 457, 467 (1999) ("A cross-racial instruction should be given only when, as in the present case, identification is a critical issue in the case, and an eyewitness's cross-racial identification is not corroborated by other evidence giving it independent reliability").

43. *See generally* Brigham, *Disputed Eyewitness Identifications: Can Experts Help?*, THE CHAMPION 10 (June 1989); Cutler, Penrod & Dexler, *The Eyewitness, the Expert Psychologist, and the Jury*, 13 LAW & HUM. BEHAV. 311 (1989); Elliot, *Expert Testimony About Eyewitness Identification: A Critique*, 17 LAW & HUM. BEHAV. 423 (1993); Geiselman, *Providing Eyewitness Expert Testimony in Los Angeles*, 3 EXPERT EVIDENCE 9 (1994) (describing L.A. court panel of eyewitness identification experts); Gross, *Loss of Innocence: Eyewitness Identifications and Proof of Guilt*, 16 J. LEGAL STUD. 395 (1987); Handberg, *Expert Testimony on Eyewitness Identification: A New Pair of Glasses for the Jury*, 32 AM. CRIM. L. REV. 1013 (1995); Holt, *Expert Testimony on Eyewitness Identification: Invading the Province of the Jury?*, 26 ARIZ. L. REV. 399 (1984); Klingsberg, *The Admissibility of Eyewitness Expert Testimony*, 25 CRIM. L. BULL. 219 (1989); Loftus & Schneider, *"Behold With Strange Surprise": Judicial Reactions to Expert Testimony Concerning Eyewitness Reliability*, 56 U. MO. K.C. L. REV. 1 (1987); Murphy, *An Evaluation of the Arguments Against the Use of Expert Testimony on Eyewitness Identification*, 8 U. BRIDGEPORT L. REV. 21 (1987); Sanders, *Expert Witnesses in Eyewitness Facial Identification Cases*, 17 TEX. TECH. L. REV. 1409 (1986); Westling, *The Case for Expert Witness Assistance to the Jury in Eyewitness Identification Cases*, 71 OR. L. REV. 93 (1992); Note, *Did Your Eyes Deceive You? Expert Psychological Testimony on the Unreliability of Eyewitness Identification*, 29 STAN. L. REV. 969 (1977); Comment, *Expert Testimony on Eyewitness Identification: The Constitution Says, "Let the Expert Speak,"* 56 TENN. L. REV. 735 (1989); Note, *Admission of Expert Testimony on Eyewitness Identification*, 73 CALIF. L. REV. 1402 (1985).

44. *E.g.*, United States v. Larkin, 978 F.2d 964, 971 (7th Cir. 1992) (The hazards of eyewitness identifications "are well within the ken of most lay jurors"), *cert. denied*, 507 U.S. 935 (1993); United States v. Curry, 977 F.2d 1042, 1051-52 (7th Cir. 1992) (not error to exclude testimony of Dr. Loftus concerning six aspects of identification), *cert. denied*, 507 U.S. 947 (1993); United States v. Holloway, 971 F.2d 675, 679 (11th Cir. 1992) ("The established rule of this circuit is that such testimony is not admissible"), *cert. denied*, 507 U.S. 962 (1993); United States v. Hudson, 884 F.2d 1016, 1023-24 (7th Cir. 1989), *cert. denied*, 496 U.S. 939 (1990); United States v. Christophe, 833 F.2d 1296, 1298-1300 (9th Cir. 1987); United States v. Blade, 811 F.2d 461, 464-65 (8th Cir. 1987), *cert. denied*, 484 U.S. 839 (1987); United States v. Langford, 802 F.2d 1176, 1179-80 (9th Cir. 1986), *cert. denied*, 483 U.S. 1008 (1987); United States v. Poole, 794 F.2d 462, 468 (9th Cir.), *opinion amended on other issues*, 806 F.2d 853 (9th Cir. 1986); United States v. Benitez, 741 F.2d 1312, 1315 (11th Cir. 1984), *cert. denied*, 471 U.S. 1137 (1985); United States v. Purham, 725 F.2d 450, 454 (8th Cir. 1984); United States v. Thevis, 665 F.2d 616, 641 (5th Cir.), *cert. denied*, 459 U.S. 825 (1982); United States v. Fosher, 590 F.2d 381, 383 (1st Cir. 1979); United States v. Brown, 540 F.2d 1048, 1054 (10th Cir. 1976), *cert. denied*, 429 U.S. 1100 (1977); United States v. Brown, 501 F.2d 146, 150 (9th Cir. 1974), *rev'd on other grounds sub nom.* United States v. Nobles, 422 U.S. 225 (1975); United States v. Amaral, 488 F.2d 1148, 1153 (9th Cir. 1973); United

have upheld a trial court's decision to exclude such testimony. As discussed later, this is true, for the most part, even after the *Daubert* decision. Courts offer various rationales to support this result.[46] First, some courts hold that expert testimony on this subject is unnecessary or at least not helpful because the jury is capable of evaluating deficiencies in eyewitness testimony. According to these courts, "effective cross-examination is adequate to reveal any inconsistencies or deficiencies in the eye-witness testimony."[47] Second, other courts question the scientific basis for such testimony. One court, for example, found that the work in the field "still remains inadequate to justify its admission into evidence."[48] Third, still other courts believe that this type of expert testimony "invade[s] the province of the jury."[49] Fourth, there is also concern that such testimony would entail a time-consuming "battle of experts" that may confuse the jury.[50] None of

---

States v. Nguyen, 793 F. Supp. 497 (D.N.J. 1992) (extensive discussion of issue); United States v. Dodson, 16 M.J. 921, 930 (N.C.M.R. 1983); United States v. Hicks, 7 M.J. 561, 566 (A.C.M.R. 1979). *See also* Annot., *Admissibility, at Criminal Prosecution, of Expert Testimony on Reliability of Eyewitness Testimony*, 46 A.L.R.4TH 1047 (1986).

45. *E.g.*, Utley v. State, 308 Ark. 622, 625, 826 S.W.2d 268, 271 (1992); Perry v. State, 277 Ark. 357, 370-71, 642 S.W.2d 865, 872 (1982); State v. Kemp, 199 Conn. 473, 474-79, 507 A.2d 1387, 1387-90 (1986); Dyas v. United States, 376 A.2d 827, 831-32 (D.C.), *cert. denied,* 434 U.S. 973 (1977); Johnson v. State, 438 So. 2d 774, 777 (Fla. 1983), *cert. denied,* 465 U.S. 1051 (1984); State v. Hoisington, 104 Idaho 153, 165, 657 P.2d 17, 29 (1983); People v. Dixon, 87 Ill. App. 3d 814, 818, 410 N.E.2d 252, 256 (1980); State v. Galloway, 275 N.W.2d 736, 741-42 (Iowa 1979); State v. Wheaton, 240 Kan. 345, 347-53, 729 P.2d 1183, 1184-88 (1986); State v. Warren, 230 Kan. 385, 395, 635 P.2d 1236, 1243 (1981); State v. Stucke, 419 So. 2d 939, 944-45 (La. 1982); State v. Rich, 549 A.2d 742, 743 (Me. 1988); State v. Fernald, 397 A.2d 194, 197 (Me. 1979); Commonwealth v. Francis, 390 Mass. 89, 95-101, 453 N.E.2d 1204, 1210 (1983); State v. Helterbridle, 301 N.W.2d 545, 547 (Minn. 1980); State v. Lawhorn, 762 S.W.2d 820, 821-23 (Mo. 1988); Porter v. State, 94 Nev. 142, 147-48, 576 P.2d 275, 278-79 (1978); People v. Gibbs, 157 A.D.2d 799, 799, 550 N.Y.S.2d 400, 400-01 (1990); State v. Porraro, 121 R.I. 882, 892-93, 404 A.2d 465, 471 (1979); State v. Ward, 712 S.W.2d 485, 487 (Tenn. Crim. App. 1986); State v. Wooden, 658 S.W.2d 553, 556-57 (Tenn. Crim. App. 1983); Pierce v. State, 777 S.W.2d 399, 415-16 (Tex. Crim. App. 1989), *cert. denied,* 496 U.S. 912 (1990); State v. Onorato, 142 Vt. 99, 104-05, 453 A.2d 393, 395-96 (1982); Rodriquez v. Commonwealth, 20 Va. App. 122, 128, 455 S.E.2d 724, 727 (1995) ("We adopt the majority approach that the decision whether to allow expert testimony concerning an eyewitness identification is a decision left to the sound discretion of the trial court"); Hampton v. State, 92 Wis. 2d 450, 461, 285 N.W.2d 868, 873 (1979).

46. At one time, United States v. Amaral, 488 F.2d 1148 (9th Cir. 1973), was considered the leading case on the subject. *See also* United States v. Christophe, 833 F.2d 1296, 1297 (9th Cir. 1987) ("Despite additional psychological studies on this subject since 1973, ... this testimony is still properly excluded if it does not meet the four criteria listed in *Amaral*...").

47. United States v. Amaral, 488 F.2d 1148, 1153 (9th Cir. 1973).

48. United States v. Watson, 587 F.2d 365, 369 (7th Cir. 1978), *cert. denied,* 439 U.S. 1132 (1979).

49. United States v. Brown, 501 F.2d 146, 150 (9th Cir. 1974), *rev'd on other grounds sub nom.,* United States v. Nobles, 422 U.S. 225 (1975).

50. United States v. Fosher, 590 F.2d 381, 384 (1st Cir. 1979).

these arguments is convincing, especially in light of the numerous documented accounts of misidentifications.

Several courts, however, adopted a more receptive attitude to expert testimony concerning the problems of eyewitness identifications. These courts questioned the principal obstacle to admissibility — the view that eyewitness identification problems are readily understood by juries, and therefore expert testimony is neither necessary nor helpful.

In *State v. Chapple*[51] the Arizona Supreme Court became the first appellate court to rule that expert testimony should be admitted in some cases. The trial court had refused to permit Dr. Loftus to testify about the "forgetting curve," the effect of stress upon perception, the problem of unconscious transfer, assimilation of post-event information, and the relationship between confidence and accuracy. On appeal, the court ruled that the trial court had abused its discretion, concluding that "[w]e cannot assume that the average juror would be aware of the variables concerning identification and memory about which Dr. Loftus was qualified to testify."[52]

Similarly, in *People v. McDonald*[53] the California Supreme Court held that "although jurors may not be totally unaware of the ... psychological factors bearing on eyewitness identification, the body of information now available on these matters is 'sufficiently beyond common experience' that in appropriate cases expert opinion thereon could at least 'assist the trier of fact.'"[54] In *People v. Sanders,*[55] the court upheld a trial court's decision to exclude expert testimony on this topic. The court did not retreat from *McDonald* but ruled that the trial court had not abused its discretion. "Although eyewitness testimony was a key element

---

51. 135 Ariz. 281, 660 P.2d 1208 (1983).

52. *Id.* at 294, 660 P.2d at 1220-21. *See also* State v. McCutcheon, 162 Ariz. 54, 56-58, 781 P.2d 31, 33-35 (1989) (distinguishing *Chapple*); State v. Poland, 144 Ariz. 388, 388-89, 698 P.2d 183, 193-94 (1985) (*Chapple* is the exception rather than the rule).

53. 37 Cal. 3d 351, 690 P.2d 709, 208 Cal. Rptr. 236 (1984).

54. *Id.* at 369, 690 P.2d at 721, 208 Cal. Rptr. at 248. *See also* People v. Sanders, 51 Cal. 3d 471, 503-06, 797 P.2d 561, 578-80, 273 Cal. Rptr. 537, 554-56 (1990) (exclusion of expert testimony on eyewitness identification requires reversal only if it results in a miscarriage of justice), *cert. denied,* 500 U.S. 948 (1991); People v. Walker, 47 Cal. 3d 605, 627-28, 765 P.2d 70, 81-82, 253 Cal. Rptr. 863, 875 (1988) (exclusion of expert testimony not an abuse of discretion).

In *McDonald* the Court also commented: "When an eyewitness identification of the defendant is a key element of the prosecution's case but is not substantially corroborated by evidence giving it independent reliability, and the defendant offers qualified expert testimony on specific psychological factors shown by the record that could have affected the accuracy of the identification but are not likely to be fully known to or understood by the jury, it will ordinarily be error to exclude that testimony." 37 Cal.3d at 377, 690 P.2d at 727, 208 Cal. Rptr. at 254. *See also* People v. Sandoval, 30 Cal. App. 4th 1288, 36 Cal. Rptr. 2d 646, 651 (1994) (not an abuse of discretion to exclude testimony in this case).

55. 11 Cal. 4th 475, 905 P.2d 420, 46 Cal. Rptr. 2d 751 (1995), *cert. denied,* 519 U.S. 838 (1996).

of the prosecution's case, here, unlike *McDonald*, eyewitness testimony was not the only evidence linking the defendant to the crime. The eyewitness identification was corroborated by other independent evidence of the crime and the conspiracy leading to it."[56]

United States v. Downing[57] is the leading federal case. As had the Arizona and California Supreme Courts, the Third Circuit found that expert testimony may enlighten the jury about the various factors that affect eyewitness testimony:

> The proffer stated that the expert would testify concerning: (1) the "forgetting curve," i.e., the fact that memory does not diminish at a uniform rate; (2) the fact that, contrary to common understanding, stress causes inaccuracy of perception and distorts one's subsequent recall; (3) the "assimilation factor," which indicates that witnesses frequently incorporate into their identifications inaccurate information gathered after the event and confused with the event; (4) the "feedback factor," which indicates that where identification witnesses discuss the case with each other they can unconsciously reinforce their individual identifications; and (5) the fact that studies demonstrate the absence of a relationship between the confidence a witness has in his or her identification and the actual accuracy of the identification. Each of these "variables" goes beyond what an average juror might know as a matter of common knowledge, and indeed some of them directly contradict "common sense."[58]

In a subsequent case, *United States v. Stevens,*[59] the Third Circuit again examined this issue. The trial court had permitted the expert to testify about cross-racial identifications, weapon focus, and stress but had barred testimony on other factors. The Third Circuit ruled that the trial court should not have excluded testimony about the relationship between confidence and accuracy. The expert would have testified that the relationship was "fairly weak"[60] and "far lower than people probably would expect."[61]

---

56. *Id.* at 509, 905 P.2d at 420, 46 Cal. Rptr. 2d at 766.

57. 753 F.2d 1224 (3d Cir. 1985).

58. *Id.* at 1230-31. On remand, the trial court held that the exclusion of expert testimony under the facts of that case was proper. United States v. Downing, 609 F. Supp. 748 (E.D. Pa.), *aff'd,* 780 F.2d 1017 (3d Cir. 1985).

59. 935 F.2d 1380 (3d Cir. 1991).

60. *Id.* at 1400.

61. *Id.* at 1401. *See also* United States v. Dowling, 855 F.2d 114 (3d Cir. 1988), *aff'd on other grounds,* 493 U.S. 342 (1990); United States v. Sebetich, 776 F.2d 412, 418-19 (3d Cir. 1985), *cert. denied,* 484 U.S. 1017 (1988).

Other courts, both federal[62] and state,[63] have also indicated that expert testimony may be admitted. The exclusion of such expert testimony, however, is not a constitutional violation.[64]

Post-Daubert Cases

Whether the *Daubert* decision will alter the judicial response to this type of testimony is unclear.[65] In *United States v. Amador-Galvan*,[66] the Ninth Circuit ruled that eyewitness identification evidence had to be evaluated under *Daubert*[67] and remanded the case for this evaluation. In *United States v. Rincon*,[68] the same court held that the exclusion of expert testimony was not an abuse of discretion. The court, however, added: "Our conclusion does not preclude the admission of such testimony when the proffering party satisfies the standard established in *Daubert* by showing that the expert opinion is based upon 'scientific knowledge' which is both reliable and helpful...."[69] In *United States v. Brien*,[70] the First

---

62. *E.g.*, United States v. Harris, 995 F.2d 532, 535 (4th Cir. 1993) ("The narrow circumstances held sufficient to support the introduction of expert testimony have varied but have included such problems as cross-racial identification, identification after a long delay, identification after observation under stress, and psychological phenomena as the feedback factor and unconscious transference"); United States v. Alexander, 816 F.2d 164, 167-68 (5th Cir. 1987); United States v. Moore, 786 F.2d 1308, 1312-13 (5th Cir. 1986); United States v. Smith, 736 F.2d 1103, 1105-07 (6th Cir.), *cert. denied*, 469 U.S. 868 (1984).

63. *E.g.*, *Ex parte* Williams, 594 So. 2d 1225, 1227 (Ala. 1992) ("[W]e hold that expert testimony on the subject of human memory can be introduced into evidence in cases turning on an eyewitness identification"); Campbell v. People, 814 P.2d 1, 7 (Colo. 1991); People v. Enis, 139 Ill. 3d 264, 288-89, 564 N.E.2d 1155, 1164-65 (1990); People v. Beckford, 141 Misc. 2d 71, 72-77, 532 N.Y.S.2d 462, 462-65 (Crim. Term 1988); People v. Lewis, 137 Misc. 2d 84, 85-86, 520 N.Y.S.2d 125, 126-27 (Co. Ct. 1987); People v. Brooks, 128 Misc. 2d 608, 609-21, 490 N.Y.S.2d 692, 694-702 (Co. Ct. 1985); State v. Buell, 22 Ohio St. 3d 124, 129-33, 489 N.E.2d 795, 801-04, *cert. denied*, 489 U.S. 871 (1986); State v. Whaley, 305 S.C. 138, 406 S.E.2d 369, 371-72 (1991); Nations v. State, 944 S.W.2d 795, 799 (Tex. App. 1997) (Expert "would testify that when given a chance to respond more than once to an inquiry about identification, the respondent's first response ('that could be him') is probably the most accurate, while subsequent responses ('I'm sure it was him') could be influenced by the respondent's desire for certainty or by an unconscious desire to give her questioners the answer they want to hear"); State v. Moon, 45 Wash. App. 692, 697-700, 726 P.2d 1263, 1265-68 (1986); State v. Taylor, 50 Wash. App. 481, 488-89, 749 P.2d 181, 183-85 (1988).

64. *E.g.*, Moore v. Tate, 882 F.2d 1107, 1109-11 (6th Cir. 1989); Rodriguez v. Wainwright, 740 F.2d 884, 885 (11th Cir. 1984), *cert. denied*, 469 U.S. 1113 (1985).

65. For a discussion of *Daubert*, *see* Chapter 1. *See generally* Penrod, Solomon, Fulero & Cutler, *Expert Psychological Testimony on Eyewitness Reliability Before and After Daubert: The State of the Law and the Science*, 13 BEHAV. SCI. & LAW 229 (1995).

66. 9 F.3d 1414, 1417-18 (9th Cir. 1993).

67. For a discussion of *Daubert*, *see* § 1-7 *supra*.

68. 28 F.3d 921 (9th Cir. 1994), *cert. denied*, 513 U.S. 1029 (1994).

69. *Id.* at 926.

Circuit acknowledged that "several circuits have suggested that such evidence warrants a more hospitable reception. There is more expert literature on the subject, more experts pressing to testify, and possibly more skepticism about the reliability of eyewitnesses.... It may be that a door once largely shut is now somewhat ajar. We are unwilling to adopt a blanket rule...."[71] The court went on to hold that a sufficient basis had not been laid to satisfy the *Daubert* standard in this case. The Eleventh Circuit bluntly rejected the notion that the landscape had been changed: "[I]t is as true after *Daubert* as it was before that a district court does not abuse its discretion in excluding such testimony."[72] Other federal courts have also upheld the exclusion of eyewitness identification testimony by an expert witness.[73]

In contrast, the district court in *United States v. Norwood*[74] ruled that the defense expert could testify on a number of issues: (1) cross-racial identifications, (2) weapon focus, (3) stress, (4) the forgetting curve, (5) "relation back" phenomenon, (6) confidence-accuracy correlation, (7) suggestiveness of pre-trial identification procedures, and (8) exposure duration.

Research Findings

Many researchers believe that expert testimony would assist jurors in evaluating eyewitness testimony. For example, Brigham and Bothwell (1983) concluded that

> the present data refute the claim that expert psychological testimony on eyewitness identifications would not tell the jury members anything they do not already know. Not only do jury members overestimate the accuracy of

---

70. 59 F.3d 274 (1st Cir.), *cert. denied*, 516 U.S. 953 (1995).

71. *Id.* at 277.

72. United States v. Smith, 122 F.3d 1355, 1359 (11th Cir.), *cert. denied*, 118 S. Ct. 614 (1997).

73. *E.g.*, United States v. Hall, 165 F.3d 1095, 1104 (7th Cir.) ("This Court has a long line of cases which reflect our disfavor of expert testimony on the reliability of eyewitness identification"), *cert. denied,* 119 S. Ct. 2381 (1999); United States v. Smith, 156 F.3d 1046, 1053-54 (10th Cir. 1998) ("[E]xpert testimony on eyewitness identification may properly be admitted under *Daubert* in certain circumstances .... In this admittedly close case, we hold only that the district court did not abuse its discretion in excluding the testimony under the circumstances"), *cert. denied,* 119 S. Ct. 844 (1999); United States v. Hicks, 103 F.3d 837, 847 (9th Cir. 1996), *cert. denied*, 520 U.S. 1193 (1997); United States v. Kime, 99 F.3d 870, 883-85 (8th Cir. 1996), *cert. denied*, 519 U.S. 1141 (1997); United States v. Ginn, 87 F.3d 367, 370 (9th Cir. 1996); United States v. Jackson, 50 F.3d 1335, 1340 (5th Cir. 1995) ("[W]hether to admit expert testimony on eyewitness reliability 'is squarely within the discretion of the trial judge'"); United States v. Burrous, 934 F. Supp. 525 (E.D.N.Y. 1996).

74. 939 F. Supp. 1132 (D.N.J. 1996). *See also* United States v. Jordan, 924 F. Supp. 443 (W.D.N.Y. 1996) (expert testimony admissible in bank robbery case based largely on the identification by teller who had a short time to observe and did not identify the accused until 47 days after the robbery).

> eyewitness identifications in target-present lineups, they also appear unaware, to some extent, of the sources of error associated with this type of evidence.[75]

Subsequently, Penrod and Cutler (1989) concluded that the "studies indicate that expert psychological testimony can improve jury decisionmaking by assisting jurors in the task of appropriately evaluating eyewitness evidence, and that the improvements in juror sensitivity can be secured without increasing juror skepticism."[76] In particular, they concluded that jurors "were insensitive to the effects of disguise, weapon presence, retention interval, suggestive lineup instructions, and procedures used for constructing and carrying out the lineup."[77] Moreover, jurors "gave disproportionate weight to the confidence of the witness."[78]

This view, however, is not universally accepted. McCloskey and Egeth (1983) have written that "the available evidence fails to demonstrate that expert psychological testimony will routinely improve juror's ability to evaluate eyewitness testimony."[79] Moreover, they believe that the proponents fail "to take account of the possibility that expert testimony about eyewitness research may add little to jurors' knowledge or, more importantly, of the possibility that expert testimony may have detrimental effects (*e.g.*, by making jurors overly skeptical of eyewitnesses)."[80]

---

75. Brigham & Bothwell, *The Ability of Prospective Jurors to Estimate the Accuracy of Eyewitness Identifications*, 7 LAW & HUM. BEHAV. 19, 29 (1983).

76. Penrod & Cutler, *Eyewitness Expert Testimony and Jury Decisionmaking*, 52 LAW & CONTEMP. PROBS. 43, 83 (Autumn 1989).

77. *Id.* at 62.

78. *Id. See also* Lindsay, MacDonald & McGarry, *Perspective on the Role of the Eyewitness Expert*, 8 BEHAV. SCI. & LAW 457, 463 (1990) ("The performance of the public and prosecutors in the Knowledge of Eyewitness Behavior test suggest that expert testimony on many issues is required to avoid errors; that is, eyewitness performance still is not a matter of common sense").

79. McCloskey & Egeth, *Eyewitness Identification: What Can a Psychologist Tell a Jury?*, 38 AM. PSYCHOLOGIST 550, 558 (1983). *See also* McCloskey, Egeth & McKenna, *The Experimental Psychologist in Court: The Ethics of Expert Testimony*, 10 LAW & HUM. BEHAV. 1 (1986); Egeth & McCloskey, *Expert Testimony About Eyewitness Behavior: Is It Safe and Effective?*, *in* EYEWITNESS TESTIMONY: PSYCHOLOGICAL PERSPECTIVES 283 (G. Wells & E. Loftus eds. 1984).

80. McCloskey & Egeth, *A Time to Speak, or a Time to Keep Silence?*, 38 AM. PSYCHOLOGIST 573, 575 (1983). *See also* Kassin, Ellsworth & Smith, *Déjà vu All Over Again: Elliott's Critique of Eyewitness Experts*, 18 LAW & HUMAN BEHAV. 203 (1994) (criticizing Elliott's attack on the use of psychological experts on eyewitness identification); Elliott, *Expert Testimony About Eyewitness Identification: A Critique*, 17 LAW & HUM. BEHAV. 423 (1993).

§ 9-3. Battered Woman Syndrome.

The Battered Woman Syndrome (BWS) describes a pattern of violence inflicted on a woman by her mate. In 1979 Dr. Lenore Walker, one of the principal researchers in this field, published her seminal text, *The Battered Woman*. She described a battered woman as follows:

> A battered woman is a woman who is repeatedly subjected to any forceful physical or psychological behavior by a man in order to coerce her to do something he wants her to do without any concern for her rights. Battered women include wives or women in any form of intimate relationships with men. Furthermore, in order to be classified as a battered woman, the couple must go through the battering cycle at least twice. Any woman may find herself in an abusive relationship with a man once. If it occurs a second time, and she remains in the situation, she is defined as a battered woman.[81]

Dr. Walker's initial findings were based on a nonrandom sample of 110 battered women who were mostly white and middle-class. A later study (1984) involved a more representative sample of 435 women. In her second book, *The Battered Woman Syndrome*, Walker defined the syndrome by incidents of violence: "A battered woman is a woman ... who is or has been in an intimate relationship with a man who repeatedly subjects or subjected her to forceful physical and/or psychological abuse."[82] Two acute battering incidents qualified as "repeated" incidents.

Cycle of Violence

According to Dr. Walker, the violence associated with this type of relationship is neither constant nor random. Instead, it follows a pattern. Dr. Walker identified a three-stage cycle of violence.[83] The first stage is the "tension building" phase, during which small abusive episodes occur. These episodes gradually escalate over a period of time. The tension continues to build until the second stage — the acute battering phase — erupts. During this phase, in which most injuries occur, the battering is out of control. Psychological abuse in the form of threats of future harm is also prevalent. The third phase is a calm, loving period during which the batterer is contrite, seeks forgiveness, and promises to refrain from future violence. This phase provides a positive reinforcement for the woman to continue

---

81. L. WALKER, THE BATTERED WOMAN xv (1979).

82. L. WALKER, THE BATTERED WOMAN SYNDROME 203 (1984). *See also* L. WALKER, TERRIFYING LOVE: WHY BATTERED WOMEN KILL AND HOW SOCIETY RESPONDS (1989).

83. L. WALKER, THE BATTERED WOMAN, *supra* note 68, at 55-70.

the relationship in the hope that the violent behavior will not recur. The cycle then repeats itself.

In addition, the batterer is often extremely jealous of the spouse's time and attention, a factor that further isolates her from friends and outside support.[84] Moreover, numerous obstacles, both psychological and economic, often prevent the battered spouse from leaving her mate. Walker used Martin Seligman's theory of "learned helplessness" to explain the woman's condition.[85]

In sum, the battered woman feels "trapped in a deadly situation."[86] Caught in this cycle, she sometimes strikes back and kills.

Criticism

The BWS is not without its critics. In 1984 Professor Faigman questioned the validity of the underlying research:

> The prevailing theories of battered woman syndrome have little evidentiary value in self-defense cases. The work of Lenore Walker, the leading researcher on battered woman syndrome, is unsound and largely irrelevant to the central issues in such cases. The Walker cycle theory suffers from significant methodological and interpretative flaws that render it incapable of explaining why an abused woman strikes out at her mate when she does. Similarly, Walker's application of learned helplessness to the situation of battered women does not account for the actual behavior of many women who remain in battering relationships.[87]

A decade later, he and a colleague would write: "The syndrome, first proposed in the 1970's and based on the clinical observations of a single researcher, has yet to be corroborated by serious and rigorous empirical work.... Given the lack of a scientific basis and its failure to achieve specific political and policy goals, the battered woman syndrome can be expected to soon pass from the legal scene."[88]

---

84. Note, *Self-Defense: Battered Woman Syndrome on Trial*, 20 CAL. W. L. REV. 485, 487 (1984).

85. L. WALKER, THE BATTERED WOMAN, *supra* note 81, at 43.

86. Walker, Thyfault & Browne, *Beyond the Juror's Ken: Battered Women*, 7 VT.L. REV. 1, 12 (1982).

87. Faigman, *The Battered Woman Syndrome and Self-Defense: A Legal and Empirical Dissent*, 72 VA. L. REV. 619, 647 (1986).

88. Faigman & Wright, *Battered Woman Syndrome in the Age of Science*, 39 ARIZ. L. REV. 67, 114 (1997). They also write that the only research on BWS is seriously flawed. The experiments were designed to prove/confirm set ideas, rather than to objectively test a given hypothesis. Further, based on the research done, "[i]t is not obvious that the psychological profile of most battered women generalizes to the small number of battered women who kill." *Id.* at 79. "[L]earned helplessness as a psychological construct, is fundamentally at odds with a situation in which a woman has exercised the degree of control reflected in the act of self defense, [killing]." *Id.* at 82.

Another critic wrote: "Reduced to its essence, battered-woman syndrome is not a physicians' diagnosis but an advocate's invention. It means: Blame the deceased."[89]

A 1992 review of the research literature indicated that BWS had attained, to a large extent, scientific acceptance. Citing a survey involving experts in the field,[90] Schuller and Vidmar concluded:

> The degree of expert consensus shown in the Dodge and Greene survey tends to suggest that the scientific literature bearing on a battered woman's circumstances and situation is sound. There are, however, some aspects of the testimony — the cycle pattern of violence and the development of learned helplessness — that are not universal across battering relationships.[91]

The widespread legal acceptance of BWS is a product of the work of feminist scholars, who have attacked the traditional law of self-defense as based upon a male-oriented perspective. Such scholarship, however, also recognizes that BWS may perpetuate stereotypes: "Dueling stereotypes are likely to become the focus of the trial process. While the prosecution attempts to discredit the defendant for not living up to the standard of a 'good wom[a]n,' the defense counters with an equally distorted portrayal of the defendant as ultra-feminine: passive, helpless victim."[92] Another author suggested that most proposals for law reform concerning this subject are based on two assumptions, both of which are wrong. The first assumption is that a majority of cases involve nonconfrontational

---

89. Caplan, *Battered Wives, Battered Justice*, NAT'L REV. 49, 40 (Feb. 1991).

90. Dodge & Greene, *Jurors and Expert Conceptions of Battered Women*, 6 VICTIMS & VIOLENCE 271 (1991) (eighteen-item survey of forty-five professionals who have published in the field).

91. Schuller & Vidmar, *Battered Woman Syndrome Evidence in the Courtroom: A Review of the Literature*, 16 LAW & HUM. BEHAV. 273, 281 (1992). In 1992 Congress passed the Battered Women's Testimony Act of 1992, P.L. 102-527, which authorizes the State Justice Institute to conduct research concerning the admissibility of BWS testimony.

92. Jenkins & Davidson, *Battered Women in the Criminal Justice System: An Analysis of Gender Stereotypes*, 8 BEHAV. SCI. & LAW 161, 169 (1990). *See also* Crocker, *The Meaning of Equality for Battered Women Who Kill Men in Self-Defense*, 8 HARV. WOMEN'S L.J. 121, 150 (1985) ("She is held liable for having lived as a woman, and she is held responsible for having reacted, even if only once, as a man"); Schneider, *Describing and Changing Women's Self-Defense Work and the Problem of Expert Testimony on Battering*, 9 WOMEN'S RIGHTS L. REP. 195, 216-17 (1986) ("Yet, to the degree that the explanation is perceived to focus on her suffering from a 'syndrome,' a term which suggests a loss of control and passivity, the testimony seems to be inconsistent with the notion of reasonableness"). *See also* Mahoney, *Legal Images of Battered Women: Redefining the Issue of Separation*, 90 MICH. L. REV. 1, 4 (1991) ("Yet the expert testimony on battered woman syndrome and learned helplessness can interact with and perpetuate existing oppressive stereotypes of battered women").

situations (*e.g.*, spouse asleep or hired killer); however, a survey of the cases reveals that approximately 75% of the cases involve confrontations.[93] The second assumption is that traditional self-defense law excluded a female perspective. The author argues that while it is true that self-defense law developed in cases with male defendants, it is not true that the law ignored "the context of battered women's actions."[94]

Several studies on the impact of BWS evidence on juries have been reported.[95]

§ 9-3(A). Admissibility: Self-defense.

The admissibility of expert testimony on BWS has produced much commentary[96] and initially divided the courts. It was first introduced in the 1979

---

93. Maguigan, *Battered Women and Self-Defense: Myths and Misconceptions in Current Reform Proposals*, 140 U. PA. L. REV. 379, 397 (1991) (surveying appellate decisions).

94. *Id.* at 405.

95. *See* Kasian, Spanos, Terrance & Peebles, *Battered Women Who Kill: Jury Simulation and Legal Defenses*, 17 LAW & HUM. BEHAV. 289 (1993); Schuller & Cripps, *Expert Evidence Pertaining to Battered Women: The Impact of Gender of Expert and Timing of Testimony*, 22 LAW & HUMAN BEHAV.17, 28 (1998) ("[T]he pattern of results identified across the various measures suggests that the presentation of the female expert compared to her male counterpart was more favorable to the defendant's case, and that this was especially so when the testimony was presented early and when the evaluators were male as opposed to female"); Schuller, *The Impact of Battered Woman Syndrome Evidence on Jury Decision Processes*, 16 LAW & HUM. BEHAV. 597 (1992).

96. *See generally* REPRESENTING BATTERED WOMEN WHO KILL (S. Johann & I. Osanka eds. 1989); C. EWING, BATTERED WOMEN WHO KILL (1987); C. GILLESPIE, JUSTIFIABLE HOMICIDE: BATTERED WOMEN, SELF-DEFENSE, AND THE LAW (1989); Ammons, *Discretionary Justice: A Legal and Policy Analysis of a Governor's Use of the Clemency Power in the Cases of Incarcerated Battered Women*, 3 J. LAW & POLICY 1 (1994); Byrd, *Till Death Do Us Part: A Comparative Law Approach to Justifying Lethal Self-Defense By Battered Women*, 1991 DUKE J. COMP. & INT'L L. 169; Crocker, *The Meaning of Equality For Battered Women Who Kill Men in Self-Defense*, 8 HARV. WOMEN'S L.J. 121 (1985); Dutton & Goodman, *Posttraumatic Stress Disorder Among Battered Women: Analysis of Legal Implications*, 12 BEHAV. SCI. & LAW 215 (1994); Kinports, *Defending Battered Women's Self-Defense Claims*, 67 OR. L. REV. 393 (1988); Mather, *The Skeleton in the Closet: The Battered Woman Syndrome, Self-Defense, and Expert Testimony*, 39 MERCER L. REV. 545 (1988); Rosen, *The Excuse of Self-Defense: Correcting a Historical Accident on Behalf of Battered Women Who Kill*, 36 AM. U. L. REV. 11 (1986); Rosen, *On Self-Defense, Imminence, and Women Who Kill Their Batterers*, 71 N.C. L. REV. 371 (1993); Schopp, Sturgis & Sullivan, *Battered Woman Syndrome, Expert Testimony, and the Distinction Between Justification & Excuse*, 1994 U. ILL. L. REV. 45; Schulhofer, *The Feminist Challenge in Criminal Law*, 143 U. PA. L. REV. 2151 (1995); Schuller & Hastings, *Trials of Battered Women Who Kill: The Impact of Alternative Forms of Expert Evidence*, 20 LAW & HUM. BEHAV. 167 (1996); Tinsley, *Criminal Law: The Battered Woman Defense*, 34 AM. JUR. PROOF OF FACTS 2D 1 (1983); Vidmar & Schuller, *Juries and Expert Evidence: Social Framework Testimony*, 52 LAW & CONTEMP. PROBS. 133, 148-55 (Autumn 1989); Lenore Walker, *Understanding Battered Woman Syndrome*, 31 TRIAL 30 (Feb. 1995); Comment, *The Defense of Battered Women Who Kill*, 135 U. PA. L. REV. 427 (1987).

case of *Ibn-Tamas v. United States.*[97] Several different evidentiary issues are raised.

Relevancy

The first issue concerns the relevancy of BWS evidence. Typically, the evidence is offered in support of a self-defense claim in a homicide prosecution. A few courts have declared that BWS evidence is simply irrelevant to a self-defense claim.[98] This seems wrong. While being a battered woman by itself is no defense to homicide, the syndrome may assist a jury in understanding two elements of a self-defense claim: (1) the defendant's subjective fear of serious injury or death and (2) the reasonableness of that belief.[99] Similarly, this evidence also would be admissible on the subjective fear element in a jurisdiction that recognized "imperfect self-defense," which reduces murder to voluntary manslaughter.[100]

Numerous courts have recognized the relevancy of BWS evidence for this purpose.[101] For example, the evidence may explain why a battered woman has

97. Ibn-Tamas v. United States, 407 A.2d 626, 634-35 (D.C. 1979), *appeal after remand,* 455 A.2d 893 (D.C. 1983).

98. *See* People v. White, 90 Ill. App. 3d 1067, 1072-73, 414 N.E.2d 196, 200-06 (1980); State v. Necaise, 466 So. 2d 660, 663-65 (La. App. 1985); State v. Thomas, 66 Ohio St. 2d 518, 521, 423 N.E.2d 137, 140 (1981).

99. *See* People v. Humphrey, 13 Cal. 4th 1073, 1076-77, 921 P.2d 1, 2, 56 Cal. Rptr. 2d 142 (1996) ("The trial court should have allowed the jury to consider [BWS] testimony in deciding the reasonableness as well as the existence of defendant's belief that killing was necessary"). *See generally* W. LAFAVE & A. SCOTT, CRIMINAL LAW § 53 (2d ed. 1984); 2 P. ROBINSON, CRIMINAL LAW DEFENSES § 132 (1984).

100. People v. Erickson, 57 Cal. App. 4th 1391, 1399, 67 Cal. Rptr. 2d 740 (1997) ("[B]attered women's syndrome evidence may be relevant to establish 'imperfect self-defense,' i.e., that the defendant actually believed in the need to defend against imminent death or serious bodily injury, but the belief was objectively unreasonable"); People v. Aris, 215 Cal. App. 3d 1178, 1199, 264 Cal. Rptr. 167, 181 (1989) (BWS evidence is relevant "to prove the honest belief requirement for both perfect and imperfect self-defense"). *See also* Note, *Partially Determined Imperfect Self-Defense: The Battered Wife Kills and Tells Why,* 34 STAN. L. REV. 615 (1982).

101. *E.g.,* People v. Aris, 215 Cal. App. 3d 1178, 1196-99, 264 Cal. Rptr. 167, 179-81 (1989); Terry v. State, 467 So. 2d 761, 763-64 (Fla. App. 1985); Hawthorne v. State, 408 So. 2d 801, 806-07 (Fla. App. 1982); State v. Hundley, 236 Kan. 461, 693 P.2d 475, 479 (1985); State v. Anaya, 438 A.2d 892, 894 (Me. 1981); Commonwealth v. Rodriquez, 418 Mass. 1, 7, 633 N.E.2d 1039, 1042 (1994) ("[W]here the claim of self-defense is in issue, and there is evidence of a pattern of abuse of the defendant by the victim, expert testimony on common patterns in abusive relationships and the typical emotional and behavioral responses of persons who are battered may be admissible"); State v. Kelly, 97 N.J. 178, 202-05, 478 A.2d 364, 375-77 (1984); People v. Torres, 488 N.Y.S.2d 358, 362 (N.Y. Sup. 1985); State v. Leidholm, 334 N.W.2d 811, 820 (N.D. 1983); State v. Riley, 201 W. Va. 708, 714, 500 S.E.2d 524, 530 (1997) ("[E]xpert testimony can be utilized to explain the psychological basis for the battered woman's syndrome and to offer an opinion that the defendant meets the requisite profile of the syndrome") (citing State v. Steele, 178

not left her mate. According to the New Jersey Supreme Court, "[o]nly by understanding these unique pressures that force battered women to remain with their mates, despite their long-standing and reasonable fear of severe bodily harm and the isolation that being a battered woman creates, can a battered woman's state of mind be accurately and fairly understood."[102] Another court admitted BWS evidence to help explain a battered woman's conduct after killing her mate.[103] The Georgia Supreme Court summed up the majority view as follows:

> [T]he battered person syndrome is not a separate defense, but ... evidence of battered person syndrome is relevant in a proper case as a component of justifiable homicide by self-defense.... [E]vidence that a defendant suffered from battered person syndrome is only another circumstance which, if believed by the jury, would authorize a finding that a reasonable person, who had experienced prior physical abuse such as was endured by the defendant, would reasonably believe that the use of force against the victim was necessary, even though that belief may have been, in fact, erroneous.[104]

The court also ruled that a special jury instruction in BWS cases is required.

W. Va. 330, 359 S.E.2d 558 (1987); State v. Richardson, 189 Wis. 2d 418, 525 N.W.2d 378, 382 (App. 1994) ("The confrontational nature of an incident where a battered woman kills her abuser might only become apparent when viewed in the context of a pattern of violent behavior rather than as an isolated incident"). *See also* May v. State, 460 So. 2d 778, 785 (Miss. 1984) ("[T]he battered wife syndrome has important informational and explanatory power ...").

102. State v. Kelly, 97 N.J. 178, 196, 478 A.2d 364, 372 (1984). *See also* State v. Hines, 303 N.J. Super. 311, 696 A.2d 780, 785-87 (A.D. 1997) (reversible error excluding expert testimony relating to post traumatic stress disorder (PTSD); expert's excluded "testimony was relevant to defendant's contention that even if the killing was not an act of self-defense, it constituted passion/provocation manslaughter rather than purposeful or knowing murder or reckless manslaughter"; "Dr. Hall further testified that the PTSD from which defendant was suffering when she killed her father was similar to 'Battered Woman's Syndrome' in that she acted in a way which was consistent with the belief 'that there was no way of escaping, that there was going to take tremendous force in order to stop someone from hurting her'"); State v. J.Q., 130 N.J. 554, 574, 617 A.2d 1196, 1206 (1993) ("[E]xpert scientific evidence concerning 'battered-woman's syndrome' does not aid a jury in determining whether a defendant had or had not behaved in a given manner on a particular occasion; rather, the evidence enables the jury to overcome common myths or misconceptions that a woman who had been the victim of battering would have surely left the batterer. Thus, the evidence helps the jury to understand the battered woman's state of mind"); Fielder v. State, 756 S.W.2d 309, 319 (Tex. Crim. App. 1988).

103. People v. Minnis, 118 Ill. App. 3d 345, 356-57, 455 N.E.2d 209, 218 (1983) (BWS "might extend to [explain] dismemberment" of husband after killing, a point which the prosecution legitimately exploited).

104. State v. Smith, 268 Ga. 196, 486 S.E.2d 819, 822 (1997). *See also* People v. Humphrey, 13 Cal. 4th 1073, 921 P.2d 1, 56 Cal. Rptr. 2d 142 (1996).

Beyond Jurors' Knowledge

A second issue is whether BWS evidence is a proper subject for expert testimony. The Ohio Supreme Court held that this subject is "within the understanding of the jury"[105] and thus inappropriate for expert testimony. Most courts disagree, finding that "a battering relationship embodies psychological and societal features that are not well understood by lay observers."[106] The research appears to support this conclusion; it "suggests that jurors are misinformed on some aspects of wife abuse and that some jurors are likely to be more misinformed than others. Nevertheless, the surveys have not found overwhelming endorsement of the 'myths' about abuse."[107]

Scientific Basis

A final issue relates to the scientific basis for BWS evidence. Some courts excluded expert testimony on this subject because its scientific validity had not been sufficiently established.[108] Rejecting this argument, other courts have concluded that a "sufficient scientific basis" has been established.[109] According to a federal district court, "[t]he general acceptance of expert testimony on the battered woman syndrome has been acknowledged by legal authorities as well as the scientific community."[110]

---

105. State v. Thomas, 66 Ohio St. 2d 518, 521, 423 N.E.2d 137, 140 (1981).

106. State v. Kelly, 97 N.J. 178, 209, 478 A.2d 364, 379 (1984). *Accord* Ibn-Tamas v. United States, 407 A.2d 626, 634-35 (D.C. 1979), *appeal after remand*, 455 A.2d 893 (D.C. 1983); Hawthorne v. State, 408 So. 2d 801, 806 (Fla. App.), *appeal dismissed,* 415 So. 2d 1361 (Fla. 1982); Smith v. State, 247 Ga. 612, 618-19, 277 S.E.2d 678, 683 (1981); People v. Torres, 128 Misc. 2d 129, 134, 488 N.Y.S.2d 358, 362 (Sup. Ct. 1985); State v. Hill, 287 S.C. 398, 399, 339 S.E.2d 121, 122 (1986); State v. Allery, 101 Wash. 2d 591, 597, 682 P.2d 312, 316 (1984).

107. Schuller & Vidmar, *Battered Woman Syndrome Evidence in the Courtroom: A Review of the Literature*, 16 LAW & HUM. BEHAV. 273, 283 (1992).

108. Ibn-Tamas v. United States, 455 A.2d 893 (D.C. 1983); State v. Thomas, 66 Ohio St. 2d 518, 521-22, 423 N.E.2d 137, 140 (1981) (BWS not sufficiently developed as scientific knowledge); Buhrle v. State, 627 P.2d 1374, 1378 (Wyo. 1981) (record did not establish scientific basis).

109. State v. Kelly, 97 N.J. 178, 211, 478 A.2d 364, 380 (1984); People v. Christel, 449 Mich. 578, 592, 537 N.W.2d 194, 202 (1995) (BWS "is from a recognized discipline").

110. Fennell v. Goolsby, 630 F. Supp. 451, 459 (E.D. Pa. 1985). *See also* State v. Hodges, 241 Kan. 183, 191-92, 734 P.2d 1161, 1164-66 (1987); State v. Hodges, 239 Kan. 63, 75, 716 P.2d 563, 567-68 (1986); State v. Hennum, 441 N.W.2d 793, 797-99 (Minn. 1989); State v. Gallegos, 104 N.M. 247, 253, 719 P.2d 1268, 1274 (N.M. App. 1986); Bechtel v. State, 840 P.2d 1 (Okla. Crim. App. 1992) (BWS is a scientifically accepted theory).

Trend Toward Acceptance

After the initial setbacks, the trend favored admissibility of BWS evidence.[111] For example, the Ohio Supreme Court reversed its earlier position and admitted BWS evidence.[112] Several states, including Ohio, enacted statutes admitting BWS evidence.[113] Nevertheless, refusal to admit BWS evidence is probably not unconstitutional.[114]

Several limitations on admissibility should be noted. First, some courts permit experts to explain the syndrome only in general terms, describing the salient characteristics of BWS. Accordingly, the expert "should not be allowed to testify as to the ultimate fact that the particular defendant actually suffers from battered woman syndrome."[115]

Second, the substantive law of self-defense may limit admissibility. Traditional self-defense law requires "imminent" danger of death or serious bodily injury. Typically, a killing in the absence of a confrontation falls outside this rule. Accordingly, several courts have held that a battered woman who kills a sleeping spouse cannot claim self-defense.[116] Similarly, some courts refuse to

---

111. *See* Note, *A Trend Emerges: A State Survey on the Admissibility of Expert Testimony Concerning the Battered Woman Syndrome*, 25 J. FAM. L. 373, 396 (1986-87) ("The trend ... appears to be in the direction of admissibility ..."); Annot., *Admissibility of Expert or Opinion Testimony on Battered Wife or Battered Woman Syndrome*, 18 A.L.R.4TH 1153 (1982). *See also* Moran v. Ohio, 469 U.S. 948, 950 (1984) (Brennan, J., dissenting) (noting that battered woman's syndrome has gained support as a self-defense theory).

112. State v. Koss, 49 Ohio St. 3d 213, 217, 551 N.E.2d 970, 974 (1990); State v. Thomas, 77 Ohio St. 3d 323, 331, 673 N.E.2d 1339, 1346 (1997) ("Appellant's requested instructions would attempt to more precisely define battered woman syndrome.... Adding these proposed instructions would therefore set up an entirely separate defense, rather than charge the jury to consider the syndrome when the jury determines appellant's state of mind regarding the second element of self-defense").

113. *See* CAL. EVID. CODE § 1107(a); MO. ANN. STAT. § 563.033; OHIO REV. CODE ANN. §§ 2901.06, 2945.39, 2945.392; WYO. STAT. § 6-1-203 (1994). *See also* Commonwealth v. Crawford, 429 Mass. 60, 706 N.E.2d 289, 294 n.15 (1999) (Expert testimony on BWS has been determined to be appropriate by the Legislator and should be presented to the fact finder if it would help determine a "defendant's state-of-mind and intent at the time of a killing"); State v. Williams, 787 S.W.2d 308, 311-12 (Mo. App. 1990) (statute applies to unmarried as well as married victims); Witt v. State, 892 P.2d 132, 137 (Wyo. 1995) (statute permits syndrome evidence but not expert testimony that a particular defendant in fact believed that she was in imminent danger of death or great bodily injury).

114. Tourlakis v. Morris, 738 F. Supp. 1128, 1140 (S.D. Ohio 1990). *See also* Lumpkin v. Ray, 977 F.2d 508 (10th Cir. 1992) (no equal protection violation due to state's imminence requirement).

115. State v. Hennum, 441 N.W.2d 793, 799 (Minn. 1989).

116. *E.g.*, State v. Stewart, 243 Kan. 639, 648, 763 P.2d 572, 577 (1988); State v. Norman, 324 N.C. 253, 261-68, 378 S.E.2d 8, 13-16 (1989). *See generally* Comment, *Rendering Each Woman Her Due: Can a Battered Woman Claim Self-Defense When She Kills Her Sleeping Batterer?*, 38 U. KAN. L. REV. 169 (1989).

recognize the use of BWS evidence in "murder-for-hire" cases.[117] The opposing view is that the battered woman may justifiably believe she is in "imminent" danger, even though she is not being beaten or threatened at the time of the killing.[118]

To solve these problems, one commentator argued that the legal definition of self-defense was too restrictive and should be modified to recognize "psychological self-defense."[119]

§ 9-3(B). Admissibility: Duress Defense.

Several courts have held that BWS evidence is relevant to establish the defense of duress.[120] Nevertheless, the majority of courts that have considered the issue have taken the opposite view.[121] For example, in *United States v. Willis*[122] the Fifth Circuit commented:

---

117. *E.g.*, People v. Yaklich, 833 P.2d 758 (Colo. App. 1991); State v. Martin, 666 S.W.2d 895, 899-900 (Mo. App. 1984).

118. *But see* Lentz v. State, 604 So. 2d 243, 247 (Miss. 1992) (BWS evidence would not assist in determining whether a reasonable person would perceive that she was in "imminent" danger); State v. Burtzlaff, 493 N.W.2d 1, 5 (S.D. 1992) (Expert testimony that "battered women perceive imminent danger differently than the average person" is inadmissible under the facts of this case).

119. Ewing, *Psychological Self-Defense: A Proposed Justification for Battered Women Who Kill*, 14 LAW & HUM. BEHAV. 579 (1990). *But see* Morse, *The Misbegotten Marriage of Soft Psychology and Bad Law*, 14 LAW & HUM. BEHAV. 595, 595-96 (1990) ("The psychological justification for the defense employs unacceptably soft science, and its legal support is confused and regressive"). *See also* Greenwald, Tomkins, Kenning & Zavodny, *Psychological Self-Defense Jury Instructions: Influence on Verdicts for Battered Women Defendants*, 8 BEHAV. SCI. & LAW 171 (1990).

120. *E.g.*, Dunn v. Roberts, 963 F.2d 308 (10th Cir. 1992) (accused entitled to expert assistance to raise duress defense); United States v. Marenghi, 893 F. Supp. 85, 95-96 (D. Me. 1995) ("[T]his expert testimony may be characterized as explaining how a reasonable person can nonetheless be trapped and controlled by another at all times even if there is not overt threat of violence at any given moment.... This Court cannot envision that such evidence should be excluded in a duress defense when it is admitted in an overwhelming majority of state courts in self-defense cases"); United States v. Brown, 891 F. Supp. 1501, 1505, 1508 (D. Kan. 1995) (BWS "is not a defense.... It is some evidence to be considered to support a defense, such as self-defense, duress, compulsion, and coercion") (BWS evidence satisfies *Daubert* standard); Zelenak v. Commonwealth, 23 Va. App. 259, 475 S.E.2d 853 (1996) (BWS evidence admissible in support of duress defense).

121. *See generally* Faigman & Wright, *Battered Woman Syndrome in the Age of Science*, 39 ARIZ. L. REV. 67 (1997) (Although the defense of duress is similar to self-defense, the use of BWS has received much less acceptance in duress cases. Duress is based on the actions of a reasonable person. Therefore, BWS testimony fails because it focuses on the reasonableness of the act based on the fact that she is battered and deserves a subjective evaluation of her acts); Boland, *Battered Women Who Act Under Duress*, 28 NEW ENG. L. REV. 603 (1994); Note, *Beyond Self-Defense: The Use of Battered Woman Syndrome in Duress Defenses*, 1994 U. ILL. L. REV. 955. *See also* Jacobs, *Requiring Battered Women Die: Murder Liability for Mothers Under Failure to Protect Statutes*, 88 J. CRIM. L. & CRIMINOLOGY 579, 642 (1998) ("Duress is also predicated upon the defendant

> [W]e hold that such evidence is not relevant. This is because in order for a duress defense to criminal liability to succeed, the coercive force of the threat must be sufficient such that a person of *ordinary* firmness would succumb. Additionally, there must be no *reasonable* legal alternative to violating the law. These requirements set out an objective test. To consider battered woman's syndrome evidence in applying that test, however, would be to turn the objective inquiry that duress has always required into a subjective one.[123]

§ 9-3(C). Admissibility: Other Cases.

BWS syndrome evidence has been offered in other types of prosecutions.[124] Several cases have concerned the criminal responsibility of a woman for the protection of her child, an issue that may arise in neglect or child endangerment prosecutions or in a murder or assault case under a failure to protect theory ("omission" liability). One commentator suggested "that the mother should be able to assert that she is justified in not protecting the child because of the risk of death or serious bodily injury to herself."[125]

In *Barrett v. State*,[126] the Indiana court of appeals rejected the state's argument that BWS evidence is admissible only in self-defense cases. The court ruled that the evidence was relevant to a neglect-of-dependent charge, and its exclusion violated the defendant's constitutional right to present a defense.

---

being a person of reasonable firmness. Here the battered mother confronts the troublesome issue of whether someone who 'allows' themselves and their children to be battered can be found to be reasonable").

122. 38 F.3d 170 (5th Cir. 1994) (citations omitted), *cert. denied*, 515 U.S. 1145 (1995).

123. *Id.* at 176. *Accord* United States v. Smith, 987 F.2d 888, 890 (2d Cir.), *cert. denied*, 510 U.S. 875 (1993); United States v. Johnson, 956 F.2d 894, 898 (9th Cir.), *supplemented on denial of reh'g sub nom.* United States v. Emelio, 969 F.2d 849 (9th Cir. 1992); United States v. Sixty Acres in Etowah County, 930 F.2d 857, 860 (11th Cir. 1991). *See also* United States v. Nelson, 966 F. Supp. 1029, 1033 (D. Kan. 1997) (Defendant did not establish that her counsel was ineffective by not incorporating a BWS defense; evidence was "so overwhelming that no reasonable probability exists that the results of the proceeding would have been different had counsel pursued a trial strategy incorporating BWS"); State v. Riker, 123 Wash. 2d 351, 363, 869 P.2d 43, 50 (1994) (en banc) (duress defense in cocaine prosecution; battered person syndrome generally accepted but only in a long-term relationship).

124. *See* McMaugh v. State, 612 A.2d 725 (R.I. 1992) (BWS evidence offered in post-conviction proceeding to show defendant unable to assist counsel at trial with her codefendant husband).

125. Jacobs, *Requiring Battered Women Die: Murder Liability for Mothers Under Failure to Protect Statutes*, 88 J. CRIM. L. & CRIMINOLOGY 579, 586 (1998). "Courts cannot continue to refuse to recognize that a battered mother cannot shrug off her own abuse simply because the batterer also abuses her child. The evidence of the batterer's history of abuse is relevant to her mental state at the time the child is killed." *Id.* at 656.

126. 675 N.E.2d 1112 (Ind. App. 1996).

In *State v. Wyatt*,[127] the West Virginia Supreme Court held that BWS evidence was not admissible on the issue of intent in a prosecution against a woman for murder of a child by failure to provide medical care. The court found that there was no direct connection between the BWS and the neglect of the child. In addition, a proper foundation under *Daubert* had not been laid.[128]

The BWS evidence has also been introduced in sentencing proceedings.[129]

§ 9-3(D). Admissibility: Offered by Prosecution.

In later cases, prosecutors began to offer BWS evidence in a variety of contexts.[130] Perhaps the most common example involves the prosecution of a batterer.[131] Here, BWS evidence may be offered to explain the victim's behavior—*i.e.*, delay in reporting, recantation, and continued habitation with the abuser.

In *State v. Grecinger*[132] the Minnesota Supreme Court ruled BWS evidence admissible against the alleged batterer in an attempted murder and assault case if the defense attacks the credibility of the victim in its opening statement and during cross-examination. At this point in the state's case-in-chief, expert testimony of BWS may be admitted under Evidence Rule 608(a). The defense had already impeached the victim by pointing out her delay in prosecuting, her return to the defendant, and her recanting of the accusation when she had sought an order of protection. The expert's testimony was limited to a description of the syndrome and its characteristics.

In *State v. Ciskie*[133] BWS evidence was admitted in a rape prosecution to explain why the victim had not left the defendant or reported the abuse.[134]

---

127. 482 S.E.2d 147 (W.Va. 1996).

128. *See also* State v. Mott, 931 P.2d 1046 (Ariz.) (en banc), (1997) (ruling that evidence offered to establish a "diminished capacity" defense, which is not recognized in Arizona), *cert. denied*, 520 U.S. 1234 (1997).

129. *E.g.,* United States v. Johnson, 956 F.2d 894, 901-02 (9th Cir. 1992); United States v. Whitetail, 956 F.2d 857, 864 (8th Cir. 1992) (Sentencing guidelines "permits consideration of battered-woman syndrome as a basis for departure from the guidelines"). *See also* Knock v. Knock, 224 Conn. 776, 621 A.2d 267 (1993) (BWS testimony admissible on custody issue in a divorce case).

130. *See* Faigman & Wright, *Battered Woman Syndrome in the Age of Science*, 39 ARIZ. L. REV. 67, 98 (1997) (A prosecution's use of BWS testimony is problematic because the theory of BWS "was not designed with this use in mind," and there is no research to support the prosecution's use of the syndrome to explain a witness's conflicting testimony).

131. *See generally* Note, *Using Battered Woman Syndrome Evidence in the Prosecution of a Batterer*, 76 IOWA L. REV. 553 (1991).

132. 569 N.W.2d 189 (Minn. 1997). *See also* United States v. Taylor, 820 F. Supp. 124, 129 (S.D.N.Y. 1993) (BWS evidence admissible in a conspiracy and bribery case to rehabilitate the defendant if she is impeached for not remembering a conversation).

133. 110 Wash. 2d 263, 281, 751 P.2d 1165, 1170-71 (1988).

In *Arcoren v. United States*[135] the defendant was charged with aggravated sexual abuse. His estranged wife reported the assault but then recanted her grand jury testimony at trial. The prosecution introduced BWS evidence to explain the wife's conduct. The Eighth Circuit affirmed, finding "no persuasive reason" to limit BWS testimony "to cases in which it is offered to bolster a claim of self-defense."[136]

In *State v. Stringer*[137] the prosecution offered BWS evidence in a kidnapping and assault case. The Montana Supreme Court ruled that the evidence was relevant; it "was offered by the prosecution, to provide an understanding as to why the complaining witness might recant her earlier statement that she suffered abuse at the hands of her spouse. The overwhelming trend of other jurisdictions is to allow evidence regarding the battered woman syndrome."[138] Moreover, the evidence was not offered to bolster the woman's testimony but "to provide the jury with an explanation for the inconsistencies in her testimony."[139]

---

134. *See* State v. Frost, 242 N.J. Super. 601, 612, 577 A.2d 1282, 1287 (A.D.) ("It would seem anomalous to allow a battered woman, where she is a criminal defendant, to offer this type of expert testimony in order to help the jury understand the actions she took, yet deny her that same opportunity when she is the complaining witness and/or victim and her abuser is the criminal defendant"), *cert. denied,* 127 N.J. 321, 604 A.2d 596 (1990).

135. 929 F.2d 1235 (8th Cir. 1991), *cert. denied,* 502 U.S. 913 (1991).

136. *Id.* at 1241. *See also* People v. Dillard, 45 Cal. App. 4th 1417, 53 Cal. Rptr. 2d 456, 461 (1996) (Battered women commonly blame themselves for the abuse, develop "compassion for [the abuser],...believe his promise[s] ... [and] recant her allegations of violent conduct by the man"; expert testimony is needed to explain these behavior characteristics and dispel popular misconceptions about battered women being free to leave anytime or even enjoying and provoking the abuse); State v. Borrelli, 227 Conn. 153, 629 A.2d 1105 (1993) (BWS evidence admissible to explain recanted prior inconsistent statement); People v. Ellis, 650 N.Y.S.2d 503, 504-06 (Sup. Ct. 1996) (wife compelled to testify but recants or minimizes her grand jury testimony); State v. Bednarz, 179 Wis. 2d 460, 466, 507 N.W.2d 168, 171 (App. 1993) (expert testimony concerning recantation of domestic assault accusation admissible), *rev. denied*, 513 N.W.2d 406 (Wis. 1994). *But see* State v. Pargeon, 64 Ohio App. 3d 679, 582 N.E.2d 665 (1991) (error to admit BWS evidence during prosecution case-in-chief in a domestic violence case for injuries to defendant's wife).

137. 271 Mont. 367, 897 P.2d 1063 (1995).

138. *Id.* at 375, 897 P.2d at 1068. *See also* Commonwealth v. Goetzendanner, 42 Mass. App. 637, 679 N.E.2d 240 (1997) (BWS evidence admissible against the batterer in rape, kidnapping, and assault case), *cert. denied*, 425 Mass. 1105, 682 N.E.2d 1362 (1997).

139. *Id.* at 377, 897 P.2d at 1069. The Court went on to hold, however, that "the State [had] failed to lay an appropriate foundation establishing that Kathy was a battered spouse.... Many jurisdictions considering the admissibility of expert testimony on the battered woman syndrome require proof that the witness was the victim of two cycles of abuse." *Id* at 377-78, 897 P.2d at 1069-70. In People v. Christel, 449 Mich. 578, 537 N.W.2d 194 (1995), the Michigan Supreme Court ruled that BWS evidence may be admissible in a sexual assault case under limited circumstances, which were not present in that case. "In this case, the expert testimony was arguably relevant and helpful in understanding the complainant's actions in tolerating physical abuse over a period of years. Moreover, it may have been relevant in explaining why complainant did not report

Miscellaneous Cases

Other cases do not fall within any particular pattern. In *State v. Baker*[140] the court upheld the introduction of BWS evidence to rebut an insanity defense in the trial of a husband for the attempted murder of his wife. Another court has ruled it error for the prosecution to rebut BWS evidence with evidence of the defendant's prior aggressive acts toward the victim.[141] This type of rebuttal evidence is inadmissible because it is character evidence.

§ 9-3(E). Battered Children.

The phrase "Battered Child Syndrome" has two meanings. First, it may refer to physical evidence in a child abuse prosecution, in which case it is offered by the prosecution to suggest that injuries to the child were not accidental. Second, the phrase may be used as an analogue of the battered woman syndrome but involving a child who kills his or her parent.[142]

In *State v. Janes*[143] the arguments supporting BWS evidence were applied to a "battered child." The court reasoned that "[n]either law nor logic suggests any reason to limit to women recognition of the impact a battering relationship may have on the victim's actions or perceptions.... [C]hildren are both objectively and subjectively more vulnerable to ... violence than are adults."[144] Other cases are in accord.[145]

---

similar incidents earlier." *Id.* at 580, 537 N.W.2d at 196. The court adopted a cautious attitude in this context: "[W]e do not adopt the battered spouse syndrome, but will permit testimony regarding specific behavior where relevant and helpful to the factfinder. Furthermore, ... the expert cannot opine that complainant was a battered woman, may not testify that defendant was a batterer or that he is guilty of the crime, and cannot comment on whether complainant was being truthful." *Id.* at 591, 537 N.W.2d at 201. The court found that BWS "is from a recognized discipline," but that it was questionable under the facts of the case that the complainant's testimony and actions would be incomprehensible to average people. *Id.* at 592, 537 N.W.2d at 202.

140. 120 N.H. 773, 775-76, 424 A.2d 171, 172-73 (1980).

141. State v. Kelly, 102 Wash. 2d 188, 193-99, 685 P.2d 564, 569-71 (1984).

142. *See generally* P. MONES, WHEN A CHILD KILLS: ABUSED CHILDREN WHO KILL THEIR PARENTS (1991); Azarcon, *Battered Child Defendants in California: The Admissibility of Evidence Regarding the Effects of Abuse on a Child's Honest and Reasonable Belief of Imminent Danger*, 26 PAC. L.J. 831 (1995); Van Sambeek, *Parricide as Self-defense*, 7 LAW & INEQUALITY 87 (1988-89); Comment, *Killing Daddy: Developing a Self-Defense Strategy for the Abused Child*, 137 U. PA. L. REV. 1281 (1989).

143. 64 Wash. App. 134, 822 P.2d 1238 (1992), *aff'd*, 121 Wash. 2d 220, 850 P.2d 495 (1993).

144. 822 P.2d at 1243.

145. *See* State v. Hines, 303 N.J. Super. 311, 324, 696 A.2d 780, 787 (1997); State v. Nemeth, 82 Ohio St.3d 202, 207, 694 N.E.2d 1332, 1336 (1998) ("Expert testimony on battered child syndrome would, in this case, tend to enhance the probability that [defendant's] accounts of the facts leading up to the killing was truthful and would lend credibility to his assertion that he was in a state of rage and dissociation at the time of the killing"). *.But see* Whipple v. Duckworth, 957 F.2d 418, 421-24 (7th Cir. 1992) (exclusion of syndrome evidence did not violate constitution

§ 9-3(F). Related Issues.

Several other issues concerning the Battered Wife Syndrome have arisen in the court cases.

Ineffective Assistance of Counsel

Several cases raise claims of ineffective assistance of counsel. In *Meeks v. Bergen*[146] the Sixth Circuit ruled that a defense counsel's failure to introduce expert testimony on the battered woman syndrome did not constitute ineffective assistance. In *Commonwealth v. Stonehouse,*[147] however, the Pennsylvania Supreme Court reached the opposite result. A California appellate court concurred in *People v. Day*[148] where defense counsel admitted that he had "never heard" of such a defense, and BWS evidence would have helped dispel "many of the commonly held misconceptions about battered women. As the record reflect[ed], the prosecutor exploited several of these misconceptions in urging the jury to reject appellant's self-defense claim."[149]

Victim Examinations

The courts are split on whether a defendant who intends to introduce BWS evidence is required to submit to an examination by prosecution experts. In *United States v. Vega-Penarete*[150] the district court ruled that the prosecution "should have the opportunity to respond to the defendant's expert testimony on

---

because accused offered no evidence that he was in immediate danger), *cert. denied*, 506 U.S. 876 (1992); Jahnke v. State, 682 P.2d 991, 1008 (Wyo. 1984) ("battered son" testimony rejected because the defendant was not under attack at the time of the killing).

146. 749 F.2d 322, 328-29 (6th Cir. 1984).

147. 521 Pa. 41, 57-58, 555 A.2d 772, 781 (1989) (failure to introduce BWS evidence constituted ineffective assistance of counsel).

148. 2 Cal. App. 4th 405, 2 Cal. Rptr. 2d 916 (1992).

149. *Id.* at 416, 2 Cal. Rptr. 2d at 922. *See also* Comment, *Criminal Law: Marshaling the Defense — Indigent Defendants Guaranteed Psychiatric Assistance at Trial to Explain Battered Woman Syndrome*, 32 WASHBURN L.J. 249 (1993); Annot., *Ineffective Assistance of Counsel: Battered Spouse Syndrome as Defense to Homicide or Other Criminal Offense*, 11 A.L.R.5TH 871 (1993).

150. 137 F.R.D. 233 (E.D.N.C. 1991). *See also* United States v. Williams, 163 F.R.D. 249, 250 (E.D.N.C. 1995) ("FED. R. CRIM. P. 12.2(c) and 18 U.S.C. §§ 4241 and 4242 do not provide a basis for requiring defendant to undergo a psychiatric or psychological evaluation under the present circumstances [BWS defense]"); United States v. Bell, 855 F. Supp. 239, 240 (N.D. Ill. 1994) ("[T]he BWS does not excuse criminal conduct because a defendant was incapable of formulating a requisite mental state. Rather, it presumes such mental state to exist but offers a legally recognizable justification for the conduct").

the Battered Wife Syndrome with testimony of its expert who has also examined the defendant."[151]

The Minnesota Supreme Court in *State v. Hennum*[152] resolved the issue on different grounds. The court ruled that only generalized information about BWS is admissible, and thus a defense expert is not permitted to express an opinion about the particular defendant. This rule of limited admissibility obviates the need for an examination by prosecution experts inasmuch as the defense expert will not be allowed to testify based upon a defense examination of the accused.

Right to Expert Assistance

Finally, an indigent defendant may have the right to expert assistance when offering BWS evidence.[153] In *Dunn v. Roberts*[154] the Tenth Circuit ruled that the accused had such a right in support of a duress defense.

§ 9-4. Rape Trauma Syndrome.

Burgess and Holmstrom coined the phrase Rape Trauma Syndrome (RTS) to describe the behavioral, somatic, and psychological reactions of rape and attempted rape victims.[155] Based on interviews with 146 women, they found that victims usually progress through a two-phase process — an acute phase and a long-term reorganization phase. Impact reactions in the acute phase involved either an "expressed style" in which fear, anger and anxiety were manifested, or a "controlled style" in which these feelings were masked by a composed or subdued behavior. Somatic reactions include physical trauma, skeletal muscle tension, gastrointestinal irritability, and genitourinary disturbance. In addition, a wide gamut of emotional reactions, ranging from fear, humiliation, and embarrassment to anger, revenge, and self-blame were exhibited.

The second phase, the reorganization phase, typically began two to six weeks after the attack and was a period in which the victim attempted to reestablish her life. This period was characterized by activity, such as changing residences, changing telephone numbers, or visiting family members. Nightmares and dreams were common. Rape-related phobias, such as fear of being alone or fear

---

151. *Id.* at 235. *See also* Hickson v. State, 630 So. 2d 172, (Fla. 1993); State v. Briand, 130 N.H. 650, 657-58, 547 A.2d 235, 240 (1988) (independent evaluation required); State v. Myers, 239 N.J. Super. 158, 169-70, 570 A.2d 1260, 1266 (same), *cert. denied,* 127 N.J. 323, 604 A.2d 598 (1990).

152. 441 N.W.2d 793, 799-800 (Minn. 1989). *See generally* Comment, *A Critique and Proposed Solution to the Adverse Examination Problem Raised by Battered Woman Syndrome Testimony in State v. Hennum,* 74 MINN. L. REV. 1023 (1990).

153. For a discussion of this subject, *see* Chapter 4.

154. 963 F.2d 308 (10th Cir. 1992).

155. Burgess & Holmstrom, *Rape Trauma Syndrome*, 131 AM. J. PSYCHIATRY 981 (1974). *See also* Burgess, *Rape Trauma Syndrome*, 1 BEHAV. SCI. & LAW 97 (Summer 1983).

of having people behind their back, and difficulties in sexual relationships also were prominent.

Other studies elaborated on the initial research, sometimes confirming the earlier studies and sometimes providing additional insights.[156] "Subsequent research, which is much more rigorous, conceptualizes rape trauma in terms of specific symptoms rather than more general stages of recovery."[157]

RTS is now recognized as a type of Post-Traumatic Stress Disorder (PTSD), and such disorders are included in the most recent edition of the American Psychiatric Association's Diagnostic and Statistical Manual of Mental Disorders.[158] This approach to RTS, however, does not focus on the two-stage model of recovery posited by Burgess and Holmstrom, but rather on specific symptoms.[159]

---

156. *See generally* Buchele & Buchele, *Legal and Psychological Issues in the Use of Expert Testimony on Rape Trauma Syndrome*, 25 WASHBURN L.J. 26 (1985); Freckelton, *When Plight Makes Right: The Forensic Abuse Syndrome*, 18 CRIM. L.J. 29 (1994); Massaro, *Experts, Psychology, Credibility, and Rape: The Rape Trauma Syndrome Issue and Its Implications for Expert Psychological Testimony*, 69 MINN. L. REV. 395 (1985); McCord, *The Admissibility of Expert Testimony Regarding Rape Trauma Syndrome in Rape Prosecutions*, 26 B.C. L. REV. 1143 (1985); Mosteller, *Legal Doctrines Governing the Admissibility of Expert Testimony Concerning Social Framework Evidence*, 52 LAW & CONTEMP. PROBS. 85, 125-28 (Autumn 1989); Ross, *The Overlooked Expert in Rape Prosecutions*, 14 U. TOL. L. REV. 707 (1983); Stefan, *The Protection Racket: Rape Trauma Syndrome, Psychiatric Labeling, and Law*, 88 NW. U. L. REV. 1271 (1994); Vidmar & Schuller, *Juries and Expert Evidence: Social Framework Testimony*, 52 LAW & CONTEMP. PROBS. 133, 155-60 (Autumn 1989); Comment, *Making the Woman's Experience Relevant to Rape: The Admissibility of Rape Trauma Syndrome in California*, 39 UCLA L. REV. 251 (1991); Note, *Defining the Boundaries of Admissible Expert Psychological Testimony on Rape Trauma Syndrome*, 1989 U. ILL. L. REV. 691; Annot., *Admissibility, at Criminal Prosecution, of Expert Testimony on Rape Trauma Syndrome*, 42 A.L.R.4TH 879 (1985).

157. Frazier & Borgida, *Rape Trauma Syndrome: A Review of Case Law and Psychological Research*, 16 LAW & HUM. BEHAV. 293, 299 (1992).

158. A.P.A. DIAGNOSTIC AND STATISTICAL MANUAL OF MENTAL DISORDERS 424 (4th ed. 1994) ("Posttraumatic Stress Disorder"). Another disorder sometimes mentioned in these cases is "conversion disorder." *Id.* at 452. *See* State v. Hall, 330 N.C. 808, 822-23, 412 S.E.2d 883, 891 (1992) (discussing conversion disorder and RTS).

159. *See* Boeschen & Sales, *Rape Trauma Experts in the Courtroom*, 4 PSYCH. PUB. POL. & L. 414 (1998) ("PTSD, rather than RTS, is now more commonly measured in the aftermath of rape because PTSD is the primary trauma-related diagnosis included in the DSM-IV"; PTSD and RTS are not the same. Many common symptoms of RTS are not part of PTSD. However, PTSD testimony is more widely accepted than RTS testimony. The problem is that rape victims who do not fit the mold for PTSD can be unfairly jeopardized by judges and jurors, who believe that all "real" victims of rape will fit the criteria for PTSD. "Although RTS has historical importance, it makes for confusing and potentially unscientific expert testimony and should no longer be used in the courtroom. PTSD although far from being a perfect diagnosis for rape survivors, looks to be a more reliable and valid diagnosis for expert testimony.... If used cautiously and appropriately, expert testimony on PTSD can help to educate the judge or jury about common reactions to rape").

Critics have questioned the scientific basis for RTS evidence. After surveying the literature (1984), one commentator concluded that "definitional problems, biased research samples, and the inherent complexity of the phenomenon vitiate all attempts to establish empirically the causal relationship implicit in the concept of a rape trauma syndrome."[160] Some of the research problems included (1) unrepresentative samples, (2) failure to distinguish between victims of rapes, attempted rapes, and molestation, and (3) failure to account for individual idiosyncratic and incident-specific reactions.[161] In 1989 a psychologist concluded that "research on the rape trauma syndrome is not probative on prior consent, prior trauma, nor the cause of the complainant's current behavior."[162]

A 1992 review of the literature by Frazier and Borgida included a number of findings: Although victims experienced a range of symptoms, only a few symptoms have been studied consistently — fear and anxiety, depression, social maladjustment, and sexual dysfunction. Later studies also documented symptoms identified for PTSD — recurrent nightmares, irritability, and hypervigilance.[163] They concluded:

> In our opinion, although early studies were plagued by numerous methodological problems ... , several studies have since been conducted that are much more sophisticated methodologically ... These studies have assessed victim recovery at several points after the assault using standardized assessment measures and have employed carefully matched control groups. This research has established that rape victims experience more depression, anxiety, fear, and social adjustment and sexual problems than women who have not been victimized. Research on PTSD among rape victims is more recent but consistently suggests that many victims experience PTSD symptoms following an assault. Initially high symptom levels generally abate by 3 to 4 months postassault, although significant levels of distress continue for many victims.[164]

The focus of much of the research was to understand the victim's reactions in order to provide assistance to the victim. The focus was not on the evaluation of victims' reactions in order to establish the fact that a rape had occurred, which is how RTS evidence is sometimes used at trial. There is an accepted body of

160. Note, *Checking the Allure of Increased Conviction Rates: The Admissibility of Expert Testimony on Rape Trauma Syndrome in Criminal Proceedings*, 70 VA. L. REV. 1657, 1678 (1984).

161. *Id.* at 1678-80.

162. Graham, *Rape Trauma Syndrome: Is It Probative of Lack of Consent?*, 13 LAW & PSYCHOL. REV. 25, 41-42 (1989).

163. Frazier & Borgida, *Rape Trauma Syndrome: A Review of the Case Law and Psychological Research*, 16 LAW & HUM. BEHAV. 293, 300 (1992).

164. *Id.* at 301.

research concerning the aftereffects of rape. The critical issue, however, is how the research is used in court.

Frazier and Borgida also reviewed expert testimony in the reported cases. In several instances they found testimony that was unsupported by research. For example, in *Lessard v. State*[165] the expert testified that it is "very common" for a victim to ask an assailant not to tell anyone about the assault. Frazier and Borgida concluded that "this particular behavior has not been documented in the research literature."[166] Their conclusions concerning court testimony are noteworthy:

> In sum, experts in recent cases have described a broad range of symptoms and behaviors as consistent with RTS, some of which do not appear to be based on research. Testimony that is not research based often seems to be prompted by a defendant's claims that a complainant's behavior was inconsistent with having been raped. If virtually any victim behavior is described as consistent with RTS, the term soon will have little meaning. Indeed, some critics have argued that this already is the case ....[167]

Jury Studies

Social scientists have also attempted to determine whether the typical jury is generally knowledgeable about the aftereffects of rape, and what the impact of expert testimony on this subject will have on a jury. In 1988 Frazier and Borgida administered an eighteen-item questionnaire on sexual assault to two groups of experts: rape and PTSD experts.[168] The responses of the experts were then compared to the responses of two nonexpert groups (students and nonacademic university staff). The nonexpert groups scored markedly lower on the questionnaire than did the experts — near chance levels (57% and 58% correct).[169] Significantly, the nonexperts were unaware of the behavioral changes a victim often experiences following a rape.[170] This study suggests that jurors often need to be informed about this subject in order to understand the evidence.

Other studies by Brekke and Borgida[171] focused on the impact RTS testimony has on jurors. These experiments suggest that RTS testimony has a greater

---

165. 719 P.2d 227, 233 (Wyo. 1986).

166. Frazier & Borgida, *Rape Trauma Syndrome: A Review of the Case Law and Psychological Research*, 16 LAW & HUM. BEHAV. 293, 304 (1992).

167. *Id.* at 304-05.

168. Frazier & Borgida, *Juror Common Understanding and the Admissibility of Rape Trauma Syndrome Evidence in Court*, 12 LAW & HUM. BEHAV. 101 (1988).

169. *Id.* at 112.

170. *Id.* at 114.

171. Brekke & Borgida, *Expert Psychological Testimony in Rape Trials: A Social-Cognitive Analysis*, 55 J. PERSONALITY & SOC. PSYCHOL. 372 (1988); Borgida & Brekke, *Psycholegal*

impact when introduced earlier rather than later in the trial: "Expert testimony, when presented early in the trial, may serve as a powerful organizing theme or basis for a juror's initial impression of the case. When presented later in the trial, by contrast, the expert testimony may be treated merely as additional information to be integrated into an existing, well-organized impression."[172]

A second finding was that expert testimony had a greater impact if it was "concretized" through the use of a case-specific hypothetical question. The more general testimony consisted of an attempt to debunk many of the common myths about rape. The expert in the experiments testified that (a) few women falsely accuse men of rape, (b) rape is a highly underreported crime, (c) a large proportion of rapes involve casual acquaintance of the victim rather than strangers, (d) rape is a crime of violence rather than a crime of passion, and (e) it is often better for a woman to submit than to risk the additional violence that could result from ineffective resistance. When this testimony was followed by a hypothetical question incorporating the important features of the case, it had a greater impact.[173]

The studies also indicated that jurors did not automatically accept the expert's testimony, and that expert testimony was important in acquaintance rape and lack of physical resistance situations.

§ 9-4(A). Admissibility: Lack of Consent.

The prosecution may offer RTS evidence at trial for two different purposes: (1) to prove lack of consent by the alleged victim, and (2) to explain post-incident conduct by a victim that a jury might perceive as inconsistent with the claim of rape. The courts divide over the first use but generally accept the second use.

A number of courts permit RTS evidence to be introduced at trial to establish lack of consent, an element of the crime of rape. The inference may be stated as a syllogism: (1) Rape victims manifest certain characteristics known as RTS; (2) the alleged victim has these symptoms; and (3) therefore, she has been raped.

In 1982 in *State v. Marks*[174] the Kansas Supreme Court became the first state supreme court to uphold the admission of RTS evidence. A psychiatrist, who examined the victim two weeks after the attack, testified that the victim had suffered a "frightening assault" and was "suffering from the post-traumatic stress disorder known as rape trauma syndrome."[175] The Court concluded: "An

---

Research on Rape Trials, *in* RAPE AND SEXUAL ASSAULT: A RESEARCH HANDBOOK 313 (A. Burgess ed. 1985).

172. *Id.*, 55 J. PERSONALITY & SOC PSYCHOL. at 383.

173. *Id.*

174. 231 Kan. 645, 647 P.2d 1292 (1982).

175. *Id.* at 654, 647 P.2d at 1299.

examination of the literature clearly demonstrates that the so-called 'rape trauma syndrome' is generally accepted to be a common reaction to sexual assault .... As such, qualified expert psychiatric testimony regarding the existence of rape trauma syndrome is relevant and admissible in a case such as this where the defense is consent."[176] Other courts followed this precedent.[177] In addition, Illinois enacted a statute that permits the admission of evidence of post-traumatic stress syndrome in illegal sex acts prosecutions.[178]

Different courts imposed a variety of limitations on this use of RTS evidence. Some courts permitted the expert to testify that the victim's behavior was consistent with RTS but not that the victim had been raped.[179] Other courts prohibited (1) comment on the credibility of the alleged victim,[180] (2) use of the term "rape trauma syndrome,"[181] or (3) any reference to the accused.[182] In addition, the witness's qualifications may influence admissibility. In *State v.*

---

176. *Id. See also* United States v. Carter, 22 M.J. 771, 775 (A.C.M.R. 1986) (RTS satisfied *Frye*), *aff'd in part,* 26 M.J. 428 (C.M.A. 1988). For discussion of *Frye*, *see* Chapter 1.

177. *E.g.*, State v. Huey, 145 Ariz. 59, 64, 699 P.2d 1290, 1295 (1985); State v. Gettier, 438 N.W.2d 1, 6 (Iowa 1989); State v. McQuillen, 239 Kan. 590, 593, 721 P.2d 740, 741-42 (1986); State v. McQuillen, 236 Kan. 161, 171, 689 P.2d 822, 829 (1984); State v. Allewalt, 308 Md. 89, 109, 517 A.2d 741, 751 (1986); State v. Liddell, 211 Mont. 180, 186-89, 685 P.2d 918, 922-23 (1984); State v. Whitman, 16 Ohio App. 3d 246, 247, 475 N.E.2d 486, 488 (1984); State v. Schumpert, 435 S.E.2d 859, 862 (S.C. 1993) ("[E]xpert testimony and behavioral evidence are admissible as rape trauma syndrome to prove a sexual offense occurred where the probative value of such evidence outweighs its prejudicial effect").

See also Server v. Mizell, 902 F.2d 611, 615 (7th Cir. 1990) (admission of RTS evidence to rebut defense case did not violate due process).

178. 725 ILL. COMP. STAT. 5/115-7.2.

179. *See* People v. Eiskant, 253 Ill. App. 3d 773, 625 N.E.2d 1018, 1021 (1993) ("The preferred testimony is whether or not the victim exhibited symptoms, behaviors, or characteristics consistent with the syndrome in question"); State v. Alberico, 116 N.M. 156, 861 P.2d 192, 210 (1993) ("[Post Traumatic Stress Disorder] testimony is admissible for establishing whether the alleged victim exhibits symptoms of PTSD that are consistent with rape or sexual abuse"; however, this testimony may not be offered to show that the victim is telling the truth, and the expert may not testify about the identity of the perpetrator or mention rape trauma syndrome); Taylor v. Commonwealth, 21 Va. App. 557, 564-65, 466 S.E.2d 118, 122 (1996) (The expert "did not testify about any details of the attack, give the victim's version of the offense, or testify that she believed that the victim was telling the truth.... We hold that evidence of an emotional or psychological injury such as posttraumatic stress disorder, like medical evidence of physical injury, is relevant as circumstantial evidence of the occurrence of a traumatizing event"); State v. McCoy, 179 W. Va. 223, 229-30, 366 S.E.2d 731, 737 (W. Va. 1988).

180. State v. Brodniak, 221 Mont. 212, 217-18, 718 P.2d 322, 326-29 (1986) (RTS evidence admissible but expert may not comment on victim's credibility).

181. State v. Allewalt, 308 Md. 89, 109, 517 A.2d 741, 751 (1986) (Avoiding the term RTS is "more than cosmetic").

182. State v. Huang, 99 N.C. App. 658, 665-66, 394 S.E.2d 279, 284 (1990) (RTS evidence admissible, but expert's repeated implication of defendant was prejudicial error), *rev. denied,* 327 N.C. 639, 399 S.E.2d 127 (1990).

Willis[183] the Kansas Supreme Court ruled that a licensed social worker was not qualified "to diagnose medical and psychiatric conditions such as post-traumatic stress disorder.... Such testimony should be limited to experts with training in the field of post-traumatic stress disorder and rape trauma syndrome and possessing the professional qualifications to make appropriate diagnoses thereof."[184]

Courts rejecting RTS as proof of lack of consent disputed the scientific validity of the syndrome when offered for this purpose. In *State v. Saldana*[185] the Minnesota Supreme Court ruled that "[r]ape trauma syndrome is not the type of scientific test that accurately and reliably determines whether a rape has occurred."[186] Other courts exclude RTS evidence because it has not been generally accepted by the scientific community as required by the *Frye* test.[187] For example, in *People v. Bledsoe*[188] the California Supreme Court noted that "rape trauma syndrome was not devised to determine the 'truth' or 'accuracy' of a particular past event — *i.e.*, whether, in fact, a rape in the legal sense occurred — but rather was developed by professional rape counselors as a therapeutic tool, to help identify, predict and treat emotional problems experienced by the counselors' clients or patients."[189] Thus, according to the court, although generally accepted by the scientific community for a therapeutic purpose, expert testimony on RTS was not generally accepted "to prove that a rape, in fact, occurred."[190] The court commented:

> [A]s a rule, rape counselors do not probe inconsistencies in their clients' descriptions of the facts of the incident, nor do they conduct independent investigations to determine whether other evidence corroborates or contradicts their clients' renditions. Because their function is to help their clients deal with the trauma they are experiencing, the historical accuracy of the client's descriptions of the details of the traumatizing events is not vital in their task.[191]

Other courts accepted this rather persuasive reasoning.[192]

---

183. 256 Kan. 837, 888 P.2d 839 (1995).

184. *Id.* at 846, 888 P.2d at 845.

185. 324 N.W.2d 227 (Minn. 1982).

186. *Id.* at 229. *Accord* State v. McGee, 324 N.W.2d 232, 233 (Minn. 1982).

187. For a discussion of the *Frye* test, *see* Chapter 1.

188. 36 Cal. 3d 236, 681 P.2d 291, 203 Cal. Rptr. 450 (1984).

189. *Id.* at 249-50, 681 P.2d at 300, 203 Cal. Rptr. at 459.

190. *Id.* at 251, 681 P.2d at 301, 203 Cal. Rptr. at 460.

191. *Id.* at 250, 681 P.2d at 300, 203 Cal. Rptr. at 459. *See also* People v. Coleman, 48 Cal. 3d 112, 142-44, 768 P.2d 32, 48-49, 255 Cal. Rptr. 813, 829-30 (1990) (reaffirming *Bledsoe*).

192. *E.g.*, Spencer v. General Elec. Co., 688 F. Supp. 1072, 1075-77 (E.D. Va. 1988); State v. Hall, 330 N.C. 808, 821, 412 S.E.2d 883, 890 (1992); People v. Pullins, 145 Mich. App. 414, 421-22, 378 N.W.2d 502, 505 (1985) (RTS fails *Frye* test); State v. Taylor, 663 S.W.2d 235, 240 (Mo. 1984); State v. Ogle, 668 S.W.2d 138, 143-44 (Mo. App.), *cert. denied*, 469 U.S. 845 (1984);

§ 9-4(B). Admissibility: Explaining Behavior.

As noted above, the California Supreme Court rejected RTS evidence when offered to prove lack of consent. The court, however, approved the admissibility of RTS evidence where the defendant suggests to the jury that the conduct of the victim after the incident is inconsistent with the claim of rape. In this situation, the court wrote, "expert testimony on rape trauma syndrome may play a particularly useful role by disabusing the jury of some widely held misconceptions about rape and rape victims, so that it may evaluate the evidence free of popular myths."[193]

Most courts accepted this position. For example, expert testimony has been admitted to explain a victim's (1) passive resistance during a rape,[194] (2) delay in reporting the crime,[195] (3) failure to attempt to escape,[196] and (4) calm demeanor after an attack.[197] RTS evidence has also been introduced to explain that "in the context of a trust relationship, such as a doctor-patient relationship, some victims may return to the trusted relationship for further contact with the perpetrator of the assault."[198]

In *People v. Yates*,[199] the court admitted RTS evidence to explain the behavior of a male defendant's reaction to an alleged homosexual attack. The court noted: "A review of literature describing the effect of sexual assault on men reveals that male victims, both heterosexual and homosexual, exhibit a well defined trauma

---

People v. Taylor, 75 N.Y.2d 277, 293, 552 N.E.2d 131, 138, 552 N.Y.S.2d 883, 890 (1990) (RTS "is inadmissible when it inescapably bears solely on proving that a rape occurred"); State v. Black, 109 Wash. 2d 336, 346-49, 745 P.2d 12, 15-18 (1987) (RTS fails *Frye* test).

193. 36 Cal. 3d at 247-48, 681 P.2d at 298, 203 Cal. Rptr. at 457.

194. *E.g.*, Perez v. State, 653 S.W.2d 878, 882 (Tex. App. 1983) (in rebuttal, expert explained alleged victim's passive resistance during rape).

195. *E.g.*, United States v. Peel, 29 M.J. 235, 241 (C.M.A. 1989) (RTS evidence admitted to explain postattack behavior — delay in reporting and attempts to normalize life), *cert. denied,* 493 U.S. 1025 (1990); People v. Hampton, 746 P.2d 947, 951-52 (Colo. 1987) (RTS evidence admissible to explain delay in reporting); State v. Roles, 122 Idaho 138, 832 P.2d 311 (1992). *See also* DeLuca v. Lord, 858 F. Supp. 1330, 1340 (S.D. 1994) (expert testimony that "rape victims often do not 'cry out' to the first person they see following a rape, and initially try to resume their normal activities with no mention of the assault" held inadmissible in homicide trial because a justification defense was not offered), *cert. denied*, 519 U.S. 824 (1996).

196. *See* State v. Freeney, 228 Conn. 582, 592, 637 A.2d 1088, 1093 (1994) (expert testimony in an kidnapping and sexual assault case that complainant's conduct (*e.g.*, failing to make escape attempts) was consistent with that of other assault victims).

197. *E.g.*, People v. Taylor, 75 N.Y.2d 277, 293, 552 N.E.2d 131, 138, 552 N.Y.S.2d 883, 890 (1990) ("[H]alf of all women who have been forcibly raped are controlled and subdued following the attack"); State v. Robinson, 146 Wis. 2d 315, 333-35, 431 N.W.2d 165, 172 (1988) (many victims are "emotionally flat" immediately after assault).

198. Commonwealth v. Mamay, 407 Mass. 412, 421, 553 N.E.2d 945, 951 (1990). *See also* Simmons v. State, 504 N.E.2d 575, 579 (Ind. 1987) (initial false report consistent with RTS).

199. 637 N.Y.S.2d 625 (N.Y. Sup. Ct. 1995).

syndrome similar to and parallel to that found in female victims of rape."[200] The court also commented that a "common characteristic of male and female rape victims is delay in reporting the crime."[201]

RTS evidence has also been admitted for sentencing purposes.[202]

§ 9-4(C). Admissibility: Offered by the Defense.

In *Henson v. State*[203] the Indiana Supreme Court held that a defendant may offer RTS evidence to show that the victim had not been raped. The alleged victim claimed that she had been raped at knifepoint after leaving a bar. She returned to the same bar the next evening for a drink and remained for two hours. The defendant offered the testimony of an expert to comment on her postattack conduct. The trial court excluded the evidence, but the Supreme Court reversed: "Here, Dr. Gover's testimony would have tended to prove that J.O.'s behavior after the incident was inconsistent with that of a victim who had suffered a traumatic rape such as that J.O. recounted. The evidence therefore would have a tendency to make it less probable that a rape in fact occurred ...."[204]

A related issue is whether a defendant has a right to have the alleged victim examined psychologically in order to contest RTS evidence. This issue is discussed in section 3-10.

§ 9-5. Child Sexual Abuse: Syndrome & Related Issues.

Frequently, child sexual abuse cases are difficult to prosecute.[205] One commentator summarized the problems as follows:

> The sexual offender is often a relative or a trusted adult with whom the child spends time alone. Eyewitnesses to the molestation are therefore rare. In addition, sexual abuse is typically a nonviolent crime. Children who are abused by a trusted adult usually are manipulated psychologically and do

---

200. *Id.* at 627.

201. *Id.* at 628.

202. United States v. Hammond, 17 M.J. 218 (C.M.A. 1984). *See also* People v. Mathews, 91 Cal. App. 3d 1018, 1025, 154 Cal. Rptr. 628, 632 (1979) (RTS admitted to support self-defense and diminished capacity claim).

203. 535 N.E.2d 1189 (Ind. 1989).

204. *Id.* at 1191. *See generally* Note, *Defense Expert Testimony on Rape Trauma Syndrome: Implications for the Stoic Victim*, 42 HASTINGS L.J. 1143 (1991). *But see* State v. Jones, 83 Ohio App. 3d 723, 731, 615 N.E.2d 713, 718-19 (1992) ("While it appears that testimony regarding rape trauma syndrome can be useful in explaining the unusual behaviors that the syndrome comprises, especially where those behaviors would mislead the jury, it does not follow that the converse is true.... [S]ome victims exhibit few, if any, symptoms, and ... different victims exhibit symptoms during vastly different time frames").

205. An issue of BEHAVIORAL SCIENCES & THE LAW is devoted to child abuse: 9 BEHAV. SCI. & L. 1-84 (Winter 1991).

> not resist their abusers. Physical injury can provide valuable medical evidence of the sexual abuse, but this evidence often is lacking because the abuse is committed without force. Furthermore, the sexual abuse may involve an act other than penetration of the vagina or anus. Crimes such as petting, fondling or oral copulation usually do not involve forceful physical contact and do not leave physical scars. A lapse of time between the sexual abuse and disclosure may also contribute to the lack of medical evidence.[206]

In cases where there is no independent evidence of the abuse, the credibility of the child complainant and the defendant often becomes determinative. However, the typical responses of child sexual abuse victims are counterintuitive in many respects. Delayed disclosure, conflicting testimony, and retraction suggest fabrication by the complainant unless an explanation is offered for this anomalous behavior.

Because of these problems, prosecutors have sought other types of evidence to substantiate sex abuse claims. The "Child Sexual Abuse Accommodation Syndrome" (CSAAS) is an example. Dr. Roland Summit coined the phrase "Child Sexual Abuse Accommodation Syndrome" in 1983 to describe five factors typical of child sexual abuse.[207] The first two are preconditions to child sexual abuse; the last three are "sequential contingencies" that vary in both form and degree. The five categories identified are:

> (1) *Secrecy:* The child receives the message, either explicitly through threats or admonishments or implicitly, that the subject is to be kept secret. An aura of danger and secrecy surrounds the incidents.[208]
>
> (2) *Helplessness:* The imbalance of power that exists between child and adult makes the child feel powerless to resist. The feeling of helplessness is increased when the abuser is a trusted friend or family member.[209]
>
> (3) *Entrapment and Accommodation:* The child who does not seek or receive intervention learns to live with the sexual abuse in order to survive. In addition to submission, other survival mechanisms include turning to imaginary friends, developing multiple personalities, taking refuge in altered states of consciousness or substance abuse, running away, promiscuity, hysterical phenomena, delinquency, sociopathy, projection of rage, and self-mutilation.[210]

---

206. Note, *The Admissibility of "Child Sexual Abuse Accommodation Syndrome" in California Criminal Courts*, 17 PAC. L.J. 1361, 1368-69 (1986).

207. Summit, *The Child Sexual Abuse Accommodation Syndrome*, 7 CHILD ABUSE & NEGLECT 177 (1983).

208. *Id.* at 181.

209. *Id.* at 182-83.

210. *Id.* at 184-86.

(4) *Delayed, Conflicting and Unconvincing Disclosure:* Rarely will the child report incidents of sexual abuse immediately upon their occurrence. Because of the time lapse before report occurs and the emotional upheaval experienced by the child, the disclosure is likely to contain contradictions and misstatements. Often the disclosure is greeted by disbelief.[211]

(5) *Retraction:* "Whatever a child says about sexual abuse, she is likely to reverse it."[212] Particularly if the abuser is a family member, the child will attempt to undo the disintegration of the family caused by the disclosure.[213]

Dr. Summit developed the syndrome to assist professionals in treating abused children. The syndrome is not a diagnostic tool. "The syndrome does not detect sexual abuse. Rather, it assumes the presence of abuse, and explains the child's reactions to it. Thus, [CSAAS] is not the sexual abuse analogue of battered child syndrome, which is diagnostic of physical abuse."[214] Consequently, the use of the term syndrome in court should be avoided.

Nevertheless, sexually abused children do react to the abuse. Anxiety, depression, nightmares, enuresis, regression, and acting out are some of the reactions. Many of these responses, however, are associated with other psychological problems that are unrelated to sexual abuse. In addition, apparently 20% of abused children show no observable reactions.[215] Some reactions are strongly suggestive of abuse: "Examples of behaviors that have greater specificity for sexual abuse include age-inappropriate knowledge of sexual acts or anatomy, sexualization of play and behavior in young children, the appearance of genitalia in young children's drawings, and sexually explicit play with anatomically detailed dolls."[216]

Research concerning child sexual abuse evidence[217] and its impact on a jury continues to be reported.[218] Controversy about its use also continues.[219] In

---

211. *Id.* at 186.

212. *Id.* at 188.

213. *Id.*

214. Myers, Bays, Becker, Berliner, Corwin & Saywitz, *Expert Testimony in Child Sexual Abuse Litigation*, 68 NEB. L. REV. 1, 67 (1989) [hereinafter cited as Myers]; Steward v. State, 652 N.E.2d 490, 493 (Ind. 1995) ("The syndrome was not intended as a diagnostic device and does not detect sexual abuse.... Rather, the syndrome was designed for purposes of treating child victims and offering them more effective assistance 'within the family and within the systems of child protection and criminal justice'") (quoting Dr. Summit's article). *See also* Mosteller, *Syndrome and Politics in Criminal Trials and Evidence Law*, 46 DUKE L.J. 461 (1996) ("The terminology – Child Sexual Abuse Accommodation Syndrome or Rape Trauma Syndrome – may cause the jury to conclude that the expert reached a legal conclusion when the clinical evaluation of the behavior observed is not diagnostic or goes to a different issue").

215. *Id.* at 64.

216. *Id.* at 62-63.

217. *See* Anson, Golding & Gully, *Child Sexual Abuse Allegations: Reliability of Criteria-Based Content Analysis*, 17 LAW & HUM. BEHAV. 331 (1993); Gabora, Spanos & Joab, *The Effects*

addition, articles on "repressed memory" have been published.[220] A consensus statement of a group of experts contained the following statements: (1) "Cultures (and families within them) vary widely in their attitudes and behavioral responses to both nudity and sexuality and these difference are known to affect children's behavior." (2) "No specific behavioral syndromes characterize victims of sexual abuse." (3) "The most reliable and accurate information is obtained from children who are responding to open-ended questions designed to elicit free narrative accounts of events that they have experienced." (4) "Over the last 15 years, there have been dramatic changes in the evaluation of medical evidence suggestive of child sexual abuse."[221]

§ 9-5(A). Admissibility: Fact of Abuse.

Expert testimony on child sexual abuse may be offered at trial for several distinct purposes:[222] (1) as substantive evidence to prove that the child had been abused; (2) to explain conduct of the child that a jury might perceive as inconsistent with a claim of abuse; or (3) to bolster or impeach the child's credibility.

---

of Complainant Age and Expert Psychological Testimony in a Simulated Child Sexual Abuse Trial, 17 LAW & HUM. BEHAV. 103 (1993); Goleman, *Studies Reveal Suggestibility of Very Young as Witnesses*, N.Y. TIMES, Jun. 11, 1993, at A1.

218. *See* Crowley, O'Callaghan & Ball, *The Juridical Impact of Psychological Expert Testimony in a Simulated Child Sexual Abuse Trial*, 18 LAW & HUM. BEHAV. 89 (1994); Kovera, Levy, Borgida & Penrod, *Expert Testimony in Child Sexual Abuse Cases: Effects of Expert Evidence Type and Cross-Examination*, 18 LAW & HUM. BEHAV. 653 (1994) (study suggests that syndrome evidence is less persuasive than case history data (credibility or anatomically correct doll; strength of cross-examination not significant; women more likely than men to be pro-prosecution)).

219. *See* Gardner, *Modern Witch Hunt — Child Abuse Charges*, WALL ST. J., Feb. 22, 1993, at A10; Sherman, *Gardner's Law: A Controversial Psychiatrist and Influential Witness Leads the Backlash Against Child Sex Abuse "Hysteria,"* NAT'L L.J., Aug. 16, 1993, at 1; Gardner, *Child Sexual Abuse*, THE CHAMPION 42 (Nov. 1994).

220. *See* § 12-8 *infra*.

221. Lamb, *The Investigation of Child Sexual Abuse: An Interdisciplinary Consensus Statement*, 2 EXPERT EVIDENCE 151, 152-54 (1994).

222. *See generally* Mason, *A Judicial Dilemma: Expert Witness Testimony in Child Sex Abuse Cases*, 19 J. PSYCHOL. & LAW 185 (Fall-Winter 1991); McCord, *Expert Psychological Testimony About Child Complainants in Sexual Abuse Prosecutions: A Foray Into the Admissibility of Novel Psychological Evidence*, 77 J. CRIM. L. & CRIMINOLOGY 1 (1986); Note, *The Unreliability of Expert Testimony on the Typical Characteristics of Sexual Abuse Victims*, 74 GEO. L.J. 429 (1985); Note, *Child Sexual Abuse Accommodation Syndrome: Curing the Effects of a Misdiagnosis in the Law of Evidence*, 25 TULSA L.J. 143 (1989); Note, *Expert Testimony in Child Sexual Abuse Prosecutions: A Spectrum of Uses*, 68 B.U. L. REV. 155 (1988); Note, *Child Sexual Abuse Accommodation Syndrome: Admissibility Requirements*, 23 AM. J. CRIM. L. 171 (1995); Comments, *Restricting the Admissibility of Expert Testimony in Child Sexual Abuse Prosecutions: Pennsylvania Takes It to the Extreme*, 47 MIAMI L. REV. 201 (1992).

In addition to these purposes, the form of the testimony may vary. For example, expert testimony offered to establish abuse could take three different forms: (1) general testimony about the behavioral characteristics of abused children; (2) testimony that a particular child's behavior is consistent with that of abused children; or (3) an opinion that a particular child has been abused.

Characteristics of Abused Children

Some courts permit expert testimony "regarding the behavioral and emotional indicia of child sexual abuse victims" as well as testimony that "an alleged victim exhibits behavior consistent with such a profile."[223] Some courts go further. In *People v. Fasy,*[224] the Colorado Supreme Court upheld testimony that the alleged "victim suffered from a post-traumatic stress disorder."[225]

Other courts prohibit "consistent with" testimony. For example, the Arizona Supreme Court ruled: "Once the jury has learned the victim's behavior from the evidence and has heard experts explaining why sexual abuse may cause delayed reporting, inconsistency, or recantation, we do not believe the jury needs an expert to explain that the victim's behavior is consistent or inconsistent with the crime having occurred."[226]

Still other courts reject the substantive use of expert testimony to prove the fact of abuse. In adopting this position, the Utah Supreme Court questioned the scientific basis of this type of evidence.

> [T]he child abuse profile consists of a long list of vague and sometimes conflicting psychological characteristics that are relied upon to establish the fact of injury in a specific case as well as the cause....
>
> Not only is there lack of any consensus about the ability of the profile to determine abuse, but the scientific literature raises serious doubts as to the reliability of profile testimony when used for forensic purposes to demonstrate abuse actually occurred.[227]

---

223. State v. Charles L., 183 W. Va. 641, 659, 398 S.E.2d 123, 141 (W. Va. 1990). *See also* State v. Fairweather, 116 N.M. 456, 460, 863 P.2d 1077, 1081 (1993) (PTSD testimony may be offered to show that the victim suffered from symptoms that are consistent with sexual abuse but not to show the victim is telling the truth); State v. Koepsell, 508 N.W.2d 591, 594 (S.D. 1993) (expert testimony comparing specific and general characteristics of sexually abused children admissible).

224. 829 P.2d 1314 (Colo. 1992).

225. *Id.* at 1317. *Accord* State v. Myers, 359 N.W.2d 604, 609-10 (Minn. 1984); Hayes v. State, 935 P.2d 700, 704 (Wyo. 1997) ("Dr. Fall's opinion that the victim was sexually abused did not constitute inappropriate expert testimony in this case").

226. State v. Moran, 151 Ariz. 378, 385, 728 P.2d 248, 255 (1986).

227. State v. Rimmasch, 775 P.2d 388, 401 (Utah 1989).

The Pennsylvania Supreme Court reached the same conclusion: "According to the literature on the subject, there is no one classical or typical personality profile for abused children. The difficulty with identifying a set of behaviors exhibited by abused children is that abused children react in a myriad of ways that ... may be the very same behaviors as exhibit who are not abused."[228]

Furthermore, several courts have ruled that the use of "art therapy" as a diagnostic tool is unreliable.[229]

Physical Evidence

The psychological evidence of sexual abuse should be distinguished from medical evidence of abuse. For example, in *United States v. Whitted*[230] the Eighth Circuit stated:

> A doctor can ... summarize the medical evidence and express an opinion that the evidence is consistent or inconsistent with the victim's allegations of sexual abuse.... [H]owever, a doctor's opinion that sexual abuse has in fact occurred is ordinarily neither useful to the jury nor admissible.... A

228. Commonwealth v. Dunkle, 529 Pa. 168, 174, 602 A.2d 830, 832 (1992) (CSAAS evidence is not generally accepted by the scientific community). *See also* Hadden v. State, 690 So. 2d 573 (Fla. 1997) (child sexual abuse accommodation syndrome not generally accepted as a diagnostic tool); Irving v. State, 705 So. 2d 1021 (Fla. App. 1998) ("Even though Dr. Hord never used the magic words 'syndrome' or 'profile,' his testimony may have been based upon CSAAS evidence, which was specifically found to be inadmissible in *Hadden*"); Fleener v. State, 656 N.E.2d 1140, 1141 (Ind. 1995) ("error to permit further testimony of this nature following the objection, particularly in light of the questionable reliability of child sexual abuse syndrome evidence for purposes of proving abuse"); Steward v. State, 652 N.E.2d 490, 496 (Ind. 1995) ("The reliability of syndrome evidence, although highly questionable for purposes of affirmatively proving sexual abuse, is generally accepted for purposes of helping the jury to understand that a complainant's reactions are not atypical of a young sexual assault victim"); Lantrip v. Commonwealth, 713 S.W.2d 816, 817 (Ky. 1986); State v. York, 564 A.2d 389, 391 (Me. 1989) (no empirical research supports reliability of diagnosing sexual abuse based on subsequent behavior); State v. Peterson, 450 Mich. 349, 370, 537 N.W.2d 857, 866 (1995) ("[T]he majority of jurisdictions considering the proper use of expert syndrome evidence testimony in child sexual abuse cases have limited its admissibility.... Most courts will not allow expert testimony in this area if offered to prove that the abuse occurred"); Baine v. State, 604 So. 2d 249 (Miss. 1992) (expert testimony that a child was the victim of abuse is inadmissible); Goodson v. State, 566 So. 2d 1142, 1146-47 (Miss. 1990); State v. Hudnall, 293 S.C. 97, 99-100, 359 S.E.2d 59, 61-62 (1987); State v. Ballard, 855 S.W.2d 557 (Tenn. 1993) (evidence about the characteristics of abused children is inadmissible because it intrudes upon the jury's function of deciding credibility and because the reliability of such evidence is suspect).

229. *See* Staggs v. Commonwealth, 877 S.W.2d 604, 606-07 (Ky. 1993) (use of art therapy by an expert to conclude that child had been sexually abused by her father failed *Frye* test); State v. Cressey, 137 N.H. 402, 628 A.2d 696, 698-99 (1993) (expert testimony based in part on "art therapy" not sufficiently reliable).

230. 11 F.3d 782 (8th Cir. 1993).

> doctor also cannot pass judgment on the alleged victim's truthfulness in the guise of a medical opinion, because it is the jury's function to decide credibility.[231]

The court went on to rule that a physician's diagnosis of "repeated child sexual abuse" was improper.

Expert testimony that the absence of physical trauma may be consistent with sexual assault is admissible.[232]

§ 9-5(B). Admissibility: Explaining Behavior.

Virtually all courts admit evidence derived from research on child sexual abuse when offered in response to a defense suggestion that specific behavior is inconsistent with a claim of abuse. For example, courts have admitted expert testimony to explain why a sexually abused child would delay making an accusation,[233] retract an accusation,[234] provide inconsistent statements,[235] remain

231. *Id.* at 785-86.

232. Commonwealth v. Johnson, 690 A.2d 274, 277 (Pa. Super. 1997). *See also* Turner v. Commonwealth, 914 S.W.2d 343, 346 (Ky. 1996) (experts who examined victim testified that the physical findings (scarring, tears, etc.) were negative but that such findings did not necessarily mean that sexual abuse had not occurred; "Today, we walk a fine line, but a line nonetheless ... [T]he physicians herein did not testify to support the truthfulness of the allegation of the child/victim").

233. *E.g.,* United States v. Bighead, 128 F.3d 1329, 1330 (9th Cir. 1997) (In rebuttal, an expert "testified about 'delayed disclosure' and 'script memory,' which are typical characteristics she has observed among the more than 1300 persons she has interviewed who say they are victims of child abuse"); United States v. Suarez, 35 M.J. 374, 376 (C.M.A. 1992) ("[S]ome forms of this testimony are apparently admissible, in that it helps explain why many sexually abused children delay reporting their abuse, and why many children recant allegations of abuse and deny that anything occurred"); People v. Patino, 26 Cal. App. 4th 1737, 1744, 32 Cal. Rptr. 2d 345, 349 (1994) (Expert's "testimony was offered for the limited purpose of explaining why Dorena did not immediately inform anyone of her molestation and why she slowly revealed the details of the molestation"); Wheat v. State, 527 A.2d 269, 273 (Del. 1987); Commonwealth v. Dockham, 405 Mass. 618, 628, 542 N.E.2d 591, 597 (1989) (expert explained that sexually abused children "often delay disclosure of sexual abuse or make gradual disclosures, retract their statements, and repress the abuse"); State v. Peterson, 450 Mich. 349, 380, 537 N.W.2d 857, 871 (1995) ("Showing that the victim's delay[ed] inconsistent reporting was consistent with other sexual assault victims was mere background information that allowed the jury to better understand the victim's testimony.... [T]his evidence did not improperly bolster the child witness' testimony"); State v. Myers, 359 N.W.2d 604, 610 (Minn. 1984); State v. Carlson, 360 N.W.2d 442, 442-43 (Minn. App. 1985); Smith v. State, 100 Nev. 570, 572-73, 688 P.2d 326, 327 (Nev. 1984); State v. MacRae, 141 N.H. 106, 677 A.2d 698, 701 (1996) (The expert's "testimony was carefully limited to informing the jury about characteristics and behaviors exhibited by victims of child sexual abuse [including delay in reporting] in order to rebut the inference that the victim's testimony was not credible").

234. *E.g.,* State v. Moran, 151 Ariz. 378, 384, 728 P.2d 248, 254 (1986) (factors that lead a victim to recant and attempt to return home are admissible); Steward v. State, 652 N.E.2d 490, 499

with the offender,[236] and the like.[237] Commentators have pointed out that such "expert testimony is needed to disabuse jurors of commonly held misconceptions about child sexual abuse, and to explain the emotional antecedents of abused children's seemingly self-impeaching behavior."[238]

(Ind. 1995) ("[I]f the defense discusses or presents evidence of such unexpected behavior by the child, or if during trial testimony the child recants a prior allegation of abuse, a trial court may consider permitting expert testimony, if based upon reliable scientific principles, regarding the prevalence of the specific unexpected behavior within the general class of reported child abuse victims"); State v. Foret, 628 So. 2d 1116, 1130 (La. 1993) ("So long as the expert limits the testimony to general characteristics that would explain delays in reporting, recantations, and omission of details, the testimony" is admissible); People v. Reid, 123 Misc. 2d 1084, 1085-86, 475 N.Y.S.2d 741, 741-42 (Crim. Ct. 1984); State v. Middleton, 294 Or. 427, 437-38, 657 P.2d 1215, 1220-21 (1983); Frenzel v. State, 849 P.2d 741, 749 (Wyo. 1993) ("[E]vidence of CSAAS characteristics of sexually abused children for the sole purpose of explaining a victim's specific behavior which might be incorrectly construed as inconsistent with an abuse victim or to rebut an attack on the victim's credibility. For example, ... the victim delayed reporting the abuse, recanted the allegations, kept the abuse secretive, or was accommodating to the abuse..."), *cert. denied*, 118 S. Ct. 388 (1997).

But see Newkirk v. Commonwealth, 937 S.W.2d 690 (Ky. 1996) (expert testimony concerning the phenomenon of recantation in child sexual abuse cases is inadmissible).

235. *E.g.*, People v. Housley, 6 Cal. App. 4th 947, 954, 959, 8 Cal. Rptr. 2d 431, 435, 438-49 (1992) (Testimony that "victims commonly and falsely recant their stories of abuse, and often tell conflicting versions of a true story of abuse" is admissible; "[I]n all cases in which an expert is called to testify regarding CSAAS we hold the jury must sua sponte be instructed that (1) such evidence is admissible solely for the purpose of showing the victim's reactions as demonstrated by the evidence are not inconsistent with having been molested; and (2) the expert's testimony is not intended and should not be used to determine whether the victim's molestation claim is true"); Duckett v. State, 797 S.W.2d 906, 915-17 (Tex. Crim. App. 1990) (numerous inconsistencies and delayed reporting are elements of CSAAS).

236. *E.g.,* United States v. Johns, 15 F.3d 740, 743 (8th Cir. 1994) (Expert "described emotional and psychological traits of abuse victims that often account for behavior such as delay in reporting the abuse or failure to 'escape' the abusive situation"); State v. J.Q., 130 N.J. 554, 617 A.2d 1196, 1211 (1993) (CSAAS evidence is not admissible to establish abuse but may be admitted "to counter the mythology that if the abuse had occurred, the children surely would have complained sooner and would not have put up with repeated visits to [the accused's] apartment"); Griego v. State, 761 P.2d 973, 978 (Wyo. 1988) (expert testified that "it was common for adolescent victims to remain in the area of the offender").

237. *See* Commonwealth v. Hudson, 417 Mass. 536, 541, 631 N.E.2d 50, 53 (1994) (Expert "testimony was admissible to rebut the defendant's suggestions made during cross-examination that the victim was a troubled teenager, whose medical problems were related to menstruation, and whose unhappy home life could lead to false claims of rape"); State v. Jensen, 147 Wis. 2d 240, 252, 432 N.W.2d 913, 918 (1988) (expert testimony that it is common for sexual assault victims to be emotionally flat admitted when defense suggested such conduct was inconsistent with assault claim).

238. Myers, *supra* note 214, at 89. *See also* State v. Peterson, 450 Mich. 349, 373-79, 537 N.W.2d 857, 868 (1995) ("[T]he prosecution may present evidence [in its case-in-chief], if relevant and helpful, to generally explain the common postincident behavior of children who are victims of sexual abuse.... Unless a defendant raises the issue of the particular child victim's postincident

Expert testimony that would explain why a mother would refrain from reporting the sex abuse of her child to the police is also admissible.[239]

§ 9-5(C). Admissibility: Credibility.

Several courts have admitted expert testimony on credibility in this context. For example, the Montana Supreme Court held that expert testimony is admissible "for the purpose of helping the jury to assess the credibility of a child sexual assault victim."[240] This rule includes testimony that a particular child is telling the truth.[241]

Most courts, however, prohibit this type of expert testimony. The Arizona Supreme Court concluded: "Opinion evidence on who is telling the truth in cases such as this is nothing more than the expert's opinion on how the case should be decided.... [S]uch testimony is inadmissible, both because it usurps the jury's traditional functions and roles and because, when given insight into the behavioral sciences, the jury needs nothing further from the expert."[242] The prohibition on comments on credibility may extend to expert testimony concerning whether the child's statements were the result of manipulation or fantasizing, or that the child lacked the capacity for truth-telling.[243]

---

behavior or attacks the child's credibility, an expert may not testify that the particular child victim's behavior is consistent with that of a sexually abused child").

239. People v. McAlpin, 53 Cal. 3d 1289, 1302, 812 P.2d 563, 283 Cal. Rptr. 382, 389 (1991).

240. State v. Geyman, 224 Mont. 194, 200, 729 P.2d 475, 479 (1986).

241. *See* State v. Hall, 244 Mont. 161, 172-74, 797 P.2d 183, 190-91 (1990); State v. French, 233 Mont. 364, 368, 760 P.2d 86, 88-89 (1988).

242. State v. Lindsey, 149 Ariz. 472, 475, 720 P.2d 73, 76 (1986) ("Thus, even where expert testimony on behavioral characteristics that affect credibility or accuracy of observation is allowed, experts should not be allowed to give their opinion of the accuracy, reliability or credibility of a particular witness in the case being tried"). *Accord* Lickey v. State, 108 Nev. 191, 827 P.2d 824, 826 (1992) (psychologist may not testify about veracity of a victim); Commonwealth v. Seese, 512 Pa. 439, 444, 517 A.2d 920, 922 (1986) (pediatrician may not testify concerning credibility of eight-year-old alleged victim); State v. Stowers, 81 Ohio St.3d 260, 690 N.E.2d 881 (1998) (expert is not allowed to give a direct opinion about the child's truthfulness; however, an expert is allowed to give generalizations about "behavioral characteristics observed in sexually abused children"); Yount v. State, 872 S.W.2d 706, 711 (Tex. Crim. App. 1993) (en banc) ("[E]xpert testimony that a particular witness is truthful is inadmissible under Rule 702.... An expert who testifies that a class of persons to which the victim belongs is truthful is essentially telling the jury that they can believe the victim in the instant case as well. This is not 'expert' testimony of the kind which will assist the jury under Rule 702"); State v. Sims, 608 A.2d 1149 (Vt. 1991) (expert may not give testimony that is tantamount to a direct comment on the victim's credibility).

243. *See* Shutz v. State, 957 S.W.2d 52 (Tex. Crim. App. 1997) (exhaustively discussing the cases on this issue). *See generally* Dunn, *Questioning the Reliability of Children's Testimony: An Examination of the Problematic Elements*, 19 LAW & PSYCH. REV. 203 (1995).

Federal Rule 608

Federal Evidence Rule 608, which governs the impeachment use of character evidence, has sometimes played a role in the cases. Rule 608(a) permits opinion and reputation evidence concerning the truthful character of a witness after that witness has been impeached. In *State v. Kim*[244] the Hawaii Supreme Court concluded that an expert's testimony that he found the complaining witness "believable" was admissible under Hawaii Rule 608(a), which is patterned after the federal rule.[245]

Most courts, however, reject this view. The Utah Supreme Court concluded that the traditional view "represents an important policy choice" that "prevents trials from being turned into contests between what would amount to modern oath-helpers who would largely usurp the fact-finding function of judge or jury."[246] The court went on to embrace the position of the majority of courts that have "rejected *Kim*" and bar such testimony under Rule 608.[247] Indeed, the Hawaii Supreme Court subsequently overruled *Kim.*[248]

Due Process

In *Snowden v. Singletary,*[249] the Eleventh Circuit found a due process violation because an expert in the prosecution's case-in-chief testified that 99.5% of children tell the truth and the expert had never encountered a child who invented a lie about abuse. At the time of trial, the oldest of the alleged victims was six years of age, testifying about an incident two years before. There was little independent evidence of abuse. The court concluded: "Permitting an expert to vouch forcefully for the children's credibility in this case was a 'crucial, critical, highly significant factor.' In addition, there was no adequate means to counter

---

244. 64 Haw. 598, 645 P.2d 1330 (1982).

245. *Id.* at 610 n.14, 645 P.2d at 1339 n.14 ("While [the expert's] opinion was not couched in terms of character, its function and effect were indistinguishable from traditional character evidence .... Essentially, the difference between an opinion as to character for truthfulness and an opinion as to the believability of a witness' statements is the difference between 'I think X is believable' and 'X's statement is believable.' We feel the admissibility of either statement should turn not on niceties of phraseology but on the probative value of the testimony").

246. State v. Rimmasch, 775 P.2d 388, 392 (Utah 1989).

247. *Id. Accord* United States v. Azure, 801 F.2d 336, 341 (8th Cir. 1986); United States v. Binder, 769 F.2d 595, 602 (9th Cir. 1985), *cert. denied,* 484 U.S. 1073 (1988); Hutton v. State, 339 Md. 480, 503, 663 A.2d 1289, 1300 (1995) ("In any event, it is certain that, no matter how learned in his or her field of expertise, no expert is in a better position to assess the credibility of a witness than is the jury").

248. State v. Batangan, 71 Haw. 552, 563, 799 P.2d 48, 54 (1990) (expert may not testify child is "believable," and *Kim* is overruled).

249. 135 F.3d 732 (11th Cir. 1998), *cert. denied,* 119 S. Ct. 405 (1998).

such a contention: it truly was this expert's opinion that child witnesses in sexual abuse cases tell the truth."[250]

§ 9-5(D). Child Interviewing Techniques.

The admissibility of expert testimony on interviewing techniques in child abuse cases has raised additional issues.[251] In *State v. Gersin*,[252] the trial court refused to permit the defendant to introduce the testimony of a psychologist about established protocols for interviewing children who may have been sexually abused. The Ohio Supreme Court concluded that the testimony should have been permitted:

> [T]estimony on these protocols is admissible as expert testimony. ... [A]n expert may testify on the ultimate question of whether sexual abuse has occurred in a given case because most people are unfamiliar with the nuances of a child sexual abuse case. Similarly, most jurors are unaware of how such child abuse experts arrive at their conclusions. Necessarily, in child sexual abuse cases, experts must rely on the version of events given to them by small children. Special interviewing processes are necessary to get information from child victims, who are often immature, inarticulate, frightened, and confused about the abuse they have received. Most jurors lack the knowledge of accepted practices in interviewing child victims, and expert testimony on the issue is therefore admissible.[253]

Similarly, in *Barlow v. State*,[254] the Georgia Supreme Court ruled that expert testimony concerning the techniques used in a videotaped interview of the victim "involves an area of expertise beyond the ken of the average layman and,

---

250. *Id.* at 739. *See also* People v. Loomis, 172 Misc. 2d 265, 658 N.Y.S.2d 787 (Co. Ct. 1997) (excluding evidence of "Parental Alienation Syndrome" offered to determine whether a child's accusations are true or false).

251. *See* Thompson, Clarke-Steward & Lepore, *What Did The Janitor Do? Suggestive Interviewing And The Accuracy Of Children's Accounts*, 21 LAW & HUM. BEHAV. 405, 414, 424 (1997) ("Children questioned in a neutral manner consistently gave accurate accounts of what they had seen, but those questioned in a suggestive manner gave accounts that, over time, became consistent with the interviewers' suggestions regardless of what they had seen"; this experiment suggest "that 5- and 6- year-old children can provide reliable information about a complex event when they are interviewed properly. On the other hand, the study also shows that a suggestive interview can alter children's subsequent accounts of the event"). *See generally* D. BROWN, A. SCHEFLIN & D. HAMMOND, MEMORY, TRAUMA TREATMENT, AND THE LAW ch. 9 (1998) (interrogatory suggestion and coercive persuasion).

252. 76 Ohio St. 3d 491, 668 N.E.2d 486 (1996).

253. *Id.* at 494, 668 N.E.2d at 488. *See also* United States v. Rouse, 111 F.3d 561 (8th Cir. 1997) (excluding expert testimony harmless error), *superseding panel decision*, 100 F.3d 560 (8th Cir. 1996).

254. 270 Ga. 54, 55, 507 S.E.2d 416, 417 (1998).

therefore, ... the defendant in a child molestation case is entitled to introduce expert testimony for the limited purpose of providing the jury with information about proper techniques for interviewing children and whether interviewing techniques actually utilized were proper."[255]

The research that supports these cases has not gone unchallenged. One commentator has written that "the scientific stance of the new wave of suggestibility research conceals questionable empirical assumptions and subjective value judgments. Although the new wave asserts that one can generalize its findings to actual abuse allegations, the new wave's research ignores the realities of sexual abuse and of actual abuse investigation. These shortcomings render the new-wave criticism of limited applicability to real-world abuse cases."[256]

§ 9-5(E). Anatomically Correct Dolls.

A number of courts have considered expert testimony based on the use of "anatomically correct" dolls. The critical issue is how the dolls are used, whether as a scientific tool for determining abuse or merely as illustrative evidence.

In *United States v. Gillespie*[257] an expert (child therapist) testified that "the child's behavior with anatomically correct dolls showed she had been abused by a man using his penis and not by a woman."[258] The Ninth Circuit ruled that this use of the dolls failed to satisfy the *Frye* general acceptance test and was thus inadmissible.[259] Similarly, the Eighth Circuit has cautioned that the "empirical

---

255. "Child sexual abuse cases are a special lot. ... [A]n expert witness for the defense cannot give an opinion that the victim made false allegations of molestation, because such testimony directly addresses the credibility of the victim. However, the fact that limited expert testimony regarding proper interview techniques indirectly involves the child's credibility does not render it inadmissible." *Id.* at 418 (citations omitted). *See also* Pyron v. State, 237 Ga. App. 198, 514 S.E.2d 51, 53 (1999) ("Unlike *Barlow*, this case involves physical rather than sexual abuse. This distinction, however, does not warrant a different result since the underlying concerns remain the same"); State v. Sloan, 912 S.W.2d 592, 596 (Mo. App. 1995) ("Opinions of experts on improper or suggestive techniques employed by individuals investigating allegations of sexual abuse of children have been allowed in several jurisdictions"); State v. Michaels, 136 N.J. 299, 642 A.2d 1372 1384 (1994) (defense may offer expert testimony to explain the coercive or suggestive propensities of interviewing techniques employed but may not comment on the credibility of the child witness); State v. Kirschbaum, 195 Wis. 2d 11, 25, 535 N.W.2d 462, 467 (App. 1995) ("a subject with which a lay juror may be unfamiliar"), *rev. denied*, 537 N.W.2d 571 (Wis.1995). *But see* State v. Ellis, 669 A.2d 752, 753-54 (Me. 1996).

256. Lyon, *The New Wave in Children's Suggestibility Research: A Critique*, 84 CORNELL L. REV. 1004, 1084 (1999).

257. 852 F.2d 475 (9th Cir. 1988).

258. *Id.* at 480.

259. *Id.* at 481. *Accord In re* Amber B., 191 Cal. App. 3d 682, 690-91, 236 Cal. Rptr. 623, 629 (1987). *See* Chapter 1 (discussing *Frye*).

literature clearly reflects a concern that repeated use of the dolls can be highly suggestive."[260]

Other courts disagree. In *Reyna v. State*[261] a Texas appellate court ruled that the dolls were "not used as a scientific method of proof, but merely as a tool to aid the jury with the witness' testimony."[262] Accordingly, their use was permissible.

The commentators are also divided. Many believe that the "danger in the use of the dolls is that they will stimulate fantasy and not recall, and plant a falsified memory of fantasy to be recalled later as truth."[263] In contrast, others opine that "[r]ecent research indicates that the dolls can be helpful in evaluating suspected abuse."[264]

§ 9-5(F). Related Issues.

Another issue concerns whether the defendant has a right to have the alleged victim examined by defense experts. This issue is discussed in § 3-10 *supra*.

§ 9-6. Syndrome Evidence.

"Syndrome" evidence of all kinds has been offered at criminal trials[265] – for example, fight-flee syndrome,[266] Vietnam veterans syndrome,[267] Holocaust

---

260. United States v. Spotted War Bonnet, 882 F.2d 1360, 1370 (8th Cir. 1989), *vacated on other grounds,* 497 U.S. 1021 (1990).

261. 797 S.W.2d 189 (Tex. App. 1990).

262. *Id.* at 193. *See also* Stevens v. People, 796 P.2d 946, 955 (Colo. 1990) (dolls provide corroboration for admissibility of child hearsay statements); State v. Oslund, 469 N.W.2d 489, 494-95 (Minn. App. 1991).

263. Christiansen, *The Testimony of Child Witnesses: Fact, Fantasy, and the Influence of Pretrial Interviews*, 62 WASH. L. REV. 705, 711 (1987). *See also* Levy, *Using "Scientific" Testimony to Prove Child Sexual Abuse*, 23 FAM. L.Q. 148, (1989) ("[T]estimony about anatomically correct dolls should be inadmissible"); Sagatun, *Expert Witnesses in Child Abuse Cases*, 9 BEHAV. SCI. & L. 201, 210-12 (Spring 1991) ("little scientific" literature on subject); J. MYERS, CHILD WITNESS LAW AND PRACTICE § 4.17L (1992 Supp.) (discussing literature on use of dolls); Skinner & Berry, *Anatomically Detailed Dolls and the Evaluation of Child Sexual Abuse Allegations: Psychometric Considerations*, 17 LAW & HUM. BEHAV. 399 (1993).

264. Myers, *supra* note 214, at 63 n.259.

265. *See generally* Edwards, *Behavior and the Law Reconsidered: Psychological Syndromes and Profiles*, 43 J. FORENSIC SCI. 141 (1998); Mosteller, *Syndromes and Politics in Criminal Trials and Evidence Law*, 46 DUKE L.J. 461 (1996); McCord, *Syndromes, Profiles and Other Mental Exotica: A New Approach to the Admissibility of Nontraditional Psychological Evidence in Criminal Cases*, 66 OR. L. REV. 19 (1987); Note, *"Lies, damned Lies, and Statistics?" Psychological Syndrome Evidence in the Courtroom After Daubert*, 71 IND. L. REV. 753 (1996).

266. State v. Nazario, 726 So. 2d 349 (Fla. App. 1999) (expert testimony regarding human behavior and brain functioning while experiencing the fight/flee syndrome, the factors that trigger the syndrome, and physical symptoms experienced during the syndrome are inadmissible because the purpose was to show that the accused was precluded from forming an intent to kill and acted

syndrome,[268] confusional arousal syndrome,[269] lying child syndrome,[270] parental alienation syndrome,[271] fetal alcohol syndrome[272] — to name but a few.[273] Several syndromes are briefly noted below.

§ 9-6(A). Neonaticide Syndrome; Postpartum Psychosis.

Neonaticide is the killing of a newborn child within twenty-four hours of birth.[274] Neonaticide syndrome is an expression used to describe the feelings of isolation and denial that afflict a young women (usually between fifteen and thirty-eight years of age) who conceals her pregnancy from her friends and family, gives birth alone (usually in an isolated bathroom), and then kills and discards her baby. Neonaticide is not a distinct crime; therefore offenders are charged with varying offenses from murder or manslaughter to gross abuse of a corpse.

Some medical literature attempts to explain the patterns of behavior and mental reactions of neonaticide offenders. Expert testimony may help the jury understand the defendant's state of mind at the time of the alleged neonaticide, a concept that is beyond the scope of an average juror's knowledge. However, courts have been reluctant to allow expert testimony on neonaticide syndrome,[275] causing discrepancy in charges and sentences in cases with similar facts.

---

out of an involuntary survival instinct, which amounts to a diminished capacity defense that is not recognized under Florida law).

267. *See* United States v. Gowen, 32 F.3d 1466, 1469-70 (10th Cir. 1994) (diagnostic interview and testing results of expert on post-traumatic stress disorder [PTSD]), *cert. denied*, 513 U.S. 1173 (1995). *See generally* Erlinder, *Paying the Price for Vietnam: Post-Traumatic Stress Disorder and Criminal Behavior*, 25 B.C. L. REV. 305 (1984); Symposium, *Post-Traumatic Stress Disorders*, 1 BEHAV. SCI. & LAW 7-129 (Summer 1983).

268. Werner v. State, 711 S.W.2d 639 (Tex. Crim. App. 1986).

269. People v. Cegers, 7 Cal. App. 4th 988, 9 Cal. Rptr. 2d 297 (1992).

270. Jennette v. State, 197 Ga. App.580, 398 S.E.2d 734 (1990).

271. People v. Loomis, 172 Misc. 2d 265, 658 N.Y.S.2d 787 (Co. Ct. 1997) (excluding evidence of "Parental Alienation Syndrome" offered to determine whether a child's accusations are true or false).

272. Ferry, *Fetal Alcohol Syndrome: An Effective Capital Defense*, 24 CACJ/FORUM 42 (1997). FAS refers to the damage done to a child by its mother's drinking. General characteristics are "1) growth deficiencies, 2) a specific cluster of facial anomalies [and] 3) central nervous system disorder." Not all FAS victims exhibit all characteristics, nor is there a medical test to confirm a FAS diagnosis. However, it may affect a defendant's ability to stand trial or even form the required mens rea to commit the charged offense.

273. *See also* Leong, Silva, Garza-Trevino, Oliva, Ferrari, Komanduri & Caldwell, *The Dangerousness of Persons with the Othello Syndrome*, 39 J. FORENSIC SCI. 1445 (1994).

274. Note, *Throwing The Bath Water Out With The Baby: Wrongful Exclusion Of Expert Testimony On Neonaticide Syndrome*, 78 B.U. L. REV. 1185, 1186 (1998).

275. *See* People v. Wernick, 89 N.Y.2d 111, 674 N.E.2d 322, 651 N.Y.S.2d 392 (1996) (neonaticide syndrome not generally accepted).

Postpartum psychosis, an extreme form of postpartum depression, also involves the death of a child at the hands of his or her mother, although the etiology differs from neonaticide.[276]

§ 9-6(B). Premenstrual Stress Syndrome.

Premenstrual Dysphoric Disorder (PMDD), severe Premenstrual Stress Syndrome (PMS), is characterized by extreme anger and depression. PMDD is a recognized depressive disorder in the DSM-IV;[277] however, there is no agreed upon clinical cause.[278] In general, American courts have been reluctant to accept the PMS defense.[279] Some commentators fear that the use of this defense will increase discrimination and undermine women's credibility. Furthermore, PMS could be viewed as an aggravating, rather than a mitigating, factor; if the defendant knows that she is effected by PMS, she should be more cautions during that time period.[280]

§ 9-6(C). Urban Rage Syndrome; Cultural Defenses.

"Urban Rage" or "Black Rage" is a defense asserted by victims of racism or environmental violence at the hands of white people.[281] Black Rage is not a separately recognized mental illness in DSM-IV, but it has been linked to the insanity defense as a means of finding its way into the courtroom.[282] The theory

---

276. *See* Dent, *Postpartum Psychosis and the Insanity Defense*, U. CHI. LEGAL F. 355 (1989); Note, *Postpartum Psychosis: A Way Out for Murderous Moms?*, 18 HOFSTRA L. REV. 1133 (1990); Comment, *Mothers Who Kill: Postpartum Disorders and Criminal Infanticide*, 38 UCLA L. REV. 699 (1991).

277. Comment, *Premenstrual Syndrome: The Debate Surrounding Criminal Defense*, 54 MD. L. REV. 571, 571 (1995).

278. Note, *Premenstrual Dysphoric Disorder As A Mitigating Factor In Sentencing: Following The Lead Of English Criminal Courts*, 33 VAL. U. L. REV. 201, 205 (1998).

279. *See* Holtzman, *Premenstrual Syndrome: The Indefensible Defense*, 7 HARV. WOMEN'S L.J. 1 (1984); Keye & Trunnell, *Premenstrual Syndrome: A Medical Perspective*, 9 HAMLINE L. REV. 165 (1986); Kendall, *The Politics of Premenstrual Syndrome: Implications for Feminist Justice*, 2 J. HUM. JUST. 77 (Spring 1991); Lewis, *Premenstrual Syndrome as a Criminal Defense*, 19 ARCHIVES OF SEXUAL BEHAV. 425 (1990).

280. Note, *Has The PMS Defense Gained A Legitimate Toehold In Virginia Criminal Law? Commonwealth v. Richter*, 14 GEO. MASON U. L. REV. 427, 445 (1991).

281. Mosteller, *Syndrome and Politics in Criminal Trials and Evidence Law*, 46 DUKE L.J. 461 (1996) ("True 'trash' syndromes should not threaten justice; they can and should be excluded as scientifically invalid. The Urban Survival Syndrome should be excluded on the basis of well-established principles of evidence law. Admission of such evidence requires a showing that some real science exists to support the expert testimony; no reliable theory or methodology supports Urban Survival Syndrome").

282. Foster, *From Fear to Rage As A Natural Progression From Functional Equivalent Of Battered Women Syndrome*, 38 WM. & MARY L. REV. 1851, 1868 (1997).

that racism can harm an individual's psychological development is generally accepted; however, the issue is whether this harm can ever rise to the level of a legally recognized mental illness.[283]

Defense counsel have attempted to use Black Rage ("Urban Psychosis," "Urban Survival Syndrome," "Rotten Social Background") as an excuse for criminal behavior and as a mitigating factor. The argument asserted is that Black Rage is a subset of PTSD.[284] The traumatic stressor is not necessarily one distinct episode of abhorrent racism, but rather a lifetime of oppression and fear, which ultimately culminates in criminal behavior.[285] Critics are concerned that the use of Black Rage as part of an insanity defense will lead to an increase in racism and negative stereotypes. To date, Black Rage has not gained legal acceptance.

A related issue concerns various cultural defenses, which may take several forms: "[1] justification argument that the offense charged is not criminal in the actor's original culture; [2] a mitigation excuse argument that the offense charged is criminal but punished much less severely in the original culture than the new culture, and that the actor is therefore entitled to the more lenient punishment; [3] and an excuse argument (complete in some cases, mitigating in others) that the actor does not deny knowledge that the offense charged was a crime, but that the actions are the involuntary result of the stress of acculturation or assimilation into a new culture."[286] Such defenses have typically failed.[287]

§ 9-6(D). Munchausen Syndrome by Proxy.

Munchausen Syndrome is a clinical term that refers to a patient who invents medical symptoms or actively causes them, resulting in multiple hospitalizations, in order to gain attention. Munchausen Syndrome By Proxy (MSBP) means that the offender victimizes another person,[288] usually a young, pre-verbal child in order to receive attention.[289] The symptoms are extraordinary, often confusing medical personnel, which results in excessive testing and thereby contributes to

---

283. Note, *Post-Traumatic Stress Disorder And Black Rage: Clinical Validity, Criminal Responsibility*, 5 VA. J. SOC. POL'Y & L. 213, 221 (1997).

284. Falk, *Novel Theories Of Criminal Defense Based Upon The Toxicity Of The Social Environment: Urban Psychosis, Television Intoxication, And Black Rage*, 74 N.C. L. REV. 731, 736 (1996).

285. Book Review, *"Black Rage" Confronts The Law*, 7 B.U. PUB. INT. L.J. 181, 184 (1998) (reviewing Paul Harris's book).

286. Maguigan, *Cultural Evidence and Male Violence: Are Feminist and Multiculturalist Reformers on a Collision Course in Criminal Courts?*, 70 N.Y.U. L. REV. 36, 48-49 (1999).

287. *See also* Note, *The Availability of the "Cultural Defense" as an Excuse for Criminal Behavior*, 16 GA. J. INT'L & COMP. L. 335 (1986); Note, *The Cultural Defense in the Criminal Law*, 99 HARV. L. REV. 1293 (1986).

288. People v. Phillips, 122 Cal. App. 69, 175 Cal. Rptr. 703, 703 (1981).

289. *In re* C.M., 236 Ga. App. 874, 513 S.E.2d 773, 776 (1999).

the attention and sympathy given to the victim's caretaker.[290] The offender is typically the child's primary caretaker (mother) and has some type of medical/health education.[291] In most cases, the symptoms stop as soon as the child is separated from his caretaker.[292] MSBP is an identifiable, medical condition that has been recognized by the DSM-IV.

§ 9-6(E). Stockholm Syndrome; Captivity Syndrome.

The Stockholm Syndrome refers to the phenomenon of hostages and hostage takers developing positive feelings for each other and negative feelings and frustration towards officers of the law.[293] This syndrome is an exception to the norm. In order for it to develop, according to FBI research, the hostages must be captive for an extended period of time, in close connection with the captors, and the captors must treat the hostages with an element of respect, or at least not abuse or threaten them.[294]

Expert testimony concerning "captivity syndrome" has also been offered.[295] For example, in *United States v. Alzanki*,[296] the First Circuit ruled that a "victimologist" expert could testify in an involuntary servitude case that physical abuse victims do not always flee from the abuser at the first opportunity.

§ 9-7. Profile Evidence.

Along with syndrome evidence, courts have been confronted with the task of determining the admissibility of a variety of profiles. "A criminal psychological profile attempts to provide investigators with specific information about an offender based on an examination of a crime scene."[297] The profile does not attempt to identify any one particular person, but rather the type of person who would commit the crime. Most often, such evidence is inadmissible.[298] For

---

290. Reid v. State, 964 S.W.2d 723, 729 (Tex. App. 1998).

291. Artingstall, *Munchausen Syndrome By Proxy*, FBI LAW ENFORCEMENT BULL. 6 (Aug. 1995).

292. *In re* of C.M., 236 Ga. App. 874, 513 S.E.2d 773, 775 (1999).

293. United States v. Peralta, 941 F.2d 1003 (9th Cir. 1991) (FBI psychologist testified about Stockholm Syndrome to explain to jury why a daughter did not attempt to escape from her captors).

294. Fuselier, *Placing the Stockholm Syndrome in Perspective*, FBI LAW ENFORCEMENT BULL. 24 (July 1999).

295. *See* United States v. Kozmininski, 771 F.2d 125 (6th Cir. 1985).

296. 54 F.3d 994 (1st Cir. 1995), *cert. denied*, 516 U.S. 1111 (1996).

297. Note, *If The Profile Fits: Admitting Criminal Psychological Profiles Into Evidence In Criminal Trials*, 54 WASH. U. J. URB. & CONTEMP. L. 239, 242 (1998).

298. *Id.* ("Judicial use of criminal psychological profiling has a poor track record as a result of misunderstanding, misuse, and misapplication, and, thus, such testimony will usually not be admitted at trial.... Courts' refusal to admit into evidence criminal psychological profiles is based on the grounds that they constitute impermissible character testimony, improper subjects for scientific or expert testimony, and unduly prejudicial evidence").

example, arsonist profiles are generally not considered to be reliable and are therefore inadmissible.[299]

§ 9-7(A). Battering Parent Profile.

The Battering Parent Profile must be distinguished from the Battered Child Syndrome.[300] Both issues may arise in cases in which a parent is prosecuted for inflicting injury to or causing the death of a child. Typically, evidence of the Battered Child Syndrome involves medical testimony based on the victim's medical history and injuries; it is admissible to show that the injuries to the child were intentional rather than accidental[301] or to show that "the parent's explanation of the child's injuries is a fabrication."[302] Many courts permit this type of expert testimony.[303]

In contrast, the Battering Parent Profile involves the psychological and demographic characteristics of typical abusing parents. It is offered to show that the defendant (the parent) fits the profile and thus is more likely to have battered the child. In sum, the Battered Child Syndrome focuses on the child's physical condition, while the Battering Parent Profile focuses on the parent's characteristics.

The Battering Parent Profile is an offshoot of the research on the Battered Child Syndrome.[304] Researchers have attempted to identify not only the physical attributes of an abused child but also the characteristics of parents who abuse their children. One expert testified that the profile of a battering parent consists of the following characteristics: (1) the parent herself is the product of a violent, abusive environment; (2) the parent is under some kind of chronic environmental

299. *See* People v. Avellanet, 242 A.D.2d 865, 865, 662 N.Y.S.2d 345 (1997) (not generally accepted).

300. For a discussion of the Battered Child Syndrome, *see* Chapter 19 (forensic pathology).

301. *See* State v. Heath, 264 Kan. 557, 568, 957 P.2d 449, 459 (1998) ("Dr. Thomas, over objection, testified that based upon his autopsy findings, Cain suffered from battered child syndrome.... According to Dr. Thomas, the major diagnostic feature of battered child syndrome is a discrepancy between the history given by the caretaker and the physical findings, as well as no injury occurring during the time the child is in a protected environment"); State v. Atkins, 349 N.C. 62, 505 S.E.2d 97 (1998) (medical experts testified that the physical injuries varied in age and that the types of injuries were consistent with BCS); State v. Tanner, 675 P.2d 539, 543 (Utah 1983) ("[T]he pattern of abuse is relevant to show that *someone* injured the child intentionally, rather than accidentally").

302. United States v. Bowers, 660 F.2d 527, 529 (5th Cir. 1981).

303. *E.g.,* State v. Durfee, 322 N.W.2d 778, 783-84 (Minn. 1982); State v. Holland, 346 N.W.2d 302, 307-08 (S.D. 1984); Annot., *Admissibility of Expert Medical Testimony on Battered Child Syndrome*, 98 A.L.R.3D 306 (1980).

304. *See* McCoid, *The Battered Child and Other Assaults Upon the Family: Part One*, 50 MINN. L. REV. 1, 18-19 (1965); John, *Child Abuse — The Battered Child Syndrome*, 2 AM. JUR. 2D PROOF OF FACTS 365 (1974).

stress, caused, for example, by money or housing problems, and is frequently a single parent; (3) the parent has a history of poor social adjustment, tending to be impulsive or explosive under stress; (4) the abused child is the product of an unplanned or difficult pregnancy; and (5) the abused child is a chronically difficult child.[305]

Admissibility

Several courts have treated the profile as evidence of the defendant's character; that is, to show that the defendant matches the profile and therefore is more likely to have committed the particular abuse charged. Generally, character evidence is inadmissible unless the defendant first introduces evidence of his own good character.[306] Since the defendants in these cases had not introduced character evidence, the courts have excluded expert testimony concerning the Battering Parent Profile.[307]

Other courts have ruled such testimony inadmissible because it lacks probative value and entails a risk of unfair prejudice. As one court has noted, such "evidence invites a jury to conclude that because the defendant has been identified by an expert with experience in child abuse cases as a member of a

---

305. Sanders v. State, 251 Ga. 70, 73-74, 303 S.E.2d 13, 16 (1983). A commentator summarized the profile as follows:

> [A]busing parents seem to have low self esteem, poor impulse control, low empathy, low frustration tolerance, and inadequate knowledge of basic child development and of parenting skills. In addition, they are more likely than non-abusers to manifest diagnosable psychopathology, or other serious emotional problems.
>
> Apart from such personality characteristics, abusing parents in the reported studies were themselves almost universally abused or neglected as children. As adults, they tend to social isolation, and are likely to be under environmental stress, often belonging to lower socioeconomic groups.

Note, *The Battering Parent Syndrome: Inexpert Testimony as Character Evidence*, 17 MICH. J. L. REFORM 653, 658-59 (1984).

306. *See* FED. R. EVID. 404(a) ("Evidence of a person's character or a trait of character is not admissible for the purpose of proving action in conformity therewith on a particular occasion ...").

307. "[U]nless a defendant has placed her character in issue or has raised some defense which the battering parent syndrome is relevant to rebut, the state may not introduce evidence of the syndrome, nor may the state introduce character evidence showing a defendant's personality traits and personal history as its foundation for demonstrating the defendant has the characteristics of a typical battering parent." Sanders v. State, 251 Ga. 70, 76, 303 S.E.2d 13, 18 (1983). *Accord* State v. Durfee, 322 N.W.2d 778, 785 (Minn. 1982); State v. Loebach, 310 N.W.2d 58, 64 (Minn. 1981). *See also* Annot., *Admissibility at Criminal Prosecution of Expert Testimony on Battering Parent Syndrome*, 43 A.L.R.4TH 1203 (1986).

group having a higher incidence of child sexual abuse, it is more likely the defendant committed the crime."[308]

In addition, there seems little scientific support for the profile: "Regardless of which party offers battering parent syndrome evidence, serious questions persist about the syndrome's reliability."[309]

One court has held expert testimony on the Battering Parent Profile admissible in limited circumstances. In *State v. Conlogue*[310] the defendant attempted to show that the mother of the child, and not he, had injured the child. The mother had initially admitted that she had injured the child but later recanted and testified as a prosecution witness. A prosecution expert testified that the child was a victim of the Battered Child Syndrome and on cross-examination stated that the mother had admitted striking the child. The defense, however, was precluded from eliciting additional testimony from the expert that would have shown that the mother had also admitted that she herself had been abused and that abused children often become abusive parents. The Maine Supreme Court reversed, holding that the evidence was relevant to show that the mother and not the defendant had committed the crime: "[A] description of battered child syndrome and the likelihood that [the mother's] own history of child abuse would predispose her to abuse her own child, would have allowed the jury to weigh the credibility of [the mother's] confession against the credibility of her later retraction."[311]

§ 9-7(B). Sex Offender Profiles.

Profiles of rapists, child molesters, and pedophiles have been proffered as evidence. Sometimes prosecutors have offered such evidence, other times the defense. In either case, such profiles are generally inadmissible.

Most courts exclude evidence of a child molester profile. For example, in *United States v. Gillespie*[312] the prosecution in rebuttal called an expert who testified about the characteristics of a typical child molester. These included "an early disruption in the family environment, often with one parent missing; a relationship with the parent of the opposite sex who is dominant; unsuccessful relationships with women; a poor self-concept; and general instability in the

---

308. State v. Maule, 35 Wash. App. 287, 293, 667 P.2d 96, 99 (1983). *Accord* Sloan v. State, 70 Md. App. 630, 639, 522 A.2d 1364, 1368 (1987), *cert. denied,* 310 Md. 276, 528 A.2d 1287 (1987); Duley v. State, 56 Md. App. 275, 281, 467 A.2d 776, 780 (1983); Commonwealth v. Day, 409 Mass. 719, 723, 569 N.E.2d 397, 399 (1991) ("The use of criminal profiles as substantive evidence of guilt is inherently prejudicial to the defendant").

309. Myers, *supra* note 214, at 142.

310. 474 A.2d 167 (Me. 1984).

311. *Id.* at 173.

312. 852 F.2d 475 (9th Cir. 1988).

background."[313] The Ninth Circuit ruled this testimony inadmissible. The defendant had not offered any character evidence, and thus rebuttal on this score was impermissible. The court also commented that "testimony of criminal profiles is highly undesirable as substantive evidence because it is of low probativity and inherently prejudicial."[314]

The California Supreme Court in *People v. McAlpin*[315] upheld the admission of expert testimony concerning child abusers to rebut the notion that there was a profile. The expert testified that there was no profile of a typical abuser. He testified that a child molester can be from any social or financial status, race, age, occupation, geographic origin, or religious group. They can also be persons with impeccable reputations. The court held that this testimony was helpful to the jury because it debunked common myths about abusers—*i.e.*, that abusers are strangers, old, gay, alcoholic, or retarded.

Profiles Offered by Defense

Most courts prohibit defense evidence offered to show that the accused did not fit a profile. For example, in *State v. Cavaliere*[316] the New Hampshire Supreme Court upheld the exclusion of expert testimony that the defendant did not fit a "sexual offender profile." The published studies agreed with the prosecution's expert, who "testified that there is no test or group of tests which can determine if a person is a sexual offender."[317] Similarly, the Iowa Supreme Court ruled that a trial judge did not abuse his discretion in excluding such evidence on the grounds that it would not assist the jury.[318] Moreover, the New Jersey Supreme Court held that a psychological profile of rapists was not generally accepted in the scientific

---

313. *Id.* at 480.

314. *Id. See also* Hall v. State, 15 Ark. App. 309, 316-17, 692 S.W.2d 769, 773 (1985); State v. Pulizzano, 155 Wis. 2d 633, 657, 456 N.W.2d 325, 355 (1990) (error for prosecutor to argue that the accused's history as a victim of child sexual abuse increased likelihood that she committed the alleged acts). *See generally* Myers, *supra* note 214, at 144 ("The relevant scientific literature does not support the conclusion that there is a reliable profile of a 'typical' sex offender").

315. 53 Cal. 3d 1289, 1302-04, 812 P.2d 563, 569-72, 283 Cal. Rptr. 382, 389-90 (1991).

316. 140 N.H. 108, 663 A.2d 96 (1995).

317. 663 A.2d at 99. *See also* Flanagan v. State, 625 So. 2d 827 (Fla. 1993) ("[S]exual offender profile evidence is not generally accepted in the scientific community and does not meet the *Frye* test for admissibility").

318. State v. Hulbert, 481 N.W.2d 329, 332 (Iowa 1992). *Accord* United States v. St. Pierre, 812 F.2d 417, 420 (8th Cir. 1987) (sex offender profile not generally accepted in the scientific community); State v. Hardwick, 905 P.2d 1384, 1388 (Ariz. App. 1995) (child molester profile not generally accepted); State v. Tucker, 165 Ariz. 340, 346, 798 P.2d 1349, 1353-55 (App. 1990).

community.[319] The same exclusionary rule applies to expert testimony concerning pedophiles.[320]

In *People v. Stoll*[321] the California Supreme Court adopted a minority position. The court held that a defendant charged with child molesting may introduce expert character evidence establishing that he is not a deviant.

§ 9-7(C). Drug Courier Profile.

"A drug courier profile is a loose assortment of general, often contradictory, characteristics and behaviors used by police officers to explain their reasons for stopping and questioning a person about possible illegal drug activity."[322] The profile is often used in suppression hearings to establish or buttress probable cause.[323] However, when offered at trial as substantive evidence, the majority of jurisdictions reject such expert testimony.[324] If offered for another purpose, this

---

319. State v. Cavallo, 88 N.J. 508, 517, 443 A.2d 1020, 1024 (1982).

320. *See* United States v. Powers, 59 F.3d 1460 (4th Cir. 1995) (excluding evidence that the defendant did not fit the profile of a fixated pedophile, on the grounds that the evidence was irrelevant; the defendant was charged with statutory rape of his daughter (incest abuse) and not with being a pedophile), *cert. denied*, 516 U.S. 1077 (1996); Mendoza v. Leapley, 5 F.3d 341, 342 (8th Cir. 1993) (denial of request for appointment of psychologist to testify that accused's personality was inconsistent with that of a child rapist; "The State did not present psychological evidence, so Mendoza did not need an expert in order to respond to damaging evidence of the same type"); People v. Ruiz, 222 Cal. App. 3d 1241 1243, 272 Cal. Rptr. 368, 370 (1990) (scientific community has not developed a standard pedophile profile); Tungate v. Commonwealth, 901 SW.2d 41 (Ky. 1995) ("indicators for pedophilia" are unscientific).

321. 49 Cal. 3d 1136, 1152-53, 783 P.2d 698, 707-08, 265 Cal. Rptr. 111, 120-21 (1989). *See also* People v. McAlpin, 53 Cal. 3d 1289, 1304, 812 P.2d 563, 576-78, 283 Cal. Rptr. 382, 391-95 (1991).

322. State v. Lee, 191 Ariz. 542, 544, 959 P.2d 799, 801 (1998) (citing Kadish, *The Drug Courier Profile: In Planes, Trains, and Automobiles; And Now in the Jury Box*, 46 AM. U. L. REV. 747, 748 (1997)).

323. *See* Reid v. Georgia, 448 U.S. 438, 440-41 (1980); Florida v. Royer, 460 U.S. 491, 493 (1983).

324. *E.g.,* United States v. Jones, 913 F.2d 174 (4th Cir. 1990); United States v. Hernandez-Cuartas, 717 F.2d 552, 555 (11th Cir. 1983) ("Every defendant has a right to be tried based on the evidence against him or her, not on the techniques utilized by law enforcement officers in investigating criminal activity. Drug courier profile evidence is nothing more than the opinion of those officers conducting an investigation. Although this information is valuable in helping drug agents to identify potential drug couriers, we denounce the use of this type of evidence as substantive evidence of a defendant's innocence or guilt"); State v. Lee, 191 Ariz. 542, 545, 959 P.2d 799, 802 (1998) ("Notwithstanding these exceptions, a significant majority of jurisdictions have condemned the use of drug courier profile evidence as substantive proof of guilt"); People v. Salcedo, 1998 Colo. App. LEXIS 120 *7 (1998) ("We agree that the use of drug courier profiles as substantive evidence of guilt is improper"); Dean v. State, 690 So. 2d 720 (Fla. App. 1997); People v. Hubbard, 209 Mich. App. 234, 530 N.W.2d 130 (Mich. App. 1995), *app. denied,* 548 N.W.2d 634 (Mich.1996). *But see* Untied States v. Foster, 939 F.2d 445 (7th Cir. 1991).

type of profile evidence may be admissible. For example, courts have admitted this type of evidence as background evidence for a police stop and search,[325] as a foundation for expert opinions,[326] to explain a method of operation,[327] and as rebuttal evidence.[328]

In *United States v. Jackson*[329] the Seventh Circuit held that a written summary concerning the drug courier profile met the minimum requirements ("barely") of Rule 16(a)(1)(E), which governs discovery of proposed expert testimony. The court noted: "[W]e strongly encourage the government to offer more specific descriptions of the opinions of the witnesses, foundations for their testimony, and their qualifications."[330]

§ 9-8. Penile Plethysmograph.

In *United States v. Powers*[331] the Fourth Circuit ruled that the penile plethysmograph as a method to measure sexual arousal failed the *Daubert* test. The evidence was offered by the defense. "First, the Government proffered evidence that the scientific literature addressing penile plethysmography does not regard the test as a valid diagnostic tool because, although useful for treatment of sex offenders, it has no accepted standards in the scientific community. Second, the government also introduced evidence before the judge that a vast majority of incest offenders who do not admit their guilt, such as Powers, show a normal reaction to the test."[332] Other court decisions are in accord.[333]

---

325. United States v. Gomez-Norena, 908 F.2d 497, 501 (9th Cir.) (finding no error in using profile to provide jurors with a full portrayal of events surrounding an arrest), *cert. denied,* 498 U.S. 947 (1990).

326. United States v. Webb, 115 F.3d 711, 715 (9th Cir.) (permitting profile testimony of police expert to assist jury in understanding why a person would conceal a weapon in a car's engine), *cert. denied,* 118 U.S. 947 (1997).

327. United States v. Cordoba, 104 F.3d 225, 230 (9th Cir. 1997) (approving the use of profile testimony to "assist the jury in understanding modus operandi in a complex criminal case").

328. United States v. Beltran-Rios, 878 F.2d 1208, 1213 (9th Cir. 1989) ("The Government may introduce profile testimony ... only to rebut specific attempts by the defense to suggest innocence based on the particular characteristics described in the profile").

329. 51 F.3d 646 (7th Cir. 1995).

330. *Id.* at 651.

331. 59 F.3d 1460 (4th Cir. 1995), *cert. denied,* 516 U.S. 1077 (1996).

332. *Id.* at 1471.

333. *See* Nelson v. Jones, 781 P.2d 964, 968 (Alaska 1989) ("often give false results, both positive and negative"); *In re* Mark C., 7 Cal. App. 4th 433, 8 Cal. Rptr. 2d 856 (1992); People v. John W., 185 Cal. App. 3d 801, 803, 229 Cal. Rptr. 783, 783 (1986); Gemry v. State, 443 S.E.2d 667, 669 (Ga. App. 1994); Cooke v. Naylor, 573 A.2d 376, 379 (Me. 1990); Dutchess Cty. Dep't Social Serv. v. G., 141 Misc. 2d 641, 647, 534 N.Y.S.2d 64 (1988); State v. Spencer, 119 N.C. App. 662, 667-68, 459 S.E.2d 812, 815-16 (1995) (rejecting defense expert's claim that device is 95 percent accurate; court's review of professional literature shows penile plethysmograph is not a

The scientific validity of the technique as a diagnostic tool is suspect.[334] Nevertheless, courts continue to uphold the use of the device as a condition of parole.[335]

§ 9-9. False Confessions.

A growing body of literature is focusing on false confessions.[336] Confessions are incriminating and compelling.[337] Confessions often increase the likelihood of conviction even when claimed false because people do not believe that a person would confess to a crime he or she did not commit.

Studies show that various factors may influence an innocent person to confess, including drug intoxication, lie detector failure, misperception of proof, guilt arising from not helping the victim, and mental deficiency.[338] Some suspects confess because of the stress or pressure of the interrogation or because of implied threats. Often suspects are promised leniency if they confess or are convinced they do not remember committing the crime so they should just confess to relieve their guilt. False confessions also arise from poor police practice, over-zealousness, criminal misconduct, misdirected training, improper use of psychological interrogation techniques and a refusal to believe a suspect may be innocent.[339]

A bright line rule on dealing with false confession defenses is not apparent from court decisions. Defendants usually attempt to introduce expert testimony concerning the effects of the interrogation on a suspect and the disputed

---

reliable indicator of sexual deviancy), *rev. denied*, 341 N.C. 655 (1995); *In re* A.V., 849 S.W.2d 393 (Tex. App. 1993). *See also* Harrington v. Almy, 977 F.2d 37 (1st Cir. 1992).

334. *See* Grossman, *Deviant Sexual Responsiveness on Penile Plethysmography Using Visual Stimuli: Alleged Child Molesters Vs. Normal Control Subjects*, 3 BEHAV. SCI. & LAW 207 (1985); Simon & Schouten, *Plethysmography in the Assessment and Treatment of Sexual Deviance: An Overview*, 20 ARCH. SEXUAL BEHAV. 75 (1991).

335. *E.g.*, Walrath v. Getty, 71 F.3d 679 (7th Cir. 1995); State v. Emery, 593 A.2d 77 (Vt. 1991).

336. *See generally* D. BROWN, A. SCHEFLIN & D. HAMMOND, MEMORY, TRAUMA TREATMENT, AND THE LAW ch. 9 (1998) (interrogatory suggestion and coercive persuasion).

337. *See* Kassin & Neumann, *On the Power of Confession Evidence: An Experiment Test of the Fundamental Difference Hypothesis*, 21 LAW & HUM. BEHAV. 469 (1997); Kassin & Sukel, *Coerced Confessions and the Jury: A Test of the "Harmless Error"*, 21 LAW & HUM. BEHAV. 27 (1997); Leo & Ofshe, *The Consequences of False Confessions: Deprivations of Liberty and Miscarriages of Justice in the Age of Psychological Interrogation*, 88 J. CRIM. L. & CRIMINOLOGY 429 (1998).

338. *See* Leo & Ofshe, *supra* note 337. *See also* Sigurdsson & Gudjonsson, *The Relationship Between Types of Claimed False Confessions Made and the Reasons Why Suspects Confess to the Police According to the Gudjonsson Confession Questionnaire (GCQ)*, 1 LEGAL & CRIMINOLOGICAL PSYCHOLOGY 259 (1996); Hansen, *Untrue Confession*, 85 A.B.A. J. 50 (July 1999).

339. Leo & Ofshe, *supra* note 337, at 440.

confession or false confessions in general. In *Bullard v. State*,[340] a Florida appellate court held that the trial court did not abuse its discretion in refusing to appoint an expert on police "thought control" and coercion because no facts besides Bullard's testimony supported the claims of police misconduct or threats. Similarly, in *People v. Page*,[341] a California appellate court found no abuse in prohibiting a social psychologist from testifying about factors that could make the defendant's confession unreliable. In *Kolb v. State*,[342] the Wyoming Supreme Court held that "the district court did not abuse its discretion by prohibiting [expert] testimony after concluding that 'false confession syndrome' was unreliable based on the proffered evidence."[343]

In *Commonwealth v. Crawford*,[344] the Supreme Judicial Court of Massachusetts found error in a refusal to allow expert testimony because "[t]he testimony of experts may provide invaluable help to judges and to juries in making a determination of voluntariness."[345] In *United States v. Roark*,[346] the Eleventh Circuit concluded that refusal to admit expert testimony concerning the defendant's confession was more than harmless error.[347] In *United States v. Hall*,[348] the Seventh Circuit ruled that the trial court erred when it excluded expert testimony on false confessions:

> This ruling overlooked the utility of valid social science. Even though the jury may have had beliefs about the subject, the question is whether those beliefs were correct. Properly conducted social science research often shows that commonly held beliefs are in error. Dr. Ofshe's testimony, assuming its scientific validity, would have let the jury know that a phenomenon known as false confessions exists, how to recognize it, and how to decide whether it fits the facts of the case being tried.[349]

---

340. 650 So. 2d 631, 632 (Fla. App. 1995).

341. 2 Cal. App. 4th 161, 2 Cal. Rptr. 2d 898 (1991).

342. 930 P.2d 1238 (Wyo. 1996).

343. *Id.* at 1242.

344. 429 Mass. 60, 706 N.E.2d 289 (1999).

345. *Id.* at 293.

346. 753 F.2d 991, 995 (11th Cir. 1985).

347. *See also* State v. Buechler, 253 Neb. 727, 739, 572 N.W.2d 65 (1998) ("While ordinary citizens might understand that drug withdrawal is uncomfortable, without expert evidence ordinary citizens would not be expected to understand that in Buechler's case, withdrawal, combined with his disorders, may have made him suggestible, may have caused him to process information haphazardly, and may have caused him to reach faulty conclusions. Under that state of the record, we must conclude that the district court abused its discretion in excluding the proffered testimony").

348. 93 F.3d 1337 (7th Cir. 1996).

349. *Id.* at 1345.

Similarly, in *United States v. Shay*[350] the First Circuit reversed the trial court's exclusion of psychiatric testimony that the defendant's inculpatory statements were caused by pseudologia fantastica, a mental disorder that makes the person a pathological liar who makes false statements without regard to their consequences.[351]

§ 9-10. Future Dangerousness.

The issue of future dangerousness arises in a number of different legal contexts: preventive detention,[352] sexual predator hearings,[353] civil commitment proceedings,[354] and the like. It also arises in death penalty cases. In *Barefoot v. Estelle*[355] the defendant was convicted of capital murder in Texas. In the penalty phase of the trial, the prosecution offered the testimony of two psychiatrists who testified about Barefoot's future dangerousness, a qualifying factor under the Texas death penalty statute.[356] One psychiatrist, Dr. James Grigson, without ever examining Barefoot, testified that there was a "'*one hundred percent and absolute*' chance that Barefoot would commit future acts of criminal violence."[357]

---

350. 57 F.3d 126 (1st Cir. 1995). *But see* Bixler v. State, 582 N.W.2d 252 (Minn. 1998) (upholding exclusion of psychological testimony that because of his low intelligence the accused is susceptible to coercion, is vulnerable to suggestion and intimation, and has a tendency to say what authority figures want to hear in order to bring an end to the pressure he feels from persons in authority).

351. *See also* United States v. Gonzalez-Maldonado, 115 F.3d 9 (1st Cir. 1997) (expert testimony could be relevant to the credibility of statements and could support the theory that the defendant suffered from a mental illness that caused him to exaggerate).

352. *See* United States v. Salerno, 481 U.S. 739 (1987); Schall v. Martin, 467 U.S. 253 (1984).

353. *See* People v. Ward, 71 Cal. App. 4th 368, 83 Cal. Rptr. 2d 828, 831(1999) ("*Kelly-Frye* applies to cases involving novel devices or processes, not to expert medical testimony, such as a psychiatrist's prediction of future dangerousness or a diagnosis of mental illness") (citations omitted).

354. *See* People v. Ward, 71Cal. App. 4th 368, 83 Cal. Rptr. 2d 828, 832 (1999) ("In civil commitment cases, where the trier of fact is required by statute to determinate whether a person is dangerous or likely to be dangerous, expert prediction may be the only evidence available").

355. 463 U.S. 880 (1983). *See also* Morris & Miller, *Predictions of Dangerousness*, *in* 6 CRIME AND JUSTICE 1 (M. Tonry & N. Morris eds. 1985); Dix, *Expert Prediction Testimony in Capital Sentencing: Evidentiary and Constitutional Considerations*, 19 AM. CRIM. L. REV. 1, 12-15 (1981); Green, *Capital Punishment, Psychiatric Experts, and Predictions of Dangerousness*, 13 CAP. U. L. REV. 533 (1984); Marquart, Ekland-Olson & Sorensen, *Gazing into the Crystal Ball: Can Jurors Accurately Predict Dangerousness in Capital Cases?*, 23 LAW & SOC'Y REV. 449 (1989); Note, *People v. Murtishaw: Applying the Frye Test to Psychiatric Predictions of Dangerousness in Capital Cases*, 70 CALIF. L. REV. 1069, 1084-90 (1982).

356. TEX. CODE CRIM. PROC. art. 37.071(b)(2) (requiring a jury finding that "there is a probability that the defendant would commit criminal acts of violence that would constitute a continuing threat to society"). *See also* Jurek v. Texas, 428 U.S. 262 (1976) (upholding the constitutionality of the Texas statute).

357. 463 U.S. at 919 (Blackmun, J. dissenting) (quoting from record).

Barefoot argued before the Supreme Court that admission of this evidence violated the Due Process and Cruel and Unusual Punishment Clauses due to its unreliability.

In an amicus brief, the American Psychiatric Association (APA) stated that the "unreliability of psychiatric predictions of long-term future dangerousness is by now an established fact within the profession" and the "APA's best estimate is that two out of three predictions of long-term future violence made by psychiatrists are wrong."[358] The APA position was supported by a substantial body of research[359] and misstated by Dr. Grigson at trial.[360] Nevertheless, the Court ruled that such testimony was not constitutionally infirm. Writing for the Court, Justice White noted that "[n]either petitioner nor the [APA] suggests that psychiatrists are always wrong with respect to future dangerousness, only most of the time."[361]

Some commentators believe that testimony concerning future dangerousness is so lacking in reliability that it is unethical.[362] Indeed, the APA reprimanded Dr. Grigson for claiming 100% accuracy in capital cases in which he did not examine the defendant.[363] Nevertheless, Dr. Grigson continued to testify. By May 1990, juries had returned death penalties in 118 of the 127 cases in which he had testified.[364]

---

358. *Id.* at 920 (quoting brief).

359. *See* Ewing, *Preventive Detention and Execution: The Constitutionality of Punishing Future Crimes*, 15 LAW & HUM. BEHAV. 139 (1991); Radelet & Marquart, *Assessing Nondangerousness During Penalty Phases of Capital Trials*, 54 ALB. L. REV. 845 (1990); Slobogin, *Dangerousness and Expertise*, 133 U. PA. L. REV. 97 (1984).

360. Defense counsel cross-examined Dr. Grigson concerning studies that demonstrated the inherent unreliability of predictions of future dangerousness. In response, Dr. Grigson testified that only a small minority of psychiatrists accepted these studies and these studies did not represent the view of the APA. 463 U.S. at 919.

361. *Id.* at 901. At another point the Court wrote: "We are not persuaded that such testimony is almost entirely unreliable . ..." *Id.* at 899.

362. "[There] is good reason to conclude that psychologists and psychiatrists act unethically when they render predictions of dangerousness that provide a legal basis for restricting another person's interest in life or liberty." Ewing, *supra* note 359, at 162. *See also* Ewing, *"Dr. Death" and the Case for an Ethical Ban on Psychiatric and Psychological Predictions of Dangerousness in Capital Sentencing Proceedings*, 8 AM. J.L. & MED. 407 (1983); Grisso & Appelbaum, *Is it Unethical to Offer Predictions of Future Violence?*, 16 LAW & HUM. BEHAV. 621, 629 (1992) ("The ethics of predictions of future violence in such a context indeed are questionable"); Litwack, *On the Ethics of Dangerousness Assessments*, 17 LAW & HUM. BEHAV. 479 (1993).

363. Radelet & Marquart, *supra* note 359, at 851 n.31; ROSENBAUM, TRAVELS WITH DR. DEATH 218 (1991) (The APA "sent me a letter saying that this will serve as a reprimand") (quoting Dr. Grigson). The chapter on Dr. Grigson in Rosenbaum's book was originally published as an article. Ron Rosenbaum, *Travels With Dr. Death*, VANITY FAIR, May 1990, at 141.

364. ROSENBAUM, *supra* note 363, at 206. It is essentially the same testimony in every case:

> He'll take the stand, listen to a recitation of facts about the killing and the killer, and then – usually without examining the defendant, without ever setting eyes on him until the day of

Dr. Grigson gained notoriety, if not fame, as "Dr. Death" in the documentary film, *The Thin Blue Line*,[365] which concerned the capital trial of Randall Adams. Grigson also testified about Adams' future dangerousness.[366] Even though Adams was subsequently released due to innocence, the Doctor has not changed his mind.[367] According to Grigson, "Adams 'will kill again.'"[368]

§ 9-11. Psychological Mental States.

Throughout this chapter expert testimony relating to a defendant's or witness's mental state has been examined. Several other examples are worth noting.

The first deals with the entrapment defense. This defense took root in state courts in the late 19th Century[369] but is now dominated by United States Supreme Court cases.[370] In *United States v. Sorrells,*[371] decided in 1932, and a quarter century later, in *United States v. Sherman,*[372] the majority adopted the "subjective" approach, which focuses on the defendant's predisposition to commit the crime.[373] The subjective approach "has two related elements: [1] government inducement of the crime, and [2] a lack of predisposition on the part

---

> the trial – tell the jury that, *as a matter of medical science*, he can assure them the defendant will pose a continuing danger to society as defined by [the Texas statute]. That's all it takes.

Id. at 210.

365. *The Thin Blue Line* (1988) was made by New York filmmaker Errol Morris, who originally planned to do a film on Dr. Grigson but changed his mind after investigating the Adams case. ROSENBAUM, *supra* note 363, at 219.

366. Adams's death penalty was overturned by the U.S. Supreme Court because the jury selection process was defective. Adams v. Texas, 448 U.S. 38 (1980), *rev'g* Adams v. State, 577 S.W.2d 717 (Tex. Crim. App. 1979). The Governor commuted Adams's death penalty, thereby depriving Adams of a new trial. Adams v. State, 624 S.W.2d 568 (Tex. Crim. 1981). Adams eventually was granted a new trial. *Ex parte* Adams, 768 S.W.2d 281 (Tex. Crim. App. 1989). Adams recounts his ordeal in Adams et al., *Adams v. Texas* (1991).

367. After an extensive Texas habeas proceeding, in which Adams again claimed his innocence, the judge wrote: "Although the court cannot determine the applicant is 'innocent' of the Wood murder ["Since innocence is not a basis in Texas for a new trial . . ."], on the basis of the evidence presented at the habeas corpus hearing, applying the law which places the burden of proof on the State beyond a reasonable doubt, the court would have found applicant not guilty at a bench trial." *Ex parte* Adams, 768 S.W.2d 281, 285 (Tex. Crim. App. 1989) (quoting habeas record).

368. ROSENBAUM, *supra* note 363, at 220 (quoting Dr. Grigson).

369. 1 LAFAVE & SCOTT, SUBSTANTIVE CRIMINAL LAW § 5.2(a), at 597 (1986).

370. *Id.* ("Beginning with the decision in Sorrells v. United States in 1932, the development of the law of entrapment became largely an activity of the federal courts, with the states then adopting the doctrine thereby created").

371. United States v. Sorrells, 287 U.S. 435 (1932).

372. Sherman v. United States, 356 U.S. 369, 372-73 (1958).

373. United States v. Russell, 411 U.S. 423, 429 (1973) ("Thus, the thrust of the entrapment defense was held to focus on the intent or predisposition of the defendant to commit the crime").

of the defendant to engage in the criminal conduct."[374] In *State v. Shuck*,[375] the Tennessee Supreme Court ruled that a neuropsychologist's testimony concerning a defendant's acute susceptibility to inducement in support of an entrapment defense was admissible. Other cases are in accord.[376]

The second concerns the defense of duress. Duress, also known as coercion or compulsion, is recognized as a defense to criminal liability under some circumstances. "The rationale of the defense of duress is that, for reasons of social policy, it is better that the defendant, faced with a choice of evils, choose to do the lesser evil (violate the criminal law) in order to avoid the greater evil threatened by the other person."[377] The defense is judged by an objective standard. Not only must the defendant have a subjective (good faith) belief but that belief must be reasonable.[378] In *State v. VanNatta*,[379] the Oregon court of appeals ruled that expert testimony of the defendant's submissive personality in support of a duress defense was inadmissible because a defendant's individual personality was not the relevant issue.

Finally, defendants have offered a "brainwashing" defense.[380]

---

374. Matthews v. United States, 485 U.S. 58, 63 (1988).

375. 953 S.W.2d 662 (Tenn. 1997).

376. *See* United States v. Nunn, 940 F.2d 1148, 1149 (8th Cir. 1991); United States v. Newman, 849 F.2d 156, 165 (5th Cir. 1988); United States v. McLernon, 746 F.2d 1098, 1115 (6th Cir. 1984) ("expert testimony concerning a defendant's predisposition may be invaluable in an entrapment case"); United States v. Benveniste, 564 F.2d 335, 339 (9th Cir. 1977); United States v. Hill, 655 F.2d 512, 516 (3d Cir. 1981) ("Testimony by an expert concerning a defendant's susceptibility to influence may be relevant to an entrapment defense"), *cert. denied*, 464 U.S. 1039 (1984).

377. 1 LAFAVE & SCOTT, *supra* note 369, § 5.3, at 614 (1986). *See also* 2 ROBINSON, CRIMINAL LAW DEFENSES § 177 (1994); AMERICAN LAW INSTITUTE, MODEL PENAL CODE AND COMMENTARIES § 2.09 (1985) (duress).

378. *See* United States v. Bailey, 444 U.S. 394, 410-11 (1980) ("Clearly, in the context of prison escape, the escapee is not entitled to claim a defense of duress or necessity unless and until he demonstrates that, given the imminence of the threat, violation of § 751(a) was his only reasonable alternative").

379. 149 Or. App. 587, 945 P.2d 1062 (1997).

380. *See* Delgado, *Ascription of Criminal States of Mind: Toward a Defense Theory for the Coercively Persuaded ("Brainwashed") Defendant*, 63 MINN. L. REV. 1 (1978).

CHAPTER 10

VOICE IDENTIFICATION*

§ 10-1. In General.

The identification of a person's voice is often important in criminal cases.[1] Courts have long admitted testimony of voice recognition by lay persons. Aural identifications by experts is an extension of this line of cases.

Methods of voice identification are not limited to aural recognition. If a voice is recorded, for example, in cases involving the use of a telephone to transmit bomb threats, kidnapping ransom demands, or extortion threats, additional methods of identification may be used. Voice identification by spectrographic examination of speech samples is such a method. It is often referred to as "voiceprint" evidence.

§ 10-2. Human Voice.

Voice identification by aural and spectrographic examination of speech samples is based upon the resonant characteristics of the individual human speech tract. Speech is produced by a source of power, vibrations of vocal folds or turbulence of air flow, and resonance of this source sound in the vocal tract

---

*The sections in this chapter were revised and renumbered in this edition. The authors wish to express their appreciation to Bruce E. Koenig, of BEK TEK, Clifton, Virginia, retired Supervisory Special Agent, FBI Technical Services Division, who reviewed this chapter in the second and third edition. The authors also wish to express their appreciation to the late Dr. Oscar Tosi, Professor, Michigan State University and Director Emeritus, Speech, Hearing Sciences & Voice Identification Laboratories, who reviewed this chapter in the first two editions.

1. In addition to voice identification, a person's voice may be analyzed for other evidentiary purposes. Voice stress analysis, such as Psychological Stress Evaluation, is discussed in Chapter 8. Recent research also claims that intoxication can be determined from acoustic analysis of voice recordings. Tanford, Pisoni & Johnson, *Novel Scientific Evidence of Intoxication: Acoustic Analysis of Voice Recordings from the Exxon Valdez*, 82 J. CRIM. L. & CRIMINOLOGY 579 (1992). *See generally* H. HOLLIEN, THE ACOUSTICS OF CRIME: THE NEW SCIENCE OF FORENSIC PHONETICS (1990).

and nasal cavities.[2] Differences in the vocal tract anatomy, together with learned differences in the use of the vocal mechanism in speech production, cause dissimilarities in the way different people pronounce identical words. This dissimilarity is called interspeaker variability.

Speech scientists also recognize the existence of intraspeaker variability; that is, a speaker will not pronounce the same word in exactly the same way twice. Time lapse, psychological and physiological changes, and articulatory dynamics are some of the sources of intraspeaker variability.[3] Speaker recognition by aural and spectrographic examination depends on the extent that interspeaker variability is greater or different than intraspeaker variability,[4] an issue about which there is much debate.[5] The technique also depends on whether this assumed uniqueness of the human voice can be adequately portrayed and detected by means of aural and spectrographic analysis.[6]

§ 10-3. Aural Examinations.

Voice recognition by persons familiar with another's voice should be distinguished from voice identification by strangers. After reviewing the literature on the subject, one commentator wrote: "This research reflects that the identification accuracy rate for familiar voice samples lasting 1 second or longer ranged from 92% to 100% and averaged 95% to 100%."[7]

Voice recognition by a stranger presents more difficulties. A distinction between short- and long-term aural memory is important. An expert listening to two tape recordings uses short-term aural memory when comparing the voices on the two tapes. In contrast, a witness who hears a criminal speak during the commission of a crime and then is asked to identify a suspect's voice months later uses long-term memory. The accuracy of this type of voice identification

---

2. *See* O. Tosi, Voice Identification: Theory and Legal Application 35 (1979) [hereinafter cited as Tosi Text].

3. Tosi, *Voice Identification*, *in* Practising Law Institute, Scientific and Expert Evidence 971, 983 (2d ed. 1981).

4. Tosi, Oyer, Lashbrook, Pedrey, Nicol & Nash, *Experiment on Voice Identification*, 51 J. Acoustical Soc'y Am. 2030, 2031 (1972).

5. *See* Manning, *Understanding Speaker Identification Techniques*, 17 Trial 61, 63 (Oct. 1981) ("A basic assumption in all techniques of speaker identification procedures is that intra-speaker variability will be less (or can be made to be less) than inter-speaker variability. To date, however, this has not been satisfactorily demonstrated").

6. *See* Hennessy & Romig, *Sound, Speech, Phonetics, and Voiceprint Identification*, 16 J. Forensic Sci. 438, 449 (1971) ("Another assumption made is that the sound spectrograph and the spectrograms adequately portray the uniqueness of the individual voice which is the first principle of the theory of invariant speech").

7. Koenig, *Selected Topics in Forensic Voice Identification*, 20 Crime Lab. Digest 78, 79 (Oct. 1993).

has been questioned. After reviewing the literature on this subject, one authority commented:

> While voice memory is a demonstrable fact, good voice memory under all but super-optimal conditions of encoding, storage, and retrieval, is the exception rather than the rule. The implication for the criminal justice system is thus fairly straightforward: voice identification by a witness concerning a stranger should be treated with the utmost caution, both in its informational and its evidential aspects.[8]

§ 10-4. Admissibility & Weight of Aural Identifications.

Typically, the testimony of a person familiar with a speaker's voice is sufficient to identify that voice.[9] Federal Evidence Rule 901(b)(5) provides for the identification of a person's voice, "whether heard firsthand or through mechanical or electronic transmission or recording, by opinion based upon hearing the voice at any time under circumstances connecting it with the alleged speaker."[10] The federal drafters commented:

> Since aural voice identification is not a subject of expert testimony, the requisite familiarity may be acquired either before or after the particular speaking which is the subject of the identification, in this respect resembling visual identification of a person rather than identification of handwriting.[11]

---

8. Clifford, *Memory for Voices: The Feasibility and Quality of Earwitness Evidence*, in EVALUATING WITNESS EVIDENCE 189, 214 (S. Lloyd-Bostock & B. Clifford eds. 1983). *See also* Koenig, *Selected Topics in Forensic Voice Identification*, 20 CRIME LAB. DIGEST 78, 79 (Oct. 1993) ("[T]he range of expected correct identifications of unfamiliar voices would be 78% to 90%, with most identifications in the 78% to 83% range"); Yarmey & Matthys, *Voice Identification of an Abductor*, 6 APPLIED COGNITIVE PSYCHOL. 367 (1992) (identification of a stranger's voice is a very difficult task). *See also* Van Wallendael, Surace, Parsons & Brown, *"Earwitness" Voice Recognition: Factors Affecting Accuracy and Impact on Jurors*, 8 APPLIED COGNITIVE PSYCHOL. 661 (1994).

9. Voice recognition is only one method of authenticating a speaker's voice. For example, Federal Rule 901(B)(6) recognizes a special rule for telephone conversations. In addition, Rule 901(B)(4) recognizes speaker identification by content—for example, a "telephone conversation may be shown to have emanated from a particular person by virtue of its disclosing knowledge of facts known peculiarly to him." FED. R. EVID. 901 advisory committee's note.

10. *See generally* 2 MCCORMICK, EVIDENCE § 226 (4th ed. 1992); 2 WIGMORE, EVIDENCE § 660, 669 (Chadbourn rev. 1979); 7 *Id.* § 2155 (Chadbourn rev. 1978); Annotation, *Identification of Accused by His Voice,* 70 A.L.R.2D *995 (1960); Walter, Cautionary Instructions to Jury as to Reliability of, or Factors to be Considered in Evaluating, Voice Identification Testimony*, 17 A.L.R.5TH 851 (1994).

11. FED. R. EVID. 901 advisory committee's note.

State v. Parker,[12] a decision by the Ohio Supreme Court, is illustrative. It involved voice recognition by a rape victim: "Her voice identification of defendant was based on her previous contacts with him, the last of which was two days before the crime. The facts also show that Karen had ample opportunity to listen to defendant's voice during the commission of the crimes and thus was in a position to identify him."[13]

In-Court Identifications

Obtaining voice exemplars pre-trial does not violate the Self-incrimination Clause because the exemplars are physical, not testimonial, evidence within the meaning of the fifth amendment,[14] and courts have extended this rule to compelling a defendant to speak in front of the jury for the purpose of voice identification by a witness.[15] For example, in *Hopkins v. State*[16] the court wrote: "[W]e discern little difference in a Fifth Amendment analysis of whether the voice exemplar was testimonial in nature because of the context in which it was given, here during the trial. ... [T]hat petitioner was required to give an exemplar in court as opposed to pre-trial is of no consequence; his statement was not testimonial because it was used for identification purpose only ...."[17]

Moreover, a defendant's refusal to provide in-court voice exemplars of specific words is a proper subject of a jury instruction or prosecutorial comment concerning such refusal.[18] Since the defendant does not have a self-incrimination right in this context, commenting on the refusal to speak does not penalize the exercise of a constitutional right.

---

12. 53 Ohio St.3d 82, 558 N.E.2d 1164 (1990).

13. *Id.* at 87-88, 558 N.E.2d at 1169. *See also* United States v. Puentes, 50 F.3d 1567, 1577 (11th Cir. 1995) ("[R]ule 901(b)(5) does not require Inspector Perez to have been familiar with Puentes's voice prior to commencing the wiretap activity. At trial, Inspector Perez testified that he became familiar with Puentes's voice during the two-month wiretap surveillance. This testimony satisfied the requirement of rule 901(b)(5)"), *cert. denied*, 515 U.S. 933 (1995); United States v. Saulter, 60 F.3d 270, 276 (7th Cir. 1995) ("minimal familiarity is sufficient").

14. *See* § 10-7 *infra.*

15. *E.g.*, Burnett v. Collins, 982 F.2d 922, 927 (5th Cir. 1993) ("Fifth Amendment ... was not violated because he was not compelled to utter words to 'speak his guilt' but rather to utter words as to an identifying characteristic. The fact that he did so in front of a jury does not alter this assessment") (speaking words uttered by robber); United States v. Williams, 704 F.2d 315, 320 (6th Cir.) (live voice exemplar in presence of jury permitted) (citing state cases), *cert. denied,* 464 U.S. 991 (1983).

16. 352 Md. 146, 721 A.2d 231 (1998).

17. *Id.* at 156, 721 A.2d at 236.

18. State v. Hubanks, 173 Wis. 2d 1, 496 N.W.2d 96 (App. 1992), *cert. denied*, 510 U.S. 830 (1993).

However, in *United States v. Olvera,*[19] the Ninth Circuit ruled that requiring the defendant to speak the words uttered during a robbery in the presence of the jury violated due process under the facts of this case. In the court's view, "requiring a defendant to speak a criminal's words does not convey a message of guilt where the prosecution makes clear that the procedure is necessary for witness identification and the prosecutor carries out the procedure in a manner consistent with this objective. In such circumstances, the jury is aware that the procedure is not intended to communicate a message regarding the defendant's culpability."[20] The procedure in this case, however, fell short of these requirements.

Voice Lineups

On rare occasions "voice spreads" (voice lineups) are used for identification purposes.[21] Some commentators have warned that voice showups (one-on-one encounters) are a highly biased identification procedure.[22]

If a voice identification is made at a lineup or other pretrial identification procedures, due process and right to counsel issues may arise as in the eyewitness identification cases.[23] The Third Circuit took this position in *Government of*

---

19. 30 F.3d 1195 (9th Cir.), *cert. denied,* 513 U.S. 1031 (1994). The court also wrote: "Compelling a defendant to utter a criminal's words clearly has the potential to violate due process. ... Much like the wearing of prison clothes, the uttering of a criminal's statements isolates the defendant from all others in a courtroom and inevitably associates him or her with the charged conduct, thus tending to 'brand [him or her in the jurors'] eyes with an unmistakable mark of guilt.' The potential for influencing the jurors' judgment is particularly acute when a defendant invokes his or her Fifth Amendment right not to testify. In such a situation, the only statements by the defendant that the jury ever will hear are those in which he or she mimics the criminal. These statements thus are likely to remain prominent in the jurors' memories and to dominate their perception of the defendant." *Id.* at 1197 (citations omitted).

20. *Id.*

21. *See* § 9-2 *infra* (discussing eyewitness identifications and lineups). *See also* N. SOBEL, EYEWITNESS IDENTIFICATION: LEGAL AND PRACTICAL PROBLEMS § 5.6 (1991) (voice identification); Estrella, *Admissibility of Evidence of Voice Identification of Defendant as Affected by Allegedly Suggestive Voice Lineup Procedures,* 55 A.L.R.5TH 423 (1998) (impermissibly suggestive voice lineup procedure may result in exclusion of the voice identification; generally, voice identifications are accepted subject to the same due-process safeguards as visual identification).

22. Yarmey, Yarmey & Yarmey, *Face and Voice Identifications in Showups and Lineups,* 8 APPLIED COGNITIVE PSYCHOL. 453 (1994).

23. *See* Macias v. State, 673 So. 2d 176 (Fla. App. 1996) (victim made two pretrial voice identifications and one in-court identification; one-person voice identifications are inherently suggestive and should be avoided; voice identification reliability can be shown if (1) there was ample time to hear the assailant at the time of the crime, (2) there was a high degree of attention on the victim's part, (3) the victim provides a detailed account of the voice before hearing the sample voices, and (4) there is a high level of certainty in identifying the voice. In this case all of these factors were satisfied); Campbell v. State, 228 Ga. App. 258, 491 S.E.2d 477 (1997) (victim identified the defendant's voice from an audio recording with various voice samples; voice

Virgin Islands v. Sanes,[24] commenting: "Although voice identification obviously differs from eyewitness identification ... we conclude that the [due process] eyewitness identification test, adapted to voice identification, provides a standardized source of guidance to district courts for assessing the reliability of voice identification as well."[25] The court went on to hold that the procedure used satisfied due process requirements.

A second issue in *Sanes* involved the scope of a defense expert's testimony. The expert, a professor of linguistics, testified before the jury concerning the suggestiveness and distinguishing characteristics of the voice exemplar. However, the expert was not permitted to testify that voice comparisons were not as accurate as eyewitness identifications.[26]

Sound Recordings

Audiotape or sound recordings may be admissible under several theories. A sound recording may be authenticated under Federal Rule 901(b)(9), if the process or system used to produce the recording is shown to be reliable.[27] The use of audiotapes that are inaudible and the use of transcripts of the tapes present additional problems, which are entrusted to the trial court's discretion under Rules 403 and 611(a).[28] One court commented:

> In order to be admissible, audio recordings must be authentic, accurate and trustworthy. Admission into evidence of tape recordings containing inaudible portions is a matter within the sound discretion of the trial court.

---

identification is generally acceptable; any error in the voice lineup is harmless since the victim also identified the defendant by photo and again in the courtroom by sight); Commonwealth v. DeMaria, 46 Mass. App. 114, 703 N.E.2d 1203 (1999) (Nine days after crime a physical line-up at which each man read from a newspaper article; victim immediately identified the defendant's voice as that of her attacker; she also confirmed the voice with her visual identification); State v. Parker, 53 Ohio St.3d 82, 87, 558 N.E.2d 1164, 1169 (1990) (constitutional challenge to voice identification; victim identified rapist from tape recording of police interview two days after the incident).

24. 57 F.3d 338 (3rd Cir. 1995).

25. *Id.* at 340 (citations omitted) ("[S]he listened to the voice array three times. ... [and] then positively identified the fourth voice as that of her attacker. Sample No. 4 was Sanes' voice").

26. *Id.* at 341 ("The district court properly held a *Daubert* hearing in which the nature of Dr. Hollien's testimony was fully considered. We conclude that the district court appropriately limited Dr. Hollien's expert testimony to the pertinent issue of whether the distinguishing factors on Sample No. 4 unduly influenced [the victim's] selection").

27. *See* United States v. Carbone, 798 F.2d 21 (1st Cir. 1986), *cert. denied*, 493 U.S. 1078, (1990).

28. *See* 2 McCormick, Evidence § 214, at 20 (4th ed. 1992) ("Clearly such transcripts can serve a beneficial demonstrative function where no question exists as to the accuracy of the transcription, but serious theoretical and practical problems arise when a legitimate question is presented as to what words the recording contains").

> In determining whether to admit tape recordings, the trial court must assess whether the unintelligible portions are so substantial as to render the recordings as a whole untrustworthy.[29]

The principal risk is jury confusion. If a foundation is laid and the opponent is afforded the right to cross-examine the witnesses, the jurors can decide for themselves what is on the tape.[30]

In *United States v. Patrick*[31] a defense expert testified at a *Daubert* hearing that a tape had been "dubbed." A prosecution expert disagreed. The court ruled that "tape authentication is a subject of scientific knowledge"[32] and that the defense expert was qualified in this field.

§ 10-5. Spectrographic Examinations.

As noted above, voice identification by spectrographic examination of speech samples is another method of voice identification. It is often referred to as "voiceprint" evidence. It has been one of the most controversial types of scientific evidence that the courts have confronted. Even the name "voiceprint," which was initially used to describe this technique, has sparked controversy because it suggests an unwarranted comparison with fingerprint identification.[33] Speech scientists have noted that fingerprints and voiceprints are "fundamentally different from each other"[34] and that "the differences between them seem to exceed the similarities."[35] Courts also have criticized the term, noting that the "use of the term 'voiceprint,' with its overtones of 'fingerprint,' gives voice

29. State v. Gotsis, 13 Ohio App.3d 282, 283, 469 N.E.2d 548, 551 (1984) (citations omitted) (state provided extensive testimony concerning the recording and subsequent custody of the tapes; agent who recorded the conversations testified to content before each tape was played).

30. *See also* State v. Rodriquez, 66 Ohio App.3d 5, 15, 583 N.E.2d 384, 391 (1990) (state presented testimony of the recording and chain of custody; informant testified extensively to content of tapes; opportunity for cross-examination afforded; tapes but not transcripts sent to jury room).

31. 6 F. Supp. 2d 51 (D. Mass. 1998).

32. *Id.* at 55.

33. For a discussion of fingerprints, *see* Chapter 16.

34. National Research Council, On the Theory and Practice of Voice Identification 6 (1979) [hereinafter cited as NAS Report].

35. Bolt, Cooper, David, Dens, Picketed & Stevens, *Speaker Identification by Speech Spectrograms; A Scientist's View of its Reliability for Legal Purposes*, 47 J. Acoustical Soc'y Am. 597, 599 (1970). *See also* Rafferty, *Anything You Say Can And Will Be Used Against You: Spectrographic Evidence In Criminal Cases*, 36 Am. Crim. L. Rev. 291, 294 (1999) ("[A] fingerprint is static and will not change its physical characteristics over time. A person's voice, on the other hand, will evolve and can be affected by environmental conditions or even excitement level. Finally, a person has the capability to disguise or alter his voice deliberately, while a fingerprint cannot be altered").

spectrographic identification an aura of absolute certainty and accuracy which is neither justified by the facts nor claimed by experts in the field."[36] In this chapter, the term voicegram evidence is used in lieu of "voiceprint" evidence.

Procedures

This method of identification involves the matching of known and unknown voice samples by means of sound spectrography. It, however, is typically supplemented by an aural examination. In addition, computers are used to produce the voicegram display and to allow editing of the voice samples. In contrast, computer-assisted voice comparison procedures are neither permitted by the International Association of Identification (IAI) Standards nor used by the FBI because there are no digital algorithms that can reliably compare voices under forensic conditions.

The technique uses a sound spectrograph, an electromagnetic instrument that is widely used by speech specialists for research,[37] or a computer workstation with a high-resolution laser printer. The sound spectrograph consists of four main parts: a magnetic recording device, a variable electronic filter, a paper-carrying drum that is attached to the magnetic recorder, and an electric stylus that marks the paper as the drum rotates.[38] When a magnetic tape containing a speech sample is placed in the spectrograph, the instrument converts acoustical signals of selected words into a visual display called a spectrogram, which consists of a sequence of short term spectra. Three parameters of speech are depicted on the spectrogram: frequency (vertical axis), time (horizontal axis), and amplitude (relative darkness).[39] The spectrograms of a known voice and an unknown voice saying the same words are visually compared to determine if they were made by the same speaker.

There are two different types of examinations: open tests and closed tests. In a closed test, the examiner must determine which of several unknown voice samples is the same as a known voice sample. An open test is similar, except the

36. United States v. Baller, 519 F.2d 463, 465 n.1 (4th Cir.), *cert. denied,* 423 U.S. 1019 (1975). *Accord* United States v. Williams, 583 F.2d 1194, 1197 n.5 (2d Cir. 1978), *cert. denied,* 439 U.S. 1117 (1979); State v. Gortarez, 141 Ariz. 254, 262 n.2, 686 P.2d 1224, 1233 n.2 (1984); Cornett v. State, 450 N.E.2d 498, 500 (Ind. 1983).

As discussed in this section, the developer of the technique, Lawerence Kersta, did claim such certainty and accuracy.

37. Bolt, Cooper, David, Dens, Picketed & Stevens, *supra* note 35, at 597. The sound spectrograph is recognized as an accurate instrument, and its reliability has not been a factor in the voicegram cases.

38. Thomas, *Voiceprint — Myth or Miracle, in* PRACTISING LAW INSTITUTE, SCIENTIFIC AND EXPERT EVIDENCE 1015, 1031 (2d ed. 1981).

39. Tosi, Oyer, Lashbrook, Pedrey, Nicol & Nash, *supra* note 4, at 2031.

examiner does not know if any of the unknown samples were made by the speaker of the known sample.[40]

Subjectivity

The sound spectrograph does not make the comparison; it only produces spectrograms, which are then used by the examiner in reaching a conclusion. The examiner determines whether there are sufficient points of similarity (dissimilarity) on the known and unknown spectrograms to warrant a conclusion that both were produced by the speech of the same (or different) person.[41] Thus, although based on objective data (the spectrogram), the examiner's conclusions represent a subjective evaluation: "[T]he decisions are 'subjective' and therefore likely to be variable, even though such 'objective' aids as a spectrograph and voicegrams are used."[42]

Qualifications

Accordingly, even if the validity of the technique were established, its application would depend heavily on the qualifications of the particular examiner. The proponents of the technique have repeatedly emphasized this factor: "[T]he crucial problem with subjective methods consists in testing the honesty and reliability of the examiner."[43] In 1972, the International Association of Voice Identification was established as a certifying body for examiners. In 1980 the Voice Identification and Acoustic Analysis Subcommittee (VIAAS) of the International Association for Identification (IAI) was formed by integrating the International Association of Voice Identification into the IAI.

Early Research

Researchers (Drs. Potter, Knopp, and Green) at Bell Telephone Laboratories invented the sound spectrograph in 1941 as a means of identifying enemy radio operators during World War II. After the war, the spectrograph became available to speech scientists for general research. In the early 1960s Lawrence Kersta initiated investigations into the "voiceprint technique" while at Bell Laboratories. He soon began to champion the technique as a means of voice identification. According to Kersta, the technique was "[m]uch like fingerprint identification"[44]

---

40. Tosi Text, *supra* note 2, at 4-5.

41. In United States v. Wright, 17 C.M.A. 183, 37 C.M.R. 447, 453 (1967), Lawrence Kersta, the developer of the voicegram technique, testified that a minimum of sixteen points of identity in the sound pattern on the spectrograms was necessary for voice identification.

42. NAS Report, *supra* note 34, at 21.

43. Tosi, *supra* note 3, at 993.

44. Kersta, *Speaker Recognition and Identification by Voiceprints*, 40 CONN. B.J. 586, 586 (1966).

and his experiments showed that the technique's accuracy for correct identifications was "greater than 99 per cent."[45]

By 1966 Kersta had left Bell Laboratories and had established Voiceprint Laboratories, of which he was President. He also began testifying as an expert witness.[46] In one case he claimed that "voiceprints are practically the equivalent of fingerprints in reliability"[47] and that the voicegram technique "is virtually infallible in producing voice identification."[48]

News accounts, however, reported that Kersta had misidentified a voice in at least one case.[49] More importantly, speech scientists were skeptical about Kersta's claims. In a 1970 article, several prominent scientists wrote that "[t]oday's consensus suggests that speaker identification by voice patterns is subject to error at a high, and as yet undetermined, rate"[50] and that "the available results are inadequate to establish the reliability of voice identification by spectrograms."[51]

Michigan State Study

An extensive study on the voicegram technique was reported in 1972. This study, which was sponsored by the LEAA, was conducted at Michigan State University under the supervision of Dr. Oscar Tosi.[52] Over a two-year period, 34,992 experimental trials involving 250 male speakers and 29 examiners were conducted. False identification errors occurred in approximately 6% of the trials

---

45. *Id.* at 591. Kersta's other articles include: Kersta, *Voiceprint Identification*, 196 NATURE 1253 (1962); Kersta, *Voiceprint Identification Infallibility*, 34 J. ACOUSTICAL SOC'Y AM. 1978 (1962).

46. *See* cases cited in § 10-6 *infra.*

47. United States v. Wright, 17 U.S.C.M.A. 183, 37 C.M.R. 447, 455 (1967) (dissenting opinion).

48. 37 C.M.R. at 457. *See also* People v. King, 266 Cal. App. 2d 437, 441-42, 72 Cal. Rptr. 478, 481 (1968) ("Mr. Kersta defended his 'voiceprint' method of identification as having the infallibility of fingerprints....").

49. Burnham, *Voiceprint Mistake Conceded in Tying Inspector to Gambler*, N.Y. TIMES, Mar. 27, 1971, at 57, col. 2; Graham, *Use of "Voiceprints" in Court Proceedings Creates Legal Debate*, WALL ST. J., Mar. 13, 1972, at 1, col. 1.

50. Bolt, Cooper, David, Dens, Picketed & Stevens, *supra* note 35, at 602.

51. *Id.* at 603. *See also* Bolt, Cooper, David, Dens, Picketed & Stevens, *Identification of a Speaker by Speech Spectrograms*, 166 SCIENCE 388 (1969); Hennessy & Romig, *supra* note 6, at 452-53 ("The theory of invariant speech upon which voiceprint identification is based hypothesizes the uniqueness of the individual's speech pattern. This uniqueness, though, must be established before voiceprint identification is validated").

52. NATIONAL INSTITUTE OF LAW ENFORCEMENT AND CRIMINAL JUSTICE, VOICE IDENTIFICATION RESEARCH (February 1972) (submitted to L.E.A.A. by Department of Michigan State Police). The results of the research are also reported at Tosi, Oyer, Lashbrook, Pedrey, Nicol & Nash, *supra* note 4, and Tosi Text, *supra* note 2, at 72-75.

which most closely resembled the forensic situation.[53] The error rate was reduced to approximately 2% if the trials in which the examiners expressed "uncertainty" about their conclusions were eliminated.[54] The forensic model involved (1) "open trials," in which the examiner was not told if the unknown voice was in the known recordings, (2) noncontemporary spectrograms (one month apart), and (3) clue words which were in context rather than in isolation.

According to Dr. Tosi's court testimony, the error rate would be "negligible"[55] in a real-life situation for several reasons: First, while his examiners had only a month's training, a professional examiner would be thoroughly trained and tested to be certified. Second, Tosi's examiners had only fifteen minutes in which to render a decision, whereas a professional examiner would have unlimited time to compare the spectrograms. Third, the experimental examiners' conclusions were based only on a visual examination of spectrograms, but the professional examiner would compare the exemplars aurally as well as visually. Fourth, the professional could use the complete text of a conversation, while the experimental examiners considered only a limited number of clue words. Fifth, the professional would not have to render a conclusion if not certain; in contrast, the experimental examiners were required to make a decision. Finally, the professional examiner would be more conscientious in light of the possible consequences of the conclusions; no direct consequences resulted from the experimental examiners' conclusions.[56]

Despite the favorable results of this study, some speech scientists still questioned the validity of the technique. The scientists who had earlier criticized Kersta's claims also found problems with Tosi's conclusions. While acknowledging the contributions made by the Michigan State study, they still questioned the adequacy of the research supporting the technique: "[P]resent methods for [legal] use lack an adequate scientific basis for estimating reliability in many practical situations and ... laboratory evaluations of these methods show increasing errors as the conditions for evaluation move toward real-life situations."[57]

---

53. Errors of false elimination were reported to be approximately 13%. Tosi, Oyer, Lashbrook, Pedrey, Nicol & Nash, *supra* note 4, at 2041. Proponents argued that false eliminations should not be considered in evaluating the accuracy of the technique inasmuch as the consequence of convicting an innocent person is not raised by such errors.

54. *Id.*

55. People v. Law, 40 Cal. App. 3d 69, 78, 114 Cal. Rptr. 708, 713 (1974).

56. *Id.* at 78, 114 Cal. Rptr. at 714.

57. Bolt, Cooper, David, Dens, Picketed & Stevens, *Speaker Identification by Speech Spectrograms: Some Further Observations*, 54 J. ACOUSTICAL SOC'Y AM. 531, 534 (1973). *See also* Hazen, *Effects of Differing Phonetic Contexts on Spectrographic Speaker Identification*, 54 J. ACOUSTICAL SOC'Y AM. 650, 659 (1973) ("The data presented here indicate that the forensic value of sound spectrograms for speaker identification purposes is quite limited").

Dr. Tosi and others responded to these criticisms. They emphasized that when recording conditions deviated from laboratory conditions, the percentage of "no opinion" conclusions would increase, that a professional examiner would give a "no opinion" when in doubt, and that a positive decision was reached by the Michigan State Police only 43% of the time.[58] At about the same time (1972) the proponents of the technique established the International Association of Voice Identification as a certifying body for examiners. It was also during this period, from the publication of the Michigan State study in 1972 until 1979, that most of the court cases on the technique were decided.[59] Dr. Tosi and Lt. Nash, of the Michigan State Police, were the principal witnesses in these cases.

NAS Study

In 1976 the FBI requested the National Academy of Sciences (NAS) to evaluate the validity of voicegram evidence. The Academy appointed a Committee on Evaluation of Sound Spectrograms, which included in its membership Dr. Tosi as well as some of the critics. The Committee published its report in 1979. The NAS Report took "no position" regarding the admissibility of evidence, which it considered a legal, not a scientific, issue.[60] Nevertheless, the report played a role in later cases. The Report concluded:

> The practice of voice identification rests on the assumption that intraspeaker variability is less than or different from interspeaker variability. However, at present the assumption is not adequately supported by scientific theory and data. Viewpoints about probable errors in identification decisions at present result mainly from various professional judgments and fragmentary experimental results rather than from objective data representative of results in forensic applications.
>
> The Committee concludes that the technical uncertainties concerning the present practice of voice identification are so great as to require that forensic applications be approached with great caution.[61]

---

58. Black, Lashbrook, Nash, Oyer, Pedrey, Tosi & Truby, *Reply to Speaker Identification by Speech Spectrograms: Some Further Observations*, 54 J. ACOUSTICAL SOC'Y AM. 535 (1973).

Dr. Tosi considered the inconclusive option critical. A distorted, noisy unknown sample cannot be compared to the natural utterances of a speaker. This type of sample should be designated "inconclusive." Fifty percent of the analyses done in Dr. Tosi's laboratory were inconclusive. An inexperienced examiner might designate such a sample as an elimination, which could be a false negative but not a false positive. Letter from Dr. Tosi, dated May 31, 1992.

59. *See* § 10-6 *infra.*

60. *See* Rothstein, *Book Review*, 17 AM. CRIM. L. REV. 153, 154 (1979) ("The [NAS] report is a scientific work, not a legal document").

61. NAS Report, *supra* note 34, at 2.

In another passage the Committee wrote: "Estimates of error rates now available pertain to only a few of the many combinations of conditions encountered in real-life situations. These estimates do not constitute a generally adequate basis for a judicial or legislative body to use in making judgments concerning the reliability and acceptability of aural-visual voice identification in forensic applications."[62] The report included several recommendations for future research and use.[63]

Following the publication of this report, the FBI continued its policy of not permitting its voicegram experts to testify in court to comparison results.[64]

1986 FBI Survey

In 1986 the FBI conducted a survey of 2000 voice identification comparisons that its examiners had made over a fifteen-year period to determine the error rate under field conditions.[65] Meaningful decisions were made in 34.8% of the comparisons (696 cases).[66] The false identification error rate was reported at

---

62. *Id.* at 60. The NAS Report's other conclusions concerning the validity of the technique include: "The presently available experimental evidence about error rates consists of results from a relatively small number of separate, uncoordinated experiments. These results alone cannot provide estimates of error rates that are valid over the range of conditions usually met in practice." *Id.* at 58. "All the scientific results and forensic experiences to date, taken together, do not constitute an adequate objective basis for determining the error rates to be expected for voice identification testimony given in forensic cases generally." *Id.* at 68-69.

63. The NAS Report contained four recommendations:

> [1] We recommend that a mechanism be established to stimulate, guide, and coordinate a broad national program of scientific research on the processes of speech generation, transmission, and analysis as they pertain to the practice of voice identification.
>
> [2] We recommend that a national mechanism be established to develop objective standards and methods for testing the performance of voice identification examiners and to certify their competence as examiners.
>
> [3] We recommend that practitioners of aural-visual voice identification make full use of certain available knowledge and techniques that could improve the voice identification method.
>
> [4] We recommend that if evidence on voice identification is admitted in court — and we take no position on admissibility — then the inherent limitations in the method and in the performance of examiners should be explained to the fact finder, whether the judge or the jury, in order to protect against overvaluation of such evidence.

Id. at 63-68.

64. Koenig, *Speaker Identification (Part 2)*, FBI LAW ENFORCEMENT BULL. 20, 22 (Feb. 1980) ("The FBI conducts voice identification examinations for Federal, State, and local law enforcement authorities for investigative guidance only and will not provide expert testimony").

65. Koenig, *Spectrographic Voice Identification: A Forensic Survey*, 79 J. ACOUSTICAL SOC'Y AM. 2088 (1986) (Letters to the Editor).

66. "Most of the no or low confidence decisions were due to poor recording quality and/or an insufficient number of comparable words. Decisions were also affected by high-pitched voices (usually female) and some forms of voice disguise." *Id.* at 2090.

0.31% (one case), and the false elimination error rate was 0.53% (two cases). Two limitations were noted. First, the error rates were determined by accepting the opinions of the field investigators, and "investigators are not always correct in their evaluation of a suspect's involvement."[67] Second, the training and procedures used by the FBI were more rigorous than those of some other examiners.[68] The same article acknowledged that voicegram identification "has yet to find approval among most scientists in phonetics, linguistics, engineering, and related disciplines as a positive test in comparing voice samples."[69] In addition, the FBI continued to preclude its examiners from testifying in court.[70]

The publication of this survey prompted a response. Several speech scientists criticized the survey. One point involved the failure of the survey to specify the precise method used by the FBI examiners and the criteria for determining examiner proficiency: "To date, no evidence has been published to suggest that *any* examiner has passed objective and independent evaluations before being certified."[71] A more fundamental objection concerned the criterion for determining "ground truth":

> Identification or elimination "consistent with interviews and other evidence in the investigation" is not an adequate standard to confirm the accuracy of such decision. Any technique such as this must be proven to be valid and reliable by some independent means before it can be used. Here, the technique is used to support the guilt or innocence of an individual, while the determination of such guilt or innocence is then used to show that the technique is proper. The data provided in this report cannot do both.[72]

The FBI responded to many of these points, but its position remained unchanged. The Bureau did not support the "spectrographic (voiceprint) method" as a "positive, or conclusive, technique of comparing voices in legal applications." However, it is an "excellent investigative aid" in numerous cases.[73]

---

67. *Id.*

68. "[T]he educational and training requirements of the FBI examiners, the criteria for quality and quantity of comparable words and the sophisticated scientific procedures available to the FBI exceed the standards normally used and/or available to most other practitioners in the field." Koenig, *Spectrographic Voice Identification*, 13 CRIME LAB. DIGEST 105 (Oct. 1986).

69. Koenig, *supra* note 65, 79 J. ACOUSTICAL SOC'Y AM. at 2088.

70. Koenig, *supra* note 68, 13 CRIME LAB. DIGEST at 116. An FBI expert, however, did testify in rebuttal (against FBI policy, but required by subpoena) after the court ruled that a defense expert would be allowed to testify. United States v. Maivia, 728 F. Supp. 1471 (D. Hawaii 1990).

71. Shipp, Doherty & Hollien, *Some Fundamental Considerations Regarding Voice Identification*, 82 J. ACOUSTICAL SOC'Y AM. 687 (1987).

72. *Id.*

73. Koenig, Ritenour, Kohus & Kelly, *Reply to "Some Fundamental Considerations Regarding Voice Identification,"* 82 J. ACOUSTICAL SOC'Y AM. 688, 689 (1987). *See also* Melvin, Nakasone & Tosi, *More Fundamental Considerations Regarding Voice Identification*, 84 J. ACOUSTICAL SOC'Y

1993 FBI Article

A 1993 article by an FBI examiner contained the following comments: "When properly conducted, spectrographic voice identification [including aural comparison] is a relatively accurate but not conclusive examination for comparing a recorded unknown voice sample with a suspect repeating the identical contextual information over the same type of transmission system...."[74] The article also noted that:

> The scientific support of this [spectrographic technique] examination is limited, and the actual error rate under most investigative conditions is unknown. The research to date indicates that the technique has a certain error rate that is independent of examiner-induced errors, with errors of false elimination (voice samples were actually from the same person, but the examination found that they did not match) appreciably higher than false identification (the voice samples were actually from different persons, but the examinations found that the samples matched).[75]

The article also noted that the FBI and New York City Police Department were the only government laboratories using the technique on a regular basis. Moreover, the courtroom testimony of some experts continued to be troublesome:

> Problems still persist in the spectrographic voice identification field. Examples of these problems include the following: (1) separate sets of certified examiners making high-confidence decisions for both identification and elimination in the same case; (2) individuals with no experience, training, or education in the voice identification discipline making conclusive decisions under oath in court; and (3) examiners testifying that an unknown voice is not the defendant's, although admitting their decisions are really inconclusive based upon accepted standards.[76]

Standards

Prior to 1992, there were no universally accepted qualification standards for examiners or standard procedures for conducting an examination. In some respects the FBI's qualification requirements were more demanding than those of

---

AM. 1943 (1988) (also commenting on the FBI survey). These authors wrote: "It is true that use of forensic decisions or self-incrimination to verify the validity of a [voice identification] technique is not a scientific method, but this is the best or only direct means for verification in real-life cases."

74. Koenig, *Selected Topics in Forensic Voice Identification*, 20 CRIME LAB. DIGEST 78, 79 (Oct. 1993).

75. *Id.* at 79-80.

76. *Id.* at 80.

the Voice Identification and Acoustic Analysis Subcommittee (VIAAS) of the International Association Identification (IAI), the group that replaced the International Association of Voice Identification in 1980. The FBI required a B.S. degree, periodic hearing tests, two years of training, examination of 100 comparisons, attendance at a spectrographic school, and continuous recertification. VIAAS certification did not require a B.S. degree or a periodic hearing test. Moreover, fifty rather than 100 comparisons were required for certification.

Similarly, the FBI's minimum criteria for comparisons were more stringent. The Bureau required twenty rather than ten words for comparison and typically the original tape. It also made speed corrections and track determinations of recordings, as well as enhancement and equalization adjustments.[77] Both organizations required a second, affirming, independent opinion. Standards are important because "some practitioners have blatantly ignored all standards and criteria by conducting some examinations with only one-word comparisons, very poor quality samples, different languages on the two samples, no spectrographic training, etc., and then testifying in court to their positive, unrefutable decisions."[78]

The VIAAS adopted new standards, effective January 1, 1992.[79] These standards incorporated many of the FBI's requirements. The standards continued the oversight of a Voice Identification Certification Board. They also set forth the conclusions that may be reached in an examination: (1) Identification, (2) Probable Identification, (3) Possible Identification, (4) Inconclusive, (5) Possible Elimination, (6) Probable Elimination, and (7) Elimination. A second independent opinion is required, except for conclusions of Possible Identification, Inconclusive, and Possible Elimination. The standards took no position on whether a certified examiner should provide testimony concerning examination results. For the first time, the VIAAS required that a "statement of accuracy" be included in all reports and testimony. The statement reads: "The spectrographic/aural technique is not completely conclusive; however, an examination following the International Association for Identification Standards does allow for a meaningful voice comparison."

---

77. "If the quality is too poor, enhancement procedures using analog and/or digital filters and equalizers are sometimes tried in an attempt to meaningfully improve the intelligibility." Koenig, *supra* note 68, 13 CRIME LAB. DIGEST at 109.

78. *Id.* at 116.

79. VIAAS, *Voice Comparison Standards, reprinted in* 41 J. FORENSIC IDENTIFICATION 373 (1991).

Automated methods of voice identification[80] have been mentioned in the literature, and Dr. Tosi had used a computer-assisted method of voice identification since 1978.[81] Nevertheless, computer-assisted voice comparison procedures are neither permitted by the International Association of Identification (IAI) Standards nor used by the FBI because there are no digital algorithms that can reliably compare voices under forensic conditions.

§ 10-6. Admissibility & Weight of Spectrographic Identifications.

The principal issue concerning the admissibility of voicegram evidence has been the validity of the technique.[82] Two factors influenced how the courts decided the early cases.

The first factor was the evidentiary standard used to determine admissibility of scientific evidence. For the most part, those courts that applied the *Frye* test,[83] which requires general acceptance of a novel technique in the relevant scientific community, tended to exclude voicegram evidence. Courts that adopted a less stringent standard of admissibility tended to admit voicegram evidence.[84]

The second factor related to the publication of the various scientific reports on voicegrams. For example, the publication of the Michigan State study played a

---

80. *See* NAS Report, *supra* note 34, at 34 ("Automated methods of voice identification are being developed and are yielding information of benefit to the strengthening of the aural-visual method"). For a further discussion of automated methods, *see* Tosi Text, *supra* note 2, at 81-97.

81. *See* Tosi & Nakasone, *A Computer Assisted Method of Voice Identification; Context Independent*, 39 J. FORENSIC IDENTIFICATION 1 (1989); Tosi, *New Developments in Voice Identification, in* PRACTISING LAW INSTITUTE, SCIENTIFIC AND EXPERT EVIDENCE 1005, 1007 (2d ed. 1981) (citing State v. Weatherford, No. C4116 (Ind. 1978)).

82. *See generally* Bessner, *The Admissibility of Novel Scientific Techniques in Criminal Trials: Voice Spectroscopy*, 30 CRIM. L.Q. 294 (1988); Decker & Handler, *Voiceprint Identification Evidence — Out of the Frye Pan and into Admissibility*, 26 AM. U. L. REV. 314 (1977); Greene, *Voiceprint Identification: The Case in Favor of Admissibility*, 13 AM. CRIM. L. REV. 171 (1975); Gregory, *Voice Spectrography Evidence: Approaches to Admissibility*, 20 U. RICH. L. REV. 357 (1986); Jones, *Danger — Voiceprints Ahead*, 11 AM. CRIM. L. REV. 549 (1973); Siegel, *Cross-Examination of a "Voiceprint" Expert: A Blueprint for Trial Lawyers*, 12 CRIM. L. BULL. 509 (1976); Note, *Voiceprints in the Courtroom — Scientific and Evidentiary Problems*, 21 ARIZ. L. REV. 1163 (1979); Note, *The Admissibility of Spectrographic Voice Identification in the State Courts*, 70 J. CRIM. L. & CRIMINOLOGY 349 (1979); Note, *The Voiceprint Dilemma: Should Voices Be Seen and Not Heard?*, 35 MD. L. REV. 267 (1975).

83. Frye v. United States, 293 F. 1013 (D.C. Cir. 1923). For a further discussion of the *Frye* test, *see* Chapter 1.

84. *See* State v. Gortarez, 141 Ariz. 254, 266 n.6, 686 P.2d 1224, 1236 n.6 (1984) ("Some courts, generally following the *Frye* rule, refuse to allow spectrographic evidence.... Other courts, generally following modifications of *Frye* or not mentioning it at all, have allowed spectrographic evidence"); State v. Free, 493 So. 2d 781, 785 (La. App. 1986) ("[W]hen the *Frye* test has been applied, courts have tended to exclude expert voice identification evidence based on spectrography. The courts are equally likely to admit the evidence when the *Frye* test is not applied"), *cert. denied*, 499 So. 2d 83 (1987).

major role in gaining judicial acceptance of voicegram evidence. As one commentator noted, "The Tosi study was to become the most influential factor in changing the judicial attitude from scorn to endorsement of spectrographic voice identification."[85] Similarly, the NAS Report and the 1986 FBI survey influenced later decisions.[86]

Early Cases

The judicial decisions on voicegrams can be grouped into four periods. The first period covers cases decided prior to 1972.[87] Until the Michigan State study was published in that year, the validity of the technique was supported only by the claims of its developer, Lawrence Kersta. Because speech scientists questioned these claims,[88] two of the three initial appellate courts that considered voicegram evidence rejected it for lack of "general acceptance."[89] One of these courts even questioned Kersta's qualifications to testify about the validity of the technique. According to the court, Kersta's engineering background was insufficient; communication by speech required an understanding of other subjects, including anatomy, physiology, physics, psychology, and linguistics.[90]

1972-1979

The second period covers the cases decided between 1972 and 1979, after the completion of the Michigan State study but before the publication of the National Academy of Sciences Report. Most of the reported cases were decided during this period. The publication of the Michigan State study resulted in the acceptance of voicegram evidence by a number of courts.[91] However, as noted earlier, certain sectors of the scientific community expressed serious reservations about the adequacy of this study.[92] Other courts interpreted these reservations as a failure of the technique to gain general acceptance in the scientific community. For example, the D.C. Circuit, applying a strict *Frye* test, held that "voiceprint

---

85. Note, *The Admissibility of Spectrographic Voice Identification in the State Courts*, 70 J. Crim. L. & Criminology 349, 351 (1979).

86. *See* § 10-5 *supra* (discussing these reports).

87. People v. Straehle, No. 9323/64 (Sup. Ct. Westchester Cty. 1966), appears to be the first case to admit voicegram evidence. It is noted in 12 N.Y.L.F. 501 (1966).

88. *See* § 10-5 *supra.*

89. *Compare* People v. King, 266 Cal. App. 2d 437, 72 Cal. Rptr. 478 (1968) (voicegram evidence not admissible); State v. Cary, 49 N.J. 343, 230 A.2d 384 (1967), *on remand,* 99 N.J. Super. 323, 239 A.2d 680 (N.J. Super. Ct. 1968), *appeal granted,* 53 N.J. 256, 250 A.2d 15 (1969), *aff'd,* 56 N.J. 16, 264 A.2d 209 (1970) (voicegram evidence not admissible), *with* United States v. Wright, 17 U.S.C.M.A. 183, 37 C.M.R. 447 (1967) (voicegram evidence admitted).

90. People v. King, 266 Cal. App. 2d 437, 456, 72 Cal. Rptr. 478, 490 (1968).

91. *See* cases cited in notes 101-13 *infra.*

92. *See* § 10-5 *supra.*

identification is not now sufficiently accepted by the scientific community as a whole."[93]

Similarly, the California Supreme Court rejected voicegram evidence. The court offered three grounds for its decision. First, the court questioned "whether the testimony of a single witness [Lt. Nash] alone is ever sufficient to represent, or attest to, the views of an entire scientific community regarding the reliability of a new technique."[94] Second, the impartiality of Lt. Nash, a leading proponent of the technique, "to assess the position of the scientific community" troubled the court.[95] Third, Lt. Nash's qualifications to testify about the general acceptance of the technique in the scientific community was raised. According to the court, his "qualifications are those of *a technician and law enforcement officer, not a scientist.*"[96]

Other courts echoed similar concerns. For example, the Pennsylvania Supreme Court ruled voicegram evidence inadmissible, commenting that the "testimony of one expert [Lt. Nash] cannot satisfy [the *Frye*] standard."[97] The Michigan Supreme Court also rejected voicegram evidence because the "reputations and careers"[98] of the experts (Dr. Tosi and Lt. Nash) were "built on their voiceprint work" and therefore they were not "impartial and disinterested."[99] Other courts reached the same result.[100]

In contrast, different courts responded to the Michigan State study by modifying the *Frye* test. The Supreme Judicial Court of Massachusetts limited the "field" in which general acceptance was required to "those who would be expected to be familiar with its use"[101] and gave "greater weight to those experts who have had direct and empirical experience in the field of spectrography."[102] The Sixth Circuit took the position that "general acceptance" was "nearly

93. United States v. Addison, 498 F.2d 741, 745 (D.C. Cir. 1974). In a later case the court indicated a willingness to reexamine *Addison* "in light of the apparently increased reliability and general acceptance in the scientific community of using spectrographic analysis techniques for voice identification purposes." United States v. McDaniel, 538 F.2d 408, 413 (D.C. Cir. 1976).

94. People v. Kelly, 17 Cal. 3d 24, 37, 130 Cal. Rptr. 144, 152, 549 P.2d 1240, 1248 (1976).

95. *Id.* at 38, 130 Cal. Rptr. at 153, 549 P.2d at 1249.

96. *Id.* at 39, 130 Cal. Rptr. at 154, 549 P.2d at 1250.

97. Commonwealth v. Topa, 471 Pa. 223, 232, 369 A.2d 1277, 1282 (1977).

98. People v. Tobey, 401 Mich. 141, 146, 257 N.W.2d 537, 539 (1977).

99. *Id.*

100. *See* People v. Law, 40 Cal. App. 3d 69, 114 Cal. Rptr. 708 (1974); Brown v. United States, 384 A.2d 647 (D.C. 1978); Reed v. State, 283 Md. 374, 391 A.2d 364 (1978); People v. Collins, 94 Misc. 2d 704, 405 N.Y.S.2d 365 (1978). *See also* United States v. Baynes, 687 F.2d 659, 671 (3d Cir. 1982) (admissibility not yet decided in the Third Circuit); D'Arc v. D'Arc, 157 N.J. Super. 553, 385 A.2d 278 (1978) (civil case).

101. Commonwealth v. Lykus, 367 Mass. 191, 203, 327 N.E.2d 671, 677 (1975). *See also* Commonwealth v. Vitello, 367 Mass. 224, 234, 327 N.E. 2d 819, 827 (1975).

102. 367 Mass. at 204 n.6, 327 N.E.2d at 678 n.6.

synonymous with reliability;"[103] in a later voicegram case the court did not refer to the *Frye* standard at all.[104] Both courts admitted voicegram evidence.

Still other courts used the voicegram cases as the vehicle to reject the *Frye* general acceptance test. For example, the Fourth Circuit rejected *Frye* and adopted a relevancy approach:[105]

> Unless an exaggerated popular opinion of the accuracy of a particular technique makes its use prejudicial or likely to mislead the jury, it is better to admit relevant scientific evidence in the same manner as other expert testimony and allow its weight to be attacked by cross-examination and refutation.[106]

Following this approach, a number of other courts also admitted voicegram evidence.[107]

United States v. Williams (1978)[108] is illustrative. In evaluating the reliability of the technique, the Second Circuit rejected *Frye* as the controlling standard. Instead, the court cited a number of factors, which it believed established the reliability of voicegram analysis. The court recognized "the potential rate of error" as "[o]ne indicator of evidential reliability."[109] This factor, as well as *Williams*, was later cited by the U.S. Supreme Court in *Daubert*.[110] Citing the Michigan State study, the *Williams* court noted that the false identification error rate was 6.3%, a rate reduced to 2.4% when doubtful comparisons were eliminated.[111] This error rate, however, was undercut by the NAS Report, which was published the following year. The Report concluded that the reported error

---

103. United States v. Franks, 511 F.2d 25, 33 n.12 (6th Cir.), *cert. denied,* 422 U.S. 1042 (1975).

104. United States v. Jenkins, 525 F.2d 819, 827 (6th Cir. 1975).

105. For a discussion of the relevancy approach, *see* Chapter 1.

106. United States v. Baller, 519 F.2d 463, 466 (4th Cir.), *cert. denied,* 423 U.S. 1019 (1975).

107. *See* United States v. Sample, 378 F. Supp. 44 (E.D. Pa. 1974) (admissible in probation revocation hearing); Hodo v. Superior Court, 30 Cal. App. 3d 778, 106 Cal. Rptr. 547 (1973); Alea v. State, 265 So. 2d 96 (Fla. App. 1972); Worley v. State, 263 So. 2d 613 (Fla. App. 1972) (as corroborative evidence); State v. Williams, 388 A.2d 500, 503 (Me. 1978); State *ex rel.* Trimble v. Hedman, 291 Minn. 442, 192 N.W.2d 432 (1971) (as corroborative evidence); State v. Olderman, 44 Ohio App. 2d 130, 336 N.E.2d 442 (1975); People v. Rogers, 86 Misc. 2d 868, 385 N.Y.S.2d 228 (1976); R. v. Medvedew, 6 Crim. Rep. 3d 185 (Manitoba App. Ct. 1978).

In addition, the New Jersey Supreme Court seemed disposed to reconsider its earlier position on voicegrams after the Michigan State study. State v. Andretta, 61 N.J. 544, 296 A.2d 644 (1972). However, in Windmere, Inc. v. International Ins. Co., 105 N.J. 373, 387, 522 A.2d 405, 412 (1987), the court again rejected voicegram results.

108. 583 F.2d 1194 (2d Cir. 1978), *cert. denied,* 439 U.S. 1117 (1979).

109. *Id.* at 1198.

110. For a discussion of *Daubert*, *see* Chapter 1.

111. 583 F.2d at 1198.

rates were generally inadequate for forensic applications[112] and not "valid over the range of conditions usually met in practice."[113] Thus, the question was not whether error rates were important (they are), but rather how to determine whether they were valid. Unfortunately, the Second Circuit accepted the proffered error rates without question.

As a second reliability factor, the Second Circuit pointed to the "existence and maintenance of standards"[114] in the relevant field. The U.S. Supreme Court also adopted this factor in *Daubert*.[115] The *Williams* court cited the certification procedures of the International Association of Voice Identification. Most members of this group, however, were police officers, not scientists.[116] As the NAS Report later noted, this Association "as presently constituted does not possess the broad base of representation usually considered appropriate and perhaps essential for a national certifying board."[117] The Second Circuit simply did not appreciate that it was citing an association of technicians rather than scientists.

1980-1993

The third period of voicegram cases covers decisions decided after the publication of the National Academy of Sciences Report and before the *Daubert* opinion was rendered in 1993. The Ohio Supreme Court, rejecting the *Frye* test, admitted voicegram evidence in 1983.[118] Two points about this case are noteworthy. First, no expert testimony challenging the validity of the technique was offered at trial.[119] Second, the NAS report, published four years earlier, was not mentioned by the court. *State v. Wheeler*[120] is similar. Rejecting the *Frye* test, the Rhode Island Supreme Court ruled in favor of admissibility. The NAS report was not cited. Four prosecution experts testified, while an electrical engineer testified for the defense.

Other courts, however, excluded voicegram evidence. The Indiana Supreme Court excluded this type of evidence, concluding that the technique had not yet gained general acceptance in the scientific community.[121] The Arizona Supreme

---

112. *See* § 10-5 *supra*.

113. NAS Report, *supra* note 34, at 58.

114. 583 F.2d at 1198.

115. For a discussion of *Daubert, see* Chapter 1.

116. *See* MOENSSENS & INBAU, SCIENTIFIC EVIDENCE IN CRIMINAL CASES 580 (2d ed. 1978) ("Except for [Dr.] Tosi, no scientists were among its early members; the majority of them are still police officers who have been trained by either Kersta or Tosi to become 'voiceprint' technicians").

117. NAS Report, *supra* note 34, at 65.

118. State v. Williams, 4 Ohio St. 3d 53, 446 N.E.2d 444 (1983).

119. *Id.* at 59, 446 N.E.2d at 448.

120. 496 A.2d 1382, 1389 (R.I. 1985).

121. Cornett v. State, 450 N.E.2d 498, 503 (Ind. 1983).

Court reached the same result, ruling that voicegram identification had failed to achieve general acceptance.[122] The court relied primarily on the NAS Report, calling it "particularly persuasive."[123] The New Jersey Supreme Court again held that voicegram evidence had yet to gain sufficient scientific acceptance.[124] A Louisiana appellate court reached the same result.[125]

Nevertheless, some courts continued to admit voicegram evidence. In *United States v. Smith,*[126] decided in 1989, the Seventh Circuit found that the voicegram technique had been generally accepted by the scientific community, despite the NAS report. The *Smith* court discounted the report by pointing out that it took no position on the admissibility issue.[127] Indeed, the NAS committee believed its report should be limited to scientific, not legal, issues; the latter were beyond its expertise.[128] This point did not, however, undermine the report's largely negative conclusions.[129]

In addition, the Seventh Circuit relied on the 1986 FBI survey. The court accepted the survey at face value. No attempt to evaluate its limitations was undertaken. The court was apparently unaware that some speech scientists had criticized the survey for failing to specify the precise method used by the FBI examiners and the criteria for determining examiner proficiency. A more fundamental objection concerned the criterion for determining "ground truth."[130] Apparently, the court was also unaware that the FBI precluded its examiners from testifying in court, a fact that places the FBI survey in a different light.

There were other problems. The *Smith* court did not recognize the factual differences between its case and the prior voiceprint cases. The defendant, Tamara Smith, had an identical twin named Tanya. The expert testified that it was "highly probable" that the voice on several recordings was one twin and not the other. In other words, the examination involved a closed test, one in which the examiner determines which of several known voice samples is the same as an unknown sample. In contrast, the research cited by the court involved open tests, in which the examiner did not know if the unknown sample was made by the speaker of the known sample. In addition, unlike the research relied upon by the court, the expert did not make a positive identification. If anything, these factors

122. State v. Gortarez, 141 Ariz. 254, 686 P.2d 1224 (1984).

123. *Id.* at 265, 686 P.2d at 1235.

124. Windmere, Inc. v. International Ins. Co., 105 N.J. 373, 387, 522 A.2d 405, 412 (1987).

125. State v. Free, 493 So. 2d 781, 789 (La. App. 1986).

126. 869 F.2d 348 (7th Cir. 1989).

127. *Id.* at 353 n.7.

128. *See* Rothstein, *Book Review*, 17 AM. CRIM. L. REV. 153, 154 (1979) ("The [NAS] report is a scientific work, not a legal document").

129. The expert, Dr. Nakasone, acknowledged that "no one's voice is one-hundred percent unique, and that the field of voice identification is not one-hundred percent reliable." 869 F.2d at 354.

130. For a discussion of the FBI Survey, *see* § 10-5 *supra.*

support admissibility. The important point, however, is that the court was unaware of them.[131]

In *United States v. Maivia*[132] a federal district court also admitted voicegram evidence. In this case, an FBI examiner testified (against FBI policy, but required by subpoena) for the prosecution after the court ruled that the defense could introduce voicegram evidence through its expert. At one point in its opinion, the court wrote: "Thus it would appear that inasmuch as the admissibility of spectrographic evidence to identify voices has received general judicial recognition, it is no longer considered novel within the *Frye* test and consequently the test is inapplicable."[133]

Smith and *Mavia* are noteworthy for another reason. In *Smith* the federal prosecutor argued that voicegram evidence was reliable. Indeed, the court found that the "government presented ample evidence of the reliability of spectrographic voice identification at trial."[134] In *Maivia* a different federal prosecutor moved to exclude voicegram evidence "because spectrographic analysis is a novel scientific technique which has not gained sufficient acceptance in its field."[135] The only difference between the two cases was the offering party — the defendant proffered the evidence in *Maivia.* In sum, Assistant U.S. Attorneys, both representing the Department of Justice, argued both for and against admissibility in these cases.

The New York Court of Appeals addressed the admissibility issue in *People v. Jeter* (1992).[136] Jeter, a murder defendant, claimed that the voice on two taped confessions was not his. In rebuttal, a prosecution expert testified, based on spectrographic analysis, that the voice was Jeter's. Despite a motion by the defense, the trial court refused to hold an out-of-court hearing on admissibility. The Court of Appeals ruled that the trial court erred, finding that a hearing should have been held. The Court wrote:

> We do not agree that the [trial] court could properly have determined that voice spectrography is generally accepted as reliable based on the case law and existing literature on the subject.... In this instance, there is marked conflict in the judicial and legal authorities as to the reliability of the procedure. New York courts are split on the issue of admissibility ....

---

131. Interestingly, the court admitted the evidence under the *Frye* test. 869 F.2d at 351 ("[T]his circuit has continued to affirm (and to apply) the *Frye* standard"). This result is surprising because the FBI survey had acknowledged that voiceprint identification "has yet to find approval among most scientists in phonetics, linguistics, engineering, and related disciplines as a positive test in comparing voice samples," *FBI Survey*, *supra* note 65, at 2088.

132. 728 F. Supp. 1471 (D. Hawaii 1990).

133. *Id.* at 1478.

134. 869 F.2d at 353.

135. 728 F. Supp. at 1473.

136. 80 N.Y.2d 818, 600 N.E.2d 214, 587 N.Y.S.2d 583 (1992).

> Moreover, while several jurisdictions have held that voice spectrography evidence is sufficiently reliable to be admissible ..., others have reached just the opposite conclusion.... The legal scholarship on the admissibility of voice spectrograph is likewise conflicting.... We conclude that the trial court lacked a proper basis to admit the voice spectrographic evidence without a preliminary inquiry into reliability.[137]

Post-Daubert Cases

In *Daubert v. Merrell Dow Pharmaceuticals, Inc.*,[138] the U.S. Supreme Court rejected the *Frye* test as the applicable standard in federal trials. In its place, the Court substituted a reliability test. Surprisingly, the Court cited two voiceprint cases to support its analysis, both of which are discussed earlier in this section: *United States v. Williams* and *United States v. Smith.*

Few voicegram cases have been decided since *Daubert.*[139] In one, *State v. Coon*,[140] the Alaska Supreme Court adopted the *Daubert* test and then admitted voicegram evidence under that standard: "The scientific literature cited by the APDA permits a conclusion that there is significant disagreement among experts in the field of voice spectrographic analysis regarding the reliability of the technique. As the State notes, no scientific literature was submitted to the trial court for review, but Cain [the expert] testified about several articles and studies addressing voice spectrographic analysis, and conceded that the reliability of the technique was disputed among members of the relevant scientific community."[141]

Weight of the Evidence

Even if a jurisdiction admits voicegram evidence, the application of the technique under certain circumstances may present problems. Since the Michigan State study attempted to establish the validity of the technique *inferentially*,[142] any significant changes between the test conditions and an actual case may affect the admissibility of the evidence. Some scientists have argued that "[f]urther studies are needed, with particular attention to the examiner's decision criteria,

---

137. *Id.* at 820-21, 600 N.E.2d at 216, 587 N.Y.S.2d at 585. The Court, however, ruled the error harmless.

138. 509 U.S. 579 (1993).

139. A Fourth Circuit opinion, handed down in 1994, referred to voicegram cases: "Voice spectrograph technology, a method by which an expert can compare a known voice to an unknown voice within a small margin of error, is admissible at criminal trials in this circuit and has been for years." Sanders v. Robert Bosch Corp., 38 F.3d 736, 746 (4th Cir. 1994) (Widener, J., concurring in part and dissenting in part) (citing *Baller* case).

140. 974 P.2d 386 (Alaska 1999) (voice exemplars left on answering machine, accused charged with making terroristic telephone calls).

141. *Id.* at 402.

142. Tosi, Oyer, Lashbrook, Pedrey, Nicol & Nash, *supra* note 4, at 2031.

the selection of speaker population, the time lapse between voice samples, background-noise conditions, and the psychological condition of the speaker."[143]

Moreover, the examiner's conclusions in a particular case may be subject to attack. Dr. Tosi wrote: "Distortions due to the transmission and recording systems, background noise, or psychological or physiological alterations of the speakers will greatly decrease the percentage of cases in which an honest and well-trained examiner can reach a positive identification using these subjective methods."[144] In some cases experts have disagreed on whether a positive identification could be made;[145] in another case, the expert misidentified a spectrogram during an in-court test.[146] In a "threatening telephone call" case heard before the Los Angeles Board of Civil Service Commissioners, decided on March 25, 1992, five certified IAI examiners conducted a spectrographic voice comparison. Three examiners made an identification at a high confidence level, while two examiners eliminated the suspect with a high to very high confidence level. The Board accepted the identification opinions.[147]

These cases illustrate the importance of contesting expert testimony, especially in light of the number of juries that acquitted defendants in spite of the introduction of voicegram evidence.[148]

---

143. *See also* Bolt, Cooper, David, Dens, Picket & Stevens, *supra* note 57, at 534.

144. Tosi, *supra* note 3, at 993. *See also* Koenig, *supra* note 68, 13 CRIME LAB. DIGEST at 111 ("Forensic applications have additional problems with voice disguise, limited band width and signal-to-noise, telephone channel effects, altered psychological states, electronic manipulation, etc.").

145. Tosi, *supra* note 3, at 998 ("In March 1974, in *Michigan v. Chaisson,* the court ordered Tosi to analyze the samples presented by Nash as evidence against the defendant. Tosi was unable to use the samples as the basis of examination; he was able to offer a probability of identification on the basis of new samples obtained from the defendant, ordered by the court. The prosecution then dismissed the case").

146. People v. Chapter, 13 Crim. L. Rptr. (BNA) 2479 (Cal. Super. 1973). In his book, Dr. Tosi wrote: "The strong personality and absolute statements of Nash in the trials in which he acted as an expert witness produced strong reactions from the opponents as well as from some advocates of voice identification by spectrography. Drs. G. Papun and P. Ladefoged (1973) presented a paper at the eighty-sixth meeting of the Acoustical Society of America, reviewing two cases examined by Nash and criticizing the quality of the samples used by this officer. Poza (1974) published a paper containing similar criticisms." Tosi Text, *supra* note 2, at 141.

See also supra note 49 for another misidentification.

147. Koenig, *Selected Topics in Forensic Voice Identification*, 20 CRIME LAB. DIGEST 78, 81 n.1 (Oct. 1993) (noting the L.A. Board of Civil Service Commissioners case).

148. *See* Tosi Text, *supra* note 2, at 142 ("The verdicts from all these trials varied; in about 46 cases (since December 1970) the defendants were found guilty, in 19 cases the defendants were acquitted; in 4 cases there were hung juries; in 8 cases the defendants pleaded guilty"); Greene, *Voiceprint Identification: The Case in Favor of Admissibility*, 13 AM. CRIM. L. REV. 171, 190-91 (1975).

In United States v. Goldstein, 532 F.2d 1305 (9th Cir.), *cert. denied,* 429 U.S. 960 (1976), the defendant argued that the trial court erred in not requiring voicegram identification instead of aural

Other Proceedings

The stage of a prosecution at which voicegram evidence is offered also may affect admissibility. Although such evidence may be inadmissible at trial, it may be admissible to establish probable cause[149] or at a probation revocation hearing.[150] It also may be admissible in posttrial proceedings.[151] This approach finds some support in the NAS Report: "[A]n error rate that is judged acceptable for use in resolving a dispute over a contract or will might be judged much too large to accept for use in deciding who committed a serious crime."[152]

§ 10-7. Obtaining Voice Exemplars from Suspects.

Although defendants have challenged on constitutional grounds the methods that the police have used to obtain voice samples, these challenges have failed. The U.S. Supreme Court has ruled that the fifth amendment privilege against compulsory self-incrimination extends to testimonial, but not physical, evidence. Accordingly, in *United States v. Dionisio*[153] the Court ruled that compelling a defendant to speak for the purpose of voice analysis did not violate the fifth amendment because the "voice recordings were to be used solely to measure the physical properties of the witnesses' voices, not for the testimonial or communicative content of what was to be said."[154]

The Court also addressed a fourth amendment challenge. There are two distinct search and seizure issues. First, there may be a "seizure" of the person, which brings the suspect under the control of the police. Second, there may be a subsequent search and seizure of evidence from that person. The Court ruled against Dionisio on both issues. The accused had been summoned to appear before a grand jury to provide the voice exemplars, and the Court ruled that a grand jury subpoena was not a "seizure" within the meaning of the fourth amendment.[155] A different issue would have been presented had Dionisio been arrested or otherwise detained by the police.

On the second issue, the Court held that a person's voice is not protected by the fourth amendment:

---

identification of a taped voice. The court rejected this argument.

149. *See* State *ex rel.* Trimble v. Hedman, 291 Minn. 442, 192 N.W.2d 432 (1971).

150. *See* United States v. Sample, 378 F. Supp. 44 (E.D. Pa. 1974).

151. *See* State v. Free, 493 So. 2d 781, 789 (La. App. 1986) ("[O]ur conclusion does not prevent the use of such evidence in post trial proceedings, within the trial judge's discretion, whenever the evidence is reliable and will aid in a decision").

152. NAS Report, *supra* note 34, at 27.

153. 410 U.S. 1 (1973). *See also* United States v. Franks, 511 F.2d 25, 32 (6th Cir. 1975).

154. 410 U.S. at 7.

155. *Id.* at 10.

> The physical characteristics of a person's voice, its tone and manner, as opposed to the content of a specific conversation, are constantly exposed to the public. Like a man's facial characteristics, or handwriting, his voice is repeatedly produced for others to hear. No person can have a reasonable expectation that others will not know the sound of his voice, any more than he can reasonably expect that his face will be a mystery to the world.[156]

Accordingly, there was no search.

The constitutional aspects of obtaining evidence for forensic analysis are discussed in Chapter 2.

§ 10-8. Defense Experts.

Perhaps the most important aspect of the voicegram cases involves the failure of defense counsel to contest the validity of the evidence. One court noted that in 80% of the cases no opposing expert had testified on the issue of reliability and general acceptability of the technique.[157] The NAS Report also took note of this fact: "A striking fact about the trials involving voicegram evidence to date is the very large proportion in which the only experts testifying were those called by the state."[158] Moreover, one court found an abuse of discretion where a trial court failed to appoint a defense expert to conduct a voice spectrographic analysis of a tape allegedly containing the defendant's confession.[159]

The right to expert assistance is discussed in Chapter 4.

§ 10-9. Selected Bibliography

Bessner, *The Admissibility of Novel Scientific Techniques in Criminal Trials: Voice Spectroscopy*, 30 CRIM. L.Q. 294 (1988).

Gregory, *Voice Spectrography Evidence: Approaches to Admissibility*, 20 U. RICH. L. REV. 357 (1986).

H. HOLLIEN, THE ACOUSTICS OF CRIME: THE NEW SCIENCE OF FORENSIC PHONETICS (1990).

Kent & Chial, *Talker Identification*, *in* 2 MODERN SCIENTIFIC EVIDENCE ch. 25 (D. Faigman et al. eds 1997).

Koenig, *Selected Topics in Forensic Voice Identification*, 20 CRIME LAB. DIGEST 78 (Oct. 1993).

Koenig, *Spectrographic Voice Identification*, 13 CRIME LAB. DIGEST 105 (Oct. 1986).

Koenig, *Spectrographic Voice Identification: A Forensic Survey*, 79 J. ACOUSTICAL SOC'Y AM. 2088 (1986).

A. MOENSSENS, J. STARRS, C. HENDERSON & F. INBAU, SCIENTIFIC EVIDENCE IN CIVIL AND CRIMINAL CASES ch. 10 (4th ed. 1995).

NATIONAL RESEARCH COUNCIL, ON THE THEORY AND PRACTICE OF VOICE IDENTIFICATION (1979).

---

156. *Id.* at 14.

157. People v. Chapter, 13 Crim. L. Rptr. (BNA) 2479 (Cal. Super. 1973).

158. NAS Report, *supra* note 34, at 49.

159. People v. Tyson, 209 A.D.2d 354, 618 N.Y.S.2d 796 (1994).

Rafferty, *Anything You Say Can And Will Be Used Against You: Spectrographic Evidence In Criminal Cases*, 36 AM. CRIM. L. REV. 291, 294 (1999).

Seigal, *Cross-examination of a "Voiceprint" Expert: A Blueprint for Trial Lawyers*, 12 CRIM. L. BULL. 509 (1976).

Spectrographic Voice Identifications, 19 AM. JUR. PROOF OF FACTS 423 (1967).

Tobin, Segev & Levinson, *Forensic Voice Identification*, *in* FORENSIC SCIENCE ch. 28c (C. Wecht ed. 1998).

O. TOSI, VOICE IDENTIFICATION: THEORY AND LEGAL APPLICATIONS (1979).

Tosi, *New Developments in Voice Identification*, *in* PRACTISING LAW INSTITUTE, SCIENTIFIC AND EXPERT EVIDENCE 1005 (2d ed. 1981).

Note, *The Admissibility of Spectrographic Voice Identification in the State Courts*, 70 J. CRIM. L. & CRIMINOLOGY 349 (1979).

Annotations

Annot., *Admissibility and weight of voiceprint evidence*, 97 A.L.R.3D 294 (1980).

Annot., *Cautionary instructions to jury as to reliability of, or factors to be considered in evaluating, voice identification testimony*, 17 A.L.R.5TH 851 (1994).

Estrella, *Admissibility of evidence of voice identification of defendant as affected by allegedly suggestive voice lineup procedures*, 55 A.L.R.5TH 423 (1998).

CHAPTER 11

NEUTRON ACTIVATION ANALYSIS*

§ 11-1. In General.

Neutron activation analysis (NAA) is a qualitative and quantitative method for determining the elemental composition of substances.[1] It is one of the most sophisticated scientific techniques used in criminal trials. NAA analysis of gunshot residues, bullets, hair, glass, paint, and other substances has been admitted at trial.[2] Although well established in the scientific community for many years, the courtroom use of NAA dates back only to the mid-1960s.

The most publicized use of NAA may have occurred during the investigation into the assassination of President John F. Kennedy. Sparked by the movie *JFK,* a renewed interest in the assassination resulted in a number of news accounts on the subject in 1991. One *Time* magazine article discussed the "magic-bullet" theory, a theory which questioned whether the same bullet could have hit both President Kennedy and Governor Connally. The article states that "[n]eutron activation tests indicate that the fragments in Connally's wrist did come from the bullet in question."[3]

As a method of instrumental analysis, NAA has several advantages. First, it is extremely sensitive. Detection limits are in the microgram and nanogram range and often lower. Consequently, minute samples such as a single hair or a paint chip can be analyzed. Second, NAA is an accurate method and also permits the simultaneous analysis of many elements. Third, one type of activation analysis (purely instrumental NAA) is essentially nondestructive; therefore, in most cases the evidence subjected to analysis can be reexamined or introduced undamaged at trial.

---

*The authors wish to express their appreciation to Dr. S.S. Krishnan, Scientific Director (retired), Medical Physics Laboratory, The Toronto General Hospital, Canada, (retired), who reviewed this chapter in the first and second editions.

1. For a discussion of other instrumental techniques, *see* Chapter 25.

2. *See* § 11-4 *infra.*

3. Corliss, *Who Killed J.F.K.?*, TIME, Dec. 23, 1991, at 68. *See also* Weisberg v. United States Dep't of Justice, 438 F. Supp. 492, 499-503 (D.D.C. 1977) (Freedom of Information Act request for NAA lab results on Kennedy assassination).

NAA's major disadvantage is the expense associated with operating a nuclear reactor. Another disadvantage is that although NAA can detect most elements, there are some elements, such as lead, which are not easily detected by NAA.[4]

§ 11-2. Activation Analysis.

The atom is the smallest particle of any element that can exist independently and at the same time retain those qualities that mark it as a specific element.[5] It consists of a nucleus, which contains protons and neutrons, and electrons which circle the nucleus. Protons possess a positive electric charge, electrons possess a negative electric charge, and neutrons possess no charge. Each element has a different number of protons (atomic number). Most elements can absorb additional neutrons and thus become radioactive; when this occurs the element is called a radioisotope. In this state, however, the chemical properties of the element have not changed.

In activation analysis a sample is subjected to neutron bombardment[6] in a nuclear reactor.[7] The irradiation time, the intrinsic ability for neutron capture, and the density of the neutron bombardment (neutron flux) are among the factors that determine the sensitivity of detection. As a result of the bombardment, some of the nuclei of each stable element in the sample capture neutrons, thereby becoming artificially radioactive. These irradiated elements tend to return to a stable atomic state (radioactive decay) during which time particles and/or protons are emitted from the sample.[8] One such emanation is a gamma ray.[9] Since each element has a characteristic energy level of gamma radiation and a known rate of decay (half-life), these two indicia are used to determine the elemental composition of the sample.

---

4. NAA "has a number of drawbacks: it is much more costly; it is usually much more time consuming; and in order to perform the separations it is necessary to destroy the sample, so that it is not preserved for presentation in court or for further testing by the adverse party." Comment, *The Evidentiary Uses of Neutron Activation Analysis*, 59 CAL. L. REV. 997, 1009 (1971).

5. The description of NAA in the text is, of necessity, oversimplified and general. For a detailed discussion, *see* Watkins & Watkins, *Identification of Substances by Neutron Activation Analysis*, 15 AM. JUR. PROOF OF FACTS 115 (1964), and Comment, *supra* note 4. *See also* Katz, *Neutron Activation Analysis*, AMERICAN LABORATORY 16 (June 1985).

6. Slow (thermal) neutrons, those with relatively low energy, are used in NAA.

7. Usually, the core or neutron source in the reactor is uranium-235. After the samples are prepared, they are placed in plastic containers, which are then often placed in a specimen rack that rotates around the core. The rack equalizes the exposure of the specimens to neutron bombardment during irradiation.

8. Radioisotopes begin to decay as soon as they are created. The rate of decay is described in terms of the nuclide's half-life. The half-life is the period of time required for half the atoms of a radioisotope to disintegrate.

9. Gamma rays are a type of high-energy electromagnetic radiation. In addition to gamma rays, other subatomic particles, such as beta particles, are emitted during this process.

After the sample is removed from the reactor, the gamma rays are detected and counted by means of gamma-ray spectrometry. In addition, the respective half-lives of the emitting radionuclides often are determined. Two types of devices are used to detect gamma radiation: a scintillator[10] and a semiconductor radiation detector.[11] The latter has better resolution[12] than the former but is not as sensitive. The gamma-ray spectrometer produces a graph (spectrum), which can be compared to standard spectra of the same element. Known samples are analyzed at the same time.

Activation analysis may be purely instrumental or may involve radiochemical separation (wet chemistry). For example, when using NAA for the analysis of gunshot residues, the elements barium and antimony are chemically separated from the sample after irradiation but prior to gamma-ray detection.[13] The separation eliminates other elements that may emit gamma-rays of nearly the same energy level and thus produce overlapping spectra that interfere with the analysis.[14] It also eliminates other elements which overload the instruments.[15] The chemicals used in the separation process will not be detected because they are nonradioactive. Radiochemical separation results in the destruction of the sample.[16] In contrast, the sample is not damaged in purely instrumental analysis.

As with any type of instrumentation, errors in the analysis are possible if proper procedures are not followed. For example, as one commentator has pointed out, quantitative analysis may be flawed if there is an uneven neutron flow inside the reactor, if the known and unknown samples are not the same size and shape, if sufficient counts for the measurement are not recorded, or if two radionuclides that emit gamma rays of very nearly equal energies are involved.[17] In addition, due to its great sensitivity, NAA will detect the presence of dirt or other contaminants that are present prior to irradiation. Such contaminants can produce erroneous results.[18]

---

10. The scintillator, typically a sodium iodide crystal, converts the energy of the gamma rays into a pulse of light, which is then converted into an electrical pulse by a photomultiplier tube. The electrical pulses are measured by a multichannel analyzer.

11. The semiconductor radiation detector, typically a germanium crystal with a small amount of lithium, absorbs and converts gamma rays into electrical pulses.

12. Resolution refers to the capability of the device to distinguish gamma rays at different energy levels. The better the resolution, the less is the need to use radiochemical separation or other techniques to remove interfering spectra.

13. Krishnan, *Detection of Gunshot Residue: Present Status*, *in* 1 FORENSIC SCI. HANDBOOK 573, 575 (R. Saferstein ed. 1982).

14. Overlapping spectra also may be eliminated by spectrum stripping, a process by which the masking spectra are subtracted.

15. Krishnan, *supra* note 13, at 575.

16. Comment, *supra* note 4, at 1009.

17. *Id.* at 1012.

18. *Id.* at 1012-13.

Forensic Applications

NAA is forensically applied in two types of examinations. First, it is used in situations in which only the presence or absence of one or more elements is significant. For example, in the detection of gunshot residues, NAA is used to detect the presence and quantity of the elements antimony and barium on the hands of a person suspected of discharging a firearm.[19] These elements are constituents of many cartridges, and their presence in certain concentrations on the hand is indicative of a deposition of gunshot residue. Barium and antimony may be present on the hands of persons who have not fired a weapon but at much lower levels. Therefore, the use of NAA is based on the detection of significantly greater amounts of these elements than normally occur.[20] Several methods, including swabbing and washing techniques, have been used to remove the residues from the hands.[21]

NAA has also been used to identify bullet holes and to determine firing (muzzle-to-target) distances.[22] The presence of antimony and other residues in a definitive pattern near a hole in a garment indicates that the hole was made by a bullet. Using the same weapon and similar ammunition as that used in the crime, an experiment can be conducted in an effort to replicate the dispersion pattern of the residues found on the garment. The dispersion pattern permits the determination of the firing distance.[23]

Second, NAA is used for comparative purposes. Trace elements in hair,[24] paint,[25] soil,[26] glass,[27] and other substances discovered at a crime scene may be

---

19. For a further discussion of gunshot residue examinations, *see* Chapter 14.

20. Krishnan, *supra* note 13, at 579-80. *See generally* Kilty, *Activity After Shooting and Its Effect on the Retention of Primer Residue*, 20 J. FORENSIC SCI. 219 (1975); Krishnan, *Detection of Gunshot Residues on the Hands by Trace Element Analysis*, 22 J. FORENSIC SCI. 304 (1977); Midkiff, *Detection of Gunshot Residues: Modern Solutions for an Old Problem*, 3 J. POLICE SCI. & ADMIN. 77 (1975).

21. *See* Pillay, Jester & Fox, *New Method for the Collection and Analysis of Gunshot Residues as Forensic Evidence*, 19 J. FORENSIC SCI. 768 (1974); Pillay & Sagans, *Gunshot Residue Collection Using Film-Lift Techniques for Neutron Activation Analysis*, 2 J. POLICE SCI. & ADMIN. 388 (1974).

22. *See* Krishnan & Nichol, *Identification of Bullet Holes by Neutron Activation Analysis and Autoradiography*, 13 J. FORENSIC SCI. 519 (1968); Krishnan, *Determination of Gunshot Firing Distances and Identification of Bullet Holes by Neutron Activation Analysis*, 12 J. FORENSIC SCI. 112 (1967); Krishnan, *Firing Distance Determination by Neutron Activation Analysis*, 12 J. FORENSIC SCI. 471 (1967).

23. For a further discussion of firing distance determinations, *see* Chapter 14.

24. *See* Bate, *The Use of Activation Analysis in Procedures for the Removal and Characterization of the Surface Contaminants of Hair*, 10 J. FORENSIC SCI. 60 (1965); Cornelis, *Is It Possible to Identify Individuals by Neutron Activation Analysis of Hair?*, 12 MED. SCI. & L. 188 (1972); Forslev, *"Nondestructive" Neutron Activation Analysis of Hair*, 11 J. FORENSIC SCI. 217 (1966); Perkons & Jervis, *Trace Elements in Human Head Hair*, 11 J. FORENSIC SCI. 50 (1966);

compared with similar items obtained from a suspect. For example, even though the major constituents of two pieces of glass may be the same, impurity trace elements in each may be different because manufacturers cannot control the quantities of these elements in their products.[28] Therefore, if two pieces of glass contain the same trace elements in the same concentrations and if the presence of these elements in these concentrations is unusual, then there is a high probability that the two pieces have a common source. Determining how "unusual" a "match" may be is discussed in the next section.

§ 11-3. Interpretation of Results.

The theory upon which NAA is based is well accepted by the scientific community. Moreover, the technique — the use of a nuclear reactor for irradiation and gamma-ray spectrometry for detection — is recognized as an accurate method for analyzing elements.[29] The principal difficulty with NAA evidence involves the interpretation of the test results, not the validity of the underlying theory or instrumental technique. As one commentator has noted: "[M]ost of the legal problems surrounding NAA do not involve its validity as a technique of chemical analysis. Rather, *interpretation* of the results of the chemical analysis — the relevance of the results to a particular legal issue — causes most of the difficulties."[30]

If NAA is used, for example, to determine whether a person has recently discharged a firearm, the analysis may reveal that 1.67 micrograms of barium and 1.33 micrograms of antimony were present on the hand of a suspect.[31] This evidence, however, has no probative value unless the detected amounts differ from normal concentrations of these elements in the general population. The relevancy of this type of information, therefore, depends on the validity of

---

Perkons & Jervis, *Application of Radio-Activation Analysis in Forensic Investigations*, 7 J. Forensic Sci. 449 (1962).

25. *See* Krishnan, *Examination of Paints by Trace Element Analysis*, 21 J. Forensic Sci. 908 (1976); Snow & Washington, *Comparison of Paints by Neutron Activation Analysis II. Colored Paints*, 54 J. Assoc. Official Analytical Chemists 917 (1971).

26. *See* Hoffman, Brunelle & Snow, *Forensic Comparisons of Soils by Neutron Activation and Atomic Absorption Analysis*, 60 J. Crim. L., Criminology & Police Sci. 395 (1969).

27. *See* Pitts & Kratochivil, *Statistical Discrimination of Flat Glass Fragments by Instrumental Neutron Activation Analysis Methods for Forensic Science Applications*, 36 J. Forensic Sci. 122 (1991); Schmitt & Smith, *Identification of Origin of Glass by Neutron Activation Analysis in a Forensic Case*, 15 J. Forensic Sci. 252 (1970).

28. Comment, *supra* note 4, at 997.

29. *Id.* at 998 (NAA is a "well-established scientific technique").

30. *Id.*

31. *See* State v. Spencer, 298 Minn. 456, 459, 216 N.W.2d 131, 134 (1974).

background studies of the general population to determine handblank levels[32] and the proper correlation of these studies with the data derived from the analysis in the particular case.[33] In addition, such a study would have to account for occupational contamination; painters, plumbers, automobile mechanics, and graphic artists may have considerably higher handblank values than the general population.[34]

Similarly, if NAA is used for comparative purposes, such as hair analysis, the matching of certain elements, both qualitatively and quantitatively, in two samples becomes relevant only if the detected distribution differs from hair samples in the general population.[35] In other words, the result of activation analysis by itself is insufficient to establish the relevancy of the evidence; additional data is necessary to evaluate the significance of the results.

In short, establishing the probative value (relevance) of NAA evidence involves a problem of statistical probability.[36] Consequently, NAA evidence typically does not positively identify a defendant but only places him in a restricted subclass, and "the *size* of the subclass varies greatly with the type of thing being compared."[37] Thus, describing NAA evidence as a "nuclear fingerprint" is misleading.[38]

United States v. Stifel,[39] a leading case on the admissibility of NAA, illustrates these issues. The prosecution charged Stifel with murdering his former girlfriend's fiancé by sending a bomb through the mail. Crucial prosecution evidence involved activation analysis performed on bomb debris (vinyl tape, metal cap, cardboard mailing tube, and paper gummed label) and similar items obtained from Stifel's place of employment. The prosecution expert testified that

---

32. Handblank values are the levels of barium and antimony on the hands of persons who have not recently fired a weapon.

33. Comment, *supra* note 4, at 1075-76.

34. *Id.* at 1077.

35. The examination of hair by NAA raises a multitude of problems. *See* Cornelis, *Truth Has Many Facets: The Neutron Activation Analysis Story*, 20 J. FORENSIC SCI. SOC'Y 93, 95 (1980) ("I am convinced that irrefutable hair identification from its trace element composition still belongs to the realm of wishful thinking"); Comment, *supra* note 4, at 1039-55. For a further discussion of hair analysis by NAA, *see* § 24-2(L) *infra*.

36. *See* Broun & Kelly, *Playing the Percentages and the Law of Evidence*, 1970 U. ILL. L.F. 23, 46-48; Tribe, *Trial by Mathematics: Precision and Ritual in the Legal Process*, 84 HARV. L. REV. 1329, 1342 n.40 (1971); Comment, *supra* note 4, at 1013-14.

37. Comment, *supra* note 4, at 1016.

38. *See* State v. Coolidge, 109 N.H. 403, 420, 260 A.2d 547, 560 (1969) (NAA of hair "presented as being 'as infallible as that of fingerprints'"), *rev'd on other grounds,* 403 U.S. 443 (1971); Comment, *supra* note 4, at 1021 (fingerprints "differ in a fundamental way from a comparison of the results of an NAA measurement"); *id.* at 1029 (phrase "nuclear fingerprint" is "quite misleading").

39. 433 F.2d 431 (6th Cir. 1970), *cert. denied,* 401 U.S. 994 (1971).

the label and cardboard tube were "of the same type and same manufacture."[40] The metal cap and tape were "of the same manufacture" and from the "same batch" — one day's manufacturing production.[41]

However, any similarity between the tape recovered from the crime scene and the tape from Stifel's place of employment is not probative if most tape is similarly composed. Consequently, additional data was necessary to evaluate the significance of the NAA results; the analysis "depends on the existence of sufficient background information."[42] The background studies are critical, and testimony about "matches" and "same batch" is often misleading.

A commentator criticized the defense strategy in *Stifel* for its broadbased attack on the scientific validity of NAA:

> A better defense strategy probably would have been to stipulate to the elemental composition measurement. The jury could then have focused its attention on what apparently should have been the primary issue, namely, the invalidity of the expert's claims that "within a reasonable scientific certainty" the items measured were of the same manufacture and that he had identified the metal cap and vinyl tape fragments to within one day's production batch. No comprehensive background studies have been published on any of the materials involved in this case. The expert was an employee of the Post Office Department Inspection Service and the case involved the United States as a party. The Sixth Circuit opinion does not say whether the expert attempted to substantiate his claims with purported background studies carried out in government laboratories, but the available evidence indicates that such studies should in any event be regarded with suspicion.[43]

After his conviction, Stifel filed a request under the Freedom of Information Act. The FOIA material revealed the existence of another suspect in the bombing and discrepancies about the background tests on the vinyl tape.[44] As a result, Stifel filed a post-conviction petition, alleging a due process violation. He argued that the prosecution expert, when cross-examined, had failed to disclose that additional tests had been performed on the tape. The court disagreed that the expert had misrepresented the facts on this issue, but nevertheless noted the misleading character of this information in granting relief: "[H]ad the defense

---

40. *Id.* at 436.

41. *Id.*

42. Comment, *supra* note 4, at 1014 ("In neither of these cases is the NAA evidence sufficient in itself; additional data are needed to evaluate the significance of the chemical analyses done by neutron activation techniques").

43. Comment, *supra* note 4, at 1070-71.

44. United States v. Stifel, 594 F. Supp. 1525 (N.D. Ohio 1984).

known of the November 1968 tests performed by [the expert] on tape obtained from Plymouth Rubber Company, it could have used this evidence to further impeach the credibility of [the expert's] scientific methods."[45]

Similarly, in *People v. Collins*[46] the prosecution expert testified that there was "a distinct and high level of probability" that hair samples had a common source.[47] The defense objected to the method of testing. The case has been criticized because "[n]either the court nor, apparently, the defense, considered the question of how unique the hairs were."[48] The crucial issue was "the validity of the reasoning that leads to the conclusion that an identification has been made, rather than ... the analytical technique used to make the comparison."[49] In another case an expert testified that the chance of the resemblance he found between hair samples was one in 15,000,000,000.[50] Here, again, the underlying basis for this testimony apparently was not challenged.

§ 11-4. Admissibility.

Expert testimony based on activation analysis of gunshot residues,[51] bullets,[52] hair,[53] glass,[54] paint,[55] and other substances[56] has been admitted as evidence.

---

45. *Id.* at 1543.

46. 43 Mich. App. 259, 204 N.W.2d 290 (1972), *cert. denied,* 419 U.S. 866 (1974).

47. *Id.* at 264, 204 N.W.2d at 293.

48. Black, *A Unified Theory of Scientific Evidence*, 56 FORDHAM L. REV. 595, 636 (1988).

49. *Id.*

50. Lopez v. State, 643 S.W.2d 431, 433 (Tex. App. 1982).

51. *See* Government of Virgin Islands v. Benjamin, 736 F. Supp. 1337, 1341 (D.V.I.) ("[A] police officer obtained a swab sample for a neutron activation test from Benjamin's hands. At trial, an expert testified that the test indicated that Benjamin had either fired a gun or had been very close to a gun that had been discharged"), *aff'd,* 922 F.2d 831 (3d Cir. 1990); Mills v. State, 476 So. 2d 172, 176-77 (Fla. 1985), *cert. denied,* 475 U.S. 1031 (1986); Troedel v. State, 462 So. 2d 392, 396 (Fla. 1984); People v. Salazar, 162 Ill. 2d 513, 529, 643 N.E.2d 698, 706 (1994) (Bilandic, C.J., concurring) ("A neutron activation analysis revealed that Officer Murrin's left hand was on or near the muzzle of the gun when it discharged..."), *cert. denied,* 515 U.S. 1116 (1995); State v. Boyer, 406 So. 2d 143, 146-48 (La. 1981); Kelly v. State, 16 Md. App. 533, 535, 544-45, 298 A.2d 470, 472, 477 (1973); State v. Spencer, 298 Minn. 456, 460-61, 216 N.W.2d 131, 134 (1974); State v. Jackson, 566 S.W.2d 227, 228-29 (Mo. App. 1978); State v. Major, 564 S.W.2d 79, 81-82 (Mo. App. 1978); State v. Montgomery, 545 S.W.2d 655, 655-56 (Mo. App. 1976); State v. Duncan, 540 S.W.2d 130, 135 (Mo. App. 1976) (shotgun residue); State v. Johnson, 539 S.W.2d 493, 501-02 (Mo. App. 1976), *cert. denied,* 430 U.S. 934 (1977); State v. Toney, 537 S.W.2d 586, 597-99 (Mo. App. 1976); State v. Ross, 523 S.W.2d 841, 844-46 (Mo. App. 1975); People v. Pieropan, 72 Misc. 2d 770, 771-72, 340 N.Y.S.2d 31, 32-33 (1973); Commonwealth v. Sero, 478 Pa. 440, 449-50, 387 A.2d 63, 68 (1978).

See also Keith v. State, 612 P.2d 977, 980 (Alaska 1980) (grand jury); State v. Warden, 100 Idaho 21, 22-24, 592 P.2d 836, 837-39 (1979); Commonwealth v. Sangricco, 475 Pa. 179, 379 A.2d 1342 (1977) (search warrant issued for gunshot residues).

52. *See* People v. Johnson, 114 Ill. 2d 170, 194-98, 499 N.E.2d 1355, 1366-67 (1986), *cert. denied,* 480 U.S. 951 (1987); Jones v. State, 425 N.E.2d 128, 130-31 (Ind. 1981); Mark v. State,

Several courts have ruled that NAA evidence has been generally accepted by the scientific community and thus satisfies the *Frye* test.[57] In the leading case, *United States v. Stifel,*[58] the Sixth Circuit upheld a trial court's admission of a comparative analysis of bomb debris with materials found at the defendant's place of employment. Citing *Frye,* the court held that the "record in this case affords support for the proposition that neutron activation analysis has gained 'general acceptance in the particular field in which it belongs.'"[59] Most courts

---

568 N.W.2d 820, 826-27 (Iowa 1997) ("Neutron Activation Analysis (NAA) tests conducted in 1976 revealed similarities between the bullets purchased by Mark in California and the bullets found at the crime scene. An FBI agent testified one similarity between the samples was that neither sample contained any arsenic. The postconviction court ordered the bullets taken from the former Olson's Boat House be tested and compared to the crime scene bullets. The court also appointed an expert, Dr. Vincent Guinn, to assist Mark. These tests revealed arsenic in both the crime scene samples and the samples from Ken's Sport Shop. Mark claims this disclosure justifies the postconviction relief requested"); State v. Krummacher, 269 Or. 125, 143, 523 P.2d 1009, 1017 (1974); State v. Reynolds, 307 N.C. 184, 186, 297 S.E.2d 532, 534 (1982) (bullets "were of the same chemical composition, consistent with their having come from the same box of ammunition"); State v. Strain, 885 P.2d 810, 817 (Utah App. 1994) (FBI agent "employed two techniques in comparing the bullets, a 'neutron activation analysis' to analyze for antimony, copper, and arsenic; and an 'ICP' (an acronym for 'inductibly coupled plasma atomic emissions patromotry') to analyze for silver, bismuth, and tin. [He] testified that through analysis of these trace elements, it is possible to determine whether a bullet could have come from a specific box of ammunition, or whether two or more bullets could have come from the same box of ammunition").

53. *See* State v. Breest, 116 N.H. 734, 749-50, 367 A.2d 1320, 1332-33 (1976); People v. Collins, 43 Mich. App. 259, 265, 204 N.W.2d 290, 293 (1972), *appeal denied,* 391 Mich. 798, *cert. denied,* 419 U.S. 866 (1974); State v. Stevens, 467 S.W.2d 10, 22-24 (Mo.), *cert. denied,* 404 U.S. 994 (1971); State v. Smith, 637 S.W.2d 232, 234-38 (Mo. App. 1982); Lopez v. State, 643 S.W.2d 431, 433 (Tex. App. 1982); Ward v. State, 427 S.W.2d 876, 884 (Tex. Crim. App. 1968).

See also Long v. State, 739 S.W.2d 98, 103 (Tex. App. 1987) ("[U]nlike the microscopic analysis, neutron activation allowed the examiner to determine with reasonable accuracy that a given hair came from a given source").

54. *See* State v. Cox, 542 S.W.2d 40, 46 (Mo. App. 1976).

55. *See* State v. Breest, 116 N.H. 734, 748-50, 367 A.2d 1320, 1332-33 (1976).

56. *See* United States v. Stifel, 433 F.2d 431 (6th Cir. 1970) (bomb debris), *cert. denied,* 401 U.S. 994 (1971); United States v. Kelly, 420 F.2d 26, 28 (2d Cir. 1969) (narcotics); State v. Coolidge, 109 N.H. 403, 260 A.2d 547 (1969) (particle analysis admitted; hair analysis excluded), *rev'd on other grounds,* 403 U.S. 443 (1971). *See also* United States v. Wolfson, 297 F. Supp. 881, 888 (S.D.N.Y. 1968) (authenticity of documents), *aff'd,* 413 F.2d 804 (2d Cir. 1969). For a list of unreported cases, *see* Watkins & Watkins, *supra* note 5, at 43-51 (Supp. 1991); Guinn & Demiralp, *Arsenic in Hair by NAA — A Major Recent Murder Case,* 168 J. RADIOANAL. NUCL. CHEM. 249 (1993) (discussing the use of NAA to detect chronic arsenic induced death).

57. Frye v. United States, 293 F. 1013 (D.C. Cir. 1923). For a discussion of the *Frye* test, *see* Chapter 1.

58. 433 F.2d 431 (6th Cir. 1970), *cert. denied,* 401 U.S. 994 (1971). The defendant's conviction was later vacated. United States v. Stifel, 594 F. Supp. 1525 (N.D. Ohio 1984).

59. 433 F.2d at 441. *See also* Jones v. State, 425 N.E.2d 128, 131 (Ind. 1981) (NAA generally recognized as reliable); State v. Boyer, 406 So. 2d 143, 146-47 (La. 1981) (NAA "is the subject of

have ruled that attacks on the procedures used in conducting activation analysis, as well as the interpretation of the results, raise jury issues that do not affect admissibility.[60] In a habeas proceeding, the Sixth Circuit has ruled that refusing to take judicial notice of NAA is not constitutional error.[61]

Exclusion of NAA Evidence

Three appellate courts have rejected the results of activation analysis of certain substances.[62] The New Hampshire Supreme Court upheld a trial court's exclusion of testimony based on a comparative analysis of hair samples.[63] In the same case, however, the court upheld the admissibility of a comparative analysis of particles obtained from the victim's clothing and the defendant's car. By upholding the admission of the results of the particle examination and by citing *Frye* as the controlling authority, the court obviously found the underlying principle and the technique valid as well as accepted by the scientific community. The hair analysis was rejected for two reasons. First, it was presented as being as infallible as fingerprints.[64] Second, the method employed by the government expert would "not be acceptable to scientists in the field."[65] In contrast, the particle examination was offered to establish a similarity, rather than an identity, between samples. Moreover, according to the court, the analysis was conducted "by means of procedures sufficiently accepted by scientists familiar with this limited

---

widespread acceptance"); State v. Johnson, 539 S.W.2d 493, 501 (Mo. App. 1976) (NAA generally recognized as reliable), *cert. denied,* 430 U.S. 934 (1977).

60. *See* United States v. Stifel, 433 F.2d 431, 438 (6th Cir. 1970), *cert. denied,* 401 U.S. 994 (1971); United States v. Kelly, 420 F.2d 26, 28 (2d Cir. 1969); State v. Breest, 116 N.H. 734, 750, 367 A.2d 1320, 1333 (1976); State v. Johnson, 539 S.W.2d 493, 501 (Mo. App. 1976), *cert. denied,* 430 U.S. 934 (1977); People v. Collins, 43 Mich. App. 259, 265, 204 N.W.2d 290, 293 (1972), *cert. denied,* 419 U.S. 866 (1974); State v. Krummacher, 269 Or. 125, 143, 523 P.2d 1009, 1017 (1974).

61. *See* Hanna v. Jabe, 1995 U.S. App. LEXIS 32105, 66 F.3d 326 (6th Cir.1995) ("Hanna contends that the trial court abused its discretion by requiring Hanna to produce expert testimony to qualify a neutron activation analysis. Hanna contends that the trial court and Michigan appellate courts should have taken judicial notice of the validity of the analysis and should not have required expert testimony. The Michigan Court of Appeals held as a matter of state law that the state courts of Michigan do not accept this test as a reliable scientific procedure. ...An issue concerning the admissibility of evidence does not rise to a level of constitutional magnitude unless it can be viewed as so egregious that the petitioner was denied a fundamentally fair trial").

62. The prosecution's failure to comply with pretrial discovery requirements also has led to reversals. *See* § 11-5 *infra.*

63. State v. Coolidge, 109 N.H. 403, 260 A.2d 547 (1969), *rev'd on other grounds,* 403 U.S. 443 (1971).

64. *Id.* at 420, 260 A.2d at 560.

65. *Id.*

field."[66] In a later case, the court upheld the admissibility of activation analysis of hair and paint samples.[67]

The Missouri Supreme Court rejected activation analysis of blood because the technique — the use of a cadmium shield to remove the interfering elements from the gamma-ray spectrum — had not gained general acceptance.[68] Nevertheless, the court approvingly cited an earlier case,[69] in which it had upheld the admissibility of activation analysis of hair. Thus, the court did not reject NAA, but only its application to blood. In subsequent cases, the Missouri courts upheld the admissibility of activation analysis of gunshot residues[70] and glass.[71]

Finally, the Ohio Supreme Court rejected expert testimony based on activation analysis of hair because the expert testified that samples of the defendant's and the victim's hair "are similar *and are likely* to be from the same source."[72] According to the court, expert testimony is admissible only if the opinion is based upon "reasonable scientific certainty." For the court, reasonable scientific certainty meant that the expert had to testify that the hair sample probably came from the defendant and not that it possibly came from him. This requirement seems questionable. Frequently, experts testify that two samples "could have come from the same source" or "were likely to come from the same source." Such testimony satisfies the standard of relevancy required for admissibility.[73] Moreover, the expert was attempting to limit the conclusions that could be drawn from the analysis, a practice that should be encouraged. Other courts have rejected the reasonable scientific certainty requirement as interpreted by the Ohio Supreme Court. As one court has noted: "[N]o other jurisdiction has adopted [*Holt*'s] rationale in excluding the results of a neutron-activation analysis."[74]

Qualifications

The qualifications of the expert are critical. For the most part, the experts' qualifications have not been an issue in the reported cases. The experts have been

---

66. *Id.* at 422, 260 A.2d at 561.

67. State v. Breest, 116 N.H. 734, 749, 367 A.2d 1320, 1332-33 (1976).

68. State v. Stout, 478 S.W.2d 368, 371 (Mo. 1972).

69. State v. Stevens, 467 S.W.2d 10 (Mo.), *cert. denied,* 404 U.S. 994 (1971).

70. *See* cases listed in note 51 *supra.*

71. State v. Cox, 542 S.W.2d 40, 46 (Mo. App. 1976).

72. State v. Holt, 17 Ohio St. 2d 81, 85, 246 N.E.2d 365, 368 (1969).

73. *See* FED. R. EVID. 401 (Relevant evidence "means evidence having any tendency to make the existence of any fact that is of consequence to the determination of the action more probable or less probable than it would be without the evidence").

74. People v. Johnson, 114 Ill. 2d 170, 194-93, 499 N.E.2d 1355, 1366-67 (1986), *cert. denied,* 480 U.S. 951 (1987). *Accord* State v. Boyer, 406 So. 2d 143, 148 (La. 1981). For a further discussion of this issue, *see* § 5-6 *supra.*

associated with major federal or university laboratories.[75] In one case, however, the expert was employed by a city crime laboratory.[76] It is unlikely that he had the educational and practical background to conduct this type of sophisticated examination.[77] Nevertheless, the court accepted him as an expert.[78] More importantly, the qualifications necessary to conduct NAA differ from the qualifications necessary to interpret the results of the analysis. As noted earlier, NAA principally involves problems of statistical probability. Accordingly, the "qualifications of the expert as an analytical chemist do not necessarily establish his competence to interpret the legal relevance of his measurements."[79]

Contamination

Because of the sensitivity of NAA, care in handling the evidence prior to analysis is required: "If two unknowns that are compared to determine whether they came from a common source have both been contaminated in a similar way, it is clear that completely false points of similarity can result."[80]

Limitations

Because of the statistical basis underlying NAA evidence, the expert's opinions must be carefully circumscribed. The experts in the reported cases have sometimes overstated the results obtainable by activation analysis[81] or used terms

---

75. *E.g.,* United States v. Stifel, 433 F.2d 431 (6th Cir. 1970) (Postal Inspection Service Laboratory), *cert. denied,* 401 U.S. 994 (1971); Jones v. State, 425 N.E.2d 128 (Ind. 1981) (FBI Laboratory); State v. Stevens, 467 S.W.2d 10 (Mo.) (University of Missouri Laboratory), *cert. denied,* 404 U.S. 994 (1971); State v. Coolidge, 109 N.H. 403, 260 A.2d 547 (1969) (U.S. Treasury Laboratory), *rev'd on other grounds,* 403 U.S. 443 (1971).

76. Ward v. State, 427 S.W.2d 876 (Tex. Crim. App. 1968).

77. *See* Comment, *supra* note 4, at 1036 n.216 (questioning the qualifications of the expert in *Ward* as well as his conclusions).

78. 427 S.W.2d at 884.

79. Comment, *supra* note 4, at 1031.

80. Comment, *supra* note 4, at 1013. *See also* Giannelli, *Chain of Custody and the Handling of Real Evidence*, 20 AM. CRIM. L. REV. 527, 538 (1983). Chain of custody issues were raised in Jones v. State, 425 N.E.2d 128, 131-32 (Ind. 1981) (bullets); State v. Johnson, 539 S.W.2d 493, 505 (Mo. App. 1976) (gunshot residue), *cert. denied,* 430 U.S. 934 (1977).

For a further discussion of chain of custody, *see* Chapter 7.

81. *E.g.,* State v. Spencer, 298 Minn. 456, 459, 216 N.W.2d 131, 134 (1974) ("The presence of these elements, in the opinion of [the expert], was conclusive that defendant's right hand was associated with firing a gun"); State v. Stevens, 467 S.W.2d 10, 22 (Mo.) (Hair samples "were all from the same source, that is, the same person"), *cert. denied,* 404 U.S. 994 (1971); Ward v. State, 427 S.W.2d 876, 883-884 (Tex. Crim. App. 1968) (Hair samples were "identical and probably came from the same person").

such as "match" or "common origin,"[82] which could easily mislead a jury. One commentator has noted that "few experts have used appropriate care in limiting their testimony."[83] For example, one court has written:

> We are concerned ... about the sweeping and unqualified manner in which [the expert's] testimony was offered .... An expert witness could be permitted to testify that in his opinion the chemicals present on defendant's hand may have resulted from the firing of a gun. He should not have been permitted to state, as he did, that this defendant had definitely fired a gun.[84]

Experts in other cases have also overstated their findings. In one case the NAA expert indicated that the defendant had fired a handgun "not more than two hours before the time of the analysis."[85] In another case the NAA expert testified that two bullets "had been made by the same manufacturer on the same day and at the same hour."[86]

State v. Troedel[87] offers a stark illustration of misleading evidence. Defendants Troedel and Hawkins were convicted of capital murder in separate trials. A report of a gunshot residue test using neutron activation analysis concluded that swabs "from the hands of Troedel and Hawkins contained antimony and barium in amounts typically found on the hands of a person who has discharged a firearm or has had his hands in close proximity to a discharging firearm."[88] The expert testified in accordance with this report at Hawkins' trial, but he enhanced his testimony at Troedel's trial, where he testified that "Troedel had fired the murder weapon." Troedel's conviction was upheld by the state courts. During federal habeas proceedings, the expert's deposition was taken. In the deposition, he testified that "he could not, from the results of his tests, determine or say to a scientific certainty who had fired the murder weapon" and the "amount of barium and antimony on the hands of Troedel and Hawkins were basically insignificant."[89]

---

82. *E.g.,* United States v. Stifel, 433 F.2d 431, 436 (6th Cir. 1970) (samples "were 'of the same type and same manufacture'"), *cert. denied,* 401 U.S. 994 (1971); People v. Collins, 43 Mich. App. 259, 264, 204 N.W.2d 290, 293 (1972) (hair samples "came from the same source"), *appeal denied,* 391 Mich. 798, *cert. denied,* 419 U.S. 866 (1974); State v. Stout, 478 S.W.2d 368, 368 (Mo. 1972) (blood analysis revealed "match of the materials"); State v. Cox, 542 S.W.2d 40, 46 (Mo. App. 1976) (glass samples had "common origin"); State v. Coolidge, 109 N.H. 403, 421, 260 A.2d 547, 560 (1969) (samples had "common origin or source"), *rev'd on other grounds,* 403 U.S. 443 (1971).

83. Comment, *supra* note 4, at 1024.

84. State v. Spencer, 298 Minn. 456, 461, 216 N.W.2d 131, 134 (1974).

85. State v. Warden, 100 Idaho 21, 22, 592 P.2d 836, 837 (1979).

86. Brown v. State, 601 P.2d 221, 224 (Alaska 1979).

87. 462 So. 2d 392 (Fla. 1984).

88. Troedel v. Wainwright, 667 F. Supp. 1456, 1458 (S.D. Fla. 1986), *aff'd,* 828 F.2d 670 (11th Cir. 1987).

89. *Id.* at 1459.

The district court found this testimony "at the very least" misleading. The expert claimed that the prosecutor had "pushed" him further in Troedel's trial, a claim the prosecutor substantiated. In granting habeas relief, the court found:

> In light of this admission, the above testimony received at the evidentiary hearing and the inconsistent positions taken by the prosecution at Hawkins' and Troedel's trials, respectively, the Court concludes that the opinion Troedel had fired the weapon was known by the prosecution not to be based on the results of the neutron activation analysis tests, or on any scientific certainty or even probability. Thus, the subject testimony was not only misleading, but also was used by the State knowing it to be misleading.[90]

The court also found Troedel's counsel ineffective. Because the counsel knew that the gunshot residue testimony was "critical," his "failure either to depose the State's expert witness or, more importantly, to consult with any other expert in the field, fell outside the scope of reasonably professional assistance."[91]

In *Meis v. Wyoming Dep't of Corrections*,[92] the defendant argued that his counsel's performance was ineffective for failing to cross-examine adequately the FBI agent who used neutron activation analysis to determine the presence of gunpowder residue on the victim's hands. The court rejected this claim because the expert's testimony did not conflict with the defendant's version of the facts.

§ 11-5. Procedural Issues.

Procedural as well as evidentiary problems have arisen in the NAA cases. In *United States v. Kelly*[93] activation analysis was conducted after the trial court had ordered discovery of scientific reports. The defense, however, was not informed of the tests until trial. The Second Circuit reversed because the prosecution had failed to disclose the results of the analysis. According to the court, the "course of the government smacks too much of a trial by ambush, in violation of the spirit of the [discovery] rules. A new trial is required, with a fair opportunity for the defense to run its own neutron activation tests of the material...."[94]

---

90. *Id.* at 1459-60.

91. *Id.* at 1461.

92. 9 F.3d 695, 698-99 (8th Cir. 1993), *cert. denied,* 511 U.S. 1072 (1994).

93. 420 F.2d 26 (2d Cir. 1969).

94. *Id.* at 29. *See also* Smith v. Stewart, 140 F.3d 1263, 1274 (9th Cir. 1998) ("[W]e are told that trial counsel should have had a neutron activation test performed, even though Smith did not want it, and even though it could have (in hindsight probably would have) sunk Smith's case. Instead, trial counsel carried on about the prosecution's failure to have the test performed. Of course, he knew that the reason for the failure was that the samples were collected improperly. Well, counsel can listen to his client and often should. And Smith still does not tell us what the results of the test would have been. Those results may well have been just as devastating as counsel (and, perhaps, Smith) feared they would be").

In *State v. Wilson*[95] a laboratory report indicated that a NAA gunshot residue test was "inconclusive." However, at trial the expert testified that evidence of barium alone was consistent with the firing of a gun. The defense was never informed of this opinion and thus was misled by the report. The Ohio Supreme Court criticized the prosecutor's conduct as the type of "trial by ambush" condemned in *Kelly*.[96]

In *Stifel v. United States*[97] the Sixth Circuit went further and held that because of the expense associated with NAA, the government would be responsible for providing NAA to indigent defendants: "[I]f the government sees fit to use this time consuming, expensive means of fact finding, it must both allow time for a defendant to make similar tests, and in the instance of an indigent defendant, a means to provide for payment for same."[98] In a subsequent collateral proceeding Stifel's conviction was vacated, in part, because the prosecution had failed to disclose the results of NAA tests that its expert had conducted in connection with the case. The court wrote that "had the defense known of the November 1968 tests performed by [the expert] on tape obtained from Plymouth Rubber Company, it could have used this evidence to further impeach the credibility of [the expert's] scientific methods."[99]

§ 11-6. Obtaining Samples from Suspects.

The constitutionality of seizing evidence for the purpose of activation analysis has arisen in several cases.[100] In one case, the Montana Supreme Court held that the seizure of gunshot residues from the defendant's hands did not violate the privilege against self-incrimination, the prohibition against unreasonable searches and seizures, or the right to counsel.[101] The right to counsel did not apply because the evidence was seized before the right had attached. The fifth amendment privilege does not apply because gunshot residues are physical evidence, and the privilege covers only testimonial evidence.[102]

---

95. 30 Ohio St. 3d 99, 507 N.E.2d 1109 (1987).

96. *Id.* at 102, 507 N.E.2d at 1111. *Wilson* appears to overrule an earlier Ohio case. State v. Kassow, 28 Ohio St. 2d 141, 277 N.E.2d 435 (1971), *modified,* 408 U.S. 939 (1972).

Pretrial discovery is especially important with a complex process such as NAA. Comment, *supra* note 4, at 1036. For a further discussion of discovery, *see* Chapter 3.

97. 433 F.2d 431 (6th Cir. 1970), *cert. denied,* 401 U.S. 994 (1971).

98. *Id.* at 441.

99. United States v. Stifel, 594 F. Supp. 1525, 1543 (N.D. Ohio 1984).

100. For a discussion of the constitutional issues relating to the seizure of evidence for forensic analysis, *see* Chapter 2.

101. State v. Ulrich, 187 Mont. 347, 352-55, 609 P.2d 1218, 1221-22 (1980). *See also* Commonwealth v. Sangricco, 475 Pa. 179, 379 A.2d 1342 (1977) (search warrant issued for gunshot residues).

102. *See also* Lopez v. State, 643 S.W.2d 431, 433 (Tex. App. 1982) (hair sample subjected to NAA "is an identifying physical characteristic unprotected by the fifth amendment").

Moreover, evidence of a defendant's refusal to permit swabbings for a gunshot residue test also falls outside fifth amendment protection.[103]

§ 11-7. Selected Bibliography.

Watkins & Watkins, *Identification of Substances by Neutron Activation Analysis*, 15 Am. Jur. Proof of Facts 115 (1964) (listing numerous technical articles on NAA).

Comment, *The Evidentiary Uses of Neutron Activation Analysis*, 59 Calif. L. Rev. 997 (1971).

Note, *Identification of Evidence by Neutron Activation Analysis*, 37 Mo. L. Rev. 295 (1972).

Comment, *Evidence — Admissibility of the Neutron Activation Analysis Test*, 18 St. Louis L.J. 235 (1973).

Annotations

Annot., *Admissibility of evidence of neutron activation analysis*, 50 A.L.R.3d 117 (1973).

---

103. Commonwealth v. Monahan, 378 Pa. Super. 623, 632, 549 A.2d 231, 235-36 (1988).

CHAPTER 12

HYPNOSIS*

§ 12-1. In General.

The courts rejected hypnotic evidence when first offered at trial. In 1897 the California Supreme Court wrote: "The law of the United States does not recognize hypnotism."[1] The issue remained dormant until the 1970s when the use

---

*The sections in this chapter were revised and renumbered in this edition. The authors would like to express their appreciation to Dr. Martin Orne, Institute of Pennsylvania Hospital and University of Pennsylvania, who reviewed the second edition. The authors would like to express their appreciation to Robert A. Karlin, Ph.D., Rutgers University, and Anita Lipton, False Memory Foundation, who reviewed this edition.

1. People v. Ebanks, 117 Cal. 652, 665, 49 P. 1049, 1053 (1897). *See generally* Ladd, *Legal Aspects of Hypnotism*, 11 YALE L.J. 173 (1902).

of hypnosis in criminal investigations increased dramatically.[2] Indeed, it was "hailed as a major breakthrough in police investigation."[3]

Several factors may have accounted for this trend. First, the seminal case permitting hypnotically refreshed testimony was decided in 1968.[4] Second, by the 1960s professional organizations, such as the American Medical Association and the American Psychiatric Association, had recognized the validity of hypnosis for therapeutic purposes. Third, hypnotic induction is easily learned: "A police officer can become a reasonably skilled hypnotist in a few hours of practice, with or without formal instruction."[5] Fourth, a number of books and articles on hypnosis had advocated its use, often claiming that hypnosis provided valuable leads in many investigations: "In 77% of cases, important information was elicited that had not been available by routine interrogation."[6]

The increased use of hypnosis in criminal investigations sparked controversy. The Society for Clinical and Experimental Hypnosis and the International Society of Hypnosis passed resolutions "strongly opposing" the training of police officers as hypnotists.[7] Moreover, some books were criticized for making "extravagant claims of the usefulness and reliability of hypnosis for criminal investigative purposes."[8] Other commentators pointed out instances where hypnotically recalled information proved erroneous: "[I]n *State v. Mack* (1980), a hypnotized person remembered eating a pizza in a restaurant that did not serve pizza, seeing tattoos on someone who had none, and having been stabbed with

---

2. *See* People v. Lucas, 107 Misc. 2d 231, 232, 435 N.Y.S.2d 461, 462 (Sup. Ct. 1980) ("The past ten years have seen a dramatic rise in the use of hypnotism as an aid in criminal investigations").

3. Orne, Soskis, Dinges & Orne, *Hypnotically Induced Testimony, in* EYEWITNESS TESTIMONY: PSYCHOLOGICAL PERSPECTIVES 171, 171 (G. Wells & E. Loftus eds. 1984).

4. Harding v. State, 5 Md. App. 230, 246 A.2d 302 (1968), *cert. denied*, 395 U.S. 949 (1969). *See* § 12-5(B) *infra* (discussing *Harding*). *See also* Scheflin, *Commentary on Borawick v. Shay: The Fate of Hypnotically Retrieved Memories*, 13 CULTIC STUDIES J. 26, 26 (1996) ("In 1968 the first American court in this century permitted a previously hypnotized person to testify on the witness stand about hypnotically refreshed memories (*Harding v. State*, 1968)").

5. Diamond, *Inherent Problems in the Use of Pretrial Hypnosis on a Prospective Witness*, 68 CALIF. L. REV. 313, 314 (1980).

6. Reiser & Nielson, *Investigative Hypnosis: A Developing Specialty*, 23 AM. J. CLINICAL HYPNOSIS 75, 76 (1980). *See generally* M. ORNE, D. SOSKIS, D. DINGES, E. ORNE & M. TONRY, HYPNOTICALLY REFRESHED TESTIMONY: ENHANCED MEMORY OR TAMPERING WITH EVIDENCE? 13 (Nat'l Inst. of Justice 1985).

7. *Resolution Adopted October 1978 by the Society For Clinical and Experimental Hypnosis*, 27 INT'L J. CLINICAL & EXPERIMENTAL HYPNOSIS 452 (1979); *Resolution Adopted August 1979 by the International Society of Hypnosis*, *id.* at 453.

8. Diamond, *supra* note 5, at 313 n.3.

scissors or a knife where there was no evidence that a weapon was involved."[9] Finally, the lack of research was cited by some commentators: "[I]t is a provable fact that the law about forensic hypnosis developed before the science of forensic hypnosis was developed."[10]

Chowchilla Case (1976)

The proponents of hypnosis often cite the Chowchilla, California, case in which a busload of school children and their driver were kidnaped. The kidnapers transported the children and driver 100 miles by car to a quarry and imprisoned them in a van that had been buried in the ground. They escaped sixteen hours later but could not provide meaningful leads to identify their kidnapers. Under hypnosis, the driver was able to recall all but one digit of the license number of the culprit's car.[11]

The Chowchilla case is easily misread. First, the case is atypical in that the driver had "tried desperately to memorize" the license plate numbers during captivity. Second, the driver provided two license plate numbers, one of which was totally wrong.[12] Third, the hypnotically refreshed testimony was never introduced at trial. The defendants pleaded guilty and appealed on a sentencing issue.[13] Fourth, several facts in the case undercut the importance of the hypnotically refreshed recall. The quarry where the van was buried was "a business enterprise owned and operated by defendant Woods' father" and the buried "van had been acquired in relatively good condition by defendant Woods during the previous November."[14] These facts associating one of the defendants with the secondary crime scene indicate that the hypnotically refreshed testimony would not have been needed at trial. Indeed, they suggest that the FBI would have soon focused on Woods even without the license plate number.

Of course, if the facts are changed, a more cogent case for hypnosis as an *investigative* tool could be made — for example, assume that the driver had been separated from the children at the primary crime scene and then escaped. Under these assumed facts, the need to find the children (in contrast to the need to find the criminals) would present a compelling case to try all available investigative methods — including hypnosis.

---

9. Orne, Whitehouse, Dinges & Orne, *Reconstructing Memory Through Hypnosis: Forensic and Clinical Implications, in* HYPNOSIS AND MEMORY 21, 41 (H.M. Pettinati ed. 1988) (citing State v. Mack, 292 N.W.2d 764, 768 (Minn. 1980)).

10. Scheflin, *supra* note 4, at 37.

11. *See* Kingston, *Admissibility of Post-Hypnotic Testimony*, 55 F.B.I. LAW ENFORCEMENT BULL. 22 (April 1986).

12. Kroger & Douce, *Hypnosis in Criminal Investigation*, 27 INT'L J. CLINICAL & EXPERIMENTAL HYPNOSIS 358 (1979).

13. People v. Schoenfeld, 111 Cal. App. 3d 671, 168 Cal. Rptr. 762 (1980).

14. *Id.* at 678, 168 Cal. Rptr. at 765.

Evidentiary Issues

Because police investigations were the focus of the renewed interest in hypnosis, criminal prosecutions presented the courts with the first opportunity to address this controversy. The principal evidentiary issues concern the admissibility of (1) statements made by a person while under hypnosis, whether exculpatory or incriminatory, (2) testimony of a witness whose memory has been "refreshed" by hypnosis, and (3) testimony of an expert concerning an accused's mental state based, in part, on observations of the accused while hypnotized. Additional legal issues concern repressed memories, the hypnosis defense, and related topics. A wide range of constitutional issues are addressed in the case law.

§ 12-2. Nature of Hypnosis.

Hypnosis has been defined in a variety of ways.[15] One court has written: "Hypnosis is a state of heightened concentration with diminished awareness of peripheral events."[16] Hypnosis has also been defined as "a special psychological state with certain physiological attributes, resembling sleep only superficially and marked by a functioning of the individual at a level of awareness other than the ordinary conscious state."[17] The differences in definition reflect an underlying disagreement about the nature of hypnosis.[18] According to the Council on Scientific Affairs of the American Medical Association, there "is no single, generally accepted theory of hypnosis, nor is there consensus about a single definition."[19]

Although individuals differ in their ability to experience hypnosis, most people are able to experience some degree of hypnosis.[20] One study suggests that even persons of low hypnotizability are vulnerable to memory distortions.[21]

---

15. A comprehensive survey of hypnosis is found in Orne, Soskis, Dinges & Orne, *supra* note 3.

16. State v. Hurd, 86 N.J. 525, 534, 432 A.2d 86, 90 (1981).

17. *Hypnosis,* 6 ENCYCLOPAEDIA BRITANNICA 133 (15th ed. 1989) (Dr. Martin Orne & A. Gordon Hammer).

18. *See* Note, *The Admissibility of Testimony Influenced by Hypnosis*, 67 VA. L. REV. 1203, 1206-14 (1981). *See also* Diamond, *supra* note 5, at 316-21; Orne, *The Use and Misuse of Hypnosis in Court, in* 3 CRIME AND JUSTICE: AN ANNUAL REVIEW OF RESEARCH 61 (M. Tonry & N. Morris eds. 1982).

19. Council on Scientific Affairs, *Scientific Status of Refreshing Recollection by the Use of Hypnosis*, 253 J.A.M.A. 1918, 1919 (1985) [hereinafter cited as *AMA Scientific Status*].

20. *Id. See also* Karlin & Orne, *Commentary on Borawick v. Shay: Hypnosis, Social Influence, Incestuous Child Abuse, and Satanic Ritual Abuse: The Iatrogenic Creation of Horrific Memories for the Remote Past,* 13 CULTIC STUDIES J. 26, 34 (1996) ("Hypnotizability, as measured by response to standardized inductions and suggestions, is a stable personality trait. The test-retest reliability of the Stanford Scale of Hypnotic Susceptibility, Form A, is approximately .70 when individuals, originally measured when undergraduates at Stanford University, were measured again between 10 and 25 years later").

The various techniques of hypnotic induction typically involve establishing rapport between the hypnotist and subject; inducing a passiveness that makes the subject receptive to suggestion, often by engendering eye fatigue through the focusing on a close object; and inducing a trance-like state through a series of suggestions. One widely employed procedure is hypnotic age regression, during which the subject relives an event that has occurred in the past, sometimes to the extent of behaving in a manner appropriate to the age the subject had been at the time of the event.[22]

Another procedure for refreshing memory is the "television technique." Once hypnotized, the subject is told to imagine a television screen on which he will see a documentary of the "to-be-remembered event."[23] The subject is then directed to the event and asked to describe the documentary as he views it. The theory underlying this technique is that human memory functions much like a videotape recorder, receiving and storing all sensory impressions. Under this theory, these impressions can be retrieved through hypnosis. This theory of memory, however, has been challenged as "not consistent with research findings or with current theories of memory."[24] The research indicates that neither perception nor memory functions like a videotape recorder; both are subject to numerous influences that may affect what impressions are perceived and the content of the memory retained.[25] In particular, confabulation — the "filling in" of gaps in the memory with fantasies — is a significant problem with hypnotized subjects.

Hypnosis has been recognized as a legitimate subject of clinical and laboratory research. In addition, the American Medical Association has recognized hypnosis as an accepted medical technique for psychotherapy, treatment of psychosomatic illnesses, and amnesia.[26] Nevertheless, distinguishing between the clinical and forensic uses of hypnosis is critical. In its forensic application, hypnosis is concerned with establishing past facts, and thus its reliability is paramount. The nonforensic uses of hypnosis are quite different. "Psychiatrists and psychologists use hypnosis in an effort to alleviate distress.... It can help the patient work out symptoms even though his or her beliefs about his or her illness are entirely erroneous. Dentists, obstetricians, and anesthesiologists use hypnosis entirely for

---

21. Orne, Whitehouse, Dinges & Orne, *Memory Liabilities Associated With Hypnosis: Does Low Hypnotizability Confer Immunity?*, 44 INT'L J. CLINICAL & EXPERIMENTAL HYPNOSIS 354 (1996).

22. *AMA Scientific Status*, *supra* note 19, at 1919..

23. *Id.*

24. *Id.* at 1920. *See also* Scheflin, *supra* note 4, at 37 ("While some experts do hold this [tape recorder] position, most do not. The 'constructionist' model, whereby memory is a continual process of reconstruction, is generally accepted by memory experts").

25. For a further discussion of perception and memory, *see* § 9-2 *supra* (eyewitness identifications).

26. *See* Council on Mental Health, *Medical Use of Hypnosis*, 168 J.A.M.A. 186 (1958).

the control of pain."[27] Thus, hypnosis may be valid for therapeutic purposes and yet invalid for forensic purposes. As noted by one court, for hypnosis to be "therapeutically useful, it need not produce historically accurate memory."[28]

The clinical and forensic uses of hypnosis also differ in another respect. If therapeutic hypnosis (*e.g.*, to reduce pain or anxiety) is unsuccessful, little harm may be done. If forensic hypnosis is invalid, an erroneous conviction may result.

§ 12-3. Forensic Use of Hypnosis.

In *People v. Shirley*[29] the California Supreme Court enumerated the dangers associated with hypnotically influenced testimony. The first danger is hypersuggestibility: "Hypnosis is by its nature a process of suggestion, and one of its primary effects is that the person hypnotized becomes extremely receptive to suggestions that he perceives as emanating from the hypnotist."[30] A second danger is hypercompliance: "The person under hypnosis experiences a compelling desire to please the hypnotist by reacting positively to these suggestions, and hence, to produce the particular responses he believes are expected of him."[31] The third danger is the inability to differentiate accurate from inaccurate recall: "During the hypnotic session, neither the subject nor the hypnotist can distinguish between true memories and pseudomemories of various kinds in the reported recall; and when the subject repeats that recall in the waking state (*e.g.*, in a trial), neither an expert witness nor a lay observer (*e.g.*, the judge or the jury) can make a similar distinction."[32] The fourth danger is enhanced confidence: "[A] witness who is uncertain of his recollections before being hypnotized will become convinced by that process that the story he told under hypnosis is true and correct in every respect."[33] There is, however, no correlation between confidence and accuracy in this context.

A fifth danger, as stated by the U.S. Supreme Court, is confabulation — "fill[ing] in details from the imagination in order to make an answer more coherent and complete."[34]

---

27. Levitt, *The Use of Hypnosis to "Freshen" the Memory of Witnesses or Victims*, 17 TRIAL 56, 58 (April 1981).

28. State v. Mack, 292 N.W.2d 764, 768 (Minn. 1980). *See* Karlin & Orne, *supra* note 20, at 80 ("In recent years, scholars of psychotherapy have increasingly described historical reconstruction during psychotherapy in terms of the creation of a fictive narrative").

29. 31 Cal. 3d 18, 641 P.2d 775, 181 Cal. Rptr. 243, *cert. denied*, 459 U.S. 860 (1982).

30. *Id.* at 63, 641 P.2d at 802, 181 Cal. Rptr. at 271.

31. *Id.* at 64, 641 P.2d at 802-03, 181 Cal. Rptr. at 271.

32. *Id.* at 65, 641 P.2d at 803, 181 Cal. Rptr. at 271-72.

33. *Id.*, 181 Cal. Rptr. at 272.

34. Rock v. Arkansas, 483 U.S. 44, 60 (1987). The Court also commented: (1) "the subject becomes 'suggestible' and may try to please the hypnotist with answers the subject thinks will be met with approval" and "the subject experiences 'memory hardening,' which gives him great

The rejection of hypnotically refreshed testimony is supported by several authorities. Dr. Bernard Diamond, a critic of hypnotically refreshed testimony, wrote:

> I believe that once a potential witness has been hypnotized for the purpose of enhancing memory his recollections have been so contaminated that he is rendered effectively incompetent to testify. Hypnotized persons, being extremely suggestible, graft onto their memories fantasies or suggestions deliberately or unwittingly communicated by the hypnotist. After hypnosis the subject cannot differentiate between a true recollection and a fantasy or a suggested detail. Neither can any expert or the trier of fact. This risk is so great, in my view, that the use of hypnosis by police on a potential witness is tantamount to the destruction or fabrication of evidence.[35]

Dr. Martin Orne, another authority, originally proposed a number of safeguards that should be followed before such testimony is admitted.[36] In his later writings, however, he and his colleagues recommended that the safeguards be used only in investigative situations and wrote that "hypnotically induced testimony is not reliable and ought not be permitted to form the basis of testimony in court."[37]

The report of the A.M.A. Council on Scientific Affairs (1985) lends further support to this view. According to the Council:

---

confidence in both true and false memories, making effective cross-examination more difficult." *Id.* at 59-60.

35. Diamond, *supra* note 5, at 314.

36. *See* § 12-5(C) *infra* (procedural safeguards).

37. Orne, Soskis, Dinges & Orne, *Hypnotically Induced Testimony*, *in* EYEWITNESS TESTIMONY: PSYCHOLOGICAL PERSPECTIVES 171, 211 (G. Wells & E. Loftus eds. 1984). In a later publication, Dr. Orne and his colleagues wrote:

> In the present chapter, we have cited from a number of scientific studies that establish (1) the fundamental unreliability of recollections elicited in hypnosis; (2) the persistence of these recollections in the waking condition, whereupon they may be impossible for the individual to distinguish from memories that existed prior to hypnosis; and (3) the unwarranted increase or maintenance of confidence in the accuracy of hypnotically elicited recall, which thereby reinforces its credibility. These conditions compel the conclusion that hypnotically induced memories should *never* be permitted to form the basis for testimony by witnesses or victims in a court of law.

Orne, Whitehouse, Dinges & Orne, *Reconstructing Memory Through Hypnosis: Forensic and Clinical Implications*, *in* HYPNOSIS AND MEMORY 21, 50 (H.M. Pettinati ed. 1988). *See also* Orne, *Comments on the Draft Home Office Guidelines*, 5 BRITISH J. EXPERIMENTAL & CLINICAL HYPNOSIS 37, 42 (1988) ("I now take the position — shared by the majority of colleagues who constituted the review panel for the American Medical Association's Council on Scientific Affairs — that the use of hypnosis for memory should *never* be permitted with individuals who may later be asked to provide testimony in court").

> Review of the scientific literature indicates that when hypnosis is used to refresh recollection, one of the following outcomes occurs: (1) hypnosis produces recollections that are not substantially different from nonhypnotic recollections; (2) it yields recollections that are more inaccurate than nonhypnotic memory; or, most frequently, (3) it results in more information being reported, but these recollections contain both accurate and inaccurate details. When the third condition results, the individual is less likely to be able to discriminate between accurate and inaccurate recollections. There are no data to support a fourth alternative, namely, that hypnosis increases remembering of only accurate information.[38]

The Society for Clinical and Experimental Hypnosis and the International Society of Hypnosis subsequently adopted the A.M.A. position.[39] The A.M.A. report, however, has not gone unchallenged. According to two commentators: "[T]he AMA panel's report drew mixed reviews."[40] The A.M.A. reaffirmed its position in 1994.[41] However, the American Society of Clinical Hypnosis took a different position, noting that "we disagree with this item in the AMA report."[42]

A 1994 meta-analysis review of twenty-four research studies concluded that: (1) increased recall accuracy for hypnotized subjects has not been substantiated at this time; (2) control subjects had a higher accuracy rate for lineup identifications than hypnotized subjects, who had more false alarms; and (3) hypnotized subjects are more confident about their recall accuracy.[43]

§ 12-4. Hypnotically Induced Statements.

Courts uniformly reject the admissibility of statements made by a subject while hypnotized. Because these statements are made out of court and are

---

38. *AMA Scientific Status*, *supra* note 19, at 1921.

39. Orne, Whitehouse, Dinges & Orne, *supra* note 37, at 51.

40. SCHEFLIN & SHAPIRO, TRANCE ON TRIAL 109 (1989).

41. Council on Scientific Affairs, *Memories of Childhood Abuse*, (1994), *reprinted in* 43 INT'L J. CLINICAL & EXPERIMENTAL HYPNOSIS 114 (1995) ("[T]he Council concluded that hypnosis-induced recollections actually appear to be less reliable than nonhypnotic recall. That statement remains an accurate summary of the empirical literature").

42. AMERICAN SOCIETY OF CLINICAL HYPNOSIS, CLINICAL HYPNOSIS AND MEMORY: GUIDELINES FOR CLINICIANS AND FOR FORENSIC HYPNOSIS 6 (1995). *See also* D. BROWN, A. SCHEFLIN & D. HAMMOND, MEMORY, TRAUMA TREATMENT, AND THE LAW (1998).

43. Steblay & Bothwell, *Evidence for Hypnotically Refreshed Testimony: The View From the Laboratory*, 18 LAW & HUMAN BEHAV. 635, 649 (1994) ("Hypnosis is not necessarily a source of accurate information; at worst it may be a source of inaccurate information provided with confident testimony"). *See also* Karlin & Orne, *supra* note 20, at 80 ("Hypnosis increases productivity, certainty, and believability without a corresponding increment in historically correct information. ...There are rare instances in which hypnosis may stimulate the return of historically accurate memory that has been blocked for emotional reasons ...").

typically offered for the truth of the matters asserted, they are hearsay.[44] Not only do they raise the typical dangers associated with hearsay evidence — perception, memory, narration, and sincerity problems untested by cross-examination — but also additional problems such as confabulation.

The court decisions are supported by research data. For example, one authority has written:

> [E]xperience with a research design where deeply hypnotized subjects and unhypnotizable subjects instructed to feign hypnosis are seen by hypnotists who are unaware of the subject's actual status ... has shown that it is possible to deceive even highly experienced hypnotists.... Not only can individuals fake hypnosis, but even subjects who are generally in deep hypnosis are nonetheless able to willfully lie....[45]

Hypnotic statements may be exculpatory or incriminator; the latter includes police-obtained confessions.

§ 12-4(A). Exculpatory Statements.

Typically, hypnotically elicited statements have been offered by an accused as exculpatory evidence. In a leading case, *Greenfield v. Commonwealth*,[46] the defendant, who claimed no recollection of the charged offense, offered statements he had made concerning the crime while under hypnosis. The Virginia Supreme Court held the statements inadmissible due to their unreliability: "Most experts agree that hypnotic evidence is unreliable because a person under hypnosis can manufacture or invent false statements.... A person under a hypnotic trance is also subject to heightened suggestibility."[47]

Numerous other courts have also excluded hypnotically induced statements as unreliable,[48] including expert opinion testimony concerning the truthfulness of a

---

44. *See* FED. R. EVID. 801(a)-(c).

45. Orne, *supra* note 18, at 64. *See also* Orne, Whitehouse, Dinges & Orne, *Reconstructing Memory Through Hypnosis: Forensic and Clinical Implications*, *in* HYPNOSIS AND MEMORY 21, 24 (H.M. Pettinati ed. 1988) ("Without any special knowledge or training, individuals can successfully simulate being hypnotized and it is exceedingly difficult to detect such purposive simulation.... Moreover, subjects who are in fact deeply hypnotized are still able to lie").

46. 214 Va. 710, 204 S.E.2d 414 (1974). In a subsequent habeas proceeding, a federal district court agreed. Greenfield v. Robinson, 413 F. Supp. 1113 (W.D. Va. 1976).

47. 214 Va. at 715, 204 S.E.2d at 419.

48. *See* Sprynczynatyk v. General Motors Corp., 771 F.2d 1112, 1117 (8th Cir. 1985), *cert. denied*, 475 U.S. 1046 (1986); Shockey v. State, 338 So. 2d 33, 37 (Fla. App.), *cert. denied*, 345 So. 2d 427 (Fla. 1976); Rodriguez v. State, 327 So. 2d 903, 904 (Fla. App.), *cert. denied*, 336 So. 2d 1184 (Fla. 1976); Collier v. State, 244 Ga. 553, 557-58, 261 S.E.2d 364, 370 (1979), *cert. denied*, 445 U.S. 946 (1980); Alderman v. State, 241 Ga. 496, 510-11, 246 S.E.2d 642, 651 (1978); Emmett v. State, 232 Ga. 110, 115, 205 S.E.2d 231, 235 (1974); People v. Duckett, 133 Ill. App. 3d

subject's responses while hypnotized.[49] The rule of exclusion, in the view of one court, also applied to situations where a defense counsel attempted to use the statement to refresh a witness's recollection: "Mills presents us with no authority for why statements of a witness made under hypnosis should be relevant, reliable, or otherwise admissible."[50] This decision goes against the traditional view that anything may be used to refresh a witness's memory and may be explained as precluding the introduction of the statement through the back door.

Constitutional Right to Present a Defense

The admissibility of hypnotically induced statements may also raise constitutional issues. In several cases, defendants, citing *Chambers v. Mississippi*,[51] have argued that the Constitution requires the admission of hypnotically-influenced statements. *Chambers* did not involve the admissibility of an out-of-court hypnotic statement. Rather, it involved a now-discredited hearsay exception (the failure of the common law to recognize the admissibility of declarations against penal interests). The U.S. Supreme Court's opinion in *Chambers*, however, can be read broadly to recognize a due process right to introduce defense evidence at trial, notwithstanding a state evidentiary rule of exclusion.[52]

Even a broad reading of *Chambers*, however, must recognize a significant limitation. The Court in *Chambers* required the proffered evidence to be *reliable*. Accordingly, in *Greenfield v. Robinson*[53] a federal district court focused on this aspect of the due process argument: "[T]he very reason for excluding hypnotic

---

639, 640, 479 N.E.2d 355, 356 (1985); People v. Kester, 78 Ill. App. 3d 902, 910, 397 N.E.2d 888, 894 (1979); Strong v. State, 435 N.E.2d 969, 970 (Ind. 1982); State v. Conley, 6 Kan. App. 2d 280, 285, 627 P.2d 1174, 1178 (1981); People v. Hangsleben, 86 Mich. App. 718, 727-30, 273 N.W.2d 539, 543-44 (1978); House v. State, 445 So. 2d 815, 821 (Miss. 1984); State v. Pusch, 77 N.D. 860, 886-88, 46 N.W.2d 508, 521-22 (1950); State v. Harris, 241 Or. 224, 237, 405 P.2d 492, 498 (1965); State v. Pierce, 263 S.C. 23, 30, 207 S.E.2d 414, 418 (1974).

See also Annot., *Admissibility of Hypnotic Evidence at Criminal Trial*, 92 A.L.R.3D 442 (1979).

49. *See* House v. State, 445 So. 2d 815, 822 (Miss. 1984); Jones v. State, 542 P.2d 1316, 1328 (Okla. Crim. App. 1975).

50. Mills v. State, 322 Ark. 647, 662, 910 S.W.2d 682, 690 (1995) ("Here, the statements allegedly made by Robbins were not recalled by her and were presumably made while she was in a hypnotic trance").

51. 410 U.S. 284 (1973).

52. One legal commentator stated it this way: "Broadly construed, [*Chambers*] appears to recognize that the accused in a criminal proceeding has a constitutional right to introduce any exculpatory evidence, unless the state can demonstrate that it is so inherently unreliable as to leave the trier of fact no rational basis for evaluating its truth." Westen, *The Compulsory Process Clause*, 73 MICH. L. REV. 71, 151-152 (1974).

53. 413 F. Supp. 1113 (W.D. Va. 1976).

evidence is due to its potential unreliability."[54] Similarly, in *People v. Blair*[55] the California Supreme Court rejected the constitutional argument that the exclusion of hypnotic statements violated the right to present defense evidence under *Chambers.* According to the court, "the trial court's ruling [of exclusion] did not elevate a fastidious adherence to the technicalities of the law of evidence over the right to a fair trial. For here, unlike *Chambers*, there was no solid assurance that the hearsay statements were reliable."[56] Most courts, including the U.S. Supreme Court,[57] have reached the same result when defendants have used the *Chambers'* argument to support the admission of polygraph evidence.[58]

Neither of these cases is affected by the U.S. Supreme Court's subsequent decision in *Rock v. Arkansas.*[59] *Rock* involved the trial testimony of a defendant whose memory had been refreshed by hypnosis. It did not involve the admission of the accused's out-of-court hypnotic statements, and *Rock's* rationale — an accused's constitutional right to testify — would not extend to out-of-court statements.[60]

§ 12-4(B). Incriminatory Statements.

The evidentiary rule excluding hypnotically elicited statements applies to incriminatory as well as exculpatory statements made by an accused. For example, in *People v. Schreiner* [61] the accused recounted, during the course of a compelled mental examination, that three years previously, following a self-hypnotic episode, he remembered involvement in a murder. Out-of-court statements made by an accused, *if* offered by the prosecution, are admissible under a long-recognized exception to the hearsay rule (party admissions).[62] Nevertheless, the New York Court of Appeals ruled the defendant's statement inadmissible because "his recollection was the result of hypnotic therapy and posthypnotic suggestion" and "such recollections are inherently unreliable."[63]

---

54. *Id.* at 1120.

55. 25 Cal. 3d 640, 602 P.2d 738, 159 Cal. Rptr. 818 (1979).

56. *Id.* at 665, 602 P.2d at 753, 159 Cal. Rptr. at 833.

57. United States v. Scheffer, 523 U.S. 303 (1998).

58. For a discussion of the *Chambers* due process analysis, *see* Chapter 1.

59. 483 U.S. 44 (1987).

60. *Rock* is discussed in § 12-6(A) *infra.*

61. 77 N.Y.2d 733, 573 N.E.2d 552, 570 N.Y.S.2d 464 (1991).

62. In other words, the hearsay rule permits incriminatory statements of the accused to be admitted against the accused; these are party admissions. Exculpatory statements offered by the accused, however, are not admissible under the party admission rule.

63. 77 N.Y.2d at 740, 573 N.E.2d at 556, 570 N.Y.S.2d at 468.

§ 12-4(C). Confessions.

A constitutional issue arises if the prosecution proffers incriminatory statements obtained by the police. The use of hypnosis in obtaining a confession played a role in *Leyra v. Denno*,[64] where the U.S. Supreme Court held that a confession obtained by a "psychiatrist with considerable knowledge of hypnosis" was involuntary and thus violative of due process. The Court noted that the "suspect's ability to resist interrogation was broken to almost trancelike submission by use of the arts of a highly skilled psychiatrist."[65]

The use of hypnosis to elicit incriminatory statements remains a problem. Authorities have noted that "the most serious problem that can arise when hypnosis is used by the prosecution with defendants concerns elicitation of false confessions."[66]

§ 12-5. Hypnotically Refreshed Testimony.

Unlike the uniformly negative judicial response to out-of-court hypnotic statements,[67] the courts divided sharply over the admissibility of hypnotically-refreshed testimony. These cases provide a rich tapestry for studying the sometimes troubled interaction between law and science. The case law reflects several different positions. Many courts adopted a per se rule of exclusion. This approach, however, recognized several exceptions. The two most important concern (1) the testimony of a witness based on prehypnotic memory and (2) the testimony of the accused. The U.S. Supreme Court in *Rock v. Arkansas*[68] ruled that the exclusion of the testimony of a defendant, whose memory has been refreshed by hypnosis, raised constitutional issues.[69]

Other courts permitted previously hypnotized witnesses to testify, albeit under different conditions. First, some of these courts ruled that hypnosis affects the weight, not the admissibility, of the testimony, thus leaving the reliability issue to the jury — *i.e.*, "credibility" approach. Second, some courts admitted hypnotically refreshed testimony if certain "procedural safeguards" were satisfied. Finally, still other courts recognized a trial judge's discretion to admit the testimony if the judge finds the testimony reliable. These approaches are discussed later in this section.

---

64. 347 U.S. 556 (1954).

65. *Id.* at 561.

66. Orne, Dinges & Orne, *Rock v. Arkansas: Hypnosis, The Defendant's Privilege*, 38 INT'L J. CLINICAL & EXPERIMENTAL HYPNOSIS 250, 256 (1990).

67. *See* § 12-4 *supra*.

68. *Id.*

69. *Rock* is discussed in § 12-6(A) *infra*.

Admissibility Standard

The initial question in determining the admissibility of hypnotically enhanced testimony concerns the applicable standard for admitting scientific evidence. Many jurisdictions followed the general acceptance standard first set forth in *Frye v. United States*.[70] Under the *Frye* test, evidence derived from a new scientific technique is admissible only if the technique is "sufficiently established to have gained general acceptance in the particular field in which it belongs."[71] As noted in Chapter 1, however, a number of courts had rejected the *Frye* test prior to 1993, when the U.S. Supreme Court also rejected *Frye* in *Daubert v. Merrell Dow Pharmaceuticals, Inc.*[72] Nevertheless, a significant minority of jurisdictions have retained the *Frye* test.

Moreover, the admissibility of hypnotically refreshed testimony did not depend entirely on whether a jurisdiction had adopted or rejected *Frye*. There was disagreement over the applicability of the *Frye* test to hypnotically refreshed statements even in jurisdictions that followed the general acceptance standard. For example, soon after the Michigan Supreme Court held that hypnotically refreshed testimony did not satisfy the *Frye* test,[73] the Wisconsin Supreme Court ruled that *Frye* was limited to *expert* testimony and thus not applicable to hypnotically refreshed testimony, which involves the testimony of lay witnesses.[74] Furthermore, in a footnote, the court indicated that had *Frye* been applicable, hypnotically refreshed testimony would have satisfied the general acceptance standard.[75]

Even those courts that agreed on *Frye*'s applicability to hypnotically refreshed testimony disagreed on its precise application. For example, the New Jersey Supreme Court held that to satisfy *Frye*, hypnosis need not be "generally accepted as a means of reviving truthful or historically accurate recall" but need only be "generally accepted as a reasonably reliable method of restoring a person's memory."[76] Most courts applying *Frye* rejected this interpretation.[77]

---

70. 293 F. 1013 (D.C. 1923).

71. *Id.* at 1014.

72. 509 U.S. 579 (1993).

73. People v. Gonzales, 415 Mich. 615, 627, 329 N.W.2d 743, 748 (1982), *modified on other grounds*, 417 Mich. 968, 336 N.W.2d 751 (1983).

74. State v. Armstrong, 110 Wis. 2d 555, 567-68, 329 N.W.2d 386, 393, *cert. denied*, 461 U.S. 946 (1983). *See also* United States v. Valdez, 722 F.2d 1196, 1201 (5th Cir. 1984); State v. Long, 32 Wash. App. 732, 735-36, 649 F.2d 845, 846 (1982).

75. 110 Wis. 2d at 567 n.14, 329 N.W.2d at 393 n.14.

76. State v. Hurd, 86 N.J. 525, 538, 432 A.2d 86, 92 (1981). *Accord* United States v. Harrington, 18 M.J. 797, 802 (A.C.M.R. 1984).

77. *E.g.*, People v. Shirley, 31 Cal. 3d 18, 37-39, 641 P.2d 775, 786-87, 181 Cal. Rptr. 243, 254-55, *cert. denied*, 459 U.S. 860 (1982); State v. Collins, 296 Md. 670, 680-81, 464 A.2d 1028, 1034 (1983); Commonwealth v. Kater, 388 Mass. 519, 527, 447 N.E.2d 1190, 1195 (1983); People v.

The adoption of the *Daubert* approach, which replaced *Frye* with a reliability test, does not necessarily mean that a jurisdiction's position on hypnotically refreshed testimony will change. Instead of excluding such testimony as not "generally accepted," a court could exclude it as "unreliable" pursuant to the *Daubert* analysis. Several non-*Frye* jurisdictions had rejected hypnotically-refreshed testimony even before *Daubert* was decided. For example, a Delaware court excluded this type of evidence because the "State has not demonstrated that hypnotic recall is sufficiently reliable to be admitted as evidence."[78] Nonetheless, *Daubert* may open the door to relitigation of this issue because some courts have interpreted it as providing a lower standard than the *Frye* test. "Police hypnotists, in particular, are hoping that prosecutors will push hard for the repeal or overruling of anti-hypnosis rulings."[79]

§ 12-5(A). Per Se Exclusion & Exceptions.

Numerous courts have adopted a per se rule excluding the testimony of a witness (other than the accused) who has been hypnotized.[80] "Beginning in 1980

Hughes, 59 N.Y.2d 523, 537-43, 453 N.E.2d 484, 490-95, 466 N.Y.S.2d 255, 261-65 (1983); Commonwealth v. Nazarovitch, 496 Pa. 97, 101-02, 436 A.2d 170, 172-73 (1981).

78. State v. Davis, 490 A.2d 601, 605 (Del. Super. 1985).

79. Scheflin, *Hypnosis and the Law in the U.S.*, *in* HYPNOSIS AND THE LAW: PRINCIPLES AND PRACTICE 25, 45 (Australian Society of Hypnosis 1994) ("Thus, in all federal trials, hypnotically refreshed recollection may find an easier avenue to testimonial admissibility. ...States will be tempted to follow the federal model. Police hypnotists, in particular, are hoping that prosecutors will push hard for the repeal or overruling of anti-hypnosis rulings").

80. *E.g.*, Contreras v. State, 718 P.2d 129, 133 (Alaska 1986); State *ex rel.* Collins v. Superior Court, 132 Ariz. 180, 207, 644 P.2d 1266, 1294 (1982); State v. Mena, 128 Ariz. 226, 231, 624 P.2d 1274, 1279 (1981); State v. Davis, 490 A.2d 601, 605 (Del. Super. 1985); Stokes v. State, 548 So. 2d 188, 195-96 (Fla. 1989); Bundy v. State, 471 So. 2d 9, 18 (Fla. 1985), *cert. denied*, 479 U.S. 894 (1986); Walraven v. State, 255 Ga. 276, 282, 336 S.E.2d 798, 804 (1985); State v. Moreno, 68 Haw. 233, 236, 709 P.2d 103, 105 (1985); People v. Zayas, 131 Ill. 2d 284, 295, 546 N.E.2d 513, 518 (1989); State v. Haislip, 237 Kan. 461, 482, 701 P.2d 909, 926 (1985), *cert. denied*, 474 U.S. 1022 (1985); State v. Collins, 296 Md. 670, 701-02, 464 A.2d 1028, 1044 (1983); People v. Gonzales, 415 Mich. 615, 627, 329 N.W.2d 743, 748 (1982), *modified on other grounds*, 417 Mich. 968, 336 N.W.2d 751 (1983); State v. Blanchard, 315 N.W.2d 427, 430 (Minn. 1982); State v. Koehler, 312 N.W.2d 108, 110 (Minn. 1981); State v. Mack, 292 N.W.2d 764, 772 (Minn. 1980); Alsbach v. Bader, 700 S.W.2d 823, 825 (Mo. 1985); Palmer v. State, 210 Neb. 206, 218, 313 N.W.2d 648, 655 (1981); People v. Hughes, 59 N.Y.2d 523, 545, 453 N.E.2d 484, 495, 466 N.Y.S.2d 255, 266 (1983); Harmon v. State, 700 P.2d 212, 216 (Okla. Crim. App. 1985); Robison v. State, 677 P.2d 1080, 1085 (Okla. Crim. App.), *cert. denied*, 467 U.S. 1246 (1984); Commonwealth v. Nazarovitch, 496 Pa. 97, 110, 436 A.2d 170, 177 (1981); State v. Tuttle, 780 P.2d 1203, 1211-12 (Utah 1989), *cert. denied*, 494 U.S. 1018 (1990); Hall v. Commonwealth, 12 Va. App. 198, 403 S.E.2d 362, 370 (1991); State v. Coe, 109 Wash. 2d 832, 837, 750 P.2d 208, 211 (1988); State v. Martin, 101 Wash. 2d 713, 722, 684 P.2d 651, 654 (1984).

See also Prewitt v. State, 460 So. 2d 296, 302-04 (Ala. Crim. App. 1984) (*Frye* not satisfied under facts presented).

in Minnesota's *Mack* case ..., but most importantly in the California Supreme Court's majority decision two years later in *Shirley*, courts began to shut down the growing police practice of training police hypnotists."[81] As one court observed: "The exclusion of hypnotically-enhanced testimony was stated in the form of a per se exclusion; it did not depend on who the witness was, who called the witness to testify, or the circumstances of the case."[82] For the most part, these courts applied the *Frye* general acceptance test. The unreliability of hypnotically refreshed testimony and the inadequacy of cross-examination in exposing the suggestive aspects of hypnosis (as discussed in § 12-3) are the principal reasons given for exclusion.

The Maryland Court of Appeals revisited the issue in *Burral v. State.*[83] The court commented that the "fact is that both the scientific community and a majority of the courts continue to view hypnosis, when used as a memory enhancer, as unreliable and, in terms of testimony in court, as likely to produce false recollections and inaccurate testimony that cross-examination may be unable to expose. The same deficiencies that were prevalent in 1983 appear to remain prevalent today."[84]

Nevertheless, some authorities argue that the current majority rule — the per se rule of exclusion — also rests on shaky scientific foundations. They point out that memory itself is often unreliable, as demonstrated by eyewitness identification testimony. In their view, the critical question is whether hypnotically-enhanced memory is *less* reliable than other types of courtroom evidence.[85] While this may be true, it does not answer the question. Although the problems with eyewitness identifications are well-documented,[86] the response should be to improve the way in which the legal system deals with such

81. Scheflin, *supra* note 79, at 25. *See* People v. Shirley, 31 Cal. 3d 18, 641 P.2d 775, 181 Cal. Rptr. 243, *cert. denied*, 459 U.S. 860 (1982); State v. Mack, 292 N.W.2d 764, 772 (Minn. 1980). *See also* Scheflin, *supra* note 4, at 29 ("[M]ore than 95% of the forensic cases involving hypnosis decided since 1968 have been criminal matters. Whether the same exclusion rule should be applied in civil cases is not yet resolved by the courts, though the trend appears to be for each state to adopt the same rule in civil cases that it adopted in criminal cases").

82. Burral v. State, 352 Md. 707, 708, 724 A.2d 65, 65 (1999).

83. 342 Md. 707, 708, 724 A.2d 65, 65 (1999).

84. *Id.* at 740, 724 A.2d at 81.

85. Sheflin, *False Memory and Buridan's Ass: A Response to Karlin and Orne*, 14 CULTIC STUDIES J. 207, 272 (1997) ("The fact that with hypnosis may come false information as well as accurate information, and the fact that no one can tell the difference without independent corroboration, is meaningless because the same is true of every memory retrieval technique, and of memory itself").

86. *See* § 9-2 *supra*.

identifications, not to add more problems; several cases in which convicts were subsequently exonerated involved the prosecution use of hypnotized witnesses.[87]

Whether Subject Hypnotized

The per se rule can be avoided if a trial court decides that the witness had not in fact been hypnotized.[88] This approach makes sense, as long as it is not transformed into an automatic loophole for a trial court that disagrees with the per se approach. In addition, there are times when it is not clear whether a witness had been hypnotized, a question that raises difficult factual issues.[89]

Prehypnotic Testimony

Courts adhering to the per se rule of exclusion, however, recognize exceptions. One exception concerns testimony based on prehypnotic memory. For example, in *State ex rel. Collins v. Superior Court*[90] several rape victims were hypnotized in an attempt to discover more information about the identity of their assailant. Although no new information developed from this process, the defendant was later apprehended as he approached a police decoy. The defense moved to disqualify the victims as witnesses. On appeal, the Arizona Supreme Court reaffirmed its earlier position,[91] ruling that the testimony of a hypnotized witness is inadmissible. On a motion for rehearing, however, the court modified this ruling:

---

87. *See* E. Connors, T. Lundregan, N. Miller & T. McEwen, Convicted by Juries, Exonerated by Science: Case Studies in the Use of DNA Evidence to Establish Innocence After Trial 15-18 (1996) ("In *Honaker*, the defendant's attorney alleged that the government intentionally kept exculpatory evidence from the defense, including information that two of the government's witnesses were secretly hypnotized to enhance their testimony and the prosecution's criminalist was never told that Honaker had a vasectomy (and could not have been the source of the sperm in the victim"); Fricker, *State Falters in Retrial of Escaped Con*, 81 A.B.A. J. 38, 40 (June 1995) ("The defense was not told of the hypnosis during the first trial, and the tape of that session has since been erased").

88. *See* Scheflin, *supra* note 4, at 28 ("Courts have accepted expert opinion, based on objective tests of hypnotizability, to show that the hypnosis was ineffectual and therefore the witness may testify about posthypnotic recollections") (citing People v. Caro, 46 Cal. 3d 1035, 761 P.2d 680, 251 Cal. Rptr. 757 (1988)).

89. *See* State v. Joly, 219 Conn. 234, 593 A.2d 96 (1991); Partin v. State, 318 Ark. 312, 316, 885 S.W.2d 21, 22-23 (1994) ("[T]he trial court specifically found there was no clear evidence that Trevor had been hypnotized.... [B]ased on the record before it, we cannot say the trial court erred in finding Trevor had not been hypnotized"); Annot., *Sufficiency of evidence that witness in criminal case was hypnotized, for purposes of determining admissibility of testimony given under hypnosis or of hypnotically enhanced testimony*, 16 A.L.R.5th 841 (1993).

90. 132 Ariz. 180, 644 P.2d 1266 (1982).

91. *See* State v. Mena, 128 Ariz. 226, 624 P.2d 1274 (1981).

> [A] witness will be permitted to testify with regard to those matters which he or she was able to recall *and* relate prior to hypnosis. Thus, for example, the rape victim would be free to testify to the occurrence of the crime, the lack of consent, the injury inflicted and the like, assuming that such matters were remembered and related to the authorities prior to use of hypnosis.[92]

Although *Collins II* represents the prevailing view on this issue,[93] this approach is not without problems. First, the hypnotic session may affect the witness's manner and confidence. "Once hypnosis is used, the witness' prehypnotic memory is tampered with irreparably. Not only are new 'memories' brought forth in hypnosis unreliable, but the process confounds the manner in which the witness perceives and recounts prehypnotic memories."[94] Second, one study established that a person cannot reliably distinguish between memories retrieved prior to hypnosis and those that occurred during hypnosis. The investigators found "very clear evidence that subjects' retrospective statements concerning the occasion of their prior recall productions are quite fallible."[95] Consequently, unless the witness's prehypnotic memory is accurately and fully recorded, there is no reliable way to determine after hypnosis what the witness knew at the earlier time.

The *Collins II* approach is a compromise position between total disqualification of eyewitness testimony, which may be both reliable and critical, and the introduction of tainted evidence. It does, however, erect a substantial barrier to the admissibility of prehypnotic testimony. In a later case, the Arizona Supreme

92. 132 Ariz. at 209, 644 P.2d at 1295.

93. *See* State v. Poland, 144 Ariz. 388, 400, 698 P.2d 183, 195-96 (1985); Elliotte v. State, 515 A.2d 677, 681 (Del. 1986); State v. Bainbridge, 117 Idaho 245, 253, 787 P.2d 231, 239 (1990); People v. Wilson, 116 Ill. 2d 29, 45-49, 506 N.E.2d 571, 578-80 (1987); Calhoun v. State, 297 Md. 563, 577-78, 468 A.2d 45, 51 (1983), *cert. denied*, 466 U.S. 993 (1984); State v. Collins, 296 Md. 670, 702-03, 464 A.2d 1028, 1044-45 (1983); Commonwealth v. Kater, 394 Mass. 531, 532, 476 N.E.2d 593, 594 (1985); Commonwealth v. Kater, 388 Mass. 519, 529, 447 N.E.2d 1190, 1197 (1983); People v. Nixon, 421 Mich. 79, 86, 364 N.W.2d 593, 598-99 (1984); State v. Koehler, 312 N.W.2d 108, 110 (Minn. 1981); State v. Patterson, 213 Neb. 686, 692-93, 331 N.W.2d 500, 504 (1983); People v. Tunstall, 63 N.Y.2d 1, 6, 468 N.E.2d 30, 33, 479 N.Y.S.2d 192, 195 (1984) (defendant entitled to a hearing on the admissibility of prehypnotic testimony); People v. Hughes, 59 N.Y.2d 523, 545, 453 N.E.2d 484, 495, 466 N.Y.S.2d 255, 266 (1983); State v. Cook, 65 Ohio St.3d 516, 605 N.E.2d 70, 77 (1992) (witness had "identified appellant prior to any hypnosis"), *cert. denied*, 510 U.S. 1040 (1994); Commonwealth v. Romanelli, 522 Pa. 222, 229, 560 A.2d 1384, 1388 (1989) (*Smoyer* safeguards satisfied); Commonwealth v. Smoyer, 505 Pa. 83, 89-90, 476 A.2d 1304, 1307-08 (1984); Hopkins v. Commonwealth, 230 Va. 280, 292, 337 S.E.2d 264, 272 (1985), *cert. denied*, 475 U.S. 1098 (1988); Hall v. Commonwealth, 12 Va. App. 198, 403 S.E.2d 362, 370 (1991); State v. Martin, 101 Wash. 2d 713, 727, 684 P.2d 651, 656 (1984).

94. Orne, Dinges & Orne, *supra* note 66, at 259.

95. Whitehouse, Orne, Orne & Dinges, *Distinguishing the Source of Memories Reported During Prior Waking and Hypnotic Recall Attempts*, 5 APPLIED COGNITIVE PSYCHOL. 51, 58 (1991).

Court wrote: "We adhere to our holding in *Collins II* that post-hypnotic testimony must have been demonstrably recalled and recorded prior to hypnosis in order to be admissible."[96] Michigan required a higher burden of proof (persuasion) — *i.e.*, "clear and convincing evidence that the testimony being offered was based on facts recalled and related prior to hypnosis."[97] Other courts required compliance with the procedural safeguards discussed in section 12-5(C) *infra*.[98]

Commonwealth v. Kater[99] illustrates the problems the prosecution faces in establishing prehypnotic memories. The prosecution had to establish the witnesses' prehypnotic memories by a "preponderance of evidence." The trial court ruled that the evidence had not demonstrated that the witnesses could identify the defendant's car prior to hypnosis. The Supreme Judicial Court of Massachusetts affirmed:

> In effect, the judge ruled that the witnesses did not identify the automobile prior to hypnosis; that prior to hypnosis their descriptions of the automobile were not specific enough to indicate an ability to identify the automobile; that no new credible evidence was introduced tending to show the extent of their prehypnosis memories; and, therefore, he had no evidentiary basis to conclude that they could have identified the automobile prior to hypnosis. We agree.[100]

At one time California precluded the admission of all testimony, including testimony consistent with the witness's prehypnotic statements.[101] A subsequently-enacted statute altered this result, permitting a witness who has been hypnotized to testify if (1) the testimony is limited to matters that the witness recalled and related prior to hypnosis, (2) the substance of the prehypnotic memory was preserved in written, audiotape, or videotape form prior to hypnosis, and (3) specified procedural safeguards were followed.[102] The

---

96. State *ex rel.* Neely v. Sherrill, 165 Ariz. 508, 513, 799 P.2d 849, 854 (1990).

97. People v. Lee, 434 Mich. 59, 84-85, 450 N.W.2d 883, 895 (1990), *cert. denied*, 498 U.S. 879 (1990). The typical burden of persuasion for evidence issues is a preponderance of evidence (more probable than not).

98. *E.g.*, Hall v. Commonwealth, 12 Va. App. 198, 211-12, 403 S.E.2d 362, 370-71 (1991) (recommending *Hurd* safeguards).

99. 412 Mass. 800, 592 N.E.2d 1328 (1992).

100. *Id.* at 1330.

101. People v. Guerra, 37 Cal. 3d 385, 690 P.2d 635, 663-65, 208 Cal. Rptr. 162, 190-92 (1984).

102. CAL. EVID. CODE § 795. *See* People v. Clark, 3 Cal. 4th 41, 833 P.2d 561, 10 Cal. Rptr. 2d 554, 615 (1992) (Witness's "photographic-lineup and in-court identifications of defendant – which postdate the hypnotic session – were inadmissible..."), *cert. denied*, 507 U.S. 993 (1993); People v. Hayes, 49 Cal. 3d 1260, 1262, 783 P.2d 719, 720-21, 265 Cal. Rptr. 132, 134 (1989) (prehypnotic safeguards require (a) recording the subject's prehypnotic description of the event and the information provided to the hypnotist, (b) obtaining the subject's informed consent, and (c) videotaping the session, including the pre- and posthypnosis interviews. Further, the hypnotist must be a licensed physician, psychologist, or other licensed professional who is independent of the police. In addition, the hypnotic session is not to be conducted in the presence of the police. Finally, admissibility is determined at an out-of-court hearing at which the proponent must establish the reliability of the prehypnotic recollections by "clear and convincing evidence."

Conduct During Hypnosis

Several other exceptions to the per se exclusionary rule may develop. First, Professor Scheflin makes a convincing argument for an exception in cases in which the crime occurs while the victim is hypnotized —"suppose the therapist uses hypnosis to induce trance and then has sexual relations with the patient."[103]

Therapeutic Hypnosis

Some courts recognize an exception for nonforensic hypnosis. For example, in *McGlauflin v. State*[104] the court considered the admissibility of a child abuse victim's testimony. The hypnotic session was intended to focus on her weight problem. The court noted the lack of cases "in which a witness hypnotized for a non-forensic purpose was later called to testify in a criminal case."[105] The court ruled that there is no presumption of unreliability in this type of case because "the circumstances and results of the hypnosis session make it likely that the witness's memories have not been enhanced or altered by hypnosis."[106]

---

evidence admissible); People v. Alcala, 4 Cal. 4th 742, 842 P.2d 1192, 15 Cal. Rptr. 2d 432 (1992) (prehypnotic evidence admissible), *cert. denied*, 510 U.S. 877 (1993); People v. Miller, 50 Cal. 3d 954, 984, 790 P.2d 1289, 1304, 269 Cal. Rptr. 492, 507 (1990) ("[N]o real 'prehypnotic evidence' within the meaning of *Hayes* which the witness had recalled and related prior to hypnosis"), *cert. denied*, 498 U.S. 1041 (1991); Schall v. Lockheed Missiles and Space Co., 37 Cal. App. 4th 1485, 44 Cal. Rptr. 191, 196 (1995) ("Section 795 has no application to civil actions.... *Shirley* precludes hypnotically restored testimony in civil cases").

103. Scheflin, *Forensic Hypnosis: Unanswered Questions*, 22 AUSTRALIAN J. CLINICAL & EXPERIMENTAL HYPNOSIS 25, 26 (1994). *See also* Scheflin, *supra* note 79, at 31 ("It makes little judicial sense, and serves no cause of justice, to exclude post-hypnotic recollections in these sex cases") (citing People v. Sorscher, 151 Mich. App. 122, 391 N.W.2d 365 (1986) ("We perceive that the thrust of *Gonzales* is to exclude testimony which has been obtained through hypnosis as a method for improving a witness's memory ... In the case at bar, hypnosis was not used as a scientific technique to obtain evidence against defendant ... Rather it was used by defendant as an aid in the commission of a sexual assault")).

104. 857 P.2d 366 (Alaska App. 1993).

105. *Id.* at 375.

106. *Id.* at 378.

This position overlooks several of the dangers of hypnotically enhanced testimony and, in the absence of corroborating evidence, is problematic.[107] In *Borawick v. Shay*,[108] the Second Circuit rejected this view: "[E]ven though there may be important distinctions between the use of hypnosis to enhance memories of witnessed events and the use of hypnosis to retrieve repressed memories, given the lack of empirical studies as to the latter and the complicated nature of hypnotically-induced recall, we are not willing to assume that the risks of suggestibility, confabulation, and memory hardening are significantly reduced when the hypnosis that triggers the testimony is used for therapeutic purposes."[109]

The dilemma here is that the patient is seeking help from a counselor, and therefore the deterrent value of the per se rule will not be effective.

§ 12-5(B). Admission: Credibility Approach.

Courts admitting hypnotically refreshed testimony have adopted three different positions, one of which is a credibility or open admissibility approach — hypnosis does not affect admissibility, only the weight of the evidence. Historically, the credibility of a witness is a jury issue.[110]

The initial cases that considered the admissibility of hypnotically refreshed testimony took this position. Under this view, the use of hypnosis to stimulate recall is treated no differently than other methods of refreshing recollection.[111] Accordingly, cross-examination, the presentation of expert testimony on the dangers of hypnosis, and cautionary instructions are thought to provide sufficient guarantees to permit a jury to evaluate the credibility of previously hypnotized witnesses.[112] "From 1968 to 1978, the 'open admissibility' rule was so popular with the courts that it was the only rule applied by them."[113]

The seminal case is *Harding v. State* (1968).[114] In the case, the victim of a rape and shooting was unable to remember many of the details of the attack until she was hypnotized by a psychologist employed by a state hospital. A Maryland

---

107. *See* Karlin & Orne, *supra* note 20, at 51 ("When hypnotically influenced recall emanates from a clinical setting, it may often pose as great or even greater risks to the fact-finding process than if it originates during an investigation").

108. 68 F.3d 597 (2d Cir. 1995), *cert. denied*, 517 U.S. 1219 (1996).

109. *Id.* at 607. The court ruled the evidence inadmissible under a "totality of circumstances" approach. *See also* Hoult v. Hoult, 57 F.3d 1 (1st Cir. 1995). *See* § 12-5(D) *infra*.

110. The other approaches are: (1) The *procedural safeguards* approach — admissibility is conditioned on adherence to specified procedural safeguards designed to reduce suggestiveness. (2) The *discretionary admission* approach — the trial judge has discretion on a case-by-case basis to exclude hypnotically-refreshed testimony as unreliable. These are discussed in the following sections.

111. *See* FED. R. EVID. 612 (refreshing recollection).

112. *See* United States v. Valdez, 722 F.2d 1196, 1199 (5th Cir. 1984).

113. Scheflin, *supra* note 79, at 27.

114. 5 Md. App. 230, 246 A.2d 302 (1968), *cert. denied*, 395 U.S. 949 (1969).

appellate court wrote: "The fact that [the witness] had told different stories or had achieved her present knowledge after being hypnotized concerns the question of the weight of the evidence which the trier of facts, in this case the jury, must decide."[115] Similarly, an early federal case tracked *Harding*: "Wyller testified from his present recollection, refreshed by the [hypnotic] treatments. His credibility and the weight to be given such testimony were for the jury to determine."[116]

Other courts, both federal[117] and state,[118] followed the *Harding* approach. The precedential value of many of these cases, especially the early ones, is suspect. They were decided before the courts began to view hypnotically refreshed testimony critically and before the publication of the views of several authorities who questioned the reliability of such testimony.[119] Indeed, *Harding*, as well as one of the other early cases, was subsequently overruled.[120]

There seems little dispute that the *Harding* credibility approach rested on dubious scientific grounds.[121] One commentary pointed out that there "were serious shortcomings in this early decision [*Harding*], notably its failure to take adequate account of scientific evidence on the reliability of hypnotically refreshed recall."[122] In discussing *Harding* and its progeny, another commentary

---

115. *Id.* at 236, 246 A.2d at 306.

116. Wyller v. Fairchild Hiller Corp., 503 F.2d 506, 509-10 (9th Cir. 1974).

117. *E.g.*, United States v. Awkard, 597 F.2d 667, 669 (9th Cir.), *cert. denied*, 444 U.S. 885 (1979); United States v. Adams, 581 F.2d 193, 198 (9th Cir.), *cert. denied*, 439 U.S. 1006 (1978); Kline v. Ford Motor Co., 523 F.2d 1067, 1069 (9th Cir. 1975) ("That [a witness's] present memory depends upon refreshment claimed to have been induced under hypnosis goes to the credibility of her testimony not to the competence as a witness"); United States v. Narciso, 446 F. Supp. 252, 277-82 (E.D. Mich. 1977). *See also* United States v. Waksal, 539 F. Supp. 834, 838 (S.D. Fla. 1982), *rev'd*, 709 F.2d 653 (11th Cir. 1983). *See generally* Annot., *Necessity and Admissibility, in Federal Trial, of Expert or Opinion Testimony Regarding Use or Reliability of Hypnotically Refreshed Recollections,* 50 A.L.R. FED. 602 (1980).

118. *E.g.*, State v. Brown, 337 N.W.2d 138, 151 (N.D. 1983); State v. Jorgensen, 8 Or. App. 1, 9, 492 P.2d 312, 315 (1971); State v. Glebock, 616 S.W.2d 897, 903-04 (Tenn. Crim. App. 1981); Prime v. State, 767 P.2d 149, 153 (Wyo. 1989); Chapman v. State, 638 P.2d 1280, 1282 (Wyo. 1982). *See also* State v. Seagar, 341 N.W.2d 420, 431 (Iowa 1983); State v. Wren, 425 So. 2d 756, 759 (La. 1983).

119. *See* § 12-3 *supra*.

120. Collins v. State, 296 Md. 670, 464 A.2d 1028 (1983) (overruling *Harding*); State v. Peoples, 311 N.C. 515, 319 S.E.2d 177 (1984) (overruling State v. McQueen, 295 N.C. 96, 244 S.E.2d 414 (1978)).

121. *See* Burral v. State, 352 Md. 707, 720, 724 A.2d 65, 71 (1999) ("After a decade or so of success, the *Harding* approach came under greater scrutiny and was increasingly rejected, as the psychology of memory and the theory and practice of hypnosis in a forensic setting became better understood, in part as the result of greater attention being given to those matters in the scientific literature and in part through more extensive expert testimony in cases where previously hypnotized witnesses were called to testify").

122. ORNE, DINGES & ORNE, THE FORENSIC USE OF HYPNOSIS 2 (N.I.J. Dec. 1984).

noted: "Little attention was paid to the scientific literature on hypnosis and memory; legal discussions were brief."[123] Some of these courts simply failed to appreciate that the forensic use of hypnosis differed significantly from other uses. Hypnosis had long been recognized as a legitimate subject of clinical and laboratory research. The American Medical Association had recognized hypnosis as an accepted medical technique for psychotherapy, treatment of psychosomatic illnesses, and amnesia.[124] As the court in *State v. Mack*[125] remarked, however, for hypnosis to be "therapeutically useful, it need not produce historically accurate memory."[126]

A series of bizarre Wyoming cases illustrates the problems associated with this approach. In *Gee v. State*[127] even the prosecutor had difficulty listing the expert's qualifications. Nevertheless, the majority held the evidence admissible. The dissent replied:

> It follows, therefore, that a hobo passing through town or a derelict in the county jail could hypnotize a potential witness, and the witness' testimony would be admissible at trial.... There is a man in Oakland, California, who is the dean and lone 'professor' at 'Croaker College.' For the sum of $150 each, this man trains frogs to jump.... As part of his rigid training curriculum, the 'professor' claims that he hypnotizes the frog; while they are in their hypnotic trance, he plays an attitude-improvement tape to them. Under our present standards the dean of 'Croaker College' would be over-qualified as a hypnotist.[128]

In a later case, *Haselhuhn v. State*[129] the hypnotist, according to majority, was a non-professional with meager training in hypnotic techniques. From the dissent we learn that the "meager training" was a 32-hour home course and the hypnotist was a maintenance man at the Pacific Power and Light Company.[130]

Even proponents of admissibility believe that "[t]he 'open admissibility' rule is too lenient, yet it is still the law in Wyoming."[131]

---

123. SCHEFLIN & SHAPIRO, *supra* note 40, at 73.
124. *See* text accompanying note 38, *supra.*
125. 292 N.W.2d 764 (Minn. 1980).
126. *Id.* at 768.
127. 662 P.2d 103 (Wyo. 1983).
128. *Id.* at 105-06 & n.3.
129. 727 P.2d 280 (Wyo. 1986), *cert. denied*, 479 U.S. 1098 (1987).
130. *Id.* at 288.
131. Scheflin, *supra* note 79, at 28.

§ 12-5(C). Admission: Procedural Safeguards.

By 1980, the courts were taking a closer look at hypnotically-enhanced testimony. Some admitted hypnotically refreshed testimony provided that certain procedural safeguards were satisfied. The leading case was *State v. Hurd*,[132] decided by the New Jersey Supreme Court in 1981. Although recognizing the dangers associated with hypnotically refreshed testimony, the court in *Hurd* did not rule such evidence inadmissible. Instead, the court held that hypnotically refreshed testimony may be admitted if the party seeking admission establishes the reliability of the testimony by "clear and convincing evidence"[133] and the trial court finds that the procedures followed in the particular case were a reasonably reliable means of restoring the witness's recollection.[134]

In addition, the *Hurd* court adopted a number of procedural safeguards[135] that had been proposed by Dr. Martin Orne.[136]

> (1) A psychiatrist or psychologist experienced in the use of hypnosis must conduct the session. (2) The hypnotist must be independent of and not regularly employed by the prosecutor, investigator, or defense. (3) Any information provided the hypnotist prior to the hypnotic session must be recorded. (4) Before inducing hypnosis, the hypnotist must obtain from the subject a detailed description of the facts as the subject remembers them. (5) All contacts between the hypnotist and the subject must be recorded. The use of videotape is strongly encouraged but not mandatory. (6) Only the hypnotist and the subject should be present during the hypnotic session, including the prehypnotic testing and the posthypnotic interview.

These requirements were designed to prevent suggestion, either intentional or unintentional, and to preserve a record for review. The safeguards also applied to defense witnesses.[137] As noted earlier, Dr. Orne's present position is that

---

132. 86 N.J. 525, 432 A.2d 86 (1981).

133. *Id.* at 546, 432 A.2d at 97. The "clear and convincing evidence" standard is a more rigorous standard of proof than the typical preponderance of evidence (more probable than not) used for evidentiary issues.

134. *Id.* at 538, 432 A.2d at 92.

135. *Id.* at 545-46, 432 A.2d at 96-97.

136. The safeguards were first incorporated in an amicus curiae affidavit that was filed in Quaglino v. California, 23 Crim. L. Rep. (BNA) 4018 (Cal. App. 1977), *cert. denied*, 439 U.S. 875 (1978). *See* Orne, *supra* note 18; Orne, *The Use and Misuse of Hypnosis in Court*, 27 INT'L J. CLINICAL & EXPERIMENTAL HYPNOSIS 311, 335-36 (1979).

137. State v. L.K., 244 N.J. Super. 261, 271, 582 A.2d 297, 302 (A.D. 1990) ("[T]he procedural safeguards articulated in *Hurd* are applicable to both the defendant and the State").

hypnotically refreshed testimony should not be admitted at trial and therefore the safeguards are relevant for investigative purposes only.[138]

Fifteen years later, in *State v. Fertig*,[139] the New Jersey Supreme Court elaborated on the *Hurd* requirements. Perhaps more significantly, the court invited a reconsideration of *Hurd* in future cases. The court first explained *Hurd*:

> Under *Hurd* ... the proponent of hypnotically-refreshed testimony bears the burden of proving its reliability. The *Hurd* guidelines apply, even to hypnotic sessions that fail. Allowing the proponent of post-hypnotic testimony to sidestep *Hurd* by contending that the session failed invites abuse.... *Hurd* guidelines apply even if the State played no role in [the witness's] hypnosis.[140]

The court also stated that "when trial courts admit hypnotically-refreshed testimony, they should instruct the jury of the effect that hypnosis may have on that testimony."[141]

While the court declined to replace *Hurd* with the per se rule of exclusion as the defendant had requested, the court noted "several significant developments since we decided *Hurd*."[142] When *Hurd* was decided, a majority of courts had admitted hypnotically refreshed testimony. That had changed. Twenty-six jurisdictions exclude the evidence under the per se rule, and only four states consider such testimony generally admissible. Also, Dr. Orne, on whom the *Hurd* court had relied, has written that the procedural safeguards do not fully protect against the risks associated with this testimony. "Although mindful of the problems posed by hypnotically-refreshed testimony, we decline to abandon *Hurd* in the absence of a more complete record."[143]

Other courts adopted the *Hurd* safeguards, although strict compliance with all the safeguards was not always required by these courts.[144] Some courts added

---

138. *See* text accompanying notes 37 & 38, *supra*. *See also* Karlin & Orne, *supra* note 20, at 58 n.5 ("Unfortunately, the Hurd safeguards do not prevent the subject from being influenced by other postevent information and turning such information into 'memory' during hypnosis. Nor do they protect the process from the creation of confident errors nor from the effects of self-serving motivation, simulation, or lying").

139. 143 N.J. 115, 668 A.2d 1076 (1996).

140. *Id.* at 124, 668 A.2d at 1080.

141. *Id.* at 127, 668 A.2d at 1082.

142. *Id.* at 124, 668 A.2d at 1081.

143. *Id.* at 125, 668 A.2d at 1081.

144. *See* Sprynczynatyk v. General Motors Corp., 771 F.2d 1112, 1123 (8th Cir. 1985) (adopting a version of *Hurd* safeguards), *cert. denied*, 475 U.S. 1046 (1986); United States v. Harrington, 18 M.J. 797, 803 (A.C.M.R. 1984) (adequate but not strict compliance required); Brown v. State, 426 So. 2d 76, 91 (Fla. App. 1983) (approving some but not all safeguards); House v. State, 445 So. 2d 815, 826-27 (Miss. 1984) (substantial compliance required); State v. Beachum, 97 N.M. 682, 689-90, 643 P.2d 246, 253-54 (N.M. App. 1981), *writ quashed*, 98 N.M. 51, 644 P.2d

other safeguards. For example, the Eighth Circuit cited two additional considerations: (1) the appropriateness of using hypnosis for the kind of memory loss involved, and (2) whether there is any evidence to corroborate the hypnotically enhanced testimony.[145] To the extent that courts deviate from the *Hurd* safeguards they move toward the category of discretionary admissibility, also known as the "totality of circumstances" approach.[146]

Courts following the per se exclusion approach rejected the *Hurd* approach, finding the safeguards inadequate. For example, in *People v. Shirley* the California Supreme Court wrote:

> [V]irtually all of the [safeguards] are designed to prevent the hypnotist from exploiting the suggestibility of the subject; none will directly avoid the additional risks ... that the subject (1) will lose his critical judgment and begin to credit "memories" that were formerly viewed as unreliable, (2) will confuse actual recall with confabulation and will be unable to distinguish between the two, and (3) will exhibit an unwarranted confidence in the validity of his ensuing recollection.[147]

Nevertheless, even the courts that reject the procedural safeguards and follow the per se rule of exclusion often find the safeguards useful in addressing two of the exceptions to the per se rule: (1) determining the admissibility of a witness's prehypnotic testimony,[148] and (2) determining the admissibility of a defendant's hypnotically refreshed testimony.[149]

1040 (1982); State v. Weston, 16 Ohio App. 3d 279, 317, 475 N.E.2d 805, 813 (1984) (no single safeguard determinative); State v. Adams, 418 N.W.2d 618, 622-24 (S.D. 1988) (substantial compliance).

See also OR. REV. STAT. § 136.675 (videotape of hypnotic session required); State v. Varela, 112 N.M. 538, 541-42, 817 P.2d 731, 735-36 (1991) (safeguards not required when statements about sex abuse made during therapeutic session were not anticipated), *cert. denied*, 112 N.M. 440 (1991).

145. Sprynczynatyk v. General Motors Corp., 771 F.2d 1112, 1123 (8th Cir. 1985), *cert. denied*, 475 U.S. 1046 (1986).

146. The *Hurd* safeguards are one of a number of circumstances considered in that approach. *See* § 12-5(D) *infra*. *See also* Sheflin, *supra* note 79, at 29 ("These courts evolved a related rule called the 'totality of the circumstances' rule").

147. 31 Cal. 3d at 39, 641 P.2d at 787, 181 Cal. Rptr. at 255. *Accord* State *ex rel.* Collins v. Superior Court, 132 Ariz. 180, 207-08, 644 P.2d 1266, 1293-94 (1982); State v. Collins, 296 Md. 670, 700-02, 464 A.2d 1028, 1044 (1983); People v. Hughes, 59 N.Y.2d 523, 544, 453 N.E.2d 484, 495, 466 N.Y.S.2d 255, 265 (1983).

148. *See* § 12-5(A) *supra*.

149. *See* § 12-6(A) *infra*.

§ 12-5(D). Admission: Discretionary Admissibility.

Later cases admitting hypnotically refreshed testimony embraced another approach. They recognized a trial court's discretion to exclude hypnotically influenced testimony if it is found to be unreliable.[150] For example, the Fifth Circuit excluded hypnotically refreshed testimony in one case and admitted it in another. In the first case the procedures used during the hypnotic session were "unduly suggestive" and involved the "identification of a person known by the witness to be under suspicion, whom the witness had nevertheless been *unable* to identify before being hypnotized."[151] These problems were not present in the second case.[152]

This category is also known as the "totality of circumstances" or "case by case" approach.[153] This approach is the one "most frequently taken by the federal courts."[154]

These cases view the *Hurd* safeguards as relevant, but not determinative, factors in evaluating admissibility. For example, in *Zani v. State*[155] the Texas Court of Criminal Appeals ruled that the proponent must show, by "clear and convincing evidence," that the testimony was trustworthy in light of the totality of the circumstances. The court cited ten factors: (1) The level of the hypnotist's training in the clinical uses and forensic applications of hypnosis. (2) The hypnotist's independence from law enforcement investigators, the prosecution, and the defense. (3) The existence of a record of any information given or known by the hypnotist concerning the case prior to the session. (4) The existence of a written or recorded account of the facts as the subject remembered them prior to undergoing hypnosis. (5) The creation of recordings of all contacts between the hypnotist and the subject. (6) The presence of persons other than the hypnotist and the subject during any phase of the session. (7) The appropriateness of the

---

150. *See* United States v. Charles, 561 F. Supp. 694, 697 (S.D. Tex. 1983) (exclusion under FED. EVID. R. 403); State v. Armstrong, 110 Wis. 2d 555, 571-73, 329 N.W.2d 386, 394-95, *cert. denied*, 461 U.S. 946 (1983).

151. United States v. Valdez, 722 F.2d 1196, 1202-03 (5th Cir. 1984).

152. United States v. Harrelson, 754 F.2d 1153 (5th Cir. 1985) (admissible).

153. *E.g.*, People v. Romero, 745 P.2d 1003, 1016-17 (Colo. 1987) ("totality of circumstances" approach), *cert. denied*, 485 U.S. 990 (1988); State v. Iwakiri, 106 Idaho 618, 625-26, 682 P.2d 571, 578-79 (1984) ("totality of circumstances" approach); State v. Johnston, 39 Ohio St. 3d 48, 64, 529 N.E.2d 898, 905 (1988).

154. Borawick v. Shay, 68 F.3d 597, 605 (2d Cir. 1995) ("While recognizing the benefits of the *Hurd* guidelines, these courts conclude that the district court should be given discretion to balance all of the factors to determine the reliability of the evidence and the probative versus prejudicial effect of the testimony"), *cert. denied*, 517 U.S. 1219 (1996).

155. 758 S.W.2d 233, 243-44 (Tex. Crim. App. 1988). *See also* Soliz v. State, 961 S.W.2d 545, 549 (Tex. App. 1997) (hypnotically-refreshed testimony excluded because the police officer was not independent, other persons were present at the session, and the session were not properly videotaped).

induction and memory retrieval techniques used. (8) The appropriateness of using hypnosis on the kind of memory loss involved. (9) The existence of any evidence to corroborate the hypnotically-enhanced testimony. (10) The presence or absence of overt or subtle cuing or suggestion of answers during the hypnotic session.

In *Soliz v. State*,[156] another Texas appellate court ruled that a police officer was not qualified under a state statute that prohibited hypnotic interviews by the police unless the officer had completed a training course approved by a state commission and passed an examination designed to test the officer's knowledge of investigative hypnosis.

Some commentators recommend this approach: "The present majority rule, which automatically disqualifies any post-hypnotic recollection, is unfair, unjust, and unnecessary."[157] Others reject it: "While the totality-of-circumstances test is the only reasonable alternative to a per se exclusion, to paraphrase the *Shirley* court, the game is really not worth the candle."[158]

§ 12-5(E). Notice, Discovery & Defense Experts.

In jurisdictions that admit hypnotically refreshed testimony, the prosecution is required to notify the defense that the witness has been hypnotized. For example, in *United States v. Miller*[159] a new trial was granted because the prosecution failed to inform the defense that a key witness had undergone hypnosis. Similarly, in *Orndorff v. Lockhart*[160] the Eighth Circuit ruled that the failure to notify the defense that a witness had been hypnotized violated the Confrontation

---

156. 961 S.W.2d 545, 549 (Tex. App. 1997) (citing Tex. Gov't Code Ann. § 415.036(a) (Vernon 1990)).

157. Scheflin, *supra* note 79, at 30.

158. Karlin & Orne, *supra* note 20, at 82 (citing People v. Shirley, 723 P.2d at 1366, 181 Cal. Rptr. at 256).

159. 411 F.2d 825 (2d Cir. 1969). *See also* Brown v. State, 426 So. 2d 76, 80 (Fla. App. 1983) ("[D]ue process demands that counsel be afforded a fairer means by which to prepare his defense to this critical evidence").

160. 998 F.2d 1426 (8th Cir. 1993) (error harmless as to murder conviction but not as to death penalty), *cert. denied*, 511 U.S. 1060 (1994). *See also* E. Connors, T. Lundregan, N. Miller & T. McEwen, Convicted by Juries, Exonerated by Science: Case Studies in the Use of DNA Evidence to Establish Innocence After Trial 15-18 (1996) ("In *Honaker*, the defendant's attorney alleged that the government intentionally kept exculpatory evidence from the defense, including information that two of the government's witnesses were secretly hypnotized to enhance their testimony and the prosecution's criminalist was never told that Honaker had a vasectomy (and could not have been the source of the sperm in the victim"); Fricker, *State Falters in Retrial of Escaped Con*, 81 A.B.A. J. 38, 40 (June 1995) ("The defense was not told of the hypnosis during the first trial, and the tape of that session has since been erased").

Clause because it deprived the accused of the opportunity to cross-examine the witness on this issue. Other cases are in accord.[161]

In addition, all statements and proceedings concerning pretrial hypnosis are discoverable; that is, they must be disclosed to the opposing party before trial.[162] In *Emmett v. Ricketts*[163] the court held that the failure of the prosecution to disclose prior statements of a government witness, including hypnotic interviews, violated due process under *Brady v. Maryland.*[164] Similarly, the court in *Jean v. Rice*[165] held the failure to disclose a tape of a hypnotic session violated *Brady*.

A defendant also has the right to attack the credibility of a witness who has been hypnotized and the right to introduce expert testimony on this issue.[166] Because most defendants are indigent, the right to the appointment of a defense expert is often critical. In *Little v. Armontrout*[167] the Eighth Circuit recognized this right: "[T]he denial of a state-provided expert on hypnosis to assist this indigent defendant rendered the trial fundamentally unfair and requires that the conviction be set aside."[168]

§ 12-6. Constitutional Issues.

Hypnotically refreshed testimony raises a number of different constitutional issues, some of which have been discussed in the preceding sections. This section considers several other issues.

§ 12-6(A). Accused's Right to Testify.

In *Rock v. Arkansas*[169] the U.S. Supreme Court considered the admissibility of the testimony of a defendant whose memory had been refreshed by hypnosis. *Rock* was charged with the death of her husband but could not remember the precise details of the incident. After hypnosis, she recalled that she did not have

---

161. *See also* State v. Armstrong, 110 Wis. 2d 555, 571-73, 329 N.W.2d 386, 395, *cert. denied*, 461 U.S. 946 (1983); State *ex rel.* Collins v. Superior Court, 132 Ariz. 180, 210, 644 P.2d 1266, 1296 (1982); People v. Tait, 99 Mich. App. 19, 26-27, 297 N.W.2d 853, 856 (1980); State v. Hurd, 86 N.J. 525, 543, 432 A.2d 86, 95 (1981); Gee v. State, 662 P.2d 103, 105 (Wyo. 1983).

162. Gee v. State, 662 P.2d 103, 104 (Wyo. 1983). *See also* OR. REV. STAT. § 136.675-.695 (videotape of hypnotic session is discoverable); State v. Hurd, 86 N.J. 525, 543, 432 A.2d 86, 95 (1981).

163. 397 F. Supp. 1025 (N.D. Ga. 1975).

164. 373 U.S. 83 (1963). For a further discussion of *Brady, see* Chapter 3.

165. 945 F.2d 82, 87 (4th Cir. 1991). In later proceedings involving the same case, Jean v. Collins, 155 F.3d 701 (4th Cir. 1998), the court ruled that the police officers had immunity in a civil rights case for failing to turn over audiotapes of the hypnosis sessions.

166. State v. Armstrong, 110 Wis. 2d 555, 560, 329 N.W.2d 386, 389, *cert. denied*, 461 U.S. 946 (1983).

167. 835 F.2d 1240 (8th Cir. 1987), *cert. denied*, 487 U.S. 1210 (1988).

168. *Id.* at 1243. For a discussion of the right to a defense expert, *see* Chapter 4.

169. 483 U.S. 44 (1987).

her finger on the trigger at the time the gun discharged. She also recalled that the weapon fired when her husband grabbed her. Based on this information, her attorney had the gun examined by a firearms expert, who concluded that it was defective and prone to fire, when hit or dropped, without the trigger being pulled. The trial court excluded her testimony because she had been hypnotized, a ruling that was upheld by the Arkansas Supreme Court under the per se rule of exclusion.

The U.S. Supreme Court reversed. The Court began its analysis by recognizing an accused's right to testify: "At this point in the development of our adversary system, it cannot be doubted that a defendant in a criminal case has the right to take the witness stand and to testify in his or her own defense."[170] This right is based on due process, the right of compulsory process, the right to counsel, and the privilege against self-incrimination. Although the Court recognized the problems associated with hypnotically refreshed testimony, it found the Arkansas per se rule of inadmissibility an arbitrary restriction on the defendant's right to testify.

Two limitations in the Court's opinion are noteworthy. First, the Court explicitly limited its decision to the testimony of the accused: "This case does not involve the admissibility of testimony of previously hypnotized witnesses other than criminal defendants and we express no opinion on that issue."[171] In *Burral v. State*[172] the Maryland Court of Appeals refused to extend the *Rock* rationale to defense witnesses, noting that "[t]here is no doubt but that *Rock* itself was carefully confined to the testimony of the defendant."[173] The court went on to find that the "same deficiencies" concerning hypnotically-refreshed testimony "that were prevalent in 1983 appear to remain prevalent today."[174]

---

170. *Id.* at 49. *See also* United States v. Scheffer, 523 U.S. 303, 118 S. Ct. 1261, 1268 (1998) ("In holding that the exclusion of [Rock's testimony] violated the defendant's 'right to present a defense,' we noted that the rule deprived the jury of the testimony of the only witness who was at the scene and had firsthand knowledge of the facts. Moreover, the rule infringed upon the accused's interest in testifying in her own defense — an interest that we deemed particularly significant, as it is the defendant who is the target of any criminal prosecution. For this reason, we stated that an accused ought to be allowed 'to present his own version of the events in his own words'") (citations omitted).

171. *Id.* at 58 n.15. *See generally* Note, *Rock v. Arkansas: Hypnotically "Refreshed" Testimony or Hypnotically "Manufactured" Testimony?*, 74 CORNELL L. REV. 136 (1988); Note, *Fifth, Sixth, and Fourteenth Amendments — Constitutional Paradigm for Determining the Admissibility of Hypnotically Refreshed Testimony*, 78 J. CRIM. L. & CRIMINOLOGY 858 (1988).

172. 352 Md. 707, 724 A.2d 65 (1999).

173. *Id.* at 736, 724 A.2d at 79.

174. *Id.* at 740, 724 A.2d at 81. *See also* Giuliana, *Between Rock and a Hurd Place: Protecting the Criminal Defendant's Right to Testify after Her Testimony Has Been Hypnotically Refreshed*, 65 FORDHAM L. REV. 2151, 2186 (1997).

Second, the *Rock* Court did not rule that the defendant's testimony was automatically admissible. It recognized that an approach less restrictive than Arkansas' rule of per se exclusion may satisfy constitutional guarantees: "The State would be well within its powers if it established guidelines to aid trial courts in the evaluation of posthypnosis testimony and it may be able to show that testimony in a particular case is so unreliable that exclusion is justified."[175]

Several courts have addressed this aspect of *Rock*. For example, the Kansas Supreme Court adopted the *Hurd* safeguards for determining the admissibility of hypnotically refreshed testimony by an accused.[176] The court also added a new safeguard: that the hypnosis be conducted in a neutral setting.[177] Moreover, the prosecution must be notified and an out-of-court hearing held to determine whether the accused has "substantially" complied with the guidelines by a "preponderance of evidence." The Louisiana court of appeals required the defendant to demonstrate "strict compliance" with the *Hurd* safeguards by "clear and convincing evidence."[178] Wisconsin used a "totality of circumstances" approach to determine reliability in this context.[179]

In *Rault v. Butler*[180] the Fifth Circuit ruled that *Rock* did not apply where the defendant proposed to testify while hypnotized, noting "that in *Rock* the defendant was *not* going to testify *while* in a state of hypnosis which is what Rault's counsel proposed having Rault do in this case. Here the defense proposed to have Dr. Steck hypnotize Rault in open court before the jury, and then have Rault testify while thus hypnotized."[181]

Two commentators observed: "The *Rock* case finally ended in a plea bargain, and many found Rock's hypnotically influenced memory that the shooting was accidental both self-serving and improbable."[182]

§ 12-6(B). Right of Confrontation & Due Process.

In adopting the per se rule of exclusion, some courts based their decisions on constitutional, rather than evidentiary, grounds. According to the Arizona Supreme Court, "there is a strong belief among several authorities that hypnotism of a witness renders subsequent cross-examination ineffective.... Until the general scientific reliability of hypnotism ... [is] established and/or the barriers

---

175. 483 U.S. at 61.

176. State v. Butterworth, 246 Kan. 541, 552-54, 792 P.2d 1049, 1057 (1990).

177. *Id.* at 554, 792 P.2d at 1058.

178. State v. Holden, 554 So. 2d 121, 126 (La. App. 1989); State v. Woodfin, 539 So. 2d 645, 649 (La. App. 1989). *See also* State v. L.K., 244 N.J. Super. 261, 276, 582 A.2d 297, 305 (1990).

179. State v. Coogan, 154 Wis. 2d 387, 395-96, 453 N.W.2d 186, 188 (App.), *review denied*, 454 N.W.2d 806 (1990).

180. 826 F.2d 299 (5th Cir. 1987), *cert. denied*, 483 U.S. 1042 (1987).

181. *Id.* at 303.

182. Karlin & Orne, *supra* note 20, at 181.

which it raises to effective cross-examination are somehow overcome, we think the confrontation clause of the Sixth Amendment ... requires [exclusion]."[183] Other courts concurred.[184] There is support for this view in the scientific literature. Some commentators believed that the adversary process and the right of cross-examination "can be subverted by a technique, such as hypnosis, that greatly facilitates the reconstruction of history, that allows an individual to be influenced unwittingly, and that may catalyze beliefs into 'memories.' The resultant testimony may then be presented under oath by an honest individual who is convinced of the accuracy of what may well be pseudomemories."[185]

In contrast, most courts reject the confrontation argument. In *Rock v. Arkansas*[186] the U.S. Supreme Court recognized that hypnosis made "effective cross-examination more difficult."[187] In a later passage, however, the Court wrote that "[c]ross-examination, even in the face of a confident defendant, is an effective tool for revealing inconsistencies."[188] *Rock* involved the testimony of an accused who had been hypnotized; the Court, as explained earlier, was not concerned with the testimony of a prosecution witness. Nevertheless, the Eleventh Circuit subsequently wrote that *Rock* "teaches that, although hypnosis may make effective cross-examination more difficult, it does not always make it impossible, thereby preserving the opportunity for effective cross-examination safeguarded by the Sixth Amendment."[189]

---

183. State v. Mena, 128 Ariz. 226, 232, 624 P.2d 1274, 1280 (1981).

184. Contreras v. State, 718 P.2d 129, 139 (Alaska 1986) (violation of state constitution); State *ex rel.* Collins v. Superior Court, 132 Ariz. 180, 189, 644 P.2d 1266, 1275 (1982); State v. Gonzales, 415 Mich. 615, 626-27, 329 N.W.2d 743, 748 (1982), *modified on other grounds*, 417 Mich. 968, 336 N.W.2d 751 (1983).

185. Orne, Whitehouse, Dinges & Orne, *Reconstructing Memory Through Hypnosis: Forensic and Clinical Implications, in* HYPNOSIS AND MEMORY 21, 55 (H.M. Pettinati ed. 1988).

186. 483 U.S. 44 (1987).

187. *Id.* at 60.

188. *Id.* at 61.

189. Bundy v. Dugger, 850 F.2d 1402, 1415 (11th Cir. 1988), *cert. denied*, 488 U.S. 1034 (1989). *Accord* Pruett v. Norris, 153 F.3d 579, 589 (8th Cir. 1998) ("The admission of hypnotically refreshed testimony does not invariably result in constitutional error"); Armstrong v. Young, 34 F.3d 421, 429-30 (7th Cir. 1994) (confrontation rights not infringed but recommending *Hurd* safeguards to make judicial task of evaluating reliability easier), *cert. denied*, 514 U.S. 1021 (1995); Boykin v. Leapley, 28 F.3d 788, 793-94 (8th Cir. 1994) (no confrontation violation on facts of case); White v. Ieyoub, 25 F.3d 245, 247 (5th Cir. 1994) ("We reject the proposition that either due process or confrontation guarantees require a *per se* bar to the admission of post-hypnosis testimony"); Biskup v. McCaughtry, 20 F.3d 245, 255 (7th Cir. 1994), *cert. denied*, 516 U.S. 1172 (1996); Beachum v. Tansy, 903 F.2d 1321, 1327-28 (10th Cir. 1990), *cert. denied*, 498 U.S. 904 (1990); McQueen v. Garrison, 814 F.2d 951, 961-62 (4th Cir. 1987), *cert. denied*, 484 U.S. 944 (1987); Beck v. Norris, 801 F.2d 242, 245 (6th Cir. 1986); Harker v. Maryland, 800 F.2d 437, 443 (4th Cir. 1986); Wicker v. McCotter, 783 F.2d 487, 493 (5th Cir.), *cert. denied*, 478 U.S. 1010 (1986); United States v. Kimberlin, 805 F.2d 210, 219 (7th Cir. 1986), *cert. denied*, 483 U.S. 1023 (1987); Clay v. Vose, 771 F.2d 1, 5 (1st Cir. 1985), *cert. denied*, 475 U.S. 1022 (1986); United

In addition, several courts have ruled that per se exclusion is not required by the Due Process Clause.[190] They also indicate, however, that a due process and confrontation violation may arise from the circumstances of a particular case.[191]

§ 12-6(C). Pretrial Identifications.

The U.S. Supreme Court has held that pretrial identification procedures that create a "substantial likelihood of misidentification"[192] violate due process. This constitutional rule predates the controversy over hypnotically-refreshed testimony; it arose in lineup and photographic identification cases.[193] However, it is also applicable if an identification follows hypnosis.[194] For example, in *Hurd* the New

---

States v. Adams, 581 F.2d 193, 199 (9th Cir.), *cert. denied*, 439 U.S. 1006 (1978); Davis v. Singletary, 853 F. Supp. 1492, 1529 (M.D. Fla. 1994); Stafford v. Maynard, 848 F. Supp. 946, 958 (W.D. Okla. 1994), *appeal dismissed*, 60 F.3d 837 (10th Cir. 1995); Chamblee v. State, 527 So. 2d 173, 177 (Ala. Crim. App. 1988); State v. Evans, 316 S.C. 303, 309, 450 S.E.2d 47, 51 (1994) ("If post-hypnotic testimony is shown to be independent of the dangers associated with hypnosis, the admission of the testimony does not violate the Confrontation Clause"); State v. Armstrong, 110 Wis. 2d 555, 569-70, 329 N.W.2d 386, 393-94, *cert. denied*, 461 U.S. 946 (1983); Pote v. State, 695 P.2d 617, 627 (Wyo. 1985);

190. *See* White v. Ieyoub, 25 F.3d 245, 247 (5th Cir. 1994) ("We reject the proposition that either due process or confrontation guarantees require a *per se* bar to the admission of post-hypnosis testimony"); Biskup v. McCaughtry, 20 F.3d 245, 252 (7th Cir. 1994) ("The long and the short of this discussion is that there is no *per se* rule bottomed in the due process clause of the Fourteenth Amendment"), *cert. denied*, 516 U.S. 1172 (1996).

191. The Fifth Circuit has written:

> We are persuaded that on a case-by-case basis the court should determine whether the defendant has shown, from the totality of the circumstances, that the post-hypnosis testimony is unreliable.... [I]t is preferable, although not constitutionally mandated, that the hypnosis be performed by a professional trained in hypnosis; that the hypnotist be independent of either party; that the hypnotist's pre-session knowledge of the case be kept to a minimum and recorded as a check on suggestion; that the hypnotist obtain a description of the case from the subject before inducing hypnosis as a check on confabulation; that the session be recorded, preferably videotaped; and that only participants in the hypnotic session be present.

White v. Ieyoub, 25 F.3d 245, 248-49 (5th Cir. 1994).

192. Neil v. Biggers, 409 U.S. 188, 201 (1972). *See also* Manson v. Brathwaite, 432 U.S. 98, 114 (1977) ("[R]eliability is the linchpin in determining the admissibility of identification testimony ..."); Watkins v. Sowders, 449 U.S. 341, 347 (1981) ("It is the reliability of identification evidence that primarily determines its admissibility ...").

193. *See* § 9-2, *supra.*

194. *E.g.*, Armstrong v. Young, 34 F.3d 421, 428 (7th Cir. 1994) (even if lineup identification after hypnosis was unduly suggestive, no due process violation in this case), *cert. denied*, 514 U.S. 1021 (1995); United States v. Narciso, 446 F. Supp. 252, 279-82 (E.D. Mich. 1977); State v. Greer, 609 S.W.2d 423, 433-35 (Mo. App. 1980), *vacated on other grounds*, 450 U.S. 1027 (1981); State v. Beachum, 97 N.M. 682, 691-92, 643 P.2d 246, 255-56 (N.M. App. 1981), *writ quashed*, 98 N.M.

Jersey Supreme Court acknowledged: "[W]here the use of hypnosis results in a subsequent out-of-court or in-court identification of the defendant, the defendant may also challenge on constitutional grounds the admissibility of testimony concerning the identification."[195] In some decisions courts excluded evidence of identifications on this ground,[196] while in other cases courts have held that in-court identification derived from a source independent of the hypnotically influenced identification.[197]

Several courts have ruled that, in contrast to the typical identification case, the prosecution bears the burden of proving that the hypnotically influenced identification is reliable. For example, in *State v. Armstrong*[198] the Wisconsin Supreme Court wrote: "[B]ecause of the great susceptibility a hypnotized subject has to suggestions made by the hypnotist, ... the burden should be on the proponent to demonstrate that the hypnotic session was not affected by impermissible suggestiveness such as to render the subsequent testimony inadmissible."[199]

§ 12-6(D). Impeachment.

A different constitutional issue is raised when the defendant seeks to cross-examine a prosecution witness concerning inconsistent statements made by the witness while under hypnosis. Here, the defendant is asserting the right to confront adverse witnesses under the sixth amendment. The New York Court of Appeals has rejected such an argument, at least in cases where the defendant has conceded that the hypnotized statements were unreliable.[200]

51, 644 P.2d 1040 (1982); People v. McDowell, 103 Misc. 2d 831, 837, 427 N.Y.S.2d 181, 184 (Sup. Ct. 1980); Vester v. State, 684 S.W.2d 715, 722 (Tex. App. 1983).

195. State v. Hurd, 86 N.J. 525, 547, 432 A.2d 86, 97 (1981).

196. *E.g.*, People v. Clark, 3 Cal. 4th 41, 833 P.2d 561, 10 Cal. Rptr. 2d 554, 615 (1992) (Witness's "photographic-lineup and in-court identifications of defendant — which postdate the hypnotic session — were inadmissible..."), *cert. denied*, 507 U.S. 993 (1993); People v. Cohoon, 104 Ill. 2d 295, 472 N.E.2d 403 (1984).

197. *See* Strong v. State, 435 N.E.2d 969 (Ind. 1982); Merrifield v. State, 272 Ind. 579, 400 N.E.2d 146 (1980). *But see* People v. Cohoon, 104 Ill. 2d 295, 472 N.E.2d 403 (1984).

198. 110 Wis. 2d 555, 329 N.W.2d 386, *cert. denied*, 461 U.S. 946 (1983).

199. *Id.* at 571, 329 N.W.2d at 394. *Accord* United States v. Gatto, 924 F.2d 491, 500 (3d Cir. 1991) ("[T]he government introduced clear and convincing evidence showing that [the witness's] prospective trial testimony had an independent basis..."); Commonwealth v. Juvenile, 381 Mass. 727, 734-35, 412 N.E.2d 339, 344 (1980). *But see* State v. Hurd, 86 N.J. 525, 548, 432 A.2d 86, 97-98 (1981) (burden on defendant on constitutional issue).

200. People v. Hults, 76 N.Y.2d 190, 199, 556 N.E.2d 1077, 1082, 557 N.Y.S.2d 270, 275 (1990).

§ 12-7. Testifying While Hypnotized.

There are only a few cases in which a witness proposed to testify while in a trance,[201] and the courts overwhelming reject this type of testimony. In *Rault v. Butler*[202] the Fifth Circuit ruled that *Rock* did not apply where the defendant proposed to testify while hypnotized, noting "that in *Rock* the defendant was *not* going to testify *while* in a state of hypnosis which is what Rault's counsel proposed having Rault do in this case. Here the defense proposed to have Dr. Steck hypnotize Rault in open court before the jury, and then have Rault testify while thus hypnotized."[203]

§ 12-8. Repressed Memories.

Issues concerning the repressed memory controversy often, but not always, involve the use of hypnosis.[204] A number of books[205] and articles[206] have

---

201. *But see* Dorsey v. State, 206 Ga. App. 709, 426 S.E.2d 224, 227 (1993) (A victim of sex abuse had developed a "dissociative disorder in which she had two different personalities" and was permitted to testify in a dissociative state; court distinguished hypnosis cases; "Perhaps not surprisingly, we could find no law in any jurisdiction regarding the admissibility of testimony of a witness in a dissociative state").

202. 826 F.2d 299 (5th Cir. 1987), *cert. denied*, 483 U.S. 1042 (1987).

203. *Id.* at 303. *See* § 12-6(A) *supra* (discussing *Rock*).

204. *See* Scheflin, *supra* note 4, at 34 ("Beginning in 1986, when the first appellate court decided the first repressed memory case (*Tyson v. Tyson*, 1986), a fierce debate has raged in scientific and public circles about two issues: Do repressed memories exist? And, if so, are they accurate?") (citing Tyson v. Tyson, 107 Wash.2d 72, 727 P.2d 226 (1986)).

205. *E.g.*, E. LOFTUS & K. KETCHAM, THE MYTH OF REPRESSED MEMORY: FALSE MEMORIES AND ALLEGATIONS OF SEXUAL ABUSE (1994); M. PENDERGRAST, VICTIMS OF MEMORY (1995); L. TERR, UNCHAINED MEMORIES: TRUE STORIES OF TRAUMATIC MEMORIES, LOST AND FOUND (1994).

206. *E.g.*, Ernsdorff & Loftus, *Let Sleeping Memories Lie? Words of Caution About Tolling the Statute of Limitations in Cases of Memory Repression*, 84 J. CRIM. L. & CRIMINOLOGY 129 (1993); Golding, Sego, Sanchez & Hasemann, *The Believability of Repressed Memories*, 19 LAW & HUM. BEHAV. 569 (1995); Hakim, *Admissibility Of Testimony Following Hypnosis*, 18 J. JUV. L. 215 (1997); Hough, *Recovered Memories of Childhood Sexual Abuse: Applying the Daubert Standard in State Courts*, 69 S. CAL. L. REV. 855 (1996); Loftus, *The Reality of Repressed Memories*, 48 AM. PSYCHOLOGIST 518 (1993); Lustberg, *Hypnotic Memories of Childhood Sexual Abuse: An Argument For Liberal Admissibility In Civil Cases*, 22 VT. L. REV. 655 (1998); Pope & Hudson, *Can Memories of Childhood Sexual Abuse Be Repressed?*, 25 PSYCHOL. MED. 121 (1995); Note, *The Necessity of Memory Experts for the Defense in Prosecutions for Child Sexual Abuse Based Upon Repressed Memories*, 32 AM. CRIM. L. REV. 69 (1994); Note, *Recovered Memories of Childhood Abuse: Should Long-Buried Memories Be Admissible Testimony?*, 37 B.C. L. REV. 591 (1996).

See also Symposium, *Delayed Memory Evidence*, 2 SHEPARD'S EXPERT & SCI. EVID. Q. 389-468 (Fall 1994).

addressed the subject. Most of the cases are civil actions, either against the alleged abuser or against the therapist for allegedly planting false memories.[207]

Borawick v. Shay[208] is a leading and controversial case.[209] The alleged victim had no memory of sexual abuse for twenty years and then, after hypnotic therapy, she accused her aunt and uncle of abusing her when she was four and seven years of age. The court recognized that it was dealing with a case of first impression – *i.e.*, "the admissibility of testimony about memories of childhood sexual abuse that are recalled for the first time in adulthood following the use of hypnosis as part of psychotherapy."[210] The court ruled the evidence inadmissible under a "totality of circumstances" approach.[211] First, the court held that "it is beyond question that [the hypnotist] lacked adequate professional qualifications."[212] Second, "no videotapes, audiotapes, or event contemporaneously-drafted medical reports existed."[213] Moreover, the "inherent incredibility of Borawick's allegations"[214] influenced the court. The court also observed: "We do not believe that *Daubert* is directly applicable to the issue here since *Daubert* concerns the admissibility of data derived from scientific techniques or expert opinions."[215] Nevertheless, "[e]ven though *Daubert* does not provide direct guidance, our

---

207. A number of courts have found that repressed memories do exist. *See* Isely v. Cauchin Province, 877 F. Supp. 1055 (E.D. Mich. 1995); Shahzade v. Gregory, 923 F. Supp. 286 (D. Mass. 1996).

208. 68 F.3d 597 (2d Cir. 1995), *cert. denied*, 517 U.S. 1219 (1996). *See also* Topham, *Borawick v. Shay: The Admissibility Of Hypnotically-Induced Memories*, 27 GOLDEN GATE U. L. REV. 423 (1997).

209. *Compare* Karlin & Orne, *Hypnosis and the Iatrogenic Creation of Memory: On the Need for a Per Se Exclusion of Testimony Based on Hypnotically Influenced Memory*, 14 CULTIC STUDIES J. 172, 176, 187 (1997) ("[T]he present authors do not believe that all recovered memories, even all those elicited with hypnosis, are false"; "[A] good deal of what is said to be independent confirmation proves ephemeral when considered seriously"), *with* Scheflin, *supra* note 4, at 33 ("Let Ms. Borawick have her hearing so we see what she can prove").

210. 68 F.3d at 600.

211. *Id. See also* Hoult v. Hoult, 57 F.3d 1, 3 (1st Cir. 1995) ("Plaintiff alleged that she had repressed all memory of the abuse until she began to recapture those memories during therapy sessions in October 1985, when she was twenty four"), *cert. denied*, 119 S. Ct. 2367 (1999).

212. 68 F.3d at 609.

213. *Id.*

214. "Borawick has levelled fanciful accusations of sexual abuse against numerous persons other than the defendants in this matter that include persons both familiar and unfamiliar to her. For example, Borawick allegedly recalls being raped and sexually abused at the age of three during rituals by men who she believed to be members of the Masons. She also purports to recollect several incidents in which she was drugged by injection as well as an incident in which she was forced to drink blood at a ritual involving a dead pig, incense, chanting, and people dressed in black gowns." *Id.*

215. *Id.* at 610.

decision today is informed by the principles underlying the Supreme Court's holding."[216]

Similarly, in *Ramona v. Superior Court*,[217] a civil action against a father, a California appellate court held that "the use of sodium amytal to retrieve repressed memories of child sexual molestation is a scientific technique or method which is subject to the *Kelly* requirements of reliability and acceptance by the relevant scientific community."[218] The court went on to hold that general acceptance did not exist.[219]

There are several criminal cases. Perhaps the most notorious was *Franklin v. Duncan*,[220] where the defendant was accused of a 1969 murder. His daughter did not recall the event until twenty years later.[221] The conviction was overturned on constitutional, not evidentiary, grounds.[222]

In *State v. Hungerford*[223] the New Hampshire Supreme Court ruled that evidence based on repressed memories (self-induced trance, visualization techniques, flashbacks, inner-child therapy) had not been shown to be reliable.

---

216 *Id.*

217. 57 Cal. App. 4th 107, 66 Cal. Rptr. 2d 766 (1997). After a counselor told her mother "that up to 80 percent of persons with eating disorders have been sexually abused, Stephanie asked Holly whether Gary had sexually abused her. At that time, Holly did not claim to have been abused." *Id.* at 769.

218. *Id.* at 121, 66 Cal. Rptr. 2d at 776.

219. "Even though she may have recalled and related certain events before the sodium amytal interview, she was uncertain whether they were actual events until after the interview, thus rendering her memories uncertain and subject to contamination during the interview." *Id.* at 778. *See also* Franklin v. Stevenson, 1999 Utah LEXIS 95 (June 18, 1999) ("[B]ecause the scientific reliability of the foundations on which these so-called 'relaxation techniques' are based was not established, the testimony based on memories recovered through use of those techniques is thereby tainted").

220. 884 F. Supp. 1435 (N. Cal. 1995), *aff'd*, 70 F.3d 75, 78 (9th Cir. 1995) ("The prosecutor's comments regarding Franklin's post-*Miranda* silence and the jury instruction regarding adoptive admissions in the context of the facts of this case had a substantial and injurious effect or influence on the jury's verdict"). *See also* MACLEAN, ONCE UPON A TIME: A TRUE STORY OF MEMORY, MURDER, AND THE LAW (1993); FRANKLIN & WRIGHT, SINS OF THE FATHER (1991) (witness's book).

221. 884 F. Supp. at 1441 ("Franklin-Lipsker admitted that she had made statements about being hypnotized to her brother and mother, but said that she had lied to her brother and mother in making such statements"). *See also Repressed Memory Case Unravels*, A.B.A. J. 40 (Nov. 1996) ("But [the prosecutor's] case was seriously jeopardized when Eileen Franklin also accused her father of two other murders he couldn't have committed. And it may have suffered a fatal blow earlier this year when Franklin's other daughter, Janice, revealed that both she and her sister had been hypnotized prior to their father's trial").

222. 884 F. Supp. at 1438 ("This is a 'recovered memory' case in that Franklin-Lipsker explained that twenty years after the event, one afternoon in early 1989 after looking at her daughter, she first remembered what she had seen in 1969. ...[R]eliance by a jury on 'recovered memory' testimony does not, in and of itself, violate the Constitution").

223. 142 N.H. 110, 121, 697 A.2d 916, 922 (1997).

"Although there are skeptics, it does seem to be accepted in the psychological community that people are capable of repressing or dissociating conscious recollection of all or part of certain traumatic events. ...There is, however, a vigorous debate on the questions of how the process of repression occurs, how the process of retrieval occurs, and indeed if in fact retrieval is possible at all."[224] After reviewing the scientific and legal literature, the court concluded: "The phenomenon of recovery of repressed memories has not yet reach the point where we may perceive these particular recovered memories as reliable."[225]

In contrast, in *People v. Murphy*[226] a New York court ruled that a spontaneous recovery of a repressed memory was admissible if independently corroborated. Here, an assault victim recovered her memory after seeing a newspaper account of the crime illustrated by the defendant's photograph.

In *Commonwealth v. Crawford*[227] a murder arrest was not made until twenty years after the victim's body had been found. The witness claimed that his "flashback" occurred when he saw a person who resembled the victim while shopping. The Pennsylvania Supreme Court ruled that the exclusion of the testimony of a defense expert was proper because it invaded the jury's province of evaluating credibility. The expert would have testified that the witness's memory was inaccurate. The court noted that the prosecution had not introduced expert testimony on revived memory and had not sought to establish the scientific validity of repressed memory. Here, the defense attorney should have proffered the expert testimony on the dangers of this type of flashback without proposing to have the expert directly comment on the witness's credibility.

§ 12-9. Basis of Expert Opinion on Mental State.

The admissibility of expert testimony concerning a defendant's mental state, based on observations of the defendant while hypnotized,[228] has been considered in several cases.[229] For example, in *People v. Modesto*[230] the California Supreme Court held that it was proper for a qualified expert to base her opinion on hypnotic interviews of the defendant. In addition, the court held it was error to

---

224. *Id.* at 119, 697 A.2d at 921.

225. *Id.* at 133, 697 A.2d at 930.

226. 235 A.D.2d 933, 654 N.Y.S.2d 187, *app. denied*, 662 N.Y.S.2d 439 (1997).

227. 553 Pa. 195, 199, 718 A.2d 768, 770 (1998) ("For the most part, these phenomena consisted of hallucinatory visions or voices where [the victim] urged Mr. Reed that he must tell the truth and reveal his long suppressed knowledge and thereby obtain justice for her murder by Frank Crawford").

228. *See* Kline, *Defending the Mentally Ill: The Insanity Defense and the Role of Forensic Hypnosis*, 27 INT'L J. CLINICAL & EXPERIMENTAL HYPNOSIS 375 (1979).

229. *See generally* Annot., *Admissibility of Physiological or Psychological Truth and Deception Test or Its Results to Support Physician's Testimony*, 41 A.L.R.3D 1369 (1972).

230. 59 Cal. 2d 722, 382 P.2d 33, 31 Cal. Rptr. 225 (1963).

exclude expert testimony concerning the use of hypnosis as an analytical tool in making such a mental evaluation.[231] Similarly, in *People v. Santana*[232] the court ruled psychiatric testimony of the defendant's mental condition, based partly on hypnotic statements of the accused, was admissible: "While hypnosis may not be introduced as direct evidence of the truth of the matter asserted, a testifying psychiatrist may, nevertheless, rely on hypnosis for the purpose of assessing the subject's state of mind."[233]

Admission of the tapes of the hypnotic session upon which the expert based her opinion, however, was held in *Modesto* to fall within the discretion of the trial court.[234] Here, the principal problem is the hearsay rule. These out-of-court statements are offered only to establish the basis for the expert's opinion and not for the truth of the assertions contained therein.[235] Consequently, they are not hearsay, and a jury instruction limiting the jury's use of the evidence should be given. Nevertheless, a trial judge may believe that the jury would not be able to adhere to such a fine distinction, even if instructed on this point. In such a case, the expert's opinion may be admitted but the contents of the tapes used in forming that opinion may be excluded.

Several other courts have followed this path.[236] In contrast, some courts have rejected this position.[237]

---

231. *Id.* at 722-33, 382 P.2d at 39-40, 31 Cal. Rptr. at 231-32. ***But see*** People v. Parnell, 16 Cal. App. 4th 862, 20 Cal. Rptr. 2d 302, 306 (1993) (expert opinion excluded because there was no showing that hypnotic statements were used by experts in the field of post-traumatic stress disorder to determine an accused's mental state at the time of the crime, nor was there any showing that the expert was "familiar with hypnosis and its use in psychotherapy").

In *Modesto* the court distinguished a prior case, People v. Busch, 56 Cal. 2d 868, 366 P.2d 314, 16 Cal. Rptr. 898 (1961), in which it had held that it was not error to exclude expert testimony based, in part, on a hypnotic interview, on the ground that a proper foundation had not been laid to show the reliability of hypnosis or that the expert was qualified.

232. 159 Misc.2d 301, 604 N.Y.S.2d 1016 (Sup. Ct. 1993) (recognizing hypnosis as a well-established therapeutic and diagnostic tool).

233. *Id.* at 1018.

234. People v. Modesto, 59 Cal. 2d at 732-33, 382 P.2d at 39, 31 Cal. Rptr. at 231. *Accord* People v. Hiser, 267 Cal. App. 2d 47, 61-62, 72 Cal. Rptr. 906, 915-16 (1968); State v. Alley, 776 S.W.2d 506, 515-16 (Tenn. 1989) (exclusion of videotaped hypnotic session within trial court's discretion), *cert. denied*, 493 U.S. 1036 (1990). *See also* Rault v. Butler, 826 F.2d 299, 304 (5th Cir.) (exclusion of tapes of hypnotic session not unconstitutional), *cert. denied*, 483 U.S. 1042 (1987).

235. *See* Rault v. Butler, 826 F.2d 299, 303 (5th Cir.) ("[T]he defense did not tender the tapes or the hypnotized testimony of Rault for the truth of the matter recited, but rather as demonstrative evidence of Rault's mental condition at the time of the offense"), *cert. denied*, 483 U.S. 1042 (1987).

236. *E.g.*, Morgan v. State, 537 So. 2d 973 (Fla. 1989) (expert may express an opinion on defendant's mental state based on hypnotic interview); State v. Harris, 241 Or. 224, 241-42, 405 P.2d 492, 500 (1965); State v. Pierce, 263 S.C. 23, 30, 207 S.E.2d 414, 417-18 (1974).

§ 12-10. Hypnosis Defense.

Hypnosis may be raised as a defense to a criminal charge. Under Anglo-American law, there is no criminal liability without a voluntary act.[238] An act that is not the product of the actor's conscious determination is not a voluntary act. For example, a reflexive or convulsive act is not a voluntary act and thus cannot be the basis for criminal liability. Similarly, acts performed while unconscious or sleep-walking are not voluntary acts.

The Model Penal Code treats the acts of a hypnotized person as involuntary and thus not subject to criminal liability.[239] The basis for this position is questionable. According to Dr. Orne, the scientific evidence indicates that hypnosis alone does not make it possible for a subject to be compelled to carry out behavior that is repugnant to him.[240] The hypnosis defense has been raised unsuccessfully in several cases.[241]

§ 12-11. Related Issues.

Hypnosis has surfaced in a variety of other legal contexts, some of which are briefly noted in this section. First, several cases have considered a defendant's right to have his recollection refreshed through hypnosis. In *Cornell v. Superior Court*[242] the California Supreme Court held that the right to effective assistance of counsel encompassed the right to have the defendant placed under hypnosis for the purpose of refreshing his memory concerning the events surrounding the commission of the charged offense.[243] In *State ex rel. Sheppard v. Koblentz*[244] the Ohio Supreme Court rejected such an argument when the request for a hypnotic interview had been made in a posttrial motion.

---

237. *E.g.*, Adams v. State, 484 So. 2d 1160, 1164 (Ala. Crim. App. 1985); Commonwealth v. Langley, 468 Pa. 392, 363 A.2d 1126 (1976).

238. *See* 1 LAFAVE & SCOTT, SUBSTANTIVE CRIMINAL LAW § 3.2 (1986) (the requirement of an act).

239. MODEL PENAL CODE § 2.01(2)(c) (Proposed Official Draft 1962) ("conduct during hypnosis or resulting from hypnotic suggestion" is not a voluntary act). *See also* 2 P. ROBINSON, CRIMINAL LAW DEFENSES § 191 (1984); Comment, *"Trance on Trial": An Exegesis of Hypnotism and Criminal Responsibility*, 39 WAYNE L. REV. 1299 (1993).

240. Orne, *Can A Hypnotized Subject Be Compelled To Carry Out Otherwise Unacceptable Behavior?*, 20 INT'L J. CLINICAL & EXPERIMENTAL HYPNOSIS 101 (1972); Orne, *Antisocial Behavior and Hypnosis: Problems of Control and Validation in Empirical Studies*, *in* HYPNOSIS: CURRENT PROBLEMS 137 (G. Estabrooks ed. 1962).

241. *See* People v. Marsh, 170 Cal. App. 2d 284, 338 P.2d 495 (1959). *See also* United States v. McCollum, 732 F.2d 1419, 1423 (9th Cir.), *cert. denied*, 469 U.S. 920 (1984); United States v. Phillips, 515 F. Supp. 758, 760 (E.D. Ky. 1981); People v. Worthington, 105 Cal. 166, 172, 38 P. 689, 691 (1894).

242. 52 Cal. 2d 99, 338 P.2d 447 (1959).

243. *Id.* at 102-03, 338 P.2d at 449.

244. 174 Ohio St. 120, 187 N.E.2d 40 (1962), *cert. denied*, 373 U.S. 911 (1963).

Second, in *Burnett v. State*[245] the court held that a tape of a prehypnotic interview of a defendant by his attorney fell within the attorney-client privilege.

Third, in *People v. Renslow*[246] the court upheld a trial court's ruling refusing to order that a prosecution witness be hypnotized.

Finally, in *State v. Poland*[247] the court upheld the use of hypnotically influenced evidence in establishing probable cause to search.

§ 12-12. Selected Bibliography.

American Society of Clinical Hypnosis, Clinical Hypnosis and Memory: Guidelines for Clinicians and for Forensic Hypnosis 6 (1995).

D. Brown, A. Scheflin & D. Hammond, Memory, Trauma Treatment, and the Law (1998).

Council on Scientific Affairs, *Scientific Status of Refreshing Recollection by the Use of Hypnosis*, 253 J.A.M.A. 1918 (1985).

Diamond, *Inherent Problems in the Use of Pretrial Hypnosis on a Prospective Witness*, 68 Calif. L. Rev. 313 (1980).

J. Laurence & C. Perry, Hypnosis, Will, and Memory: A Psycho-Legal History (1988).

Orne, Dinges & Orne, *Rock v. Arkansas: Hypnosis, The Defendant's Privilege*, 38 Int'l J. Clinical & Experimental Hypnosis 250, 256 (1990).

Orne, *The Use and Misuse of Hypnosis in Court*, *in* 3 Crime and Justice: An Annual Review of Research 61 (M. Tonry & N. Morris eds. 1982).

Orne, Soskis, Dinges & Orne, *Hypnotically Induced Testimony*, *in* Eyewitness Testimony: Psychological Perspectives (G. Wells & E. Loftus eds. 1984).

M. Orne, D. Soskis, D. Dinges, E. Orne & M. Tonry, Hypnotically Refreshed Testimony: Enhanced Memory or Tampering With Evidence? (Nat'l Institute of Justice 1985).

Orne, Whitehouse, Dinges & Orne, *Reconstructing Memory Through Hypnosis: Forensic and Clinical Implications*, *in* Hypnosis and Memory 21 (H. Pettinati ed. 1988).

Perry, Orne, London & Orne, *Rethinking Per Se Exclusions of Hypnotically Elicited Recall as Legal Testimony*, 44 Int'l J. Clinical & Experimental Hypnosis 66 (1996).

A. Scheflin & J. Shapiro, Trance on Trial (1989).

Steblay & Bothwell, *Evidence for Hypnotically Refreshed Testimony: The View From the Laboratory*, 18 Law & Human Behav. 635 (1994).

Symposium on Hypnosis and Delayed Recall: Part I, 42 Int'l J. Clinical & Experimental Hypnosis 259-455 (Oct. 1994).

Symposium on Hypnosis and Delayed Recall: Part II, 43 Int'l J. Clinical & Experimental Hypnosis 114-248 (April 1995).

Legal

Belasic, *Trial by Trance: The Admissibility of Hypnotically Enhanced Testimony*, 20 Colum. J.L. & Soc. Probs. 237 (1986).

Beaudine, *Growing Disenchantment With Hypnotic Means of Refreshing Witness Recall*, 41 Vand. L. Rev. 379 (1988).

Boggs, *Rethinking the Ban on Hypnotically Enhanced Testimony*, 81 Ill. B.J. 136 (1993).

---

245. 642 S.W.2d 765 (Tex. Crim. App. 1982).

246. 98 Ill. App. 3d 288, 293, 423 N.E.2d 1360, 1364 (1981).

247. 132 Ariz. 269, 279-80, 645 P.2d 784, 794-95 (1982).

Fox & Fox, *Reciprocal Hypnosis: A New Standard for the Admission of Posthypnotic Testimony*, 20 PAC. L.J. 815 (1989).

D. FAIGMAN, D. KAYE, M. SAKS & J. SANDERS, MODERN SCIENTIFIC EVIDENCE ch. 12 (1997).

Giannelli, *The Admissibility of Hypnotic Evidence in U.S. Courts*, 43 INT'L J. CLINICAL & EXPERIMENTAL HYPNOSIS 212, 213 (1995).

Giuliana, *Between Rock and a Hurd Place: Protecting the Criminal Defendant's Right to Testify after Her Testimony Has Been Hypnotically Refreshed*, 65 FORDHAM L. REV. 2151, 2186 (1997).

Mickenberg, *Mesmerizing Justice: The Use of Hypnotically-Induced Testimony in Criminal Trials*, 34 SYRACUSE L. REV. 927 (1983).

A. MOENSSENS, J. STARRS, & C. HENDERSON, SCIENTIFIC EVIDENCE: CIVIL AND CRIMINAL § 20.17 (4th ed. 1995).

Scheflin, *Forensic Hypnosis and the Law: The Current Situation in the United States*, *in* HYPNOSIS AND THE LAW: PRINCIPLES AND PRACTICE (Evan & Stanley eds., 1994).

Shaw, *The Admissibility of Hypnotically Enhanced Testimony in Criminal Trials*, 75 MARQ. L. REV. 1 (1991).

Note, *Fifth, Sixth, and Fourteenth Amendments — A Constitutional Paradigm for Determining the Admissibility of Hypnotically Refreshed Testimony*, 78 J. CRIM. L. & CRIMINOLOGY 853 (1988).

Comment, *Hypnotically Enhanced Testimony: Has It Lost Its Charm?*, 15 S. ILL. U. L.J. 289 (1991).

Note, *Rock v. Arkansas: Hypnotically "Refreshed" Testimony or Hypnotically "Manufactured" Testimony?*, 74 CORNELL L. REV. 136 (1988).

Note, *The Use of Hypnosis in Criminal Trials: The Black Letter of the Black Art*, 21 LOY. L.A. L. REV. 635 (1988).

Comment, *The Admissibility of Hypnotically Influenced Testimony*, 55 TENN. L. REV. 785 (1988).

Note, *Awakening from the Exclusionary Trance: A Balancing Approach to the Admissibility of Hypnotically Refreshed Testimony*, 61 TEX. L. REV. 719 (1982).

Note, *The Admissibility of Testimony Influenced by Hypnosis*, 67 VA. L. REV. 1203 (1981).

Annotations

Annot., *Admissibility of hypnotically refreshed or enhanced testimony*, 77 A.L.R.4TH 927 (1990).

Annot., *Admissibility of hypnotic evidence at criminal trial*, 92 A.L.R.3D 442 (1979).

Annot., *Necessity and admissibility, in federal trial, of expert or opinion testimony regarding use or reliability of hypnotically refreshed recollections*, 50 A.L.R. FED. 602 (1980).

Annot., *Fact that witness undergoes hypnotic examination as affecting admissibility of testimony in civil cases*, 31 A.L.R.4TH 1239 (1984).

Annot., *Sufficiency of evidence that witness in criminal case was hypnotized, for purposes of determining admissibility of testimony given under hypnosis or of hypnotically enhanced testimony*, 16 A.L.R.5TH 841 (1994).

CHAPTER 13

BITE MARK AND DENTAL IDENTIFICATION*

§ 13-1. In General.

Forensic dentistry, also known as forensic odontology, concerns the application of dentistry to law.[1] In criminal trials, forensic dentistry typically is used in two ways: (1) to establish the identity of a homicide victim through an examination of dentition and (2) to connect a defendant with a crime by means of bite mark analysis.

§ 13-2. Dental Identification.

The identification of deceased persons by means of their dentition is sometimes the only method by which identity can be established. Although identification by fingerprints is often used to establish identity,[2] that method cannot be used when the skin tissue of the decedent's fingers is no longer available or when the decedent's fingerprints have never been previously recorded. In contrast to skin tissue, human dentition (as well as dental restorations and prostheses) remains long after death.[3] Moreover, in some cases certain types of dental evidence may be just as useful as fingerprints in establishing identity. For example, radiographs, casts, and photographs may establish that an individual's dentition is so unique and distinctive that a positive

---

*The sections in this chapter were revised and renumbered in this edition. The authors wish to express their appreciation to Lowell J. Levine, D.D.S., Medicolegal Investigations Unit, New York State Police, who reviewed this chapter.

1. *See* I. SOPHER, FORENSIC DENTISTRY vii (1976) ("the application of dentistry to the legal structure"); Keiser-Nielsen, *Forensic Odontology*, 1 U. TOLEDO L. REV. 633, 634 (1969) ("Forensic odontology is that branch of odontology which ... deals with the proper handling and examination of dental evidence and with the proper evaluation and presentation of dental findings").

2. For a discussion of fingerprints, *see* Chapter 16.

3. I. SOPHER, *supra* note 1, at 40-41.

identification is possible.[4] For this reason, dental examinations are often used to identify individuals in mass disasters.[5]

Dental identification is based on the assumption that every person's dentition is unique.[6] The human adult dentition consists of thirty-two teeth, each with five anatomic surfaces.[7] Thus, there are 160 dental surfaces that may contain identifying characteristics. Restorations alone, with varying shapes, sizes, and restorative materials, may offer numerous points of individuality.[8] In addition to restorations, the number of teeth, prostheses, decay, malposition, malrotation, peculiar shapes, root canal therapy, bone patterns, bite relationship, and oral pathology may all provide identifying characteristics.[9] One study established the uniqueness of human dentition through a statistical analysis of a general population sample.[10]

---

4. Digital radiographs and images are the diagnostic choice today.

5. *See* Brannon & Kessler, *Problems in Mass-Disaster Dental Identifications: A Retrospective Review*, 44 J. FORENSIC SCI. 123, 126 (1999) (analyzing 50 mass disasters) ("[F]ragmented dental remains, unrecovered dental structures, and inadequate AM [antemortem] dental records are the most commonly encountered problems in mass-disaster dental identification"). Criminal cases differ from mass disaster situations in that the latter often involve a limited group of persons — for example, an airline will have a manifest of the crew and passengers. In contrast, in a skeletal remains case the universe of possible persons may be extremely large. *See also* P. STIMSON & C. MERTZ, FORENSIC DENTISTRY chs. 9 & 10 (1997).

6. "The premise that human dentition is unique to each individual is widely accepted. ...The randomness of filling locations and shapes are unique identifying features which can be compared to preexisting dental records and radiographs." Sweet, *Human Bitemarks: Examination, Recovery, and Analysis, in* MANUAL OF FORENSIC ODONTOLOGY 148 (3d. ed 1997) (C. Bowers & G. Bell eds.) (American Society of Forensic Odontology) [hereinafter cited as ASFO MANUAL].

7. There are four types of teeth: incisors, cuspids or canines, bicuspids, and molars. The five surfaces are the buccal, distal, lingual, mesial, and occlusal/incisal. I. SOPHER, *supra* note 1, at 20-25. The occlusal is the surface of the tooth that comes into contact with the opposing teeth when the mouth is closed; the term "incisal" is used for the anterior teeth. The lingual is the surface facing the inside of the mouth, while the buccal faces the outside of the mouth (*i.e.*, the cheek). The distal and mesial surfaces contact adjacent teeth. The upper jaw is called the maxilla. The lower jaw is the mandible. The latter is movable; the former is not.

8. *See* Silverstein, *Comparison of Antemortem and Postmortem Findings*, ASFO MANUAL, *supra* note 6, at 31 ("It is increasingly more common to see people totally devoid of dental caries. This results in decreasing amounts or complete absence of any dental restorations. The forensic odontologist must then rely more heavily on anatomical landmarks, tooth and bone anatomy to attempt an identification").

9. I. SOPHER, *supra* note 1, at 82. *See also* Hubar & Carr, *Computed Dental Radiography Used to Reproduce Antemortem Film Position*, 44 J. FORENSIC SCI. 401, 401 (1999) ("Typically, a forensic scientist looks for missing or supernumerary teeth, malformed or ectopic teeth, existing dental restorations and their features, and atypical anatomical features or landmarks, any or all of which may assist in positively identifying a decedent").

10. Rawson, Ommen, Kinard, Johnson & Yfantis, *Statistical Evidence for the Individuality of the Human Dentition*, 29 J. FORENSIC SCI. 245, 252 (1984) ("This mathematical evaluation of a

The identification of a decedent involves a comparison of antemortem records with postmortem findings to determine points of identity. Antemortem records may consist of written records (including charts), X rays, and casts. Radiographs are particularly helpful because they provide details not usually present in dental charts, and they do not contain the errors that are often found in charts.[11] Without a putative identity, however, obtaining these records is difficult because dental records, until recently,[12] were not maintained in a central depository like fingerprints.[13] Even when records are available, a positive identification may not be possible if the records are incomplete or inaccurate. Moreover, the amount and condition of the postmortem dentition available for comparison also affects whether a positive identification can be made.[14]

There is no minimum number of characteristics necessary to establish a positive identification.[15] The number and quality of characteristics determine whether a positive identification may be made; a few points involving unusual characteristics may be sufficient: "[T]he recovery of only a single tooth or jaw fragment may bear the degree of specificity necessary for positive identification."[16] However, there must be no unexplained inconsistencies.[17] For example, a missing tooth in the postmortem dentition is not necessarily

---

general population sample demonstrates the uniqueness of the human dentition beyond any reasonable doubt ...").

11. Stimson, *Radiology in Forensic Odontology*, 48 DENTAL RADIOGRAPHY & PHOTOGRAPHY 51, 53-55 (1975). *See also* Hubar & Carr, *supra* note 9, at 401 ("A digitized image is produced on a computer monitor that can then be stored, printed onto paper or transmitted via modem to another distant location"); MacLean, Kogon & Stitt, *Validation of Dental Radiographs for Human Identification*, 39 J. FORENSIC SCI. 1195 (1994).

12. The FBI maintains records in a central databank, Missing Persons and Unidentified Deceased records. Several states also require records. *See* CAL. HEALTH & SAFETY CODE § 102870 (Department of Justice acts as repository or computer center for unidentified person's dental examination records); LA. REV. STAT. § 33: 1563(H) (dental examination records for missing children clearinghouse); MASS. GEN. ANN. ch. 22A, § 5 (medical examiner shall forward dental records to Department of Public Safety); N.Y. MCKINNEY'S EXEC. LAW § 838(6) (Division of Justice shall compare the dental records received to dental records of missing persons on file); WEST'S WASH. REV. CODE § 68.50.310 (establishing a dental identification section in state patrol to compare records).

13. I. SOPHER, *supra* note 1, at 41 ("Antemortem dental records, unlike fingerprints, are not easily obtained and recorded, are not centrally classified and are not readily retrievable for comparison"); O'Shaughnessy, *The Theory of Human Identification, in* ASFO MANUAL, *supra* 6, at 4, 6 ("Dental identification, as good as it is, requires one basic element that may *not* always be readily available — antemortem records").

14. I. SOPHER, *supra* note 1, chs. 5 and 7.

15. Stimson, *supra* note 11, at 53 ("There are no specific number of concordant points necessary for positive identification").

16. I. SOPHER, *supra* note 1, at 41. *See also* Stimson, *supra* note 11, at 53 ("If one filling is extremely unique, it could be specific").

17. I. SOPHER, *supra* note 1, at 107.

inconsistent with the presence of that tooth in the antemortem records; the tooth may have come out after the records were prepared, including after death. In contrast, a missing tooth in the antemortem records is inconsistent with the presence of that tooth in the postmortem dentition.[18]

Estimating Age

The adult dentition is the second set of teeth, which replace deciduous (baby) teeth during childhood. Forensic odontologists may be able to estimate the age of a victim by an examination of dentition. The estimate is more precise for young people than for adults.[19] This subject is discussed in § 19-4(B) *infra*.

§ 13-3. Admissibility of Dental Identifications.

The courts have accepted dental identification as a means of establishing the identity of a homicide victim,[20] with some cases going back to the 19th Century.[21] According to one court, "it cannot be seriously disputed that a dental structure may constitute a means of identifying a deceased person ... where there is some dental record of that person with which the structure may be compared."[22] In another case, the court upheld the identification of skeletal remains by a forensic odontologist based on a comparison of the remains and inter vivos photographs

---

18. Sperber, *Forensic Odontology, in* PRACTISING LAW INSTITUTE, SCIENTIFIC AND EXPERT EVIDENCE 721, 731 (E. Imwinkelried ed. 1981).

19. *See* Bowers, *Determining Age From Teeth: The Estimation of Age From Dental Development, in* ASFO MANUAL, *supra* note, 6, ch. 3. *See also* Xiaohu, Philipsen, Jablonski, Pang, & Jiazhen, *Age Estimation From the Structure of Adult Human Teeth: Review of the Literature*, 54 FORENSIC SCI. INT'L 23 (1992); Mincer, Harris & Berryman, *The A.B.F.O. Study of Third Molar Development and Its Use As an Estimator of Chronological Age*, 38 J. FORENSIC SCI. 379 (1993); Skinner & Dupras, *Variation in Birth Timing and Location of the Neonatal Line in Human Enamel*, 38 J. FORENSIC SCI. 1383 (1993); Solheim, *A New Method for Dental Age Estimation in Adults*, 59 FORENSIC SCI. INT'L 137 (1992).

20. *See* People v. Westlake, 106 Cal. App. 247, 289 P. 212 (1930); Wooley v. People, 148 Colo. 392, 367 P.2d 903 (1961) (dentist compared his patient's record with dentition of a corpse); State v. Johnston, 62 Idaho 601, 113 P.2d 809 (1941); Martin v. State, 636 N.E.2d 1268, 1272 (Ind. App. 1994) (dentist who had been out of dental school for approximately 3 months was qualified to compare X rays of one of his patients with skeletal remains of murder victim and make a positive identification); State v. Goodson, 299 Mo. 321, 252 S.W. 389 (1923); Hawkins v. State, 60 Neb. 380, 83 N.W. 198 (1900); Fields v. State, 322 P.2d 431, 446 (Okla. Crim. App. 1958) (murder case in which victim was burned beyond recognition); Williamson v. State, 679 S.W.2d 523, 529-30 (Tex. Ct. App.), *rev'd on other grounds,* 672 S.W.2d 484 (Tex. Crim. App. 1984). *See also* Annot., *Homicide: Identification of Victim as Person Named in Indictment or Information*, 86 A.L.R.2D 722 (1962).

21. *See* Commonwealth v. Webster, 59 Mass. (5 Cush.) 295, 52 Am. Dec. 711 (1850) (remains of the incinerated victim, including charred teeth and parts of a denture, were identified by the victim's dentist); Lindsay v. People, 63 N.Y. 143 (1875).

22. People v. Mattox, 96 Ill. App. 2d 148, 150-51, 237 N.E.2d 845, 846 (1968).

of the victim. According to the expert, the facial structure, occlusion, and the shape of the teeth and jaw permitted an identification.[23] In addition, courts have held that a decedent's dental records are admissible under the business records exception to the hearsay rule.[24]

§ 13-4. Bite Mark Analysis.

Bite mark analysis has been used for the last thirty years[25] to establish a connection between a defendant and a crime.[26] Bite marks occur primarily in sex-related crimes, child abuse cases, and offenses involving physical altercations, such as homicide. Male victims are most often bitten on the arms and shoulders, while female victims are most commonly bitten on the breasts, arms, and legs. Multiple bites occur in 40% of the cases.[27]

Theory of Uniqueness

Identification of a suspect by matching his dentition with a bite mark found on the victim of a crime rests on the theory that each person's dentition is unique.[28]

---

23. *Ex parte* Dolvin, 391 So. 2d 677 (Ala. 1980).

24. *E.g.,* Williamson v. State, 679 S.W.2d 523, 529 (Tex. Ct. App. 1983), *rev'd on other grounds,* 672 S.W.2d 484 (Tex. Crim. App. 1984).

25. *See* Dinkel, *The Use of Bite Mark Evidence as an Investigative Aid,* 19 J. Forensic Sci. 535 (1973); De Vore, *Bitemarks for Identification?—A Preliminary Report,* 11 Med. Sci. & Law 144 (July 1971); Luntz & Luntz, *A Case in Forensic Odontology: A Bite Mark in a Multiple Homicide,* 36 Oral Surg. 72 (1972) (trial of John Rice).

The use of bite marks at earlier times has been noted. *See* Humble, *Identification by Means of Teeth,* 154 Brit. Dent. J. 528 (1933); Keyes, *Teeth Marks on the Skin as Evidence in Establishing Identity,* 67 Dent. Cosmos. 1165 (1925); Rothwell, *Bite Marks in Forensic Dentistry: A Review of Legal, Scientific Issues,* 126 J. Am. Dental Assoc. 223 (Feb. 1995) ("Debtors coming from Britain or Europe to America to work as servants verified their agreements by biting the seal on the pact in lieu of a signature and became known as *indentured servants*"); Strom, *Dental Aspects of Forensic Medicine,* 4 Int'l Dent. J. 527 (1954).

26. *See* Sweet, Parhar & Wood, *Computer-Based Production of Bite Mark Comparison Overlays,* 43 J. Forensic Sci. 1050, 1051 (1998) ("Bite mark physical evidence may be highly significant in that it may closely reproduce the characteristics of the biter's teeth. This evidence may be crucial to identify a suspect in a crime, or to exclude an innocent person"); Vale, *Bite Mark Evidence in the Investigation of Crime,* 14 J. Calif. Dent. Ass'n 36 (1986).

27. Vale & Noguchi, *Anatomical Distribution of Human Bite Marks in a Series of 67 Cases,* 28 J. Forensic Sci. 61, (1983).

28. One study attempted to establish the individuality of bite marks by comparing the bite marks of identical twins by means of a computer technique. Sognnaes, Rawson, Gratt & Nguyen, *Computer Comparison of Bitemark Patterns in Identical Twins,* 105 J. Am. Dental Assoc. 449 (1982). *See also* Rawson, Ommen, Johnson & Yfantis, *Statistical Evidence for the Individuality of the Human Dentition,* 29 J. Forensic Sci. 245 (1984). *But see* Sweet & Bowers, *Accuracy of Bite Mark Overlays: A Comparison of Five Common Methods to Produce Exemplars from a Suspect's*

In this respect, bite mark comparisons are based on the same principle as the identification of a deceased person.[29] Although the courts have accepted this theory,[30] there are significant differences in the application of these two uses of forensic dentistry. In 1976, when bite mark comparisons were first studied, one authority raised the following problems:

> [Bite]marks can never be taken to reproduce accurately the dental features of the originator. This is due partially to the fact that bite marks generally include only a limited number of teeth. Furthermore, the material (whether food stuff or human skin) in which the mark has been left is usually found to be a very unsatisfactory impression material with shrinkage and distortion characteristics that are unknown. Finally, these marks represent only the remaining and fixed picture of an action, the mechanism of which may vary from case to case. For instance, there is as yet no precise knowledge of the possible differences between biting off a morsel of food and using one's teeth for purposes of attack or defense.[31]

None of these problems is involved with dental identifications.[32] In addition, thirty-two teeth are not used in bite mark comparisons; often only four to eight

---

Dentition, 43 J. FORENSIC SCI. 362, (1998) ("Neither study examines the resultant transference of the hypothesized individual characteristics to skin or similar media").

29. *See* People v. Milone, 43 Ill. App. 3d 385, 397, 356 N.E.2d 1350, 1358 (1976) ("The concept of identifying a suspect by matching his dentition to a bite mark found at the scene of a crime is a logical extension of the accepted principle that each person's dentition is unique").

30. *See* People v. Milone, 43 Ill. App. 3d 385, 396-97, 356 N.E.2d 1350, 1358 (1976); State v. Sager, 600 S.W.2d 541, 573 (Mo. App. 1980), *cert. denied,* 450 U.S. 910 (1981); People v. Smith, 110 Misc. 2d 118, 125, 443 N.Y.S.2d 551, 556-57 (Cty. Ct. 1981) ("The basic premise is the unique nature of individual dentition .... and the virtually infinite number of individual bite configurations"); State v. Green, 305 N.C. 463, 471, 290 S.E.2d 625, 630 (1982); State v. Temple, 302 N.C. 1, 11-13, 273 S.E.2d 273, 280-81 (1981).

31. Keiser-Nielson, *supra* note 1, at 636. In an early experiment, a commentator concluded that expert witnesses "should be aware that at the present state of our knowledge there are problems not only in determining the incidence of identical or near identical occlusions but also in interpreting the bite marks made under standardized laboratory conditions." Whittaker, *Some Laboratory Studies on the Accuracy of Bite Mark Comparison*, 25 INT'L DENTAL J. 166, 170 (1975).

32. Another problem plagued the early cases. In one of the first books in the field, published in 1976, Dr. Sopher noted:

> The problem of specificity in the bite mark analysis results from the lack of a scientific core of basic data for comparison. The results of the bite mark comparison may indicate a perfect or reasonably perfect fit between the bite mark and a suspect's dentition; however, how can one be absolutely or even perhaps reasonably certain that no other individual could have produced a particular bite? Classified bite mark characteristics on large segments of the population are unavailable; therefore, an absolute scientific estimation of specificity regarding the particular bite mark/suspect comparison is not possible. The situation is comparable to the point in the distant past when the 100th set of fingerprints was classified.

teeth are biting teeth. Similarly, five anatomic surfaces are not used in biting; only the edges of the front teeth are used. In sum, bite mark identification depends not only on the uniqueness of each person's dentition but also on "whether there is a [sufficient] representation of that uniqueness in the mark found on the skin or other inanimate object."[33]

Nevertheless, some experts believe that bite marks in skin can capture the unique and individual characteristics of teeth with good fidelity, at least in some cases. Others disagree. Two commentators have written:

> There is effectively no valid documented scientific data to support the hypothesis that bite marks are demonstrably unique. Additionally, there is no documented scientific data to support the hypothesis that a latent bite mark, like a latent fingerprint, is a true and accurate reflection of this uniqueness. To the contrary, what little scientific evidence that does exist clearly supports the conclusion that crime-related bite marks are grossly distorted, inaccurate, and therefore unreliable as a method of identification.[34]

Methods of Comparison

Several methods of bite mark analysis have been reported.[35] All methods involve three steps: (1) registration of the bite mark and the suspect's dentition, (2) comparison of the dentition and bite mark, and (3) evaluation of the points of similarity or dissimilarity.

Registration of the bite mark by photography is used in all cases; the photographs are then enlarged to life-size proportion for comparison.[36] "For bites

---

> At that time, it was known that the set of prints did not match the ninety-nine others previously recorded, but it was not known if the set of prints were specific for only the one individual fingerprinted.

I. SOPHER, *supra* note 1, at 140.

33. Rawson, Ommen, Kinard, Johnson, & Yfantis, *supra* note 10, at 252. *See also* Sweet, Parhar & Wood, *supra* note 26, at 1050 ("The foundation of bite mark analysis lies in the following premises: (a) each individual's dentition is presumed to be unique, and (b) this presumed uniqueness is accurately recorded in the characteristics of the injury on the skin or object").

34. Wilkinson & Gerughty, *Bite Mark Evidence: Its Admissibility is Hard to Swallow*, 12 W. ST. U. L. REV. 519, 560 (1985).

35. *See* I. SOPHER, *supra* note 1, at 125-26; State v. Sager, 600 S.W.2d 541, 569-70 (Mo. App. 1980) (outlining different methods), *cert. denied,* 450 U.S. 910 (1981).

36. *See* Rawson, Vale, Herschaft, Sperber & Dowell, *Analysis of Photographic Distortion in Bite Marks: A Report of the Bite Mark Guidelines Committee*, 31 J. FORENSIC SCI. 1261 (1986) (presenting a method for analyzing photographically distorted bite marks); Hyzer & Krauss, *The Bite Mark Standard Reference Scale ABFO No. 2*, 33 J. FORENSIC SCI. 498 (1988) (offering a scale of spatial reference for bite mark photography); Robinson & Wentzel, *Toneline Bite Mark Photography*, 37 J. FORENSIC SCI. 195 (1992); West & Frair, *The Use of Videotape to Demonstrate*

on human skin, a potential bite must be recognized early, as the clarity and shape of the mark may change in a relatively short time in both living and dead victims."[37] Where bite indentations (three-dimensional bite marks) are present in the skin tissue, impressions may be obtained; these are used to reproduce models of the bite mark, which can then be used for comparison.[38] In deceased persons, the bite marks should be excised.[39] The suspect's dentition is reproduced by means of models.[40] Errors can be introduced at any stage.[41] Typically, salivary trace evidence is collected at this time for DNA[42] and serological testing.[43]

---

the Dynamics of Bite Marks, 34 J. FORENSIC SCI. 88 (1989) (presenting videotaped bite marks as an alternative to still photography).

37. Rothwell, *supra* note 25, at 226.

38. *See* Benson, Cottone, Bomberg & Sperber, *Bite Mark Impressions: A Review of Techniques and Materials*, 33 J. FORENSIC SCI. 1238 (1988) (describing techniques and material used to make impressions for comparison). *See also* West, Barsley, Frair & Seal, *The Use of Human Skin in the Fabrication of a Bite Mark Template: Two Case Reports*, 35 J. FORENSIC SCI. 1477 (1990).

39. *See* Dorion, *Excision of Bitemarks, in* ASFO MANUAL, *supra* note 6, at 171; Dorion, *Preserving, Storing and Transporting Excised Skin, id.* at 172.

40. *See* Sweet & Bowers, *supra* note 28, at 362 ("There are numerous methods available to the odontologist to reproduce two- or three-dimensional examples of the suspected dentition. These include styrofoam to record the shape and position of tooth surfaces, scanning electron microscopy, hand-traced outlines, wax impressions, xerographic images, videotapes, computer imaging, and computerized axial tomography. This reflects the current freedom allowed by the discipline to permit the expert to use a 'personal' preference for this phase of bite mark analysis").

41. *See* Sweet, Parhar & Wood, *supra* note 26, at 1050 ("Several methods which are widely utilized by odontologists exist to produce these overlays. However, each of these methods involves some degree of subjective input by the odontologist. This may lead to significant errors being incorporated into the overlays which may make it difficult to reach a valid conclusion. Additionally, there are often limitations to the use of bite mark evidence. Bitemarks on skin may be ill-defined due to bruising or substrate curvature. Inaccurate reproductions of the tooth markings may be present due to tissue distortion. Healing in the living victim or postmortem changes in the deceased victim may subject the injury to color changes over time. Compounded errors may result in substantial difficulties in reaching conclusions with a high degree of confidence") (citations omitted).

42. Smith, Hollard, Sweet & Dizinno, *DNA and Forensic Odontology, in* ASFO MANUAL, *supra* note 6, 283 ("[I]t has been shown that under experimental conditions and in forensic casework, the DNA contained in teeth, oral soft tissues, and saliva can be extracted and typed"). *See also* State v. Lyons, 324 Or. 256, 924 P.2d 802, 804 (1993) (Criminalist "tested the saliva sample taken from bite marks on the victim's body" and "tested a sample of defendant's blood and determined that he is a type-A secretor"; "Blake, a forensic evidence consultant, conducted PCR-based DNA tests on the hair and saliva samples").

43. Sweet, *Human Bitemarks: Examination, Recovery, and Analysis, in* ASFO MANUAL, *supra* note 6, 148, 151 ("Serologists estimate that 80-85% of the human population secrete agglutinins in their body fluids (saliva, seminal fluid, tears, and perspiration) which can be used to determine the person's ABH blood group classification").

The reproductions of the bite mark and the suspect's dentition are then analyzed through a variety of different methods,[44] including transparent overlays,[45] direct comparison of photographs, or direct comparison of photographs with models.[46] New techniques, including computerized bite analysis, have been reported.[47] The use of scanning electron microscopy,[48] CAT scanning,[49] digital imagining,[50] and ultraviolet forensic imaging[51] also have been reported.

Conclusions

It is easier to conclude that a person's dentition and a bite mark do not match than it is to find a match.[52] This is due to the fact that any *unexplained* inconsistency between the bite mark and the dentition means that the suspect could not have made the bite mark.[53] A positive identification, however, may still be possible even though some inconsistencies are present, provided the inconsistencies can be explained. One commentator has written:

> There may, of course, be slight variations that are consistent — i.e., all of the bite marks are on a larger (or smaller) arch than the teeth themselves. In other words, depending on the location of the bite marks, whether the person (victim or suspect) was passive, unconscious, or struggling, the

44. *Id.* at 162 ("The analytical protocol for bitemark comparison is made up of two broad categories. Firstly, the measurement of specific traits and features called a *metric analysis*, and secondly, the physical matching or comparison of the configuration and pattern of the injury called a *pattern association*").

45. *See* Sweet & Bowers, *supra* note 28, at 362 (1998) ("A review of the forensic odontology literature reveals multiple techniques for overlay production. There is an absence of reliability testing or comparison of these methods to known or reference standards").

46. Sperber, *supra* note 18, at 744-47.

47. *See* Beckstead, Rawson & Giles, *Review of Bite Mark Evidence*, 99 J. AM. DENTAL ASSOC. 69, 72 (1979); Sognnaes, Rawson, Gratt & Nguyen, *supra* note 28, at 450 (citing a case in which computerized bite analysis was admitted in evidence).

48. David, *Adjunctive Use of Scanning Electron Microscopy in Bite Mark Analysis: A Three Dimensional Study*, 31 J. FORENSIC SCI. 1126 (1986).

49. Farrell, Rawson, Steffens & Stephens, *Computerized Axial Tomography as an Aid in Bite Mark Analysis: A Case Report*, 32 J. FORENSIC SCI. 266 (1987).

50. Naru & Dykes, *The Use of a Digital Imaging Technique to Aid Bite Mark Analysis*, 36 SCIENCE & JUSTICE 47 (1995).

51. West & Barsley, *Ultraviolet Forensic Imaging*, 61 FBI LAW ENFORCEMENT BULL. 14, (May 1992) ("[U]ltraviolet light provides more detail and contrast to an injured area than standard lighting techniques").

52. *See* Keiser-Nielson, *supra* note 1, at 637-38; I. SOPHER, *supra* note 1, at 140; Sperber, *supra* note 18, at 752.

53. *See* Sperber, *supra* note 18, at 747. *See also* Litaker v. State, 784 S.W.2d 739, 743 (Tex. App. 1990) (board certified forensic odontologist "affirmed that if there were just one inconsistency in the bite mark pattern, that would exclude the individual as being the biter").

degree of sucking that occurred during the biting and manual manipulation, the forensic odontologist may be able to explain "consistent variations" in the comparison.[54]

The conclusions that an expert can draw from the evaluation depend on the number and quality of the points of comparison. In the reported cases, experts have expressed their opinions in a variety of ways, some testifying that the suspect dentition was "consistent with" the bite mark, others that the dentition probably made the bite mark, and still others that the match was a positive identification (to the exclusion of all other persons).[55]

Subjectivity

Although the expert's conclusions are based on objective data, the opinion is essentially a subjective one.[56] There is no accepted minimum number of points of identity required for a positive identification.[57] The experts who have testified in reported bite mark cases have used a low of eight points of comparison to a high of fifty-two points.[58] Like fingerprint and firearms identifications (which also have a subjective aspect), the conclusions are based on the examiner's experience and expertise. Not surprisingly, this aspect opens the door to criticism: "Recently, criticism of bite mark evidence as a reliable scientific tool has been expressed due to the subjective nature of the comparative analysis."[59]

Moreover, disagreements between experts in court appear commonplace because agreements between prosecution and defense experts typically do not

---

54. Sperber, *supra* note 18, at 747-48.

55. The cases are discussed in § 13-5 *infra.*

56. *See* Sobel, *Forensic Odontology, in* 2 FORENSIC SCIENCES 28-32 (C. Wecht ed. 1984); I. SOPHER, *supra* note 1, at 140.

57. *See* Keiser-Nielson, *supra* note 1, at 637-38.

58. *E.g.*, State v. Garrison, 120 Ariz. 255, 258, 585 P.2d 563, 566 (1978) (10 points); People v. Slone, 76 Cal. App. 3d 611, 621, 143 Cal. Rptr. 61, 62 (1978) (10 points); People v. Milone, 43 Ill. App. 3d 385, 393, 356 N.E.2d 1350, 1356 (1976) (29 points); State v. Sager, 600 S.W.2d 541, 564 (Mo. App. 1980) (52 points), *cert. denied*, 450 U.S. 910 (1981); State v. Green, 305 N.C. 463, 471, 290 S.E.2d 625, 630 (1982) (14 points); State v. Temple, 302 N.C. 1, 10, 273 S.E.2d 273, 279 (1981) (8 points); Kennedy v. State, 640 P.2d 971, 976 (Okla. Crim. App. 1982) (40 points); State v. Jones, 273 S.C. 723, 732, 259 S.E.2d 120, 124 (1979) (37 points).

59. Sweet, Parhar & Wood, *supra* note 26, at 1050 (1998) (citing Rothwell, *Bite Marks in Forensic Odontology: Fact or Fiction?, in* ORAL AND MAXILLOFACIAL SURGERY (P. Worthington & J.R. Evans eds. 1994), and Zarkowski, *Bite Mark Evidence: Its Worth in the Eyes of the Expert*, J. LAW & ETHICS IN DENT. 47 (1988)). *See also* Bowers, *A Statement Why Court Opinions on Bitemark Analysis Should be Limited*, 4(2) ABFO NEWSLETTER 5 (1996); Rothwell, *Bitemarks in Forensic Dentistry: A Review of Legal, Scientific Issues*, 126 J. AM. DENT. ASS'N 223 (1995).

result in a trial.[60] "Although bite mark evidence has demonstrated a high degree of acceptance, it continues to be hotly contested in 'battles of the experts.' Review of trial transcripts reveals that distortion and the interpretation of distortion is a factor in most cases."[61] One commentator observed:

> Forensic odontologists note that it is easier to observe dissimilarity between bitemarks and suspect dentition, and harder to identify uniqueness. It is this difficulty that often results in disagreements among bitemark experts. Disagreements are common for at least four basic reasons: 1) bites are not accurate reproductions of dentition; 2) bites include a limited number [of] teeth; 3) skin is not suitable impression material; and 4) similar results may have different mechanisms.[62]

ABFO Guidelines

The development of an objective scoring system would overcome, to a significant degree, the subjectivity problem. In 1984, the American Board of Forensic Odontology (ABFO) adopted guidelines for bite mark analysis, including a uniform scoring system.[63] According to the drafting committee, "The scoring system ... has demonstrated a method of evaluation that produced a high degree of reliability among observers."[64] Moreover, "[t]he scoring guide ... is the beginning of a truly scientific approach to bite mark analysis."[65] In a subsequent letter, however, the drafting committee wrote:

> While the Board's published guidelines suggest use of the scoring system, the authors' present recommendation is that all odontologists await the results of further research before relying on precise point counts in evidentiary proceedings.... [T]he authors believe that further research is

60. Silverstein, ASFO MANUAL, *supra* note 6, at 31 ("To avoid creating bias, many forensic odontologists suggest restricting the amount of the information they receive concerning the circumstances surrounding the death of the decedent").

61. Rawson, Vale, Herschaft, Sperber & Dowell, *Analysis of Photographic Distortion in Bite Marks: A Report of the Bite Mark Guidelines Committee*, 31 J. FORENSIC SCI. 1261, 1261-62 (1986). The Committee noted: "[P]hotographic distortion can be very difficult to understand and interpret when viewing prints of bite marks that have been photographed from unknown angles." *Id.* at 1267.

62. Nordby, *Can We Believe What We See, If We See What We Believe? — Expert Disagreement*, 37 J. FORENSIC SCI. 1115, 1118 (1992).

63. A.B.F.O., *Guidelines For Bite Mark Analysis*, 112 J. AM. DENTAL ASS'N 383 (1986). For a discussion of the ABFO guidelines, *see* McClure, *Odontology: Bite Marks as Evidence in Criminal Trials*, 11 SANTA CLARA COMPUTER & HIGH TECH. L. J. 269, 275-77 (1995).

64. Rawson, Vale, Sperber, Herschaft & Yfantis, *Reliability of the Scoring System of the American Board of Forensic Odontology for Human Bite Marks*, 31 J. FORENSIC SCI. 1235, 1256 (1986).

65. *Id.* at 1259.

needed regarding the quantification of bite mark evidence before precise point counts can be relied upon in court proceedings.[66]

Qualifications

While the American Dental Association does not recognize Forensic Dentistry as a specialty, it provides materials and sponsors courses on the topic.[67] Forensic dentistry, much less bite mark comparison, is often not taught in dental school.[68] The Armed Forces Institute of Pathology, Washington, D.C., offered courses on forensic dentistry in the 1960s. The American Academy of Forensic Sciences created an Odontology Section in 1970.[69] The American Society of Forensic Odontology (ASFO) was organized later that same year.[70] In 1976, the American Board of Forensic Odontologists was incorporated to established certification standards.[71]

Other Procedures

In some cases the age of a bite mark may be important.[72] Unfortunately, "forensic experts have very little scientific research to support opinions regarding the aging of bruises either visually or microscopically."[73]

Distinguishing adult and juvenile bite marks may be possible, depending on the particular bite mark.[74]

---

66. Letter, *Discussion of "Reliability of the Scoring System of the American Board of Forensic Odontology for Human Bite Marks,"* 33 J. FORENSIC SCI. 20 (1988).

67. ADA may be contacted at (800) 621-8099.

68. *See* Hershaft & Rasmussen, *The Teaching of Forensic Dentistry: A Status Report*, 42 DENT. EDUC. J. 532 (1978) (of 60 dental schools surveyed, 42% of respondents did not offer formal courses in forensic dentistry).

69. *See* Aksu & Gobetti, *The Past and Present Legal Weight of Bite Marks as Evidence*, 17 AM. J. FORENSIC MED. & PATH. 136 (1996) (also mentioning the National Board of Forensic Dentistry & the American Academy of Oral Pathology).

70. The Forensic Science Foundation, Inc., received federal funds through the Law Enforcement Assistance Administration, Department of Justice, to develop certification procedures. The ABFO telephone number is: (719) 636-1100.

71. Bowers, *Starting a Career as a Forensic Dentist*, ASFO MANUAL, *supra* note 6, at 3 ("There are currently 94 Diplomates in the US and Canada").

72. *See* People v. Noguera, 4 Cal. 4th 599, 842 P.2d 1160, 1165 n.1, 15 Cal. Rptr. 2d 400, 405 n.1 (1992) ("At trial, extensive testimony by forensic odontologists was presented by both sides, pro and con, as to whether the wounds were human bite marks and, if so, when they were inflicted"), *cert. denied*, 512 U.S. 1253 (1994).

73. Dailey & Bowers, *Aging of Bitemarks: A Literature Review, in* ASFO MANUAL, *supra* note 6, at 184, 189.

74. *See* Whittaker, Brickley & Evans, *A Comparison of the Ability of Experts and Non-Experts to Differentiate Between Adult and Child Human Bite Marks Using Receiver Operating Characteristics (ROC) Analysis*, 92 FORENSIC SCI. INT'L 11 (1998).

§ 13-5. Admissibility & Weight of Bite Mark Evidence.

Courts have admitted bite mark comparison evidence in homicide,[75] rape,[76] and child abuse cases.[77] In virtually all the cases, the evidence was first offered by the prosecution.[78] The typical bite mark case has involved the identification of the defendant by matching his dentition with a mark left on the victim. In several cases, however, the victim's teeth have been compared with marks on the defendant's body.[79] One bite mark case involved dentures,[80] another braces.[81] A few cases have involved bite impressions on foodstuff found at a crime scene: apple,[82] piece of cheese,[83] and sandwich.[84] Another case involved a dog bite.[85]

---

75. *E.g.,* State v. Garrison, 120 Ariz. 255, 585 P.2d 563 (1978); People v. Marx, 54 Cal. App. 3d 100, 126 Cal. Rptr. 350 (1975); People v. Milone, 43 Ill. App. 3d 385, 356 N.E.2d 1350 (1976); State v. Temple, 302 N.C. 1, 273 S.E.2d 273 (1981); State v. Howe, 136 Vt. 53, 386 A.2d 1125 (1978).

76. *E.g.,* People v. Johnson, 8 Ill. App. 3d 457, 289 N.E.2d 722 (1972); State v. Routh, 30 Or. App. 901, 568 P.2d 704 (1977); People v. Bethune, 105 A.D.2d 262, 484 N.Y.S.2d 577 (1984); State v. Green, 305 N.C. 463, 290 S.E.2d 625 (1982); State v. Jones, 273 S.C. 723, 259 S.E.2d 120 (1979).

77. *E.g.,* People v. Stanciel, 153 Ill. 2d 218, 606 N.E.2d 1201, 1205 (1992) ("According to Dr. Kenney, these [26 bite] marks showed that the victim had been abused over a long period of time"); Bludsworth v. State, 98 Nev. 289, 291 n.1, 646 P.2d 558, 559 n.1 (1982). *See generally* Vale, *Dentistry's Role in Detecting and Preventing Child Abuse, in* FORENSIC DENTISTRY ch. 8 (P. Stimson & C. Mertz eds. 1997).

78. *But see* State v. Stokes, 433 So. 2d 96, 103 (La. 1983) (expert report on bite mark evidence offered by the defense was excluded as inadmissible hearsay).

79. *See* Rogers v. State, 256 Ga. 140, 344 S.E.2d 644, 647 ("Bite marks on one of Rogers' arms were consistent with the dentures worn by the elderly victim"), *cert. denied*, 479 U.S. 995 (1986); Bradford v. State, 460 So. 2d 926, 929-30 (Fla. App. 1984); Davis v. State, 611 So. 2d 906, 910 (Miss. 1992); State v. Schaefer, 855 S.W.2d 504, 506 (Mo. App. 1993); People v. Bethune, 105 A.D.2d 262, 265-67, 484 N.Y.S.2d 577, 580-83 (1984); State v. Warness, 77 Wash. App. 636, 893 P.2d 665, 669 (1995) ("[T]he expert testified that his opinion was not conclusive, but the evidence was consistent with the alleged victim's assertion that she had bitten Warness.... Its probative value was therefore limited, but its relevance was not extinguished. The trial court correctly found that the expert's uncertainty relevant to the weight and not the admissibility of his testimony").

80. *See* Rogers v. State, 256 Ga. 140, 344 S.E.2d 644, 647 ("Bite marks on one of Rogers' arms were consistent with the dentures worn by the elderly victim"), *cert. denied*, 479 U.S. 995 (1986).

81. *See* People v. Shaw, 278 Ill. App. 3d 939, 945, 948, 664 N.E.2d 97, 101, 103 (1996) (In a murder and aggravated sexual assault prosecution, the forensic odontologist opined that the mark on the defendant was caused by the orthodontic braces on the victim's teeth; "Dr. Kenney admitted that he was not a certified toolmark examiner"; no abuse of discretion to admit evidence).

82. State v. Ortiz, 198 Conn. 220, 502 A.2d 400 (1985).

83. *See* Doyle v. State, 159 Tex. Crim. 310, 263 S.W.2d 779 (1954). *See also* Kogon, Johnson, Koval & Wainright, *Selection of the Appropriate Impression and Casting Materials for Reproduction of Bitemarks from Foodstuff for Forensic Dental Investigation*, 23 CANADIAN SOC'Y FORENSIC SCI. J. 147, 148 (1990) ("The literature is replete with cases of bitemarks found in cheese, pencils, pipe stems, soap, gum, and other materials"); Corbett & Spence, *A Forensic Investigation of Teeth Marks in Soap*, 157 BRIT. DENT. J. 270 (1984).

In addition to establishing identity, bite mark evidence has been introduced to show unfitness to be a parent,[86] aggravating circumstances ("torture") in a capital case,[87] and as uncharged misconduct evidence.[88]

Lay Testimony

Some courts have admitted evidence of a bite mark on the defendant without expert testimony.[89] These cases do not invoke comparisons, only that a mark is or appears to be a bite mark. Federal Rule of Evidence 701 permits lay witness opinions if the testimony is rationally based on the witness's perception and is helpful to the jury's understanding of the case.[90] In one case, a police officer testified that a mark he had observed on a defendant's penis was a bite mark.[91] The court ruled that the evidence was an opinion based upon personal

---

84. Banks v. State, 725 So. 2d 711 (Miss. 1997) (due process violation when prosecution expert threw sandwich away after finding the accused's teeth consistent with the sandwich bite).

85. Davasher v. State, 308 Ark. 154, 166, 823 S.W.2d 863, 870 (expert testified that victim's dog could be eliminated as the source of mark found on defendant), *cert. denied,* 504 U.S. 976 (1992).

86. Rimer v. Rimer, 395 N.W.2d 390, 391, 393 (Minn. 1986) (child custody case) ("In the one substantiated incident, in which Robbie reported a bite mark on the child's arm, Regina admitted biting the child as a disciplinary measure to teach him not to bite others"; "However inappropriate, that alone will not support a finding of unfitness").

87. Commonwealth v. Edwards, 521 Pa. 134, 157, 162, 555 A.2d 818, 822, 833 (1989) ("The rest of her body was marked by at least thirty-five human bite wounds. The victim had been bitten on her chest, breasts, stomach, thighs, pelvis, arms and hands. The bite marks were vicious, deep and penetrating. ... The bites ... were not random bites. Except for the defensive wounds, the bites were systematically inflicted in sexual areas of the victim's body").

88. United States v. Dia, 826 F. Supp. 1237, 1241 (D. Ariz. 1993) (applying FED. R. EVID. 404(b); "both [victims] sustained bites on their breasts during the assault"); State v. Fortin, 318 N.J. Super. 577, 589, 724 A.2d 818, 824 (1999) ("The bite marks on both women of the left breast, outer aspect, chin, and nipple exhibit segments which have similarities when compared to each other. ...Based upon the comparison revealing similarities among the bite marks, it is my opinion that the bite marks on both women could have been caused by Steven Fortin. Dr. Levine could not conclude within a reasonable degree of scientific certainty that the bite marks to Padilla's chin were caused by defendant").

89. *See Ex parte* Smith, 72 F. Supp. 935, 940 (M.D. Pa. 1947) ("The British Constable examined Smith's hand for tooth marks"), *aff'd,* 336 U.S. 695 (1949); People v. Stewart, 110 Ill. App. 2d 435, 249 N.E.2d 725, 726, 728 (1969) ("During the struggle the victim bit the assailant's right hand. ... Officer Marshall noted that the defendant had an oval scar on his right hand which looked as if it could have been caused by a bite"; "The scar on the defendant's right hand further corroborates her identification"), *aff'd,* 46 Ill. 2d 125, 262 N.E.2d 911 (1970); State v. McClinton, 265 S.C. 171, 217 S.E.2d 584, 585 (1975) ("She managed to scream, to kick her attacker, and to bite her assailant's hand"; "We do not think that the [the arresting officer's] descriptions of the injury as a 'cut, as though it had been bitten;' 'a mark was similar to a tooth'" were improper).

90. *See generally* 1 E. IMWINKELRIED, P. GIANNELLI, F. GILLIGAN & F. LEDERER, COURTROOM CRIMINAL EVIDENCE ch. 14 (3d ed. 1998).

91. Mobley v. State, 212 Ga. App. 293, 441 S.E.2d 780, 782 (1994).

observation of a physical fact and not an expert opinion. Given the disagreements by experts on this issue, these cases are troublesome if such evidence is going to play an important role at trial.

Early Bite Mark Cases

The first reported bite mark case appears to be *Doyle v. State,*[92] decided in 1954 by the Texas Court of Criminal Appeals. The court devoted only twelve lines of its opinion to this issue. Moreover, the bite mark in *Doyle* was left on a piece of cheese by a burglar, unlike the later cases where the mark was left on human tissue, a substance far more subject to distortion. Further, the two experts were a dentist and a firearms identification ("ballistics") expert. There is no indication that either had any experience in this field.[93]

Two decades later, *Patterson v. State,*[94] another Texas case, was decided. In this trial, prosecution experts matched the defendant's teeth with a mark found on the murder victim. These experts conceded that the dentition of others might also match the mark.[95] The defense expert testified that he could not see a "match." However, he was able to match the cast of one his patient's teeth to the mark. The appellate court rejected Patterson's attack on the reliability of the bite mark evidence by merely noting that it had previously admitted "similar evidence" in *Doyle.*

The next case, *People v. Marx* (1975),[96] is the leading bite mark case. The court in *Marx* avoided applying the *Frye* test, which requires acceptance of a novel technique by the scientific community as a prerequisite to admissibility.[97] According to the court, the *Frye* test "finds its rational basis in the degree to which the trier of fact must accept, on faith, scientific hypotheses not capable of proof or disproof in court and not even generally accepted outside the courtroom."[98] The court went on to hold that bite mark evidence did not involve blind acceptance by the jury. The basis on which the expert reached his

---

92. 159 Tex. Crim. 310, 263 S.W.2d 779 (1954).

93. Zarkowski, *Bite Mark Evidence: Its Worth in the Eyes of the Expert*, 1 J. LAW & ETHICS IN DENTISTRY 47, 52 (1988) ("The acceptance of bite mark analysis as a scientific procedure evolved from a weak beginning. ...Experiments were not conducted, nor were techniques tested, to apply the theory of bite mark analysis and evaluate the concept. ...The acceptance of bite mark evidence seemed to be premised on the assumption than anatomical configurations, like fingerprints, are unique to each individual, although support for this belief was not apparent"); Saks, *Merlin And Solomon: Lessons From The Law's Formative Encounters With Forensic Identification Science*, 49 HASTINGS L.J. 1069 (1998).

94. 509 S.W.2d 857, 862 (Tex. Crim. App. 1974).

95. One dentist testified that bite marks were as unique as fingerprints. *Id.* at 862.

96. 54 Cal. App. 3d 100, 126 Cal. Rptr. 350 (1975). This case is discussed in Note, *The Admissibility of Bite Mark Evidence*, 51 SO. CAL. L. REV. 309 (1978).

97. For a discussion of the *Frye* test, *see* Chapter 1.

98. 54 Cal. App. 3d at 110, 126 Cal. Rptr. at 355-56.

conclusions — models, photographs, and X-rays — were shown to the trier of fact, and the expert's conclusions were verifiable by the court. Thus, the "court did not have to sacrifice its independence and common sense in evaluating" the evidence.[99] Whether the *Frye* test should be so easily avoided is less than clear.

Moreover, the precedential value of *Marx* is undercut, at least to a certain degree, because the case involved an exceptional three-dimensional bite mark. Indeed, the court noted that the experts used a "virtually unprecedented three-dimensional approach."[100] A scientific article about the case uses the term "unusual" in the title.[101]

Judicial Acceptance

Despite these shortcomings,[102] until recently, no reported case had rejected bite mark evidence.[103] One commentator wrote: "As of March, 1992, there [have] been one hundred and ninety-three reported cases where human bite mark evidence has been introduced or noted in appeal.... Furthermore, bite mark evidence has been accepted as admissible in thirty-five states."[104] Some courts follow *Marx* and admit such evidence without applying the *Frye* test.[105] In any

---

99. *Id.* at 111, 126 Cal. Rptr. at 356.

100. *Id.* at 107, 126 Cal. Rptr. at 353.

101. Vale, Sognnaes, Felando & Noguchi, *Unusual Three-Dimensional Bite Mark Evidence in a Homicide Case*, 21 J. FORENSIC SCI. 642 (1976). In addition, the victim had been embalmed and buried for three months.

102. Two Australian cases, however, excluded bite mark evidence. *See* Lewis (1987), 29 A. CRIM. R. 267 (odontological evidence was improperly relied on, in that this method has not been scientifically accepted); Carroll (1985), 19 A. CRIM. R. 410 ("[T]he evidence given by the three odontologist is such that it would be unsafe or dangerous to allow a verdict based upon it to stand").

103. *See* FORENSIC DENTISTRY (P. Stimson & C. Merts eds. 1997) (app. A, listing 226 cases, including unreported cases).

104. Weigler, *Bite Mark Evidence: Forensic Odontology and the Law*, 2 HEALTH MATRIX: J.L.-MED. 303, (1992).

105. *See* Handley v. State, 515 So. 2d 121, 130-31 (Ala. Crim. App. 1987); State v. Garrison, 120 Ariz. 255, 585 P.2d 563 (1978); Verdict v. State, 315 Ark. 436, 868 S.W.2d 443 (1993) (bite mark evidence "widely accepted by the courts"); People v. Watson, 75 Cal. App. 3d 384, 142 Cal. Rptr. 134 (1977); Bundy v. State, 455 So. 2d 330, 348-49 (Fla. 1984); People v. Holmes, 234 Ill. App. 3d 931, 601 N.E.2d 985, 991-93 (1992), *app. denied*, 622 N.E.2d 1217 (Ill. 1993); People v. Milone, 43 Ill. App. 3d 385, 356 N.E.2d 1350 (1976); People v. Johnson, 8 Ill. App. 3d 457, 289 N.E.2d 722 (1972); Niehaus v. State, 265 Ind. 655, 359 N.E.2d 513, *cert. denied,* 434 U.S. 902 (1977); State v. Peoples, 227 Kan. 127, 605 P.2d 135 (1980); Commonwealth v. Cifizzari, 397 Mass. 560, 569-72, 492 N.E.2d 357, 362-64 (1986); People v. Marsh, 177 Mich. App. 161, 166-67, 441 N.W.2d 33, 35-36 (1989); Bludsworth v. State, 98 Nev. 289, 646 P.2d 558 (1982); State v. Green, 305 N.C. 463, 290 S.E.2d 625 (1982); State v. Temple, 302 N.C. 1, 273 S.E.2d 273 (1981); Kennedy v. State, 640 P.2d 971 (Okla. Crim. App. 1982); State v. Routh, 30 Or. App. 901, 568 P.2d 704 (1977); State v. Jones, 273 S.C. 723, 259 S.E.2d 120 (1979); State v. Cazes, 875 S.W.2d 253 (Tenn. 1994), *cert. denied*, 513 U.S. 1086 (1995); Spence v. State, 795 S.W.2d 743, 750-52

event, the *Frye* rule has not played a determinative role in the bite mark cases. Courts applying the *Frye* general acceptance standard have reached the same result.[106] It is not unusual for courts to speak of bitemark comparison as a "science."[107]

Indeed, its acceptance is so well-established that the New York Court of Appeals held that its validity need not be proved in every case:

> The reliability of bite mark evidence as a means of identification is sufficiently established in the scientific community to make such evidence admissible in a criminal case, without separately establishing scientific reliability in each case, but subject, of course, to the establishment by foundation evidence of the authenticity of the materials used and propriety of the procedure followed in the particular case and to cross-examination intended to test the reliability of the conclusion reached in that case.[108]

In short, courts may judicially notice the general validity of bite mark evidence.[109] Judicial notice, however, does not extend to the validity of an identification in a particular case.

Post-Daubert Cases

One commentator has stated that "the *Daubert* decision is likely to have little effect on bite mark admissibility."[110] In light of later developments in other fields, however, this statement seems highly debatable. The reliability standard

---

(Tex. Crim. App.), *cert. denied*, 499 U.S. 932 (1990); Patterson v. State, 509 S.W.2d 857 (Tex. Crim. App. 1974); State v. Howe, 136 Vt. 53, 386 A.2d 1125 (1978).

106. *See* United States v. Martin, 13 M.J. 66, 67-68 (C.M.A. 1982); People v. Slone, 76 Cal. App. 3d 611, 623-24, 143 Cal. Rptr. 61, 68-69 (1978); State v. Hodgson, 512 N.W.2d 95, 98 (Minn. 1994) (bite mark analysis routinely used); State v. Kleypas, 602 S.W.2d 863, 868-70 (Mo. App. 1980); State v. Sager, 600 S.W.2d 541, 573 (Mo. App. 1980), *cert. denied,* 450 U.S. 910 (1981); People v. Middleton, 54 N.Y.2d 42, 49-50, 429 N.E.2d 100, 103-04, 444 N.Y.S.2d 581, 584-85 (1981); People v. Bethune, 105 A.D.2d 262, 267, 484 N.Y.S.2d 577, 581 (1984); People v. Smith, 110 Misc. 2d 118, 124-26, 443 N.Y.S.2d 551, 556-57 (Cty. Ct. 1981).

107. *See* People v. Marsh, 177 Mich. App. 161, 164, 441 N.W.2d 33, 35 (1989) ("the science of bite mark analysis has been extensively reviewed in other jurisdictions"); State v. Sager, 600 S.W.2d 541, 569 (Mo. App. 1980) ("an exact science"), *cert. denied*, 450 U.S.910 (1981).

108. People v. Middleton, 54 N.Y.2d 42, 45, 429 N.E.2d 100, 101, 444 N.Y.S.2d 581, 582 (1981). *See also* State v. Richards, 166 Ariz. App. 576, 579, 804 P.2d 109, 112 (1990) ("[B]ite mark evidence is admissible without a preliminary determination of reliability..."); People v. Smith, 63 N.Y.2d 41, 63, 468 N.E.2d 879, 889, 479 N.Y.S.2d 706, 716 (1984), *cert. denied*, 469 U.S. 1227 (1985); State v. Armstrong, 369 S.E.2d 870, 877 (W. Va. 1988) (judicially noticing the reliability of bite mark evidence).

109. For a discussion of judicial notice, *see* Chapter 1.

110. McClure, *Odontology: Bite Marks as Evidence in Criminal Trials*, 11 SANTA CLARA COMPUTER & HIGH TECH. L.J. 269, 281 (1995).

adopted in *Daubert* has been applied to exclude some types of evidence that had previously been admitted at trial.[111]

One of the few reported cases excluding bite mark evidence is *Howard v. State*,[112] in which Dr. Michael West made a "positive match" of a bitemark on the victim with the defendant's teeth. "Dr. West testified that the science of dentistry recognized that teeth are unique, and that bite marks can 'be identified back to the perpetrator or biter.' Dr. West also stated that bite-mark evidence is similar to fingerprint identification."[113] The Mississippi Supreme Court reversed, noting: "While few courts have refused to allow some form of bite-mark comparison evidence, numerous scholarly authorities have criticized the reliability of this method of identifying a suspect." The court went on to observe: "There is little consensus in the scientific community on the number of points which must match before any positive identification can be announced. ... Suffice it to say that testimony concerning bite marks in soft, living flesh has not been scientifically accredited at this time."[114] Nevertheless, the same court later admitted bitemark evidence through the testimony of Dr. West.[115]

Specificity of Opinion

In some cases experts have testified only that a bite mark is "consistent with" the defendant's teeth.[116] In other cases experts have testified that it is "highly

---

111. For a discussion of *Daubert, see* Chapter 1.

112. 697 So. 2d 415 (Miss. 1997).

113. *Id.* at 428.

114. *Id.* at 429.

115. State v. Brewer, 725 So. 2d 106 (Miss. 1998). *See infra. See also* Keko v. Hingle, 1999 WL 155945 (E.D. La.) (Civil rights action against law enforcement officials for using Dr. West, who testified on the state's behalf as an expert witness. West had developed "a novel process" ("radical and innovative methods"). By means of his own controversial technique, he "concluded that the teeth marks on [the victim's] body were made by the plaintiff." Due to Dr. West's conclusions, the defendants sought an arrest warrant against plaintiff. The plaintiff was subsequently convicted of murder. Defendants "supplied Dr. West with evidence which would only allow him to find that plaintiff had made the bite marks which only Dr. West could see through his 'technique'.... Taking all of the plaintiff's allegations as true, the defendants should have known that the allegations they were making in the requests for warrants were unfounded").

116. *E.g.*, Handley v. State, 515 So. 2d 121, 129 (Ala. Crim. App. 1987); People v. Watson, 75 Cal. App. 3d 384, 400-01, 142 Cal. Rptr. 134, 143 (1977); Rogers v. State, 256 Ga. 140, 344 S.E.2d 644, 647 (1986) ("Bite marks on one of Rogers' arms were consistent with the dentures worn by the elderly victim"), *cert. denied*, 479 U.S. 995 (1986); People v. Williams, 128 Ill. App. 3d 384, 398, 470 N.E.2d 1140, 1150 (1984) ("could have"); People v. Marsh, 177 Mich. App. 161, 164, 441 N.W.2d 33, 35 (1989); State v. Hodgson, 512 N.W.2d 95, 98 (Minn. 1994) (en banc) (Board-certified forensic odontologist testified that "there were several similarities between the bite mark and the pattern of [the victim's] teeth, as revealed by known molds of his mouth"); Bludsworth v. State, 98 Nev. 289, 292 n.1, 646 P.2d 558, 559 n.1 (1982); People v. Bethune, 105 A.D.2d 262, 266, 484 N.Y.S.2d 577, 580-81 (1984); State v. Routh, 30 Or. App. 901, 903, 568 P.2d 704, 705

probable" or "very highly probable" that the defendant made the mark.[117] In still other cases experts have made positive identifications (to the exclusion of all other persons).[118]

Disagreements Among Experts

Given the subjective character of bite mark comparisons, it is not surprising to find qualified experts disagreeing in individual cases.[119] In some cases the experts

(1977) ("similarity"); Litaker v. State, 784 S.W.2d 739, 743 (Tex. App. 1990); Williams v. State, 838 S.W.2d 952, 954 (Tex. App. 1992) ("One expert, a forensic odontologist, testified that Williams's dentition was consistent with the injury (bite mark) on the deceased. On cross-examination, the expert said, 'I did not say that to a reasonable certainty or a positive certainty that [Williams] did it'"); State v. Warness, 77 Wash. App. 636, 893 P.2d 665, 669 (1995) ("[T]he expert testified that his opinion was not conclusive, but the evidence was consistent with the alleged victim's assertion that she had bitten Warness.... Its probative value was therefore limited, but its relevance was not extinguished. The trial court correctly found that the expert's uncertainty relevant to the weight and not the admissibility of his testimony").

117. *E.g.,* People v. Slone, 76 Cal. App. 3d 611, 621, 143 Cal. Rptr. 61, 67 (1978); People v. Johnson, 8 Ill. App. 3d 457, 461, 289 N.E.2d 722, 726 (1972).

118. *E.g.,* DuBoise v. State, 520 So. 2d 260, 261 (Fla. 1988) (Expert "testified at trial that within a reasonable degree of dental certainty DuBoise had bitten the victim"); Morgan v. State, 639 So. 2d 6, 9 (Fla. 1994) ("[T]he testimony of a dental expert at trial positively matched the bite marks on the victim with Morgan's teeth"); People v. Gallo, 260 Ill. App. 3d 1032, 1038, 632 N.E.2d 99, 103 (forensic dentist testified that the injury to the murder victim's "breast was caused by human teeth and that it was the defendant's teeth that made the teeth mark"), *app. denied,* 645 N.E.2d 1362 (Ill. 1994); People v. Milone, 43 Ill. App. 3d 385, 392-93, 356 N.E.2d 1350, 1355-56 (1976); Commonwealth v. Cifizzari, 397 Mass. 560, 564, 492 N.E.2d 357, 360 (1986); Brewer v. State, 725 So. 2d 106, 116 (Miss. 1998) ("Dr. West opined that Brewer's teeth inflicted the five bite mark patterns found on the body of Christine Jackson. The doctor further concluded that it was 'highly consistent and probable' that the other fourteen bite mark patterns were also inflicted by Brewer"), *cert. denied,* 119 S. Ct. 1270 (1999); Davis v. State, 611 So. 2d 906, 910 (Miss. 1992) (prosecution expert had "no doubt"); State v. Schaefer, 855 S.W.2d 504, 506 (Mo. App. 1993) ("[A] forensic dentist testified that the bite marks on Schaefer's shoulder matched victim's dental impression, and concluded that victim caused the marks"); State v. Sager, 600 S.W.2d 541, 564 (Mo. App. 1980), *cert. denied,* 450 U.S. 910 (1981); State v. Temple, 302 N.C. 1, 10, 273 S.E.2d 273, 279 (1981); State v. Lyons, 324 Or. 256, 924 P.2d 802, 804 (1993) (Forensic odontologist "had no doubt that the wax models were made from the same person whose teeth marks appeared on the victim's body"); State v. Cazes, 875 S.W.2d 253, 258 (Tenn. 1994) (A forensic odontologist "concluded to a reasonable degree of dental certainty that Cazes' teeth had made the bite marks on the victim's body at or about the time of her death"), *cert. denied,* 513 U.S. 1086 (1995).

119. *E.g.,* Czapleski v. Woodward, 1991 U.S. Dist. LEXIS 12567 (N.D. Cal. Aug. 30, 1991) (Dentist's initial report concluded that "bite" marks found on child were consistent with dental impressions of mother; several experts later established that the marks on child's body were postmortem abrasion marks and not bite marks); Kinney v. State, 315 Ark. 481, 868 S.W.2d 463 (1994) (disagreement that marks were human bite marks); Harris v. State, 1992 Ark. App. LEXIS 728, at *5 (Nov. 18, 1992) ("Appellant also points to the testimony of Dr. Thomas Krauss, a forensic odontologist, who disputed the opinion of Dr. West that the bite mark was made by the appellant"); People v. Noguera, 4 Cal. 4th 599, 842 P.2d 1160, 1165 n.1, 15 Cal. Rptr. 2d 400, 405

have arrived at diametrically opposed conclusions, while in others they disagree only on whether the data is sufficient to support a positive identification.

People v. Milone[120] is an example. In that case three experts testified for the prosecution and four experts testified for the defense. The prosecution experts all positively identified the defendant's teeth as the source of the bite mark found on the victim. The defense experts testified either that a positive identification could not be made or that the defendant's teeth did not make the mark.[121] Despite this disagreement, the defendant was convicted. Interestingly, one of the experts in that case subsequently wrote that "[r]ecently discovered evidence proves that Milone ... is innocent."[122] Milone subsequently filed a federal habeas corpus petition, once again challenging the admissibility of the bite mark evidence and offering the testimony of a new expert. The federal court, however, ruled this testimony merely cumulative and therefore not a basis for habeas relief: "The bite mark testimony of Milone's new expert, Dr. Campbell, would merely be one more expert opinion added to the numerous opinions before the court."[123] The Seventh Circuit upheld the district court's ruling that Milone's constitutional rights had not been violated. Nevertheless, the court also added that "Milone has made a credible claim that newly discovered evidence would not only cast a doubt upon his guilt but in fact would exonerate him."[124]

Similarly, in *People v. Smith*[125] seven experts testified, four for the prosecution and three for the defense. While the prosecution experts found that the bite mark on a murder victim had been made by the accused, the defense experts testified that not only was the mark not made by the defendant but that it "was not a bite mark at all."[126] In addition, the experts disagreed about the proper methods that may be used for the comparison. The prosecution experts used two methods of comparison. First, they compared a stone model of the defendant's dentition and

---

n.1 (1992) ("At trial, extensive testimony by forensic odontologists was presented by both sides, pro and con, as to whether the wounds were human bite marks and, if so, when they were inflicted"), *cert. denied*, 512 U.S. 1253 (1994); State v. Sager, 600 S.W.2d 541, 563-67 (Mo. App. 1980), *cert. denied*, 450 U.S. 910 (1981); People v. Bethune, 105 A.D.2d 262, 266-71, 484 N.Y.S.2d 577, 580-83 (1984); Spence v. State, 795 S.W.2d 743, 750-52 (Tex. Crim. App.), *cert. denied*, 499 U.S. 932 (1990); Patterson v. State, 509 S.W.2d 857, 862 (Tex. Crim. App. 1974); State v. Howe, 136 Vt. 53, 65, 386 A.2d 1125, 1132 (1978).

120. 43 Ill. App. 3d 385, 356 N.E.2d 1350 (1976).

121. *Id.* at 393, 356 N.E.2d at 1356.

122. Levine, *Forensic Dentistry: Our Most Controversial Case, in* LEGAL MEDICINE ANNUAL 73 (C. Wecht ed. 1978).

123. Milone v. Camp, No. 85C10098, 1992 U.S. Dist. LEXIS 14615, at *16 (N.D. Ill., Sept. 29, 1992) (also noting that the "trial judge reviewed over 1300 pages of bite mark evidence"). *See also* Milone v. Camp, 643 F. Supp. 679 (N.D. Ill. 1986).

124. Milone v. Camp, 22 F.3d 693, 705 (7th Cir. 1994), *cert. denied*, 513 U.S. 1076 (1995).

125. 63 N.Y.2d 41, 468 N.E.2d 879, 479 N.Y.S.2d 706 (1984), *cert. denied*, 469 U.S. 1227 (1985).

126. *Id.* at 58, 468 N.E.2d at 886, 479 N.Y.S.2d at 713.

impressions made in aluwax from the model with life-size photographs of the mark on the victim. Second, they made photo-to-photo comparisons of the victim's mark and a bite mark known to have been made by the defendant on human tissue four years earlier.[127] In contrast, the defense experts compared transparencies made from a model of the defendant's teeth with a photograph of the mark on the victim. The transparencies were then laid over the photograph.[128] The defense experts, however, conceded that there was no completely objective method for identifying bite marks and that each method ultimately relied on the judgment of the individual expert.

In still another case, two odontologists made a positive identification of bite marks in a murder trial. Defense experts, however, showed that the mark had been misinterpreted — that it was not even a bite mark.[129] The jury acquitted the accused.

These types of disagreements continue in later cases. In *State v. Holmes*[130] two prosecution experts testified that the defendant inflicted the bite marks found on the victim. Then, two defense experts testified that the marks were not bite marks and thus were not made by the defendant.[131] In *Davis v. State*[132] the prosecution expert had "no doubt" that the victim's teeth made the bite mark on the defendant's arm, whereas the defense expert testified that the mark "was not a bite mark, but even if it were, it was inconsistent with [the victim's] teeth."[133]

In *Brewer v. State*[134] Dr. West opined that Brewer's teeth inflicted the five bite mark patterns found on the victim's body. "The doctor further concluded that it was 'highly consistent and probable' that the other fourteen bite mark patterns

---

127. *Id.*

128. *Id.*

129. Sperry & Campbell, *An Elliptical Incised Wound of the Breast Misinterpreted as a Bite Injury*, 35 J. FORENSIC SCI. 1226 (1990). *See also* Sperber, *Lingual Markings of Anterior Teeth As Seen in Human Bite Marks*, 35 J. FORENSIC SCI. 838, 838 (1990) ("In a recent California case, it was necessary to perform a histologic examination in order to demonstrate conclusively that the lesion identified by a forensic dentist as a bite mark was, in fact, a postmortem artifact"); Karazulas, *The Presentation of Bite Mark Evidence Resulting in the Acquittal of a Man After Serving Seven Years in Prison for Murder*, 29 J. FORENSIC SCI. 355 (1984) (After three trials, defendant finally acquitted where bite mark evidence was the main issue in the third trial); Nordby, *Can We Believe What We See, If We See What We Believe? — Expert Disagreement*, 37 J. FORENSIC SCI. 1115, 1122 n.16 (1992) ("The trial ... involved disagreements among reputable forensic odontologists ranging from those unwilling to identify the injury as a bite mark to the exclusion of other mechanisms, to those willing to identify the injury as a bite inflicted by a specific individual to the exclusion of all other individuals"; citing State v. Kendrick, 47 Wash. App. 620, 736 P.2d 1079 (1987)).

130. 234 Ill. App. 3d 931, 601 N.E.2d 985 (1992), *app. denied*, 622 N.E.2d 1217 (Ill. 1993).

131. *Id.* at 991-93.

132. 611 So. 2d 906 (Miss. 1992).

133. *Id.* at 910.

134. 725 So. 2d 106 (Miss. 1998), *cert. denied*, 119 S. Ct. 1270 (1999).

were also inflicted by Brewer."[135] In contrast, Dr. Souviron, a founding member of the ABFO, testified that "none of the wounds on the child's body were bite marks ... because there were no corresponding lower teeth prints found on the child's body. Dr. West explained that, for some unknown reason, Brewer's lower teeth were not very sharp."[136]

Expert Qualifications

Although the qualifications of experts who have testified in the bite mark cases have been challenged in some prosecutions, these challenges typically have failed.[137] Most of the experts have been experienced forensic odontologists. In one case, however, a court ruled that a pathologist's testimony that a bruise discovered during an autopsy was consistent with a bite mark was improper because he was not qualified in forensic dentistry.[138] In another case, a dentist was considered qualified even though the bite mark comparison in issue was the first he had made.[139]

In *Brewer v.* State,[140] the defense challenged the qualifications of Dr. Michael West because he had been suspended by the American Board of Forensic Odontology, and had resigned from the International Association of Identification and the American Academy of Forensic Sciences. The court rejected the challenge, pointing out that West's "fiasco" in a prior case involved his "blue light" technique, through which he claimed that he could perfectly match a bruise on the accused's palm with the murder weapon.[141] Moreover, West had testified in seven cases after his suspension. Finally, the defense expert conceded that West was qualified and that West's direct comparison technique was an acceptable method.[142]

Statistical Evidence

In *State v. Garrison*,[143] the expert was permitted to state his conclusion in terms of probability theory, testifying that "there is an eight in one million probability that the teeth marks found on the deceased's breast were not made by

---

135. *Id.* at 116.

136. *Id.*

137. *See* People v. Williams, 128 Ill. App. 3d 384, 397, 470 N.E.2d 1140, 1149-50 (1984); State v. Peoples, 227 Kan. 127, 132-33, 605 P.2d 135, 139-40 (1980); State v. Temple, 302 N.C. 1, 12-13, 273 S.E.2d 273, 280 (1981).

138. State v. Adams, 481 A.2d 718, 727-28 (R.I. 1984).

139. Niehaus v. State, 265 Ind. 655, 359 N.E.2d 513, *cert. denied,* 434 U.S. 902 (1977).

140. 725 So. 2d 106 (Miss. 1998).

141. *See* Giannelli, *The Abuse of Scientific Evidence: The Need for Independent Crime Laboratories*, 4 VA. J. L. & SOC. POLICY 439, 454-55 (1997) (discussing the blue-light technique).

142. 725 So. 2d at 125-26.

143. 120 Ariz. 255, 585 P.2d 563 (1978).

appellant."[144] Such a statement appears to be without scientific foundation. The expert did not perform any of his own mathematical calculations, was unaware of the formula used to arrive at that figure other than that it was "computerized," and was ignorant of the statistical weight assigned to each variable used in the equation.[145] The dissent commented: "[W]hile Dr. Campbell may have a great deal of expertise in the actual comparison techniques of bite-mark identification, he is totally out of his field when the discussion turns to probability theory."[146]

Microorganism

In *Washington v. State*,[147] a capital case, the prosecution expert conceded that he had used a novel method of comparison that no one else had ever used. The expert testified that:

> he used two types of analyses to identify appellant as the assailant: bitemark/dentition comparison and a comparison of microorganisms found in the wound and in appellant's mouth. The doctor placed primary identification emphasis on the microorganism "aspergillus" being present in both the bitemark and in appellant's mouth. At trial, the doctor testified that aspergillus would be found in the mouths of only "one in a billion people." Although the doctor claimed that his tests were "accepted," he admitted that he was aware of no other persons who either used or advocated the use of microbiological analysis in bitemark comparisons.[148]

The basis for this astounding statistic is not revealed. The court, nevertheless, ruled that the defendant was not entitled to a defense expert.

---

144. *Id.* at 258, 585 P.2d at 566.

145. "As indicated in the majority opinion, Dr. Campbell was unsure as to precisely where he obtained the figure 'eight in one million.' My independent research reveals that of the two treatises which he could name as containing statistical information, only ... [one] lists any figures on the uniqueness of a bite-mark. Rather than the eight in one million figure vouched for by Dr. Campell, though, that treatise ... contains the figure eight in one hundred thousand." *Id.* at 260-61, 585 P.2d at 568-69. "Moreover, the applicability of even an eight in one hundred thousand figure to the defendant is dubious." *Id.* at n.1, 585 P.2d at 569 n.1.

146. *Id.* at 260, 585 P.2d at 568. *See also* McCord, *A Primer For the Nonmathematically Inclined on Mathematical Evidence in Criminal Cases: People v. Collins and Beyond*, 47 WASH. & LEE L. REV. 741, 801 (1990) ("A blistering and convincing dissent [in *Garrison*] showed the probability to be without foundation and thus unfairly prejudicial").

147. 836 P.2d 673 (Okla. Crim. App. 1992).

148. *Id.* at 678 (Parks, J., concurring in part, dissenting in part).

Characterization of Bite Marks

In *Commonwealth v. Henry,*[149] the expert went beyond a comparison and characterized a bite mark as "sadistic" rather than a "sexual" or "fighting" mark. "The essence of the distinction is that fighting bite marks are less well defined because they are done carelessly and quickly, whereas attacking and sadistic bite marks are made slowly and produce a clearer pattern ...."[150] According to the expert, "the sadistic bite mark is one of the most well defined. Sexual bite marks are also well defined, but usually have a red center, produced by sucking tissue into the mouth."[151] The testimony characterizing the mark as a "sadistic" mark was relevant on the issue of whether the homicide was committed by means of torture. It seems doubtful that a bite mark can be characterized as sexual or fighting by an examination of the mark alone. Surrounding circumstances, including an autopsy, may permit such a characterization.

Destruction of Evidence

In *Banks v. State,*[152] a capital murder case, the State's expert witness testified that although Banks' teeth correlated with the bite marks in the remaining portion of a sandwich found at the crime scene he could not say with any degree of certainty that Banks had bitten the sandwich. The defense expert had to use photographs of the bologna sandwich because the sandwich had been destroyed. Consequently, he was unable to make any definite conclusions. The court stated that "the prejudicial impact of the State's destruction of the sandwich on the persuasive value of Banks' case is plainly apparent, and Dr. West's destruction of the sandwich was unnecessary and inexcusable."[153] Both experts should be afforded a comparable vantage point, otherwise the evidence presented by the "advantaged" expert is fundamentally unfair.

Spoliation Evidence

Evidence that a defendant has attempted to alter his teeth after learning of the prosecution's intention to introduce bite mark evidence is admissible as spoliation evidence. In *State v. Turner,*[154] the expert detected new tooth fractures when he attempted to cast the defendant's dentition. The defendant was aware that impressions of his teeth would be taken but claimed that the fractures occurred when he bit a bone during a meal. The expert testified that the fractures

---

149. 524 Pa. 135, 569 A.2d 929 (1990), *cert. denied,* 499 U.S. 931 (1991).

150. *Id.* at 146, 569 A.2d at 934.

151. *Id.*

152. 725 So. 2d 711 (Miss. 1997).

153. *Id.* at 716.

154. 633 S.W.2d 421 (Mo. App. 1982).

resulted in some other way. The court held that evidence of the defendant's conduct was admissible: "The spoliation of evidence evinces a consciousness of guilt and is admissible for that reason."[155]

§ 13-6. Obtaining Dental Impressions from Suspects.

Defendants have challenged the admissibility of bite mark evidence on a number of constitutional grounds.[156] The U.S. Supreme Court has ruled that the fifth amendment privilege against compelled self-incrimination extends to testimonial, but not physical, evidence. Accordingly, a suspect may be compelled to provide bite impressions.[157]

The sixth amendment right to counsel is inapplicable for two reasons. First, the right to counsel does not attach with an arrest; it attaches only when judicial adversary proceedings have commenced.[158] Second, taking bite impressions is not a critical stage of a criminal prosecution requiring the assistance of an attorney.[159]

The fourth amendment prohibits unreasonable searches and seizures. There are two distinct fourth amendment issues. First, there may be a "seizure" of the person which brings the suspect under the control of the police. Second, the taking of a bite impression from that person is a distinct additional search.

---

155. *Id.* at 424.

156. For a detailed discussion of the constitutional aspects of obtaining evidence from suspects, *see* Chapter 2.

157. *See* United States v. Maceo, 873 F.2d 1, 5-6 (1st Cir.) (examination of teeth), *cert. denied,* 493 U.S. 840 (1989); United States v. Holland, 378 F. Supp. 144, 154-55 (E.D. Pa.), (obtaining dental impressions from a defendant is not compelled self-incrimination), *aff'd sub nom.* Appeal of Ehly, 506 F.2d 1050 (3d Cir. 1974), *cert. denied,* Ehly v. United States, 420 U.S. 994 (1975); State v. Evans, 44 Conn. App. 307, 689 A.2d 494, 501 ("[B]ecause the order to display one's teeth, whether prior to or at trial, does not involve communications or testimony, the defendant's claim is not of constitutional magnitude ..."), *app. denied,* 692 A.2d 819 (1997); State v. Asherman, 193 Conn. 695, 715, 478 A.2d 227, 240 (1984) (state constitution); State v. Thornton, 253 Ga. 524, 525, 322 S.E.2d 711, 712 (1984) (state constitution); People v. Milone, 43 Ill. App. 3d 385, 392, 356 N.E.2d 1350, 1355 (1976); Brewer v. State, 725 So.2d 106, 130 (Miss. 1998) ("[T]he trial court's admission of the dental impression into evidence was proper as the impression was nothing more than evidence identifying a physical characteristic — very similar to fingerprints"), *cert. denied,* 119 S. Ct. 1270 (1999); People v. Smith, 110 Misc. 2d 118, 121-22, 443 N.Y.S.2d 551, 554-55 (Cty. Ct. 1981); People v. Allah, 84 Misc. 2d 500, 502, 376 N.Y.S.2d 399, 401 (Sup. Ct. 1975); State v. Sapsford, 22 Ohio App. 3d 1, 3, 488 N.E.2d 218, 220 (1983); Patterson v. State, 509 S.W.2d 857, 862-63 (Tex. Crim. App. 1974).

158. State v. Howe, 136 Vt. 53, 63, 386 A.2d 1125, 1131 (1978) (right to counsel had not attached at time dental impressions taken); Spence v. State, 795 S.W.2d 743, 752-53 (Tex. Crim. App. 1990) (same), *cert. denied,* 499 U.S. 932 (1991).

159. Brewer v. State, 725 So. 2d 106, 130 (Miss. 1998) ("[T]he taking of the dental impression was like the taking of fingerprints — which this court has held not be a critical stage so as to require counsel's presence"), *cert. denied,* 119 S. Ct. 1270 (1999).

Generally, searches and seizures must be based on probable cause and a warrant, unless there is consent or some other exception to the warrant requirement.[160]

§ 13-7. Defense Experts.

An indigent defendant has the right to the appointment of an defense expert in this field under certain circumstances.[161]

In *Washington v. State*,[162] a capital case, the Oklahoma Court of Criminal Appeals ruled that a defendant was not entitled to the appointment of a defense expert, even though a prosecution expert had testified that the defendant had made the bite mark found on the murder victim. Moreover, the prosecution expert conceded that he had used a novel method of comparison that no one else had ever used. He also testified that only "one in a billion people" had a particular characteristic shared by the defendant.[163] The basis for this astounding statistic is not revealed. The need for a defense expert under these circumstances is compelling.

Another bite mark case, *Harrison v. State*,[164] involved the death penalty for the murder of a ten-year-old girl. A prosecution expert testified that the defendant

---

160. In the following cases the courts ruled that obtaining dental impressions from a defendant did not violate the fourth amendment: United States v. Holland, 378 F. Supp. 144, 154-55 (E.D. Pa.), *aff'd sub nom.* Appeal of Ehly, 506 F.2d 1050 (3d Cir. 1974), *cert. denied*, Ehly v. United States, 420 U.S. 994 (1975); DuBoise v. State, 520 So. 2d 260, 261 (Fla. 1988) (accused consented to providing stone cast model of his impression); People v. Milone, 43 Ill. App. 3d 385, 390-91, 356 N.E.2d 1350, 1354 (1976); People v. Smith, 110 Misc. 2d 118, 122-23, 443 N.Y.S.2d 551, 554-55 (Cty. Ct. 1981); State v. Sapsford, 22 Ohio App. 3d 1, 3, 488 N.E.2d 218, 220 (1983); State v. Howe, 136 Vt. 53, 64, 386 A.2d 1125, 1131-32 (1978).

But see People v. Dace, 153 Ill. App. 3d 891, 896-99, 506 N.E.2d 332, 335-37 (warrant for bite impression and photographs lacked probable cause), *cert. denied,* 116 Ill. 2d 565, 515 N.E.2d 116 (1987).

161. *See* Thornton v. State, 255 Ga. 434, 435, 339 S.E.2d 240, 241 (1986) (indigent accused entitled to state funds for court-appointed expert to examine dental impressions linking accused to murder). For a further discussion of this issue, *see* Chapter 4.

162. 836 P.2d 673 (Okla. Crim. App. 1992).

163. *Id.* at 678. The prosecution's expert testified that:

> he used two types of analyses to identify appellant as the assailant: bitemark/dentition comparison and a comparison of microorganisms found in the wound and in appellant's mouth. The doctor placed primary identification emphasis on the microorganism "aspergillus" being present in both the bitemark and in appellant's mouth. At trial, the doctor testified that aspergillus would be found in the mouths of only "one in a billion people." Although the doctor claimed that his tests were "accepted," he admitted that he was aware of no other persons who either used or advocated the use of microbiological analysis in bitemark comparisons.

Id. (Parks, J., concurring in part, dissenting in part).

164. 635 So. 2d 894 (Miss. 1994). For a further discussion, *see* Moss, *Death, Habeas and Good Lawyers: Balancing Fairness and Finality*, 78 A.B.A. J. 83, 85 (Dec. 1992). John Holdridge also

had bitten the victim more than forty times, but the trial court nevertheless rejected a defense request for an expert. To demonstrate a "particularized need" for a defense expert, the trial judge required that the expert first review the evidence and write an affidavit. Without pay, however, most experts will not review the evidence or prepare an affidavit. By the time of the appeal, an expert had been found, and he had concluded that the "marks were not from bites."[165] The Mississippi Supreme Court reversed on another issue.[166]

§ 13-8. Ineffective Assistance of Counsel.

In *People v. Blommaert*,[167] the accused argued that defense counsel was ineffective for failing to investigate the bite mark evidence. A report by a forensic odontologist indicated a sibling had caused bite marks on a ten-month-old homicide victim. Counsel had not contacted this expert. The appellate court, however, concluded that counsel's performance was not ineffective because he was aware of the bite mark evidence and did not pursue the issue due to discussions with the accused.

§ 13-9. Selected Bibliography.

Books

J. CAMERSON & B. SIMS, FORENSIC DENTISTRY (1974).

MANUAL OF FORENSIC ODONTOLOGY (3d. ed 1997) (C. Bowers & C. Bell eds.) (ASFO publication).

PRACTICAL FORENSIC ODONTOLOGY (D. Clark ed. 1992).

G. GUSTAFSON, FORENSIC ODONTOLOGY (1966).

W. HARVEY, DENTAL IDENTIFICATION AND FORENSIC ODONTOLOGY (1976).

S. KEISER-NIELSON, PERSON IDENTIFICATION BY MEANS OF THE TEETH (1980).

L. LUNTZ & P. LUNTZ, HANDBOOK FOR DENTAL IDENTIFICATION (1973).

I. SOPHER, FORENSIC DENTISTRY (1976).

P. STIMSON & C. MERTZ, FORENSIC DENTISTRY (1997).

OUTLINE OF FORENSIC DENTISTRY (J. Cottone & S. Standish eds. 1982).

Chapters in Books

A. MOENSSENS, J. STARRS, & C. HENDERSON, SCIENTIFIC EVIDENCE: CIVIL AND CRIMINAL ch. 16 (4th ed. 1995).

Identification of Tooth Marks, 25 AM. JUR. PROOF OF FACTS 765 (1970).

Rawson, *Identification from Bite Marks*, *in* MODERN SCIENTIFIC EVIDENCE ch. 24 (D. Faigman, D. Kaye, M. Saks & J. Sanders eds. 1997).

---

noted that it is difficult to obtain good lawyers for three reasons: "Fees may be restricted, judges are reluctant to spend money on experts, and standards are lax for trial counsel." *Id.* at 84.

165. *Id.* at 85.

166. Harrison v. State, 635 So. 2d 894 (Miss. 1994) (reversed due to trial court's failure to appoint defense pathologist).

167. 237 Ill. App. 3d 811, 604 N.E.2d 1054 (1992), *app. denied*, 612 N.E.2d 516 (Ill. 1993).

Articles

McClure, *Odontology: Bite Marks as Evidence in Criminal Trials*, 11 SANTA CLARA COMPUTER & HIGH TECH. L.J. 269 (1995).

Weigler, *Bite Mark Evidence: Forensic Odontology and the Law*, 2 HEALTH MATRIX: J.L.-MED. 303 (1992).

Wilkerson & Gerughty, *Bite Mark Evidence: Its Admissibility is Hard to Swallow*, 12 W. ST. U. L. REV. 519 (1985).

Note, *Forensic Dentistry and the Law: Is Bite Mark Evidence Here to Stay?*, 24 AM. CRIM. L. REV. 983 (1987).

Comment, *Bite Mark Evidence: Hocus Pocus or Science*, 16 CUMB. L. REV. 127 (1985).

Comment, *Evidence: The Erosion of Legal Safeguards on the Admissibility of Bitemark Evidence in Criminal Trials: Bradford v. State*, 37 U. FLA. L. REV. 889 (1985).

Note, *The Admissibility of Bite Mark Evidence*, 51 S. CAL. L. REV. 309 (1978).

Annotations

Annot., *Admissibility of evidence tending to identify accused by his own bite marks*, 77 A.L.R.3D 1122 (1977).

CHAPTER 14

FIREARMS, TOOLMARK AND RELATED EXAMINATIONS*

§ 14-1. In General.

"Firearms identification is a discipline of forensic science which has as its primary concern to determine if a bullet, cartridge case or other ammunition component was fired by a particular firearm."[1] Apparently, the first written

---

*The sections in this chapter were revised and renumbered in this edition. The authors wish to express their appreciation to John Cayton, Chief, Firearms Section, Regional Criminalistics Laboratory, Kansas City, Missouri, who reviewed this chapter. The authors also want to thank Robert D. Koons and Donald G. Havekost, FBI Laboratory, who reviewed parts of this chapter.

1. Association of Firearm and Tool Mark Examiners, Glossary 80 (1980) [hereinafter AFTE Glossary]. *See also* FBI Handbook of Forensic Science 57 (rev. ed. 1994) ("Firearms identification is the forensic science discipline that identifies a bullet, cartridge case or other ammunition component as having been fired by a particular firearm to the exclusion of all other firearms").

reference to the subject appeared in 1900.[2] The topic gained considerable attention in the 1920s due to the work of Calvin Goddard[3] and played a controversial role in the Sacco and Vanzetti case during the same decade.[4] In 1923, the Illinois Supreme Court wrote that positive identification of a bullet was not only impossible but "preposterous."[5] Seven years later that court became one of the first courts in this country to admit firearms identification evidence.[6]

Although this subject is popularly known as "ballistics," that term is not correct. Ballistics is the study of the motion of a projectile. Interior ballistics concerns the study of the projectile within the firearm;[7] exterior ballistics concerns the study of the projectile after it leaves the firearm;[8] and terminal (wound) ballistics concerns the study of the effects of the projectile on a target. Firearms identification does not directly involve ballistics. Accordingly, a true "ballistics" expert may know very little about firearms identification. Similarly, a firearms expert — a person knowledgeable about weapons and ammunition — may know little about firearms identification.[9]

---

2. *See* Hall, *The Missile and the Weapon*, 39 BUFFALO MED. J. 727 (1900).

3. Calvin Goddard, often credited as the "father" of firearms identification, was responsible for much of the early work on the subject. *E.g.*, Goddard, *Scientific Identification of Firearms and Bullets*, 17 J. CRIM. L., CRIMINOLOGY & POLICE SCI. 254 (1926).

For a brief history of firearms identification, *see* J. HATCHER, F. JURY & J. WELLER, FIREARMS INVESTIGATION IDENTIFICATION AND EVIDENCE ch. 1 (1957); Dougherty, *Report on Two Early United States Firearms Identification Cases*, 14 J. FORENSIC SCI. 453 (1969); Springer, *Toolmark Examinations — A Review of its Development in the Literature*, 40 J. FORENSIC SCI. 964 (1995); Thomas, *Comments on the Discovery of Striation Matching and on Early Contributions to Forensic Firearms Identification*, 12 J. FORENSIC SCI. 1 (1967).

4. *See* L. JOUGHIN & E. MORGAN, THE LEGACY OF SACCO & VANZETTI 15 (1948) (The firearms identification testimony was "carelessly assembled, incompletely and confusedly presented, and ... beyond the comprehension" of the jury); Starrs, *Once More Unto the Breech: The Firearms Evidence in the Sacco and Vanzetti Case Revisited*, 31 J. FORENSIC SCI. 630 (1986) (Part I); 31 J. FORENSIC SCI. 1050 (1986) (Part II).

5. People v. Berkman, 307 Ill. 492, 501, 139 N.E. 91, 94 (1923).

6. People v. Fisher, 340 Ill. 216, 239, 172 N.E. 743, 753 (1930).

7. Interior ballistics has been defined as the "study of the motion of the projectile(s) within the firearm from the moment of ignition until it leaves the barrel." AFTE GLOSSARY at 13. Interior ballistics includes such matters as chamber configuration, chamber pressure, and rifling.

8. Exterior ballistics has been defined as the "study of the motion of the projectile(s) after it leaves the barrel of the firearm." AFTE GLOSSARY at 13. Exterior ballistics includes such matters as velocity and trajectory. People v. Bloyd, 43 Cal. 3d 333, 356-57, 729 P.2d 802, 816-17, 233 Cal. Rptr. 368, 381-82 (1987) (firearms identification examiner qualified to testify about "trajectory" of bullet).

9. *See* State v. Leonard, 243 N.W.2d 887, 892 (Iowa 1976) (distinguishing between "ballistics" and "firearms" expert); *Firearms Identification*, 29 AM. JUR. PROOF OF FACTS 65, 66-67 (1972). *See also* United States v. Bonavia, 927 F.2d 565, 567 n.2 (11th Cir. 1991) (firearms expert permitted to testify where a particular weapon had been manufactured to establish required interstate nexus for federal prosecution).

Two newspaper accounts demonstrate the importance of this subject. In a Los Angeles murder trial the jury forewoman said that the "jurors reached the guilty verdict by relying heavily on the ballistics evidence."[10] In a New York murder case, however, the jury acquitted. One juror later told the press that "a number of [my] colleagues were skeptical of the ballistics evidence."[11]

§ 14-2. Firearms & Ammunition.

An understanding of firearms identification requires some appreciation of firearms and ammunition.[12] Typically, three types of firearms — rifles, handguns, and shotguns — are examined.[13]

Rifles & Handguns

The barrels of modern rifles and handguns are *rifled;* that is, parallel spiral grooves are cut into the inner surface (bore) of the barrel.[14] The surfaces between the grooves are called *lands.* The lands and grooves twist in a direction: right twist or left twist. Each manufacturer specifies the number of lands and grooves, the direction of twist, the angle of twist (pitch), the depth of the grooves, and the width of the lands and grooves. As a bullet passes through the bore, the lands and grooves force the bullet to rotate, giving it stability in flight and thus increased accuracy. Because the lands "bite" into the bullet surface, land and groove impressions are imprinted on the bullets and microscopic details in the land and groove impressions play an important role in firearms identification.

Rifles and handguns are classified according to their caliber. The caliber is the diameter of the bore of the firearm; it is expressed in either hundredths or thousandths of an inch (*e.g.*, .22, .45, .357 caliber) or millimeters (*e.g.*, 7.62

---

10. Rainey, *"Nightmare" Killer Is Convicted of All Charges*, L.A. TIMES, Jan. 26, 1989, pt. 2 (Metro), at 1, col. 1.

11. Levitt, *Davis Juror Fed Up Following Acquittal*, NEWSDAY, Mar. 5, 1988 (News Section), at 10.

12. *See* Hamby & Thorpe, *Firearms Reference Collections — Their Size, Composition, and Use*, 42 J. FORENSIC SCI. 461 (1997).

13. Other types of firearms, such as machine guns, tear gas guns, zip guns, and flare guns, may also be examined. *See generally* Koffler, *Zip Guns and Crude Conversions — Identifying Characteristics and Problems*, 61 J. CRIM. L., CRIMINOLOGY & POLICE SCI. 115 (1970).

14. The end of the bore from which the projectile emerges is the muzzle; the end of the bore into which the cartridge is inserted is the breech.

mm).[15] In addition to caliber designation, rifles are classified by their loading mechanism — for example, semiautomatic, pump, bolt, or lever action.[16]

The two major types of handguns[17] are revolvers[18] and semiautomatic pistols.[19] One difference between these two types of handguns is that the cartridge case is automatically ejected when a semiautomatic pistol is fired. If recovered at the crime scene, it may be possible to identify the cartridge case with the firearm from which it was fired.[20] The case is not ejected when a revolver is discharged.

Ammunition

Rifle and handgun cartridges (ammunition) consist of the projectile (bullet),[21] case,[22] propellant (powder), and primer. The primer contains a small amount of an explosive mixture, which detonates when struck by the firing pin. If the primer is located in the center of the base of the cartridge case, the cartridge is called a center fire cartridge. If the primer is in the rim of the base, the cartridge is called a rimfire cartridge. When the firing pin detonates the primer, an explosion occurs which ignites the propellant. Modern propellant is smokeless

---

15. The caliber is measured from land to land in a rifled weapon. Typically, the designated caliber is more an approximation than an accurate measurement. *See* 1 J. MATHEWS, FIREARMS IDENTIFICATION 17 (1962) ("'nominal caliber' would be a more proper term").

16. Rifles may also be classified according to their purpose — for example, sporting, military, or target.

17. Some handguns, such as single shot pistols, are neither revolvers nor semiautomatic pistols.

18. Revolvers have a cylindrical magazine which rotates behind the barrel. The cylinder typically holds five to nine cartridges, each within a separate chamber. When a revolver is fired, the cylinder rotates and the next chamber is aligned with the barrel. A single action revolver requires the manual cocking of the hammer; in a double action revolver the trigger cocks the hammer. Revolvers may also be classified by their loading mechanism — swing-out cylinder, removable cylinder, or top-break cylinder.

19. Unlike revolvers, semiautomatic (self-loading) pistols do not have cylinders. The cartridges are contained in a vertical magazine, which is typically loaded into the grip of the pistol. When the pistol is fired, the spent cartridge case is ejected, the firing mechanism is cocked, and a new cartridge is chambered. Although pistols are often referred to as "automatic" firearms, this label is incorrect. An automatic firearm permits continuous firing; a semiautomatic firearm, although self-loading, requires the trigger to be squeezed each time it is fired. A machine gun is an example of an automatic firearm.

20. *See* § 14-4 *infra* for a discussion of cartridge case identification.

21. Bullets are generally composed of lead and small amounts of other elements (hardeners). They may be completely covered with another metal (jacketed) or partially covered (semijacketed). Bullets may also be classified according to their shape. Different types of bases, such as flat base, hollow base, or boattail, and different types of noses, such as round nose, flat nose, or hollow point, are manufactured.

22. Cartridge cases are generally made of brass. Several different shapes — straight, tapered, or bottleneck — are manufactured. The type of rim may also differ — for example, rimmed, semi-rimmed, rimless, belted, or rebated (rim diameter less than case diameter).

powder, either single base (nitrocellulose) or double base (nitrocellulose and nitroglycerin).[23]

Shotguns

Shotguns are smooth bore firearms; they do not have lands and grooves. They can be double or single barrel and can be semiautomatic, pump, bolt, or break open firearms. Shotgun shells most often consist of a case,[24] primer, propellant, projectiles, and wadding. Generally, the projectiles in a shot shell are spherical balls (pellets). Shotguns, however, can also fire bullets, called slugs.[25] Except for the .410 caliber shotgun, shotguns and shot shells are classified according to their gauge — for example, 12, 16, or 20 gauge. The gauge is the number of spherical balls of pure lead, each exactly fitting the bore, that equals one pound. The wadding keeps the powder and the pellets in position inside the shell.[26]

§ 14-3. Bullet Identification.

Firearms identifications may be based on either bullet or cartridge case examinations. Two types of identifying characteristics are used: class characteristics and individual characteristics.[27]

Class Characteristics

The class characteristics of a firearm result from design factors and are determined prior to manufacture. They include the caliber and rifling specifications: (1) the land and groove diameters, (2) the direction of rifling (left or right twist), (3) the number of lands and grooves, (4) the width of the lands and grooves, and (5) the degree of the rifling twist.[28] A .38 caliber bullet with six land and groove impressions and with a right twist could have been fired only from a firearm with those same characteristics. It could not have been fired from a .32 caliber firearm, or from a .38 caliber firearm with a different number of

---

23. Prior to the development of smokeless powder, black powder, a mixture of potassium nitrate, charcoal, and sulfur, was used. Black powder is sometimes still used today.

24. The case has a brass head and a tube of either paper or plastic.

25. *See generally* Townshend, *Identification of Rifled Shotgun Slugs*, 15 J. FORENSIC SCI. 173 (1970).

26. Wadding may be plastic or a paper material.

27. The discussion in the text focuses on the typical case. Sometimes the examiner is faced with an atypical case — for example, one in which the firearm has been altered or an undersized bullet has been used. *See generally* 1 J. MATHEWS, *supra* note 15, ch. 6 (*Pitfalls for the Unwary*); Munhall, *Firearms Identification Problems Pertaining to Supplemental Chambers, Auxiliary Cartridges, Insert Barrels and Conversion Units*, 5 J. FORENSIC SCI. 319 (1960); Goddard, *The Unexpected in Firearms Identification*, 1 J. FORENSIC SCI. 57 (1956).

28. 1 J. MATHEWS, *supra* note 15, at 17.

lands and grooves or a left twist. In sum, if the class characteristics do not match, the firearm could not have fired the bullet.

Class characteristics play another role in criminal investigations. Frequently, the bullet is recovered before the firearm comes into the possession of the police. In this situation, the class characteristics provide significant information concerning the type of firearm that could have fired the bullet.

Individual Characteristics

If the class characteristics of a firearm and an evidence bullet match, a positive identification may be possible. Bullet identification involves a comparison of the evidence bullet and a test bullet fired from the firearm.[29] The two bullets are examined by means of a comparison microscope, which permits a split-screen view of the two bullets and manipulation so that the striations (marks) on both bullets may be aligned.[30] A camera, attached to the microscope, can be used to take photomicrographs.[31]

A positive identification of a bullet as having been fired from a particular firearm is based on individual barrel characteristics. Barrels are machined during the manufacturing process[32] and imperfections in the tools used in the machining process are imprinted on the bore. The subsequent use of the firearm adds additional individual imperfections. For example, mechanical action (erosion) caused by the friction of bullets passing through the bore of the firearm produces accidental imperfections. Similarly, chemical action (corrosion) caused by moisture (rust), as well as primer and propellant chemicals, produces other imperfections.

When a bullet is fired, microscopic striations are imprinted on the bullet surface as it passes through the bore of the firearm.[33] These bullet markings are produced by the individual imperfections of the bore, and since these bore

---

29. Test bullets are obtained by firing a firearm into a recovery box or bullet trap, which is usually filled with cotton, or a recovery tank, which is filled with water.

30. In effect, the comparison microscope is two microscopes, optically paired. Both microscopes are connected so that two objects may be viewed at the same time. For a description of the comparison microscope, *see* 1 J. MATHEWS, *supra* note 15, ch. 4 (*Instrumentation*).

31. *See generally* 1 J. MATHEWS, *supra* note 15, at 43; 1 C. SCOTT, PHOTOGRAPHIC EVIDENCE ch. 15 (2d ed. 1969).

32. Methods of rifling, such as the scrape cutter, hook cutter, broaching, and swaging methods, are described in 1 J. MATHEWS, *supra* note 15, at 4-9.

33. *See* Tontarski & Thompson, *Automated Firearms Evidence Comparison: A Forensic Tool for Firearms Identification — An Update*, 43 J. FORENSIC SCI. 641, 642 (1998) ("When a cartridge is fired in a firearm, the generated forces act on both the casing in the firearm's chamber and the bullet being driven down the barrel. The microscopic imperfections made during the manufacture of the firearm's barrel, breech face, firing pin, and action leave toolmarks on the softer bullet and cartridge casing metals. ...Experience has shown that for bullets, the most reproducible marks are normally found in the land impressions near the base").

imperfections are randomly produced, they are considered unique to each firearm.[34] The probability that another firearm would have identical bore imperfections is considered so remote that firearms identification examiners often conclude that a bullet has been fired from a particular firearm and could not have been fired by any other firearm. In effect, this opinion is based on probability theory. As McCormick has noted:

> [A]ny expert giving any opinion on whether the scientific test identifies the defendant as being the person who left the incriminating trace, such as a ... bullet, ... necessarily bases this conclusion on an understanding or impression of how similar the items being compared are and how common it is to find items with these similarities. If these beliefs have any basis in fact, it is to be found in the general experience of the criminalists or more exacting statistical studies of these matters.[35]

Firearms identification falls into the former category; it is based on the "general experience" of firearms identification examiners and not statistical studies.[36]

The condition of a firearm or evidence bullet may preclude a positive identification. For example, there may be insufficient marks on the bullet or, due to mutilation, an insufficient amount of the bullet may have been recovered. Similarly, if the barrel of the firearm has changed significantly, due to erosion or corrosion, a positive identification may be impossible. In these situations, the examiner may render a "no conclusion" determination.[37] Such a conclusion, however, may have some evidentiary value; that is, the firearm could have fired the bullet because the class characteristics match.[38]

---

34. "No two barrels are microscopically identical, as the surfaces of their bores all possess individual and characteristic markings." G. BURRARD, THE IDENTIFICATION OF FIREARMS AND FORENSIC BALLISTICS 138 (1962); 1 J. MATHEWS, *supra* note 15, at 3 ("Experience has shown that no two firearms, even those of the same make and model and made consecutively by the same tools, will produce the same markings on a bullet or a cartridge").

35. 1 C. MCCORMICK, EVIDENCE § 210, at 951 (4th ed. 1992).

36. For articles on the statistical basis of firearms identification, *see* Biasotti, *A Statistical Study of the Individual Characteristics of Fired Bullets*, 4 J. FORENSIC SCI. 34 (1959); Biasotti, *The Principles of Evidence Evaluation as Applied to Firearms and Tool Mark Identification*, 9 J. FORENSIC SCI. 428, 432 (1964) ("[W]e lack the fundamental statistical data needed to develop verifiable criteria"); Deinet, *Studies of Models of Striated Marks Generated by Random Processes*, 26 J. FORENSIC SCI. 35 (1981).

37. FBI, *supra* note 1, at 57 ("Exams may also conclude that there are not sufficient individual microscopic marks of value on the bullet or cartridge case for identification purposes or that the condition of the firearm precludes the possibility of making an identification").

38. *See* § 14-6 *infra* (admissibility).

Subjectivity

Although a positive identification is based on objective data (the striations on the bullet surface), the examiner's conclusion is essentially a subjective judgment. This judgment rests on the reproducible points of identity. There are no objective criteria used for this determination: "Ultimately, unless other issues are involved, it remains for the examiner to determine for himself the modicum of proof necessary to arrive at a definitive opinion."[39] In this sense, firearms identification is more of an art than a science.[40]

Given the subjective aspect of the comparison, it is not surprising that examiners may disagree and also be mistaken.[41] Also, the Crime Laboratory Proficiency Testing Program (1978) raised questions about the competence of some firearms identification examiners. In one test 5.3% of the participating laboratories misidentified firearms evidence, and in another test 13.6% erred. These tests involved bullet and cartridge case comparisons. The Project Advisory Committee considered these errors "particularly grave in nature" and concluded that they probably resulted from carelessness, inexperience, or inadequate supervision.[42] A third test required the examination of two bullets and two cartridge cases to identify the "most probable weapon" from which each was fired. The error rate was 28.2%. There were significant limitations in these studies. In later tests, "[e]xaminers generally did very well in making the comparisons. For all fifteen tests combined, examiners made a total of 2106 [bullet and cartridge case] comparisons and provided responses which agreed with the manufacturer responses 88% of the time, disagreed in only 1.4% of responses, and reported inconclusive results in 10% of cases."[43]

---

39. J. Peterson, E. Fabricant & K. Field, Crime Laboratory Proficiency Testing Research Program 207 (October 1978) [hereinafter cited as Laboratory Proficiency Test]. *See* also Biasotti, *The Principles of Evidence Evaluation as Applied to Firearms and Tool Mark Identification*, 9 J. Forensic Sci. 428, 429 (1964) ("In general, the texts on firearms identification take the position that each practitioner must develop his own intuitive criteria of identity gained through practical experience").

40. "From the number of texts devoted exclusively to the subject of firearms and tool mark identification, it might appear that this specialized area of physical comparison is a highly developed science with well defined criteria for evidence evaluation. On the contrary, a review of the literature reveals a very superficial treatment of this basic problem of evaluating results and establishing identity." Biasotti, *supra* note 39, at 428. *See also* Springer, *Toolmark Examinations — A Review of its Development in the Literature*, 40 J. Forensic Sci. 964, 966-67 (1995) ("According to the Association of Firearms and Toolmarks Examiners' Criteria for Identification Committee, interpretation of toolmark individualization and identification is still considered to be subjective in nature, based on one's training and experience").

41. *See* § 14-6 *infra* (discussing disagreements & mistakes).

42. Laboratory Proficiency Test, *supra* note 39, at 207-08.

43. Peterson & Markham, *Crime Laboratory Proficiency Testing Results, 1878-1991, II: Resolving Questions of Common Origin*, 40 J. Forensic Sci. 1009, 1018 (1995). The authors also

An analogy between firearms identification and fingerprint identification may be more misleading than helpful. A person's fingerprints do not change, whereas the markings on the bore of a firearm may change every time the weapon is fired. For example, rust or dirt in the bore may leave a mark on one bullet that will not be found on a subsequently fired bullet because the rust or dirt may have been dislodged from the barrel when the first bullet was fired. Metal fouling, which is common with lead bullets, may also change the interior surface of the barrel.[44] The examiner, therefore, must distinguish unimportant dissimilar markings from significant dissimilar markings. One commentator has written:

> [O]ne of the most surprising things which must strike any observer who is examining fired bullets is the astonishing differences which seem to be present on bullets which are known to have been fired through the same barrel. These differences are due to the sliding imprint, but with practice it is possible to detect the difference between variations resulting from the sliding imprint and variations due to different barrels.[45]

§ 14-4. Cartridge Case Identification.

Cartridge cases are most often identified by breech face,[46] firing pin impression,[47] extractor,[48] ejector,[49] or chamber marks. Cartridge case identification is based on the same theory as bullet identification:

---

stated: "The performance of laboratories in the firearms tests was comparable to that of the earlier LEAA study, although the rate of successful identifications actually was slightly over—88% vs. 91%. Laboratories cut the rate of errant identifications by half (3% to 1.4%) but the rate of inconclusive responses doubled, from 5% to 10%." *Id.* at 1019.

44. *See* 1 J. MATHEWS, *supra* note 15, at 21 ("If a test bullet is fired through a barrel which has become fouled subsequent to the passage of the evidence bullet through it, the markings on the test and evidence bullets may be quite different").

45. G. BURRARD, *supra* note 34 , at 145. *See also* Goddard, *Scientific Identification of Firearms and Bullets*, 17 J. CRIM. L., CRIMINOLOGY & POLICE SCI. 254, 262 (1956) ("All the fine striations will not match together by any means, but enough will do so to dispel any doubt as to the fact that their arm of origin was identical").

46. *See* Sinha, Mehrotra & Kumar, *Direct Breech Face Comparison*, 4 J. POLICE SCI. & ADMIN. 261 (1976).

47. The firing pin or striker has a distinctive shape. *See also* Grove, Judd & Horn, *Evaluation of SEM Potential in the Examination of Shotgun and Rifle Firing Pin Impressions*, 19 J. FORENSIC SCI. 441 (1974); Grove, Judd & Horn, *Examination of Firing Pin Impressions by Scanning Electron Microscopy*, 17 J. FORENSIC SCI. 645 (1972).

48. The extractor is the mechanism that withdraws the cartridge case from the chamber after the firearm has been fired. *See generally* Wilson, *The Identification of Extractor Marks on Fired Shells*, 29 J. CRIM. L. & CRIMINOLOGY 724 (1939).

49. The ejector is the mechanism that throws or "kicks out" the cartridge case from the firearm after it has been fired.

> [T]he whole principle of identification is based on the fact that since the breech face of every weapon must be individually distinct, the cartridge cases which it fires are imprinted with this individuality. The imprints on all cartridges fired from the same weapon are the same, and those on cartridges fired from different weapons must always be different.[50]

As with barrels, defects produced in the manufacturing process leave distinctive characteristics on the breech face, firing pin, chamber, extractor, and ejector. The subsequent use of the firearm produces additional distinctive defects. When the trigger is pulled, the firing pin strikes the primer of the cartridge, causing the primer to detonate. This detonation ignites the propellant (powder). In the process of combustion, the powder is converted rapidly into gases. The pressure produced by this process propels the bullet from the weapon and also forces the base of the cartridge case backwards against the breech face, imprinting breech face marks on the base of the cartridge case. Similarly, the firing pin, ejector, and extractor may leave characteristic marks on a cartridge case.[51]

Cartridge case identification involves a comparison of the cartridge case recovered at the crime scene and a test cartridge case obtained from the firearm after it has been fired. Shot shell casings as well as cartridge cases inserted into handguns and rifles may be identified in this way.[52] As in bullet identification, the comparison microscope is used for the examination. "According to the Association of Firearms and Toolmarks Examiners' Criteria for Identification Committee, interpretation of toolmark individualization and identification is still considered to be subjective in nature, based on one's training and experience."[53]

Bullet and cartridge case identifications differ in several respects. Since the bullet is traveling through the barrel at the time it is imprinted with the bore imperfections, these marks are "sliding" imprints, called striated marks. In contrast, the cartridge case receives "static" imprints, called impressed marks.[54] Thus, cartridge case marks may be easier to match. Nevertheless, since some firearms, such as revolvers, do not automatically eject the cartridge case at the

---

50. G. BURRARD, *supra* note 34, at 107.

51. *See* Tontarski & Thompson, *supra* note 33, at 642 ("When a cartridge is fired in a firearm, the generated forces act on both the casing in the firearm's chamber and the bullet being driven down the barrel. The microscopic imperfections made during the manufacture of the firearm's barrel, breech face, firing pin, and action leave toolmarks on the softer bullet and cartridge casing metals. ...[T]he breech face and firing pin impressions found on an expended casing are primary areas for comparison of identifiable microscopic marks").

52. Ejector and extractor marks by themselves may indicate only that the cartridge case had been *loaded in,* not fired from, a particular firearm.

53. Springer, *Toolmark Examinations — A Review of its Development in the Literature,* 40 J. FORENSIC SCI. 964, 966-67 (1995).

54. G. BURRARD, *supra* note 34, at 145.

scene when fired, cartridge case identification is probably not as common as bullet identification.

As with bullet identification, cartridge case identification was part of the Laboratory Proficiency Testing Program (1978). Two cartridge cases, each fired in a different firearm, were tested. The test required the comparison of both cartridge cases to determine if they had been fired in the same firearm. Five laboratories, representing 3.8% of those participating in the test, misidentified a cartridge case.[55] In later proficiency tests, examiners did very well.[56]

§ 14-5. Automated Identification Systems.

Automated firearms identification systems are operating in numerous locations. One system, "Bulletproof," analyzes bullets and was sponsored in part by the Bureau of Alcohol, Tobacco, and Firearms. Another system, "Drugfire," analyzes cartridge cases; this program was sponsored by the F.B.I.[57] "These ballistic imaging systems use the powerful searching capabilities of the computer to match the images of recovered crime scene evidence against digitized images stored in a computer database."[58] The two systems were combined into a program called the National Integrated Ballistics Information Network (NIBIN) Program.[59] The automated systems "give[] firearms examiners the ability to screen virtually unlimited numbers of bullets and cartridge casings for possible matches."[60] These systems do not replace the examiner, who still must make the final comparison: "'High Confidence' candidates (likely hits) are referred to a firearms examiner for examination on a comparison microscope."[61]

---

55. LABORATORY PROFICIENCY TEST, *supra* note 39, at 207-08.

56. *See* text accompany note 43, *supra*.

57. Sibert, *Drugfire: Revolutionizing Forensic Firearms Identification and Providing the Foundation for a National Firearms Identification Network*, 21 CRIME LAB. DIGEST 63 (Oct. 1994); Sibert, *Drugfire: Responding to Gang and Drug-Related Shootings*, 19 CRIME LAB. DIGEST 6 (Jan. 1992).

58. *Benchmark Evaluation Studies of the Bulletproof and Drugfire Ballistic Imaging Systems*, 22 CRIME LAB. DIGEST 51 (April 1995). *See also* Kinder & Bonfanti, *Automated Comparisons of Bullet Striations Based on 3D Topography*, 101 FORENSIC SCI. INT'L 85, 86 (1999) ("[A]n automatic system will cut the time demanding and tedious manual searches for one specific item in large open case files").

59. *FBI and BATF Collaborate on Ballistics Network*, 24 CRIME LAB. DIGEST 2 (Spring 1997).

60. Tontarski & Thompson, *Automated Firearms Evidence Comparison: A Forensic Tool for Firearms Identification — An Update*, 43 J. FORENSIC SCI. 641 (1998).

61. *Id.*

§ 14-6. Admissibility & Weight of Firearms Evidence.

Firearms identification developed in the early part of this century, and by 1930 courts were admitting firearms identification evidence.[62] Subsequent cases have followed these precedents, admitting evidence of bullet,[63] cartridge case,[64] and shot shell[65] identifications. The test bullet itself, however, need not be admitted in evidence.[66] If the firearm used in the crime is not recovered and therefore a test

---

62. *E.g.,* People v. Fisher, 340 Ill. 216, 172 N.E. 743 (1930); Evans v. Commonwealth, 230 Ky. 411, 19 S.W.2d 1091 (1929); Burchett v. State, 35 Ohio App. 463, 172 N.E. 555 (1928). *But see* People v. Berkman, 307 Ill. 492, 501, 139 N.E. 91, 94 (1923) (positive identification of bullet "preposterous").

63. *E.g.,* United States v. Wolff, 5 M.J. 923, 926 (N.C.M.R. 1978), *petition denied,* 6 M.J. 305 (C.M.A. 1979); State v. Nemeth, 182 Conn. 403, 408, 438 A.2d 120, 123 (1980); People v. Torres, 100 Ill. App. 3d 931, 937, 427 N.E.2d 329, 334-35 (1981); State v. Harriman, 469 So. 2d 298, 306-07 (La. App. 1985), *cert. denied,* 476 U.S. 1109 (1986); Commonwealth v. Ellis, 373 Mass. 1, 5-6, 364 N.E.2d 808, 811-12 (1977); State v. Hill, 294 N.C. 320, 332-33, 240 S.E.2d 794, 802-03 (1978); State v. Mack, 73 Ohio St. 3d 502, 512, 653 N.E.2d 329, 337 (1995) (The examiner "compared the test shot with the morgue bullet recovered from the victim, ... and the spent shell casings recovered from the crime scene, concluding that all had been discharged from appellant's gun"), *cert. denied,* 516 U.S. 1096 (1996); State v. Benton, 413 A.2d 104, 112-13 (R.I. 1980); State v. Schreuder, 712 P.2d 264, 268-69 (Utah 1985); McDaniel v. State, 632 P.2d 534, 536-37 (Wyo. 1981). *See generally* Annot., *Expert Evidence to Identify Gun From Which Bullet or Cartridge Was Fired,* 26 A.L.R.2D 892 (1952).

64. *E.g.,* Bentley v. Scully, 41 F.3d 818, 825 (2d Cir. 1994) ("[A] ballistic expert found that the spent nine millimeter bullet casing recovered from the scene of the shooting was fired from the pistol found on the rooftop"), *cert. denied,* 516 U.S. 1152 (1996); State v. Gonzales, 92 Idaho 152, 155, 158, 438 P.2d 897, 900, 903 (1968); State v. Goyette, 407 A.2d 1104, 1113-14 (Me. 1979); State v. Thomas, 299 A.2d 919, 920 (Me. 1973); Edwards v. State, 198 Md. 132, 143-44, 81 A.2d 631, 635-36 (1951); People v. King, 58 Mich. App. 390, 398-99, 228 N.W.2d 391, 396 (1975); State v. Hindman, 543 S.W.2d 278, 284 (Mo. App. 1976); State v. Williams, 73 Ohio St. 3d 153, 155, 652 N.E.2d 721, 725 (1995) (The witness, "a ballistics and firearms expert from BCI, testified that all three of the cartridge casings had at one time been loaded in, chambered in, and extracted from the same firearm. [His] testimony indicated that although he could not conclusively determine whether the cartridge casings had been *fired* from the same firearm, they had been *extracted* from the same firearm") (emphasis added), *cert. denied,* 516 U.S. 1161 (1996); Goins v. Commonwealth, 251 Va. 442, 449-50, 470 S.E.2d 114, 120 (1996) (Expert "testified that she compared the markings on one of the cartridge casings found at the crime scene with the markings on the unfired .45 caliber cartridge found in the home of ... Goins' girlfriend... and [the expert] concluded that both items had been in the same weapon"); State v. Aiken, 72 Wash. 2d 306, 352, 434 P.2d 10, 39 (1967), *vacated on other grounds,* 392 U.S. 652 (1968).

65. *E.g.,* Williams v. State, 384 So. 2d 1205, 1210-11 (Ala. Crim. App. 1980); Lewis v. State, 335 So. 2d 426, 428 (Ala. App. 1975), *cert. denied,* 335 So. 2d 429 (Ala. 1976); Douglas v. State, 314 Ala. App. 329, 163 So. 2d 477, 492 (1963), *cert. denied,* 163 So. 2d 496 (Ala. 1964); Burge v. State, 282 So. 2d 223, 229 (Miss. 1973), *cert. denied,* 415 U.S. 985 (1974).

66. *See* Hinton v. State, 548 So. 2d 562, 568 (Ala.), *cert. denied,* 493 U.S. 969 (1989).

bullet or cartridge case cannot be obtained, a bullet or cartridge case fired by that firearm at a different time may be used for comparison.[67]

In *People v. Hawkins*,[68] a 1995 decision, the defendant challenged the scientific basis of firearms identification evidence. The experts

> conceded that ballistics identification is not an exact science. Rather, ballistics experts develop proficiency by microscopically observing a large number of bullets known to have been fired from the same gun, and from different guns, so that they acquire knowledge of when the similarities of the bullets' striations are sufficient to establish that the bullets were discharged from the same firearm.[69]

In rebuttal, the defense introduced two articles by Alfred Biasotti that called for reforming firearms identifications by developing a statistical data base.[70] One expert "conceded that ballistics identification was to some extent more of a skill than a science, an intuition informed by extensive experience."[71] The California Supreme Court upheld admissibility. Nevertheless, in the post-*Daubert* world more challenges of this sort are to be expected.[72]

Federal Rules

The Federal Rules of Evidence treat this issue as one of authentication. Rule 901(b)(3) provides that an item of evidence may be identified by an expert witness through a comparison of the item and specimens that have been authenticated. The federal drafters specifically mentioned "ballistics" comparisons.[73] Under the Federal Rule, bullet or cartridge case identification

67. *E.g.,* State v. Lane, 72 Ariz. 220, 225-26, 233 P.2d 437, 440-41 (1951); Commonwealth v. Ellis, 373 Mass. 1, 5-6, 364 N.E.2d 808, 811-12 (1977); People v. Williams, 15 Mich. App. 683, 687-88, 167 N.W.2d 358, 360 (1969); State v. Boccadoro, 105 N.J.L. 352, 354-55, 144 A. 612, 613 (1929); Goins v. Commonwealth, 251 Va. 442, 449-50, 470 S.E.2d 114, 120 (1996) (Expert "testified that she compared the markings on one of the cartridge casings found at the crime scene with the markings on the unfired .45 caliber cartridge found in the home of ... Goins' girlfriend... and [the expert] concluded that both items had been in the same weapon"). *See also* United States v. Bowers, 534 F.2d 186, 193-94 (9th Cir.), *cert. denied,* 429 U.S. 942 (1976).

68. 10 Cal. 4th 920, 897 P.2d 574, 42 Cal. Rptr. 2d 636 (Cal. 1995), *cert. denied,* 517 U.S. 1193 (1996). Two experts testified that "bullet fragments found in Hedlund's body were fired from the same gun as the fragments recovered from the Sonny's Market crime scene. These experts explained that the copper jackets of the respective bullets were examined under a microscope to compare the striations or lines imprinted on the jackets. The striations are produced when the bullet is fired, and thus reflect the unique characteristics of each gun barrel." *Id.* at 649-50.

69. 42 Cal. Rptr. 2d at 650.

70. These articles are cited in note 36 *supra.*

71. 42 Cal. Rptr. 2d at 650.

72. For a discussion of *Daubert, see* Chapter 1.

73. FED. R. EVID. 901 advisory committee's note.

evidence is admissible if evidence sufficient to *support* a finding of identification has been introduced.[74]

Lack of Positive Identification

A number of courts have also permitted an expert to testify that a bullet *could have been fired* from a particular firearm;[75] that is, the class characteristics of the bullet and the firearm are consistent.[76] Although this type of evidence is not as probative as a positive identification, it nevertheless has some probative value and satisfies the evidentiary test for relevancy.[77] As one court commented, the expert's "testimony, which established that the bullet which killed [the victim] could have been fired from the same caliber and make of gun found in the possession of [the defendant], significantly advanced the inquiry."[78]

Errors & Disagreements

Given the subjective nature of the identification process, it is not surprising that experts might disagree. In *State v. Nemeth*[79] one expert testified "that he was unable to determine whether the bullets had been fired from the same gun," whereas another "testified that both bullets had been fired from the same gun."[80]

---

74. FED. R. EVID. 901(a).

75. *E.g.,* State v. Edgin, 110 Ariz. 416, 418-19, 520 P.2d 288, 290-91 (1974); Ruiz v. State, 265 Ark. 875, 896, 582 S.W.2d 915, 925 (1979), *cert. denied,* 454 U.S. 1093 (1981); State v. Hatton, 95 Idaho 856, 861, 522 P.2d 64, 69 (1974); People v. Singletary, 73 Ill. App. 3d 239, 248, 391 N.E.2d 440, 447 (1979); Luttrell v. Commonwealth, 952 S.W.2d 216, 218 (Ky. 1997) (expert "testified only that the bullets which killed the victim could have been fired from Luttrell's gun"); State v. Reynolds, 307 N.C. 184, 196-97, 297 S.E.2d 532, 539-40 (1982); State v. Ward, 300 N.C. 150, 153-54, 266 S.E.2d 581, 583-84 (1980); State v. Bayless, 48 Ohio St. 2d 73, 111, 357 N.E.2d 1035, 1058-59 (1976), *vacated on other grounds,* 438 U.S. 911 (1978); State v. Courtney, 25 Ohio App. 3d 12, 14-15, 495 N.E.2d 472, 475-76 (1985); Commonwealth v. Moore, 462 Pa. 231, 237-38, 340 A.2d 447, 451 (1975); Commonwealth v. Pierce, 453 Pa. 319, 324-25, 309 A.2d 371, 373-74 (1973); Commonwealth v. Hoss, 445 Pa. 98, 115-16, 283 A.2d 58, 67-68 (1971). *See generally* Annot., *Admissibility of Testimony That Bullet Could or Might Have Come From a Particular Gun,* 31 A.L.R.4TH 486 (1984).

76. *See also* State v. Treadwell, 217 Wis. 2d 290, 577 N.W.2d 387, 1998 WL 50138 (App. 1998) ("[T]he bullets found in Powell's car were analyzed and a ballistics report was issued which stated that, although the bullets found in Powell's car could not be positively identified as coming from [the defendant's] gun, the bullets were consistent with bullets fired from [the defendant's] gun"; defendant's attorney informed him that the ballistics report showed a "match" between the defendant's bullets and the bullets in the car; he then pled guilty).

77. *See* FED. R. EVID. 401: "'Relevant evidence' means evidence having any tendency to make the existence of any fact that is of consequence to the determination of the action more probable or less probable than it would be without the evidence."

78. Commonwealth v. Hoss, 445 Pa. 98, 115-16, 283 A.2d 58, 68 (1971).

79. 182 Conn. 403, 438 A.2d 120 (1980).

80. *Id.* at 408, 438 A.2d at 123.

The court held that such a disagreement did not affect the admissibility of the evidence, only the weight of the evidence (*i.e.*, an issue for the jury). In another case, *Commonwealth v. Ellis*,[81] the "Commonwealth's two experts did not fully agree."[82]

Mistaken identifications have also occurred. In *People v. Kirschke*[83] a prosecution expert testified that an evidence bullet had been fired by a particular firearm and that "no other in the world was the murder weapon."[84] However, in post-conviction proceedings court-appointed experts testified that a positive identification could not be made.[85] Although the court found that the expert had "negligently presented false demonstrative evidence in support of his ballistics testimony,"[86] it denied post-conviction relief because the defendant had failed to challenge the testimony at trial, even though he had the opportunity to do so.

Another case involved the 1989 arrest of Rickey Ross for the murder of three prostitutes. An expert, the head of a firearms identification unit, made a *positive* identification after comparing the murder bullets and a bullet fired from Ross' 9mm Smith & Wesson. One of the defense attorneys later admitted, "I suppose I was like the average citizen .... They said it was a match, I thought it was like a fingerprint."[87] Based on the same evidence, however, a defense expert reached the opposite conclusion — Ross' gun could *not* have fired the fatal bullets. Two independent experts came to yet another conclusion: there was insufficient evidence to reach any definite conclusion. The case against Ross was dropped.

A misidentification also occurred in the investigation of Sirhan Sirhan for the assassination of Bobby Kennedy:

> In [*People v. Sirhan*] seven independent examiners were appointed by the presiding judge of the Superior Court of Los Angeles County to reexamine the purported firearms bullet comparison post trial. The examiners were unanimous in their findings that the identification[s] testified to at the grand jury indictment and in the trial were misrepresented in that the purported identification[s] of bullets lodged in victim Kennedy ... with Sirhan's gun

---

81. 373 Mass. 1, 364 N.E.2d 808 (1977).

82. *Id.* at 5, 364 N.E.2d at 812. *See also* Hinton v. State, 548 So. 2d 562, 565 (Ala.) (defense expert disagreed with prosecution experts' positive identification), *cert. denied,* 493 U.S. 969 (1989).

83. 53 Cal. App. 3d 405, 125 Cal. Rptr. 680 (1975), *cert. denied,* 429 U.S. 820 (1976).

84. *Id.* at 410, 125 Cal. Rptr. at 683.

85. *Id.* at 411, 125 Cal. Rptr. at 684 ("were not able to make a positive identification").

86. *Id.* at 408, 125 Cal. Rptr. at 682.

87. Baker & Lieberman, *Faulty Ballistics in Deputy's Arrest; Eagerness to "Make" Gun Cited in LAPD Lab Error*, L.A. TIMES, May 22, 1989, at 1, col. 1; Freed, *LAPD Probing What Went Wrong With Ballistics Tests on Ross' Gun*, L.A. TIMES, May 16, 1989, § 1, at 26, col. 1.

were non-existent. In both of these cases discovery and cross examination were lacking.[88]

Other, more disturbing, problems have surfaced. For example, a grand jury report noted that the "testimony of the firearms examiner that he could not have refused to sign what he believed was an inadequate and preliminary report on pain of potential discharge is highly alarming. If true, it could undermine public confidence in all scientific analysis performed by this agency."[89]

Examiner Qualifications

Determining whether a witness is qualified to testify concerning a firearms identification is a decision entrusted to the discretion of the trial court and will be reversed on appeal only for an abuse of discretion: "Unless the trial court's exercise of discretion is clearly erroneous, its decision as to the qualifications of an expert witness should not be disturbed."[90] Although rare, appellate courts have found an abuse of discretion, especially when a defense expert's testimony has been excluded for lack of qualifications.[91] One appellate court stated that the trial judge should not declare the witness to be an expert in the presence of the jury.[92] In addition, several cases have involved "firearms" experts who misrepresented their credentials.[93]

The last section illustrates the importance of the examiner's qualifications. Generally, this expertise is obtained through on-the-job training and experience,

---

88. Bradford, *Forensic Firearms Identification: Competence or Incompetence*, 5 FORUM 14 (July/August 1978).

89. Bradford, *Problems of Ethics and Behavior in the Forensic Sciences*, 21 J. FORENSIC SCI. 763, 767 (1976) (quoting *Report of January 1970 Grand Jury*, U.S. District Court, Northern District of Illinois, Eastern Div., at 121).

90. Ignacio v. Territory of Guam, 413 F.2d 513, 520 (9th Cir. 1969), *cert. denied,* 397 U.S. 943 (1970). *Accord* Brown v. State, 245 Ga. 588, 589, 266 S.E.2d 198, 200 (1980); State v. Zigler, 42 N.C. App. 148, 156, 256 S.E.2d 479, 484 (1979). *See generally* Joling & Stern, *An Overview of Firearms Identification Evidence for Attorneys. III: Qualifying and Using the Firearms Examiner as a Witness*, 26 J. FORENSIC SCI. 166 (1981).

91. State v. Macumber, 112 Ariz. 569, 570-71, 544 P.2d 1084, 1085-86 (1976) (en banc). *But see* People v. Williams, 790 P.2d 796, 798-800 (Colo. 1990) (en banc) (detailed examination of qualifications of proposed defense expert before upholding trial court's finding that witness was not qualified).

92. Luttrell v. Commonwealth, 952 S.W.2d 216, 218 (Ky. 1997) ("Great care should be exercised by a trial judge when the determination has been made that the witness is an expert. If the jury is so informed such a conclusion obviously enhances the credibility of that witness in the eyes of the jury. All such rulings should be made outside the hearing of the jury and there should be no declaration that the witness is an expert").

93. *E.g.,* State v. DeFronzo, 59 Ohio Misc. 113, 394 N.E.2d 1027 (C.P. 1978); Starrs, *Mountebanks Among Forensic Scientists, in* 2 FORENSIC SCIENCE HANDBOOK 1, 18, 20 (R. Saferstein ed. 1988).

not formal academic training.[94] The Association of Firearm and Tool Mark Examiners (AFTE) is the most important professional association in this field. Founded in 1969, AFTE publishes a *Training Manual, Glossary*, and a quarterly journal.[95] It also conducts annual training seminars.

AFTE has adopted a code of ethics and a quality assurance program, which requires minimum training standards, case documentation, proficiency testing, and continuing education.[96] It is studying the implementation of a certification program for firearm and toolmark examiners. An applicant for regular membership must have practiced in the field for three years and be sponsored by three experienced members.

Defense Experts

Under some circumstances, an indigent defendant would have a right to the appointment of a firearms identification expert.[97]

Photomicrographs

Courts have admitted photomicrographs in connection with the testimony of firearms identification examiners.[98] As with other types of photographs, the offering party must lay a foundation establishing that the photograph is an accurate representation of the object depicted. If photomicrographs of the comparison are not offered, the expert may still testify concerning the identification.[99]

There is disagreement about the value of photomicrographs.[100] Since the identification is based on the overall length and circumference of the bullet — each land and groove impression — and juries are not trained to interpret

---

94. Darby, *Firearms Identification, in* 3 FORENSIC SCIENCE § 38.02(a)(1) (C. Wecht ed. 1992).

95. ASSOCIATION OF FIREARM AND TOOL MARK EXAMINERS, GLOSSARY (1980); ASSOCIATION OF FIREARM AND TOOL MARK EXAMINERS, TRAINING MANUAL (1982).

96. ASSOCIATION OF FIREARM AND TOOL MARK EXAMINERS, QUALITY ASSURANCE PROGRAM (1986).

97. The right to expert assistance is discussed in Chapter 4. *See also* Annot., *Right of Indigent Defendant in State Criminal Case to Assistance of Ballistics Experts*, 71 A.L.R.4TH 638 (1989).

98. *E.g.*, Redus v. State, 243 Ala. 320, 325, 9 So. 2d 914, 918 (1942), *cert. denied,* 318 U.S. 774 (1943); State v. Jefferson, 204 Kan. 50, 54, 460 P.2d 610, 614 (1969); Commonwealth v. Giacomazza, 311 Mass. 456, 470-71, 42 N.E.2d 506, 514-15 (1942); State v. Hackett, 215 S.C. 434, 447, 55 S.E.2d 696, 702 (1949). *See generally* 2 C. SCOTT, PHOTOGRAPHIC EVIDENCE ch. 39 (2d ed. 1969); Annot., *Admissibility in Evidence of Enlarged Photographs or Photostatic Copies*, 72 A.L.R.2D 308, 331 (1960).

99. *E.g.*, People v. Buckowski, 37 Cal. 2d 629, 631, 233 P.2d 912, 913 (1951), *cert. denied,* 342 U.S. 928 (1952); People v. O'Neal, 118 Ill. App. 2d 116, 123, 254 N.E.2d 559, 562 (1969); State v. White, 321 So. 2d 491, 496 (La. 1975); State v. Harriman, 469 So. 2d 298, 306-07 (La. App. 1985), *cert. denied,* 476 U.S. 1109 (1986); State v. Schreuder, 712 P.2d 264, 268-69 (Utah 1985).

100. 1 J. MATHEWS, *supra* note 15, at 46-47.

photomicrographs, photomicrographs are often not taken or brought to court. One commentator, however, has rejected this practice:

> When a firearms identification expert testifies in court and does not produce photographs to demonstrate his opinion the defense attorney should cross-examine him vigorously as to why no photographs were made.... Always regard as suspect the statement that the ballistics expert could see the identity or nonidentity under the microscope but that it was impossible to photograph it. Ordinarily anything that can be seen can be photographed.[101]

Photomicrographs should be sought through discovery.[102]

§ 14-7. Muzzle-to-Target Distance.

Determining the distance between a firearm and a target at the time of discharge is often important in cases in which suicide, self-defense, or accident are issues. Under certain circumstances, it may be possible to ascertain the *approximate* firing distance.

§ 14-7(A). Shotgun Dispersion Patterns.

When a shot shell is fired from a shotgun, the pellets generally emerge from the muzzle grouped together and then disperse in an ever-increasing pattern as the distance from the muzzle increases. At a very close range the pellets will leave a single hole in the target surface. At greater ranges, multiple single holes are present and the radius of the pattern increases. In sum, the closer the shotgun is to the target, the smaller the dispersion pattern.

By firing a shotgun at different distances, the dispersion pattern for a particular distance may be ascertained and compared to the dispersion pattern present at the crime scene.[103] The relevancy of these experiments depends on the extent to which the conditions existing at the crime can be replicated in the experiment. Because the dispersion pattern differs for different shotguns and different types

---

101. 2 C. Scott, *supra* note 98, at 657-58.

102. For a discussion of discovery, *see* Chapter 3.

103. *See generally* Chugh, *Mathematical Analysis of Dispersion of Pellets Fired From a Shot Gun*, 32 Forensic Sci. Int'l 93 (1986); Fann, Ritter, Watts & Rowe, *Regression Analysis Applied to Shotgun Range-of-Fire Estimations: Results of a Blind Study*, 31 J. Forensic Sci. 840 (1986); Guerin, *Shotgun Wounds*, 5 J. Forensic Sci. 294 (1960); Jauhari, Chatterjee & Ghosh, *Statistical Treatment of Pellet Dispersion Data for Estimating Range of Firing*, 17 J. Forensic Sci. 141 (1972); Mattoo & Nabar, *Evaluation of Effective Shot Dispersion in Buckshot Patterns*, 14 J. Forensic Sci. 263 (1969); Nag & Sinha, *An Investigation into Pellet Dispersion Ballistics*, 55 Forensic Sci. Int'l 105 (1992); Rios, Thornton & Guarino, *Multivariate Statistical Analysis of Shotgun Pellet Dispersion*, 32 Forensic Sci. Int'l 21 (1986).

of ammunition, the identical weapon and the same type of ammunition used in the crime typically are required for this type of test.[104]

For example, the choke of a shotgun affects the dispersion pattern. The choke refers to the constriction of a shotgun barrel; that is, the diameter of the barrel is smaller at the muzzle end than at the breech end. The purpose of the choke is to produce a smaller dispersion pattern at greater distances. Several types of chokes are used: full choke, modified choke, improved cylinder, and cylindrical bore (no choke). The greater the choke, the smaller the dispersion pattern. Accordingly, the dispersion patterns of shotguns with different chokes cannot be compared.

Similarly, the type of ammunition affects the dispersion pattern; the pattern changes depending on the size of the pellets and the type of wadding used in the shot shell.

One study reported that shell temperature significantly reduced pattern diameter.[105] This study was undertaken because firearms examiners had disagreed about firing distances and each examiner's conclusion was supported by the actual sample data. The only difference was temperature. The study confirmed earlier studies that statistical treatment of shotgun pellet patterns is desirable but ecological factors also influence the tests: The "findings are clear that it is also important to ensure that the test ammunition had been stored in the same conditions as that used in the crime."[106] Another study concluded that lots of ammunition "manufactured months apart have very different ballistic performances."[107]

§ 14-7(B). Handgun & Rifle Residue Tests.

Firing distance determinations for bullets and shot shells differ. When a bullet is fired, unburned or partially burned powder and soot are propelled from the muzzle along with the bullet. Primer particles and bullet fragments may also be ejected from the muzzle.[108] At close ranges these materials will strike the target,

---

104. *See* FBI, *supra* note 1, at 58 (Shot pattern examinations "[c]an be conducted for muzzle-to-garment distance determination if a suspect shotgun is recovered and type of ammunition (shotshells) used is identified").

105. Horvath, Gardner & Siegel, *Range of Fire Estimates from Shotgun Pellet Patterns: The Effect of Shell and Barrel Temperature*, 38 J. FORENSIC SCI. 585 (1993).

106. *Id.* at 592.

107. Halvorsen & Rowe, *Comparison of Sizes of Pellet Patterns Fired with Different Lots of 0.410 Gauge No. 4 Shotshells*, 57 FORENSIC SCI. INT'L 175 (1992).

108. Carreras & Palma, *Ejection Patterns of Shot Residues Made from 9mm Parabellum Gun, 9 mm Short Gun, .38 Revolver and 7.62 mm Cetme Rifle*, 96 FORENSIC SCI. INT'L 143, 166 (1998):

> In shots with firearms with a rifled barrel, the residues which are formed from the combustion of gunpowder initially acquire a greater velocity than the bullet due to the notable rubbing of the bullet with the inner surface of the barrel. The advance of a large part of the soot is slowed down by the base of the bullet which acts as a plug, another small part

causing smudging (blackening) and stippling or tattooing.[109] Accordingly, the presence of these effects is indicative of a close range shot and may permit the muzzle-to-target distance to be approximated.[110]

Testimony concerning the range of fire may involve different types of experts. A pathologist, based on an autopsy and an examination of a homicide victim's clothing, may offer an opinion on the approximate muzzle-to-target distance.[111] A firearms identification expert, based on an examination of the clothing, may also offer an opinion.[112] The examination of the clothing may be visual, microscopic, or involve chemical tests for the presence of gunshot residues.[113] In addition,

---

> of the soot passes through the grooves of the barrel overtaking the bullet and therefore, being the first to come outside, and so they are called the primary residues, which form the first cloud, situated in a distal position.
>
> Then the bullet leaves, together with most of the gunpowder combustion residues, which were impeded from reaching the outside by the projectile: these residues, which are clustered or denser than the primary ones, are called secondary residues, because they are expelled in second place. While the secondary residues, when leaving the muzzle of the barrel, advance surrounding the bullet, over several milliseconds the rest of the residues, which remained in the barrel and which are called tertiary, are expelled, and which together with the secondary ones, form a proximal cloud which is more voluminous that the distal one. The bullet, which due to its greater mass has far more energy than the soot, preserves its muzzle exit velocity, whereas the soot rapidly loses its velocity, and so the projectile advances between the soot residues until abandoning them.

Using this information, the investigators classified shot-distances as follows: (1) contact wound shots, (2) shots at close range with dense or clustered soiling, (3) shots at close range with medium concentration soiling, (4) shots as close range with blurred or low density soiling, (5) shots at close range with gunpowder tattoo, (6) short distances shots, and (7) long distance shots.

109. Spitz, *Gunshot Wounds*, *in* MEDICOLEGAL INVESTIGATION OF DEATH 216 (W. Spitz & R. Fisher eds. 1980). *See also* Goins v. Commonwealth, 251 Va. 442, 448, 470 S.E.2d 114, 119 (1996) (victim's "wounds showed evidence of 'stippling,' consisting of burned and unburned gun powder, which indicated that the gun was fired within a few feet of her head").

110. Sometimes identifying a hole as a bullet hole is important. *See* Steinberg, Leist & Tassa, *A New Field Kit for Bullet Hole Identification*, 29 J. FORENSIC SCI. 169 (1984).

111. Spitz, *supra* note 109, at 227-28; DiMaio, Petty & Stone, *An Experimental Study of Powder Tattooing of the Skin*, 21 J. FORENSIC SCI. 367 (1976). For a further discussion of this subject, *see* Chapter 19 (forensic pathology).

112. FBI, *supra* note 1, at 58 ("On evidence, such as clothing, can be conducted for muzzle-to-garment distance determination. Microscopic exams and chemical processing of the area surrounding the hole to produce patterns of gunshot residues are compared to test patterns that are shot using the suspect firearm and ammunition like that used in the crime. These tests can only be conducted if a suspect firearm is recovered, and the type of ammunition used is identified").

113. *See* Walker, *Chemistry and Legal Medicine*, 216 NEW ENGLAND J. MED. 1024 (1937); Walker, *Bullet Holes and Chemical Residues in Shooting Cases*, 31 J. CRIM. L. & CRIMINOLOGY 497 (1940). *See also* Stahling, *Modified Sheet Printing Method (MSPM) for the Detection of Lead in Determination of Shooting Distance*, 44 J. FORENSIC SCI. 179, 181 (1999) ("The modification of the SPM method (MSPM) ... has several advantages. Colored spots, indicating a positive reaction

instrumental analysis, such as neutron activation analysis, may be used to detect the presence of bullet and primer residues.[114]

As with shotguns, the particular firearm and the same type of ammunition used in the incident should be used in the tests.[115] The residue pattern is affected by numerous factors: distance, barrel length, propellant burning rate, propellant type, caliber, muzzle-to-target angle, target material, primer, propellant charge weight, and weapon type.[116] Most of these factors are accounted for if the same weapon and similar ammunition are used in the experimental tests. The target material will rarely be the same, and thus this factor may affect the conclusions that may be drawn from the tests. As one authority has noted:

> A frequent source of error with respect to the evaluation of the distance from which a gun was fired is the comparison of a test pattern on a white paper or cloth with the pattern of the wound on the skin. Scattered specks of gunpowder are certainly not as conspicuous on the skin as they are on a smooth white background such as cloth or paper.[117]

The results of proficiency testing in this area reveals the limitations of these types of experiments.[118]

---

for lead, appear clearly on the white paper background; even weak spots are visible. The time needed to perform the test is much lower compared with the original methods").

114. *See* Krishnan, *Determination of Gunshot Firing Distances and Identification of Bullet Holes by Neutron Activation Analysis*, 12 J. FORENSIC SCI. 112 (1967); Krishnan, *Firing Distance Determination by Neutron Activation Analysis*, 12 J. FORENSIC SCI. 471 (1967); Gapannesi, Ciavola & Sedda, *Determination of Firing Distance and Firing Angle by Neutron Activation Analysis in a Case Involving Gunshot Wounds*, 61 FORENSIC SCI. INT'L 75 (1993). For a discussion of neutron activation analysis, *see* Chapter 11.

See also Stone & Petty, *Examination of Gunshot Residues*, 19 J. FORENSIC SCI. 784 (1974) (discussing other instrumental techniques); Andrasko, *Characterization of Smokeless Powder Flakes from Fired Cartridge Cases and from Discharge Patterns on Clothing*, 37 J. FORENSIC SCI. 1030 (1992); Nag & Sinha, *A Note on Assessability of Firing Distance from Gunshot Residues*, 56 FORENSIC SCI. INT'L 1 (1992).

115. Munhall, *Fundamental Ballistics Pertaining to Investigations Involving Firearms*, 6 J. FORENSIC SCI. 215, (1961) ("It is well recognized that different guns and different ammunition will vary widely in their residue distribution patterns ...").

116. Barnes & Helson, *An Empirical Study of Gunpowder Residue Patterns*, 19 J. FORENSIC SCI. 448, 449 (1974).

117. Spitz, *supra* note 109, at 228.

118. *See* Peterson & Markham, *supra* note 43, at 1018 ("Two scenarios (81-5 and 90-3) also asked laboratories to make a target/muzzle distance-of-fire determination. ...All laboratories (17) reporting the target to muzzle distance in 81-5 produced results in conformity with the manufacturer's specifications. Approximately one-quarter of these, however, reported distances that were at the outer limits of acceptability. In addition about one-quarter of the laboratories did not attempt or report results on this test. In 90-3, while about 90% of the mean target value estimates were within a 'reasonable' range of 6"–12" (9" was the actual muzzle-to-target distance), in about half these replies one of the estimates (near or far) was outside the reasonable range").

§ 14-7(C). Admissibility of Muzzle-to-Target Distance Evidence.

The results of tests conducted to determine muzzle-to-target distance have been admitted in cases involving rifles and handguns[119] as well as shotguns.[120] As one court has remarked:

> The results of tests to determine the distance from which a weapon had been fired are admissible into evidence provided the test was conducted under conditions sufficiently similar to the actual conditions involved in the case that they can be fairly said to have probative value and will enlighten, not confuse the jury.[121]

If the conditions are not "substantially" similar, the results are not admissible.[122] For example, some courts have excluded dispersion pattern tests on the ground that the target material used in the test was not shown to be similar to human skin tissue.[123] In contrast, other courts have held that admissibility is not affected by this factor.[124]

In *State v. Barnes*,[125] the testimony of a defense expert about a pellet dispersion pattern test was excluded because the expert was not qualified. He "became a gunsmith after completing a correspondence course. He had never received training in forensic science, firearms identification or ballistics. He had

---

119. *E.g.,* State v. Castagna, 170 Conn. 80, 90-91, 364 A.2d 200, 206 (1976); People v. Carbona, 27 Ill. App. 3d 988, 1004, 327 N.E.2d 546, 561 (1975), *cert. denied,* 424 U.S. 914 (1976); State v. Jiles, 258 Iowa 1324, 1328-32, 142 N.W.2d 451, 453-56 (1966); State v. Galvan, 368 N.W.2d 400, 403 (Minn. App. 1985), *cert. denied,* 475 U.S. 1097 (1986); State v. Atwood, 250 N.C. 141, 108 S.E.2d 219 (1959); State v. Goins, 24 N.C. App. 468, 472, 211 S.E.2d 481, 483-84, *cert. denied,* 287 N.C. 262, 214 S.E.2d 434 (1975); State v. Kahan, 268 S.C. 240, 245-46, 233 S.E.2d 293, 294 (1977); State v. Brooks, 16 Wash. App. 535, 540, 557 P.2d 362, 366 (1976). *See also* Annot., *Admissibility, in homicide prosecution, of evidence as to tests made to ascertain distance from gun to victim when gun was fired,* 11 A.L.R.5TH 497 (1993); Annot., *Admissibility in homicide prosecution of evidence as to tests made to ascertain distance from gun to victim when gun was fired,* 86 A.L.R.2D 611 (1962).

120. *E.g.,* State v. Polan, 78 Ariz. 253, 258-59, 278 P.2d 432, 436 (1954); West v. State, 200 Ga. 566, 571, 37 S.E.2d 799, 801-02 (1946); State v. Tourville, 295 S.W.2d 1, 6-7 (Mo. 1956), *cert. denied,* 352 U.S. 1018 (1957); State v. Bates, 48 Ohio St. 2d 315, 321-22, 358 N.E.2d 584, 588-89 (1976), *vacated on other grounds,* 438 U.S. 910 (1978); Andrews v. State, 555 P.2d 1079, 1083-84 (Okla. Crim. App. 1976); Williams v. State, 147 Tex. Crim. 178, 184, 179 S.W.2d 297, 300 (1944).

121. Andrews v. State, 555 P.2d 1079, 1083 (Okla. Crim. App. 1976). *See generally* § 5-8 *supra* (admissibility of evidence of out-of-court experiments).

122. *E.g.,* Miller v. State, 250 Ind. 656, 236 N.E.2d 585 (1968); Roberts v. State, 117 Tex. Crim. 418, 424-25, 35 S.W.2d 175, 178 (1931).

123. *E.g.,* Roberts v. State, 189 So. 2d 543, 546 (Fla. App. 1966); People v. Cohen, 50 N.Y.2d 908, 409 N.E.2d 921, 431 N.Y.S.2d 446 (1980).

124. *E.g.,* State v. Brooks, 16 Wash. App. 535, 540, 557 P.2d 362, 366 (1976).

125. 597 So. 2d 1109 (La. App. 1992).

never testified as an expert in any area. He worked as a sales clerk at a hardware store and in his own gun repair business."[126]

§ 14-8. Time of Firearm Discharge.

The estimation of the time lapse since a firearm has been discharged would often be of great value in criminal investigations. The detection of combustion products in the barrel may be the basis for this estimation. One study used solid phase microextraction (SPME) for this purpose. If the actual shotgun and ammunition is available, decay curves may be used.[127] For unknown ammunition, repetitive sampling of other ammunition must be employed. An indication that the weapon had been fired from (1) two-three days, (2) one-two weeks, or (3) more than three weeks may be obtained. This method was used to undercut a self-defense claim, by showing that a double-barreled shotgun had been fired sequentially from the same barrel rather than simultaneously.[128]

§ 14-9. Accidental Firings.

If a defendant claims that a weapon fired accidentally, the condition of the weapon may be an issue. In such a case, a firearms examiner may check the weapon to determine whether any parts are worn, broken, or missing.[129] In particular, the functioning of the safety, hammer, and trigger may be tested. The pressure required to pull the trigger can be measured and compared with other weapons of the same make.[130] Evidence of accidental shootings has been admitted at trial.[131]

---

126. *Id.* at 1112.

127. Andrasko, Norberg & Stahling, *Time Since Discharge of Shotguns*, 43 J. FORENSIC SCI. 1005, 1013 (1998) ("Not only does the type of ammunition, the temperature of storage, the cleaning of the barrel after the shooting and the number of shots fired influence the results, but even using the same type of ammunition can give significant differences in amount of decomposition compounds detected inside the barrel at a certain time after the shooting").

128. Andersson & Andrasko, *A Novel Application of Time Since the Latest Discharge of a Shotgun in a Suspect Murder*, 44 J. FORENSIC SCI. 211 (1999).

129. FBI, *supra* note 1, at 58 (Alteration examination "[c]an be conducted to determine if a firearm has been altered to fire in the automatic mode and if the firearm actually can fire in the automatic mode; function examinations can be conducted to determine if a firearm is capable of firing as it was designed and if all safeties are properly operating. Examinations can be conducted to determine if a firearm can be made to fire accidentally, that is, without pulling the trigger").

130. FBI, *supra* note 1, at 58 (Trigger pull examinations "[c]an be conducted to determine the amount of pressure necessary to fire a firearm").

131. *See* Hilburn v. State, 166 Ga. App. 357, 357, 304 S.E.2d 480, 482 (1983).

§ 14-10. Serial Number Restoration.

Serial number restoration is another procedure often conducted by firearms identification examiners. Firearms, as well as numerous other metal objects, such as typewriters and automobiles, are imprinted with serial numbers. Various procedures, such as rolling, stamping, and engraving, are used to imprint the serial number at the time of manufacture. Sometimes a firearm or other object recovered in a criminal investigation has had its serial number obliterated by filing or grinding. Even though the number is visually removed, it may be possible to restore it. When the serial number is originally stamped, for example, the stamping process strains the metal to a depth greater than the visual number. If the filing does not penetrate to this depth, restoration procedures, such as chemical etching and electrolytic processing, may be used to restore the number.[132] Evidence of serial number alteration has been admitted at trial.[133]

§ 14-11. Bullet & Cartridge Composition Analysis.

The chemical analysis of bullets to ascertain their elemental composition has been conducted for over three decades. Courts have admitted evidence identifying bullets by their elemental composition—using a variety of techniques, such as spectrographic analysis,[134] neutron activation analysis,[135] and Inductively

---

132. *See* 1 J. MATHEWS, *supra* note 15, ch. 5. *See also* Mongan, *Visualization of a Restored Serial Number Using Scanning Electron Microscopy (SEM)*, 41 J. FORENSIC SCI. 1074 (1996); Young, *The Restoration of Obliterated Stamped Serial Numbers by Ultrasonically Induced Cavitation in Water*, 19 J. FORENSIC SCI. 820 (1974).

133. *See* People v. Snow, 21 Ill. App. 3d 873, 876-77, 316 N.E.2d 216, 218-19 (1974) (expert testimony concerning alteration of serial number on automobile admitted).

134. *See* Medley v. United States, 155 F.2d 857, 860 (D.C. Cir.), *cert. denied,* 328 U.S. 873 (1946).

135. *E.g.,* People v. Johnson, 114 Ill. 2d 170, 194-98, 499 N.E.2d 1355, 1366-67 (1986), *cert. denied,* 480 U.S. 951 (1987); Jones v. State, 425 N.E.2d 128, 130-31 (Ind. 1981); Mark v. State, 568 N.W.2d 820, 826-27 (Iowa 1997) ("Neutron Activation Analysis (NAA) tests conducted in 1976 revealed similarities between the bullets purchased by Mark in California and the bullets found at the crime scene. An FBI agent testified one similarity between the samples was that neither sample contained any arsenic. The postconviction court ordered the bullets taken from the former Olson's Boat House be tested and compared to the crime scene bullets. The court also appointed an expert, Dr. Vincent Guinn, to assist Mark. These tests revealed arsenic in both the crime scene samples and the samples from Ken's Sport Shop. Mark claims this disclosure justifies the postconviction relief requested"); State v. Krummacher, 269 Or. 125, 143, 523 P.2d 1009, 1017 (1974); State v. Reynolds, 307 N.C. 184, 186, 297 S.E.2d 532, 534 (1982) (bullets "were of the same chemical composition, consistent with their having come from the same box of ammunition"); State v. Strain, 885 P.2d 810, 817 (Utah App. 1994) (FBI agent "employed two techniques in comparing the bullets, a 'neutron activation analysis' to analyze for antimony, copper, and arsenic; and an 'ICP' (an acronym for 'inductibly coupled plasma atomic emissions patromotry') to analyze for silver, bismuth, and tin. [He] testified that through analysis of these trace elements, it is possible to determine whether a bullet could have come from a specific box of

Coupled Plasma-Atomic Emission Spectrometry (ICP) among others.[136] It is one thing to say that two bullets have the same elemental composition (and in the same percentages); it is quite another thing to say how rare these findings are.[137] In one case, a NAA expert testified that two bullets "had been made by the same manufacturer on the same day and at the same hour."[138]

Information on ammunition other than headstamps and ballistic information is not readily available: "There are no databases available, which list both chemical and physical characteristics of cartridges from different manufactures."[139] Nevertheless, the FBI laboratory has analyzed thousands of bullets and has significant experience in this field.

In *State v. Noel,*[140] the New Jersey Supreme Court ruled that expert opinion testimony concerning similarity in the composition of bullets based on ICP was admissible even in the absence of statistical evidence. An FBI expert testified that bullets that come from the same box have the same composition of lead and bullets that come from different boxes have different compositions. He also acknowledged, however, that mixing may occur during storage and that fifty thousand bullets may have the same composition.[141]

---

ammunition, or whether two or more bullets could have come from the same box of ammunition"). For a further discussion of neutron activation analysis, *see* Chapter 11.

136. *See* United States v. Davis, 103 F.3d 660, 673-74 (8th Cir. 1996) ("Mr. Riley testified that ICP, an analysis that the FBI has been using for approximately 10 years, is a generally accepted scientific technique that has been subjected to testing, publication, and peer review, and the technique is the same no matter who performs it. Another procedure used to accomplish the same basic analysis is neuron [neutron] activation analysis. The FBI has been using the neuron [neutron] activation analysis since the mid-1960s but now favors ICP for trace elemental analysis because ICP is more sensitive. ICP can determine trace elements down to parts per million (.0001 percent). The procedure determines which of five trace elements are present in the bullets to be compared. If the same elements are present in each, then the procedure determines the percentage of each element present. If the same elements are present in the same amounts then they are analytically indistinguishable"), *cert. denied,* 520 U.S. 1258 (1997).

137. FBI, *supra* note 1, at 57-58 ("Lead samples from the bullet and/or fragment are compared with ammunition recovered from the suspect's possession. Analysis may determine that the composition of the bullet and/or fragment is identical to the composition of the recovered ammunition. Although circumstantial, lead composition information is often useful to link a suspect to a shooting, and similar information may be determined from an analysis of shotpellets and slugs").

138. Brown v. State, 601 P.2d 221, 224 (Alaska 1979).

139. Wrobel, Millar & Kijek, *Identification of Ammunition from Gunshot Residues and Other Cartridge Related Materials — A Preliminary Model Using .22 Caliber Rimfire Ammunition,* 43 J. FORENSIC SCI. 324, 324 (1998).

140. 157 N.J. 141, 723 A.2d 602 (1999).

141. *Id.* at 149, 723 A.2d at 606. "He based his testimony on years of analyzing boxes of bullets and on a tour of the Speer plant"). *See also* Commonwealth v. Daye, 411 Mass. 719, 742, 587 N.E.2d 194, 207 (1992).

In *Slocum v. State*[142] the expert testified that the unfired bullet and the one found in the victim "were of the same manufacturing process by weight and design. The expert said, '[T]hey both have the same weight, that being 230 [grams]. They both are full metal copper jacketed. They both have open exposed lead on the base."[143] The court ruled the testimony admissible as circumstantial evidence.

§ 14-12. Toolmark Identification.

§ 14-12(A). Class & Individual Characteristics.

"Toolmark identification is a microscopic side-by-side comparison that attempts to link a particular tool with a particular mark to the exclusion of any other tool produced."[144] Toolmark identifications are based on the same theory as firearms identifications:[145] Tools have both (1) class characteristics and (2) individual characteristics; the latter are accidental imperfections produced in the machining process and also by subsequent use. When the tool is used, these characteristics are often imparted onto the surface of another object.

Firearms identification could be considered a subspecialty of toolmark identification; the firearm (tool) imprints its individual characteristics on the bullet. Toolmark identification, however, is often more difficult than firearms identification. The markings on a bullet or cartridge case are imprinted in the same way every time a firearm is fired. In contrast, a tool can be used in a variety of different ways, each producing a different mark: "[I]n toolmark work the angle at which the tool was used must be duplicated in the test standard, pressures must be dealt with, and the degree of hardness of metals and other materials must be taken into account."[146]

---

142. 325 Ark. 38, 924 S.W.2d 237 (1996).

143. *Id.* at 41, 924 S.W.2d at 239.

144. FBI, *supra* note 1, at 60 ("The term 'tool' is used in a very broad sense. It could mean a screwdriver blade, vice grips, a knife or a pry tool. It could also be the comparison of a piece of paint on the tool with the surface upon which that tool was used. Further, it could be the comparison of two pieces of rubber that have been pulled apart from each other, as can happen in a car stripping operation"). *See also* Springer, *Toolmark Examinations — A Review of its Development in the Literature*, 40 J. FORENSIC SCI. 964 (1995) ("The identification is based ... on a series of scratches, depressions, and other marks which the tool leaves on the object it comes into contact with. The combination of these various marks have been termed toolmarks and the claim is that every instrument can impart a mark individual to itself").

145. *See* Biasotti, *The Principles of Evidence Evaluation as Applied to Firearms and Tool Mark Identification*, 9 J. FORENSIC SCI. 428 (1964).

146. Flynn, *Toolmark Identification*, 2 J. FORENSIC SCI. 95, 105 (1957). *See also* Darby, *supra* note 94, § 38.10.

Toolmarks may be impressions (compression marks) or striations (friction or scrape marks) or a combination of both.[147] Fracture matches are another type of examination.[148] The marks may be left on a variety of different materials, such as wood or metal. In some cases, only class characteristics can be matched. For example, it may be possible to identify a mark (impression) left on a piece of wood as having been produced by a hammer, punch, or screwdriver. A comparison of the mark and the evidence tool may establish that the size of the tool (another class characteristic) and the mark also match. Unusual features of the tool, such as a chip, may permit a positive identification. Striations caused by scraping with a tool may also produce individual characteristic marks in much the same way that striations are imprinted on a bullet when a firearm is discharged. This type of examination has the same limitations as firearms identification: "[T]he characteristics of a tool will change with use."[149]

As with firearms identification testimony, toolmark identification testimony is based on the subjective judgment of the examiner; the expert determines whether sufficient marks of similarity are present to permit a positive identification.[150] There are no objective criteria. As one commentator has noted: "[I]t is not possible at present to categorically state the number and percentage of the [striation] lines which must correspond."[151] Proficiency testing on toolmark examinations have been reported.[152]

The comparison microscope is also used in this examination. The use of scanning electron microscopy[153] and automated systems have been reported; the latter systems use a computer and digitized striation patterns.[154]

---

147. Burd & Greene, *Tool Mark Examination Techniques*, 2 J. FORENSIC SCI. 297, 298 (1957).

148. FBI, *supra* note 1, at 61 ("Fracture examinations are conducted to ascertain if a piece of material from an item such as a metal bolt, plastic automobile trim, knife, screwdriver, wood gunstock, rubber hose, etc., was or was not broken from a like damaged item available for comparison").

149. Flynn, *supra* note 146, at 102.

150. *See* Springer, *Toolmark Examinations — A Review of its Development in the Literature*, 40 J. FORENSIC SCI. 964, 966-67 (1995) ("According to the Association of Firearms and Toolmarks Examiners' Criteria for Identification Committee, interpretation of toolmark individualization and identification is still considered to be subjective in nature, based on one's training and experience").

151. Burd & Greene, *supra* note 147, at 310. For other articles on toolmark identification, *see* Burd & Greene, *Tool Mark Comparisons in Criminal Investigations*, 39 J. CRIM. L. & CRIMINOLOGY 379 (1948); Burd & Kirk, *Tool Marks: Factors Involved in Their Comparison and Use as Evidence*, 32 J. CRIM. L. & CRIMINOLOGY 679 (1942); Greene & Burd, *Special Techniques Useful in Tool Mark Comparisons*, 41 J. CRIM. L. & CRIMINOLOGY 523 (1950); Meyers & Kivela, *Interesting Applications of Tool Mark Identification*, 6 J. FORENSIC SCI. 316 (1961).

152. *See* Peterson & Markham, *supra* note 43, at 1025 ("Overall, laboratories performed not as well on the toolmark tests as they did on the firearms tests").

153. *See* Sehgal, Singh, Dey, Kumar, Jain, Grover & Dua, *Tool Marks Comparison of a Wire Cut Ends by Scanning Electron Microscopy — A Forensic Study*, 36 FORENSIC SCI. INT'L 21 (1988).

§ 14-12(B). Admissibility of Toolmark Evidence.

Courts have often admitted toolmark identification evidence. The cases have involved screwdrivers,[155] crowbars,[156] punches,[157] knives,[158] as well as other objects.[159] As the Ninth Circuit has noted, toolmark identification "rests upon a scientific basis and is a reliable and generally accepted procedure."[160] An expert's opinion is admissible even if not a positive identification. For example, in *United States v. Murphy*,[161] an FBI expert "testified that the tools such as the screwdriver associated with Murphy 'could' have made the marks on the ignitions but that he could not positively attribute the marks to the tools identified with Murphy."[162]

In *State v. Genrich*,[163] the Colorado Court of Appeals allowed expert testimony that three different sets of pliers recovered from the accused's house were used to cut wire and fasten a cap found in the debris from pipebombs. The lack of a databank as used in fingerprints and firearms identifications was not a

---

154. Geradts, Keijzer & Keereweer, *A New Approach to Automatic Comparison of Striation Marks*, 39 J. FORENSIC SCI. 974 (1994).

155. *E.g.*, State v. Dillon, 161 N.W.2d 738, 741 (Iowa 1968) (screwdriver and nail bar fit marks on door frame); State v. Hazelwood, 209 Kan. 649, 655-56, 498 P.2d 607, 612 (1972) (screwdriver and imprint on window molding); State v. Wade, 465 S.W.2d 498 (Mo. 1971) (screwdriver and pry marks on door jamb); State v. Brown, 291 S.W.2d 615, 618-19 (Mo. 1956) (crowbar and screwdriver marks on window sash and door); State v. Eickmeier, 187 Neb. 491, 493, 191 N.W.2d 815, 816 (1971) (screwdriver and marks on door); State v. Wessling, 260 Iowa 1244, 150 N.W.2d 301 (1967) (screwdriver).

156. *E.g.*, People v. Perroni, 14 Ill. 2d 581, 591-92, 153 N.E.2d 578, 583 (1958) (crowbar matched marks on safe); State v. Brown, 291 S.W.2d 615, 618-19 (Mo. 1956) (crowbar and screwdriver marks on window sash and door); State v. Raines, 29 N.C. App. 303, 224 S.E.2d 232, *cert. denied*, 290 N.C. 311, 225 S.E.2d 831 (1976).

157. *E.g.*, State v. Montgomery, 175 Kan. 176, 180, 261 P.2d 1009, 1011-12 (1953) (punch and marks on safe).

158. *E.g.*, State v. Baldwin, 36 Kan. 1, 12 P. 318 (1886) (experienced carpenters could testify that wood panel could have been cut by accused's knife); Graves v. State, 563 P.2d 646, 650 (Okla. Crim. App. 1977) (blade and knife handle matched); State v. Clark, 156 Wash. 543, 549, 287 P. 18, 20 (1930) (knife and cuts on tree branches); State v. Bernson, 40 Wash. App. 729, 735, 700 P.2d 758, 764 (1985) (knife tip comparison).

159. *E.g.*, United States v. Taylor, 334 F. Supp. 1050, 1056-57 (D.C. Pa. 1971) (impressions on stolen vehicle and impressions made by dies found in defendant's possession), *aff'd*, 469 F.2d 284 (3d Cir. 1972); State v. McClelland, 162 N.W.2d 457, 462 (Iowa 1968) (pry bar and marks on "jimmied" door); Adcock v. State, 444 P.2d 242, 243-44 (Okla. Crim. App. 1968) (tool matched pry marks on door molding); State v. Olsen, 212 Or. 191, 195-96, 317 P.2d 938, 940 (1957) (hammer and marks on safe). *See also* Allgeier v. Commonwealth, 915 S.W.2d 745, 747 (Ky. 1996) (testimony that "gouge mark on the door did not indicate force sufficient to force the door open" admitted).

160. United States v. Bowers, 534 F.2d 186, 193 (9th Cir.), *cert. denied*, 429 U.S. 942 (1976).

161. 996 F.2d 94 (5th Cir. 1993), *cert. denied*, 510 U.S. 971 (1993).

162. *Id.* at 99.

163. 928 P.2d 799 (Colo. App. 1996).

bar to admissibility. The fact that other experts disagreed (finding that the marks were inconclusive in two instances) affected the weight, not admissibility, of the evidence. Finally, the court observed: "The expert's premise, that no two tools make exactly the same mark, is not challenged by any evidence in this record. Hence, the lack of a database and points of comparison does not render the opinion inadmissible."[164] The accused also challenged the expert's qualifications, noting that (1) the expert did not have any post-high school formal education, (2) there was no standard curriculum to train toolmark examiners, and (3) there was no national certification program. Rejecting this attack, the court ruled that neither a college degree nor formal training in an established curriculum is necessarily required for an expert.[165]

Two cases have involved toolmark (knife) impressions discovered in the cartilage of the victim. One court admitted the evidence,[166] while the other rejected such testimony.[167]

§ 14-13. Gunshot Residue Tests.

Determining whether a person has recently fired a firearm is important in (1) identifying an assailant, (2) proving or rebutting a self-defense claim, or (3) distinguishing a suicide from a homicide.[168] When a firearm is discharged, a backblast of gases escape and gunshot residues (GSR) may be deposited on the hand of the person firing the weapon or any other person or surface in the vicinity. Both propellent (smokeless powder) and primer residues are discharged.

Consequently, a number of techniques designed to detect gunshot residues on the hands of a suspect (which is rare)[169] or victim have been developed.[170] These

---

164. *Id.* at 802.

165. *See* § 5-3 *supra* (qualifications).

166. State v. Churchill, 231 Kan. 408, 413-14, 646 P.2d 1049, 1054 (1982).

167. Ramirez v. State, 542 So. 2d 352, 354-55 (Fla. 1989). *See also* Rao & Hart, *Toolmark Determination in Cartilage of Stabbing Victim*, 28 J. FORENSIC SCI. 794 (1983) (*e.g.*, where striations on rib cartilages were conclusively matched with a knife).

168. *See* State v. Shapiro, 431 So. 2d 372, 378 (La. 1982) ("There was no indication of suicide ... there was no gunshot residue on the victim's hands ..."); Reed, McGuire & Boehm, *Analysis of Gunshot Residue Test Results in 112 Suicides*, 35 J. FORENSIC SCI. 62 (1990).

169. *See generally* Aaron, *Gunshot Primer Residue: The Invisible Clue*, 60 FBI LAW ENFORCEMENT BULL. 19 (June 1991); DeGaetano & Siegel, *Survey of Gunshot Residue Analysis in Forensic Science Laboratories*, 35 J. FORENSIC SCI. 1087 (1990); Krishnan, *Detection of Gunshot Residue: Present Status*, *in* 1 FORENSIC SCIENCE HANDBOOK 572 (R. Saferstein ed. 1982); Midkiff, *Detection of Gunshot Residues: Modern Solutions for an Old Problem*, 3 J. POLICE SCI. & AD. 77 (1975); Stone, *Evidence of Firearms Discharge Residues*, 33 BAYLOR L. REV. 285 (1981); Annot., *Admissibility, in Criminal Case, of Results of Residue Detection Test to Determine Whether Accused or Victim Handled or Fired Gun*, 1 A.L.R.4TH 1072 (1980).

170. Obtaining gunshot residues from a suspect may raise constitutional issues. In State v. Ulrich, 187 Mont. 347, 609 P.2d 1218 (1980), the court held that taking residue samples at the time

techniques range from the controversial paraffin test to the more modern techniques, which use instrumental analysis or scanning electron microscopy.[171] The modern GSR tests focus on primer residues (antimony, barium, and lead) and the detection of these elements in sufficient quantity to infer recent proximity to a discharging firearm or ammunition component.[172]

Limitations

All GSR techniques have limitations. First, the residues can be removed by rubbing or washing the hands and thus usually must be collected soon after the firearm is fired.[173] This also means that the absence of residues is not very

---

of arrest did not violate the fourth amendment prohibition against unreasonable searches and seizures, the fifth amendment prohibition against self-incrimination, or the sixth amendment right to counsel. *See also* State v. Odom, 303 N.C. 163, 277 S.E.2d 352 (evidence of the defendant's refusal to provide gunshot residue samples did not violate the right to counsel or due process), *cert. denied,* 454 U.S. 1052 (1981); Commonwealth v. Monahan, 378 Pa. Super. 623, 632-33, 549 A.2d 231, 235-36 (1988) (evidence of defendant's refusal to submit to GSR test admissible).

The Supreme Judicial Court of Massachusetts has ruled that evidence of a defendant's refusal to submit to a gunshot residue test violated the state constitution: "If the fact that the defendant refused to allow the hand-swabbing demonstrates consciousness of guilt, such refusal rises to the level of a self-accusation." Commonwealth v. Lydon, 413 Mass. 309, 597 N.E.2d 36, 40 (1992).

For a further discussion of the constitutional issues, *see* Chapter 2.

171. There is some disagreement concerning the mechanism of GSR deposition, that is, whether the residues are blasted onto the hand or settle from airborne gases. Moreover, whether the source of the residues is only the breech or the breech and muzzle is another source of disagreement. One study of these issues concluded: "When a firearm is discharged, the GSR issuing through the breeches of the firearm are blown at once on the immediate surfaces of the firearm, including any hand in contact with, or in close proximity to, the firearm. This forced deposition is essentially a blasting mechanism in which the rapidly cooled down GSR impart only momentum but no heat energy to the surfaces these strike. Thus the hand deposits of the shooter are mainly the trigger-blast residues. The rate of deposition of these residues is not influenced by the substrate surface characteristics." Basu, Boone, Denio & Miazga, *Fundamental Studies of Gunshot Residue Deposition by Glue-Lift*, 42 J. FORENSIC SCI. 571, 580 (1997). "If the gun is pre-cleaned and the ammunition and the hand grasp on the firearm remain unchanged, a reasonably constant amount of residues is deposited per firing on the back of the firing hand. This density distribution of GSR is the most practical criterion required to reconstruct a shooting crime, and for such reconstruction the gun must be pre-cleaned." *Id.*

172. *See* Zeichner & Levin, *More on the Uniqueness of Gunshot Residue (GSR) Particles*, 42 J. FORENSIC SCI. 1027 (1997) ("Their [early investigators] definition of unique was based on the experimental fact that those compositions have thus far been observed only in GSR. Particularly it was based on their examination of about 80 hand samples from people whose occupation involved the metals or compounds of lead, barium and antimony. ...However, the definition 'unique' to describe material compositions should be applied cautiously").

173. *See* Kilty, *Activity After Shooting and Its Effect on the Retention of Primer Residue*, 20 J. FORENSIC SCI. 219, 230 (1975) ("As the time after the shooting passes, the possibility decreases that significant amounts of [antimony] and [barium] will be detected"); Wainwright v. Norris, 872 F. Supp. 574, 585 (E.D. Ark. 1994) (Expert "testified that gunshot residue deposited by a firearm can

probative. Second, even valid GSR tests are not conclusive; the value of the GSR test is that it can associate an individual with a GSR environment.

In *People v. Gutierrez*,[174] an expert testified that GSR test results did not permit a conclusion as to whether the accused had handled or fired a gun. The prosecution and defense stipulated to the introduction of the test results. The defense, however, objected to several hypothetical questions posed by the prosecution:

> The People asked whether the delay in residue testing, the effect of the wind while riding on the motorcycle, the result of removing a long-sleeved shirt or jacket, and the effect of having contact with beer could have reduced the gunshot residue on the defendant's hands. The expert testified that assuming a person fired a gun and given the above mentioned factors it would not be unusual to find an insignificant amount of gunshot residue on the person's hands.[175]

The appellate court ruled the evidence admissible: "[I]f the defendant was entitled to introduce evidence [that] the test did not suggest he had fired a gun, the People were entitled to elicit evidence showing why the test did not rule out that possibility."[176]

§ 14-13(A). Paraffin Test.

The "paraffin"[177] or dermal nitrate test was introduced in this country in the early 1930s[178] and was adopted quickly by law enforcement agencies.[179] The test

---

be easily removed by washing the hands or even rubbing them vigorously. Even normal activity, within three hours, may remove the residue"), *cert. denied*, 519 U.S. 968 (1996).

Failure to protect the hands also affects the use of GSR tests in suicide cases. *See* Reed, McGuire & Boehm, *Analysis of Gunshot Residue Test Results in 112 Suicides*, 35 J. FORENSIC SCI. 62, 66 (1990) ("The single most important factor in obtaining accurate results is condition of the hands before swabbing.... Cases in which the hands were not safeguarded before transportation to the hospital or morgue resulted in low positive test results").

174. 10 Cal. App. 4th 1729, 13 Cal. Rptr. 2d 464 (1992), *cert. denied*, 516 U.S. 1049 (1995).

175. *Id.* at 1734, 13 Cal. Rptr. 2d at 467.

176. *Id.* at 1735, 13 Cal. Rptr. 2d at 467.

177. The term "paraffin test" is misleading because the paraffin cast technique is merely a method for removing the residues from the hands. The test is also known as the "dermal nitrate test," "diphenylbenzidine test," or the "diphenylamine test." Nitrate is the residue detected; diphenylamine and diphenylbenzidine are the reagents used in the test.

178. *See* Mathews, *The Paraffin Test*, 102 AMERICAN RIFLEMAN 20 (1954).

179. *See Diphenylamine Test for Gun Powder*, 4 FBI LAW ENFORCEMENT BULL. 5 (1935) ("current widespread use"); Castellanous & Plasencia, *The Paraffin Gauntlet: A New Technique for the Dermo-Nitrate Test*, 32 J. CRIM. L., CRIMINOLOGY & POLICE SCI. 465 (1943) ("For a number of years the National Bureau of Identification, Cuba, has used the so-called Paraffin or Dermo-Nitrate

was designed to detect the presence of nitrate residues, which, due to the backblast of gases that escape during discharge, may be deposited on the hand of the person firing the firearm. These substances are residues from smokeless powder, the propellant used in cartridges. The term "paraffin test" derives from the paraffin cast technique, which was used to remove the residues from the hands.[180] After the paraffin cast was removed from the hand, it was tested with a reagent, either diphenylamine or diphenylbenzidine. A color reaction — "dark blue spots" — indicated the presence of nitrate residues.[181]

The principal problem with the "paraffin" test was its nonspecificity. A significant number of substances other than gunpowder residues contain nitrates and therefore also produce a positive reaction.[182] One study concluded that a positive reaction is produced by tobacco or tobacco ash, fertilizer, pharmaceuticals, leguminous plants, and urine.[183] A more comprehensive study found that "'rust,' colored fingernail polishes, residue from evaporated urine, soap and tap water"[184] all produce a positive reaction. In other words, the test detected nitrate residues, but the source of these residues could not be determined. Consequently, the probative value of a positive reaction was marginal at best. If, however, a positive reaction was accompanied by microscopic identification of gunpowder particles, the nonspecificity problem may be overcome.[185] Because of its nonspecificity, the test is not used today.[186]

Test ..."; also, editor notes limitations and advises caution); Crane, *The Paraffin Test*, 14 TRIAL 36 (Mar. 1978).

180. The backs of the hands were coated with molten paraffin. After the paraffin cooled, it solidified into a thin cast, which was lifted from the hands. Midkiff, *supra* note 169, at 77.

181. *Id.*

182. The first FBI report on the paraffin test noted that the test revealed only the presence of nitrates and there were a "large number of substances with a nitrate content other than gunpowder"; concluding that test "is of some value in criminal investigations"), 4 FBI LAW ENFORCEMENT BULL., *supra* note 179. Soon thereafter the FBI concluded that the test was unreliable. *See Further Observations on the Diphenylamine Test for Gunpowder Residue*, 9 FBI LAW ENFORCEMENT BULL. 10 (June 1940) ("Recently there have been additional experiments conducted ... which corroborate the unreliability of the ... test for gunpowder residue"); *Gunpowder Tests*, 18 FBI LAW ENFORCEMENT BULL. 2, 3 (Aug. 1949) ("Despite the unreliability of the diphenylamine test for gunpowder, it does have some investigative value. It may have a psychological effect upon a suspect when he is confronted with the positive results of such a test. The limitations to the test, however, are most definite").

183. Turkel & Lipman, *Unreliability of Dermal Nitrate Test for Gunpowder*, 46 J. CRIM. L., CRIMINOLOGY & POLICE SCI. 281, 282 (1955).

184. Cowan & Purdon, *A Study of the "Paraffin Test,"* 12 J. FORENSIC SCI. 19, 23 (1967).

185. *E.g.*, State v. Fields, 434 S.W.2d 507, 516 (Mo. 1968); Commonwealth v. Westwood, 324 Pa. 289, 300, 188 A. 304, 309 (1936).

186. *See* Krishnan, *supra* note 169, at 573 ("The paraffin cast method has ... been abandoned as a means of detecting GSR"). *But see* Conrad, *Evidential Implications of the Dermal Nitrate Test for Gunpowder Residues*, 44 MARQ. L. REV. 500 (1961).

The first reported case admitting testimony based on the paraffin test was decided in 1936.[187] In 1959, the first case rejecting the test was reported.[188] Although several courts followed suit and also rejected the paraffin test,[189] evidence based on the paraffin test continued to be admitted in other courts.[190] Indeed, in 1979 the Oklahoma Court of Criminal Appeals overruled an earlier decision and held evidence based on the test admissible, at least where the result of the test was negative.[191]

§ 14-13(B). Harrison-Gilroy Test.

In 1959, Harrison and Gilroy developed a new chemical method (color test) for gunshot residue detection.[192] Unlike the paraffin test which detected propellant residues, this test was designed to detect primer residues — antimony, barium, and lead. Accordingly, the presence of nitrates was immaterial and the nonspecificity of that substance, the principal problem with the paraffin test, was avoided. In addition, the simplicity of the Harrison-Gilroy test made it suitable for field use. Nevertheless, it is not used today due to its inadequate sensitivity and other drawbacks.[193] Today, the test is important primarily because it focused attention on primer residues rather than powder residues.

Few reported cases considered the admissibility of evidence based on the Harrison-Gilroy test. In one case, the court excluded evidence of the test because the analyst modified the test procedure.[194] In another case, the evidence was

---

187. Commonwealth v. Westwood, 324 Pa. 289, 188 A. 304 (1936).

188. Brooke v. People, 139 Colo. 388, 339 P.2d 993 (1959).

189. *See* Born v. State, 397 P.2d 924, 939 (Okla. Crim. App. 1964), *cert. denied,* 379 U.S. 1000 (1965); Clarke v. State, 218 Tenn. 259, 270, 402 S.W.2d 863, 869, *cert. denied,* 385 U.S. 942 (1966). *See also* Fowler v. State, 512 P.2d 238, 244 (Okla. Crim. App. 1973) ("zinc oxide" test for gunshot residue inadmissible).

Both *Born* and *Fowler* were overruled in Brookins v. State, 602 P.2d 215, 217 (Okla. Crim. App. 1979).

190. *See* Harris v. State, 239 Ark. 771, 778, 394 S.W.2d 135, 140 (1965), *cert. denied,* 386 U.S. 964 (1967); State v. Hoy, 199 Kan. 340, 348, 430 P.2d 275, 281 (1967); People v. Simpson, 5 Mich. App. 479, 486-87, 146 N.W.2d 828, 831 (1966); State v. Fields, 434 S.W.2d 507 (Mo. 1968); Henson v. State, 159 Tex. Crim. 647, 655-56, 266 S.W.2d 864, 869 (1953). *See also* United States v. Snook, 31 C.M.R. 199, 203 (C.M.A. 1962) (paraffin test was negative); State v. Foster, 44 Hawaii 403, 354 P.2d 960 (1960).

191. Brookins v. State, 602 P.2d 215, 217 (Okla. Crim. App. 1979).

192. *See* Harrison & Gilroy, *Firearms Discharge Residues,* 4 J. Forensic Sci. 184 (1959).

193. *See* Krishnan, *supra* note 169, at 574 ("This method did not gain wide acceptance in crime laboratories for field use because of a lack of specificity of the color reaction for the trace elements, inadequate sensitivity, interference of the color reactions among the three elements themselves, and the instability of the colors developed").

194. State v. Smith, 50 Ohio App. 2d 183, 193-94, 362 N.E.2d 1239, 1246 (1976).

admitted but the court apparently believed it was considering the paraffin test, which it had earlier approved.[195]

§ 14-13(C). Neutron Activation Analysis.

Neutron activation analysis (NAA) is a qualitative and quantitative method for determining the elemental composition of substances. It is extremely sensitive and accurate. "[A] modified version of this procedure [NAA] remained the predominant analytical method in the FBI Laboratory for about 20 years. ... NAA is not widely used because most laboratories lack access to a high-flux neutron source."[196] NAA is discussed in detail in Chapter 11.

In the detection of gunshot residues, NAA is used to detect the presence and quantity of the elements antimony and barium on the hands.[197] These elements are the primer constituents of most cartridges, and their presence in certain concentrations on the hands is indicative of a recent discharge of a firearm. Barium and antimony, however, may be present on the hands of persons who have not fired a firearm; thus NAA is based on the detection of significantly greater amounts of these elements than normally occur:

> The presence of [antimony and barium] together and in amounts significantly higher than those normally found on the hands of the general population (hand blanks) is taken as indicative of the presence of GSR. Hand blank levels have been collected and reported by a number of laboratories. The actual levels depend on the area of the hands sampled and to some extent on the sampling method used.[198]

Another disadvantage (besides access to a nuclear reactor) is that NAA cannot easily detect lead.

Several methods, including swabbing and washing techniques, have been used to remove the residues from the hands.[199] Typically, antimony and barium are chemically separated from the sample before detection.[200]

---

195. Commonwealth v. Farrior, 446 Pa. 31, 34, 284 A.2d 684, 685 (1971).

196. *See* Koons, *Analysis of Gunshot Primer Residue Collection Swabs by Inductively Coupled Plasma-Mass Spectrometry*, 43 J. FORENSIC SCI. 748 (1998).

197. *See* Midkiff, *supra* note 169, at 78-79; Kilty, *A Review of the FBI Laboratory's Gunshot Primer Residue Program*, 13 CRIME LAB. DIGEST 54 (April 1986); Krishnan, *Detection of Gunshot Residues on the Hands by Trace Elemental Analysis*, 22 J. FORENSIC SCI. 304, 306 (1977); Comment, *The Evidentiary Uses of Neutron Activation Analysis*, 59 CAL. L. REV. 997, 1074-78 (1971).

198. Krishnan, *supra* note 169, at 579-80; Havekost, Peters & Koons, *Barium and Antimony Distributions on the Hands of Nonshooters*, 35 J. FORENSIC SCI. 1096 (1990).

199. *See* Pillay, Jester & Fox, *New Method for the Collection and Analysis of Gunshot Residues as Forensic Evidence*, 19 J. FORENSIC SCI. 768 (1974); Krishnan, *supra* note 169, at 577-79; Pillay & Sagans, *Gunshot Residue Collection Using Film-Lift Techniques for Neutron Activation*

Courts have admitted expert testimony, based on NAA, when offered to show the recent firing of a firearm.[201] In one case, however, the court criticized the expert for overstating the conclusions that can be drawn from the test:

> We are concerned ... about the sweeping and unqualified manner in which [the expert's] testimony was offered.... An expert witness could be permitted to testify that in his opinion the chemicals present on defendant's hand may have resulted from the firing of a gun. He should not have been permitted to state, as he did, that this defendant had definitely fired a gun.[202]

Experts in other cases have also overstated their findings. In one case the NAA expert indicated that the defendant had fired a handgun "not more than two hours before the time of the analysis."[203]

State v. Troedel[204] offers a stark illustration of misleading evidence. Defendants Troedel and Hawkins were convicted of capital murder in separate trials. A report of a gunshot residue test using neutron activation analysis concluded that swabs "from the hands of Troedel and Hawkins contained antimony and barium in amounts typically found on the hands of a person who has discharged a

---

Analysis, 2 J. POLICE SCI. & AD. 388 (1974). *See also* Lewis, *The Element of Subjectivity in Interpreting Instrumental Test Results*, *in* PRACTICING LAW INSTITUTE, SCIENTIFIC AND EXPERT EVIDENCE 409, 423 (Imwinkelried ed. 1981) ("[T]he method by which the residue is collected may determine the outcome of the experiment").

200. Krishnan, *supra* note 169, at 575.

201. *See* Government of Virgin Islands v. Benjamin, 736 F. Supp. 1337, 1341 (D.V.I.) ("[A] police officer obtained a swab sample for a neutron activation test from Benjamin's hands. At trial, an expert testified that the test indicated that Benjamin had either fired a gun or had been very close to a gun that had been discharged"), *aff'd*, 922 F.2d 831 (3d Cir. 1990); Mills v. State, 476 So. 2d 172, 176-77 (Fla. 1985), *cert. denied,* 475 U.S. 1031 (1986); Troedel v. State, 462 So. 2d 392, 396 (Fla. 1984); People v. Salazar, 162 Ill. 2d 513, 529, 643 N.E.2d 698, 706 (1994) (Bilandic, C.J., concurring) ("A neutron activation analysis revealed that Officer Murrin's left hand was on or near the muzzle of the gun when it discharged..."), *cert. denied*, 515 U.S. 1116 (1995); State v. Boyer, 406 So. 2d 143, 146-48 (La. 1981); Kelly v. State, 16 Md. App. 533, 535-36 & 544-45, 298 A.2d 470, 472 & 477, *aff'd,* 270 Md. 139, 310 A.2d 538 (1973); State v. Spencer, 298 Minn. 456, 459-62, 216 N.W.2d 131, 134-35 (1974); State v. Jackson, 566 S.W.2d 227, 228-29 (Mo. App. 1978); State v. Major, 564 S.W.2d 79, 81-82 (Mo. App. 1978); State v. Montgomery, 545 S.W.2d 655, 655-56 (Mo. App. 1976); State v. Duncan, 540 S.W.2d 130, 134-35 (Mo. App. 1976) (shotgun residue); State v. Johnson, 539 S.W.2d 493, 501-02 (Mo. App. 1976), *cert. denied,* 430 U.S. 934 (1977); State v. Toney, 537 S.W.2d 586, 597-99 (Mo. App. 1976); State v. Ross, 523 S.W.2d 841, 844-46 (Mo. App. 1975); People v. Pieropan, 72 Misc. 2d 770, 340 N.Y.S.2d 31 (1973); Commonwealth v. Sero, 478 Pa. 440, 449-50, 387 A.2d 63, 68 (1978).

See also United States v. Barton, 731 F.2d 669, 671-72 (10th Cir. 1984) (unspecified "primer residue test" admitted).

202. State v. Spencer, 298 Minn. 456, 461, 216 N.W.2d 131, 134 (1974).

203. State v. Warden, 100 Idaho 21, 22, 592 P.2d 836, 837 (1979).

204. 462 So. 2d 392 (Fla. 1984).

firearm or has had his hands in close proximity to a discharging firearm."[205] The expert testified in accordance with this report at Hawkins' trial, but he enhanced his testimony at Troedel's trial, where he testified that "Troedel had fired the murder weapon." Troedel's conviction was upheld by the state courts. During federal habeas proceedings, the expert's deposition was taken. In the deposition, he testified that "he could not, from the results of his tests, determine or say to a scientific certainty who had fired the murder weapon" and that the "amount of barium and antimony on the hands of Troedel and Hawkins were basically insignificant."[206] The district court found this testimony "at the very least" misleading. The expert claimed that the prosecutor had "pushed" him further in Troedel's trial, a claim the prosecutor substantiated. In granting habeas relief, the court remarked:

> In light of this admission, the above testimony received at the evidentiary hearing and the inconsistent positions taken by the prosecution at Hawkins' and Troedel's trials, respectively, the Court concludes that the opinion Troedel had fired the weapon was known by the prosecution not to be based on the results of the neutron activation analysis tests, or on any scientific certainty or even probability. Thus, the subject testimony was not only misleading, but also was used by the State knowing it to be misleading.[207]

The court also found Troedel's counsel ineffective. Because the counsel knew that the gunshot residue testimony was "critical," his "failure either to depose the State's expert witness or, more importantly, to consult with any other expert in the field, fell outside the scope of reasonably professional assistance."[208]

In *Meis v. Wyoming Dep't of Corrections*,[209] the defendant argued that his counsel's performance was ineffective for failing to cross-examine adequately a prosecution expert who used neutron activation analysis to detect the presence of gunshot residues on the victim's hands. The court rejected this claim because the expert's testimony did not conflict with the defendant's version of the facts.

§ 14-13(D). Atomic Absorption.

Atomic absorption spectroscopy (AAS) and flameless atomic absorption spectroscopy (FAAS) are instrumental techniques used for elemental analysis. These techniques are discussed in detail in Chapter 25.

---

205. Troedel v. Wainwright, 667 F. Supp. 1456, 1458 (S.D. Fla. 1986), *aff'd,* 828 F.2d 670 (11th Cir. 1987).

206. *Id.* at 1459.

207. *Id.* at 1459-60.

208. *Id.* at 1461.

209. 9 F.3d 695, 698-99 (8th Cir. 1993), *cert. denied,* 511 U.S. 1650 (1994).

In the detection of gunshot residues, AAS and FAAS are used to detect the elements antimony, barium, and lead. The greater availability of these instrumental techniques and their capability of detecting lead, in comparison to neutron activation analysis, have made them an attractive method for analyzing GSR.[210] An FBI report stated that "the AAS method has been adopted for use in the FBI Laboratory on all submitted GSR swab evidence kits. Results of the interlaboratory portion of this study show that the accuracy and precision achieved using the tested procedure in various settings with analysts of diverse backgrounds and levels of training is generally suitable for proper interpretation of GSR swab data."[211] The report also noted that "[f]lameless AAS offers advantages over NAA to most forensic laboratories in its excellent sensitivity for Ba (barium) and SB (antimony), ready availability, ease of use, and its applicability to other elements, particularly lead."[212]

Several courts have admitted expert testimony, based on these techniques, in gunshot residue cases.[213]

---

210. *See* Koons, Havekost & Peters, *Analysis of Gunshot Primer Residue Collection Swabs Using Flameless Atomic Absorption Spectrophotometry and Inductively Coupled Plasma-Atomic Emission Spectrometry: Effects of a Modified Extraction Procedure and Storage of Standards*, 34 J. FORENSIC SCI. 218 (1989); Krishnan, *Detection of Gunshot Residues on the Hands by Neutron Activation Analysis and Atomic Absorption Analysis*, 19 J. FORENSIC SCI. 789 (1974); Midkiff, *supra* note 169, at 80-82; Newton, *Rapid Determination of Antimony, Barium, and Lead in Gunshot Residue Via Automated Atomic Absorption Spectrophotometry*, 26 J. FORENSIC SCI. 302 (1981); Rudzitis, *Analysis of the Results of Gunshot Residue Detection in Case Work*, 25 J. FORENSIC SCI. 839 (1980).

211. Koons, *Flameless Atomic Absorption Spectrophotometric Determination of Antimony and Barium in Gunshot Residue Collection Swabs: A Collaborative Study*, 20 CRIME LAB. DIGEST 19, 23 (Jan. 1993). *See also* Koons, *Analysis of Gunshot Primer Residue Collection Swabs by Inductively Coupled Plasma-Mass Spectrometry*, 43 J. FORENSIC SCI. 748 (1998) ("Graphite furnace atomic absorption spectrophotometry (GFAAS) found acceptance in many crime laboratories because of its relatively low cost, ease of use, wide availability, and the added capability of determining Pb [lead]. ...GFAAS methods are relatively time consuming and are subject to some interferences resulting from the presence of high concentrations of nonanalyte constituents").

212. *Id.*, 20 CRIME LAB. DIGEST at 19.

213. *See* Chatom v. State, 348 So. 2d 838, 842 (Ala. 1977); Bell v. State, 339 So. 2d 96, 99 (Ala. Crim. App. 1976); People v. Cole, 170 Ill. App. 3d 912, 524 N.E.2d 926, 936-37 (1988) ("[T]he results of atomic absorption analysis are admissible in Illinois for the purpose of determining whether a suspect handled or fired a weapon"; Expert "conceded that the test is not conclusive as to whether a person has actually fired a weapon"), *cert. denied*, 530 N.E.2d 253 (1988); State v. Chatman, 156 N.J. Super. 35, 38-40, 383 A.2d 440, 441-42 (1978); State v. Crowder, 285 N.C. 42, 53-55, 203 S.E.2d 38, 46-47 (1974), *modified on other grounds,* 428 U.S. 903 (1976); State v. Sparks, 297 N.C. 314, 326-28, 255 S.E.2d 373, 381-82 (1979); State v. McCall, 698 S.W.2d 643, 651 (Tenn. Crim. App. 1985).

§ 14-13(E). Scanning Electron Microscopy.

The scanning electron microscope (SEM) uses a high energy electron beam to produce magnification significantly greater than that which is possible with an optical microscope.[214] This increased magnification, as well as greater depth of field, permits the identification of gunshot particles by their characteristic morphology. In addition, scanning with an electron beam causes the emission of X-rays. Since each element produces characteristic X-rays, an elemental analysis of the substances under examination is possible through the use of an X-ray analyzer. Barium, antimony, and lead are the elements that are indicative of a firearm discharge. In sum, SEM permits the identification of gunshot particles by their unique morphological characteristics and by elemental analysis. The particles are removed from the hands by an adhesive lift technique.[215] SEM is discussed in Chapter 25.

The principal disadvantages of this technique are the cost of the instruments and the time-consuming nature of the analysis. Other reported problems concern the "variation between laboratories in determining the minimum number of particles analyzed to confirm gunshot residue" and the fact that cigarette lighter flint particles "mimic GSR in morphology"[216] but not in composition.

Although the use of SEM for the detection of gunshot residues is widely used,[217] there have been few legal challenges. In *People v. Palmer*,[218] a 1978

---

214. Judd, *Scanning Electron Microscopy as Applied to Forensic Evidence Analysis, in* PRACTISING LAW INSTITUTE, SCIENTIFIC AND EXPERT EVIDENCE 873, 878-80 (Imwinkelried ed. 1981). *See also* Korda, MacDonell & Williams, *Forensic Applications of the Scanning Electron Microscope*, 61 J. CRIM. L., CRIMINOLOGY & POLICE SCI. 453 (1970).

215. *See* Tassa, Adan, Zeldes & Leist, *A Field Kit for Sampling Gunshot Residue Particles*, 27 J. FORENSIC SCI. 671 (1982); Zeichner & Levin, *Collection Efficiency of Gunshot Residue (GSR) Particles from Hair and Hands Using Double-Side Adhesive Tape*, 38 J. FORENSIC SCI. 571 (1993) (describing an alternative to automated methods for collection of GSR particles). The article notes: "A major disadvantage of the SEM/DEX technique is the time needed for carrying out a test [sometimes up to 8 hours].... One solution for this problem has been to automate the search and analysis procedures. Recently, a number of fully automatic methods, based on commercially available equipment, have been described." *Id.* at 571.

216. DeGaetano & Siegel, *Survey of Gunshot Residue Analysis in Forensic Science Laboratories*, 35 J. FORENSIC SCI. 1087, 1090, 1092 (1990).

217. *See* Andrasko & Maehly, *Detection of Gunshot Residues on Hands by Scanning Electron Microscopy*, 22 J. FORENSIC SCI. 279 (1977); Basu, *Formation of Gunshot Residues*, 27 J. FORENSIC SCI. 72 (1982); Germani, *Evaluation of Instrumental Parameters for Automated Scanning Electron Microscopy/Gunshot Residue Particle Analysis*, 36 J. FORENSIC SCI. 331 (1991); Hellmiss, Lichtenberg & Weiss, *Investigation of Gunshot Residues by Means of Auger Electron Spectroscopy*, 32 J. FORENSIC SCI. 747 (1987); Matricardi & Kilty, *Detection of Gunshot Residue Articles from the Hands of a Shooter*, 22 J. FORENSIC SCI. 725 (1977); Nesbitt, Wessel & Jones, *Detection of Gunshot Residue by Use of the Scanning Electronic Microscope*, 21 J. FORENSIC SCI. 595 (1976); White & Owens, *Automation of Gunshot Residue Detection and Analysis by Scanning Electron Microscopy/Energy Dispersive X-Ray Analysis (SEM/EDX)*, 32 J. FORENSIC SCI. 1595

decision, expert testimony identifying gunshot particles based on SEM was upheld. According to the court, the technique has been generally accepted by the scientific community.[219]

§ 14-13(F). Miscellaneous Techniques.

A number of other GSR techniques have been reported. Several are discussed in this section.

ICP-AES

Inductively coupled plasma-atomic emission spectroscopy (ICP-AES) has been used by the FBI and other laboratories to detect barium in GSR cases.[220] It is used in conjunction with atomic absorption, which detects antimony and lead. It has some drawbacks. "ICP-AES is a rapid, multi-element technique that is relatively free of matrix interferences, but commercial instruments lack the sensitivity required for accurate determinations of Sb (antimony) at relevant levels."[221]

ICP-MS

Inductively Coupled Plasma-Mass Spectrometry (ICP-MS), a new GSR method, is being researched by the FBI. The use of ICP-MS instrumentation for numerous tasks has increased since its commercial introduction in the early 1980s. It can handle large-volume caseloads, has the required sensitivity to detect GSR elements (antimony, barium, and lead), and is faster than many other methods. The MS component permits monitoring for spectral interferences.[222]

(1987); Wolten, Nesbitt, Calloway, Loper & Jones, *Particle Analysis for the Detection of Gunshot Residue*, 24 J. FORENSIC SCI. 409, 423, 864 (1979) (3 part article); Wolten & Nesbitt, *On the Mechanism of Gunshot Residue Particle Formation*, 25 J. FORENSIC SCI. 533 (1980); Zeichner, Levin & Dvorachek, *Gunshot Residue Particles Formed by Using Ammunitions That Have Mercury Fulminate Based Primes*, 37 J. FORENSIC SCI. 1567 (1992) (describing GSR problems when analyzing mercury fulminate-based primers that are commonly made by Eastern Bloc countries).

218. 80 Cal. App. 3d 239, 145 Cal. Rptr. 466 (1978).

219. *Id.* at 252-54, 145 Cal. Rptr. at 472-73.

220. Koons, Havekost & Peters, *Determination of Barium in Gunshot Residue Collection Swabs Using Inductively Coupled Plasma-atomic Emission Spectrometry*, 33 J. FORENSIC SCI. 35 (1988).

221. Koons, *Analysis of Gunshot Primer Residue Collection Swabs by Inductively Coupled Plasma-Mass Spectrometry*, 43 J. FORENSIC SCI. 748 (1998).

222. There are other potential, but yet unexplored, advantages: "First, the ICP-MS procedure allows the determination of the levels of additional elements which may be associated with handling of a weapon or ammunition component, or elements which may be present in specific ammunitions, such as strontium in some nontoxic primers, cobalt in Nyclad bullets, or copper, nickel, or zinc in jacketed bullets. Second, the use of MS detection also allows the possibility of some sourcing of primer-derived Pb [lead] by isotope distributions." *Id.* at 753-54.

Anodic Stripping Voltammetry

Anodic Stripping Voltammetry (ASV) has been used for detecting gunshot residues in a limited number of cases.[223] It provides a simultaneous qualitative and quantitative method for detecting copper, lead, and antimony. Whether ASV alone is sufficient for the detection of GSR is questionable. In one article the researchers used ASV to detect lead and antimony and atomic absorption to detect barium.[224] Barium, one of two elements in modern primer residue, is used in other instrumental techniques for the detection of GSR. Other researchers have not used barium in detecting gunshot residues by ASV. Apparently, they rely primarily on the presence of antimony.[225] Reliance on antimony alone, however, is debatable.[226] This method is not widely used.

Several Missouri cases admitted GSR testimony based on ASV. Defense experts, however, apparently did not testify in any of the cases.[227]

Lead-Free Primers

Manufacturers have begun to reformulate their primers to decrease the amount of lead, antimony, and barium. Airborne lead from the primer and bullet is considered a health hazard, especially in an indoor firing range. Jacketed or coated bullets reduce this hazard. Removal of lead from primers was achieved with the introduction of "Sintox" in Europe in the 1980s (and later Blazer "clean

---

223. Two authors described the theory underlying ASV as follows:

> In the ASV method, metals are preconcentrated (reduced) from an electrolyte solution in a thin-film of mercury which has been deposited on a carbon-based electrode. The metals are then "stripped" (oxidized) from the mercury layer by changing the applied potential on the electrode. Since each metal has a characteristic potential at which it strips from the mercury layer and since the current required to remove the particular amount of metal from the mercury film is proportional to the original concentration, both qualitative and quantitative information can be obtained from a single experiment.

Choucholy & Briner, *An Inexpensive Approach to Inorganic Gunshot Residue Analysis Using Anodic Stripping Voltammetry*, 4 CURRENT SEPARATIONS 20 (1982); Briner, *An Interesting Gunshot Residue Pattern*, 30 J. FORENSIC SCI. 945 (1985).

224. Brihaye, Machiroux & Gillain, *Gunpowder Residues Detection by Anodic Stripping Voltammetry*, 20 FORENSIC SCI. INT'L 269, 271 (1982).

225. Choucholy & Briner, *supra* note 223; BRINER, BRATIN & LONGWELL, EXPLOSIVES AND GUNSHOT RESIDUE DETECTION BY APPLICATIONS OF ELECTROCHEMISTRY (1982). *See also* Liu, Lin & Nicol, *The Application of Anodic Stripping Voltammetry to Forensic Science. II. Anodic Stripping Voltammetric Analysis of Gunshot Residues*, 16 FORENSIC SCI. INT'L 53 (1980); Liu & Lin, *The Application of Anodic Stripping Voltammetry to Forensic Science. I. The Construction of a Low-Cost Polarograph*, 16 FORENSIC SCI. INT'L 43 (1980).

226. Starrs, *In the Land of Agog: An Allegory for the Expert Witness*, 30 J. FORENSIC SCI. 289, 297 (1985) (relying on antimony alone is not accepted by the scientific community).

227. State v. Cooper, 691 S.W.2d 353, 356-57 (Mo. App. 1985); State v. Williams, 659 S.W.2d 309, 310-11 (Mo. App. 1983); State v. Walker, 654 S.W.2d 129, 131-32 (Mo. App. 1983).

fire" in the U.S.). The new primers also eliminate antimony and barium.[228] As noted above, these elements form the basis for most GSR tests. Accordingly, false negatives will result if traditional techniques are employed with this ammunition. New methods to deal with this problem are being developed.[229]

Photoluminescence

Other GSR techniques, such as photoluminescence,[230] have been reported[231] but are apparently not in current use.

§ 14-14. Trace Metal Detection Technique.

The trace metal detection technique (TMDT) is designed to determine whether a person has recently handled a metallic object, including a firearm. In this respect, it differs from gunshot residue tests that are designed to determine whether a person has recently *fired* (or had contact with a recently fired) firearm.

In 1970, LEAA-sponsored research first described TMDT.[232] This research showed that metal objects leave traces (metallic ions) when they come in contact with skin and clothing surfaces. When sprayed with a reagent and exposed to ultraviolet light, the metal traces can be detected by their fluorescent colors. In

228. *See* Gunaratnam & Himberg, *The Identification of Gunshot Residue Particles from Lead-Free Sintox Ammunition*, 39 J. FORENSIC SCI. 532 (1994); Harris, *Analysis of Primer Residue from CCI Blazer Lead Free Ammunition by Scanning Electron Microscopy/Energy Dispersive X-ray*, 40 J. FORENSIC SCI. 27 (1995); Zeichner, Schecter & Brener, *Antimony Enrichment of the Bullets' Surfaces and the Possibility of Finding It In Gunshot Residue (GSR) of the Ammunition Having Antimony-Free Primers*, 43 J. FORENSIC SCI. 493 (1998) ("It was found that there is a small probability of finding GSR containing a considerable concentration of antimony if the primer of the fired ammunition is antimony-free, even when the surface of the bullet is highly enriched by this element").

229. MacCrehan, Smith & Rowe, *Sampling Protocols for the Detection of Smokeless Powder, Residues Using Capillary Electrophoresis*, 43 J. FORENSIC SCI. 119 (1998). *See also* Sanders, *Forensic Testing: Gunshot Residue Findings*, LAW ENFORCEMENT TECH. BULL. 36 (Feb. 1991) (Micellar Electrokinetic Capillary Electrophoresis).

230. *E.g.*, Jones & Nesbitt, *A Photoluminescence Technique for Detection of Gunshot Residue*, 20 J. FORENSIC SCI. 231 (1975); Nesbitt, Wessel, Wolten & Jones, *Evaluation of a Photoluminescence Technique for the Detection of Gunshot Residue*, 22 J. FORENSIC SCI. 288 (1977);

231. *See* Bohannan & Van Galen, *A Sensitive Electrochemical Method for the Analysis of Nitrite Ion and Metals in Gunshot Residue*, 36 J. FORENSIC SCI. 886 (1991); Meng & Caddy, *Gunshot Residue Analysis — A Review*, 42 J. FORENSIC SCI. 533 (1997); Singer, Davis & Houck, *A Survey of Gunshot Residue Analysis Methods*, 41 J. FORENSIC SCI. 195 (1996); Sen, Panigrahi, Rao, Varier, Sen & Mehta, *Application of Proton-Induced X-Ray Emission Technique to Gunshot Residue Analysis*, 27 J. FORENSIC SCI. 330 (1982).

232. NATIONAL INSTITUTE OF LAW ENFORCEMENT AND CRIMINAL JUSTICE, TRACE METAL DETECTION TECHNIQUE IN LAW ENFORCEMENT (Oct. 1970).

addition, characteristic patterns, such as those left by the handling of a firearm, sometimes can be identified:

> Examination by ultraviolet light of the metal trace patterns which appear as fluorescent colors on the hands or clothing of the suspect allows a police officer to determine whether a suspect has been in contact with certain metal objects, the type of metal or metals in the objects; and also to infer what type of weapon or metal object was probably involved.[233]

In sum, the color of the pattern provides information about the identity of the metal, and the location, size, and shape of the pattern provides information about the type of object that the test surface came in contact with.[234] According to the research, metal traces may be detected up to thirty-six to forty-eight hours after contact with a firearm, even if normal routine washings have occurred.

Further research disclosed that TMDT is not as straightforward a procedure as the LEAA research indicated — that the amenability of subjects to the test varied and that the test "involves highly subjective judgments."[235] Thus, the successful use of the technique "hinges upon the acquisition of considerable personal experience, augmented by the accumulation of an extensive photographic file of patterns characteristic of as many different weapons and tools as possible."[236]

Later, commercial products, based on the PDT iron (II), came on the market: "The commercial pre-packaged aerosol devices, Ferroprint and Ferrotrace, which contain a solution of PDT and ascorbic acid, provide good means to link ... suspect and weapon by developing the iron imprints on the hand."[237] These products are designed as field tests. When used as evidence at trial, they have important limitations:

> First the object held must have a distinctive or characteristic morphology and the pattern produced on the skin must reflect this if this is to be used as associative evidence. Several factors can adversely affect the fidelity of the

---

233. *Id.* at 1.

234. Stevens & Messler, *The Trace Metal Detection Technique (TMDT): A Report Outlining a Procedure for Photographing Results in Color, and Some Factors Influencing the Results in Controlled Laboratory Tests*, 19 J. FORENSIC SCI. 496, 497 (1974).

235. Stevens & Messler, *Trace Metal Detection Technique*, *in* PRACTISING LAW INSTITUTE, SCIENTIFIC AND EXPERT EVIDENCE 1075, 1088 (Imwinkelried ed. 1981). *See also* Lee, *The Detection of Iron Traces on Hands by Ferrozine Sprays: A Report on the Sensitivity and Interference of the Method and Recommended Procedure in Forensic Science Investigations*, 31 J. FORENSIC SCI. 920 (1986); Kokocinski, Brundage & Nicol, *A Study of the Use of 2-Nitroso-1-Naphthol as a Trace Metal Detection Reagent*, 25 J. FORENSIC SCI. 810 (1980); Goldman & Thornton, *A New Trace Ferrous Metal Detection Reagent*, 21 J. FORENSIC SCI. 625 (1976).

236. Stevens & Messler, *supra* note 234, at 497.

237. Almog & Glattstein, *Detection of Firearms Imprints on Hands of Suspects: Study of the PDT-Based Field Test*, 42 J. FORENSIC SCI. 993, 996 (1997).

pattern. In the more commonly encountered situation where there is a reaction but where the pattern is less distinct, the results may be useful, but only as investigative aids. If the circumstances are favorable and the results are to be used as associative evidence, it is important that they be documented photographically so that they can be evaluated independently later.[238]

Admissibility of TMDT Evidence

Of the few courts that have considered the admissibility of TMDT evidence, most have admitted the evidence.[239] One court, however, has ruled TMDT evidence inadmissible for lack of general acceptance by the scientific community.[240] In addition, the state's failure to use TMDT, upon a defense request, has been held to violate due process.[241]

A striking aspect of the TMDT cases has been the lack of scientific testimony regarding the technique. In one case the technician who administered the test and testified at trial "admitted that he had no understanding of the reason for the reaction that occurred when [the] test was administered."[242] In another case the expert admitted on cross-examination that he "had 'no idea' of the scientific community's acceptance of the trace metal test, he was unaware of any statistics supporting the test's reliability, and he had no knowledge of the chemical composition of the reagent spray used in the test."[243] Despite these admissions, the evidence was admitted in both cases.

§ 14-15. Glossary.

The following definitions are reprinted with permission from the Association of Firearm and Tool Mark Examiners, *Glossary* (1980).

---

238. *Id.*

239. *See* Reid v. State, 267 Ind. 555, 558-60, 372 N.E.2d 1149, 1151-52 (1978); State v. Snyder, 190 N.J. Super. 626, 631-33, 464 A.2d 1209, 1211-12 (1983); State v. Daniels, 37 Ohio App. 2d 4, 5-6, 305 N.E.2d 497, 498 (1973); Brotherton v. State, 666 S.W.2d 126, 129-30 (Tex. App. 1983).

Other cases mention TMDT but do not address its admissibility. Tucker v. State, 261 Ark. 505, 507, 549 S.W.2d 285, 286 (1977); People v. Level, 103 Cal. App. 3d 899, 902, 162 Cal. Rptr. 682, 684, *vacated,* 449 U.S. 945 (1980); People v. Marioneaux, 44 Colo. App. 213, 215-17, 618 P.2d 678, 680-81 (1980); State v. Jackson, 226 Kan. 302, 303, 597 P.2d 255, 256 (1979), *cert. denied,* 445 U.S. 952 (1980); Giles v. State, 325 So. 2d 120, 122 (Miss. 1975); State v. Journey, 201 Neb. 607, 614, 271 N.W.2d 320, 324 (1978) (TMDT apparently described as a gunshot residue test).

240. People v. Lauro, 91 Misc. 2d 706, 712-13, 398 N.Y.S.2d 503, 507 (1977). *See also* Esquivel v. State, 595 S.W.2d 516, 528-29 (Tex. Crim. App.) (second TMDT test not admitted because it was not conducted under similar conditions as first test), *cert. denied,* 449 U.S. 986 (1980).

241. People *ex rel.* Gallagher v. District Court, 656 P.2d 1287, 1290-92 (Colo. 1983).

242. Reid v. State, 267 Ind. 555, 559, 372 N.E.2d 1149, 1152 (1978).

243. Brotherton v. State, 666 S.W.2d 126, 129 (Tex. App. 1983).

Action: The working mechanism of a firearm.

Ammunition: One or more loaded cartridges consisting of a primed case, propellant, and with or without one or more projectiles. Also referred to as fixed or live ammunition.

Backthrust: The force exerted on the breechblock by the head of the cartridge case during propellant burning.

Ballistics: The study of a projectile in motion. Often confused with Firearms Identification.

Ballistics, Exterior: The study of the motion of the projectile(s) after it leaves the barrel of the firearm.

Ballistics, Interior: The study of the motion of the projectile(s) within the firearm from the moment of ignition until it leaves the barrel.

Ballistics, Terminal: The study of the projectile's impact on the target.

Barrel: That part of a firearm through which a projectile or shot charge travels under the impetus of powder gases, compressed air, or other like means. May be rifled or smooth.

Bore: The interior of a barrel forward of the chamber.

Breech: The part of a firearm at the rear of the bore into which the cartridge or propellant is inserted.

Breech Face: That part of the breechblock or breech bolt which is against the head of the cartridge case or shotshell during firing.

Bullet: A non-spherical projectile for use in a rifled barrel.

Bullet, Copper Jacketed: A bullet having an outer jacket of copper or copper alloy and containing a lead alloy core.

Bullet, Full Metal Jacket: A projectile in which the bullet jacket encloses the core, usually with the exception of the base. Also called "Full Jacketed," "Full Patch," and "Full Metal Case."

Bullet Jacket: A usually metallic cover over the core.

Caliber:

Firearms: The approximate diameter of the circle formed by the tops of the lands of a rifled barrel.

Ammunition: A numerical term, without the decimal point, included in a cartridge name to indicate a rough approximation of the bullet diameter.

Cartridge: A single unit of ammunition consisting of the case, primer, and propellant with or without one or more projectiles. Also applies to a shotshell.

Chamber: The rear part of the barrel bore that has been formed to accept a specific cartridge. Revolver cylinders are multi-chambered.

Chamber Marks: Individual microscopic marks placed upon a cartridge case by the chamber wall as a result of any or all of the following: (1) chambering (2) expansion during firing (3) extraction.

Choke: An interior constriction at or near the muzzle end of a shotgun barrel bore for the purpose of controlling shot dispersion.

Class Characteristics: Measurable features of a specimen which indicate a restricted group source. They result from design factors, and are therefore determined prior to manufacture.

Comparison Microscope: Essentially two microscopes connected to an optical bridge which allows the viewer to observe two objects simultaneously with the same degree of magnification. This instrument can have a monocular or binocular eyepiece. Sometimes referred to as "Comparison Macroscope."

Cylinder: The rotatable part of a revolver that contains the chambers.

Distance Determination: The process of determining the distance from the firearm, usually the muzzle, to the target based upon patterns of gunpowder or gunshot residues deposited upon that target. Where multiple projectiles, such as shot, have been fired the spread of those projectiles is also indicative of distance.

Double Action: A handgun mechanism in which a single pull of the trigger cocks and releases the hammer.

Ejector: A portion of a firearm's mechanism which ejects or expels cartridges or cartridge cases from a firearm.

Ejector Marks: Toolmarks produced upon a cartridge or cartridge case on the head, generally at or near the rim, from contact with the ejector.

Extraction: The act of withdrawing a cartridge or cartridge case from the chamber of a firearm.

Extractor: A mechanism for withdrawing the cartridge or cartridge case from the chamber.

Extractor Marks: Toolmarks produced upon a cartridge or cartridge case from contact with the extractor. These are always found on or just ahead of the rim.

Firearm: An assembly of a barrel and action from which a projectile(s) is propelled by products of combustion.

Firearms Identification: Firearms identification is a discipline of forensic science which has as its primary concern to determine if a bullet, cartridge case, or other ammunition component was fired by a particular firearm.

Firing Pin: That part of a firearm mechanism which strikes the primer of a cartridge to initiate ignition. Sometimes called hammer nose or striker.

Firing Pin Impression: The indentation in the primer of a centerfire cartridge case or in the rim of a rimfire cartridge case caused when it is struck by the firing pin.

Gauge: A term used in the identification of a shotgun bore. The number of round lead balls of bore diameter that equal one pound. Thus 12 gauge is the diameter of a round lead ball weighing 1/12 of a pound.

Gunpowder: Any of various powders used in firearms as a propellant charge.

Gunpowder Pattern:

1. The spatial distribution of gunpowder residues deposited upon a surface.
2. The test firing of a firearm for a muzzle-to-target distance determination.

Gunshot Residues: The total residues resulting from the discharge of a firearm. It includes both gunpowder and primer residues, plus metallic residues from projectiles, fouling, etc.

Hammer: A component part of the firing mechanism which gives impulse to the firing pin or primer.

Handgun: A firearm designed to be held and fired with one hand.

Identifiable Striae: Striations in the evidence mark which can be identified with reproduced striations in the test marks. *See* Striations.

Impression: Surface contour variations on an object caused by applying force without motion, or where the motion is approximately perpendicular to the plane being marked. *See* Striations.

Land: The raised portion between the grooves in a rifled bore.

Land and Groove Impressions: The negative impressions on the bearing surface of a bullet caused by the rifling in the barrel from which it was fired.

Magazine:

1. A container for cartridges which has a spring and follower to feed those cartridges into the chamber of a firearm. The magazine may be detachable or an integral part of the firearm.
2. A secure storage place for gunpowder, ammunition, or explosives.

Metal Fouling: Metallic bullet material left in the bore after firing.

Microscopic Marks: Striae or patterns of minute lines or grooves in an object. In firearm and toolmark identification these marks are characteristic of the object which produced them and are the basis for identification.

Muzzle: The end of a firearm barrel from which the bullet or shot emerges.

Pistol: A handgun in which the chamber is part of the barrel. A term sometimes used for handgun.

Powder: Commonly used term for the propellant in a cartridge or shotshell.

Powder Burn: The charring or singeing of a surface from contact with gunshot residues....

Powder, Smokeless: A propellant containing mainly nitrocellulose (single base) or both nitrocellulose and nitroglycerin (double base).

Primer: The ignition component of a cartridge.

Primer Residues: The components of gunshot residue which contain elements which were originally part of the primer mixture of a cartridge. Neutron Activation Analysis, Atomic Absorption and Energy Dispersive X-ray are used to analyze for some of the elements in primer residue, such as antimony and barium.

Propellant: In a firearm, the chemical composition, which when ignited by a primer, generates gas. The gas propels the projectile(s). Also called powder; gunpowder; powder, smokeless.

Revolver: A firearm, usually a handgun, with a cylinder having several chambers so arranged as to rotate around an axis and be discharged successively by the same firing mechanism.

Rifle: A firearm having rifling in the bore and designed to be fired from the shoulder.

Rifling: Helical grooves in the bore of a firearm barrel to impart rotary motion to a projectile.

Shot: Spherical pellets used in loading shotshells or cartridges.

Shotgun: A smooth bore shoulder firearm designed to fire shotshells containing numerous pellets or sometimes a single projectile.

Shotshell: A cartridge containing projectile(s) designed to be fired in a shotgun. The cartridge body may be metal, plastic, or paper.

Striations: Parallel surface contour variations on the surface of an object caused by a combination of force and motion where the motion is approximately parallel to the plane being marked. These striations are accidental in nature and unique to a common origin, (a particular firearm or tool). Also called striae. *See* Impression.

Test Bullet: A bullet fired into a bullet recovery system in a laboratory for comparison or analysis.

Toolmark Identification: Toolmark identification is a discipline of forensic science which has as its primary concern to determine if a toolmark was produced by a particular tool.

Toolmark, Impressed: A tool is placed against an object and enough pressure is applied to the tool so that it leaves an impression in the object. The shape and any individual characteristics can be used to identify the tool with the mark it left on the object. Also called Compression Marks.

Toolmark, Striated: A tool is placed against an object softer than itself and with pressure applied the tool is moved across the object producing a scrape. The parallel surface irregularities produced by this scraping action are known as a striated toolmark. Friction marks, abrasion marks, and scratch marks are terms commonly used when referring to striated marks.

Trigger: That part of a firearm mechanism which is moved manually to cause the firearm to discharge.

§ 14-16. Selected Bibliography.

ASSOCIATION OF FIREARM AND TOOL MARK EXAMINERS, GLOSSARY (1980).

ASSOCIATION OF FIREARM AND TOOL MARK EXAMINERS, TRAINING MANUAL (1982).

G. BURRARD, THE IDENTIFICATION OF FIREARMS AND FORENSIC BALLISTICS (1962).

V. DiMaio, Gunshot Wounds — Practical Aspects of Firearms, Ballistics, and Forensic Techniques (1985).

D. Faigman, D. Kaye, M. Saks & J. Sanders, Modern Scientific Evidence ch. 23 (1997).

J. Hatcher, F. Jury, & J. Weller, Firearms Investigation, Identification, and Evidence (1957).

B. Heard, Handbook of Firearms and Ballistics (1996).

J. Mathews, Firearms Identification (1962) (3 volumes).

A. Moenssens, J. Starrs, & C. Henderson, Scientific Evidence: Civil and Criminal ch. 6 (4th ed. 1995).

Nicols, *Firearm and Toolmark Identification Criteria: A Review of the Literature*, 42 J. Forensic Sci. 466 (1997).

Springer, *Toolmark Examinations — A Review of its Development in the Literature*, 40 J. Forensic Sci. 964 (1995).

Amburgh, *Common Sources of Error in the Examination and Interpretation of Ballistics Evidence*, 26 B.U. L. Rev. 207 (1946).

Darby, *Firearms Identification*, 3 Forensic Sciences ch. 38 (C. Wecht ed. 1984).

Firearms Identification, 29 Am. Jur. Proof of Facts 65 (1972).

Hays, *Ballistics: A Study of the Expert Witness*, 2 Wm. & Mary L. Rev. 61 (1959).

Rowe, *Firearms Identification*, *in* 2 Forensic Science Handbook 393 (R. Saferstein ed. 1988).

Wilhelm, *General Considerations of Firearms Identification and Ballistics*, *in* Practising Law Institute, Scientific and Expert Evidence 675 (Imwinkelried ed. 1981).

Annotations

Annot., *Expert evidence to identify gun from which bullet or cartridge was fired*, 26 A.L.R.2d 892 (1952).

Annot., *Admissibility of testimony that bullet could or might have come from a particular gun*, 31 A.L.R.4th 486 (1984).

Annot., *Admissibility, in homicide prosecution, of evidence as to tests made to ascertain distance from gun to victim when gun was fired*, 86 A.L.R.2d 611 (1962).

Annot., *Admissibility, in homicide prosecution, of evidence as to tests made to ascertain distance from gun to victim when gun was fired*, 11 A.L.R.5th 497 (1993).

CHAPTER 15

STATISTICAL EVIDENCE*

§ 15-1. In General.

Statistical techniques are in wide use in the physical and social sciences. The last three decades have witnessed expanding use of those techniques in the law.[1] Several factors have facilitated that expansion. One is that law and business schools increasingly employ those techniques in their curricula.[2] Another is the growing availability of computer programs for performing statistical analyses.[3] A further consideration is the public's growing familiarity with statistical evidence. The public was exposed to a good deal of statistical testimony about random match probabilities in the *Simpson* prosecution, and some observers now believe

*The authors wish to express their appreciation to Professor Edward Spitznagel, Jr. of the Mathematics Department, Washington University, who reviewed this chapter in all three editions of the treatise, and David Kaye, Regents Professor, of the Arizona State University College of Law, who reviewed this chapter in the first two editions.

1. *Foreword*, 46 LAW & CONTEMP. PROBS. 1 (Autumn 1983).

2. *Id.* at 2.

3. *Id.* at 1.

that many jurors expect statistical testimony. These factors have accelerated the trend toward wider use of statistical evidence in court.[4] These factors are helping to fulfill Holmes' prophecy that "the man of the future is the man of statistics...."[5]

However, perhaps the most important factor paving the way for judicial reliance on statistical techniques has been the realization of the tremendous utility of the legal applications of the techniques. A defense attorney may use a survey of local opinion as the basis for a change of venue; the survey may show that there is such hostility against the defendant in the community that the defendant cannot obtain a fair trial in a local court. In a gambling prosecution, the prosecution may offer a statistician's probability analysis to show that the defendant's apparent handicapping skill was due to cheating rather than chance.[6] The Solicitor General has offered the Supreme Court log-linear regression studies to support his position that the death penalty deters crime.[7] In obscenity prosecutions, counsel have attempted to introduce surveys to establish the community standards.[8] The attorney may also offer statistical analyses to support or attack the validity of other scientific techniques such as breathalyzer evidence.[9] The central issue in the recent dispute over the forthcoming Census was whether either the Census Act or the Census Clause in the Constitution precludes the Census Bureau from employing statistical sampling techniques in determining population for purposes of apportioning the House of Representatives.[10]

4. Koehler, *The Probity/Policy Distinction in the Statistical Evidence Debate*, 66 TUL. L. REV. 141 (1991) ("the use of statistical testimony at trial has increased dramatically during the past two decades"); Montlack, *Using Statistical Evidence to Enforce the Laws Against Discrimination*, 22 CLEV. ST. L. REV. 259, 268 (1973). The proposed Racial Justice Act would have legislatively authorized the admission of statistical evidence to support an inference that a death penalty was "imposed based on race." However, the Senate voted to oppose inclusion of the act in the omnibus crime bill passed in 1994. 55 Crim. L. Rep. (BNA) 1161 (May 18, 1994).

5. Holmes, *The Path of the Law*, 10 HARV. L. REV. 457, 469 (1897). *But see* West v. Swift, Hunt & Wesson, 847 F.2d 490, 492 n.2 (8th Cir. 1988) ("In Benjamin Disraeli's famous philippic against the use of statistics, he characterized an opponent as employing 'lies, damn lies, and statistics'").

6. United States v. Gerry, 515 F.2d 130 (2d Cir.), *cert. denied,* 423 U.S. 832 (1975).

7. Fisher, *Multiple Regression in Legal Proceedings*, 80 COLUM. L. REV. 702 (1980).

8. Keller v. State, 606 S.W.2d 931 (Tex. Crim. App. 1980).

9. Bass, Gesser & Mount, *Scientific Statistical Methodology and the Doctrine of "Reasonable Doubt" in Criminal Law; (With Specific Reference to the Breath Analysis for Blood Alcohol) Empirical Fact or Legal Fiction?*, 5 DALHOUSIE L.J. 350 (1979). *See also* Cortez III Service Corp. v. Nat. Aeronautics & Space Admin., 950 F. Supp. 357 (D.D.C. 1996) (use of statistical evidence to justify a set aside contract for disadvantaged small businesses).

10. Department of Commerce v. U.S. House of Representatives, 525 U.S. 316 (1999) (the Census Act prohibited the proposed use of statistical sampling in connection with the decennial census, whether as a substitute for or supplement to the traditional enumeration method for calculating the population for apportionment purposes). *See also* Glavin v. Clinton, 19 F. Supp. 2d 543 (E.D. Va. 1998) (the 1976 Census Act forbids using statistical sampling to even supplement an actual head count).

Initially, courts were content to analyze raw numbers and percentages;[11] they engaged in straight comparisons of numbers[12] and relied on purely intuitive assessments of the disparities.[13] However, more recently, courts have tended to insist upon more sophisticated statistical analyses.[14] As the Fourth Circuit has remarked,

> Courts ... from time to time, have used straight percentage comparisons without the necessary standard deviation analysis in proving and rebutting discrimination cases. Statisticians do not simply look at two statistics, such as the actual and expected percentage of blacks on a grand jury, and make a subjective conclusion that the statistics are significantly different. Rather,

11. Pouncy v. Prudential Ins. Co., 668 F.2d 795 (5th Cir. 1982). *E.g.,* E.E.O.C. v. Local 14, Int'l Union of Operating Eng'rs, 553 F.2d 251 (2d Cir. 1977); Spratley v. Paderick, 528 F.2d 733 (4th Cir. 1975); Buck v. Green, 690 F. Supp. 1034 (M.D. Ga. 1988), *vacated on other grounds,* 874 F.2d 1578 (11th Cir. 1989); Pina v. City of East Providence, 492 F. Supp. 1240 (D.R.I. 1980).

12. Hazelwood School Dist. v. United States, 433 U.S. 299, 307-08 (1977) ("There is no doubt that '[w]here gross statistical disparities can be shown, they alone in a proper case may constitute prima facie proof of a pattern or practice of discrimination' under Title VII"). United States v. Alvarado, 923 F.2d 253 (2d Cir. 1991) ("a statistical disparity"); Moultrie v. Martin, 690 F.2d 1078 (4th Cir. 1982); Harris v. Delchamps, Inc., 5 F. Supp. 2d 1316, 1333 (M.D. Ala. 1998); Mayfield v. Thornburgh, 741 F. Supp. 284, 286 n.3 (D.D.C. 1990) (disparity); United States v. Turner, 901 F. Supp. 1491, 1497 (C.D. Cal. 1995) ("the Ninth Circuit held that a colorable basis existed statistically based on ... the Federal Public Defender's showing that 24 out of 24 defendants whom it had defended on crack charges in 1991 were black."), *rev'd,* 104 F.3d 1180 (9th Cir.), *cert. denied sub nom.* Jones v. United States, 117 S. Ct. 1566 (1997); *But see* United States v. Olvis, 97 F.3d 739 (4th Cir. 1996) ("an informal statistical study" showing that "in the Norfolk-Newport News area, of all the federal crack cocaine trafficking prosecutions in federal court since 1992 in which the defendant's race was apparent, over 90% involved black defendants").

13. C. McCormick, Evidence §209 (5th ed. 1999); Walter v. Lone Star Gas Co., 977 F.2d 161 (5th Cir. 1992) (gross statistical disparities); United States v. Gault, 973 F. Supp. 1309 (D.N.M. 1997) (absolute disparity figure), *aff'd,* 141 F.3d 1399 (10th Cir. 1998); Mitchell v. Carrier Corp., 954 F. Supp. 1568 (M.D. Ga. 1995) (gross statistical disparities alone), *aff'd,* 108 F.3d 343 (11th Cir. 1997).

Many courts attach little weight to gross disparities which have not been evaluated statistically. *E.g.,* United States v. Contreras, 108 F.3d 1255, 1269 n.8 (10th Cir. 1997); United States v. Olvis, 97 F.3d 739 (4th Cir. 1996); Middleton v. City of Flint, Mich., 92 F.3d 396 (6th Cir. 1996) (raw percentages alone), *cert. denied,* 520 U.S. 1196 (1997); United States v. Cannon, 88 F.3d 1495 (8th Cir. 1996); United States v. Reyes, 934 F. Supp. 553 (S.D.N.Y. 1996); United States v. Rioux, 930 F. Supp. 1558 (D. Conn. 1995), *aff'd,* 97 F.3d 648 (2d Cir. 1996); Scanlan, *Mired in Numbers: Statistical tendencies, rather than bias, explain much racial disproportionality in the criminal justice system,* Legal Times, Oct. 21, 1996, at 23 ("Sometimes stark racial disparities in criminal justice statistics are not exactly what they seem.").

14. United States v. Holloway, 29 F. Supp. 2d 435 (M.D. Tenn. 1998) (statistical evidence offered in support of a claim of selective prosecution). *See* McAdams, *Race and Selective Prosecution: Discovering the Pitfalls of Armstrong,* 73 Chi.-Kent L. Rev. 605, 624-25 (1998).

statisticians compare figures through an objective process known as hypothesis testing.[15]

This chapter discusses some of the statistical techniques such as hypothesis testing commonly used in court. It is only an introduction and thus is both selective and somewhat oversimplified. There are numerous useful techniques not covered here, including the Fisher Exact test,[16] the Gamma measure,[17] the Poisson Distribution Formula,[18] the Spearman Rank Correlation Coefficient,[19] and the Lagrangian Interpolation.[20] The purpose of this chapter is not to prepare the reader to independently perform statistical analyses. Rather, the objective is to acquaint the reader with enough of the basic concepts and terminology to intelligently question a statistician serving as a consultant.

§ 15-2. Descriptive Statistics.

A complete set or collection of numbers is called a universe or population. A subset of the population would be called a sample. When the statistician knows or has conducted a census of all the elements of a particular sample or population, the statistician may be content to use descriptive or summary statistics. As the term suggests, these statistics merely summarize characteristics of the set of numbers; the statistician is not drawing any inference such as when the statistician uses statistics about a known sample to estimate the corresponding parameters of an unknown population. The average value in the sample is verifiable, but to an extent the statistician may have to speculate about the average value in the population. The statistics are shorthand overviews of the set.[21] There are two primary types of descriptive statistics: measures of central tendency and measures of dispersion.

---

15. Moultrie v. Martin, 690 F.2d 1078, 1082 (4th Cir. 1982). *See also* Wingfield v. United Techs. Corp., 678 F. Supp. 973 (D. Conn. 1988) (although the plaintiff in a discrimination suit presented statistics about promotions, the plaintiff failed to present an expert interpretation of the statistics).

16. Smith & Abram, *Quantitative Analysis and Proof of Employment Discrimination*, 1981 U. ILL. L. REV. 33, 65. *See* Victory v. Hewlett-Packard Co., 34 F. Supp. 2d 809, 823 (E.D.N.Y. 1999).

17. L. LOEWEN, SOCIAL SCIENCE IN THE COURTROOM 222 (1982).

18. Braun, *Quantitative Analysis and the Law: Probability Theory as a Tool of Evidence in Criminal Trials*, 4 UTAH L. REV. 41, 81 (1982).

19. D. BARNES, STATISTICS AS PROOF: FUNDAMENTALS OF QUANTITATIVE EVIDENCE 284 (1983).

20. United States *ex rel.* Barksdale v. Blackburn, 610 F.2d 253, 266 (5th Cir. 1980), *cert. denied,* 454 U.S. 1056 (1981). A purist might argue that Lagrangian Interpolation belongs to the discipline of numerical analysis rather than statistics.

21. W. CURTIS, STATISTICAL CONCEPTS FOR ATTORNEYS 21 (1983).

§ 15-2(A). Measures of Central Tendency.

When the elements in a set are arranged in numerical order, measures of central tendency describe numbers about which the elements are arranged.[22] There are many measures of central tendency, including the increasingly popular geometric means. There are currently three common measures of central tendency: the mode, the median, and the mean. Each statistic has its utility and its limitations.

Mode

The mode is the number that occurs most frequently in a set of data. If the set contains a single mode, the array is called unimodal; when there are two modes, bimodal; and if there are several modes, multimodal.[23] When each value in the set occurs with the same frequency, some statisticians say that the set has no mode.[24] The mode is a poor measure of central tendency. That certainly holds true when the set has no mode. Even when there is a mode, the mode may be unrepresentative of the data as a whole. Consequently the modal value may be extremely large or small in comparison to the rest of the data.

Median

The median is a positional figure. When the elements are arranged in order of numerical size, the median is the figure in the middle. Half the observations will lie above the median and half below. When the number of elements in the set is odd, the median is the value exactly in the middle of the set. When the number of elements in the set is even, the statistician uses this formula to determine the median:

$$\text{Md} = \frac{N+1}{2}$$

In the formula, N is the number of elements in the set.[25] The median is the value halfway between the two middle values. The median is more representative of the set than the mode. However, the data on one or both sides of the median may be much larger or smaller than the median.

---

22. *Id.* Of course, the central tendencies exist whether or not the sample is ordered.

23. *Id.*

24. *Id.*

25. *Id.* at 23.

Mean

The mean is the arithmetic average. It is a computational figure, and the formula for computing the mean is

$$\mu = \frac{\Sigma x}{N}$$

In this formula, μ is the mean; Σ is the summation notation indicating that the values should be added or summed; x indicates all the values of x, the elements in the set; and N is the number of elements in the set.[26] If the three values of x were 3, 6, and 9, N would be 3; Σx would be 18; and μ would be 6.

For many purposes, the mean is the best and most important measure of central tendency. It can be the best measure because it is the most representative. The formula for computing the mean takes into account every value in the set. The only weakness is that an extremely large or small value in the set, an "outlier," may unduly influence the mean. Furthermore, the mean is the most important measure of centrality. This is so in two senses. First, it is the measure used most often. Second, many more sophisticated statistical techniques, such as the standard deviation, incorporate the mean value.

Although the concepts of mode, median, and mean are distinct, in a given set of numbers the three figures can coincide. The next section discusses the normal distribution. The normal distribution can be visualized as Figure 15-1, the familiar bell-shaped curve.

The normal distribution is only one of a family of bell-shaped, unimodal, symmetric curves. In a normal distribution, the values are distributed symmetrically with a single peak. In such a distribution, the mode, median, and mean are identical. (In a finite population, even though idealized to be normal, the mean, median, and mode may differ slightly. If the measurements made are very precise, no value may occur twice; and hence, there would be no mode.)

Courts have readily recognized the validity and utility of these concepts. Like statisticians, the courts have most frequently employed the mean. The mean has been used in civil damage computations[27] and actions alleging racial discrimination.[28] In criminal cases, the courts have relied on means to determine

---

26. *Id.* at 25.

27. L.C.L. Theatres, Inc. v. Columbia Pictures Indus., 421 F. Supp. 1099 (N.D. Tex. 1976), *modified,* 566 F.2d 494 (5th Cir. 1978); W. CURTIS, *supra* note 21, at 29-31.

28. Pettway v. American Cast Iron Pipe Co., 494 F.2d 211 (5th Cir. 1974), *cert. denied,* 439 U.S. 1115 (1979); W. CURTIS, *supra* note 21, at 31. *See also* Pargo v. Elliott, 894 F. Supp. 1242, 1258 n.20 (S.D. Iowa 1995) (sex discrimination), *aff'd,* 69 F.3d 280 (8th Cir.), *cert. denied,* 519 U.S. 831 (1996).

whether there has been discrimination in the selection of a grand or petit jury.[29] Similarly, testimony about the median is sometimes relevant and admissible.[30]

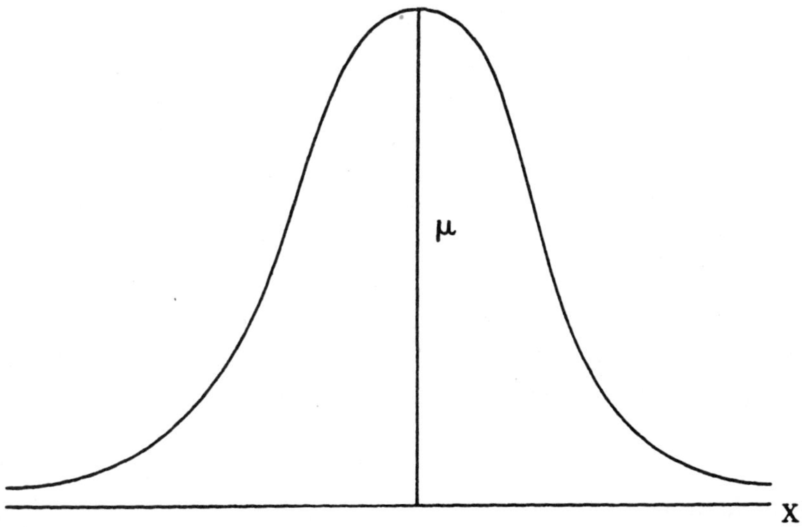

Figure 15-1[31]

§ 15-2(B). Measures of Dispersion.

In contrast to measures of central tendency, measures of dispersion assess the spread or variation in a set of numbers. Four measures of dispersion — the range, the variance, the standard deviation, the coefficient of variation — as well as a related concept, the coefficient of skewness are considered.

Range

The range is sometimes defined as the difference between the largest and the smallest values in a set of numbers. At other times the range is described as the largest and smallest values themselves. Suppose, for example, that the following table lists the number of minority jurors in 10 recent trials:

---

29. United States *ex rel.* Barksdale v. Blackburn, 610 F.2d 253 (5th Cir. 1980), *cert. denied,* 454 U.S. 1056 (1981). The courts sometimes explicitly analyze the proportion, but the proportion is simply a special case of the mean.

30. CSX Transp. v. Board of Pub. Works of W. Va., 871 F. Supp. 897, 901 (S.D. W. Va. 1995), *aff'd in part, rev'd in part,* 95 F.3d 318 (4th Cir. 1996).

31. The drawing is a rough rendering of a normal distribution. More exact renditions are found in T. WONNACOTT & R. WONNACOTT, INTRODUCTORY STATISTICS 92 (3d ed. 1977) and W. CURTIS, *supra* note 21, at 72. In the drawing, x represents all the values that the variable can assume; μ signifies the mean or average value.

trial number	number of minority jurors
1	0
2	2
3	3
4	4
5	2
6	5
7	3
8	9
9	2
10	1

In this hypothetical example, the range runs from nine to zero.

The range is a poor measure of dispersion. It sheds little or no light on the values falling between the largest and smallest values.

Variance and Standard Deviation

The formula for computing the variance is the following:

$$\sigma^2 = \frac{\Sigma(x - \mu)^2}{N}$$

σ^2 is the variance, x is each individual value in the set, μ is the mean, 2 indicates that the value should be squared, and N is the number of elements in the array. The statistician takes the difference between each value and the mean and then squares the difference, adds these squares, and divides by N (or N-1). Squaring the value is critical. If the statistician simply took the differences and added them, the sum would be zero; there would be some values higher than the mean and others lower. The zero would give no insight into the dispersion. However, squaring the difference yields a positive number. The problem with the variance is that it is stated in squared units such as squared feet. If the statistician were investigating jury discrimination, the variance might be expressed in terms of (the number of minority jurors per panel)^2.

To remedy this problem, statisticians developed the standard deviation.[32] The standard deviation is the square root of the variance:

$$\sigma = \sqrt{\sigma^2}$$

σ^2 is the variance; σ is the standard deviation, and indicates the process of taking the square root such as extracting 2 as the square root of 4. The advantage of the

32. E.E.O.C. v. Warshawsky & Co., 768 F. Supp. 657, 652 n.4 (N.D. Ill. 1991).

standard deviation is that it is stated in the original units of measurement such as feet or minority jurors per panel.

Although statisticians sometimes use the original formula,

$$\sigma^2 = \frac{\Sigma(x-\mu)^2}{N}$$

to compute the variance, it is more common to use an algebraically equivalent expression:

$$\sigma^2 = \frac{\Sigma x^2}{N} - \left(\frac{\Sigma x_1}{N}\right)^2$$

The notation to the immediate right of the equals signs indicates that the statistician squares each value; adds those values; and then divides by N, the number of elements in the set. This notation is equivalent to μ^2. The statistician then subtracts the notation on the extreme right. That notation indicates that the statistician adds all the individual values of x, divides that sum by N, and then squares the number resulting from the division. In our hypothetical example, both formulas yield the result that the standard deviation is 2.39 minorities per panel:

$$\sigma^2 = \frac{153}{10} - \left(\frac{31}{10}\right)^2$$
$$= 15.3 - 9.61$$
$$= 5.69\,(\text{minorities per panel})^2$$

The square root of 5.69, the standard deviation, is 2.39.

The standard deviation is the counterpart to the mean. Just as the mean is the most popular measure of central tendency, the standard deviation is the most popular measure of dispersion. The standard deviation incorporates all the elements of the set in its computation, and its magnitude is directly related to the amount of variation in the data. Moreover, the standard deviation is the most important measure of dispersion. Just as the mean figures in many of the more sophisticated statistical formulae, many such formulae incorporate the standard deviation. For instance, as noted later in this chapter, knowing the standard deviation of a normal distribution and assuming normality, the statistician can predict the percentage of the values in the array that should fall within one, two, or three deviations from the mean.

Coefficient of Variation

The statistician uses the variance and standard deviation when the question is the spread within a set of data. However, sometimes the issue turns on a comparison between the spread of two different sets of data. For example, suppose that the statistician wants to compare the variation in the number of minority jurors on federal and state juries. Assume that the mean for state juries is 8.9 minority members per panel, while the mean for federal juries is 5.9. Further suppose that the standard deviation for state juries is 1.73 minority members per panel, and the figure for federal juries is 1.2 minority members. The analyst might be tempted to leap to the conclusion that there is much greater spread on state juries. However, add the facts that the federal panels include 20 jurors while the state panels include 30. It is misleading to make a direct comparison between the standard deviations of two sets of data of different size. Any meaningful comparison must account for the difference in panel size.

To take this factor into account, statisticians developed the coefficient of variation, V.[33] To use the coefficient, the statistician follows these steps:

— Find the mean, μ_a, and standard deviation, σ_a, of the first population.
— Compute the coefficient of variation for that population:

$$V_a = \frac{\sigma_a}{\mu^a}$$

— Find the mean, μ^b, and standard deviation, σ^b, of the second population.
— Compute the coefficient of variation for that population:

$$V_b = \frac{\sigma_b}{\mu_b}$$

— Compare the two coefficients.

Following this procedure, the statistician would find that the coefficient for federal panels is .295 and the coefficient for state panels .297. In short, the spread is almost identical. Relative to its population mean, the dispersion of each population is similar to the other.

---

33. N. Channels, Social Science Methods in the Legal Process 206-07 (1985) ("This coefficient describes the size of the standard deviation of a sample as a percentage of the mean of the sample and thus has the effect of putting the standard deviation into the context of the size of the mean"). There is a further difference between the variance and skewness. Since the formula for variance squares the deviations, that formula measures the overall size of the deviations from the mean. In contrast, skewness measures the tendency of the deviations to be larger in one direction than in the other.

Coefficient of Skewness

The coefficient of skewness relates to the shape of the distribution of numbers in the set. As noted earlier, Figure 15-1 represents a classic, normal distribution. However, the distribution could be positively skewed as in Figure 15-2,

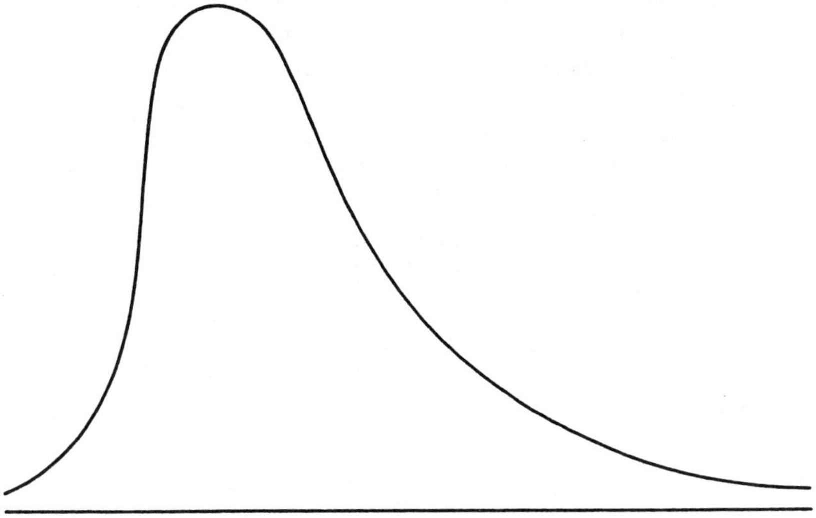

Figure 15-2.[34]

or negatively skewed as in Figure 15-3.

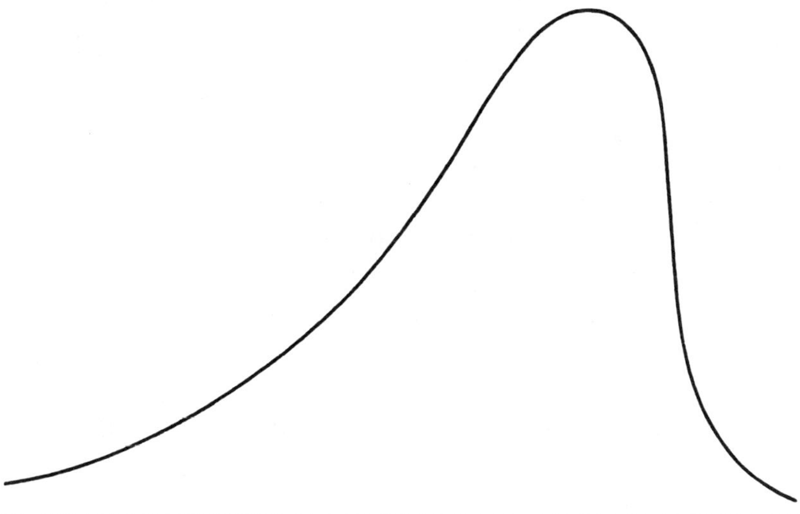

Figure 15-3.[35]

34. For another depiction of a positively skewed distribution, *see* W. CURTIS, *supra* note 21, at 9.

One formula for measuring the coefficient of skewness is:

$$sk = \frac{3(\mu - Md)}{\sigma}$$

In the formula, sk signifies the coefficient of skewness, μ is the mean, Md is the median, and σ is the standard deviation. The formula uses the median rather than the mode because, as previously stated, some sets of data have no mode.[36] (For that matter, a set can be multimodal). If the distribution is skewed to the right, the mean is greater than the median, and sk will be a positive value.[37] If the distribution skews to the left, the mean is less than the median, and sk will be negative.

Although the above formula for skewness is sometimes used, the most popular statistics packages, SAS and SPSS, employ different formulae. SAS uses

$$\frac{n}{(n-1)(n-2)}$$

while SPSS utilizes 1/n in the numerator. The factor

$$\frac{n}{(n-1)(n-2)}$$

is a bias adjustment similar to the division by (n–1) in calculating the sample variance.

Just as the courts have admitted testimony based on measures of central tendency, the courts appreciate the validity of the measures of dispersion. A leading Supreme Court jury discrimination case, *Castaneda v. Partida,*[38] and a leading precedent on discrimination in teacher hiring, *Hazelwood Sch. Dist. v. United States,*[39] consider testimony based on an analysis of standard deviations. Lower courts and tribunals have also resorted to the coefficient of variation.[40]

§ 15-3. Inferential Statistics — An Introduction.

The discussion of descriptive statistics sets the stage for an analysis of the second major area of statistics, inferential statistics. Even when the data are incomplete, the statistician may be interested in estimating the parameters of the population or determining whether the observed values could occur randomly, that is, by chance. Whatever the inference, an essential step in the statistician's

---

35. For a more exact rendition, *see id.*

36. *Id.* at 38.

37. *Id.* at 40.

38. 430 U.S. 482 (1977).

39. 433 U.S. 299 (1977); W. CURTIS, *supra* note 21, at 40-41.

40. *In re* Forte-Fairbairn, Inc., 62 F.T.C. 1146, 1167 (1963); D. BARNES, *supra* note 19, at 13.

analysis consists in generating an expected value. The expected value serves as the estimate, and the contrast between the expected and observed values enables the statistician to determine whether chance would explain the observed value. To generate expected values, statisticians sometimes rely on two distributions: the binomial distribution and the normal distribution.

§ 15-3(A). Binomial Distribution.

The statistician can use the binomial distribution to predict expected values.[41] The predictions forecast the distribution that should exist if there are random draws.[42] As the term "binomial" suggests, "this distribution results from repeated independent trials of an experiment in which there are only two possible mutually exclusive outcomes on each trial."[43]

The statistician can employ the binomial distribution to predict expected values when three conditions are present.

First, each trial can result in one of two possible outcomes.[44] The binomial distribution assumes this dichotomy.[45] One outcome can be termed a success, while the other can be described as a failure. These designations are arbitrary. The success might be choosing a minority juror for a trial, and the failure might be selecting a non-minority juror.

Second, the probability of success on any given trial must remain constant throughout the sequence of trials.[46] Theoretically the probability will remain constant only when the population that the choice is made from is infinite or if the chosen element is replaced after the draw. If the population is finite and there is no replacement (as when a white juror is chosen for one trial and not reinserted into the jury pool), the probability changes; there should be a slightly greater probability of choosing a minority juror on the subsequent draws. However, when the population is large, the change is slight. For all practical purposes, the assumption of a constant probability works well.

Third, the trials must be statistically independent.[47] In any given trial, the outcome does not depend on any prior or subsequent trials. Some statisticians list independence as a separate condition, but others take the position that the first two conditions imply the independence of the trials. (One of our reviewers, Professor Spitznagel, questions whether dichotomous outcomes and constant probability imply independence.)

---

41. Smith & Abram, *supra* note 16, at 64.

42. *Id.* at 40.

43. W. CURTIS, *supra* note 21, at 62.

44. *Id.* at 63.

45. Shoben, *Differential Pass-Fail Testing in Employment Testing: Statistical Proof Under Title VII*, 91 HARV. L. REV. 793, 796 (1978).

46. *Id.*

47. W. CURTIS, *supra* note 21, at 63.

When these three conditions are present, the events are called Bernoulli trials. The statistician can use the binomial distribution to predict the probability of *r* successes in *n* Bernoulli trials given the probability of success in any given trial.[48] The distribution predicts how likely it is to obtain that value by chance.[49] Consider the example of flipping a fair coin. The conditions are present here: There are two possible outcomes — heads and tails; the probability of a head remains constant throughout any number of trials — namely, 0.50; and the outcome of any given flip is independent of the outcome of prior and subsequent flips. Using the binomial distribution, the statistician can predict the probability of obtaining any possible number of heads in five tosses of a fair coin.[50] Figure 15-4 depicts the binomial distribution for this experiment.

There is a formula[51] for computing binomial probabilities:

$$P(r/n, p) = \frac{n!}{r!(n-r)!} p^r (1-p)^{n-r}$$

In the formula, r is the number of successes (or heads or minority jurors), n is the number of trials, and p is the constant probability (such as the probability of a head or the probability of a minority juror). Since the only two sides of a coin are

48. *Id.* at 64-65.
49. J. LOEWEN, *supra* note 17, at 219.
50. W. CURTIS, *supra* note 21, at 61.
51. *Id.* at 65.

Probabilities for the Possible Outcomes of an Experiment Consisting of Five Tosses of a Fair Coin

Values of Random Variable (x)	Outcomes			Probability of x (P(x))
0	(TTTTT)			(½ · ½ · ½ · ½ · ½) = .03125
1	(HTTTT)	(THTTT)	(TTHTT)	
	(TTTHT)	(TTTTH)		5(½ · ½ · ½ · ½ · ½) = .15625
2	(HHTTT)	(HTHTT)	(HTTHT)	
	(HTTTH)	(THHTT)	(THTHT)	
	(THTTH)	(TTHHT)	(TTHTH)	
	(TTTHH)			10(½ · ½ · ½ · ½ · ½) = .31250
3	(HHHTT)	(HHTHT)	(HHTTH)	
	(TTHHH)	(THTHH)	(THHHT)	
	(THHTH)	(HTHHT)	(HTHTH)	
	(HTTHH)			10(½ · ½ · ½ · ½ · ½) = .31250
4	(HTHHH)	(HHTHH)	(HHHTH)	
	(HHHHT)	(THHHH)		5(½ · ½ · ½ · ½ · ½) = .15625
5	(HHHHH)			(½ · ½ · ½ · ½ · ½) = .03125
	Total			1.00000

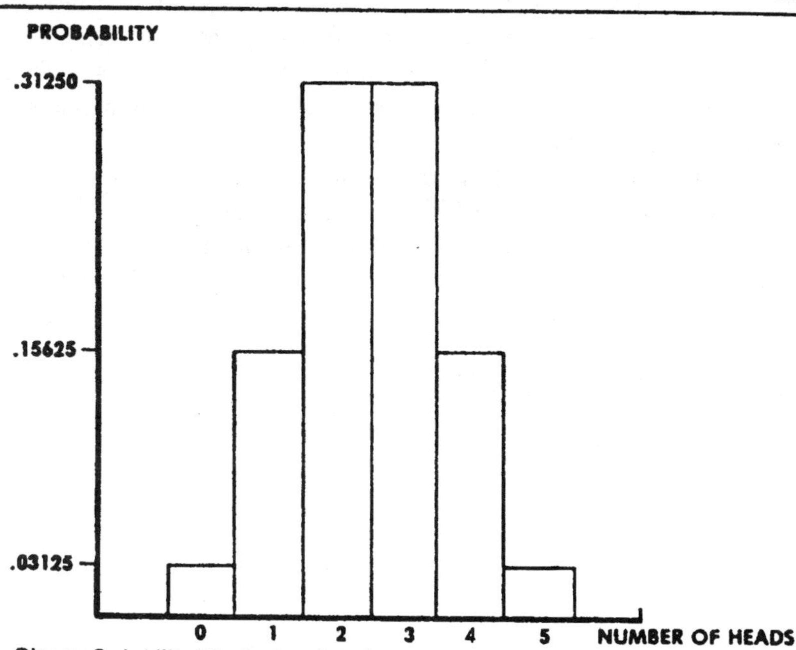

Discrete Probability Distribution of the Experiment Involving Five Tosses of a Fair Coin

Figure 15-4.[52]

52. *Id.* at 61. The table is reprinted from WAYNE C. CURTIS, STATISTICAL CONCEPTS FOR ATTORNEYS: A REFERENCE GUIDE, Quorum Books, Westport, CT, 1983. Used with permission of the publisher.

a head and a tail, the probability of a head would be 0.5. If the minority population in a large metropolitan area were 10%, the probability of randomly drawing a minority juror would be 0.1. The symbol ! is called a factorial.[53] If n is 4, n! means 4 times 3 times 2 times 1. This computation can be time-consuming.[54] Fortunately, there are both computer programs and published tables of binomial probabilities.[55]

There is a family of binomial distributions.[56] The statistician might resort to a computer program or consult a table. There is a separate table for each n, that is, each number of trials.[57] The statistician first finds the right table, depending on the n. Suppose, for example, that there are two flips of the coin and the question is the probability of two heads in a row. The statistician turns to the n=2 table. The top, horizontal margin of the table lists the possible values for p, the constant probability. The statistician reads across from left to right until he or she comes to the appropriate p. In our case, the statistician would read across until he or she came to .50, the probability of a head. The left-hand, vertical margin of the table lists the possible number of successes the statistician is interested in — the values for 4. Since the statistician wants to know the likelihood of two heads in two trials, he reads down the margin until he comes to 2. The statistician then finds the entry for the intersection between p equals .50 and r equals 2. The entry would be .2500. There is a 25% probability that two flips of a fair coin will randomly produce two heads.[58]

The courts acknowledge the utility of the binomial distribution. The Supreme Court has relied on binomial probabilities in discrimination cases.[59] The lower courts have followed suit.[60] If the statistician can establish the assumptions of the binomial distribution (two possible outcomes, independent trials, and a constant probability of success), courts routinely permit the statistician to use binomial probabilities.

---

53. *Id.* at 64.

54. *Id.* at 67.

55. *Id.* at 189.

56. *Id.* at 65.

57. *Id.* at 189.

58. *See also* Sugrue & Fairley, *A Case of Unexamined Assumptions: The Use and Misuse of Statistical Analysis of Casteneda/Hazelwood in Discrimination Litigation*, 24 B.C. L. Rev. 925 (1983).

59. Castaneda v. Partida, 430 U.S. 482 (1977). Professor Spitznagel comments that there is a difference between point probabilities and interval probabilities. In his view, only interval probabilities are appropriate for judging how unusual a given imbalance is, particularly when n is large and all individual frequencies have small probability.

60. *E.g.*, E.E.O.C. v. Federal Reserve Bank, 698 F.2d 633 (4th Cir. 1983), *rev'd on other grounds*, 467 U.S. 867 (1984).

§ 15-3(B). Normal Distribution.

In addition to its other uses, a normal distribution can be employed as a model for predicting expected values. Curtis describes the origin of the normal distribution:

> Study of the normal distribution began during the 1700s, when it was found that when physical characteristics such as weights, speeds, length, and volumes were measured repeatedly, variations occurred in the measurements. Carl Friedrich Gauss ... theorized that successive measurements yielding different values had a "normal" curve of error distributed around the true value. Hence, the normal distribution, a bell-shaped curve, was known for many years as the normal curve of error or the Gaussian curve.[61]

Figure 15-1 exemplifies the curve.[62] In Figure 15-1, μ represents the mean, and x signifies the various values that the variable can assume.

The mean and the standard deviation are the two parameters of the distribution. In fact, there is a different normal distribution for every combination of mean and standard deviation. Furthermore, the normal distribution is symmetric, and the mode, median, and mean coincide.[63] Finally, as Figure 15-5 indicates, "[a]reas of the normal distribution are customarily related to standard deviations from the mean. For example, approximately 68.26 percent of the area under the normal curve lies within $\pm 1\sigma_x$, 95.44 percent lies within $\pm 2\sigma_x$, and 99.73 percent lies within $\pm 3\sigma_x$ of the mean."[64] Thus, the "area under the curve over any interval on the horizontal axis represents the probability of the random variable, x, taking on a value in that interval."

The statistician uses the z statistic to determine probabilities based on normal distributions. The formula[65] for computing the Z statistic is:

$$Z = \frac{x - \mu}{\sigma}$$

x is the value that the variable has assumed, μ is the mean, and σ is the standard deviation. The z value "tells the number of standard deviations away from the

61. W. CURTIS, *supra* note 21, at 71-72.

62. *See id.* at 92.

63. *Id.* at 73.

64. *Id.*

65. D. BARNES, *supra* note 19, at 199; N. CHANNELS, *supra* note 33, at 195 (a certain number had "a Z-score of .89 .... That is, it falls less than one standard deviation from the mean score — about 89% of one standard deviation ...").

mean any particular ... sample lies."[66] The z value is "the number of standard deviations our observed value is from the mean."[67] Suppose that the statistician computes the z value to two decimal points such as 1.33.

After calculating the z value, the statistician can use a computer or a published table such as Figure 15-6 to convert the z value into a probability.

Suppose again that the z value is 1.33. The statistician first reads down the left-hand margin of the table to find 1.3 and then reads across to the .03 column. The number at the intersection of the two columns is .0918. Thus, there would be little more than a 9% probability that the normal random variable would assume a value that large.

What does the statistician do if for some reason he cannot use the z statistic? In some such cases, the statistician will be able to employ the t or student's t statistic. For example, the statistician can use the t statistic rather than the z statistic when the sample size is small.[68] It is based on a distribution with more area under the tails (the extreme ends of the distribution) than the standard normal distribution. Theoretically the t statistic can always be utilized, but in practice some statisticians use t rather than z only when n, the sample size, is 30 or fewer.[70] As the sample size increases, the z and t statistics come closer to coinciding. Our reviewer, Professor Kaye, cautions that the fundamental distinction between z-scores and t-statistics is not that z-scores are inapplicable to

---

66. Idaho State Tax Comm'n v. Staker, 104 Idaho 734, 749, 663 P.2d 270, 285 (1982); Webb v. Missouri Pac. R.R. Co., 826 F. Supp. 1192, 1202 (E.D. Ark. 1993); Stender v. Lucky Stores, Inc., 803 F. Supp. 259, 323 (N.D. Cal. 1992).

67. D. BARNES, *supra* note 19, at 199; Ross v. Buckeye Cellulose Corp., 733 F. Supp. 344, 353 (M.D. Ga. 1989), *rev'd*, 980 F.2d 648 (11th Cir. 1993), *cert. denied*, 513 U.S. 814 (1994).

68. T. WONNACOTT & R. WONNACOTT, *supra* note 29, at 210; Ross v. Buckeye Cellulose Corp., 733 F. Supp. 344, 355 n.14 (M.D. Ga. 1989) ("The T Test is similar to the Z test, but is allegedly more accurate on smaller pools of variables"), *rev'd*, 980 F.2d 648 (11th Cir. 1993), *cert. denied*, 513 U.S. 814 (1994).

70. D. BARNES, *supra* note 19, at 260.

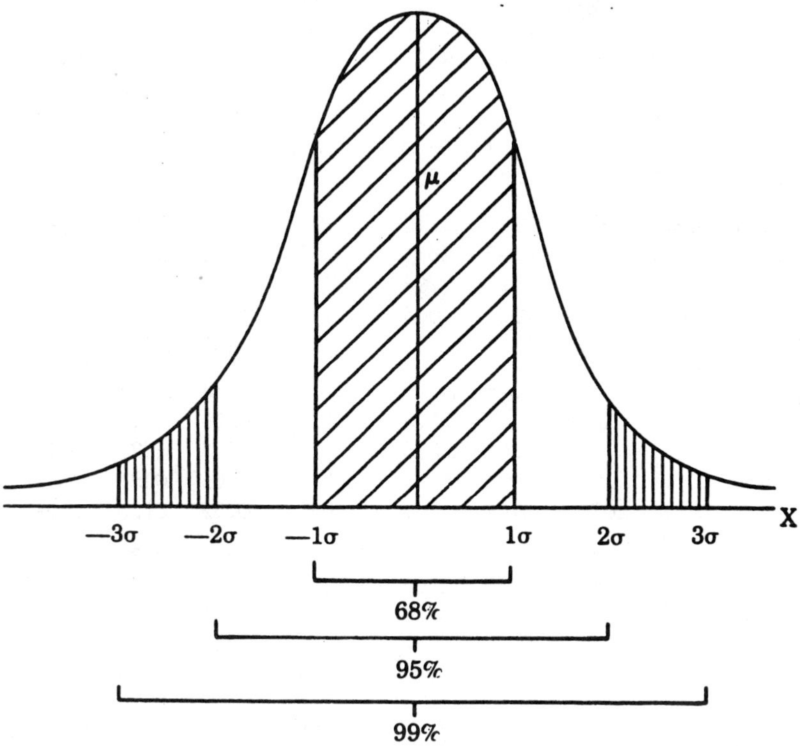

Figure 15-5[69]
Statistics for Determining Normal Probabilities

small samples; rather, the distinction is whether the population standard deviation is known. A z-score is correctly used only when the population standard deviation is known. However, a t-statistic may be employed whenever the population standard deviation can be estimated. For large samples, the difference between the z- and the t-distribution is slight; and the former may be used as an approximation for the latter.

69. This rough drawing is based on the depiction of the relationship in W. CURTIS, *supra* note 21, at 73.

	Second Decimal Place of z_0									
$\downarrow z_0$ $\rightarrow$	*.00*	*.01*	*.02*	*.03*	*.04*	*.05*	*.06*	*.07*	*.08*	*.09*
0.0	.5000	.4960	.4920	.4880	.4840	.4801	.4761	.4721	.4681	.4641
0.1	.4602	.4562	.4522	.4483	.4443	.4404	.4364	.4325	.4286	.4247
0.2	.4207	.4168	.4129	.4090	.4052	.4013	.3974	.3936	.3897	.3859
0.3	.3821	.3783	.3745	.3707	.3669	.3632	.3594	.3557	.3520	.3483
0.4	.3446	.3409	.3372	.3336	.3300	.3264	.3228	.3192	.3156	.3121
0.5	.3085	.3050	.3015	.2981	.2946	.2912	.2877	.2843	.2810	.2776
0.6	.2743	.2709	.2676	.2643	.2611	.2578	.2546	.2514	.2483	.2451
0.7	.2420	.2389	.2358	.2327	.2296	.2266	.2236	.2206	.2177	.2148
0.8	.2119	.2090	.2061	.2033	.2005	.1977	.1949	.1922	.1894	.1867
0.9	.1841	.1814	.1788	.1762	.1736	.1711	.1685	.1660	.1635	.1611
1.0	.1587	.1562	.1539	.1515	.1492	.1469	.1446	.1423	.1401	.1379
1.1	.1357	.1335	.1314	.1292	.1271	.1251	.1230	.1210	.1190	.1170
1.2	.1151	.1131	.1112	.1093	.1075	.1056	.1038	.1020	.1003	.0985
1.3	.0968	.0951	.0934	.0918	.0901	.0885	.0869	.0853	.0838	.0823
1.4	.0808	.0793	.0778	.0764	.0749	.0735	.0722	.0708	.0694	.0681
1.5	.0668	.0655	.0643	.0630	.0618	.0606	.0594	.0582	.0571	.0559
1.6	.0548	.0537	.0526	.0516	.0505	.0495	.0485	.0475	.0465	.0455
1.7	.0446	.0436	.0427	.0418	.0409	.0401	.0392	.0384	.0375	.0367
1.8	.0359	.0352	.0344	.0336	.0329	.0322	.0314	.0307	.0301	.0294
1.9	.0287	.0281	.0274	.0268	.0262	.0256	.0250	.0244	.0239	.0233
2.0	.0228	.0222	.0217	.0212	.0207	.0202	.0197	.0192	.0188	.0183
2.1	.0179	.0174	.0170	.0166	.0162	.0158	.0154	.0150	.0146	.0143
2.2	.0139	.0136	.0132	.0129	.0125	0122	.0119	.0116	.0113	.0110
2.3	.0107	.0104	.0102	.0099	.0096	.0094	.0091	.0089	.0087	.0084
2.4	.0082	.0080	.0078	.0075	.0073	.0071	.0069	.0068	.0066	.0064
2.5	.0062	.0060	.0059	.0057	.0055	.0054	.0052	.0051	.0049	.0048
2.6	.0047	.0045	.0044	.0043	.0041	.0040	.0039	.0038	.0037	.0036
2.7	.0035	.0034	.0033	.0032	.0031	.0030	.0029	.0028	.0027	.0026
2.8	.0026	.0025	.0024	.0023	.0023	.0022	.0021	.0021	.0020	.0019
2.9	.0019	.0018	.0017	.0017	.0016	.0016	.0015	.0015	.0014	.0014

Figure 15-6[71]

As in the case of z statistics, there is a formula for computing the t value and tables to simplify the computation. The formula[72] is:

$$t - \frac{x - \mu}{s / \sqrt{n}}$$

71. *Id.*

72. T. WONNACOTT & R. WONNACOTT, *supra* note 31, at 208.

x is the observed value, μ is the mean, σ is the standard deviation estimate, and $\sqrt{n}$ is the square root of n, the number of elements in the sample.[73] Once the t value is determined, the statistician can then use tables such as Figure 15-7 to determine the probability.

Critical Values of the *t* Distribution, One-Tail Area

	Level of Significance, α				
df	.10	.05	.025	.010	.005
1	3.078	6.314	12.706	31.821	63.657
2	1.886	2.920	4.303	6.965	9.925
3	1.638	2.353	3.182	4.541	5.841
4	1.533	2.132	2.776	3.747	4.604
5	1.476	2.015	2.571	3.365	4.032
6	1.440	1.943	2.447	3.143	3.707
7	1.415	1.895	2.365	2.998	3.499
8	1.397	1.860	2.306	2.896	3.355
9	1.383	1.833	2.262	2.821	3.250
10	1.372	1.812	2.228	2.764	3.169
11	1.363	1.796	2.201	2.718	3.106
12	1.356	1.782	2.179	2.681	3.055
13	1.350	1.771	2.160	2.650	3.012
14	1.345	1.761	2.145	2.624	2.977
15	1.341	1.753	2.131	2.602	2.947
16	1.337	1.746	2.120	2.583	2.921
17	1.333	1.740	2.110	2.567	2.898
18	1.330	1.734	2.101	2.552	2.878
19	1.328	1.729	2.093	2.539	2.861
20	1.325	1.725	2.086	2.528	2.845
21	1.323	1.721	2.080	2.518	2.831
22	1.321	1.717	2.074	2.508	2.819
23	1.319	1.714	2.069	2.500	2.807
24	1.318	1.711	2.064	2.492	2.797
25	1.316	1.708	2.060	2.485	2.787
26	1.315	1.706	2.056	2.479	2.779
27	1.314	1.703	2.052	2.473	2.771
28	1.313	1.701	2.048	2.467	2.763
29	1.311	1.699	2.045	2.462	2.756
30	1.310	1.697	2.042	2.457	2.750
∞	1.28155	1.64485	1.95996	2.32634	2.57582

Figure 15-7[74]

73. Idaho State Tax Comm'n v. Staker, 104 Idaho 734, 749, 663 P.2d 270, 285 (1982). Professor Spitznagel points out that s involves dividing by degrees of freedom (n – 1) rather than sample size. That can make a major difference when sample size is very small, for example, only two or three.

74. Table A.3, reprinted from WAYNE C. CURTIS, STATISTICAL CONCEPTS FOR ATTORNEYS: REFERENCE GUIDE, Quorum Books, Westport, CT, 1983. Reprinted with permission of the publisher.

The symbol "df" in the left-hand margin of the table means degree of freedom. Degree of freedom is a technical concept, but it is sufficient for present purposes to understand that in this context, the degrees of freedom are $n-1$ and the size of the sample minus one.[75] The upper margin of the table refers to levels of significance, a concept that is discussed in the next section on estimation.

As in the case of the binomial distribution, the courts will not permit the statistician to use the normal distribution or the related z statistic unless the appropriate assumptions are satisfied. Some contend that if it is clear that a population is probably not distributed normally, z statistics should not be used.[76] However, our reviewer, Professor Kaye, states that samples drawn from non-normal distributions can yield approximately normal distributions of certain statistics. For example, although a population is not normally distributed, the sampling distribution of the proportion might be binomially distributed in a manner approximated by a normal distribution. Even assuming that the distribution must be normal, the courts have permitted the use of z statistics so long as the statistician can plausibly assume that the population will be distributed normally.[77] They have also approved the use of t statistics.[78]

§ 15-3(C). Use of Normal Distribution to Approximate Binomial Distribution.

If the sample is small, a binomial distribution is subject to chance fluctuations.[79] However, as the sample size increases, the chance factor averages out.[80] When n, the sample size, is large, the statistician can use the normal distribution to approximate the binomial distribution.[81] The two distributions overlap — at least they come closer and closer together.[82] Think back to Figure 15-1 and the histogram in the lower half of Figure 15-4. Visualize superimposing

---

75. W. CURTIS, *supra* note 21, at 103.

76. T. WONNACOTT & R. WONNACOTT, *supra* note 31, at 492. Professor Spitznagel states that while this generalization holds true for estimating population percentages, the generalization is not true when you are dealing with an inference regarding the population mean.

77. Craik v. Minnesota State Univ. Bd., 731 F.2d 465 (8th Cir. 1984); United States v. Georgia Power Co., 474 F.2d 906 (5th Cir. 1973); Gay v. Waiters & Dairy Lunchmen's Union, 489 F. Supp. 282 (N.D. Cal. 1980), *aff'd,* 694 F.2d 605 (9th Cir. 1982); W. CURTIS, *supra* note 21, at 79; C. MCCORMICK, *supra* note 13, at §209; Barnes, *A Common Sense Approach to Understanding Statistical Evidence*, 21 SAN DIEGO L. REV. 809, 830 (1984).

78. E.E.O.C. v. International Bus. Machs. Corp., 583 F. Supp. 875, 897 (D. Md. 1984).

79. T. WONNACOTT & R. WONNACOTT, *supra* note 31, at 89-91 ("With a small sample size, chance fluctuations influence the picture. But as sample size increases, chance is averaged out, and relative frequencies settle down to probabilities. At the same time, the increase in sample size allows a finer definition of cells").

80. *Id.*

81. W. CURTIS, *supra* note 21, at 77.

82. *Id.* at 78.

Figure 15-1 over the histogram in Figure 15-4. The curve in Figure 15-1 would cut through the middle of the top of almost all the rectangles in the histogram.

§ 15-4. Inferential Statistics — Estimating Parameters.

It is often too costly or time-consuming to conduct a complete census or enumeration of a population. In this situation, the statistician may sample a subset of the universe and infer the population parameters from the sample data. For example, at a defense counsel's behest, a statistician may sample a small number of local residents to estimate the local community's hostility to the defendant.[83] The sampling may serve as the basis for a change of venue. Estimating parameters is one of the key tasks of inferential statistics. This section reviews the scientific and legal restrictions on estimating parameters.

§ 15-4(A). Process of Estimating Parameters.

Estimating population parameters entails three steps: conducting the sampling, computing statistics for the sample (the mean, the standard deviation, and the standard error of the mean), and finally using the statistics as a basis for estimating the parameters.[84]

Conducting the Sampling

There are quantitative and qualitative concerns about the sample. Quantitatively, the statistician wants a sample large enough to generate reliable statistics. Although many statisticians do not agree, some have asserted a rule of thumb that "a sample size numbering 30 (N = 30) provides stable statistics ...."[85] Our reviewer, Professor Kaye, though, states that he is aware of no textbook on sampling which approves of this asserted rule of thumb. "[D]oubling a sample size does not halve the error of the estimate."[86] As noted later in this section, one indicator of the sampling error is the standard error.[87] The standard error is inversely proportional to the square root of the sample size.[88] "Thus, to double the precision of the estimate of the parameter ... sample size must be increased not by a factor of 2 but by its square, 4."[89] "Students of sampling know that the famous survey fiascos of the past were based on samples that were too large, not

---

83. United States v. Kouri-Perez, 985 F. Supp. 25 (D.P.R. 1997).

84. Gomes v. Avco Corp., 816 F. Supp. 131, 133 (D. Conn. 1993).

85. J. LOEWEN, *supra* note 17, at 129. Professor Spitznagel takes issue with this rule of thumb. He states that the stability of the mean depends on how variable the data are rather than on how large the sample size is.

86. W. CURTIS, *supra* note 21, at 111.

87. *Id.*

88. *Id.*

89. *Id.*

too small. For example, when the *Literary Digest* predicted in 1936 that FDR would lose, the prediction was based on a survey of more than 50,000 persons....”[90] A large sample, like any other sample, can be obtained in a biased manner.

Qualitatively, the sample must be unbiased. In some cases, the statistician attempts to ensure that the sample is representative by consciously including in the sample persons whose backgrounds embody the principal characteristics of the population. This is sometimes termed representative or purposive sampling.[91]

However, statisticians often use simple random sampling. In this type of random sampling, each element of the population is just as likely to be observed; every element has the same, equal chance of being included.[92] For example, the statistician might assign a number to each element and direct a computer to apply a list of random numbers to choose the elements to be sampled. In other cases in which simple random sampling is inefficient, statisticians use different types of random sampling such as stratified random sampling. Even in these other types of random sampling, each unit in the sampling frame has a known probability of being selected.

It is equally critical that the sampling be unbiased. Bias can arise from several sources. The phrasing of the questions might be slanted or leading.[93] Or the

---

90. J. LOEWEN, *supra* note 17, at 128. J. WITMER, DATA ANALYSIS: AN INTRODUCTION 97-98 (1992) (as the basis for the prediction in its October 31, 1936 issue, the *Digest* polled a large number of people and according to this author, there were 2.4 million returned questionnaires. However, they “did not send questionnaires to a random sample of potential voters; rather, they drew their sample from such sources as telephone books and lists of automobile owners. This sampling scheme under-represented the poor and introduced a selection bias in favor of the Republican candidate, Landon.” The author cites a further example of the problem: “[i]n 1987 Shere Hite reported the results of a survey she made of 4,500 women. Among her findings was that 70% of the women married five years or more said they had had an extramarital affair. She gathered her data by mailing questionnaires to 100,000 members of various women’s groups. At roughly the same time, advice columnist Abigail Van Buren ... asked her readers, ‘Have you ever cheated on your mate?’ She heard from 150,000 women, only 15% of whom said they had cheated. [B]oth of these surveys have massive selection and nonresponse biases....”).

91. Wishard, *Admissibility of Opinion Survey*, 18 AM. JUR. PROOF OF FACTS 2D 305, 317 (1979). Miller, *Facts, Expert Facts and Statistics: Descriptive and Experimental Research Methods in Litigation*, 40 RUTGERS L. REV. 101, 117-19 (1987), discusses the various types of sampling, including stratified, systematic, and quota sampling.

92. W. CURTIS, *supra* note 21, at 92.

93. Dutka, *The Use of Survey Research in Legal Proceedings*, 68 A.B.A. J. 1508, 1510 (1982). Miller, *Facts, Expert Facts, and Statistics: Descriptive and Experimental Research Methods in Litigation*, 40 RUTGERS L. REV. 101, 144-45 (1987), lists seven different ways in which the phrasing of a survey question can be biased. Arche, Inc. v. Azaleia, U.S.A., Inc., 882 F. Supp. 334, 335 (S.D.N.Y. 1995) (citing the FEDERAL JUDICIAL CENTER’S REFERENCE MANUAL ON SCIENTIFIC EVIDENCE); Southland Sod Farms v. Stover Seed Co., 108 F.3d 1134 (9th Cir. 1997) (the methodology of a consumer survey); Blum, *Once Shunned Surveys Gain Favor of Courts*, NAT’L L.J., Oct. 30, 1995, at A17 (“After 1975, the use of surveys and polls snowballed”; however, in

sequence may be leading. "For example, asking, 'What brand do you think of when you hear this slogan?' is apt to be slanted if the brand was mentioned in the previous question."[94] Furthermore, the persons conducting the survey "should have no knowledge of the client's identity or the purpose of the survey."[95]

A final qualitative concern is the caliber of the recordation and measurements themselves. An interviewer may incorrectly record the respondent's statement. Or the respondent may have misunderstood the question or misspoken in answering. Lastly, the overall data must be correctly tabulated.

Computing the Sample Statistics

After tabulating the results of the sample, the statistician can compute three statistics for the sample: the sample mean, the sample standard deviation, and the standard error of the mean.

For a finite population, the formula for the sample mean is the same as the formula for the population mean, discussed in § 15-2. The sample mean formula is:

$$\overline{X} = \frac{\Sigma x_i}{n}$$

The formula uses n rather than N because we are dealing with a sample rather than the universe or population. The population mean uses the Greek letter μx, but the sample mean is designated by the Roman letter $\overline{X}$.[96]

The formula for the sample standard deviation differs slightly from the standard deviation formula discussed in § 15-2. The formula for the sample variance is

$$\Sigma = \frac{\Sigma x^2}{n-1} - \frac{(\Sigma x)^2/n}{n-1}$$

The sample standard deviation is then

$$s = \sqrt{s^2}$$

Indianapolis Colts Inc. v. Metropolitan Baltimore Football Club L.P., 34 F.3d 410, Judge Posner of the Seventh Circuit questioned the reliability of survey evidence); Becker, *Public Opinion Polls and Surveys as Evidence: Suggestions for Resolving Confusing and Conflicting Standards Governing Weight and Admissibility*, 70 OR. L. REV. 463 (1991) (reviewing the case law and proposing a statute to govern the admissibility of survey evidence); Keller, *A Survey of Survey Evidence*, 19 LITIG. 23, 24 (Fall 1992) (the foundation for survey evidence). *See also* Lipton, *Trademark Litigation: A New Look at the Use of Social Science Evidence*, 29 ARIZ. L. REV. 639, 646-49 (1987).

94. *Id. See also* Haller, *Using Public Opinion Surveys*, LITIG., Winter 1982, at 19.

95. Dutka, *supra* note 93, at 1510.

96. W. CURTIS, *supra* note 21, at 96.

The population standard deviation is designated by the Greek letter σ_x, and the sample standard deviation is designated with the Roman letter s. Moreover, the denominator is n - 1, one less than the sample size.

The third statistic is the standard error of the sample mean. This statistic measures the sampling error, the imprecision inherent in estimating population parameters from samples. The formula for the standard error is

$$S_{\bar{x}} = \frac{s}{\sqrt{n}}$$

$S_{\bar{x}}$ is the standard error, s is the standard deviation, and n is the sample size. When the sample is drawn from a finite sample without replacement, the researcher usually modifies the equation by a finite correction factor. The modified equation reads

$$S_{\bar{x}} = \frac{s}{\sqrt{n}}\sqrt{\frac{N-n}{N-1}}$$

In the modified formula, N is the population size and n is still the sample size. Many statisticians use the correction factor only if the sample size, n, is at least 5% of the population size, N.[97]

Estimating the Population Parameters

The statistician is now ready to use the sample statistics as proxies for the population parameters. The final phase is the actual estimation. The estimation requires several steps.

Initially, the statistician chooses a confidence coefficient. The most commonly encountered confidence coefficients are .90, .95, and .99. If, as is often the convention, the statistician chooses a .95 confidence coefficient, the statistician might report that there should be only a 5% chance that the actual population parameter such as the actual mean lies outside the confidence interval. Our reviewer, Professor Kaye, disputes this interpretation of confidence coefficients; he has written:

> The ninety-five percent "confidence" pertains only to the statistical procedure that generates an interval estimate. The confidence co-efficient of ninety-five percent means that if a great many simple random samples had been taken and a different confidence interval computed for each such sample, about ninety-five percent of these intervals would have included the

---

97. *Id.* at 102.

> unknown parameter. [T]his does not imply that the parameter has a ninety-five percent chance of being in any particular interval ....[98]

The statistician next decides whether to use a Z test or a t test. Some assert that the normality of the distribution and the sample size determine which statistic is appropriate. When the degrees of freedom (n−1) exceed 30, the statistician normally uses the Z test. However, our reviewer, Professor Kaye, states that the determinative factor in the decision is whether the population standard deviation is known. As previously stated, a Z test is correctly used only when the standard deviation is known.

The statistician uses the formula set out below to calculate the confidence interval:

$$\overline{X} \pm \left(t \cdot s_{\overline{X}}\right)$$

In this formula, μ is the population parameter being estimated (here the mean), X is the sample mean, t is the t value, and $s_{\overline{X}}$ is the standard error of the sample mean. If a Z test were appropriate, the statistician would replace the t value with the Z score.

Consider this example. Assume that after sampling the minority representation on 15 local juries, the statistician computes the following sample statistics: the sample mean, $\overline{X}$, is 3.67; the sample standard deviation, 1.39; and a standard error of the sample mean of .88. The estimation proceeds in this fashion:

- — The statistician chooses a confidence coefficient such as .95.
- — Since the sample size is small (n = 15) and the population standard deviation must be estimated from the sample variance, the statistician would use a student's t distribution.[99]

---

98. Kaye, *Is Proof of Statistical Significance Relevant?*, 61 WASH. L. REV. 1333, 1348-49 (1986). Knapp Shoes, Inc. v. Sylvania Shoe Mfg. Corp., 72 F.3d 190, 202 n.8 (1st Cir. 1995) ("'a 95 percent level of confidence'"), *cert. denied*, 517 U.S. 1245 (1996); *In re* Estate of Marcos Human Rights Litigation, 910 F. Supp. 1460, 1464-65 (D. Haw. 1995) ("a 95% statistical confidence level that all claims would fall within the ambit of the 137 randomly selected claims"), *aff'd*, 103 F.3d 767 (9th Cir. 1996); Gacy v. Welborn, 994 F.2d 305, 309 (7th Cir.) (a confidence interval), *cert. denied*, 510 U.S. 899 (1993); United States *ex rel.* Free v. McGinnis, 818 F. Supp. 1098, 1105 (N.D. Ill. 1992) (confidence interval), *aff'd in part, rev'd in part*, 12 F.3d 700 (7th Cir. 1993). *See also* Kaye, *Apples and Oranges: Confidence Coefficients and the Burden of Persuasion*, 73 CORNELL L. REV. 54, 62 (1987) ("the confidence coefficient is not the probability that [the value] lies within the lonely interval we observed. Rather, it is the long run frequency with which various and varied CIs would cover the unknown value .... Confidence pertains not to any specific interval estimate, but to the process for constructing CIs").

99. D. BARNES, *supra* note 19, at 258.

The table would be a bit more complex than Figure 15-7. In this instance, the statistician could use a table that distinguished between one-tailed and two-tailed tests. That distinction is explained in the next section on hypothesis testing. For now it is sufficient to state that in the present hypothetical, the statistician might employ a two-tailed test. The table would be similar to Figure 15-7 in that the statistician would read degrees of freedom down the left-hand, vertical margin and significance levels along the top, horizontal margin. Reading left to right, on the top of the table the statistician first finds the significance level .05 for two-tailed tests. Since the sample size is 15, the degrees of freedom are 14 (n, 15, minus one). Therefore, the statistician next locates 14 degrees of freedom on the left-hand margin. The intersection of the two columns is 2.145, the critical t score for this estimation.

The statistician can now apply the formula:

$$\overline{X} \pm \left(t \cdot s_{\overline{X}}\right)$$

Substituting for the variables, the formula becomes

$$\mu = 3.67 \pm (21.4 \cdot .88) = 3.67 \pm 1.89$$

The common interpretation of a confidence interval would be that there is a 95% probability that the true number of minorities per panel (the population parameter or mean) lies within the interval 3.67 minorities per panel plus or minus 1.89 minorities.

§ 15-4(B). Legal Restrictions on Parameter Estimates.

The courts have accepted the validity of the statistical techniques used in estimating parameters.[100] We have already seen that the courts have recognized Z and t statistics, and they acknowledge the validity of the formulae for computing the sample mean, the sample standard deviation, the standard error of the sample mean, and the confidence interval. So long as the sampling is conducted properly, parameter estimates are admissible.[101]

The most fruitful attacks on the admissibility of parameter estimates are usually on the preliminary sampling process. Especially when samples were used to determine public opinions such as public hostility toward a criminal defendant,

---

100. *Id.*

101. Guardians Ass'n of New York City Police Dep't, Inc. v. Civil Serv., 633 F.2d 232 (2d Cir. 1980), *aff'd,* 463 U.S. 582 (1983). *See also* Davis & Abbott, *How to Use Expert Public Opinion Testimony*, 35 PRAC. LAW. 21 (Dec. 1989); Ostberg & Christopher, *Survey Evidence: A Lawyer's Secret Weapon*, 22 TRIAL 74 (Nov. 1986).

the early courts frequently excluded the sample evidence on hearsay grounds.[102] However, the contemporary view is that the hearsay objection is unsound; the respondents' answers are either nonhearsay or exceptionally admissible as declarations of state of mind or under the residual exception.[103] The Advisory Committee Note to Federal Rule of Evidence 703 states that contemporary courts focus on "the validity of the techniques employed rather than [on] relatively fruitless inquiries whether hearsay is involved."[104]

However, the proponent must lay a proper foundation for the sample. Many courts assert that a complete foundation includes evidence that: The population was properly defined; a representative sample was selected; the questions were phrased in a clear, non-leading fashion; competent interviewers used sound interviewing procedures; and the data was accurately recorded.[105] The proponent has the burden on each foundational element.[106] A successful attack on any element of the foundation may lead to the exclusion of the sample.[107]

By way of example, a court may exclude the sample if the statistician chooses the wrong population. Suppose that the defendant claims discrimination in jury selection. "In recent years ... a number of courts have accepted the prosecution's argument that the proper comparison is between the percentage of majority jurors and the percentage of minorities among the population eligible for jury service, not the population as a whole."[108] If the statistician does not limit the sample to

---

102. Ziesel, *The Uniqueness of Survey Evidence*, 45 CORN. L.Q. 322 (1960); Note, *Public Opinion Surveys as Evidence: The Pollsters Go to Court*, 66 HARV. L. REV. 498 (1953); Annot., 76 A.L.R.2D 619 (1961).

103. Brokerage Concepts, Inc. v. U.S. Healthcare, Inc., 140 F.3d 494, 516 n.14 (3d Cir. 1998) (the residual hearsay exception, now codified in Federal Rule of Evidence 807); Opuki-Boateng v. State of Cal., 95 F.3d 1461 (9th Cir. 1996) (invoking the residual hearsay exception codified in Federal Rule of Evidence 803(24)), *cert. denied*, 520 U.S. 1228 (1997); Prudential Ins. Co. v. Gibraltar Fin. Corp., 694 F.2d 1150, 1156 (9th Cir. 1982), *cert. denied*, 463 U.S. 1208 (1983); Lubbock Radio Paging v. Southwestern Bell Tel., 607 S.W.2d 29, 32 (Tex. Civ. App. 1980).

104. Brokerage Concepts, Inc. v. U.S. Healthcare, Inc., 140 F.3d 494, 516 n.14 (3d Cir. 1998) ("generally accepted survey principles").

105. Toys R Us, Inc. v. Canarsie Kiddie Shop, Inc., 559 F. Supp. 1189, 1205 (E.D.N.Y. 1983); Liberty Fin. Mgt. Co. v. Beneficial Data Processing Corp., 670 S.W.2d 40 (Mo. App. 1984). For lists of foundational elements, *see* Lutheran Mut. Life Ins. Co. v. United States, 816 F.2d 376, 378 (8th Cir. 1987) (citing HANDBOOK OF RECOMMENDED PROCEDURES FOR THE TRIAL OF PROTRACTED CASES, 25 F.R.D. 351, 429 (1960)); Inc. Pub. Corp. v. Manhattan Magazine, Inc., 616 F. Supp. 370, 390 (S.D.N.Y. 1985), *aff'd*, 788 F.2d 3 (2d Cir. 1986).

106. National Football League Properties, Inc. v. Wichita Falls Sportswear, Inc., 532 F. Supp. 651 (W.D. Wash. 1982).

107. *E.g.*, Ways & Means, Inc. v. IVAC Corp., 506 F. Supp. 697 (N.D. Cal. 1979), *aff'd on other grounds*, 638 F.2d 143 (9th Cir.), *cert. denied*, 454 U.S. 895 (1981); Washington v. Vogel, 880 F. Supp. 1545, 1547 (M.D. Fla. 1995) ("unrepresentative").

108. Beale, *Integrating Statistical Evidence and Legal Theory to Challenge the Selection of Grand and Petit Jurors*, 46 L. & CONT. PROB. 269, 271 (Autumn 1983).

eligible persons, the court may exclude the sample on the ground of an incorrect comparison.[109]

In some cases, courts have barred samples when in the court's judgment, the sample was too small to yield reliable statistics.[110] The courts have also excluded

---

109. Note, *Statistics in the Law: Potential Problems in the Presentation of Statistical Evidence*, 40 WASH. & LEE L. REV. 313, 317, 328 (1983). E.E.O.C. v. American Airlines, 48 F.3d 164, 172-73 (5th Cir. 1995). *See also* Tinker v. Sears, Roebuck & Co., 127 F.3d 519, 524 (6th Cir. 1997) ("the statistical evidence is rendered suspect when the sample includes persons leaving their employment under incentive programs or to take new jobs"); Forehand v. Florida State Hosp. at Chattahoochee, 89 F.3d 1562, 1574 (11th Cir. 1996) ("the 'proper comparison'"); Engineering Contractors Ass'n v. Metro Dade County, 943 F. Supp. 1546 (S.D. Fla. 1996) (the relevant pool), *aff'd*, 122 F.3d 895 (11th Cir. 1997), *cert. denied*, (1998). E.E.O.C. v. United Ass'n of Journeymen, Apprentices, 9 F. Supp. 2d 836, 844 (N.D. Ohio 1998) ("when special qualifications are required to fill particular jobs, 'comparisons to the general population (rather than to the smaller group of individuals who possess the necessary qualifications) may have little probative value"); N.A.A.C.P. v. Town of East Haven, 998 F. Supp. 176, 183 (D. Conn. 1998) ("the proper comparison [is] between the racial composition of [the at-issue jobs] and the racial composition of the qualified ... population in the relevant labor market"); Longariello v. School Bd. of Monroe County, Fla., 987 F. Supp. 1440, 1446 (S.D. Fla. 1997) ("Where plaintiffs use statistical evidence to challenge an employer's hiring practices, that evidence, to be probative of discriminatory intent, must compare the relevant portion of the employer's work force with the qualified portion in the relevant labor market"), *aff'd*, 161 F.3d 21 (11th Cir. 1998); BEW v. City of Chicago, 979 F. Supp. 693 (N.D. Ill. 1997) (the correct pool); Hiller v. County of Suffolk, 977 F. Supp. 202, 206 (E.D.N.Y. 1997) ("when special qualifications are required to fill particular jobs, comparisons to the general population may have little probative value").

110. Mayor of Philadelphia v. Educational Equality League, 415 U.S. 605, 620-21 (1974) (a sample of only 13 people); Brune v. BASF Corp., 41 F. Supp. 2d 768, 772-73 (S.D. Ohio 1999) ("a four person sample is statistically unreliable;" the court cites cases involving samples of 17 and 18 persons); Blue Cross & Blue Shield of N.J. v. Philip Morris, 36 F. Supp. 2d 560, 575 (E.D.N.Y. 1999) ("a large statistical base can be expected to yield more accurate results. 'In a large population, random variations tend to cancel each other out, yielding an overall observed distribution that is far more useful in evaluating correlations, relationships and probabilities'"); Barnett v. Technology Int., Inc., 1 F. Supp. 2d 572, 579 (E.D. Va. 1998) ("[G]iven that small changes in the numbers will have a potentially huge effect on the statistical showing[,] ... it [is] improper to rely on the results of statistical analyses which will involve too small a sample size," quoting Birkbeck v. Marvel Lighting Corp., 30 F.3d 507, 511 (4th Cir. 1994)); Reynolds v. Alabama Dept. of Transp., 996 F. Supp. 1156, 1191 (M.D. Ala. 1998) ("in general, statistical tests are more accurate when performed on large samples. In other words, a larger number of people in the sample pool will result in 'greater statistical power'"); Gray v. Robert Plan Corp., 991 F. Supp. 94, 104 (E.D.N.Y. 1998) ("statistical significance becomes harder to attain as the sample size shrinks"); Tinker v. Sears, Roebuck & Co., 127 F.3d 519, 524 (6th Cir. 1997) ("A sample which is too small can undermine the probative value of statistical evidence"; Tinker's "sample was only 13 employees"); Lewis v. Aerospace Community Credit Union, 114 F.3d 745, 750 (8th Cir. 1997) ("The sample size of three nonbargaining-unit employees over the age of fifty is simply too small independently to support a discrimination claim"; the court cites "Harper v. Trans World Airlines, 525 F.2d 409, 412 (8th Cir. 1975) (sample of five too small)"), *cert. denied*, 523 U.S. 1062 (1998); Shutt v. Sandoz Crop Protection Corp., 934 F.2d 186, 189 (9th Cir. 1991) (a group of only 11 employees; "here, there existed no necessity to employ a small group"), *cert. denied*, 503 U.S. 937

sample evidence on qualitative grounds. For example, courts have cited the following grounds for barring sampling data: The sample was not chosen at random;[111] the sample was designed or executed in a biased manner;[112] the

(1992); Frazier v. Consolidated Rail Corp., 851 F.2d 1447 (D.C. Cir. 1988) (small sample size); Simpson v. Midland-Ross Corp., 823 F.2d 937, 943 (6th Cir. 1987) (a 17-person sample); Hair v. Helena Chem. Co., 732 F. Supp. 1515, 1520 (E.D. Ark.) (the "statistical evidence is unreliable because of the small sample size. This small size detracts from the value of the evidence and is too small to give rise to any statistically reliable references"), *aff'd,* 915 F.2d 1579 (8th Cir. 1990); E.E.O.C. v. Carolina Freight Carriers Corp., 723 F. Supp. 734, 751 (S.D. Fla. 1989) ("The EEOC's focus on one terminal for a limited four-year period where only six driving positions were open is an inadequate sample to conduct a statistically significant study"); United States v. Lansdowne Swim Club, 713 F. Supp. 785, 809 (E.D. Pa. 1989) ("The Supreme Court has recognized that small sample size may detract from the value of statistical evidence. The danger posed by small samples is that they may produce short-term results that would not hold over the long run .... Recognizing this danger, a number of courts have invalidated or failed to give weight to statistics derived from small samples"), *aff'd,* 894 F.2d 83 (3d Cir. 1990); People v. Bell, 49 Cal. 3d 502, 527 n.14, (1989) ("Use of more complex tests than the absolute disparity method ... has been criticized ... when the [sample] is very small"), *cert. denied,* 495 U.S. 963 (1990); E.E.O.C. v. H.S. Camp & Sons, 542 F. Supp. 411 (M.D. Fla. 1982); Kelley v. American Heyer-Schulte Corp., 957 F. Supp. 873, 880 n.8 (W.D. Tex. 1997) ("Adequacy of a sample size is an important consideration in assessing the validity of a study, and the adequacy of a sample size must be viewed in terms of a specified level of statistical significance, the chance of missing a real effect, the estimated magnitude of disease risk, and the background rate of disease."); Fisher v. Vassar College, 66 F.3d 379, 404 (2d Cir. 1995) ("the small size of the 'hard' sciences sample"); Myree v. Local 41, IBEW, 789 F. Supp. 597, 611 (W.D.N.Y. 1992) ("'[S]mall or incomplete data sets ...' are 'typical examples' of unreliable statistical data."); Maidenbaum v. Bally's Park Place, Inc., 870 F. Supp. 1254, 1259 (D.N.J. 1994) (collecting cases holding sample sizes to be too small), *aff'd,* 67 F.3d 291 (3d Cir. 1995); W. CURTIS, *supra* note 21, at 114-15. *But see* E.E.O.C. v. Steamship Clerks Union, Local 1066, 48 F.3d 594, 604 (1st Cir.) ("'[e]ven small samples are not per se unacceptable'"), *cert. denied,* 516 U.S. 814 (1995). *See* Allen v. United States, 588 F. Supp. 247, 418 (D. Utah 1984), *rev'd,* 816 F.2d 1416 (10th Cir. 1987), *cert. denied,* 484 U.S. 1004 (1988); Pope, *Statistical Evidence as Proof of Causation,* DEF. COUNS. J., Apr. 1988, at 139 ("In Mayor v. Educational Equality League, the Supreme Court concluded that no significant findings could be based on a sample of 13 people. Other courts in employment discrimination cases also have refused to infer discrimination on the basis of statistical evidence when only small samples were examined"). *But see* Texpor Traders, Inc. v. Trust Company Bank, 720 F. Supp. 1100, 1105 n.2 (S.D.N.Y. 1989) ("The court takes judicial notice that in statistical analysis, using a well known mathematical theorem, viz., the Central Limit Theorem, a sample size of thirty or more is generally recognized as sufficient to guarantee normality of the distribution of sample means"); Freeman v. Package Mach. Co., 865 F.2d 1331, 1342 n.5 (1st Cir. 1988).

111. Wishard, *supra* note 91, at 317; Annot., 76 A.L.R.2D 619, 638-39 (1979); *In re* Chevron, U.S.A., Inc., 109 F.3d 1016 (5th Cir. 1997) (over 3,000 individuals filed personal injury, wrongful death, and property damage claims against Chevron for alleged soil contamination; the district judge developed a trial plan to resolve several common issues of liability; the plan entailed a hearing on 30 cases, 15 selected by each side; the court of appeals invalidated the plan; the court ruled that to be used as a basis for deciding common issues, the sample of cases "must be one that is a randomly selected, statistically significant" one).

phrasing of questions in the survey was leading[113] or the respondents knew the purpose of the survey;[114] the survey included ambiguous, undefined terms;[115] or the interviewers were unqualified.[116] However, the courts have been liberal in sustaining the qualifications of persons and organizations conducting sampling. In the past, they have accepted samples prepared by "advertising agencies, ... a college psychology department and the professors working in it, personnel of a college statistical laboratory and an industrial science research institution, an economist, ... an expert in marketing and marketing psychology, an expert pollster in a large industrial city, ... an independent statistical research organization, and psychological corporations."[117]

The courts will tolerate some flaws in sampling technique. Some courts assert that sample data can be reliable even if the sample is not drawn randomly.[118] They have accepted samples in which the data was obviously flawed[119] or incomplete.[120] As one court declared, "The conclusion that flaws in the data deprived it of any probative value is itself flawed."[121] Courts are increasingly exercising independent judgment in assessing the probative value of sampling evidence and holding that minor errors affect the weight, rather than the admissibility, of the evidence.[122]

---

112. *Id.* at 635-36; Wishard, *supra* note 91, at 319, 329; United States v. Local 560 of Int'l Bhd. of Teamsters, Inc., 780 F.2d 267, 277 (3d Cir. 1985), *cert. denied,* 476 U.S. 1140 (1986).

113. Hutchinson v. Essence Commun., Inc., 769 F. Supp. 541, 564-65 (S.D.N.Y. 1991); Blum, *Once Shunned Surveys Gain Favor of Courts,* NAT'L L.J., Oct. 30, 1995, p. A17 (in a Seventh Circuit case, Indianapolis Colts Inc. v. Metropolitan Baltimore Football Club L.P., 94-2578, Judge Posner faulted certain questions as loaded and slanted); American Home Products v. Proctor & Gamble Co., 871 F. Supp. 739, 761 (D.N.J. 1994) (even though certain questions were open-ended, their repetition was suggestive and leading).

114. Liberty Fin. Mgt. Co. v. Beneficial Data Processing Corp., 670 S.W.2d 40, 54 (Mo. App. 1984).

115. Porter v. United States, 409 F. Supp. 757 (Cust. Ct. 1976).

116. Wishard, *supra* note 91, at 319; Annot., 76 A.L.R.2D 619, 636 (1961).

117. Wishard, *supra* note 91, at 318-19.

118. Boehringer Ingelheim G.m.b.H. v. Pharmadyne Labs., 532 F. Supp. 1040 (D.N.J. 1980).

119. Detroit Police Officers Ass'n v. Young, 608 F.2d 671, 687 (6th Cir. 1979), *cert. denied,* 452 U.S. 938 (1981).

120. Clark v. Chrysler Corp., 673 F.2d 921, 926 (7th Cir. 1982), *cert. denied,* 459 U.S. 873 (1982).

121. Detroit Police Officers Ass'n v. Young, 608 F.2d 671, 687 (6th Cir. 1979), *cert. denied,* 452 U.S. 938 (1981).

122. International Bhd. of Teamsters v. United States, 431 U.S. 324, 340 (1977); Harolds Stores, Inc. v. Dillard Department Stores, 82 F.3d 1533, 1544 (10th Cir.) ("Technical and methodological deficiencies in the survey, including the sufficiency of the universe sampled, bear on the weight of the evidence, not the survey's admissibility"), *cert. denied*, 519 U.S. 928 (1996); McNeilab, Inc. v. American Home Prods. Corp., 848 F.2d 34, 38 (2d Cir. 1988) (survey admissible notwithstanding defendant's challenges to the use of leading questions and the interpretation of the test results; the limitations affected only the weight of the evidence); Chase Fed. Sav. & Loan

§ 15-5. Inferential Statistics — Hypothesis Testing.

The last section discussed the use of expected values to estimate the parameters of a population; the estimation techniques allow the statistician to draw reliable inferences about the population from data about the sample. Expected values have another important use in inferential statistics. By contrasting the observed values with the expected values that should be generated by random chance, the statistician can assess whether the difference between the expected and observed values is a product of random chance.[123] If the difference between the observed and expected values is too great, for example, if the disparity between the observed number of minority jurors and the expected number is too substantial, the statistician can infer that some other factor, perhaps discrimination, accounts for the observed values.[124] The process of deciding whether to draw such an inference is known as hypothesis testing. The purpose of hypothesis testing is to determine whether random chance adequately explains the observed values. There are several techniques for hypothesis testing.

§ 15-5(A). Standard Deviation.

At least when a population is normally distributed, the statistician can predict the percentage of values that should fall within a particular number of standard deviations from the mean. Sixty-eight percent of the observations ought to fall

---

Ass'n v. Chase Manhattan Fin. Servs., 681 F. Supp. 771 (S.D. Fla. 1987) (survey admissible despite failure to properly define universe in the survey); Consumers Union of U.S., Inc. v. New Regina Corp., 664 F. Supp. 753, 768-69 (S.D.N.Y. 1987) ("Technical deficiencies in surveys conducted by reputable professionals usually go to the weight to be accorded the survey results rather than to its admissibility"); *See also* Hutchinson v. Essence Commun., Inc., 769 F. Supp. 541, 564-65 (S.D.N.Y. 1991).

123. Harolds Stores, Inc. v. Dillard Department Stores, 82 F.3d 1533, 1544 (10th Cir.) ("Technical and methodological deficiencies in the survey, including the sufficiency of the universe sampled, bear on the weight of the evidence, not the survey's admissibility"), *cert. denied*, 519 U.S. 928 (1996); Daniels v. Pipefitters Ass'n Local Union No. 597, 945 F.2d 906, 923-24 (7th Cir. 1991) (the expert "concluded that the probability that this disparity in referrals would arise by chance was less than one in a trillion ..."), *cert. denied*, 503 U.S. 951 (1992); Bouman v. Block, 940 F.2d 1211, 1225 n.1 (9th Cir.) ("For example, plaintiff's expert showed that the violations of the 80 percent rule were significant at the .05 level. This means that the disparate success rates of men and women 'would be the result of chance only one time in twenty'"), *cert. denied*, 502 U.S. 1005 (1991); Silver v. City University of New York, 767 F. Supp. 494, 498 (S.D.N.Y.) ("The purpose of statistical evidence in employment discrimination cases is to analyze differences between actual employment data and projections of what would exist in the absence of discrimination. When differences between actual and projected values grow great enough, the likelihood that the difference is merely due to chance diminishes"), *aff'd*, 947 F.2d 1021 (2d Cir. 1991); Allen v. United States, 588 F. Supp. 247, 416-17 (D. Utah 1984), *rev'd*, 816 F.2d 1417 (10th Cir. 1987), *cert. denied*, 484 U.S. 1004 (1988); W. CURTIS, *supra* note 21, at 117.

124. Smith & Abram, *supra* note 16, at 40; Silver v. City University of New York, 767 F. Supp. 494, 498 (S.D.N.Y.), *aff'd*, 947 F.2d 1021 (2d Cir. 1991).

within one standard deviation, 95.4% within two deviations, 99.7% within three deviations, and 99.99% within four standard deviations.[125] This technique is sometimes used as a rough method of hypothesis testing. If, for instance, the observed number of minority jurors is more than two standard deviations away from the expected number of minority jurors, some would be inclined to treat that as proof there is a 95% likelihood that some factor other than random, innocent chance accounts for the inordinately small number of minority jurors.[126]

However, our reviewer, Professor Kaye, states that treating standard deviations in this fashion rests on a misinterpretation of a significance level. In his view, the statistician should report only the probability that an observed value would arise for an assumed mean (the null hypothesis). If, for instance, the number of minority jurors follows a normal distribution and the expected number (the mean) corresponds to the proportion in the population at large, and the observed number is two standard deviations from the expected number, the statistician may report that *if* the number hypothesis is true, the probability of such a large discrepancy is only 5%. However, the statistician cannot specify the probability that the null hypothesis is true given the observed discrepancy. He or she can only calculate the probability of so large a discrepancy if the null hypothesis is true. When that probability is very small, it may be reasonable to conclude that the null hypothesis is small — because if it were true, the observed discrepancy would be very uncommon.

The Supreme Court employed the standard deviation technique as a method of hypothesis testing in a famous jury discrimination case, *Castaneda v. Partida.*[127] The case arose in a county in Texas. In that county, 79.1% of the population was Mexican-American. During the period in question, 870 persons had been summoned as grand jurors. Only 339 were Mexican-Americans. The Court accepted the use of binomial probabilities to estimate the number of Mexican-

125. D. Barnes, *supra* note 19, at 140; Ottavani v. State University of New York, 875 F.2d 365, 372 n.7 (2d Cir. 1989) ("two standard deviations corresponds roughly to a 1 in 20 chance that the outcome is a random fluctuation. Three standard deviations corresponds to approximately a 1 in 384 chance of randomness. Finally, a range of four to five standard deviations corresponds to a probability range of 1 chance in 15,786 to 1 chance in 1,742,160"), *cert. denied,* 493 U.S. 1021 (1990); Bouman v. Block, 940 F.2d 1211, 1225 n.1 (9th Cir.), *cert. denied*, 502 U.S. 1005 (1991); United States v. Warren, 759 F. Supp. 355, 360-61 (E.D. Mich. 1991); Lopez v. Laborers Int'l Union Local No. 18, 987 F.2d 1210 (5th Cir. 1993).

126. W. Curtis, *supra* note 21, at 72; Waisome v. Port Auth. of New York & New Jersey, 758 F. Supp. 171, 175-76 (S.D.N.Y.) ("The greater the number of standard deviations, the less likely it is that chance is the cause of any difference between the expected and observed results"), *rev'd,* 948 F.2d 1370, 1376 (2d Cir. 1991) ("Standard deviation analysis measures the probability that a result is a random deviation from the predicted result — the more standard deviations the lower the probability the result is a random one"); Kincade v. Firestone Tire & Rubber Co., 694 F. Supp. 368, 381 (M.D. Tenn. 1987).

127. 430 U.S. 482 (1977).

Americans who should have been summoned by random chance. The Court stated that "[g]iven that 79.1% of the population is Mexican-American, the expected number of Mexican-Americans among the 870 persons summoned to serve as grand jurors over the 11-year period is approximately 688." The Court found that the standard deviation "is approximately 12." The Court then stated:

> As a general rule for large samples, if the difference between the expected value and the observed number is greater than two or three standard deviations, then the hypothesis that the jury drawing was random would be suspect to a social scientist. The 11-year data here reflect a difference between the expected and observed number of Mexican-Americans of approximately 29 standard deviations.[128]

Barnes has reconstructed the Court's statistical reasoning into a nine-step process. Note that Barnes uses a special formula, $\sigma = \sqrt{N \times P_1 \times P_2}$ to compute the standard deviation for a binomial distribution. As Barnes defines P_2, it is algebraically equivalent to $(1-P_1)$. The formula for the standard deviation for a binomial distribution is sometimes stated in these terms: $\sigma = \sqrt{N \times P_1 \times (1-P)}$. With that formula in mind, Barnes' description of the Court's reasoning is self-explanatory:

Step 1. Find N. N is the size of the group which is the result of discrimination. In *Castaneda,* N is the number of people in the jury pool for the 11-year period, 870. The jury pool is the "group of suspect composition" because we suspect there was discrimination in selecting the members of this group.

Step 2. Find P_1. P_1 is the underlying percentage of the allegedly discriminated-against group in the population. In *Castaneda* 79.1% of the population was Spanish-surnamed, so $P_1 = .791$.

Step 3. Find P_2. P_2 is the percentage of the underlying population not in P_1. In *Castaneda,* P_2 is the percentage of non-Spanish-surnamed people, so P_2 equals 1 minus .791, or .209.

Step 4. Find the number of the allegedly discriminated-against group you would expect to find in the group of suspect composition if there were no discrimination. The expected number is always P_1 times N. In *Castaneda* we would expect .791 times 870 Spanish-surnamed people in the jury pool if the jury pool reflected the underlying population, so the expected number is 688.

Step 5. Find the number of the allegedly discriminated-against group you actually observed in the group of suspected composition. You would find this as part of the discovery process. The

---

128. *Id.* at 496 n.17.

Castaneda opinion reports that 339 Spanish-surnamed people were actually chosen for this group, so the observed number is 339.

Step 6. Calculate the disparity by subtracting the expected number from the observed number. In *Castaneda* 339 minus 688 is minus 349, so the disparity is –349 people. The minus sign indicates an underrepresentation.

Step 7. Calculate one standard deviation by the formula $SD = \sqrt{N \times P_1 \times P_2}$. In *Castaneda* this figure amounts to $\sqrt{870 \times .791 \times .209} = 12$, so one standard deviation is 12 people.

Step 8. Calculate the number of standard deviations the observed is from the expected by dividing the disparity by 12 people in one standard deviation: –349/12 equals –29. The observed number is 29 standard deviations below what we expected.

Step 9. Compare the calculated number of standard deviations to the two-or-three-standard-deviations guideline. For *Castaneda* 29 is greater than two or three, so we suspect that the jury pool members were selected discriminatorily.[129]

---

129. D. Barnes, *supra* note 19, at 91-92. Reprinted by permission of Little, Brown, and Company, Inc. Maddow v. Proctor & Gamble, Inc., 107 F.2d 846, 852 (11th Cir. 1997) (3.83 standard deviations). African-American Voting Rights v. State of Mo., 994 F. Supp. 1105, 1117 (E.D. Mo. 1997) ("the basic statistical tool of standard deviations"). Proof of three standard deviations is not invariably required. Ottavani v. State University of New York, 875 F.2d 365, 372 (2d Cir. 1989) ("several courts have accepted two standard deviations as prima facie proof of discrimination. 'Most courts and commentators have accepted the .05 level,' or 1 in 20 probability, as indicative of statistical significance. [W]e reject ... a formal 'litmus' test for assessing the legitimacy of Title VII claims"), *cert. denied,* 493 U.S. 1021 (1990). Rendon v. AT & T Technologies, 883 F.2d 388, 398 (5th Cir. 1989) ("Two standard deviations are ... sufficient to establish liability in our sister circuits"); Gay v. Waiters & Dairy Lunchmen's Union, 694 F.2d 531, 551 (9th Cir. 1982) ("courts should be extremely cautious of drawing any inferences from standard deviations in the range of 1 to 3"); Berger v. Iron Workers Reinforced Rodmen Local 201, 843 F.2d 1395, 1412 (D.C. Cir. 1988) ("Under this circuit's precedent, in most instances a difference of just under two standard deviations has been deemed sufficient to establish a prima facie case"), *cert. denied*, 490 U.S. 1105 (1989); E.E.O.C. v. Jordan Graphics, Inc., 769 F. Supp. 1357, 1383 (W.D.N.C. 1991) ("The Fourth Circuit has cautioned against attaching significance to standard deviations between one and three"); Groves v. Alabama State Bd. of Educ., 776 F. Supp. 1518, 1527 (M.D. Ala. 1991) ("Although no particular number of standard deviations automatically translates into a finding of disparate impact, a difference between the observed and expected values of more than three standard deviations is usually recognized as statistically significant — in other words, adequate to support an inference that a racially differential selection pattern is a consequence of the challenged practice rather than a random distribution"); Santiago v. Miles, 774 F. Supp. 775, 799 (W.D.N.Y. 1991) ("Federal cases have recognized that statistical differences greater than two or three standard deviations provide an acceptable basis to infer discrimination"); Daines v. Mankato, 754 F. Supp. 681 (D. Minn. 1990) (2.71 to 3.11 standard deviations); Chicago

Following the Supreme Court lead, many lower courts approved of similar uses of the standard deviation. The courts have accepted the technique in civil actions alleging discriminatory employment practices[130] and post– *Castaneda* criminal cases in which the defense challenged the method of jury selection.[131] Defense attorneys have also employed the technique in attempts to establish that prosecutors have used peremptory challenges for discriminatory purposes.[132]

§ 15-5(B). Z and t Statistics.

The statistician can use Z and t statistics in hypothesis testing. *Castaneda* employed a Z statistic. When a statistician uses the statistics for this purpose, the testing proceeds through six stages.

Fire Fighters Local No. 2 v. Washington, 736 F. Supp. 923, 930 (N.D. Ill. 1990) ("a difference of greater than two or three standard deviations between the expected percentage and the observed percentage of minorities in a relevant labor pool can be sufficient to support an inference of discrimination"), *aff'd*, 962 F.2d 1269 (7th Cir. 1992), *cert. denied*, 510 U.S. 908 (1993); Richardson v. Lamar Cty. Bd. of Educ., 729 F. Supp. 806, 816 (M.D. Ala. 1989) ("There is no set mathematical threshold that must be met ..."), *aff'd*, 935 F.2d 1240 (11th Cir. 1991); Rossini v. Ogilvy & Mather, Inc., 615 F. Supp. 1520, 1527 (S.D.N.Y. 1985), *rev'd on other grounds*, 798 F.2d 590 (2d Cir. 1986); Palmer v. Shultz, 662 F. Supp. 1551 (D.D.C. 1987) (in a two-tailed test, 1.96 standard deviations suffices while 1.645 standard deviations are needed in a one-tailed test), *aff'd in part, rev'd in part sub nom.* Palmer v. Baker, 905 F.2d 1544 (D.C. Cir. 1990); Shuford v. Alabama State Bd. of Educ., 897 F. Supp. 1535, 1566 (M.D. Ala. 1995) ("As a general rule, a disparity greater than two or three standard deviations establishes a prima facie case of discrimination"); E.E.O.C. v. Sheet Metal Workers' Intern., 889 F. Supp. 642, 660 (S.D.N.Y. 1995) ("When a disparity is represented by two or more units of standard deviation, there is less than a five percent chance that the variation occurred randomly, and social scientists and courts commonly deem the disparity statistically significant"), *aff'd in part, rev'd in part*, 81 F.3d 1162 (2d Cir.), *cert. denied*, 519 U.S. 945 (1996).

130. Harrell v. Northern Elec. Co., 672 F.2d 444, 446 n.4 (5th Cir.), *modified*, 679 F.2d 31 (5th Cir.), *cert. denied*, 459 U.S. 1037 (1982); Wilmore v. City of Wilmington, 533 F. Supp. 844, 853 n.24 (D. Del. 1982), *rev'd*, 699 F.2d 667 (3d Cir. 1983); Jones v. Pepsi-Cola Metropolitan Bottling Co., Inc., 871 F. Supp. 305 (E.D. Mich. 1994); Beggs, *Novel Expert Evidence in Federal Civil Rights Litigation*, 45 AMER. U. L. REV. 1, 4-5 (1995).

131. Boykins v. Maggio, 715 F.2d 995, 996 (5th Cir. 1983), *cert. denied*, 466 U.S. 940 (1984); Ford v. Commonwealth, 665 S.W.2d 304, 307 (Ky. 1983), *cert. denied*, 469 U.S. 984 (1984).

132. Edwards v. Thigpen, 682 F. Supp. 1374 (S.D. Miss. 1987), *aff'd*, 849 F.2d 204 (5th Cir. 1988), *cert. denied*, 489 U.S. 1059 (1989). *See also* Geressy v. Digital Equip. Corp., 980 F. Supp. 640 (E.D.N.Y. 1997) (Judge Weinstein adapted the two standard deviation norm to the evaluation of awards of damages for pain and suffering; if the defendant claims that the award is excessive, the judge considers a pool of awards in similar cases and then reduces awards that stray more than two standard deviations from the mean), *aff'd in part*, 152 F.3d 919 (2d Cir. 1998); Higgins, *Homogenized Damages: Judge Suggests Using Statistical Norms to Determine Whether Pain and Suffering Awards Are Excessive*, 83 A.B.A. J. 22 (Sep. 1997); Brienza, *Putting a Price on Pain Can Be More Objective, Federal Judge Says*, TRIAL, Sept. 1997, at 14.

Establishing Null and Alternative Hypotheses

At the outset, the statistician constructs two hypotheses: the null hypothesis, H_o, and the alternate hypothesis, H_a. The hypotheses are assumptions about values of unknown parameters of the population.[133] The null hypothesis "means nothing unusual is going on ... and the results could have occurred by chance."[134] The null hypothesis represents the expected value that should obtain if the values were determined by chance. Suppose, for example, that the minority population in a county represents 50% of the population. If there is no discrimination in petit jury selection and the jury selection is chosen randomly in the long term, 50% of jury panel members would be minority persons. Since in this county there are 20 members on each panel, the null hypothesis would be

$$H_o : \mu = 10$$

On the average (the mean), there should be ten minority jurors on each panel. The alternative hypothesis would be

$$H_o : \mu = 10$$

However, the hypotheses can be formulated even more specifically. Under the substantive law, a client may be entitled to relief only if he can show that minorities are discriminated against. Thus, we would really be interested in learning only whether minorities are underrepresented on the panels. Hence, the pivotal question is whether the mean is ten or fewer. If there are ten or more minority members on each panel, there is little evidence of discrimination against minorities. For that reason, the null hypothesis can be rephrased:

$$H_o : \mu > 10$$

The symbol > means equal to or greater than. Similarly, the alternative hypothesis would be

$$H_o : \mu < 10$$

The symbol < indicates that the alternative hypothesis is that the mean is fewer than 10 minority members on each panel. The symbol, > or <, points toward the smaller figure.

In the section on estimating parameters, one- and two-tailed tests were mentioned. This test is one-tailed. We are interested in determining solely whether the mean falls at one end of the distribution, underrepresentation of minorities. In a two-tailed test, we are interested in determining whether the

---

133. W. CURTIS, *supra* note 21, at 119.

134. J. LOEWEN, *supra* note 17, at 223; Allard v. Indiana Bell Telephone Co., 1 F. Supp. 2d 898, 907 (S.D. Ind. 1998).

mean differs from a particular value; and it is immaterial whether the mean is larger or smaller than that value. It would obviously make no sense to use a two-tailed test when at most a mean larger than 10 would prove a type of discrimination that did not entitle a client to relief. In the hypothetical, the only means probative of discrimination entitling our client to relief are those under 10.

Selecting Significance Level

There is a good deal of confusion about significance levels. For example, some authorities assert that the significance level measures the "strength of a scientist's confidence that she is right in rejecting the null hypothesis, for example, and asserting that some factor, perhaps discrimination, must be involved to explain the observed difference between two groups."[135] However, our reviewer, Professor Kaye, states that it is a mistake to equate the significance level with any degree of subjective belief on the statistician's part. Likewise, the significance level can be loosely described as a measurement of the likelihood that a finding did not occur by chance.[136] However, Professor Kaye cautions that this description is loose to the point of being wrong. A special variation of the significance level technique is sometimes referred to as the sign test.[137]

Three frequently used significance levels are .10, .05, and .01.[138] The choice of a level is essentially arbitrary, but "[i]t has become a convention in social sciences to accept as statistically significant values which have a probability of occurring by chance 5% of the time or less."[139] A 5% significance level means that the disparity observed should occur by chance only one out of twenty times.[140] If the significance level were 1% and the confidence level 99%, the observed value should occur by chance only one out of a hundred times.[141] Assume for hypothetical purposes that the statistician selects a .05 significance level.

---

135. *Id.* at 224.

136. *Id.* at 227.

137. *Id.* at 95.

138. C. McCormick, *supra* note 13, at §209. United States *ex rel.* Free v. Peters, 806 F. Supp. 705, 713 (N.D. Ill. 1992), *aff'd in part, rev'd in part*, 12 F.3d 700 (7th Cir. 1993), *cert. denied*, 513 U.S. 967 (1994).

139. Brown v. Delta Air Lines, Inc., 522 F. Supp. 1218, 1228 n.13 (S.D. Tex. 1980), *aff'd*, 673 F.2d 1325 (5th Cir. 1982).

140. Sobel v. Yeshiva Univ., 566 F. Supp. 1166, 1173 n.22 (S.D.N.Y. 1983), *rev'd*, 797 F.2d 1478 (2d Cir. 1986), *cert. denied*, 490 U.S. 1105 (1989); Bouman v. Block, 940 F.2d 1211, 1225 n.1 (9th Cir.), *cert. denied*, 502 U.S. 1005 (1991).

141. Sobel v. Yeshiva Univ., 566 F. Supp. 1166, 1173 n.22 (S.D.N.Y. 1983), *aff'd*, 673 F.2d 1325 (5th Cir. 1982, *rev'd*, 797 F.2d 1478 (2d Cir. 1986), *cert. denied*, 490 U.S. 1105 (1989). *See also* Smith & Abram, *supra* note 16, at 41, 52.

Specifying Test Statistic

If the statistician can plausibly assume that the values will be distributed normally, the statistician can use either a Z or t statistic. If the degrees of freedom exceed 30, the statistician will employ the Z statistic. In this context of hypothesis testing, the degrees of freedom are (n – 1); thus, if the set of data includes 31 or more elements, the Z statistic is appropriate. If the set is smaller, the statistician might resort to the t statistic. In our hypothetical, assume that we have data for minority representation on 15 jury panels. Some would assert that since the hypothetical sample is small, the statistician could use the t statistic. (Again, our reviewer, Professor Kaye, states that the choice between a Z or t statistic turns on whether the population standard deviation is known. A Z test is correctly used only when the standard deviation is known.) To determine the critical t value, the statistician turns to the appropriate table.[142]

The test is one-tailed; we are concerned only with underrepresentation of minorities. The statistician reads across on the top margin of the table from left to right until he finds the .05 significance level for one-tailed tests. Since n is 15, the degrees of freedom on the left-hand margin are 14. The two columns would intersect at the t value of 1.761.

Formulating a Decision Rule

The decision rule is a statement about the action to be taken, that is, the acceptance or rejection of the null hypothesis.[143] The null hypothesis is rejected if there is too great a disparity between the expected or hypothesized minority representation and the observed minority representation. To visualize the decision process, we can divide the distribution into acceptance and rejection regions,[144] as in Figure 15-8.

In a one-tailed test such as our hypothetical, there would be only one rejection region. In a two-tailed test, there would be a rejection region at each end of the distribution. "For any given level of statistical significance, ... the two-tailed test has a smaller area of rejection at a given tail of the curve and thus requires a greater difference from the mean to qualify."[145]

The statistician uses the t value to define the border between the acceptance and rejection regions. To determine the overall size of the acceptance region, the statistician multiplies the t value, t_c, by the standard error of the sample mean, s_x. The formula is (t_c/s_x). One border of the region is set at the upper critical value, x_u; x_u is the sum of the expected or hypothesized value and (t_c/s_x).The lower

---

142. *E.g.*, D. BARNES, *supra* note 19, at 258.

143. W. CURTIS, *supra* note 21, at 120.

144. *Id.* at 121.

145. N. CHANNELS, *supra* note 33, at 233.

critical value, x_l, is ascertained by subtracting (t_c/s_x) from the expected value.[146] In our hypothetical, the expected value is 10 minority members per panel. Figure 15-9 illustrates the distribution divided into two rejection regions by x_u and x_l for a two-tailed test.[147]

The procedure is similar for a one-tailed test. In a one-tailed test, the statistician is interested in a disparity in only one direction. In our hypothetical, we are concerned only if the mean is under 10 minority members per panel. When we are trying to prove reverse discrimination, again our test would be one-tailed; but we would be concerned only if the mean exceeds 10 minority members per panel. Depending on the nature of the inequality, the statistician defines the border of the one rejection region by adding or subtracting the product of the standard error and the t value, (t_c/s_x), from the expected value.[148]

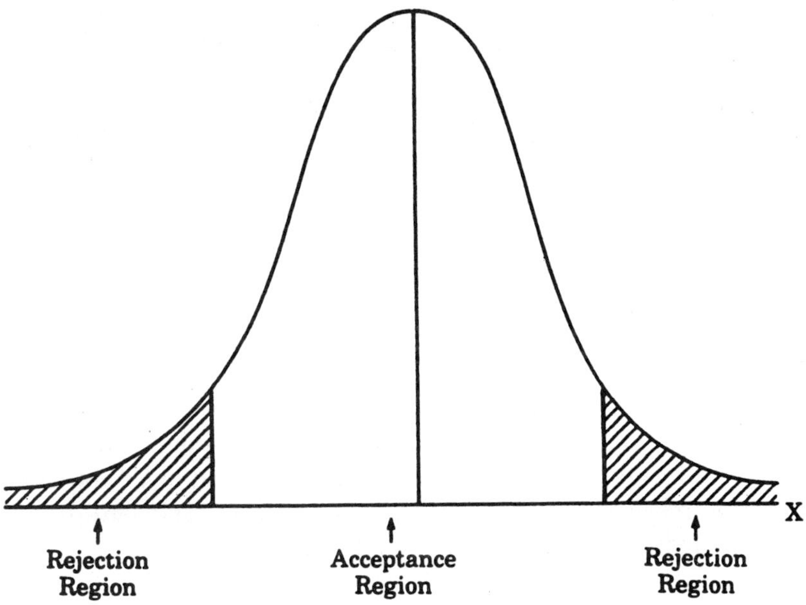

Figure 15-8

146. W. CURTIS, *supra* note 21, at 121.

147. *See* H. CASSIDY, USING ECONOMETRICS: A BEGINNER'S GUIDE 133-37 (1981).

148. In Palmer v. Shultz, 815 F.2d 84 (D.C. Cir. 1987), a sex discrimination suit, the court opted for a two-tailed test of statistical significance. The court stated that a one-tailed test addresses the question whether one group is favored over another. However, the court asserted that the hypothesis to be tested is whether the two groups are treated in the same fashion. The court concluded that a two-tailed test is preferable to test that hypothesis.

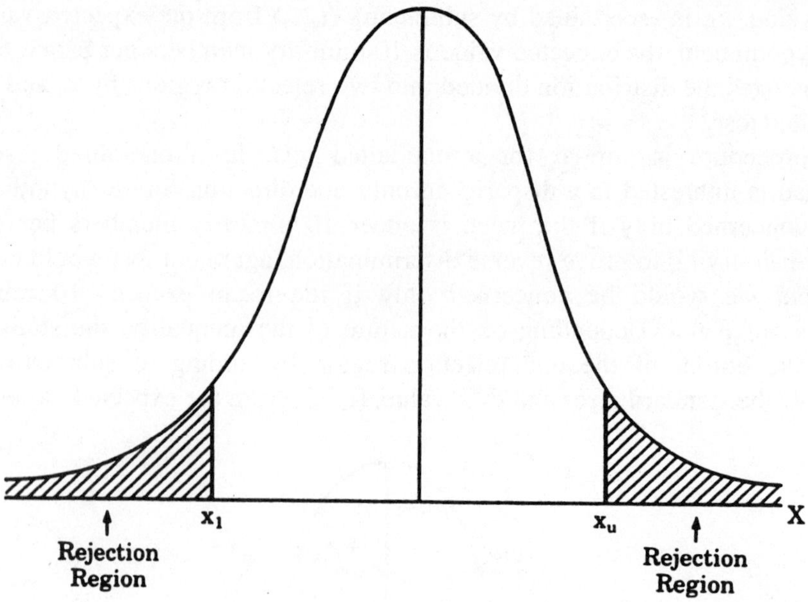

Figure 15-9

Selecting Sample Observations from Population and Computing Sample Statistics

The researcher resorts to sampling as he or she does in estimating parameters. The statistician calculates the sample mean, the sample standard deviation, and the standard error of the sample mean. In our hypothetical in § 15-4, we assumed that the sample mean was 3.67 minorities per panel, the standard deviation was 1.39, and the standard error of the sample mean was .88.

Accepting or Rejecting Null Hypothesis

The statistician next determines whether the sample statistic falls within the acceptance region. If it does, the statistician accepts the null hypothesis and concludes that the population parameter probably equals the hypothesized value. A small discrepancy between the expected value and the observed value in the sample can be attributed to chance. However, when the sample statistic falls in the rejection region, the statistician rejects the null hypothesis; the disparity is too large to be attributed to random chance.

In our hypothetical, the use of the above formulae results in a lower limit, x_1, of 8.45 minorities per panel. That is the border of the rejection region. However, the sample mean is only 3.67 minorities per panel. The sample statistic thus falls in the rejection region and necessitates rejecting the null hypothesis. The statistician concludes that the observed number of minorities per panel is statistically different from the expected or hypothesized number of 10 minorities per panel. The disparity is too great to be attributed to chance.[149]

There are two types of errors that the statistician might commit at this stage of hypothesis testing: Type I and Type II errors. A Type I error is the erroneous rejection of the null hypothesis. This is sometimes referred to as an alpha risk. A Type II error is the erroneous acceptance of the null hypothesis. This type of mistake is sometimes called a beta risk.[150]

The courts have admitted expert opinion testimony on hypothesis testing. In a leading case challenging racial discrimination in teacher hiring, *Hazelwood School District v. United States,*[151] the Supreme Court accepted such evidence. The Court approved the use of inferential statistics to establish that the disparity between the observed number of minority teachers and the expected number was not due to chance alone. The lower courts have followed the Court's lead, and their opinions often contain sophisticated discussions of the meaning of the various significance levels used in hypothesis testing.[152]

Although the admissibility of hypothesis testing techniques is well-settled, some authorities such as Professor Kaye have questioned the courts' routine,

149. The probability is that the data did not "result[] from 'the luck of the draw.'" Allard v. Indiana Telephone Co., Inc., 1 F. Supp. 2d 898, 907 (S.D. Ind. 1998). In reviewing this chapter, Professor Spitznagel pointed out one weakness in using this approach to the discrimination problem. In his words, "If I were an attorney attempting to lower minority representation in juries, I could defeat this hypothesis test by underrepresenting minorities but making sure that individual panels varied more than the binomial model allows. That would raise the standard error and drop the value of the t statistic. Rather than the t-test, I would favor a simple binomial that looks at all panels combined. That test would pick up a much smaller difference, and one could also look at unusual types of spread." Notwithstanding this weakness, the authors chose to retain the hypothesis testing example because it does illustrate all the essential steps in testing.

150. T. Wonnacott & R. Wonnacott, *supra* note 31, at 255; Radford, *Statistical Error and Legal Error: Type One and Two Type Errors and the Law*, 21 Loy. L.A. L. Rev. 843, 851-52 (1988).

151. 433 U.S. 299 (1977).

152. Alston v. Manson, 791 F.2d 255 (2d Cir. 1986), *cert. denied,* 479 U.S. 1084 (1987) (statistical decision theory); Moultrie v. Martin, 690 F.2d 1078, 1083 (4th Cir. 1982); United States v. Georgia Power Co., 474 F.2d 906 (5th Cir. 1973); Allard v. Indiana Bell Telephone Co., Inc., 1 F. Supp. 2d 898, 907-08 (S.D. Ind. 1998); Boston Chapter, NAACP, Inc. v. Beecher, 371 F. Supp. 507 (D. Mass.), *aff'd,* 504 F.2d 1017 (1st Cir. 1974), *cert. denied,* 421 U.S. 910 (1975); Chance v. Board of Exmrs., 330 F. Supp. 203 (S.D.N.Y. 1971), *aff'd,* 458 F.2d 1167 (2d Cir. 1972); W. Curtis, *supra* note 21, at 137-40. The lower court opinion, Alston v. Lopes, 621 F. Supp. 992 (D. Conn. 1985), *aff'd,* 791 F.2d 255 (2d Cir. 1986), *cert. denied,* 479 U.S. 1084 (1987), also approves of the use of statistical decision theory. A Woman's Choice – East Side Women's Clinic v. Newman, 904 F. Supp. 1434, 1455 n.10 (S.D. Ind. 1995) ("All of these data were significant at a level of at least 95 percent, and most to higher degrees of significance. *See* Pl. Ex. 4 (values of '*p*' ranging from less than 0.05 to less than 0.0001)").

uncritical acceptance of such evidence. Moreover, the sufficiency of hypothesis testing evidence to sustain the proponent's initial burden of going forward is a controversial issue.[153] Even if the evidence is admissible, it might be legally insufficient to support a required finding. For instance, in civil toxic tort cases, can the plaintiff defeat a summary judgment or directed verdict motion without epidemiological studies that find a causal link that is statistically significant at the 0.05 (or 5%) level?[154] Or, should the burden of proof in criminal cases be equated with a significance level of .05 (or 5%), thereby seemingly assuring 95% probability of guilt? Professor Kaye has addressed this question:

> The difficulty is that this interpretation of the result of the hypothesis testing is wrong. The test was structured so as to retain the null hypothesis unless the chance of getting the evidence under the hypothesis fell below 5%. The test focused exclusively on the probability of the evidence given the null hypothesis. Nothing was said about the probability of the hypothesis in light of the experimental evidence. It may be tempting to call the probability of 0.055 the chance of a coincidence, and to say that the probability of something other than a coincidence — of foul play — must be what is left over, namely 0.945. But this only shows that one can "prove" anything with words. The more precise mathematical notation makes it plain that the burden of persuasion refers to one probability — Pr (Alternative hypothesis/Evidence) — while the hypothesis test looks to another — Pr (Evidence/Null hypothesis).[155]

---

153. Kaye, *Statistical Significance and the Burden of Persuasion*, 46 LAW & CONTEMP. PROBS. 13 (Autumn 1983).

154. *Compare* DeLuca v. Merrell Dow Pharmaceuticals, 922 F.2d 941, 955 (3d Cir. 1990) ("the confidence level or 'significance' of a statistical analysis is but a part of a meaningful evaluation of [the] reliability" of an epidemiological study), Christophersen v. Allied-Signal Corp., 902 F.2d 362 (5th Cir. 1990), *reh'g*, 939 F.2d 1106 (5th Cir. 1991), Werlein v. United States, 746 F. Supp. 887, 898-900 (D. Minn. 1990), and Longmore v. Merrell Dow Pharmaceuticals, Inc., 737 F. Supp. 1117, 119 (D. Idaho 1990) ("the scientific standard for determining causation is much stricter than the standard employed in this Court. While the epidemiologist may conclude that the observed association is insignificant, the 'certainty that the observed increase is related to its hypothetical cause rather than mere chance is still far more likely than not.' '[A] distinction exists between legal sufficiency and scientific certainty'"), *with* Brock v. Merrell Dow Pharmaceuticals, Inc., 874 F.2d 307 (5th Cir.), *modified*, 884 F.2d 166 (5th Cir. 1989), *cert. denied*, 494 U.S. 1046 (1990). *See also* Dore, *A Proposed Standard for Evaluating the Use of Epidemiological Evidence in Toxic Tort and Other Personal Injury Cases*, 28 HOW. L.J. 677 (1985); Feldman & Del Giorno, *Toxic-Tort Case: Court Eases Standard of Proof*, NAT'L L.J., Mar. 18, 1991, at 19; Nace, *Epidemiological Evidence: Its Use and Misuses in Toxic Tort Cases*, 24 TRIAL 62 (Oct. 1988); Nace & Bleakley, *How Much Evidence Is Enough?*, 26 TRIAL 38 (Aug. 1990); Roisman, *"Junk Law": Defense Attack on Causation*, 27 TRIAL 51 (Sep. 1991).

155. Kaye, *Statistical Significance and the Burden of Persuasion*, 46 LAW & CONTEMP. PROBS. 13, 22 (Autumn 1983).

In an article on the issue, Professor Kaye points out that social scientists borrowed the 0.05 convention from those "who were concerned primarily with problems in biology."[156] He argues that explicit testimony about hypothesis testing presents such grave dangers of confusion and distraction that it "should not survive a well-developed [Federal] Rule [of Evidence] 403 objection."[157]

In toxic tort cases, the issue is legal sufficiency rather than admissibility: Can the plaintiff defeat a summary judgment or directed verdict motion without epidemiological studies that find a causal link which is statistically significant at the 0.05 (or 5%) level?[158] Subsection 15–5(D) discusses epidemiology.

§ 15-5(C). Chi-Square Distribution.

Some hypothesis testing techniques, notably the use of Z statistics, rest on several assumptions, particularly the assumption that the sample comes from a normally distributed population.[159] When the necessary assumptions do not apply, those techniques cannot be used.[160] In that event, statisticians can use another parametric technique based on the actual population distribution or resort

---

156. Kaye, *Is Proof of Statistical Significance Relevant?*, 61 WASH. L. REV. 1333, 1343-44 (1986).

157. *Id.* at 1362. *See also* DeLuca v. Merrell Dow Pharmaceuticals, Inc., 911 F.2d 941, 955 (3d Cir. 1990) (citing Professor Kaye's article, the court stated that "a poorly conceived or conducted study that disproves the null hypothesis at a .01 level of significance may be far less reliable than a well conceived and conducted study that is significant at a .1 level").

158. *Compare* DeLuca v. Merrell Dow Pharmaceuticals, Inc., 911 F.2d 941, 955 (3d Cir. 1990) ("the confidence level or 'significance' of a statistical analysis is but a part of a meaningful evaluation of [the] reliability" of an epidemiological study), Christophersen v. Allied-Signal Corp., 902 F.2d 362 (5th Cir. 1990), *reh'g*, 939 F.2d 1106 (5th Cir. 1991), *cert. denied*, 503 U.S. 912 (1992), Werlein v. United States, 746 F. Supp. 887, 898-900 (D. Minn. 1990), *vacated in part*, 793 F. Supp. 898 (D. Minn. 1992) and Longmore v. Merrell Dow Pharmaceuticals, Inc., 737 F. Supp. 1117, 1119 (D. Idaho 1990) ("the scientific standard for determining causation is much stricter than the standard employed in this Court. While the epidemiologist may conclude that the observed association is insignificant, the 'certainty that the observed increase is related to its hypothetical cause rather than mere chance is still far more likely than not.' '[A] distinction exists between legal sufficiency and scientific certainty'") *with* Brock v. Merrell Dow Pharmaceuticals, Inc., 874 F.2d 307 (5th Cir.), *modified*, 884 F.2d 166 (5th Cir. 1989), *cert. denied*, 494 U.S. 1046 (1990). *See also* Dore, *A Proposed Standard for Evaluating the Use of Epidemiological Evidence in Toxic Tort and other Personal Injury Cases*, 28 HOW. L.J. 677 (1985); Feldman & Del Giorno, *Toxic-Tort Case: Court Eases Standard of Proof*, NAT'L L.J., Mar. 18, 1991, at 19; Nace, *Epidemiological Evidence: Its Use and Misuses in Toxic Tort Cases*, 24 TRIAL 62 (Oct. 1988); Nace & Bleakley, *How Much Evidence Is Enough?*, 26 TRIAL 38 (Aug. 1990); Roisman, *"Junk Law": Defense Attack on Causation*, 27 TRIAL 51 (Sept. 1991).

159. W. CURTIS, *supra* note 21, at 141.

160. *Id.*

to nonparametric methods of hypothesis testing, including the chi-square distribution.[161]

The symbol for chi-square is x^2, the square of the Greek letter chi. The chi-square distribution makes no assumptions about the population from which the statistician draws the sample. The distribution's lower limit is zero, and it extends to infinity in the right-hand direction,[162] as illustrated by Figure 15-10. X^2 cannot have a negative value. As in the case of the binomial and normal distributions, the chi-square distribution compares the expected or presupposed frequencies to the observed frequency. The formula[163] for computing x^2 is

$$x^2 = n \sum \frac{(O_i - E_i)^2}{E_i}$$

In this formula, n is the number of elements in the sample, O is the observed frequency, and E is the expected frequency.[164] Barnes described the procedures for using the test in this fashion:

Step 1. Subtract the expected number from the observed number.
Step 2. Square the difference.
Step 3. Divide by the expected number.
Step 4. Add these values together to get the chi-square value.[165]

Chi-square can be used in hypothesis testing. Suppose, for example, that the issue is whether two variables or classifications are independent. Curtis gives an excellent illustration. Suppose that a criminal defense counsel hires a statistician to assist the attorney to select jurors.[166] The statistician surveys 400 local adults. One thing the defense attorney wants to learn is whether jurors associate the defendant's name with the crime he is charged with. In particular, the defense attorney wants to know whether male or female jurors are more likely to associate the defendant's name with the crime. The null hypothesis, then, is that the respondent's sex and name association are independent.[167] The alternative

---

161. *Id.*; N. CHANNELS, *supra* note 33, at 238 ("The chi-square statistic indicates whether there is a relationship between two variables ... greater than expected by chance alone. [T]his procedure begins with a null hypothesis of no association between the variables and, if rejected, leads to acceptance of the alternative that there exists a relationship that is not likely to be a mere fluke of sampling. [T]he chi-square does not indicate either the strength or direction of the association between the variables, only whether ... it is likely to have occurred by chance").

162. W. CURTIS, *supra* note 21, at 142.

163. *Id.*

164. Finkelstein, *The Application of Statistical Theory to the Jury Discrimination Cases*, 80 HARV. L. REV. 338, 366 (1966).

165. D. BARNES, *supra* note 19, at 173.

166. W. CURTIS, *supra* note 21, at 144.

167. *Id.* at 145.

hypothesis is that the person's sex affects the probability that he or she associates the defendant's name with the crime.

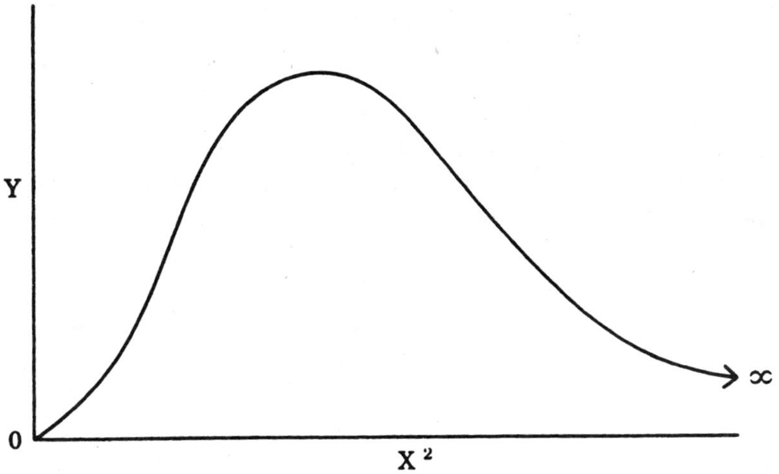

Figure 15-10

After conducting the sampling, the statistician displays the results in the following manner:

Response	Male	Female	Total
Yes	99	121	220
No	42	114	156
Total	141	235	376

These are the observed values. The figures reading across are said to be in rows. The figures reading down are said to be in columns. This format is called a contingency table.

What are the expected values to be contrasted with the observed values? If sex and name association are independent, "one would expect the proportion of 'yes' responses and the proportion of 'no' responses to be the same for both sexes."[168] On this assumption, the expected frequency for any classification, E_{ij}, would be the product of the total of the ith row and the jth column, divided by the sample size:

$$E_{ij} = \frac{t_{i+}t_{+j}}{n}$$

168. *Id.*

Thus, the expected number of 'yes' responses from males in the hypothetical would be:

$$E_{ij} = \frac{(220)\text{ times }(141)}{376} = 82.5$$

220/376 is the percent of yes responses in the total sample. That figure is multiplied by the number of males in the sample, 141.

After determining the observed and expected values, the statistician can use the chi-square formula. Since there are only two rows and two columns in the hypothetical, the statistician must employ a special correction factor to compute x^2.[169] In our hypothetical, x^2 would be 11.967.

To evaluate the significance of the x^2 score, the statistician now turns to a chi-square table.[170] The format of a chi-square table is very similar to a t statistic table such as Figure 15-7. The top, horizontal margin of the table represents the significance level. The vertical, left-hand margin represents degrees of freedom. For chi-square computations, the degrees of freedom are $(r-1)(c-1)$, that is, (the number of rows minus one) times (the number of columns minus one). In our hypothetical, the formula yields 1 degree of freedom, (2–1) times (2–1).[171]

Suppose that the statistician wants to test the null hypothesis at a .01 significance level. Finding that value in the top margin and 1 degree of freedom in the left margin, the statistician locates the intersection, 6.635. 6.635 is the chi-square value. "Since the calculated value of 11.967 is greater than the critical value, N_o (the null hypothesis) is rejected. It can be concluded that sex of respondent and association of the name of the defendant with the crime are not independent. Based on the results of the survey, males were much more likely to associate the defendant's name with the crime."[172]

Like the other hypothesis testing techniques, the chi-square formula has been accepted by the courts. Federal courts of appeal[173] and district courts[174] have recognized the validity of the technique.[175]

---

169. *Id.* at 146. Professor Spitznagel points out that many statisticians disagree with the use of the correction term.

170. D. BARNES, *supra* note 19, at 176.

171. W. CURTIS, *supra* note 21, at 146.

172. *Id.*

173. Barnes v. GenCorp, Inc., 896 F.2d 1457, 1463 (6th Cir.), *cert. denied,* 498 U.S. 878 (1990); Smith v. Western Elec. Co., 770 F.2d 520 (5th Cir. 1985); Bilingual Bicultural Coalition on Mass Media, Inc. v. FCC, 595 F.2d 621 (D.C. Cir. 1978).

174. Tagatz v. Marquette Univ., 681 F. Supp. 1344, 1349 (E.D. Wis.), *aff'd,* 861 F.2d 1040 (7th Cir. 1988); Chance v. Board of Exmrs., 330 F. Supp. 203 (S.D.N.Y. 1971), *aff'd,* 458 F.2d 1167 (2d Cir. 1972); Harper v. Godfrey Co., 839 F. Supp. 583, 600 (E.D. Wis. 1993), *aff'd in part, rev'd in part,* 45 F.3d 143 (7th Cir. 1995). *See also* United States v. Lansdowne Swim Club, 713 F. Supp. 785, 809 (E.D. Pa. 1989) (Baldus and Cole "state that for comparing selection rates the chi-square

§ 15-5(D). Epidemiology.

Epidemiology studies the incidence of diseases and attempts to identify causal factors.[176] Epidemiologists contrast the rate of disease in an exposed population to that in an unexposed population.[177] Even if there is a difference in rates, is the difference so small that it can be attributed to random chance?

There are various types of studies. Epidemiological studies are generally conducted in one of two ways. One type is a cohort study comparing the incidence of defects in a group of persons in a population exposed to a drug (the exposed group) to a group of persons who are members of the same population but have not been exposed (the cohort group). Cohort studies are prospective; after the event exposing the group, the researchers monitor the exposed and cohort groups to determine the proportion of each group which develops the disease. A cohort study can be both expensive and prolonged. The second type of study is case-control. Case-control studies are retrospective in nature. In this type of study, the researchers compare a group of persons who were exposed in the past to a group which presumably has not been exposed. The researchers compare the two groups' frequency of the disease or illness. The comparisons are measured in terms of relative risk (RR), odds ratio (OR), and attributable risk (AR).[178]

As indicated, the comparison yields a relative risk or risk ratio.[179] The RR is the ratio of the incidence of the effect in the exposed group to the incidence in the cohort group. When the rates for the two groups are identical, there is a one to one ratio; and the relative risk is 1.0. The AR is the proportion of the effect in the exposed group that is associated with the exposure. When the relative risk (RR) is 1.0 and the incidence in the two groups is identical, the attributable risk (AR) — the incidence caused by the drug — is zero. When the relative risk exceeds 1.0, the risk in exposed individuals is greater than the risk in the unexposed population; as the *Reference Manual on Scientific Evidence* indicates, the

---

test will generally be preferred 'if the sample sizes are not too small'"), *aff'd,* 894 F.2d 83 (3d Cir. 1990).

175. *See* D. BARNES, *supra* note 19, at 163-82; Barnes, *A Common Sense Approach to Understanding Statistical Evidence*, 21 SAN DIEGO L. REV. 809, 831 (1984). *But see* People v. Louie, 158 Cal. App. 3d Supp. 28, 205 Cal. Rptr. 247 (1984) (rejecting the use of hypothesis testing in a prosecution).

176. Dore, *A Proposed Standard for Evaluating the Use of Epidemiological Evidence in Toxic Tort and Other Personal Injury Cases*, 28 HOW. L.J. 677 (1985).

177. Green, *Expert Witnesses and Sufficiency of Evidence in Toxic Substances Litigation: The Legacy of Agent Orange and Bendectin Litigation*, 86 NW. U. L. REV. 643, 647 (1992).

178. Sanders, *From Science to Evidence: The Testimony on Causation in the Bendectin Cases*, 46 STAN. L. REV. 1, 22 (1993).

179. ANGELL, SCIENCE ON TRIAL 164 (1996).

enhanced risk suggests a positive association between the agent and disease.[180] When the relative risk is even higher and exceeds 2.0, the attributable risk is greater than fifty percent.[181] As Judge Sparr remarked in a 1998 breast implant decision,

> The threshold for concluding that an agent was more likely the cause of a disease than not is a relative risk greater than 2.0. Recall that a relative risk of 1.0 means that the agent has no effect on the incidence of disease. When the relative risk reaches 2.0, the agent is responsible for an equal number of cases of disease as all other background causes. Thus, a relative risk of 2.0 implies a 50% likelihood that an exposed individual's disease was caused by the agent.[182]

Admissibility

As in the case of other types of hypothesis testing, today the courts are receptive to epidemiological evidence.[183] In *Daubert*, the Supreme Court indicated that even an epidemiological reanalysis would be admissible if it passed the empirical validation test. However, the courts have imposed limitations on the introduction of such evidence.[184] In its 1997 decision in *General Electric Co. v. Joiner*,[185] the Supreme Court indicated that trial judges should consider the following factors in determining the admissibility of proffered epidemiological studies:

— The studies must be relevant and their methodology reliable;
— The subject of the studies must be similar to the case on trial;

---

180. Bailey, Gordis & Green, *Reference Guide on Epidemiology, in* REFERENCE MANUAL ON SCIENTIFIC EVIDENCE 121, 148 (Fed. Jud. Ctr. 1994).

181. Note, *Evidence--Scientific Testimony--Epidemiological Evidence May Be Used to Establish Causation in Toxic Tort Litigation Provided That The Applicable Standards of Admissibility Are Met--Landrigan v. Celotex Corp., 127 N.J. 404, 605 A.2d 1079 (1992)*, 24 SETON HALL L. REV. 447, 451 (1993).

182. *In re*: Breast Implant Litigation, No. 96-S-9260 (D. Colo., June 3, 1998) (Sparr, J.), quoting Hall v. Baxter Healthcare Corp., 947 F. Supp. 1387, 1403 (D. Or. 1996). In turn, the *Hall* court was quoting REFERENCE MANUAL ON SCIENTIFIC EVIDENCE 168 (1994).

183. Karns, *Understanding Epidemiological Evidence*, 30 TRIAL 46, 51 (Sep. 1994) ("Most courts in the country seem to be admitting epidemiological evidence"); Comment, *How to Tell the Truth with Statistics: A New Approach to Analyzing the Bendectin Epidemiological Data in the Aftermath of Daubert v. Merrell Dow Pharmaceuticals*, 31 HOUS. L. REV. 1241 (1994). *See also* Raynor v. Merrell Pharmaceuticals, Inc., 104 F.3d 1371 (D.C. Cir. 1997).

184. Kelley v. American Heyer-Schulte Corp., 957 F. Supp. 873, 878 (W.D. Tex. 1997) ("With regard to the Rule 703 standard, the Fifth Circuit has held that epidemiological studies with lower-end confidence intervals less than one are not reasonably relied upon by experts to form opinions about causation").

185. 522 U.S. 136 (1997).

— The authors of the study should be qualified to draw conclusions from the statistics;
— The studies should suggest a link between the increase of the incidence of illness and exposure to the product at issue;
— The studies should not involve exposure to more than one potentially toxic product as a cause of the illness; and
— In the study, there should not be too great an analytical gap between the underlying data and the expert opinion proffered.[186]

At the lower court level, the critical question appears to be whether an epidemiological study, yielding a relative risk exceeding 1.0 but less than 2.0, is admissible. A growing number of cases hold that to be admissible, much less legally sufficient to sustain a verdict, an epidemiological study must yield a relative risk exceeding 2.0.[187] It has been argued that that holding confuses the admissibility issue with the question of whether, standing alone, the epidemiological evidence should be deemed legally sufficient to support a finding of general causation.[188] In *Daubert*,[189] Justice Blackmun emphasized the distinction between the admissibility and legal sufficiency questions. If a study shows an enhanced risk, that is, one higher than 1.0, it is arguably relevant and presumptively admissible under Federal Rule of Evidence 402. However, the most recent cases set the bar for admissibility at a finding of a relative risk exceeding 2.0.

Assume *arguendo* that those decisions set the admissibility bar too high; that is, assume that an RR exceeding 1.0 but less than 2.0 should be considered relevant, admissible evidence on the issue of causation. However, distinguish that question from another admissibility issue. Suppose that an expert contemplates testifying to "probable" causation and proposes to do so solely on the basis of an epidemiological study yielding an RR exceeding 1.0 but less than 2.0. That presents a radically different question. In the preceding paragraphs, the proffered item of evidence was the study itself. Given the minimal standard of logical relevance codified in Federal Rule of Evidence 401, even an epidemiological study generating an RR slightly greater than 1.0 ought arguably to be deemed relevant and admissible. The study is the proffered evidence; and so long as the methodology of the study is sound, the foundation for the proffered evidence is both proper and adequate. However, when the expert contemplates basing an

---

186. Tyler by and through Tyler v. Sterling Drug, Inc., 19 F. Supp. 2d 1239, 1242-43 (N.D. Okla. 1998).

187. Daubert v. Merrell Dow Pharmaceuticals, Inc., 43 F.3d 1311 (9th Cir.), *cert. denied*, 516 U.S. 869 (1995); Hall v. Baxter Healthcare Corp., 947 F. Supp. 1387 (D. Or. 1996).

188. Imwinkelried, *Forensic Science: The Second Prong of the Daubert Test: Disturbing Implications of Two Recent Civil Cases*, 33 CRIM. L. BULL. 570 (Nov.-Dec. 1997).

189. Daubert v. Merrell Dow Pharmaceuticals, Inc., 509 U.S. 579 (1993).

opinion of probable causation on the solitary basis of such an epidemiological study, the proffered evidence changes; and a stronger foundation is required. The expert should not be allowed to opine to probable causation unless the RR is greater than 2.0.

Legal Sufficiency

Just as there are disputes over the admissibility of epidemiological studies, there are questions about the significance of such studies in legal sufficiency analysis. One question that has arisen is whether a proponent must submit an epidemiological study in order to make out a legally sufficient showing of general medical causation. In the 1989 district court opinion in *Daubert*, the trial judge ruled that a finding of "causation in this area" cannot be deemed admissible unless it is supported by epidemiological studies demonstrating a statistically significant connection.[190] However, there is a substantial body of authority that proof of an epidemiological study is not invariably necessary.[191] These decisions recognize that it can be time-consuming and expensive to conduct epidemiological studies. Further, in some cases, there are practical considerations which render it infeasible to conduct such studies.[192]

The second question is whether, without more, an epidemiological study finding an enhanced risk but an RR less than 2.0 makes out a submissible case. As the preceding paragraphs pointed out, some jurisdictions have gone to the length of holding that an epidemiological study is not even admissible unless it yields an RR exceeding 2.0. That holding is debatable, but it seems more justifiable to conclude that standing alone such a study lacks sufficient probative worth to carry a case to the jury. In the vast majority of civil cases, the plaintiff's burden is the measure of a preponderance of the evidence. The conventional understanding is that to satisfy the burden, the plaintiff must establish a probability exceeding 50%. As previously stated, many authorities assert that to create that probability, an epidemiological study must yield an RR greater than 2.0.

---

190. Daubert v. Merrell Dow Pharmaceuticals, Inc., 727 F. Supp. 570, 572 (S.D. Cal. 1989).

191. Kennedy v. Collagen Corp., 161 F.3d 1226 (9th Cir. 1998); Benedi v. McNeil-P.P.C., Inc., 66 F.3d 1378, 1384 (4th Cir. 1995).

192. Kenney v. Collagen Corp., 161 F.3d 1226 (9th Cir. 1998) ("Dr. Spindler explained that epidemiological studies linking an increased incidence of SLE to patients injected with collagen would be almost impossible to perform because patients who have collagen injections normally do not seek treatment from rheumatologists for their reactions. Patients who have collagen injections usually consult the injecting doctor when any subsequent problems arise. Because the injecting doctor typically is a plastic surgeon or dermatologist, he is not trained to recognize autoimmune or immune disorders. Thus, the causal connection goes unrecognized").

§ 15-6. Inferential Statistics — Association Analysis.

At the risk of oversimplification, some say that the hypothesis testing techniques described in the last section have an essentially negative thrust; they help the statistician eliminate random chance as the explanation for the observed values. Those tests can help demonstrate that something besides chance probably accounts for the observed values. However, the techniques do not affirmatively identify the cause of the observed phenomena.[193] The techniques discussed in this section, correlation and regression, supposedly can aid making that affirmative determination. Our reviewer, Professor Kaye, adds two caveats. First, the term "help" is used advisedly; statistics alone cannot establish causality. Second, the affirmative-negative distinction is a false dichotomy. In his judgment, the real distinction is between continuous and categorical variables. In a grand jury discrimination case, the question would be whether a change in one variable (race) causes a change in the value of another variable (selection to serve on the grand jury). The variables are binary, and the statistician can use hypothesis testing previously discussed to investigate the association between the variables. In another case, if the statistician were testing for an association between the height of dogs and their weight, one might inquire whether a change in height corresponds to a change in weight. Here, the variables are continuous, and for that reason the statistician would employ a different test statistic, such as the slope of a regression line discussed below. Simply stated, different statistics are appropriate for examining the association between continuous as opposed to categorical variables.

§ 15-6(A). Correlation.

The correlation coefficient is a measure of the inter-relatedness of two factors.[194] Suppose that a prosecutor hires a statistician to determine whether there is a correlation between income level and intelligence. The prosecutor contemplates presenting a complex case, and she wants extraordinarily intelligent jurors. The prosecutor fears that she will not have sufficient time to investigate each member of the venire after it is announced, and she wants to know in general whether there is a correlation between the two variables. The statistician would select a number of members of the local population as a sample. For each member of the sample, the statistician determines the income level (variable x) and the intelligence quotient (variable y). The statistician then computes a correlation coefficient between the two variables.

---

193. D. BARNES, *supra* note 19, at 93; Smith & Abram, *supra* note 16, at 53.
194. W. CURTIS, *supra* note 21, at 153.

The correlation coefficient is designated r.[195] The coefficient depends not only on whether two variables move in the same direction but also how much they move. The value of r can range between – 1 and +1. An r value of – 1 indicates a perfect negative correlation; when one variable, x, increases, the other, y, invariably decreases. An r value of +1 indicates a perfect positive correlation; when x increases, y always increases. An r value of 0 means that the variables are independent; the movement of x does not predict y's movement, at least linearly. One authority has proposed the following scheme to evaluate the common intermediate r scores:

less than .20 ....slight, negligible relationship
.20-.40 ....low correlation, definite but small relationship
.40-.70 ....moderate correlation, substantial relationship
.70-.90 ....high correlation, marked relationship
.90-1.00 ....very high correlation, very dependable relationship[196]

Other statisticians believe that it is arbitrary to assign such interpretations to intermediate scores. There is no scientific justification, for example, for labelling a correlation "marked" rather than "substantial."

The formula[197] for computing r is:

$$r = \frac{n\Sigma xy - \Sigma x \Sigma y}{\sqrt{(n\Sigma x^2 - (\Sigma x)^2)\ (n\Sigma y^2 - (\Sigma y)^2)}}$$

Σ is the summation notation. Hence, Σxy means that the statistician must multiply each x value by the corresponding y value and then sum the products of all the multiplications.

There are several caveats about correlations. One is that the correlation measured in the sample might be an artifact. There may be no correlation. A high r value could occur by chance.[198] Even a strong positive correlation does not necessarily mean that there is a true cause-and-effect relationship between the two variables. As one authority has noted, there is "a strong positive correlation between teachers' salary increases and sales of liquor."[199] Even if there is a

---

195. *Id.* at 154. *See also* BARNES, *supra* note 19, at 817.

196. GUILFORD, CORRELATION IN FUNDAMENTAL STATISTICS IN PSYCHOLOGY AND EDUCATION 154 (1950). If the statistician prepared a scatter diagram for r = .2, the reader would see that the diagram exhibits a weak upward trend that the reader must look hard to find.

197. W. CURTIS, *supra* note 21, at 156.

198. *Id.* at 157.

199. *Id.* at 158; Ottavani v. State Univ. of New York at New Paltz, 875 F.2d 365, 372 n.6 (2d Cir. 1989) ("no matter how great the number ... is, statistical tests can never entirely rule out the possibility that chance caused the disparity"), *cert. denied,* 493 U.S. 1021 (1990); Heafey, *Trial by Lottery: The Misuse of Epidemiology and Statistics to Prove Causation in Drug and Chemical Litigation*, 12 AM. J. TRIAL ADVOC. 19, 24 (1988) ("An association is a correlation of one thing

cause-and-effect relationship, correlation testing does not tell the statistician which variable is the cause and which the effect.[200]

Notwithstanding these limitations, correlation testing is a valuable statistical technique. The courts have recognized its value and admitted evidence based on correlation testing.[201]

§ 15-6(B). Regression Analysis.

In the physical sciences, there are often exact cause-and-effect relationships between variables.[202] The scientist can define the relationship in precise, mathematical terms. Indeed, the relationships are often linear.[203] As one variable, x, increases, the other, y, increases. When the combinations of x and y variables are plotted on a chart such as Figure 15-11, the analyst can draw a straight line connecting the plots.[204]

---

with another. For example, the increased consumption of soft drinks during the summer months was associated with an increased incidence of polio. In fact, the incidence of polio and soft drink consumption had nothing to do with each other, but the fact that both increased during summer months accounted for their 'association.' An association is merely a correlation and does not prove a causal fact"); Pope, *Statistical Evidence as Proof of Causation*, DEF. COUNS. J., Apr. 1988, at 140 ("For example, there may be a high degree of association or correlation between the movement of the temperature in Phoenix and the movement of stock prices on the New York Stock Exchange.... It would be ludicrous, however, to suggest that changes of temperature in Phoenix cause changes in stock prices in New York. If statistical evidence is relied on to establish causation, a showing of statistical association is only the first, not the final, step").

200. W. CURTIS, *supra* note 21, at 154-55; Tagatz v. Marquette Univ., 861 F.2d 1040, 1044 (7th Cir. 1988) ("Correlation is not causation"); Waisome v. Port Auth. of New York & New Jersey, 758 F. Supp. 171, 176 (S.D.N.Y.) ("Statistical significance is not the same as practical significance..."), *rev'd,* 948 F.2d 1370 (2d Cir. 1991).

201. Adams v. Indiana Bell Telephone Co., Inc., 2 F. Supp. 2d 1077, 1095 (S.D. Ind. 1998) ("correlation coefficients"); United States v. Chicago, 385 F. Supp. 543 (N.D. Ill. 1974); Boston Chapter, NAACP, Inc. v. Beecher, 371 F. Supp. 507 (D. Mass.), *aff'd,* 504 F.2d 1017 (1st Cir. 1974), *cert. denied,* 421 U.S. 910 (1975); D. BARNES, *supra* note 19, at 272-77; W. CURTIS, *supra* note 21, at 167-68. Harvell v. Blytheville School Dist. #5, 71 F.3d 1382, 1397 (8th Cir. 1995), *cert. denied*, 517 U.S. 1233 (1996). *See also* LeFevre v. Secretary, Dept. of Veterans Affairs, 66 F.3d 1191, 1993 (Fed. Cir. 1995) (discussing 38 U.S.C. § 1116, a legislative mandate that the National Academy of Science determine "whether a statistical association with herbicide exposure exists" for Vietnam veterans exposed to Agent Orange), *cert. denied*, 517 U.S. 1188 (1996).

202. M. LEWIS-BECK, APPLIED REGRESSION — AN INTRODUCTION 9 (1980).

203. *Id.* at 11.

204. *Id.* at 9-11.

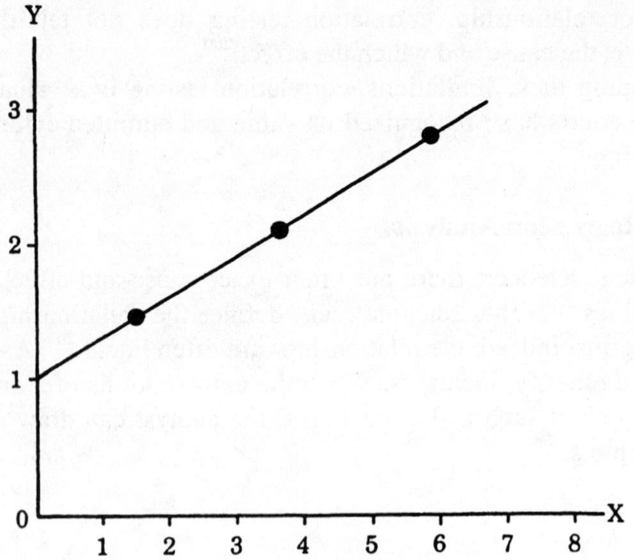

Figure 15-11

Unfortunately, the law is usually concerned about the relationship of variables in the social sciences. Those relationships are ordinarily neither capable of description in precise, mathematical terms nor exactly linear.[205] Even when two variables in the social sciences are strongly related, a chart depicting their relationship is more likely to resemble the scattergram shown in Figure 15-12.

205. *Id.* at 11.

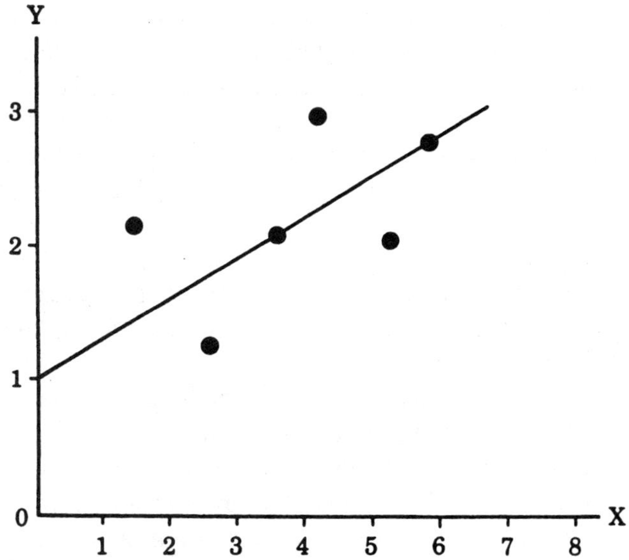

Figure 15-12

The purpose of regression analysis is to cut through the "noise" in a set of data (depicted as a scattergram) and determine whether it is possible to extract a signal from the noise. The signal the statistician seeks is a straight line that comes so close to connecting all the plots that the line suggests a causal relationship between the two variables.[206] There are four steps in regression analysis.

Constructing Model of Behavior of Variables

The initial task facing the statistician is to develop a model or hypothesis explaining the behavior in question. The statistician must not only identify the dependent variable but all the independent variables that influence the effect.[207]

206. Armour v. State of Ohio, 775 F. Supp. 1044, 1057 n.14 (N.D. Ohio 1991).

207. Note, *Title VII, Multiple Linear Regression Models, and the Courts: An Analysis*, 46 LAW & CONTEMP. PROBS. 283, 284, 286 (Aut. 1983). In Barrett & Doiverspike, *Fundamental Errors and Erroneous Beliefs in Using Regression Analysis as a Test for Sex Discrimination*, 13 LAW & PSYCHOLOGY REV. 1 (1989), the authors argue that in developing a model in a sex discrimination case, the expert should use only the legitimate personnel factors actually considered by the allegedly discriminating organization. *Id.* at 7. "[A]n organization does not have to follow any abstract economic theory concerning the factors to be used in determining individual salary levels...." *Id.* at 6. "An organization ... is not required to have a compensation policy which fits the model of the plaintiff's expert or some abstract economic theory." *Id.* at 16-17. Professor Spitznagel points out that in social science statistics, there are many models in which an independent variable is not assumed to be a cause. For example, race is strongly related to many outcome measures, but race is often not the cause. Rather, income levels associated with race are

While this terminology does not imply a simple causal relationship, it may be helpful to think of the dependent variable as the effect and the independent variables as the causes. The model should incorporate all the major potentially contributory factors to the effect.

One error that the statistician can commit at this stage is misspecification, that is, omitting a relevant independent variable.[208] The inclusion of unnecessary variables is rarely fatal to the regression analysis. However, the omission of an explanatory independent variable can badly distort the analysis.[209] Thus, in evaluating a regression analysis, the opponent must always force the proponent to disclose the underlying model of the behavior. After disclosure, the opponent can review the model for completeness.

Suppose that a defense counsel wants to challenge the jury selection in a particular case. The defense counsel contends that it is the prosecutor's routine practice to exercise peremptory challenges to strike all minority members of the jury panel when the defendant is a member of a minority race. The defense counsel hires a statistician to develop a regression analysis to support the contention. At the outset, the statistician could conceivably approach the problem by developing the following model of the relevant behavior:

dependent variable	(JUR) —	the number of minority persons serving on the jury
independent variables	(1) VEN —	the number of minorities on the venire
	(2) PCD—	the number of peremptory challenges cast against minority members
	(3) RAD —	the defendant's race
	(4) RAV —	the victim's race
	(5) PCP —	the number of peremptory challenges possessed by the prosecutor
	(6) CRM —	the type of crime

The statistician cannot be content to test only the dependent variable and independent variable (3), the defendant's race. That model would be obviously incomplete. Any regression analysis based on that model would be unreliable and probably inadmissible. Note that some of the variables such as race are not inherently numerical. They are termed dummy variables. They are qualitative variables, but they can be incorporated in a regression analysis by arbitrarily

---

frequently the cause. League of United Latin Am. Citizens v. Clements, 986 F.2d 728, 774 (5th Cir. 1993) (the independent variable), *cert. denied*, 510 U.S. 1071 (1994).

208. Note, *supra* note 207, at 286.

209. Vuyanich v. Republic Nat'l Bank, 505 F. Supp. 224, 255-56 (N.D. Tex. 1980), *vacated,* 723 F.2d 1195 (5th Cir.), *cert. denied*, 469 U.S. 1073 (1984). *See also* E.E.O.C. v. Chicago Miniature Lamp Works, 947 F.2d 292, 300-02 (7th Cir. 1991).

assigning values to the categories. For example, one might indicate black or female while zero could indicate white or male.

Collecting Data to Test Model

Refer back to the material on sampling included in § 15-4. The statistician must gather data to test the validity of the model. The statistician must: Define the relevant population or universe; select a random sample of the population; ensure that there is no bias in the design or execution of the sampling plan; and guard against mismeasurement of the data. If the sample is seriously deficient in any respect, the sample and the related regression analysis may be inadmissible.[210]

In our hypothetical, the statistician would have to research earlier trials in the jurisdiction. The statistician would have to consult court records to determine the number of strikes and the composition of each petit jury. Moreover, he would probably review other official records such as driver's license applications and birth certificates to determine the jurors' race. Alternatively, the statistician could conduct a telephone poll, contact the former jurors directly, and ascertain their race in that fashion.

Calculating Regression Relationship

The purpose of regression analysis is to determine whether the relationship between the dependent and independent variables is linear enough to serve as some evidence of a cause-effect relationship. Regression analysis poses this question: Does a change in the independent variable cause a change in the dependent variable? Regression analysis is based on a more sophisticated version of the charts depicted earlier. Figure 15-13 shows how the chart relates to the formula used for computing regression analyses:[211]

210. *See* cases cited in note 209, *supra.*

211. *See* W. CURTIS, *supra* note 21, at 159.

$$Y = a + bX$$

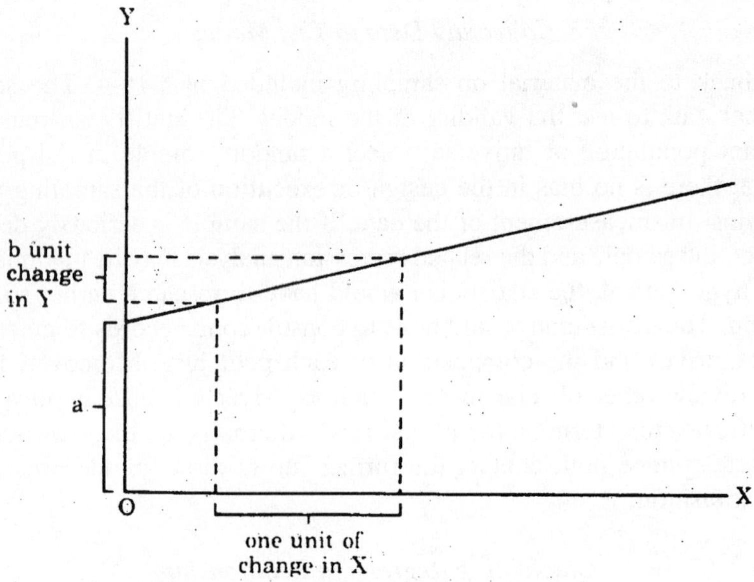

Figure 15-13

The vertical axis measures the values of y, the dependent variable (the effect). The horizontal axis measures the values of x, the independent variable (the cause). The coefficient, a, is the y intercept. When the x value is zero, the y variable equals a. The coefficient, b, is the slope of the line (the sloper). The slope indicates how much change in y is associated with a change in x. The slope is the average change in y associated with a change in x; x and y will assume various values in the regression analysis — the values found during the sampling. In contrast, a and b, the intercept and sloper, are constants.

Figure 15-13 depicts a simple geometric relationship between two variables, x and y. When the regression model is this simple, it is easy to visualize the attempt to draw a straight line through the scattergram. However, in our hypothetical, as in most cases, there is more than one independent variable. "When there are two independent variables, one is fitting a plane to a scatter of points in space. When there are more than two independent variables, one is fitting a hyperplane (the generalization of a plane to more than three dimensions), but the principles are still the same, although the visualization is no longer immediate."[212] This mode of analysis is called multiple regression.

The chart discussed above is reducible to the following formula:

$$y = a + bx + u\,.$$

This formula regresses y on x.[213] In multiple regression, the formula might read:

$$y = a + b_1x_1 + b_2x_2 + b_3x_3 + u\,.$$

Y is the dependent variable or effect that the statistician is investigating, a is the intercept, b is the slope, x is the independent variable, and u is termed the disturbance term or residual. Since the relationship will probably not be perfectly linear, the straight line will not cut exactly through each point on the scattergram. The regression analysis will estimate where the point should fall if it fell exactly on the line, but the values observed during the sampling are likely to fall above or below the line. The deviation between the observed and expected value of y falls into the residual in the equation.

The key to the regression analysis is generating values for a and b. To identify those values, the statistician relies on the least square principle:

> The total deviation of the points on the scatter diagram from the regression line is the sum of all the vertical distances between the points and the line. Least squares analysis assures that the sum of the squared deviations of the plotted points from the regression line is less than any other line.[214]

---

212. Fisher, *Multiple Regression in Legal Proceedings*, 80 COLUM. L. REV. 702, 712 (1980). A. SYKES, AN INTRODUCTION TO REGRESSION ANALYSIS, University of Chicago Law and Economics Working Paper No. 20 (2d Series), p. 9 (1993) ("we lack the capacity to visualize in more than three dimensions," but the multiple regression analysis can construct a hyperplane).

213. W. CURTIS, *supra* note 21, at 160.

214. *Id.*

The statistician wants to identify the line that best fits the values plotted on the scattergram. The statistician wants to identify the line that will produce the least deviation between expected y values and observed y values, the line that produces the smallest sum when the deviations are squared. A square is always a positive value, and the least squares principle maximizes the goodness of fit.

Given the least squares principle, the statistician computes the values for a and b in the following fashion:[215]

$$b = \frac{\Sigma xy - n\overline{x}\overline{y}}{\Sigma x^2 - n\overline{x}^2}$$

Notice the squared figures in the denominator of the equation. Having computed b, the statistician can calculate a:[216]

$$a = y - b\overline{x}$$

The use of the regression equation permits the statistician to predict values of y given the a, b, and x. The above formulae supply the a and b while the statistician can select any point on the x axis.[217]

However, the equation can be used properly only when certain assumptions are met. Just as the statistician cannot resort to the binominal or normal distributions unless the relevant assumptions are satisfied, the regression equation cannot be used with full confidence unless several assumptions are met.[218] The assumptions include the following premises:

— The residual term is independent from the independent variables. The size of any particular deviation between the expected and observed y values should be a product of chance. This assumption will not hold true when the model is misspecified. For instance, if the statistician omits a relevant independent variable, the formula will in effect place that factor in the residual term.[219]

— The residual for one observation is independent of the residual for any other observation. If the residuals are dependent, they are said to be autocorrelated.[220]

— The residual terms are homoskedastically distributed.[221] Regardless of the size of x, the degree of dispersion of the residual term around the line must be constant.

---

215. *Id.*

216. *Id.*

217. *Id.* at 161.

218. H. CASSIDY, USING ECONOMETRICS: A BEGINNER'S GUIDE 104 (1981).

219. Fisher, *supra* note 212, at 707, 709-10.

220. *Id.* at 710.

221. H. CASSIDY, *supra* note 218, at 107.

— The independent variables must be independent of each other. If they are not, they are said to be multicollinear.[222]

It would be a mistake to think that regression is useless unless all the conditions are satisfied. However, the violation of any assumption can reduce the explanatory power of the regression analysis and produce spurious results. There are other assumptions in addition to those listed above.[223] In addition to asking his statistician to review the completeness of the opposing expert's model and the accuracy of the opposing expert's sampling, the attorney should direct the expert to ensure that all the assumptions of regression analysis are present in the case.

Interpreting Regression Analysis

To interpret the analysis, the statistician can consider the degree of goodness of the fit of the line or plane to the observed values.[224] The goodness of the fit indicates the strength of the supposed causal relation between the dependent and independent variables. There are a number of methods of testing the goodness of fit, including the use of statistics and standard error.[225] A common method is the use of R^2, the coefficient of determination.[226] In the last subsection, we discussed r, the coefficient of correlation. R^2 is the symbol for the coefficient of determination. The formula[227] for computing this coefficient is:

$$R^2 = \frac{SSR}{SST}$$

In the formula, SSR means the sum of the squares explained by the regression line while SST is the total sum of squares of y about the mean.[228] In turn, there are formulae for computing SSR and SST.[229]

$$SSR = b\left[\Sigma xy - \frac{\Sigma x \Sigma y}{n}\right]$$

222. *Id.* at 107-08. According to Professor Spitznagel, the absence of multicollinearity should not be treated as a requirement. Economists frequently deal with highly collinear data. The standard errors of the slopes automatically adjust upward, the more collinearity there is.

223. *Id.* at 104-09.

224. Fisher, *supra* note 212, at 710.

225. *Id.* at 717-24.

226. W. Curtis, *supra* note 21, at 162. Nipper v. Chiles, 795 F. Supp. 1525, 1533 n.2 (M.D. Fla. 1992), *rev'd*, 1 F.3d 1171 (11th Cir. 1993), *cert. denied*, 514 U.S. 1083 (1995); Williams v. Orange Cty., Fla., 783 F. Supp. 1348, 1366 (M.D. Fla.), *aff'd*, 979 F.2d 1504 (11th Cir. 1992), *cert. denied*, 509 U.S. 905 (1993).

227. W. Curtis, *supra* note 21, at 163.

228. *Id.*

229. *Id.*

In the formula, n is the number of observations in the sample, b is the slope, x is the observed value of the independent variable, and y is the observed value for each corresponding y variable. The SST formula reads:[230]

$$SST = \Sigma y^2 - n\bar{y}^2$$

Suppose that R^2 yields the number .866.[231] That number is the coefficient of determination or the proportion of the variance explained. In very rough terms, the number means that the movement of the independent variable accounts for or explains almost 87% of the movement of the dependent variable. An R^2 that high strongly suggests a cause-effect relationship. However, there is a distinction between statistical and practical significance. There is always the possibility that the high R^2 is a product of happenstance. The R^2 is evidence of a cause-effect relationship between the independent and dependent variables, but the R^2 is not dispositive. The R^2 may be persuasive circumstantial evidence, but it is not conclusive. The volume of ice cream consumption might be linearly related to the number of homicides because both grow in proportion to the size of the population.

The courts have been increasingly receptive to regression analyses.[232] The analysis does not have to be complete[233] in the sense that the model includes

---

230. *Id.*

231. *Id.*

232. *E.g.*, Thornburg v. Gingles, 478 U.S. 30, 52-53 (1986); Albemarle Paper Co. v. Moody, 422 U.S. 405 (1975); Craik v. Minnesota State Univ. Bd., 731 F.2d 465 (8th Cir. 1984); Solomon v. Liberty Cty., 865 F.2d 1566, 1577 (11th Cir. 1988) ("Bivariate regression analysis is widely used to show racial polarization in vote dilution cases"), *vacated on other grounds*, 873 F.2d 248 (11th Cir. 1989), *cert. denied*, 498 U.S. 1023 (1991); Segar v. Smith, 738 F.2d 1249 (D.C. Cir. 1984), *cert. denied*, 471 U.S. 1115 (1985); Adams v. Indiana Bell Telephone Co., Inc., 2 F. Supp. 2d 1077, 1095 (S.D. Ind. 1998) ("slopes of regression lines"); African-American Voting Rights v. State of Mo., 994 F. Supp. 1105, 1117-18 (E.D. Mo. 1997) ("Following the statistical techniques recognized by the Supreme Court in Thornburg v. Gingles, 478 U.S. 30, 52-53, Bivariate Ecological Regression Analysis...."); African Ewing v. Monroe Cty., 740 F. Supp. 417 (N.D. Miss. 1990) (the use of ecological regression analysis to demonstrate racial voting patterns); Brown v. Board of Comm'rs, 722 F. Supp. 380, 391 (E.D. Tenn. 1989) (the use of ecological regression analysis in a Voting Rights Act case); Gunn v. Chickasaw Cty., 705 F. Supp. 315, 319 (N.D. Miss. 1989) (the use of ecological regression analysis to show racial bloc voting); Hill v. City of Greenville, 696 F. Supp. 1123, 1130 (N.D. Tex. 1988); Martin v. Allain, 658 F. Supp. 1183 (S.D. Miss. 1987); Vuyanich v. Republic Nat'l Bank, 505 F. Supp. 224 (N.D. Tex. 1980), *vacated,* 723 F.2d 1195 (5th Cir.), *cert. denied*, 469 U.S. 1073 (1984); Boston Chapter, NAACP, Inc. v. Beecher, 371 F. Supp. 507 (D. Mass.), *aff'd,* 504 F.2d 1017 (1st Cir. 1974), *cert. denied,* 421 U.S. 910 (1975); City & Cty. of San Francisco v. F.E.H.C., 191 Cal. App. 3d 976, 987-88, 236 Cal. Rptr. 716, 724 (1987); W. CURTIS, *supra* note 21, at 168-70; Barnes, *supra* note 175, at 820. Regression analysis can also be used to establish the amount of damages in civil cases. Weese, *Employing Financial Expertise*, NAT'L L.J., Mar. 18, 1991, at 21. Barnett v. City of Chicago, 969 F. Supp. 1359, 1442 (N.D. Ill. 1997) (ecological regression), *aff'd in part, vacated in part*, 141 F.3d 699 (7th

every relevant variable.[234] However, if the court decides that a major[235] variable has been omitted from the underlying model[236] or that an essential assumption of

---

Cir. 1998), *cert. denied sub nom.* Bialczak v. Barnett, 118 S. Ct. 2372 (1998); Cofield v. City of LaGrange, Ga., 969 F. Supp. 749, 760 (N.D. Ga. 1997) (regression analysis of elections); Rollins v. Fort Bend Indep. Sch. Dist., 89 F.3d 1205, 1218 (5th Cir. 1996) (ecological regressions); State of Ohio *ex rel.* Mont. v. Louis Trauth Dairy, 925 F. Supp. 1247 (S.D. Ohio 1996) (multiple regression analysis); Reed v. Town of Babylon, 914 F. Supp. 843 (E.D.N.Y. 1996) (ecological regression analysis to establish the voting behavior of distinct population groups); Lulac v. North East Indep. Sch. Dist., 903 F. Supp. 1071, 1076 (W.D. Tex. 1995) (multivariate statistical analysis); Flavel v. Svedala Indust., 875 F. Supp. 550 (E.D. Wis. 1994) (multivariate analysis); Meek v. Metropolitan Dade County, Fla., 985 F.2d 1471, 1484 (11th Cir. 1993) (bivariate regression analysis); Hall v. Holder, 955 F.2d 1563, 1571 (11th Cir. 1992), *cert. granted in part*, 507 U.S. 959 (1993); AFSCME v. County of Nassau, 799 F. Supp. 1370 (E.D.N.Y. 1992) (multiple regression); Trout v. Garrett, 780 F. Supp. 1396 (D.D.C. 1991) (multiple regression); Jenkins v. Red Clay Consol. Sch. Dist., 780 F. Supp. 221, 231 (D. Del. 1991), *rev'd*, 4 F.3d 1103 (3d Cir. 1993), *cert. denied*, 512 U.S. 1252 (1994); A. Sykes, An Introduction to Regression Analysis, University of Chicago Law and Economics Working Paper No. 20 (2d Series), at 1 (1993) ("Regression analyses have been offered as evidence of liability under Title VII of the Civil Rights Act of 1964, as evidence of racial bias in death penalty litigation, as evidence of damages in contract actions, as evidence of violations under the Voting Rights Act, and as evidence of damages in antitrust litigation...."); Sherman & Richmond, *Reading the Numbers*, Legal Times, Nov. 21, 1994, at 28 (the use of multiple regression analysis to estimate damages); Schwartz & Goodman, *Expert Testimony on Decision Processes in Employment Cases*, 16 Law & Hum. Behav. 337 (1992).

233. McMillan v. Mass. Soc. Prev. of Cruelty to Animals, 140 F.3d 288, 303 (1st Cir. 1998) ("such analyses are admissible even in disparate impact cases unless they are 'so incomplete as to be inadmissible as irrelevant'"); Bazemore v. Friday, 751 F.2d 662 (4th Cir. 1984) ("a statistical model need not be completely specified, and some arguably relevant variables can be omitted in certain cases"), *aff'd in part, vacated in part*, 478 U.S. 385 (1986).

234. E.E.O.C. v. Local 638, 81 F.3d 1162, 1173 (2d Cir. 1996) (refusing to exclude regression analysis for alleged failure "to include . . . several important variables"); E.E.O.C. v. General Tel. Co. of Northwest, 885 F.2d 575, 579-81 (9th Cir. 1989) (the majority view is that the opponent must not only point to the omitted variable but also demonstrate that the inclusion of the missing factor would significantly affect the analysis), *cert. denied*, 498 U.S. 950 (1990); Rendon v. A.T. & T. Technologies, 883 F.2d 388, 396 (5th Cir. 1989) (A.T. & T. complained that the expert failed to control for certain factors, but "AT & T did not present evidence at trial detailing the effects of these variables"); Bazemore v. Friday, 751 F.2d 662 (4th Cir. 1984), *aff'd in part, vacated in part*, 478 U.S. 385 (1986); Hughes v. Alabama Dept. of Public Safety, 994 F. Supp. 1395, 1402 (M.D. Ala. 1998) ("not all variables must be accounted for....").

235. Coward v. ADT Sec. Systems, Inc., 140 F.3d 271, 274 (D.C. Cir. 1998).

236. United States v. Artero, 121 F.3d 1256 (9th Cir. 1997) (a statistical study that fails to correct for salient explanatory variables has no value as a causal explanation and is therefore inadmissible), *cert. denied*, 522 U.S. 1133 (1998); Sobel v. Yeshiva Univ., 656 F. Supp. 587, 591-92 (S.D.N.Y. 1987), *rev'd on other grounds*, 839 F.2d 18 (2d Cir. 1988), *cert. denied*, 490 U.S. 1105 (1989); McCleskey v. Zant, 580 F. Supp. 338 (N.D. Ga. 1984), *rev'd on other grounds sub nom.* McCleskey v. Kemp, 753 F.2d 877 (11th Cir. 1985) (en banc), *aff'd*, 481 U.S. 279 (1987); Denniston, *New Appeals from Death Row*, Cal. Law., July 1984, at 52-53; Smith v. Virginia Commonwealth Univ., 62 F.3d 659, 663 (4th Cir. 1995) ("Although failure to include some factors affect a study's weight, not its admissibility, a study must include all major factors"; this study did

regression analysis does not hold true in a particular case,[237] the analysis may be excluded. As in the case of errors in sampling, not every technical error automatically leads to the exclusion of regression evidence.[238] However, the model's omission of an obviously influential variable or the absence of a major assumption of regression analysis often results in the inadmissibility of the evidence. Even if testimony about the regression analysis is admissible, the trier of fact must decide how much weight to assign to the testimony.

In the past, neither the courts[239] nor the commentators[240] have insisted that the regression have a high R-squared value. However, the value is a measure of the explanatory power of the model.[241] Some commentators favor placing greater importance on the value.[242] In *McCleskey v. Kemp,*[243] the challenge to Georgia's capital punishment system, the defense relied on a regression analysis. The Supreme Court was willing to assume that the study was valid and admissible.[244] However, the Court depreciated the study because the R-squared value was "between .46 and .48. Thus, ... the ... model does not predict the outcome in half of the cases."[245] In light of *McCleskey,* the lower courts now seem to be placing greater emphasis on the explanatory power of the model.[246]

---

not account for a professor's status as a former administrator, the amount of time actually spent teaching, and productivity measures such as teaching loads and publications; the court stressed "the number of important variables omitted from the multiple regression analysis, and the evidence presented by the appellants that these variables are crucial."), *rev'd,* 894 F.3d 672 (4th Cir. 1996).

237. Wilkins v. University of Houston, 662 F.2d 1156, 1157 n.3 (5th Cir. 1981), *vacated,* 459 U.S. 809 (1982); E.E.O.C. v. Sears, Roebuck & Co., 628 F. Supp. 1264 (N.D. Ill. 1986) (invalid assumption that women and men employees were equally interested in commission sales positions), *aff'd,* 839 F.2d 302 (7th Cir. 1988); Fisher, *supra* note 212, at 702.

238. *See generally* Vuyanich v. Republic Nat'l Bank, 505 F. Supp. 224 (N.D. Tex. 1980), *vacated,* 723 F.2d 1195 (5th Cir.), *cert. denied,* 469 U.S. 1073 (1984); E.E.O.C. v. Chicago Miniature Lamp Works, 947 F.2d 292, 300-02 (7th Cir. 1991).

239. Fogel, *Class Pay Discrimination and Multiple Regression Proofs*, 65 NEB. L. REV. 289, 324 (1986) (collecting the cases).

240. C. MCCORMICK, EVIDENCE §209 (5th ed. 1999); Gross, *Race and Death: The Judicial Evaluation of Evidence of Discrimination in Capital Sentencing*, 18 U.C. DAVIS L. REV. 1275, 1291 n.83 (1985).

241. Griffin v. Board of Regents of Regency Univ., 795 F.2d 1281, 1291 (7th Cir. 1986); Windy Boy v. County of Big Horn, 647 F. Supp. 1002, 1010 (D. Mont. 1986); Palmer v. Shultz, 616 F. Supp. 1540 (D.D.C. 1985), *rev'd on other grounds,* 815 F.2d 84 (D.C. Cir. 1987).

242. Fogel, *supra* note 239, at 324.

243. 481 U.S. 279 (1987).

244. *Id.* at 291 n.7.

245. *Id.* at 288-89 n.6.

246. Mister v. Illinois Cent. Gulf R.R., 832 F.2d 1427, 1437 (7th Cir. 1987) ("Perhaps a court should say that only statistical models explaining a substantial portion of the variance may be used to infer discrimination ..."), *cert. denied,* 485 U.S. 1035 (1988).

§ 15-7. Inferential Statistics — The Calculus of Probabilities.

As a matter of historical fact, probability theory emerged before much of the theory of statistical inference. However, it may be useful to think of the calculus of probabilities as a subdivision of inferential statistics. This section reviews the various formulae used in this calculus and the legal restrictions on the admission of evidence based on the formulae.

§ 15-7(A). Formulae for Computing Probabilities.

The threshold question is always the source of the individual probabilities used in the various formulae. There are three theories for deriving the individual probabilities. One theory is Laplace's classical model.[247] Under this theory, the statistician identifies all the possible outcomes and assumes that they are equiprobable; that is, all outcomes have the same likelihood of occurring. A second theory is the subjective model.[248] This model directs the trier of fact to convert his degree of belief into a number. The third model is the objective or frequency model.[249] The statistician conducts sampling or a review of past historical experience to determine how frequently the outcome has occurred in the past.[250]

No matter how the individual probabilities are derived, there is agreement on the formulae that may be used to manipulate and combine the individual probabilities. The most commonly encountered formulae are listed below.

---

247. Braun, *Quantitative Analysis and the Law: Probability Theory as a Tool of Evidence in Criminal Trials*, 4 UTAH L. REV. 41, 46 (1982); McCord, *A Primer for the Nonmathematically Inclined on Mathematical Evidence in Criminal Cases: People v. Collins and Beyond*, 47 WASH. & LEE L. REV. 741, 745-46 (1990) ("The classical theory is quite limited in application because its results are rationally acceptable only when one is willing to assume that each of the possible outcomes is equally likely. In non-game-like-real-world situations, ... outcomes are rarely equally likely ...").

248. Braun, *supra* note 247, at 48; McCord, *supra* note 247, at 746, 781 ("The third probability model — the subjective model — had its origins in the work of James Bernoulli in the early eighteenth century, and was popularized by an influential work published by Professor Leonard Savage in 1950. Savage demonstrated that given a few simple and relatively noncontroversial assumptions, a probability subjectively developed by an individual can still meaningfully be called a 'probability.' Such a probability can ... be used as a meaningful input into Bayes' Theorem"; some refer to this theory as "Pascalian"). Our reviewer, Professor Kaye, cautions that Professor McCord appears to be the only commentator using the expression "Pascalian" in this fashion. Professor Kaye points out that Jonathan Cohen, who popularized the expression, uses it to refer generally to the probability calculus.

249. Braun, *supra* note 247, at 45; McCord, *supra* note 247, at 746 ("The frequency model bases its predictions on the relative frequency with which particular outcomes are expected to result from repeated trials").

250. W. CURTIS, *supra* note 21, at 45.

General Law of Addition

This law enables the statistician to compute the probability that several events will occur either separately or jointly.[251] The formula provides:

$$P(A \text{ or } B) = P(A) + P(B) - P(A \text{ and } B)$$

Curtis gives the simple example of computing the probability that a person will draw a jack or a diamond from a standard deck of 52 playing cards. The probability of a diamond is 13/52, the probability of a jack is 4/52, and one card will be the jack of diamonds. Hence, the formula yields the result:

$$P(A \text{ or } B) = 13/52 + 4/52 - 1/52 = .3077$$

Special Law of Addition

This law applies when the two events are mutually exclusive.[252] The formula reads:

$$P(A \text{ or } B) = P(A) + P(B)$$

In a standard deck, hearts and spades are mutually exclusive categories; a card cannot be both a heart and a spade. Hence, the statistician deletes the last element, $-P(A \text{ and } B)$, from the general law of addition. The statistician merely sums the two probabilities.

Rule of Complements

Suppose that the outcomes are not only mutually exclusive; together they are exhaustive.[253] Then the formula reads:

$$P(A) + P(B) = 1$$

General Rule of Multiplication

Some probabilities are conditional.[254] The happening of one event affects the probability that the other will occur. We can identify two separate probabilities, for example, the probability that a person chosen for a jury will be a woman and the likelihood that the person will be a college graduate.[255] These categories are not mutually exclusive; the person could be a female college graduate. Consequently, if we know that the person chosen is a woman, the occurrence of that event affects the probability that that person is a college graduate.

---

251. *Id.* at 51.
252. Braun, *supra* note 247, at 71.
253. *Id.* at 75 n.153.
254. W. CURTIS, *supra* note 21, at 49.
255. *Id.*

Statisticians usually express this relationship by the symbol P(A B). The symbol means the probability of A given that event B has already occurred.

When two probabilities are conditional, the general law of multiplication applies. The formula for the general law[256] is as follows:

$$P(A \text{ and } B) = P(A) \times P(B|A)$$

Suppose, for instance, that the attorney wants to know the likelihood of two successive jurors who are male college graduates.[257] The attorney knows that there are only 15 such jurors in a group of 100. The probabilities are conditional. If one is chosen, that choice reduces the number of male college graduates in the remaining pool. Hence, the formula would yield:

$$15/100 \times 14/99 = .021$$

Special Law of Multiplication

Assume alternatively that the probabilities are mutually independent. The statistician might employ regression analysis to test the hypothesis of independence.[258] If the probabilities are independent, the statistician can compound the probabilities by using the multiplication or product rule:[259]

$$P(A \text{ and } B) = P(A) \times P(B)$$

The simplest example is the likelihood of tails on two successive coin tosses.[260] On each toss, the probability is .50, and the events are independent. Thus, the formula converts into:

$$.50 \times .50 = .25$$

This is the formula used to generate random match probabilities in genetic marker cases. If the genetic markers identified are independent, the application of this formula to their population frequencies will yield the random match probability for that genetic profile.

Bayes' Theorem

In the 18th century, the Reverend Thomas Bayes devised a formula that serves two purposes.[261] First, the formula allows the statistician to adjust or modify a

---

256. *Id;* McCord, *supra* note 247, at 747.

257. W. CURTIS, *supra* note 21, at 50.

258. Braun, *supra* note 247, at 79 n.134.

259. W. CURTIS, *supra* note 21, at 51; Even, Bergman, Springer & Feingold, *Probability Analysis and the Evidential Value of Bolt Arrangements*, 33 J. FORENSIC SCI. 1278 (1988) ("A commonly used approach is to apply the well-known rule: the probability of two independent events happening is equal to the product of their separate probabilities").

260. W. CURTIS, *supra* note 21, at 50.

prior probability in light of new evidence. The revision of the prior probability results in a posterior probability. Second, when a trier of fact converts a subjective degree of belief into a prior probability, the formula allows the trier of fact to combine mathematical and nonmathematical evidence in a case. The formula "can accommodate any combination of subjective or frequency-derived inputs as the prior or new-evidence probabilities...."[262] In the simplest case, the formula permits the combination of an objectively ascertained prior probability with objectively ascertained likelihoods. No one seriously questions the propriety of that use of the formula. However, as we shall see, the other applications of the formula have proven to be controversial.

Bayes derived his formula by combining the laws of addition and multiplication discussed above.[263] It is unnecessary to go through the derivation in this text. There are several algebraically equivalent versions of the formula.[264] However, a common version is stated in this manner:

$$P(D|S) = \frac{P(S|D) \times P(D)}{(P(S|D) \times P(D)) + (P(S|\text{not - }D) \times P(\text{not - }D))}$$

A concrete example may make the formula more understandable. Suppose that the prosecutor wants to use Bayes' theorem to help the jury quantify their certitude that the defendant is guilty. The prosecutor has some nonmathematical evidence such as lay eyewitness testimony. The prosecutor also has a laboratory analysis showing that the defendant's blood matches a blood type found on the victim's clothing. In this example, the elements of the formula would signify the following:

P(D) — This is the prior probability that the defendant was at the crime scene. This probability is based on the testimony other than the blood evidence.

P(D | S) — This is the posterior probability. This is the probability that the defendant was at the crime scene, given the blood evidence (S).

To get from P(D) to P(D | S), the statistician must assign values to the other elements of the formula. The remaining elements are:

P(S | D) — This is the probability that the defendant's blood type would match that found at the crime scene if the defendant was at the scene. This

---

261. Bayes, *An Essay Toward Solving a Problem in the Doctrine of Chances*, 53 PHIL. TRANSACTIONS ROYAL SOC'Y 370 (1763), *reprinted in* U.S. DEP'T OF AGRICULTURE, FACSIMILES OF TWO PAPERS BY BAYES (1940).

262. McCord, *supra* note 247, at 749.

263. W. CURTIS, *supra* note 21, at 52-53.

264. Ellman & Kaye, *Probabilities and Proof: Can HLA and Blood Group Testing Prove Paternity?*, 54 N.Y.U. L. REV. 1131, 1148-49 (1979).

is the complement of the probability that the blood test will yield a false negative result. For example, the historical experience of the specific test used may be that in 15% of the cases, there is a false negative. If the result is a false negative, the defendant's blood will seem to differ even though the defendant was present and left the blood stain.

P(S not-D) — This is the probability that the defendant's blood type will match the type at the crime scene even though the defendant was not there. This represents the probability of a false positive result. A false positive is quite probable in the ABO system because many other persons undoubtedly share the same blood type. (The probability would be much lower in the case of HLA or DNA testing.) The possibility of a false positive thus corresponds to the frequency of that blood type in the population.

P(not-D) — This is the probability that the defendant was not at the crime scene. Since P(D) and P(not-D) are mutually exclusive and exhaustive, the rule of complements applies; the two probabilities total one. The statistician can easily derive P(not-D) by subtracting P(D) from one.

To work the hypothetical, we must assign values to the variables. Initially assume that the test yields no false negatives. If the test is so reliable that it will always reveal the true blood type, there is no chance of a false negative. Then $P(S \mid D)$ becomes one. If $P(S \mid D)$ is one, we can simplify the formula:

$$\frac{P(D)}{P(D) + (P(S \mid \text{not - D}) \times P(\text{not - D}))}$$

Now assume that the incidence of the blood type in the population is relatively rare; the frequency is only .07. The statistician inserts .07 as the value for $P(S \mid \text{not-D})$. The formula now reads:

$$\frac{P(D)}{P(D) + (.07 \times P(\text{not - D}))}$$

The next step is for the trier of fact to determine a prior probability, P(D). Since P(D) and P(not-D) equal one, after assigning a value to P(D), the trier subtracts that value from one to determine P(not-D). The trier now has a value for every variable in the formula. The following chart indicates the posterior probabilities that will result from assigning particular values to the prior probability with a .07 frequency for the blood type:

P(D)	P(D | S)
.05	.43
.25	.83
.50	.93
.75	.98
.95	.99

§ 15-7(B). Legal Restrictions on Use of Formulae.

At first, the courts were reluctant to admit statistical testimony, especially in criminal cases.[265] They feared that the testimony would overwhelm or confuse the lay jurors.[266] However, as we shall see, the empirical studies of the impact of statistical evidence have not borne out that fear for the most part;[267] and modern courts are more receptive to statistical testimony.[268] Most courts no longer endorse a blanket renunciation of statistical evidence or bar the evidence altogether.[269] Some courts have even permitted the use of Bayes' theorem in a

---

265. *See generally* C. McCormick, *supra* note 13, at §210; Annot., 36 A.L.R.3d 1194 (1971).

266. *See generally* C. McCormick, *supra* note 13, at §210. Duncan v. State, 828 S.W.2d 847, 850 (Ark. App. 1992) ("the probability of one key fitting two cars was 1 in 7500").

267. Imwinkelried, *The Next Step in Conceptualizing the Presentation of Expert Evidence as Education: The Case for Didactic Trial Procedures*, 1 Internat'l J. Evidence & Proof 128, 135-36 (1997) (collecting the studies).

268. Braun, *supra* note 247, at 86-87; Koehler, *The Probity-Policy Distinction in the Statistical Evidence Debate*, 66 Tul. L. Rev. 141 (1991) ("the use of statistical testimony at trial has increased dramatically during the past two decades"); McCord, *supra* note 247, at 793, 800-06 (the recent case law evidences "a distinct tendency" toward adopting the probabilist position); Rachals v. State, 184 Ga. App. 420, 361 S.E.2d 671 (1987) (a number of patients seemingly died of accidental cardiac arrest while the defendant nurse was on duty; after citing statistics on the incidence of cardiac arrest, a U.S. Centers for Disease Control epidemiologist testified that the probability of so many deaths occurring accidentally was "less than one in a trillion;" Professor Spitznagel points out that if SIDS is genetic, that is, a familial or inherited tendency, one cannot properly calculate the probability by multiplication), *aff'd*, 258 Ga. 48, 364 S.E.2d 867, *cert. denied*, 487 U.S. 1238 (1988); State v. Pankow, 144 Wis. 2d 23, 422 N.W.2d 913, 917-18 (Ct. App. 1988) (several children died while in the care of the defendant babysitter; a sociological statistician testified that the statistical probability of so many children dying of sudden infant death syndrome in the same household within such a short period of time was "one thousand times smaller than 9.1 in one trillion .... [S]uch an event would occur by chance every 600,000 years"); United States v. Shonubi, 895 F. Supp. 460, 514, 517-19 (E.D.N.Y. 1995) (Weinstein, J.) ("Today, complex statistical evidence is being introduced in American courts in a wide variety of both civil and criminal matters. [A] Lexis search of district court opinions using the words 'statistic,' 'statistics,' or 'statistical' turned up 608 examples in the years 1960 to 1969; 2,786 cases from 1970 to 1979; 4,364 cases from 1980 to 1989; and 3,015 from 1990 thru July 31, 1995;" "In mass torts, proof of causation often requires the use of statistically based epidemiological proof. 'Naked' statistical evidence has also been decisive in discrimination cases;" "no special rule of exclusion is required in criminal cases"), *vacated*, 103 F.3d 1085 (2d Cir. 1997).

criminal case.[270] Indeed, the courts' new attitude has spilled over to the question of whether the witness qualifies as an expert on the topic of statistics; the courts have frequently accepted statistical testimony from psychologists, sociologists, economists, and physicians who have had some formal training in statistics but who may be far out of date in their methodology. In light of this new attitude, the opponent of statistical evidence must rely upon a more specific objection to the proffered testimony. A discussion of the admissibility attacks on testimony based on the special multiplication rule and Bayes' theorem will serve to illustrate the most important objections to statistical evidence.

Special Multiplication Rule

The first possible objection to the use of the multiplication rule is that the proponent has not presented trustworthy evidence of the individual probabilities inserted in the formula. Chapter 17, devoted to genetic markers, discusses the famous *Collins* case.[271] One of the errors that the California Supreme Court found in *Collins* was that the prosecutor invented the probabilities without any foundational evidence. A long line of cases following *Collins* mandates that the proponent document the individual probabilities.[272] To satisfy this requirement, the statistician could conduct sampling to establish the probability. Or the statistician could rely on probabilities set out in standard, authoritative texts falling within the learned treatise hearsay exception.[273] Under Federal Rule of Evidence 703, some judges would probably even allow the statistician to rely on probabilities figures that did not satisfy the requirements of the hearsay exception so long as the data was "of a type reasonably relied upon by experts in the particular field in forming opinions or inferences upon the subject...."[274]

Another objection is that there is inadequate proof that the probabilities are independent. As noted in Chapter 17, in *Collins* there was not only no proof that the factors were independent; it was obvious that they were not independent. One factor included persons with beards while another included persons with moustaches. Those two probabilities are clearly interdependent to a degree. The California court stressed that there was no "proof of the statistical independence

---

269. Braun, *supra* note 247, at 86-87; Davis v. State, 476 N.E.2d 127 (Ind. App. 1985) (Bayes' theorem); State v. Jackson, 320 N.C. 452, 358 S.E.2d 679 (1987).

270. McCord, *supra* note 247, at 814 (citing State v. Jackson, 320 N.C. 452, 358 S.E.2d 679 (1987)).

271. People v. Collins, 68 Cal. 2d 319, 438 P.2d 33, 66 Cal. Rptr. 497 (1968).

272. Miller v. State, 240 Ark. 340, 399 S.W.2d 268 (1966); State v. Sneed, 76 N.M. 349, 414 P.2d 858 (1966); People v. Risley, 214 N.Y. 75, 108 N.E. 200 (1915). *But see* Roach v. State, 451 N.E.2d 388 (Ind. App. 1983).

273. FED. R. EVID. 803(18). *See* Imwinkelried, *A Comparativist Critique of the Interface Between Hearsay and Expert Opinion in American Evidence Law*, 33 B.C. L. REV. 1, 20-22 (1991).

274. FED. R. EVID. 703.

of the ... factors."[275] Before invoking the special multiplication rule, the proponent must show the independence of the factors. Absent that showing, the foundation should be ruled inadequate as a matter of law.

Still another objection arises not from the formula itself but rather from the proponent's misuse of the formula. Suppose that as in *Collins*, the prosecutor uses the product rule to establish the likelihood that another random couple would have the same characteristics as the defendants, characteristics that lay eyewitnesses have attributed to the perpetrators of the crime. The formula may yield the probability of another couple possessing that set of characteristics, but neither in testimony nor in closing argument may the prosecutor equate that probability with the ultimate probability of guilt. In *Collins,* the court pointed out:

> [N]o mathematical formula could ever establish beyond a reasonable doubt that the prosecutor's witnesses correctly observed and accurately described the distinctive features which were employed to link defendants to the crime. Conceivably, for example, the guilty couple might have included a light-skinned Negress with bleached hair rather than a Caucasian blond; or the driver of the car might have been wearing a false beard as a disguise; or the prosecution witness might simply have been unreliable.[276]

The proponent may not ask the statistician to opine on the probability of guilt, and the proponent may not characterize the likelihood as the probability of guilt during summation.[277] The prosecutor must not confuse "the probability of concurrence of the identifying marks with the probability of mistaken identification" of the defendant.[278]

It is critical to avoid confusing a random match probability, generated by the special multiplication rule, with a source probability. Suppose that after ascertaining the population frequencies for certain DNA markers, the witness applies the special multiplication rule and determines that for the Caucasian population, the random match probability is only 1 in 100,000. At first blush, that figure seems impressive. However, assume further that in a given metropolitan area, there are one million Caucasians. In light of the size of the population, there should be nine other Caucasians with the same DNA profile. In short, to compute the source probability, the expert needs data as to population size as well as population frequency.

The last objection to testimony based on the multiplication rule relates to the fears that originally inspired the wholesale exclusion of statistical testimony. In

---

275. People v. Collins, 68 Cal. 2d 319, 328-29, 438 P.2d 33, 39, 66 Cal. Rptr. 497, 503 (1968).

276. *Id.* at 330, 438 P.2d at 40, 66 Cal. Rptr. at 504.

277. United States v. Massey, 594 F.2d 676, 681 (8th Cir. 1979).

278. *Id. See also* Hicks v. Scurr, 671 F.2d 255, 259 (8th Cir.), *cert. denied,* 459 U.S. 968 (1982).

Collins, the California Supreme Court used the colorful language that "in our computerized society," mathematics is "a veritable sorcerer."[279] The court's argument sounds in legal relevance, the doctrine stated in Federal Rule of Evidence 403.[280] The argument is that there is an intolerable danger that the statistical testimony will awe the lay jurors. That risk is certainly present in cases like *Collins* when the expert quotes a staggering random match probability such as 1 in 12,000,000. In the DNA cases, some experts are quoting probabilities in the billions. Although this generalized objection may occasionally succeed to block the admission of statistical testimony[281] or persuade the judge to give the jury a cautionary instruction about the testimony,[282] support for this view is eroding. Commentators have pointed out that lay jurors are often asked to evaluate complex material in medical malpractice, antitrust, and patent cases.[283] More and more courts have faith in jurors' ability to critically evaluate statistical testimony.[284] Some empirical studies indicate that rather than being overwhelmed by statistical evidence, jurors tend to underutilize the evidence during their deliberations.[285]

---

279. People v. Collins, 68 Cal. 2d 319, 438 P.2d 33, 66 Cal. Rptr. 497 (1968).

280. Vaughan v. Metrahealth Companies, Inc., 145 F.3d 197, 203 (4th Cir. 1998) ("statistical evidence is inherently malleable and it is thus subject to careful scrutiny"); Blancha v. Raymark Indus., 972 F.2d 507, 516 (3d Cir. 1992) ("evidence of statistical probabilities" is a "likely subject [ ] of exclusion" under Rule 403). *See also* United States v. State of Or., 782 F. Supp. 502, 513 (D. Or. 1991) ("Statistics ... are subject to a wide range of manipulation"), *aff'd,* 28 F.3d 110 (9th Cir. 1994.

281. State v. Carlson, 267 N.W.2d 170, 176 (Minn. 1978).

282. McAlester v. United Air Lines, Inc., 851 F.2d 1249 (10th Cir. 1988) (the judge instructed the jury that statistics are inherently slippery in nature).

283. Braun, *supra* note 247, at 44 n.1.

284. State v. Clayton, 646 P.2d 723, 727 n.1 (Utah 1982). *See also* United States *ex rel.* DiGiacomo v. Franzen, 680 F.2d 515 (7th Cir. 1982.

285. *E.g.,* Schklar & Diamond, *Juror Reactions to DNA Evidence: Errors and Expectancies,* 23 LAW & HUM. BEHAV. 159 (1999) ("participants in our study . . . afforded probabilitistic evidence less weight than would be expected...."); Cecil, Hans & Wiggins, *Citizen Comprehension of Difficult Issues: Lessons from Civil Jury Trials,* 40 AM. U. L. REV. 727, 744-45, 751, 754, 758 (1991); Faigman & Baglioni, *Bayes' Theorem in the Trial Process: Instructing Jurors on the Value of Statistical Evidence,* 12 LAW & HUM. BEHAV. 1, 13-16 (1988); Kaye & Koehler, *Can Jurors Understand Probabilistic Evidence?,* 154 J. ROYAL STAT. SOC'Y 75 (1991); Thompson, *Are Juries Competent to Evaluate Statistical Evidence?,* 52 LAW & CONTEMP. PROBS. 9 (1989); Thompson & Schumann, *Interpretation of Statistical Evidence in Criminal Trials: The Prosecutor's Fallacy and the Defense Attorney's Fallacy,* 11 LAW & HUM. BEHAV. 167, 183 (1987); Goodman, *Jurors' Comprehension and Assessment of Probabilistic Evidence,* 16 AM. J. TRIAL ADVOC. 361, 386 (1992) ("[F]inal judgments of guilt ... tended to be significantly lower than a Bayesian analysis suggests they should have been").

Bayes' Theorem

There are numerous objections to the courtroom use of Bayes' theorem. One objection to the use of Bayes' theorem is similar to the initial objection to the use of the special multiplication rule. Under Bayes' theorem, the trier of fact must use a prior probability; the prior probability can be subjective or frequency-based. The trier then alters that probability in light of the new, mathematical evidence. In some reported cases, the proponent's expert used the theorem without explaining to the trier of fact that a prior probability was being assumed or making it clear that the trier of fact could disagree with the expert's assessment of the prior probability.[286] It would be preferable if the proponent presented the jury with a chart, including a range of prior probabilities and associated posterior probabilities and informed the jury that they were not bound by the expert's choice of a prior probability.[287] Otherwise, the statistician usurps the jury's role in assessing the weight of nonmathematical evidence in the case.

Another objection is that the lay jurors are ill-equipped to convert their subjective beliefs into a numerical, prior probability.[288] Cognitive psychology indicates that jurors typically decide cases by in effect viewing the two sides' positions as hypotheses and inquiring which hypothesis better accounts for the evidence. Jurors are not accustomed to thinking in numerical terms.[289] Their translation of subjective belief into probabilities may be arbitrary and unreliable.

---

286. *See* Ellman & Kaye, *supra* note 264, at 1149.

287. *Id.*

288. Braun, *supra* note 247, at 50-53. *See generally* Tribe, *Trial by Mathematics: Precision and Ritual in the Legal Process*, 84 HARV. L. REV. 1329 (1971); McCord, *supra* note 220, at 750-52, 775, 781 (relying on the inductive theories of Sir Francis Bacon, the anti-probabilists reject the assumption "that all evidence is in essence probabilistic" and that "each item's evidentiary value can be expressed in terms of the subjective probability of its being true;" in their view, nonstatistical testimony cannot be "probabilized;" "each piece of evidence ... is ultimately an all-or-nothing proposition" for the trier of fact, and after deciding which items of evidence to believe the trier "consider[s] alternative hypotheses that would explain the [believable] evidence, and chooses the most plausible explanation"). *See also* Jaffee, *Prior Probability — A Black Hole in the Mathematician's View of the Sufficiency and Weight of Evidence*, 9 CARDOZO L. REV. 967, 968, 1010 (1988) (Bayes' theorem cannot be used in the courtroom because, in principle, the jury should employ a zero prior probability).

289. Ellman & Kaye, *supra* note 264, at 1153. Twining, *Narrative and Generalisations in Argumentation About Questions of Fact, in* FESTSKRIFT TILL STIG STROMHOLM 821, 824-25 (1997) (there is "compelling evidence that in practice jurors and other triers of fact reach judgements about particular past events by assessing the plausibility of stories. Jurors, it is said, proceed 'holistically' by comparing competing stories or by deciding on the plausibility of the story...;" jurors do not engage in "atomistic," statistical reasoning to reconstruct particular past events); Allen, *Factual Ambiguity and a Theory of Evidence*, 87 NW. U. L. REV. 604, 604-05 (1994) ("cognitive psychology generally, and research into jury decisionmaking specifically, ... have made it rather plain that virtually no one thinks" as the probabilitists assume; rather than "deciding the truth or falsity of particular elements," the lay jurors adopt "holistic perspectives, ... deciding the relative

A further objection is that the numerical evidence may tend to obscure the non-numerical evidence — dwarf the soft variable, to use Professor Tribe's expression.[290] The fear is that especially when the numbers are impressive, the lay jurors may overemphasize the statistical evidence during their deliberations.[291]

There is also a risk of double counting.[292] To properly apply Bayes' theorem, the trier of fact must assess the prior probability without considering the numerical evidence. The difficulty is that at trial, the jury hears all the evidence, mathematical and nonmathematical, before beginning its deliberations. The jury hears all the statistical testimony before it begins applying the theorem. When the numbers are impressive, the numbers may subconsciously influence the jurors and lead them to inflate the prior probability.

As in the case of the special multiplication rule, there is a risk of misuse when the court admits testimony about Bayes' theorem. The testimony can establish the likelihood of the defendant's presence at a crime scene by combining the nonmathematical evidence with, for example, expert testimony that the defendant's blood type matches a blood stain at the scene.[293] However, the posterior probability is not the probability of guilt.[294] "Neither the fingerprint expert nor [a] statistician could possibly testify to the guilt of the accused, for this would be a matter wholly outside his competence."[295]

The opponent can also make the same legal relevance objection to the admission of an impressive posterior probability generated by Bayes' theorem that he can urge under *Collins:* The admission of the posterior probability will overwhelm the jury.

The opponents of reliance on Bayes' theorem are especially insistent that a "naked statistical evidence" case is legally insufficient and should not even be submitted to the jury.[296] There is case law generally indicating that a jury may not

---

plausibility of opposing stories"); Callen, *A Brief Word on the Statistical Evidence Debate*, 66 TUL. L. REV. 1405 (1992) ("Bayesian ... theory is an inaccurate model of human inference under uncertainty"); United States v. Hannigan, 27 F.3d 890, 897 (3d Cir. 1994) (collecting cases).

290. Tribe, *supra* note 288, at 1366. *See also* Note, *Statistics in the Law: Potential Problems in the Presentation of Statistical Evidence*, 40 WASH. & LEE L. REV. 313, 334 (1983).

291. *Id.* at 337.

292. Ellman & Kaye, *supra* note 264, at 1156.

293. *Id.* at 1155.

294. *Id.*

295. Finkelstein & Fairley, *A Comment on "Trial by Mathematics,"* 84 HARV. L. REV. 1801, 1805 (1971).

296. Jaffee, *Of Probativity and Probability: Statistics, Scientific Evidence, and the Calculus of Chance at Trial*, 46 U. PITT. L. REV. 925 (1985); Dant, *Gambling on the Truth: The Use of Purely Statistical Evidence as a Basis for Civil Liability*, 22 COLUM. J.L. & SOC. PROBS. 31, 69 (1988) (although conceding that statistical analysis should inform such decisions as gambling, the author argues that "[t]he analogy between judicial factfinding and the gambler's decision to place a bet is improper because the goals ... are ... different. In gambling, the only rational goal is to maximize winnings over time. Whether or not the gambler has reason to think she will win any particular bet

base a verdict on statistical evidence alone; there must be some individualized evidence about the parties' conduct.[297] Suppose, for example, that a personal injury plaintiff proves that she was struck by a blue bus and that the defendant company owns most of the blue busses in that city. It is generally assumed that based on that evidence, a jury could not return a verdict for the plaintiff.[298] The argument is that the plaintiff's evidence is so obviously incomplete that a rational juror would not find for the plaintiff.[299]

However, there are counterarguments. One commentator argues that "[s]upport for the proposition that courts are reluctant to allow cases to be decided on the basis of 'statistical evidence' is greatly exaggerated in the literature."[300] Professor Kaye concedes that the trier of fact ought to consider gaps in the plaintiff's or prosecutor's case,[301] but he believes that the Bayesian formula can be modified to

---

is unimportant. What is important is that she follows rules that will allow her to come out ahead in the long run. In judicial factfinding, ... the goal is not to maximize the number of correct guesses. The goal is to determine the truth in the individual case before the court. Fairness and respect for individuals demand that juries appeal to evidence rather than to rules for maximizing the number of correct verdicts in the long run"). Wright, *Causation, Responsibility, Risk, Probability, Naked Statistics, and Proof: Pruning the Bramble Bush by Clarifying the Concepts*, 73 IOWA L. REV. 1001, 1050-51 (1988).

297. Smith v. Rapid Transit, Inc., 317 Mass. 469, 58 N.E.2d 754 (1945); Baker v. Bridgestone/Firestone Co., 966 F. Supp. 874, 876 (W.D. Mo. 1996) ("As a general rule, statistical evidence alone is insufficient to avoid a motion for directed verdict.... This rule is founded in large part on the desirability of forcing plaintiffs to identify specific and particularized evidence to support their case. Otherwise, Plaintiffs could merely show that 95 per cent of replacement wheels are sold by one Defendant and therefore in 100 per cent of all cases that Defendant would be liable unless there was definitive evidence that the defendant did not sell the wheel."); United States v. Hannigan, 27 F.3d 890, 897 (3d Cir. 1994) (citing *Smith*).

298. Brilameyer, *Second-Order Evidence and Bayesian Logic*, 66 B.U. L. REV. 673, 674-75 (1986); Nesson, *The Evidence or the Event? On Judicial Proof and the Acceptability of Verdicts*, 98 HARV. L. REV. 1357, 1379-80 (1985).

299. Cohen, *The Role of Evidential Weight in Criminal Proof*, 66 B.U. L. REV. 635, 638-39, 649 (1986).

300. Allen, *A Reconceptualization of Civil Trials*, 66 B.U. L. REV. 401, 429 n.67 (1986); Allen, *On the Significance of Batting Averages and Strikeout Totals: A Clarification of the "Naked Statistical Evidence" Debate, the Meaning of "Evidence," and the Requirement of Proof Beyond a Reasonable Doubt*, 65 TUL. L. REV. 1093, 1096 (1991) ("statistical evidence is admissible, and heavily statistical cases may be sufficient"). Baker v. Bridgestone/Firestone Co., 966 F. Supp. 874, 876 (W.D. Mo. 1996) ("Not all commentators have agreed on this approach. This reluctance to recognize statistical probability as a basis for a verdict has been eroded in recent times when there are insurmountable obstacles to producing particularized proof."). *See also* Kaye, *Apples and Oranges: Confidence Coefficients and the Burden of Persuasion*, 73 CORNELL L. REV. 54, 56 n.7 (1987) ("The notion that the law clearly and categorically forbids naked statistical evidence ... is largely a myth").

301. Kaye, *Do We Need a Calculus of Weight to Understand Proof Beyond a Reasonable Doubt?*, 66 B.U. L. REV. 657, 658, 664 (1986).

take that factor into consideration.[302] Another commentator contends that there is no principled difference between statistical evidence and individualized evidence. According to this commentator, the only superficial distinction is that in the case of statistical evidence, the risk of error is more overt.[303] The lay public may be squeamish about confronting the risk of error so openly; but in this commentator's view, the opponents of reliance on Bayes' theorem elevate symbolism over reality.[304] In *Daubert*, Justice Blackmun frankly confronted the uncertainty of the scientific enterprise; he wrote that even in the hard sciences, "arguably, there are no certainties...."[305] The justice's endorsement of this realistic view should lead the courts to be more receptive to overly uncertain scientific evidence such as probability testimony.[306]

The last possible objection is the most philosophic, and perhaps the most important: the possible dehumanization of the justice process.[307] To the extent that the admission of statistical evidence encourages or impels a jury to use strictly mathematical reasoning, the evidence robs the legal process of a subjective, humane quality. We ordinarily rely on a general verdict and under Federal Rule of Evidence 606(b) cloak jury deliberations with secrecy to protect that quality. The liberal admission of statistical testimony, based on any of the formulae discussed in this section, may imperil this quality. For their part, utilitarian probabilists favor the admission of statistical evidence because, in their view, it maximizes the number of correct decisions,[308] but the anti-probabilists counter that there are important legal values other than accuracy and efficiency.[309]

In the main, though, the courts appear to be growing more receptive to the admission of statistical testimony. Indeed, in some cases they have virtually demanded that type of evidence. In one case, a prosecution expert testified that the chemical composition of a crime scene bullet matched that of lead in bullets possessed by the defendant.[310] The expert testified that in the process of bullet

---

302. *Id.* at 666.

303. Shaviro, *Statistical-Probability Evidence and the Appearance of Justice*, 103 HARV. L. REV. 530, 534, 538, 547 (1989).

304. *Id.* at 535, 542, 545, 547, 553-54. *But see* Callen, *Adjudication and the Appearance of Statistical Evidence*, 65 TUL. L. REV. 457 (1991); Shaviro, *A Response to Professor Callen*, 65 TUL. L. REV. 499 (1991).

305 Daubert v. Merrell Dow Pharmaceuticals, Inc., 509 U.S. 579, 590 (1993).

306. Imwinkelried, *Evidence Law Visits Jurassic Park: The Far-Reaching Implications of the Daubert Court's Recognition of the Uncertainty of the Scientific Enterprise*, 81 IOWA L. REV. 55, 65-67 (1995).

307. *See generally* Tribe, *supra* note 288, at 1329.

308. Callen, *Adjudication and the Appearance of Statistical Evidence*, 65 TUL. L. REV. 457, 462-64 (1991); McCord, *supra* note 247, at 752-53.

309. *Id.* at 754-55.

310. State v. Noel, 303 N.J. Super. 435, 697 A.2d 157 (App. Div. 1997).

manufacturing, molten lead is poured into 70-pound blocks called billets and that approximately 43,000 9 mm bullets could be made from a single billet. Nevertheless, the intermediate appellate court found the foundation inadequate for the expert's testimony about a "match." The court commented that the jury's assessment of the probative value of the testimony

> must necessarily depend on how many nine-millimeter bullets could have been produced from a single batch, what the likelihood is that those same bullets wound up for sale in the same geographical area, and what percentage of nine-millimeter bullets marketed in the Newark area came from Speers [the manufacturer].[311]

Since the expert could not supply that data, his opinion might have misled the jury. It is true that the state supreme court reversed the intermediate appellate court.[312] The supreme court ruled that more extensive statistical evidence was not a prerequisite to the admission of testimony about a match in chemical composition. However, the court acknowledged the relevance of the missing statistics; the court commented that the lack of the data affected the weight of the prosecution testimony.

§ 15-8. Summary.

This chapter covers much complex material. However, most of the points made in this chapter are reducible to a few, common-sense questions that should always be asked when a proponent offers statistical testimony:

- Is the witness qualified as an expert?[313]
- What formula did the expert use to generate the final number?
- Has the expert shown that the formula itself is valid? Does the formula satisfy *Daubert*[314] or *Frye*?

---

311. *Id.*

312. State v. Noel, 157 N.J. 141, 723 A.2d 602 (1999).

313. Melendez v. Illinois Bell Tel. Co., 79 F.3d 661, 669 n.9 (7th Cir. 1996) (although the plaintiff's expert "had never previously validated an employment test," he had "a doctorage in social psychology and has published in the area of statistical analysis"); Berkovich v. Hicks, 922 F.2d 1018, 1025 (2d Cir. 1991) ("Berkovich's witness was not an expert in statistics ..."); IMPACT v. Firestone, 893 F.2d 1189 (11th Cir. 1990) (the witness was a political scientist rather than a statistician), *cert. denied sub nom.* Secretary of State of Florida v. Walker, 498 U.S. 847 (1990); Randall v. Howard University, 941 F. Supp. 206 (D.D.C. 1996) (a university administrator was not qualified as an expert to provide statistical evidence of discriminatory practices), *aff'd*, 132 F.3d 1482 (D.C. Cir. 1997).

314. Adams v. Indiana Bell Telephone Co., Inc., 2 F. Supp. 2d 1077, 1094 (S.D. Ind. 1998) (the application of Rule 702 and the *Daubert* standard to statistical evidence). *See also* Coastal Fuels of Puerto Rico v. Caribbean Petroleum, 175 F.3d 18, 33-34 (1st Cir. 1999) (the application of *Daubert* and *Kumho* to economic testimony).

— What does each variable in the formula represent?
— Does the proper use of the statistical technique, such as the binomial distribution, the normal distribution, and regression analysis, depend on any assumptions? If so, has the proponent shown that the assumptions are satisfied in the instant case?
— What is the source for every number that the expert inserted in a variable in the formula? Is the source itself trustworthy?[315] Is the source admissible?
— Did the proponent misuse the final number during the trial? For example, did the proponent characterize a probability of the defendant's mere presence at the crime scene as the likelihood of guilt? Does the final number represent a random match probability or a source probability?
— Is the statistical testimony so complex and the final number so impressive that the jury may be overwhelmed or confused?
— Did the witness exceed his or her expertise by attempting to draw an inference on a question of law?[316]

§ 15-9. Selected Bibliography.

C. G. AITKEN, STATISTICS AND THE EVALUATION OF EVIDENCE FOR FORENSIC SCIENTISTS (1995).

D. BALDUS & J. COLE, STATISTICAL PROOF OF DISCRIMINATION (1980).

D. BARNES, STATISTICS AS PROOF: FUNDAMENTALS OF QUANTITATIVE EVIDENCE (1983).

D. BARNES & J. CONLEY, STATISTICAL EVIDENCE IN LITIGATION: METHODOLOGY, PROCEDURE, AND PRACTICE (1986).

J. BROOK, A LAWYER'S GUIDE TO PROBABILITY AND STATISTICS (1990).

H. CASSIDY, USING ECONOMETRICS: A BEGINNER'S GUIDE (1981).

W. CURTIS, STATISTICAL CONCEPTS FOR ATTORNEYS (1983).

M. DEGROOT, S. FIENBERG & J. KADANE, STATISTICS AND THE LAW (1986).

S. FIENBERG, THE EVOLVING ROLE OF STATISTICAL ASSESSMENT AS EVIDENCE IN THE COURTS (1989).

M. FINKELSTEIN, QUANTITATIVE METHODS IN LAW: STUDIES IN THE APPLICATION OF MATHEMATICAL PROBABILITY AND STATISTICS TO LEGAL PROBLEMS (1978).

M. FINKELSTEIN & B. LEVIN, STATISTICS FOR LAWYERS (1990).

D. FREEDMAN, R. PISANI, R. PURVES & A. ADHIKARI, STATISTICS (2d ed. 1991).

M. GASTWIRTH, STATISTICAL REASONING IN LAW AND PUBLIC POLICY (1988).

R. HY, D. FEIG & R. REGAL, RESEARCH METHODS AND STATISTICS — A PRIMER FOR CRIMINAL JUSTICE AND RELATED SCIENCES (1983).

---

315. Ruiz v. Johnson, 37 F. Supp. 2d 855, 891 (S.D. Tex. 1999) ("An axiom of statistical analysis is that utility of statistically valid conclusions is wholly dependent on the trustworthiness of the underlying data"); Nakajima v. General Motors Corp., 857 F. Supp. 100, 105 (D.D.C. 1994) ("Where, as here, the expert's opinion is based on an incorrect assumption ..., the testimony should not be permitted....").

316. Mahan v. Farmers Union Cent. Exch., Inc., 235 Mont. 410, 768 P.2d 850, 857 (1989) ("statisticians may testify that their statistical tests show or do not show patterns of discrimination based on age, but may not testify to the ultimate conclusion that age discrimination in his termination was or was not exercised against Wayne Mahan in this case. The jury should be the final arbiter of that issue").

D. Kaye & D. Freeman, *Reference Guide on Statistics*, *in* REFERENCE MANUAL ON SCIENTIFIC EVIDENCE 331 (1994).

D. KAYE & M. AICKIN, STATISTICAL METHODS IN DISCRIMINATION LITIGATION (1986).

J. LOEWEN, SOCIAL SCIENCE IN THE COURTROOM (1982).

D. MOORE, STATISTICS: CONCEPTS AND CONTROVERSIES (2d ed. 1985).

D. MOORE & G. MCCABE, INTRODUCTION TO THE PRACTICE OF STATISTICS (1989).

B. ROBERTSON & G. VIGNAUX, INTERPRETING EVIDENCE: EVALUATING FORENSIC SCIENCE IN THE COURTROOM (1995).

H. SAHAI & A. KHURSHID, STATISTICS IN EPIDEMIOLOGY: METHODS, TECHNIQUES, AND APPLICATIONS (1996).

A. Sykes, *An Introduction to Regression Analysis*, UNIVERSITY OF CHICAGO LAW & ECONOMICS WORKING PAPER No. 20 (2d Series) (1993)

D. VINSON & P. ANTHONY, SOCIAL SCIENCE RESEARCH METHODS FOR LITIGATION (1984).

R. WEHMOEFER, STATISTICS IN LITIGATION: PRACTICAL APPLICATIONS FOR LAWYERS (1985).

T. WONNACOTT & R. WONNACOTT, INTRODUCTORY STATISTICS (3d ed. 1977).

CHAPTER 16

FINGERPRINTS*

§ 16-1. In General.

Impressions left at a crime scene can often link a suspect to the crime. The impressions may have been made by an object associated with the perpetrator of the crime — for instance, a shoe[1] or tire impression.[2] Or the impression may have

---

*The authors wish to express their appreciation to Mr. Clarence Phillips of Printrak International, Inc., retired Senior Fingerprint Instructor, Federal Bureau of Investigation, who reviewed this chapter in the second and third editions. The authors would also like to thank Mr. Robert Hazen, also retired from the Federal Bureau of Investigation, who reviewed this chapter in the first edition of this treatise.

1. People v. Lucero, 64 Cal. App. 4th 1107, 75 Cal. Rptr. 2d 806 (1998); People v. Campbell, 146 Ill. 2d 363, 583 N.E.2d 1261 (1992); People v. Edelbacher, 47 Cal. 3d 983, 766 P.2d 1, 254 Cal. Rptr. 586 (1989) (shoe tracks); State v. Ingold, 450 N.W.2d 344, 348 (Minn. App. 1990)

been created by part of the perpetrator's skin surface.[3] These impressions can take the form of bare footprints from the foot's sole or plantar surface,[4] toe

---

("Expert testimony on whether a defendant's shoe made a print found at a crime scene is admissible"); State v. Gardner, 700 S.W.2d 172 (Mo. App. 1985); State v. Dees, 639 S.W.2d 149, 153 (Mo. App. 1982), ; Commonwealth v. Ellis, 354 Pa. Super. 11, 510 A.2d 1253 (1986) (sneaker print); Shor & Weisner, *A Survey of the Conclusions Drawn on the Same Footwear Marks Obtained in Actual Cases by Several Experts Throughout the World*, 44 J. FORENSIC SCI. 380, 383 (1999) (on the one hand, there is a "lack of common standards in shoeprint examiner;" on the other hand, in a 1995 proficiency test 95% "gave the 'right' answer," and in a 1996 test "93% of the participants answered correctly"); von Bremen, *The Comparison of Brake and Accelerator Pedals with Marks on Shoe Soles*, 35 J. FORENSIC SCI. 14 (1990); Music & Bodziak, *Evaluation of the Air Bubbles Present in Polyurethane Shoe Outsoles as Applicable in Footwear Impression Comparisons*, 33 J. FORENSIC SCI. 1185 (1988); Rao, *Patterned Injury and Its Evidentiary Value*, 31 J. FORENSIC SCI. 768 (1986); Bodziak, *Manufacturing Processes for Athletic Shoe Outsoles and Their Significance in the Examination of Footwear Impression Evidence*, 31 J. FORENSIC SCI. 153 (1986); Bodziak, *Shoe and Tire Impression Evidence*, 53 FBI LAW ENF. BULL. 2 (July 1984); Davis, *An Intelligence Approach to Footwear Marks and Toolmarks*, 21 J. FORENSIC SCI. SOC'Y 183 (1981); Petraco, Resua & Harris, *A Rapid Method for the Preparation of Transparent Footwear Test Prints*, 27 J. FORENSIC SCI. 935 (1982); Rose, *Interpretation of Shoe Wear Patterns in a Personal Injury Case*, 26 J. FORENSIC SCI. 608 (1981); W. BODZIAK, FOOTWEAR IMPRESSION EVIDENCE. *But see* Bird v. State, 594 So. 2d 644 (Ala. Crim. App. 1990) (a podiatrist was prepared to testify that the defendant had not made the shoeprints at the murder scene, but the defense failed to show that the podiatrist's method of comparison was based upon a reasonably sound scientific approach); W. BODZIAK, FOOTWEAR IMPRESSION EVIDENCE (1992); Shor, Vinokurov & Glattstein, *The Use of an Adhesive Lifter and pH Indicator for the Removal and Enhancement of Shoeprints in Dust*, 43 J. FORENSIC SCI. 182 (1998); Zugibe, Costello & Breithaupt, *Identification of a Killer by a Definitive Sneaker Pattern and His Beating Instruments by Their Distinctive Patterns*, 41 J. FORENSIC SCI. 310 (1996); Glattstein, Shor, Levin & Zeichner, *ph Indicators as Chemical Reagents for the Enhancement of Footwear Marks*, 41 J. FORENSIC SCI. 23 (1996); Mikkonen & Astikainen, *Databased Classification System for Shoe Sole Patterns — Identification of Partial Footwear Impression Found at a Scene of Crime*, 39 J. FORENSIC SCI. 1227 (1994); Hall & Nolan, *An Improved Technique to Enable 2-Dimensional Shoe Sole Impression Evidence to Be Photographically Recorded "To Scale,"* 39 J. FORENSIC SCI. 1094 (1994); Wilshire & Hurley, *Development of Two-Dimensional Footwear Impressions Using Magnetic Flake Powders*, 41 J. FORENSIC SCI. 678 (1996); Commonwealth v. Billings, 42 Mass. App. Ct. 261, 676 N.E.2d 62 (1997).

2. State v. Farris, 639 S.W.2d 279 (Mo. App. 1982); Cook, *Footprints and Tire Tracks (Class or Individual Characteristics?)*, 31 IDENT. NEWS 7 (July 1981). One of the foremost tireprint experts in America is Peter McDonald who heads Tire Footprint Identification, 333 Boston Mills Road, Hudson, Ohio 44236. Mr. McDonald is a former manager of tire design for Firestone. *See* P. MCDONALD, TIRE IMPRINT EVIDENCE (1989). P. MCDONALD, TIRE IMPRINT EVIDENCE (1992), reviewed in DeForest, *Book Review*, 37 J. FORENSIC SCI. 663 (1992).

3. Steyer, *Sci-Fi Security*, AMERICAN WAY, Mar. 15, 1987, at 76. Biometrics manufacturers are now developing machines to measure identifying human characteristics. For example, they are already marketing retinal scanners and hand geometry equipment.

4. United States v. Ferri, 778 F.2d 985 (3d Cir. 1985), *cert. denied*, 476 U.S. 1172 (1986); People v. Farmer, 47 Cal. 3d 888, 765 P.2d 940, 254 Cal. Rptr. 508 (footprint impressions), *cert. denied*, 490 U.S. 1107 (1989); People v. Corral, 224 Cal. App. 2d 300, 36 Cal. Rptr. 591 (1964);

prints,[5] lip prints,[6] earprint,[7], fingernail impressions,[8] palm prints,[9] impressions left by the pores on the skin,[10] an impression left by a face[11] or glove,[12] or impressions left by the edges of the friction ridges on hands.[13]

Annot., *Admissibility of expert testimony that item of clothing or footgear belonged to, or was worn by, particular individual*, 71 A.L.R.4TH 1148 (1989); Annot., *Admissibility of bare footprint evidence*, 45 A.L.R.4TH 1178 (1986); L. ROBBINS, FOOTPRINTS: COLLECTION, ANALYSIS AND INTERPRETATION (1985); Laskowski & Kyle, *Barefoot Impressions — A Preliminary Study of Identification Characteristics and Population Frequency of Their Morphological Features*, 33 J. FORENSIC SCI. 378 (1988). However, a controversy has arisen over the question of whether a person can be identified on the basis of wear patterns in shoes. *Compare* Thiel v. State, 762 P.2d 478 (Alaska App. 1988) (yes) and State v. Hasan, 205 Conn. 485, 534 A.2d 877 (1987) (yes) *with* People v. Ferguson, 172 Ill. App. 3d 1, 122 Ill. Dec. 266, 526 N.E.2d 525, *app. denied*, 122 Ill. 2d 583, 530 N.E.2d 254, 125 Ill. Dec. 226 (1988) (no). Stapleton, *Best Foot Forward: Infant Footprints for Personal Identification*, 63 FBI LAW ENF. BULL. 14 (Nov. 1994); Hansen, *Believe It or Not*, 79 A.B.A. J. 64 (June 1993) (discussing the controversy over the late Louise Robbins' theory that a person can be identified on the basis of wear patterns in shoes).

5. A. MOENSSENS, J. STARRS, C. HENDERSON & F. INBAU, SCIENTIFIC EVIDENCE IN CRIMINAL CASES § 8.10 (4th ed. 1995).

6. Kasprzak, *Possibilities of Cheiloscopy*, 46 FORENSIC SCI. INT'L 145 (1990) (reviewing the history of the development of this study, beginning with Fischer's identification of systems of furrows on the red part of human lips in 1902); Burns, *A "Kiss" for the Prosecution*, 31 IDENT. NEWS 3 (July 1981).

7. *Earprint Is Pivotal Evidence in Trial*, THE RECORDER, July 17, 1997, p. 6 ("A jury convicted a man of killing his ex-wife's fiancee in a trial that included the rare evidence of an earprint taken from the crime scene;" in part on the basis of the evidence, David Kunze was convicted in Clark County, Washington Superior Court; "The pivotal evidence was an earprint lifted from [the victim's] bedroom door. A Dutch crime expert, Cor van der Lugt, testified that he was '100 percent certain' that the earprint belonged to Kunze. He did acknowledge that no scientific studies prove earprints are unique. Defense experts said the earprint could not be positively linked to Kunze. The use of earprints as evidence at a criminal trial is unusual in the United States. In 1986, a murder defendant was convicted based partly on earprint evidence in a California case").

8. Diaz, Boehm & Rowe, *Comparison of Fingernail Ridge Patterns of Monozygotic Twins*, 35 J. FORENSIC SCI. 97 (1990); Stone & Wilimovsky, *Evidentiary Basis for Fingernail Striation Association*, 12 J. POLICE SCI. & ADMIN. 201 (1984); Apolinar & Rowe, *Examination of Human Fingernail Ridges by Polarized Light*, 25 J. FORENSIC SCI. 154 (1980); Stone, *Fingernail Associations in Murder Cases*, AFTE J. 39 (Jan. 1981); Thomas & Baert, *The Longitudinal Striation of the Human Nails as a Means of Identification*, 14 J. FORENSIC MED. 113 (1967); Thomas & Baert, *A New Means of Identification of the Human Being: The Longitudinal Striation of the Nails*, 5 MED. SCI. & LAW 39 (1965). *But see* People v. Wesley, 103 Mich. App. 240, 303 N.W.2d 194 (1981), *aff'd*, 421 Mich. 375, 365 N.W.2d 692 (1984). Several courts have now admitted fingernail comparison testimony. Commonwealth v. Graves, 310 Pa. Super. 184, 456 A.2d 561 (1983); State v. Shaw, 124 Wis. 2d 363, 369 N.W.2d 772 (Ct. App. 1985); Annot., *Admissibility of evidence of fingernail comparisons in criminal cases*, 40 A.L.R.4TH 575 (1985); Kempton, Sirignano, DeGaetano, Yates & Row, *Comparison of Fingernail Striation Patterns in Identical Twins*, 37 J. FORENSIC SCI. 1534 (1992) (even identical twins' ridge patterns are distinguishable). *But see* Starrs, *Judicial Control Over Scientific Supermen: Fingerprint Experts and Others Who Exceed the Bounds*, 35 CRIM. L. BULL. 234, 240 (May-June 1999) (discussing a

Although all these objects and parts of the skin surface leave impressions, no impression is as important as a fingerprint. This chapter focuses on fingerprints for two reasons. First, crime laboratories rely on fingerprints more heavily than on any other type of impression. Second, most of the techniques for detecting and analyzing fingerprints are transferable to the other impressions. The initial sections of this chapter are devoted to the scientific state of the art: the scientific premises underlying fingerprint evidence; the visualization, photographing, lifting, classification, and identification of fingerprints; and determining the age of fingerprints. The final three sections of the chapter review the legal restrictions on fingerprint evidence.

Developments since the release of the second edition of this treatise have underscored the importance of fingerprint evidence. To begin with, as § 16-4(A) points out, there has been a notorious scandal involving the New York State Police. The investigation of the scandal unearthed evidence that in several cases between 1982 and 1992, New York State Police Troopers had tampered with fingerprint evidence.

Furthermore, both here and abroad there have been alarming disclosures of errors by fingerprint examiners. In Britain, there was a revelation of the mistaken fingerprint identification of Neville Lee — despite the fact that the British examiners insist on 16 points for an identification and triple check fingerprint identifications.[14] A similar fingerprint misidentification occurred in England in 1997 in the case of Andrew Chiory — despite England's "rigid and conservative

---

case of Jimmy Mankins who was erroneously indicted for murder based on fingernail identification but was later cleared by DNA testing).

9. United States v. Moore, 936 F.2d 1508, 1519-20 (7th Cir.), *cert. denied*, 502 U.S. 991 (1991); State v. Johnson, 634 S.W.2d 492 (Mo. App. 1982); Shimoda & Franck, *Writer's Palmar Impressions*, 34 J. FORENSIC SCI. 468 (1989).

10. Ashbaugh, *Ridgeoscopy — The Time Is Now*, 32 IDENT. NEWS 11 (June 1982). The study is known as poroscopy. However, some authorities emphasize that a fingerprint examiner does not consider pores in making a fingerprint identification. In correspondence with the authors, Frankie Franck stated: "Fingerprint identifications are based upon a finding of sufficient number of ridge characteristics in the same relative position in both the inked print and the latent print. Pores are not considered ridge formations and poroscopy is not used to identify or classify fingerprints ...." Letter from Frankie E. Franck to Professor Imwinkelried (Aug. 16, 1988) (available in Professor Imwinkelried's office).

11. United States v. Gillette, 22 M.J. 840 (A.F.C.M.R. 1986), *aff'd.* 25 M.J. 243 (C.M.A. 1987), *cert. denied*, 484 U.S. 1011 (1988).

12. Lambourne, *Glove Print Identification*, 38 J. FORENSIC IDENT. 7 (Jan./Feb. 1988); Starrs, *The Erumpent Quality of Bones: Part Three*, 18 SCIENCE SLEUTHING 7 (Spr. 1994) (Professor Eugene Giles, a University of Illinois anthropologist, was prepared to give "his opinion on the identity of the person who had left ... gloved 'handprint smudges' on" an automobile).

13. *Id.*; Ashbaugh, *Ridgeology: Our Next Evaluative Step*, 45 R.C.M.P. GASETTE 10 (May 1983). This study is termed ridgeology or edgescopy.

14. Starrs, *A Colossal Blunder Under the Union Jack*, 22 SCI. SLEUTHING REV. 10 (Sum. 1998).

standard for reporting a fingerprint identification."[15] In the United States, Collaborative Testing Services, Inc. released the results of a 1995 proficiency study of fingerprint examiners, reviewed by the International Association for Identification.[16] In the test, seven supposed latent crime scene prints were provided, and the participating examiners were asked to compare them with four inked ten-print cards. Five of the seven latents originated from persons whose cards were furnished. "156 examiners were tested. Of these, only 68, or 44%, ... correctly noted the five latent impressions as well as correctly noted the two eliminations. 88 or 56% provided divergent (read as wrong, incorrect, erroneous) answers. Six respondents were declared to have failed to identify any of the latent prints. [O]f the 156 examiners, 58 included erroneous identifications."[17] "Six persons failed to make any correct identifications. Erroneous identifications constituted 22% of the total."[18] Fingerprint identification is not as infallible as many laypersons assume it to be.

§ 16-2. Scientific Premises.

The science of fingerprint examination or dactylography rests on the basis that fingerprints are unchanging, unique, and transferable to surfaces.

The friction ridges that leave impressions are found on the fingers and palmar surfaces of the hands and on the toes and plantar areas of the feet. These ridges begin to form in the third and fourth months of fetal life. It is often said that once formed, the fingerprint pattern is "immutable."[19] There are two main layers of friction skin: the outer skin (epidermis) and the lower layer (dermis). There are furrows or grooves in the friction skin. Between the grooves there are friction ridges. As a person's body grows, the friction pattern expands. When the person becomes elderly, the pattern shrinks. However, even while the pattern is expanding or shrinking, the position of the ridge characteristics relative to each other remains constant. Although there is one report to the contrary,[20] the almost

---

15. Starrs, *Judicial Control Over Scientific Supermen: Fingerprint Experts and Others Who Exceed the Bounds*, 35 CRIM. L. BULL. 234, 245 (May-June 1999).

16. Starrs, *Forensic Science on the Ropes: An Upper Cut to Fingerprinting*, 20 SCI. SLEUTHING REV. 1 (Wint. 1996); Grieve, *Possession of Truth*, 46 J. FORENSIC IDENT. 521 (1996). The report was entitled *Latent Prints Examination, Report No. 9508.*

17. Starrs, *Forensic Science on the Ropes: An Upper Cut to Fingerprinting*, 20 SCI. SLEUTHING REV. 1, 2 (Wint. 1996).

18. *Id.* at 3. An especially "troubling" aspect of the test was that it was not blind, since the participating examiners "were surely on notice that they were being tested and such notice should have put them on their guard to do their very best." *Id.*

19. *But see* Starrs, *Judicial Control Over Scientific Supermen: Fingerprint Experts and Others Who Exceed the Bounds*, 35 CRIM. L. BULL. 234, 241-42 (May-June 1999).

20. Caarick, *Ridge Count Reduction*, 7 FINGERPRINT WHORLD 71 (1982), describes the case of a person whose ridge count evidently decreased during a 12-year period although there was no skin damage to explain the change in ridge count.

universal belief is that the ridge pattern never changes during life. If there is a superficial abrasion or laceration of the epidermis (damage to a depth of less than one millimeter), the epidermis will be temporarily scarred; but the scar will soon heal, and the original pattern will return. When there is a deeper injury to the dermal layer, permanent scars that will interfere with the classification of the pattern may result. However, if sufficient distinctive ridge detail remains, it is still possible to identify the fingerprint. The pattern lasts until after death, when decomposition sets in. Even years after death, if mummification occurs as it would in a hot, dry environment, the pattern may persist.

The pattern is considered unique as well as unchanging. On the one hand, there are commonly recurring types of patterns (loops, arches, and whorls) which permit the systematic classification of fingerprints. On the other hand, the set of minutiae or fine ridge details, such as ridge endings, bifurcations, and dots on each person's fingers, is individualistic. One estimate is that the odds of fingerprint duplication are only one in 64 billion.[21]

These unique features can be detected at a crime scene because of the peculiar characteristics of fingerprints and their transferability from the friction skin to other surfaces. At irregular intervals on the ridges, there are pore openings. Sweat glands in the dermis discharge perspiration through these openings, and this discharge is deposited on surfaces that the friction skin contacts. The deposit or residue contains water and solids. Most of the deposit — roughly 98.5% — is water. However, the water evaporates. Roughly one third of the remaining deposit consists of inorganic salts such as sodium chloride while the other two thirds is organic in nature, including amino acids.

---

21. Braun, *Quantitative Analysis and the Law: Probability Theory as a Tool of Evidence in Criminal Trials*, 1982 UTAH L. REV. 41, 57 n.82. *See also* Stoney & Thornton, *A Critical Analysis of Quantitative Fingerprint Individuality Models*, 31 J. FORENSIC SCI. 1187 (1986). *But see* Starrs, *Forensic Science on the Ropes: An Upper Cut to Fingerprinting*, 20 SCI. SLEUTHING REV. 1 (Winter 1996) (The author describes another article, David L. Grieve, *Possession of Truth*, 46 J. FORENSIC IDENT. 521 (1996). The article reports on the results of a report entitled LATENT PRINTS EXAMINATION, REPORT NO. 9508, conducted by Collaborative Testing Services, Inc., which describes a 1995 proficiency test sponsored by the International Association of Identification. In the test, seven supposed latent crime scene prints were provided, and the participating examiners were asked to compare them with four inked ten-print cards. Five of the seven latents originated from persons whose cards were provided. "156 fingerprint examiners were tested. Of these, 'only 68, or 44%, had correctly noted the five latent impressions as well as correctly noted the two eliminations.' 88 or 56% 'provided divergent (read as wrong, incorrect, erroneous) answers.' Six respondents were declared to have 'failed to identify any of the latent prints.' [O]f the 156 examiners 48 included 'erroneous identifications'" (*id.* at 2). "Six persons failed to make any correct identifications. Erroneous identifications constituted 22% of the total" (*id.* at 3). An especially "troubling" aspect of the test was that it was not blind, since the participating examiners "were surely on notice that they were being tested and such notice must have put them on their guard to do their very best." *Id.*).

When the transfer occurs, a latent impression of the friction skin is left on the surface that the skin contacted. The impression can take one of three forms. If at the time of contact the skin was clean and the surface was clean and smooth — even a pop can or a bamboo plant — the impression is generally invisible to the naked eye. A laser or other special forensic lights (Alternate Light Source [ALS]), powders, or chemical treatments are needed to visualize the impression. However, if the surface was covered with a wet foreign substance, such as blood, grease, ink, paint, or mud, the impression will be visible. Finally, if the surface was part of a soft material, such as butter, thick dust, putty, or wax, a plastic impression will remain.

There are indications that latent fingerprints left by children last a shorter period of time — and must consequently be detected and visualized more quickly — than those left by adults. Some police departments have encountered particular difficulty visualizing prints of children.[22] The question requires much more extensive research, but the suspicion is that children's fingerprint residue contains more volatile components which evaporate faster.[23]

§ 16-3. Detection and Visualization of Crime Scene Impressions.

As noted in the last section, there are three types of latent fingerprint impressions: invisible, visible, and plastic. Accordingly, the crime scene investigators often conduct a two-phase search for fingerprints. One phase is a visual search intended to locate visible and plastic impressions. The investigator may use a flashlight beam to provide oblique light to make faint prints more visible. The second phase is blind development. This phase extends to any area where invisible impressions may have been left, including likely entry and exit points and furniture and other objects that seem to have been disturbed. At these locations powder and chemical techniques are used to visualize impressions. There are also several novel visualization procedures under study.

§ 16-3(A). Conventional Procedures.

The type of surface suspected of containing the impression determines the kind of visualization procedure used.[24]

---

22. Starrs, *The Durability of Children's and Adult's Prints Examined*, 22 SCI. SLEUTHING REV. 5 (Sum. 1998), discussing Focus, *Vanished Into Thin Air: The Search for Children's Fingerprints*, ANAL. CHEM., July 1, 1995, pp. 435A-438A.

23. Starrs, *The Durability of Children's and Adult's Prints Examined*, 22 SCI. SLEUTHING REV. 5 (Sum. 1998).

24. *See generally* Menzel, *The Development of Fingerprints, in* SCIENTIFIC AND EXPERT EVIDENCE 619 (2d ed. 1981).

Nonporous Surfaces

On surfaces such as finished wood, glass, and metal,[25] a powder technique is ordinarily used. The basic principle underlying the various powder techniques is preferential adherence. When applied to the area containing a latent impression, the powder tends to adhere to the residue deposited by the friction skin. The investigator can either spread the powder over the area with a special fingerprint brush or spray magnetized powder over the area and collect the excess with a magnet. The brush can be made of camelhair, squirrelhair, or fiberglass. Numerous fingerprint powders, including aluminum,[26] black, Dragon's blood, gold bronze, gray, and red bronze are available. The choice of powder depends upon the color and nature of the surface. A powder that will contrast with the surface is preferred; for example, a black powder on a white or light-colored surface or a gray powder on a dark-colored surface.

Porous Surfaces

Surfaces such as cardboard, paper, fabrics, and unfinished wood do not generally lend themselves to powder techniques. For these surfaces, it is possible to use a chemical technique such as ANS[27] or liquid crystals.[28] However, our reviewer informs us that those techniques are not used in real forensic work. Rather, chemical methods such as a physical developer, iodine fuming, silver nitrate, or ninhydrin are employed. The visualization is a result of a chemical reaction between the reagent used (iodine, silver nitrate, or ninhydrin) and chemicals present in the fingerprint residue.

In iodine fuming, the reaction occurs when fats and oily substances in the residue absorb iodine fumes. The residue can be exposed to iodine fumes in two ways. The object suspected to have the fingerprint residue can be inserted in a glass tank containing iodine crystals, or the analyst may use a fuming pipe to spread the iodine vapor onto the surface. The absorption of the iodine causes the print to turn brown. The fuming pipe is an effective procedure for detecting prints on cardboard and paper. The F.B.I. has developed a liquid formula of iodine for

---

25. In the case of metallic objects such as cartridge cases, it may be necessary to initially remove material which covers the fingerprint and would otherwise preclude visualizing the print. Cantu, Leben, Ramotowski, Kopera & Simms, *Use of Acidified Hydrogen Peroxide to Remove Excess Gun Blue from Gun Blue-Treated Cartridge Cases and to Develop Latent Prints on Untreated Cartridge Cases*, 43 J. FORENSIC SCI. 294 (1998).

26. James, Pounds & Wilshire, *Flake Metal Powders for Revealing Latent Fingerprints*, 36 J. FORENSIC SCI. 1368 (1991). James, Pounds & Wilshire, *Magnetic Flake Powders for Fingerprint Development*, 38 J. FORENSIC SCI. 391 (1993).

27. Cheng, *ANS (8-Anilinonaphthalene-1-Sulfonate) — A New Reagent for Detection of Latent Fingerprints*, 33 J. FORENSIC SCI. 527 (1988).

28. Bladek & Moszczynski, *Analysis of the Possible Use of Liquid Crystals in Fingerprinting*, 50 FORENSIC SCI. INT'L 87 (1991) (fabrics).

visualizing prints. The liquid solution is made by dissolving one gram of iodine in one liter of cyclohexane. 100 ml of that solution is then mixed with 2 ml of another solution composed of 5 grams of napthoanone in 40 ml of mithyline chloride. The two solutions are mixed with a magnetic stirrer.

In the silver nitrate technique, there is a reaction between chloride ions of salt in the residue and silver ions.[29] The silver nitrate method works well for impressions left on cardboard, paper, some porous plastics, and unfinished wood.

Although iodine fuming and silver nitrate are in widespread use, the most commonly employed chemical technique is ninhydrin.[30] This technique is based

---

29. Kerr, Westland & Hague, *Observations on the Use of Silver Compounds for Fingerprint Visualization*, 18 FORENSIC SCI. INT'L 209 (1981). Migron & Mandler, *Development of Latent Fingerprints on Unfired Cartridges by Palladium Deposition: A Surface Study*, 42 J. FORENSIC SCI. 986 (1997) ("ammoniacal solution of silver nitrate and gun-blue are frequently used as a means of visualizing latent fingerprints on unfired brass cartridge cases. In both methods, developed images on brass cartridges show the valleys as black lines whereas the ridges as golden brass-colored lines"; these researchers developed a new technique, namely, palladium deposition; palladium was found to deposit onto both valleys and ridges).

30. *E.g.*, Almog, Frank, Sterling & Leonov, *Aminoninhydrins: Fingerprint Reagents with Direct Fluorogenic Activity — Preliminary Studies*, 36 J. FORENSIC SCI. 104 (1991); Lennard, Margot, Stoilovic & Warrener, *Synthesis and Evaluation of Ninhyrdrin Analogues as Reagents for the Development of Latent Fingerprints on Paper Surfaces*, 28 J. FORENSIC SCI. SOC'Y 3 (1988); Lennard, Margot, Sterns & Warrener, *Photoluminescent Enhancement of Ninhydrin Developed Fingerprints by Metal Complexation: Structural Studies of Complexes Formed Between Ruhemann's Purple and Group IIb Metal Salts*, 32 J. FORENSIC SCI. 597 (1987); Everse & Menzel, *Sensitivity Enhancement of Ninhydrin-Treated Latent Fingerprints by Enzymes and Metal Salts*, 31 J. FORENSIC SCI. 446 (1986); Stoilovic, Kobus, Margot & Warrener, *Improved Enhancement of Ninhydrin Developed Fingerprints by Cadmium Complexation Using Low Temperature Photoluminescence Techniques*, 31 J. FORENSIC SCI. 432 (1986); Almog, Hirshfeld & Klug, *Reagents for the Chemical Development of Latent Fingerprints: Synthesis and Properties of Some Ninhydrin Analogues*, 27 J. FORENSIC SCI. 912 (1982) ("Ninhydrin was adopted for the detection of latent fingerprints on paper in 1954 ... and since then has become the most common reagent for the chemical development of latent fingerprints"); Lee & Arrard, *Comparison of Fluorescamine, O-phthalaldehyde, and Ninhydrin for the Detection and Visualization of Latent Fingerprints*, 7 J. POLICE SCI. & AD. 333 (1979) ("The most widely used chemical reagent for developing latent fingerprints is ninhydrin"). Hewlett, Winfield & Clifford, *The Ninhydrin Process in Supercritical Carbon Dioxide*, 41 J. FORENSIC SCI. 487 (1996); *New Reagents for Development of Latent Fingerprints*, NAT'L INSTIT. JUST. UPDATE, Sep. 1995 (NIJ-sponsored research has assisted in developing synthetic approaches to yield "a total of 21 new ninhydin analogs;" for example, the researchers "reported novel approaches to the synthesis of benzo[f]-ninhydrin, 5-methoxy-ninhydrin, 5-(methylthio)-ninhydrin [and] thenino[f]ninhydrin;" some of these new analogs "displayed properties (*i.e.* brighter fluorescence, better line resolution) superior to ninhydrin's as fingerprint developing agents"); Cantu, *A Comparative Examination of Several Amino Acid Reagents for Visualizing Amino Acids (Glycine) on Paper*, 43 J. FORENSIC IDENT. 44 (1993); Almog, Hirshfeld, Frank, Grant, Harel & Ittah, *5-Methylthio Ninhyrdrin and Related Compounds: A Novel Class of Flurogenic Fingerprint Reagents*, 37 J. FORENSIC SCI. 688 (1992).

on a reaction between the ninydrin reagent and amino acids in the fingerprint residue.

Iodine, silver nitrate, and ninhydrin are the chemical reagents in general use for visualizing latent prints, but special techniques are needed for peculiar surfaces. One such surface is black electrical tape.[31] Iodine, silver nitrate, and ninhydrin produce dark stains that yield poor contrast on black tape. However, a crystal violet technique is available.[32] Crystal violet is dissolved in a mixture of ethanol and phenol. The object suspected of supporting the impression is floated in the solution. The crystal violet visualizes the impression by staining the residue. Paper can also be a troublesome surface. DFO and diketones can be effective in developing latent fingerprints on paper.[33] It can also be difficult to visualize latents on fired cartridge cases. Several conventional techniques, including silver nitrate, have been adapted to that challenge.[34]

§ 16-3(B). Novel Procedures.

Researchers have developed new techniques for visualizing impressions on surfaces such as fabrics that have proven to be difficult for conventional powder and chemical methods.[35] Some techniques have even been proposed for lifting fingerprint impressions from human skin.

---

31. Menzel, *Fingerprint Development*, *in* SCIENTIFIC AND EXPERT EVIDENCE 619, 627 (2d ed. 1981); Howard, *Basic Fuchsin — A Guide to One-Step Processing Technique for Black Electrical Tape*, 38 J. FORENSIC SCI. 1391 (1993). *See also* Bratton & Gregus, *Development of a Black Powder Method to Process Adhesive Tapes*, 23 FINGERPRINT WHORLD 21 (1997) (prints on the backing of tape are typically latent while prints on the sticky side are generally plastic; when the print is on the sticky side, the most widely used approach is to stain the cellular material with gentian violet; Japanese researchers have developed "Sticky Side Powder" for prints on the sticky side; however, that commercial product is quite expensive; these researchers developed their own powder/surfactant combination for prints on the sticky side).

32. Menzel, *Fingerprint Development*, *in* SCIENTIFIC AND EXPERT EVIDENCE 619, 627 (2d ed. 1981).

33. Almog, Springer, Weisner, Frank, Khodzhaev, Lidor, Badhar, Varkony, Dayan & Rozen, *Latent Fingerprint Visualization by 1,2-Indanedione and Related Compounds: Preliminary Results*, 44 J. FORENSIC SCI. 114 (1999).

34. Migron, Hocherman, Springer, Almog & Mandler, *Visualization of Sebaceous Fingerprints on Fired Cartridge Cases: A Laboratory Study*, 43 J. FORENSIC SCI. 543 (1998).

35. United States v. Riley, 906 F.2d 841, 853-55 (2d Cir. 1990). *See generally* Menzel, *The Development of Fingerprints*, *in* SCIENTIFIC AND EXPERT EVIDENCE 619, 628-45 (2d ed. 1981); Fincher, *Lifting "Latents" Is Now Very Much a High-Tech Matter*, 20 SMITHSONIAN MAGAZINE 201 (Oct. 1989); Haque, Westland, Milligan & Kerr, *A Small Particle (Iron Oxide) Suspension for Detection of Latent Fingerprints on Smooth Surfaces*, 41 FORENSIC SCI. INT'L 73 (1989).

Surfaces Other Than Human Skin

Several new fingerprint development techniques have emerged in recent decades.

One is metal deposition. Fingerprint residue on a surface can prevent or limit the deposition of metal on the surface. Metal is spread over a surface through a process of vacuum evaporation. The metal film adheres to the clean surface areas, but the film does not deposit on the residue outlining the friction ridges. Gold is one of the best metals for deposition.[36]

Another technique is autoradiography. This technique consists of labeling the fingerprint residue with a beta-emitting radioisotope. There are several labeling methods. The technician can treat the residue containing the radioisotope. Alternatively, the technician can insert the object containing the impression in a nuclear reactor and generate the radioisotope in the residue through neutron activation analysis (NAA), discussed in Chapter 11. The technician next brings the labeled residue into contact with X-ray film. The beta energy emitted by the radioisotope produces an image of the friction ridge pattern on the film.

Still another method is laser illumination.[37] The Ontario Provincial Police in Canada and the F.B.I. have already used a variation of this method for

36. Kent, *Latent Fingerprints and Their Detection*, 21 J. FORENSIC SCI. SOC'Y 15 (1981).

37. Hooker, Creer & Brennan, *Microspectrophotometry in the Development and Photography of Fluorescing Marks*, 51 FORENSIC SCI. INT'L 297 (1991); Kaminski, *Development of Fingerprints with Laser*, 46 FORENSIC SCI. INT'L 111 (1990) (the experience of the Department of Criminalistics in Poland confirms that the use of the laser permits examination of fingerprints "on a variety of substrates such as aluminum foil, different sorts of paper, clothes, plastics, and wood," but some of the Department's findings were at odds with those reported in the foreign literature); Pearson, *Latent Evidence*, 46 FORENSIC SCI. INT'L 41 (1990) (summarizing the experience of London's Metropolitan Police Forensic Science Laboratory in using an argon ion laser); Pounds, Grigg & Mongkolaussavaratana, *The Use of 1,8-Diazafluoren-9-one (DFO) for the Fluorescent Detection of Latent Fingerprints on Paper — A Preliminary Evaluation*, 35 J. FORENSIC SCI. 169 (1990); Menzel & Mitchell, *Intramolecular Energy Transfer in the Europium-Ruhemann's Purple Complex: Application to Latent Fingerprint Detection*, 35 J. FORENSIC SCI. 35 (1990); Menzel, Bartsch & Hallman, *Fluorescent Metal-Ruhemann's Purple Coordination Compounds: Applications to Latent Fingerprint Detection*, 35 J. FORENSIC SCI. 25 (1990); Meylan, Lennard & Margot, *Use of a Gaseous Electrical Discharge to Induce Luminescence in Latent Fingerprints*, 45 FORENSIC SCI. INT'L 73 (1990); Almog & Hirschfeld, *5-Methoxyninhydrin: A Reagent for the Chemical Development of Latent Fingerprints That is Compatible with the Copper-Vapor Laser*, 33 J. FORENSIC SCI. 1027 (1988); Cheng, *The Use of Frequency-Doubled Neodymium:Yttrium Aluminum Garnet (Nd:YAG) Laser for Enhancement of Weak Bloody Fingerprints*, 33 J. FORENSIC SCI. 1022 (1988); Menzel, *Laser Detection of Latent Fingerprints — Treatment with Phosphorescers*, 14 J. FORENSIC SCI. 582 (1979). The police employed laser illumination during the "Night Stalker" investigation. THE DAVIS ENTERPRISE, Aug. 30, 1985, at 4. Siegel, *Applications of Fluorescence Spectroscopy to Forensic Sciences*, 8 FOR. SCI. REV. 1 (1996); Beesley, Damaskinos & Dixon, *Fingerprint Imaging with a Confocal Scanning Laser Macroscope*, 40 J. FORENSIC SCI. 10 (1995); Bramble, Creer, Quiang & Sheard, *Ultraviolet Luminescence from Latent Fingerprints*, 59 FORENSIC SCI. INT'L 3 (1993); Kaymaz & Mitra, *A Novel Approach to Fourier Spectral*

investigative purposes.[38] There are two modes of laser illumination. In one mode, the technician capitalizes on the inherent luminescence of some elements in fingerprint residue. The investigator employs a laser[39] to produce the luminescence. While luminescent, the latent impression can be photographed with special equipment. There have been mixed reports on the effectiveness of this mode. The initial reports were favorable.[40] However, subsequent researchers were less enthusiastic.[41] These researchers found that: The technique produced detectable impressions in only a small percentage of the cases; and even in these cases, the luminescence is weak and cannot be detected at a distance beyond three meters.[42]

Another mode of this technique is treating fingerprint residue with luminescent substances.[43] Some surfaces such as cardboard, paper, and varnish display strong luminescence. If the fingerprint impression rests on such a surface, the surface's own background luminescence may overwhelm the residue's luminescence. Treating the residue with luminescent material may accentuate its luminescence and permit the visualization of the impression. The technician can effect the treatment in several ways: dusting the residue with luminescent powder; staining the residue with fluorescent dye; or adding chemicals such as fluorescamine that react with the residue to create luminescent reaction products.

An additional technique is Super Glue fuming.[44] Super Glue Corporation of Ridgewood, New York, was one of the first to manufacture Super Glue fuming

---

Enhancement of Laser-Luminescent Fingerprint Images, 38 J. FORENSIC SCI. 530 (1993). One of the problems with the laser technique is that the laser excites background luminescence which may make it difficult to obtain the necessary contrast. However, the background luminescence is shorter-lived than that of the fingerprint; and researchers are now developing time-resolved imaging systems to detect the fingerprint. Mekkaoui & Menzel, *Spectroscopy of Rare Earth-Ruhemann's Purple Complexes*, 38 J. FORENSIC SCI. 506 (1993); Murdock & Menzel, *A Computer Interfaced Time-Resolved Luminescence Imaging System*, 38 J. FORENSIC SCI. 521 (1993); Wenchong, Chunhua, Hong, Chengbai, Zhiming, Bangrui & Bingqun, *Laser Fingerprint Detection Under Background Light Interference*, 37 J. FORENSIC SCI. 1076 (1992).

38. Dempewolff, *How Lab Sleuths Use Science to Fight Crime*, POPULAR MECHANICS, June 1981, at 70; Ridgely, *Latent Print Detection by Laser*, 54 FBI LAW ENF. BULL. 1 (June 1985).

39. Copper vapor and YAG lasers are employed for this purpose

40. Dalrymple, Duff & Menzel, *Inherent Luminescence of Fingerprints by Laser*, 22 J. FORENSIC SCI. 106 (1977).

41. Salares, Eves & Carey, *On the Detection of Fingerprints by Laser Excited Luminescence*, 14 FORENSIC SCI. INT'L 229 (1979).

42. *Id.* at 233-34.

43. Ben Yosef, Almog, Frank, Springer & Cantu, *Short UV Luminescence for Forensic Applications: Design of a Real-Time Observation System for Detection of Latent Fingerprints and Body Fluids*, 43 J. FORENSIC SCI. 299 (1998).

44. Burns, *Base-Activated Latent Fingerprints Fumed with Cyanoacrylate Monomer. A Quantitative Study Using Fourier-Transform Infra-red Spectroscopy*, 362 ANAL. CHEM. ACTS 171 (1998); Alomog & Gabay, *A Modified Super Glue Technique — The Use of Polycyanoarylate for Fingerprint Development*, 31 J. FORENSIC SCI. 250 (1986); Siegel, *Fingerprint Process May Aid Criminal Investigation*, FORUM, Sept./Oct. 1986, at 40; Olenik, *Super Glue, A Modified Technique*

kits, entitled "Dura-Print Fuming Process."[45] Super Glue products are now available from most vendors of forensic identification supplies and equipment. The principal component of the reagent is cyanoacrylate. Cyanoacrylate esters react with other chemicals or heat to produce fumes that will expose fingerprints on difficult surfaces such as ceramics, plastics, and foliage.[46]

Another technique is the use of the plastic impression material typically utilized to register dental impressions.[47] The materials include dental wax, silicone, and alginate. When these techniques are available, the investigator can register the fingerprint in three dimensions.

Finally, researchers are now combining some novel techniques with more conventional methods and with other novel techniques. For example, some researchers have used ninhydrin in conjunction with laser excitation.[48] Other laboratories are combining the laser and Super Glue fuming techniques.[49] For that matter, image enhancement techniques are being employed to complete partial prints.[50]

---

for the Development of Latent Fingerprints, 29 J. FORENSIC SCI. 881 (1984); Kendall & Rehn, *Rapid Method of Super Glue Fuming Application for the Development of Latent Fingerprints*, 28 J. FORENSIC SCI. 777 (1983).

45. Siegel, *New Fingerprint Process May Aid Criminal Investigation*, 19 TRIAL 104 (Sept. 1983).

46. *Id.* at 106; Jian & Dao-An, *A Modified Cyanoacrylate Technique Utilizing Treated Neutral Filter Paper for Developing Latent Fingerprints*, 52 FORENSIC SCI. INT'L 31 (1991); Howorka & Kretschmer, *Experimental Study of Using Cyanoacrylate Ester Vapour for Developing Latent Fingerprints*, 46 FORENSIC SCI. INT'L 31 (1990); Karlinszky & Harkai, *Detection of Latent Fingerprints: Application of Cyanoacrylate for the Inside of Cars*, 46 FORENSIC SCI. INT'L 29 (1990); Nielson & Katz, *A Processing Protocol for Drug Residue and Latent Fingerprint Evidence*, 33 J. FORENSIC SCI. 1463 (1988) (discussing the use of cyanoacrylate vapors); Nielson & Katz, *Recovery of Latent Prints and Drug Residues from a Problem Porous Surface*, 33 J. FORENSIC SCI. 1506 (1988); Onstwedder & Gamboe, *Small Particle Reagent: Developing Latent Prints on Water-Soaked Firearms and Effect on Firearms Analysis*, 34 J. FORENSIC SCI. 321 (1989) (discussing another use of cyanoacrylate ester fuming). One problem with this technique is that it can be difficult to obtain the necessary contrast, since the color of the developed latent fingerprint is white. However, there are several methods of improving the contrast. Chesher, Stone & Rowe, *Use of the Omniprint 1000 Alternative Light Source to Produce Fluorescence in Cyanoacrylate-Developed Latent Fingerprints Stained with Biological Stains and Commercial Fabric Dyes*, 57 FORENSIC SCI. INT'L 163 (1992); Kempton & Rowe, *Contrast Enhancement of Cyanoacrylate-Developed Latent Fingerprints Using Biological Stains and Commercial Fabric Dyes*, 37 J. FORENSIC SCI. 99 (1992).

47. Ulmansky, Fogelman, Degany & Bab, *Registration of Fingertip Pattern with Dental Impression Materials: A Scanning Electron Microscope Study*, 32 FORENSIC SCI. INT'L 237 (1986).

48. Herod & Menzel, *Laser Detection of Latent Fingerprints: Ninhydrin Followed by Zinc Chloride*, 27 J. FORENSIC SCI. 513 (1982); Herod & Menzel, *Laser Detection of Latent Fingerprints*, 27 J. FORENSIC SCI. 200 (1982).

49. Menzel, Burt, Sinor, Tubach-Ley & Jordan, *Laser Detection of Latent Fingerprints: Treatment with Glue Containing Cyanoacrylate Ester*, 28 J. FORENSIC SCI. 307 (1983).

50. Moler, Ballarin, Pessana, Torres & Olmo, *Fingerprint Identification Using Image Enhancement Techniques*, 43 J. FORENSIC SCI. 689 (1998).

Human Skin

It would be a landmark breakthrough if a technique could be perfected to visualize fingerprints left on human skin. However, there are major impediments to perfecting such a technique. Fingerprint residue contains many of the same chemicals found in human skin. Hence, it is difficult to develop good contrast between the fingerprint residue and the skin. In addition, it appears that after deposition on human skin, fingerprint residue quickly disperses, blurring ridge detail. An hour and a half or two hours after deposition may be the maximum period of time in which to detect clear ridge detail.[51] Finally, the impression must be left on a relatively smooth, clean portion of the skin surface. The inner thigh yields some of the best impressions.[52] There are a number of promising techniques, but to date they have been only occasionally successful.

While today magnetic powder is the most extensively used and most successful method for developing latent prints on human skin, at one time the most widely used technique was iodine silver transfer.[53] In this technique, an iodine fuming pipe is used to spread fumes over the fingerprint residue. The technician then presses a silver plate against the fumed area. The pressure transfers the fingerprint pattern to the plate. The plate is then exposed to ultraviolet light for visualization.

Another method is direct transfer from the skin onto a mineral-coated card. Krome-Kote paper is commercially available.[54] After pressing the card against the skin, the technician dusts the card with iodine or fingerprint powder.

---

51. Feldman, Meloan & Lambert, *A New Method for Recovering Latent Fingerprints from Skin*, 27 J. FORENSIC SCI. 806 (1982).

52. *Rape Victims, Investigations Are Focus of Workshop at IACP Convention*, 30 CRIM. L. REP. (BNA) 2042, 2043 (1981).

53. Gelinas, *The Iodine Silver Transfer Method for Obtaining Fingerprints from Skin*, 25 LAW & ORDER 72 (1977). Futrell, *Hidden Evidence: Latent Prints on Human Skin*, 65 FBI LAW ENF. BULL. 21 (Apr. 1996) (in the initial phase of this study, the researchers used the iodine/silver transfer method; the researchers ultimately found that "[t]he one technique that developed identifiable latent prints most often was glue fuming in conjunction with magnetic fingerprint powder"; at first, the researchers used "an airtight plastic tent over a small area of skin or [the] entire body" to spread the fumes; a portable "glue fuming chamber" proved to be more effective; it has "a built-in heat source and a small electric fan"). *See also* Allred, Lin & Menzel, *Lipid-Specific Latent Fingerprint Detection: Fingerprints on Currency*, 42 J. FORENSIC SCI. 997 (1997) ("Lanthanide-based methods of latent fingerprint detection are intended to allow processing of surfaces that display intense background fluorescence. The lanthanides exhibit long luminescence lifetimes.... The long lanthanide lifetimes permit one to suppress background fluorescence via time-resolved imaging. The lanthanide of choice is usually europium.... We emphasize that the described chemical methodology has yet to reach the maturity, with older latent prints in particular, for routine case work. It is nonetheless promising and worth further pursuit....").

54. Feldman, Meloan & Lambert, *supra* note 51, at 806.

Still another method is the use of a polyethylene terephthalate (PET) sheet.[55] This method capitalizes on the phenomenon that static electricity attracts dust. Fingerprint secretions also attract dust. The sheet produces static electricity which then attracts both the dust and the fingerprint oil onto the sheet. Sidelighting can then be employed to visualize the fingerprint impression.

In one case, Amido Black was used successfully to visualize a latent impression on the right inner thigh of the victim of a sexual assault and homicide.[56] Amido Black is a protein dye which is sensitive to the protein in blood. It can cause the fingerprint to turn a blue-black color. This technique requires the preparation of three solutions. The first is created by mixing one gram of Amido Black with 50 ml of Glacial Acetic Acid with a magnetic stirrer. The second solution consists of 100 ml of Glacial Acetic Acid and 900 ml of Methanol. The third solution is comprised of 50 ml of Glacial Acetic Acid and 950 ml of distilled water.[57]

A further method is electronography. Here the skin is dusted with lead powder and then exposed to X-ray. The X-rays excite the powder and cause electron emissions. The emissions create an image of the ridge detail on the X-ray film.

Autoradiography, discussed earlier, can also be used to visualize fingerprint impressions left on human skin.[58]

A final method is the use of the laser or alternate light source. It has been employed to detect fingerprints on both living skin and cadavers.[59] The technician dusts the skin area with fluorescent powder or stains the area with fluorescent dyes[60] and then subjects the area to laser examination.

---

55. Guo & Xing, *Visualization Method for Fingerprints on Skin by Impression on a Polyethylene Terephthalate (PET) Semigrid Sheet*, 37 J. FORENSIC SCI. 604 (1992).

56. Jernigan, *Amido Black Treatment of a Murder Victim Fingerprint Examination Undertaken by Charles Counts, Newberry County, S.C.*, 19 FINGER. WHORLD 55 (1993).

57. Once the three solutions are prepared, the analyst uses the following protocol:

— The evidence is initially immersed in the methanol solution in a covered tray for an hour. The used methanol is then discarded.

— In a glass tray, the evidence is covered with the working solution. It is soaked for two to three minutes or until the latent prints become a blue-black color.

— The evidence is next immersed in enough of the Glacial Acetic Acid-methanol solution to cover.

— The evidence is rinsed with the distilled water solution.

— The evidence is permitted to dry.

— Lastly, the developed latent prints are photographed.

58. Jernigan, *Amido Black Treatment of a Murder Victim Fingerprint Examination Undertaken by Charles Counts, Newberry County, S.C.*, 19 FINGER. WHORLD 55 (1993).

59. Dalrymple, Duff & Menzel, *supra* note 40, at 114.

60. Menzel, *Laser Detection of Latent Fingerprints on Skin*, 27 J. FORENSIC SCI. 918 (1982).

§ 16-4. Permanent Recordation of Crime Scene Impressions.

It is not enough to temporarily visualize the impression; the impression must be permanently recorded in a fashion that will permit proof of the impression at trial. There are two methods of permanent recordation: photographing and lifting.

§ 16-4(A). Photographing.

Before attempting to lift the visualized impression, the print should be photographed in its original location. Special cameras and filters are available for this purpose.[61] In some cases, the photograph must be taken immediately after visualization. For instance, iodine is volatile; and if the technician uses an iodine technique to visualize the impression, the impression may fade quickly.

In the past, development of the final print of the impression in some instances required reversing the negative.[62] However, Kodak has marketed a new film, Kodak Professional Direct Duplicating Film, that eliminates the need to reverse the negative.[63] Although the use of the new film saves time, the film has a disadvantage; it lacks a high degree of contrast.[64]

The New York State Police Department now requires that all fingerprints be photographed at the crime scene before removal.[65]

Fingerprint evidence can be fabricated.[66] In large part, the adoption of the requirement was the result of an evidence tampering scandal.[67] Six New York State Police troopers were involved in the scandal:

> Their basic modus operandi was to wait until a crime scene investigation produced a primary suspect, and then lift that suspect's fingerprints from a police station booking card or a foreign object which the trooper knew the suspect had touched. Soon thereafter the trooper would confront the suspect with his fingerprints, stating that it had been lifted from the crime scene or a murder weapon. On occasion this confrontation was sufficient to coerce a confession. Whether or not the suspect confesses, the trooper would repeat the lies at trial and help secure a wrongful conviction.[68]

---

61. FBI, THE SCIENCE OF FINGERPRINTS ch. 16 (1977).

62. Kutz, *Photographing Light Powder Latent Prints*, 50 FBI LAW ENF. BULL. 20 (July 1981).

63. *Id.* at 21.

64. *Id.*

65. Hansen, *Troopers' Wrongdoing Taints Cases*, 80 A.B.A. J. 22 (Mar. 1994).

66. Starrs, *Fingerprints: Preventing Fabrication*, 22 SCI. SLEUTHING REV. 13 (Fall 1998); Wertheim, *Integrity Assurance: Policies and Procedures to Prevent Fabrication of Latent Print Evidence*, 48 J. FORENSIC IDENT. 431 (1998).

67. Wertheim, *Integrity Assurance: Policies and Procedures to Prevent Fabrication of Latent Print Evidence*, 48 J. FORENSIC IDENT. 431 (1998).

68. Tarlow, *Fingerprints Don't Lie — But Liars Take Fingerprints*, 19 THE CHAMPION 28 (Jan.-Feb. 1995). *See also* Tarlow, *The Truth May Set You Free*, 22 C.A.C.J. FORUM 66, 67 (Mar. 1995)

§ 16-4(B). Lifting.

After photographing the impression, either an opaque or a transparent lift is used to make a second permanent record of the impression.[69] The most common opaque lift is rubber tape, which has an adhesive surface protected by a sheet of plastic material. It is ideal for lifting impressions from curved or uneven surfaces such as light bulbs. Before attempting to lift an impression, the technician peels the plastic cover from the tape and applies the tape's adhesive side to the impression. The technician now peels the tape from the surface and replaces the plastic cover to protect the impression. Identification data is written on the back of the tape.

A transparent lift may also be used. One advantage of a transparent lift is that it permits immediate comparison with an inked fingerprint because the impression can be viewed in its correct position. After using the transparent tape to lift the impression, the technician mounts the tape on a material such as card stock.

§ 16-5. Taking Known Impressions.

In the first and second editions of this treatise, this section was entitled "Taking Inked Impressions." Inking is the traditional method of obtaining a known impression, and the following subsections deal with inking procedures in detail. However, our reviewer has pointed out to us that many departments now use "Live Scan Systems" to record known exemplars. Live Scan systems scan fingers and/or palms and store the fingerprint/palm print information in digital form. Live Scan data representing the prints can be routed electronically to an Automated Fingerprint Identification System (AFIS)[70] to be searched through a database of previously recorded known fingerprints. If needed, hard copies of Live Scan prints can be produced on standard fingerprint card forms.

In the past, though, to identify the defendant as the source of the impressions found at the crime scene, an inked impression of the defendant's fingerprints was always required. The inked impression is compared with the impression visualized at the crime scene.

("Since 1992, six New York State Police Troopers have been convicted or are being prosecuted for their participation in an evidence tampering ring which operated between 1982 and 1992. Their basic modus operandi was to wait until a crime scene investigation produced a primary suspect, and then lift that suspect's fingerprints from a police station booking card or a foreign object which the trooper knows the suspect had touched. Soon thereafter the trooper would confront the suspect with his fingerprints, stating that it had been lifted from the crime scene or a murder weapon"); Taylor, *Fake Evidence Becomes Real Problem*, NAT'L L.J., Oct. 9, 1995, p. A28.

69. FBI, *Lifting Latent Fingerprints*, FBI LAW ENF. BULL. REPRINT, June 1965.

70. *See* § 16-7(B), *infra*.

If the police have focused on a particular suspect but cannot locate an existing set of his inked impressions, they will have to obtain a new set from him. In doing so, the police must comply with the constitutional limitations set out in Chapter 2. There are general procedures for taking inked impressions and special techniques for troublesome cases such as cadavers and persons with abnormal fingers.

§ 16-5(A). General Procedures.

In the run-of-the-mill case, taking inked or rolled impressions from a suspect is a simple matter. Most police agencies follow the procedures recommended by the Federal Bureau of Investigation and use the 8" by 8" card developed by the F.B.I.[71] As shown in Figure 16-1, the card has three rows for inked impressions.[72]

The top two rows are intended for rolled impressions. The very top row is for rolled impressions of the individual fingers on the right hand, and the middle row on the card is for rolled impressions of the individual fingers on the left hand. Reading from left to right, each row includes: the thumb, the index finger, the middle finger, the ring finger, and the little finger. The technician lightly inks the suspect's finger and, with even pressure, rolls the fingertip from side to side onto the card. This technique ensures that the block for each finger contains all the identifying ridge detail of that fingertip.

The bottom row of the card is for flat, plain, or simultaneous inked impressions. These impressions are smaller than the rolled impressions in the top two rows. In the middle of the third row, the technician presses down the impressions of the two thumbs. At the extreme left end of the row the technician simultaneously presses down the left hand's fingers, excluding the thumb. At the extreme right end of this row, the technician presses down the four right-hand fingers other than the thumb.

In most police departments, the standing operating procedure is to take three complete sets of inked impressions. The department retains one set for its dababase and forwards the other two sets to the F.B.I. for classification and filing. Some departments forward the sets directly to the F.B.I. while others route the two sets through a state agency.

---

71. FBI, *supra* note 61, at chs. 9-10.

72. *Id.* at 165. Reprinted with permission of the Federal Bureau of Investigation.

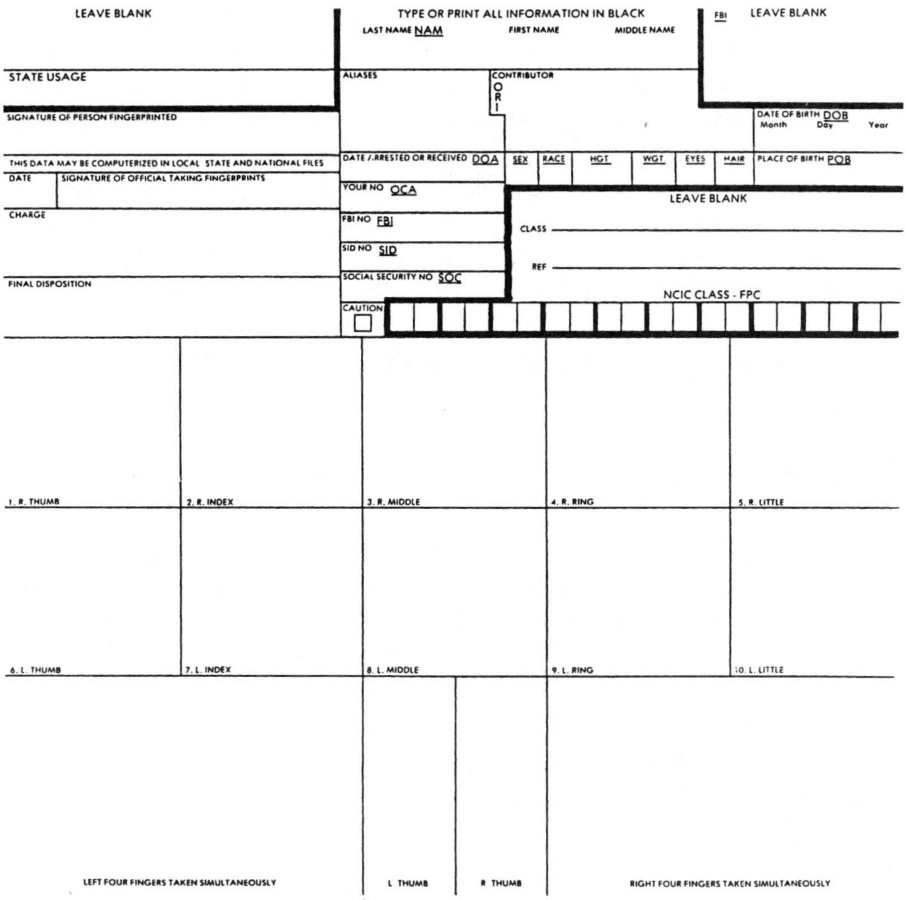
LEAVE BLANK

TYPE OR PRINT ALL INFORMATION IN BLACK

LAST NAME NAM FIRST NAME MIDDLE NAME

FBI LEAVE BLANK

STATE USAGE

ALIASES

CONTRIBUTOR O R I

SIGNATURE OF PERSON FINGERPRINTED

DATE OF BIRTH DOB Month Day Year

THIS DATA MAY BE COMPUTERIZED IN LOCAL STATE AND NATIONAL FILES

DATE ARRESTED OR RECEIVED DOA | SEX | RACE | HGT. | WGT. | EYES | HAIR | PLACE OF BIRTH POB

DATE | SIGNATURE OF OFFICIAL TAKING FINGERPRINTS

YOUR NO. OCA

LEAVE BLANK

CHARGE

FBI NO. FBI

CLASS

SID NO. SID

REF

SOCIAL SECURITY NO. SOC

FINAL DISPOSITION

NCIC CLASS - FPC

CAUTION

1. R. THUMB | 2. R. INDEX | 3. R. MIDDLE | 4. R. RING | 5. R. LITTLE

6. L. THUMB | 7. L. INDEX | 8. L. MIDDLE | 9. L. RING | 10. L. LITTLE

LEFT FOUR FINGERS TAKEN SIMULTANEOUSLY | L. THUMB | R. THUMB | RIGHT FOUR FINGERS TAKEN SIMULTANEOUSLY

Figure 16-1

§ 16-5(B). Special Procedures.

The suspect may have a deformed or abnormal finger. For example, the finger may be bent or crippled. Fingerprint technicians have developed special procedures for obtaining inked impressions from such suspects.[73] The technicians may use a spatula to apply the printer's ink to the finger in question. The technicians will have a curved holder and block cardstock for each finger. The technician inserts the cardstock in the curved holder and then presses the finger against the cardstock. Each individual finger block is then pasted onto a fingerprint card in the normal sequence.

---

73. FBI, *Ways of Obtaining Good Fingerprints, Insuring Legibility*, FBI LAW ENF. BULL. REPRINT, July 1961.

Cadavers pose special problems. If the epidermis has begun to come loose, the technician can use dusting tape to obtain an impression of the decedent's fingerprints.[74] The tape is mounted on transparent vinyl for preservation. If the skin has begun to wrinkle badly, the technician can inject a tissue builder such as air or gelatin into the finger's bulb to smooth the skin surface.[75]

Members of certain occupations, including bricklayers, cement workers, and carpenters, create unique problems. In their work, they may wear down their ridge detail. The technician can apply a softening agent to the skin to enhance the detail or fingerprint at a later time when the ridges have reformed.

§ 16-6. Locating Existing Inked Impressions — Classification of Fingerprints.

In many cases, the investigator does not have a suspect or believes that the suspect has already been fingerprinted. In either event, the investigator will attempt to locate an existing inked impression that matches the crime scene impression. The F.B.I. has over 198,000,000 fingerprint cards with sets of inked impressions in its files. To understand the process of locating a matching, existing inked impression, two subjects must be considered: the types of fingerprint patterns and the classification systems for fingerprints.

§ 16-6(A). Types of Patterns.

There are three basic fingerprint patterns: loops, arches, and whorls. A loop looks something like a jump rope; a ridge line enters from one side of the fingerprint pattern, recurves, and either exits or tends to exit on the same side as it entered on. A whorl tends to make a complete circuit in the middle of its pattern. In contrast, arches tend to be straight lines with upthrusts in the center. These are very rough definitions of the patterns. To understand these patterns, some technical concepts of fingerprint patterns must be reviewed:

—*Pattern area.* The pattern area is the part of the impression that the technician examines in classification.[76] The area is present in all patterns. However, it is more readily defined in the case of loops and whorls. In those cases, the area is enclosed by type lines.

---

74. Principe & Verbeke, *Fingerprinting of the Deceased by the Dusting-Tape Method*, 63 J. CRIM. L., CRIMINOLOGY & POLICE SCI. 439 (1972).

75. *Id.* at 440. *See also* Haglund, *A Technique to Enhance Fingerprinting of Mummified Fingers*, 33 J. FORENSIC SCI. 1244 (1988); Zugibe & Costello, *A New Method for Softening Mummified Fingers*, 31 J. FORENSIC SCI. 726 (1985); Keating & Miller, *A Technique for Developing and Photographing Ridge Impressions on Decomposed Water-Soaked Fingers*, 38 J. FORENSIC SCI. 197 (1993).

76. FBI, *supra* note 61, at 4.

—*Type lines*. These are the innermost ridges which start parallel, diverge, and then either surround or tend to surround the pattern area.[77] In fingerprinting, "diverge" has a technical meaning. Two parallel lines can diverge when they begin to move apart. In contrast, when one line breaks into two lines, that line is said to bifurcate. Type lines diverge in the technical sense.[78]

—*Delta*. A delta is the point on a ridge that is at or in front and nearest the center of the divergence of the type lines.[79] Figure 16-2 illustrates a delta.[80]

Figure 16-2

Deltas can take many forms: a bifurcation, an abrupt ending ridge, a dot, a short ridge, or a meeting of two ridges.[81] It is sometimes difficult to identify the delta; there may be two or more features that satisfy the above definition of a delta.[82] For those cases, the science of fingerprinting has developed a set of rules for selecting the delta.[83]

—*The core*. The core is the approximate center of the fingerprint pattern.[84] Like the identification of the delta, the selection of the core can sometimes be troublesome. As in the case of the delta, there are rules for identifying the core of a pattern.[85] In the case of a loop, the core is often the uppermost

77. *Id.* at 6.
78. *Id.* at 8.
79. *Id.*
80. *Id.* at 9. Reprinted with permission of the Federal Bureau of Investigation.
81. *Id.*
82. *Id.* at 11.
83. *Id.* at 11-17.
84. *Id.* at 13.
85. *Id.* at 13-17.

portion of the ridge in the very center of the loop, as illustrated by Figure 16-3.[86]

Figure 16-3

—*Ridge count.* The count is the number of ridges intervening between the pattern's delta and core.[87] The technician draws an imaginary line between the delta and the core and counts the number of ridges that cross or touch the line.[88] Neither the delta nor the core is included in the count.

—*Ridge tracing.* Ridge tracing is a concept in the classification of whorls.[89] A whorl has two or more deltas. The technician first locates the friction skin detail that constitutes the delta which is farthest left. He next traces that detail toward the delta which is farthest right. The technician uses the following conventions: "If the traced ridge flows above or to the inside of the right delta by three or more ridges the whorl is called 'inner' (symbol I); if the traced ridge meets the right delta or passes either over or under it with not more than two intervening ridges, the whorl is called 'meeting' (symbol M); if the ridge traced from the left delta flows under or to the outside of the right delta by three or more ridges, the pattern is 'outer' (symbol O)."[90]

Arches

Arches represent only 5% of the patterns encountered. Arches are plain or tented. The ridges of a plain arch look like straight lines slightly arched. The ridge lines enter on one side of the pattern and tend to flow out the opposite side

86. *Id.* at 13. Reprinted with permission of the Federal Bureau of Investigation.
87. *Id.* at 23.
88. *Id.*
89. A. Moenssens, J. Starrs, C. Henderson & F. Inbau, *supra* note 5, at §8.06.
90. *Id.*

of the pattern. Figure 16-4 depicts a tented arch.[91] There are several types of

Figure 16-4

tented arches. In some, the ridges at the center form a definite angle, even 90 degrees; in others, there is an ending ridge or upthrust in the center that rises at an angle of 45 degrees or more; and in still others, the pattern is similar to a loop — the pattern may possess one of the three essential loop characteristics listed below.[92]

Loops

Loops constitute between 60 and 70% of the patterns encountered. A loop has three required characteristics: a delta, a recurve, and a ridge count across a looping ridge.[93] There are two categories of loops: radial and ulnar. These categories take their names from the radius and ulna bones of the forearm.[94] If the loop flows toward the ulna in the direction of the little finger, the loop is called ulnar. If the loop flows toward the radius in the direction of the thumb, the loop is called radial.

Whorls

Between 25 and 35% of the patterns encountered consist of whorls. A whorl has at least two deltas with a recurve in front of each.[95] Whorls can be subdivided a number of ways.

---

91. FBI, *supra* note 61, at 34. Reprinted with permission of the Federal Bureau of Investigation.
92. *Id.* at 34.
93. *Id.* at 18.
94. *Id.* at 30.
95. *Id.* at 48.

In one subdivision, the categories are: plain whorl, central pocket loop, double loop, and accidental. A plain whorl is shown in Figure 16-5.[96] A plain whorl has

Figure 16-5

two deltas and at least one ridge making a complete circuit.[97] An imaginary line between the two deltas touches or crosses at least one of the recurving ridges.

Figure 16-6 illustrates a central pocket loop.[98] A central pocket loop also has two deltas and at least one ridge making a complete circuit.[99] However, an imaginary line between the two deltas cannot touch or cross any of the recurving ridges.

Figure 16-6

96. *Id.* at 49. Reprinted with permission of the Federal Bureau of Investigation.

97. *Id.*

98. *Id.* at 53. Reprinted with permission of the Federal Bureau of Investigation.

99. *Id.* at 52.

Figure 16-7 is an example of a double loop whorl.[100]

Figure 16-7

This type of whorl has two separate loop formations; the pattern has two deltas and two distinct sets of shoulders.[101]

An accidental whorl is a combination of two different types of patterns.[102] The pattern has two or more deltas. It displays some of the characteristics of two or more different types but does not satisfy all the requirements of any type.

The second subdivision of whorls is made on the basis of ridge tracing. As previously noted, ridge tracing results in the categorization of whorls as inner, meeting, or outer. This subdivision is also used in the classification of fingerprint patterns.

§ 16-6(B). Classification of Patterns.

This subsection and § 16-7(A) discuss the traditional methods of classifying and matching fingerprints. However, at the outset it should be emphasized that automated systems are of growing importance. Subsection 16-7(B) presents an overview of computer comparison. The latest information about the F.B.I.'s Integrated Automated Fingerprint Identification System (IAFIS) can be obtained from its Criminal Justice Information Service (CJIS) Division. Most states and some local law enforcement agencies have similar automated systems. To fully appreciate the utility of automated systems, though, it is necessary to understand the traditional methods.

Agencies like the F.B.I. usually have several filing systems for sets of inked fingerprint impressions. For example, the F.B.I. has both name files and fingerprint files. If the local or state agency has a particular suspect in mind, the

---

100. *Id.* at 60. Reprinted with permission of the Federal Bureau of Investigation.
101. *Id.* at 60.
102. *Id.* at 63.

F.B.I. fingerprint technician can go straight to the name files to determine if there is already a set of inked impressions in the files.[103] However, when the agency requesting a search of the files does not have a particular suspect, the F.B.I. must search through its fingerprint files. A manual search of all 198,000,000 files would obviously be infeasible. For that reason, the F.B.I. has a classification system for sorting sets of inked impressions. The F.B.I. system is a modified and extended version of the classification scheme developed by Sir Edward Henry, a British civil servant in India in the 1890s. This scheme is dominant in most European and English-speaking countries.

Henry's classification scheme is based on the characteristics of all 10 fingers. When a fingerprint technician initially receives an 8" by 11" card for classification, he "blocks out" the card. "Blocking out" is the process of placing a symbol for the appropriate pattern type under each impression on the card. For example, the symbol for a tented arch is "t." If the technician decides that the correct classification of an impression on the top row of the card is a tented arch, he writes "t" directly under the impression. After each impression has been blocked out, the technician can prepare the classification of the card. The easiest method of understanding the classification system is to study a classification element by element. The following is an illustrative classification formula:

$$\frac{6 \quad \text{I} \quad 6 \quad \text{U} \quad \text{I00} \quad 11}{\text{O} \quad 18 \quad \text{Ur} \quad \text{OOM}}$$

Starting on the extreme left, "6" is the key classification, "I/O" the major division, "6/18" the primary classification, "U/Ur" the secondary classification, "I00/OOM" the subsecondary classification, and "11" the final classification.[104]

Key Classification

By convention, the fingers of the hands are considered in a predetermined sequence during classification: (1) right thumb, (2) right index, (3) right middle, (4) right ring, (5) right little, (6) left thumb, (7) left index, (8) left middle, (9) left ring, and (10) left little. In the key classification, the technician disregards the little fingers, that is, fingers (5) and (10). The technician then reviews the remaining fingers one by one to identify the first finger with a loop pattern. The technician next determines the ridge count of that loop. The technician enters that

103. Of course, this procedure is available only when the suspect is currently using the name under which the set is filed.

104. *See generally* FBI, *supra* note 61, at ch. 4. Our reviewer informs us that in the current FBI classification system, a small letter (a for plain arch, t for tented arch, or r for radial loop) does away with the major division (if it is in finger 1 or 6) or the subsecondary classification (if it appears in fingers 3, 4, 5, 8, 9, or 10).

number, the ridge count, as the numerator for the key classification. If there is no loop, there is no key.

Major Division

The major classification depends upon the pattern of the thumbs, fingers (1) and (6). The classification for the right thumb appears in the numerator while the classification for the left thumb serves as the denominator. The classifications are determined in the following fashion:

—If the pattern is a plain arch, tented arch, or radial loop, there is no major division.
—If the pattern is a whorl, the technician traces the whorl and enters I (inner), M (meeting), or O (outer) as the classification.
—If the pattern is a loop, the technician records S (small), M (medium), or L (large) as the classification.

To decide which entry is appropriate for the left thumb, the technician initially determines the ridge count. If the ridge count is from 1 to 11, the entry is S; from 12 to 16, M; and 17 or higher, L.

When the left thumb is L, the technician employs the following rules to determine the correct entry for the right thumb. If the right count is 1 to 17, the entry is S; from 18 to 22, M; and 23 or higher, L.

Primary Classification

For this classification, the technician uses the sequence of fingers described under the key classification. The even numbered fingers, (2), (4), (6), (8), and (10), are grouped in the numerator and the odd numbers in the denominator. In making this classification, only whorls are considered. Depending on the finger they occur in, whorl patterns are assigned arbitrary numerical values: a whorl on fingers (1) or (2) has a value of 16, a value of 8 on fingers (3) and (4), a value of 4 on fingers (5) and (6), a value of 2 on fingers (7) and (8), a value of one on fingers (9) and (10), and a value of 0 if the pattern is not a whorl. After assigning the values to the fingers in the numerator and denominator, the numerator and denominator values are totaled. The technician then adds 1 to the sum in both the numerator and the denominator. The resulting fraction is the primary classification.

There are 1,024 possible primary classifications.[105] The distribution of fingerprint patterns into the various classifications is not even. In fact, nearly 50% of the fingerprint cards tend to fall into 10 of the 1,024 classifications.[106]

---

105. New York State Identification and Intelligence System, Fingerprinting Techniques 5 (1967).

Secondary Classifications

The secondary classification is based primarily on the pattern of the index fingers, fingers (2) and (7). The symbols for the right index finger appear in the numerator, and the symbols for the left index finger are placed in the denominator. The following capital letter symbols are used: A for plain arch, T for tented arch, R for radial loop, U for ulnar loop, and W for whorls.

Plain arches, tented arches, and radial loops occurring on other fingers are also indicated in this classification. The indication is made by lower case symbols: a for plain arch, t for tented arch, and r for radial loop. The order of the lower case symbols is determined by their order of occurrence on the fingerprint card. If intervening fingers have other patterns such as whorls or ulnar loops, the intervening fingers are represented by dashes. The lower case symbols for the right middle, right ring, and right little fingers are written to the right of the capital letter in the numerator, and the lower case symbol for the right thumb is written to the left. Similarly, lower case symbols for the left middle, left ring, and left little fingers are written to the right of the capital letter in the denominator, and the lower case symbol for the left thumb is written to the left.

Subsecondary Classification

This classification is based on the ridge count and/or whorl tracings of the index, middle, and ring fingers. The possible entries are I, M, and O. The entries for right-hand fingers appear in the numerator while left-hand symbols are placed in the denominator. If one of these fingers has a plain or tented arch pattern or radial loop, a dash is entered in the appropriate position. If the pattern is a whorl, ridge tracing determines the entry: I for inner, M for meeting, and O for outer. If the pattern is a loop, the ridge count is determinative. The following rules apply: I (1 to 9 for an index finger, 1 to 10 for a middle finger, and 1 to 13 for a ring finger) or O (10 or higher for an index finger, 11 or higher for a middle finger, and 14 or higher for a ring finger).

Final Classification

This classification is based on the patterns of the little fingers. The entry represents the ridge count of the loops on the little fingers. In the F.B.I. system, though, you do not bring up the ridge count in finger #10 if there is a ridge count on finger #5. The count for the right little finger is written in the numerator, and the count for the left in the denominator. With one exception, there is no entry for a finger if the pattern is not a loop. The exception applies in certain circumstances when both little fingers are whorls. In that event, the ridge count of the right little finger is placed in the numerator.

---

106. *Id.*

The above classifications exhaust the traditional Henry system. However, the F.B.I. has so many sets of inked fingerprint impressions that it has found it necessary to modify and extend the Henry scheme. The F.B.I. has developed a number of extensions.

Second Subsecondary Classification

Until recently, the F.B.I. entered a second subsecondary classification immediately above the subsecondary classification in the Henry formula.[107] This classification was based on the index, middle, and ring fingers. The possible entries were S, M, and L. The numerical rules governing the entry were as follows:

Index Finger	Middle Finger	Ring Finger
1 to 5, S	1 to 8, S	1 to 10, S
6 to 12, M	9 to 14, M	11 to 18, M
13 or more, L	15 or more, L	19 or more, L

The letter system is now being replaced by an explicitly numerical system.

WCDX Extension

This extension is based on the whorl patterns of the various fingers. The technician uses capital letters for whorls on the index finger and small letter symbols for whorls on all other fingers.[108] W or w (or dashes) is a plain whorl, C or c a central pocket whorl, D or d a double loop whorl, and X or x an accidental pattern.

Special Loop Extension

If all fingers have loop patterns, the technician can subdivide the classification by a special loop extension. The entry represents the ridge count for fingers (2), (3), (4), (7), (8), (9), and (10). The count is arbitrarily converted into a value:

107. FBI, *supra* note 61, at 95.
108. *Id.*

Ridge Count	Value
1 to 4	1
5 to 8	2
9 to 12	3
13 to 16	4
17 to 20	5
21 to 24	6
25 and over	7

The right-hand values are written in the numerator, and the left-hand values in the denominator.

The Henry classification system as well as the F.B.I. extensions are based on an analysis of the patterns on all 10 fingers. Unfortunately, in investigative work, police often encounter latent impressions including fewer than 10 fingers. For that reason, many depositories of inked impressions have created other systems for filing five finger or single finger impressions. The Battley single-print system is in widespread use. In this system, the technician measures the distance between a core and the delta. Depending upon the distance, the print receives a classification letter value between A and H.

§ 16-7. Comparison — Identification of Fingerprints.

In fingerprinting, classification and identification are distinct concepts. The two functions may and often are performed by different personnel. In some police departments, the division of labor may be so sharp that a person skilled in fingerprint classification may not be qualified to identify suspects based on fingerprint examination. The examination may be conducted manually or by computer followed by manual comparison.

§ 16-7(A). Manual Comparison.

The fingerprint examiner studies the latent and inked impressions with a 4X magnifier or a five to ten power magnifying glass. The examiner usually begins with a detailed study of the latent impression and then compares the latent with the inked impression. The purpose of the examination is to determine whether there is sufficient similarity between the two impressions to support an opinion that both impressions were made by the same person.[109]

In conducting the examination, the analyst considers not only the general pattern that determines the print's classification but also the fine ridge detail. A single inked fingerprint may have between 100 and 175 fine details. These details can be short ridges, ridge endings, bifurcations (a single ridge splitting

109. *See generally* J. COWGER, FRICTION RIDGE SKIN (1983).

into two), trifurcations, enclosures, dots, and islands.[110] One leading authority has stated that in evaluating the details, the analyst should consider four factors,[111] which are discussed below.

General Pattern Agreement

The impression's general pattern determines its classification. At the outset of the examination, the analyst should determine whether the general pattern of the latent impression matches that of the inked impression. However, the general pattern is only a class characteristic; it is not the type of individual characteristic needed for identification. Thus, agreement between the general patterns is not sufficient for an identification. Moreover, in one sense, agreement is not necessary for identification. The latent impression may be partial, and consequently it may be impossible to determine its general pattern. It is nevertheless conceivable that the partial latent and inked impressions will have a sufficient number of points of identity for an identification.

Qualitative Concordance

The next factor is the qualitative agreement between the two impressions. Qualitative agreement denotes that individual ridge characteristics in one impression have the same type and shape as corresponding characteristics in the other impression.

Relationship of Ridge Characteristics

It is not enough that each fine detail on one impression has a counterpart in the other impression; the various details on each impression must stand in the same relationship. For example, the analyst must determine whether there is the same number of ridges intervening between two details on the latent and the corresponding details on the inked impression. It has been said that the analyst can sometimes assess the relationship among details on each impression by drawing geometric designs connecting the details and discovering whether a similar design connects the corresponding details on the other impression;[112] but, according to our reviewer, this technique is rarely, if ever, used by experienced fingerprinter experts. The analyst usually will not

---

110. Some fingerprint experts contend that there are only three basic characteristics — ridge endings, bifurcations, and dots — and that all other ridge details are merely combinations of these characteristics. Olsen, *The Philosophy of the Field of Identification*, 32 IDENT. NEWS 14 (March 1982).

111. *See* A. MOENSSENS, FINGERPRINT TECHNIQUES (1971); A. MOENSSENS, FINGERPRINTS AND THE LAW 27 (1969).

112. Engert, *Statement, in A.B.A. Section of Criminal Justice*, SCIENTIFIC ADVANCES IN CRIME DETECTION 16 (1973).

attempt to superimpose one impression on the other.[113] When the impression was made, either the latent or the inked impression could have been distorted by pressure or twisting.[114] Hence, even if the two impressions originate from the same person, the impressions may not perfectly superimpose.

Quantitative Factors

The final factor is the number of points of identity shared by the two impressions. A large number of points of similarity between the impressions of even one finger will suffice for an identification.[115]

There is no consensus on the number of points necessary for an identification. In the United States, one often hears that eight or ten points are "ordinarily" required. Some local police departments generally require 12 points.[116] In England, many examiners use 16 points as the rule of thumb.[117] In France, the required number used most often is 24 while the number is 30 in Argentina and Brazil. After studying the issue at length, the International Association for Identification concluded that there is no justification for mandating a particular number of points of similarity.

Since there is no numerical standard, to some extent fingerprint identification is an evaluative art.[118] The weight the analyst assigns to a point of identity depends in large part on how rare he considers that characteristic.[119] If the characteristic is common, the analyst attaches less weight to the match. However, if the characteristic occurs less frequently, as in the case of trifurcations, the analyst attaches greater weight to the match; and seven such matches might persuade the examiner that there is a positive identification. Fingerprint examiners vary in their estimates of the incidence of particular fingerprint details.[120]

After surveying the literature, Professor Moenssens reports that in tens of thousands of comparisons, "experts have been unable to find more than four

---

113. FBI, *supra* note 61, at 194.

114. *Id.*

115. Petersilia, *Processing Latent Fingerprints — What Are the Payoffs?*, 6 J. POLICE SCI. & ADMIN. 157, 161 n.5 (1978).

116. State v. Lambert, 475 So. 2d 791, 796 (La. App. 1985), *writ denied,* 481 So. 2d 1345 (La. 1986); State v. Sanders, 619 S.W.2d 344, 350 (Mo. App. 1981) (the standard of the St. Louis Police Department).

117. Menzel, *supra* note 24, at 652-54; Starrs, *A Colossal Blunder under the Union Jack*, 22 SCI. SLEUTHING REV. 10 (Sum. 1998); Campbell, *Fingerprints: A Review*, 1985 CRIM. L. REV. 195, 199. The author adds that the standard in Australia is 12 points of agreement. *Id.*

118. Ashbaugh, *Fingerprint Identification Today*, 33 IDENT. NEWS 8 (Sept. 1983).

119. *Id.*

120. Osterburg, *An Inquiry into the Nature of Proof*, 9 J. FORENSIC SCI. 413, 420-26 (1984); C. MCCORMICK, EVIDENCE § 210, at 655 n.18 (3d ed. 1984). *See also* Starrs, *A Miscue in Fingerprint Identification: Causes and Concerns*, 12 J. POLICE SCI. & ADMIN. 287 (1984).

clearly defined characteristics that are quantitatively and qualitatively the same in two prints known to be from different fingers."[121] Thus, even a standard of seven or eight points of identity provides an ample safety margin. Examiners can distinguish between the fingerprints of twins.[122] This also helps to explain why, at least until recently, it has been assumed that fingerprint examiners rarely disagree. The International Association of Identification insists that certified fingerprint analysts opine only when they can be relatively certain; the only permissible opinions are a match, no match, or inconclusive result. Under I.A.I. Resolution VII, certified examiners may not testify to possible, probable, or likely identifications; an examiner who does so runs the risk of decertification.

Even a single unexplained point of dissimilarity between the latent and inked impressions establishes that the impressions came from different fingers. Of course, explanations are frequently possible. The explanation might be that: (1) the inked impression was taken carelessly; (2) when the inked impression was made, the suspect's finger was over- or under-inked; (3) when the latent impression was made, uneven pressure resulted in distortion or blurring; (4) the surface was dirty; or (5) the person's skin was dirty. If a solitary point of dissimilarity cannot be explained, the examiner's opinion is effectively impeached.

A caveat is necessary, though. As § 16-1 pointed out, the 1995 proficiency study of fingerprint examiners calls into question both the assumption that examiners routinely agree and that they reach the correct finding in the overwhelming majority of cases. Again, 156 examiners participated in that study.[123] Only 44% of the examiners reached the correct conclusion on all the identification tasks. "88 or 56% provided divergent (read as wrong, incorrect, erroneous) answers."[124] Six examiners failed to identify any of the latent prints. "[O]f the 156 examiners 48 included erroneous identifications.[125] "Erroneous identifications constituted 22% of the total."[126] Those results should give either a judge or an attorney pause before facilely assuming that fingerprint identifications are both consistent and accurate.

---

121. A. Moenssens, J. Starrs, C. Henderson & F. Inbau, *supra* note 5, at § 8.08.

122. Lin, Liu, Osterburg & Nicol, *Fingerprint Comparison I: Similarity of Fingerprints*, 27 J. Forensic Sci. 290 (1982).

123. Starrs, *Forensic Science on the Ropes: An Upper Cut to Fingerprinting*, 20 Sci. Sleuthing Rev. 1 (Wint. 1996); Grieve, *Possession of Truth*, 46 J. Forensic Ident. 521 (1996).

124. Starrs, *Forensic Science on the Ropes: An Upper Cut to Fingerprinting*, 20 Sci. Sleuthing Rev. 2 (Wint. 1996).

125. *Id.*

126. *Id.*

§ 16-7(B). Computer Comparison.

National, state, and local police agencies now use computerized methods to search fingerprint files for inked impressions that match latent impressions.[127] The F.B.I. has a computerized fingerprint system,[128] as do most states, including Minnesota,[129] California,[130] and Utah[131] and some local agencies, such as those in Houston, San Francisco,[132] Chicago,[133] and New York.[134] Cogent, Morpho, NEC Information Systems of Boxboro, Massachusetts, and Printrak International Inc. of Anaheim, California, have made such systems commercially available.[135] Six western states (Idaho, Montana, Nevada,

---

127. Brotman & Pavel, *Identification: A Move Toward the Future*, 60 FBI LAW ENF. BULL. 1 (July 1991); Fitzpatrick, *Selecting an Automated Fingerprint Identification System*, 57 FBI LAW ENF. BULL. 7 (Jan. 1988); Buracker & Storer, *Automated Fingerprint Identification*, 53 FBI LAW ENF. BULL. 1 (Aug. 1984).

128. Brotman & Pavel, *Identification: A Move Toward the Future*, 60 FBI LAW ENF. BULL. 1 (July 1991); Neudorfer, *Fingerprint Automation: Progress in the FBI's Identification Division*, 55 FBI LAW ENF. BULL. 3 (Mar. 1986) (working with Rockwell International and Calspan Corporation, the FBI is developing computer hardware, fingerprint readers, and computer logic software); Reed, *Automated Fingerprint Identification: From Will West to Minnesota Nine-Fingers and Beyond*, 9 J. POLICE SCI. & ADMIN. 317, 320 (1981). Sargeant, *New Fingerprint Technology Revitalizes Forensic Mainstay*, 28 TRIAL 98, 99 (Dec. 1992) ("The FBI plans to computerize its 40 million fingerprint files ... by the end of the decade."). The FBI hopes to have its system completed by July 1999. The system is being built in six increments. The FBI opted for the incremental approach to reduce the technological risks associated with attempting to develop a complex system all at once. The first two increments have already been finished. As a result, the FBI has a database of 5,000,000 sets of prints for specific crime categories.

129. *Id.*

130. The California system is called CAL-ID. *New Crime Detection Tool Approved*, SAN JOSE POST-RECORD, Oct. 16, 1985, at 1. The system conducts automated searches of a collection of 7.5 million files. Like the laser technique, this computer system was utilized in the "Night Stalker" investigation. Elias, *Super Computer Fights Crime*, THE DAVIS ENTERPRISE, Nov. 28, 1985, at 8. *See* CAL. DEPT. JUSTICE, AFIS PATTERN RECOGNITION MANUAL (1997).

131. Rogers, *Utah's Computerized Technical Fingerprint Search System*, 27 IDENT. NEWS 7 (Nov. 1977).

132. Sanger, *Technology: Fingerprinting and Computers*, N.Y. TIMES, April 26, 1984, at 28Y. *See* Perkey v. Department of Motor Vehicles, 42 Cal. 3d 185, 196 n.2, 721 P.2d 50, 57 n.2, 228 Cal. Rptr. 169, 176 n.1 (1986).

133. Kolarik, *Fingerprints Exonerate Convict*, 81 A.B.A. J. 20 (May 1995) (the use of AFIS helped exonerate James Newsome who had been wrongfully convicted of a murder). *See also* People v. Newsome, 443 N.E.2d 634 (Ill. App. 1982), *cert. denied*, 464 U.S. 934 (1983); CHICAGO TRIBUNE, Aug. 9, 1995, *Tempo* section, at 1. Newsome filed a 42 U.S.C. § 1983 claim. In that litigation, the trial judge ordered the Chicago police to run the fingerprints found at the murder scene through an automated fingerprint identification system. Newsome v. James, 968 F. Supp. 1318, 1325-26 (N.D. Ill. 1997).

134. Barbanel, *Fingerprints Still Top Identification Means*, ST. LOUIS POST-DISPATCH, Oct. 13, 1980, at 4D.

Oregon, Wyoming, and Utah) formed WIN (Western Identification Network), a nonprofit corporation to provide AFIS (automated fingerprint identification system) technology in that region.[136]

The principal problem in adapting computer technology to fingerprint identification is that when the latent impression is laid down, there may be distortion caused by many factors such as uneven pressure. As noted in the last section, during manual examination the analyst cannot simply superimpose the two impressions. The difficulty is programming the computer to compensate for an expectable degree of difference between the latent and inked impressions. If the computer searches for a perfect match, it is likely to reach a false negative conclusion. There is seldom a perfect match.

Some early researchers proceeded on the assumption that the computer could use the traditional classification system described in the last section.[137] However, the likelihood of distortion in the latent impression makes it impractical to rely on the traditional classification system.[138] The computer may not find the same ridge detail in exactly the same position in both impressions and may erroneously report that there is no matching inked impression in the files.

Other researchers have abandoned the traditional classification scheme and are programming computers to: (1) search for specified characteristics in the latent and inked impressions, (2) digitize this information, and (3) report matches when the digital information satisfies certain statistical decision rules. For example, the F.B.I.'s automatic system measures approximately 20 variables in each impression.[139] The computer converts these measurements into a digital code for the impression.[140]

Perhaps the most advanced research is testing the applicability of graph theory to computerized fingerprint identification.[141] Graph theory is the study of patterns and their properties.[142] Suppose, for example, that the figure being studied is a rectangle, as in Figure 16-8.[143]

---

135. Armstrong, *Fingerprints: With New Technology, a Better Crime-Buster*, CHRISTIAN SCIENCE MONITOR, July 10, 1984, at 21.

136. *WIN: AFIS Technology for Rural States*, 59 FBI LAW ENF. BULL. 24-25 (Nov. 1990). The corporation has since been expanded to include additional states.

137. Seufert & Cote, *Automated Identification and Analysis of Fingerprints by Interferometry*, 29 J. FORENSIC SCI. 486, 487 (1984).

138. *Id.;* Sparrow, *Digital Coding of Single Fingerprints: A New Approach for the Computer Age*, 10 J. POLICE SCI. & ADMIN. 206, 207 (1982).

139. Reed, *supra* note 128, at 320.

140. Liu, Lin, Osterburg & Nicol, *supra* note 122, at 316; Sparrow, *supra* note 138, at 207.

141. *Id.* at 209-12.

142. *Id.* at 209.

143. *Id.* Reprinted with permission of the author and the Journal of Police Science and Administration.

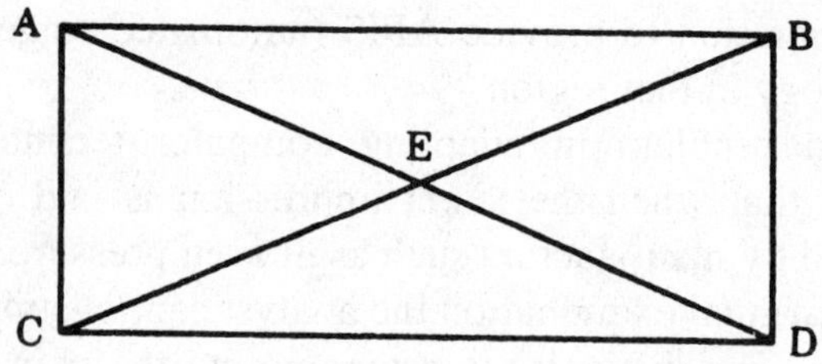

Figure 16-8

An analyst could describe the figure spatially with references to lengths such as four inches and directions such as north. However, a purely graphic analysis would describe the same figure without any references to distance or direction: "There are five vertices A, B, C, D, and E. A is linked by a single edge to B, C, D, and E. A is linked by single ... lines ... to B, C, and E; B is similarly joined to A, E, and D; C to A, E, and D; D to B, E, and C; and E is joined to all the others by one line."[144] This manner of describing a fingerprint pattern is relatively immune to the problem of distortion caused by pressure variation.[145] Pressure might change the apparent distance or direction of a ridge detail, but graphical descriptions do not depend on distance or direction.[146] Of course, the computer must still convert the graphical information into digital form.[147] Researchers have developed a digital code to facilitate comparison of the graphical description of fingerprint patterns.[148]

Automated fingerprint comparison is proving to be an effective investigative tool for the police. The computer can check hundreds of prints per second. After doing so, it provides the examiner with a ranked series of possible matches, ranging from the most likely match to the least likely. In "cold hit" cases, in which the police investigation has not uncovered any suspects and a search of all fingerprint files would theoretically be needed, a manual search is infeasible. When manual searches are undertaken in these cases, they are rarely productive. In Houston, before the police implemented an automated system, manual searches turned up suspects in "cold hit" cases only once a year.[149] Houston's automated system is identifying 30 or more suspects each month.[150] In San Francisco where the police department operates a similar automated system, the arrest rate for cold searches now approaches

144. *Id.*
145. *Id.*
146. *Id.*
147. *Id.* at 210-12.
148. *Id.* at 210-14.
149. Armstrong, *supra* note 135, at 21.
150. *Id.*

19%.[151] One San Francisco police sergeant commented that nothing "that has come about in the last 50 ... years ... has had this much impact on solving crimes."[152]

Computers, however, have not eliminated the need for human fingerprint examiners. AFIS technology has limitations:

—"The AFIS system does not know which way is up. Therefore, a fingerprint recorded in a more slanted position on the fingerprint card than the latent print lifted from the crime scene will not 'hit' a correct respondent.

—"The AFIS system does not know left from right. Therefore, if some ... law enforcement officer allowed a fingerprint card to be submitted in which the hands were reversed (the left thumb recorded in the right thumb block and so on) a latent print lifted from a crime scene which could be determined as a right thumb would never be matched.

—"The AFIS system does not know a thumb print from a little fingerprint or any of the other digits for that matter. Therefore if a ... law enforcement officer did not check the correct order in which the fingerprints were recorded and a latent print lifted from a crime scene was determined to be a right forefinger, for example, a correct respondent could not be obtained."[153] To date, police have used computers only as an investigative tool. At trial, the prosecutor calls a fingerprint examiner to testify to the comparison and identification. It is conceivable that eventually a prosecutor will attempt to offer both the examiner's live testimony and a report of the computer's identification of a particular suspect. The proffer of the computer evidence would raise many of the admissibility questions discussed in Chapter 1. In a *Frye* jurisdiction, the prosecutor would have to demonstrate the general acceptance of the technology as a means of identifying the source of the fingerprint impression. Even if the case arose in a *Daubert* jurisdiction, the prosecutor would have to lay a detailed foundation, including proof of the experimentation conducted to validate the computer's identification program.

---

151. *Id.*

152. *Id. See also* Buracker and Storer, *supra* note 127, at 4-5. *But see* Skees & Skees, *Forensic Science: The Automated Fingerprint Identification System (AFIS)*, THE ADVOCATE 58 (Oct. 1990) (the number of "hits" in Kentucky "has not been impressive since the database has a lot of garbage entered into it;" in the authors' opinion, many of the fingerprints in the Kentucky database are of poor quality). The Advocate is a publication of the Kentucky Department of Public Advocacy.

153. Skees & Skees, *Forensic Science: The Automated Fingerprint Identification System (AFIS)*, THE ADVOCATE 58-59 (Oct. 1990). The Advocate is a publication of the Kentucky Department of Public Advocacy.

§ 16-8. Age Determinations.

In addition to eliciting expert testimony as to the identity of the source of a fingerprint impression, the prosecutor often would like to elicit testimony about the age of the impression. The prosecutor wants to demonstrate not only that the defendant was at the crime scene but that he was there when the crime was committed. In a number of cases, fingerprint experts have presented such testimony.[154] The experts have testified in both relative terms that the print was fresh[155] or recent[156] and in numerical terms that the print was only one day[157] or five days[158] old. In another case, an expert was permitted to testify that a fingerprint on a bathtub "had been left after the tub had last been [thoroughly] cleaned."[159]

Trial courts sometimes permit testimony along these lines.[160] Expressions such as "fresh" and "recent" are ambiguous from a lay perspective and imprecise in a scientific sense.[161] Perhaps in these cases, the expert meant only that the print had been left since the last time the surface had been cleaned[162] or that the print was of high quality — "one which is capable of easy comparison, with good contrast between the latent fingerprint and the surface from which it is lifted."[163] However, the term "fresh" seems to connote more; and if the trier of fact adopts

---

154. State v. Cline, 909 P.2d 1171 (Mont. 1996) (although the age of the latent print could not be established with complete accuracy and the subject was one on which experts might disagree, the weight of the opinion was for the jury, not the judge); State v. Kitt, 231 Neb. 52, 434 N.W.2d 543 (1989) (on direct examination, the state's fingerprint expert testified that prints were "fairly fresh" and could have been as fresh as one hour old; on cross-examination, the expert admitted that "the prints could have been two days old").

155. People v. Dotson, 635 N.E.2d 559, 562 (Ill. App. 1994); People v. King, 481 N.E.2d 1074, 1075 (Ill. App. 1985); Edwards v. State, 660 S.W.2d 622 (Tex. App. 1983).

156. State v. Thompson, 610 S.W.2d 629 (Mo.), *cert. denied,* 454 U.S. 840 (1981); State v. Alston, 81 N.C. App. 459, 344 S.E.2d 339 (1986). *See also* People v. Donaldson, 107 A.D.2d 758, 484 N.Y.S.2d 123 (1985) (the crime occurred on a rainy day, and the expert testified that the finger of the person who left the impression was wet at the time the impression was made).

157. Couser v. State, 4 Md. App. 543, 243 A.2d 639 (1968). *See also* People v. Fitzgerald, 29 Cal. App. 3d 296, 105 Cal. Rptr. 458 (1972) (the expert opined that the fingerprint was fresh — one day old — because "a fresh print usually grabs the powder readily").

158. State v. Turner, 90 N.M. 79, 559 P.2d 1206 (1976), *cert. denied,* 90 N.M. 6, 558 P.2d 621 (1977).

159. Starrs, *The Aging of Fingerprints*, 22 SCI. SLEUTHING REV. 1 (Sum. 1998) (describing a Louisiana decision).

160. *But see* Roberson v. State, 569 So. 2d 691, 696 (Miss. 1990); Starrs, *Judicial Control Over Scientific Supermen: Fingerprint Experts and Others Who Exceed the Bounds*, 35 CRIM. L. BULL. 234, 246-50, 257-73 (May-June 1999) (questioning the reliability of such testimony).

161. Starrs, *Judicial Control Over Scientific Supermen: Fingerprint Experts and Others Who Exceed the Bounds*, 35 CRIM. L. BULL. 234, 246-50, 257-73 (May-June 1999).

162. Starrs, *The Aging of Fingerprints*, 22 SCI. SLEUTHING REV. 1 (Sum. 1998).

163. State v. Phillips, 1981 Ohio App. LEXIS 13473.

that connotation, the testimony can be misleading.[164] The available data points to the conclusion that "no method exists to scientifically determine when ... fingerprints were placed on a particular surface."[165] Determining the age of a fingerprint impression is subject to so many environmental and physiological variables that any opinion on the subject is at best a rough approximation.[166] One variable is the smoothness of the surface; impressions tend to last longer on smooth surfaces. The humidity and temperature in the surrounding environment have a major effect on the permanency of fingerprints.[167] Persons vary in the amount of perspiration they produce; an old fingerprint left by a person who perspires profusely may have the same appearance as a fresh impression from a person who perspires lightly. An individual's rate of perspiration varies from time to time; the individual may produce much perspiration when he experiences nervous tension.

However, there are three methods of estimating the age of an impression within broad time parameters. The techniques for visualizing latent impressions vary in their periods of effectiveness.[168] The iodine method rarely develops identifiable latent prints regardless of the age of the latent print. Silver nitrate infrequently develops latent prints which are more than a few months old. Ninhydrin develops new prints, aged prints, and occasionally very old prints (more than 30 years old). The components of the latent print residue (salt, amino acid, oil, etc.) determine which chemicals will be successful, not necessarily the age of the print. Not all latent print residue components are present in every print.

Another promising technique is fingerprint luminescence.[169] As fingerprints age, their luminescence changes from greenish-yellow to orange.[170] This color change occurs in a year or less.[171] To date, there has been no detailed study of

---

164. Starrs, *The Aging of Fingerprints*, 22 SCI. SLEUTHING REV. 1-2 (Sum. 1998).

165. *Id.*, citing State v. Phillips, 1981 Ohio App. LEXIS 13473; Starrs, *Judicial Control Over Scientific Supermen: Fingerprint Experts and Others Who Exceed the Bounds*, 35 CRIM. L. BULL. 234, 246-50, 257-73 (May-June 1999).

166. People v. Robinson, 61 Cal. 2d 373, 392 P.2d 970, 38 Cal. Rptr. 890 (1964) (the expert was unable to fix the date of the fingerprint). Baniuk, *Determination of the Age of Fingerprints*, 46 FORENSIC SCI. INT'L 133 (1990); Dikshitulu et al., *Aging Studies on Fingerprint Residues Using Thin-Layer and High Performance Liquid Chromatography*, 31 FORENSIC SCI. INT'L 261 (1986); Santamaria, *The Extrinsic Value of Fingerprints*, 14 INT'L CRIM. POL. REV. 87 (1959).

167. Barnett & Berger, *The Effects of Temperature and Humidity on the Permanency of Latent Fingerprints*, 16 J. FORENSIC SCI. SOC'Y 249 (1976).

168. *See* A. MOENSSENS, FINGERPRINT TECHNIQUES (1971).

169. Dalrymple, Duff & Menzel, *supra* note 40, at 114.

170. Menzel, *supra* note 24, at 645.

171. *Id.*

this technique.[172] Even one of the researchers who urges further study of the technique concedes that "prospects for success may not be good."[173]

A third technique involves the use of both thin layer and high performance liquid chromatography.[174] The researchers working with this technique believe that as fingerprints age, some components disappear and the ratios of the remaining components change.[175] These changes can be detected by chromatographic analysis. With further experimentation, this technique may make it "possible to determine the age of [a] fingerprint ...."[176]

The Dactyloscopy Department of the Main Police Headquarters in Warsaw, Poland, claims to have had considerable success with a fourth technique for determining the age of fingerprints:[177]

> The ageing process can be divided into two stages: (1) Drying of the sweat-grease substance, [and] (2) Loss of the legibility of the traces. In the first stage the following phases can be differentiated: ... Dulling of the sweat-grease substance, ... Loss of stickiness, ... Narrowing of the fingerprints, ... [and] Loss of the continuity of the fingerprints.[178]

Based on its empirical research, the Department has calculated normal "life spans" for fingerprint traces under various sets of conditions.[179] However, this research leaves our reviewer unconvinced. In his view, there is simply no scientific method of determining the age of latent prints. The Polish study leaves many questions unanswered: What are the components of this latent print residue? Was the touching finger heavily or lightly covered with residue? Under what conditions was the surface touched? What was the condition of the finger? What were the conditions affecting the evidence before and after the latent print was deposited? Was the pressure applied by the finger to the surface when the print was deposited firm or light? What was the condition of the surface? In his judgment, there are so many variables that the test is unhelpful.

§ 16-9. Admissibility of Fingerprint Evidence.

The foundational evidence for fingerprint identification often follows this pattern. The proponent, usually the prosecutor: introduces a record of the impression visualized at the crime; then offers a record of the defendant's inked

---

172. *Id.* at 646.

173. *Id.*

174. Dikshitulu, Prasad, Pal & Rao, *Aging Studies of Fingerprint Residues Using Thin-Layer and High Performance Liquid Chromatography*, 31 FORENSIC SCI. INT'L 261 (1986).

175. *Id.* at 266.

176. *Id.*

177. Baniuk *Determination of the Age of Fingerprints*, 46 FORENSIC SCI. INT'L 133 (1990).

178. *Id.* at 134.

179. *Id.*

impression; qualifies a witness as a fingerprint examiner; has the witness testify to the general validity of fingerprint identification; and finally elicits the witness's opinion that the latent and inked impressions belong to the same person. Sometimes the examiner does not appear in person, and the proponent offers a report in lieu of the examiner's live testimony. The proponent can request that the impressions be sent to the jury room during deliberations. The proponent may even request that the judge provide the jurors with a magnifying glass.[180] This line of testimony raises several admissibility issues.

§ 16-9(A). Authentication of Crime Scene Prints.

The witness establishing this element of the foundation initially testifies that he visualized the latent impression at the crime scene. At this point, the opponent may challenge the validity of the technique that the witness used to visualize the latent. Conventional techniques such as powder and ninhydrin are generally accepted and pass muster under *Frye*.[181] However, the more novel techniques may be subject to a *Frye* objection. Some techniques such as autoradiography have yet to surface in reported American cases. In one published opinion involving luminescence, the evidence was admitted without objection.[182] There have been trial court decisions admitting fingerprints developed by Super Glue fuming[183] and on human skin.[184] There is one appellate decision approving the Super Glue fuming technique.[185] So long as the technique has been empirically validated, its use is permissible under *Daubert*.

---

180. United States v. Young, 814 F.2d 392 (7th Cir.), *cert. denied*, 484 U.S. 838 (1987).

181. Hutcherson v. State, 677 So. 2d 1174 (Ala. Crim. App. 1994) (ninhydring), *rev'd*, 677 So. 2d 1205 (Ala. 1996); Johnson v. State, 620 So. 2d 679, 693-94 (Ala. Crim. App. 1992), *rev'd on other grounds*, 620 So. 2d 709 (Ala.), *cert. denied*, 510 U.S. 905 (1993).

182. State v. Jackson, 308 N.C. 549, 304 S.E.2d 134 (1983), *appeal after remand*, 317 N.C. 1, 343 S.E.2d 814 (1986), *vacated*, 479 U.S. 1077 (1987).

183. Siegel, *supra* note 45, at 107 (trial court decisions in Florida, Louisiana, and Virginia).

184. Hall, *Latent Skin Print Identification Solves Homicide*, 48 FBI LAW ENF. BULL. 9 (Oct. 1979) (Dade County, Florida prosecution). In Cavazos v. State, 779 P.2d 987 (Okla. Crim. App. 1989), the technician developed a latent fingerprint in blood on the victim's back. To do so, the technician used ortho-toluidine. The technician conceded that she had never used the technique on a human body before. The court refused to apply the *Frye* test to the use of ortho-toluidine to develop latents; the court distinguished this development technique from hypnosis and polygraph, subject to *Frye*, on the ground that this technique merely enhances evidence which is already present.

185. In People v. Eyler, 133 Ill. 2d 173, 549 N.E.2d 268, 139 Ill. Dec. 756 (1989), *cert. denied*, 498 U.S. 993 (1990), the court found that the use of cyanoacrylate ester fumes to enhance latent prints is generally accepted in the scientific community. The court cited testimony that the Chicago police have regularly used Super Glue fuming since the early 1980s and that the technique is employed by the FBI and in other countries. There was defense testimony that the application of excessive fumes can obliterate latents and cause false positives. However, the court ruled that these problems affected only the weight of the evidence, not its admissibility.

The witness next offers sponsoring testimony for the permanent record of the latent impression. This record can take two forms: a photograph or a lift. If the proponent offers a photograph of the latent, the witness must be prepared to testify that the photograph is a true and accurate depiction of the impression observed at the crime scene.[186] When the proponent offers the lift, the lift must be authenticated as an item of physical evidence. If the witness added unique marks such as the case number and date to part of the lift itself, the court may treat the lift as a readily identifiable article.[187] On this assumption, the witness's recognition of the lift, based on the distinctive marks, is sufficient authentication. On the other hand, if the witness made the marks on a separate identification tag or the lift was made on delicate material, the trial court may insist on proof of a chain of custody.[188]

Federal Rule of Evidence 901 governs the question of the sufficiency of the authentication of the crime scene prints.[189] Under Rule 901, the test is whether the proponent of the evidence has presented "evidence sufficient to support a finding that the matter in question is what its proponent claims." The witness on the stand need not have personally lifted the print; it is sufficient if the witness was present and saw the print lifted.[190] The print is admissible even if the prosecution cannot show that the print was impressed at the time of the crime.[191]

§ 16-9(B). Admissibility of Inked Impressions.

There are several possible objections to the admission of the record of the inked impression.

As in the case of the latent impression, authentication of the record may be an issue. There are several methods of establishing the genuineness of the record. When the witness took the inked impression or was present when it was rolled, he can testify from personal knowledge and identify the inked impression.[192] Furthermore, if the person who took the inked impression did so in the normal

---

186. *See generally* 2 C. McCormick, Evidence § 214 (5th ed. 1999).

187. *See* Imwinkelried, *The Identification of Original Real Evidence*, 61 Mil. L. Rev. 145, 147-53 (1973).

188. *Id.* at 153-55, Giannelli, *Chain of Custody and the Handling of Real Evidence*, 20 Am. Crim. L. Rev. 527 (1983); People v. Williams, 48 Cal. 3d 1112, 774 P.2d 146, 259 Cal. Rptr. 473 (1989) (a business card containing the defendant's fingerprints was properly admitted at trial despite some mishandling of the evidence before trial); State v. Vampran, 491 So. 2d 1356 (La. App.) (the chain of custody for the murder victim's fingerprint comparison card was inadequate), *writ denied*, 496 So. 2d 347 (La. 1986).

189. United States v. Vasquez, 858 F.2d 1387, 1392 (9th Cir. 1988), *cert. denied*, 488 U.S. 1034 (1989).

190. *Id.* at 1393.

191. United States v. Dorsey, 852 F.2d 1068, 1069 (8th Cir. 1988).

192. C. McCormick, *supra* note 186, at §§ 219-20. United States v. Abreu, 952 F.2d 1458, 1468-69 (1st Cir.), *cert. denied*, 503 U.S. 994 (1992).

course of the activities of a police department or other regularly conducted activity, the impression would qualify as a business record. Business records can be authenticated on the basis of proper custody; anyone familiar with the business' filing system can vouch that the record was obtained from the appropriate file.[193] The custodian of the records can lay the foundation.[194] Lastly, if the activity that initially obtained the inked impression was a government agency, the impression may constitute a public record. In many jurisdictions, public records can be authenticated without live testimony; the only requirement is that the record must be accompanied with a properly executed certificate.[195] In many reported opinions, the prosecutor has offered inked impressions from a defendant's official penitentiary packet,[196] county jail records or corrections records,[197] and attesting certificates were attached to the official record.[198]

The opponent may argue that there is insufficient proof that the person fingerprinted was the defendant. There are several methods of establishing the

---

193. C. McCormick, *supra* note 186, at § 224. *But see* United States v. Dockins, 986 F.2d 888, 895 (5th Cir.) (the exhibit was not self-authenticating, the witness was not the custodian, and there was "no circumstantial evidence at trial to support a finding that Exhibit 5a came from the Denver Police Department"), *cert. denied*, 510 U.S. 850 (1993). In Federal Rules of Evidence News 93-160, the editor speculates:

> Suppose that Exhibit 5a was a printed form identifying the Denver Police Department. The odds that someone in Mississippi fabricated this printed form purporting to originate in Colorado seem extremely low. Moreover, I would expect that there must have been some testimony that the federal authorities in Mississippi had communicated with the Denver Police and received this card in response to their request. Under the "reply doctrine," it would seem to be adequate circumstantial showing of origin.

194. State v. Schneider, 585 S.W.2d 114 (Mo. App. 1979).

195. C. McCormick, *supra* note 186, at § 224. *See* Fed. R. Evid. 902, 28 U.S.C.A.

196. United States v. Dancy, 861 F.2d 77 (5th Cir. 1988) (citing Federal Rule of Evidence 902(4)); Rodasti v. State, 749 S.W.2d 161 (Tex. App. 1988) (the certificate on the pen packet was signed and accompanied by the imprint of an official seal); Felton v. State, 659 S.W.2d 482, 486 (Tex. App. 1983); Loftin v. State, 624 S.W.2d 351 (Tex. App. 1981); *But see* United States v. Dockins, 986 F.2d 888, 895 (5th Cir.) (the exhibit was not self-authenticating, the witness was not the custodian, and there was "no circumstantial evidence at trial to support a finding that Exhibit 5a came from the Denver Police Department"), *cert. denied*, 510 U.S. 850 (1993). In Federal Rules of Evidence News 93-160, the editor speculates:

> Suppose that Exhibit 5a was a printed form identifying the Denver Police Department. The odds that someone in Mississippi fabricated this printed form purporting to originate in Colorado seem extremely low. Moreover, I would expect that there must have been some testimony that the federal authorities in Mississippi had communicated with the Denver Police and received this card in response to their request. Under the "reply doctrine," it would seem to be adequate circumstantial showing of origin.

197. Lyle v. State, 669 S.W.2d 853 (Tex. App. 1984) (county jail records); Phillips v. State, 654 S.W.2d 846 (Tex. App. 1983) (corrections records).

198. State v. McMillan, 593 S.W.2d 629, 635 (Mo. App. 1980); Phillips v. State, 654 S.W.2d 846 (Tex. App. 1983); United States v. Taylor, 4 U.S.C.M.A. 232, 15 C.M.R. 232 (1954).

defendant's identity. To begin with, the person who took the inked impressions may identify the defendant as the person he fingerprinted. Although there is contrary authority,[199] the majority view is that identity between the defendant's name and the name on the record is sufficient to identify the defendant as the person fingerprinted.[200] For example, Oregon Rule of Evidence 311(r) recognizes a presumption that a "person is the same if the name is identical." The more unusual the name, the stronger is the inference of identity.[201] The proponent may rely on the fact that the defendant matches any physical description[202] or photograph accompanying the fingerprint record. To support the inference, the proponent may also point out that the defendant's address matches the address listed in the record for the person fingerprinted.[203]

Finally, the opponent may object that the fingerprint record is hearsay. Given the typical use of fingerprint evidence, the record seems to constitute hearsay.[204] It is offered to prove the assertion that the inked fingerprints belong to the person whose name is listed in the record. However, there are available hearsay exceptions. The record may qualify as a business entry[205] under Federal Rule of Evidence 803(6) or a public record[206] under Rule 803(8).

The above paragraphs discuss common-law and statutory attacks on the admissibility of the inked impressions. Of course, those attacks do not exhaust the universe of possibilities. For example, an accused might contend that the police obtained the inked impressions by virtue of an illegal warrantless arrest.[207] Chapter 2 discusses the relevant constitutional limits.

---

199. State v. Forteson, 8 Ariz. App. 468, 474, 447 P.2d 560, 566 (1968).

200. Corona-Palomera v. Immigration & Naturalization Serv., 661 F.2d 814 (9th Cir. 1981); State v. Mays, 622 S.W.2d 21, 23 (Mo. App. 1981); State v. Patterson, 598 S.W.2d 483, 489 (Mo. App. 1980); State v. Winters, 579 S.W.2d 715 (Mo. App.1979).

201. State v. Mays, 622 S.W.2d 21, 23 (Mo. App. 1981).

202. State v. Barry, 605 S.W.2d 148 (Mo. App. 1980).

203. Rogers v. State, 598 S.W.2d 258, 262 (Tex. Crim. App. 1980).

204. FED. R. EVID. 801(c).

205. Smith v. State, 650 S.W.2d 476, 479 (Tex. App. 1983).

206. United States v. Taylor, 4 U.S.C.M.A. 232, 15 C.M.R. 232 (1954). *See also* United States v. Gilbert, 774 F.2d 962 (9th Cir. 1985). Rule 803(8)(C) purports to prohibit the prosecution from offering a report of "matters observed by ... law enforcement personnel." The courts have held that this prohibitory language does not apply to fingerprint cards in pen packets. United States v. Dancy, 861 F.2d 77 (5th Cir. 1988); United States v. Vidaure, 861 F.2d 1337 (5th Cir. 1988), *cert. denied*, 489 U.S. 1088 (1989).

207. *But see* United States v. Ortiz-Gonzalbo, 946 F. Supp. 287 (S.D.N.Y. 1996) (even if the police obtained the inked impressions after an illegal warrantless arrest, the impressions are admissible so long as the police did not arrest the accused in order to secure the fingerprint evidence), *aff'd*, 133 F.3d 908 (2d Cir. 1997).

§ 16-9(C). Examiner Qualifications.

To testify to a comparison of two impressions, the witness must qualify as an expert on the identification of fingerprints. An expert in the detection or classification of prints is not necessarily qualified to identify prints.[208] In a particular police agency, there may be a sharp division of labor; even persons who are skilled and proficient in detection and classification may have no training or experience in identification. The opponent should never stipulate to the qualification of a "fingerprint expert" until it is clear that the purported expert is skilled in the function of fingerprint identification rather than some other phase of fingerprint processing.

However, the standard for expertise in identification is minimal. No college awards a degree in fingerprint identification, although some offer criminalistics courses that touch or even concentrate on fingerprint analysis. Experience in fingerprint identification is typically sufficient expertise.[209] It is helpful if the witness has also had formal training either on-the-job,[210] at a police academy,[211] or at a specialized course.[212]

At the urging of the American Academy of Forensic Sciences, in 1977 the International Association for Identification created a certification board for fingerprint examiners.[213] Moreover, Professor Moenssens has proposed that the courts follow a general rule that only certified examiners may qualify as experts in court.[214] Although this proposal has merit, to date no court has adopted it.

§ 16-9(D). Validity of Fingerprinting.

The introduction to this chapter noted that fingerprints are only one type of impression that can be used as a means of personal identification. Other impressions include lip and fingernail impressions. Until recently the admissibility of lip prints has never been litigated in the United States, but in

---

208. A. Moenssens, J. Starrs, C. Henderson & F. Inbau, *supra* note 5, at § 8.11.

209. State v. Carter, 591 S.W.2d 219, 221 (Mo. App. 1979).

210. *Id.* State v. Usenia, 599 A.2d 1026, 1032-33 (R.I. 1991).

211. Jiminez v. State, 630 S.W.2d 776, 777 (Tex. App. 1982).

212. Cobb v. State, 655 S.W.2d 276 (Tex. App. 1983).

213. The I.A.I. guidelines for certification state that the candidate must: Be of good moral character, have completed 40 hours of formal training in classification and 40 hours of classroom training in latent prints, possess three years of experience, pass an examination, submit an example of his or her courtroom testimony for review or subject himself or herself to questions about a case, and have a B.S. or B.A. degree. Reneau, *The Legal Profession, the Dactylography Profession and Certification*, Forum, Sept./Oct. 1986, at 39. Approximately 1,000 latent print examiners have already been certified. *Id.*

214. A. Moenssens, J. Starrs, C. Henderson & F. Inbau, *supra* note 5, at § 8.11.

1999 one case ruled lip print evidence admissible.[215] Although there is contrary authority, in one court test of fingernail evidence the appellate court held the evidence inadmissible.[216] There is limited authority sustaining the admission of testimony about earprints.[217] In contrast, fingerprints,[218] palm prints,[219] and bare footprints[220] all have been repeatedly recognized as valid scientific techniques.[221] The Illinois court broke ground by sustaining the admission of fingerprint evidence in a case near the turn of the century.[222] One court has declared that modernly fingerprints are regarded as the strongest evidence of a person's

---

215. People v. Davis, 304 Ill. App. 3d 427, 710 N.E.2d 1251, 238 Ill. Dec. 149 (1999) (an expert testified that lip print comparison is a known and accepted form of scientific comparison; both the Federal Bureau of Investigation and the Illinois State Police consider lip prints to be a positive means of identification).

216. People v. Wesley, 103 Mich. App. 240, 303 N.W.2d 194 (1981), *aff'd*, 421 Mich. 375, 365 N.W.2d 692 (1984). *But see* Commonwealth v. Graves, 310 Pa. Super. 184, 456 A.2d 561 (1983); State v. Shaw, 124 Wis. 2d 363, 369 N.W.2d 772 (Ct. App. 1985); State v. Shaw, No. 82-Cr.-266 (Wis. Cir. 1982), discussed in Stone, *Capabilities of Modern Forensic Laboratories*, 25 WM. & MARY L. REV. 659, 670 (1984). *See generally* Annot., *Admissibility of evidence of fingernail comparisons in criminal cases*, 40 A.L.R.4TH 575 (1985).

217. *Earprint Is Pivotal Evidence in Trial*, THE RECORDER, July 17, 1997, at 6 ("A jury convicted a man of killing his ex-wife's fiancee in a trial that included the rare evidence of an earprint taken from the crime scene"; based in part on the evidence, David Kunze was convicted in Clark County, Washington Superior Court; "The pivotal evidence was an earprint lifted from [the victim's] bedroom door. A Dutch crime expert, Cor van der Lugt, testified that he was '100 percent certain' that the earprint belonged to Kunze. He did acknowledge that no scientific studies prove earprints are unique. Defense experts said the earprint could not be positively linked to Kunze. The use of earprints as evidence at a criminal trial is unusual in the United States. In 1986, a murder defendant was convicted based partly on earprint evidence in a California case.").

218. People v. Adamson, 27 Cal. 2d 478, 168 P.2d 3 (1946), *aff'd*, 332 U.S. 46 (1947); People v. Jennings, 252 Ill. 534, 96 N.E. 1077 (1911); Rivas v. State, 627 S.W.2d 494 (Tex. App. 1981); Grice v. State, 142 Tex. Crim. 4, 151 S.W.2d 211 (1941); United States v. Sherwood, 98 F.3d 402 (9th Cir. 1996).

219. United States v. Moore, 936 F.2d 1508, 1519-20 (7th Cir.), *cert. denied*, 502 U.S. 991 (1991); People v. Buckowski, 37 Cal. 2d 629, 233 P.2d 912 (1951), *cert. denied*, 342 U.S. 928 (1952); Paschall v. State, 152 Ind. App. 408, 283 N.E.2d 801 (1972); Roberts v. State, 268 So. 2d 578 (Fla. App. 1972); Chandler v. State, 267 Ind. 610, 372 N.E.2d 465 (1978); Williams v. State, 210 So. 2d 780 (Miss. 1968); Sharp v. State, 115 Neb. 737, 214 N.W. 643 (1927); State v. Kuhl, 42 Nev. 185, 175 P. 190 (1918); People v. Gates, 24 N.Y.2d 666, 301 N.Y.S.2d 597, 249 N.E.2d 450 (1969); State v. Pittman, 10 N.C. App. 508, 179 S.E.2d 198, *later app.*, 12 N.C. App. 401, 183 S.E.2d 307 (1971), *later app.*, 14 N.C. App. 588, 188 S.E.2d 694 (1972); Clark v. State, 500 S.W.2d 107 (Tex. Crim. App. 1973); Galvan v. State, 461 S.W.2d 396 (Tex. Crim. App. 1970).

220. Paschall v. State, 152 Ind. App. 408, 283 N.E.2d 801 (1972); Chandler v. State, 267 Ind. 610, 372 N.E.2d 465 (1978); State v. Jells, 53 Ohio St. 3d 22, 559 N.E.2d 464 (1990) (citing numerous cases from other jurisdictions, the court rules that a police officer could give nonexpert opinion testimony about the identification of a footprint), *cert. denied*, 498 U.S. 1111 (1991). *See also* Dees v. Caspiri, 904 F.2d 452, 454-55 (8th Cir.), *cert. denied*, 498 U.S. 970 (1990).

221. *See generally* Annot., 28 A.L.R.2D 1115 (1953).

222. People v. Jennings, 96 N.E. 1077, 1078 (Ill. 1911).

identity.[223] So long as the foundation is otherwise complete, any uncertainty in the expert's opinion tends to cut to the weight of the evidence rather than its admissibility.[224] In the case of fingerprints[225] and palm prints,[226] the courts have judicially noticed the technique's validity. Those techniques are so well accepted that the proponent need not present live testimony vouching for the technique.

For that matter, even though their use is rather novel, the use of super glue and lasers has been upheld.[227] In addition, a state intermediate appellate court has sustained testimony based on digital enhancement of fingerprints.[228] There is also authority permitting expert testimony that based on the location of the fingerprints on a notebook, a person was probably holding the notebook in a particular way.[229]

In the present state of the law, there are only two situations in which there should be a serious challenge to the validity of the technique. One situation would be a case in which evidence of a truly novel means of identification such as lip or fingernail impression is offered. The other case would be a situation in which a computerized identification of finger, palm, or bare footprints is offered.

---

223. People v. Adamson, 27 Cal. 2d 478, 165 P.2d 3 (1946), *aff'd,* 332 U.S. 46 (1947).

224. United States v. Jones, 72 F.3d 1324 (7th Cir. 1995) (the witness conceded that he could not identify the points of similarity without the benefit of a magnifying glass or enlarged photograph); Schneider v. Delo, 890 F. Supp. 791, 835-36 (E.D. Mo. 1995) (although "there were not enough prints to make a conclusive identification," the witness testified that "the latent print was probably that of Thompson;" "the fact that she could not make a conclusive match ... does not render her testimony inadmissible. Whatever weaknesses there were in her opinion go[ ] to the weight of her testimony, an issue for the jury to consider"), *aff'd,* 85 F.3d 335 (8th Cir.), *cert. denied sub nom.* Schneider v. Bowersox, 117 S. Ct. 530 (1996).

225. State v. Rodgers, 233 N.C. 390, 64 S.E.2d 572 (1951); Grice v. State, 142 Tex. Crim. 4, 151 S.W.2d 211 (1941); People v. Figueroa, 2 Cal. App. 4th 1584, 4 Cal. Rptr. 2d 40 (1992).

226. State v. Inman, 350 A.2d 582 (Me. 1976).

227. People v. Webb, 6 Cal. 4th 494, 862 P.2d 779, 24 Cal. Rptr. 2d 779 (1993), *cert. denied,* 513 U.S. 839 (1994). *Webb* was handed down by the California Supreme Court which still adheres to the traditional *Frye* standard for determining the admissibility of scientific evidence. However, the court ruled that there was no need for a full foundation, establishing the general acceptance of the laser technique. The court reasoned that the rationale for *Frye* is the fear that the purportedly scientific testimony will overwhelm the jury. The court asserted that the technique in question did not pose that risk to any significant degree, since the jury could view and second guess the prints being compared.

228. State v. Hayden, 90 Wash. App. 100, 950 P.2d 1024 (1998) ("Enhanced digital imaging technology used to enhance photographs of latent prints evolved from efforts in the NASA space program.... No court has ruled in a published appellate decision on the admissibility of latent prints processed by enhanced digital imaging. Certainly digital photography is not a novel process. Neither is the use of computer software to enhance images"; "digital image processing has been used as a means of enhancing latent fingerprints by the Los Angeles County Sheriff's Department since at least 1987"; the court cites a number of scientific journal articles discussing the technique).

229. United States v. Salameh, 152 F.3d 88, 128-29 (2d Cir. 1998).

However, the critical question is whether the state of the law will change. In *Daubert*,[230] the Supreme Court announced that the proponent of scientific evidence must demonstrate the empirical validation of the technique in order to establish that the technique qualifies as reliable "scientific ... knowledge" under Federal Rule of Evidence 702. In 1999, in *Kumho*,[231] the Court declared that the reliability of even non-scientific expert testimony is subject to "*Daubert*-style scrutiny."[232] The results of the 1995 proficiency study, mentioned in § 16-1, raise serious questions about the trustworthiness of fingerprint analysis. It has been said that the criteria used by examiners are "the product of probabilistic intuitions widely shared among fingerprint examiners, not of scientific research."[233] One of leading commentators on expert testimony, Professor David Faigman, has written that if a court rigorously examined the fingerprint literature, the court would find "little if any" of the indicia of empirical validity demanded by *Daubert*.[234] It remains to be seen whether the courts will rethink their position on fingerprint evidence,[235] as some jurisdictions have done in other areas of forensic science such as questioned document examination and trace analysis.

§ 16-9(E). Fingerprint Reports.

In some cases, the fingerprint examiner is unavailable to give live testimony at trial. In that event, the proponent may offer the examiner's written report.[236] The report may fall within the business entry or public record hearsay exception. Federal Rule of Evidence 803(6) embodies the business entry exception, and Rule 803(8) similarly codifies the public record exception. However, Rule 803(8) excludes "in criminal cases matters observed by police officers and other law enforcement personnel ...." If the court construes "law enforcement personnel" as including fingerprint technicians working on crime laboratory staffs, the rule would arguably bar the prosecution from introducing a fingerprint report. It is becoming common practice in some jurisdictions to include testimony about the

---

230. Daubert v. Merrell Dow Pharmaceuticals, Inc., 509 U.S. 579 (1993).

231. Kumho Tire Co., Ltd. v. Carmichael, 119 S. Ct. 1167 (1999).

232. *Id.* at 1179.

233. Stoney, *The Scientific Questions*, *in* 2 MODERN SCIENTIFIC EVIDENCE: THE LAW AND SCIENCE OF EXPERT TESTIMONY 55, 70 (D. Faigman et al, eds. 1997).

234. *Id.* at 55.

235. Starrs, *Judicial Control Over Scientific Supermen: Fingerprint Experts and Others Who Exceed the Bounds*, 35 CRIM. L. BULL. 234, 273-76 (May-June 1999).

236. *E.g.*, United States v. Gilbert, 774 F.2d 962 (9th Cir. 1985); Bradford Trust Co. v. Merrill Lynch, Pierce, Fenner & Smith, Inc., 805 F.2d 49 (2d Cir. 1986); United States v. Taylor, 4 U.S.C.M.A. 232, 15 C.M.R. 232 (1954); People v. Champion, 9 Cal. 4th 879, 891 P.2d 93, 39 Cal. Rptr. 2d 547 (1995) ("the report itself was properly admissible under the business records exception to the hearsay rule. Evid. Code, § 1271"), *cert. denied*, 516 U.S. 1051 (1996).

original examiner's qualifications in the foundation for the examiner's report.[237] As previously stated, fingerprint examiners rarely disagree over identifications. Given the supposed reliability of fingerprint evidence, the admission of fingerprint reports may not violate the confrontation clause.[238]

§ 16-10. Sufficiency of Fingerprint Evidence.

When the prosecutor relies solely or heavily on fingerprint evidence, two questions arise: What is the legal standard for assessing the sufficiency of the fingerprint evidence? And do the circumstances set out in the record meet the standard?

§ 16-10(A). Legal Test for Sufficiency.

Fingerprints can be offered for a number of purposes at trial. For example, they may be presented to corroborate either a defendant's confession[239] or an accomplice's testimony.[240] When the prosecutor offers fingerprint evidence for these limited purposes, the evidence must merely satisfy the minimal tests for corroborative proof.[241]

In many cases, though, the prosecutor offers fingerprints for broader purposes. In some instances, the prosecutor tenders the proof to establish only the defendant's identity. For example, the prosecution may be attempting to show that the defendant was the same person who suffered a prior conviction; at the sentencing phase of a trial, proof of a prior conviction may be required to establish the defendant's status as an habitual offender[242] or to enhance the maximum imposable punishment.[243] In these cases, the only inference the prosecutor must establish is one of identity. Standing alone, the fingerprint evidence may be sufficient to support the inference.

---

237. State v. Hamilton, 612 S.W.2d 141 (Mo. App. 1980); State v. Carter, 591 S.W.2d 219, 221 (Mo. App.1979).

238. Imwinkelried, *The Constitutionality of Introducing Evaluative Laboratory Reports Against Criminal Defendants*, 30 HAST. L.J. 621, 638-39 (1979). For a discussion of the admissibility of laboratory reports, *see* Chapter 6.

239. Rodriguez v. State, 452 S.W.2d 457 (Tex. Crim. App. 1970).

240. Merriweather v. State, 364 So. 2d 374 (Ala. App.), *writ denied,* 364 So. 2d 377 (Ala. 1978); People v. Manson, 61 Cal. App. 3d 102, 132 Cal. Rptr. 265 (1976), *cert. denied,* 430 U.S. 986 (1977).

241. *See generally* E. IMWINKELRIED, P. GIANNELLI, F. GILLIGAN & F. LEDERER, COURTROOM CRIMINAL EVIDENCE §§ 718, 2321 (3d ed. 1998).

242. State v. Muse, 367 So. 2d 789 (La. 1979).

243. Johnson v. State, 435 S.W.2d 512 (Tex. Crim. 1969). *See also* United States v. Canady, 126 F.3d 352 (2d Cir. 1997) (the defendant was charged with "carrying" a firearm; the defendant's fingerprint was found on the gun), *cert. denied*, 522 U.S. 1134 (1998).

However, in many cases, when other evidence is lacking, at the guilt phase of the trial the prosecutor relies solely or primarily on the fingerprint evidence to satisfy the burden of production or going forward.[244] Chapter 23, devoted to drug identification, notes that until recently the American courts were split over the question of the standard for assessing the initial burden in criminal cases; some courts were satisfied with a scintilla of evidence, others required substantial evidence, and still others required evidence to remove any lingering doubt from the mind of a hypothetical, rational juror. This split of authority is reflected in the cases on fingerprint evidence. A number of courts insisted that the circumstances surrounding the fingerprint evidence exclude every reasonable hypothesis other than the assumption that the defendant impressed his fingers at the scene during the crime.[245] Yet other jurisdictions applied tests, accepting any evidence.[246]

As noted in Chapter 23, the Supreme Court's 1979 decision in *Jackson v. Virginia*[247] seems to resolve the split of authority in favor of the strictest view. Some courts have already acknowledged the pertinence of *Jackson* in fingerprint cases[248] In the future, courts should use the standard of whether the fingerprint evidence and the surrounding circumstances are sufficient to permit a rational trier of fact to find guilt beyond a reasonable doubt.[249]

§ 16-10(B). Illustrative Fact Patterns.

"[F]ingerprint evidence alone may under certain circumstances support a conviction."[250] It is impossible to state hard-and-fast rules for evaluating the sufficiency of the evidence in fingerprint cases. Each case has some peculiar facts, and the court must look to the cumulative probative value of all the facts in the record. For example, the courts have refused to announce that any particular number of points of similarity is necessary to uphold a conviction.[251] However,

---

244. For a discussion of the initial burden, *see* E. IMWINKELRIED, P. GIANNELLI, F. GILLIGAN & F. LEDERER, *supra* note 241, at §§ 2903-2907.

245. *See generally* A. MOENSSENS, J. STARRS, C. HENDERSON & F. INBAU, *supra* note 5, at § 8.09, at 522 n.28, *citing* People v. Rodis, 145 Cal. App. 2d 44, 301 P.2d 886 (1956); People v. Daly, 168 Cal. App. 2d 169, 335 P.2d 503 (1959); Anthony v. State, 85 Ga. App. 119, 68 S.E.2d 150 (1951); State v. Helms, 218 N.C. 592, 12 S.E.2d 243 (1940); Lawless v. State, 3 Md. App. 652, 241 A.2d 155 (1968); Fladung v. State, 4 Md. App. 664, 244 A.2d 909 (1968); Grice v. State, 142 Tex. Crim. 4, 151 S.W.2d 211 (1941).

246. Mason v. Commonwealth, 357 S.W.2d 667 (Ky. 1962).

247. 443 U.S. 307 (1979).

248. Colvin v. State, 299 Md. 88, 472 A.2d 953, *cert. denied*, 469 U.S. 873 (1984).

249. Gibson v. Collins, 947 F.2d 780, 784-85 (5th Cir. 1991), *cert. denied*, 506 U.S. 833 (1992); Mikes v. Borg, 947 F.2d 353, 356-57 (9th Cir. 1991), *cert. denied*, 505 U.S. 1229 (1992).

250. Mikes v. Borg, 947 F.2d 353, 356 (9th Cir. 1991). *See also* United States v. Canady, 126 F.3d 352 (2d Cir. 1997) (the defendant was charged with "carrying" a firearm; the defendant's fingerprint was found on the gun), *cert. denied*, 118 S. Ct. 1092 (1998).

251. People v. Campbell, 146 Ill. 2d 363, 586 N.E.2d 1261 (1992) (shoeprint).

there are recurring fact patterns in which the courts tend to hold either that the evidence is sufficient or insufficient. Listing those fact patterns may provide some insights into the sufficiency problem.

Factual Showings Held Sufficient

The key fact persuading a court to find the evidence sufficient may be the location where the fingerprint is found. The courts tend to uphold the sufficiency of the evidence when:

—The owner of the property testifies that he never granted the defendant access to the location where the fingerprint was found and where the crime was committed.[252] For example, the print is found on an interior portion of the house such as an inside door[253] or the inside surface of a window.[254]

—The defendant would necessarily have had to commit a trespass to reach the location where the fingerprint was found and where the crime occurred.[255]

—The fingerprint was found on a part of the building high off the ground where the perpetrator evidently entered or exited the building.[256]

—There was a physical barrier denying the general public access to the place where the fingerprint was found and where the criminal obviously spent some time during the crime.[257]

—The fingerprint was found on a part of the building such as a window, that was first exposed during the criminal's entry, exit, or commission of the crime.[258]

---

252. Summerson v. State, 200 So. 2d 594 (Fla. App. 1967); Stacy v. State, 49 Okla. Crim. 154, 292 P. 885 (1930); State v. Berry, 58 N.C. App. 355, 357, 293 S.E.2d 650, 651 (1982), *aff'd,* 307 N.C. 463, 298 S.E.2d 386 (1983).

253. People v. Adamson, 27 Cal. 2d 478, 165 P.2d 3 (1946), *aff'd,* 332 U.S. 46 (1947).

254. Jones v. State, 156 Ga. App. 823, 824, 275 S.E.2d 712, 713 (1980).

255. Colvin v. State, 299 Md. 88, 472 A.2d 953, *cert. denied,* 469 U.S. 873 (1984). *Cf.* Gibson v. Collins, 947 F.2d 780, 785 (5th Cir. 1991) ("In a criminal case in which the only evidence is the discovery of the defendant's fingerprints at the scene of the crime, a reasonable juror may find guilt beyond a reasonable doubt only if the evidence indicates that the imprinted object was generally inaccessible to the defendant except during the commission of the crime"), *cert. denied,* 506 U.S. 833 (1992).

256. State v. Pittman, 10 N.C. App. 508, 179 S.E.2d 198, *later app.,* 12 N.C. App. 401, 183 S.E.2d 307 (1971), *later app.,* 14 N.C. App. 588, 188 S.E.2d 694 (1972) (10 feet); People v. Rodis, 145 Cal. App. 2d 44, 301 P.2d 886 (1956) (nine feet); Avent v. Commonwealth, 209 Va. 474, 164 S.E.2d 655 (1968).

257. Merriweather v. State, 364 So. 2d 374 (Ala. App.), *cert. denied,* 364 So. 2d 377 (Ala. 1978) (counter in store); State v. Pryor, 306 So. 2d 675 (La. 1975) (counter).

258. United States v. Butler, 390 F.2d 620 (4th Cir.), *cert. denied,* 392 U.S. 915 (1968) (window previously covered by wire mesh); People v. Matthews, 102 Cal. App. 3d 704, 162 Cal. Rptr. 615 (1980) (window behind screen removed); Couser v. State, 4 Md. App. 543, 243 A.2d 639 (1968) (side of sign that had been against the building); State v. Allen, 420 S.W.2d 330 (Mo. 1967) (glass

—The fingerprint was found on the interior framing of a broken store window, and the print was pointing downward.[259]

If the fingerprint is found on an item of personal property, the courts tend to uphold the sufficiency of the evidence when there is an inference that the defendant could have had access to the object only during the crime:[260]

—The fingerprint was found on a wine bottle that had been stolen and had been wrapped when stolen.[261]
—The fingerprint was found on an object that was previously secured in a container broken into during the crime.[262]
—The fingerprint was found on the inside of a container that previously housed the stolen property and was broken into during the crime.[263]
—The fingerprint was found on an object that was obviously moved during the criminal's entry, exit, or commission of the crime.[264]
—The fingerprint was found on debris such as glass fragments that the criminal made in forcing entry.[265]
—The fingerprint was found in blood left by the crime.[266]
—The fingerprint was found on an object that was recently painted[267] or cleaned.[268]

---

previously covered by molding); Anderson v. State, 672 S.W.2d 14 (Tex. App. 1984) (window previously covered by screen); Grice v. State, 142 Tex. Crim. 4, 151 S.W.2d 211 (1941) (glass previously covered by molding).

259. Miles v. State, 466 So. 2d 239 (Fla. App. 1984).

260. United States v. Seawood, 172 F.3d 986 (7th Cir. 1999); Gibson v. Collins, 947 F.2d 780, 785 (5th Cir. 1991) ("In a criminal case in which the only evidence is the discovery of the defendant's fingerprints at the scene of the crime, a reasonable juror may find guilt beyond a reasonable doubt only if the evidence indicates that the imprinted object was generally inaccessible to the defendant except during the commission of the crime"), *cert. denied*, 506 U.S. 833 (1992).

261. Hamilton v. H.M. Advocate, JC (Scot) 1 (1934).

262. United States v. Lamartina, 584 F.2d 764, 765 (6th Cir. 1978) (voucher inside milk machine), *cert. denied,* 440 U.S. 928 (1979); United States v. Jones, 433 F.2d 1107 (D.C. Cir. 1979) (money box inside meter box); Shuemak v. State, 254 Ind. 117, 258 N.E.2d 158 (1970) (coin box locked in vending machine).

263. State v. McGriff, 7 Ariz. App. 498, 441 P.2d 264 (1968) (inside of telephone).

264. State v. Miller, 49 Ohio St. 2d 198, 3 Ohio Op. 3d 321, 361 N.E.2d 419 (1977) (hacksaw blade and display package moved near point of exit), *vacated in part*, 438 U.S. 911 (1978); Rushing v. State, 88 Okla. Crim. 82, 199 P.2d 614 (1948) (slats removed from door panel to effect entry); Jamison v. State, 209 Tenn. 426, 354 S.W.2d 252 (1962) (ditto machine moved next to window where entry made).

265. People v. Rhodes, 85 Ill. 2d 241, 52 Ill. Dec. 603, 422 N.E.2d 605 (1981) (shard of glass); People v. King, 88 Ill. App. 3d 548, 43 Ill. Dec. 937, 410 N.E.2d 1070 (1980) (shard of glass).

266. State v. Phillips, 15 N.C. App. 74, 189 S.E.2d 602, *cert. denied,* 281 N.C. 762, 191 S.E.2d 359 (1972).

267. Brunson v. State, 9 Md. App. 1, 261 A.2d 794 (1970) (three weeks before housebreaking).

If the object was generally inaccessible to the defendant, the mere existence of other possible hypotheses as to how the fingerprints got on the object does not require a judgment of acquittal.[269]

Another fact situation routinely held sufficient by the courts is a case in which there is expert testimony that the fingerprints were fresh or recent. We saw earlier in this chapter that such testimony is suspect.[270] Environmental and physiological factors make it difficult for any expert to estimate the age of fingerprints. Nevertheless, age estimates are sometimes admitted. Experts have been permitted to testify that a fingerprint was only 24 hours old,[271] not more than one day old,[272] or no more than five days old.[273] Other experts have testified more generally that the print was so fresh and strong that it was apparently the last impression placed on the object.[274] Like the freshness of the print, its unsmudged condition can sometimes constitute compelling evidence that the print was left at the time of the crime.[275]

Factual Showings Held Insufficient

In a fair number of cases, the courts have found the prosecution's evidence to be insufficient.[276] *Borum v. United States*[277] may be the high water mark for

---

268. State v. Penson, 351 So. 2d 1181 (1977) (weekly); Reynolds v. State, 368 So. 2d 596 (Fla. App. 1978) (day and a half earlier); Hack v. Commonwealth, 433 S.W.2d 877 (Ky. 1968) (day before crime); State v. Crawford, 619 S.W.2d 735 (Mo. 1981) (minutes before robbery); State v. Clemmons, 579 S.W.2d 682 (Mo. App. 1979) (same day); Campbell v. State, 493 P.2d 1126 (Okla. Crim. 1972) (night of the crime).

269. Gibson v. Collins, 947 F.2d 780, 785 (5th Cir. 1991) (a "theoretical[] possib[ility]" does not preclude conviction), *cert. denied*, 506 U.S. 833 (1992); State v. Watson, 224 N.J. Super. 354, 540 A.2d 875, *cert. denied*, 488 U.S. 983 (1988).

270. *See* Roberson v. State, 569 So. 2d 691 (Miss. 1990); Starrs, *Judicial Control Over Scientific Supermen: Fingerprint Experts and Others Who Exceed the Bounds*, 35 CRIM. L. BULL. 234 (May-June 1999).

271. Hervey v. People, 178 Colo. 38, 495 P.2d 204 (1972).

272. Couser v. State, 4 Md. App. 543, 243 A.2d 639 (1968).

273. State v. Turner, 90 N.M. 79, 559 P.2d 1206 (App. 1976), *cert. denied,* 90 N.M. 9, 558 P.2d 621 (1977).

274. State v. Wynn, 666 S.W.2d 862 (Mo. App. 1984).

275. Hall v. DiPaolo, 72 F.3d 243, 245 (1st Cir.) ("Where ... there is no evidence linking defendant to the crime other than his fingerprint at the scene, our question is whether it could be found beyond a reasonable doubt that defendant left his print at the time of the robbery. The evidence must foreclose all reasonably viable possibilities that he could have left it at some other time"; the state court reasoned that "because the fingerprint lifted from the doorknob was unsmudged and since the bathroom was used regularly by all the store's employees, the print was likely put there by one of the last people to touch the knob"), *cert. denied*, 518 U.S. 1010 (1996).

276. *See* Annot., 28 A.L.R.2D 1115, 1155-57 (1953); Mikes v. Borg, 947 F.2d 353 (9th Cir. 1991), *cert. denied*, 505 U.S. 1229 (1992); People v. Trevino, 39 Cal. 3d 667, 697, 704 P.2d 719, 737, 217 Cal. Rptr. 652, 670 (1985) (a "solitary fingerprint of some unknown vintage").

277. 380 F.2d 595 (D.C. Cir. 1967).

defense attacks on the legal sufficiency of fingerprint evidence. In that case, the defendant's fingerprints were detected on a jar that had contained a coin collection. A burglar had broken into the victim's house and stolen the collection. The record contained expert testimony that fingerprints could remain on objects such as the jar indefinitely. On appeal, the majority held the prosecution's proof insufficient; the majority faulted the prosecutor for failing to show that the defendant had no access to the jar. The majority reversed over a vigorous dissent by then Circuit Judge Burger. He charged that there was no need for the prosecution to trace the history of the jar on which the defendant's fingerprint was found. Some cases follow the lead of the *Borum* majority when the item is small and easily moveable,[278] but most subsequent decisions seem more in accord with the *Borum* dissent.[279]

Exceptional circumstances sometimes persuade appellate courts that fingerprint evidence is insufficient. A fingerprint found in a stolen car may be insufficient if there is undisputed evidence that the defendant was previously a lawful occupant of the car.[280] If other unidentified fingerprints are found near the defendant's and the surrounding circumstances suggest a lone criminal, the fingerprint evidence again may be insufficient.[281]

The testimony may be insufficient even when the owner of a house testifies that he never granted the defendant permission to enter the area where the fingerprint was found; the evidence may indicate that there were other lawful occupants of the premises such as children who frequently extended permission to third parties to enter.[282]

Note the relationship between the court's legal sufficiency ruling and the court's appreciation of the difficulty of time dating a fingerprint.[283] The more difficult the court believes it is to age a print, the longer the period of time the print may have remained on the surface where it was found; and the longer the period of time within which the defendant would have had to innocently plant his

---

278. United States v. Corso, 439 F.2d 956 (4th Cir. 1971). *See also* Mikes v. Borg, 947 F.2d 353 (9th Cir. 1991) (the defendant's fingerprints were found on three items at the murder scene; the testimony indicated that the victim had purchased the items four months before the killing; the prosecution neglected to adduce any proof that the items were inaccessible to the defendant before the crime; the court cites *Borum*), *cert. denied*, 505 U.S. 1229 (1992).

279. *E.g.*, People v. Rhodes, 85 Ill. 2d 241, 52 Ill. Dec. 603, 422 N.E.2d 605 (1981) (Simon, J., dissenting) (criticizing the majority for declining to require the prosecution to establish the history of the clock radio on which the defendant's fingerprint was found).

280. Mobley v. State, 363 So. 2d 170 (Fla. App. 1978).

281. Anthony v. State, 85 Ga. App. 119, 68 S.E.2d 150 (1951).

282. State v. Berry, 58 N.C. App. 355, 359, 293 S.E.2d 650, 652 (1982), *aff'd,* 307 N.C. 463, 298 S.E.2d 386 (1983) (Whichard, J., dissenting) (citing State v. Scott, 296 N.C. 519, 251 S.E.2d 414 (1979)).

283. Starrs, *Judicial Control Over Scientific Supermen: Fingerprint Experts and Others Who Exceed the Bounds*, 35 CRIM. L. BULL. 234, 246-73 (May-June 1999).

or her fingerprint at the crime scene.[284] In short, to persuade the court to sustain a legal sufficiency attack, the defense may initially have to educate the court about the difficulty of time dating the print.

§ 16-11. Lack of Fingerprint Evidence.

Fingerprint evidence is so highly regarded and so frequently offered at trial that the defense may attempt to capitalize on the absence of fingerprint evidence in a particular case. To what extent may the defense do so? If the defense opens the issue, how may the prosecution respond?

Defense Attacks

The defense may raise the issue in several fashions. The defense may simply question the witness to establish that there is no fingerprint evidence in the case.[285] This line of inquiry seems unobjectionable unless the defense attempts to elicit improper opinions such as whether the lack of fingerprint evidence shakes the witness's confidence in the defendant's guilt.[286]

A step beyond mere questioning is arguing in summation that the lack of fingerprint evidence shows that the prosecution case is weak.[287] Some courts generally permit the defense to highlight gaps in the prosecution case such as the lack of fingerprint evidence.[288] The leading defense precedent is *Eley v. State*,[289] a 1980 Maryland decision. There the court asserted that the "unexplained silence concerning a routine and reliable method of identification especially in a case where the identification testimony is at least subject to some question ... is within the scope of permissible argument." In an analogous case, one court permitted the prosecution to comment on the defense's failure to call its fingerprint

284. *Id.* at 249.

285. State v. Olsen, 135 Wash. 240, 237 P. 502 (1925); United States v. Rose, 104 F.3d 1408, 1417 (1st Cir.) ("Rose's counsel was free to argue that, in the absence of [fingerprint] evidence, the government had not sufficiently linked Rose to the crime"), *cert. denied*, 520 U.S. 1258 (1997); United States v. Poindexter, 942 F.2d 354, 358-60 (6th Cir.) (it was error to prohibit defense counsel from pointing out the lack of fingerprints), *cert. denied*, 502 U.S. 994 (1991); Squires v. Dugger, 794 F. Supp. 1568, 1578-79 (M.D. Fla. 1992).

286. *E.g.,* Treats v. State, 280 Ark. 319, 657 S.W.2d 556 (1983).

287. *E.g.*, State v. Williams, 623 S.W.2d 552, 553 (Mo. 1981); United States v. Thompson, 37 F.3d 450 (9th Cir. 1994).

288. Eley v. State, 288 Md. 548, 419 A.2d 384 (1980). *See also* McInnes v. Yamaha Motor Corp., 659 S.W.2d 704, 712 (Tex. App. 1983) (failure to call expert in civil cases), *aff'd*, 673 S.W.2d 185 (Tex. 1984), *cert. denied*, 469 U.S. 1107 (1985).

289. 288 Md. 548, 419 A.2d 384 (1980). In 1988, the Maryland Court of Appeals extended the *Eley* doctrine. The court held that during closing argument, the defense may comment on the lack of fingerprint evidence even if the defendant did not inquire about fingerprint evidence during the examination of witnesses. Sample v. State, 314 Md. 202, 550 A.2d 661 (1988).

expert.[290] Other courts follow a general rule prohibiting the defense from drawing an adverse inference from the lack of fingerprint evidence.[291] Other jurisdictions permit defense comment only when there is evidence that a search for fingerprints or similar physical evidence was in fact made.[292]

The defense may not be content with the negative remark that fingerprint evidence is lacking. The defense may want to assert that if the fingerprint evidence had been produced, it might have been exculpatory.[293] The defense may even request a jury instruction to that effect.[294] It is doubtful whether the comment and instruction are proper if there was no search for fingerprints. Even if there has been a search, many courts bar the comment and deny the instruction. In civil cases, the courts are reluctant to allow the "absent" or "missing" witness comment on the opposing party's failure to call a medical witness.[295] The courts have exhibited a similar reluctance in criminal cases.[296]

---

290. United States v. Grammer, 513 F.2d 673 (9th Cir. 1975).

291. *See* United States v. Hoffman, 964 F.2d 21 (D.C. Cir. 1992) (in summation, the defense counsel argued the non-record facts that the police did not search for fingerprints and that in failing to do so, they violated standard police procedure; "*Eley* may be distinguishable from the case at bar, because it appears that the defense lawyer's argument in that case was limited to the contention that the absence of fingerprint evidence weakened the prosecution's case against his client — an argument that the Government concedes to be appropriate. However, ...some of the language in *Eley* seems to go further, suggesting that the kinds of inferences urged by Hoffman's counsel in this case would be permissible even in the absence of any evidentiary foundation. To the extent that *Eley* so holds, we part company with the Maryland Court of Appeals and instead join ranks with the numerous other courts, federal and state, that have reached a contrary conclusion"); Henderson v. State, 51 Md. App. 152, 155 n.4, 441 A.2d 1114, 1116 n.4 (Md. 1982) (citing cases).

292. State v. Holmes, 654 S.W.2d 133 (Mo. App. 1983); United States v. Hoffman, 964 F.2d 21, 24-26 (D.C. Cir. 1992) (there must be an "evidentiary foundation" for the defense argument; the court added that "*Eley* may be distinguishable from the case at bar, because it appears that the defense lawyer's argument in that case was limited to the contention that the absence of fingerprint evidence weakened the prosecution's case.... However, ... some of the language in *Eley* seems to go further, suggesting ... that unexplained absence of fingerprint evidence 'permit[s] the adverse inference that the evidence would have been unfavorable to the State.' To the extent that *Eley* so holds, we part company with the Maryland Court of Appeals and instead join ranks with the numerous other courts, federal and state, that have reached a contrary conclusion").

293. *E.g.*, State v. Williams, 623 S.W.2d 552 (Mo. 1981).

294. *E.g.*, United States v. Anders, 602 F.2d 823 (8th Cir. 1979).

295. Coons v. Washington Mirror Works, Inc., 477 F.2d 864 (2d Cir. 1973); Oglesby v. Conger, 31 Colo. App. 504, 507 P.2d 883 (1972); Levin v. Arrabal, 11 Md. App. 89, 272 A.2d 818 (1971); Bay St. Louis v. Johnson, 222 So. 2d 841 (Miss. 1969); La Lima v. Fath, 36 A.D.2d 923, 320 N.Y.S.2d 882 (1971); Rice v. Ninacs, 34 A.D.2d 388, 312 N.Y.S.2d 246 (1970); Silveous v. Rensch, 20 Ohio St. 2d 82, 49 Ohio Op. 2d 355, 253 N.E.2d 758 (1969); Downey v. Weston, 451 Pa. 259, 301 A.2d 635 (1973); Martin v. Estrella, 107 R.I. 247, 266 A.2d 41 (1970); Schemenauer v. Travelers Indem. Co., 34 Wis. 2d 299, 149 N.W.2d 644 (1967). Herbert v. Wal-Mart Stores, Inc., 911 F.2d 1044 (5th Cir. 1990), indicates that the "missing witness" doctrine is no longer good law, since contemporary procedure permits any litigant to subpoena any potential witness and modern

Another defense attack is the argument that the police failure to search for fingerprints violated the due process clause by denying the defendant potentially exculpatory evidence. The courts have uniformly rejected this argument.[297] It is one thing if the police deliberately or negligently destroy fingerprint evidence before trial.[298] It is quite another matter to impose upon the police an affirmative duty to search for potentially exculpatory evidence. Chapter 22, devoted to intoxication testing, discusses the 1984 Supreme Court decision in the *Trombetta* case.[299] *Trombetta* makes it patent that the Supreme Court is not about to impose that affirmative duty on the police.

Prosecution Responses

If the defense broaches the issue of lack of fingerprint evidence, the prosecution may respond. For example, the prosecution may show that a person accompanying the defendant had a pair of gloves.[300] The defendant's easy access to gloves is relevant to explain the lack of fingerprints. The prosecutor may present the testimony of a sheriff, an experienced law enforcement officer, to explain the absence of fingerprints[301] or the unidentifiability of the prints found at

---

evidentiary rules such as Federal Rule of Evidence 607 permit any litigant to impeach any trial witness. Note, 37 LOY. L. REV. 387 (1991).

296. United States v. Anders, 602 F.2d 823 (8th Cir. 1979).

297. State v. Wells, 103 Idaho 137, 645 P.2d 371 (Ct. App. 1982); People v. Levario, 169 Cal. App. 3d 306, 215 Cal. Rptr. 157 (1985). However, the *Levario* opinion was later ordered depublished. Villafuerte v. Lewis, 75 F.3d 1330, 1341 (9th Cir. 1996) ("With regard to fingerprints, the officers did not have a constitutional duty to perform all tests desired by Villafuerte. Villafuerte does not specify why he believes the failure to test for fingerprints in certain areas constitutes bad faith"); Banks v. Powell, 917 F. Supp. 414, 418 (E.D. Va. 1996) ("The absence of fingerprints is a fact the jury may consider, but there is no constitutional or statutory requirement that police take fingerprints or employ every investigative technique known for each crime suspected").

298. *Cf.* State v. Wells, 103 Idaho 137, 138, 645 P.2d 371, 373 (Ct. App. 1982).

299. California v. Trombetta, 467 U.S. 479 (1984). *See* People v. Galindo, 229 Cal. App. 3d 1529, 281 Cal. Rptr. 155, 159-60 (1991) (citing *Trombetta*, the court stated that "[i]n the absence of any showing regarding the exculpatory value of the forfeited evidence or of bad faith on the part of the People, defendant was not entitled to sanctions, let alone an instruction concerning the failure of the People to preserve such evidence").

300. State v. Singleton, 654 S.W.2d 344 (Mo. App.), *rereported*, 660 S.W.2d 13 (Mo. App. 1983).

301. United States v. Burdeau, 168 F.3d 352, 357 (9th Cir. 1999) ("On redirect, the state elicited testimony that identifiable fingerprints are almost never found on guns and only rarely found on other objects submitted for testing. The witness also offered possible explanations for the absence of such identifiable prints: the surface might not be conducive to fingerprints, skin can be too dry to leave a print, or fingers may be moved in a manner that smudges a print"); United States v. Darland, 659 F.2d 70 (5th Cir. 1981), *cert. denied,* 454 U.S. 1157 (1982); Scott v. Henrich, 978 F.2d 481, 485 (9th Cir. 1992) ("It's true that, in the popular mythology, people leave telltale fingerprints on everything they touch. But in real life that's just not so. 'Experience has shown that it is possible to examine quite a number of articles which have been recently handled with the result

the crime scene.[302] However, the prosecutor must offer admissible evidence to establish the explanation; the prosecutor may not simply assert during summation, "In 98% of the cases we do not find a print on a stolen car."[303] The prosecutor certainly may not insinuate that any partial prints were inculpatory without supporting evidence.[304] Moreover, the witness's attempted explanation is opinion testimony, and the witness must qualify as an expert.[305] Unless the witness has the necessary expertise, he may be limited to testifying that there were no fingerprints; the witness's opinion that the criminal used gloves or wiped away the prints may be objectionable.[306] In addition to presenting responsive testimony, the prosecutor may point out during summation that the defense did not offer any fingerprint evidence.[307] Furthermore, the judge may comment on the lack of fingerprint evidence and give the jurors guidance on the proper inferences from the lack of such evidence.[308]

---

that there is a surprising lack of anything approaching even the suggestion of a finger mark'"), *opinion withdrawn*, 994 F.2d 1343 (9th Cir. 1993), *superseded,* 39 F.3d 912 (9th Cir. 1994), *cert. denied*, 515 U.S. 1159 (1995). *But see* State v. Roberson, 409 S.E.2d 288, 301 (N.C. 1991) (the officer may give the jury "scientific explanations regarding why a fingerprint may ... not be found at a crime scene, [but] it is simply not relevant to the issues in this case that Sergeant Lance has found identifiable prints in only three percent of the cases he has personally investigated").

302. United States v. Burdeau, 168 F.3d 352, 357 (9th Cir. 1999) ("fingers may be moved in a manner that smudges a print"); James, Pounds & Wilshire, *Obliteration of Latent Fingerprints*, 36 J. FORENSIC SCI. 1376 (1991) (the type of brush or brushing procedure may result in smearing ridges, and overpowdering or overbrushing can render a print partially or totally unidentifiable).

303. People v. Martinez, 82 Cal. App. 3d 1, 147 Cal. Rptr. 208 (1978). *See also* United States v. Thomas, 864 F.2d 843, 847-48 (D.C. Cir. 1989) ("the inherent difficulty of obtaining fingerprint evidence from the surfaces of the items seized"); United States v. Feldman, 788 F.2d 544 (9th Cir. 1986), *cert. denied,* 479 U.S. 1067 (1987) (FBI agent testified that fingerprints are recovered less than 5% of the time); State v. Walker, 489 So. 2d 353 (La. App.) (it is common to find only unidentifiable smudges), *cert. denied,* 493 So. 2d 1215 (La. 1986).

304. United States v. Manning, 23 F.3d 570, 573 (1st Cir. 1994), *cert. denied,* 519 U.S. 853 (1996).

305. United States v. Booth, 669 F.2d 1231, 1240 (9th Cir. 1981); State v. Aaron, 57 Wash. App. 277, 787 P.2d 949 (1990) (a police detective was qualified to explain the absence of fingerprints at the burglary scene; testimony that gloves, socks, and handkerchiefs can be used to prevent the deposition of latent prints "is not sophisticated expert testimony and need not meet the rigors of a scientific theory").

306. *Id.*

307. United States v. Alvarez, 837 F.2d 1024 (11th Cir.) (the trial judge clearly instructed the jury that the prosecution had the burden of proof on the issue of identity, and the prosecutor's remarks at least did not amount to reversible error), *cert. denied,* 486 U.S. 1026 (1988); Benson v. State, 636 A.2d 907 (Del. 1994) (the comment is proper so long as the defendant never requested funds to obtain an expert).

308. United States v. Quinn, 901 F.2d 522, 532 (6th Cir. 1990).

§ 16-12. Selected Bibliography.

W. BODZIAK, FOOTWEAR IMPRESSION EVIDENCE: DETECTION, RECOVERY, AND EXAMINATION (2d ed. 1999).

W. CLEMENT, STUDY OF LATENT FINGERPRINTS — A SCIENCE (1987).

J. COWGER, FRICTION RIDGE SKIN: COMPARISON AND IDENTIFICATION OF FINGERPRINTS (1992)

J. COWGER, FRICTION RIDGE SKIN (1983).

Darby, *Criminalistics, in* 3 FORENSIC SCIENCES ch. 36 (C. Wecht ed. 1983).

FEDERAL BUREAU OF INVESTIGATION, THE SCIENCE OF FINGERPRINTS (1977).

H. LEE & R. GAENSSLEN, ADVANCES IN FINGERPRINT DEVELOPMENT (1992).

P. MCDONALD, TIRE IMPRINT EVIDENCE (1989).

Menzel, *The Development of Fingerprints, in* SCIENTIFIC AND EXPERT EVIDENCE ch. 20 (2d ed. 1981).

A. MOENSSENS, FINGERPRINT TECHNIQUES (1971).

A. MOENSSENS, FINGERPRINTS AND THE LAW (1969).

CHAPTER 17

GENETIC MARKERS OTHER THAN DNA*

§ 17-1. In General.

This chapter discusses the analysis of genetic markers, including blood types. This subject is important for three reasons. First, no area of forensic science progressed as rapidly since the 1970s as serological analysis. The analysis of genetic markers underwent a virtual revolution during the past three decades.[1] Second, the advances in serology epitomize one of the major trends in contemporary forensic science: the effort to explain the significance of test results in statistical terms. Thus, the statistical techniques for evaluating test results disclosing the presence of genetic markers are also considered in this chapter. As in many areas of modern forensic science, the most important ongoing research is directed at "defin[ing] in statistical terms the meaning and

*The authors wish to express their appreciation to Dr. Robert Allen, Director, Human Identification Laboratory, H.A. Chapman Institute of Medical Genetics, Children's Medical Center, Tulsa, Oklahoma, who reviewed this chapter in the second and third editions of the treatise. The authors would also like to express their gratitude to Professor David Kaye of the Arizona State University College of Law, who reviewed this chapter in the second edition. The authors would similarly like to thank Dr. Hugh Chaplin, Jr., of the Washington University School of Medicine who reviewed this chapter in our first edition.

1. Jonakait, *Will Blood Tell? Genetic Markers in Criminal Cases*, 31 EMORY L.J. 833 (1982).

significance of the data" generated by tests for the presence of genetic markers.[2] Third, there are indications that there may be a significant error rate in genetic marker analysis.[3]

Blood is complex material. If a tube of blood is allowed to sit for a period of time, the blood tends to separate into two parts.[4] One part is liquid called plasma. The liquid is called serum when the proteins responsible for blood clotting are removed. The second part is cellular material[5] which includes: erthrocytes (red blood cells), leucocytes (white blood cells), and platelets or thrombocytes. The red blood cells contain the hemoglobin that carries oxygen throughout the body. The white blood cells are responsible for maintaining the body's immune system that helps the body defend itself against attacking diseases. Each component of blood lends itself to a number of tests and helps the expert reach several conclusions.

With one exception, this chapter presents an overview of genetic marker analysis and the admissibility of testimony based on those analytic techniques. That exception is DNA analysis. The literature on DNA typing has become so voluminous and the issue of the admissibility of DNA typing testimony looms so large in the cases that the second and current editions of this treatise devote an entire chapter to that topic. Thus, Chapter 18 discusses DNA typing. However, it would be a mistake to leap to the conclusion that the advent of DNA typing has eclipsed the other genetic marker systems. Systems such as ABO blood grouping remain "an indispensable part of routine medicolegal examinations."[6] In some cases, if DNA testing is prohibitively expensive, other systems are used rather than DNA. In other cases, when the litigant wants to spare no expense, other systems can be used in addition to DNA.

§ 17-2. Expert Qualifications.

The type of expertise required depends upon the content of the proposed testimony. Assume, for example, that the expert intends to testify only that: He or

---

2. Saferstein, *Criminalistics — A Look Back at the 1970s, A Look Ahead at the 1980s*, 24 J. FORENSIC SCI. 925, 930 (1979).

3. Pearsall, *DNA Printing: The Unexamined "Witness" in Criminal Trials*, 77 CALIF. L. REV. 665, 673 (1989) (on a Collaborative Testing Services test of the proficiency of laboratories performing electrophoresis testing, "[o]f the sixty-eight laboratories that returned results, sixteen (23.5%) were in error on one or both samples"); Grunbaum, *Problems Inherent in the Analysis of Rape Evidence — State of the Art*, FORM 31, 34-36 (Sept.-Oct. 1986) (summarizing the results of various proficiency tests, including tests conducted by Collaborative Testing Services).

4. Gaensslen & Camp, *Forensic Serology: Analysis of Bloodstains and Body Fluid Stains, in* 2 FORENSIC SCIENCES 29-9 (C. Wecht ed. 1983).

5. *Id.* at 29-10.

6. Bunai, Nakamura, Nagai, Yamada, Watanabe, Takayama & Ohya, *Blood Grouping of Mixed Bloodstains Using Immunocytochemical Methods*, 44 J. FORENSIC SCI. 100 (1999).

she conducted certain tests for the presence of genetic markers; the tests revealed that particular markers were present or absent; and a certain percentage of the population has or lacks that genetic marker. On this assumption, the expert needs only a background in genetic marker testing. In one case, a trial judge ruled a person incompetent as an expert on blood typing when she had twice failed proficiency tests on the subject.[7] However, cases holding the witness unqualified are the exception rather than the rule. The courts have held that the witness can acquire this expertise solely through experience; academic training is unnecessary.[8] The standard for the admissibility of the testimony is relatively lax; the court may rule the witness qualified as an expert even if the witness says he considers himself "[un]qualified to answer" the particular question.[9]

However, to make a persuasive courtroom presentation, the proponent should call a better trained expert. One possibility is a medical technologist. To become a certified medical technologist, a person must: possess a B.S. degree; complete a one-year internship; and pass the National Registration Examination administered by the American Society for Clinical Pathology. In 1997, the National Certification Agency (NCA) began certifying technologists through an examination for expertise in molecular biology. As in the case of a medical technologist, one must have a bachelor's degree, complete one year of internship, and pass a certifying examination. Those who pass are designated as Certified Laboratory Specialists (Molecular Biology).[10] Even better, the proponent could call a physician or a Ph.D. with formal training in genetics and immunology.[11]

Suppose alternatively that the proponent is not content to elicit only the genetic marker test results or the population frequencies. The proponent also wants to present a statistical evaluation of the test results. It would be ideal if the proponent called a statistician and furnished him with the necessary data in the form of a hypothetical question. However, many physicians, Ph.D.s, and

7. Madsen v. Dormire, 137 F.3d 602, 603 (8th Cir. 1998).

8. State v. Hanson, 587 S.W.2d 895 (Mo. App. 1979). *See also* Graunbaum, *Admissibility of Biochemical Analyses Results from Sexual Assault Evidence in the United States Courts*, 8 MED. LAW 485 (1989) ("In many US crime laboratories there are no professional qualifications or requirements for the analysts assigned to this type of work").

9. People v. Rich, 45 Cal. 3d 1036, 1087-88, 755 P.2d 960, 992, 248 Cal. Rptr. 510, 543 (1988), *cert. denied*, 488 U.S. 1051 (1989). *See also* Spencer v. Commonwealth, 238 Va. 563, 385 S.E.2d 850 (1989) (the witness was qualified to testify about molecular and population genetics; the witness had a bachelor's degree in biology with minors in chemistry and pathology, a master's degree in molecular, cellular, and developmental biology with a specialty in genetics, and a doctorate in molecular and population genetics), *cert. denied*, 493 U.S. 1093 (1990). *But see* State v. Madsen, 772 S.W.2d 656 (Mo. 1989) (the witness did not qualify as an expert in serology; she had been denied certification as a qualified serologist, since she had not passed typing proficiency tests), *cert. denied*, 493 U.S. 1046 (1990).

10. CLSp(MB).

11. *See* Gaensslen & Camp, *supra* note 4, at 29-89.

technologists have had some formal training in statistics during their academic education; and that training suffices to persuade most trial courts to allow them to offer a statistical interpretation of the test results.

§ 17-3. Blood Determinations.

If the police find a fluid or stain at a crime scene and are interested in typing the material,[12] they preserve it and forward it to the laboratory. When the laboratory receives fluid or a stain, the threshold question is whether the material is blood. The expert usually runs, in sequence, a preliminary, presumptive, or screening test followed by a confirmatory test.

---

12. Stoilovic, *Detection of Semen and Blood Stains Using Polilight as a Light Source*, 51 FORENSIC SCI. INT'L 289 (1991). Of course, the analyst may be interested in making determinations other than whether blood of a certain type is present. In sexual assault cases, the analyst may be searching for indications of intercourse. To do so, the analyst can employ morphological and chemical tests. Chen, Kobilinsky, Wolosin, Shaler & Baum, *A Physical Method for Separating Spermatozoa from Epithelial Cells in Sexual Assault Evidence*, 43 J. FORENSIC SCI. 114 (1998).

Ejaculate contains a solid fraction (spermatazoa) and a liquid fraction (seminal fluid/plasma). To begin with, the analyst may analyze the morphology of the suspected spermatazoa in the specimen. An intact sperm has a head containing the paternal DNA, a middle piece, and a tail which provides its motility. The analyst might find intact spermatazoa, only heads, or no spermatazoa at all. Several components of the liquid fraction can be tested. First, the analyst can test for acid phosphatase, an enzyme produced by the prostate. On the average, acid phosphatase persists 24-72 hours post-coitus vaginally. Bey v. Morton, 124 F.3d 524, 532 (3d Cir. 1997) ("the forensic scientist's uncontested testimony that sperm may remain in the body for up to 48 hours after sexual intercourse, although it is rarely discovered later than 16 hours after such activity"), *cert. denied*, 522 U.S. 1081 (1998). Second, the analyst can test for choline which originates in the seminal vesicles and epididymis. Choline can be detected by the Florence test. The test is a microcrystalline method forming brown rhombic-like crystals. Third, the specimen might contain spermine originating in the prostate gland. It can be detected by the Barberios test, a microcrystalline method which forms yellow needle-like crystals. In addition, the analyst can test for p-30 or Prostatic Antigen (PA). Glycoprotein is produced by the epithelial cells lining the ducts in the prostate gland. Whichever test the analyst uses, the outcome will often be negative if there is a delay between the assault and the administration of the test. The incidence of recovering sperm is particularly low in cases of ejaculation into the victim's oral cavity. With its natural cleansing process, the cavity is a hostile environment for sperm. Moreover, the victim often washes out his or her mouth after the assault. Hence, a delay of even an hour or two may result in a negative outcome.

In one case, the witness employed the Phadebas methodology to detect saliva on a vaginal swab. The court upheld the admissibility of the testimony. State v. Dennis, 129 N.C. App. 686, 500 S.E.2d 765 (1998).

Screening Tests

One type of screening test is a microscopic method.[13] In this method, the expert stains the blood cells and observes the reaction between the cells and the stain. The test is catalytic, that is, based on the catalytic activity of the heme in hemoglobin.[14] The oxidation reaction entails the loss of electrons. The heme triggers an oxidation reaction leading to a color change. The most common tests are benzidine,[15] phenolphthalein,[16] orthotolidine, leucomalachite green, luminol,[17] and tetramethyl-benzidine.[18] These tests are very sensitive.[19] For example, some of these tests can detect blood diluted 1:1,000,000 in water.[20] Thus, a negative test result is almost conclusive evidence that blood is absent. However, it is disputed whether these are specific for blood.[21] Some authorities flatly assert that the tests are nonspecific.[22] False positives have been reported with samples from apple, cabbage, radish, grass, lettuce, celery, potato, tomato, corn, onion, rust, and bleach.[23] Although testimony about "presumptive tests for

---

13. Lee, *Identification and Grouping of Bloodstains, in* FORENSIC SCIENCE HANDBOOK 267, 271 (R. Saferstein ed. 1982).

14. Gaensslen & Camp, *supra* note 4, at 29-14.

15. Clark v. Moran, 942 F.2d 24 (1st Cir. 1991).

16. Cox, *A Study of the Sensitivity and Specificity of Four Presumptive Tests for Blood*, 36 J. FORENSIC SCI. 1503 (1991) ("the phenolphthalein test is the best single test for evaluating suspected bloodstains"); Clark v. Moran, 749 F. Supp. 1186, 1190 (D.R.I. 1990) ("[P]henolphthalein ... turns pink when it comes into contact with blood. Pyridine ... crystallize[s] the elements of blood present. The person doing the test would look at the solution under the microscope and [see] if the crystals appear ...."), *aff'd*, 942 F.2d 24 (1st Cir. 1991).

17. Laux, *Effects of Luminol on the Subsequent Analysis of Bloodstains*, 36 J. FORENSIC SCI. 1512 (1991); Thornton, Guarino, Rios & Cashman, *Enhancement of the Luminol Test by Means of Light Amplification*, 31 J. FORENSIC SCI. 254 (1986) (the use of a "starlight scope"). Luminol is 3-aminopthalhydrazine. The technique has numerous advantages: It is highly sensitive, can be used rapidly, and does not contaminate the sample so as to interfere with subsequent testings for typing. The test kit includes two components: (1) 0.7 grams of sodium perborate; and (2) 0.1 grams of 3-aminophthalhydrazine and five grams of sodium carbonate thoroughly dissolved in 100 ml of water. The reagent is prepared by mixing the two components. The reagent should be used within an hour of mixing. The area is darkened, and then the reagent is sprayed. Luminescence indicates the presence of blood; the blood oxidizes luminol, thereby generating visible luminescence.

18. Lee, *supra* note 13, at 272. *See also* Fox v. State, 779 P.2d 562 (Okla. Crim. App. 1989), *cert. denied*, 494 U.S. 1060 (1990).

19. Gaensslen & Camp, *supra* note 4, at 29-15.

20. *Id.*

21. *Id.* at 29-17.

22. Lee, *supra* note 13, at 275.

23. Sutton, *Serological Evidence, in* VIOLENT CRIMES 2 (unpublished manuscript on file with the National College of District Attorneys, Bates College of Law, University of Houston, Houston, Texas).

blood [is] generally accepted," the proponent of the testimony must establish the reliability of the specific test employed in the case.[24]

Confirmatory Tests

There are numerous confirmatory tests for the presence of blood. One of the most popular is a crystal method. The reaction between blood and the test reagent forms crystals with a distinctive shape and color.[25] The heme (oxygen-carrying) portion of the red blood cell reacts with the reagent. The expert can use the Teichmann, Wagenaar, or Takayama crystal test.[26] These tests are based upon a reaction between the crystal and the heme (oxygen-carrying) portion of the red blood cell. The crystal tests are less sensitive than the catalytic tests but are far more specific.[27] Some authorities declare that the crystal tests "are specific for the heme portion of the hemoglobin molecule. No false positives are generally encountered ...."[28]

There are confirmatory tests in addition to the crystal methods. For example, the expert can use spectrophotometric and chromatographic methods[29] discussed in Chapter 23 on drug identification. The expert can also employ electrophoresis,[30] discussed later in this chapter as a method of grouping. Finally, the expert can use an immunological technique.[31] This technique is based on a reaction between blood and anti-hemoglobin serum. Unfortunately, the serum is in short supply, and consequently this technique is rarely used.

The courts are liberal in admitting testimony on the question of whether material is blood. Some courts even declare that no expertise is necessary to

---

24. People v. Coleman, 46 Cal. 3d 749, 775, 759 P.2d 1260, 1277, 251 Cal. Rptr. 83, 100 (1988) ("[B]ecause we have no information as to the type of presumptive test the 'hemostick' was, we cannot ... assume it is one of the generally accepted presumptive tests for blood. The hemostick test should not, therefore, have been admitted"), *cert. denied*, 489 U.S. 1100 (1989). *See also* Young v. State, 316 Ark. 225, 871 S.W.2d 373 (1994) (the admission of luminol test results without follow-up tests confirming the presence of human blood was error; follow-up tests did not confirm the presence of human blood).

25. Lee, *supra* note 13, at 276.

26. *Id.* at 276-79. *See also* Young v. State, 316 Ark. 225, 871 S.W.2d 373 (1994) (the admission of luminol test results without follow-up tests confirming the presence of human blood was error; follow-up tests did not confirm the presence of human blood).

27. Gaensslen & Camp, *supra* note 4, at 29-20.

28. Sutton, *supra* note 23, at 3.

29. Lee, *supra* note 13, at 280-83. Espinoza, Kirms & Filipek, *Identification and Quantitation of Source from Hemoglobin of Blood and Blood Mixtures by High Performance Liquid Chromatography*, 41 J. FORENSIC SCI. 804 (1996); Andrasko & Rosen, *Sensitive Identification of Hemoglobin in Bloodstains from Different Species by High Performance Liquid Chromatography with Combined UV and Fluorescence Detection*, 39 J. FORENSIC SCI. 1018 (1994).

30. *Id.* at 280-81.

31. Lee, *supra* note 13, at 283.

identify blood and, hence, that lay opinion is permissible on that subject.[32] If a medical technologist offers testimony about preliminary tests, confirmatory tests, or a combination of such tests, the testimony is routinely admissible.

§ 17-4. Human or Animal Blood.

The next step in analyzing blood is determining the species of the blood: Is the blood of human or animal origin? In some cases, this type of testing cannot be performed. For example, the stain might have been denatured by exposure to the elements.[33] Assuming that the sample is suitable, there are a number of tests for making this determination. The earliest tests were based on measurements of the average size of the blood cells; it was believed that the size of human blood cells differed from that of the cells of other species.[34] However, the contemporary tests rest on differences between the proteins and other components of the blood of various species.[35]

One procedure is the ring precipitin test. If an animal is exposed to an antigen (any substance that would harm the animal), the animal's immune system will tend to develop an antibody to the antigen. Serologists capitalize on this principle by injecting animals (often rabbits) with human blood. The human blood functions as an antigen, and the animal develops an antibody to the human blood. The serologist subsequently bleeds the animal and isolates the anti-human antiserum. The expert places both the suspected human blood and the anti-human antiserum in a test tube. If the blood is human, a ring will form at the interface between the blood and the antiserum. The blood of the higher apes, including gorilla, chimpanzee, and orangutan, will also produce a positive test result.[36] There are antisera to detect the species of other animals, such as dogs, cats, chickens, pigs, and horses.[37]

There is also a diffusion test for determining whether blood is human.[38] There are several variations of the test: single diffusion in one dimension, single diffusion in two dimensions, and double diffusion in one dimension.[39] In all variations of the test, the expert studies the movement of the suspected human

---

32. Farmer v. State, 623 S.W.2d 788 (Tex. App. 1981).

33. Whelchel v. Wood, 996 F. Supp. 1019, 1040 (E.D. Wash. 1997).

34. Gaensslen & Camp, *supra* note 4, at 29-26.

35. Comment, *Scientific Evidence: The Nebraska Game and Parks Commission Explores New Blood and Tissue Identification Techniques for Game Law Enforcement*, 57 NEB. L. REV. 1062, 1064 (1978).

36. Sutton, *supra* note 23, at 4. The blood of old world monkeys is also closely related to that of human beings. However, the blood of marmosets and new world monkeys is not.

37. *Id. See also* Smith, *Chemicals Reacting with Various Forms of Hemoglobin: Biological Significance, Mechanisms, and Determination*, 31 J. FORENSIC SCI. 662 (1990).

38. Lee, *supra* note 13, at 284.

39. *Id.* at 284-86.

blood in a gel. The reaction between antigen in the blood and antibody in the gel determines the movement of the blood.

A recent variation of diffusion is immunodiffusion.[40] In this technique, a glass slide with three spots containing antiserum and three spots of suspected human blood is prepared.[41] The expert places the spots to form a circular pattern, and the antiserum and blood spots alternate. When the blood is human blood, the bands form a hexagon shape.[42] However, if the blood does not match the antiserum, a triangular pattern emerges.[43]

Laboratories are now using immunoelectrophoresis for species determinations.[44] In this technique, the expert divides a slide in two with a trough in the middle.[45] Known human blood samples and the suspected human samples are placed on opposite sides of the trough. An electric current is passed through the slide. Antiserum is placed in the trough. If the two samples match, that is, if the unknown blood is also human, "the precipitate arcs on the right side of the trough will be exactly the same as the precipitate arcs on the left side ...." — "mirror image precipitin arcs."[46]

Further, some laboratories employ isoelectric focusing (IEF) as a species test.[47] IEF is an advanced form of electrophoresis. In one experiment, researchers attempted to differentiate the hemoglobin (Hb) of 34 other species from that of human blood.[48] The researchers concluded that IEF could ultimately "offer a significant advance for differentiation of human and animal Hbs ...."[49]

---

40. *Id.* at 286.

41. Comment, *supra* note 35, at 1067. All these immunodiffusion techniques work with hemolyzed blood.

42. *Id.* at 1068.

43. *Id.*

44 Lee, *supra* note 13, at 287; Harrington, Heaney, McSweeney, Quarino, Schwartz & Versoza, *Haptoglobin Typing in Canine Bloods*, 36 J. FORENSIC SCI. 1561 (1991) (vertical electrophoresis); Marbach, *Isoelectrophoretogram of Gazelle Hemoglobin -- A Suggested Tool for Proving Hunting Offenses*, 34 J. FORENSIC SCI. 475 (1989); Alsawaf & Tu, *Isotachophoretic Analysis of Bloodstains: Differentiation of Human, Menstrual, Bovine, and Ovine Bloods*, 30 J. FORENSIC SCI. 922 (1985).

45. Comment, *supra* note 35, at 1068.

46. *Id.*

47. Oshima, Inoue & Hara, *Identification of Species Specific Hemoglobin by Isoelectric Focusing*, 20 FORENSIC SCI. INT'L 277 (1982).

48. *Id.* at 279.

49. *Id.* at 283. *See also* Itoh & Matsuzawa, *Detection of Human Hemoglobin A (HbA) and Human Hemoglobin F (HbF) in Biological Stains by Microtiter Latex Agglutination-Inhibition Test*, 47 FORENSIC SCI. INT'L 79 (1990) (listing the various techniques for detecting HbA and HbF); Quarino & Kobilinsky, *Development of a Radioimmunoassay Technique for the Detection of Human Hemoglobin in Dried Bloodstains*, 33 J. FORENSIC SCI. 1369 (1988) (traditionally, experts have run first a presumptive test for blood, next a confirmatory test, and then a test determining whether the blood is of human origin; the authors have devised a procedure for simultaneously identifying blood and determining that the blood is human); Yamamoto, Tsutumi & Ishizu, *Species Identification of Blood and Bloodstains by Enzyme-Linked Immunosorbent Assay (ELISA) Using*

Finally, the newest technique is immunochromatography.[50] A few police laboratories in Germany and Switzerland are currently using the Hexagon OBTI test to identify human fecal occult blood. The test is designed to detect the presence of human hemoglobin in stool samples. The test employs an anti-human hemoglobin antibody in an immunochromatographic procedure. The test is "human specific (or at least primate specific) . . . ."[51] In addition, the test appears to be more sensitive than the procedures currently in widespread use.[52]

With the possible exception of the novel techniques of isoelectric focusing and immunochromatography, these techniques are generally well accepted in scientific circles.[53] At this point, it is probably fair to say that even isoelectric focusing is widely accepted. Courts frequently admit expert testimony that blood is of human origin.[54] Even if the jurisdiction follows the *Frye* test discussed in Chapter 1, the proponent should have little difficulty if the expert is qualified and relies on a conventional method of species determination. Likewise, these methods have been validated by extensive empirical testing, and they consequently should also be admissible under *Daubert*.

§ 17-5. Age of Human Bloodstain.

Several techniques have been proposed for dating the age of a bloodstain.[55] Marsters describes the techniques in this fashion:

> Progressive change in color from red to brown affords a means of distinguishing a relatively fresh stain from an old one. A study conducted on dried bloodstains prepared in the laboratory proposed a spectrophotometric method that could provide an objective assessment of the color change.

Anti-Human Immunoglobin Kappa Light Chain Monoclonal Antibody, 40 FORENSIC SCI. INT'L 85 (1989).

50. Hochmeister, Budowle, Sparkes, Rudin, Gehrig, Thali, Schmidt, Cordier & Dirnhofer, *Validation Studies of an Immunochromatographic l-Step Test for the Forensic Identification of Human Blood*, 44 J. FORENSIC SCI. 597 (1999).

51. *Id.* at 602.

52. *Id.*

53. *See generally* Comment, *supra* note 35, at 1062.

54. Linder v. State, 273 Ark. 470, 620 S.W.2d 944 (1981). *But see* State v. Walker, 239 Kan. 635, 722 P.2d 556 (1986) (the forensic examiners could not determine whether the blood was of human or animal origin). In one recent case, a defense witness was permitted to testify that a substance previously identified by Fred Zain as human blood was not of human origin. MacCormack, *Zain Says He's Fall Guy in Evidence Scandals*, SAN ANTONIO EXPRESS-NEWS, Apr. 1, 1997, at 1 (describing the testimony of a defense witness, Dr. Moses Schanfield); Pauza, *Forensic Expert: Blood on Ax Not Human*, LAREDO MORNING TIMES, Apr. 1, 1997, at 1 (Moses Schanfield, a principal of an analytical genetic testing laboratory based in Denver, testified "that a test for blood of human species on the ax revealed that the blood was not of human origin").

55. Marsters, *Medicolegal Aspects of Blood and Other Biologic Stains*, *in* HANDBOOK OF LEGAL MEDICINE 120, 156-57 (5th ed. 1979).

> Decrease of solubility in water with increased lapse of time has been the basis for various tests for indicating the relative age of bloodstains. A recent study indicates that the albumin and the globulin fractions of human serum deteriorate at different rates and that the A/G ratio may provide an indicator of the age of a stain.[56]

Although these techniques have been proposed, they have yet to surface in an American courtroom. Marsters states skeptically that the techniques have "not been evaluated by sufficient application to casework ...."[57] Experts have rarely attempted to offer opinions on the age of bloodstains. In one case, *State v. Abbott,*[58] the expert estimated that the stain was only one month old. The expert based that opinion on "our experience here (in this geographic area) that in the summer months the genetic markers in dried blood which has not been refrigerated will last less than one month .... Genetic markers ... were developed from this blood sample."[59] The testimony was evidently admitted without objection.[60] Thus, the *Abbott* decision has no precedential value.

§ 17-6. Sex of Source.

Just as there are experimental techniques for dating human bloodstains, there are new techniques for sexing the blood.[61] The techniques include the following methods:

—The presence of Barr bodies in the nuclei of a mammalian cell is characteristic of the female.[62]

---

56. *Id.* Andrasko, *The Estimation of Age of Bloodstains by HPLC Analysis*, 42 J. FORENSIC SCI. 601 (1997) ("The first techniques for the estimation of bloodstain age were based on the decreased solubility of bloodstains in various aqueous solvents with age.... It has been known for a long time that bloodstains change in color from red to brown with increasing age, caused mainly by the oxidation of hemoglobin to methemoglogin. Patterson measured the color changes with a reflectance colorimeter and was able to produce an objective method for color assessment. A new HPLC system is described for estimating the age of bloodstains deposited on clothing. In addition to the decomposition peak designed as 'X' and reported earlier in the literature, several other ageing processes were studied and found suitable for estimation of age of the stains. The various processes can be used independently of each other for estimation of bloodstain age when the storing temperature is known"; the area of the peak in question increases with the age of the bloodstain).

57. Marsters, *supra* note 55 at 157.

58. 654 S.W.2d 260 (Mo. App. 1983).

59. SCIENTIFIC SLEUTHING NEWSLETTER, Jan. 1984, at 5.

60. *Id.*

61. Graham & Kochanski, *Move Over, Quincy,* NATIONAL INSTITUTE OF JUSTICE REPORTS, NOV. 1983, at 6; Hillman & Shaler, *The Rehydration and Isolation of Leukocytes from Dried Bloodstains*, 26 J. FORENSIC SCI. 543 (1981).

—The presence of fluorescent Y chromosomes (F bodies) also indicates the sex of the source of the blood.[63] There has been extensive experimentation with this technique.[64]

—The level of a particular type of seminoprotein can also indicate the sex of the source.[65] Its level is 3.3-fold higher in male adults than in female adults.

—Analysis of X-Y homologous amelogenin gene codes also are indicative of sex.[66] The determination of the Y/X ratio is useful in typing for gender.

—The level of sex hormones present can serve as an indicator.[67] Researchers have tested hormones such as testosterone, progesterone, and estradiol; they measure the levels present and determine the ratios.[68] Testosterone is considered a male sex steroid hormone while progesterone and estradiol are female sex steroids.[69] In a blind study, researchers relying on this technique reached no incorrect conclusions.[70] However, the data base was limited and all the research subjects in that study were healthy persons.[71] Chapter 18 discusses DNA typing. One of our reviewers informs us that the newest technique for sexing biological stains is based on the amplification of small regions of DNA contained on the Y chromosome.

There is a further parallel to the new techniques for aging human stains: The admissibility of these sexing techniques is not yet well settled. Expert testimony sexing a bloodstain was offered in one New York case.[72] However,

---

62. Gaensslen & Camp, *supra* note 4, at 29-75. *See also* Duffy, Waterfield & Skinner, *Isolation of Tooth Pulp Cells for Sex Chromatin Studies in Experimental Dehydrated and Cremated Remains*, 49 FORENSIC SCI. INT'L 127 (1991).

63. Gaensslen & Camp, *supra* note 4, at 29-75. *See also* Duffy, Waterfield & Skinner, *Isolation of Tooth Pulp Cells for Sex Chromatin Studies in Experimental Dehydrated and Cremated Remains*, 49 FORENSIC SCI. INT'L 127 (1991).

64. Thomsen, *An Investigation of Some of the Factors Influencing the Results of Y-Chromosome Detection in Blood Stains*, 17 FORENSIC SCI. INT'L 111 (1980). Pettenati, Rao, Schnell, Hayworth-Hodge, Lantz & Geisinger, *Gender Identification of Dried Human Bloodstains Using Fluorescence in Situ Hybridization*, 40 J. FORENSIC SCI. 885 (1995).

65. Yukama, Kohno, Ishikawa & Takahama, *A Sensitive Sandwich Enzyme Immunoassay for y-Seminoprotein and Its Application to Sex Discrimination of Blood and Bloodstains*, 55 FORENSIC SCI. INT'L 161 (1992).

66. LaFountain, Schwartz, Cormier & Buel, *Validation of Capillary Electrophoresis for Analysis of the X-Y Homologous Amelogenin Gene*, 43 J. FORENSIC SCI. 1188 (1998).

67. Gaensslen & Camp, *supra* note 4, at 29-75.

68. Brown, *The Determination of the Sex of an Individual from a Dried Bloodstain Using Radioimmunoassay of Testosterone, Progesterone, and Estradiol-17B*, 26 J. FORENSIC SCI. 766 (1981).

69. *Id.* at 767.

70. *Id.* at 779.

71. *Id.* at 778.

72. People v. Alston, 79 Misc. 2d 1077, 362 N.Y.S.2d 356 (Sup. Ct. 1974), *discussed in* Gaensslen & Camp, *supra* note 4, at 29-76.

the evidence was excluded on the ground that the technique has not yet gained sufficient acceptance to satisfy *Frye.* The court was troubled by the fact that the stains in question were 22 months old and that expert testimony questioned the reliability of an analysis of such old stains.[73]

§ 17-7. Race of Source.

A third developing area is the determination of the race of the person who was the source of the stain.[74] Researchers have discovered that some genetic markers serve to identify the race of the source. For example, in the MNSs system, the Su marker is found almost exclusively among blacks;[75] in the Duffy system the presence of $Fy^{aÀbÀ}$ is "strong evidence" that the source was black;[76] the $C3^f$ form of the serum protein C3 is almost completely absent among Asians;[77] Gc (group-specific component) and A2HS can be employed to identify Afro-Caribbeans;[78] all Caucasians are Pep A while black persons are Pep A 1-1, 2-1, and 2-2; the PLG system is useful in identifying Mongolians and Africans;[79] and the markers in the Gm system are also of assistance in identifying the racial origins of a stain.[80]

§ 17-8. Blood Groups.

We have reviewed the serological procedures for determining the race and sex of the source of a human bloodstain. To some extent, each determination narrows the class of possible sources of the blood. The class can be narrowed further by conducting tests to determine the group or category of the blood. For example, the expert can type the blood in the ABO system, discover that the blood group is type AB, and inform the jury that only 3% of the population has type AB blood. Three percent is the population frequency for type AB. In some jurisdictions the proponent may also invite the expert to make a more sophisticated statistical

---

73. *See* the discussion of *Alston* in People v. Borcsok, 114 Misc. 2d 810, 813-14, 452 N.Y.S.2d 814, 816 (Sup. Ct. 1982).

74. Graham & Kochanski, *supra* note 61, at 6.

75. Sussman, *Up-To-Date Blood Testing for Paternity and Nonpaternity*, 24 TRAUMA 12 (June 1982).

76. *Id.* at 13.

77. Eberhard & Kobilinsky, *The Electrophoretic Analysis of the Third Component of Complement (C3) in Dried Bloodstains*, 29 J. FORENSIC SCI. 774, 778 (1984).

78. Westwood, Seaman, O'Brien & Thorogood, *The Phenotypic Frequencies of Group Specific Component and a-2-HS-Glycoprotein in Three Ethnic Groups. The Use of These Proteins as Racial Markers in Forensic Biology*, 35 FORENSIC SCI. INT'L 197 (1987).

79. Gamero, Romero, Viscaya & Arufe, *Polymorphism of the Plasminogen (PLG) System in Cadiz Province, Southern Spain*, 36 J. FORENSIC SCI. 226, 228 (1991).

80. Shaler, *Interpretation of Gm Testing Results: Two Case Histories*, 27 J. FORENSIC SCI. 231 (1982).

evaluation of the test result. This section focuses on the scientific basis and legal acceptability of the various systems of genetic markers used to type blood.

There is a compelling need for this sort of evidence in legal proceedings, including criminal cases. Probably the most acute need is in paternity actions. Paternity suits often degenerate into swearing contests. Perjury is rampant in these cases. In one study, polygraph experts determined that 93% of the subjects (complainants and defendants) lied in some respect about their sexual activity during the paternity action.[81] The study indicated that 48% of the mothers questioned lied when they denied intercourse with other men during the possible period of conception.[82]

In contrast, blood grouping evidence is grounded on scientific fact. Each person inherits 23 chromosomes from each parent.[83] The chromosomes carry genes, which determine a person's characteristics such as height and hair color. A gene's position on a chromosome is termed a locus. (Alternatively, a locus can be defined as the chromosomal address for a genetic marker). Genes come in pairs; a pair of chromosomes (one paternal and the other maternal) is inherited. Alleles are variations in a genetically controlled trait; and as Chapter 18 points out, they are now used as well to denote variations in DNA sequences at the locus for a gene. In short, they are specific forms of a gene.[84] Alleles can be codominant, dominant, or recessive. If an allele is dominant, when the allele is paired with a recessive allele, the dominant allele determines the characteristic expressed in the person. For example, if the allele for one hair color is dominant and the other recessive, the person will have the hair color dictated by the dominant allele. The complete set of alleles is called the person's genotype; the genotype may include both dominant and recessive alleles. Half of the genotype — the paternal haplotype — comes from the person's father while the other half — the maternal haplotype — comes from the person's mother. In the genotype, if the dominant allele suppresses the trait associated with the recessive allele, the observed characteristic — the phenotype — is the one dictated by the dominant allele. When the two alleles are identical, the person is said to be homozygous. When the alleles differ, the person is heterozygous.

There are other features of the blood grouping system that are critical underpinnings of the evidence offered in court. One feature is polymorphism. A genetic marker is polymorphic if there are a number of possible forms of the marker that perform the same function. Polymorphisms in markers reflect polymorphisms in genes, that is, multiple alleles. For example, in the Rh system,

---

81. Arthur & Reid, *Utilizing the Lie Detector Technique to Determine the Truth in Disputed Paternity Cases*, 45 J. CRIM. L., CRIMINOLOGY & POLICE SCI. 213, 215 (1954).

82. *Id. See also* Ellman & Kaye, *Probabilities and Proof: Can HLA and Blood Group Testing Prove Paternity?*, 54 N.Y.U. L. REV. 1131, 1134 (1979).

83. Gaensslen & Camp, *supra* note 4, at 29-34.

84. *Id.* at 29-35.

a person may have type C, C^W, C^X, or C^G. The various types are different forms of the same genetic marker. In the current state of the art, serologists can work with tens of different marker systems. All the systems are polymorphic. "[I]t is estimated that there are well over 500 billion possible known blood group phenotypes, and other undiscovered blood group systems undoubtedly exist."[85] The second critical feature is that the passing of the genes from one generation to another follows the Mendelian laws of inheritance. Barring the remote possibility of mutation, the child cannot have characteristics that neither parent possesses. Moreover, knowing the genotype of the child and one parent, the expert can make certain deductions about the other parent's genotype. Because of these features, the father of blood grouping, Karl Landsteiner, predicted that a person's blood grouping would one day be as demonstrably unique as the person's fingerprint. Some serologists believe that that day is near at hand.

Although this chapter concentrates on blood analysis, these genetic markers often appear in other body tissues and fluids. Between 75 and 80% of the population secretes many of its genetic markers into other body fluids such as saliva[86] and semen.[87] Consequently, even if the police do not recover blood at a crime scene, the discovery of other biological material may permit testing for genetic markers.

Blood grouping evidence can be used in two ways in a legal proceeding. First, assuming that the evidence is not barred by a rule such as a conclusive

85. Lee, *supra* note 13, at 269-70.

86. Iida, Sawazaki, Yasuda, Tsubota, Aoyama, Matsuki & Kishi, *Deoxyribonuclease I Phenotyping from Saliva Stains*, 44 J. FORENSIC SCI. 175 (1999).

87. McCloskey, *Dealing with the Forensic Serologist in the Defense of Alleged Sexual Assault*, 10 CRIM. DEF. 18 (May-June 1983); *See also* Hofft & van de Voorde, *The Zinc Test as an Alternative for Acid Phosphatase Spot Tests in the Primary Identification of Seminal Traces*, 47 FORENSIC SCI. INT'L 269 (1990); Grispino, *Serological Evidence in Sexual Assault Investigations*, 59 F.B.I. LAW ENF. BULL. 14, 17 (Oct. 1990) ("Semen is identified where sperm cells are microscopically identified and/or a semen-specific protein associated with human semen, known as p30 or prostatic antigen, is determined to be present in extracts of dried stains upon examination"); Keating, *Information from Penile Swabs in Sexual Assault Cases*, 43 FORENSIC SCI. INT'L 63 (1989); Mudd, *The Detection of Soluble ABH Blood Group Substances in Semen and Saliva Using Monoclonal Blood Grouping Reagents*, 34 J. FORENSIC SCI. 1082 (1989); Rordorf, Dimo-Simonin, Brandt-Casadevall & Gujer, *A, B, and H Group Specific Substances in Human Vitreous Humor*, 41 FORENSIC SCI. INT'L 111 (1989); Koblinsky & Harrington, *Detection and Use of Salivary Hemagglutins for Forensic Blood Grouping*, 33 J. FORENSIC SCI. 396 (1988); Oepen, *Identification of Characteristics in Blood and Semen Stains — A Review*, 36 FORENSIC SCI. INT'L 183 (1988); Annot., *Admissibility, in prosecution for sex-related offense, of results of tests on semen or seminal fluids*, 75 A.L.R.4TH 897 (1990). Persons who do not secrete their markers into their body fluids are termed non-secretors. Coleman v. O'Leary, 845 F.2d 696, 697 n.1 (7th Cir.) ("About 22% of Caucasians are 'nonsecretors'"), *cert. denied*, 488 U.S. 972 (1988); People v. Coleman, 46 Cal. 3d 749, 793, 759 P.2d 1260, 1289, 251 Cal. Rptr. 83, 113 (1988), *cert. denied*, 489 U.S. 1100 (1989). Washington v. Hargett, 889 F. Supp. 260, 263 (S.D. Miss. 1995) ("twenty percent (20%) of the population are non-secretors and ... eighty percent (80%) are secretors").

presumption of parentage,[88] otherwise relevant blood grouping evidence can be used to exclude an alleged parent. There is a first-order exclusion if the child possesses an allele that neither parent possesses.[89] A second-order exclusion occurs when the child lacks an allele that any child would necessarily have inherited from a particular parent.[90] If a complainant alleges that a particular man is the father, it is logically relevant to introduce genetic markers showing that the paternity is impossible. However, the courts are split over the question of whether such test results are conclusive.[91] Some jurisdictions hold that even test results positively excluding the alleged parent are not conclusive.[92] However, other courts, perhaps a majority, accord such test results conclusive weight.[93] Some courts even take judicial notice that such test results are conclusive.[94]

Second, if the tests do not positively exclude the alleged source, the proponent may offer the test results to increase the probability that the person was indeed the source. Although the expert cannot conclusively say that a particular person was the source of a drop or stain of blood, he can narrow the class of possible sources. In some jurisdictions inclusionary test results are not only legally inconclusive; they are also inadmissible. These courts fear that the trier of fact may misestimate the probative value of test results that merely include the subject within a class of possible sources. However, the support for barring inclusionary test results in criminal cases is eroding.[95] There is growing support for the view that so long as the genetic marker evidence passes the jurisdiction's normal evidentiary standards for scientific proof such as *Daubert* or *Frye,*[96] inclusionary test results are as admissible as exclusionary results.

The following subsections review the various genetic marker systems that are used to reach exclusionary and inclusionary results.

---

88. Miller v. Miller, 64 Cal. App. 4th 111, 74 Cal. Rptr. 2d 797 (1998), *cert. denied*, 119 S. Ct. 904 (1999); Amrhein v. Cozad, 714 A.2d 409, 1998 Pa. Super. LEXIS 858 (Pa. Super. Ct, 1998).

89. Armitage & Cross, *Paternity Testing in a Judicial Setting*, 39 J. MO. BAR 478-79 (Oct.-Nov. 1983).

90. Marsters, *supra* note 55, at 134-35.

91. Sawyer & Vander Jagt, *Evidentiary Problems of Medical Tests*, 8 THE PRACTICAL LAWYER 57 (Apr. 1962).

92. B.S.H. v. J.J.H., 613 S.W.2d 453, 461 (Mo. App. 1981).

93. Comment, *Proving Paternity by Means of Serological Testing: Should It Be Admitted as Evidence by the Courts?*, 1981 DET. COL. L. REV. 47, 64. *E.g.*, C.G.W. v. B.F.W., 675 S.W.2d 323, 330-31 (Tex. App. 1984).

94. R. HUNTER, FEDERAL TRIAL HANDBOOK § 62.19, at 540 (1974). *Cf.* R. HUNTER, FEDERAL TRIAL HANDBOOK § 62.19, at 730 (2d ed. 1984).

95. Annot., 2 A.L.R.4TH 500 (1980).

96. State v. Onken, 660 S.W.2d 312 (Mo. App. 1983).

§ 17-8(A). Red Blood Cell (RBC).

The red blood cells or erthyrocytes carry oxygen throughout the body. Certain antigens are found on the surface of these cells. These antigens are determined by the person's alleles on the chromosomes inside the cells. RBC testing identifies the antigens and thus allows the expert to deduce the alleles. Although many RBC antigens are undetectable in the newborn, the antigens are usually fully expressed and testable by the time the child is six months old.

Serology laboratories work with six primary RBC systems: ABO,[97] MNSs, Rh, Kell, Kidd, and Duffy. The ABO system is the system that Landsteiner discovered when he pioneered blood grouping at the turn of the century. The Rh system is particularly complex. To begin with, the nomenclature for the system varies from country to country. Some countries use the terminology coined by Wiener while others follow the Fisher-Race CDE systems.[98] The system has at least 39 recognizable specificities.[99] There are RBC systems in addition to these six;[100] but in light of the "availability of the necessary ... testing antisera ... and the gene frequency of the types of each system," these six are the most useful.[101]

There are numerous methods of testing for RBC antigens. In most methods, however, the primary mechanism is the agglutination or clumping phenomenon. Landsteiner observed that when blood was transfused into a donor, the donor sometimes experienced a violent reaction. The purpose of Landsteiner's research — for which he was awarded a Nobel Prize in 1930 — was to determine when such reactions would occur and thereby prevent the reaction. He discovered that the blood of certain persons agglutinated or clumped when it was mixed with

---

97. Smeets, van de Voorde & Hooft, *ABO Bloodgrouping on Tooth Material*, 50 FORENSIC SCI. INT'L 277 (1991); Lee, Berka, Folk, Pagliaor, Carroll-Reho, Brubaker & Gaensslen, *Genetic Markers in Human Bone: II. Studies on ABO (and IGH) Grouping*, 36 J. FORENSIC SCI. 639 (1991); Roy, *Concentration of Urine Samples by Three Different Procedures: ABO Typing from Concentrated Urine Samples*, 35 J. FORENSIC SCI. 1133 (1990); Zhou, Guo, Wang & Chen, *The Rapid Determination of the ABO Group from Body Fluids (or Stains) by Dot Enzyme-Linked Immunoabsorbent Assay (Dot-ELISA) Using Enzyme-Labeled Monoclonal Antibodies*, 35 J. FORENSIC SCI. 1125 (1990); Thomsen & Adamzik, *Immunocytochemical Determination of ABH and MN Antigens on Dried Blood Traces in the Nanoliter Range*, 48 FORENSIC SCI. INT'L 59 (1990); Sato, Higashide & Katsumata, *A Sensitive Enzyme-Linked Immunoasbsorbent Assay Used to Differentiate Type AB Specimen from a Mixture of Type A and Type B Specimens*, 46 FORENSIC SCI. INT'L 231 (1990); Wegener & Bulnheim, *Determination of ABO Antigens in Fingernails Using the APAAP (Immunoalkaline Phosphatase) Technique*, 46 FORENSIC SCI. INT'L 11 (1990). Salaru, *Paternity Investigation Among Known False Trios: ABO, Rh, MNSs, Kell, Duffy, Kidd, and HLA Systems*, 38 J. FORENSIC SCI. 1482 (1993); Xingshi, Ji, Hao, Ming & Zhuyao, *ABO Blood Grouping on Dental Tissue*, 38 J. FORENSIC SCI. 956 (1993).

98. Marsters, *supra* note 55, at 139.

99. Gaensslen & Camp, *supra* note 4, at 29-54-55.

100. Sussman, *supra* note 75, at 10.

101. *Id.*

other blood.[102] He observed a visible clumping and theorized that the clumping was due to a reaction between an antigen in one blood sample and an antibody in the other. "The combination of an antigen and an antibody may be visualized diagrammatically as the interlocking of two pieces of a jigsaw puzzle. Red blood cells clump together (agglutinate) when red blood cell antigens and their corresponding specific antibodies combine. Clumping can be seen with the naked eye, and means that the antigen tested for is present on the surface of the red blood cells. No clumping indicates that the antigen tested for is absent."[103] The testing proceeds as a process of elimination until the expert hits upon the correct antibody and agglutination occurs.

Although agglutination is the heart of most RBC testing, there are different methods of preparing the sample before testing for the agglutination reaction. One method, illustrated by Figure 17-1, is absorption inhibition:

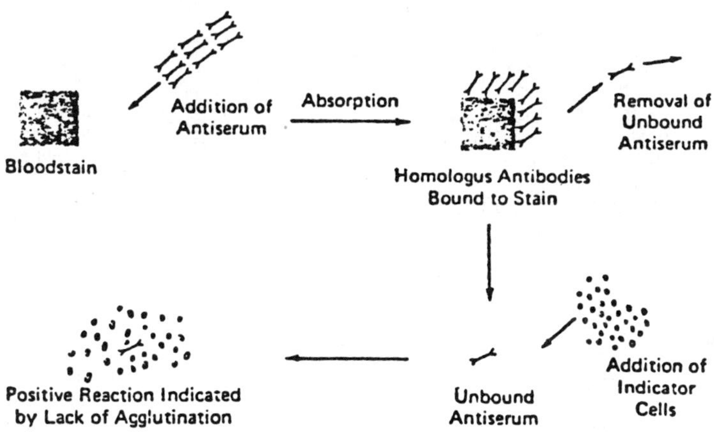

Figure 17-1[104]

102. Stroud, Bundrant & Galindo, *Paternity Testing: A Current Approach*, 16 TRIAL 47 (Sept. 1980).

103. *Id.* Driscoll v. Delo, 71 F.3d 701, 707 (8th Cir. 1995) ("Dr. Su testified that blood can be type A, type B, type AB, or type O. Using a 'thread' or 'antigen' test, Dr. Su explained, a reagent called anti-A is added to the blood and agglutination (clumping) occurs if the blood is type A. Similar reagents signal the presence of type B and of type AB. Using this methodology, however, the presence of type O blood is signaled only by the absence of a reaction to anti-A and anti-B reagents. Thus, when type A and type O blood are mixed, the antigen test will not reveal the presence of type O blood because the agglutination showing type A will occur. Dr. Su testified that with the antigen test type A blood 'masks' the presence of type O blood"), *cert. denied*, 519 U.S. 910 (1996).

104. Lee, *supra* note 13, at 308. Copyright 1982. Reprinted with permission of Prentice-Hall, Inc.

In this method, known antiserum (containing a blood group antibody of known strength and specificity) is added and absorbed into the unknown blood stain (containing an antigen). The analyst then removes the stain-absorbed antiserum from the stain and adds indicator red cells to the absorbed antiserum.[105] If the stain contained the same antigen as the indicator cells, it will have absorbed the antibody from the known antiserum; as a result, the absorbed antiserum will fail to react (or will react only weakly) with the indicator cells. Weakening of the reaction is determined by titrating the unabsorbed antiserum against the indicator cells and comparing the result with the reaction obtained with the stain-absorbed serum. Thus, a negative or weak reaction in the final step with indicator cells is a positive test, indicating that the antigen was in the stain. The weakness of the absorption-inhibition method is that it is relatively insensitive.[106]

A second method is mixed agglutination, depicted in Figure 17-2:

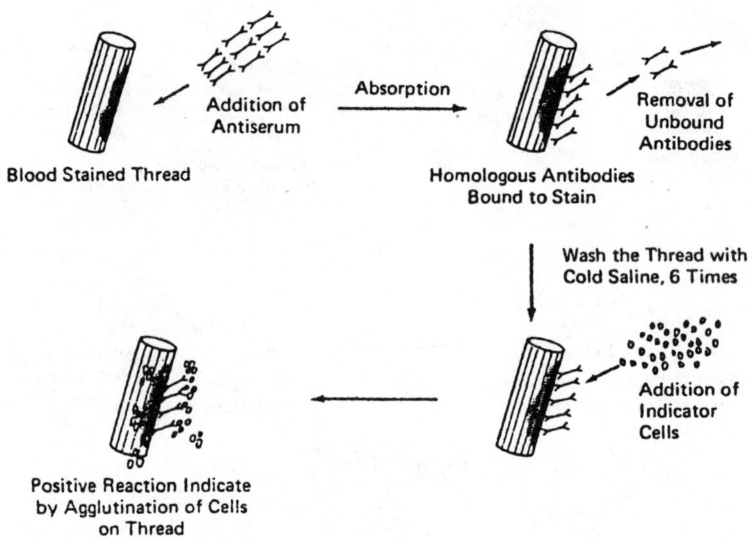

Figure 17-2[107]

This technique is simpler than absorption-inhibition.[108] There is no need to carefully measure the titer of antiserum used in the method. In this technique, known antiserum is added to the bloodstain. The analyst next washes away any excess antiserum. Only antibody which has reacted with antigen in the stain

---

105. *Id. See also* Lee, Gaensslen, Pagliaro & Novitch, *Two-Dimensional Absorption-Inhibition*, 33 J. Forensic Sci. 1127 (1988); People v. Yorba, 209 Cal. App. 3d 1017, 257 Cal. Rptr. 641 (1989) (the admission of agglutination inhibition testing of blood stains).

106. Lee, *supra* note 13, at 308.

107. *Id.* at 312. Reprinted with permission of Prentice-Hall, Inc.

108. *Id.* at 311.

remains in the stain. The analyst then adds indicator cells. If the antigen of the indicator cells corresponds to the antibody remaining in the stain, the indicator cells will attach to the stain. The attachment of indicator cells of a known antigen indicates that the blood in the original stain has the same antigen. This method is very sensitive.[109] However, although this method is simpler than absorption-inhibition, it is still a time-consuming, complicated procedure.[110]

The disadvantages of absorption-inhibition and mixed agglutination account for the widespread use of the third method, absorption-elution, shown in Figure 17-3:

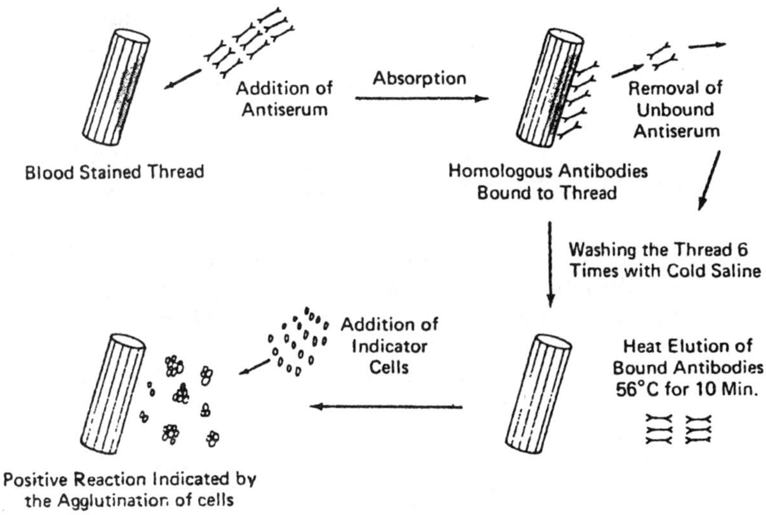

Figure 17-3[111]

Absorption-elution has been described in the following fashion:

> This technique utilizes the principle that antisera can be absorbed by corresponding antigens, and, after washing away the unbound antiserum, the bound antibody can be eluted (removed) by heating to participate in an agglutination reaction with the cells of a known type.[112]

Figure 17-3 is a bit misleading because it suggests the continued presence of the thread. The analyst removes the thread by centrifugation or filtration to prevent the antibody molecules from reattaching to the thread. Absorption-elution is not

109. *Id.*

110. *Id.*

111. *Id.* at 316. Reprinted with permission of Prentice-Hall, Inc.

112. Dixon & Tahir, *A Modified Technique for Rho(D) Typing of Dried Bloodstains*, 8 J. POLICE SCI. & ADMIN. 145, 145-46 (1980).

only a simple method; it "represents an increase in sensitivity of almost 100-fold over the absorption-inhibition method."[113]

Enzyme-linked immunosorbent assay (ELISA) is also becoming a popular method for determining genetic markers in the ABO system.[114] In rape cases, it can be critical to differentiate between an AB specimen and a mixture of A and B specimens; a seminal stain may become mixed with vaginal secretion. Some of the other tests used to identify markers in this system have difficulty distinguishing an AB specimen from a mixture of type A and type B specimens, but this assay can be used to make that distinction.[115]

As we shall see in the next chapter, PCR (polymerase chain reaction) is a widely used methodology for testing DNA. It has been adapted for testing ABO blood groupings.[116] Thus, a cutting-edge technology is being utilized to improve the testing of one of the oldest genetic marker systems.

The RBC systems have great forensic utility because they can be applied to dried bloodstains.[117] Many RBC markers, including those in the ABO system,

---

113. *Id.* at 146. *See also* Thomsen & Adamzik, *Immunocytochemical Determination of ABH and MN Antigens on Dried Blood Traces in the Nanoliter Range*, 48 Forensic Sci. Int'l 59 (1990) ("The absorption-elution test is the preferred method for detecting ABH and MN antigens on small blood traces").

114. de Soyza, *Evaluation of an Enzyme Linked Immunosorbent Assay (ELISA) Method for ABO and Lewis Typing of Body Fluids in Forensic Samples*, 52 Forensic Sci. Int'l 65 (1991); Stowell, Sharman & Hamel, *An Enzyme-Linked Immunosorbent Assay (ELISA) for Prostate-Specific Antigen*, 50 Forensic Sci. Int'l 125 (1991); Zhou, Gou, Wang & Chen, *The Rapid Determination of the ABO Group from Body Fluids (or Stains) by Dot Enzyme-Linked Immunoabsorbent Assay (Dot-ELISA) Using Enzyme Labeled Monoclonal Antibodies*, 35 J. Forensic Sci. 1125 (1990); Sato, Higashide & Katsumata, *A Sensitive Enzyme-Linked Immunoabsorbent Assay Used to Differentiate Type AB Specimen from a Mixture of Type A and Type B Specimens*, 46 Forensic Sci. Int'l 231 (1990). Matsubara, Tanabe, Yuasa, Nakamura, Tanabe, Idzu, Takahashi & Kimura, *A Unique and Sensitive ELISA Technique for Typing ABH Antigens in Bloodstains Using UEA-1 Lectin — The Removal of Detergent with a Sephadex G-25 Mini-Column Improves Sensitivity*, 41 J. Forensic Sci. 35 (1996); Parigan, *An ELISA Procedure for the Detection of Soluble ABH Blood Group Substance in Semen, Saliva, and Vaginal Samples*, 40 J. Forensic Sci. 122 (1995).

115. *Id.*

116. Tun, Honda, Nakatome, Islam, Bai, Ogura, Kuroki, Yamazaki, Terada & Wakasugi, *Rapid and Clear Detection of ABO Genotypes by Simultaneous PCR-RFLP Method*, 41 J. Forensic Sci. 1027 (1996); Liechti-Gallati & Neeser, *Efficient and Reliable PCR-Based Detection of the ABO Blood Group Alleles: Genotyping on Stamps and Other Biological Evidence Samples*, 41 J. Forensic Sci. 653 (1996); Herrin, *A Simplified Amplification Procedure for Two Regions of the Glycosyl Transferase (ABO Blood Group) Gene*, 41 J. Forensic Sci. 138 (1996).

117. Jonakait, *supra* note 1, at 837. *See also* Mudd & Adams, *A Modification of the Microplate Method for Reverse ABO Typing of Bloodstains and Additional Validation Studies*, 35 J. Forensic Sci. 447 (1990); Pflug, Bassler & Eberspacher, *ABO and Lewis Typing of Secretion Stains on Nitrocellulose Membranes Using a New Dot-Blot-ELISA Technique*, 43 Forensic Sci. Int'l 171 (1989); Harrington, Martin & Kobilinsky, *Detection of Hemagglutinins in Dried Saliva Stains and Their Potential Use in Blood Typing*, 33 J. Forensic Sci. 628 (1988).

seem to persist without deterioration for substantial periods of time.[118] However, one research project, the Denault study, reported false positives with ABO markers after the stains had been left for 26 weeks.[119] The same study discovered some false positives in the Rh system when the stains remained for two weeks.[120] Doubts have also been raised about the possibility of false positives in the MN system with dried stains.[121]

Like older dried stains, mixed stains pose a challenge for the analyst. If the analyst suspects that more than one person has contributed to a given stain, the analyst must resort to special procedures to identify all the markers present. In ABO testing, immunocytochemical methods have been used for this purpose.[122]

The principles underlying the RBC systems are well accepted in scientific and legal circles. If a jurisdiction admits inclusionary test results and the analyst properly conducts an accepted test for an RBC marker, most courts will admit the test result.[123]

§ 17-8(B). Human Leukocyte Antigens (HLA).

The white blood cells are known as leukocytes or lymphocytes.[124] The red blood cells outnumber the white cells 500 to one. Nevertheless, the white cells perform a vital function; they regulate the body's immune system, a line of defense against infection.[125] They determine whether the body will accept grafted tissue in a transplant.[126] If the genetic markers of the body and tissue do not match, the white cells may attempt to repel the new tissue, leading to the

---

118. Jonakait, *supra* note 1, at 881-82. *See also* Kubo, *Changes in the Specificity of Blood Groups Induced by Enzymes from Soil Fungi*, 34 J. Forensic Sci. 96 (1989) (describing the effect which soil bacteria have on the blood groupings of material buried in soil).

119. Jonakait, *supra* note 1, at 887.

120. *Id.* at 891.

121. *Id.* at 892. *But see* Berns & Lotterle, *Micromethod for MN Antigen Grouping of Dried Bloodstains*, 33 J. Forensic Sci. 230 (1988).

122. Bunai, Nakamura, Nagai, Yamada, Watanabe, Takayama & Ohya, *Blood Grouping of Mixed Bloodstains Using Immunocytochemical Methods*, 44 J. Forensic Sci. 100 (1999).

123. Annot., *Admissibility or compellability of blood test to establish testee's nonpaternity for purpose of challenging testee's parental rights*, 87 A.L.R.4th 572 (1991); Annot., *Admissibility in prosecution for sex related offense of results of test on semen or seminal fluids*, 75 A.L.R.4th 897 (1990); Annot., *Admissibility and weight of blood grouping tests in disputed paternity cases*, 43 A.L.R.4th 579 (1986); Annot., 46 A.L.R.2d 1000, 1022 (1956); People v. Hill, 17 Cal. 4th 800, 952 P.2d 673, 72 Cal. Rptr. 2d 656, 667 (1998); People v. Banks, 804 P.2d 203, 205 (Colo. App. 1990) ("Many jurisdictions have recognized that the absorption inhibition test is generally relied upon by the scientific community to establish an individual's blood type and have admitted the results of such testing for this purpose"). People v. Morganti, 43 Cal. App. 4th 643, 50 Cal. Rptr. 2d 837 (1996) (an agglutination inhibition test).

124. Sussman, *supra* note 75, at 9.

125. *Id.*

126. *Id.*

rejection of the graft and the possible death of the recipient. The white cells play a major role in determining the compatibility of grafted tissue, and the antigens they express are sometimes referred to as Human Leukocyte Antigens (HLA).

In HLA testing, the analyst is concerned with four loci on chromosome #6.[127] The loci are called HLA-A, HLA-B, HLA-C, and HLA-D. Since the genes at the A and B loci are the most polymorphic, most testing concentrates on those two loci.[128] Although these antigens are found in white blood cells, white blood cells are not their only repository. The same antigens can be found in almost all body tissues, including the liver and kidneys.

The mechanics of HLA testing differ from the procedures for RBC and DNA[129] testing. The analyst initially separates the white cells by centrifuging the blood sample. The red cells spin to the bottom of the test tube while the white cells remain on top of the red cells. The analyst then removes the white cells and tests them against known HLA antisera. The test is called a lymphocytotoxicity test. In a positive test, the white cells die; the effect of the corresponding antiserum on the white cell antigen is toxic. The various known HLA antisera are arranged in trays. There may be 60 wells per tray, and the analyst may use two or three trays. Each well contains a different antiserum. The Food and Drug Administration has promulgated potency and specificity requirements for HLA antisera. The analyst can test the white blood cells against 120 or 180 different known antisera. After mixing the white blood cells and antisera, the analyst applies a vital dye to each well. If the antiserum does not match the antigen, the white cells remain viable and repel the dye. On the other hand, when the antiserum matches, the white cells are killed and swell in size; they will be stained by the dye.[130] The analyst reads each well microscopically. If, in his judgment, 80 to 100% of the cells are dead, a positive test result is reported. In some laboratories, the analysis and grading of the wells are done by computer.

The HLA system has numerous advantages. While some RBC antigens are not fully developed until six months after birth, HLA antigens are completely expressed at birth. At one time, critics contended that HLA tests had a high error rate on the order of two percent.[131] However, proponents of HLA testing contend

---

127. *Id.*

128. *Id.*

129. However, some DNA testing procedures can be adapted to analyze HLA loci. Comey & Budowle, *Validation Studies on the Analysis of the HLA DQ Locus Using the Polymerase Chain Reaction*, 36 J. FORENSIC SCI. 1633 (1991); Harrington, Dunaiski, Williams & Fowler, *HLA DQ Typing of Forensic Specimens by Amplification Restriction Fragment Polymorphism (ARFP) Analysis*, 51 FORENSIC SCI. INT'L 147 (1991).

130. Stroud, Bundrant & Galindo, *supra* note 102, at 47.

131. Note, *Blood Test Evidence in Disputed Paternity Cases: Unjustified Adherence to the Exclusionary Rule*, 59 WASH. U. L.Q. 977, 994 (1981).

that the error rate has now fallen to 0.35%.[132] Most importantly, the HLA system is extremely polymorphic. The World Health Organization (WHO) Terminology Committee has officially recognized HLA-A and -B antigens that can exist in hundreds of combinations in all ethnic groups.[133] HLA testing will positively exclude a falsely accused defendant in many cases in which RBC testing fails to exclude.[134]

However, HLA testing suffers from some disadvantages. There are practical limitations on the use of HLA procedures. Depending upon the laboratory, HLA testing may be five times as expensive as RBC testing.[135] An HLA test may take two and one-half times longer to complete than an RBC test.[136] Furthermore, it may be impossible to locate a local laboratory conducting HLA tests. In one national survey of laboratories, only 17% of the AABB (American Association of Blood Bank) Reference Laboratories and 2% of all laboratories contacted reported HLA capability.[137] White cells also tend to be less durable and stable than red cells. Many HLA laboratories insist on fresh blood samples; they will test only if they receive the sample within 24 to 72 hours after the sample is drawn.[138] Similarly, some laboratories either refuse to accept samples sent by mail or demand that the sample be packaged in special insulated boxes protecting the sample from extreme temperatures.[139]

Because of the delicacy of white cells, there are doubts about the applicability of HLA procedures to the analysis of dried bloodstains. There has been some experimentation to determine the feasibility of typing dried stains for HLA

---

132. Terasaki, *Resolution by HLA Testing of 1000 Paternity Cases Not Excluded by ABO Testing*, 16 J. FAM. L. 543, 548 (1978).

133. Young & Simsteim, *The Medicolegal Implications of the HLA System*, 27 RESIDENT & STAFF PHYSICIAN 74 (June 1981).

134. Terasaki, *supra* note 132, at 543; Boonlayangoor, *True Paternity or Exclusion: Analysis in the Case of a Deceased Person*, 34 J. FORENSIC SCI. 703, 705 (1989) ("HLA is the most powerful single system and can exclude a falsely accused man above 85% of the time"). According to our reviewer, Dr. Allen, in a paternity testing for HLA, A, B, and C procedures, approximately 90% of falsely accused men will be excluded. In contrast, testing for six red blood cell antigen systems will collectively exclude only approximately 60% of falsely accused men. Salaru, *Evaluation of HLA in Detection of Non-Parentage Among Known False Trios*, 38 J. FORENSIC SCI. 1478 (1993).

135. Note, *Use of Human Leukocyte Antigen Test Results to Establish Paternity*, 14 IND. L. REV. 831, 855 (1981).

136. Note, *supra* note 131, at 991.

137. Camp & Gaensslen, *Forensic Serology: Paternity Testing (and Transfusion Reactions)*, *in* 2 FORENSIC SCIENCES 30-52 (C. Wecht ed. 1983).

138. Note, *Human Leukocyte Antigen Testing: Technology Versus Policy in Cases of Disputed Parentage*, 36 VAND. L. REV. 1587, 1592 (1983).

139. *Id.*

antigens,[140] but critics question the adequacy of the experiments conducted to date.[141]

As the previous subsection noted, PCR is now being used to improve RBC testing. PCR is also being employed in conjunction with HLA testing.[142]

Admissibility of HLA Test Results

In the past, when a proponent offered HLA test results, the proponent sometimes encountered two objections. One objection was that the state paternity statute barred merely inclusionary test results. The other objection was that HLA testing had not gained sufficient scientific acceptance to satisfy *Frye*. Those objections to HLA evidence are on the wane. One authority asserts that the admissibility of HLA test results is well-settled in at least 34 states.[143] In 1983, the Family Law Reporter published a detailed, jurisdiction-by-jurisdiction survey of the admissibility of HLA evidence.[144] The 1983 survey documented a strong trend toward the admission of HLA evidence. Even at that early date the survey asserted that the admissibility of HLA evidence was well established in 35 jurisdictions.[145]

Until recently, many states had statutes that purported to bar the admission of merely inclusionary test results: results that did not positively exclude but placed the subject within a class of potential parents or sources. Legislatures and courts have gradually eroded objections based on such statutes. In many states, legislatures have amended the statutes to permit inclusionary evidence.[146] Some statutes specifically refer to HLA evidence.[147] In other jurisdictions, the courts

---

140. Nelson, Turner & Reisner, *A Feasibility Study of Human Leukocyte Antigen (HLA) Typing for Dried Bloodstains*, 28 J. FORENSIC SCI. 608 (1983).

141. *See generally* Jonakait, *supra* note 1, at 833.

142. Del Rio, Marino & Belgrader, *PCR-Based Human Leukocyte Antigen (HLA) DQa Typing of Blood Stained Light and Dark Blue Denim Fabric*, 41 J. FORENSIC SCI. 490 (1996).

143. Lauter, *Paternity: The Final Word*, NAT'L L. J., Sept. 12, 1983.

144. Kolko, *Admissibility of HLA Test Results to Determine Paternity*, 9 FAM. L. REP. (BNA) 4009-19 (Feb. 15, 1983). Reprinted by permission from THE FAMILY LAW REPORTER, copyright 1983 by the Bureau of National Affairs, Inc., Washington, D.C. *See also* County of El Dorado v. Schneider, 183 Cal. App. 3d 732, 744, 228 Cal. Rptr. 531, 539-40 (1986), *sub. op. on reh'g.*, 191 Cal. App. 2d 1263, 237 Cal. Rptr. 51 (1987); State v. Spann, 219 N.J. Super. 85, 529 A.2d 1039 (1987), *rev'd*, 236 N.J. Super. 13, 563 A.2d 1145 (1989); Lemmon & Murphy, *The Evidentiary Use of the HLA Blood Test in Virginia*, 19 U. RICH. L. REV. 235 (1985); Note, *Establishing Paternity Through HLA Testing: Utah Standards for Admissibility*, 1988 UTAH L. REV. 717.

145. *Id.*

146. *Id. See also* Annot., *Admissibility and weight of blood grouping tests in disputed paternity cases*, 43 A.L.R.4TH 579 (1985); Annot., *Weight and sufficiency of Human Leukocyte Antigen (HLA) tissue typing tests in paternity cases*, 37 A.L.R.4TH 167 (1985).

147. Note, *supra* note 131, at 1003, quotes GA. CODE ANN. § 74-306 (1981) and IND. CODE ANN. § 31-6-6.1-8 (Burns 1980). Both statutes expressly sanction the receipt of HLA evidence.

have undercut the objection by statutory construction. Some courts have overruled the objection in criminal cases by confining the operation of the paternity statute to civil actions.[148] This argument is especially strong if the jurisdiction has a provision such as Federal Rule of Evidence 402, abolishing all non-statutory bars to the admission of relevant evidence.[149] The existence of a provision such as Rule 402 cuts in favor of a narrow construction of the statutory limitation on relevant inclusionary test results.[150] In several states, the courts have concluded that the statute is inapplicable to HLA evidence.[151] These courts reason that the original statute was aimed only at RBC tests. The RBC systems are not as polymorphic as HLA, RBC tests do not narrow the class of possible sources as radically as HLA tests, and hence HLA tests have far more probative value.[152] Based on this reasoning, the courts concluded that the state legislature never intended to extend the statutory ban to evidence as probative as HLA. In the late 1980s, two authors, our reviewer, Professor Kaye, and Ronald Kanwischer, published a comprehensive survey of the state statutes.[153] The latest such survey appears in a 1998 issue of Jurimetrics.[154] That survey includes the following three tables. The tables demonstrate that HLA evidence is now routinely admissible in most jurisdictions.

Tables I and III provide detailed information about the admissibility of scientific paternity tests under the statutes of the various jurisdictions in the United States. Table III uses the abbreviations defined in Table I as well as the following:

Under the "R" column:

P – Rebuttable by a preponderance of the evidence.
C – Rebuttable by clear and convincing evidence.
N – The required level of proof is not specified.

---

148. People v. Vallez, 80 Cal. App. 3d 46, 143 Cal. Rptr. 914 (1978).

149. Cramer v. Morrison, 88 Cal. App. 3d 873, 153 Cal. Rptr. 865 (1979) (CAL. EVID. CODE § 351). *See* Imwinkelried, *A Brief Defense of the Supreme Court's Approach to the Interpretation of the Federal Rules of Evidence*, 27 IND. L. REV. 267 (1993); Imwinkelried, *Federal Rule of Evidence 402: The Second Revolution*, 6 REV. LITIG. 129 (1987). In 1978, the former Reporter for the Advisory Committee, Professor Edward Cleary, wrote that "[i]n principle, under the Federal Rules no common law of evidence remains." Cleary, *Preliminary Notes on Reading the Rules of Evidence*, 57 NEB. L. REV. 908, 915 (1978). On two occasions, the Supreme Court has approvingly quoted that passage. Daubert v. Merell Dow Pharmaceuticals, Inc., 509 U.S. 579 (1993); United States v. Abel, 469 U.S. 45 (1984).

150. *Id.*

151. Kolko, *supra* note 144, at 4009.

152. *Id.*

153. Kaye & Kanwischer, *Admissibility of Genetic Testing in Paternity Litigation: A Survey of State Statutes*, 22 FAM. L.Q. 109 (Summer 1988).

154. Litovsky & Schultz, *Scientific Evidence of Paternity: A Survey of State Statutes*, 39 JURIMETRICS J. 79 (Fall 1998). Reprinted by permission.

Under the "M" column:

PoP – Probability of paternity.
PoE – Probability of exclusion.
PoI – Probability of inclusion.
PI – Paternity Index
U – Unspecified.

TABLE I.
General Categories of Statutes

CATEGORIES OF THE STATUTES ON SCIENTIFIC EVIDENCE OF PATERNITY	Number of States with Statutes in Category
Specifically allows the admission of blood test results. (B)	39
Specifically allows admission of DNA test results. (DNA)	16
Not definite on what types of tests may be used or specifically allows the admission of results other than blood tests. (OT)	48
Allows for the admission of biostatistical analysis to include a man as a possible father. (SSA)	50
Allows for the inclusion of a man as a possible father of a child, but does not specifically allow for admissibility of biostatistical analysis. (NSA)	1
Specifically allows the admission of biostatistical analyses even if no rebuttable presumption of paternity is established. (I)	11
Clearly specifies methods of biostatistical analysis to be used in processing the results of scientific tests. (M)	49
Provides for use of biostatistical analysis to trigger a rebuttable presumption of paternity. (P)	47
Specifies the burden of proof or production needed to rebut a presumption of paternity. (R)	33
Provides for a conclusive presumption of paternity. (CP)	8
Provides for a conclusive presumption of non-paternity. (CNP)	22

TABLE II.

Statutes Governing Admissibility of Genetic Tests of Parentage by State.

STATE	Statutes Governing Admissibility of Paternity Tests	Year of Last Revision
Alabama	ALA CODE §§ 26-17-12 to 13, 26-7-19 (1992 & Supp. 1997)	1997
Alaska	ALASKA STAT. § 25.20.050 (Michie 1997)	1997
Arizona	ARIZ. REV. STAT. ANN. §§ 25-807, 25-814 (West 1993 & Supp. 1997)	1995
Arkansas	ARK. CODE ANN. §§ 9-10-103, 9-10-108, 9-10-115 (Michie Supp. 1997)	1997
California	CAL. FAM. CODE §§ 895.5, 7004, 7541,7552.5, 7554, 7555 (West 1994 & Supp. 1997)	1997
Colorado	COLO. REV. STAT. §§ 13-25-126, 19-4-105, 19-4-109, 19-4-113 (1997)	1994
Connecticut	CONN. GEN. STAT. § 46b-168 (1995 & Supp. 1997)	1997
Delaware	DEL. CODE ANN. tit. 13, §§ 804, 810 (1993 & Supp. 1996)	1994
D.C.	D.C. CODE ANN. §§ 16-909, 16-909.1, 16-2343, 16-2343.1 (1997)	1997
Florida	FLA. STAT. ANN. §§ 742.031, 742.12 (West Supp. 1997)	1997
Georgia	GA. CODE ANN. § 19-7-46 (1994 & Supp. 1997)	1997
Hawaii	HAW. REV. STAT. §§ 584-4, 584-6, 584-11 (Supp. 1997)	1997
Idaho	IDAHO CODE §§ 7-1115, 7-1116, 7-1118 (1990 & Supp. 1997)	1994
Illinois	750 ILL. COMP. STAT. ANN. 45/11 (West Supp. 1997)	1995
Indiana	IND. CODE §§ 1637-2-10, 31-14-6-3 (1997)	1997
Iowa	IOWA CODE ANN. § 600B.41 (West 1996 & Supp. 1997)	1995
Kansas	KAN. STAT. ANN. §§ 38-1114, 38-1119 (Supp. 1996)	1994
Kentucky	KY. REV. STAT. §§ 406.081, 406.091, 406.111 (Banks-Baldwin 1997)	1994
Louisiana	LA. REV. STAT. ANN. §§ 9:396, 397.3 (West Supp. 1997)	1995
Maine	ME. REV. STAT. tit. 19 §§ 1561, 1564, 1601 (West Supp. 1997)	1997

STATE	Statutes Governing Admissibility of Paternity Tests	Year of Last Revision
Maryland	MD. CODE ANN. [FAM. LAW] § 5-1029 (Supp. 1997)	1997
Massachusetts	MASS. GEN. LAWS ch. 209C § 17 (Supp. 1997)	1995
Michigan	MICH. COMP. LAWS § 722.716 (1997)	1996
Minnesota	MINN. STAT. ANN. §§ 257.55, 257.62, 257.63 (West Supp. 1997)	1995
Mississippi	MISS. CODE ANN. §§ 93-9-91 to 93-9-27 (Supp. 1997)	1997
Missouri	MO. REV. STAT. §§ 210.822, 210.832, 210.834, 210.836, 210.839 (1996)	1994
Montana	MONT. CODE ANN. §§ 40-5-232, 40-5-234, 40-5-237, 40-6-112, 40-6-105 (1996 & Supp. 1997)	1995
Nebraska	NEB. REV. STAT. §§ 43-1414, 43-1415 (Supp. 1996)	1994
Nevada	NEV. REV. STAT. §§ 126.051, 126.121, 126.131 (Supp. 1997)	1997
New Hampshire	N.H. REV. STAT. ANN. § 522:1 to :4 (1997)	1997
New Jersey	N.J. STAT. ANN. § 9:17-52 (West Supp. 1997)	1994
New Mexico	N.M. STAT. ANN. §§ 40-11-5, 40-11-12, 40-11-13 (Michie Supp. 1994)	1993
New York	N.Y. FAM. CT. ACT. § 532 (Consol. 1997)	1997
North Carolina	N.C. GEN. STAT. § 8-50.1 (Supp. 1994)	1994
North Dakota	N.D. CENT. CODE §§ 14-17-04, 14-17-10, 14-17-11, 14-17-17 (Supp. 1997)	1997
Ohio	OHIO REV. CODE ANN. §§ 3111.03, 3111.09, 3111.10 (West Supp. 1997)	1996
Oklahoma	OKLA. STAT. ANN. tit. 10, §§ 501 & 504 (West Supp. 1994)	1994
Oregon	OR. REV. STAT. §§ 109.251, 109.258 (1995)	1995
Pennsylvania	23 PA. CONS. STAT. §§ 4343, 5104 (Supp. 1997)	1994
Rhode Island	R.I. GEN. LAWS §§ 15-8-3, 15-8-1, 15-8-11, 15-8-15 (1997)	1997
South Carolina	S.C. CODE ANN. §§ 20-7-954, 20-7-955, 20-7-956 (Law Co-op. Supp. 1997)	1991
South Dakota	S.D. CODIFIED LAWS ANN. §§ 15-6-35, 25-8-7.1, 25-8-58 (Michie Supp. 1997)	1994
Tennessee	TENN. CODE ANN. §§ 24-7-112, 36-2-309 (1997)	1994

STATE	Statutes Governing Admissibility of Paternity Tests	Year of Last Revision
Texas	TEX. FAM CODE ANN §§ 160.101 to 160 110 (1996 & West Supp 1997)	1994
Utah	UTAH CODE ANN §§ 78-45a-7, 78-45a-10 (Supp. 1997)	1997
Vermont	VT. STAT. ANN. tit 15, §§ 304, 308 (Supp. 1997)	1997
Virginia	VA. CODE ANN. §§ 20-49.1 to 20-49.4, 64.1-5.2 (Michie 1995 & Supp. 1997)	1997
Washington	WASH. REV. CODE ANN. §§ 26.26.040, 26.26.100 & 26.26.110 (West Supp. 1997)	1997
West Virginia	W. VA. CODE § 48A-6-3 (1997)	1997
Wisconsin	WIS. STAT. ANN. §§ 767.47, 767.48 (West Supp. 1997)	1995
Wyoming	WYO. STAT. ANN. §§ 14-2-109 & 14-2-110 (Michie 1997)	1997

TABLE III.

Statutory Provisions Concerning Effects of the Evidence.

State	Types of Tests			Admissibility of Tests			Effects of the Evidence				
	B	DNA	OT	SSA	NSA	I	M	P	R	CP	CNP
Connecticut		x[ii]		x			PoP	99	N		
Delaware	x		x	x			PoP	99	C		x
D.C.	x		x[iii]	x			PoP	.99		x	x
Florida			x	x			PoP	.95	N		x
Georgia	x	x	x	x			PoP	.97	C		
Hawaii	x		x	x			PoE	.99[iv]	C		x
Idaho			x	x			PoP	.98	N		x
Illinois	x	x	x	x		x[v]	PI	500[vi]	C		
Indiana	x	[vii]	x	x		x	U				x
Iowa	x		x	x		x	PoP	.95	C		
Kansas			x	x			PoP	.97	C		
Kentucky			x	x			PoP	.99	P		
Louisiana	x		x	x			PoP	.999	N		x
Maine	x		x	x		x	PoP	.97	C		x

State	Types of Tests			Admissibility of Tests			Effects of the Evidence				
	B	DNA	OT	SSA	NSA	I	M	P	R	CP	CNP
Maryland	x		x	x		x[viii]	PoE	.973	[ix]		
Massachusetts	x		x	x			PoP	.97	N		
Michigan	x	x	x	x			PoP	.99	C		
Minnesota	x		x	x			PoP	.99	C		
Mississippi	x		x	x			PoP	.98	P		x
Missouri	x	x	x	x			PoP	.98	C	x	x
Montana	x	x	x	x			PoP	.95	P	x	x
Nebraska	x		x	x			PoP	.99	N		
Nevada	x		x	x			PoP	.99	C		
New Hampshire	x	x	x	x		x	PoP	.97	C		x
New Jersey	x		x	x			PoP				
New Mexico	x	x	x	x			PoP	.99		x	
New York	x	x	x	x			PoP	.95	N		
North Carolina	x		x[x]	x		x[xi]	PoP	.97[xii]	C		x
North Dakota			x	x			PoP	.95	C		
Ohio	x	x		x			PoP	.95	C		
Oklahoma			x	x		x	PoP	.95	[xiii]	x	x
Oregon	x			x[xiv]			PI	99			x
Pennsylvania	x		x	x			PoP	.99	C		x
Rhode Island	x	x	x	x			PoI	.97	C	x	
South Carolina			x	x			PoP	.95	N		
South Dakota	x		x	x			PoP	.95	N		
Tennessee	x	x	x	x			PoP	.99	P	[xv]	x
Texas	x		x	x			PoE	.99	C		x
Utah			x	x			PI	150	[xvi]	[xvii]	x
Vermont			x		[xviii]		PoP	.98	N		
Virginia	x		x	x			U				
Washington	x		x	x			PoP		C		
West Virginia	x		x	x		x	PoP	.98	P		
Wisconsin			x	x			PoP	.99	N		x
Wyoming	x	x	x	x		x	PoP	.97	C		x[xix]

Once a court concludes that there is no statutory ban to admitting HLA evidence, the issue becomes whether the evidence satisfies the jurisdiction's common-law standards. There is already a wealth of case law attesting to the accuracy of HLA tests.[155] If the jurisdiction follows *Daubert*, the proponent must establish the empirical validation of HLA testing; but there have been numerous studies pointing to the validity of the technique. If the jurisdiction adheres to *Frye,* the proponent will have to demonstrate general acceptance of HLA testing.[156] Many courts have already concluded that HLA testing satisfies the *Frye* standard.[157] This conclusion seems sound, since the medical community uses HLA tests extensively in determining whether a proposed tissue graft will be compatible with the intended recipient's tissue. *Frye* should pose a major barrier to the admission of HLA test results only when the analyst employs serologically based HLA testing to analyze old stains.[158]

§ 17-8(C). Red Cell Enzymes and Serum Proteins.

In addition to analyzing the antigens on the surface of the red cells, the expert can examine red cell enzymes and serum proteins.[159] The detectability of such enzymes and proteins does not depend upon whether the person is a "secretor." Many laboratories commonly test for four serum proteins and seven red cell enzymes: haptoglobin (Hp),[160] transferrin (Tf),[161] group specific component (Gc), properdin factor B (Bf), acid phosphatase (AcP), 6-phosphogluconate dehydrogenase (6-PGD), phosphoglucomutase-1 (PGM1),[162] adenylate kinase (AK), glutamic pyruvic transaminase (GPT), and esterase-D (EsD). If an abbreviation consists entirely of capital letters, it ordinarily represents a red cell enzyme. When an abbreviation includes both capital and lower case letters, the

---

155. Note, *supra* note 131, at 1000-01.

156. Cramer v. Morrison, 88 Cal. App. 3d 873, 153 Cal. Rptr. 865 (1979).

157. Wright v. Hughes, 52 U.S.L.W. (BNA) 2051 (Okla. App. June 14, 1983). *See also* Shipp v. State, 713 P.2d 10, 11 (Okla. 1986); Callison v. Callison, 687 P.2d 106, 111 (Okla. 1984); Kolko, *supra* note 144, at 4009.

158. Chapter 18 deals with PCR based testing for HLA-D (DQA testing). That is a commonly used forensic test and, as Chapter 18 notes, has passed muster under both *Frye* and *Daubert* on many occasions. The comment in text refers to serologically based HLA tests rather than PCR based HLA tests.

159. Yamada, Hirata, Tsugawa, Bunai & Ohya, *Vomit Identification by a Pepsin Assay Using a Fibrin Blue-Agarose Gel Plate*, 52 FORENSIC SCI. INT'L 215 (1992); Tsutsumi, Higashide, Mizuno, Tamaki & Katsumata, *Identification of Saliva Stains by Determination of the Specific Activity of Amylase*, 50 FORENSIC SCI. INT'L 37 (1991).

160. Roy, *Detection of Haptoglobin from Concentrated Urine Samples by Enzyme Immunoassay*, 36 J. FORENSIC SCI. 1580 (1991).

161. Yamaba, Sawazaki, Yasuda, Nadano, IIda & Kishi, *Transferrin Subtyping of Bloodstains and Semen Using Isoelectric Focusing and Immunoblotting*, 50 FORENSIC SCI. INT'L 187 (1991).

162. Washington v. Murray, 952 F.2d 1472, 1476-77 (4th Cir. 1991).

abbreviation signifies a serum protein.[163] These markers can be found not only in blood, but also in tissue such as dental pulp,[164] hair bulbs,[165] muscle,[166] and hair-root tissue,[167] and other liquids such as semen,[168] inner ear fluid,[169] and saliva.[170]

The technique for testing enzymes and proteins is electrophoresis.[171] The most popular mode of electrophoretic analysis is horizontal gel electrophoresis.[172] In this mode, the electrophoretic system includes five components: a buffer solution, a positive electrode tank, a negative electrode tank, a power supply, and a support medium. The most commonly used support media are cellulose acetate membranes, agar or agarose gels, starch gels, and acrylamide gels.[173] The expert moistens the support medium with the buffer and places the sample to be tested on the medium.[174] The sample and medium are then subjected to an electric current. The composition of the sample, in particular its amino acids and sugars, determines the charge that the sample takes.[175] The enzymes and proteins take positive, negative, or neutral charges. Positively charged samples are attracted toward the negative electrode, while negatively charged samples migrate toward

---

163. Gaensslen & Camp, *supra* note 4, at 29-35-38. *See also* OFFICE OF CHILD SUPPORT ENF., U.S. DEP'T HEALTH, EDUCATION & WELFARE, TEMPO NO. FOUR 7 (1980).

164. Kido, Komatsu, Ose & Oya, *Fucosidase Phenotyping in Human Tissues, Dental Pulps and Hair Roots*, 33 FORENSIC SCI. INT'L 53 (1987); Turowska & Trela, *Studies on the Isoenzymes PGM, ADA, and AK in Human Teeth*, 9 FORENSIC SCI. 45 (1977).

165. Parkitna-Cegla & Dobosz, *Determination of Phosphoglucomutase Phenotypes in Hair Bulbs*, 46 FORENSIC SCI. INT'L 87 (1990).

166. Szczerkowska, *Polymorphism of Isoenzymes in Preserved Muscle Tissues*, 46 FORENSIC SCI. INT'L 95 (1990).

167. Scott, *Electrophoretic Typing of Glyoxalase I (GLO I) Isoenzymes Using a Mixed Starch/Agarose Gel*, 20 FORENSIC SCI. INT'L 287 (1982).

168. Budowle, Murch, Davidson, Gambel & Kearney, *Subtyping Phosphoglucomutase-1 in Semen Stains and Bloodstains: A Report on the Method*, 31 J. FORENSIC SCI. 1341 (1986); Blake & Sensabaugh, *Genetic Markers in Human Semen: A Review*, 21 J. FORENSIC SCI. 784 (1976).

169. Turowka & Trela, *The Gm(2) and Ivn(1) Factors in Human Inner Ear Fluid*, 9 FORENSIC SCI. 43 (1977).

170. Caeiro, Boan & Carracedo, *A Simplified Procedure for Simultaneous Detection of Salivary Proteins and Its Application in Paternity Testing*, 33 FORENSIC SCI. INT'L 47 (1987); Hayashi & Hayashi, *Determination of Phenotypes of Esterases (Set) in Fresh Saliva and Saliva Stains by Disc Electrophoresis and the Distribution of Set Phenotypes in the Japanese Population*, 14 FORENSIC SCI. INT'L 57 (1979).

171. *See generally* Sensabaugh, *Biochemical Markers of Individuality*, *in* FORENSIC SCIENCE HANDBOOK 338, 352-58 (R. Saferstein ed. 1982). Cox & Thomas, *The Application of Immunoblotting to the Phenotyping of Haptoglobin*, 37 J. FORENSIC SCI. 1652 (1992); Lopez-Abadia, Arroyo, Gremo & de la Cuesta, *An Improved Method for Subtyping Pi in Old Bloodstains*, 37 J. FORENSIC SCI. 323 (1992).

172. *Id.* at 353.

173. *Id.*

174. Stroud, Bundrant & Galindo, *supra* note 102, at 47.

175. Sensabaugh, *supra* note 171, at 355.

the positive electrode. The positive electrode is called an anode while the negative electrode is called a cathode. Thus, the sample tends to migrate and separate into bands. The mobility of each sample depends on its charge, density, shape, and size. Some samples are visible, but most must be stained.[176] The location and number of the bands are clues to the identity of the enzyme or protein.[177] The expert compares the pattern with known standards to confirm the identification.[178]

At first researchers were content to use electrophoresis to test for one enzyme or protein at a time. However, there were major disadvantages to this approach.[179] Multiple tests were costly, and the initial tests often necessitated the destruction of scarce samples and thereby precluded other tests.[180] For that reason, the National Institute of Justice sponsored research to develop a system for conducting multiple electrophoretic analyses simultaneously.[181] This research led to the development of the so-called multi-system.[182] The proponents of the system claim that the system permits the expert to "analyze 10 genetic markers, not in a matter of a week or more, but within a 24-hour period."[183]

A variation of electrophoresis is isoelectric focusing (IEF).[184] In IEF, the expert sets up a pH gradient between two electrodes. The low end of the gradient

---

176. *Id.* at 357.

177. Stroud, Bundrant & Galindo, *supra* note 102, at 47-48. *See also* Destro-Bisol & Spinella, *Non-Equilibrium pH Gradient Electrophoresis (NEPHGE) on Ultrathin Polyacrylamide Gels Containing Separators: Improved Erythrocyte Phosphoglucomutase (PGM1) and Esterase D (EsD) in Red Cell Lysates and Bloodstains*, 42 FORENSIC SCI. INT'L 43 (1989) ("The introduction of non-equilibrium pH gradient electrophoresis (NEPHGE) ... and of chemical spacers or separators ... has allowed" researchers to effect "increased separations of the bands ...").

178. *Id.*

179. Graham & Kochanski, *supra* note 61, at 5.

180. *Id.*

181. *Id. See* Wraxall & Stolorow, *The Simultaneous Separation of the Enzymes Glyoxalase 1, Esterase D, and Phosphoglucomutase*, 31 J. FORENSIC SCI. 1439 (1986); Wolson & Stuver, *Simultaneous Electrophoretic Determination of Phosphoglucomutase Subtypes, Adenoise Deaminase, Erthrocyte Acid Phosphatase, and Adenylate Kinase Enzyme Pheontypes*, 30 J. FORENSIC SCI. 904 (1985).

182. Jonakait, *supra* note 1, at 867.

183. Graham & Kochanski, *supra* note 61, at 5.

184. Sensabaugh, *supra* note 171, at 356. *See* Harada, Umetsu, Yuasa, Ikeda & Suzuki, *Orosomucoid 1 Phenotyping from Human Urine by Isoelectric Focusing*, 35 J. FORENSIC SCI. 1191 (1990); Kido & Oya, *PGD Phenotyping in Bloodstains, Organ Tissues, Dental Pulps and Hair Roots by Isoelectric Focusing*, 48 FORENSIC SCI. INT'L 185 (1990); Thomas & Asskov, *Routine Phenotyping of Native and Desialyzed a2HS-Clycoprotein from Blood Stains*, 47 FORENSIC SCI. INT'L 173 (1990); Iida, Sawazaki, Ikehara, Yasuda, Mizuta & Kishi, *GC Polymorphism Detected in Human Urine by Isoelectric Focusing and Immunoblotting*, 47 FORENSIC SCI. INT'L 71 (1990); Kishi, Ikehara, Toshihiro, Mizuta & Sato, *Transferrin Polymorphism Detected in Human Urine Using Isoelectric Focusing Followed by Immunoblotting*, 45 FORENSIC SCI. INT'L 225 (1990); Qingen, Qiuju, Rongzhi & Kun, *Typing Study of Human Semen DIA3 by Isoelectric Focusing —*

is the positive pole, and the high end the negative pole.[185] Suppose, for example, that a sample with a negative charge is analyzed. The expert places the sample near the negative pole. The sample is attracted toward the positive pole and migrates in that direction. However, the sample will reach a point in the gradient

---

Distribution in the Wuhan Population, China, 44 FORENSIC SCI. INT'L 203 (1990); Butler, DeForest & Kobilinsky, *The Use of Isoelectric Focusing to Identify Rhinoceros Keratins*, 35 J. FORENSIC SCI. 336 (1990); Stockwell, Gregonis & Jones, *Evaluation of a Nonequilibrium Isoelectric Focusing (IEF) Method for the Simultaneous Typing of Esterase D (EsD), Red Cell Acid Phosphatase (AcP1), Phosphoglucomutase (PGM1), Adenylate Kinase (AK), and Adenosine Deaminase (ADA)*, 35 J. FORENSIC SCI. 46 (1990); Lopez-Rodriguez, Munoz-Barus, Carracedo, Montiel & Cocheiro, *The Use of Hybrid Isoelectric Focusing for the Detection of Polymorphic Proteins in Bloodstains*, 43 FORENSIC SCI. INT'L 239 (1989); Pawlowski, *A Method of Human Diaphorase Locus 3 Phenotyping in Human Semen by Isoelectric Focusing*, 42 FORENSIC SCI. INT'L 131 (1989); Arndt, *Group Specific Component: Isoelectric Focusing Subtyping and Immunoblot Detection*, 34 J. FORENSIC SCI. 1318 (1989); Garg & Kobinlinsky, *Determination of C3 Phenotype in Dried Bloodstains Using Isoelectric Focusing*, 34 J. FORENSIC SCI. 980 (1989); Garg & Kobilinsky, *Simultaneous Identification of Alpha-L-Fucosidase and Phosphoglucomutase (PGM) Subtyping in Semen Stains*, 34 J. FORENSIC SCI. 336 (1989); Alonso, *Group Specific Component Subtyping in Bloodstains by Separator Isoelectric Focusing in Micro-Ultrathin Polyacrylamide Gels Followed by Immunoblotting*, 33 J. FORENSIC SCI. 1267 (1988); Carracedo, Andrade-Vide, Rodriguez-Calvo, Montiel & Lareu, *Fast Isoelectric Focusing of Some Polymorphic Proteins and Enzymes in Miniaturized Gels Using an Automated System*, 33 J. FORENSIC SCI. 1379 (1988); Sebetan, *A Simple Pattern Method for Alpha HS-Glycoprotein Typing*, 33 J. FORENSIC SCI. 1031 (1988); Nakamura, Ohue, Akiyama & Abe, *Genetic Polymorphism of Human CIR Subcomponent of the First Complement Component in the Japanese Population*, 39 FORENSIC SCI. INT'L 71 (1988); Shutler & Tompkins, *Bloodstain Characterization in the EAP, Hp, Hb, AK, and GLO 1 Systems Using Minigels and the Phastsystem*, 39 FORENSIC SCI. INT'L 97 (1988); Budowle & Gambel, *A Hybrid Ampholyte Focusing Technique for Esterase D Subtyping of Evidentiary Material*, 33 J. FORENSIC SCI. 738 (1988); Murch & Budowle, *Applications of Isoelectric Focusing in Forensic Serology*, 31 J. FORENSIC SCI. 869 (1986). Dulmer, Reker, Nguyen, Henke & Henke, *Human Orosomucoid (ORM1) Subtyping: Further Population Genetic Data and Reports on the Feasibility to Type Aged Blood Samples and Stains*, 43 J. FORENSIC SCI. 413 (1998); Sebetan, Oshida & Tie, *An Improved High Resolution Single Method for Orosomucoid ORM1 and ORM2 Phenotyping*, 42 J. FORENSIC SCI. 115 (1995) (isoelectric focusing); Miller, Stern & Schanfield, *Simultaneous Subtyping of Group Specific Component and Esterase D by Isoelectric Focusing on Agarose Gels*, 38 J. FORENSIC SCI. 1488 (1993); Kido, Kimura & Oya, *Transferrin Subtyping in Dental Pulp*, 38 J. FORENSIC SCI. 1063 (1993); Lopez-Abadia & de la Cuesta, *A Simplified Method for Phenotyping Alpha-2-HS-glycoprotein*, 38 J. FORENSIC SCI. 1183 (1993); Sawazaki, Yasuda, Nadano, Tenjo, Iida, Takeshita & Kishi, *A New Individualization Marker of Semen: Deoxyribonuclease I (DNase I) Polymorphism*, 57 FORENSIC SCI. INT'L 39 (1992); Rodriguez-Calvo, Carracedo, Munoz & Concheiro, *Isoelectric Focusing of Human Hair Keratins: Correlation with Sodium Dodecyl Sulfate-Polyacrylamide Gel Electrophoresis (SDS-PAGE) Patterns and Effect of Cosmetic Treatments*, 37 J. FORENSIC SCI. 425 (1992); Sawazaki, Eng, Yasuda, Nadano, Iida & Kishi, *Transferrin (TF) Typing from Semen Stains Using Isoelectric Focusing and Immunoblotting: Correlation of TF Types Among Blood, Semen, Urine, and Vaginal Secretion*, 37 J. FORENSIC SCI. 1514 (1992).

185. Sensabaugh, *supra* note 171, at 357.

at which the sample has no net charge[186] — its isoelectric point.[187] When the sample reaches that point, it stops. IEF produces more complex patterns[188] and very sharp bands.[189] IEF offers "the ultimate in protein separation."[190] "Because of its superior resolution, isoelectric focusing has revealed hitherto unrecognized genetic variation in several proteins."[191]

Electrophoretic testing of cell enzymes and serum proteins has many advantages. Since red cells are hardier and more stable than white cells, electrophoresis is not subject to some of the practical restraints of HLA testing.[192] For instance, the samples may be sent through the mail.[193] Electrophoretic testing is ordinarily less expensive than HLA testing.[194] Finally, electrophoretic testing is quite accurate; the reported overall error rate is only one-half of one percent.[195]

However, electrophoresis has weaknesses. It is sometimes claimed that HLA testing can positively exclude a falsely accused father in over 90% of the cases.[196] In contrast, the probability of exclusion for eleven enzymes and proteins is 85%.[197]

Furthermore, there are questions about the precision of the population frequencies for the various alleles in the enzyme-protein system. As of the late 1970s a number of laboratories were just beginning to collect data on the frequencies of enzymes and proteins in the local populations.[198] In some states, the experts rely on data collected in California; but other experts charge that "the California data is nonapplicable ...."[199] It is clear that frequencies vary from country to country.[200] In North Carolina, when experts have attempted to testify on the basis of population frequencies gathered in other states, opposing counsel

---

186. The number of positive and negative charges is equal.

187. Wraxall, *Forensic Serology, in* SCIENTIFIC AND EXPERT EVIDENCE 897, 923 (2d ed. 1981).

188. Welch, Wood & Dodd, *Red Cell PGM1 (Phosphoglucomutase) Phenotyping by Isoelectric Focusing and Starch Gel Electrophoresis in Cases of Disputed Paternity in the United Kingdom. An Evaluation of the Results Obtained in 95 Cases*, 13 FORENSIC SCI. INT'L 87 (1979).

189. Sensabaugh, *supra* note 171, at 356.

190. *Id.*

191. *Id.* at 357.

192. Note, *supra* note 131, at 994.

193. *Id.*

194. *Id.*

195. *Id.*

196. *Id.* at 988. *But see* Boonlayangoor, *True Paternity or Exclusion: Analysis in the Case of a Deceased Person*, 34 J. FORENSIC SCI. 703, 705 (1989) ("above 85% of the time").

197. Note, *supra* note 131, at 993.

198. Hagins, Shaler, Mortimer, Stuver & Neilson, *Population Frequencies of Forensically Important Genetic Markers: Phosphoglucomutase, Erythrocyte Acid Phosphatase and Haptoglobin*, 23 J. FORENSIC. SCI. 563 (1978).

199. Juriek, *Electrophoresis: A Continuation of the Discussion*, 29 J. FORENSIC SCI. 704 (1984).

200. Eberhart & Kobilinsky, *supra* note 77, at 778.

have often objected.[201] However, "[t]o date, these objections have been overruled and all appeals have been denied."[202] A New York court permitted an expert to rely on population frequency studies conducted in Miami, Detroit, Los Angeles, Seattle, Austin, Pittsburgh, and England.[203]

A further challenge to electrophoretic evidence is the contention that there has been insufficient experimental verification of the technique's application to dried stains.[204] There has been some experimentation to verify the hypothesis that even aged stains can be accurately tested for enzymes and proteins.[205] The researchers report correctly typing stains as old as two years.[206] However, there has been

---

201. Nelson, *A Computer-Assisted Population Frequency Study of 14 Polymorphic Blood Grouping Systems in North Carolina*, 29 J. FORENSIC SCI. 762 (1984).

202. *Id.*

203. People v. Borcsok, 114 Misc. 2d 810, 811, 452 N.Y.S.2d 814, 815 (Sup. Ct. 1982). Population frequency studies are under way both in the United States and abroad. Gamero-Lucas, Romero, Vizcaya & Arufe, *Polymorphisms of the Enzyme Systems Galactose-1-Phosphate Uridyltransferase (GALT) and Esterase D (EsD) in the Province of Cadiz, Southern Spain*, 36 J. FORENSIC SCI. 880, 882 (1991) ("With the GALT system, it was significant that very few differences were observed between the frequencies recorded in our province for the Gt1 allele and those observed for this variant among the greater part of European populations. The similarities between the frequencies of the alleles EsD1 and EsD2 observed in our province and those recorded for these variants in the majority of European populations ... are ... remarkable"); Gamero, Romero, Vizcaya & Arufe, *Polymorphism of the Plasminogen (PLG) System in Cadiz Province, Southern Spain*, 36 J. FORENSIC SCI. 226, 228 (1991) ("we ... underline the similarities observed between the distribution of gene frequencies found in our province and those found in the majority of populations of Latin origin, as well as the existing differences between the populations of Northern and Central Europe and the Mongolian and Black African races"); Roy & Roy, *Haptoglobin Phenotyping from Older Bloodstains by Enzyme Immunoassay and Haptoglobin Phenotypes Within a Nebraska Caucasian Population*, 36 J. FORENSIC SCI. 571, 574 (1991) ("The frequencies resemble those of other Caucasian populations in the United States"); Smith & Myers, *The Detection of Group Specific Component (Gc) in the General Population of West Virginia*, 35 J. FORENSIC SCI. 1436 (1990) ("the occurrence of Gc phenotypes in the population of West Virginia is consistent with established frequencies for the system"); Roy, Schmidt & Gaensslen, *Distributions of Genetic Markers in a Nebraska Population*, 35 J. FORENSIC SCI. 1207 (1990) ("the phenotypic frequencies are generally in agreement with frequencies reported in other populations in the United States").

204. *See generally* Jonakait, *supra* note 1, at 833.

205. Eberhart & Kobilinsky, *supra* note 77, at 778; Budowle & Allen, *Electrophoresis Reliability: I. The Contaminant Issue*, 32 J. FORENSIC SCI. 1537, 1546 (1987) ("There should be no doubt that even though body fluid stains may be exposed to a myriad of environmental insults, when placed in its proper perspective, electrophoretic analyses of evidentiary material are valid and reliable"); Nelson, *Detection of the Rare PGM13 Allele. Further Biochemical and Genetic Characterization of the PGM13 Isoenzymes*, 26 J. FORENSIC SCI. 75 (1981); Noppinger & Morrison, *The Determination of Carbonic Anhydrase-2 Phenotypes in Dried Bloodstains by Cellulose Acetate Electrophoresis*, 26 J. FORENSIC. SCI. 176 (1981); Stolorow & Wraxall, *An Efficient Method to Eliminate Streaking in the Electrophoretic Analysis of Haptoglobin in Bloodstains*, 24 J. FORENSIC SCI. 863 (1979).

206. Stolorow & Wraxall, *supra* note 205, at 863.

criticism of the application of electrophoresis to dried stains.[207] Critics argue that the markers may not persist and may change. Although an expert may be able to subsequently read a pattern, the pattern may not be the same pattern that would have been observed if a fresh sample had been tested.[208] The critics point to evidence that PGM,[209] AK,[210] ADA,[211] EsD,[212] and EAP[213] may be subject to aging effects. Some experts have asserted that when the possibilities of aging effects, contamination, and heat effects come into play, "the probability of error in identification of type approaches 100%."[214] Other experts counter that these possible sources of error produce only limited, recognizable changes in electrophoretic patterns.[215] Furthermore, the proponents of electrophoretic testing note that in proficiency testing, "[f]or the commonly used markers, the typing error rate is usually less than 1%."[216] As the following analysis of the pertinent case law indicates, for the most part the courts have sided with the proponents of electrophoretic testing.

Admissibility of Electrophoretic Test Results

In the early electrophoretic cases, the proponents succeeded in introducing the test results.[217] Courts in Kansas,[218] Maine,[219] Maryland,[220] and New York[221] accepted the evidence with little hesitation. The Kansas decision was particularly significant because the appellate court sustained the admission of the evidence in the face of extensive defense expert testimony attacking both the experimentation done to validate multi-system analysis and the assumption that aged stains can be accurately typed.

---

207. Jonakait, *supra* note 1, at 833.

208. *Id.* at 877-79.

209. *Id.* at 896.

210. *Id.* at 899.

211. *Id.*

212. *Id.* at 900.

213. *Id.* at 903-05.

214. Juriek, *The Misapplication of Genetic Analysis in* Forensic Science, 29 J. FORENSIC SCI. 8, 9 (1984). *See also* Parigian & Schaeffer, *The Effects of Heat Upon the Glyoxalase 1 Isoenzyme*, 35 J. FORENSIC SCI. 452 (1990) ("upon heating, band alterations ... occur, ... render[ing] the results inconclusive").

215. Sensabaugh, Response to *The Misapplication of Genetic Analysis in* Forensic Science, 29 J. FORENSIC SCI. 12 (1984).

216. *Id.* at 13.

217. Note, *supra* note 131, at 1004.

218. State v. Washington, 229 Kan. 47, 622 P.2d 986 (1981).

219. State v. Rolls, 389 A.2d 824 (Me. 1978).

220. Robinson v. State, 47 Md. App. 558, 425 A.2d 211 (1981).

221. People v. Borcsok, 114 Misc. 2d 810, 452 N.Y.S.2d 814 (Sup. Ct. 1982).

However, in 1982 Professor Jonakait published a major article on electrophoretic analysis of dried stains.[222] In the article, Professor Jonakait mounted several attacks on such evidence. He reiterated the questions about the adequacy of the experimentation testing the application of the technique to dried stains. He argued that since this forensic application of the technique is used almost exclusively by crime laboratories, there is insufficient proof of the general acceptance of the application in the broader, more impartial scientific community. He wrote, "The only people trying to detect genetic markers in dried blood are forensic scientists, and these scientists are almost exclusively either employees of law enforcement agencies or are funded by such governmental bodies."[223] Although civilian hospitals routinely use RBC and HLA tests for their own, non-law enforcement objectives, only crime laboratories employ electrophoresis to analyze dried blood.

In the early 1980s, some electrophoresis cases took a skeptical attitude toward the evidence. In 1983, in *People v. Young*[224] the Michigan Supreme Court excluded the evidence. The court pointed out that the prosecution's expert witness had helped develop the multi-system.[225] The court commented that the witness's testimony, standing alone, was "insufficient to determine whether the procedure enjoys general scientific acceptance among impartial and disinterested experts."[226] The court noted "the apparent growing controversy over the procedure's reliability."[227] An Illinois appellate court echoed the sentiments of the Michigan Supreme Court in 1984.[228] After reviewing the expert testimony in the court below, the appellate court concluded that there is a bona fide scientific dispute over the reliability of electrophoretic analysis of dried stains. Although the court balked at holding the evidence inadmissible as a matter of law, it made clear that the prosecutor would have to lay a more persuasive foundation to admit the evidence at the retrial in the case. In the mid-1980s, the California and Michigan Supreme Courts reaffirmed their position that electrophoretic evidence was not yet ready for admission in court,[229] and a New York court questioned the reliability of the multisystem.[230]

---

222. Jonakait, *supra* note 1, at 833.

223. *Id.* at 853.

224. 418 Mich. 1, 340 N.W.2d 804 (1983).

225. *Id.*, 340 N.W.2d at 814.

226. *Id.*

227. *Id.* at n.9.

228. People v. Harbold, 124 Ill. App. 3d 363, 79 Ill. Dec. 830, 464 N.E.2d 734 (1984). *See also* Lorraine M. v. S., 115 Misc. 2d 922, 455 N.Y.S.2d 48 (1982) (Although the scientific community generally regards enzyme and protein test results as reliable, inclusionary enzyme and protein test results are inadmissible under the Family Court Act).

229. People v. Brown, 40 Cal. 3d 512, 709 P.2d 440, 220 Cal. Rptr. 637 (1985), *rev'd on other grounds*, 479 U.S. 538 (1987); People v. Young, 425 Mich. 470, 391 N.W.2d 270 (1986).

230. People v. Seda, 139 Misc. 2d 834, 529 N.Y.S.2d 931 (Sup. Ct. 1988).

However, since the mid-1980s most courts, including intermediate appellate courts in California, continue to admit the evidence.[231] One 1986 article argued vigorously for the admission of the evidence.[232] The article relied on a report by an Ad Hoc Committee of the American Academy of Forensic Sciences.[233] Moreover, by the late 1980s, the California Supreme Court changed its position and indicated that electrophoretic testing should now be admissible in that state.[234] Throughout the 1990s, the California Supreme Court continued to adhere

231. Annot., *Admissibility, in criminal case, of evidence of electrophoresis of dried evidentiary blood stains*, 66 A.L.R.4TH 588 (1988); People v. Smith, 215 Cal. App. 3d 230, 263 Cal. Rptr. 684 (1989) (the trial judge may judicially notice the validity of electrophoresis of dried bloodstains); People v. Morris, 199 Cal. App. 3d 377, 245 Cal. Rptr. 52 (1988); People v. Reilly, 196 Cal. App. 3d 1127, 242 Cal. Rptr. 496 (1987); Correll v. State, 523 So. 2d 562 (Fla.), *cert. denied*, 488 U.S. 871 (1988); People v. Eyler, 133 Ill. 2d 173, 549 N.E.2d 268, 139 Ill. Dec. 756 (1989), *cert. denied*, 498 U.S. 881 (1990); State v. Klindt, 389 N.W.2d 670 (Iowa 1986); Smith v. State, 62 Md. App. 627, 490 A.2d 1307, *cert. denied*, 304 Md. 96, 497 A.2d 819 (1985); State v. Fenney, 448 N.W.2d 54 (Minn. 1989); Lieberman, *Blood Test Evidence Is Admissible*, MO. LAWYERS WEEKLY, June 4, 1990, at 1, 4 (in State v. Foote, the Court of Appeals for the Eastern District of Missouri upheld the admission of electrophoresis testimony); People v. Crosby, 116 A.D.2d 731, 498 N.Y.S.2d 31 (1986); Rawlings v. State, 740 P.2d 153 (Okla. Crim. App. 1987); Plunkett v. State, 719 P.2d 834 (Okla. Crim. App.), *cert. denied*, 479 U.S. 1019 (1986); State v. Adams, 418 N.W.2d 618 (S.D. 1988); State v. Dirk, 364 N.W.2d 117 (S.D. 1985). *See also* Redman v. Thieret, 666 F. Supp. 148 (C.D. Ill. 1987) (the electrophoresis technique is not so unreliable that admission of testimony based on the technique would violate due process). Pioneer Hi-Bred International v. Holden Foundation Seeds, Inc., 35 F.3d 1226 (8th Cir. 1994); Adams v. Leapley, 31 F.3d 713 (8th Cir. 1994), *cert. denied*, 513 U.S. 1091 (1995); People v. Stanley, 246 Ill. App. 3d 393, 186 Ill. Dec. 295, 615 N.E.2d 1352 (1993) (electrophoresis is generally accepted); People v. Lopez, 593 N.E.2d 647 (Ill. App. 1992) (it is judicially noticeable that electrophoresis is generally accepted by forensic scientists).

232. Note, *The Admissibility of Electrophoretic Methods of Genetic Marker Bloodstain Typing Under the Frye Standard*, 11 OKLA. CITY U. L. REV. 773 (1986).

233. *Id.* at 804 n.211 ("There is widespread agreement in the relevant scientific community that reliable, accurate determination of genetic marker ... types in dried blood and body fluid stains is possible using these techniques ....").

234. People v. Cooper, 53 Cal. 3d 771, 809 P.2d 865, 281 Cal. Rptr. 90, 112 ("Defendant challenges the general admissibility of electrophoretic testing of dried bloodstains. We recently considered and rejected this contention. People v. Morris ...."), *cert. denied*, 502 U.S. 1016 (1991); People v. Morris, 53 Cal. 3d 152, 207, 807 P.2d 949, 980, 279 Cal. Rptr. 720, 751, *cert. denied*, 502 U.S. 959 (1991) ("We ... have endorsed *Reilly*, although in dictum. Electrophoresis has been found acceptable in at least 19 appellate decisions from 11 states"); People v. Kaurish, 52 Cal. 3d 658, 690 n.5, 802 P.2d 278, 299 n.5, 276 Cal. Rptr. 788, 809 n.5 (1990), *cert. denied*, 502 U.S. 837 (1991); People v. Gallego, 52 Cal. 3d 115, 802 P.2d 169, 276 Cal. Rptr. 679 (1990) (citing *Coleman, infra*), *cert. denied*, 502 U.S. 924 (1991); People v. Coleman, 46 Cal. 3d 749, 791, 759 P.2d 1260, 1288, 251 Cal. Rptr. 83, 111 (1988) (citing the *Reilly* case mentioned in note 213, the court commented in dictum, "Recently, the Court of Appeal after an eight-day trial court hearing upheld the admissibility of electrophoretic typing of dried bloodstain evidence"), *cert. denied*, 489 U.S. 1100 (1989); People v. Yorba, 209 Cal. App. 3d 1017, 257 Cal. Rptr. 641, 644 (1989) (citing *Coleman*, the court stated, "The Supreme Court has approved the *Reilly* holding in dictum").

to that position.[235] However, Michigan stands virtually alone in steadfastly excluding the evidence.[236]

§ 17-8(D). Sperm Antibodies.

Some men carry anti-sperm antibodies in their systems. The antibodies are formed when the man's sperm leaks into his bloodstream. The blood cells react to the sperm as an antigen and produce the antibodies to fend off the antigen. There is some medical evidence that anti-sperm antibodies are particularly common among men who have had reverse vasectomies.

The defendant in *United States v. Gwaltney*[237] had had a reverse vasectomy. Gwaltney was charged with violating a woman's civil rights by murdering her in 1982. The evidence technicians found traces of semen on the victim's body and clothing. Laboratory testing revealed that the semen contained anti-sperm antibodies. The prosecution attempted to introduce evidence that: The sperm found at the crime scene contained such antibodies; reverse vasectomies can cause the formation of the antibodies; the defendant had had a reverse vasectomy; and only 12% of the male population would have the genetic markers present in the sperm, including the antibodies.[238] The defense objected on the ground that this technique is too novel, but the trial court overruled the objection and admitted the evidence. After hearing the evidence, the jury convicted. The Ninth Circuit affirmed the admission of the evidence.[239]

§ 17-8(E). Neutron Activation Analysis (NAA).

One expert, Professor Leddicotte, has urged that a person can be identified by analyzing the levels of various chemical elements in his blood.[240] Professor Leddicotte contends that the trace element levels can be measured by neutron

---

235. People v. Hart, 976 P.2d 683, 85 Cal. Rptr. 2d 132, 187-88 (1999); People v. Ashmus, 54 Cal. 3d 932, 820 P.2d 214, 2 Cal. Rptr. 2d 112 (1991), *cert. denied*, 506 U.S. 841 (1992); People v. Fierro, 1 Cal. 4th 173, 821 P.2d 1302, 3 Cal. Rptr. 2d 426, 442 (1991), *cert. denied*, 506 U.S. 907 (1992). People v. Wash, 6 Cal. 4th 215, 861 P.2d 1107, 24 Cal. Rptr. 2d 421 (1993), *cert. denied*, 513 U.S. 836 (1994).

236. People v. Stoughton, 185 Mich. App. 219, 460 N.W.2d 591 (1990) (although the court barred testimony about the Wraxall multisystem method, the court permitted the admission of evidence about a modified single-system method designed to overcome the deficiencies of the multisystem).

237. U.S. Dist. Ct., Los Angeles, Calif., 83-927.

238. Galante, *Test of Sperm Antibodies Is Admitted Into Evidence*, NAT'L L.J., Apr. 23, 1984, at 4. The *Gwaltney* prosecutor, Assistant United States Attorney Richard Kendall, was kind enough to send Professor Imwinkelried the transcripts of the pretrial motions and trial testimony about sperm antibodies. The transcripts are on file at Professor Imwinkelried's office.

239. United States v. Gwaltney, 790 F.2d 1378 (9th Cir. 1986), *cert. denied*, 479 U.S. 1104 (1987).

240. State v. Stout, 478 S.W.2d 368, 369-70 (Mo. 1972).

activation analysis (NAA). The prosecution attempted to offer Professor Leddicotte's testimony in *State v. Stout,*[241] a case discussed in Chapter 11 which is devoted to NAA.

In *Stout,* Professor Leddicotte testified that if he had not used a cadmium shield mode of NAA, the peaks for some of the stronger elements such as sodium and chlorine would have interfered with and hidden smaller peaks for other, identifying elements present in the blood sample.[242] The cadmium shielding technique filtered out the larger peaks and allowed him to see the peaks for the other elements present.[243]

The Missouri Supreme Court acknowledged that in earlier cases, it had sustained the admission of NAA evidence to identify a hair sample.[244] However, the court stated that "[t]he issue must be narrowed to whether the application of the 'Leddicotte technique' to blood samples has 'gained general acceptance in the particular field in which it belongs.'"[245] The court held that the prosecution had made an insufficient showing of general acceptance of the technique. It does not appear that evidence of the Leddicotte technique has been offered in subsequent cases.

§ 17-8(F). Chromosome Variant Analysis (CVA).

In *Cobey v. State,*[246] chromosome variant analysis (CVA) met the same fate as the Ledicotte technique in *Stout*. In *Cobey*, the defendant was charged with rape. The rape victim became pregnant as a result of the assault. She obtained an abortion, and Dr. Susan Olson, a cytogeneticist, used CVA to compare samples from the fetus and the defendant.

Dr. Olson described the technique and vouched for its accuracy. She testified that each chromosome contains an area known as heterochromatin, part of the DNA structure. Her studies indicated that the amount and shape of the heterochromatin vary from person to person. She detailed the laboratory procedures used to examine the heterochromatin or chromosome variants. She added that she had published some of her research.[247]

---

241. *Id.*

242. *Id.* at 370-71.

243. *Id.* at 371.

244. *Id.* at 369, citing State v. Stevens, 467 S.W.2d 10, 22-24 (Mo.), *cert. denied*, 404 U.S. 994 (1971).

245. *Id.* at 371.

246. 73 Md. App. 233, 533 A.2d 944, 950 (1987), *cert. denied*, 312 Md. 127, 538 A.2d 778 (1988).

247. Olson, *Human Chromosome Variation: The Discriminatory Power of Q-band Heteromorphism (Variant) Analysis in Distinguishing between Individuals, with Specific Application to Cases of Questionable Paternity*, 38 AM. J. HUM. GENETICS 235 (1986).

Nevertheless, the Maryland court held that it was error to admit Dr. Olson's testimony. The court invoked the *Frye* rule. The court noted that other researchers had found CVA to have much less discriminatory power than Dr. Olson claimed.[248] Moreover, "Dr. Olson did not refer to any published articles supporting her theories or name any of the other cytogeneticists she claims share her view."[249]

§ 17-8(G). Autoantibodies.

Researchers have long known that autoantibodies occur with high frequency in patients suffering from systemic rheumatic diseases. They have recently discovered that normal persons have a novel type of autoantibodies.[250] These autoantibodies increase in number from the person's birth and seem to remain constant for decades, perhaps lifelong. Preliminary research indicates that a person's complement of autoantibodies is unique to that individual. Miragen, Inc., of San Diego, California, has pioneered research to develop an "antibody fingerprint."[251]

§ 17-9. Statistical Evaluation.

Many trial attorneys no longer end the expert's direct examination when the expert testifies that the defendant's genetic markers match those found at the crime scene or those possessed by the defendant's alleged child. They are now attempting to take the next step and offer a statistical evaluation of the blood grouping test results. The experts employ a number of different statistics, and it is critical to understand: what formula the expert used, where the expert obtained the numbers to insert into the variables in the formula, and the significance of the final number yielded by the formula. This section reviews some of the statistics cited in court and the evidentiary limitations that courts have placed on the use of the statistics.

§ 17-9(A). Types of Statistics.

There is no one formula for evaluating the significance of a blood grouping test result. The experts use several formulae to explain the import of the test results.

---

248. Cobey v. State, 73 Md. App. 233, 533 A.2d 944, 950 (1987), *cert. denied*, 312 Md. 127, 538 A.2d 778 (1988).

249. *Id.*, 533 A.2d at 949.

250. Francoeur, *Antibody Fingerprinting: A Novel Method for Identifying Individual People and Animals*, 6 BIO/TECH. 822 (1988).

251. *Id.*

Population Frequencies Derived Empirically

In any polymorphic system, the various genetic markers are distributed in the population. For example, in the ABO system, a person can have type A, B, AB, or O. The frequency distribution is uneven. Approximately 40% of the population is type A, 14% type B, 3% type AB, and 43% type O.[252] The expert cannot deduce the frequencies a priori; the frequencies must be compiled by empirical investigation.[253]

Gathering the empirical data is sometimes difficult. The rarer the antigen, the more difficult it may be to obtain a representative sample. There has been criticism of the population frequencies used to evaluate blood grouping test results. In 1980, the United States Public Health Service declared that "although some genetic markers systems have been known for longer than 75 years ... no reliable frequency data exist on population samples for the U.S. population as a whole, for various U.S. geographic regions, or for sub-classifications by age or sex. Many frequencies reported are derived from blood donor samples that often are not representative of the total population ...."[254] Some have questioned the reliability of the DNA population frequencies.[255] Frequencies do not seem to vary markedly among ages or sexes,[256] but there apparently are significant differences among geographic areas[257] and races.[258]

---

252. A. MOENSSENS, J. STARRS, C. HENDERSON & F. INBAU, SCIENTIFIC EVIDENCE IN CIVIL AND CRIMINAL CASES §13.10. at 778 (4th ed. 1995).

253. However, when the defense has not questioned the expert about the source of the frequency, courts have upheld the admission of frequencies although the expert did not specify a source. State v. Onken, 701 S.W.2d 518, 522 (Mo. App. 1985).

254. NAT'L CENTER FOR HEALTH STATISTICS, PUBLIC HEALTH SERVICE, U.S. DEP'T HEALTH, EDUCATION, AND WELFARE, SELECTED GENETIC MARKERS OF BLOOD AND SECRETIONS FOR YOUTH 12-17 YEARS OF AGE: UNITED STATES 4 (1980), *quoted in* Jonakait, *When Blood Is Their Argument: Probabilities in Criminal Cases, Genetic Markers, and, Once Again, Bayes' Theorem*, 1983 U. ILL. L. REV. 369, 378. *But see* Davis v. State, 476 N.E.2d 127, 134-35 (Ind. App. 1985) (although an expert may not cite "unsubstantiated estimates," the expert may rely on "accepted scientific tables"); State v. Klindt, 389 N.W.2d 670, 671-72 (Iowa 1986) ("information received from a recognized data bank"); State v. Stukey, 242 Kan. 204, 747 P.2d 137 (1987) (a genetic marker expert need not specify any particular study as the source of population frequencies); Funderburk v. Commonwealth, 6 Va. App. 334, 368 S.E.2d 290 (1988) (although the study is not in evidence, the expert may rely on the study if it is the type of information customarily relied upon by specialists in that field).

255. Ingwerson, *DNA fingerprints: when the proof is in the genes*, CHRIST. SCI. MON., Apr. 12, 1988, at 4 (Hal Urhig "notes that Lifecodes projects extremely high certainties mathematically but their sample base is only about 1,000 DNA tests").

256. Jonakait, *supra* note 254, at 376.

257. Peterson, *A Few Things You Should Know About Paternity Tests (But Were Afraid to Ask)*, 22 SANTA CLARA L. REV. 667, 675 (1982).

258. *Id.* at 693; Jonakait, *supra* note 254, at 376; Walsh, Lawton, Buckleton, Seber & Woodfield, *Comments on the Use of Blood Marker Frequency Data*, 32 FORENSIC SCI. INT'L 131

On the whole, the available population frequencies qualify as "reasonably accurate approximation(s)."[259] However, many frequencies are not precise.[260] The rarer the marker, the greater is the significance of even small discrepancies.[261] For example, one study reports a population frequency of 0.1% for a rare marker in the Gc system while another study lists the figure at between 0.4 and 0.9%.[262] As one commentator noted, "although the given frequencies are all within a percentage point, [one study] indicates that this rare phenotype occurs four to nine times as often as that reported by the [other study]."[263]

Moreover, a given population frequency figure is meaningful only when it is compared to the relevant universe or population. At first blush, for instance, a population frequency of 0.1% may sound impressive to a jury; it may sound as if the odds are 1,000 to one in favor of the defendant's guilt or paternity. However, if the relevant population includes 1,000,000 persons, there are probably 1,000 persons with the same "rare" genetic marker as the defendant. The frequency must be applied to the pertinent universe to derive a source probability.[264]

Population Frequencies Derived Through Product Rule

Suppose that the expert tests the defendant's blood for two blood grouping systems. In one system, the defendant has a marker with a 10% population frequency. In the other system, the defendant's marker has a 20% population frequency. Unfortunately, there have been no empirical studies of the frequency of persons with the two markers. The expert may nevertheless derive the combined frequency by applying the product or multiplication rule. The rule is that the combined probability of the occurrence of two independent events equals the product of multiplying one probability by the other:[265]

$$Pr_{(1+2)} = Pr_1 \times Pr_2$$

(1986); Baird, Balazs, Giusti, Miyazaki, Nicholas, Wexler, Kanter, Glassberg, Allen, Rubinstein & Sussman, *Allele Frequency Distribution of Two Highly Polymorphic DNA Sequences in Three Ethnic Groups and Its Application to the Determination of Paternity*, 39 AM. J. HUM. GENETICS 489, 500 (1986) ("the analysis of the allele frequency distribution of two highly polymorphic DNA loci shows significant differences among American blacks, Caucasoids, and Hispanics from the New York metropolitan area"); Comment, *The Use of Blood Tests in Actions to Determine Paternity*, 16 WAKE FOREST L. REV. 591, 600 (1980). Our reviewer points out that while there may be significant differences for blood groups, enzymes, and proteins, the differences are less significant for DNA markers.

259. Jonakait, *supra* note 254, at 380.

260. *Id.*

261. *Id.*

262. *Id.*

263. *Id.*

264. *Id.* at 387-89.

265. E. IMWINKELRIED, THE METHODS OF ATTACKING SCIENTIFIC EVIDENCE § 6-6(d) (3d ed. 1997).

In our hypothetical, inserting 10% and 20% for the variables, the expert would derive the conclusion that the frequency is 2%:

$$.10 \times .20 = .02$$

This figure represents the random match probability or the probability of chance duplication. The leading case on the product rule is the famous California decision, *People v. Collins*.[266] Although *Collins* does not deal with the statistical evaluation of blood grouping tests, it is instructive for our purpose. In *Collins* a couple perpetrated a robbery. An eyewitness testified to the following description of the perpetrators: They drove a yellow car; the man was black with a moustache and beard; and the woman was Caucasian with blond hair and a ponytail. During the trial, the prosecutor called a mathematics professor. In a hypothetical question, the prosecutor instructed the professor to assume these probabilities:

—yellow automobile..1/10
—man with moustache...1/4
—black man with beard 1/10
—girl with blond hair..1/3
—girl with ponytail...1/10
—interracial couple...1/1000

The witness then invoked the multiplication rule and testified to a probability of 1/12,000,000. In reversing, the California Supreme Court found several flaws in the testimony. Two flaws are worth noting here. First, the prosecutor had arbitrarily assigned values to the various probabilities. In effect, the prosecutor pulled the numbers from the air and instructed the mathematics professor to assume the validity of the numbers. The court held that the proponent invoking the product rule must show that the numbers to be inserted in the variables are trustworthy. Second, some of the probabilities multiplied were not independent; for example, the fact that a person has a beard obviously affects the likelihood that he has a moustache. The proponent can apply the product rule only when the probabilities are independent; that is, the occurrence of one factor has no effect on the likelihood of the occurrence of the other factor.

How does the *Collins* analysis apply to the use of the product rule to derive population frequencies for genetic markers? Under *Collins,* the proponent has the burden of showing that the individual probabilities, that is, the empirical population frequencies, are trustworthy. Moreover, *Collins* permits the use of the product rule only if the population frequencies are independent; the person's marker in one system has no impact on the marker he possesses in another

266. 68 Cal. 2d 319, 438 P.2d 33, 66 Cal. Rptr. 497 (1968).

system. Most genetic marker systems are independent.[267] However, some of the HLA systems are "tightly linked";[268] the person's classification in one HLA may affect his classification in another system. Prior to the DNA laboratories' shift to single-locus probes, some questioned the independence of the markers used in DNA identification.[269] However, for practical purposes, most systems seem to be mutually independent.[270]

People v. Gillespie[271] illustrates the proper use of the product rule to evaluate blood test results. In *Gillespie* blood was found at the crime scene. An analysis of the blood revealed that it was type A with a positive rheumatoid arthritis factor. The expert cited the population frequencies for type A blood and for the factor. The expert then multiplied the numbers to derive the opinion that only 2.7% of the population would have that set of genetic markers. Since there was a reasonable basis in genetic theory and empirical studies for treating the two marker systems as independent, the expert correctly used the product rule.

Discriminatory Power (DP)

The discriminatory power (DP) of a genetic marker system represents the probability that samples taken from two randomly chosen persons and tested for a marker in that system will differ.[272] The DP is usually derived in two steps.

---

267. Peterson, *supra* note 257, at 692.

268. *Id.*

269. Ingwerson, *DNA fingerprints: when the proof is in the genes*, CHRIST. SCI. MON., Apr. 12, 1988, at 4 ("Mr. Uhrig questions the theory behind the high certainties offered by scientists. While geneticists treat each band of DNA like a random variable, Uhrig notes that genetic traits often go together — such as blond hair and blue eyes — and their DNA codes may not be as ... independent from each other as they are made out to be"); Kaye, *DNA Paternity Probabilities*, 24 FAM. L.Q. 279, 299 n.80 (Fall 1990) ("The underlying assumption of statistical independence of bands has been questioned on several grounds").

270. Jonakait, *supra* note 254, at 673. *See also* United States v. Garries, 19 M.J. 845, 857 (A.F.C.M.R. 1985), *aff'd*, 22 M.J. 288 (C.M.A.), *cert. denied*, 479 U.S. 985 (1986); Kaye, *The Admissibility of "Probability Evidence" in Criminal Trials — Part II*, JURIMETRICS J. 160, 163 (Winter 1987) (citing State v. Chavez, 100 N.M. 730, 676 P.2d 257 (Ct. App. 1983)).

271. 24 Ill. App. 3d 567, 321 N.E.2d 398 (1974).

272. Laux & Wurster, *The Relative Indices of Efficiency for Selected Methods of Bloodstain Analysis*, 28 J. FORENSIC SCI. 1000 (1983).

The first step is computing the likelihood of a random match.[273] That probability is the sum of the squares of the occurrence of each type in the system. Suppose, for instance, that in a particular system, there are three types with population frequencies of .79, .20, and .01.[274] The probability of a random match is

$$P = F_i^2$$

In this formula, F indicates that the figures must be summed or added. The superscript 2 means that each value must be squared. The subscript i means that all the frequencies must be squared; i represents the *i*th or last type. In our hypothetical, after inserting the proper numbers, we would obtain:

$$(.79)^2 + (.20)^2 + (.01)^2 = .66$$

0.66 is thus the probability of a random match.

The second step is subtracting that probability from 1:

$$DP = 1.00 - P$$

Here the DP is 0.34:

$$0.34 = 1.00 - 0.66$$

Given the distribution of frequencies in this system, there is roughly a one in three chance that the markers of two randomly chosen persons in the system will differ.

Knowing the frequencies for the various markers in each system, the expert can compute the DP of the system. There are also available charts listing the DP for each system.[275] The DP has limited forensic value; it may help the expert decide which systems to investigate, but it is an awkward method of expressing the probative value of the test results at trial.

Probability of Exclusion (PE)

The probability of exclusion is similar to a system's discriminatory power. The probability of exclusion (PE) represents the likelihood that the use of a particular system will exclude a falsely accused defendant.[276] To determine the PE, the expert initially lists every possible combination of markers in the system among a mother, child, and putative father.[277] The expert next identifies the combinations which would positively exclude the alleged father as the parent.[278]

---

273. Sensabaugh, *supra* note 171, at 395.

274. *Id.*

275. Gaensslen & Camp, *supra* note 4, at 29-44; Laux & Wurster, *supra* note 272, at 1001.

276. Wayne, *HLA Blood Tests: Pinpointing Paternity?*, 2 CRIM. JUST. J. 35, 39 (1978).

277. Camp & Gaensslen, *supra* note 137, at 30-12.

278. *Id.;* 1 S. SCHATKIN, DISPUTED PATERNITY PROCEEDINGS § 7.05, at 7-5-17 (1983 rev.).

A comparison between the two lists of combinations yields the PE.[279] Formulas have been developed to simplify the calculation.[280]

The expert may also be interested in the cumulative probability of exclusion (CPE) if several systems are used. The formula for calculating the CPE is as follows:[281]

$$CPE = 1 - (1 - P_1)(1 - P2) \ldots (1 - P_n)$$

In this formula, n represents the number of different systems tested. For example, when the analyst used the ABO, MNSs, Rh, Kidd, and Duffy systems, n would be 5. Each P is the probability of exclusion for an individual system. The calculation of the P or PE is discussed above.

As in the case of the discriminatory power, there are published charts for both probabilities of exclusion[282] and cumulative probability of exclusion.[283]

It is critical to understand the limited significance of the PE and CPE. Suppose that the CPE is 0.95. "This does not mean that there is a 95 percent chance that the alleged father is the true father. Of course, the higher the probability of exclusion, the greater is the likelihood of paternity for a non-excluded man. But there is no direct relationship between the probability of exclusion and the likelihood of paternity. Likelihood of paternity cannot be extrapolated from the probability of exclusion."[284] It is tempting to the lay jurors to equate the probability of exclusion and the probability of paternity, but those two probabilities are not synonymous.[285] One expert "documented 13 actual cases ... in which the probability of exclusion ranged from 80% to 96%, yet the probability of paternity ranged between 4.4% and 44%."[286]

Paternity Index (PI)

The last two statistics, the discriminatory power (DP) and the probability of exclusion (PE), are essentially negative or exclusionary. They give some insight into the capability of a marker system to find differences, sometimes differences

---

279. Camp & Gaensslen, *supra* note 137, at 30-12.

280. *Id.* citing Walker, *Probability in the Analysis of Paternity Test Results, in* PATERNITY TESTING (American Association of Blood Banks 1978).

281. *Id.* at 30-13; Wayne, *supra* note 276, at 39 n.23; Peterson, *supra* note 257, at 678; 1 S. SCHATKIN, *supra* note 278, at § 7.07, at 7-20.

282. Camp & Gaensslen, *supra* note 137, at 30-14-18.

283. *Id.* at 30-19. *See also* Peterson, *supra* note 257, at 677 n.39; Comment, *supra* note 258, at 596.

284. Stroud, Bundrant & Galindo, *supra* note 102, at 47.

285. Chakraborty, Shaw & Schull, *Exclusion of Paternity: The Current State of the Art*, 26 AM. J. HUM. GENET. 477, 484 (1974), *cited in* Peterson, *supra* note 257, at 678-79 n.43.

286. *Id.* at 679.

so marked that a defendant can confidently be eliminated as the possible father of a child.

We now shift to statistics with essentially affirmative uses. These statistics afford insights into the significance of matches between the defendant's markers and markers found in a child or in a stain at a crime scene. The first such statistic is the paternity index or PI. The PI compares the defendant alleged father to a random man; it is a ratio representing "how much more likely the alleged father is to be the true father than is an unrelated random man of the same race."[287] It is a relative likelihood;[288] as a likelihood ratio, it indicates how many more times more probable it is that certain data would arise if one hypothesis as opposed to another is true. The index is determined by the formula:[289]

$$PI = \frac{X}{Y}$$

One hypothesis is that the defendant or a phenotypically indistinguishable person (on the system tested) is the father. X is the probability that in combination with an egg from the mother, a sperm from a man phenotypically indistinguishable from the defendant would produce a zygote with the child's phenotypes. The other hypothesis is that an unrelated, random man of the same race is the father. Y is the probability that in combination with the mother's egg, a sperm from a random, unrelated man would produce the zygote.[290] Both X and Y are conditional probabilities. Thus, X is the probability that the child would have the phenotypes identified in the testing given that the father was the defendant or a phenotypically indistinguishable man. Hence, if the ratio were 100/1, "it is 100 times more likely the alleged father is the biological father than the random man."[291]

There are a number of steps in computing the PI. The initial step is identifying the obligatory genes that the biologic father must have transmitted to the child. Consider this hypothetical. After testing the alleged father, mother, and child for HLA types, the expert concludes that they have the following genotypes:[292]

---

287. Armitage & Cross, *supra* note 89, at 479.

288. Camp & Gaensslen, *supra* note 137, at 30-20. *See also* Kaye, *Plemel as a Primer on Proving Paternity*, 24 WILLAMETTE L. REV. 867, 873 (1988) ("This index is a likelihood ratio .... Odds are essentially probabilities. A likelihood is not a probability; it is a ratio of two probabilities that pertain to an outcome conditioned on different events").

289. Camp & Gaensslen, *supra* note 137, at 30-20. Our reviewer, Dr. Allen, states the formula PI = x/y. x is the likelihood of the included alleged father producing a single sperm containing the necessary genetic information inherited by the child from his or her true father. y is the probability of encountering the necessary sperm in the racially appropriate random population.

290. *Id.*

291. *Id.*

292. Sussman, *supra* note 75, at 17.

Alleged father:	(A2, B52)	(A23, B39)
Mother:	(A3, B35)	(A28, B44)
Child:	(A2, B52)	(A28, B44)

Applying the Mendelian laws of inheritance, the expert will conclude that the child must have acquired the (A2, B52) haplotype from the biological father with the (A28, B44) haplotype supplied by the mother.[293]

The second step is determining the value for X, the probability that the alleged father would transmit those genes in a mating with the mother. If the expert knows that the father is homozygous, that is, if both haplotypes are the same, the probability would be 1.00. However, the father may be heterozygous.

This step becomes a bit complex. Sussman describes the computation in this fashion:

> Since the father can be either (A2, B52) (A23, B39) or (A2, B39) (A23, B52), the frequency with which he can produce (A2, B52) is calculated from the gene frequency table.
>
> (1) (A2, B52) (A23, B39) = frequency of A2, B52 x frequency of A23, B39 = .26580 = .498 (% of 100)
> (2) (A2, B39) (A23, B52) = frequency of A2, B39 x frequency of A23, B52 = .26880 = .502 (% of 100)
>
> The chance of each haplotype is the ratio of .26580 to .26880 = .498 to .502. Since the necessary haplotype to contribute to the mother's haplotype (A28, B44) to complete the child's phenotype is (A2, B52), the frequency with which any sperm of this man could carry this haplotype is 1/2 of the (A2, B52) (A23, B39) phenotype. Therefore 1/2 of .498 = .249 = X. X = the chance that a man of HLA grouping (A2, B52) (A23, B39) would pass the (A2, B52) haplotype to his child.[294]

This step is necessary because in a random mating with the mother, the alleged father could have passed either haplotype to the child born of the mating. The expert must determine the relative likelihood that the alleged father would pass one haplotype rather than the other.

The third step is ascertaining the value of Y, the probability that the random, unrelated man of the same race would transmit the haplotype. That value is the frequency of the haplotype in the population.[295]

---

293. *Id.* at 18.
294. *Id.*
295. *Id.*

The final step is dividing X by Y. Suppose, for instance, that the gene frequency tables indicate that the incidence of the (A2, B52) haplotype in the relevant population is only .00295. The division[296] is then

$$\frac{X}{Y} = \frac{.249}{.00295} = 84.4$$

It is 84.4 times more likely that anyone with the phenotype of the alleged father is the biological father than it is that a man drawn at random from the population on which the haplotype frequency tables are based is the biological father.[297]

The PI can range from 0 to infinity.[298] In practice, most reported indices seem to range between 10 and 100.[299] Until the advent of DNA testing, many experts stated that a PI greater than 20 (PI/20) was "strong evidence of paternity."[300] In 1976, the American Bar Association and the American Medical Association approved the following guidelines for interpreting paternity indices:[301]

Index =	
5 or less (prob. 83% or less)	no significance
6 to 10 (prob. 83% to 91%)	undecided
11 to 20 (prob. 92% to 95%)	paternity likely
21 to 100 (prob. 96% to 99%)	paternity very likely
likely 101 to 200 (prob. 99% to 99.5%)	paternity extremely likely
over 200 (prob. over 99.5%)	paternity practically proven

Other authorities recommend different guidelines:[302]

Probability of Paternity	Likelihood of Paternity	Paternity Index
99.8-99.9%	practically proven	399-1
99.0-99.7%	extremely likely	95 to 1
95.0-98.9%	very likely	19 to 1
90.0 -94.9%	likely	9 to 1
80.0 -89.9%	certain hint	4 to 1
less than 80%	not useful	4 to 1

---

296. *Id.*

297. *Id. Paternity Case — Direct and Cross-Examination of Plaintiff's Expert Immunohematologist*, 1982 ANN. MED. TR. TECH. Q. 359 (Winter).

298. Peterson, *supra* note 257, at 683.

299. *Id.*

300. Camp & Gaensslen, *supra* note 137, at 30-20. One impact of DNA typing technology is that PIs are generally higher now due to the high degree of polymorphism exhibited by DNA systems. According to our reviewer, Dr. Allen, in today's paternity testing laboratory, it is unacceptable to report a PI of 20 as strong proof of paternity given the DNA systems available for extended testing.

301. Peterson, *supra* note 257, at 700.

302. *Id.*

The Nordic countries use more conservative standards in evaluating paternity indices.[303] Under the A.B.A.-A.M.A. guidelines, an index of 11 or higher makes paternity "likely."[304] The Nordic countries find a likelihood of paternity only after the index reaches 19.

There are caveats in applying the paternity index. Some haplotypes do not pass with the frequency that they theoretically should transmit with. This phenomenon is termed disequilibrium. Further, more than one nonexcluded man may have an impressively high PI. "One study found that of the nonexcluded men tested in the HLA system alone, 67% scored over 19 (prob. 95%), and 86% scored over 9 (prob. 90%). Only two cases out of 1000 scored below 1 (prob. 50%)."[305] This is understandable, since likelihood ratios such as PI relate to all men phenotypically indistinguishable from the defendant — not the defendant alone.

Plausibility of Paternity (W, PP, or RCP)

The paternity can be converted into a percentage by computing the plausibility of paternity. This figure is termed the PP,[306] W,[307] or RCP value.[308] If the expert is basing the calculation of percentage solely upon the genetic test results, then the formula is stated as[309]

$$W = \frac{PI}{PI + 1}$$

or[310]

$$W = \frac{\frac{X}{Y}}{1 + \frac{X}{y}}$$

303. *Id.*

304. *Id.*

305. *Id.* at 701.

306. Armitage & Cross, *supra* note 89, at 479.

307. *Id.;* Sussman, *supra* note 75, at 18.

308. *Paternity Case — Direct and Cross-Examination of Plaintiff's Expert Immunohematologist, supra* note 297, at 359 (relative chance of paternity).

309. *Id.*

310. Sussman, *supra* note 75, at 18.

Assume that the PI is 84.4, as in our earlier hypothetical. The computation would then be:[311]

$$W = \frac{84.4}{84.4+1} = \frac{84.4}{85.4} = 98.8\%$$

To evaluate the significance of the W, PP, or RCP value, the expert employs the percentage columns in the tables included in the discussion of the PI. These tables were developed by Professor Konrad Hummel and are usually referred to as Hummel's Verbal Predicates.[312]

Bayes' Theorem

Bayes' theorem is discussed in Chapter 15 on statistical evidence. The theorem is a method of relating conditional probabilities, even when some probabilities are based on frequency data and others rest on non-genetic, subjective estimates.[313] When the expert uses the theorem, he or she begins with a prior probability.[314] The expert then revises the probability in light of new evidence to derive a posterior probability.[315] In the context of paternity testing, the prior probability is the likelihood of paternity based on non-genetic evidence. The jury may have to determine what value to assign to that probability. The new evidence is the result of the blood grouping test. The expert employs Bayes' theorem to combine the non-genetic probability and the test result to arrive at a probability of paternity.

The latest edition of McCormick on Evidence contains an excellent discussion of Bayes' theorem.[316] The theorem can be stated in this fashion:[317]

$$\text{Odds}\,(B/T) = LR \times \text{Odds}\,(B)$$

In the formula, B represents paternity, T signifies the test, B/T is the probability of paternity revised in light of the test result, and LR is the likelihood ratio.[318] In this version of the theorem, B is the prior probability, T is the new evidence, and B/T is the posterior probability. In most paternity cases, the expert assumes that

---

311. *Id.;* Peterson, *supra* note 257, at 683.

312. Sussman, *supra* note 75, at 18. *See also* Wayne, *supra* note 276, at 39.

313. Jonakait, *supra* note 254, at 403.

314. Comment, *supra* note 258, at 602.

315. Jonakait, *supra* note 254, at 399.

316. C. McCormick, Evidence § 211 (5th ed. 1999).

317. *Id.*

318. *Id.*

the prior probability is 50%.[319] Thus, B is .5/.5 or 1. Inserting one for Odds (B), the formula becomes

$$\text{Odds}\,(B/T) = LR \times 1 = LR$$

On this assumption, the formula is reducible to the likelihood ratio. The likelihood ratio is a ratio between two probabilities. "The numerator is the probability that the phenotypes T would be found if the alleged father really were the biological father. The denominator is the probability that the phenotypes T would be found if the alleged father were not the biological father."[320] In assigning a value to the denominator, the expert normally assumes a mating between the woman and a hypothetical, random man. The expert then uses the frequency of the markers in the population as a whole as the denominator.[321] Suppose that in light of the frequency of the markers in the random population, "it is 50 times more likely to obtain a child with the observed phenotypes from a man with the alleged father's phenotype than from the imaginary 'random man.' For prior odds of 1, this means that the odds that the alleged father is the biological father are 50 to 1. The corresponding probability of paternity is 50/51 = .98, or 98%."[322]

$$\frac{g_f \times h_g}{(g_f \times h_g) + (g_p \times h_r)}$$

Other paternity experts use another version of Bayes' theorem, written in a more obscure notation:[323] In this formula, h_g is the prior probability that the defendant is the biological father, h_r is the prior probability that a random man in the population is the father, g_f is the likelihood that the defendant would have transmitted the necessary genes to the child, and g_p is the frequency of the genes among the population at large.[324] The expert can arrive at a value for g_p by multiplying the frequencies of all the relevant genes in the random population.[325]

There are two points to remember about the use of Bayes' theorem in paternity testing. The first is that there is no mathematical formula that predetermines the prior probability. By convention, many experts use the constant value of 50%.[326]

---

319. *Id.* Our reviewer, Dr. Allen, points out that the use of a prior probability of 50% puts the laboratory in a neutral position, basing its opinion only on the genetic testing results.

320. *Id.*

321. *Id.*

322. *Id.*

323. Beautyman, *Paternity Actions — A Matter of Opinion or a Trial of the Blood,* 4 J. LEGAL MED. 20-21 (Apr. 1976).

324. *Id.* at 20.

325. *Id.*

326. Comment, *supra* note 258, at 602. Some commentators describe the choice of 50-50 odds as an arbitrary choice. However, our reviewer, Dr. Allen, argues that paternity testing laboratories

However, the use of the value is not inexorable. One alternative is to present the jury with a table stating the result of blood grouping tests and indicating how the use of a range of prior probabilities (*e.g.*, .10, .20, .30, etc.), taken with the test results, would yield differing posterior probabilities.[327] Two leading authorities on statistical evidence, Finkelstein and Fairley, have prepared a table of calculations of Bayes' theorem for various prior values.[328] The jury could independently choose a prior probability, based on non-genetic evidence, and then use the chart to derive the posterior probability.

An example of how non-genetic evidence can influence the posterior probability and, hence, the opinion regarding paternity is illustrative. Suppose an alleged father is tested for genetic markers with a mother and child and is included with a PI of 99:1. The value for W at a 50% prior probability is 99%, a compelling value implicating the man as the father. However, suppose the man can prove that he was overseas during the period of conception. Given that proof, a prior probability of 10% might be assigned to reflect the non-genetic evidence against paternity. The posterior probability equation becomes:

$$W = \frac{0.1(99)}{0.1(99) + 0.9} = \frac{9.9}{10.8} = 91.7\%$$

The 10% prior probability times the genetic evidence favoring paternity (PI = 99) is divided by the sum of all the probabilities (*i.e.*, that favoring paternity plus the remaining 90% probability that he is not the father). The effect of assigning the lower prior probability is to reduce the posterior probability of paternity to a less than compelling value.

The second point is that an underlying assumption of this version is that the defendant should be compared to a random person in the population. The expert computes the likelihood of the defendant's paternity compared to a random man.[329] However, suppose that the mother in question might have had intercourse with a close relative or identical twin of the defendant.[330] The expert could no longer rely on the frequency of the markers in the random population to establish the defendant's likelihood of paternity compared to the other related,

---

assign a 50% prior probability because that probability puts the laboratory in a neutral position in the case — considering only the results of the genetic testing performed. If the probability of paternity (as a percentage) is graphed against the paternity index, there is a linear relationship only at a 50% prior probability.

327. *See generally* Ellman & Kaye, *Probabilities and Proof: Can HLA and Blood Group Testing Prove Paternity?*, 54 N.Y.U. L. REV. 1131 (1979).

328. Finkelstein & Fairley, *A Bayesian Approach to Identification Evidence*, 83 HARV. L. REV. 488, 500 (1980).

329. Comment, *supra* note 258, at 599.

330. Terasaki, *supra* note 132, at 549.

nonexcluded putative father.[331] It might be just as likely that the relative is the biological father.

Essen-Moller Derivation of Bayes' Theorem

In 1938, the Essen-Moller derivation of Bayes' theorem in different notation was published.[332] This theorem is specially adapted to evaluating the significance of paternity test results. The Essen-Moller adaptation can be derived from the second version of Bayes' theorem:[333]

$$\frac{g_f \times h_g}{(g_f \times h_g) + (g_p \times h_g)}$$

Once again the expert assumes that there is a 50% prior chance of the defendant's paternity.[334] Thus, all the h values in the formula are equal and, by division, can be eliminated from the formula. The formula then becomes:[335]

$$\frac{g_f}{g_f + g_p}$$

The expert now divides the numerator and denominator by g_f The formula transforms into:[336]

$$\frac{1}{1 + \frac{g_p}{g_f}}$$

Many experts insert X for g_f and Y for g_p. When the expert has tested the defendant for several genetic markers, the Essen-Moller formula becomes:[337]

$$\frac{1}{1 + \frac{Y_1}{X_1} \times \frac{Y_2}{X_2} \times \frac{Y_3}{X_3}}$$

The same caveats applicable to the Bayes' theorem itself apply here. First, there is an implicit assumption about the prior probability of paternity. The expert can strike the h values from the formula only if he or she assumes that there is a 50%

---

331. *Id.*

332. Peterson, *supra* note 257, at 682-83.

333. Beautyman, *supra* note 323, at 21.

334. *Id.*

335. *Id.*

336. *Id.*

337. *Id. See also* Camp & Gaensslen, *supra* note 137, at 30-23; Wayne, *supra* note 276, at 39 n.23; Comment, *supra* note 258, at 600.

prior chance.[338] Second, the formula compares the defendant to the hypothetical random man. It is only on that assumption that the expert is justified in using the gene frequencies in the random population to supply the Y values. If a relative of the defendant also had access to the mother, the formula would not be a valid basis for comparing the defendant's odds to the odds of his relative's paternity.

§ 17-9(B). Evidentiary Limitations.

One recurring theme throughout the legal limitations on statistics is the "legal" relevance doctrine. Federal Rule of Evidence 403 states a contemporary version of the doctrine:

> Although relevant, evidence may be excluded if its probative value is substantially outweighed by the danger of unfair prejudice, confusion of the issues, or misleading the jury, or by considerations of undue delay, waste of time, or needless presentation of cumulative evidence.[339]

The primary fears are confusion and misleading. Statistics may seem so arcane and complex that the jury will be confused and misled as to probative value of the statistics. That argument has been urged against the admission of many of the statistics discussed in § 17-9(A).

Population Frequencies

It would seem that the least objectionable sort of statistical evidence would be a statement of the population frequency of genetic markers possessed by the defendant and either found at the crime scene or shared by the child. Assuming that the frequency otherwise satisfies the evidentiary standards for expert testimony,[340] the frequency would appear to be clearly relevant. However, the issue of the admissibility of population frequencies has triggered a sharp split of authority among the courts.

At one extreme are decisions holding that when the blood grouping and statistical evidence merely includes the defendant within the class of potential perpetrators or fathers, the evidence is inadmissible. A leading case in this line of authority was the 1970 New York decision, *People v. Robinson.*[341] The same view was also championed by several intermediate appellate courts in

338. Armitage & Cross, *supra* note 89, at 480.

339. Fed. R. Evid. 403.

340. State v. Payne, 402 S.E.2d 582, 594 (N.C. 1991) (Federal Rule of Evidence 703 permits the expert to rely on "current authorities relied on by experts in the field of blood analysis," including statistics compiled from studies or published in scientific journals), *cert. denied*, 514 U.S. 1038 (1995).

341. 27 N.Y.2d 864, 265 N.E.2d 543, 317 N.Y.S.2d 19 (1970).

Michigan.[342] In one Michigan case, the proffered evidence would have shown that the defendant and the perpetrator were both nonsecretors, a category including roughly 20% of the population.[343] The court declared that "blood type evidence, when used solely for the purpose of including a defendant in a class of possible defendants, has no probative value."[344]

At the other extreme are decisions holding that merely inclusionary test results and the related frequencies are admissible.[345] There are two Michigan intermediate appellate courts aligned on this side of the dispute.[346] One of these courts asserts that its position is now the view of "the overwhelming majority of courts."[347] Commentators have remarked that the *Robinson* approach "has been widely rejected."[348] New York itself has abandoned that approach,[349] and the trend toward admitting inclusionary test results has accelerated.[350]

A compromise position would be possible and defensible. The compromise view would admit the inclusionary statistics when the genetic markers are rare but exclude them when the markers are so common that the evidence has only marginal probative value. In the leading Michigan opinion excluding the population frequencies, the court stated in dictum that the case might have been different if the population frequency had been markedly lower than 20%.[351] The rarity of the markers affects the probative value of the evidence, and both the common-law legal relevance doctrine and Federal Rule of Evidence 403 permit the trial court to factor the quantum of probative value into the ruling on the admissibility of the evidence.[352] If DNA testing were performed, the laboratory can almost always identify a relatively rare set of markers with a significant quantum of probative value.

---

342. People v. McMillen, 126 Mich. App. 211, 336 N.W.2d 895 (1984); People v. Sturdivant, 91 Mich. App. 128, 283 N.W.2d 669 (1979).

343. People v. Sturdivant, 91 Mich. App. 128, 283 N.W.2d 669 (1979).

344. *Id.* at 134, 283 N.W.2d at 672.

345. *See* C. McCormick, *supra* note 316, at § 210; Annot., 2 A.L.R.4th 500 (1980).

346. People v. Thorin, 126 Mich. App. 293, 336 N.W.2d 913 (1983); People v. Horton, 99 Mich. App. 40, 297 N.W.2d 857, *vacated,* 410 Mich. 865, 301 N.W.2d 775 (1980).

347. *Id.* at 50, 297 N.W.2d at 862.

348. Jonakait, *supra* note 254, at 391. *See* People v. Johnson, 37 Ill. App. 3d 328, 345 N.E.2d 531 (1976); State v. Brown, 669 S.W.2d 620, 622 (Mo. App. 1984); State v. Bolder, 635 S.W.2d 673 (Mo. 1982), *cert. denied,* 459 U.S. 1137 (1983).

349. People v. Mountain, 66 N.Y.2d 197, 486 N.E.2d 802, 495 N.Y.S.2d 944 (1985).

350. Callahan v. State, 471 So. 2d 447 (Ala. Crim. App. 1983), *rev'd on other grounds*, 471 So. 2d 463 (Ala.), *cert. denied*, 474 U.S. 1019 (1985); People v. Babbitt, 45 Cal. 3d 660, 755 P.2d 253, 248 Cal. Rptr. 69, 79 (1988), *cert. denied*, 488 U.S. 1034 (1989); Shaw v. State, 179 Ga. App. 807, 348 S.E.2d 132 (1986); Jenkins v. State, 485 N.E.2d 625 (Ind. 1985); People v. Trevino, 155 Mich. App. 10, 399 N.W.2d 424 (1986); State v. Duncan, 698 S.W.2d 63 (Tenn. 1985), *cert. denied*, 475 U.S. 1031 (1986); State v. Nicholas, 34 Wash. App. 775, 663 P.2d 1356 (1983).

351. People v. Sturdivant, 91 Mich. App. 128, 132, 283 N.E.2d 669, 671 (1979).

352. C. McCormick, *supra* note 316, at § 185.

Product Rule

Like Bayes' theorem, the product or multiplication rule is examined in Chapter 15. Earlier in this chapter we discussed the leading case of *People v. Collins.*[353] There are at least two possible objections to the use of the product rule in a particular case: The proponent has not presented trustworthy evidence of the individual probabilities, or the proponent did not establish the independence of the factors. When the proponent has surmounted these hurdles, many courts permit the use of the product rule.[354] As we shall see in Chapter 18, numerous courts have permitted the use of the product rule in DNA cases.

However, other courts refuse to sanction the use of the product rule even when the proponent overcomes both objections.[355] In addition to faulting the foundation in *Collins* for untrustworthy probabilities and lack of independence, the California Supreme Court voiced its concern that mathematics is "a veritable sorcerer in our computerized society."[356] Other courts have expressed the fear that the probability generated by the multiplication rule will have an undue "psychological impact" on the lay jurors.[357] These courts believe that the probability is inadmissible because the jury will be unable to assess its true significance. However, other courts[358] and commentators[359] have greater faith in the jurors' ability to critically evaluate statistical evidence. As the years pass, the judicial support for a ban on the product rule is dwindling.

Probability of Exclusion

The introduction of the probability of exclusion at trial poses a serious risk. The jurors may be unable to differentiate between a negative probability of exclusion and an affirmative probability of paternity.[360] For that reason, some commentators argue that the probability of exclusion should not be admitted at

---

353. 68 Cal. 2d 319, 438 P.2d 33, 66 Cal. Rptr. 497 (1968).

354. People v. Coleman, 46 Cal. 3d 749, 760, 777, 759 P.2d 1260, 1267, 1278, 251 Cal. Rptr. 83, 90, 101 (1988) ("the frequencies are independent of each other"), *cert. denied*, 489 U.S. 1100 (1989); State v. Fulton, 299 N.C. 491, 263 S.E.2d 608 (1980); People v. Gillespie, 24 Ill. App. 3d 567, 321 N.E.2d 398 (1974); C. McCormick, *supra* note 316, at § 210; Jonakait, *supra* note 254, at 392.

355. State v. Carlson, 267 N.W.2d 170, 176 (Minn. 1978); C. McCormick, *supra* note 316, at § 210.

356. 68 Cal. 2d 319, 320, 438 P.2d 33, 33, 66 Cal. Rptr. 497, 497 (1968).

357. State v. Carlson, 267 N.W.2d 170, 176 (Minn. 1978). *See also* Shines, *Blood Grouping and Genetic Marker Evidence: The Use of Electrophoretic Testing*, 24 Crim. L. Bull. 475, 482 (1988) (the Illinois cases "indicate that the use of statistics might constitute reversible error if the evidence is evenly balanced or entirely circumstantial").

358. State v. Clayton, 646 P.2d 723, 727 n.1 (Utah 1982).

359. Saks & Kidd, *Human Information Processing and Adjudication: Trial by Heuristics*, 15 Law & Soc'y Rev. 123, 125-31 (1981), *cited in* Jonakait, *supra* note 254, at 410.

360. Peterson, *supra* note 257, at 680; Ellman & Kaye, *supra* note 327, at 1144.

trial. Several courts have adopted that argument.[361] One court declared: "Simply put, evidence of the failure of a man to be excluded as the result of paternity exclusion tests is not proof of paternity.... It does not render an inference of paternity more probable than it would be without that evidence."[362] The last sentence is, of course, incorrect; the probability of an exclusion is relevant evidence given the lax standard for relevancy stated in Federal Rule of Evidence 401.[363] The court was more accurate in asserting that the probability of exclusion "is of little aid to a jury."[364] According to the court, since the statistic has slight probative value and great potential to mislead, the trial judge has discretion to exclude the evidence under Rule 403.

Paternity Index and Plausibility of Paternity

There is a trend toward the admission of statistics affirmatively indicating the defendant's paternity.[365] In some jurisdictions, statutes sanction the admission of

---

361. State *ex rel.* Hausner v. Blackman, 7 Kan. App. 2d 693, 648 P.2d 249 (1982), *aff'd,* 233 Kan. 223, 662 P.2d 1183 (1983); Commonwealth v. Beausoleil, 397 Mass. 206, 217, 490 N.E.2d 788, 795 (1986); Imms v. Clarke, 654 S.W.2d 281 (Mo. App. 1983); Note, *Establishing Paternity Through HLA Testing: Utah Standards for Admissibility*, 1988 UTAH L. REV. 717, 726 (the Utah courts bar testimony about the probability of exclusion "because of its tendency to mislead or confuse"); Kaye, *The Probability of an Ultimate Issue: The Strange Case of Paternity Testing*, 75 IOWA L. REV. 75 (1989); Kaye, *Plemel as a Primer on Proving Paternity*, 24 WILLAMETTE L. REV. 867, 875 (1988) (collecting the cases barring testimony about the probability of exclusion). However, in State v. Hartman, 145 Wis. 2d 1, 426 N.W.2d 320 (1988) and State v. Spann, 236 N.J. Super. 13, 563 A.2d 1145 (1989), *aff'd*, 130 N.J. 484, 617 A.2d 247 (1993), the courts upheld the admission of the testimony.

362. State *ex rel.* Hausner v. Blackman, 7 Kan. App. 2d 693, 648 P.2d 249 (1982), *aff'd,* 233 Kan. 223, 662 P.2d 1183 (1983). *See also* State v. Joon Kyu Kim, 398 N.W.2d 544, 547-49 (Minn. 1987); Note, *Establishing Paternity Through HLA Testing: Utah Standards for Admissibility*, 1988 UTAH L. REV. 717, 726 (the Utah courts bar testimony about the probability of exclusion "because of its tendency to mislead or confuse").

363. FED. R. EVID. 401 ("any tendency to make the existence of any fact that is of consequence to the determination of the action more probable ...").

364. Imms v. Clarke, 654 S.W.2d 281, 285 (Mo. App. 1983).

365. Mendelson, *From Here to Paternity*, THE BARRISTER, Winter 1982, at 14. *See* United States v. Kandiel, 865 F.2d 967, 971 (8th Cir. 1989) ("Dr. Polesky testified that, based on a comparison of the HLA genetic markers when applied to population frequencies of blood group typings, appellant was seventeen times more likely than someone from a random population to be the brother of Ahmed Kandiel"); People v. Alzoubi, 133 Ill. App. 3d 806, 479 N.E.2d 1208, 89 Ill. Dec. 202 (1985); State v. Thompson, 503 A.2d 689 (Me. 1986); Commonwealth v. Beausoleil, 397 Mass. 206, 490 N.E.2d 788 (1986) ("we believe it preferable that the HLA results be presented to the jury in terms of the probability of paternity .... [W]e believe that the jury may be presented with [this probability] only where the combined tests administered would exclude at least 90% of the nonfathers tested. We ... require that inculpatory blood test evidence shall be admissible only if the probability of the putative father's paternity is 95% or greater"); Camden v. Miller, 34 Ohio App. 3d 86, 517 N.E.2d 253 (1986) (the probability of paternity); Plemel v. Walter, 303 Or. 262, 735

the evidence while in other jurisdictions the courts have decided to admit the statistics as a matter of decisional law.[366] However, on the familiar ground of legal relevance the Minnesota Supreme Court has barred the admission of the paternity index and the plausibility of paternity value.[367] In doing so, the court relied heavily on Professor Tribe's critique of statistical evidence.[368] The Minnesota position, though, appears to be the minority view.[369]

Bayes' Theorem

Until recently, due in part to forceful criticism,[370] there had been only "severely limited" use of Bayes' theorem in criminal cases.[371] The fears have included concerns that: The jury would find the evidence overly impressive; the numerical evidence would "dwarf the soft variables"; the jury would count the evidence twice — once formally in the computation and once subconsciously, since the impressive number would probably influence the jury's estimate of the prior probability; and reliance on the formula would lead to the dehumanization of justice.[372] Until the recent advent of statistical evaluation of blood grouping test results, the opponents of judicial use of the theorem have been "the de facto winner[s]. [N]othing in the reported cases indicated that Bayes' Theorem has been presented to juries or applied by the triers of fact."[373]

P.2d 1209 (1987) (the court stressed that the expert must make it clear to the trier of fact that the paternity index does not directly equate with a probability of paternity); Olson v. Dietz, 347 Pa. Super. 1, 500 A.2d 125 (1985); State v. Hartman, 145 Wis. 2d 1, 426 N.W.2d 320 (1988) (admitting testimony about the paternity index but excluding testimony about the probability of paternity because the latter statistic assumes that the defendant committed the crime); Kaye, *The Probability on an Ultimate Issue: The Strange Case of Paternity Testing*, 75 IOWA L. REV. 75 (1989); Kaye, *Plemel as a Primer on Proving Paternity*, 24 WILLAMETTE L. REV. 867, 871-78 (1988); County of El Dorado v. Misura, 33 Cal. App. 4th 73, 38 Cal. Rptr. 2d 908 (1995) (paternity index), *cert. denied*, 516 U.S. 1112 (1996); Commonwealth v. Khamphouseane, 434 Pa. Super. 93, 642 A.2d 490 (paternity index), *appeal denied*, 649 A.2d 669 (Pa. 1994).

366. Mendelson, *supra* note 365, at 14.

367. State v. Boyd, 331 N.W.2d 480 (Minn. 1983).

368. *Id.* at 482. *See also* State v. Joon Kyu Kim, 398 N.W.2d 544 (Minn. 1987); State v. Spann, 236 N.J. Super. 13, 563 A.2d 1145 (1989) (testimony about the probability of paternity statistic was inadmissible because it was based on a model which assumed a 50% prior probability), *aff'd*, 130 N.J. 484, 617 A.2d 247 (1993).

369. Davis v. State, 476 N.E.2d 127, 135 (Ind. App. 1985) ("The approach taken in Minnesota... has been rejected by an impressive array of courts and commentators").

370. Tribe, *Trial by Mathematics: Precision and Ritual in the Legal Process*, 84 HARV. L. REV. 1329 (1971).

371. Braun, *Quantitative Analysis and the Law: Probability Theory as a Tool of Evidence in Criminal Trials*, 1982 UTAH L. REV. 41, 42.

372. Jonakait, *supra* note 254, at 402-05.

373. *Id.* at 411; State v. Spann, 236 N.J. Super. 13, 563 A.2d 1145 (1989), *aff'd*, 130 N.J. 484, 617 A.2d 247 (1993).

However, the attempts to introduce the theorem and the Essen-Moller adaptation of the theorem "started [the debate] anew."[374] European courts use the theorem in paternity cases, but they typically try the case to a judge without a jury.[375] The use of the theorem in paternity cases is spreading to the United States.[376] In one case, after ruling the probability of exclusion inadmissible, in virtually the next breath the court announced that "[t]he expert may ... offer an opinion on the likelihood of paternity formulated by the Bayes' Theorem from the tests and the other empirical evidence."[377] There has been noticeable movement toward the view permitting the use of the theorem in paternity cases.[378] Many statutes now authorize the admission of a "probability" of paternity.[379] In some jurisdictions, only probabilities exceeding a certain likelihood such as 75%[380] 95%,[381] or 97.3%[382] are admissible. In some jurisdictions, a probability exceeding a specified percentage such as 97% creates a presumption of paternity.[383] In other states, when the paternity exceeds a certain likelihood, such as 92%, the putative father has a duty to pay temporary child support during the proceeding.[384]

Although many courts and legislatures now seem receptive to the admissibility of paternity probabilities, the debate over the wisdom of admitting such evidence is far from over. Mikel Aickin authored an article forcefully opposing admission.[385] Aickin advanced several arguments.

First, the likelihood ratio does not establish the probability of the defendant's paternity. The ratio compares a random, unrelated man to all men phenotypically indistinguishable from the defendant. Other men will have the same serological types, and "the laboratory cannot produce any evidence suggesting that one or the other of the men is more likely to be the father."[386] Second, the phenotypically indistinguishable men should not be compared to random men in

---

374. Jonakait, *supra* note 254, at 411.

375. Peterson, *supra* note 257, at 689.

376. *See* C. McCormick, *supra* note 316, at § 211 (collecting cases).

377. Imms v. Clarke, 654 S.W.2d 281, 287 (Mo. App. 1983). *See also* Turek v. Hardy, 312 Pa. Super. 158, 458 A.2d 562 (1983); Hudson v. Capps, 651 S.W.2d 243 (Tenn. App. 1983).

378. *See generally* Ellman & Kaye, *supra* note 327, at 1131. *See also* Davis v. State, 476 N.E.2d 127 (Ind. App. 1985) (the use of the theorem in a prosecution for neglect of a dependent).

379. *E.g.*, Ark. Stat. Ann. § 34-705.1 (Supp. 1983); Mich. Comp. Laws § 25.496 (1984); N.J. Stat. Ann. § 9-17-51e (Supp. 1985); Ohio Code § 3111.10(B) (Supp. 1984).

380. W. Va. Code § 48-7-4 (Supp. 1984).

381. Massachusetts v. Beausoleil, 397 Mass. 206, 490 N.E.2d 788 (1986).

382. Md. Ann. Code FL § 5-1029(e) (1984).

383. Colo. Rev. Stat. § 19-6-105 (Supp. 1984).

384. Minn. Stat. Ann. § 257.62, Subd. 5 (Supp. 1985).

385. Aickin, *Some Fallacies in the Computation of Paternity Probabilities*, 36 Am. J. Hum. Genet. 904 (1984).

386. *Id.* at 907.

the geographic area. "What is pertinent is the population of 'plausible fathers,'"[387] and that population may be very difficult to identify.[388] Third, even if it were appropriate to compare the phenotypically indistinguishable men to random men in the geographic area, in new systems such as HLA "there may not be very good evidence about the distribution of genetic characteristics" in the area.[389] Finally, Aickin posed several hypotheticals in which he claims that assumptions used by the proponents of paternity probabilities may "swindle" jurors out of their prior belief that the defendant's paternity was unlikely.[390] Aickin concluded that "[s]ome courts may have gone too far already" in admitting paternity probabilities.[391] The discernible trend in the case law is toward the admission of such probabilities, but Aickin's article indicates that the controversy is far from over.[392]

§ 17-10. Selected Bibliography.

DNA TECHNOLOGY AND FORENSIC SCIENCE (J. Ballantyne ed. 1989).

P. DEROHANNESIAN, SEXUAL ASSAULT TRIALS (1994).

W. ECKERT & S. JAMES, INTERPRETATION OF BLOODSTAIN EVIDENCE (1989).

M. FARLEY & J. HARRINGTON, FORENSIC DNA TECHNOLOGY (1991).

R. GAENSSLEN & H. LEE, PROCEDURES AND EVALUATION OF ANTISERA FOR THE TYPING OF ANTIGENS IN BLOODSTAINS — ABO, RH, MNSS, KELL, DUFFY, AND KIDD BLOOD GROUP ANTIGENS AND GM/KM SERUM GROUP ANTIGENS (1984).

S. HUNT, INVESTIGATION OF SEROLOGICAL EVIDENCE — A MANUAL FOR FIELD INVESTIGATORS (1984).

H. LEE & R. GAENSSLEN, ADVANCES IN FORENSIC SCIENCE I: FORENSIC SEROLOGY (1985).

NAT'L ASS'N OF CRIMINAL DEFENSE LAWYERS, DNA DEFENSE NOTEBOOK (1990).

S. SCHATKIN, DISPUTED PATERNITY PROCEEDINGS (1983 rev.).

INCLUSION PROBABILITIES IN PARENTAGE TESTING (R. Walker ed. 1983).

Gaensslen & Camp, *Forensic Serology: Analysis of Bloodstains and Body Fluid Stains*, *in* 2 FORENSIC SCIENCE, ch. 29 (C. Wecht ed. 1983).

Lee, *Identification and Grouping of Bloodstains*, *in* FORENSIC SCIENCE HANDBOOK 267 (R. Saferstein ed. 1982).

---

387. *Id.* at 909.

388. *Id.* at 910.

389. *Id.* at 909.

390. *Id.* at 910-14. State v. Skipper, 228 Conn. 610, 637 A.2d 1101 (1994) (the expert assumed a 50-50 chance that the defendant had intercourse with the complainant; that assumption was antithetical to the presumption of innocence); State v. Spann, 130 N.J. 484, 617 A.2d 247 (1993) (the expert used a 50:50 prior probability; the jury should be required to use its own prior probability figure, and it should be told how to proceed if its prior probability estimate differs from the expert's), *aff'd*, 130 N.J. 484, 617 A.2d 247 (1993).

391. Aickin, *Some Fallacies in the Computation of Paternity Probabilities*, 36 AM. J. HUM. GENET. 904, 915 (1984).

392. *See also* Aickin & Kaye, *Some Mathematical and Legal Considerations in Using Serological Tests to Prove Paternity*, *in* INCLUSION PROBABILITIES IN PARENTAGE TESTING 155 (R. Walker ed. 1983).

Marsters, *Medicolegal Aspect, of Blood and Other Biologic Stains, in* HANDBOOK OF LEGAL MEDICINE (5th ed. 1979).

Sensabaugh, *Biochemical Markers of Individuality, in* FORENSIC SCIENCE HANDBOOK 338 (R. Saferstein ed. 1982).

Wraxall, *Forensic Serology, in* SCIENTIFIC AND EXPERT EVIDENCE 897 (2d ed. 1981).

Aickin, *Some Fallacies in the Computation of Paternity Probabilities*, 36 AM. J. HUM. GENET. 904 (1984).

Beautyman, *Paternity Actions — A Matter of Opinion or a Trial of the Blood*, 4 J. LEG. MED. 20 (Apr. 1976).

Brown, *DNA and Kelly-Frye: Who Will Survive in California*, 11 CRIM. JUST. J. 1 (1988).

Ellman & Kaye, *Probabilities and Proof: Can HLA and Blood Grouping Tests Prove Paternity?*, 54 N.Y.U. L. REV. 1131 (1979).

Gaensslen, *When Blood Is Their Argument: Use and Interpretation of Population Genetic Marker Frequency Data in Forensic Serology*, 12 CRIME LAB. DIG. 75 (1985).

Grunbaum, *Genetic Typing of Physiological Stain Evidence: A Proposal for Quality Assurance Guidelines*, 11 FORUM 11 (Nov. – Dec. 1984).

Hoeffel, *The Dark Side of DNA Profiling: Unreliable Scientific Evidence Meets the Criminal Defendant*, 42 STAN. L. REV. 465 (1990).

Jonakait, *Will Blood Tell? Genetic Markers in Criminal Cases*, 31 EMORY L.J. 833 (1982).

Jonakait, *When Blood Is Their Argument: Probabilities in Criminal Cases, Genetic Markers, and, Once Again, Bayes' Theorem*, 1983 U. ILL. L. REV. 369.

Stroud, Bundrandt & Galindo, *Paternity Testing: A Current Approach*, 16 TRIAL 47 (Sept. 1980).

Sussman, *Up-To-Date Blood Testing for Paternity and Nonpaternity*, 24 TRAUMA 12 (June 1982).

Thompson & Ford, *DNA Typing: Acceptance and Weight of New Genetic Identification Tests*, 75 VA. L. REV. 45 (1989).

Annotations

Annot., *Weight and sufficiency of Human Leukocyte Antigen (HLA) tissue typing tests in paternity cases*, 37 A.L.R.4TH 167 (1985).

Annot., *Admissibility and weight of blood disputed paternity cases*, 43 A.L.R.4TH 579 (1986).